3e

Physics Galaxy

Volume IV

Optics & Modern Physics

Ashish Arora
Mentor & Founder
PHYSICSGALAXY.COM

World's largest encyclopedia of online video courses on High School Students preparing for
JEE Main * JEE Advanced * NEET * NSEP/INPhO/IPhO

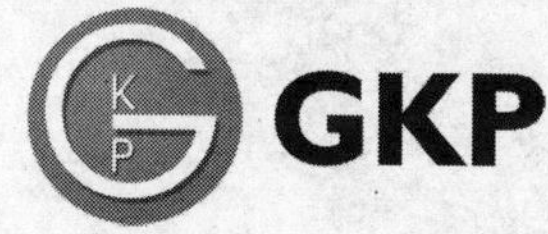

First Edition : December, 2000

Second Edition : May, 2016

Revised Edition : April, 2023

Title : Physics Galaxy : Vol. 4 - Optics & Modern Physics, 3rd edition

Language : English

Author's Name : Ashish Arora

Typeset & Published by :

Career Launcher Infrastructure (P) Ltd.

A-45, Mohan Cooperative Industrial Area, Near Mohan Estate Metro Station, New Delhi - 110044

Marketed by :

G.K. Publications (A Unit of CL Educate)

14/4, Mathura Road, Faridabad, Haryana, 121003

ISBN : **978-93-95101-02-8**

Printer's Details : Printed in India, New Delhi.

For product information :

Visit ***www.gkpublications.com*** or email to ***gkp@gkpublications.com***

Dedicated

to

My Parents, Son, Daughter

and

My beloved wife

In his teaching career since 1992 Ashish Arora personally mentored more than 10000 IITians and students who reached global heights in various career and profession chosen. It is his helping attitude toward students with which all his students remember him in life for his contribution in their success and keep connections with him live. Below is the list of some of the successful students in International Olympiad personally taught by him.

NAVNEET LOIWAL	***International GOLD Medal in IPhO-2000 at LONDON***, Also secured **AIR-4** in **IIT JEE 2000** PROUD FOR INDIA : Navneet Loiwal was the first Indian Student who won first International GOLD Medal for our country in International Physics Olympiad.
DUNGRA RAM CHOUDHARY	**AIR-1** in **IIT JEE 2002**
HARSHIT CHOPRA	***National Gold Medal in INPhO-2002*** and got **AIR-2** in **IIT JEE-2002**
KUNTAL LOYA	A Girl Student got position **AIR-8** in **IIT JEE 2002**
LUV KUMAR	***National Gold Medal in INPhO-2003*** and got **AIR-3** in **IIT JEE-2003**
RAJHANS SAMDANI	***National Gold Medal in INPhO-2003*** and got **AIR-5** in **IIT JEE-2003**
SHANTANU BHARDWAJ	***International SILVER Medal in IPhO-2002 at INDONESIA***
SHALEEN HARLALKA	***International GOLD Medal in IPhO-2003 at CHINA*** and got **AIR-46** in **IIT JEE-2003**
TARUN GUPTA	***National GOLD Medal in INPhO-2005***
APEKSHA KHANDELWAL	***National GOLD Medal in INPhO-2005***
ABHINAV SINHA	***Hon'ble Mension Award in APhO-2006*** at ***KAZAKHSTAN***
RAMAN SHARMA	***International GOLD Medal in IPhO-2007*** at ***IRAN*** and got **AIR-20** in **IIT JEE-2007**
PRATYUSH PANDEY	***International SILVER Medal in IPhO-2007*** at ***IRAN*** and got **AIR-85 in IIT JEE-2007**
GARVIT JUNIWAL	***International GOLD Medal in IPhO-2008*** at ***VIETNAM*** and got **AIR-10** in **IIT JEE-2008**
ANKIT PARASHAR	***National GOLD Medal in INPhO-2008***
HEMANT NOVAL	***National GOLD Medal in INPhO-2008*** and got **AIR-25** in **IIT JEE-2008**
ABHISHEK MITRUKA	***National GOLD Medal in INPhO-2009***
SARTHAK KALANI	***National GOLD Medal in INPhO-2009***
ASTHA AGARWAL	***International SILVER Medal in IJSO-2009*** at ***AZERBAIJAN***
RAHUL GURNANI	***International SILVER Medal in IJSO-2009*** at ***AZERBAIJAN***
AYUSH SINGHAL	***International SILVER Medal in IJSO-2009*** at ***AZERBAIJAN***
MEHUL KUMAR	***International SILVER Medal in IPhO-2010*** at ***CROATIA*** and got **AIR-19** in **IIT JEE-2010**
ABHIROOP BHATNAGAR	***National GOLD Medal in INPhO-2010***
AYUSH SHARMA	***International Double GOLD Medal in IJSO-2010*** at ***NIGERIA***
AASTHA AGRAWAL	***Hon'ble Mension Award in APhO-2011*** at ***ISRAEL*** and got **AIR-93** in **IIT JEE 2011**
ABHISHEK BANSAL	***National GOLD Medal in INPhO-2011***
SAMYAK DAGA	***National GOLD Medal in INPhO-2011***
SHREY GOYAL	***National GOLD Medal in INPhO-2012*** and secured **AIR-24** in **IIT JEE 2012**
RAHUL GURNANI	***National GOLD Medal in INPhO-2012***
JASPREET SINGH JHEETA	***National GOLD Medal in INPhO-2012***
DIVYANSHU MUND	***National GOLD Medal in INPhO-2012***
SHESHANSH AGARWAL	***International SILVER Medal in IAO-2012 at KOREA***
SWATI GUPTA	***International SILVER Medal in IJSO-2012 at IRAN***
PRATYUSH RAJPUT	***International SILVER Medal in IJSO-2012 at IRAN***
SHESHANSH AGARWAL	***International BRONZE Medal in IOAA-2013 at GREECE***
SHESHANSH AGARWAL	***International GOLD Medal in IOAA-2014 at ROMANIA***
SHESHANSH AGARWAL	***International SILVER Medal in IPhO-2015 at INDIA*** and secured **AIR-58** in **JEE(Advanced)-2015**
VIDUSHI VARSHNEY	***International SILVER Medal in IJSO-2015 at SOUTH KOREA***
AMAN BANSAL	**AIR-1 in JEE Advanced 2016**
KUNAL GOYAL	**AIR-3 in JEE Advanced 2016**
GOURAV DIDWANIA	**AIR-9 in JEE Advanced 2016**
DIVYANSH GARG	***International SILVER Medal in IPhO-2016 at SWITZERLAND***
NALIN KHANDELWAL	**AIR-1 in NEET 2019**
MRIDUL AGARWAL	**AIR-1 in JEE Advanced 2021**

ABOUT THE AUTHOR

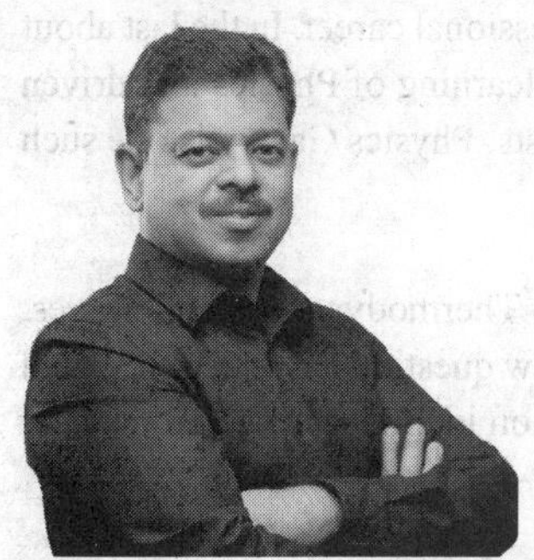

The complexities of Physics have given nightmares to many, but the homegrown genius of Jaipur- Ashish Arora has helped millions of students to live their dreams by decoding it.

Newton Law of Gravitation and Faraday's Magnetic induction force apply perfectly well with this unassuming genius. A Pied Piper of students, his webportal https://www.physicsgalaxy.com, The world's largest encyclopedia of video lectures on high school Physics possesses strong gravitational pull and magnetic attraction for students who want to make it big in life.

Ashish Arora, gifted with rare ability to train masterminds, has mentored over 10,000 IITians and Medicos in his past over three decades of teaching sojourn including lots of students made it to Top 100 in IIT-JEE/JEE(Advance) including multiple times AIR-1 and many in Top-10. Apart from that, he has also groomed hundreds of students for cracking International Physics Olympiad. No wonder his student Navneet Loiwal brought laurel to the country by becoming the first Indian to win a Gold medal at the 2000 - International Physics Olympiad in London (UK).

His special ability to simplify the toughest of the Physics theorems and applications rates him as one among the best Physics teachers in the world. With this, Arora simply defies the logic that perfection comes with age. Even at 18 when he started teaching Physics while pursuing engineering, he was as engaging as he is now. Experience, besides graying his hair, has just widened his horizon.

Now after encountering all tribes of students - some brilliant and some not-so-intelligent - this celebrated teacher has embarked upon a noble mission to make the entire galaxy of Physics inform of his webportal PHYSICSGALAXY.COM to serve and help global students in the subject. Today students from 183 countries are connected with this webportal. On any topic of physics students can post their queries in INTERACT tab of the webportal on which many global experts with Ashish Arora reply to several queries posted online by students.

Dedicated to global students of middle and high school level, his website *www.physicsgalaxy.com* also has teaching sessions dubbed in American accent and subtitles in 87 languages. For students in India preparing for JEE & NEET, his online courses will be available soon on PHYSICSGALAXY.COM.

FOREWORD

It has been pleasure for me to follow the progress Er. Ashish Arora has made in teaching and professional career. In the last about three decades he has actively contributed in developing several new techniques for teaching & learning of Physics and driven important contribution to Science domain through nurturing young students and budding scientists. Physics Galaxy is one such example of numerous efforts he has undertaken.

The third edition of Physics Galaxy provides a good coverage of various topics of Mechanics, Thermodynamics and Waves, Optics & Modern Physics and Electricity & Magnetism through dedicated volumes and many new questions included. It would be an important resource for students appearing in competitive examination for seeking admission in engineering and medical streams.

The structure of book is logical and the presentation is innovative. Importantly the book covers some of the concepts on the basis of realistic experiments and examples. The book has been written in an informal style to help students learn faster and more interactively with better diagrams and visual appeal of the content. Each chapter has variety of theoretical and numerical problems to test the knowledge acquired by students. The book also includes solution to all practice exercises with several new illustrations and problems for deeper learning.

I am sure the book will widen the horizons of knowledge in Physics and will be found very useful by the students for developing in-depth understanding of the subject.

Prof. Sandeep Sancheti
Ph. D. (U.K.), B.Tech. FIETE, FIE (I), SMIEEE

Vice-Chancellor (Provost) Marwadi University, Rajkot
Member Executive Council, Association of Commonwealth Universities, London
Former President, AIU, New Delhi
Former Vice-Chancellor, SRMIST, Chennai
Former President, Manipal University, Jaipur
Former-Director NIT Surathkal, NIT New Delhi, NIT Trichy,
NIT Calicut, SPA Delhi; Former-Mentor Director NIT Goa,
NIT Sikkim, NIT Puducherry
Former-Member JEE Apex Board (JAB), MHRD, GoI
Former-Chairman, Central Counselling Board (CCB), AIEEE, MHRD, GoI
Former-Chairman, Direct Admission of Students Abroad (DASA), MHRD, GoI

PREFACE

For a science student, Physics is the most important subject, unlike to other subjects it requires logical reasoning and high imagination of brain. Without improving the level of physics it is very difficult to achieve a goal in the present age of competitions. To score better, one does not require hard working at least in physics. It just requires a simple understanding and approach to think a physical situation. Actually physics is the surrounding of our everyday life. All the six parts of general physics-Mechanics, Heat, Sound, Light, Electromagnetism and Modern Physics are the constituents of our surroundings. If you wish to make the concepts of physics strong, you should try to understand core concepts of physics in practical approach rather than theoretical. Whenever you try to solve a physics problem, first create a hypothetical approach rather than theoretical. Whenever you try to solve a physics problem, first create a hypothetical world in your imagination about the problem and try to think psychologically, what the next step should be, the best answer would be given by your brain psychology. For making physics strong in all respects and you should try to merge and understand all the concepts with the brain psychologically.

The book PHYSICS GALAXY is designed in a totally different and friendly approach to develop the physics concepts psychologically. The book is presented in five volumes, which covers almost all the core branches of general physics. This part of book, volume 4 covers Modern Physics and Optics. These are most scoring topics of Physics for any competitive or school level exams which helps in building strong applications of the subject. The things you will learn in this book will help in building your overall strength in the branch of Modern Physics and Optics. In this book every chapter is explained in a simple, interactive and experimental way. The book is divided in the six major chapters, first chapters is covering applications of atomic structure followed by the next chapter on photoelectric effect and matter waves. Both of these initial chapters builds foundation of modern physics by understanding characteristics of an atom and atomic spectrum. This chapter also includes the calculation and analysis of electron transition between energy levels of atom and ionization of atom. Photoelectric effect builds a good level of understanding for electron transition effects by absorption of energy. Third chapter covers production and properties of X-Rays and its applications. Next chapter on radioactivity and nuclear physics forms the basis of understanding of nucleus of an atom and also the detailed analysis of stability of nucleus is discussed along with properties of radioactive radiations. The last two chapters at the end, ray optics and wave optics covers the major application of light in form of ray and a wave respectively.

The best way of understanding physics is the experiments and this methodology I am using in my lectures and I found that it helps students a lot in concept visualization. In this book I have tried to translate the things as I used in lectures. After every important section there are several solved examples included with simple and interactive explanations. It might help a student in a way that the student does not require to consult any thing with the teacher. Everything is self explanatory and in simple language.

One important factor in preparation of physics I wish to highlight that most of the student after reading the theory of a concept start working out the numerical problems. This is not the efficient way of developing concepts in brain. To get the maximum benefit of the book students should read carefully the whole chapter at least three or four times with all the illustrative examples and with more stress on some illustrative examples included in the chapter. Practice exercises included after every theory section in each chapter is for the purpose of in-depth understanding of the applications of concepts covered. Illustrative examples are explaining some theoretical concept in the form of an example. After a thorough reading of the chapter students can start thinking on discussion questions and start working on numerical problems.

Exercises given at the end of each chapter are for circulation of all the concepts in mind. There are two sections, first is the discussion questions, which are theoretical and help in understanding the concepts at root level. Second section is of conceptual MCQs which helps in enhancing the theoretical thinking of students and building logical skills in the chapter. Third section of numerical MCQs helps in the developing scientific and analytical application of concepts. Fourth section of advance MCQs with one or more options correct type questions is for developing advance and comprehensive thoughts. Last section is the Unsolved Numerical Problems which includes some simple problems and some tough problems which require the building fundamentals of physics from basics to advance level problems which are useful in preparation of NSEP, INPhO or IPhO.

In this third edition of the book I have included many new questions and solutions in different exercises at practice, conceptual, numerical and advance MCQs to support students who are dependent on their self study and not getting access to teachers for their preparation.

This book has taken a shape just because of motivational inspiration by my mother in 1997 when I just thought to write something for my students. She always motivated and was on my side whenever I thought to develop some new learning methodology for my students.

I don't have words for my best friend my wife Anuja for always being together with me to complete this book in the unique style and format.

I would like to pay my gratitude to Sh. Dayashankar Prajapati in assisting me to complete the task in Design Labs of PHYSICSGALAXY.COM and presenting the book in totally new format of third edition.

At last but the most important person, my father who has devoted his valuable time in finally presenting the book in such a format and a simple language, thanks is a very small word for his dedication in building the base structure of this book.

In this third edition I have tried my best to make this book error free but owing to the nature of work, inadvertently, there is possibility of errors left untouched. I shall be grateful to the readers, if they point out me regarding errors and oblige me by giving their valuable and constructive suggestions via emails for further improvement of the book.

Ashish Arora

PHYSICSGALAXY.COM
B-80, Model Town, Malviya Nagar, Jaipur-302017
e-mails: ashisharora@physicsgalaxy.com
ashash12345@gmail.com

CONTENTS

Chapter 6 *Wave Optics* 341-408

ANSWERS & SOLUTIONS

Atomic Physics

1

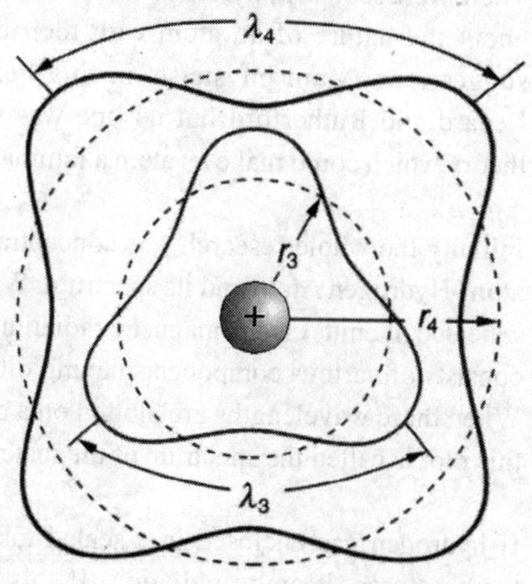

FEW WORDS FOR STUDENTS

In your previous classes from several we have studied about existence of atoms and nuclei. However most of us cannot cite much experimental evidence from them. In this chapter we will discuss the experiments that form the basis for our knowledge of atoms. Now, we examine many fundamental facts of atomic structures and our reasons for believing in them. Thus in this chapter we are going to frame our groundwork for further discussion of atomic physics in the following chapters.

CHAPTER CONTENTS

COVER APPLICATION

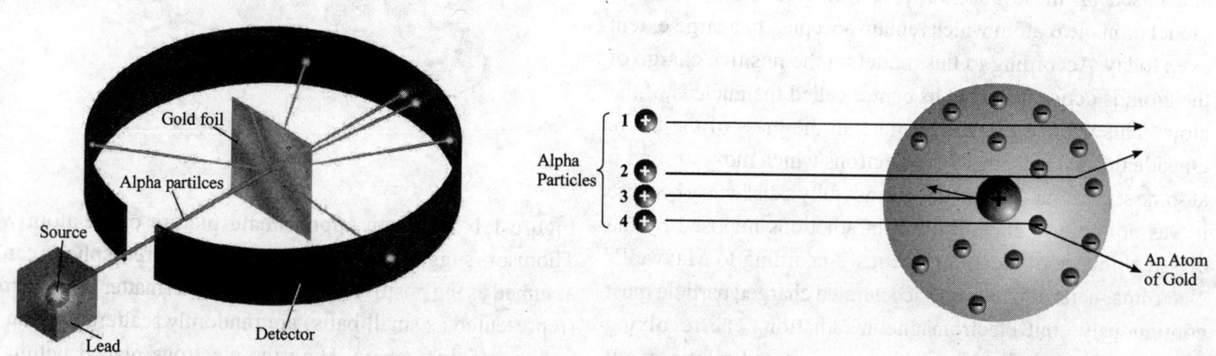

Figure (a) **Figure (b)**

Rutherford's Alpha Scattering experiment based on which atomic model was defined by Rutherford. Figure-(a) shows the experimental setup and figure-(b) shows the atomic visualization of scattering of alpha particles.

Atomic Physics is that branch of physics in which we'll deal with the properties of an atom. The whole Physics is based on our physical environment, surroundings and everything in our surroundings is the multidimensional arrangement of different atoms.

There were so many physicists who had given their explanation about the nature of an atom with their atomic models and suggestions. Main physicists in this field were Thomson, Lenard and Rutherford but no one was successful with his theory which could make an atom a familiar concept.

Initially the whole research was concentrated on the simplest atom-Hydrogen Atom and its spectrum. When a material body is heated, it emits electromagnetic radiation. The radiation may consists of various components having different wavelengths. When these wavelengths are plotted on a calibrated scale then this plot is called the spectrum of the material body.

If hydrogen gas enclosed in a sealed tube is heated to high temperatures, it emits radiation. If this radiation is passed through a prism, components of different wavelengths are deviated by different amounts and thus we get the hydrogen spectrum. When the Hydrogen spectrum was taken then the main features of this spectrum are, some sharply defined, discrete wavelengths exist in the emitted radiation. For example, the radiation of wavelength 6562 Å was observed and then the radiation of 4860 Å was observed. Hydrogen atom do not emit any radiation between 6562 Å and 4860 Å. There were also so many lines of electromagnetic radiations above and below these two lines in visible region, ultraviolet, infra red region etc.

1.1 A Brief History to Atomic Physics

In this age of classical Physics no one was present who could explain the theory of hydrogen spectrum. Although Rutherford got some interesting results with his α-scattering experiment and based on these observations, Rutherford proposed the model of nuclear atom which remain accepted to a large extent even today. According to this model all the positive charge of the atom is concentrated at its centre called the nucleus of the atom. This nucleus contains almost all the mass of the atom. Outside this nucleus, there are electrons which move around it at some separation. This model was not fully satisfactory because it was not able to explain the contradictions imposed by the classical theory of electromagnetics. According to Maxwell's electromagnetic equation any accelerated charged particle must continuously emit electromagnetic radiation. The revolving electron should therefore, always emit radiations at all temperatures and the radius of the circle should gradually decrease and the electron should finally fall into the nucleus. But this is not the case actually exist.

The actual observations are quite different. At room temperature or below normal room, hydrogen is vary stable, it neither emits radiation nor does the electron collapse into the nucleus. The Hydrogen atom emits fixed wavelengths which are observed in Hydrogen spectrum. Such observations could not be explained by classical concepts of physics.

These puzzles related to the Hydrogen atom and its spectrum was solved upto a greater extent by an atomic model which was presented by Niels Bohr, in 1913. This was the age of Modern Physics.

Now we'll discuss this "*Bohr's Model of atom*" in detail with theoretical and analytical expressions. The atomic model of Bohr is based on three assumptions, these assumptions are called Postulates of the Bohr's model. Before proceeding to Bohr's Model First we'll discuss the basic concepts of Thomson's Model and Rutherford's experiment.

1.2 Thomson's Atomic Model

In 1898, J.J. Thomson suggested an atomic model which became the most popular model of an atom in very early twentieth century. He suggested that the positive atom was spherical in shape and the positive charges were uniformly distributed in this sphere of atomic dimensions or the sphere was filled with positive charged matter of uniform density and sufficient number of negative particles, electrons are embedded randomly throughout the volume just like seeds in watermelon to balance the positive charge.

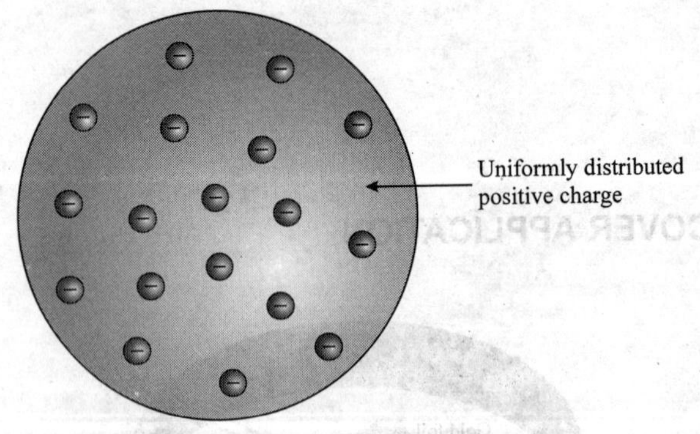

Figure 1.1

Figure-1.1 shows an approximate picture of an atom what Thomson suggested. Here the gray coloured sphere can be assumed as the positively charged uniform matter and electrons (represented as small balls) are randomly scattered within the volume of this sphere. Here the electrons placed within the positive charge resembled the plum fruit seeds in a pudding hence this atomic model is sometimes called as "*plum pudding model*".

1.3 Rutherford's Atomic Model

In 1911, Earnest Rutherford performed a critical experiment that showed that Thomson's model could not be correct. In this experiment a beam of positively charged alpha particles (helium nuclei) was projected into a thin gold foil. It is observed that most of the alpha particles passed through the foil as if it were empty space. But some surprising results are also seen. Several alpha particles are deflected from their original direction by large angles. Few alpha particles are observed to be reflected back, reversing their direction of travel as shown in figure-1.2.

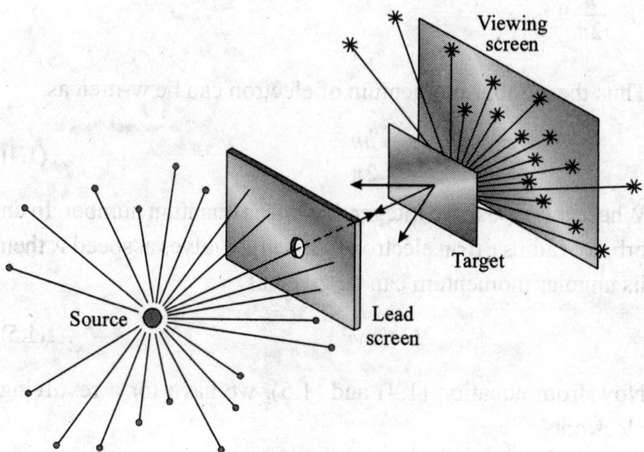

Figure 1.2

If Thomson model is assumed to be true that the positive charge is spreaded uniformly in the volume of an atom then the alpha particle can never experience such a large repulsion due to which it will be deflected by such large angles as observed in the experiment. On the basis of this experiment Rutherford presented a new atomic model.

In this new atomic model it was assumed that the positive charge in the atom was concentrated in a region that was small relative to the size of atom. He called this concentration of positive charge, the nucleus of the atom. Electrons belonging to the atom were assumed to be moving in the large volume of atom outside the nucleus. To explain why these electrons were not pulled into the nucleus, Rutherford said that electrons revolve around the nucleus in orbits around the positively charged nucleus in the same manner as the planets orbit the sun. The corresponding atomic model can be approximately shown in figure-1.3.

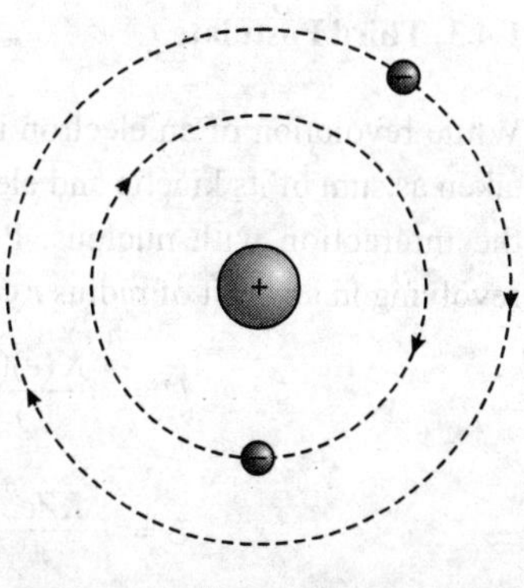

Figure 1.3

In the Rutherford's planetary model, two basic difficulties exist. First is the emission of some characteristic frequencies of electromagnetic radiation by an atom. It is observed that every atom emits some characteristic frequencies and no other frequency is emitted. Rutherford's model was not able to explain this phenomenon. Second difficulty was the revolution of electrons around the nucleus. These electrons undergo a centripetal acceleration. According to Maxwell's Theory of electromagnetism, a centripetally accelerated, charge particle should continuously radiate electromagnetic waves of same frequency as that of its revolution. In this model if we apply this classical theory it says that as electron radiates energy, the radius of its orbit steadily decreases and its frequency of revolution continuously increases. This would lead to an ever-increasing frequency of emitted radiation and ultimately atom will collapse as the electron plunges into the nucleus as shown in figure-1.4.

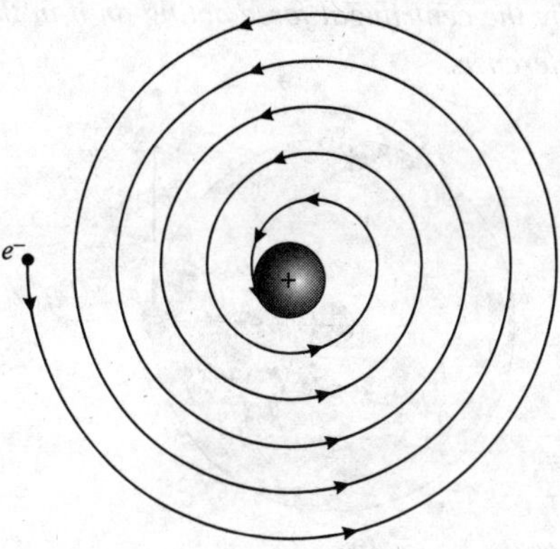

Figure 1.4

1.4 Bohr's Model of an Atom

Between 1913 and 1915 Niels Bohr developed a quantitative atomic model for the Hydrogen atom that could account for its spectrum. The model incorporated the nuclear model of the atom proposed by Rutherford on the basis of his experiments. We shall see that this model was successful in its ability to predict the gross features of the spectrum emitted by Hydrogen atom. This model was developed specifically for Hydrogenic atoms. Hydrogenic atoms are those which consist of a nucleus with positive charge + Ze (Z = atomic number, e = charge of electron) and a single electron. More complex electron-electron interactions in an atom are not accounted in the Bohr's Model that's why it was valid only for one electron system or hydrogenic atoms.

The Bohr model is appropriate for one electron systems like H, He^+, Li^{+2} etc. and it was successful upto some extent in explaining the features of the spectrum emitted by such hydrogenic atoms. However this model is not giving a true picture of even these simple atoms. The true picture is fully a quantum mechanical affair which is different from Bohr model in several fundamental ways. Since Bohr model incorporates aspects of some classical and some modern physics, it is now called semiclassical model. Bohr has explained his atomic model in three steps called postulates of Bohr's atomic model. Lets discuss these postulates one by one.

1.4.1 First Postulate

In this postulate Bohr incorporates and analyze features of the Rutherford nuclear model of atom. In this postulate it was taken that as the mass of nucleus is so much greater then the mass of electron, nucleus was assumed to be at rest and electron revolves around the nucleus in an orbit. The orbit of electron is assumed to be circular for simplicity. Now the statement of first postulate is "*During revolution of electron around the nucleus in circular orbit, the electric coulombian force on electron is balanced by the centrifugal force acting on it in the rotating frame of reference.*"

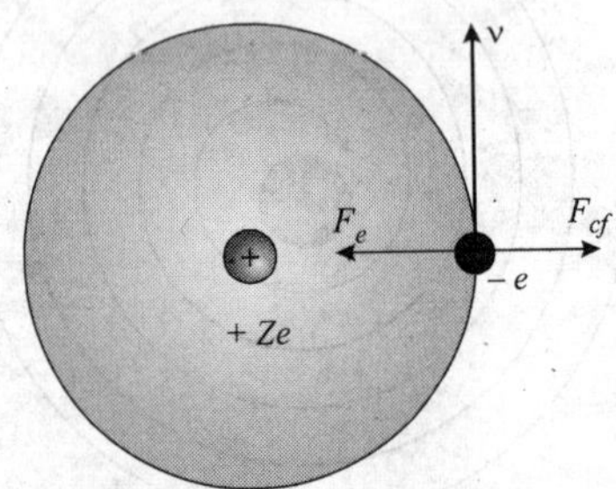

Figure 1.5

If electron revolves with speed v in the orbit of radius r. Then relative to rotating frame attached with electron, the centrifugal force acting on it is

$$F_{cf} = \frac{mv^2}{r} \quad \ldots(1.1)$$

The coulombian force acting on electron due to charge of nucleus (+ Ze) is

$$F_{\text{electric}} = \frac{K(e)(Ze)}{r^2}$$

$$\Rightarrow \quad = \frac{KZe^2}{r^2} \quad \ldots(1.2)$$

Now according to first postulate from equation-(1.1) & (1.2) we have

$$\frac{mv^2}{r} = \frac{KZe^2}{r^2}$$

$$\Rightarrow \quad mv^2 = \frac{KZe^2}{r} \quad \ldots(1.3)$$

Equation-(1.3) is called equation of Bohr's first postulate.

1.4.2 Second Postulate

In the study of atom, Bohr found that while revolving around the nucleus the orbital angular momentum of the electron was restricted to only certain values, we say that the orbital angular momentum of the electron is quantized. He therefore took this as a second postulate of the model. The statement of second Postulate is, Bohr proposed that - "*During revolution around the nucleus, the orbital angular momentum of electron L could not have just any value, it can take up only those values which are integral multiples of Plank's Constant divided by 2π i.e.* $\frac{h}{2\pi}$"

Thus the angular momentum of electron can be written as

$$L = \frac{nh}{2\pi} \quad \ldots(1.4)$$

Where n is a positive integer, known as quantum number. In an orbit of radius r, if an electron (mass m) revolves at speed v, then its angular momentum can be given as

$$L = mvr \quad \ldots(1.5)$$

Now from equation-(1.4) and (1.5), we have for a revolving electron

$$mvr = \frac{nh}{2\pi} \quad \ldots(1.6)$$

Equation-(1.6) is known as equation of second postulate of Bohr model. Here the quantity $\frac{h}{2\pi}$ occurs so frequently in modern physics that, for convenience, it is given its own designation $\hbar$, pronounced as "h-bar."

$$\hbar = \frac{h}{2\pi} \simeq 1.055 \times 10^{-34} \text{ J-s} \quad \ldots(1.7)$$

1.4.3 Third Postulate

While revolution of an electron in an orbit its total energy is taken as sum of its kinetic and electric potential energy due to the interaction with nucleus. Potential energy of electron revolving in an orbit of radius r can be simply given as

$$U = -\frac{K(e)(Ze)}{r}$$

$$\Rightarrow \quad U = -\frac{KZe^2}{r} \quad \ldots(1.8)$$

For kinetic energy of electron, we assume that relativistic speeds are not involved so we can use the classical expression for kinetic energy. Thus kinetic energy of electron in an orbit revolving at speed v can be given as

$$K = \frac{1}{2}mv^2 \quad \ldots(1.9)$$

Thus total energy of electron can be given as

$$E = K + U = \frac{1}{2}mv^2 - \frac{KZe^2}{r} \quad \ldots(1.10)$$

Here we can see that while revolving in a stable orbit, the energy of electron remains constant. From the purely classical viewpoint, during circular motion, as electron is accelerated, it should steadily loose energy by emitting electromagnetic radiations and it spiraled down into the nucleus and collapse the atom.

Bohr in his third postulate stated that "*While revolving around the nucleus in an orbit, it is in stable state, it does not emit any energy radiation during revolution. It emits energy radiation only when it makes a transition from higher energy level (upper orbit) to a lower energy level (lower orbit) and the energy of emitted radiation is equal to the difference in energies of electron in the two corresponding orbits in transition.*"

If an electron makes a transition form a higher orbit n_2 to a lower orbit n_1 as shown in figure-1.6 (b). Then the electron radiates a single photon of energy

$$\Delta E = -E_{n_2} - E_{n_1} = h\nu$$

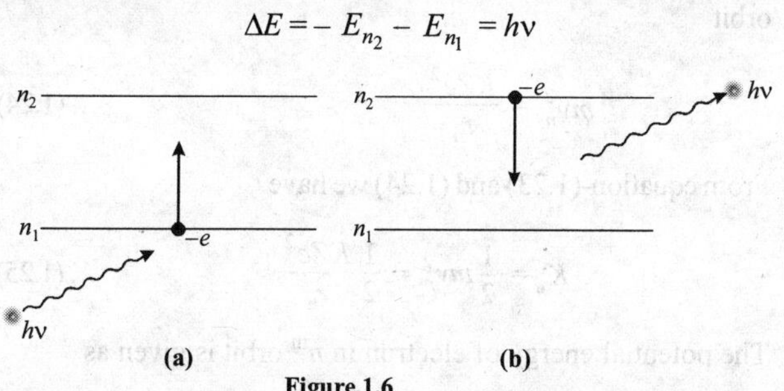

Figure 1.6

Here E_{n_2} and E_{n_1} are the total energies of electron in the two orbits n_2 and n_1. The emitted photon energy can be expressed as $h\nu$ where ν is the frequency of radiated energy photon. If λ be the wavelength of photon emitted then the energy of emitted photon can also be given as

$$\Delta E = h\nu = \frac{hc}{\lambda} \quad \ldots(1.11)$$

Similarly when energy is supplied to the atom by an external source then the electron will make a transition from lower energy level to a higher energy level as shown in figure-1.6 (a). This process is called excitation of electron from lower to higher energy level. In this process the way in which energy is supplied to the electron is very important because the behaviour of the electron in the excitation depends on the process by which energy is supplied from an external source. This we'll discuss in detail in later part of this chapter.

First we'll study the basic properties of an electron revolving around the nucleus of hydrogenic atoms.

1.5 Properties of Electron in Bohr's Atomic Model

Now we'll discuss the basic properties of an electron revolving in stable orbits. These stable orbits we call Bohr energy level. We have discussed that there are some particular orbits in which electron can revolve around the nucleus for which first and second postulates of Bohr model was satisfied. Thus only those orbits are stable for which the quantum number $n = 1, 2, 3, \ldots$. Now for n^{th} orbit if we assume its radius is denoted by r_n and electron is revolving in this orbit with speed v_n. We can represent all the physical parameters associated with the electron in n^{th} orbit by using a subscript n with the symbol of the physical parameter like r_n, v_n etc.

1.5.1 Radius of nth Orbit in Bohr Model

Radius of electron in n^{th} Bohr's Orbit can be calculated using the first two postulates of the Bohr's model, using equations-(1.3) & (1.6) we have from equation-(1.6)

$$v_n = \frac{nh}{2\pi m r_n}$$

Substituting this value of v_n in equation-(1.3), we get

$$r_n = \frac{n^2h^2}{4\pi^2 KZe^2 m} \quad \ldots(1.12)$$

$$\Rightarrow \quad r_n = \frac{h^2}{4\pi^2 Ke^2 m} \times \frac{n^2}{Z}$$

$$\Rightarrow \quad r_n = 0.529 \times \frac{n^2}{Z}\,\text{Å} \quad \ldots(1.13)$$

1.5.2 Velocity of Electron in n^{th} Bohr's Orbit

By substituting the value of r_n from equation-(1.12) in equation-(1.6) we can calculate the value of v_n as

$$v_n = \frac{2\pi KZe^2}{nh} \quad \ldots(1.14)$$

$$\Rightarrow \quad v_n = \frac{2\pi Ke^2}{h} \times \frac{Z}{n}$$

$$\Rightarrow \quad v_n = 2.18 \times 10^6 \times \frac{Z}{n}\ \text{m/s} \quad \ldots(1.15)$$

1.5.3 Angular Velocity of Electron in n^{th} Bohr's Orbit

Angular velocity of the electron in n^{th} orbit is given by

$$\omega_n = \frac{v_n}{r_n}$$

$$\Rightarrow \quad \omega_n = \frac{8\pi^3 K^2 Z^2 e^4 m}{n^3 h^3} \quad \ldots(1.16)$$

1.5.4 Frequency of Electron in n^{th} Bohr's Orbit

Frequency i.e. the number of revolution made by the electron per second in n^{th} orbit is given as

$$f_n = \frac{\omega_n}{2\pi}$$

$$\Rightarrow \quad f_n = \frac{4\pi^2 K^2 Z^2 e^4 m}{n^3 h^3} \quad \ldots(1.17)$$

1.5.5 Time period of Electron in n^{th} Bohr's Orbit

Time period of electron in n^{th} orbit is given by

$$T_n = \frac{1}{f_n}$$

$$\Rightarrow \quad T_n = \frac{n^3 h^3}{4\pi^2 K^2 Z^2 e^4 m} \quad \ldots(1.18)$$

1.5.6. Current in n^{th} Bohr's Orbit

Electrons revolve around the nucleus in the nth Bohr's Orbit then due to revolution there is current in the orbit and according to the definition of current, the current in the nth orbit will be total coulombs passing through a point in one seconds, and in an orbit an electron passes through a point f_n times in one second so the current in the nth orbit will be

$$I_n = f_n \times e$$

$$\Rightarrow \quad I_n = \frac{4\pi^2 K^2 Z^2 e^5 m}{n^3 h^3} \quad \ldots(1.19)$$

1.5.7 Magnetic Induction at the Nucleus Due to n^{th} Orbit

An electron revolving in n^{th} Bohr's Orbit is equivalent to a current carrying coil having radius r_n, and due to this electron current there is a magnetic induction at the centre of the orbit, at the nucleus and magnitude of this magnetic induction is given by

$$B_n = \frac{\mu_0 I_n}{2r_n}$$

$$\Rightarrow \quad B_n = \frac{8\pi^4 \mu_0 K^3 Z^3 e^7 m^2}{n^5 h^5} \quad \ldots(1.20)$$

1.5.8 Magnetic Moment of the nth Bohr's Orbit

The magnetic moment of the nth Bohr's Orbit due to the electron current is given by

$$M_n = I_n \times A_n$$

$$\Rightarrow \quad M_n = I_n \times \pi r^2$$

$$\Rightarrow \quad M_n = \frac{4\pi^2 K^2 Z^2 e^5 m}{n^3 h^3} \times \pi \left(\frac{n^2 h^2}{4\pi^2 K Z e^2 m}\right)^2$$

$$\Rightarrow \quad M_n = \frac{enh}{4\pi m} \quad \ldots(1.21)$$

in this equation-(1.21), for $n = 1$ the magnetic moment M_1 is also known as *"Bohr Magneton"*.

1.5.9 Energy of Electron in n^{th} Orbit

We've discussed that in n^{th} orbit during revolution the total energy of electron can be given as sum of kinetic and potential energy of the electron as

$$E_n = K_n + U_n \quad \ldots(1.22)$$

Kinetic energy of electron in n^{th} orbit can be given as

$$K_n = \frac{1}{2} m v_n^2 \quad \ldots(1.23)$$

From equation of first postulate of Bohr Model we have for n^{th} orbit

$$m v_n^2 = \frac{KZe^2}{r_n} \quad \ldots(1.24)$$

From equation-(1.23) and (1.24) we have

$$K_n = \frac{1}{2} m v_n^2 = \frac{1}{2}\frac{KZe^2}{r_n} \quad \ldots(1.25)$$

The potential energy of electron in n^{th} orbit is given as

$$U_n = -\frac{KZe^2}{r_n} \quad \ldots(1.26)$$

Thus total energy of e^- in n^{th} orbit can be given as

$$E_n = K_n + U_n$$

$$\Rightarrow \quad E_n = \frac{1}{2}\frac{KZe^2}{r_n} - \frac{KZe^2}{r_n}$$

$$\Rightarrow \quad E_n = -\frac{1}{2}\frac{KZe^2}{r_n} \quad \ldots(1.27)$$

NOTE : Here we can see that $|E_n| = |K_n| = \frac{1}{2}|U_n|$ which is a **very useful relation, always followed by a particle revolving under the action of a force obeying inverse square law.**

Now substituting the value of r_n from equation-1.12 in equation-(1.27) we get

$$E_n = -\frac{1}{2} KZe^2 \times \frac{4\pi^2 KZe^2 m}{n^2 h^2}$$

$$\Rightarrow \qquad E_n = -\frac{2\pi^2 K^2 Z^2 e^4 m}{n^2 h^2}$$

$$\Rightarrow \qquad E_n = -\frac{2\pi^2 K^2 e^4 m}{h^2} \times \frac{Z^2}{n^2}$$

Substituting the value of constants in above equation we get

$$E_n = -13.6 \times \frac{Z^2}{n^2} \text{ eV} \qquad \ldots(1.28)$$

The above equation can be used to find out energies of electron in different energy level of different hydrogenic atoms.

1.5.10 Energies of Different Energy Level in Hydrogenic Atoms

By the use of equation-(1.28) we can find out the energies of different energy levels. Students should remember these energies for first six levels as

$$\begin{aligned} E_1 &= -13.6\, Z^2 \text{ eV} \\ E_2 &= -3.40\, Z^2 \text{ eV} \\ E_3 &= -1.51\, Z^2 \text{ eV} \\ E_4 &= -0.85\, Z^2 \text{ eV} \\ E_5 &= -0.54\, Z^2 \text{ eV} \\ E_6 &= -0.36\, Z^2 \text{ eV} \end{aligned} \qquad \ldots(1.29)$$

The equation-(1.29) clearly shows that as the value of n increases, the difference between two consecutive energy levels decreases. It can be shown with the help of Figure-1.7, which shows the energy level diagram for a hydrogen atom.

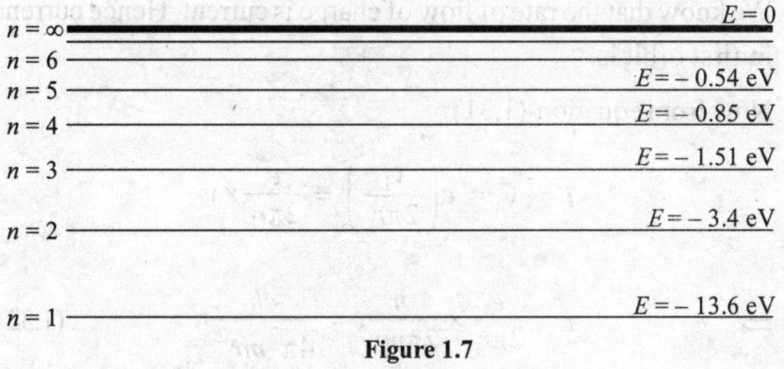

$n = \infty$ ———— $E = 0$
$n = 6$
$n = 5$ ———— $E = -0.54$ eV
$n = 4$ ———— $E = -0.85$ eV
$n = 3$ ———— $E = -1.51$ eV
$n = 2$ ———— $E = -3.4$ eV
$n = 1$ ———— $E = -13.6$ eV

Figure 1.7

Now if we multiply the numerator and denominator of equation-(1.28) by ch we get

$$E_n = -\frac{2\pi^2 K^2 e^4 m}{ch^3} \times ch \times \frac{Z^2}{n^2}$$

$$\Rightarrow \qquad E_n = -Rch \times \frac{Z^2}{n^2}\, eV \qquad \ldots(1.30)$$

Where $R = \dfrac{2\pi^2 K^2 e^4 m}{ch^3}$ is defined as Rydberg Constant and the value of it is given as $R = 10967800 \text{ m}^{-1}$, which can be taken approximately as 10^7 m^{-1}. For $n = 1$ and $Z = 1$ the energy is given as

$E = -Rch$ joules and is called as One Rydberg Energy

1 Rydberg $= 13.6$ eV $= 2.17 \times 10^{-18}$ joules

Lets discuss some examples on Bohr's atomic model to understand it better.

 # Illustrative Example 1.1

If the average life time of an excited state of hydrogen is of the order of 10^{-8} s, estimate how many orbits an electron makes when it is in the state $n = 2$ before it suffers a transition to state $n = 1$.

Solution

As we've discussed that the frequency of revolution of an electron in 4th orbit is

$$f_n = \frac{\omega_n}{2\pi}$$

$$\Rightarrow \qquad f_n = \frac{v_n}{2\pi r_n}$$

$$\Rightarrow \qquad f_n = \frac{2.18\times10^6 \times Z/n}{2\times3.14\times0.529\times10^{-10}\times n^2/Z} \text{ s}^{-1}$$

Thus number of revolutions completed in 10^{-8} second in $n = 2$ state are

$$N = f_n \times 10^{-8}$$

$$\Rightarrow \qquad N = \frac{2.18\times10^6\times10^{-8}}{2\times3.14\times0.529\times10^{-10}} \times \frac{Z^2}{n^3}$$

$$\Rightarrow \qquad N = 8.2\times10^6 \text{ revolutions}$$

 # Illustrative Example 1.2

What is the angular momentum of an electron in Bohr's hydrogen atom whose energy is -3.4 eV?

Solution

Energy of electron in n^{th} Bohr orbit of hydrogen atom is given by,

$$E = -\frac{13.6}{n^2} \text{ eV}$$

Hence, $\qquad -3.4 = -\dfrac{13.6}{n^2}$

$$\Rightarrow \qquad n^2 = 4$$

$$\Rightarrow \qquad n = 2$$

The angular momentum of an electron in n^{th} orbit is given as $L = \frac{nh}{2\pi}$. Putting $n = 2$, we obtain

$$L = \frac{2h}{2\pi} = \frac{h}{\pi}$$

Illustrative Example 1.3

The electron in a hydrogen atom makes a transition $n_1 \rightarrow n_2$ where n_1 and n_2 are the principle quantum numbers of the two states. Assume the Bohr model to be valid, the time period of the electron in the initial state is eight times that in the final state. What are the possible values of n_1 and n_2 ?

Solution

The time period T of an electron in a Bohr orbit of principal quantum number n is

$$T = \frac{n^3h^3}{4\pi^2k^2Z^2e^4m}$$

Thus, $T \propto n^3$

$$\Rightarrow \quad \frac{T_1}{T_2} = \frac{n_1^3}{n_2^3}$$

As $T_1 = 8T_2$, the above relation gives

$$\left(\frac{n_1}{n_2}\right)^3 = 8$$

$$\Rightarrow \quad n_1 = 2n_2$$

Thus the possible values of n_1 and n_2 are

$n_1 = 2, n_2 = 1;$

$n_1 = 4, n_2 = 2;$

$n_1 = 6, n_2 = 3;$ and so on....

Illustrative Example 1.4

How many times does the electron go round the first Bohr orbit of hydrogen atom in $1s$?

Solution

We know the frequency of revolution of electron is

$$f_n = \frac{v_n}{2\pi r_n}$$

it is the number of revolutions in 1 second, it can be given as for $n = 1$ orbit of hydrogen atom as

$$f_1 = \frac{2.18\times10^6}{2\times3.14\times0.529\times10^{-10}} \text{ sec}^{-1}$$

$$\Rightarrow \quad f_1 = 6.56 \times 10^{15} \text{ sec}^{-1}$$

Illustrative Example 1.5

An electron in the ground state of hydrogen atom is revolving in anticlockwise direction in the circular orbit of radius R as shown in figure-1.8.

(i) Obtain an expression for the orbital magnetic dipole moment of the electron.

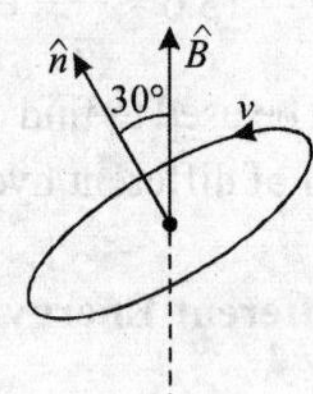

Figure 1.8

(ii) The atom is placed in a uniform magnetic induction B such that the plane normal of the electron orbit makes an angle 30° with the magnetic induction. Find the torque experienced by the orbiting electron.

Solution

(i) According to Bohr's second postulate

$$mvr = n\frac{h}{2\pi} = \frac{h}{2\pi}$$

(As for $n = 1$ first only)

$$\Rightarrow \quad v_1 = \frac{h}{2\pi m r_1} \qquad \ldots(1.31)$$

We know that the rate of flow of charge is current. Hence current in first orbit is

Now from equation-(1.31)

$$i = ev_1 = e\left(\frac{v_1}{2\pi r_1}\right) = \frac{e}{2\pi r_1} \times v_1$$

$$\Rightarrow \quad i = \frac{e}{2\pi r_1} \times \frac{h}{2\pi m r_1} = \frac{eh}{4\pi^2 m r^2} \qquad \ldots(1.32)$$

Magnetic dipole moment,

$$M_1 = i \times A_1$$

$$\Rightarrow \quad M_1 = \frac{eh}{4\pi^2 m r^2} \times \pi r_1^2 = \frac{eh}{4\pi m} \qquad \ldots(1.33)$$

(ii) Torque on the orbiting electron in uniform magnetic field is

$$\vec{\tau} = \vec{M} \times \vec{B}$$

$$\Rightarrow \quad \tau = MB \sin 30°$$

$$\Rightarrow \quad \tau = \frac{eh}{4\pi m} \times \frac{B}{2} = \frac{ehB}{8\pi m}$$

Illustrative Example 1.6

Determine the maximum wavelength that hydrogen in its ground state can absorb. What would be the next smaller wavelength that would work ?

Solution

Maximum wavelength will correspond to the minimum energy transition of an electron. From ground state of hydrogen atom the minimum energy transition is for $n = 1$ to $n = 2$, for which energy released will be

$$\Delta E_{12} = E_2 - E_1$$

$$\Rightarrow \quad \Delta E_{12} = (-3.4\,\text{eV}) - (-13.6\,\text{eV})$$

$$\Rightarrow \quad \Delta E_{12} = 10.2\,\text{eV}$$

Thus 10.2 eV energy is absorbed in the form of a photon, if λ be its wavelength then

$$\frac{hc}{\lambda} = 10.2 \times 1.6 \times 10^{-19}$$

$$\Rightarrow \quad \lambda = \frac{hc}{10.2 \times 1.6 \times 10^{-19}}$$

$$\Rightarrow \quad \lambda = \frac{(6.63 \times 10^{-34}) \times (3 \times 10^{-8})}{10.2 \times 1.6 \times 10^{-19}}$$

$$\Rightarrow \lambda = 1218\,\text{Å}$$

For next smaller wavelength the possibility is for an electron transition from $n = 1$ to $n = 3$, for which the absorbed energy photon required is

$$\Delta E_{13} = E_3 - E_1$$

$$\Rightarrow \quad \Delta E_{13} = (-1.5\,\text{kV}) - (-13.6\,\text{eV})$$

$$\Rightarrow \quad \Delta E_{13} = 12.09\,\text{eV}$$

If λ' be its wavelength then it is given as

$$\frac{hc}{\lambda'} = 12.09\,\text{eV}$$

$$\Rightarrow \quad \lambda' = \frac{(6.63 \times 10^{-34}) \times (3 \times 10^{8})}{12.09 \times 1.6 \times 10^{-19}}$$

$$\Rightarrow \quad \lambda' = 1027.5\,\text{Å}$$

Web Reference at www.physicsgalaxy.com

Age Group - High School Physics | Age 17-19 Years
Section - MODERN PHYSICS
Topic - Atomic Structure
Module Number - 1 to 18

Practice Exercise 1.1

(i) The innermost orbit of the hydrogen atom has a diameter of 1.06 Å. What is the diameter of the tenth orbit ?

[106 Å]

(ii) Which energy state of the triply ionized beryllium (Be^{+++}) has the same electron orbital radius as that of the ground state of hydrogen ? Given Z for beryllium = 4 :

[$n = 2$]

(iii) In Q. (ii), what is the ratio of the energy state of beryllium and that of hydrogen ?

[4]

(iv) The orbital speed of the electron in the ground state of hydrogen is v. What will be its orbital speed when it is excited to the energy state – 3.4 eV ?

[$\frac{v}{2}$]

(v) Which energy state of doubly ionized lithium (Li^{++}) has the same energy as that of the ground state of hydrogen ? Given Z for lithium = 3.

[$n = 3$]

(vi) In the Bohr model of the hydrogen atom, find the ratio of the kinetic energy to the total energy of the electron in a quantum state n ?

[– 1]

(vii) The total energy of the electron in the first excited state of hydrogen is – 3.4 eV. What is the kinetic energy of the electron in this state ?

[+ 3.4 eV]

1.6 Excitation and Ionization of an Atom

According to third postulate of Bohr model we've discussed when some energy is given to an electron of atom from an external source it may make a transition to the upper energy level. This phenomenon we call excitation of electron or atom and the upper energy level to which the electron is excited is called excited state. To excite an electron to a higher state energy can be supplied to it in two ways. Here we'll discuss only the energy supply by an electromagnetic photon. Other method of energy supply we'll discuss later in this chapter.

According to Plank's quantum theory photon is defined as a packet of electromagnetic energy, which when absorbed by a physical particle, its complete electromagnetic energy is converted into the mechanical energy of particle or the particle utilizes the energy of photon in the form of increment in its mechanical energy. When a photon is supplied to an atom and an electron absorbs this photon, then the electron gets excited to a higher energy level only if the photon energy is equal to the difference in energies of the two energy levels involved in the transition.

For example say in hydrogen atom an electron is in ground state (energy $E_1 = -13.6$ eV). Now it absorbs a photon and makes a transition to $n = 3$ state (Energy $E_3 = -1.51$ eV) then the energy of incident photon must be equal to

$$\Delta E_{13} = E_3 - E_1$$

$$\Rightarrow \quad \Delta E_{13} = (-1.51) - (-13.6)\text{ eV}$$

$$\Rightarrow \quad \Delta E_{13} = 12.09\text{ eV}$$

Similarly if we find the difference in energies of state $n = 1$ and $n = 4$, we get

$$\Delta E_{14} = E_4 - E_1$$

$$\Rightarrow \Delta E_{14} = (-0.85) - (-13.6)\text{ eV}$$

$$\Rightarrow \quad \Delta E_{14} = 12.75\text{ eV}$$

Thus when a photon of energy 12.75 eV incidents on a hydrogen atom, the electron may be excited to $n = 4$ level if it absorbs this photon. In the same fashion, the energy of a photon required to excite the electron of a hydrogen atom from ground state ($n = 1$) to next higher level ($n = 2$) which we call first excited state is given as

$$\Delta E_{12} = E_2 - E_1$$

$$\Rightarrow \quad \Delta E_{12} = (-3.4) - (-13.6)\text{ eV}$$

$$\Rightarrow \quad \Delta E_{12} = 10.2\text{ eV}$$

Here we have seen that in the ground state of a hydrogen atom electron can absorbs photons of energies 10.2 eV, 12.09 eV and 12.75 eV to get excited to $n = 2$, $n = 3$ and $n = 4$ levels.

Now we'll see what will happen when a photon of energy equal to 11 eV incident on this atom. From the above calculation of energy differences of different energy levels we can say that if the electron in ground state absorbs this photon it will jump to a state somewhere between energy levels $n = 2$ and $n = 3$ as shown in figure-1.9. When electron in ground state absorbs a photon of 11 eV energy, its total energy becomes

$$E = E_1 + 11$$

$$\Rightarrow \quad E = -13.6 + 11\text{ eV}$$

$$\Rightarrow \quad E = -2.6\text{ eV}$$

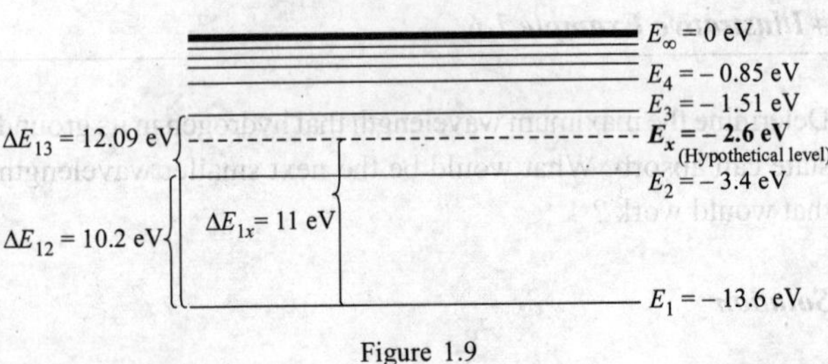

Figure 1.9

As discussed in previous sections, in an atom electron can not take up all energies. It can exist only in some particular energy levels which have energy given as $-13.6/n^2$ e V.

When a photon of energy 11 eV is absorbed by an electron in ground state. The energy of electron becomes -2.6 eV or it will excite to a hypothetical energy level X somewhere between $n = 2$ and $n = 3$ as shown in figure-1.9, which is not permissible for an electron. Thus when in ground state electron can absorb only those photons which have energies equal to the difference in energies of the stable energy levels with ground state. If a photon beam incident on H-atoms having photon energy not equal to the difference of energy levels of H-atoms such as 11 eV, the beam will just be transmitted without any absorption by the H-atoms.

Thus to excite an electron from lower energy level to higher levels by photons, it is necessary that the photon must be of energy equal to the difference in energies of the two energy levels involved in the transition.

As we know that for higher energy levels, energy of electrons is less. When an electron is moved away from the nucleus to ∞^{th} energy level or at $n = \infty$, the energy becomes O or the electron becomes free from the attraction of nucleus or it is removed from the atom. Infect when an electron is in an atom, its total energy is negative $\left(E_n = -\frac{13.6}{n^2}Z^2\right)$. This negative sign shows that electron is under the influence of attractive forces of nucleus. When energy equal in magnitude to the total energy of an electron in a particular energy level is given externally, its total energy becomes zero or we can say that electron gets excited to ∞^{th} energy level or the electron is removed from the atom and atom is said to be ionized.

We know that removal of electron from an atom is called ionization. In other words, ionization is the excitation of an electron to $n = \infty$ level. The energy required to ionize an atom is called ionization energy of atom for the particular energy level from which the electron is removed. In hydrogenic atoms, the ionization energy for n^{th} state can be given as

$$\Delta E_{n\to\infty} = E_\infty - E_n$$

$$\Rightarrow \quad \Delta E_{n\to\infty} = 0 - \left(-\frac{13.6\,Z^2}{n^2}\right)\text{eV}$$

$$\Rightarrow \quad \Delta E_{n\to\infty} = \frac{13.6\,Z^2}{n^2}\text{ eV}$$

1.6.1 Frequency and Wavelength of Emitted Radiation

When an electron absorbs a monochromatic radiation from an external energy source then it makes a transition from a lower energy level to a higher level. But this state of the electron is not a stable one. Electron can remain in this excited state for a very small internal at most of the order of 10^{-8} second. The time period for which this excited state of the electron exists is called the life time of that excited state. After the life time of the excited state the electron must radiate energy and it will jump to the ground state. Say if it was in fifth energy level then it may come to the ground state by following the path as $5 \to 3 \to 1$ or it may follow $5 \to 4 \to 2 \to 1$ or in so many ways, and in each transition it will emit a photon of energy equal to the energy difference of the two corresponding orbits according to Bohr's Third Postulate.

Let us assume that the electron is initially in n_2 state and it will jump to a lower state n_1 then it will emit a photon of energy equal to the energy difference of the two states n_1 and n_2 as

$$\Delta E = E_{n_2} - E_{n_1}$$

Where ΔE is the energy of the emitted photon. Now substituting the values of E_{n_2} and E_{n_1} in above equation, we get

$$\Delta E = -\frac{2\pi^2K^2Z^2e^4m}{n_2^2h^2} + \frac{2\pi^2K^2Z^2e^4m}{n_1^2h^2}$$

$$\Rightarrow \quad \Delta E = \frac{2\pi^2K^2Z^2e^4m}{h^2}\left(\frac{1}{n_1^2} - \frac{1}{n_2^2}\right)$$

$$\Rightarrow \quad \Delta E = 13.6\,Z^2\left(\frac{1}{n_1^2} - \frac{1}{n_2^2}\right)eV \qquad \ldots(1.34)$$

Here $13.6\,Z^2$ can be used as ionization energy for $n = 1$ state for a hydrogenic atom thus the energy of emitted photon can also be written as

$$\Delta E = IP\left(\frac{1}{n_1^2} - \frac{1}{n_2^2}\right) \qquad \ldots(1.35)$$

Equation-(1.34) can also be used to find the energy of emitted radiation when an electron jumps from a higher orbit n_2 to a lower orbit n_1. If λ be the wavelength of the emitted radiation then

$$\Delta E = \frac{hc}{\lambda}$$

This energy can be converted to eV by dividing this energy by the electronic charge e, as if wavelength is given in A, the energy in eV can be given as

$$\Delta E = \frac{hc}{\lambda e}\text{ (in eV)} \qquad \ldots(1.36)$$

Substituting the values of h, c and e we get

$$\Delta E = \frac{(6.63\times10^{-34})\times(3\times10^{8})}{\lambda\times(1.6\times10^{-19})\times10^{-10}}\text{ eV}$$

$$\Rightarrow \quad \Delta E = \frac{12431}{\lambda}\text{ eV} \qquad \ldots(1.37)$$

Here in above equation-(1.37), lambda is in Å units.

This equation is the most important in numerical calculations, as it will be very frequently used. From equation-(1.34) & (1.36) we have

$$\frac{hc}{\lambda} = -13.6\,Z^2\left(\frac{1}{n_1^2} - \frac{1}{n_2^2}\right)eV$$

$$\Rightarrow \quad \frac{1}{\lambda} = -\frac{13.6Z^2}{hc}\left(\frac{1}{n_1^2} - \frac{1}{n_2^2}\right)eV$$

$$\Rightarrow \quad \bar{\nu} = \frac{1}{\lambda} = -RZ^2\left(\frac{1}{n_1^2} - \frac{1}{n_2^2}\right) \qquad \ldots(1.38)$$

(As Rydberg Constant $R = 13.6/hc$ eV)

Here $\bar{\nu}$ is called wave number of the emitted radiation and is defined as number of waves per unit length and the above relation is used to find the wavelength of emitted radiation when an electron makes a transition from higher level n_2 to lower level n_1 is called Rydberg formula. But students are advised to use equation-(1.37) in numerical calculations to find the wavelength of emitted radiation using the energy difference in electron volt. If can be rearranged as

$$\lambda = \frac{12431}{\Delta E(\text{in eV})}\text{ Å} \qquad \ldots(1.39)$$

Above relation you can use directly for fast calculations in numerical problems. For example if we wish to find the wavelength of radiation emitted when an electron makes a transition from $n = 4$ to $n = 1$ in a hydrogen atom, we use the relation in equation-(1.39). As we know the energy released in above transition is

$$\Delta E = E_4 - E_1$$

$$\Rightarrow \quad \Delta E = (-0.85) - (3.6)\text{ eV}$$

$$\Rightarrow \quad \Delta E = 12.75\text{ eV}$$

Thus the wavelength of radiation emitted can be given by equations-(1.39) as

$$\lambda = \frac{12431}{12.75} \text{ Å}$$

$$\Rightarrow \qquad \lambda = 975 \text{ Å}$$

1.6.2 Number of Lines Emitted During, de-excitation of an Atom

When an electron is in some excited state of an atom, after its life time of excitation it will make a transition to lower states and emits electromagnetic radiations which when passed through a spectrometer, different lines are plotted in the corresponding spectrum for each radiation emitted. We know that for an electron in n^{th} state of a hydrogenic atom, it can make a transition to lower states in different possible ways and ultimately it comes back to ground state by following different possible paths. When electron makes transition to lower state then it emits a photon corresponding to each transition until it reaches ground state. Thus from n^{th} state an electron can have $^nC_2$ different possible ways to make a transition before it comes to ground state. Thus for a gas containing several atoms/ions all excited to n^{th} state when start making transition to ground state the number of maximum possible lines obtained in the resulting spectrum are

$$N = {}^nC_2 = \frac{n(n-1)}{2} \qquad \ldots(1.40)$$

When an electron makes a transition from n^{th} state to ground state then the electron during its transition to ground state it will emit a minimum one photon when it will directly transit from $n \to 1$ and will emit maximum $(n-1)$ photon when it will follow the path $n \to (n-1) \to (n-2) \to \ldots\ldots 3 \to 2 \to 1$. Thus maximum number of photons emitted by a single electron from state n are

$$N = n - 1 \qquad \ldots(1.41)$$

1.7 The Hydrogen Spectrum

It is clear that the energy of outer orbits is greater than the energy of inner orbits. When external radiation is given to the hydrogen atom then the electron in ground state jumps to a higher energy state and the atom is called now in excited state. Any excited state is an unstable state and the maximum lifetime of an excited state is of the order of 10^{-8} seconds, and after the lifetime of the excited state the electron jumps to the ground state again directly or indirectly by emitting one or more electromagnetic radiations. It may have so many paths to come to ground state.

When Hydrogen gas is discharged in a discharge tube (at High potential difference of the order of 10^4 volts), the Hydrogen atoms in the discharge tube get excited due to the high potential and there are so many infinite number of atoms in the tube and different atoms are excited to different excited states and when they again jump to their ground state after life time of the excited states, so many radiations are emitted from the discharge tube. These radiation are allowed to pass through the spectrometer and the radiation spectrum of these radiations is obtained on a fluorescent screen. It looks like the photograph shown in figure-1.10.

Figure 1.10

In the above H-spectrum, we can see that there are several group of lines between which there is a blank band in which no wavelength is emitted by *h*-atom. These groups we call spectral series of Hydrogen atom. In next section we'll discuss these spectral series in detail.

1.7.1 Spectral Series of Hydrogen Atom

The wavelength of the lines of every spectral series can be calculated using the formula given by equation-(1.37).

Five spectral series are observed in the Hydrogen Spectrum corresponding to the five energy levels of the Hydrogen atom and these five series are named as on the names of their inventors. These series are

(1) Lyman Series (2) Balmer Series
(3) Paschen Series (4) Brackett Series
(5) Pfund Series

These spectral series are shown in figure-1.11

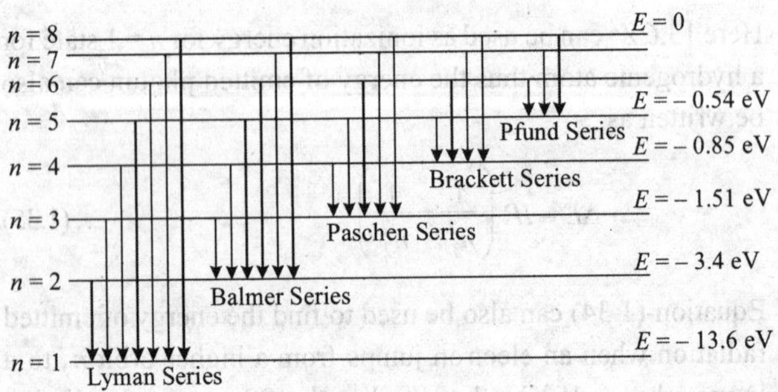

Figure 1.11

(1) Lyman Series : The series consists of wavelengths of the radiations which are emitted when electron jumps from a higher energy level to $n = 1$ orbit. The wavelengths constituting this series lie in the Ultra Violet region of the electromagnetic spectrum.

For Lyman Series

$$n_1 = 1$$

and $$n_2 = 2, 3, 4 \ldots\ldots$$

First line of Lyman series is the line corresponding to the transition $n_2 = 2$ to $n_1 = 1$, similarly second line of the Lyman series is the line corresponding to the transition $n_2 = 3$ to $n_1 = 1$.

(2) Balmer Series : The series consists of wavelengths of the radiations which are emitted when electron jumps from a higher energy level to $n = 2$ orbit. The wavelengths consisting this series lie in the visible region of the electromagnetic spectrum.

(3) Paschen Series : The series consists of wavelengths of the radiations which are emitted when electron jumps from a higher energy level to $n = 3$ orbit. The wavelengths constituting this series lie in the Near Infra Red region of the electromagnetic spectrum.

(4) Brackett Series : The series consists of wavelengths of the radiations which are emitted when electron jumps from a higher energy level to $n = 4$ orbit. The wavelengths constituting this series lie in the Infra Red region of the electromagnetic spectrum.

(5) Pfund Series : The series consists of wavelengths of the radiations which are emitted when electron jumps from a higher energy level to $n = 5$ orbit. The wavelengths constituting this series lie in the Deep Infra Red region of the electromagnetic spectrum.

We can find out the wavelengths corresponding to the first line and the last line for remaining four spectral series as mentioned in the case of Lyman Series.

Lets discuss the transition of electron between different orbits in detail with the help of some examples.

 # Illustrative Example 1.7

The wavelength of the first member of the Balmer series in hydrogen spectrum is 6563 Å. Find the wavelength of first member of Lyman series in the same spectrum.

Solution

For the first member of the Balmer series

$$\bar{v} = \frac{1}{\lambda_1} = R\left[\frac{1}{2^2} - \frac{1}{3^2}\right] = \frac{5}{36}R \qquad \ldots(1.42)$$

For the first member of Lyman series

$$\bar{v} = R\left[\frac{1}{1^2} - \frac{1}{2^2}\right] = \frac{3R}{4} \qquad \ldots(1.43)$$

Dividing equation-(1.42) by equation-(1.43), we get

$$\frac{\lambda_2}{\lambda_1} = \frac{5}{27} \quad \text{or} \quad \lambda_2 = \frac{5}{27}\lambda_1$$

$$\Rightarrow \qquad \lambda_2 = \frac{5 \times 6563}{27} = 1215.37 \text{ Å}$$

 # Illustrative Example 1.8

Find the ratio of ionization energy of Bohr's hydrogen atom and hydrogen-like lithium atom.

Solution

Energy of an electron in ground state of Bohr's hydrogen-like atom is given by,

$$E = -\frac{13.6Z^2}{n^2} \text{ eV}$$

Where Z = atomic number of the atom

The ionization energy of this atom is equal in magnitude to energy of ground state = $E_\infty = 13.6\,Z^2$

$$\Rightarrow \qquad \frac{(E_\infty)_H}{(E_\infty)_{Li}} = \frac{(Z_H)^2}{(Z_{Li})^2}$$

$$\Rightarrow \qquad \frac{(E_\infty)_H}{(E_\infty)_{Li}} = \left(\frac{1}{3}\right)^2 = \frac{1}{9}$$

 # Illustrative Example 1.9

Electrons of energies 10.20 eV and 12.09 eV can cause radiation to be emitted from hydrogen atoms. Calculate in each case, the principal quantum number of the orbit to which electron in the hydrogen atom is raised and the wavelength of the radiation emitted if it drops back to the ground state.

Solution

We know the orbital energy of an electron revolving in n^{th} orbit is given by

$$E_n = -\frac{13.6}{n^2} \text{ eV}$$

Where n is the principal quantum number.

When $n=1\ E_1=-13.6\text{ eV}$

$n=2\ E_2=-3.4\text{ eV}$

$n=3\ E_3=-1.51\text{ eV}$

Here we can see that

$$10.0\text{ eV}=E_2-E_1$$

and $12.09\text{ eV}=E_3-E_1$

Thus by absorbing a radiation photon of 10.2 eV electron will make a transition to n = 2 state and by absorbing 12.09 eV photon electron will make a transition to $n=3$ state. Now after the life time of excited states, the electron in $n=2$ and $n=3$ will make transitions to lower states and ultimately come back to ground state. In this process the possibilities of reverse transition are

$n=3$ to $n=2$

$n=3$ to $n=1$

$n=2$ to $n=1$

In above three transitions the amount of energy released will be

$$\Delta E_{32}=(-1.51\text{ eV})-(-3.4\text{ eV})$$

$$=1.89\text{ eV}$$

$$\Delta E_{31}=(-1.51\text{ eV})-(-13.6\text{ eV})$$

$$=12.09\text{ eV}$$

$$\Delta E_{21}=(-3.4\text{ eV})-(-13.6\text{ eV})$$

$$=10.2\text{ eV}$$

Thus wavelengths of radiations of corresponding transition are

$$\lambda_{32}=\frac{12431}{1.89}=6577.2\text{ Å}$$

$$\lambda_{31}=\frac{12431}{12.09}=1028.2\text{ Å}$$

$$\lambda_{21}=\frac{12431}{10.2}=1218.7\text{ Å}$$

Illustrative Example 1.10

Determine the wavelength of the first Lyman line, the transition from $n=2$ to $n=1$. In what region of the electromagnetic spectrum does this line lie ?

Solution

We know for transition n = 2 to n = 1, the energy released is

$$\Delta E_{21}=E_2-E_1$$

$$\Rightarrow \quad \Delta E_{21}=(-3.4\text{ eV})-(-13.6\text{ eV})$$

$$\Rightarrow \quad \Delta E_{21}=10.2\text{ eV}$$

The wavelength corresponding to this transition can be given as

$$\lambda=\frac{12431}{10.2}=1218.7\text{ Å}$$

This radiations is in ultraviolet region

Illustrative Example 1.11

Hydrogen atom in its ground state is excited by means of monochromatic radiation of wavelength 975 Å. How many different lines are possible in the resulting spectrum? Calculate the longest wavelength amongst them. You may assume the ionization energy for hydrogen atom as 13.6 eV.

Solution

When an electron of hydrogen atom absorbs a wavelength 975 Å. The energy in eV, it absorbs is given by

$$E=\frac{12431}{975}$$

$$\Rightarrow \quad E=12.75\text{ eV}$$

As discussed earlier that 12.75 eV is the energy difference of $n=1$ and $n=4$. Thus electron will make a transition from ground state to $n=4$ orbit. From $n=4$ when electron will start reverse transitions and ultimately comes back to ground state then the number of possible transitions are

$$N={}^nC_2=\frac{n(n-1)}{2}$$

$$\Rightarrow \quad N=\frac{n\times 3}{2}=6$$

These are also shown in figure-1.12

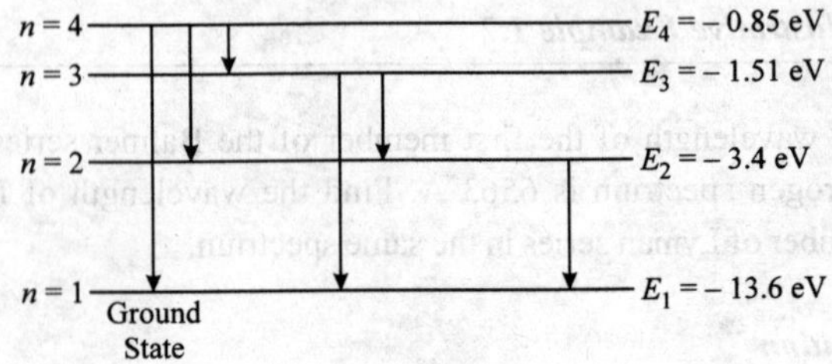

Figure 1.12

Among these six transitions, the longest wavelength will be corresponding to the minimum energy which is released for transition $n = 4$ to $n = 3$, the energy released in this transition is

$$\Delta E_{43} = E_4 - E_3$$

$$\Rightarrow \quad \Delta E_{43} = (-0.85\text{ eV}) - (-1.51\text{ eV})$$

$$\Rightarrow \quad \Delta E_{43} = 0.66\text{ eV}$$

The wavelength corresponding to this energy is

$$\lambda = \frac{12431}{0.66}\text{ Å}$$

$$\Rightarrow \quad \lambda = 18834.8\text{ Å}$$

Illustrative Example 1.12

A hydrogen atom in a state having a binding energy of 0.85 eV makes a transition to a state with excitation energy 10.2 eV.

(i) Find the energy and wavelength of the photon emitted.

(ii) Show the transition on an energy level diagram for hydrogen, indicating quantum numbers.

Solution

(i) Binding energy $= \dfrac{13.6}{n_1^2}$

$$\Rightarrow \quad 0.85\text{ eV} = \frac{13.6}{n_1^2}$$

$$n_1 = 4$$

$$E_{n_1} = -0.85\text{ eV}$$

Suppose the transition takes place to state n_2 for which excitation energy is 10.2 eV. In this case ground state energy + excitation energy $= E_{n_2}$

$$-13.6 + 10.2 = \frac{13.6}{n_2^2}$$

Solving we get $n_2 = 2$ and we have

$$E_{n_2} = -3.4\text{ eV}$$

Energy of photon emitted $= E_{n_1 \to n_2}$

$$= 3.4 - 0.85 = 2.55\text{ eV}$$

Now the wavelength emitted is

$$\lambda = \frac{hc}{E}$$

$$\Rightarrow \quad \lambda = \frac{12431}{2.55}\text{ Å}$$

$$\Rightarrow \quad \lambda = 4875\text{ Å}$$

(ii) Energy level diagram is shown in figure-1.13.

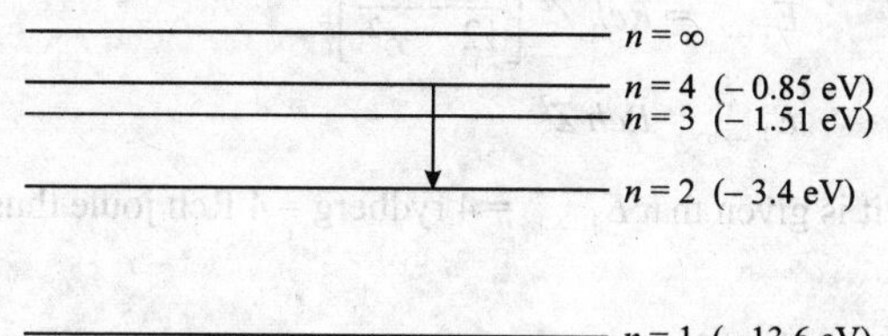

Figure 1.13

Illustrative Example 1.13

Ultraviolet light of wavelength 830 Å and 700 Å when allowed to fall on hydrogen atom in their ground state is found to liberate electrons with kinetic energy 1.8 eV and 4.0 eV respectively. Find the value of Planck's constant.

Solution

We known that

$$E = \frac{hc}{\lambda}$$

For radiation of wavelengths λ_1 and λ_2 having energies E_1 and E_2 respectively, we get

$$E_1 = \frac{hc}{\lambda_1} \text{ and } E_2 = \frac{hc}{\lambda_2}$$

$$\Rightarrow \quad E_1 - E_2 = hc\left(\frac{1}{\lambda_1} - \frac{1}{\lambda_2}\right)$$

$$h = \frac{(E_1 - E_2)\lambda_1\lambda_2}{c(\lambda_2 - \lambda_1)}$$

$$\Rightarrow \quad h = \frac{(4.0-1.8)\times 1.6\times 10^{-19}\times 700\times 10^{-10}\times 800\times 10^{-10}}{(3\times 10^8)\times 100\times 10^{-10}}$$

$$\Rightarrow \quad h = 6.57\times 10^{-34}\text{ J-s}$$

Illustrative Example 1.14

The ionization energy of a hydrogen like Bohr atom is 4 rydberg. (i) What is the wavelength of radiation emitted when the electron jumps from first excited state to the ground state ? (ii) What is the radius of first orbit for this atom ? Given that Bohr radius of hydrogen atom $= 5\times 10^{-11}$ m and 1 rydberg $= 2.2\times 10^{-18}$ J.

Solution

(i) We know that ionization energy of an hydrogen like atom is given as

$$E_{1\to\infty} = Rch\,Z^2\left[\frac{1}{12}-\frac{1}{\infty^2}\right]$$

$$\Rightarrow \quad E_{1\to\infty} = Rch\,Z^2$$

Here it is given that $E_{1\to\infty}$ = 4 rydberg = 4 Rch joule thus, we have

$$Z^2 = 4$$

$$\Rightarrow \quad Z = 2$$

Thus the wavelength emitted when e^- makes a transition from $n = 2$ to $n = 1$ is

$$\frac{1}{\lambda} = RZ^2\left[\frac{1}{12}-\frac{1}{2^2}\right]$$

$$\Rightarrow \quad \frac{1}{\lambda} = 10967800 \times 4 \times \frac{3}{4}$$

$$\Rightarrow \quad \frac{1}{\lambda} = 32903400$$

$$\Rightarrow \quad \lambda = 304 \text{ Å}$$

(ii) Radius of nth orbit of a hydrogenic atom having atomic number Z is given as

$$r_u = 0.529 \times \frac{n^2}{Z} \text{ Å}$$

Here $Z = 2$ and $n = 1$ thus radius of first orbit is

$$r = 0.529 \times \frac{1}{2} \text{ Å}$$

$$\Rightarrow \quad r = 0.2645 \text{ Å}$$

Illustrative Example 1.15

Estimate the average kinetic energy of hydrogen atoms (or molecules) at room temperature and use the result to explain why nearly all H atoms are in the ground state at room temperature and hence emit no light.

Solution

According to kinetic theory the average kinetic energy of atoms or molecules in a gas is given by,

$$\overline{K} = \frac{3}{2}KT$$

$$\Rightarrow \quad \overline{K} = \frac{3}{2} \times 1.38 \times 10^{-23} \times 300$$

$$\Rightarrow \quad \overline{K} = 6.2 \times 10^{-21} \text{ J}$$

or, in electron volt it is given as

$$\overline{K} = \frac{6.2\times10^{-21}}{1.6\times10^{-19}} = 0.04 \text{ eV}$$

The average kinetic energy is thus very small compared to the energy between the ground state and the next higher energy state (13.6 – 3.4 = 10.2 eV). Any atoms in excited state emit light and eventually fall to the ground state. Once in the ground state, collisions with other atoms can transfer energy of 0.04 eV on the average. A small fraction of atoms can have much more energy (in accordance with the distribution of molecular speeds), but even kinetic energy that is 10 times the average is not nearly enough to excite atoms above the ground state. Thus, at room temperature, nearly all atoms are in the ground state. Atoms can be excited to upper states at very high temperatures or by passing current of high energy electrons through the gas, as in a discharge tube.

Illustrative Example 1.16

The emission spectrum of hydrogen atoms has two has two lines of Balmer series with wavelength 4102 Å and 4861 Å. To what series does a spectral line belong if its wave number is equal to the difference of wave numbers of above two lines ? What is the wavelength of this line ? [Take $R = 1.097 \times 10^7$ m^{-1}]

Solution

According to given problem

$$\frac{1}{\lambda_1} = RZ^2\left[\frac{1}{n_1^2}-\frac{1}{n_2^2}\right]$$

$$\Rightarrow \quad \frac{1}{\lambda_2} = RZ^2\left[\frac{1}{2^2}-\frac{1}{n_2^2}\right] \quad \ldots(1.44)$$

and

$$\frac{1}{\lambda_2} = RZ^2\left[\frac{1}{2^2}-\frac{1}{(n_2')^2}\right] \quad \ldots(1.45)$$

$$\Rightarrow \quad \frac{1}{\lambda_1}-\frac{1}{\lambda_2} = \left[\frac{1}{(n_2')^2}-\frac{1}{n_2^2}\right]RZ^2$$

The wave numbers of above radiations are

$$\overline{\nu}_1 = \frac{1}{\lambda_1} \text{ and } \overline{\nu}_2 = \frac{1}{\lambda_2}$$

Thus

$$\overline{\nu}_1 - \overline{\nu}_2 = \left[\frac{1}{\lambda_1}-\frac{1}{\lambda_2}\right]$$

$$\Rightarrow \quad \overline{\nu}_1 - \overline{\nu}_2 = RZ^2\left[\frac{1}{(n_2')^2}-\frac{1}{n_2^2}\right]$$

Let the wave number of the third emitted line will be

$$\overline{\nu} = \overline{\nu}_1 - \overline{\nu}_2$$

$$\Rightarrow \quad \frac{1}{\lambda}=RZ^2\left[\frac{1}{(n_2')^2}-\frac{1}{n_2^2}\right] \quad \ldots(1.46)$$

From equation-(1.44), we have

$$\frac{1}{RZ^2\lambda_1}=\frac{1}{4}-\frac{1}{n_2^2}$$

$$\Rightarrow \quad \frac{1}{n_2^2}=\frac{1}{4}-\frac{1}{RZ^2\lambda_1}$$

$$\Rightarrow \quad \frac{1}{n_2^2}=\frac{1}{4}-\frac{1}{(1.097\times10^7)(1)^2(4102\times10^{-10})}$$

Solving for n_2, we get $n_2=6$

Similarly from equation-(1.45), we have $n_2'=4$

From so, the third line belongs to Brackett series because the transition is from level 6 to level 4

The wavelength is given by equation-(1.46) so

$$\frac{1}{\lambda}=(1.097\times10^7)(1)^2\left[\frac{1}{(4)^2}-\frac{1}{(6)^2}\right]$$

$$\Rightarrow \quad \lambda=2.62\times10^{-6}\text{ m}$$

Illustrative Example 1.17

Two hydrogen-lime atoms *A* and *B* are of different masses, and each atom contains equal number of protons and neutrons. The energy difference between the radiation corresponding to first Balmer lines emitted by *A* and *B* is 5.667 eV. When the atoms *A* and *B*, moving with the same velocity, strikes a heavy target they rebound back with the same velocity. In this process the atom *B* imparts twice the momentum to the target than that *A* imparts. Identify the atoms *A* and *B*.

Solution

The excitation energies corresponding to the first Balmer line ($n=3$ to $n=2$) emitted by *A* and *B* are

$$(\Delta E)_A=-13.6\,Z_A^2\left[\frac{1}{2^2}-\frac{1}{3^2}\right]$$

$$\Rightarrow \quad (\Delta E)_A=-13.6\times\frac{5}{36}\,Z_A^2\text{ eV}$$

$$(\Delta E)_B=-13.6\,Z_B^2\left[\frac{1}{2^2}-\frac{1}{3^2}\right]$$

$$\Rightarrow \quad (\Delta E)_B=-13.6\times\frac{5}{36}\,Z_B^2\text{ eV}$$

$$\Delta E=(\Delta E)_B-(\Delta E)_A$$

$$\Rightarrow \quad \Delta E=13.6\times\frac{5}{36}\,[Z_A^2-Z_B^2]$$

$$\Rightarrow \quad 5.667=13.6\times\frac{5}{36}\,[Z_A^2-Z_B^2]$$

(Given that $\Delta E=5.667$ eV)

$$\Rightarrow \quad Z_A^2-Z_B^2=3 \quad \ldots(1.47)$$

Applying the law of conservation of momentum, we have, if *P* is the momentum imparted to target

$$m_A v=P-m_A v_1$$

and $$m_B v=2P-m_B v_1$$

Here $m_A=2Z_A$ and $m_B=2Z_B$ as they contain equal number of neutrons and protons. Hence

$$2Z_A v=P-2Z_A v_1$$

and $$2Z_B v=2P-2Z_B v_1$$

$$\Rightarrow \quad 2Z_A(v+v_1)=P \quad \ldots(1.48)$$

$$\text{and } 2Z_B(v+v_1)=2P \quad \ldots(1.49)$$

Dividing equation-(1.48) and (1.49), we get

$$\frac{Z_A}{Z_B}=2 \quad \text{or} \quad Z_A=2Z_B \quad \ldots(1.50)$$

Substituting the value of Z_A in equation-(1.47), we get

$$4Z_B^2-Z_B^2=3 \quad \text{or} \quad Z_B=1 \quad \ldots(1.51)$$

From equation-(1.50),

$$Z_A=2Z_B=2 \quad \ldots(1.52)$$

Hence atoms *A* and *B* are $_1H^2$ (deuterium) and $_2He^4$ (helium) respectively.

Illustrative Example 1.18

A hydrogen-like atom of atomic number *Z* is in an excited state of quantum number 2*n*. It can emit a maximum energy photon of 204 eV. If it makes a transition to quantum state *n*, a photon of energy 40.8 eV is emitted. Find *n*, *Z* and the ground state energy (in eV) for this atom. Also, calculate the minimum energy (in eV) that can be emitted by this atom during de-excitation. Ground state energy of hydrogen atom is –13.6 eV.

Solution

The energy levels of a hydrogen like atom are governed by

$$E_n=-\frac{Z^2Rch}{n^2}=-(13.6\text{ eV})\frac{Z^2}{n^2} \quad \ldots(1.53)$$

The energy of emitted photon corresponding to transition

$n = n_2$ to $n = n_1$ with $n_2 > n_1$ is given by

$$E_{n_2 \to n_1} = -(13.6\text{ eV})Z^2\left(\frac{1}{n_2^2}-\frac{1}{n_1^2}\right) \quad \ldots(1.54)$$

If $n_2 = 2$ n, the energy of the emitted photon will be maximum for transition $n_2 = 2$ n to $n_1 = 1$. Thus

$$E_{max} = -(13.6\text{ eV})Z^2\left(\frac{1}{(2n)^2}-\frac{1}{1^2}\right)$$

$$\Rightarrow \quad E_{max} = -(13.6\text{ eV})Z^2\left(\frac{1}{4n^2}-1\right)$$

Given that $E_{max} = 204$ eV, we use

$$204\text{ eV} = -(13.6\text{ eV})Z^2\left(\frac{1}{4n^2}-1\right) \quad \ldots(1.55)$$

for the transition $n_2 = 2$ n to $n_1 = n$, we have

$$E_{2n \to n} = -(13.6\text{ eV})Z^2\left(\frac{1}{4n^2}-\frac{1}{n^2}\right)$$

Given that $E_{2n \to n} = 40.8$ eV, we use

$$40.8\text{ eV} = -(13.6\text{ eV})Z^2\left(\frac{1}{4n^2}-\frac{1}{n^2}\right) \quad \ldots(1.56)$$

Dividing (1.55) by (1.56), we get

$$\frac{204}{40.8} = \frac{\left(\frac{1}{4n^2}-1\right)}{\left(\frac{1}{4n^2}-\frac{1}{n^2}\right)}$$

$$\Rightarrow \quad 5 = \frac{1-4n^2}{1-4}$$

Which gives $4n^2 = 16$ or $n = 2$. Using this value of n in either (1.55) or (1.56) we get $Z^2 = 16$ or $Z = 4$

The ground state energy of the atom corresponds to state $n = 1$. Putting $n = 1$ and $Z = 4$ in equation-(1.53), the ground state energy of the atom is

$$E_1 = -(13.6\text{ eV}) \times \frac{(4)^2}{(1)^2} = -217.6\text{ eV}$$

Since $n = 2$, the given excited atom has $n_2 = 2n = 4$

It will emit a photon of minimum energy for a transition $n_2 = 4$ to $n_1 = 3$. Using these values in (1.54), we have

$$E_{min} = (-13.6\text{ eV})(4)^2\left(\frac{1}{4^2}-\frac{1}{3^2}\right)$$

$$= 10.58\text{ eV}$$

Illustrative Example 1.19

A single electron orbits a stationary nucleus of charge + Ze, where Z is a constant and e is the magnitude of electronic charge. It requires 47.2 eV to excite the electron from the second Bohr orbit to third Bohr orbit. Find

(i) The value of Z

(ii) The energy required to excite the electron from the third to the fourth Bohr orbit.

(iii) The wavelength of electromagnetic radiation required to remove the electron from first Bohr orbit to infinity.

(iv) The kinetic energy, potential energy and the angular momentum to the electron in first Bohr orbit.

(v) The radius of the first Bohr orbit.

(The horizontal energy of hydrogen atom = 13.6 eV, Bohr radius = 5.3×10^{-11} m, velocity of light = 3×10^8 m/s, Planck's constant = 6.6×10^{-34} J.s)

Solution

The energy required to excite the electron from n_1 to n_2 orbit revolving round the nucleus with charge + Ze is given by

$$\Rightarrow \quad E_{n_2} - E_{n_1} = 13.6\,Z^2\left[\frac{1}{n_1^2}-\frac{1}{n_2^2}\right]\text{ eV}$$

(i) According to the given problem, 47.2 eV energy is required to excite the electron from $n_1 = 2$ to $n_2 = 3$ orbit. Hence

$$47.2 = Z^2 \times 13.6\left[\frac{1}{2^2}-\frac{1}{3^2}\right]$$

$$\Rightarrow \quad Z^2 = \frac{47.2 \times 36}{13.6 \times 5} = 25$$

$$\Rightarrow \quad Z = 5$$

(ii) The energy required to excite the electron from $n_1 = 3$ to $n_2 = 4$ orbit is given by

$$E_4 - E_3 = 25 \times 13.6 \times \left[\frac{1}{3^2}-\frac{1}{4^2}\right]$$

$$\Rightarrow \quad E_4 - E_3 = \frac{25 \times 13.6 \times 7}{144} = 16.53\text{ eV}$$

(iii) The energy required to remove the electron from the first Bohr orbit to infinity (∞) is given by

$$E_\infty - E_1 = 13.6 \times Z^2\left[\frac{1}{1^2}-\frac{1}{\infty^2}\right]$$

$$\Rightarrow \quad E_\infty - E_1 = 13.6 \times 25\text{ eV}$$

In order to calculate the wavelength of radiation, we use

$$\lambda = \frac{12431}{13.6 \times 25} \text{ Å}$$

$$\Rightarrow \quad \lambda = 36.561 \text{ Å}$$

(iv) We know for a given orbit for an electron

$$\text{Total energy} = \text{Kinetic energy} = \frac{1}{2} \text{ Potential energy}$$

For $n = 1$

Total energy in n^{th} orbit is

$$E_n = -\frac{13.6Z^2}{h^2} \text{ eV}$$

Here $Z = 5$ and $n = 1$, thus

$$E_1 = -13.6 \times 25 \text{ eV}$$

$$\Rightarrow \quad E_1 = -340 \text{ eV}$$

Thus kinetic energy in first orbit is

$$K_1 = +340 \text{ eV}$$

and potential energy in first orbit is

$$P_1 = 2 \times E_1$$

$$\Rightarrow \quad P_1 = -680 \text{ eV}$$

Angular momentum of electron is

$$mv_1 r_1 = \frac{h}{2\pi}$$

$$\Rightarrow \quad mv_1 r_1 = \frac{6.63 \times 10^{-34}}{2 \times 3.14}$$

$$\Rightarrow \quad mv_1 r_1 = 1.055 \times 10^{-34} \text{ J-s}$$

(v) Radius of first Bohr orbit is given as

$$r_1 = 0.529 \times \frac{n^2}{Z} \text{ Å}$$

$$\Rightarrow \quad r_1 = 0.529 \times \frac{1}{5} \text{ Å}$$

$$\Rightarrow \quad r_1 = 0.1058 \text{ Å}$$

 # Illustrative Example 1.20

A gas of identical hydrogen like atoms has some atoms in the lowest (ground) energy level *A* and some atoms in a particular upper (excited) energy level *B* and there are no atoms in any other energy level. The atoms of the gas make transition to higher energy level by absorbing monochromatic light of photon 2.7 eV. Subsequently, the atoms emit radiation of only six different photons energies. Some of the emitted photons have energy 2.7 eV, some have energy more and some have less than 2.7 eV.

(i) Find the principal quantum number of the initially excited level *B*.

(ii) Find the ionization energy for the gas atoms.

(iii) Find the maximum and the minimum energies of the emitted photons.

Solution

(i) Figure-1.14 shows the energy level *A* and *B* of hydrogen like atom. When light of photon energy 2.7 eV is absorbed, the electrons go to excited state. Now the atom emits six different photons such that six different transitions are possible. This is only possible when the excited state corresponds to quantum number four. So the principal quantum number n_B of state *B* must lie between 1 and 4. So either $n_B = 2$ or $n_B = 3$. Given that the atoms of the gas make transition to higher energy levels by absorbing monochromatic light of photon 2.7 eV. If $n_B = 3$, there will be no subsequent radiations with energy less than 2.7 eV. But radiations with energy less than 2.7 eV are possible. This is possible when $n_B = 2$

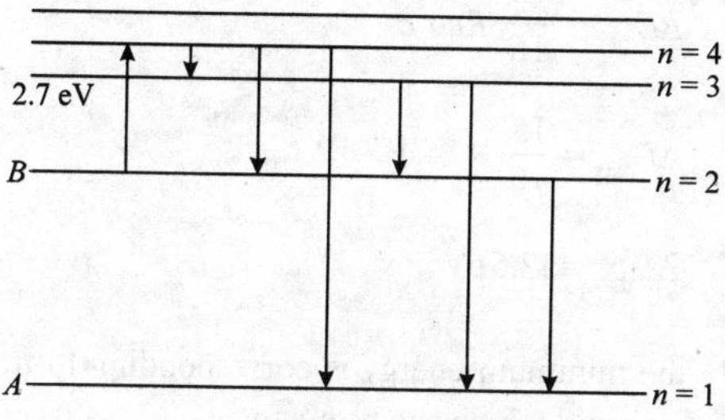

Figure 1.14

Let *Z* be the charge on the nucleus of hydrogen like atom, then

$$E_n = -Rch \frac{Z^2}{n^2}$$

Now for $n = 2$

$$E_2 = -\frac{Rch\, Z^2}{4}$$

and for $n = 4$

$$E_4 = -\frac{Rch\, Z^2}{16}$$

Thus energy released when electron makes a transition from $n = 4$ to $n = 2$ is

$$\Rightarrow \quad E_4 - E_2 = \left(-\frac{Rch\, Z^2}{16}\right) - \left(-\frac{Rch\, Z^2}{4}\right)$$

$$\Rightarrow \quad E_4 - E_2 = Rch\,Z^2\left[\frac{1}{4}-\frac{1}{16}\right]$$

$$\Rightarrow \quad E_4 - E_2 = \frac{3}{16}RchZ^2$$

Further $\quad 2.7\,\text{eV} = \frac{3}{16}RchZ^2$

(As $E_4 - E_2 = 2.7$ eV Given)

$$\Rightarrow \quad Rch\,Z^2 = 14.4\,\text{eV}$$

(ii) Thus ionization energy of atom is

$$E_{1\to\infty} = RchZ^2 = 14.4\,\text{eV}$$

(iii) When electron makes a transition from $n = 4$ then maximum energy is corresponding to transition from $n = 4$ to $n = 1$ which can be given as

$$\Delta E_{max} = \Delta E_{41} = Rch\,Z^2\left[\frac{1}{1^2}-\frac{1}{4^2}\right]$$

$$\Rightarrow \quad \Delta E_{max} = Rch\,Z^2\left[1-\frac{1}{16}\right]$$

$$\Rightarrow \quad \Delta E_{max} = \frac{15}{16}Rch\,Z^2$$

$$\Rightarrow \quad \Delta E_{max} = \frac{15}{16}\times 14.4$$

$$\Rightarrow \quad \Delta E_{max} = 13.5\,\text{eV}$$

Similarly the minimum energy is corresponding to transition from $n = 4$ to $n = 3$ which can be given as

$$\Delta E_{min} = \Delta E_{43} = Rch\,Z^2\left[\frac{1}{3^2}-\frac{1}{4^2}\right]$$

$$\Rightarrow \quad \Delta E_{min} = Rch\,Z^2\left[\frac{1}{9}-\frac{1}{16}\right]$$

$$\Rightarrow \quad \Delta E_{min} = \frac{7}{144}\times 14.4\,\text{eV}$$

$$\Rightarrow \quad \Delta E_{min} = 0.7\,\text{eV}$$

Web Reference at www.physicsgalaxy.com

Age Group - High School Physics | Age 17-19 Years

Section - MODERN PHYSICS

Topic - Atomic Structure

Module Number - 19 to 36

Practice Exercise 1.2

(i) Find the ratio of minimum to maximum wavelength of radiation emitted by electron in ground state of Bohr's hydrogen atom.

[3/4]

(ii) Determine the wavelength of light emitted when a hydrogen atom makes a transition from $n = 6$ to $n = 2$ energy level according to the Bohr model.

[4113.2 Å]

(iii) A double ionized Lithium atom is hydrogen-like with atomic number 3 :

(a) Find the wavelength of the radiation required to excite the electron in Li^{++} from the first to the third Bohr orbit. (Ionization energy of hydrogen atom equals 13.6 eV).

(b) How many spectral lines are observed in the emission spectrum of the above excited system.

[114.26 Å, 3]

(iv) An energy of 68.0 eV is required to excite a hydrogen like atom from its second Bohr orbit to the third. The nuclear charge is *Ze*. Find the value of *Z*, the kinetic energy of the electron in the first Bohr orbit and the wavelength of the electromagnetic radiation required to eject the electron from the first Bohr orbit to infinity.

[$Z = 6$, 489.6 eV, 25.39 Å.]

(v) The wavelength of the first line of Lyman series for hydrogen is identical to that of the second line of Balmer series for some hydrogen-like ion *X*. Calculate energies of the four levels of *X*. Also find its ionization potential (Given : Ground state binding energy of hydrogen atom 13.6 eV).

[– 54.4 eV, – 13.6 eV, – 6.04 eV, – 3.4 eV, 54.4 eV]

(vi) In hydrogen like atom (atomic number Z) is in a higher excited state of quantum number *n*. This excited atom can make a transition to first excited state by emitting photons of energies 10.20 eV and 17.00 eV respectively. Alternatively the atom from the same excited state can make a transition to the second excited state by successively emitting two photons of energies 4.25 eV and 5.95 eV respectively. Determine values of *n* and *Z*, (ionization energy of hydrogen atom = 13.6 eV).

[$n = 6$, $Z = 3$]

(vii) A gas of hydrogen like ions is prepared in such a way that ions are only in the ground state and the first excited state. A monochromatic light of wavelength 1218 Å is absorbed by the ions. The ions are lifted to higher excited states and emit radiation of six wavelength, some higher and some lower than the incident wavelength. Find the principal quantum number of all the excited state. Identify he nuclear charge on the ions. Calculate the values of the maximum and minimum wavelengths.

[$Z = 2$, 4708.71 Å, 243.74 Å]

1.8 Effect of Mass of Nucleus on Bohr Model

Upto this level we've discussed about the structure of a hydrogenic atom by considering nucleus at rest and electron revolving around the nucleus. In fact we know that as no external force is acting on a nucleus electron system, hence the centre of mass of the nucleus electron system must remains at rest. Theoretically mass of electron is negligible or small compared to that of nucleus and due to this we assume that centre of mass of the atom is almost situated at nucleus that's why in Bohr atomic model it was assumed that in an atom, nucleus remains at rest and electron revolves around it. But practically the situation is a bit different. Actually centre of mass of nucleus electron system is close to nucleus as it is heavy and to keep centre of mass at rest, both electron and nucleus revolve around their centre of mass like a double star system as shown in figure-1.15. If r is the distance of electron from nucleus, the distances of nucleus and electron from centre of mass r_1 and r_2 can be given as

$$r_1 = \frac{m_e r}{m_N + m_e}$$

and $$r_2 = \frac{m_N r}{m_N + m_e}$$

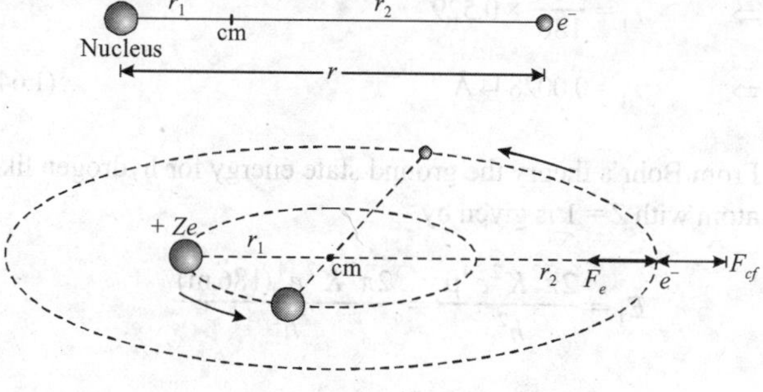

Figure 1.15

Now we can see that in the atom, nucleus and electron revolve around their centre of mass in concentric circles of radii r_1 and r_2 to keep centre of mass at rest. In above system we can analyze the motion of electron with respect to nucleus by assuming nucleus to be at rest and the mass of electron replaced by its reduced mass μ_e, given as

$$\mu_e = \frac{m_N m_e}{m_N + m_e}$$

Now the relative picture of atom will be same what we've considered earlier as shown in figure-1.16 but electron mass is replaced by its reduced mass.

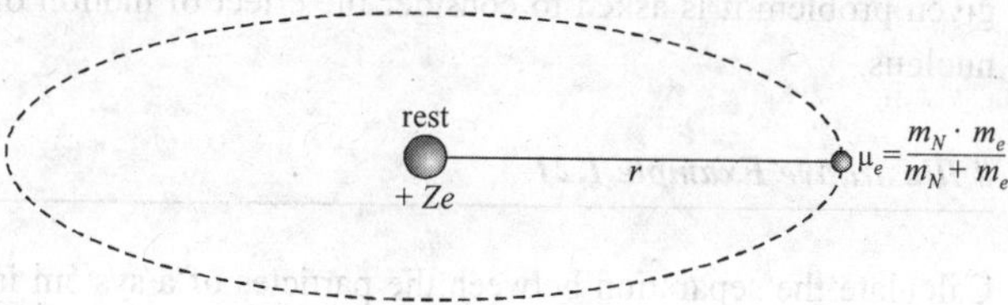

Figure 1.16

Now we can use all those relations which we've derived for Bohr model just by replacing m_e by μ_e. Such as the radius of electron in n^{th} orbit of Bohr's model is given as

$$r_n = \frac{n^2 h^2}{4\pi^2 KZe^2 m_e} \quad \dots(1.57)$$

But if we consider the motion of nucleus into account, the radius of nth orbit will be given as

$$r'_n = \frac{n^2 h^2}{4\pi^2 KZe^2 \mu_e}$$

$$\Rightarrow \quad r'_n = \frac{n^2 h^2 (m_N + m_e)}{4\pi^2 KZe^2 m_e m_N} \quad \dots(1.58)$$

$$\Rightarrow \quad r'_n = r_n \times \frac{m_e}{\mu_e} \quad \dots(1.59)$$

Similarly if we find the speed of electron in n^{th} Bohr orbit, it can be given by equation-1.14 as

$$v_n = \frac{2\pi KZe^2}{nh} \quad \dots(1.60)$$

Here we can see that in the above expression of speed no term of m_e (mass of electron) is present, hence it does not depend on electron mass, no change will be these in speed of revolution if we consider the motion of nucleus into account.

Similarly we know the expression of energy of electron in nth orbit of Bohr model is given as

$$E_n = -\frac{2\pi^2 K^2 Z^2 e^4 m_e}{n^2 h^2} \quad \dots(1.61)$$

Taking the motion of nucleus into account the expression of energy become

$$E'_n = -\frac{2\pi^2 K^2 Z^2 e^4 \mu_e}{n^2 h^2}$$

$$\Rightarrow \quad E'_n = -\frac{2\pi^2 K^2 Z^2 e^4 m_N m_e}{n^2 h^2 (m_N + m_e)} \quad \dots(1.62)$$

$$\Rightarrow \quad E'_n = E_n \times \frac{\mu_e}{m_e} \quad \dots(1.63)$$

Thus we can say that the energy of electron will be slightly less compared to what we've derived earlier. But for numerical calculations this small change can be neglected unless in a given problem it is asked to consider the effect of motion of nucleus.

Illustrative Example 1.21

Calculate the separation between the particles of a system in the ground state, the corresponding binding energy and wavelength of first line in Lyman series of such a system is positronium consisting of an electron and positron revolving round their common centre.

Solution

The reduced mass of the system (electron and positron) is given by

$$\mu = \frac{m.m}{m+m} = \frac{m}{2}$$

Where m = mass of electron or positron.

The radius of first Bohr's orbit is given by

$$r_1 = \frac{h^2}{4\pi^2 Ke^2(m/2)}$$

$\Rightarrow$ $r_1 = 2 \times$ radius of first Bohr's orbit of hydrogen

$\Rightarrow$ $r_1 = 2 \times 0.529$ Å

$\Rightarrow$ $r_1 = 1.058$ Å

Energy of first Bohr's orbit is given as

$$E_1 = \frac{2\pi^2 K^2 Z^2 e^4 (m/2)}{h^2}$$

$\Rightarrow$ $E_1 = -\frac{1}{2} \times$ ground state energy of hydrogen

$\Rightarrow$ $E_1 = -\frac{1}{2} \times 13.6$ eV

$\Rightarrow$ $E_1 = -6.8$ eV (Binding energy)

The wavelength of Lyman series is given by

$$\frac{1}{\lambda} = R_\mu \left[\frac{1}{1^2} - \frac{1}{n^2}\right] = R_\mu \left(\frac{1}{1^2} - \frac{1}{2^2}\right)$$

$$\Rightarrow \quad \lambda = \frac{4}{3R_\mu}$$

$$\Rightarrow \quad R_\mu = \frac{2\pi^2 K^2 e^4 \mu}{3} = \frac{R}{m_e}\mu = \frac{1}{2}R$$

$$\Rightarrow \quad \lambda = 10967800 \times \frac{1}{2} = 5483900 \text{ m}^{-1}$$

$$\Rightarrow \quad \lambda = \frac{4}{3 \times 5483900} \text{ m}$$

$$\Rightarrow \quad \lambda = 2430 \text{ Å}$$

Illustrative Example 1.22

A μ meson (charge – e, mass = 207 m, where m is the mass of electron) can be captured by a proton to form a hydrogen like 'mesic' atom. Calculate the radius of the first Bohr orbit, the binding energy and the wavelength of the first line in the Lyman series for such an atom. The mass of the proton is 1836 times the mass of the electron. The radius of first Bohr orbit and the binding energy of hydrogen are 0.529 Å and 13.6 eV respectively. Take $R = 109678 \text{ cm}^{-1}$.

Solution

The reduced mass of the system is given by

$$\mu = \frac{(207m)(1836m)}{(207m + 1836m)} = 186 \text{ m}$$

The radius of first orbit is given by

$$r_1 = \frac{h^2}{4\pi^2 Ke^2 (186 \text{ m})}$$

$\Rightarrow$ $r_1 = \frac{1}{186} \times$ radius of first Bohr orbit of hydrogen atom

$$\Rightarrow \quad r_1 = \frac{1}{186} \times 0.529$$

$$\Rightarrow \quad r_1 = 0.002844 \text{ Å} \qquad \ldots(1.64)$$

From Bohr's theory the ground state energy for hydrogen like atom with $Z = 1$ is given by

$$E_1 = \frac{2\pi^2 K^2 e^4 \mu}{h^2} = \frac{2\pi^2 K^2 e^4 (186 \text{ m})}{h^2}$$

$$\Rightarrow \quad E_1 = -186 \times 13.6 \text{ eV}$$

$$\Rightarrow \quad E_1 = -2530 \text{ eV} \qquad \ldots(1.65)$$

Hence the binding energy is 2530 eV

The wavelength of the Lyman lines are given by

$$\frac{1}{\lambda} = R_\mu \left(\frac{1}{1^2} - \frac{1}{n^2}\right)$$

$$n = 2, 3, 4, \ldots$$

Where R_μ = Rydberg constant for mesic atom.

For first line $\frac{1}{\lambda} = R_\mu\left(\frac{1}{1^2}-\frac{1}{2^2}\right)$

$$\Rightarrow \quad \lambda = \frac{4}{3R_\mu} \quad \ldots(1.66)$$

Now, $$R_\mu = \frac{2\pi^2K^2e^4\mu}{ch^3} = R\frac{\mu}{m}$$

$$\Rightarrow \quad = 186\,R$$

$$\Rightarrow \quad = 186\times 10967800\,\text{m}^{-1}$$

Substituting the value of R_μ in equation-(1.66), we get

$$\lambda = \frac{4}{3\times 186\times 109678}\,\text{m}$$

$$\Rightarrow \quad \lambda = 653.6\,\text{Å}$$

 # Illustrative Example 1.23

A particle of charge equal to that of an electron, – e, and mass 208 times the mass of electron (called a μ-meson) moves in a circular orbit around a nucleus of charge + 3e. (Take the mass of the nucleus to be infinite). Assuming that Bohr model of the atom is applicable to this system.

(i) Derive an expression for the radius of the nth Bohr orbit.

(ii) Find the value of n for which the radius of the orbit is approximately the same as that of the first Bohr orbit for the hydrogen atom.

(iii) Find the wavelength of the radiation emitted when the μ-meson jumps from the third orbit to the first orbit. (Rydberg's constant = 10967800 m.)

Solution

(i) We have the radius of nth orbit of a hydrogen atom as

$$r_n = \frac{n^2h^2}{4\pi^2Kze^2m}$$

If electron is replaced by a heavy particle of mass 20 times that of electron then the radius is given as

$$r_n = \frac{n^2h^2}{4\pi^2K(3)e^2(208\,m)}$$

$$\Rightarrow \quad r_n = \frac{n^2h^2}{2496\pi^2Kze^2m} \quad \ldots(1.67)$$

Here we have not used reduced mass because it is given that mass of nucleus is assumed to be infinite and here we take $z = 3$.

(ii) The radius of first Bohr orbit is given as

$$r_1 = \frac{h^2}{4\pi^2Ke^2m}$$

From equation-(1.67), we have

$$\frac{n^2h^2}{2496\pi^2Ke^2m} = \frac{h^2}{4\pi^2Ke^2m}$$

$$\Rightarrow \quad n^2 = 624$$

$$\Rightarrow \quad n \simeq 25$$

(iii) Rydberg constant for hydrogenic atoms is

$$R = \frac{2\pi^2K^2e^4m}{ch^3}$$

Now when electron is replaced by μ-meson, rydberg constant will change as

$$R' = \frac{2\pi^2K^2e^4(208\,m)}{ch^3}$$

$$\Rightarrow \quad R' = 208\,R = 208\times 10967800\,\text{m}^{-1}$$

Now the wavelength λ of the radiation emitted when μ-meson makes a transition from $n_2 = 3$ to $n = 1$ is

$$\frac{1}{\lambda} = R'Z^2\left[\frac{1}{n_1^2}-\frac{1}{n_2^2}\right]$$

$$\Rightarrow \quad \frac{1}{\lambda} = R'(3)\left[\frac{1}{1^2}-\frac{1}{3^2}\right]$$

$$\Rightarrow \quad \frac{1}{\lambda} = 8\,R'$$

$$\Rightarrow \quad \lambda = \frac{1}{8R'}$$

$$\Rightarrow \quad \lambda = \frac{1}{8\times 208\times 10967800}\,\text{m}^{-1}$$

$$\Rightarrow \quad \lambda = 0.548\,\text{Å}$$

 # Illustrative Example 1.24

A pi-meson hydrogen atom in a bound state of negatively charged pion (denoted by π^-, $m_\pi = 273\,m_e$) and a proton. Estimate the number of revolutions a π-meson make (averagely) in the ground state of the atom before it decay (mean life of a π-meson $\cong 10^{-8}$ sec). (mass of proton = 1.67×10^{-27} kg).

Solution

The frequency of revolution of an electron in hydrogen atom in first orbit is given by

$$f_1 = \frac{4\pi^2K^2e^4m}{h^3}$$

Here in case of a π meson the mass of electron is replaced by the reduced mass as

$$\mu = \frac{m_p(273\ m)}{m_p + 273\ m}$$

Thus the frequency of revolution of π meson will become

$$f_1 = \frac{4\pi^2 Ke^4 m_p(273\ m)}{h^3(m_p + 273\ m)}$$

$$\Rightarrow \quad f_1 = \frac{\begin{matrix}4\times(3.14)^2\times 9\times10^9(1.6\times10^{-19})^4\\ \times(1.67\times10^{-27})(273\times9.1\times10^{-31})\end{matrix}}{\begin{matrix}(6.63\times10^{-34})^3\\(1.67\times10^{-27}+273\times9.1\times10^{-31})\end{matrix}}$$

$$\Rightarrow \quad f_1 = 1.77\times10^{18}\ \text{sec}^{-1}$$

Thus in the life two of π meson 10^{-8} sec, number of revolutions made by it is given as

$$N = f_1 \times \Delta t$$

$$\Rightarrow \quad N = 1.77\times10^{18}\times10^{-8}$$

$$\Rightarrow \quad N = 1.77\times10^{10}\ \text{revolutions}$$

Illustrative Example 1.25

Taking into account the motion of the nucleus of a hydrogen atom, find the expressions for the electron's binding energy in the ground state and for the Rydberg constant. How much (in percent) do the binding energy and the Rydberg constant, obtained without taking into account the motion of the nucleus, differ from the more accurate corresponding value of these quantities ?

Solution

If mass of nucleus is considered (not infinity) then the reduced mass of nucleus electron system can be taken as

$$\mu = \frac{mM}{m+M}$$

Here m is mass of electron and M is that of nucleus. The binding energy in ground state of hydrogen atom can now be given as

$$E = +\frac{2\pi^2K^2e^4\mu}{h^2}$$

$$\Rightarrow \quad E = 13.6\times\frac{\mu}{m}\ \text{eV}$$

$$\Rightarrow \quad E = \frac{13.6M}{m+M}\ \text{eV}$$

We've hydrogen atom Rydberg constant is given as

$$R = \frac{2\pi^2K^2e^4m}{ch^3}$$

If effect of mass of nucleus is considered the new value of Rydberg constant can be given as

$$R_\mu = \frac{2\pi^2K^2e^4\mu}{ch^3}$$

$$\Rightarrow \quad R_\mu = \frac{RM}{m+M}$$

Percentage difference in the values of R and R_μ is given as

$$\frac{\Delta R}{R} = \frac{R_\mu - R\times100}{R_\mu}$$

$$\Rightarrow \quad \frac{\Delta R}{R} = \frac{m}{M}\times100 \simeq 0.055\%$$

Illustrative Example 1.26

Calculate the difference between the ionization potentials of atomic hydrogen and atomic deuterium.

Solution

The ionization energy for a hydrogenic atom can be given as energy required to excite electron from $n_1 = 1$ to $n_2 = \infty$ given as

$$E = Rch\left[\frac{1}{n_1^2} - \frac{1}{n_2^2}\right]$$

$$\Rightarrow \quad E = Rch\left[\frac{1}{1^2} - \frac{1}{\infty^2}\right]$$

$$\Rightarrow \quad E = Rch\ \text{Joule}$$

If motion of nucleus is considered then the value of Rydberg constant can be given as

$$R = \frac{2\pi^2K^2e^4}{ch^3}\left(\frac{mM_H}{m+M_H}\right)$$

Thus the ionization energy of hydrogen and deuterium atoms can be given as

$$E_H = \frac{2\pi^2K^2e^4}{h^2}\left(\frac{mM_H}{m+M_H}\right) \quad (\text{Here } M_H = 1840\ \text{m})$$

and

$$E_D = \frac{2\pi^2K^2e^4}{h^2}\left(\frac{mM_D}{m+M_D}\right) \quad (\text{Here } M_D = 3680\ \text{m})$$

The difference of E_D & E_H is

$$\Delta E_{1P} = E_D - E_H$$

$$\Rightarrow \quad \Delta E_{1P} = \frac{2\pi^2K^2e^4}{h^2}\left[\frac{mM_D}{m+M_D} - \frac{mM_H}{m+M_H}\right]$$

$$\Rightarrow \quad = \frac{2\pi^2 K^2 e^4}{h^2}\left[\frac{3680}{3681} - \frac{1840}{1841}\right]$$

$$\Rightarrow \quad = 5.88 \times 10^{22}\ \text{J}$$

$$\Rightarrow \quad = 6.68 \times 10^{-3}\ \text{eV}$$

Illustrative Example 1.27

A muon is an unstable elementary particle whose mass is 207 m_e and whose charge is either $+e$ or $-e$. A negative muon (μ^-) can be captured by a nucleus to form a muonic atom. Suppose a proton captures a negative muon (μ^-), find the radius of first Bohr orbit and the ionization energy of the atom. (Take mass of proton $m_p = 1836\ m_e$, where m_e is mass of electron).

Solution

Reduced mass of a system of two particles is given by

$$\mu = \frac{mM}{m+M} = \frac{(207\ m_e)(1836\ m_e)}{(207\ m_e)+(1836\ m_e)} = 186\ m_e$$

Radius corresponding to the reduced mass μ is given by

$$r'_1 = \left(\frac{m}{\mu}\right) r_1 = \left(\frac{m_e}{186 m_e}\right) a_0 = 2.85 \times 10^{-13}\ \text{m}$$

Where a_0 is the radius of first Bohr orbit of ordinary hydrogen atom.

$$a_0 = 5.29 \times 10^{-11}\ \text{m.}$$

Ionization energy is given by

$$E'_1 = \left(\frac{\mu}{m_e}\right) E_1 = 186\ E_1$$

$$\Rightarrow \quad E'_1 = -2.53 \times 10^3\ \text{eV}$$

Where E_1 is the ionization energy of ordinary hydrogen atom.

1.9 Use of Bohr Model to Define Hypothetical Atomic Energy Levels

We've already discussed that for hydrogenic atoms, Bohr model gives first and second postulates as

$$\frac{KZe^2}{r_n^2} = \frac{mv_n^2}{r_n} \qquad \ldots(1.68)$$

and

$$mv_n r_n = \frac{nh}{2\pi} \qquad \ldots(1.69)$$

Here equation-(1.68) is given by balancing the inward coulombian force on electron by the outward centrifugal force on it in the rotating frame of reference. There may be some situation in which it is given that electron of an atom is revolving under the influence of a new potential energy field given as $U = f(r)$ [Non coulombian field] and using Bohr model, we are required to develope the properties of electron in this new atom. For this first we'll develope the first postulate equation for this new atom. As electron is orbiting in a new potential energy field given as $U = f(r)$, it will experience an inward force toward the centre of orbit given as

$$F = \left|\frac{dU}{dr}\right| = \left|\frac{d}{dr}[f(r)]\right| \qquad \ldots(1.70)$$

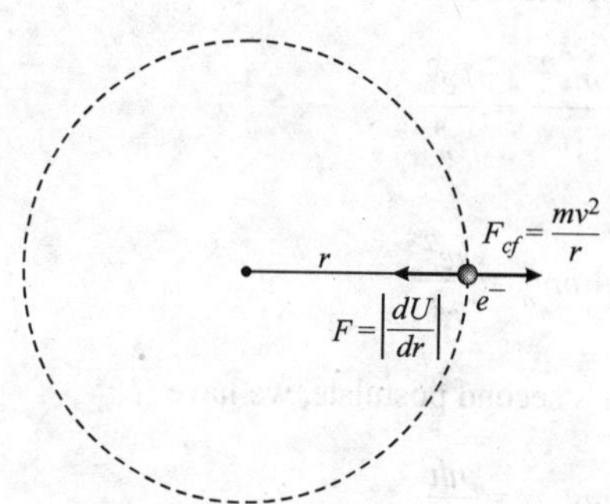

Figure 1.17

Thus for a stable n^{th} orbit if electron is moving with speed v_n in the orbit of radius r_n, we have

$$\left|\frac{d}{dr}[f(r_n)]\right| = \frac{mv_n^2}{r_n} \qquad \ldots(1.71)$$

This equation-(1.71) will be the new equation for first postulate and from Bohr model the second postulate is based on quantization of angular momentum of electron, its equation will remain same as

$$mv_n r_n = \frac{nh}{2\pi} \qquad \ldots(1.72)$$

Now using equation-(1.71) and (1.72), we can derive all the properties for electron motion like, radius of nth orbit, velocity of electron in n^{th} orbit, angular velocity, frequency, time period, current, magnetic induction, magnetic moment and the total energy of energy levels for this hypothetical atom in the same way we've derived these for properties for a general hydrogenic atom. Lets discuss few examples to understand these concepts in a better way.

Illustrative Example 1.28

Suppose the potential energy between electron and proton at a distance r is given by $-ke^2/3r^3$. Use Bohr's theory to obtain energy levels of such a hypothetical atom.

Solution

According to given situation for an electron revolving in an nth orbit the potential energy is given as

$$U = -\frac{ke^2}{3r_n^3} \quad \text{...(1.73)}$$

The centripetal force on electron due to this force is given as

$$F = -\frac{dU}{dr} = \frac{ke^2}{r_n^4} \quad \text{...(1.74)}$$

If in n^{th} orbit electron revolves at speed v_n then we have

$$\frac{mv_n^2}{r_n} = \frac{ke^2}{r_n^4}$$

$$\Rightarrow \quad mv_n^2 = \frac{ke^2}{r_n^3} \quad \text{...(1.75)}$$

From Bohr's second postulate, we have

$$mv_n r_n = \frac{nh}{2\pi} \quad \text{...(1.76)}$$

From equation-(1.75) and (1.76), we have

$$v_n = \frac{nh}{2\pi mr_n}$$

and $$m\left(\frac{nh}{2\pi mr_n}\right)^2 = \frac{ke^2}{r_n^3}$$

$$\Rightarrow \quad r_n = \frac{4\pi^2 ke^2 m}{n^2h^2} \quad \text{...(1.77)}$$

and $$v_n = \frac{n^3h^3}{8\pi^3 km^2e^2} \quad \text{...(1.78)}$$

Now energy in n^{th} orbit is

$$E_n = \frac{1}{2}mv_n^2 - \frac{ke^2}{3r_n^3}$$

$$\Rightarrow \quad E_n = \frac{1}{2}\frac{ke^2}{r_n^3}$$

$$\Rightarrow \quad E_n = \frac{1}{6}ke^2\left(\frac{n^2h^2}{4\pi^2ke^2m}\right)^3$$

$$\Rightarrow \quad E_n = \frac{n^2h^2}{384\pi^2k^2e^4m^3}$$

 # Illustrative Example 1.29

Suppose potential energy between electron and proton at separation r is given by $U = k \ln r$, where k is a constant. For such a hypothetical hydrogen atom, calculate the radius of nth Bohr's orbit and its energy levels.

Solution

In the given situation the centripetal force on electron in n^{th} orbit is given by

$$F = -\frac{dU}{dr} = \frac{k}{r_n}$$

If in n^{th} orbit speed of electron is v_n then we have

$$\frac{mv_n^2}{r_n} = \frac{k}{r_n}$$

$$\Rightarrow \quad mv_n^2 = k \quad \text{...(1.79)}$$

According to Bohr's quantization postulate, we have

$$mv_nr_n = \frac{nh}{2\pi} \quad \text{...(1.80)}$$

Solving equation-(1.79) and (1.80), we get

$$r_n = \frac{nh}{2\pi\sqrt{mk}} \quad \text{...(1.81)}$$

Energy of electron in n^{th} level is

$$E_n = kE_n + PE_n$$

$$\Rightarrow \quad E_n = \frac{1}{2}mv_n^2 - k\ln r$$

$$\Rightarrow \quad E_n = \frac{k}{2} - k\ln r$$

$$\Rightarrow \quad E_n = \frac{k}{2} - k\ln\frac{nh}{2\pi\sqrt{mk}}$$

$$\Rightarrow \quad E_n = \frac{k}{2}\left[1 - \ln\left(\frac{n^2h^2}{4\pi^2mk}\right)\right]$$

1.10 Atomic Collisions

In previous sections of the chapter we've discussed that there are two ways to excite an electron in an atom. One way, of supplying energy to an electron is by electromagnetic photons, which we've already discussed. We've also discussed that an electron absorbs a photon only when the photon energy is equal to the difference in energies of the two energy levels of atom otherwise the photon will not be absorbed.

The another way by which energy can be supplied to an electron is by collisions. To understand the energy supply by collisions we consider an example of a head on collision of a moving neutron with a stationary hydrogen atom as shown in figure-1.18. Here for mathematical analysis we can assume the masses of neutron and H-atom as same.

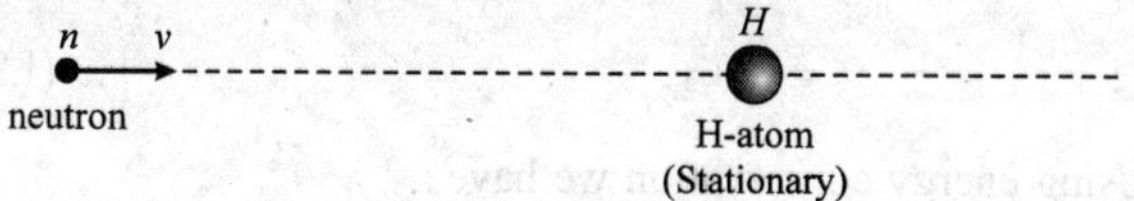

Figure 1.18

If in this case when perfectly electric collision takes place, we know for equal masses here, neutron will come to rest and hydrogen atom will move with the same speed and kinetic energy with which the neutron was moving initially as shown in figure-1.19

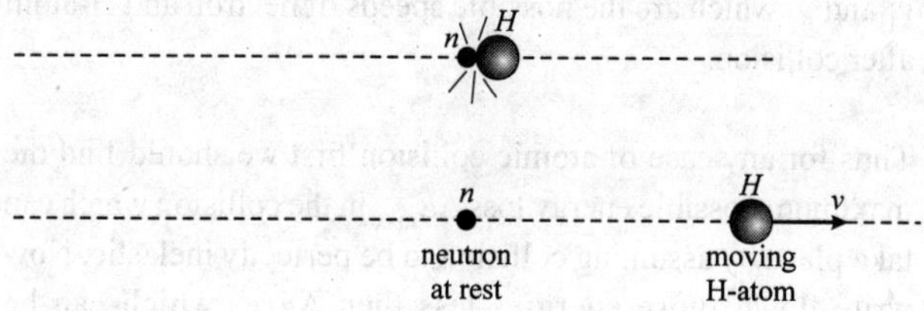

Figure 1.19

Now if we consider the collision to be perfectly inelastic, then after collision both neutron and H-atom will move together with speed v_1 which can be given by law of conservation of momentum as

$$mv_0 = 2\,mv_1$$

$$\Rightarrow \qquad v_1 = \frac{v}{2} \qquad \text{...(1.82)}$$

In this case the loss of energy can be given as the difference in initial and final kinetic energies of the neutron and H-atom, given as

$$\Delta E = E_i - E_f$$

$$\Rightarrow \qquad \Delta E = \frac{1}{2}mv^2 - \frac{1}{2}(2m)\left(\frac{v}{2}\right)^2$$

$$\Rightarrow \qquad \Delta E = \frac{1}{2}mv^2 - \frac{1}{4}mv^2$$

$$\Rightarrow \qquad \Delta E = \frac{1}{4}mv^2 = \frac{1}{2}E_i \qquad \text{...(1.83)}$$

Thus half of the initial kinetic energy will be lost in the collision. One important point which we should understand carefully is, in collisions of elementary particles and atoms, no energy can be lost as heat because here we can not consider the deformation of any lattice in the colliding body. The energy lost can only be absorbed by the atom involved in the collision and may get excited or ionized by this energy loss which take place in inelastic collision.

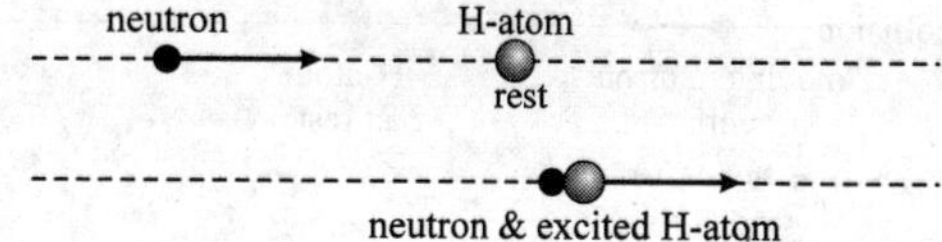

Figure 1.20

In our case of collision of a neutron with a H-atom, the energy loss is $\frac{1}{4}mv^2$ (half of initial energy of neutron). This loss in energy can be absorbed by H-atom only. We know that the minimum energy required to excite an H-atom is 10.2 eV for $n = 1$ to $n = 2$. Thus hydrogen atom can absorb only when this energy loss is equal to 10.2 eV. If this energy loss in perfectly inelastic collision is more then 10.2 eV then H-atom may absorb 10.2 eV energy for its excitation and rest of the energy will remain in the colliding particles (n & H-atom) as their kinetic energy and the collision will not be perfectly inelastic in this case.

For example say the coming neutron which is going to collide head on a stationary H-atom has initial kinetic energy 24.5 eV. In this case if perfectly inelastic collision takes place, then the maximum energy loss can be given as

$$\Delta E_{max} = \frac{1}{2}E_i = \frac{1}{2}(24.5)\,\text{eV}$$

$$\Rightarrow \qquad \Delta E_{max} = 12.25\,\text{eV}$$

From this energy H-atom can absorb either 10.2 eV or 12.09 eV for its excitation from $n = 1$ to $n = 2$ or from $n = 1$ to $n = 3$ energy level.

Thus in this case there may be three possibilities for this collision. These are :

(i) It may be possible that the collision is perfectly elastic and no energy is absorbed by H-atom as shown in figure-1.21

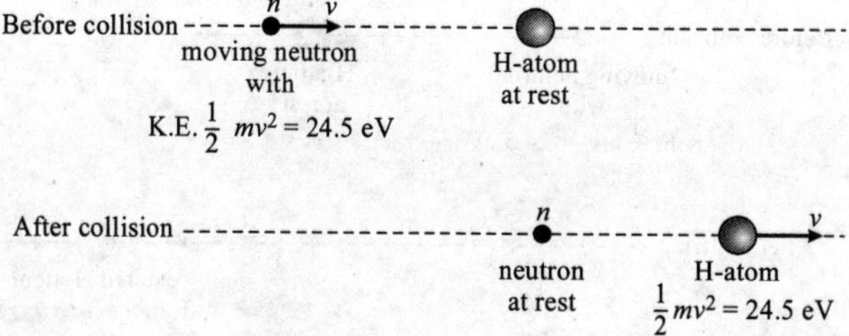

Figure 1.21

(ii) It may be possible that H-atom will absorb 10.2 eV energy during collision and both neutron and H-atom will be moving with kinetic energy 24.5 – 10.2 = 14.3 eV after collision as shown in figure-1.22. In this case the collision will be partially elastic.

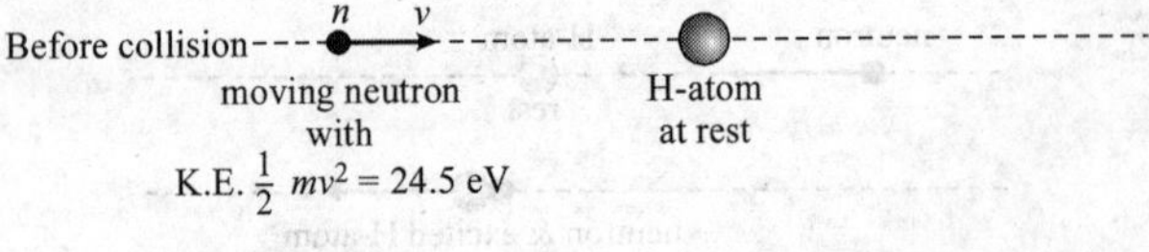

Figure 1.22

Final kinetic energy $E_f = \frac{1}{2}mv_1^2 + \frac{1}{2}mv_2^2 = 14.3$ eV

In this case the final speeds of neutron and H-atom can be obtained by using equations of law of conservation of momentum and energy. Here by momentum conservation law, we have

$$mv = mv_1 + mv_2$$

$$\Rightarrow \quad v = v_1 + v_2 \quad \ldots(1.84)$$

Using energy conservation we have

$$\frac{1}{2}mv^2 - 10.2\text{ eV} = \frac{1}{2}mv_1^2 + \frac{1}{2}mv_2^2$$

$$\Rightarrow \quad 24.5\text{ eV} - 10.2\text{ eV} = \frac{1}{2}mv_1^2 + \frac{1}{2}mv_2^2$$

$$\Rightarrow \quad \frac{1}{2}mv_1^2 + \frac{1}{2}mv_2^2 = 14.3\text{ eV} \quad \ldots(1.85)$$

Now solving equation-(1.84) and (1.85) we'll get the values of v_1 and v_2 which are the possible speeds of neutron and H-atom after collision.

(iii) It may be possible that H-atom will absorb 12.09 eV energy during collision and both neutron and H-atom will be moving with kinetic energy 24.5 – 12.09 = 12.41 eV after collision as shown in figure-1.23. In this case the collision will be partially elastic.

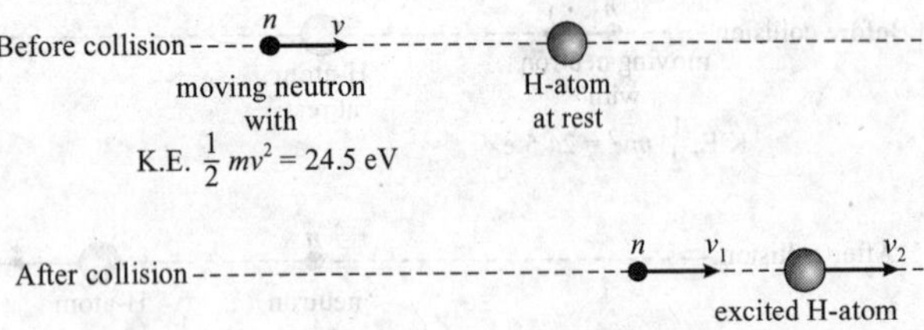

Figure 1.23

Final kinetic energy $E_f = \frac{1}{2}mv_1^2 + \frac{1}{2}mv_2^2 = 12.41$ eV

In this case the final speeds of neutron and H-atom can be obtained by using equations of law of conservation of momentum and energy. Here by momentum conservation law, we have

$$mv = mv_1 + mv_2$$

$$\Rightarrow \quad v = v_1 + v_2 \quad \ldots(1.86)$$

Using energy conservation we have

$$\frac{1}{2}mv^2 - 12.09\text{ eV} = \frac{1}{2}mv_1^2 + \frac{1}{2}mv_2^2$$

$$\Rightarrow \quad 24.5\text{ eV} - 12.09\text{ eV} = \frac{1}{2}mv_1^2 + \frac{1}{2}mv_2^2$$

$$\Rightarrow \quad \frac{1}{2}mv_1^2 + \frac{1}{2}mv_2^2 = 12.41\text{ eV} \quad \ldots(1.87)$$

Now solving equation-(1.86) and (1.87) we'll get the values of v_1 and v_2 which are the possible speeds of neutron and H-atom after collision.

Thus for any case of atomic collision first we should find the maximum possible energy loss ΔE_{max} in the collision which can take place by assuming collision to be perfectly inelastic. Now write down those energies less then ΔE_{max} which can be absorbed the atom or atoms involved in the collision, then considering possible cases of these energy absorption using momentum and energy conservation we can find the possible values of final kinetic energies of the colliding particles. Lets discuss some examples to understand this phenomenon in a better way.

 # Illustrative Example 1.30

A hydrogen atom moves with a velocity u, and makes a head on inelastic collision are in the ground state before collision. What is the minimum value of u, if one of them is to be given a minimum excitation energy ? The ionization energy is 13.6 eV. Mass of the hydrogen atom is $1.0078 \times 1.66 \times 10^{-27}$ kg.

Solution

From conservation of momentum

$$mu = 2mv$$

$$\Rightarrow \quad v = u/2 \quad \ldots(1.88)$$

The energy of excitation ΔE is given by

$$\Delta E = \frac{1}{2}mu^2 - 2 \times \frac{1}{2}m(u/2)^2$$

$$\Rightarrow \quad \Delta E = \frac{1}{4}mu^2 \quad \ldots(1.89)$$

The minimum excitation energy for a H-atom is for transition $n_1 = 1$ to $n_2 = 2$ which corresponds to an energy of 10.2 eV.

From equation-(1.89)

$$\frac{1}{4} \times (1.0078 \times 1.66 \times 10^{-27}) u^2 = 10.2 \times (1.6 \times 10^{-19})$$

$$u = 6.24 \times 10^4 \text{ m/s}$$

 # Illustrative Example 1.31

A neutron of kinetic energy 65 eV collides inelastically with a singly ionized helium atom at rest. It is scattered at an angle of 90° with respect to its original direction.

(i) Find the allowed values of the energy of the neutrons and that of the atom after the collision.

(ii) If the atoms gets deexcited subsequently by emitting radiation, find the frequencies of the emitted radiation.

[Given : Mass of He atom = 4 × (mass of neutron) Ionization energy of H atom = 13.6 eV].

Solution

(i) The situation is shown in figure-1.24.

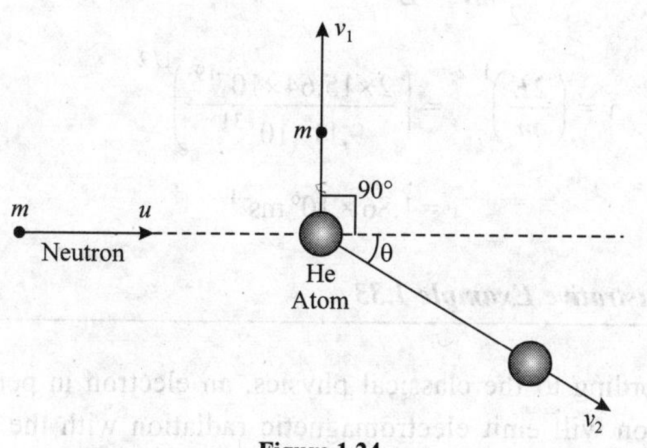

Figure 1.24

Applying the law of conservation of momentum, we have

$$mu = 4m\, v^2 \cos\theta \qquad \ldots(1.90)$$

$$mv_1 = 4\, m\, v^2 \sin\theta \qquad \ldots(1.91)$$

From these equations, we get

$$u = 4\, v^2 \cos\theta$$

and $$v_1 = 4v^2 \sin\theta$$

$$u^2 + v_1^2 = 16\, v_2^2\, [\sin^2\theta + \cos^2\theta]$$

$$= 16\, v_2^2$$

$$\Rightarrow \qquad v_2^2 = \frac{u^2 + v_1^2}{16} \qquad \ldots(1.92)$$

Let Q be the energy lost in the reaction. Then

$$65\,\text{eV} = \frac{1}{2} mv_1^2 + \frac{1}{2}(4m)v_2^2 + Q$$

$$\Rightarrow \qquad 65\,\text{eV} = \frac{1}{2} mv_1^2 + \frac{mu^2}{8} + \frac{mv_1^2}{8} + Q$$

$$\Rightarrow \qquad 65\,\text{eV} = \frac{1}{2} mv_1^2 + \frac{1}{4}\left(\frac{1}{2} mu^2\right) + \frac{mv_1^2}{8} + Q$$

$$\Rightarrow \qquad 65\,\text{eV} = \frac{5}{8} mv_1^2 + \frac{1}{4}(65\,\text{eV}) + Q \qquad \ldots(1.93)$$

Now ionization energy of He atom is

$$IE_{\text{He}^+} = 13.6 \times 4 = 54.4\,\text{eV}$$

Thus energy of electron in first orbit of He atom

$$IE_{\text{He}^+} = -54.4\,\text{eV}$$

Similarly, the energy of electron in second, third and fourth orbits would be – 13.6 eV, – 6 eV and – 3.4 eV respectively. The energy lost must have been used in exciting the atom.

First possibility : Let $Q = 54.4 - 13.6 = 40.8$ eV

$$\frac{5}{8} mv_1^2 = 65 \times \frac{3}{4} - Q = 65 \times \frac{3}{4} - 40.8$$

$$= 8\,\text{eV nearly}$$

So, $$\frac{1}{2} mv_1^2 = \frac{4}{5}(8\,\text{eV}) = 6.4\,\text{eV}$$

This will be the energy of recoil electron.

From equation-(1.92),

$$u^2 + v_1^2 = 16\, v_2^2$$

$$\Rightarrow \qquad \frac{1}{2} mu^2 + \frac{1}{2} mv_1^2 = \frac{1}{2} m \times 16 v_2^2$$

$$= 4 \times \frac{1}{2}(4\,m)\, v_2^2$$

$$65\,\text{eV} + 6.4\,\text{eV} = 4\,\text{KE of atom}$$

$$\Rightarrow \qquad \text{KE of atom} = \frac{65 + 6.4}{4} = 17.85\,\text{eV}$$

Second possibility: Let $Q = 54.4 - 6 = 48.4$ eV

Calculating in the same ways as above, we have energy of recoil neutron = 0.28 eV

energy of atom = 16.32 eV

Proceeding as above, let

$$Q = 54.4 - 3.4 = 51\,\text{eV}$$

In this case, the energy of recoil electron = – 2.25 eV (negative). This is meaningless.

Hence $Q = 40.8\ \text{eV}, 48.4\ \text{eV}$

(ii) It is obvious from first part that the atom is excited to third state or second state. The frequencies of emission can be calculated as follows :

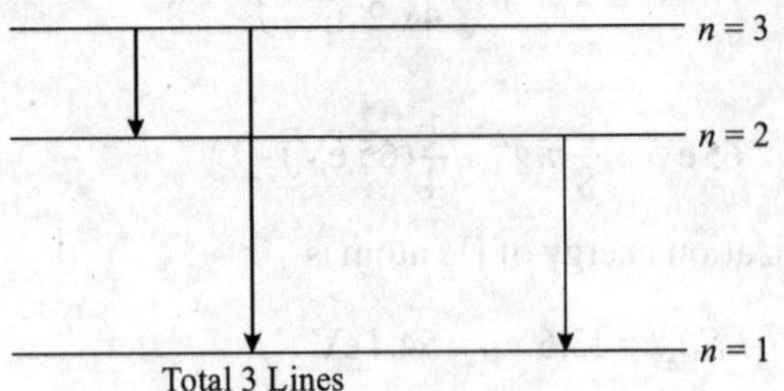

Figure 1.25

Figure-1.25 shows the number of emitted frequencies. These are

(i) $$\frac{1}{\lambda_1} = RZ^2\left[\frac{1}{1^2}-\frac{1}{2^2}\right]$$

$$\Rightarrow \quad \frac{1}{\lambda_1} = (1.097\times10^7)\times4\times\frac{3}{4}$$

$$\Rightarrow \quad \nu_1 = \frac{c}{\lambda_1} = (1.097\times10^7)\times4\times\frac{3}{4}\times(3\times10^8)$$

$$\Rightarrow \quad \nu_1 = 9.85\times10^{15}\ \text{Hz}$$

(ii) $$\frac{1}{\lambda_2} = RZ^2\left[\frac{1}{1^2}-\frac{1}{3^2}\right]$$

$$\Rightarrow \quad \frac{1}{\lambda_2} = (1.097\times10^7)\times4\times\frac{8}{9}$$

$$\Rightarrow \quad \nu_2 = \frac{c}{\lambda_2} = (1.097\times10^7)\times4\times\frac{8}{9}\times(3\times10^8)$$

$$\Rightarrow \quad \nu_2 = 11.7\times10^{15}\ \text{Hz}$$

(iii) $$\frac{1}{\lambda_3} = \left[\frac{1}{2^2}-\frac{1}{3^2}\right]$$

$$= (1.097\times10^7)\times4\times\frac{5}{36}$$

$$\nu_3 = \frac{c}{\lambda_3} = (1.097\times10^7)\times4\times\frac{5}{36}\times(3\times10^8)$$
$$= 1.827\times10^{15}\ \text{Hz}$$

Illustrative Example 1.32

An electron of energy 20 eV collides with a hydrogen atom in the ground state. As a result of the collision, the atom is excited to a higher energy state and the electron is scattered with reduced velocity. The atom subsequently returns to its ground state with emission of radiation of wavelength 1.216×10^{-7} m. Find the velocity of the scattered electron.

Solution

The energy lost by the electron in exciting the hydrogen atom equals the energy corresponding to

$$\lambda = 1.216\times10^{-7}\ \text{m},$$

$$\Rightarrow \quad \lambda = h\nu = \frac{hc}{\lambda}$$

$$\Rightarrow \quad \lambda = \frac{6.63\times10^{-34}\times3.0\times10^8}{1.216\times10^{-7}}$$

$$\Rightarrow \quad \lambda = 16.36\times10^{-19}\ \text{J}$$

Now, the initial energy of electron is 20 eV = 32×10^{-19} J. Hence the kinetic energy of the scattered electron is

$$E = 32\times10^{-19}\ \text{J} - 16.36\times10^{-19}\ \text{J}$$

$$\Rightarrow \quad E = 15.64\times10^{-19}\ \text{J}$$

The velocity v of the scattered electron is given by

$$\frac{1}{2}mv^2 = E$$

$$\Rightarrow \quad v = \left(\frac{2E}{m}\right)^{1/2} = \left(\frac{2\times15.64\times10^{-19}}{9.11\times10^{-31}}\right)^{1/2}$$

$$\Rightarrow \quad v = 1.86\times10^6\ \text{ms}^{-1}$$

Illustrative Example 1.33

According to the classical physics, an electron in periodic motion will emit electromagnetic radiation with the same frequency as that of its revolution. Compute this value for hydrogen atom in n^{th} quantum state. Under what conditions does Bohr's quantum theory permit emission of such photons due to transitions between adjoining orbits ? Discuss the result obtained.

Solution

The orbital frequency of nth orbit is given by

$$\nu_n = \frac{\text{electron speed}}{\text{orbital circumference}}$$

$$\Rightarrow \quad \nu_n = \frac{e^2}{2nh\epsilon_0}\times\frac{1}{2\pi}\times\frac{\pi me^2}{n^2\epsilon_0 h^2}$$

$$\Rightarrow \quad \nu_n = \frac{me^4}{4\epsilon_0^2 n^3 h^3} \qquad \left[\text{As } K = \frac{1}{4\pi\epsilon_0}\right]$$

From the laws of electromagnetic theory, the frequency of the radiation emitted by this electron will also be v_n.

According to Bohr's theory, the frequency of the radiation for the adjoining orbits is given by

$$v_n = \frac{E_n - E_{n-1}}{h} = \frac{me^4}{8\epsilon_0^2 h^2}\left[\frac{1}{(n-1)^2} - \frac{1}{n^2}\right]$$

$$\Rightarrow \quad v_n = \frac{me^4}{8\epsilon_0^2 h^2}\cdot\frac{(2n-1)}{(n-1)^2 \times n^2}$$

$$\Rightarrow \quad v_n = \frac{me^4}{4\epsilon_0^2 h^2}\cdot\frac{(2n-1)}{2n^2(n-1)^2}$$

A comparison of this expression with the classical expression above show that the difference in their predictions will be large for small n, i.e., for $n=2$, $1/n^3 = 1/8$ and $(2n-1)/2n^2(n-1)^2 = 3/8$, so that the frequency given by quantum theory is 3 time that calculated from classical theory. However, for very large n, the quantum expression radius to that obtained from classical theory because for $n \to \infty$

$$\frac{2n-1}{2n^2(n-1)^2} \cong \frac{2n}{2n^2 \cdot n^2} = \frac{1}{n^3}$$

Consequently, the predictions of Bohr's theory agrees with that of the classical theory in the limit of very large quantum numbers. This correspondence is called as "*Bohr's Correspondence Principle*".

Illustrative Example 1.34

A 100 eV electron collides with a stationary helium ion (He^+) in its ground state and excites to a higher level. After the collision, He^+ ions emits two photons in succession with wavelength 1085 Å and 304 Å. Find the principal quantum number of the excited state. Also calculate the energy of the electron after the collision. Given $h = 6.63 \times 10^{-34}$ Js.

Solution

The energy of the electron in the nth state of He^+ ion of atomic number Z is given by

$$E_n = -(13.6\,\text{eV})\frac{Z^2}{n^2}$$

For He^+ ion, $Z = 2$. Therefore

$$E_n = -\frac{(13.6\,\text{eV})\times(2)^2}{n^2}$$

$$\Rightarrow \quad E_n = -\frac{54.4}{n^2}\,\text{eV} \quad \ldots(1.94)$$

The energies E_1 and E_2 of the two emitted photons in eV are

$$E_1 = \frac{12431}{1085}\,\text{eV} = 11.4\,\text{eV}$$

and $$E_2 = \frac{12431}{304}\,\text{eV} = 40.9\,\text{eV}$$

Thus total energy

$$E = E_1 + E_2 = 11.4 + 40.9 = 52.3\,\text{eV}$$

Let n be the principal quantum number of the excited state. Using equation-(1.94) we have for the transition from $n = n$ to $n = 1$

$$E = -(54.4\,\text{eV})\left(\frac{1}{1^2} - \frac{1}{n^2}\right)$$

But $E = 52.3$ eV. Therefore

$$52.3\,\text{eV} = 54.4\,\text{eV} \times \left(1 - \frac{1}{n^2}\right)$$

$$\Rightarrow \quad 1 - \frac{1}{n^2} = \frac{52.3}{54.4} = 0.96$$

Which gives, $n^2 = 25$ or $n = 5$

The energy of the incident electron = 100 eV (given). The energy supplied to He^+ ion = 52.3 eV. Therefore, the energy of the electron left after the collision = 100 – 52.3 = 47.7 eV.

Web Reference at www.physicsgalaxy.com

Age Group - High School Physics | Age 17-19 Years
Section - MODERN PHYSICS
Topic - Atomic Structure
Module Number - 37 to 48

Practice Exercise 1.3

(i) Show that for large values of principal quantum number, the frequency of an electron rotating in adjacent energy levels of hydrogen atom and the radiated frequency for a transition between these levels all approach the same value.

(ii) Determine the separation of the first line of the Balmer series in a spectrum of ordinary hydrogen and tritium (mass number 3). Take Rydberg's constant $R = 10967800\,\text{m}^{-1}$

[2.387 Å]

(iii) A photon of energy 5.4852 eV liberates an electron from the Li atom initially at rest. The emitted electron moves at right angles to the direction in which photon moves. Find the speed and the direction in which the Li^{2+} ion will move. Ionization potential of Li atom = 5.3918 V. Atomic weight of Li = 6.94 g, $N_{Av} = 6.02 \times 10^{23}\ mol^{-1}$ and $m_e = 9.1 \times 10^{-31}$ kg.

[14.2 m/s, θ = 88.9°]

(iv) A neutron moving with speed v strikes a hydrogen atom in ground state moving towards it with the same speed. Find the minimum speed of the neutrons for which inelastic collision may take place. Take mass of neutrons and that of hydrogen is 1.67×10^{-27} kg.

[3.13×10^4 m/s]

(v) A uniform magnetic field B exists in a region. An electron projected perpendicular to the field goes in a circle. Assuming Bohr's quantization rule for angular momentum, calculate

(a) the smallest possible radius of the electron

(b) the radius of the nth orbit and

(c) the minimum possible speed of the electron.

[(a) $\sqrt{\frac{h}{2\pi eB}}$; (b) $\sqrt{\frac{nh}{2\pi eB}}$; (c) $\sqrt{\frac{heB}{2\pi m^2}}$]

(vi) A particle of mass m, atomic number Z', initial speed v and impact parameter b is scattered by a heavy nucleus of atomic number Z. Use the principle of conservation of angular momentum and energy to obtain a relation between the minimum distance s of the particle from the nucleus in terms of Z, Z', v and b. Show that for $b = 0$, s reduces to the distance of closest approach r_0 given by

$$r_0 = \frac{1}{4\pi\epsilon_0}\frac{2ZZ'e^2}{mv^2}$$

[$\frac{1}{2}mv^2\left(1-\frac{b^2}{s^2}\right) = \frac{1}{4\pi\epsilon_0}\frac{ZZ'e^2}{s}$]

(vii) A small particle of mass m moves in such a way that the potential energy $U = -\frac{1}{2}mb^2r^2$, where b is a constant and r is the distance of the particle from the origin (Nucleus). Assuming Bohr model of quantization of angular momentum and circular orbits, show that radius of the nth allowed orbit is proportional to $\sqrt{n}$.

Advance Illustrations Videos at www.physicsgalaxy.com

Age Group - Advance Illustrations

Section - Modern Physics

Topic - Atomic and Nuclear Physics

Illustrations - 54 In-depth Illustrations Videos

* * * * *

Discussion Questions

Q1-1 Balmer series was observed and analyzed before the other series. Can you suggest a reason for such an order ?

Q1-2 You are examining the spectrum of a particular gas that is excited in a discharge tube. You are viewing the discharge through a transparent box that contains the same gas. Under what conditions would you expect to see dark lines in the spectrum?

Q1-3 The first excited energy of a He^+ ion is the same as the ground state energy of hydrogen. Is it always true that one of the energies of any hydrogen like ion will be same as the ground state energy of a hydrogen atom ?

Q1-4 An atom is in its excited state. Does the probability of its coming to ground state depend on whether the radiation is already present or not ? If yes, does it also depend on the wavelength of the radiation present ?

Q1-5 At room temperature, most of the atoms of atomic hydrogen contain electrons that are in the ground state or $n = 1$ energy level. A tube is filled with atomic hydrogen. Electromagnetic radiation with a continuous spectrum of wavelengths, including those in the Lyman, Balmer, and Paschen series, enters one end of this tube and leaves the other end. The existing radiation is found to contain absorption lines. To which one (or more) of the series do the wavelengths of these absorption lines correspond ? Assume that once an electron absorbs a photon and jumps to a higher energy level, it does not absorb yet another photon and jump to an even higher energy level. Explain your answer.

Q1-6 When electromagnetic radiation is passed through, a sample of hydrogen gas at room temperature, absorption lines are observed in Lyman series only. Explain.

Q1-7 The difference in the frequencies of series limit of Lyman series and Balmer series is equal to the frequency of the first line of the Lyman series. Explain.

Q1-8 Bohr's model was not able to explain Zeeman and Stark effect. Discuss possible reasons for this.

Q1-9 Does it take more energy to ionize (free) the electron of a hydrogen atom that is in an excited state than one in the ground state ? Explain.

Q1-10 Galaxies tend to be strong emitters of Lyman-α photons (from the $n = 2$ to $n = 1$ transition in atomic hydrogen). But the intergalactic medium—the very thin gas between the galaxies—tends to *absorb* Lyman-α photons. What can you infer from these observations about the temperature in these two environments ? Explain.

Q1-11 The total energy of the hydrogen atom is negative. What significance does this have ?

Q1-12 Find out the wavelength of the first line of the He+ ion in a spectral series whose frequency width is $\Delta\nu = 3.3 \times 10^{15}\ s^{-1}$.

Q1-13 Very accurate measurements of the wavelengths of light emitted by a hydrogen atom indicate that all wavelengths are slightly longer than expected from the Bohr theory. How might the conservation of momentum help explain this ? [Hint: Photons carry momentum and energy, both of which must be conserved.]

Q1-14 In the Bohr model for the hydrogen atom, the closer the electron is to be nucleus, the smaller is the total energy of the atom. Is this also true in the quantum mechanical picture of the hydrogen atom ? Justify your answer.

Q1-15 The materials (phosphors) that coat the inside of a fluorescent lamp convert ultraviolet radiation (from the mercury-vapor discharge inside the tube) into visible light. Could one also make a phosphor that converts visible light to ultraviolet ? Explain.

Q1-16 Consider the line spectrum emitted from a gas discharge tube such as a neon sign or a sodium-vapor or mercury-vapor lamp. It is found that when the pressure of the vapor is increased, the spectrum lines spread out over a larger range of wavelengths, that is, are less monochromatic. Why ?

Q1-17 Which wavelengths will be emitted by a sample of atomic hydrogen gas (in ground state) if electrons of energy 12.2 eV collide with the atoms of the gas ?

Q1-18 As a body is heated to a very high temperature and becomes self-luminous, the apparent color of the emitted radiation shifts from red to yellow and finally to blue as the temperature increases. Why the color shifts ? What other changes in the character of the radiation occur ?

Q1-19 Explain why the Bohr theory is applicable only to the hydrogen atom and to hydrogen-like atoms, such as singly ionized helium, doubly ionized lithium, and other one-electron systems.

Q1-20 What are the most significant differences between the Bohr model of the hydrogen atom and the Schrodinger analysis of that atom ? What are the similarities ?

Q1-21 How many wavelengths are emitted by atomic hydrogen in visible range (380 nm – 780 nm) ? In the range 50 nm to 100 nm ?

Q1-22 Stars appear to have distinct colors. Some stars look red, some yellow, and others blue. What is a possible explanation for this ?

Q1-23 What will be the energy corresponding to the first excited state of a hydrogen atom if the potential energy of the atom is taken to be 10 eV when the electron is widely separated from the proton ? Can we still write $E_n = E_1/n^2$? $r_n = a_0 n^2$?

Q1-24 The numerical value of ionization energy in eV equals the ionization potential in volts. Does the equality hold if these quantities are measured in some other units ?

Q1-25 When the outermost electron in an atom is in an excited state, the atom is more easily ionized than when the outermost electron is in the ground state. Why ?

Q1-26 Elements in the gaseous state emit line spectra with well-defined wavelengths. But hot solid bodies always emit a continuous spectrum, that is, a continuous smear of wavelengths. Can you account for this difference ?

* * * * *

Conceptual MCQs Single Option Correct

1-1 According to Bohr's theory of the hydrogen atom, the total energy of the hydrogen atom with its electron revolving in the *n*th stationary orbit is :

(A) Proportional to n

(B) Proportional to n^2

(C) Inversely proportional to n

(D) Inversely proportional to n^2

1-2 According to Bohr's theory of the hydrogen atom, the radii r_n of stationary electron orbits are related to the principal quantum number n as :

(A) $r_n \propto 1/n^2$ (B) $r_n \propto 1/n$

(C) $r_n \propto n$ (D) $r_n \propto n^2$

1-3 The wavelengths involved in the spectrum of deuterium ($^2_1$D) are slightly different from that of hydrogen spectrum, because :

(A) Size of the two nuclei are different

(B) Nuclear forces are different in the two cases

(C) Masses of the two nuclei are different

(D) Attraction between the electron and the nucleus is different in the two cases

1-4 The energy of the electron of hydrogen orbiting in a stationary orbit of radius r_n is proportional to :

(A) r_n (B) $1/r_n$

(C) r^2_n (D) $1/r^2_n$

1-5 The shortest wavelength of the spectrum for transition of an electron to $n = 4$ energy level of a hydrogen like atom (atomic number = Z) is the same as the shortest wavelength of the Balmer series of hydrogen atom. The value of Z is :

(A) 2 (B) 3

(C) 4 (D) 6

1-6 Which of the following series in the spectrum of the hydrogen atom lies in the visible region of the electromagnetic spectrum ?

(A) Paschen series (B) Balmer series

(C) Lyman series (D) Brackett series

1-7 The angular momentum of an electron in an orbit is quantized because it is a necessary condition for the compatibility with :

(A) The wave nature of electron

(B) Particle nature of electron

(C) Pauli's exclusion behaviour

(D) None of these

1-8 In the following figure-1.26 the energy levels of hydrogen atom have been shown along with some transitions marked A, B, C, D and E. The transitions A, B and C respectively represent :

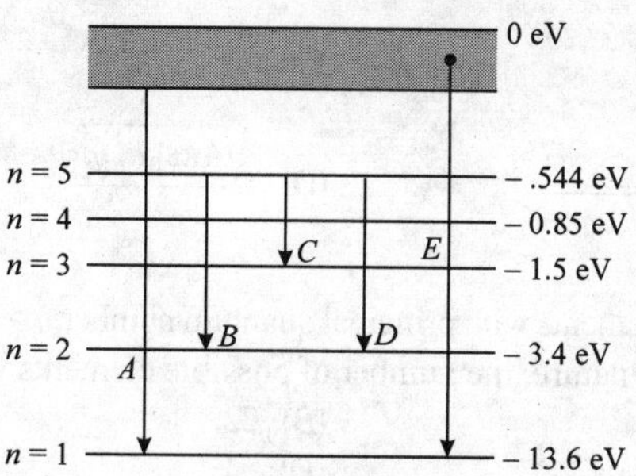

Figure 1.26

(A) The first member of Lyman series, third member of Balmer series and second member of Paschen series

(B) The ionisation potential of hydrogen, second member of Balmer series and third member of Paschen series

(C) The series limit of Lyman series, second member of Balmer series and second member of Paschen series

(D) The series limit of Lyman series, third member of Balmer series and second member of Paschen series

1-9 The electron in a hydrogen atom makes a transition from an excited state to the ground state. Which of the following statements is true ?

(A) Its kinetic energy increases and its potential and total energies decreases

(B) Its kinetic energy decreases, potential energy increases and its total energy remains the same

(C) Its kinetic and total energies decrease and its potential energy increases

(D) Its kinetic, potential and total energies decrease

1-10 A stationary hydrogen atom of mass M emits a photon corresponding to the first line of Lyman series. If R is the Rydberg's constant, the speed of recoil of the atom after the emission of the photon is :

(A) $\frac{3Rh}{4M}$ (B) $\frac{Rh}{4M}$

(C) $\frac{Rh}{2M}$ (D) $\frac{Rh}{M}$

1-11 According to Bohr's theory of the hydrogen atom, the speed v_n of the electron in a stable orbit is related to the principal quantum number n as (C is a constant) :

(A) $v_n = C/n^2$ (B) $v_n = C/n$

(C) $v_n = C \times n$ (D) $v_n = C \times n^2$

1-12 In the Bohr model of a hydrogen atom, the centripetal force is furnished by the coulomb attraction between the proton and the electron. If a_0 is the radius of the ground state orbit, m is the mass and e is the charge on the electron and ε_0 is the vacuum permittivity, the speed of the electron is :

(A) 0 (B) $\frac{e}{\sqrt{\varepsilon_0 a_0 m}}$

(C) $\frac{e}{\sqrt{4\pi\varepsilon_0 a_0 m}}$ (D) $\frac{\sqrt{4\pi\varepsilon_0 a_0 m}}{e}$

1-13 If elements with principal quantum number $n > 4$ were not allowed in nature, the number of possible elements would be :

(A) 60 (B) 32
(C) 4 (D) 64

1-14 Bohr's atomic model gained acceptance above all other models because it :

(A) Is based on quantum hypothesis
(B) Explained the constitution of atom
(C) Assumed continuous radiation of energy by orbiting electrons
(D) Explained hydrogen spectrum

1-15 Pauli's exclusion principle states that no two electrons in an atom can have identical values for :

(A) One of the four quantum numbers
(B) Two of the four quantum numbers
(C) Three of the four quantum numbers
(D) All four quantum numbers

1-16 Energy levels A, B and C of a certain atom correspond to increasing values of energy i.e. $E_A < E_B < E_C$. If $\lambda_1, \lambda_2, \lambda_3$ are the wavelengths of radiation corresponding to transition C to B, B to A and C to A respectively, which of the following statements is correct ?

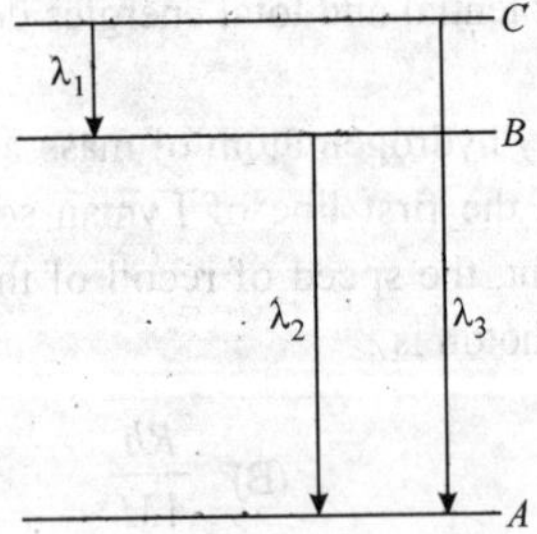

Figure 1.27

(A) $\lambda_3 = \lambda_1 + \lambda_2$ (B) $\frac{1}{\lambda_3} = \frac{1}{\lambda_1} + \frac{1}{\lambda_2}$

(C) $\lambda_1 + \lambda_2 + \lambda_3 = 0$ (D) $\lambda_3 = \sqrt{\lambda_1^2 + \lambda_2^2}$

1-17 When white light (violet to red) is passed through hydrogen gas at room temperature, absorption lines will be observed in the

(A) Lyman series (B) Balmer series
(C) Both (A) and (B) (D) Neither (A) or (B)

1-18 The difference in angular momentum associated with electron in two successive orbits of hydrogen atom is :

(A) $\frac{h}{\pi}$ (B) $\frac{h}{2\pi}$

(C) $\frac{nh}{2\pi}$ (D) $\frac{h}{2\pi}$

1-19 If radiation of all wavelengths from ultraviolet to infrared is passed through hydrogen gas at room temperature absorption lines will be observed in the

(A) Lyman series (B) Balmer series
(C) Both (A) and (B) (D) Neither (A) or (B)

1-20 Which of the following force is responsible for α-particle scattering ?

(A) Gravitational (B) Nuclear
(C) Coulomb (D) Magnetic

1-21 A Hydrogen atom and Li^{++} ion are both in the second excited state. If L_H and L_{Li} are their respective angular momenta, and E_H and E_{Li} their respective energies, then :

(A) $L_H > L_{Li}$ and $|E_H| > |E_{Li}|$
(B) $L_H = L_{Li}$ and $|E_H| < |E_{Li}|$
(C) $L_H = L_{Li}$ and $|E_H| > |E_{Li}|$
(D) $L_H < L_{Li}$ and $|E_H| < |E_{Li}|$

1-22 The minimum kinetic energy of an electron, hydrogen ion, helium ion required for ionization of a hydrogen atom is E_1 in case electron is collided with hydrogen atom. It is E_2 if hydrogen ion is collided and E_3 when helium ion is collided. Then:

(A) $E_1 = E_2 = E_3$ (B) $E_1 > E_2 > E_3$
(C) $E_1 < E_2 < E_3$ (D) $E_1 > E_3 > E_2$

1-23 The wavelength of radiation emitted due to transition of electron from energy level E to zero is equal to λ. The wavelength of radiation (λ_1) emitted when electron jumps from energy level $\frac{3E}{2}$ to zero will be :

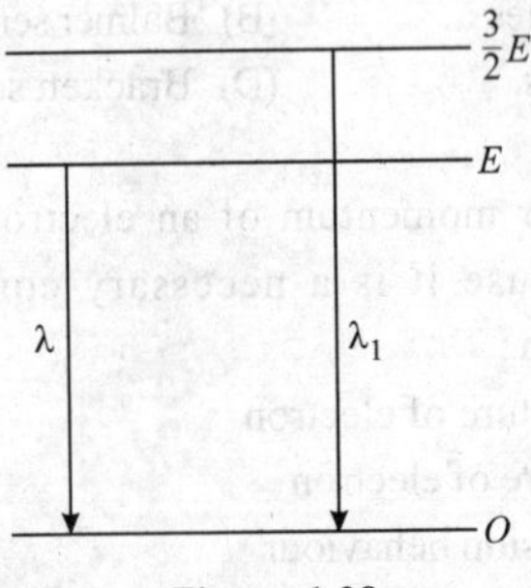

Figure 1.28

(A) $\frac{2}{3}\lambda$ (B) $\frac{3}{2}\lambda$

(C) $\frac{4}{9}\lambda$ (D) $\frac{9}{4}\lambda$

1-24 A neutron collies head-on with a stationary hydrogen atom in ground state. Which of the following statements is correct ?

(A) If kinetic energy of the neutron is less than 13.6 eV, collision must be elastic

(B) If kinetic energy of the neutron is less than 13.6 eV, collision may be inelastic

(C) Inelastic collision may take place on when initial kinetic energy of neutron is greater than 13.6 eV

(D) Perfectly inelastic collision can not take place

1-25 An electron in hydrogen atom after absorbing an energy photon jumps from energy state n_1 to n_2. Then it returns to ground state after emitting six different wavelengths in emission spectrum. The energy of emitted photons is either equal to, less than or greater than the absorbed photons. Then n_1 and n_2 are :

(A) $n_2 = 4, n_1 = 3$ (B) $n_2 = 5, n_1 = 3$

(C) $n_2 = 4, n_1 = 2$ (D) $n_2 = 4, n_1 = 1$

1-26 Mark correct statement among the following :

(A) Bohr's theory is applicable to hydrogen alone because its nucleus is most light

(B) Binding energy of electron (in ground state) of $_1H^2$ is greater than that of $_1H$ in ground state

(C) All the lines of Balmer series lie in visible spectrum

(D) None of these

1-27 Figure-1.29 represents transitions of electrons from higher to lower state of a hydrogen atom. Which transition represents the line of Balmer series :

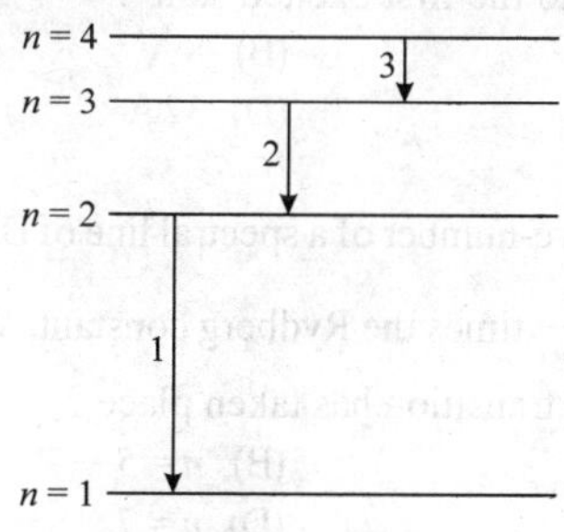

Figure 1.29

(A) 1 (B) 2

(C) 3 (D) All 1, 2, and 3

1-28 Hydrogen H, deuterium D, singly ionized helium He^+ and doubly ionized lithium Li^{++} all have one electron around the nucleus. Consider $n = 2$ and $n = 1$ transition. The wavelengths of the emitted radiations are $\lambda_1, \lambda_2, \lambda_3$ and λ_4 respectively. Then approximately :

(A) $\lambda_1 = 2\lambda_2 = 2\sqrt{2}\,\lambda_3 = 3\sqrt{2}\,\lambda_4$

(B) $\lambda_1 = \lambda_2 = 2\lambda_3 = 3\lambda_4$

(C) $\lambda_1 = \lambda_2 = 4\lambda_3 = 9\lambda_4$

(D) $4\lambda_1 = 2\lambda_2 = 2\lambda_3 = \lambda_4$

1-29 Which of the following curves may represent the energy of electron in hydrogen atom as a function of principal quantum number n :

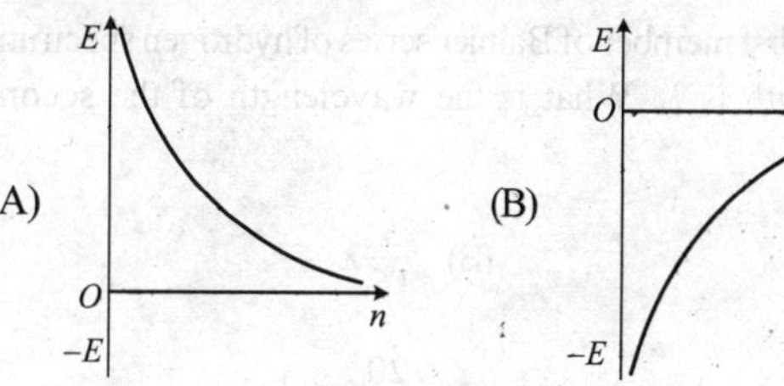

(C)

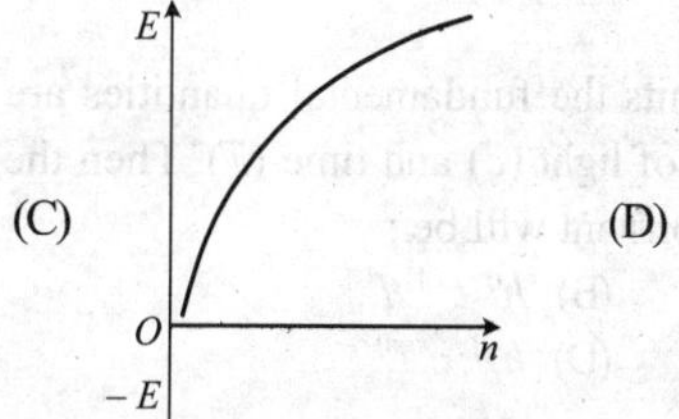

(D)

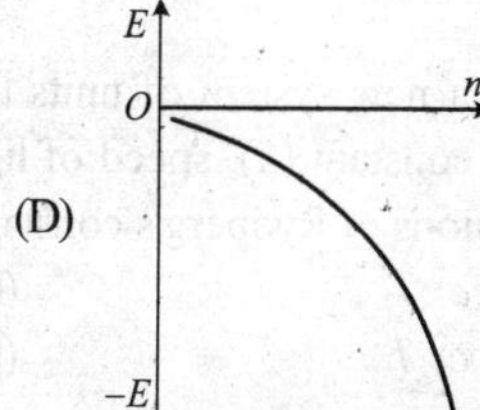

1-30 A hydrogen atom in ground state absorbs 12.1 eV energy. The orbital angular momentum of electron is increased by :

(A) $\frac{h}{2\pi}$ (B) $\frac{h}{\pi}$

(C) $\frac{3h}{2\pi}$ (D) zero

1-31 Magnetic moment due to the motion of the electron in n^{th} energy state of hydrogen atom is proportional to :

(A) n (B) n^0

(C) n^5 (D) n^3

* * * * *

Numerical MCQs Single Option Correct

1-1 The energy required to excite a hydrogen atom from $n = 1$ to $n = 2$ energy state 10.2 eV. What is the wavelength of the radiation emitted by the atom when it goes back to its ground state ?

(A) 1024 Å (B) 1122 Å
(C) 1218 Å (D) 1324 Å

1-2 Consider Bohr's theory for hydrogen atom. The magnitude of angular momentum, orbit radius and frequency of the electron in n^{th} energy state in a hydrogen atom are L, r & f respectively. Find out the value of 'x', if the product $f\,r\,L$ is directly proportional to n^x :

(A) 0 (B) 1
(C) 2 (D) 3

1-3 For the first member of Balmer series of hydrogen spectrum, the wavelength is λ. What is the wavelength of the second member ?

(A) $\frac{5}{30}\lambda$ (B) $\frac{3}{16}\lambda$
(C) $\frac{4}{9}\lambda$ (D) $\frac{20}{27}\lambda$

1-4 In a new system of units the fundamental quantities are planks constant (h), speed of light (c) and time (T). Then the dimensions of Rydberg's constant will be :

(A) $h^1\,c^1\,T^1$ (B) $h^0\,c^{-1}\,T^{-1}$
(C) $h^1\,c^0\,T^{-1}$ (D) $h^{-1}\,c\,T^0$

1-5 In a hypothetical atom, if transition from $n = 4$ to $n = 3$ produces visible light then the possible transition to obtain infrared radiation is :

(A) $n=5$ to $n=3$ (B) $n=4$ to $n=2$
(C) $n=3$ to $n=1$ (D) none of these

1-6 If first excitation potential of a hydrogen like atom is V electron volt, then the ionization energy of this atom will be:

(A) V electron volt
(B) $\frac{3V}{4}$ electron volt
(C) $\frac{4V}{3}$ electron volt
(D) cannot be calculated by given information

1-7 Ionisation energy for hydrogen atom in the ground state is E. What is the ionisation energy of Li^{++} atom in the 2nd excited state ?

(A) E (B) $3E$
(C) $6E$ (D) $9E$

1-8 The different lines in the Lyman series have their wavelengths laying between :

(A) Zero to infinite (B) 900 Å to 1200 Å
(C) 1000 Å to 1500 Å (D) 500 Å to 1000 Å

1-9 The orbital electron of the hydrogen atom jumps from the ground state to a higher energy state and its orbital velocity is reduced to one third of its initial value. If the radius of the orbit in the ground state is r, then what is the radius of the new orbit ?

(A) $2r$ (B) $3r$
(C) $4r$ (D) $9r$

1-10 If we assume that penetrating power of any radiation/particle is inversely proportional to its de-Broglie wavelength of the particle then :

(A) a proton and an α-particle after getting accelerated through same potential difference will have equal penetrating power.
(B) penetrating power of α-particle will be greater than that of proton which have been accelerated by same potential difference.
(C) proton's penetrating power will be less than penetrating power of an electron which has been accelerated by the same potential difference.
(D) penetrating powers can not be compared as all these are particles having no wavelength or wave nature.

1-11 According to Bohr's theory the ratio of time taken by electron to complete one revolution in first excited and second excited states of hydrogen will be :

(A) $1:8$ (B) $8:27$
(C) $8^2:27^2$ (D) $4:9$

1-12 The area of the electron orbit for the ground state of hydrogen atom is A. What will be the area of the electron orbit corresponding to the first excited state ?

(A) 4 A (B) 8 A
(C) 16 A (D) 32 A

1-13 If the wave-number of a spectral line of Brackett series of hydrogen is $\frac{9}{400}$ times the Rydberg constant. What is the state from which the transition has taken place ?

(A) $n=4$ (B) $n=5$
(C) $n=6$ (D) $n=7$

1-14 Ionization potential of hydrogen atom is 13.6 V. Hydrogen atom in the ground state is excited by monochromatic radiation of photons of energy 12.09 eV. The number of spectral lines emitted by the hydrogen atom, according to Bohr's theory, will be :

(A) One (B) Two
(C) Three (D) Four

1-15 An electron jumps from the first excited state to the ground stage of hydrogen atom. What will be the percentage change in the speed of electron ?

(A) 25% (B) 50%
(C) 100% (D) 200%

1-16 An energy of 24.6 eV is required to remove one of the electron from the neutral helium atom. The energy (in eV) required to remove both the electron from a neutral helium atom is :

(A) 38.2 (B) 49.2
(C) 51.8 (D) 79.0

1-17 A neutron beam, in which each neutron has same kinetic energy, is passed through a sample of hydrogen like gas (but not hydrogen) in ground state and at rest. Due to collision of neutrons with the ions of the gas, ions are excited and then they emit photons. Six spectral lines are obtained in which one of the lines is of wavelength (6200/51) nm. Which gas is this ?

(A) H (B) He^+
(C) Li^{+2} (D) Bi^{+3}

1-18 In previous question what is the minimum possible value of kinetic energy of the neutrons for this to be possible. The mass of neutron and proton can be assumed to be nearly same. Use $hc = 12400$ eVÅ.

(A) 31.875 eV (B) 63.75 eV
(C) 127.5 eV (D) 182.5 eV

1-19 In Millikan's oil drop experiment, a charged oil drop of mass 3.2×10^{-14} kg is held stationary between two parallel plates 6 mm apart by applying a potential difference of 1200 V between them. How many excess electrons does the oil drop carry ? Take $g = 10\ \text{ms}^{-2}$:

(A) 7 (B) 8
(C) 9 (D) 10

1-20 In a hydrogen like atom the energy required to excite the electron from 2nd to 3rd orbit is 47.2 eV. What is the atomic number of the atom ?

(A) 2 (B) 3
(C) 4 (D) 5

1-21 Two hydrogen atoms are in excited state with electrons in $n = 2$ state. First one is moving towards left and emits a photon of energy E_1 towards right. Second one is moving towards right with same speed and emits a photon of energy E_2 towards right. Taking recoil of nucleus into account during emission process :

(A) $E_1 > E_2$ (B) $E_1 < E_2$
(C) $E_1 = E_2$ (D) information insufficient

1-22 In a hydrogen atom following the Bohr's postulates the product of linear momentum and angular momentum is proportional to n^x where 'n' is the orbit number. Then 'x' is :

(A) 0 (B) 2
(C) –2 (D) 1

1-23 The velocity of an electron in second orbit of tenly ionized sodium atom (atomic number $Z = 11$) is v. The velocity of an electron in its fifth orbit will be:

(A) v (B) $\frac{5}{2}v$
(C) $\frac{2}{5}v$ (D) $\frac{22}{5}v$

1-24 A positronium consists of an electron and a positron revolving about their common centre of mass. If Bohr's quantization model is considered valid for this system, calculate the separation between the electron and positron in their first excited state :

(A) 0.529 A (B) 1.058 A
(C) 2.116 A (D) 4.232 A

1-25 A positronium consists of an electron and a positron revolving about their common centre of mass. If Bohr's quantization model is considered valid for this system, Calculate the kinetic energy of the electron in ground state :

(A) 1.51 eV (B) 3.4 eV
(C) 6.8 eV (D) 13.6 eV

1-26 A hydrogen atom is in an excited state of principle quantum number n. It emits a photon of wavelength λ when returns to the ground state. The value of n is :

(A) $\sqrt{\lambda R(\lambda R-1)}$ (B) $\sqrt{\frac{(\lambda R-1)}{\lambda R}}$
(C) $\sqrt{\frac{\lambda R}{\lambda R-1}}$ (D) $\sqrt{\lambda(R-1)}$

1-27 The ratio of magnitude of energies of electron in hydrogen atom in first to second excited states is :

(A) 1 : 4 (B) 4 : 9
(C) 9 : 4 (D) 4 : 1

1-28 Monochromatic radiation of wavelength λ is incident on a hydrogen sample in ground state. Hydrogen atoms absorb a fraction of light and subsequently emit radiations of six different wavelengths. Find the wavelength λ :

(A) 975 A (B) 1218 A
(C) 2248 A (D) 4316 A

1-29 Out of the following transitions, the frequency of emitted photon will be maximum for :

(A) $n=5$ to $n=3$ (B) $n=6$ to $n=2$
(C) $n=2$ to $n=1$ (D) $n=4$ to $n=2$

1-30 Imagine a neutral particle of same mass m as electron revolving around a proton of mass M_p only under newton's gravitational force. Assuming Bohr's quantum condition, the radius of electron orbit is given by :

(A) $\frac{n^2h^2}{\pi m^2 GM_p}$ (B) $\frac{n^2h^2}{4\pi^2 m^2 GM_p}$

(C) $\frac{GM_p n^2h^2}{4\pi^2 m^2}$ (D) $\frac{nhGM_p}{4\pi m}$

1-31 Determine the ratio of perimeters in 2nd and 3rd Bohr orbit in He^+ atom :

(A) $\frac{9}{4}$ (B) $\frac{9}{16}$

(C) $\frac{4}{9}$ (D) $\frac{16}{9}$

1-32 The photon radiated from hydrogen corresponding to 2nd line of Lyman series is absorbed by a hydrogen like atom 'X' in 2nd excited state. As a result the hydrogen like atom 'X' makes a transition to n^{th} orbit. Then,
(A) $X = He^+, n=4$ (B) $X = Li^{++}, n=6$
(C) $X = He^+, n=6$ (D) $X = Li^{++}, n=9$

1-33 An α particle with a kinetic energy of 2.1 eV makes a head on collision with a hydrogen atom moving towards it with a kinetic energy of 8.4 eV. The collision :
(A) must be perfectly elastic
(B) may be perfectly inelastic
(C) may be inelastic
(D) must be perfectly inelastic

1-34 A hydrogen atom is initially at rest and free to move is in the second excited state. It comes to ground state by emitting a photon, then the momentum of hydrogen atom will be approximately : (in kg-m/s)
(A) 12.1×0^{-27} (B) 6.45×10^{-27}
(C) 3×10^{-27} (D) 1.5×0^{-27}

1-35 An gas of H-atoms in excited state n_2 absorbs a photon of some energy and jump in higher energy state n_1. Then it returns to ground state after emitting six different wavelengths in emission spectrum. The energy of emitted photon is equal, less or greater than the energy of absorbed photon then n_1 and n_2 will be :
(A) $n_1 = 5, n_2 = 3$ (B) $n_1 = 5, n_2 = 2$
(C) $n_1 = 4, n_2 = 3$ (D) $n_1 = 4, n_2 = 2$

1-36 Imagine an atom made of a nucleus of charge (Ze) and a hypothetical particle of same mass but double the charge of the electron. Apply the Bohr atom model and consider all possible transitions of this hypothetical particle to the ground state. The longest wavelength of photon that will be emitted has wavelength λ (given in terms of Rydberg constant R of hydrogen atom equal to :

(A) $\frac{Z^2}{3R}$ (B) $\frac{1}{3Z^2R}$

(C) $\frac{4}{3Z^2R}$ (D) $\frac{16}{3Z^2R}$

1-37 One of the lines in the emission spectrum of Li^{2+} has the same wavelength as that of the 2nd line of Balmer series in hydrogen spectrum. The electronic transition corresponding to this line is :
(A) $n=4 \rightarrow n=2$ (B) $n=8 \rightarrow n=2$
(C) $n=8 \rightarrow n=4$ (D) $n=12 \rightarrow n=6$

1-38 In Bohr's theory the potential energy of an electron at a position is $\frac{Kr^2}{2}$ (where K is a positive constant); then the quantized energy of the electron in nth orbit is :

(A) $\frac{nh}{2\pi}\left(\frac{K}{m}\right)$ (B) $\frac{nh}{2\pi}\left(\frac{K}{m}\right)^{1/2}$

(C) $nh\left(\frac{K}{m}\right)$ (D) $\frac{nh}{2\pi}\left(\frac{m}{K}\right)^{1/2}$

1-39 If first and second frequencies in transition to 'k' orbital are related by the relation $\nu_1 = k\nu_2$, then the first frequency in the transition to second orbital will not be equal to :

(A) $\nu_1\left(\frac{1}{k}-1\right)$ (B) $(1-k)\,\nu_2$

(C) $\nu_2 - \nu_1$ (D) $k^2\nu_2$

1-40 The electron in a hydrogen atom first jumps from the third excited state to the second excited state and subsequently to the first excited state. The ratio of the respective wavelengths, λ_1/λ_2, of the photons emitted in this process is :
(A) 9/7 (B) 7/5
(C) 27/5 (D) 20/7

1-41 A monochromatic radiation of wavelength λ is incident on a sample containing He^+. As a result the Helium sample starts radiating. A part of this radiation is allowed to pass through a sample of atomic hydrogen gas in ground state. It is noticed that the hydrogen sample has started emitting electrons whose maximum Kinetic Energy is 37.4 eV. ($hc = 12400$ eV Å) Then λ is :
(A) 275 Å (B) 243 Å
(C) 656 Å (D) 386 Å

1-42 Of the following transitions in hydrogen atom, the one which gives an absorption line of highest frequency is :

(A) $n=1$ to $n=2$ (B) $n=3$ to $n=8$
(C) $n=2$ to $n=1$ (D) $n=8$ to $n=3$

1-43 An electron of the kinetic energy 10 eV collides with a hydrogen atom in 1st excited state. Assuming loss of kinetic energy in the collision to be quantized which of the following statements is INCORRECT.

(A) The collision may be perfectly inelastic
(B) The collision may be inelastic
(C) The collision may be elastic
(D) The collision must be inelastic

1-44 If in the first orbit of a hydrogen atom the total energy of the electron is -21.76×10^{-19} J, then its electric potential energy will be :

(A) -43.52×10^{-19} J (B) -21.76×10^{-19} J
(C) -10.88×10^{-19} J (D) -13.6×10^{-19} J

1-45 In the figure six lines of emission spectrum are shown. Which of them will be absent in the absorption spectrum.

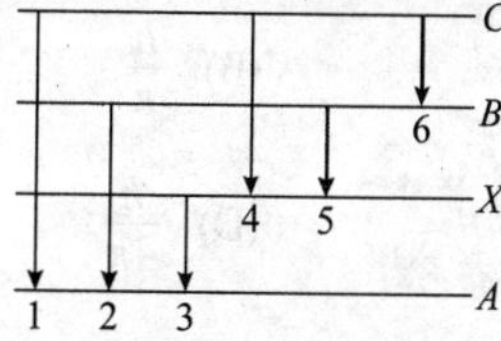

Figure 1.30

(A) 1, 2, 3 (B) 1, 4, 6
(C) 4, 5, 6 (D) 1, 2, 3, 4, 5, 6

1-46 An orbital electron in the ground state of hydrogen has an angular momentum L_1, and an orbital electron in the first orbit in the ground state of lithium (double ionised positively) has an angular momentum L_2. Then :

(A) $L_1 = L_2$ (B) $L_1 = 3L_2$
(C) $L_2 = 3L_1$ (D) $L_2 = 9L_1$

1-47 The ratio of the maximum wavelength of the Lyman series in hydrogen spectrum to the maximum wavelength in the Paschen series is :

(A) $\frac{3}{105}$ (B) $\frac{6}{15}$
(C) $\frac{52}{7}$ (D) $\frac{7}{108}$

1-48 Consider atoms H, He^+, Li^{++} in their ground states. Suppose E_1, E_2 and E_3 are minimum energies required so that the atoms H, He^+, Li^{++} can achieve their first excited states respectively, then :

(A) $E_1 = E_2 = E_3$ (B) $E_1 > E_2 > E_3$
(C) $E_1 < E_2 < E_3$ (D) $E_1 = E_2 = E_3$

1-49 The radius of first Bohr orbit of hydrogen atom is 0.53 Å. Then the radius of first Bohr-orbit of mesonic atom (negative meson has mass 207 times that of electron but same charge) is :

(A) 2.85×10^{-13} m (B) 1.06×10^{-13} m
(C) 0.53×10^{-10} m (D) 7.0×10^{-12} m

* * * * *

Advance MCQs with One or More Options Correct

1-1 The ground state and first excited state energies of hydrogen atom are -13.6 eV and -3.4 eV respectively. If potential energy in ground state is taken to be zero. Then :

(A) potential energy in the first excited state would be 20.4 eV

(B) total energy in the first excited state would be 23.8 eV

(C) kinetic energy in the first excited state would be 3.4 eV

(D) total energy in the ground state would be 13.6 eV

1-2 An electron is excited from a lower energy state to a higher energy state in a hydrogen atom. Which of the following quantity/quantities decreases/decrease in the excitation ?

(A) Potential energy (B) Angular speed

(C) Kinetic energy (D) Angular momentum

1-3 A single electron orbits a stationary nucleolus of charge $+Ze$, where Z is a constant and e is the magnitude of electronic charge. It requires 47.2 eV to excite the electron from the second Bohr orbit to third Bohr orbit :

(A) The value of Z is 2

(B) The energy required to excite the electron from third to fourth Bohr orbit is 16.53 eV

(C) The wavelength of electromagnetic radiation required to just remove electron from the first Bohr orbit to infinity is 3.65 nm

(D) The value of Z is 3

1-4 An electron in hydrogen atom first jumps from second excited state to first excited state and then from first excited state to ground state. Let the ratio of wavelength, momentum and energy of photons emitted in these two cases be, a, b and c respectively. Then :

(A) $c=1/a$ (B) $a=9/4$

(C) $b=5/27$ (D) $c=5/27$

1-5 The magnitude of energy, the magnitude of linear momentum and orbital radius of an electron in a hydrogen atom corresponding to the quantum number n are E, P and r respectively. Then according to Bohr's theory of hydrogen atom :

(A) EPr is proportional to $1/n$

(B) P/E is proportional to n

(C) Er is constant for all orbits

(D) Pr is proportional to n

1-6 The wavelengths and frequencies of photons in transitions 1, 2 and 3 for hydrogen like atom are $\lambda_1, \lambda_2, \lambda_3, \nu_1, \nu_2$ and ν_3 respectively. Then :

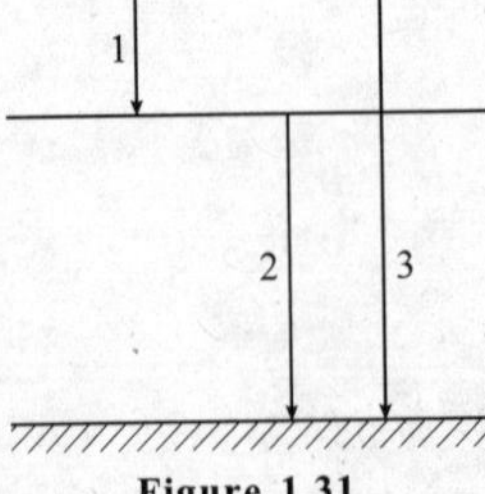

Figure 1.31

(A) $\nu_3=\nu_1+\nu_2$

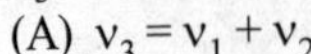

(B) $\nu_3=\dfrac{\nu_1\nu_2}{\nu_1+\nu_2}$

(C) $\lambda_3=\lambda_1+\lambda_2$ (D) $\lambda_3=\dfrac{\lambda_1\lambda_2}{\lambda_1+\lambda_2}$

1-7 Which of the following transitions in He^+ ion will give rise to a spectral line which has the same wavelength as some spectral line in the hydrogen atom ?

(A) $n=4$ to $n=2$ (B) $n=6$ to $n=2$

(C) $n=6$ to $n=3$ (D) $n=8$ to $n=4$

1-8 In the Bohr model of the hydrogen atom, let R, V and E represent the radius of the orbit, speed of the electron and the magnitude of total energy of the electron respectively. Which of the following quantities are proportional to the quantum number n?

(A) VR (B) RE

(C) $\dfrac{V}{E}$ (D) $\dfrac{R}{E}$

1-9 In an electron transition inside a hydrogen atom, angular momentum of electron may change by

(A) h (B) $\dfrac{h}{\pi}$

(C) $\dfrac{h}{2\pi}$ (D) $\dfrac{h}{4\pi}$

1-10 A beam of ultraviolet light of all wavelength passes through hydrogen gas at room temperature, in the x-direction. Assume that all photons emitted due to electron transitions inside the gas emerge in the y-direction. Let A and B denote the lights emerging from the gas in the x-and y-directions respectively :

(A) Some of the incident wavelengths will be absent in A

(B) Only those wavelengths will be present in B which are absent in A

(C) B will contain some visible light

(D) B will contain some infrared light

1-11 Whenever a hydrogen atom emits a photon in the Balmer series :

(A) It may emit another photon in the Balmer series

(B) It must emit another photon in the Lyman series

(C) The second photon, if emitted, will have a wavelength of about 122 nm

(D) It may emit a second photon, but the wavelength of this photon cannot be predicted

1-12 Which of the following statements about hydrogen spectrum is/are correct ?

(A) All the lines of Lyman series lie in ultraviolet region

(B) All the lines of Balmer series lie in visible region
(C) All the lines of Paschen series lie in infrared region
(D) none of these

1-13 The ionization energy of a Hydrogen like atom is 54.4 eV. Then which of the following statement(s) is/are true about this atom:
(A) Its first excitation potential is 40.8 V
(B) Its $Z = 2$
(C) It can absorb a photon of energy 50 eV
(D) It can absorb a photon of energy 56 eV

1-14 If, in hydrogen atom, radius of nth Bohr orbit is r_n, frequency of revolution of electron in n^{th} orbit is f_n and area enclosed by n^{th} orbit is A_n, time period of electron is T_n then which of the following graphs is/are correct ?

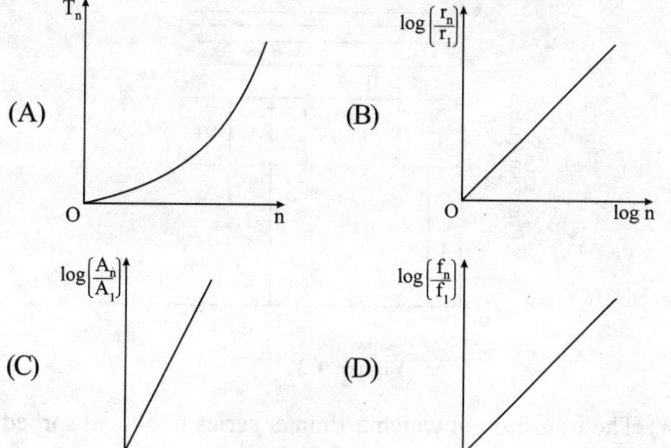

1-15 Let the energy, magnitude of linear momentum and angular frequency of an electron in hydrogen atom be E, P and ω respectively. If n be the corresponding energy level, then which of the following statement(s) is/are correct:
(A) E/ω varies as n
(B) EP/ω is independent of n
(C) $P\omega$ varies as $n^{1/2}$
(D) $EP\omega$ is independent of n

1-16 A photon of energy 10.5 eV is allowed to interact with a hydrogen atom in its ground state. Then :
(A) the photon is completely absorbed by the H-atom
(B) the photon cannot excite the H-atom and comes out with energy 10.5 eV
(C) the photon transfers 10.2 eV energy to H-atom exciting it to first excited state
(D) none of these

1-17 When a hydrogen atom is excited from ground state to first excited state :
(A) Its kinetic energy increases by 10.2 eV
(B) Its kinetic energy decreases by 10.2 eV
(C) Its potential energy increases by 20.4 eV
(D) Its angular momentum increases by 1.05×10^{-35} J-s

1-18 Suppose the potential energy between electron and proton at a distance r is given by $-\frac{Ke^2}{2r^3}$.
Using Bohr's theory choose the correct statements :
(A) Energy in the nth orbit is proportional to n^3
(B) Energy in the nth orbit is proportional to n^6
(C) Energy is proportional to m^2 (m : mass of electron)
(D) Energy is proportional to m^{-3} (m : mass of electron)

1-19 An electron in an hydrogen atom has total energy of – 3.4 eV. Choose the correct statement (s) :
(A) The kinetic energy of the electron in that orbit is 3.4 eV
(B) The potential energy of the electron in that orbit is – 6.8 eV
(C) Angular momentum of the electron in that orbit is h/π
(D) Angular momentum of the electron for that orbit is $2h/\pi$

1-20 When Z is doubled in an atom, which of the following statements are consistent with Bohr's theory ?
(A) Energy of a state is double
(B) Radius of an orbit is doubled
(C) Velocity of electrons in an orbit is doubled
(D) Radius of an orbit is halved

1-21 The electron in a hydrogen atom jumps back from an excited state to ground state, by emitting a photon of wavelength $\lambda_0 = \frac{16}{15R}$, where R is Rydberg's constant. In place of emitting one photon, the electron could come back to ground state by
(A) Emitting 3 photons of wavelengths λ_1, λ_2 and λ_3 such that $\frac{1}{\lambda_1}+\frac{1}{\lambda_2}+\frac{1}{\lambda_3}=\frac{15R}{16}$
(B) Emitting 2 photons of wavelength λ_1 and λ_2 such that $\frac{1}{\lambda_1}+\frac{1}{\lambda_2}=\frac{15R}{16}$
(C) Emitting 2 photons of wavelength λ_1 and λ_2 such that $\lambda_1+\lambda_2=\frac{16}{15R}$
(D) Emitting 3 photons of wavelength λ_1, λ_2 and λ_3 such that $\lambda_1+\lambda_2+\lambda_3=\frac{16}{15R}$

1-22 A particle P collides inelastically with a single ionized helium atom which is at rest, initially helium atom (He^+) is in ground state. After collision, the particle P is found to be scattered at an angle 90° with respect to it's initial direction of motion, and before emitting any radiation, He^+ and particle P have same kinetic energy. He^+ is observed to emit total 6 wavelengths representing all possible transitions in between

excited state to the ground state. Which of the following statement(s) is/are true:
(A) The particle P may be a sufficiently energetic electron
(B) The particle P may be a sufficiently energetic neutron
(C) Out of six wavelength only one belongs to visible region
(D) None of emitted radiations belongs to visible region

1-23 A particular hydrogen like atom has its ground state binding energy 122. 4 eV. It is in ground state. Then
(A) Its atomic number is 3
(B) An electron of 90 eV can excite it
(C) An electron of kinetic energy nearly 91.8 eV can be brought to almost rest by this atom
(D) An electron of kinetic energy 2.6 eV may emerge from the atom when electron of kinetic energy 125 eV collides with this atom
Momentum ratio of photons is

1-24 In a "Positronium" atom a pair of electron and positron orbit each other. If Bohr's atomic model is valid, then in comparison with Bohr's atomic hydrogen,
(assume that mass of proton >>> mass of electron)
(A) The Rydberg's constant for positronium is half
(B) The ionisation energy for positronium is double
(C) The radius of positronium is double
(D) The kinetic energy of electron in the center of mass frame of positronium is one fourth that of the electron w.r.t. proton in the H-atom

1-25 In the hydrogen atom, if the reference level of potential energy is assumed to be zero at the ground state level. Choose the incorrect statement.
(A) The total energy of the shell increases with increase in the value of n
(B) The total energy of the shell decrease with increase in the value of n
(C) The difference in total energy of any two shells remains the same
(D) The total energy at the ground state becomes 13.6 eV

1-26 Choose the correct statement(s) for hydrogen and deuterium atoms (considering the motion of nucleus)
(A) The radius of first Bohr orbit of deuterium is less than that of hydrogen
(B) The speed of electron in first Balmer line of deuterium is more than that of hydrogen
(C) The wavelength of first Balmer line of deuterium is more than that of hydrogen
(D) The angular momentum of electron in the first Bohr orbit of deuterium is more than that of hydrogen

1-27 A neutron collides head–on with a stationary hydrogen atom in ground state. Which of the following statements are correct (Assume that the hydrogen atom and neutron has same mass)
(A) If kinetic energy of the neutron is less than 20.4 eV collision must be elastic
(B) If kinetic energy of the neutron is less than 20.4 eV collision may be inelastic
(C) Inelastic collision may be take place only when initial kinetic energy of neutron is greater than 20.4 eV
(D) Perfectly inelastic collision can not take place

1-28 The figure-1.32 below shows an energy level diagram for the hydrogen atom. Several transitions are marked as I, II, III, ________. The diagram is only indicative and not to scale.

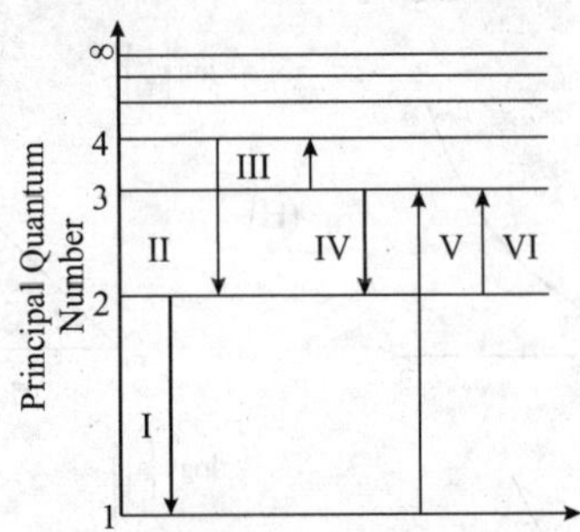

Figure 1.32

(A) The transition in which a Balmer series photon absorbed is VI.
(B) The wavelength of the radiation involved in transition II is 486 nm.
(C) IV transition will occur when a hydrogen atom is irradiated with radiation of wavelength 103 nm.
(D) IV transition will emit the longest wavelength line in the visible portion of the hydrogen spectrum.

1-29 A hydrogen atom is in the 4th excited state, then :
(A) the maximum number of emitted photons will be 10
(B) the maximum number of emitted photons will be 6
(C) it can emit three photons in ultraviolet region
(D) if an infrared photon is generated, then a visible photon may follow this infrared photon

1-30 An electron with kinetic energy E eV collides with a hydrogen atom in the ground state. The collision is observed to be elastic for :
(A) $0 < E < \infty$ (B) $0 < E < 10.2$ eV
(C) $0 < E < 13.6$ eV (D) $0 < E < 3.4$ eV

* * * * *

Unsolved Numerical Problems for Preparation of NSEP, INPhO & IPhO

For detailed preparation of INPhO and IPhO students can refer advance study material on www.physicsgalaxy.com

1-1 A positive ion having just one electron ejects it if a photon of wavelength 228 Å or less is absorbed by it. Identifying the ion.

Ans. [He^{+1}]

1-2 A hydrogen like ion has the wavelength difference between the first lines of Balmer and Lyman series equal to 59.3 nm. Identify the atomic number of ion.

Ans. [3]

1-3 A beam of ultraviolet radiation having wavelength between 100 nm and 200 nm is incident on a sample of atomic hydrogen gas. Assuming that the atoms are in ground state, which wavelengths will have low intensity in the transmitted beam? If the energy of a photon is equal to the difference between the energies of an excited state and the ground state, it has large probability of being absorbed by an atom in the ground state.

Ans. [λ_1 = 122 nm; λ_2 = 103 nm]

1-4 A hydrogen atom in $n = 6$ makes two successive transitions & reaches the ground state. In the first transition a photon of 1.13 eV is emitted. Find the energy of the photon emitted in the second transition & value of n for the intermediate state.

Ans. [12.1 eV, 3]

1-5 Demonstrate that the frequency ν of a photon emerging when an electron jumps between neighbouring circular orbits of a hydrogen like atom satisfies the inequality $\nu_{n+1} < \nu < \nu_n$ where ν_n and ν_{n+1} are the frequencies of revolution of that electron around the nucleus along the circular orbits. Also show that for large values of n all these three are almost equal.

1-6 Find the quantum number n corresponding to the excited state of He^+ ion if on transition to the ground state that ion emits two photons in succession with wave lengths 108.5 and 30.4 nm.

Ans. [n = 5]

1-7 (a) Find the maximum wavelength λ of light which can ionize a H-atom in ground state.

(b) Light of wavelength λ incident on a H-atom which is in its first excited state. Find the kinetic energy of the electron coming out.

Ans. [(a) 913 Å, (b) 10.2 eV]

1-8 A hydrogen atom in ground state absorbs a photon of ultraviolet radiation of wavelength 500 Å. Assuming that the entire photon energy is takes up by the electrons, with what kinetic energy will the electron be ejected.

Ans. [11.24 eV]

1-9 Suppose, in certain conditions only those transitions are allowed to hydrogen atoms in which the principal quantum number n changes by 2.

(a) Find the smallest wavelength emitted by hydrogen.

(b) List the wavelengths emitted by hydrogen in the visible range (380 nm to 780 nm)

Ans. [(a) 103 nm; (b) 487 nm]

1-10 A particle of mass m moves along a circular orbit in a centrosymmetrical potential field $U(r) = \frac{kr^2}{2}$. Using the Bohr's quantization condition, find the permissible orbital radii and energy levels of that particle.

Ans. [$r_n = \sqrt{\frac{n\hbar}{m\omega}}$ and E_n = where $\hbar = \frac{h}{2\pi}$ and $\omega = \sqrt{\frac{k}{m}}$]

1-11 Consider a charged particle moving in circular motion under the effect of a uniform magnetic field. If Bohr's quantization postulate is applied on this particle than calculate the ratio of its speed in third excited state to ground state.

Ans. [2]

1-12 A parallel beam, of light of wavelength 100 nm passes through a sample of atomic hydrogen gas in ground state.

(a) Assume that when a photon supplies some of its energy to a hydrogen atom, the rest of the energy appears as another photon moving in the same direction as the incident photon. Neglecting the light emitted by the excited hydrogen atoms in the direction of the incident beam, what wavelengths may be observed in the transmitted beam?

(b) A radiation detector is placed near the gas to detect radiation coming perpendicular to the incident beam. Find the wavelengths of radiation that may be detected by the detector.

Ans. [(a) 100 nm, 560 nm, 3880 nm; (b) 103 nm, 121 nm, 654 nm]

1-13 A μ-meson particle moves in a circular orbit around a very heavy nucleus (assumed to be of infinite mass compared to other surrounding particles) of charge $+3e$. Assuming Bohr's model is applicable to this system. When μ-meson jumps from 3rd orbit to 1st orbit, find the wavelength of emitted radiation. [A μ-meson is a particle, whose charge is equal to that of an electron and mass = 208 times that of an electron]

Ans. [55 pm]

1-14 A stationary He^+ ion emitted a photon corresponding to the first line of the Lyman series. That photon liberated a photoelectron from a stationary hydrogen atom in the ground state. Find the velocity of photoelectron.

Ans. [$v = 3.1 \times 10^6$ m/s, where m is the mass of the electron]

1-15 The average kinetic energy of molecules in a gas at temperature T is 1.5 KT. Find the temperature at which the average Kinetic energy of the molecules of hydrogen equals the binding energy of its atoms. Will hydrogen remain in molecular form at this temperature?

Ans. [1.05×10^5K, Yes]

1-16 A well collimated parallel pencil of cathode rays falls through a potential difference 3 kV & enters the spacing between two parallel metallic plates, parallel to their length the spacing between the plates being 0.5 cm. The pencil strikes a fluorescent screen, mounted perpendicular to the length of the plates at the farther end of the plates & produces fluorescent spot. If now a potential difference of 3 V is applied across the two plates, calculate the linear deflection of the spot on the screen. Given the length of the plates is 10 cm.

Ans. [0.05 cm]

1-17 A hydrogen in a state having a binding energy of 0.85 eV makes transition to a state with excitation energy is 10.2 eV.

(a) Identify the quantum no. n of an upper and the lower energy states involved in the transition.

(b) Find the wavelength of the emitted radiation.

Ans. [4, 2, 4870 Å]

1-18 A hypothetical, hydrogen like atom consists of a nucleus of mass m_1 and charge ($+Ze$) and a mu-meson of mass m_2 and charge ($-e$). Using Bohr's theory, derive an expression for distance between nucleus and mu-meson for principal quantum number n and derive a relation for energy also. Hence obtain expression for reduced mass.

Ans. [$r = \frac{\varepsilon_0 n^2 h^2 (m_1 + m_2)}{\pi m_1 m_2 Z e^2}$, $E = -\frac{1}{8} \cdot \frac{m_1 m_2 Z^2 e^4}{(m_1 + m_2)\varepsilon_0^2 n^2 h^2}$, $m_0 = \frac{m_1 m_2}{m_1 + m_2}$]

1-19 Whenever a photon is emitted by hydrogen in Balmer series, it is followed by another photon in Lyman series. What wavelength does latter photon correspond to ?

Ans. [1224 Å]

1-20 A particular hydrogen-like ion emits radiation of frequency 2.467×10^{15} Hz when it makes transition from $n = 2$ to $n = 1$. What will be the frequency of the radiation emitted a transition from $n = 3$ to $n = 1$?

Ans. [2.92×10^{15} Hz]

1-21 Consider a hydrogen like atom whose energy in n^{th} excited state is given by

$$E_n = -\frac{13.6}{n^2} Z^2$$

When this excited atom makes a transition from an excited state to ground state. The most energetic and least energetic photon energies emitted are given as

$$E_{max} = 52.224 \text{ eV}$$

$$E_{min} = 1.224 \text{ eV}$$

Find the atomic number of atom and the quantum number of the excited state.

Ans. [2, 5]

1-22 A single electron orbits around a stationary nucleus of charge $+Ze$, where Z is a constant and e is the magnitude of the electronic charge. It requires 47.2 eV to excite the electron from the second Bohr orbit to the third Bohr orbit. Find :

(i) The value of Z.

(ii) The energy required to excite the electrons from the third orbit to fourth.

(iii) The wavelength of the electromagnetic radiation required to remove the electron from the first Bohr orbit to infinity.

(iv) The kinetic energy, potential energy and the angular momentum of the electron in the first Bohr orbit.

(v) The radius of the first Bohr orbit.

(the ionization energy of hydrogen atom = 13.6 eV, Bohr radius = 5.3×10^{-11} m, velocity of light = 3×10^8 ms^{-1}, Planck's constant = 6.63×10^{-34} Js)

Ans. [(i) 5; (ii) 16.53 eV; (iii) 621/17 Å = 36.5 Å; (iv) 340 eV, – 680 eV, $h/2\pi$; (v) 0.106 Å]

1-23 At what minimum kinetic energy must a hydrogen atom move for its inelastic head-on collision with another, stationary, hydrogen atom to make one of them capable of emitting photon ? Both atoms are supposed to be in the ground state prior to the collision.

Ans. [T_{min} = 20.4 eV]

1-24 Atoms of a hydrogen like gas are in a particular excited energy level. When these atoms de-excite, they emit photons of different energies. Maximum and minimum energies of emitted photons are E_{max} = 52.224 eV and E_{min} = 1.224 eV respectively. Identify the gas and calculate principal quantum number of initially excited energy level. (Ionisation energy of hydrogen atom = 13.6 eV)

Ans. [He^+, 5]

1-25 A hydrogen atom moving at a speed v collides with another hydrogen atom kept at rest. Find the minimum value of v for which one of the atoms may get ionized. The mass of a hydrogen atom is 1.67×10^{-27} kg.

Ans. [7.2×10^4 m/s]

1-26 Assuming that in an at an atom, neutron with mass m_n and electron with mass m_e are bound to each other by gravitational force and assuming Bohr's quantization postulate to be valid, derive the expression for energy of election in n^{th} level.

Ans. [$-\dfrac{2\pi^2 G^2 m_e^3 m_n^2}{n^2 h^2}$]

1-27 Electrons are emitted from an electron gun at almost zero velocity and are accelerated by an electric field E through a distance of 1 m. The electrons are now scattered by an atomic hydrogen sample in ground state. What should be the minimum value of E so that red light of wavelength 6563 Å may be emitted in the hydrogen ?

Ans. [12.1 volts/m]

1-28 A hydrogen like gas emits radiation of wavelengths 460 Å, 828 Å and 1035 Å, only. Assume that the atoms have only two excited states and the difference between consecutive energy levels decreases as energy is increased. Taking the energy of the highest energy state to be zero. Find the energies of the ground state and the first excited state.

Ans. [– 27.2 eV, – 12 eV]

1-29 A gas of hydrogen-like ions is prepared in a particular excited state A. It emits photons having wavelength equal to the wavelength of the first line of the Lyman series together with photons of five other wavelengths. Identify the gas and find the principal quantum number of the state A.

Ans. [He^+, 4]

1-30 Find the temperature at which the average thermal kinetic energy is equal to the energy needed to take a hydrogen atom from its ground state to $n = 3$ state. Hydrogen can now emit red light of wavelength 653.1 nm. Because of Maxwellian distribution of speeds, a hydrogen sample emits red light at temperatures much lower than that obtained from this problem. Assume that hydrogen molecules dissociate into atoms.

Ans. [9.4×10^4 K]

1-31 A spectroscopic instrument can resolve two nearby wavelengths λ and $\lambda + \Delta\lambda$ if $\lambda/\Delta\lambda$ is smaller than 8000. This is used to study the spectral lines of the Balmer series of hydrogen. Approximately how many lines will be resolved by the instrument?

Ans. [38]

1-32 A hydrogen atom in the normal state is located at a distance $r = 2.5$ cm from a long straight conductor carrying a current $I = 10$ A. Find the maximum force acting on the atom.

Ans. [$F = 3 \times 10^{-26}$ N]

1-33 Using Bohr's theory show that when n is very large the frequency of radiation emitted by hydrogen atom due to transition of electron from n to $(n - 1)$ is equal to frequency of revolution of electron in its orbit.

1-34 In a hydrogen like ionized atom a single electron is orbiting around a stationary positive charge. If a spectral line of λ equal to 4861 Å is observed due to transition from $n = 12$ to $n = 6$. What is the wavelength of a spectral line due to transition from $n = 9$ to $n = 6$ and also identify the element.

Ans. [6563 Å, Z = 3]

1-35 The energy of an electron in an excited hydrogen atom is – 3/4 eV. Calculate the angular momentum of the electron according to Bohr's theory. Given. Rydberg's constant $R = 1.09737 \times 10^7$ m^{-1}, Planck's constant $h = 6.626176 \times 10^{-34}$ Js and speed of light $c = 3 \times 10^8$ ms^{-1}.

Ans. [2.11×10^{-34} Js]

1-36 A gas of identical hydrogen-life atoms has same atoms in the lowest energy level A and some atoms in a particular upper level B and there are no atoms in any other energy level. The atoms of the gas make transition to a higher energy level by absorbing monochromatic light of photons energy 7.56 eV. Subsequently, the atoms emit radiation of only six different photon energies. Some of emitted photons have energy 7.56 eV, some have energy more and some have less than 7.56 eV. Calculate

(i) the principal quantum number of the initially excited level B,

(ii) maximum and minimum energies of emitted photons and

(iii) ionisation energy for gas atoms

Ans. [(i) 2, (ii) 37.8 eV, 1.96 eV, (iii) 40.32 eV]

1-37 Two hydrogen like atoms A & B are of different masses & each atom contains equal number of protons & neutrons. The difference in the energies between the first Balmer lines emitted by A & B is 5.667 eV. When atoms A & B, moving with the same velocity. In the process atom B imparts twice the momentum to the target than that A imparts. Identify the atoms A & B.

Ans. [$Z_A = 1$, $Z_B = 2$]

1-38 A free electron with kinetic energy 3.4eV happens to fall into an orbit around a fixed alpha particle forming a He^+ atom in the first excited state. *A* photon of wavelength λ_1 is emitted. Then the atom comes to the ground state emitting another photon of wavelength λ_2. Calculate λ_1/λ_2.

Ans. [2.4]

1-39 A neutron strikes a hydrogen atom (Mass is considered same as that of neutron) which is initially at rest and free to move. The initial speed of the neutron is v_0. After the collision both neutron and the *H* atom move making 30° angle with the initial velocity of the neutron. Also the *H* atom if found to get excited to first excited state. If the initial kinetic energy of neutron is *K* times first excitation energy of the *H* atom, find the value of *K*.

Ans. [3]

* * * * *

Photo Electric Effect & Matter Waves

2

FEW WORDS FOR STUDENTS

To understand atomic phenomena, we need both a model of atom and a theory that describes the behaviour of atoms. In this chapter we will examine some of the experiments that led to our present understanding of the atoms. These experiments which we are going to study also contributed to the development of quantum mechanics. The ideas of Planck, Einstein and Bohr are especially important in describing the fundamental theory of atoms. You will find that ideas such as dual nature of light and concept of matter waves play a fundamental role in explaining observations in different experiments related to atomic theory.

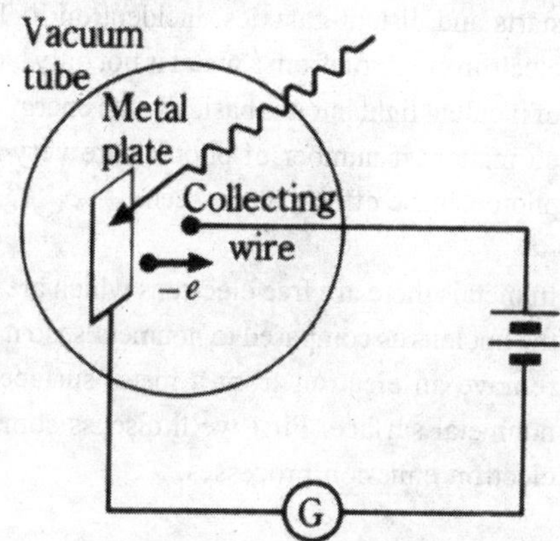

CHAPTER CONTENTS

COVER APPLICATION

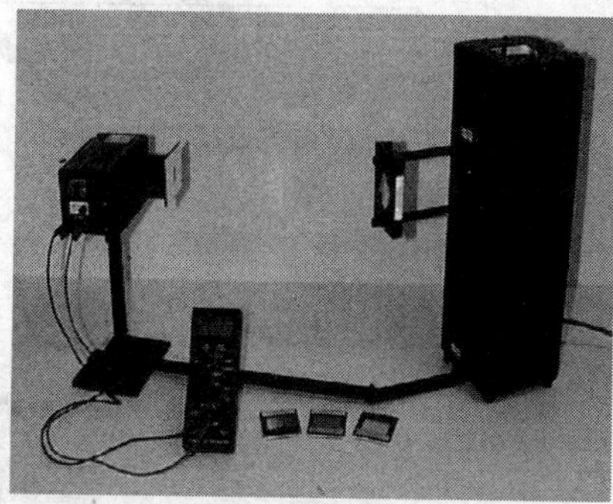

Figure (a)

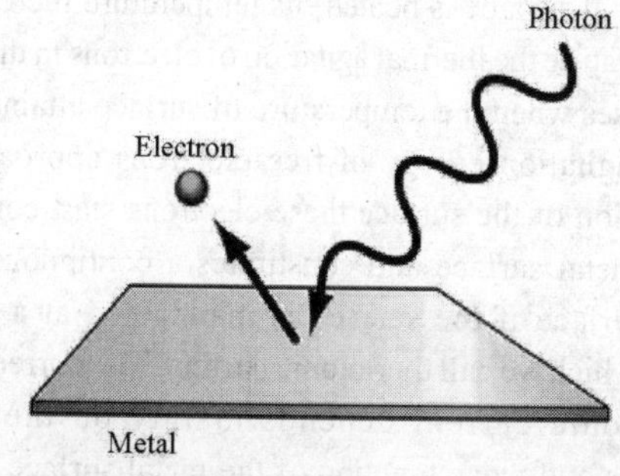

Figure (b)

Figure-(a) shows the laboratory experimental setup for study of photoelectric effect to analyze the variation of current-voltage characteristics and figure-(b) shows the microscopic view of the phenomenon of photoelectric effect how a light quanta (photon) is absorbed and without any time leg an electron is emitted under the conditions of photoelectric effect.

Planck's hypothesis about the way energy is carried in bundles by light become useful in explanation of one of the important phenomenon of modern physics-photoelectric effect. Photoelectric effect is the emission of electrons when light of an appropriate frequency is incident on a metallic surface. It was observed that electrons are ejected from a metal surface some times even when incredibly dim light such as that from starts and distant galaxies, incident on it. This shows that the electron emission from a metal is not only based on the intensity of incident light but it is basically the energy of incident photons no matters if number of photons are very less in a dim light, photoelectric effect can be seen.

In metals there are free electrons which are loosely bounded to the nucleus as compared to nonmetals, so it is relatively easy to remove an electron from a metal surface as compared to a nonmetal surface. First we'll discuss some different ways of electron emission processes.

2.1 Electron Emission Processes

We know from an atom the minimum energy required to remove an electron is called Ionization Potential. Similarly the minimum energy required to remove an electron from a metal surface is called '*Work Function*' for that metal surface.

There are several ways in which we can supply work function to a metal surface, which we call electron emission process. In general there are four electron emission processes. These are :

(1) Thermionic Emission

(2) Photoelectric Emission

(3) Secondary Emission

(4) Field Emission

2.1.1 Thermionic Emission

When a metal surface is heated, its temperature increases and with temperature the thermal agitation of electrons in the surface also increases when the temperature of surface attains a value when the agitation energy of free electrons approaches the work function of the surface these electrons start coming out from the metal surface and constitutes a continuous current into the surface if the surface is maintained at a constant potential, which we call thermionic current. The current density of thermionic current depends mainly on the surface temperature and work function of the metal surface given by "*Richardson Dushman Equation*", given as

$$J = A\,T^2\,e^{-\phi/KT} \qquad \ldots(2.1)$$

Here A is a constant called '*Richardson Constant*'.

Here if S is the surface area of the metal surface then thermionic current at the surface can be given as

$$I = JS = A\,S\,T^2\,e^{-\phi/KT} \qquad \ldots(2.2)$$

2.1.2 Photoelectric Emission

In this process, work function is provided in the form of light photons, as shown in figure-2.1. If the energy of incident photons is more then the work function of the metal surface, the free electrons of the surface absorb these photons and comes out from the surface as shown.

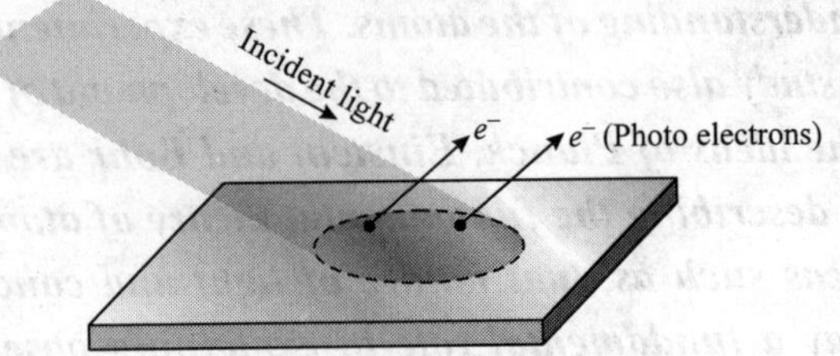

Figure 2.1

2.1.3 Secondary Emission

This is a process in which the work function is supplied to the free electrons of a metal surface by collisions with the fast moving secondary particles like neutrons. β-particles etc. For this a beam of fast moving particles is incident on a metal surface like neutrons from a neutron gun in the figure-2.2 shown. Due to high kinetic energy these neutrons penetrate the metal and during collisions with the free electrons of the metal transfer energy to these electrons, if this energy is more then work function these electrons are ejected out from the metal surface.

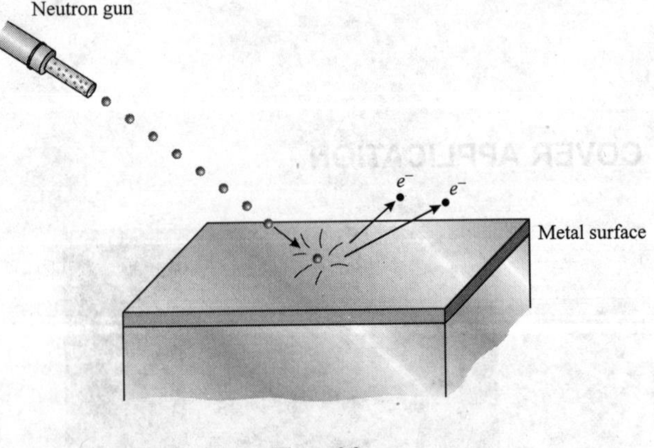

Figure 2.2

2.1.4 Field Emission

This is a process in which work function of a metal is provided to the free electron of a metal surface by applying a strong electric field on the metal surface. As shown in figure-2.3 if an electric field in downward direction is increased on the metal, the pull on electron due to this electric field increases and it increases the electrical potential energy of the free electrons, when this energy increases beyond the work function, the electron will come out from the metal surface.

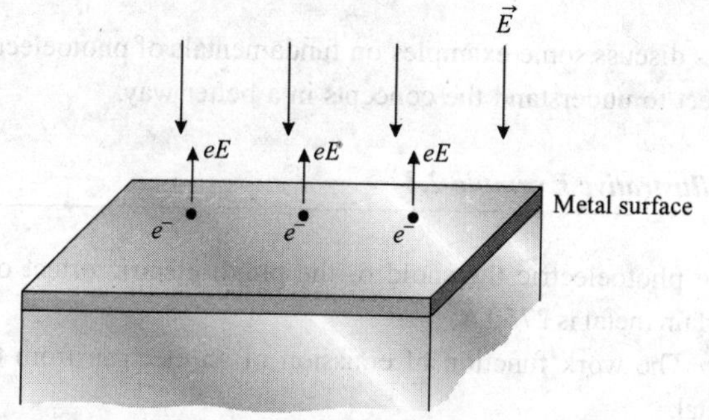

Figure 2.3

2.2 *Photoelectric Effect*

Photo electric effect is the phenomenon of photoelectric emission when a light beam having photon energy more than work function incident on a metal surface and ejects electrons from the surface.

Based on phenomenon of photoelectric effect, several experiments are done by scientists and some conclusions were made for understanding this phenomenon and its applications in detail. These conclusions are summarized in some points which are called fundamental laws of photo electric effect. Now we'll discuss these fundamental laws then later we'll discuss about the experimental study of photo electric effect.

2.2.1 Fundamental Laws of Photoelectric Effect

On the basis of Planck's idea of quantization of energy, in year 1905 Albert Einstein proposed his theory of Photoelectric Effect. 1905 was the same year in which his special theory of relativity was given. Some Sequential points are mentioned here to understand the fundamentals of photoelectric effect.

(1) "When light incident on a metal surface, photoelectric effect will start only if the frequency of incident radiation is more than a fixed frequency, which we call threshold frequency".

We have discussed that to start photoelectric emission the energy of incident photon on metal surface must be more than the work function of the metal. If ϕ is the work function of the metal then there must be a minimum frequency of the incident light photon which is just able to eject the electron from the metal surface. This minimum frequency or threshold frequency ν_{th} can be given as

$$h\nu_{th} = \phi \qquad \dots(2.3)$$

Threshold frequency ν_{th} is a characteristic property of a metal as it is the minimum frequency of the light radiation required to eject a free electron from the metal surface.

Threshold Wavelength

As the threshold frequency is defined, we can also define threshold wavelength λ_{th} for a metal surface. Threshold wavelength is also called cut off wavelength. For a given metal surface threshold wavelength is the longest wavelength at which photo electric effect is possible. Thus we have

$$\frac{hc}{\lambda_{th}} = \phi$$

So for wavelength of incident light $\lambda > \lambda_{th}$, the energy of incident photons will become less then the work function of the metal and hence photoelectric effect will not start.

Thus for a given metal surface photoelectric emission will start at $\nu > \nu_{th}$ or $\lambda < \lambda_{th}$.

(2) Following Planck's idea, Einstein suggested that the energy of photon ($h\nu > \phi$) which is more then work function of a metal when incident on the metal surface is used by the electron after absorption in two parts.

(i) A part of energy of absorbed photon is used by the free electron in work done in coming out from the metal surface as work function.

(ii) The remaining part of the photon energy will be gained by the electron in the form of kinetic energy after ejection from the metal surface.

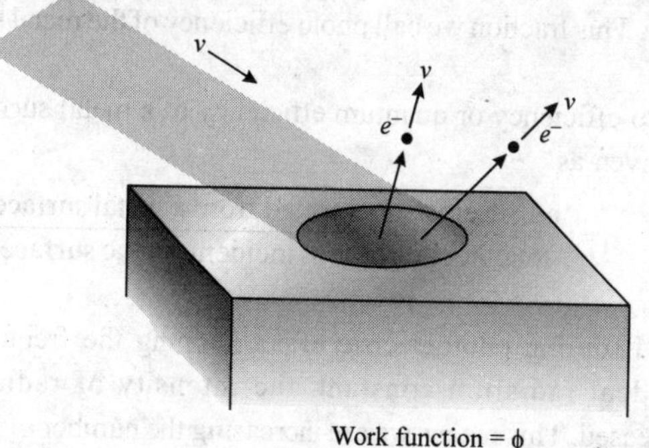

Figure 2.4

If a light beam of frequency ν (each photon energy = $h\nu$) is incident on a metal surface having work function ϕ then for $h\nu > \phi$, we have

$$h\nu = \phi + \frac{1}{2}mv_{max}^2 \qquad \dots(2.4)$$

In equation-(2.4) the second term on right hand side of equation is $\frac{1}{2}mv_{max}^2$, which is the maximum kinetic energy of the ejected electron.

In practical cases whenever an electron absorbs a photon from incident light, it comes out from the metal surface if $h\nu > \phi$ but in process of ejection it may collide with the neighbouring electrons and before ejection it may loose some energy during collisions with the neighbouring electrons. In this case after ejection the kinetic energy of ejected electrons will be certainly less then $(h\nu - \phi)$. If we assume there are some electrons which do not loose any energy in the process of ejection, will come out from the metal surface with the maximum kinetic energy given as

$$\frac{1}{2}mv_{max}^2 = h\nu - \phi \qquad \ldots(2.5)$$

Thus all the ejected electrons from the metal surface may have different kinetic energies, distributed from 0 to $\frac{1}{2}mv_{max}^2$.

(3) During the phenomenon of photoelectric effect one incident photon on metal surface $(h\nu > \phi)$ can eject at most only one electron. As according to Plank's explanation a photon is an energy packet, which if absorbed, fully absorbed not partially. Thus one photon can not be absorbed by more then one electron.

Here one more point is important that energy of photon incident on metal will not necessarily cause emission of an electron even if its energy is more then work function. In the process of ejection as discussed earlier, the electron after absorption may be involved in many other process like collisions etc. in which it can lose energy hence the ratio of number of electrons emitted to the number of photons incident on metal surface is less then unity. This fraction we call photo efficiency of the metal surface.

Photo efficiency or quantum efficiency of a metal surface can be given as

$$\eta = \frac{\text{no. of electrons ejected from a metal surface}}{\text{total no. of photons incident on the surface}}$$

(4) If during photoelectric effect keeping the frequency of incident radiation constant, the intensity of radiation is increased. This means we are increasing the number of incident photons per second in the beam. As each photon is capable to eject an electron, the number of ejected electrons per second, which we call photocurrent increases.

(5) During photoelectric effect, the rate at which the electrons are emitted from the surface is entirely independent from the temperature of the surface. This shows that the Photoelectric emission is entirely independent from the Thermionic emission.

(6) During Photoelectric Effect, there is no time lag between absorption of the photon by the surface and the emission of the photoelectron from the surface.

(7) From equation-(2.5) we can see that if the frequency of incident radiation increases, it will increase the kinetic energy of ejected, photoelectron because for a given metal surface, work function is constant.

Lets discuss some examples on fundamentals of photoelectric effect to understand the concepts in a better way.

Illustrative Example 2.1

The photoelectric threshold of the photo electric effect of a certain metal is 2750 Å. Find

(i) The work function of emission of an electron from this metal,

(ii) Maximum kinetic energy of these electrons,

(iii) The maximum velocity of the electrons ejected from the metal by light with a wavelength 1800 Å.

Solution

(i) Given that the threshold wavelength of a metal is $\lambda_{th} = 2750$ Å. Thus workfunction of metal can be given as

$$\phi = \frac{hc}{\lambda_{th}}$$

$$\Rightarrow \quad \phi = \frac{12431}{2750}\ \text{eV}$$

$$\Rightarrow \quad \phi = 4.52\ \text{eV}$$

(ii) The energy of incident photon of wavelength 1800 Å on metal in eV is

$$E = \frac{12431}{1800}\ \text{eV}$$

$$\Rightarrow \quad E = 6.9\ \text{eV}$$

Thus maximum kinetic energy of ejected electrons is

$$KE_{max} = E - \phi$$

$$\Rightarrow \quad KE_{max} = 6.9 - 4.52\ \text{eV}$$

$$\Rightarrow \quad KE_{max} = 2.38\ \text{eV}$$

(iii) If the maximum speed of ejected electrons is v_{max} then we have

$$\frac{1}{2}mv_{max}^2 = 2.38\ \text{eV}$$

$$\Rightarrow \quad v_{max} = \sqrt{\frac{2 \times 2.38 \times 1.6 \times 10^{-19}}{9.1 \times 10^{-31}}}$$

$$\Rightarrow \quad v_{max} = 9.15 \times 10^5\ \text{m/s}$$

Illustrative Example 2.2

Light quanta with an energy 4.9 eV eject photoelectrons from metal with work function 4.5 eV. Find the maximum impulse transmitted to the surface of the metal when each electrons flies out.

Solution

According to Einstein's photoelectric equation

$$E = \frac{1}{2}mv_{max}^2 = h\nu - \phi$$

$$= 4.9 - 4.5 = 0.4\,\text{eV}$$

If E be the energy of each ejected photo electron momentum of electrons is

$$P = \sqrt{2mE}$$

We know that change of momentum is impulse. Here the whole momentum of electron is gained when it is ejected out thus impulse on surface is given as

$$J = \sqrt{2mE}$$

Substituting the values, we get maximum impulse

$$J = \sqrt{2 \times 9.1 \times 10^{-31} \times 0.4 \times 1.6 \times 10^{-19}}$$

$$\Rightarrow \quad J = 3.45 \times 10^{-25}\,\text{kg m/sec}$$

Illustrative Example 2.3

In an experiment tungsten cathode which has a threshold 2300 Å is irradiated by ultraviolet light of wavelength 1800 Å. Calculate

(i) Maximum energy of emitted photoelectron and

(ii) Work function for tungsten

(Mention both the results in electron-volts)

Given Planck's constant $h = 6.6 \times 10^{-34}$ joule-sec, $1\,\text{eV} = 1.6 \times 10^{-19}$ joule and velocity of light $c = 3 \times 10^8$ m/sec

Solution

The work function of tungsten cathode is

$$\phi = \frac{hc}{\lambda_{th}}$$

$$\Rightarrow \quad \phi = \frac{12431}{2300}\,\text{eV}$$

$$\Rightarrow \quad \phi = 5.4\,\text{eV}$$

The energy in eV of incident photons is

$$E = \frac{hc}{\lambda}$$

$$\Rightarrow \quad E = \frac{12431}{1800}\,\text{eV}$$

The maximum kinetic energy of ejected electrons can be given as

$$KE_{max} = E - \phi$$

$$\Rightarrow \quad KE_{max} = 6.9 - 5.4\,\text{eV}$$

$$\Rightarrow \quad KE_{max} = 1.5\,\text{eV}$$

Illustrative Example 2.4

Light of wavelength 1800 Å ejects photoelectrons from a plate of a metal whose work function is 2 eV. If a uniform magnetic field of 5×10^{-5} tesla is applied parallel to plate, what would be the radius of the path followed by electrons ejected normally from the plate with maximum energy.

Solution

Energy of incident photons in eV is given as

$$E = \frac{12431}{1800}\,\text{eV}$$

As work function of metal is 2 eV, the maximum kinetic energy of ejected electrons is

$$KE_{max} = E - \phi$$

$$\Rightarrow \quad KE_{max} = 6.9 - 2\,\text{eV}$$

$$\Rightarrow \quad KE_{max} = 4.9\,\text{eV}$$

If v_{max} be the speed of fastest electrons then we have

$$\frac{1}{2}mv_{max}^2 = 4.9 \times 1.6 \times 10^{-19}\,\text{joule}$$

$$\Rightarrow \quad v_{max} = \sqrt{\frac{2 \times 4.9 \times 1.6 \times 10^{-19}}{9.1 \times 10^{-31}}}$$

$$\Rightarrow \quad v_{max} = 1.31 \times 10^6\,\text{m/s}$$

When an electron with this speed enters a uniform magnetic field normally it follows a circular path whose radius can be given by

$$r = \frac{mv}{qB} \qquad \left[\text{As } qvB = \frac{mv^2}{r}\right]$$

$$\Rightarrow \quad r = \frac{9.1 \times 10^{-31} \times 1.31 \times 10^6}{1.6 \times 10^{-19} \times 5 \times 10^{-5}}$$

$$\Rightarrow \quad r = 0.149\,\text{m}$$

Illustrative Example 2.5

The radiation emitted, when an electron jumps from $n = 3$ to $n = 2$ orbit is a hydrogen atom, falls on a metal to produce photo electrons. The electrons from the metal surface with maximum kinetic energy are made to move perpendicular to a magnetic field of (1/320) T in a radius of 10^{-3} m. Find (i) the kinetic energy of electrons (ii) work function of metal and (iii) wavelength of radiation.

Solution

(i) The energy of electron in the nth energy level of hydrogen atom is given by

$$E_n = -\frac{13.6}{n^2}\text{ eV}$$

For $n = 3$, we have

$$E_3 = -\frac{13.6}{(3)^2} = -1.51\text{ eV}$$

and for $n = 2$, we have

$$E_2 = -\frac{13.6}{(2)^2} = -3.4\text{ eV}$$

Now, $$\Delta E_{32} = E_3 - E_2 = -1.51 + 3.4$$

$$= 1.89\text{ eV} = h\nu$$

Now these radiations incident on a metal surface. The photo electrons emitted from the metal surface move perpendicularly in magnetic field B. Let v be the velocity of photo electrons in a circle of radius r. Then,

$$\frac{mv^2}{r} = q\,v\,B$$

$$\Rightarrow \quad mv = q\,B\,r$$

$$\Rightarrow \quad p = (1.6 \times 10^{-19})\left(\frac{1}{320}\right)(10^{-3})$$

$$p = 5 \times 10^{-25}\text{ kg-m/s}$$

The kinetic energy of photo electrons is

$$\Rightarrow \quad E_k = \frac{p^2}{2m} = \frac{(5\times10^{-25})^2}{2\times(9.1\times10^{-31})}\text{ J}$$

$$\Rightarrow \quad E_k = \frac{25\times10^{-50}}{2\times(9.1\times10^{-31})\times(1.6\times10^{-19})}\text{ eV}$$

$$\Rightarrow \quad E_k \approx 0.86\text{ eV}$$

(ii) According to Einstein's photoelectric equation

$$h\nu = \phi + \frac{1}{2}mv^2_{max}$$

$$\Rightarrow \quad 1.89 = \phi + 0.86$$

$$\Rightarrow \quad \phi = 1.03\text{ eV}$$

(iii) The energy of incident radiation is 1.89 eV thus the corresponding wavelength is

$$\lambda = \frac{12431}{1.89}\text{ Å}$$

$$\Rightarrow \quad \lambda = 6577.2\text{ Å}$$

Illustrative Example 2.6

Photoelectrons are emitted when 4000 Å radiation is incident on a surface of work function 1.9 eV. These photoelectrons pass through a region containing α-particles. A maximum energy electron combine with an α-particle to form a He^+ ion, emitting a single photon in this process. He^+ ions thus formed are in their fourth excited state. Find the energies (in eV) of the photons, lying in the 2 to 4 eV range, that are likely to be emitted during and after the combination. Take $h = 4.14 \times 10^{-15}$ eVs.

Solution

The energy of the incident photon is

$$E_i = h\nu = \frac{hc}{\lambda} = \frac{12431}{4000}\text{ eV}$$

$$\Rightarrow \quad E_i = 3.1\text{ eV}$$

From Einstein's photoelectric equation, the maximum kinetic energy of the emitted electrons is

$$KE_{max} = h\nu - \phi = 3.1\text{ eV} - 1.9\text{ eV} = 1.2\text{ eV}$$

It is given that

(electron with E_{max}) + He → He^+ + photon(in 4th excited state).

The fourth excited state corresponds to $n = 5$. For He^+ ion $Z = 2$. Now, we know that the energy of the electron in the nth state for a hydrogen like ion is

$$E_n = -(13.6\text{ eV})\frac{Z^2}{n^2} \qquad \ldots(2.6)$$

Thus, $$E_5 = -(13.6\text{ eV}) \times \frac{(2)^2}{(5)^2} = -2.18\text{ eV}$$

The energy of the emitted photon in the above combination reaction is

$$E = KE_{max} + (-E_5)$$

$$\Rightarrow \quad E = 1.2\text{ eV} + 2.18\text{ eV} = 3.38\text{ eV}$$

This energy is within the range 2 to 4 eV

After the recombination reaction, the electron may undergo transitions from a higher level to a lower level, thus emitting photons. Using Equation-(2.6), the energies in the lower electronic levels of He^+ ions are

$$E_4 = \frac{(-13.6\text{ eV})\times(2)^2}{(4)^2} = -3.4\text{ eV}$$

$$E_3 = \frac{(-13.6\,\text{eV})\times(2)^2}{(3)^2} = -6.04\,\text{eV}$$

$$E_2 = \frac{(-13.6\,\text{eV})\times(2)^2}{(2)^2} = -13.6\,\text{eV}$$

and $$E_1 = \frac{(-13.6\,\text{eV})\times(2)^2}{(1)^2} = -54.4\,\text{eV}$$

We have seen above that $E_5 = -2.18$ V. The energies of the emitted photons are given by the differences of these energies. The differences of energies lying in the range 2 to 4 eV are

(1) $\Delta E_{43} = E_4 - E_3 = -3.4 - (-6.04)$
$= 2.64\,\text{eV}$

(2) $\Delta E_{53} = E_5 - E_3 = -2.18 - (-6.04)$
$= 3.86\,\text{eV}$

In addition to $E = 3.38$ eV. Hence, the energies of the photons that are likely to be emitted with energies in the range 2 to 4 eV are 2.64 eV, 3.38 eV and 3.86 eV.

Web Reference at www.physicsgalaxy.com

Age Group - High School Physics | Age 17-19 Years
Section - MODERN PHYSICS
Topic - Photoelectric Effect
Module Number - 1 to 13

Practice Exercise 2.1

(i) Lithium has a work function of 2.30 eV. It is exposed to light of wavelength 4800 Å. Find the maximum kinetic energy with which electron leaves the surface. What is the longest wavelength which can produce the photoelectrons ?

[0.29 eV, 5404.78 Å]

(ii) A photon of wavelength 3310 Å falls on photocathode and ejects an electron of energy 3×10^{-19} joule. If the wavelength of incident photon is changed to 5000 Å, the energy of the ejected electron is 0.97×10^{-19} joule. Calculate the value of the work function of photocathode and Planck's constant. (Take speed of light $c = 3 \times 10^8$ m/sec.).

[1.88 eV, 6.634×10^{-34} J-s]

(iii) The maximum kinetic energy of the photoelectrons emitted from a metal surface of work function 1.7 eV is 10.4 eV. Find the wavelength of the radiation used. Also identify the energy levels in hydrogen atom which will emit this wavelength.

[1027.35 Å, $n = 3$ to $n = 1$]

(iv) A small metal plate (work function = ϕ) is kept at a distance d from a singly ionized, fixed ion. A monochromatic light beam is incident on the metal plate and photoelectrons are emitted. Find the maximum wavelength of the light beam so that some of the photoelectrons may go round the ion along a circle.

[$\frac{8\pi\varepsilon_0 dhc}{e^2 + 8\pi\varepsilon_0 \phi d}$]

(v) A beam of monochromatic light of wavelength λ ejects photoelectrons from a cesium surface ($\phi = 1.9$ eV). These photoelectrons are made to collide with hydrogen atoms in ground state. Find the maximum value of λ for which

(a) hydrogen atoms may be ionized.

(b) hydrogen atom get excited from the ground state to the first excited state and

(c) the excited hydrogen atoms may emit visible light.

[812.48 Å, 1044.62 Å, 901.45 Å]

(vi) A monochromatic light source of frequency ν illuminates a metallic surface and ejects photoelectrons. The photoelectrons having maximum energy are just able to ionize the hydrogen atoms in ground state. When the whole experiment is repeated with an incident radiation of frequency $5\nu/6$, the photo electrons so emitted are able to excite the hydrogen atom beam which then emit a radiation of wavelength 1218 Å. Find the work function of metal and the frequency ν.

[6.80 eV, 4.923×10^{15} Hz]

2.3 Experimental Study of Photo Electric Effect

Experiments with the photoelectric effect are performed in a discharge tube apparatus as illustrated in figure-2.5. The cathode of discharge tube is made up of a metal which shows photoelectric effect on which experiment is being carried out.

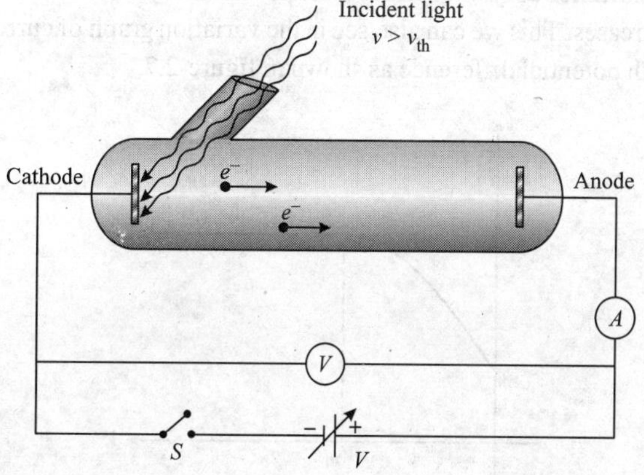

Figure 2.5

A high potential is applied to a discharge tube through a variable voltage source and a voltmeter and an ammeter are connected to measure the potential difference across the electrodes and to measure photoelectric current. Light with frequency more than threshold frequency of cathode metal is incident on it, due to which photoelectrons are emitted from the cathode. These electrons will reach the anode and constitute the photoelectric current which the ammeter will show.

Now we start the experiment by closing the switch S. Initially the variable battery source is set at zero potential. Even at zero potential variable source, ammeter will show some current because due to the initial kinetic energy some electrons will reach the anode and cause some small current will flow. But as we know majority of ejected electrons have low values of kinetic energies which are collected outside the cathode and create a cloud of negative charge, we call space charge, as shown in figure-2.6

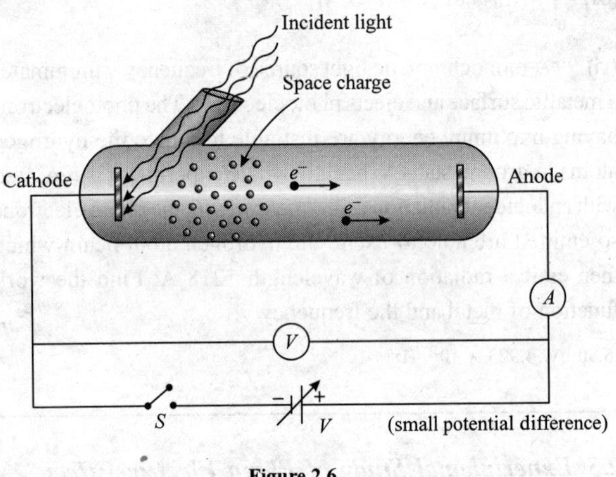

Figure 2.6

If the potential difference applied across the discharge tube is gradually increased from the variable source, positive potential of anode starts pulling electrons from the space charge. As potential difference increases, space charge decreases and simultaneously the photoelectric current in circuit also increases. This we can also see in the variation graph of current with potential difference as shown in figure-2.7.

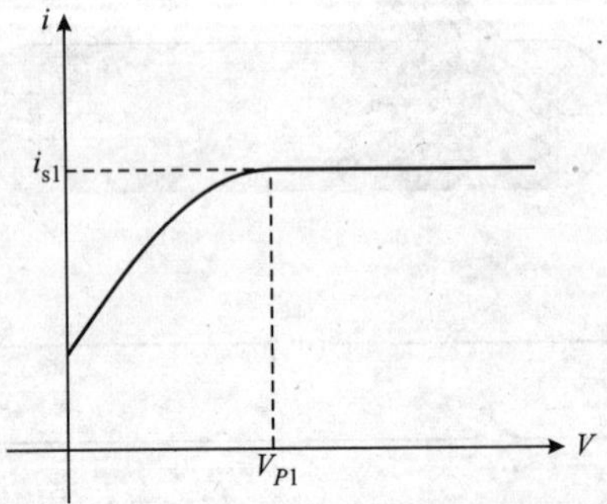

Figure 2.7

As shown in graph, we can see as potential difference increases, current in circuit increases. But at a higher voltage V_{P1} space charge vanishes and at this voltage anode is able to pull the slowest electron (zero kinetic energy) ejected by the cathode. Now as all the ejected electrons from cathode start reading anode. If further potential difference is increased, it will not make any difference in the number of electrons reaching the anode hence, further increase in potential difference will not increase the current. This we can see in figure-2.7 that beyond V_{P1} current in circuit becomes constant. This current i_{s1} is called saturation current. This potential difference V_{P1} at which current becomes saturated is called "pinch off voltage".

Now if the frequency of incident light is kept constant and its intensity is further increased, then the number of incident photons will increase which increases the number of ejected photo electrons so current in circuit increases and now in this case at higher intensity of incident light, current will not get saturated at potential difference V_{P1} as now due to more electron emission, space charge will be more and it will not vanish at V_{P1}. To pull all the electrons emitted from cathode more potential difference is required. This we can see from figure-2.8, that at higher intensity I_2 ($I_2 > I_1$) current becomes saturated at higher value of potential difference V_{P2}.

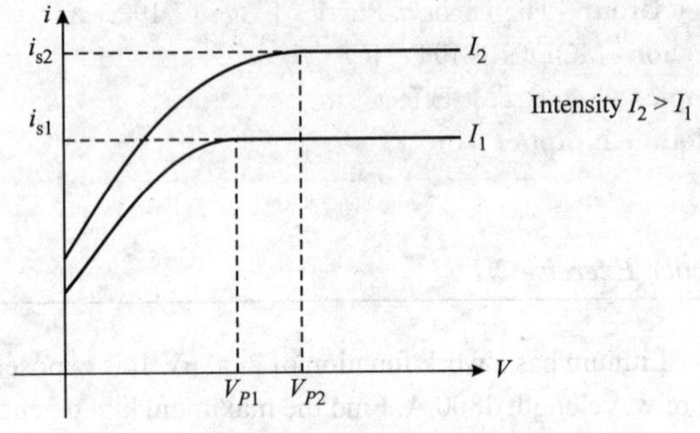

Figure 2.8

Beyond V_{P2}, we can see that all the electrons ejected from cathode are reaching the anode and current becomes saturated at i_{s2} because of more electrons. Another point we can see from figure-2.8 that when $V = 0$ then also current is more at high intensity incident radiation as the number of electrons of high kinetic energy are also more in the beginning which will reach anode by penetrating the space charge.

2.3.1 Kinetic Energies of Electrons Reaching Anode

We know that when electrons are ejected from cathode then kinetic energies may vary from 0 to $\frac{1}{2}mv_{max}^2$. If V is the potential difference applied across the discharge tube then it will accelerates the electron while reaching the anode. The electron which is ejected from cathode with zero kinetic energy will be the slowest one reaching the anode if its speed is v_1 at anode then we have

$$0+eV=\frac{1}{2}mv_1^2 \quad \ldots(2.7)$$

Similarly the electron ejected from cathode with maximum kinetic energy $\frac{1}{2}mv_{max}^2$ will be the fastest one when it will reach anode. If its speed is v_2 at anode then we have

$$\frac{1}{2}mv_{max}^2+eV=\frac{1}{2}mv_2^2 \quad \ldots(2.8)$$

Thus we can say that all the electrons reaching anode will have their speeds distributed from v_1 to v_2.

2.3.2 Reversed Potential Across Discharge Tube

Now the experiment is repeated with charging the polarity of source across the discharge tube. Now positive terminal of source is connected to the cathode of discharge tube. When a light beam incident on the cathode with ($h\nu > \phi$), photoelectrons are ejected and move toward anode with negative polarity.

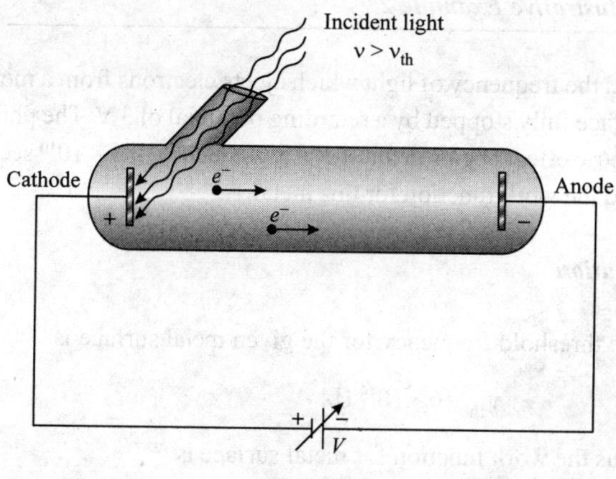

Figure 2.9

Now the electrons which are ejected with very low kinetic energy are attracted back to the cathode because of its positive polarity. Those electrons which have high kinetic energies will rush toward, anode and may constitute the current in circuit.

In this case the fastest electron ejected from cathode will be retarded during its journey to anode. As the maximum kinetic energy just after emission at cathode is $\frac{1}{2}mv_{max}^2$, if potential difference across the discharge tube is V then the speed v_f with which electrons will reach anode can be given as

$$\frac{1}{2}mv_{max}^2-eV=\frac{1}{2}mv_f^2 \quad \ldots(2.9)$$

Thus all the electrons which are reaching anode will have speed less then or equal to v_f. Remaining electrons which have relatively low kinetic energy will either be attracted to cathode just after ejection or will return during their journey from cathode to anode. Only those electrons will cause current to flow in circuit which have high kinetic energies more then eV which can overcome the electric work against electric forces on electron due to opposite polarity of source.

2.3.3 Cut off Potential or Stopping Potential

We have seen that with reverse polarity electrons are retarded in the discharge tube. If the potential difference is increased with reverse polarity, the number of electrons reaching anode will decrease hence photo electric current in circuit also decreases, this we can see from figure-2.10 which shows variation of current with increase in voltage across discharge tube in opposite direction. Here we can see that at a particular reverse voltage V_0, current in circuit becomes zero. This is the voltage at which the fastest electron from cathode will be retarded and stopped just before reaching the anode.

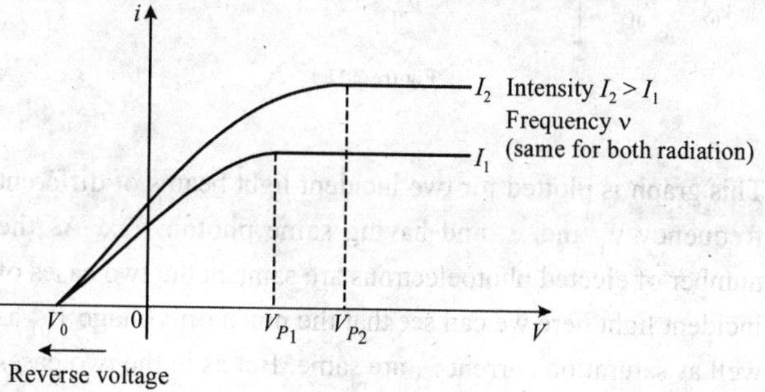

Figure 2.10

This voltage V_0, we can calculate from equation-(2.9) by substituting $v_f = 0$ hence

$$\frac{1}{2}mv_{max}^2-eV_0=0$$

$$\Rightarrow \quad eV_0=\frac{1}{2}mv_{max}^2$$

$$\Rightarrow \quad V_0=\frac{\frac{1}{2}mv_{max}^2}{e} \quad \ldots(2.10)$$

$$\Rightarrow \quad V_0=\frac{h\nu-\phi}{e} \quad \ldots(2.11)$$

We can see one more thing in figure-2.10 that the graphs plotted for two different intensities I_1 and I_2, V_0 is same. Current in both the cases in cut off at same reverse potential V_0. The reason for this is equation-(2.10) and (2.11). If is clear that the value of V_0 depends only on the maximum kinetic energy of the ejected electrons which depends only on frequency of light and not on intensity of light. Thus in above two graphs as frequency of incident light is same, the value of V_0 is also same. This reverse potential difference V_0 at which the fastest photoelectron is stopped and current in the circuit becomes zero is called cut off potential or stopping potential.

2.3.4 Effect of Change in Frequency of Light on Stopping Potential

If we repeat the experiment by increasing the frequency of incident light with number of incident photons constant, the variation graph of current with voltage will be plotted as shown in figure-2.11.

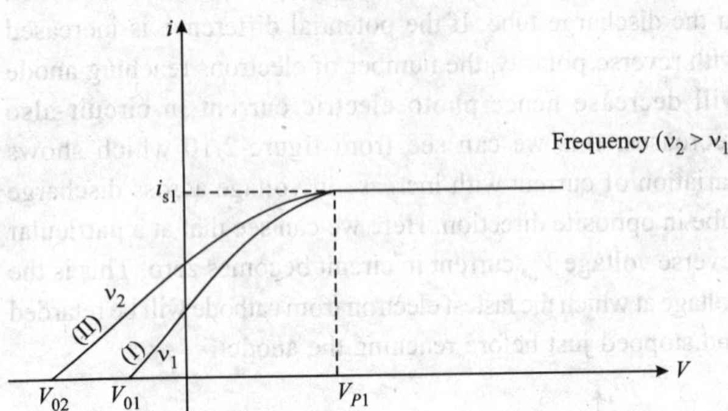

Figure 2.11

This graph is plotted for two incident light beams of different frequency ν_1 and ν_2 and having same photon flux. As the number of ejected photoelectrons are same in the two cases of incident light here we can see that the pinch off voltage V_{01} as well as saturation current i_{s1} are same. But as in the two cases the kinetic energy of fastest electron are different as frequencies are different, the stopping potential for the two cases will be different. In graph II as frequency of incident light is more, the maximum kinetic energy of photoelectron will also be high and to stop it high value of stopping potential is needed. These here V_{01} and V_{02} can be given as

$$V_{01} = \frac{h\nu_1 - \phi}{e} \quad \ldots(2.12)$$

and $$V_{02} = \frac{h\nu_2 - \phi}{e} \quad \ldots(2.13)$$

In general for a given metal with work function ϕ, if V_0 is the stopping potential for an incident light of frequency ν then we have

$$eV_0 = h\nu - \phi$$

$$\Rightarrow \quad eV_0 = h\nu - h\nu_{th} \quad \ldots(2.14)$$

$$\Rightarrow \quad V_0 = \left(\frac{h}{e}\right)\nu - \frac{h\nu_{th}}{e} \quad \ldots(2.15)$$

Equation-(2.15) shows that stopping potential V_0 is linearly proportional to the frequency ν of incident light. The variation of stopping potential with frequency ν can be shown in figure-2.12.

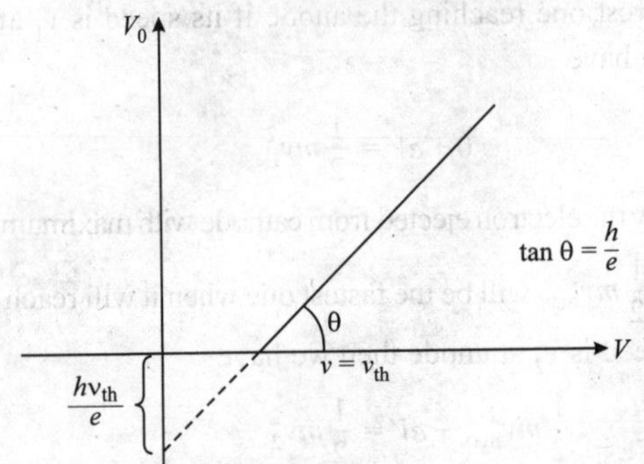

Figure 2.12

Here equation-(2.14) can be written as

$$\frac{1}{2}mv_{max}^2 = eV_0 = h(\nu - \nu_{th}) \quad \ldots(2.16)$$

This equation-(2.16) is called Einstein's Photo Electric Effect equation which gives a direct relationship between the maximum kinetic energy stopping potential frequency of incident light and the threshold frequency.

 # Illustrative Example 2.7

Find the frequency of light which ejects electrons from a metal surface fully stopped by a retarding potential of 3 V. The photo electric effect begins in this metal at frequency of 6×10^{14} sec^{-1}. Find the work function for this metal.

Solution

The threshold frequency for the given metal surface is

$$\nu_{th} = 6 \times 10^{14} \text{ Hz}$$

Thus the work function for metal surface is

$$\phi = h\nu_{th}$$

$$\Rightarrow \quad \phi = 6.63 \times 10^{-34} \times 6 \times 10^{14}$$

$$\Rightarrow \quad \phi = 3.978 \times 10^{-19} \text{ J}$$

As stopping potential for the ejected electrons is 3 V, the maximum kinetic energy of ejected electrons will be

$$KE_{max} = 3 \text{ eV}$$

$$\Rightarrow \quad KE_{max} = 3 \times 1.6 \times 10^{-19} \text{ J}$$

$$\Rightarrow \quad KE_{max} = 4.8 \times 10^{-19} \text{ J}$$

According to photo electric effect equation, we have

$$h\nu = h\nu_{th} + KE_{max}$$

$\Rightarrow$ frequency of incident light is

$$\nu = \frac{\phi + KE_{max}}{h}$$

$$\Rightarrow \quad \nu = \frac{3.978\times10^{-19} + 4.8\times10^{-19}}{6.63\times10^{-34}}$$

$$\Rightarrow \quad \nu = 1.32\times10^{15}\,\text{Hz}$$

Illustrative Example 2.8

Electrons with maximum kinetic energy 3 eV are ejected from a metal surface by ultraviolet radiation of wavelength 1500 Å. Determine the work function of the metal, the threshold wavelength of metal and the stopping potential difference required to stop the emission of electrons.

Solution

Energy of incident photon in *eV* is

$$E = \frac{12431}{1500}\,\text{eV}$$

$$\Rightarrow \quad E = 8.29\,\text{eV}$$

According to photo electric effect equation, we have

$$E = \phi + KE_{max}$$

$$\Rightarrow \quad \phi = E - KE_{max}$$

$$\Rightarrow \quad \phi = 8.29 - 3\,\text{eV}$$

$$\Rightarrow \quad \phi = 5.29\,\text{eV}$$

Threshold wavelength for the metal surface corresponding to work function 5.29 eV is given as

$$\lambda_{th} = \frac{12431}{5.29}\,\text{Å}$$

$$\Rightarrow \quad \lambda_{th} = 2349.9\,\text{Å}$$

Stopping potential for the ejected electrons can be given as

$$V_0 = \frac{KE_{max}}{e} = \frac{3eV}{e} = 3\,\text{volt}$$

Illustrative Example 2.9

Calculate the velocity of a photoelectron, if the work function of the target material is 1.24 eV and the wavelength of incident light is 4360 Å. What retarding potential is necessary to stop the emission of the electrons ?

Solution

Energy of incident photons in *eV* on metal surface is

$$E = \frac{12431}{4360}\,\text{eV}$$

$$\Rightarrow \quad E = 2.85\,\text{eV}$$

According to photo electric effect equation we have

$$E = \phi + KE_{max}$$

$$\Rightarrow \quad KE_{max} = E - \phi$$

$$\Rightarrow \quad KE_{max} = 2.85 - 1.24\,\text{eV}$$

$$\Rightarrow \quad KE_{max} = 1.61\,\text{eV}$$

The stopping potential for these ejected electrons can be given as

$$V_0 = \frac{KE_{max}}{e}$$

$$\Rightarrow \quad V_0 = \frac{1.61\,\text{eV}}{e} = 1.61\,\text{volts}$$

Illustrative Example 2.10

Determine the Planck's constant *h* if photoelectrons emitted from a surface of a certain metal by light of frequency 2.2×10^{15} Hz are fully retarded by a reverse potential of 6.6 V and those ejected by light of frequency 4.6×10^{15} Hz by a reverse potential of 16.5 eV.

Solution

From photo electric effect equation, we have

Here $\quad h\nu_1 = \phi + eV_{01} \quad$ ...(2.17)

and $\quad h\nu_2 = \phi + 2eV_{02} \quad$ ...(2.18)

Subtracting equation-(2.17) from equation-(2.18), we get

$$h(\nu_2 - \nu_1) = e(V_{02} - V_{01})$$

$$\Rightarrow \quad h = \frac{(V_{02} - V_{01})(1.6\times10^{-19})}{(\nu_2 - \nu_1)}$$

$$\Rightarrow \quad h = \frac{(16.5 - 6.6)(1.6\times10^{-19})}{(4.6 - 2.2)\times10^{15}}$$

$$\Rightarrow \quad h = 6.6\times10^{-34}\,\text{J-s}$$

Illustrative Example 2.11

When a surface is irradiated with light of wavelength 4950 Å, a photo current appears which vanishes if a retarding potential greater than 0.6 volt is applied across the photo tube. When a different source of light is used, it is found that the critical retarding potential is changed to 1.1 volt. Find the work function of the emitting surface and the wavelength of second source. If the photo electrons (after emission from the surface) are subjected to a magnetic field of 10 tesla, what changes will be observed in the above two retarding potentials.

Solution

In first case the energy of incident photon in eV is

$$E_1 = \frac{12431}{4950}\text{ eV}$$

$$= 2.51\text{ eV}$$

The maximum kinetic energy of ejected electrons is

$$KE_{\max 1} = eV_{01}$$

$$= 0.6\text{ eV}$$

Thus work function of metal surface is given as

$$\phi = E_1 - KE_{\max 1}$$

$$\Rightarrow \quad \phi = 2.51 - 0.6\text{ eV}$$

$$\Rightarrow \quad \phi = 1.91\text{ eV}$$

In second case the maximum kinetic energy of ejected electrons will become

$$KE_{\max 2} = eV_{02}$$

$$\Rightarrow \quad KE_{\max 2} = 1.1\text{ eV}$$

Thus the incident energy of photons can be given as

$$E_2 = \phi + KE_{\max 2}$$

$$\Rightarrow \quad E_2 = 1.91 + 1.1\text{ eV}$$

$$\Rightarrow \quad E_2 = 3.01\text{ eV}$$

Thus the wavelength of incident photons in second case will be

$$\lambda = \frac{12431}{3.01}\text{ Å}$$

$$\Rightarrow \quad \lambda = 4129.9\text{ Å}$$

When magnetic field is present there will be no effect on the stopping potentials as magnetic force can not change the kinetic energy of ejected electrons.

Illustrative Example 2.12

(a) If the wavelength of the light incident on a photoelectric cell be reduced from λ_1 to λ_2 Å, then what will be the change in the cutoff potential ?

(b) Light is incident on the cathode of a photocell and the stopping voltages are measured for light of two different wavelengths. From the data given below, determine the work function of the metal of the cathode in *eV* and the value of the universal constant *hc/e*.

Wavelength (Å)	Stopping voltage (volt)
4000	1.3
4500	0.9

Solution

(a) Let the work function of the surface be ϕ. If ν be the frequency of the light falling on the surface, then according to Einstein's photoelectric equation, the maximum kinetic energy $KE_{\max}$ of emitted electron is given by

$$KE_{\max} = h\nu - \phi = \frac{hc}{\lambda} - \phi$$

We know that,

$$KE_{\max} = eV_0$$

Where V_0 = cutoff potential.

$$\Rightarrow \quad eV_0 = \frac{hc}{\lambda} - \phi$$

$$\Rightarrow \quad V_0 = \frac{hc}{e\lambda} - \frac{\phi}{e}$$

Now, $\Delta V_0 = V_{02} - V_{01}$

$$\Rightarrow \quad \Delta V_0 = \left(\frac{hc}{e\lambda_2} - \frac{\phi}{e}\right) - \left(\frac{hc}{e\lambda_1} - \frac{\phi}{e}\right)$$

$$\Rightarrow \quad \Delta V_0 = \frac{hc}{e}\left(\frac{1}{\lambda_2} - \frac{1}{\lambda_1}\right)$$

$$\Rightarrow \quad \Delta V_0 = \frac{hc}{e}\left(\frac{\lambda_1 - \lambda_2}{\lambda_1\lambda_2}\right) \quad \ldots(2.19)$$

(b) From equation-(2.19), we have

$$\frac{hc}{e} = \frac{\Delta V_0(\lambda_1\lambda_2)}{\lambda_1 - \lambda_2}$$

$$\Rightarrow \quad \frac{hc}{e} = \frac{(1.3-0.9)[(4000\times10^{-10})\times(4500\times10^{-10})]}{500\times10^{-10}}$$

$$\Rightarrow \quad \frac{hc}{e} = 1.44\times10^{-6}\text{ V/m}$$

We use, $V_0 = \frac{hc}{e\lambda} - \frac{\phi}{e}$

$$\Rightarrow \quad \frac{\phi}{e} = \frac{hc}{e\lambda} - V_0 = \frac{1.44\times10^{-6}}{4000\times10^{-10}} - 1.3$$

$$\Rightarrow \quad \phi = 2.3\text{ eV}$$

Illustrative Example 2.13

A low intensity ultraviolet light of wavelength 2271 Å irradiates a photocell made of molybdenum metal. If the stopping potential is 1.3 V, find the work function of the metal. Will the photocell work if it is irradiated by a high intensity red light of wavelength 6328 Å ?

Solution

The energy in eV of incident photons is

$$E = \frac{12431}{2271} \text{ eV}$$

$$\Rightarrow \quad E = 5.47 \text{ eV}$$

As stopping potential for ejected electrons is 1.3 V, the maximum kinetic energy of ejected electrons will be

$$KE_{max} = eV_0$$

$$\Rightarrow \quad KE_{max} = 1.3 \text{ eV}$$

Now from photoelectric effect equation, we have

$$E = \phi + KE_{max}$$

$$\Rightarrow \quad \phi = E - KE_{max}$$

$$\Rightarrow \quad \phi = 5.47 - 1.3 \text{ eV}$$

$$\phi = 4.17 \text{ eV}$$

Energy in eV for photons of red light of wavelength 6328 Å is

$$E' = \frac{12431}{6328} \text{ eV}$$

$$\Rightarrow \quad E' = 1.96 \text{ eV}$$

As $E' < \phi$, photocell will not work if irradiated by this red light no matter however intense the light will be.

 # Illustrative Example 2.14

A peak emission from a black body at a certain temperature occurs at a wavelength of 9000 Å. On increasing the temperature, the total radiation emitted is increased 81 times. At the initial temperature when the peak radiation from the black body is incident on a metal surface, it does not cause any photoemission from the surface. After the increase of temperature the peak radiation from the black body caused photoemission. To bring these photoelectrons to rest, a potential equivalent to he excitation energy between the n = 2 and n = 3 Bohr levels of hydrogen atom is required. Find the work function of the metal.

Solution

Let T be the initial absolute temperature of the black body. The total energy emitted by the body per unit area per second is given by

$$E = \sigma T^4$$

Where σ is the Stefan's constant. When the temperature of the black body is raised to T'. We have

$$E' = \sigma T'^4,$$

$$\Rightarrow \quad \frac{E'}{E} = 8.1$$

$$\text{Hence,} \quad 81 = \left(\frac{T'}{T}\right)^4$$

Which gives $T' = 3T$

It is given that peak emission at temperature T occurs at a wavelength λ_m = 9000 Å. If λ'_m is the wavelength for peak emission at temperature T', then from Wien's displacement law $\lambda_m T$ = constant, we have

$$\lambda'_m T' = \lambda_m T$$

$$\Rightarrow \quad \lambda'_m = \lambda_m \frac{T}{T'} = 9000 \text{ Å} \times \frac{T}{3T} = 3000 \text{ Å}$$

According to the problem, the kinetic energy of the emitted photoelectrons = excitation energy for transition $n = 2$ to $n = 3$, which is

$$KE_{max} = E_{32} = (13.6 \text{ eV})\left(\frac{1}{2^2} - \frac{1}{3^2}\right)$$

$$\Rightarrow \quad KE_{max} = 13.6 \times \frac{5}{36} = 1.89 \text{ eV}$$

The energy of the photon of wavelength λ' = 3000 Å in eV is

$$E = \frac{12431}{3000} \text{ eV}$$

$$\Rightarrow \quad E = 4.14 \text{ eV}$$

Now, from Einstein's photoelectric equation, the work function for the metal surface is given as

$$\phi = E - KE_{max}$$

$$\Rightarrow \quad \phi = 4.14 - 1.89 \text{ eV}$$

$$\Rightarrow \quad \phi = 2.25 \text{ eV}$$

Web Reference at www.physicsgalaxy.com

Age Group - High School Physics | Age 17-19 Years

Section - MODERN PHYSICS

Topic - Photoelectric Effect

Module Number - 14 to 18

Practice Exercise 2.2

(i) The stopping potential for photoelectrons emitted from surface illuminated by light of wavelength 5896 Å is 0.36 Volt. Calculate the maximum kinetic energy of photoelectrons, the work function of the surface and the threshold frequency. (Take $h = 6.63 \times 10^{-34}$ Joule-sec, $c = 3.0 \times 10^8$ m/sec and 1 eV = 1.6×10^{-19} Joule)

[0.36 eV, 1.748 eV, 4.218×10^{14} Hz]

(ii) A vacuum photo cell consists of a central cathode and an anode. The internal surface is silver of work function 4.5 eV. The contact potential difference between the electrodes is equal to 0.6 volt. The photo cell is illuminated by light of wavelength 2300 Å,

(a) What retarding potential difference should be applied between electrodes of photocell for the photocurrent to drop to zero ?

(b) If a retarding potential of 1 volt is applied between electrodes at what limiting wavelength λ of light incident on the cathode will the photocurrent begin ?

[(a) 1.5 V (b) 2536.94 Å]

(iii) A clean metallic surface just emits electrons when irradiated by light of wavelength less than or equal to 621 nm. When it is radiated by light of wavelength 414 nm the stopping potential required is 1 V. Assuming the values of *e*, *m* & *c* as standard values, calculate :

(a) Value for Plank's constant *h*.

(b) The maximum velocity of electrons emitted in the second case.

[(a) 6.624×10^{-34} J-s (b) 5.927×10^{5} m/s]

(iv) In an experiment on photoelectric emission, following observation are made : Wavelength of incident light is given as λ = 1980 Å and stopping potential = 2.5 V. Find (a) threshold frequency (b) work function and (c) energy of photoelectrons with maximum speed.

[(a) 9.122×10^{14} Hz, (b) 3.78 eV, (c) 2.5 eV]

(v) Monochromatic light of wavelength 6402 Å irradiates a photocell made of caesium on tungsten. The stopping potential is measured to be 0.54 V. What will be the new stopping potential of the cell if it is irradiate by monochromatic light of wavelength 4272 Å ?

[1.508 V]

(vi) In a photoelectric experiment, it was found that the stopping potential decreases from 1.85 V to 0.82 V as the wavelength of the incident light is varies from 3000 Å to 4300 Å. Calculate the value of the Planck's constant from these data.

[5.451×10^{-34} J-s]

(vii) In an experiment on photoelectric effect, light of wavelength 4000 Å is incident on a cesium plate at the rate of 5 watt. The potential of the collector plate is made sufficiently positive w.r.t. the emitter so that the current reaches its saturation value, assuming that on the average one out of every 10^6 photons is able to eject a photoelectron, find the photocurrent in the circuit.

[1.6 μA]

(viii) A clean metallic surface emits electrons when irradiated by light of wavelength less than 6210 Å. When it is radiated by light of wavelength 4140 Å, the stopping potential in this case required is 1 V. Calculate :

(a) Value for Planck's constant.

(b) The maximum velocity of electrons emitted in the second case.

[(a) 6.624×10^{-34} (b) 5.927×10^{5} m/s]

2.4 No. of Photon Emitted by Source Per second

If *B* is a light bulb of power *P* watt as shown in figure. If the wavelength of light emitted by the bulb is λ then energy of each photon emitted by the bulb can be given as

$$E = \frac{hc}{\lambda} \qquad \ldots(2.20)$$

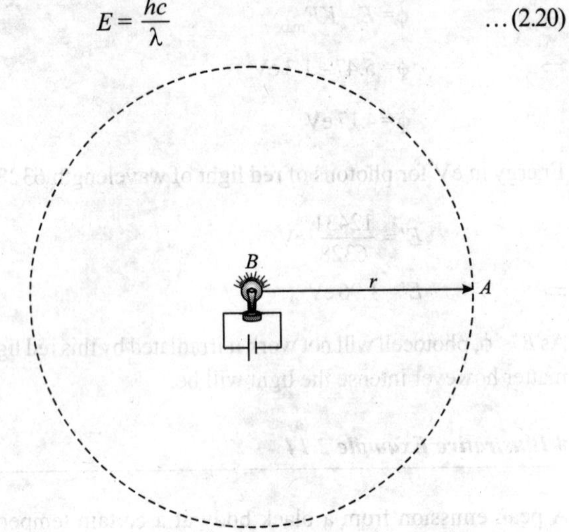

Figure 2.13

As the power of bulb is *P* watt or we can say that bulb is emitting light energy *P* joule per second in the form of photons. If it is 100% efficient. Then the number of photons emitted per second by the source (bulb) can be given as

$$n = \frac{P}{E} = \frac{P\lambda}{hc} \qquad \ldots(2.21)$$

These all photons are assumed to be emitted uniformly in all directions if bulb in figure-2.13 is taken as a point isotropic source of light. Here we can consider that all the light energy emitted by the source is uniformly distributed in the spherical region with centre at the source. As light propagates at speed of light *c*, the radius of this sphere will uniformly increase at a rate of $c = 3 \times 10^8$ m/s in free space.

2.5 Intensity of Light due to a Light Source

Figure-2.14 shows a torch which emits a uniform cylindrical light beam of cross-sectional area = *S*. If torch emits a total power *P* in the beam, the intensity of light beam can be given as the energy crossing per-second per unit cross-sectional area of the beam as

$$I = \frac{P}{S} \text{ watt/m}^2$$

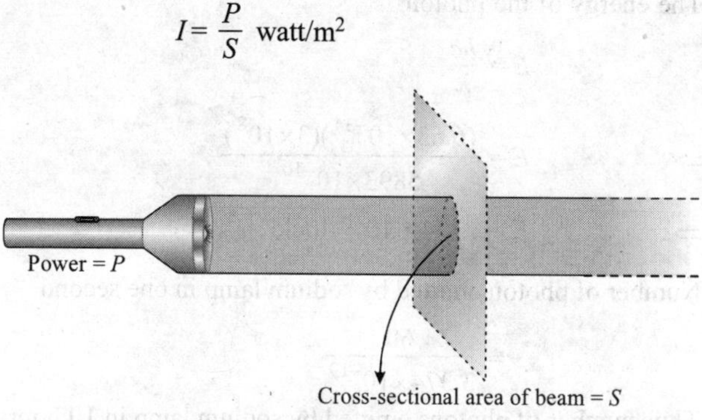

Figure 2.14

As cross-sectional area of the beam is constant throughout, the beam intensity at every point remains constant.

Similarly we can find the intensity of light due to a point isotropic source as shown in figure-2.15

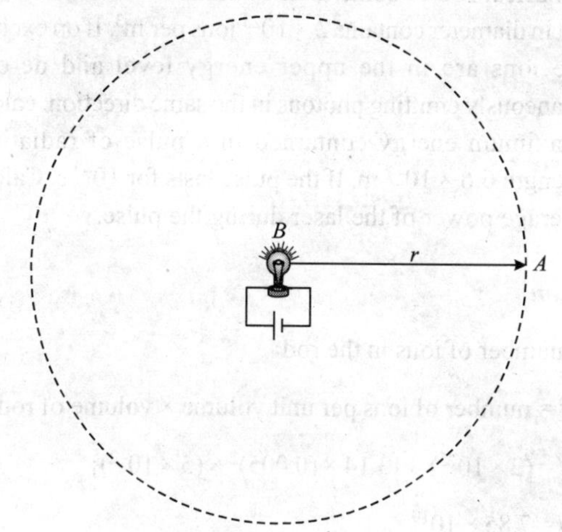

Figure 2.15

Figure-2.15 shows a bulbs B of power P watt emitting light in all directions uniformly. If we wish to find light intensity at a point A, at a distance r from the bulb B then it can be given as

$$I = \frac{P}{4\pi r^2} \text{ watt/m}^2 \quad \text{... (2.22)}$$

Here it can be assumed that the while power P is incident on the normal area of a hypothetical sphere of radius r passing through point A with centre at bulb as shown in figure. Thus energy crossing per unit area per second at point A can be given by equation-(2.22).

2.5.1 Photon Flux in a Light Beam

Photon flux is defined as the number of photons incident on a normal surface per second per unit area. If a light beam of intensity I watt/m^2 having wavelength λ incident on a surface then number of photons per second per unit area in the beam can be given as

$$\text{Photon flux} \quad \phi_N = \frac{I}{hc/\lambda} = \frac{I\lambda}{hc} \quad \text{... (2.23)}$$

If we consider a point source of power P watt which emits light in all directions, produces photons per second at a rate

$$n = \frac{P\lambda}{hc} \quad \text{... (2.24)}$$

These all photons are distributed in the three dimensional spherical space around the source. If we find the photon flux at a distance r from the point source, it can be given as

$$\phi_N = \frac{n}{4\pi r^2} \quad \text{... (2.25)}$$

2.5.2 Photon Density in a Light Beam

When photon are emitted by a light source, they move away from the source with speed of light. If we consider a uniform cylindrical beam of light as shown in figure-2.16. If the torch of power P watt is producing a uniform light beam of cross-sectional area S then the intensity of light beam is

$$I = \frac{P}{S}$$

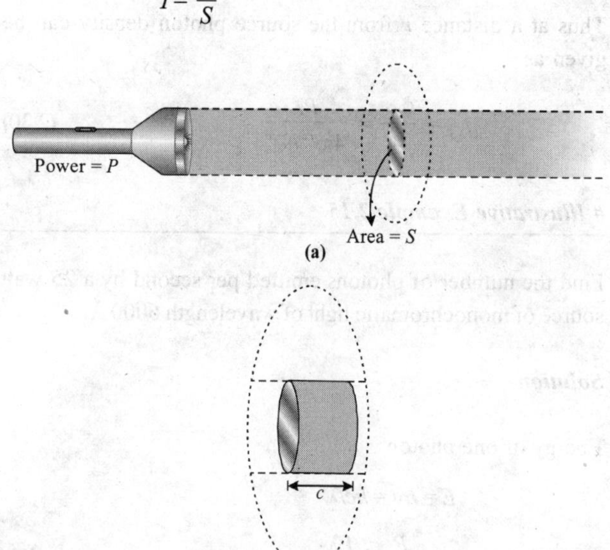

Figure 2.16

If we find the photon flux at the cross-sectional area S of light beam, it can be given as

$$\phi_N = \frac{I\lambda}{hc} \quad [\text{Here } \lambda \leftarrow \text{wavelength of light}] \quad \text{... (2.26)}$$

Equation-(2.26) gives the number of photons incident per unit area of section S. Now during one second these photons will cover a distance c and all the photons in the shaded volume Sc

of figure-2.16(b), have crossed the section in one second, thus total number of photons in this shaded volume can be given as

$$N = \frac{I\lambda}{hc} \times S$$

Thus photon density in the light beam can be given as

$$\rho_{ph} = \frac{N}{Sc} = \frac{I\lambda}{hc^2} = \frac{\phi_N}{c} \text{ photons/m}^2 \qquad \dots(2.27)$$

As the beam is uniform and cylindrical, the photon density throughout the beam remains, constant and at any point in space photon density can be given as

$$\rho_{ph} = \frac{\phi_N}{c} = \frac{\text{photon flux}}{\text{speed of light}} \qquad \dots(2.28)$$

Similarly for a point isotropic source of light we can say that as the emitted photons move away from the source, the distance between photons increases and the photon density decreases. If we wish to find photon density at a distance r from a point source of light of power P watt, then we first find the photon flux at a distance r from the source which is given as

$$\phi_N = \frac{P\lambda/hc}{4\pi r^2} \qquad \dots(2.29)$$

Thus at a distance r from the source photon density can be given as

$$\rho_{ph} = \frac{\phi_N}{c} = \frac{P\lambda}{4\pi r^2 hc^2} \qquad \dots(2.30)$$

Illustrative Example 2.15

Find the number of photons emitted per second by a 25 watt source of monochromatic light of wavelength 6000 Å.

Solution

Energy of one photon

$$E = h\nu = hc/\lambda$$

$$\text{No. of photons} = \frac{P}{E} = \frac{P\lambda}{hc}$$

Substituting the values, we get

$$\text{No. of photons} = \frac{25 \times 600 \times 10^{-10}}{6.63 \times 10^{-34} \times 3 \times 10^8}$$

$$= 7.546 \times 10^{19}$$

Illustrative Example 2.16

Calculate the number of photons emitted in 10 hours by a 60 W sodium lamp. ($\lambda = 5893$ Å)

Solution

The energy of the photon

$$E = \frac{hc}{\lambda}$$

$$\Rightarrow \quad E = \frac{(6.63 \times 10^{-34})(3 \times 10^8)}{5893 \times 10^{-10}}$$

$$\Rightarrow \quad E = 3.374 \times 10^{-19} \text{ Joule}$$

Number of photon emitted by sodium lamp in one second

$$= \frac{60}{3.374 \times 10^{-19}}$$

Thus number of photons emitted by sodium lamp in 10 hours

$$N_{\text{Total}} = Nt = \frac{60 \times 10 \times 3600}{3.374 \times 10^{-19}} = 6.40 \times 10^{24}$$

Illustrative Example 2.17

A cylindrical rod of some laser material 5×10^{-2} m long and 10^{-2} m in diameter contains 2×10^{25} ions per m^3. If on excitation all the ions are in the upper energy level and de-excite simultaneously emitting photons in the same direction, calculate the maximum energy contained in a pulse of radiation of wavelength 6.6×10^{-7} m. If the pulse lasts for 10^{-7} s. Calculate the average power of the laser during the pulse.

Solution

Total number of ions in the rod

$$N = \text{number of ions per unit volume} \times \text{volume of rod}$$

$$\Rightarrow \quad N = (2 \times 10^{25}) \times \{3.14 \times (0.005)^2 \times (5 \times 10^{-2})\}$$

$$\Rightarrow \quad N = 7.85 \times 10^{19}$$

The number of photons excited in one direction is equal to the total number of ions because all ions are excited. Now excited energy

$$E = \text{number of excited photons} \times \text{energy of photon}$$

$$\Rightarrow \quad E = (7.85 \times 10^{19}) \times \frac{hc}{\lambda}$$

$$\Rightarrow \quad E = (7.85 \times 10^{19}) \times \frac{(6.6 \times 10^{-34}) \times (3 \times 10^8)}{6.6 \times 10^{-7}}$$

$$\Rightarrow \quad E = 23.55 \text{ J}$$

Average power

$$P = \frac{\text{Energy}}{\text{Time}} = \frac{23.55 \text{ joule}}{10^{-7} \text{ second}}$$

$$\Rightarrow \quad P = 23.55 \times 10^7 \text{ W}$$

$$\Rightarrow \quad P = 235.5 \text{ MW}$$

 # Illustrative Example 2.18

A 100 watt sodium lamp is radiating light of wavelength 5890 Å, uniformly in all directions,

(i) At what rate, photons are emitted from the lamp?

(ii) At what distance from the lamp, the average flux is 1 photon/cm^2-s ?

(iii) At what distance the average density is 1 photon/cm^3 ?

(iv) What are the photon flux and photon density at 2 m from the lamp ?

Solution

(i) The energy of photon is given by

$$E = h\nu = \frac{hc}{\lambda} = \frac{1990\times10^{-28}\text{ joule}}{\lambda}$$

$$\Rightarrow \quad E = \frac{1990\times10^{-28}}{5890\text{ Å}}$$

$$\Rightarrow \quad E = 3376\times10^{-22}\text{ joule} \qquad \dots(2.31)$$

Given that the lamp is emitting energy at the rate of 100 J/s (Power = 100 watt). Hence, number of photons N emitted is given by

$$N = \frac{100}{3376\times10^{-22}} \cong 3\times10^{20}\text{ photons/sec} \qquad \dots(2.32)$$

(ii) We regard the lamp as a point source. Therefore, at a distance r from the lamp, the light energy is uniformly distributed over the surface of sphere of radius r. So N photons are crossing area $4\pi r^2$ of spherical surface per second. So flux at a distance r is given by

$$n = \frac{N}{4\pi r^2}$$

For a flux of $n = 1$ photon/cm^2-s, we have

$$1 = \frac{N}{4\pi r^2} \quad \text{or} \quad r = \sqrt{\left(\frac{N}{4\pi}\right)}$$

$$\Rightarrow \quad r = \sqrt{\left(\frac{3\times10^{20}}{4\times3.14}\right)}\text{ cm}$$

$$\Rightarrow \quad r = 4.9\times10^4\text{ km} \qquad \dots(2.33)$$

So at this distance, on the average one photon will cross through 1 cm^2 area normal to radial direction.

(iii) The number of photons crossing through surface S $(4\pi r^2)$ in time interval dt is $N\,dt$. During interval dt, the photons entering surface S has moved to a distance $dr = c\,dt$ in radial direction.

Now, they occupy a volume dV enclosed between spheres of radii r and $r + dr$. Hence the average density at r is given by

$$\rho = \frac{N\,dt}{dV} \quad \text{or} \quad dV = \frac{N}{\rho}\times\frac{dr}{c}$$

$$\Rightarrow \quad \frac{4}{3}\pi[(r+dr)^3 - r^3] = \frac{N}{\rho}\times\frac{dr}{c}$$

Taking the limit, $dr \to 0$, we have

$$\rho = \frac{N}{4\pi r^2 c} \qquad \dots(2.34)$$

For $\rho = 1$ photon/cm^3 = 10^6 photons/m^3, we get

$$r = \sqrt{\left(\frac{N}{4\pi\rho c}\right)} = \sqrt{\left(\frac{3\times10^{20}}{4\times3.14\times10^6\times3\times10^8}\right)}$$

$$\Rightarrow \quad r = 282\text{ m}$$

Thus at a distance of 282 m from 100 W lamp, there is on the average only 1 photon/cm^3 at any moment.

(iv) Photon flux at $r = 2$ m

$$n = \frac{3\times10^{20}}{4\pi(200\text{ cm})^2}$$

$$\Rightarrow \quad n = 5.9\times10^{14}\text{ photons/cm}^2$$

Average density of photons at $r = 2$ m is given by

$$\rho = \frac{3\times10^{20}}{4\times3.14\times(200)^2\times(3\times10^{10})}$$

$$\Rightarrow \quad \rho = 2\times10^4\text{ photons/cm}^2$$

 # Illustrative Example 2.19

One milliwatt of light of wavelength 4560 Å is incident on a cesium surface. Calculate the photoelectric current liberated assuming a quantum efficiency of 0.5%, given Planck's constant $h = 6.62\times10^{-34}$ J-s and velocity of light $c = 3\times10^8$ m/s.

Solution

The energy of each photon of incident light is

$$E = h\nu = \frac{hc}{\lambda} = \frac{(6.62\times10^{-34})(3\times10^8)}{(4560\times10^{-10})}$$

$$\Rightarrow \quad E = 4.35\times10^{-19}\text{ J}$$

Number of photons in one milliwatt source

$$N = \frac{10^{-3}}{4.35\times10^{-19}}$$

$$\Rightarrow \quad N = 2.29\times10^{15}\text{ /s}$$

(As power of source = 1 milliwatt = 10^{-3} W)

Number of photons released

$$N_{th} = (2.29 \times 10^{15}) \times \frac{0.5}{100}$$

$$\Rightarrow \quad N_{th} = 1.14 \times 10^{13} \text{ /s}$$

Thus photoelectric current

$$I = (1.14 \times 10^{13})(1.6 \times 10^{-9})$$

$$\Rightarrow \quad I = 1.824 \times 10^{-6} \text{ A} = 1.824 \text{ μA}$$

Illustrative Example 2.20

A uniform monochromatic beam of light of wavelength 365 × 10^{-9} and intensity 10^{-8} W/m^2 falls on a surface having absorption coefficient 0.8 and work function 1.6 eV. Determine the rate of number of electrons emitted per m^2, power absorbed per m^2 and the maximum kinetic energy of emitted photoelectrons.

Solution

The intensity of radiation I is defined as the energy passing per unit time per unit area normal to the direction of the beam. If N be the number of photons crossing unit area per unit time, then

$$I = N \times \text{energy carried by one photon}$$

$$I = N\frac{hc}{\lambda}$$

$$\Rightarrow \quad N = \frac{I\lambda}{hc}$$

If N_i be the number of incident photons per unit area per unit time, then

$$N_i = \frac{I_i\lambda}{hc} = \frac{10^{-8} \times 365 \times 10^{-9}}{6.62 \times 10^{-34} \times 3 \times 10^{8}}$$

$$\Rightarrow \quad N_i = 18.35 \times 10^9$$

The number of photons absorbed N_{ab} by the surface per unit area per unit time is given by

$$N_{ab} = \text{absorption coefficient of surface} \times N_i$$

$$\Rightarrow \quad N_{ab} = 0.8 \times 8.35 \times 10^9$$

$$\Rightarrow \quad N_{ab} = 1.47 \times 10^{10} \text{ m}^{-2}\text{ s}^{-1}$$

Now assuming that each photon ejects only one electrons, the rate of electrons emitted per unit area is given by

$$N = N_{ab} = 1.47 \times 10^{10} \text{ m}^{-2}\text{ s}^{-1}$$

Power absorbed/m^2 = Absorption coefficient

$$= \frac{\text{Incident power}}{\text{m}^2}$$

$$= 0.8 \times 10^{-8} = 8 \times 10^{-9} \text{ W/m}^2$$

From Einstein's equation, maximum kinetic energy is given by

$$KE_{max} = h\nu - W_0 = \frac{hc}{\lambda} - W_0$$

$$\Rightarrow \quad KE_{max} = \frac{(6.62 \times 10^{-34})(3 \times 10^{8})}{365 \times 10^{-9}} - 1.6 \times 1.6 \times 10^{-19}$$

$$\Rightarrow \quad KE_{max} = 2.89 \times 10^{-19} \text{ joules} = 1.80 \text{ eV}$$

Illustrative Example 2.21

When a beam of 10.6 eV photon of intensity 2.0 W/m^2 falls on a platinum surface of area 1.0 × 10^{-4} m^2 and work function 5.6 eV, 0.53% of the incident photons eject photoelectrons. Find the number of photoelectrons emitted per second and their minimum energies (in eV). Take 1 eV = 1.6 × 10^{-19} J.

Solution

Energy of the photon beam striking the platinum surface in time t = 1 second is

$$E_b = \text{intensity of beam} \times \text{area of surface} \times \text{time}$$

$$\Rightarrow \quad E_b = (2.0 \text{ Wm}^{-2}) \times (1.0 \times 10^{-4} \text{ m}^2) \times 1 \text{ s}$$

$$\Rightarrow \quad E_b = 2.0 \times 10^{-4} \text{ Ws} = 2.0 \times 10^{-4} \text{ J}$$

Energy carried by each photon

$$E_p = 10.6 \text{ eV} = 10.6 \times 1.6 \times 10^{-19}$$

$$\Rightarrow \quad E_p = 16.96 \times 10^{-19} \text{ J}$$

Thus the number of photons striking the surface per second is

$$n = \frac{E_b}{E_p} = \frac{2.0 \times 10^{-4}}{16.96 \times 10^{-19}}$$

$$\Rightarrow \quad n = 1.18 \times 10^{14}$$

It is given that 0.53% of the incident photons eject photoelectrons. The number of photoelectrons emitted photoelectrons = 0 and the maximum energy is

$$E_{max} = 10.6 \text{ eV} - 5.6 \text{ eV} = 5.0 \text{ eV}$$

Illustrative Example 2.22

A beam of light has three wavelength 4144 Å, 4972 Å and 6216 Å with a total intensity of 3.6 × 10^{-3} Wm^{-3} equally distributed amongst the three wavelengths. The beam falls normally on an area 1.0 cm^2 of a clean metallic surface of work function 2.3 eV. Assume that there is no loss of light by reflection and that each energetically capable photon ejects one electron. Calculate the number of photo electrons liberated in two seconds.

Solution

Threshold wavelength for a metal of work function 2.3 eV is

$$\lambda_{th} = \frac{12431}{2.3} \text{ Å}$$

$$\Rightarrow \quad \lambda_{th} = 5404.7 \text{ Å}$$

Thus the only wavelength 4144 Å and 4972 Å will emit electrons from the metal surface as lesser then threshold wavelength.

The energy incident on surface for each wavelength

P = intensity of each wavelength × area of the surface

$$\Rightarrow \quad P = \frac{3.6\times10^{-3}}{3}\times(1.0\,\text{cm}^2)$$

$$\Rightarrow \quad P = (1.2\times10^{-7}\,\text{W/m}^2)\times(10^{-4}\,\text{m}^2)$$

$$\Rightarrow \quad P = 1.2\times10^{-7}\,\text{watt}$$

Energy incident on surface for each wavelength in 2 seconds.

$$E = (1.2\times10^{-7})\times(2) = 2.4\times10^{-7}\,\text{joule}$$

The number of photons of wavelength λ are

$$n = \frac{E}{(hc/\lambda)} = \frac{E\lambda}{hc}$$

Number of photons n_1 due to wavelength

$$4144\,\text{Å} = (4144\times10^{-10}\,\text{m})$$

$$n_1 = \frac{(1.2\times10^{-7})(4144\times10^{-10})}{(6.63\times10^{-34})(3\times10^8)}$$

$$\Rightarrow \quad n_1 = 0.5\times10^{12}$$

Number of photons n_2 due to wavelength 4972 Å

$$n_2 = \frac{(2.4\times10^{-7})(4972\times10^{-10})}{(6.63\times10^{-34})(3\times10^8)}$$

$$\Rightarrow \quad n_2 = 0.575\times10^{12}$$

Total photons $N = n_1 + n_2 = 0.5\times10^{12} + 0.575\times10^{12}$

$$\Rightarrow \quad N = 1.075\times10^{12}$$

Illustrative Example 2.23

A small plate of a metal (work function = 1.17 eV) is placed at a distance of 2 m from a monochromatic light source of wavelength 4800 Å and power 1.0 watt. The light falls normally on the plate. Find the number of photons striking the metal plate per square meter per second. If a constant magnetic field of strength 10^{-4} tesla is applied parallel to the metal surface, find the radius of the largest circular path followed by the emitted photo electrons.

Solution

Energy of incident photon in eV is

$$E = \frac{12431}{4800}\,\text{eV}$$

$$\Rightarrow \quad E = 2.58\,\text{eV}$$

$$\Rightarrow \quad E = 2.58\times1.6\times10^{-19}\,\text{J}$$

$$\Rightarrow \quad E = 4.125\times10^{-19}$$

The rate of emission of photon from source

$$r = \frac{I}{E} = \frac{1.0\,\text{joule/sec}}{4.125\times10^{-19}\,\text{joule}}$$

$$\Rightarrow \quad r = 2.424\times10^{18}\,/\text{s}$$

Number of photons striking per square meter per second on the plate

$$N = \frac{2.425\times10^{18}}{4\times(3.14)\times(2)^2}$$

$$\Rightarrow \quad N = 4.82\times10^{16}\,\text{m}^{-2}\,\text{s}^{-1}$$

The maximum kinetic energy of the photoelectrons emitted from the plate having work function ϕ = 1.17 eV is given by

$$KE_{max} = E - \phi$$

$$\Rightarrow \quad KE_{max} = 2.58 - 1.17$$

$$\Rightarrow \quad KE_{max} = 1.41\,\text{eV}$$

The maximum velocity of photoelectrons ejected is given as

$$\frac{1}{2}mv_{max}^2 = 1.41\,\text{eV}$$

$$\Rightarrow \quad v_{max} = \sqrt{\frac{2\times1.41\times1.6\times10^{-19}}{9.1\times10^{-31}}}$$

$$\Rightarrow \quad v_{max} = 7.036\times10^5\,\text{m/s}$$

The radius of the circle traversed by photo electron in magnetic field B is given by

$$r = \frac{mv}{qB} = \frac{(9.1\times10^{-31})(7.036\times10^5)}{(1.6\times10^{-19})\times(10^{-4})} \quad \left[\text{As } qvB = \frac{mv^2}{r}\right]$$

$$\Rightarrow \quad r = 40.0\times10^{-3}\,\text{metre} = 4.0\,\text{cm}$$

Illustrative Example 2.24

A 40 W ultraviolet-light source of wavelength 2480 Å illuminates a magnesium (Mg) surface placed 2 m away. Determine the number of photons emitted from the source per second and the number incident on unit area of the Mg surface per second. The photoelectric work function for Mg is 3.68 eV. Calculate the kinetic energy of the fastest electrons ejected from the surface. Determine the maximum wavelength for which the photoelectric effect can be observed with Mg surface.

Solution

The energy of incident photon in eV is given by

$$E = \frac{12431}{2480}\,\text{eV}$$

$$\Rightarrow \quad E = 5.01\,\text{eV}$$

$$\Rightarrow \quad E = 5.01\times1.6\times10^{-19}\,\text{J}$$

$$\Rightarrow \quad E = 8\times10^{-19}\,\text{J}$$

The number of photons emitted per second by the source can be given as

$$N = \frac{P}{hc/\lambda}$$

$$\Rightarrow \quad N = \frac{40}{8 \times 10^{-19}} = 5 \times 10^{19}\ \text{s}^{-1}$$

The number of photons incident on *Mg* surface per unit area per second

$$N' = \frac{5 \times 10^{19}}{4\pi r^2} = \frac{5 \times 10^{19}}{4 \times 3.14 \times (2)^2}$$

$$\Rightarrow \quad N' = 1.04 \times 10^{18}\ \text{s}^{-1}\ \text{m}^{-2}$$

The K.E. of the fastest electron is given by

$$KE_{max} = E - \phi$$

$$\Rightarrow \quad KE_{max} = 5.01\ \text{eV} - 3.68\ \text{eV} = 1.33\ \text{eV}$$

Now the threshold wavelength for *Mg* surface can be given as for its work function 3.68 eV is

$$\lambda_{th} = \frac{12431}{3.68}\ \text{Å}$$

$$\Rightarrow \quad \lambda_{th} = 3378\ \text{Å}$$

Illustrative Example 2.25

A mercury arc lamp provides 0.10 W of *UV* radiation at a wavelength of $\lambda = 2537$ Å (all other wavelengths having been absorbed by filters). The cathode of photoelectric device (a phototube) consists of potassium and has an effective area of 4 cm². The anode is located at a distance of 1 m from radiation source. The work function for potassium is $\phi_0 = 2.22$ eV.

(a) According to classical theory, the radiation from the arc spreads out uniformly in space as spherical wave. What time of exposure to the radiation should be required for a potassium atom (radius 2 Å) in the anode to accumulate sufficient energy to eject a photoelectron ?

(b) What is the energy of a single photon from the source ?

(c) What is the flux of photons (number per second) at the cathode ? To what saturation current does this flux correspond if the photo-conversion efficiency is 5% (i.e., if each photon has a probability of 0.05 of ejecting an electron).

(d) What is the cut off potential V_0 ?

Solution

(a) The UV energy flux at a distance of one metre

$$= \frac{0.1}{4\pi}\ \text{watt per square metre}$$

Cross-sectional area of atom $A = \pi r^2$

$$\Rightarrow \quad A = \pi (2 \times 10^{-10}\ \text{m})^2 = 4\pi \times 10^{-20}\ \text{m}^2$$

Energy required to eject photoelectron E_0 is given by

$$(2.22\ \text{eV})(1.60 \times 10^{-19}\ \text{J/eV}) = 3.55 \times 10^{-19}\ \text{J}$$

Now exposure time

$$t = \frac{3.55 \times 10^{-19}\ \text{J}}{\left(\frac{0.1}{4\pi}\frac{\text{W}}{\text{m}^2}\right) \times (4\pi \times 10^{-20}\ \text{m}^2)}$$

$$\Rightarrow \quad t = 355\ \text{s}$$

(b) Incident photon energy in *eV* is $E = \frac{12431}{2537}\ eV$

$$\Rightarrow \quad E = 4.9\ \text{eV}$$

$$\Rightarrow \quad E = 4.9 \times 1.6 \times 10^{-19}\ \text{J}$$

$$\Rightarrow \quad E = 7.84 \times 10^{-19}\ \text{J}$$

(c) At the cathode (area 4×10^{-4} m²), the photon flux is

$$N = \left(\frac{0.1}{4\pi}\frac{\text{W}}{\text{m}^2}\right) \frac{4 \times 10^{-4}\ \text{m}^2}{7.84 \times 10^{-19}\ \text{J}}$$

$$\Rightarrow \quad N = 4.06 \times 10^{12}\ \text{photons/s}$$

With an efficiency of 5%, the photocurrent is

$$I = 0.05\,Ne = (0.05)(4.06 \times 10^{12})(1.60 \times 10^{-19}\ \text{C})$$

$$\Rightarrow \quad I = 3.25 \times 10^{-8}\ \text{A} = 32.5\ \text{nA}$$

(d) The stopping potential for ejected electrons can be given as

$$V_0 = \frac{h\nu - \phi_0}{e} = \frac{4.86\ \text{eV} - 2.22\ \text{eV}}{e}$$

$$\Rightarrow \quad V_0 = 2.64\ \text{V}$$

Illustrative Example 2.26

A monochromatic point source *S* radiating wavelength 6000 Å, with power 2 watt, an aperture *A* of diameter 0.1 m and a large screen SC are placed as shown in figure-2.17. A photoemissive detector *D* of surface area 0.5 cm² is placed at the centre of the screen (see the figure). The efficiency of the detector for the photoelectron generation per incident photon is 0.9.

(a) Calculate the photon flux at the centre of the screen and the photocurrent in the detector.

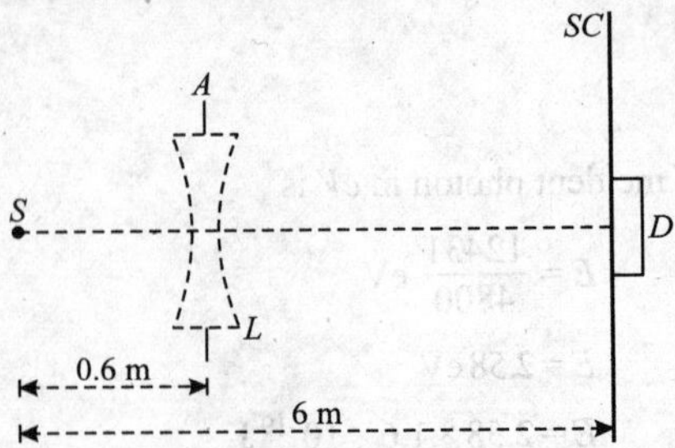

Figure 2.17

(b) If a concave lens L of focal length 0.6 m is inserted in the aperture as shown, find the new values of photon flux and photocurrent. Assume uniform average transmission of 80% from the lens.

(c) If the work function of the photoemissive surface is 1 eV, calculate the value of the stopping potential in the two cases. (without and with the lens in the aperture)

Solution

(a) Energy of Photon is

$$E = \frac{hc}{\lambda} = \frac{6.63\times10^{-34}\times(3\times10^{8})}{6000\times10^{-10}}$$

$$\Rightarrow \quad E = 3.315\times10^{-19}\text{ joule}$$

Number of photons emitted per second from the source are

$$n = \frac{\text{Power}}{\text{Energy of each photon}}$$

$$\Rightarrow \quad n = \frac{2}{3.315\times10^{-19}}$$

$$\Rightarrow \quad n = 6.033\times10^{18}\text{ photon sec}^{-1}$$

Here the solid angle subtended by detector is less than that subtended by aperture on the source. This shows that all the photons reaching the detector are allowed by aperture. In this way the number of photons reaching the detector per m^2 per second is given by

$$\text{Photon flux} \quad \phi_P = \frac{n}{4\pi r^2}$$

$$\Rightarrow \quad \phi_P = \frac{6.033\times10^{18}}{4\times(3.14)\times(6.0)^2}\text{ m}^{-2}\text{s}^{-1}$$

$$\Rightarrow \quad \phi_P = 1.33\times10^{16}\text{ photons/m}^2\text{-sec}$$

Photo current $= n\,e$

$$I = [9.0\times\text{photon flux}\times\text{area of detector}]\,e$$

$$\Rightarrow \quad I = [0.9\times\text{photon flux}\times(0.5\times10^{-4})]\times1.6\times10^{-19}\text{ Amp.}$$

$$\Rightarrow \quad I = 0.096\ \mu\text{A}$$

(b) The source is at the focus of concave lens.

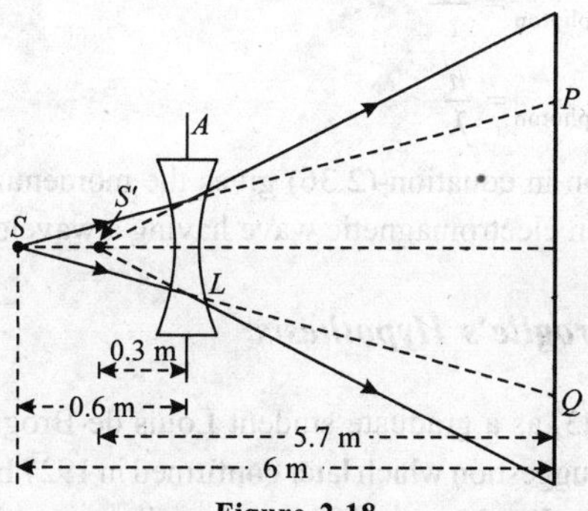

Figure 2.18

Thus the concave lens forms its image at a distance $f/2$ i.e., 0.3 metre on the left of the lens. This we get from lens formula

$$\frac{1}{f} = \frac{1}{v} - \frac{1}{u}$$

$$\Rightarrow \quad \frac{1}{v} = \frac{1}{f} + \frac{1}{u} = \frac{1}{-0.6} + \frac{1}{-0.6} = -\frac{1}{0.3}$$

$$\Rightarrow \quad v = -0.3\text{ m}$$

Now all the photons are focussed at a distance 0.3 m from the lens or 5.7 m from the detector. The detector transmits 80% of photons. So the number of photons reaching the detector

$$n' = \frac{80}{100}\times\text{photon flux}\times\frac{\text{Solid angle subtended by detector}}{\text{Solid angle subtended by aperture}}$$

$$\Rightarrow \quad n' = \frac{80}{100}\times\text{photon flux}\times\frac{(0.5\times10^{-4}/5.7)^2}{\pi\times(0.05)^2/(0.3)^2}$$

Substitute the value of photon flux and obtain the value of n'

$$\text{Photon flux} \quad \phi_P = \frac{n'}{\text{area of detector}}$$

$$\Rightarrow \quad \phi_P = \frac{n'}{0.5\times10^{-4}}\text{ per m}^2\text{ per second}$$

$$\Rightarrow \quad \phi_P = 2.956\times10^{15}\text{/m}^2\text{ sec}$$

Thus photon current $= 0.9\times\text{Photon flux}\times e$

$$\Rightarrow \quad I = 0.9\times\text{Photon flux}\times1.6\times10^{-19}\text{ Amp}$$

$$\Rightarrow \quad I = 0.0213\ \mu\text{A}$$

(c) The stopping potential V_s is independent of photocurrent. In both the cases, according to Einstein's photoelectric equation, this is given by

$$E = W + eV_s$$

$$\Rightarrow \quad 3.315\times10^{-19} = 1\,eV + eV_s$$

$$\Rightarrow \quad \frac{3.315\times10^{-19}}{1.6\times10^{-19}}\,eV = 1\,eV + eV_s$$

$$\Rightarrow \quad 2.06\,eV = 1\,eV + eV_s$$

$$\Rightarrow \quad V_s = 2.06 - 1$$

$$\Rightarrow \quad V_s = 1.06\text{ volt}$$

Web Reference at www.physicsgalaxy.com

Age Group - High School Physics | Age 17-19 Years

Section - MODERN PHYSICS

Topic - Wave Particle Duality

Module Number - 3 to 11

Practice Exercise 2.3

(i) Calculate the number of photons emitted per second by a 10 watt sodium vapour lamp. Assume that 60% of the consumed energy is converted into light. Wavelength of the sodium light = 5900 Å.

[1.7×10^{16}]

(ii) A lamp emits light of mean wavelength of 4500 Å The lamp is rated at 150 watt and 8% of the energy appears as emitted light. How many photons are emitted by the lamp per second.

[27.15×10^{18}]

(iii) 0.05 kg of ice at – 20°C is to be converted into steam at 100°C. The ice is first heated with a 420 Watts heater for 5 minutes. After this, it is heated with an infrared lamp of λ = 10000 Å for 23 minutes and 20 seconds at an efficiency of 50%. Find the rate at which the photons are striking the ice when heated with infrared lamp.

Specific heat of ice at – 20°C = 500 cal/kg

Specific heat of water = 10^3 cal/kg

Latent heat of fusion of ice = 8×10^4 cal/kg

Latent heat of vaporization of water = 5.42×10^5 cal/kg

[$1.99 \times 10^{20}\ s^{-1}$]

(iv) A light source, emitting three wavelengths 5000 Å, 6000 Å and 7000 Å has a total power of 10^{-3} Watt and a beam diameter of 0.002 m. The power density is distributed equally amongst the three wavelengths. The beam shines normally on a metallic surface of area 10^{-4} m^2 and having a work function of 1.9 eV. Assuming that each photon liberates an electron, calculate the charge emitted per unit area in one second.

[93.94 coul/m^2/s]

(v) A monochromatic light source of intensity 5 mW emits 8×10^{15} photons per second. This light ejects photoelectrons from a metal surface. The stopping potential for this setup is 2.0 V, calculate the work function of the metal.

[1.9 eV]

(vi) A potassium surface is placed 75 cm away from a 100 W bulb. It is found that the energy radiated by the bulb is 5% of the input power. Consider each potassium atom as a circular disc of diameter 1 Å & determine the time required for each atom to absorb an amount of energy equal its work function of 2.0 eV. What is the answer if the atom is assumed to be spherical.

[57.63 s]

(vii) When the sun is directly overhead, the surface of the earth receives 1.4×10^3 W/m^2 of sunlight. Assume that the light is monochromatic with average wavelength 5000 Å and that no light is absorbed in between the sun and the earth's surface. The distance between the sun and the earth is 1.5×10^{11} m.

(a) Calculate the number of the photons falling per second on each quare meter of earth's surface directly below the sun.

(b) How many photons are there in each cubic meter near the earth's surface at any instant ?

(c) How many photons does the sun emits per second ?

[3.5×10^{21}, 1.2×10^{13}, 9.9×10^{44}]

2.6 Wave Particle Duality

The true nature of light is very difficult to asses. In 1801 Young's double slit experiment it was shown that light exhibit fundamental properties like a wave diffraction and interference. After several years Maxwell discovered that light was a wave of oscillating electric and magnetic fields, an electromagnetic wave. On the other hand Plank's equation theory, photoelectric effect and compton effects indicates that light behaves like a particle, a photon, with both energy and momentum. Thus light shows wave particle duality.

2.6.1 Momentum of a Photon

According to relativistic theory the total relativistic energy E of a particle is related to the magnitude p of the momentum and mass m as

$$E^2 = p^2c^2 + m^2c^4 \qquad \dots(2.35)$$

For a photon, its mass is zero, thus we have

$$E = pc$$

$$\Rightarrow \qquad p = \frac{E}{c}$$

For a photon its energy can be given as

$$E = h\nu = \frac{hc}{\lambda}$$

Thus photon momentum is given as

$$p_{\text{photon}} = \frac{h\nu}{c}$$

$$\Rightarrow \qquad p_{\text{photon}} = \frac{h}{\lambda} \qquad \dots(2.36)$$

This relation in equation-(2.36) gives the momentum of each photon of an electromagnetic wave having a wavelength λ.

2.7 De-Broglie's Hypothesis

In year 1923, as a graduate student Louis de-Broglie made a surprising suggestion which later confirmed in 1927 by different experiments. By the year 1921 it was all accepted that light behaves like a particle, a stream of photons and the wavelength of light is related to the magnitude of its momentum as

$$\lambda = \frac{h}{p_{\text{photon}}} \quad \dots(2.37)$$

Using the above accepted fact, Broglie started thinking the reverse of it. He suggested that since light waves could exhibit particle like behaviour, particles of matter should exhibit wave like behaviour. De-Broglie proposed that all moving matter has a wavelength associated with it, just as a wave does and this wavelength is related to the magnitude of its momentum by an equation of the same form as given in equation-(2.37) as

$$\lambda = \frac{h}{p_{\text{particle}}} \quad \dots(2.38)$$

The wavelength associated with a particle is called its de-Broglie wavelength. The de-Broglie hypothesis implies that the wave particle duality has a universal and symmetrical character i.e. waves have particle properties and moving particles have wave properties.

It was also assumed that as the speed of a particle increases its wave character also increases and the wavelength associated with the particle may have a significant practical values. For particles in nature moving very slowly, the wave character associated with the particle will not have much significance.

2.7.1 Explanation of Bohr's Second Postulate

The de-Broglie hypothesis brought Bohr's second postulate in a new light. It was stated that the magnitude of angular momentum of the orbiting electron in a hydrogenic atom was an integral multiple of $h/2\pi$. Given as

$$mvr = \frac{nh}{2\pi} \quad \dots(2.39)$$

As in an orbit speed of electron is of the order of 10^6 m/s it may have a significant wave character associated with it. As we know in an atom stable orbits are those in which electron does not radiate any electromagnetic radiation. Thus if we describe electron as a wave, its stable orbits in an atom are those that satisfy the conditions for a stationary wave so that the complete wave energy is sustained in that orbit only. Thus for stationary waves to exist in an orbit the circumference of the orbit must be an integral multiple of the wavelength, which can be given for an orbit of radius r

$$2\pi r = n\lambda_e \quad \dots(2.40)$$

For electron, its de-Broglie wavelength λ_e can be given as

$$\lambda_e = \frac{h}{mv} \quad \dots(2.41)$$

Now from equation-(2.41) & (2.42) we have

$$2\pi r = n\,\frac{h}{mv}$$

$$\Rightarrow \quad mvr = \frac{nh}{2\pi} \quad \dots(2.42)$$

Thus if a wavelength is associated with the electron, the quantization of atomic orbitals leads to consider integral number of wavelengths that fit into each orbit. For example figure-2.19 shows the different orbits in which for different values of n electron wave is forming a stationary wave. Figure-2.19(a) shows an orbit in which the stationary wave is formed for the principle quantum number $n = 3$. Similarly figure-2.19(b) shows an orbit corresponding to $n = 4$ and figure-2.19(c) shows an orbit which is larger then that of $n = 3$ but smaller then that of $n = 4$ in which we can see that in this orbit wavelength is not fit properly thus standing waves can not be formed for this orbit hence the orbit is not stable.

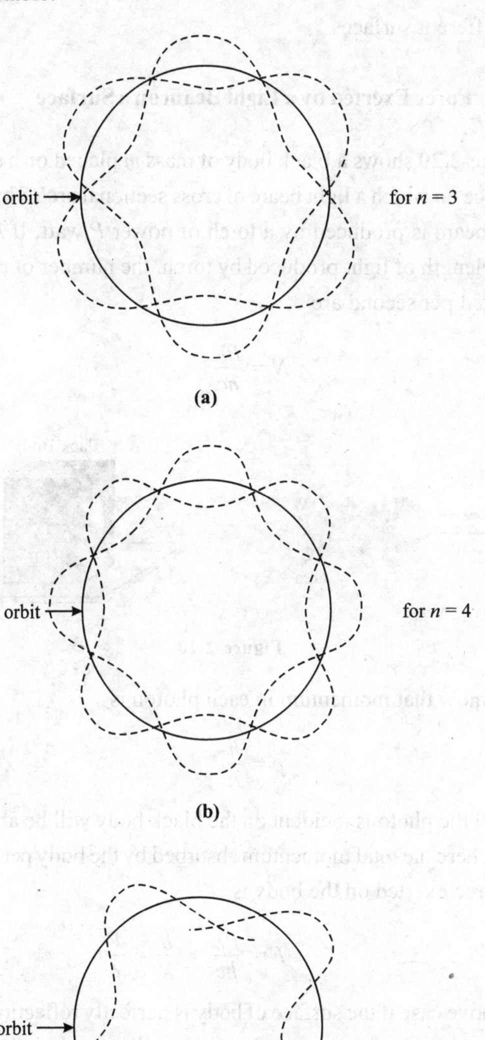

Figure 2.19

2.8 Radiation Pressure

We've discussed that a photon carries momentum, given as

$$p = \frac{h}{\lambda} \quad \ldots(2.43)$$

When a photon beam incidents on a surface and absorbed, the total momentum carried by the beam is also transferred to that surface hence a force is exerted on the surface. If the surface on which the beam incident is reflecting then due to the reflection in photon beam the change in momentum of photons will be twice the value compared to the case when it was absorbed. Thus force exerted on surface will also get almost doubled. Now we'll discuss different cases of incidence of a light beam on different surfaces.

2.8.1 Force Exerted by a Light Beam on a Surface

Figure-2.20 shows a black body of mass m placed on a smooth surface on which a light beam of cross sectional area S incident. The beam is produced by a torch of power P watt. If λ is the wavelength of light produced by torch, the number of photons emitted per second are

$$N = \frac{P\lambda}{hc} \quad \ldots(2.44)$$

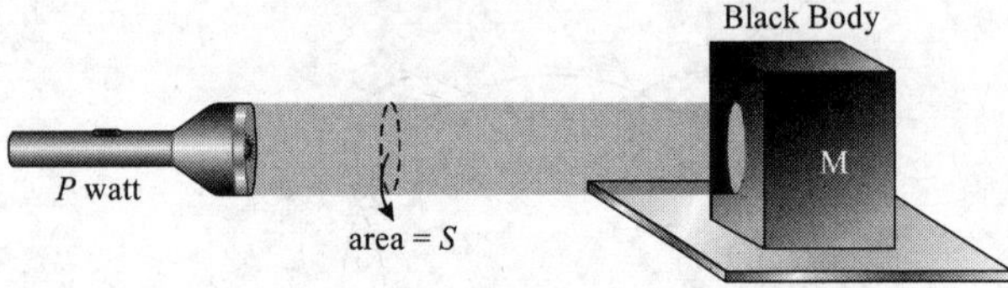

Figure 2.20

We know that momentum in each photon is

$$p = \frac{h}{\lambda} \quad \ldots(2.45)$$

As all the photons incident on the black body will be absorbed by it, here the total momentum absorbed by the body per second or force exerted on the body is

$$F = \frac{P\lambda}{hc} \times \frac{h}{\lambda} = \frac{P}{c} \quad \ldots(2.46)$$

In above case if the surface of body is perfectly reflecting like a mirror then the force exerted on body will become

$$F = \frac{2P}{c} \quad \ldots(2.47)$$

Similarly consider another case as shown in figure-2.21. Now the surface of body on which light beam is incident is having a reflection coefficient $a_r = 0.7$ and absorption coefficient $a_a = 0.3$.

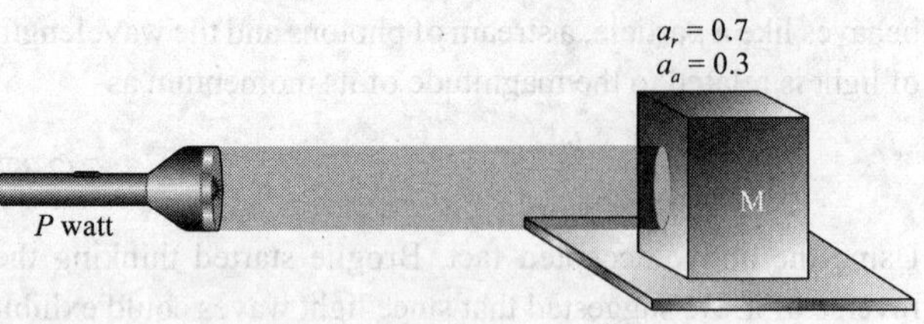

Figure 2.21

In this case 70% of the incident photons are reflected back and 30% are absorbed by the body. Thus the photon which is absorbed will impart a momentum $\frac{h}{\lambda}$ to the body and the photon which is reflected will impart the change in momentum $\frac{2h}{\lambda}$ to the body. Thus net force acting on body can be given as

$$F = \frac{0.7P\lambda}{hc} \times \frac{2h}{\lambda} + \frac{0.3P\lambda}{hc} \times \frac{h}{\lambda}$$

$$\Rightarrow \quad F = \frac{1.7P}{c} \quad \ldots(2.48)$$

If in any of the case we wish to find pressure on the surface on which light beam is incident. In above relations we can use light intensity $I = P/S$ instead of power P of the light source.

2.8.2 Force Exerted on any Object in the Path of a Light Beam

Figure-2.22 shows a big lamp of power P watt which produces a uniform parallel beam of light of cross sectional area S. Thus the intensity of this light beam will be

$$I = \frac{P}{S} \text{ w/m}^2 \quad \ldots(2.49)$$

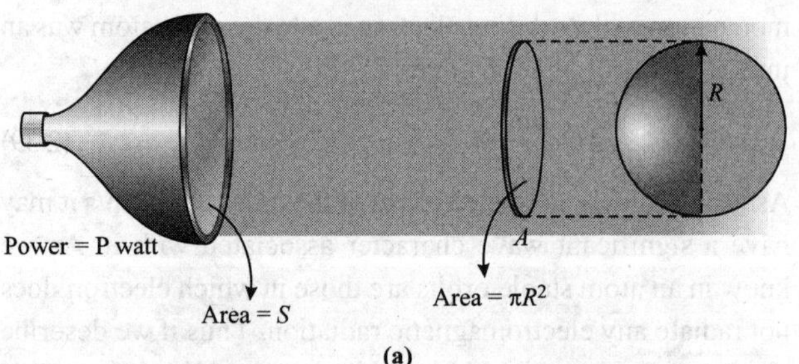

(a)

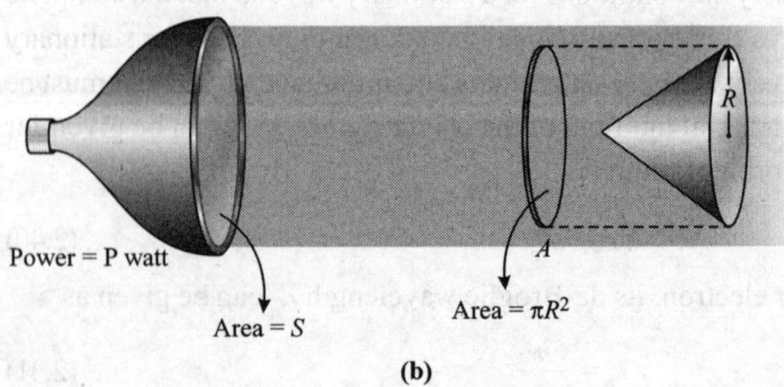

(b)

Figure 2.22

If in the path of this beam a black body sphere is placed as shown in figure-2.22(a). In this case only those photons will be incident on the sphere which pass through the cross sectional area $A = \pi R^2$ which is the projection of sphere on a cross-sectional plane. Thus the power incident on sphere is

$$P_i = IA = I\pi R^2 \quad \ldots(2.50)$$

Thus force exerted on sphere will be

$$F = \frac{P_i}{c} = \frac{I\pi R^2}{c} \quad \ldots(2.51)$$

Similarly as shown in figure-2.22(b) a black body cone is placed in the path of the light beam. Here also the projection of cone along a cross-sectional plane of beam is $A = \pi R^2$ hence the force exerted on cone due to the beam will remain same as

$$F = \frac{I\pi R^2}{c} \quad \ldots(2.52)$$

2.8.3 Force Exerted by a Light Beam at Oblique Incidence

As shown in figure-2.23 when a light beam incident on a mirror at an angle θ to normal, it will be reflected at same angle. If power of light beam is P watt, the momentum of photons in the beam per second will be

$$\Delta p = \frac{P}{c} \quad \ldots(2.53)$$

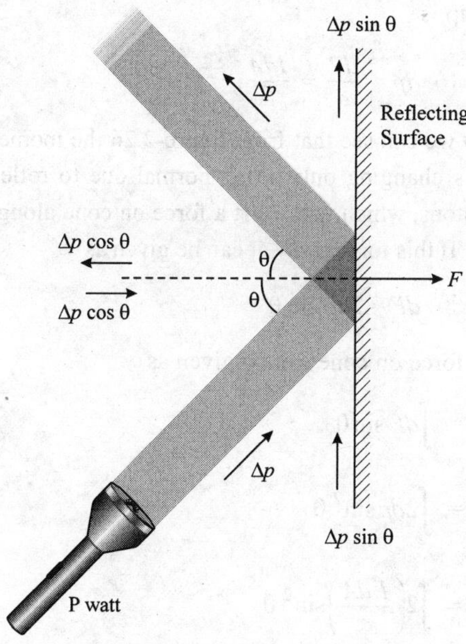

Figure 2.23

Here as shown in figure-2.23 there will be no change in the component of this momentum along the mirror due to reflection but along normal momentum of light beam is changed by $2\Delta p \cos\theta$. Thus force exerted on the mirror is along its normal and is given by

$$F = 2\,\Delta p \cos\theta = \frac{2P}{c}\cos\theta \quad \ldots(2.54)$$

Illustrative Example 2.27

In the path of a uniform light beam of large cross-sectional area and intensity I, a solid sphere of radius R which is perfectly reflecting is placed. Find the force exerted on this sphere due to the light beam.

Solution

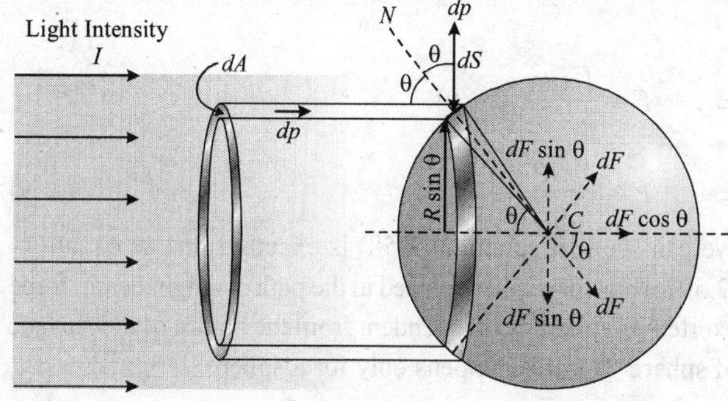

Figure 2.24

To find the force on sphere, we consider a small elemental strip of angular width $d\theta$ on its surface at an angle θ from its horizontal diameter as shown. The area dS of this strip on the surface of sphere is

$$dS = 2\pi R\sin\theta \cdot R d\theta \quad \ldots(2.55)$$

Now as shown in figure-2.24, dA is the projection of the slant strip area dS along the cross-sectional plane of the light beam and it is given as

$$dA = dS\cos\theta \quad \ldots(2.56)$$

Here the power of light incident on this strip is

$$dP = IdA$$

Thus the momentum of photons per second incident on this strip are

$$dp = \frac{dP}{c} = \frac{IdA}{c} \quad \ldots(2.57)$$

Here we can see that these photons are incident at an angle θ to the normal N of this strip and as sphere is perfectly reflecting. These are reflected at the same angle θ to N as shown in figure-2.24.

Here the change in momentum of photons is along the normal and thus force exerted on this strip along the normal is

$$dF = 2dp\cos\theta = \frac{2IdA}{c}\cos\theta \quad \ldots(2.58)$$

Thus net force on sphere will be given as

$$F = \int dF\cos\theta$$

$$\Rightarrow \quad F = \int \frac{2I\,dA}{c}\cos^2\theta$$

$$\Rightarrow \quad F = \int_0^{\pi/2} \frac{2I}{c}(2\pi R \sin\theta \cos\theta \cdot R d\theta)\cos^2\theta$$

$$\Rightarrow \quad F = \frac{4I\pi R^2}{c}\int_0^{\pi/2} \cos^3\theta \sin\theta\, d\theta$$

$$\Rightarrow \quad F = \frac{4I\pi R^2}{c}\left[-\frac{\cos^4\theta}{4}\right]_0^{\pi/2}$$

$$\Rightarrow \quad F = \frac{I\pi R^2}{c}[1-0]$$

$$\Rightarrow \quad F = \frac{I\pi R^2}{c} \qquad \ldots(2.59)$$

We can see that equation-(2.58) is exactly same as equation-(2.59). Thus for a sphere placed in the path of a light beam, force exerted on sphere is independent from the nature of the surface of sphere. But this happens only for a sphere.

Lets discuss the same for a cone with reflecting surface in the path of a light beam, illustrated in next example.

Illustrative Example 2.28

Figure-2.25 shows a cone of radius R and height H with perfectly reflecting lateral surface, is placed in the path of a light beam of intensity I. Find the force exerted on this cone.

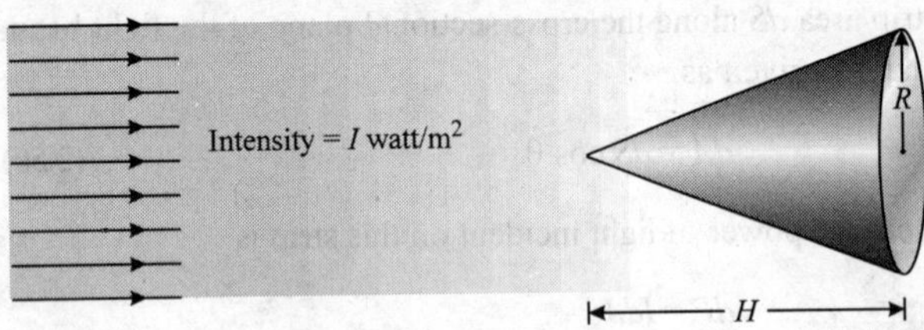

Figure 2.25

Solution

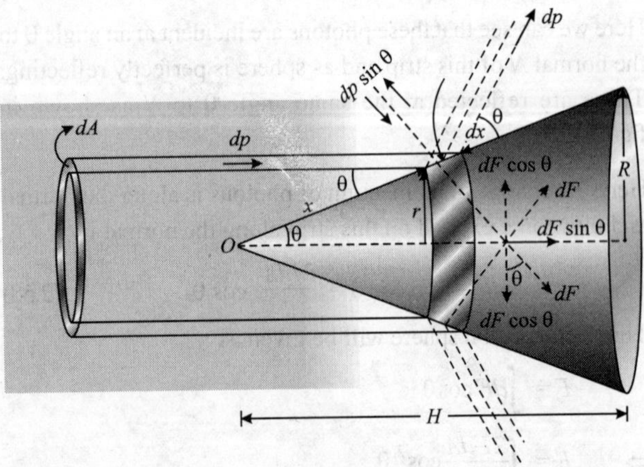

Figure 2.26

Now to find the force on the cone, we consider an elemental strip of width dx on the lateral surface of cone at a distance x from the vertex O of cone as shown in figure-2.26. If the radius of the strip is r its surface area is

$$dS = 2\pi r \cdot dx \qquad \ldots(2.60)$$

Here by similar triangles in cone we have

$$\Rightarrow \quad \frac{r}{x} = \frac{R}{\sqrt{R^2+H^2}} \qquad \ldots(2.61)$$

$$\Rightarrow \quad r = x\sin\theta$$

Thus area of strip can be given as

$$dS = 2\pi x \sin\theta \cdot dx$$

If dA be the projection of slant strip of area dS along the cross-sectional plane of the light beam, it can be given as

$$dA = dS \sin\theta \qquad \ldots(2.62)$$

If dP is the power of light beam incident on the strip then

$$dP = IdA \qquad \ldots(2.63)$$

Now the momentum per second of the light photons dp incident on the strip is

$$dp = \frac{dP}{c} = \frac{IdA}{c} \qquad \ldots(2.64)$$

Here also we can see that from figure-2.26 the momentum of photons is changing only along normal due to reflection of these photons, which will exert a force on cone along normal direction. If this force is dF, it can be given as

$$dF = 2dp\sin\theta \qquad \ldots(2.65)$$

Thus net force on cone can be given as

$$F = \int dF \sin\theta$$

$$\Rightarrow \quad F = \int 2dp\sin^2\theta$$

$$\Rightarrow \quad F = \int 2\left(\frac{I\,dA}{c}\right)\sin^2\theta$$

$$\Rightarrow \quad F = \int \frac{2I}{c} dS \sin^3\theta$$

$$\Rightarrow \quad F = \int \frac{2I}{c} 2\pi x\, dx \sin^4\theta$$

$$\Rightarrow \quad F = \frac{4I\pi\sin^4\theta}{c}\int_0^{\sqrt{R^2+H^2}} x\,dx$$

$$\Rightarrow \quad F = \frac{4I\pi}{c}\sin^4\theta\left[\frac{x^2}{2}\right]_0^{\sqrt{R^2+H^2}}$$

$$\Rightarrow \quad F = \frac{2I\pi}{c} \times \left(\frac{R}{\sqrt{(R^2+H^2)}}\right)^4 \times (R^2+H^2)$$

$$\left[\text{As } \sin\theta = \frac{R}{\sqrt{(R^2+H^2)}}\right]$$

$$\Rightarrow \quad F = \frac{2I\pi R^4}{c(R^2+H^2)} \qquad \ldots(2.66)$$

Equation-(2.66) gives the force exerted by light beam on a perfectly reflecting cone in its path.

2.8.4 Recoiling of an Atom Due to Electron Transition

We know that when an e^- in a hydrogenic atom makes a transition from a higher energy level n_2 to a lower energy level n_1, the difference of energies of the two energy level is released in the form of an electromagnetic radiation photon. As we've discussed that every photon has a momentum associated with it, we can say that when a photon is emitted from an atom, it must recoil in opposite direction as shown in figure-2.27

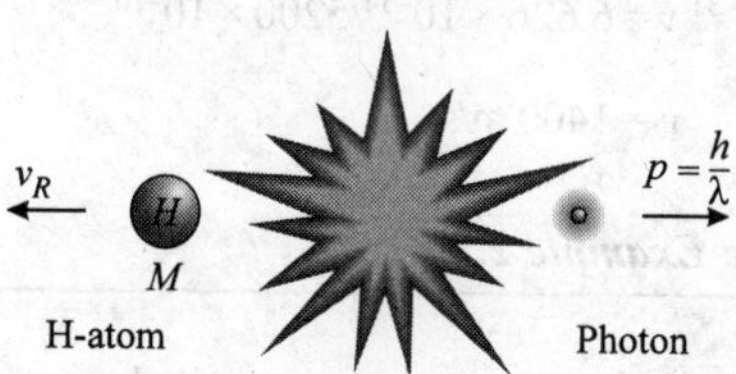

Figure 2.27

Here the wavelength of emitted photon can be given as

$$\frac{1}{\lambda} = RZ^2\left[\frac{1}{n_1^2} - \frac{1}{n_2^2}\right] \qquad \ldots(2.67)$$

The momentum of this emitted photon can be given as

$$p = \frac{h}{\lambda} = hRZ^2\left[\frac{1}{n_1^2} - \frac{1}{n_2^2}\right] \qquad \ldots(2.68)$$

If the after emission of photon the atom recoils with speed v_R, using momentum conservation principle, we can write

$$Mv_R = \frac{h}{\lambda}$$

$$\Rightarrow \quad v_R = \frac{hRZ^2}{M}\left(\frac{1}{n_1^2} - \frac{1}{n_2^2}\right) \qquad \ldots(2.69)$$

2.8.5 Variation in Wavelength of Emitted Photon with State of Motion of an Atom

As we've discussed that when a photon is emitted by transition of an electron in an atom, the atom recoils and the recoil velocity can be obtained by momentum conservation. In previous section we've discussed that the emitted photon wavelength is given by Rydberg's formula as

$$\frac{1}{\lambda} = RZ^2\left[\frac{1}{n_1^2} - \frac{1}{n_2^2}\right] \qquad \ldots(2.70)$$

This equation-(2.70) or Rydberg formula is valid only if all the energy released by electron during transition from energy level n_2 to n_1 will transform into the photon energy. But in our case if all the energy released by electron is carried by the photon then no energy is left with which the atom an recoil. If it does not recoil, the law of momentum conservation will violet. Thus in previous section equation-(2.69) only gives an approximate value of recoil velocity.

Practically we can say that the energy released by electron during transition is shared between the emitted photon and the kinetic energy of recoiled atom. If λ' is the wavelength of emitted photon and v_R is the recoil velocity of atom, we can write the energy equation as

$$RchZ^2\left[\frac{1}{n_1^2} - \frac{1}{n_2^2}\right] = \frac{hc}{\lambda'} + \frac{1}{2}mv_R^2 \qquad \ldots(2.71)$$

Using momentum conservation we can write

$$\frac{h}{\lambda'} = Mv_R \qquad \ldots(2.72)$$

Solving equation-(2.71) and (2.72), we can calculate the exact value of recoil velocity v_R and the wavelength of emitted photon λ'. Note that the value of λ' will be slightly more compared to that calculated in previous section by equation-(2.67). As the difference between the two is very small, for numerical applications students can use equation-(2.69) and (2.70) for calculations of emitted wavelength and recoil velocity if very high accuracy is not needed in the application.

2.8.6 Variation in Wavelength of Photon During Reflection

We've discussed that when light incident on a body a force is exerted due to the momentum associated with the light photons. Consider the following example. A torch of power P in front of a body of mass M is lit just for a time Δt so that torch will emit a pulse of energy ΔE which is given as

$$\Delta E = P\Delta t \qquad \ldots(2.73)$$

If wavelength light is λ, the momentum in this pulse is

$$\Delta P = \frac{\Delta E}{(hc/\lambda)} \times \frac{h}{\lambda} = \frac{\Delta E}{c} \qquad \ldots(2.74)$$

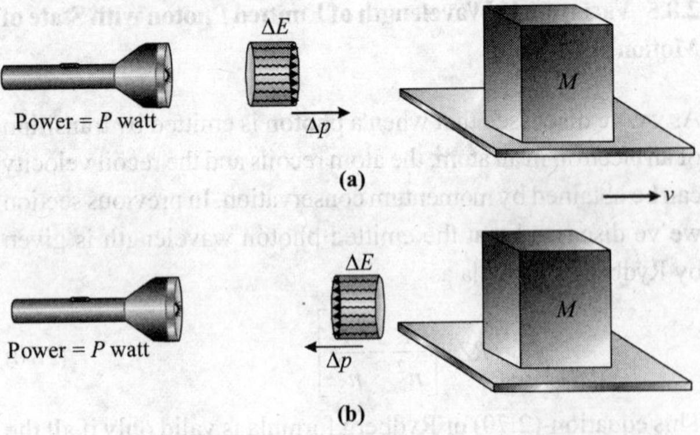

Figure 2.28

As shown in figure-2.28 we can see that when the energy pulse is reflected from the body if its surface is perfectly reflecting. Due to this the body will gain a velocity v as shown in figure-2.28(b).

Here if we assume that the wavelength of reflected and incident light are same, we can say that the momentum of reflected pulse is same in magnitude but direction is opposite. Thus by momentum conservation we can write

$$\Delta p = Mv - \Delta p$$

$$\Rightarrow \quad 2\,\Delta p = Mv$$

$$\Rightarrow \quad \frac{2\Delta E}{c} = Mv \quad \ldots(2.75)$$

Using the above equation we can find the speed of the block after reflecting the pulse. But this result will only be an approximate value. If we carefully look into the situation once again, a question arises, if whole of the energy of pulse is reflected back, how the block has gained the kinetic energy $\frac{1}{2}Mv^2$.

Thus it is sure that when the incident energy pulse is reflected from the block, some of its energy is transmitted to block as its kinetic energy and remaining is reflected as energy pulse of energy $\Delta E'$. Now the way of accurate calculations for the speed of block is given here.

The number of photons in the incident pulse are

$$N = \frac{\Delta E}{(hc/\lambda)}$$

$$\Rightarrow \quad N = \frac{\Delta E\lambda}{hc} \quad \ldots(2.76)$$

Here λ is the wavelength of incident light.

If λ' is the wavelength of reflected light, the equation for momentum conservation can be written as

$$N\frac{h}{\lambda} = Mv - N\frac{h}{\lambda'} \quad \ldots(2.77)$$

As the total energy of system is also constant, the equation for energy conservation can be given as

$$N\cdot\frac{hc}{\lambda} = \frac{1}{2}Mv^2 + N\cdot\frac{hc}{\lambda'} \quad \ldots(2.78)$$

Now solving equation-(2.77) and (2.78) we can get the value of speed of block as well as the wavelength λ' of reflected light pulse. This process gives accurate results but for numerical problems, it is relatively lengthy procedure. Students are advised to directly use equation-(2.75) or assume that the reflected wavelength is approximately same because the difference is very small which can be neglected for numerical problems.

 # Illustrative Example 2.29

With what velocity must an electron travel so that its momentum is equal to that of photon with a wavelength of $\lambda = 5200$ Å.

Solution

Momentum of photon

$$p = \frac{h}{\lambda} = \frac{6.626\times10^{-34}}{5200\times10^{-10}}\ \text{kg.m/s}$$

Momentum of electron $= mv = 9.1\times10^{-31}\,v$

Where v is the velocity of electron

Equating the two momenta, we have

$$9.1\times10^{-31}\,v = 6.626\times10^{-34}/5200\times10^{-10}$$

$$\Rightarrow \quad v = 1400\ \text{m/s}$$

 # Illustrative Example 2.30

Hydrogen gas in the atomic state is excited to an energy level such that the electrostatic potential energy of H-atom becomes – 1.7 eV. Now the photoelectric plate having work function $\phi = 2.3$ eV is exposed to the emission spectra of this gas. Assuming all the transitions to be possible, find the minimum de-Broglie wavelength of ejected photoelectrons.

Solution

Given that electrostatic potential energy of H-atom is

$$PE = -1.7\ \text{eV}$$

We know that kinetic energy is given as

$$= \left|\frac{PE}{2}\right| = \frac{1.7}{2} = 0.85\ \text{eV}$$

Thus total energy

$$E = -1.7 + 0.85 = -0.85\ \text{eV}$$

We use, $$E_n = -\frac{13.6}{n^2} = -0.85\ \text{eV}$$

$$\Rightarrow \qquad n^2 = \frac{13.6}{0.85} = 16$$

$$\Rightarrow \qquad n = 4$$

Hence the atom is excited to state $n = 4$. The maximum energy is emitted when electrons will make a transition from $n = 4$ to $n = 1$ for which energy emitted is

$$\Delta E = -0.85 - (-13.6) = 12.75 \text{ eV}$$

Now this photon energy when incident on a metal plate having work function 2.3 eV, the kinetic energy of fastest electron ejected can be given as

$$KE_{max} = \Delta E - \phi = 12.75 - 2.3 = 10.45 \text{ eV}$$

The minimum de-Broglie wavelength is given by

$$\lambda_{min} = \frac{h}{(p)_{max}} = \frac{h}{\sqrt{2m\,(K.E.)_{max}}}$$

$$\Rightarrow \quad \lambda_{min} = \frac{6.63\times10^{-34}}{\sqrt{2\times(9.1\times10^{-31})(10.45\times1.6\times10^{-19})}}$$

$$\Rightarrow \quad \lambda_{min} = 3.8\times10^{-10}\text{ m} = 3.8 \text{ Å}$$

Illustrative Example 2.31

An α-particle and a proton are fired through the same magnetic fields which is perpendicular to their velocity vectors. The α-particle and the proton move such that radius of curvature of their path is same. Find the ratio of their de-Broglie wavelengths.

Solution

Magnetic force experienced by a charged particle in a magnetic field is given by,

$$F_B = q\vec{v}\times\vec{B} = qvB\sin\theta$$

In our case, $F_B = qvB$ [As $\theta = 90°$]

Hence, $Bqv = \dfrac{mv^2}{r}$

$$\Rightarrow \qquad mv = qBr$$

The de-Broglie wavelength

$$\lambda = \frac{h}{mv} = \frac{h}{qBr}$$

$$\Rightarrow \qquad \frac{\lambda_{\alpha\text{-particle}}}{\lambda_{\text{proton}}} = \frac{q_p r_p}{q_\alpha r_\alpha}$$

Since, $\dfrac{r_\alpha}{r_p} = 1$

and $\dfrac{q_\alpha}{q_p} = 2,$

$$\Rightarrow \qquad \frac{\lambda_\alpha}{\lambda_p} = \frac{1}{2}$$

Illustrative Example 2.32

Find the ratio of de-Broglie wavelength of proton and α-particle which have been accelerated through same potential difference.

Solution

Kinetic energy gained by a charge q after being accelerated through a potential difference V volt,

$$qV = \frac{1}{2}mv^2$$

$$\Rightarrow \qquad v = \sqrt{\frac{2qV}{m}}$$

$$\Rightarrow \qquad mv = \sqrt{2mqV}$$

Now we have, de-Broglie wavelength is given as

$$\lambda = \frac{h}{mv} = \frac{h}{\sqrt{2mqV}}$$

$$\Rightarrow \qquad \frac{\lambda_p}{\lambda_\alpha} = \sqrt{\frac{m_\alpha q_\alpha V_\alpha}{m_p q_p V_p}}$$

Substituting $V_\alpha = V_p$

We get $\dfrac{\lambda_p}{\lambda_\alpha} = \sqrt{\dfrac{4\times2}{1\times1}} = 2\sqrt{2}$

Illustrative Example 2.33

Assume that the de-Broglie wave associated with an electron can form a standing wave between the atoms arranged in a one dimensional array with nodes at each of the atomic sites. It is found that one such standing wave is formed if the distance d between the atoms of the array is 2 Å. A similar standing wave is again formed if d is increase to 2.5 Å but not for any intermediate value of d. Find he energy of the electrons in electron volt and the least value of d for which the standing wave of the type described above can forms.

Solution

From the given situation it is clear that stationary waves are formed for two successive values of 2 Å and 2.5 Å thus we can directly say that

$$\frac{\lambda}{2} = 0.5 \text{ Å}$$

$$\Rightarrow \qquad \lambda = 2\times0.5 = 1 \text{ Å}$$

Thus the energy of electrons can be given as

$$E=\frac{P^2}{2m}$$

$$\Rightarrow \quad E=\frac{(h/\lambda)^2}{2m}$$

$$\Rightarrow \quad E=\frac{(6.63\times10^{-34})^2}{(10^{-10})^2\times2\times9.1\times10^{-31}}$$

$$\Rightarrow \quad E=2.41\times10^{-17}\text{ J}$$

$$\Rightarrow \quad E=\frac{2.41\times10^{-17}}{1.6\times10^{-19}}\text{ eV}$$

$$\Rightarrow \quad E=150.6\text{ eV}$$

For formation of stationary waves between two atomic sites the minimum separation must be $\frac{\lambda}{2}$ that is 0.5 Å.

Illustrative Example 2.34

In a photo electric effect setup, a point source light of power 3.2×10^{-3} W emits mono-energetic photons of energy 5.0 eV. The source is located at a distance of 0.8 m from the centre of a stationary metallic sphere of work function 3.0 eV and of radius 8.0×10^{-3} m. The efficiency of photoelectron emission is one for every 10^6 incident photons. Assume that the sphere is located and initially neutral, and that photoelectrons are instantly swept away after emission.

(a) Calculate the number of photoelectrons emitted per second.

(b) Find the ratio of the wavelength of incident light to the de-Broglie wavelength of the fastest photoelectrons emitted.

(c) It is observed that the photoelectrons emission stops at a certain time t after the light source is switched on. Why ?

(d) Evaluate the time t.

Solution

(a) The energy reaching the sphere is given by

$$E'=\frac{P}{4\pi R^2}\times\pi r^2=\frac{Pr^2}{4R^2}$$

Here $R=0.8$ m, $r=8\times10^{-3}$ m, $P=3.2\times10^{-3}$ W

$$\Rightarrow \quad E'=\frac{(3.2\times10^{-3})(8\times10^{-3})^2}{4\times(0.8)^2}$$

The number of photoelectrons emitted per second = $E'\times(\nu/E)$

$$E'=\frac{(3.2\times10^{-3})(8\times10^{-3})^2}{4\times(0.8)^2}\times\frac{10^{-6}}{(5\times1.6\times10^{-19})}$$

$$\Rightarrow \quad E'=10^5\text{ s}^{-1}$$

(b)
$$\lambda=\frac{hc}{E}=\frac{(6.63\times10^{-34})(3\times10^8)}{(5\times1.6\times10^{-19})}$$

$$\lambda=2.48625\times10^{-7}\text{ m}=2486\text{ Å}$$

$$KE_{max}=h\nu-\phi=2\text{ eV}$$

$$\lambda_{deBroglie}=\frac{h}{P}=\frac{h}{\sqrt{2mK}}$$

$$\Rightarrow \quad \lambda_{deBroglie}=\frac{6.63\times10^{-34}}{\sqrt{2\times(9.1\times10^{-31})\times(2\times1.6\times10^{-19})}}$$

$$\Rightarrow \quad \lambda_{deBroglie}=8.6877\text{ Å}$$

Now we use

$$\frac{\lambda}{\lambda_{deBroglie}}=\frac{2486}{8.6877}=286.18$$

(c) After time t, the potential V of the sphere is given by

$$V=\frac{1}{4\pi\varepsilon_0}\left(\frac{q}{r}\right)$$

where q = charge on the sphere

We also use stopping potential as

$$V_0=\frac{E_{photon}-\phi}{e}$$

When potential of sphere becomes 2 volt, photo electric emission stops as maximum kinetic energy of photoelectrons is 2 eV.

(d)
$$V_0=\frac{1}{4\pi\varepsilon_0}\left(\frac{ne}{r}\right)=2$$

$$\Rightarrow \quad \frac{(9\times10^9)\,n\,(1.6\times10^{-19})}{8\times10^{-3}}=2$$

Solving we get

$$n=1.11\times10^7$$

Now, we use $t=\frac{n}{10^5}=\frac{1.11\times10^7}{10^5}$

$$\Rightarrow \quad t=111\text{ sec}$$

Web Reference at www.physicsgalaxy.com

Age Group - High School Physics | Age 17-19 Years
Section - MODERN PHYSICS
Topic - Wave Particle Duality
Module Number - 12 to 22

Practice Exercise 2.4

(i) What is the de-Broglie wavelength of an electron in first orbit of Bohr's hydrogen atom which has radius *r*?

[$2\pi r$]

(ii) Find the ratio of de-Broglie wavelength of molecules of hydrogen and helium which are at temperatures 27°C and 127°C respectively.

[$\sqrt{\frac{8}{3}}$]

(iii) What amount of energy should be added to an electron to decrease its de-Broglie wavelength from 100 pm to 50 pm?

[0.4524 KeV]

(iv) It is desired to move a small space vehicle of mass 50 kg at rest, by a lamp of 100 Watt emitting blue light of wavelength 4700 Å. If the vehicle if in free space, find its acceleration. Assume all the photons emitted will incident on body.

[6.66×10^{-9} m/s^2]

(v) A totally reflecting, small plane mirror placed horizontally faces a parallel beam of light as shown in the figure-2.29. The mass of the mirror is 20 gm. Assume that there is no absorption in the lens and that 30% of the light emitted by the source goes through the lens. Find the power of the source needed to support the weight of the mirror.

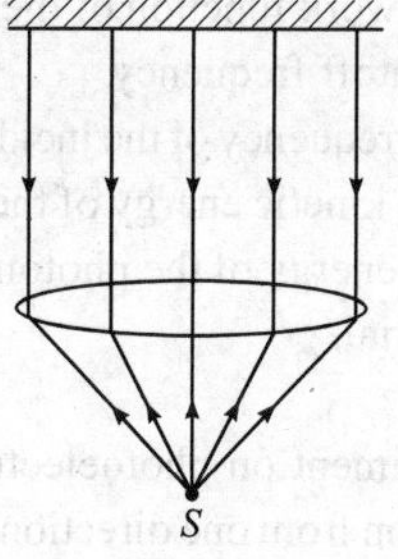

Figure 2.29

[100 MW]

(vi) Consider an excited hydrogen atom in state *n* moving with a velocity v ($v << c$). It emits a photon in the direction of its motion and changes its state to a lower state *m*. Apply momentum and energy conservation principles to calculate the frequency *f* of the emitted radiation. Compare this with the frequency f_0 emitted if the atom were at rest.

[$f = f_0\left(1+\frac{v}{c}\right)$]

(vii) Two identical nonrelativistic particles move at right angles to each other, possessing de-Broglie wavelengths, λ_1 & λ_2. Find the de-Broglie wavelength of each particle in the frame of their centre of mass.

[$\lambda = \frac{2\lambda_1\lambda_2}{\sqrt{\lambda_1^2+\lambda_2^2}}$]

Advance Illustrations Videos at www.physicsgalaxy.com

Age Group - Advance Illustrations
Section - Modern Physics
Topic - Atomic and Nuclear Physics
Illustrations - 54 In-depth Illustrations Videos

* * * * *

Discussion Questions

Q2-1 When the speed of a particle doubles, its momentum doubles, and its kinetic energy becomes four times greater. When the momentum of a photon doubles, does its energy becomes four times greater ? Provide a reason for your answer.

Q2-2 It is found that yellow light does not eject photoelectrons from a metal. Is it advisable to try with orange light? With green light?

Q2-3 It is found that photosynthesis starts in certain plants when exposed to the sunlight but it does not start if the plant is exposed only to infrared light. Explain.

Q2-4 Photon A has twice the energy of photon B.
(a) If the momentum of A less than, or equal to, or greater than that of B ?
(b) Is the wavelength of A less than, equal to, or greater than that of B ?

Q2-5 If electromagnetic radiation is made up of quanta, why don't we detect the discrete packets of energy, for example, when we listen to a radio ?

Q2-6 The threshold wavelength of a metal is λ_0. Light of wavelength slightly less than λ_0 is incident on an insulated plate made of this metal. It is found that photoelectrons are emitted for sometime and after that the emission stops. Explain.

Q2-7 Consider the de-Broglie wavelength of an electron and a proton. Which wavelength is smaller if the two particle have (a) the same speed (b) the same momentum (c) the same energy?

Q2-8 If an electron has a wavelength, does it also have a colour?

Q2-9 Human skin is relatively insensitive to visible light, but ultraviolet radiation can cause severe burns. Does this have anything to do with photon energies ? Explain.

Q2-10 Do all electrons emitted in the photoelectric effect have the same kinetic energy ?

Q2-11 If you shine ultraviolet light on an isolated metal plate, the plate emits electrons for a while. Why does it eventually stop?

Q2-12 Is it always true that for two sources of equal intensity, the number of photons emitted in a given time are equal ?

Q2-13 The wave theory of radiation cannot explain .... existence of threshold frequency, dependence of photocurrent on intensity, dependence of stopping potential on frequency, that stopping potential is independent of intensity.

Q2-14 The photoelectros emitted by an illuminated surface have a maximum kinetic energy of 3.0 eV. If the intensity of the light is tripled, what is the maximum kinetic energy of photoelectrons now ?

Q2-15 The threshold frequencies for photoemission for three metals numbered 1, 2, 3 are respectively v_1, v_2, v_3 and $v_1 > v_2 > v_3$. An incident radiation of frequency $v_0 > v_2$ .... cause the photoemission from 3 but .... cause photoemission from 1.

Q2-16 Is $p = E/c$ valid for electrons ?

Q2-17 Photon A is from an ultraviolet tanning lamp and photon B is from a television transmitter. Which has the greater
(a) wavelength (b) energy
(c) frequency and (d) momentum

Q2-18 Of the following statements about the photoelectric effect, which are true and which are false ?
(a) The greater the frequency of the incident light is, the greater is the stopping potential.
(b) The greater the intensity of the incident light is, the greater is the cutoff frequency.
(c) The greater the work function of the target material is, the greater is the stopping potential.
(d) The greater the work function of the target material is, the greater is the cutoff frequency.
(e) The greater the frequency of the incident light is, the greater is the maximum kinetic energy of the ejected electrons.
(f) The greater the energy of the photons is, the smaller is the stopping potential.

Q2-19 In an experiment on photoelectric effect, a photon is incident on an electron from one direction and the photoelectron is emitted almost in the opposite direction. Does this violate conservation of momentum.

Q2-20 Can we find the mass of a photon by the definition $p = mv$?

Q2-21 If the intensity of the light producing a photocurrent is doubled, how is that current affected ?

Q2-22 Should the energy of a photon be called its kinetic energy or its internal energy?

Q2-23 In an experiment on photoelectric effect, a photon is incident on an electron from one direction and the photoelectron is emitted almost in the opposite direction. Does this violate conservation of momentum?

Q2-24 The de-Broglie hypothesis predicts that a wave associated with any object has momentum. Why do we not observe the wave nature of a moving car ?

Q2-25 In the photoelectric effect, if the frequency of the radiation is below a certain cutoff value, no photoelectrons will be observed no matter how intense the radiation is. Why does this fact favor a particle theory of light over a wave theory ?

Q2-26 The photons emitted by a source of light do *not* all have the same energy. Is the source monochromatic ? Give your reasoning.

Q2-27 Radiation of a given wavelength causes electrons to be emitted from the surface of one metal but not from the surface of another metal. Explain why this could be.

Q2-28 Can a photon be deflected by an electric field? By a magnetic field ?

Q2-29 In the photoelectric effect, suppose that the intensity of the light is increased, while the frequency is kept constant. The frequency is greater than the minimum frequency f_0. State whether each of the following will increase, decrease, or remain constant, and explain your choice: (a) the current in the phototube, (b) the number of electrons emitted per second from the metal surface, c) the maximum kinetic energy that an electron could have, (d) the maximum momentum that an electron could have, and (e) the minimum de-Broglie wavelength that an electron could have.

Q2-30 A hot body is placed in a closed room maintained at a lower temperature. Is the number of photons in the room increasing ?

Q2-31 What is the speed of a photon with respect to another photon if (a) the two photons are going in the same direction and (b) they are going in opposite directions ?

Q2-32 Which colored light bulb, red, orange, yellow, green, or blue, emits photons with (a) the least energy and (b) the greatest energy ? Account for your answers.

Q2-33 A stone is dropped from the top of a building. As the stone falls, does its de-Broglie wavelength increase, decrease, or remain the same ? Provide a reason for your answer.

Q2-34 "If the frequency of light incident on a metallic plate be doubled, the kinetic energy of the emitted electrons is also doubled". Explian if this statement is TRUE or FALSE.

* * * * *

Conceptual MCQs Single Option Correct

2-1 The photoelectric current in a photoelectric cell depends upon :
(A) The nature of the metal used as the emitter
(B) The wavelength of the incident light
(C) The intensity of the incident light
(D) All the above parameters

2-2 In a photoelectric experiment, two metal plates *A* and *B* are used for a given light intensity *I* and frequency *f*. Work function of metal *B* is more than that of *A*. The correct variation of stopping potential difference versus frequency is given by :

(A) 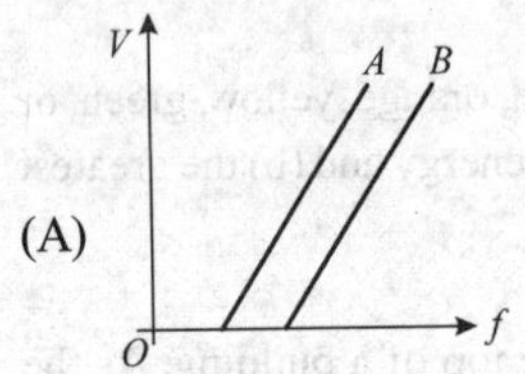

(B) 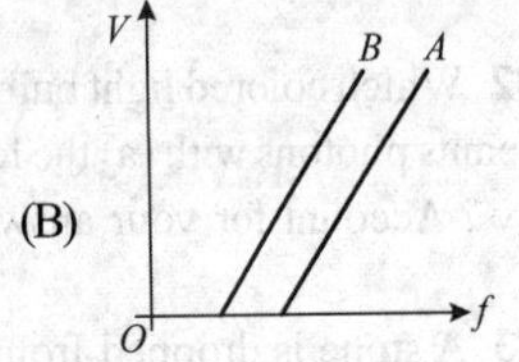

(C) 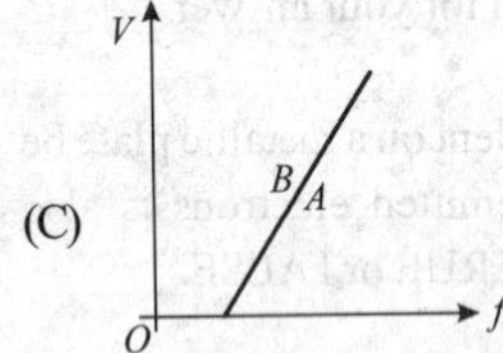

(D) 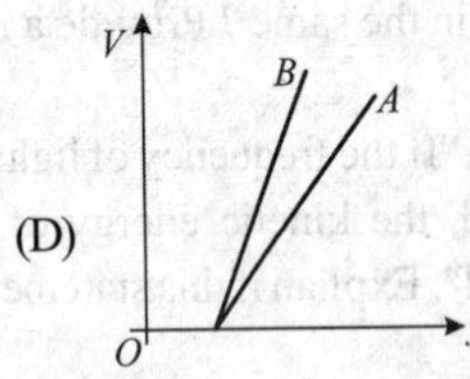

2-3 The threshold wavelength for photoelectric emission from a material is 5200 Å. Photoelectrons will be emitted when this material is illuminated with monochromatic radiation from a :
(A) 50-watt infrared lamp (B) 100-watt red neon lamp
(C) 40-watt sodium lamp (D) 5-watt ultraviolet lamp

2-4 A photon of light enters a block of glass after travelling through a vacuum. The energy of the photon on entering the glass block
(A) Increases because its associated wavelength decreases
(B) Decreases because the speed of the radiation decreases
(C) Stays the same because the speed of the radiation and the associated wavelength do not change
(D) Stays the same because the frequency of the radiation does not change

2-5 Which one of the following statements is NOT true for de-Broglie waves ?
(A) All atomic particles in motion have waves of a definite wavelength associated with them
(B) The higher the momentum, the longer is the wavelength
(C) The faster the particle, the shorter is the wavelength
(D) For the same velocity, a heavier particle has a shorter wavelength

2-6 Moving with the same velocity, which of the following has the longest de-Broglie wavelength ?
(A) β-particle (B) α-particle
(C) Proton (D) Neutron

2-7 Two photons having
(A) Equal wavelengths have equal linear momenta
(B) Equal energies have equal linear momenta
(C) Equal frequencies have equal linear momenta
(D) Equal linear momenta have equal wavelengths

2-8 A proton and an electron move with the same velocity. The associated wavelength for proton is :
(A) Shorter than that of the electron
(B) Longer than that of the electron
(C) The same as that of the electron
(D) Zero

2-9 In photoelectric effect when photons of energy $h\nu$ fall on a photosensitive surface (work function $h\nu_0$) electrons are emitted from the metallic surface with a kinetic energy. It is possible to say that :
(A) All ejected electrons have same kinetic energy equal to $h\nu - h\nu_0$
(B) The ejected electrons have a distribution of kinetic energy from zero to $(h\nu - h\nu_0)$
(C) The most energetic electrons have kinetic energy equal to $h\nu_0$
(D) All ejected electrons have kinetic energy $h\nu_0$

2-10 The photoelectric emission from the surface of a metal starts only when the light incident on the surface has a certain:
(A) Minimum frequency (B) Minimum wavelength
(C) Minimum intensity (D) Minimum speed

2-11 Photoelectric effect can be explained by assuming that light :
(A) Is a form of transverse waves
(B) Is a form of longitudinal waves
(C) Can be polarized
(D) Consists of quanta

2-12 At frequencies of the incident radiation above the threshold frequency, the photoelectric current in a photoelectric cell increases with increase in :
(A) Intensity of incident radiation
(B) Wavelength of incident radiation
(C) Frequency of incident radiation
(D) Speed of incident radiation

2-13 A metallic surface has a threshold wavelength 5200 Å. This surface is irradiated by monochromatic light of wavelength 4500 Å. Which of the following statements is true ?
(A) The electrons are emitted from the surface having energy between 0 and infinity
(B) The electrons are emitted from the surface having energy between 0 and certain finite maximum value
(C) The electrons are emitted from the surface, all having certain finite energy
(D) No electrons is emitted from the surface

2-14 Let p and E denote the linear momentum and energy of a photon. If the wavelength is decreased,
(A) Both p and E increase
(B) p increases and E decreases
(C) p decreases and E increases
(D) Both p and E decreases

2-15 The equation $E = pc$ is valid
(A) For an electron as well as for a photon
(B) For an electron but not for a photon
(C) For a photon but not for an electron
(D) Neither for an electron nor for a photon

2-16 Let n_r and n_b be respectively the number of photons emitted per second by a red bulb and a blue bulb of equal power in a given time.
(A) $n_r = n_b$ (B) $n_r < n_b$
(C) $n_r > n_b$
(D) The information is insufficient to get a relation between n_r and n_b.

2-17 The photoelectrons emitted from a metal surface :
(A) Are all at rest
(B) Have the same kinetic energy
(C) Have the same momentum
(D) Have speeds varying from zero up to a certain maximum value

2-18 The graph between, which of the following two factors for photoelectric effect, is a straight line?
(A) Intensity of radiation and photoelectric current
(B) Potential of anode and photoelectric current
(C) Threshold frequency and velocity of photoelectrons
(D) Intensity of radiations and stopping potential

2-19 When ultraviolet light is incident on a photocell, its stopping potential is V_0 and the maximum kinetic energy of the photoelectrons is K_{max}. When X-rays are incident on the same cell, then :
(A) V_0 and K_{max} both increase
(B) V_0 and K_{max} both decrease
(C) V_0 increases but K_{max} remains the same
(D) K_{max} increases but V_0 remains the same

2-20 The slope of the stopping potential versus frequency graph for photoelectric effect is equal to:
(A) h (B) he
(C) h/e (D) e

2-21 A photon of energy $h\nu$ is absorbed by a free electron of a metal having work function $\varphi < h\nu$
(A) The electron is sure to come out
(B) The electron is sure to come out with a kinetic energy $h\nu - \varphi$
(C) Either the electron does not come out or it comes out with a kinetic energy $h\nu - \varphi$
(D) It may come out with a kinetic energy less than $h\nu - \phi$

2-22 Which one of the following statements is NOT true about photoelectric emission ?
(A) For a given emitter illuminated by light of a given frequency, the number of photo-electrons emitted per second is proportional to the intensity of incident light
(B) For every emitter there is a definite threshold frequency below which no photoelectrons are emitted, no matter what the intensity of light is
(C) Above the threshold frequency, the maximum kinetic energy of photoelectrons is proportional to the frequency of incident light
(D) The saturation value of the photoelectric current is independent of the intensity of incident light

2-23 Blue light can cause photoelectric emission from a metal, but yellow light cannot. If red light is incident on the metal, then :
(A) Photoelectric current will increase
(B) Rate of emission of photoelectrons will decrease
(C) No photoelectric emission will occur
(D) Energy of the photoelectrons will increase

2-24 A proton and an electron are accelerated by the same potential difference. Let λ_0 and λ_p denote the de-Broglie wavelengths of the electron and the proton respectively.
(A) $\lambda_e = \lambda_p$ (B) $\lambda_e < \lambda_p$
(C) $\lambda_e > \lambda_p$
(D) The relation between λ_e and λ_p depends on the accelerating potential difference.

2-25 Photoelectrons are being obtained by irradiating zinc by a radiation of 3100 Å. In order to increase the kinetic energy of ejected photoelectrons:
(A) The intensity of radiation should be increased
(B) The wavelength of radiation should be increased
(C) The wavelength of radiation should be decreased
(D) Both wavelength and intensity of radiation should be increased

2-26 Which one of the following graphs in figure shows the variation of photoelectric current (I) with voltage (V) between the electrodes in a photoelectric cell ?

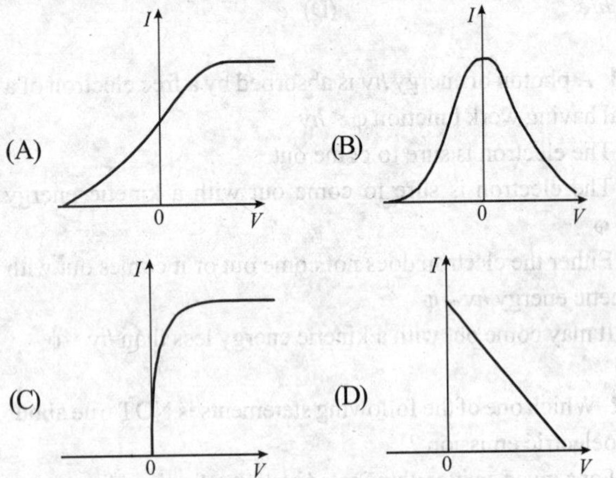

2-27 When monochromatic light falls on a photosensitive material, the number of photoelectrons emitted per second is n and their maximum kinetic energy is K_{max}. If the intensity of the incident light is doubled keeping its frequency constant, then:
(A) Both n and K_{max} are doubled
(B) Both n and K_{max} are halved
(C) n is doubled but K_{max} remains the same
(D) K_{max} is doubled but n remains the same

2-28 The frequency and the photon flux of a beam of light falling on the surface of photoelectric material are increased by a factor of two. This will
(A) Increase the maximum kinetic energy of the photoelectrons, as well as photoelectric current by a factor of two
(B) Increase the maximum kinetic energy of the photo electrons and would increase the photo electric current by a factor of two
(C) Increase the maximum kinetic energy of the photo electrons by a factor of two and will have no effect on the magnitude of the photo electrons by a factor of two and will have no effect on the magnitude of the photoelectric current produced
(D) No produce any effect on the kinetic energy of the emitted electrons but will increase the photo electric current by a factor of two.

2-29 Let K_1 be the maximum kinetic energy of photoelectrons emitted by light of wavelength λ_1 and K_2 corresponding to wavelength λ_2. If $\lambda_1 = 2\lambda_2$ then :
(A) $2K_1 = K_2$ (B) $K_1 = 2K_2$
(C) $K_1 < K_2/2$ (D) $K_1 > 2K_2$

2-30 When stopping potential is applied in an experiment on photoelectric effect, no photocurrent is observed. This means that
(A) The emission of photoelectrons is stopped
(B) The photoelectrons are emitted but are reabsorbed by the emitter metal
(C) The photoelectrons are accumulated near the collector plate
(D) The photoelectrons are dispersed from the sides of the apparatus

2-31 If the frequency of light in a photoelectric experiment is doubled, the stopping potential will
(A) Be doubled
(B) Be halved
(C) Become more than double
(D) Become less that double

2-32 A caesium photo cell, with a steady potential difference of 60 volt across it, is illuminated by a small bright light placed 50 cm away. When the same light is placed one meter away the electrons crossing the photo cell :
(A) Each carry one quarter of their previous energy
(B) Each carry one quarter of their previous momentum
(C) Are half as numerous
(D) Are one quarter as numerous

2-33 A point source of light is used in a photoelectric effect. If the source is removed farther from the emitting metal, the stopping potential
(A) Will increase
(B) Will decrease
(C) Will remain constant
(D) Will either increase or decrease

2-34 A metal surface is illuminated by a light of given intensity and frequency to cause photoemission. If the intensity of illumination is reduced to one fourth of its original value keeping frequency of radtion constant, then the maximum kinetic energy of the emitted photoelectrons would become :
(A) Unchanged (B) 1/16th of original value
(C) Twice the original value (D) Four times the original value

2-35 A point source causes photoelectric effect from a small metal plate. Which of the following curves may represent the saturation photocurrent as a function of the distance between the source and the metal?

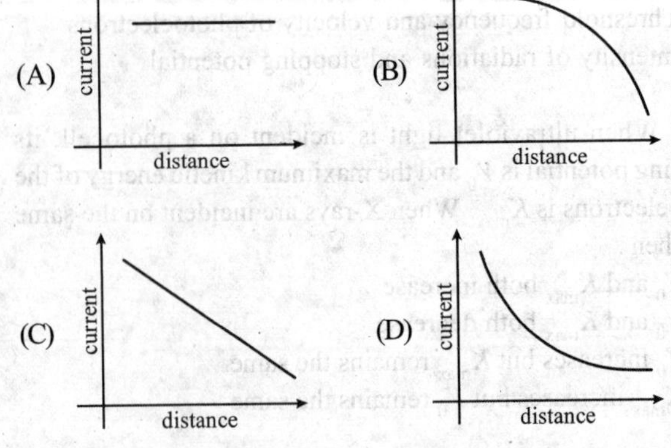

2-36 The stopping potential for a certain photosensitive metal is V_0 when the frequency of incident radiation is ν_0. When the frequency of the incident radiations is doubled, what will be the stopping potential ?
(A) V_0 (B) $2\ V_0$
(C) $4\ V_0$ (D) None of the above

2-37 The collector plate in an experiment on photoelectric effect is kept vertically above the emitter plate. Light source is put on and a saturation photocurrent is recorded. An electric field is switched on which has a vertically downward direction.
(A) The photocurrent will increase
(B) The kinetic energy of the electron will increase
(C) The stopping potential will decrease
(D) The threshold wavelength will increase

2-38 Which electrons are emitted in the photoelectric effect ?
(A) Electrons in the inner orbits of the atom
(B) Electrons in the outer most orbit of the atom
(C) Electrons from within the nucleus
(D) Electrons freely roaming about in the interatomic space

2-39 Two photons of different frequency have energies 1 eV and 2.5 eV respectively. They incident one after another on a metallic plate of work function 0.5 eV, then ratio of maximum kinetic energies of emitted photo electrons is :
(A) 4 : 1 (B) 1 : 4
(C) 1 : 5 (D) 1 : 2

2-40 The image of the sun is formed on the photosensitive metal with a convex lens and the photoelectric saturation current obtained is *I*. If, the lens is replaced by another similar lens of half the diameter and double the focal length, then photoelectric current will be (Assume all light passing through lens falling on the photosensitive metal):
(A) *I* (B) *I*/4
(C) *I*/8 (D) *I*/16

2-41 When monochromatic light of wavelength λ illuminates a metal surface, then stopping potential for photo electric current is $3\ V_0$. If wavelength changes to 2λ, then stopping potential becomes V_0. Threshold wavelength for photo electric emission is :
(A) 4λ (B) 8λ
(C) $4/3\ \lambda$ (D) 6λ

2-42 According to Einstein theory of photoelectric effect, light is not behaving like a wave because :
(A) Kinetic energy of ejected electrons does not depend on the intensity of light
(B) Energy absorbed *b* an electron from a spreading wavefront is negligible
(C) No electron is ejected if the frequency is not more than threshold frequency whatever may be the intensity of light
(D) All the above

2-43 According to Einstein's photoelectric equation, the graph between the kinetic energy of photoelectrons ejected and the frequency of incident radiation is :

(A) 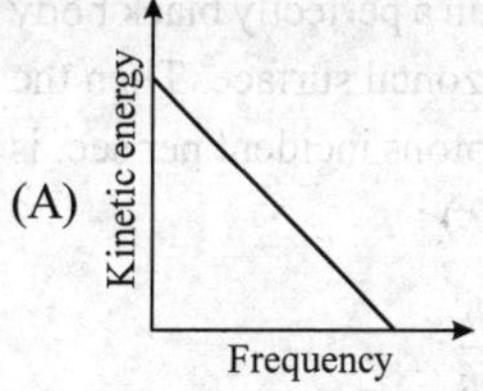

(B) 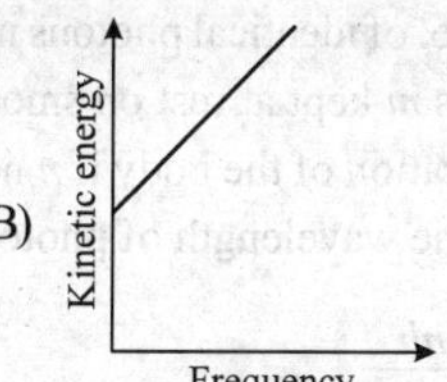

(C) 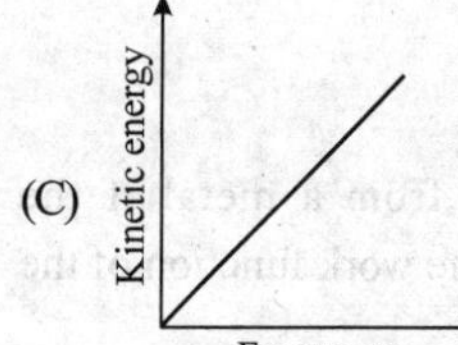

(D) 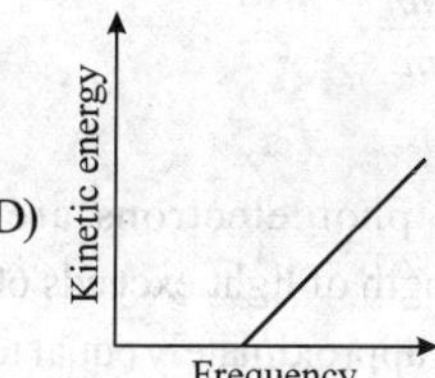

* * * * *

Numerical MCQs Single Option Correct

2-1 Light of wavelength 400 nm is incident continuously on a Cesium ball. (work function 1.9 eV). The maximum potential to which the ball will be charged is :

(A) 3.1 V (B) 1.2 V
(C) zero (D) infinite

2-2 Electrons are accelerated in television tubes through potential differences of about 10 kV. The highest frequency of the electromagnetic waves emitted when these electrons strike the screen of the tube is :

(A) 2.4×10^{18} Hz (B) 3.6×10^{18} Hz
(C) 2.2×10^{17} Hz (D) 3.2×10^{16} Hz

2-3 1.5 mW of 400 nm light is directed at a photoelectric cell. If 0.10% of the incident photons produce photoelectrons, the current in the cell is :

(A) 0.36 μA (B) 0.48 μA
(C) 0.42 mA (D) 0.32 mA

2-4 No. of identical photons incident on a perfectly black body of mass m kept at rest on smooth horizontal surface. Then the acceleration of the body if n no. of photons incident per sec. is (Assume wavelength of photon to be λ) :

(A) $\frac{nh}{2\pi\lambda m}$ (B) $\frac{nh}{\lambda m}$

(C) $\frac{2\pi nh}{\lambda m}$ (D) $\frac{\lambda m}{nh}$

2-5 No photoelectrons are emitted from a metal if the wavelength of light exceeds 6000 Å. The work function of the metal is approximately equal to :

(A) 3.315×10^{-6} J (B) 3.315×10^{-19} J
(C) 2.07×10^{-19} J (D) 2.07×10^{-22} J

2-6 5% of the energy supplied to a lamp is radiated as a visible light. How many quanta of light are emitted per second by 100 watt lamp. Assume the average wavelength of visible light as 555 nm ?

(A) 0.75×10^{19} (B) 1.39×10^{19}
(C) 2.16×10^{19} (D) 2.83×10^{19}

2-7 All electrons ejected from a surface by incident light of wavelength 2000 Å can be stopped before travelling 1 m in the direction of uniform electric field of 4 N/C. The work function of the surface is:

(A) 4 eV (B) 6.2 eV
(C) 2 eV (D) 2.2 eV

2-8 Radiation pressure on any surface is :

(A) dependent on wavelength of the light used
(B) dependent on nature of surface and intensity of light used
(C) dependent on frequency and nature of surface
(D) depends on the nature of source from which light is coming and on nature of surface on which it is falling

2-9 The maximum energy of the photoelectrons emitted in a photocell is 5 eV. For no photoelectron to reach the anode, the potential difference of the anode with respect to the photo sensitive plate should be :

(A) Zero (B) +2 V
(C) +5 V (D) None of the above

2-10 Both the frequency and the intensity of a beam of light falling on the surface of photoelectric material are increased by a factor of two. This will :

(A) increase both, the maximum kinetic energy of the photo-electrons, as well as photoelectric saturation current by a factor of two.
(B) increase the maximum kinetic energy of the photo-electrons by a factor greater than two and would increase the photoelectric saturation current by a factor of two.
(C) increase the maximum kinetic energy of the photoelectrons by a factor greater than two and will have no effect on the magnitude of the photoelectric saturation current produced.
(D) increase the maximum kinetic energy of the emitted photo-electrons by a factor of two but will have no effect on the saturation photoelectric current.

2-11 Minimum light intensity that can be perceived by normal human eye is about 10^{-10} W m^{-2}. What is the minimum number of photons of wavelength 660 nm that must enter the pupil in one second, for one to see the object ? Area of cross-section of the pupil is 10^{-4} m^2 ?

(A) 3.318×10^3 (B) 1.453×10^3
(C) 3.318×10^4 (D) 1.453×10^5

2-12 The average wavelength of de-Broglie wave associated with a thermal neutron of mass m at absolute temperature T is given by (here k is the Boltzmann constant) :

(A) $\frac{h}{\sqrt{mkT}}$ (B) $\frac{h}{\sqrt{2mkT}}$

(C) $\frac{h}{\sqrt{3mkT}}$ (D) $\frac{h}{2\sqrt{mkT}}$

2-13 What percentage increase in wavelength leads to 75% loss of photon energy in a photon-electron collision?

(A) 200% (B) 100%
(C) 67.7% (D) 300%

2-14 A parallel beam of light of intensity I and cross section area S is incident on a plate at normal incidence. The photoelectric emission efficiency is 100%, the frequency of beam is ν and the work function of the plate is φ ($h\nu > \varphi$). Assuming all the electrons are ejected normal to the plane and with same maximum possible speed. Calculate the net force exerted on the plate only due to striking of photons and subsequent emission of electrons :

(A) $\frac{IS}{h\nu}\left(\frac{h}{\lambda}+\sqrt{m(h\nu-\phi)}\right)$ (B) $\frac{IS}{h\nu}\left(\frac{h}{\lambda}+\sqrt{2m(h\nu-\phi)}\right)$

(C) $\frac{h\nu S}{I}\left(\frac{h}{\lambda}+\sqrt{2m(h\nu-\phi)}\right)$ (D) None of these

2-15 A desklamp illuminates a desk top with light of wavelength λ. The amplitude of this electromagnetic wave is E_0. Assuming illumination to be normally on the surface, the number of photons striking the desk per second per unit area N is :

(A) $N=\frac{\lambda\varepsilon_0 E_0^2}{h}$ (B) $N=\frac{2\lambda\varepsilon_0 E_0^2}{h}$

(C) $N=\frac{\lambda\varepsilon_0 E_0^2}{2h}$ (D) Data Insufficient

2-16 If a hydrogen atom at rest, emits a photon of wavelength λ, the recoil speed of the atom of mass m is given by :

(A) $\frac{h}{m\lambda}$ (B) $\frac{mh}{\lambda}$

(C) $mh\lambda$ (D) None of these

2-17 A point source of radiation power P is placed on the axis of completely absorbing disc. The distance between the source and the disc is 2 times the radius of the disc. Find the force that light exerts on the disc :

(A) $\frac{P}{c}$ (B) $\frac{P}{5c}$

(C) $\frac{P}{10c}$ (D) $\frac{P}{20c}$

2-18 A beam of light has an power of 144 W equally distributed among three wavelengths of 4100 Å, 4960 Å and 6200 Å. The beam is incident at an angle of incidence of 60° on an area of 1 cm² of a clean sodium surface, having a work function of 2.3 eV. Assuming that there is no loss of light by reflection and that each energetically capable photon ejects a photoelectron, find the saturation photocurrent. (Take $hc/e = 12400$ eVÅ)

(A) 1.76mA (B) 0.88mA

(C) 3.52mA (D) None of these

2-19 The work function of a substance is 4.0 eV. The longest wavelength of light that can cause photoelectron emission from this substance is approximately :

(A) 540 nm (B) 400 nm

(C) 310 nm (D) 220 nm

2-20 When a metallic surface is illuminated with monochromatic light of wavelength λ, the stopping potential is $5V_0$. When the same surface is illuminated with light of wavelength 3λ, the stopping potential is V_0. Then the work function of the metallic surface is :

(A) $\frac{hc}{6\lambda}$ (B) $\frac{hc}{5\lambda}$

(C) $\frac{hc}{4\lambda}$ (D) $\frac{2hc}{4\lambda}$

2-21 In a photoelectric experiment, with light of wavelength λ, the fastest electron has speed v. If the exciting wavelength is changed to $\frac{3\lambda}{4}$, the speed of the fastest emitted electron will become

(A) $v\sqrt{\frac{3}{4}}$ (B) $v\sqrt{\frac{4}{3}}$

(C) less than $v\sqrt{\frac{3}{4}}$ (D) greater than $v\sqrt{\frac{4}{3}}$

2-22 The work function of a certain metal is $\frac{hC}{\lambda_0}$. When a monochromatic light of wavelength $\lambda < \lambda_0$ is incident such that the plate gains a total power P. If the efficiency of photoelectric emission is η% and all the emitted photoelectrons are captured by a hollow conducting sphere of radius R already charged to potential V, then neglecting any interaction between plate and the sphere, expression of potantial of the sphere at time t is :

(A) $V+\frac{100\eta\lambda Pet}{4\pi\varepsilon_0 RhC}$ (B) $V+\frac{\eta\lambda Pet}{4\pi\varepsilon_0 RhC}$

(C) V (D) $\frac{\lambda Pet}{4\pi\varepsilon_0 RhC}$

2-23 Radiation of frequency 1.5 times the threshold frequency is incident on a photosensitive material. If the frequency of incident radiations is halved and the intensity is doubled, the number of photoelectron ejected per second becomes :

(A) zero

(B) half of its initial value

(C) one fourth the initial value

(D) three fourth the initial value

2-24 The maximum kinetic energy of photoelectrons emitted from a surface when photons of energy 6 eV fall on it is 4 eV. The stopping potential is :

(A) 2V (B) 4V
(C) 6V (D) 10V

2-25 When a certain metallic surface is illuminated with mono chromatic light of wavelength λ, the stopping potential for photoelectric current is $3V_0$. When the same surface is illuminated with light of wavelength 2λ the stopping potential is V_0. The threshold wavelength for this surface for photoelectric effect is :

(A) 6λ (B) 4λ
(C) $\lambda/4$ (D) 8λ

2-26 In the photoelectric experiment, if we use a monochromatic light, the I - V curve is as shown. If work function of the metal is 2eV, estimate the power of light used. (Assume efficiency of photo emission = 10^{-3}%, i.e. number of photoelectrons emitted are 10^{-3}% of number of photons incident on metal.)

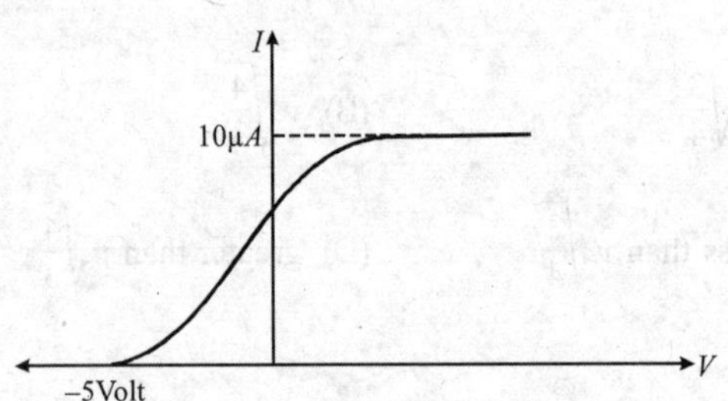

Figure 2.30

(A) 2 W (B) 5 W
(C) 7 W (D) 10 W

2-27 The eye can detect 5×10^4 photons/m^2 s of light of wavelength 500 nm. The ear can detect 10^{-13} W/m^2. As a power detector, which is more sensitive ?

(A) Sensitivity of eye is one fifth of the ear
(B) Sensitivity of eye is five times that of ear
(C) Both are equally sensitive
(D) Eye cannot be used as power detector

2-28 A metal whose work function is 3.3 eV is illuminated by light of wavelength 3×10^{-7} m. What is the threshold frequency for photoelectric emission? Planck's constant = 6.6×10^{-34} Js :

(A) 0.4×10^{15} Hz (B) 0.8×10^{15} Hz
(C) 1.6×10^{15} Hz (D) 3.2×10^{15} Hz

2-29 In Q. 28, the maximum energy of photoelectrons is :

(A) 0.84 eV (B) 1.05 eV
(C) 1.25 eV (D) 1.54 eV

2-30 In Q. 28, what is the stopping potential ?

(A) 0.84 V (B) 1.05 V
(C) 1.25 V (D) 1.54 V

2-31 A point source of radiation power P is placed on the axis of an ideal plane mirror. The distance between the source and the mirror is n times the radius of the mirror . Find the force that light exerts on the mirror :

(A) $\dfrac{2P}{C(n^2+1)}$ (B) $\dfrac{P(n^2+1)}{2C}$
(C) $\dfrac{P}{2C(n^2+1)}$ (D) $\dfrac{P}{4C(n^2+1)}$

2-32 A sensor is exposed for time t to a lamp of power P placed at a distance l. The sensor has an opening that is $4d$ in diameter. Assuming all energy of the lamp is given off as light, the number of photons entering the sensor if the wavelength of light is λ is :

(A) $N=\dfrac{P\lambda d^2 t}{hcl^2}$ (B) $N=\dfrac{4P\lambda d^2 t}{hcl^2}$
(C) $N=\dfrac{P\lambda d^2 t}{4hcl^2}$ (D) $N=\dfrac{P\lambda d^2 t}{16hcl^2}$

2-33 The de-Broglie wavelength of an electron moving with a velocity 1.5×10^8 ms^{-1} is equal to that of a photon. The ratio of the kinetic energy of the electron to that of the photon is :

(A) 2 (B) 4
(C) $\dfrac{1}{2}$ (D) $\dfrac{1}{4}$

2-34 Monochromatic light of frequency ν_1 irradiates a photocell and the stopping potential is found to be V_1. What is the new stopping potential of the cell if it is irradiated by monochromatic light of frequency ν_2 ?

(A) $V_1+\dfrac{h}{e}(\nu_2-\nu_1)$ (B) $V_1-\dfrac{h}{e}(\nu_2-\nu_1)$
(C) $V_1+\dfrac{h}{e}(\nu_1+\nu_2)$ (D) $V_1-\dfrac{h}{e}(\nu_1+\nu_2)$

2-35 An electromagnetic radiation of frequency 3×10^{15} cycles per second falls on a photo electric surface whose work function is 4.0 eV. Find out the maximum velocity of the photo electrons emitted by the surface :

(A) 13.4×10^{-19} m/s (B) 19.8×10^{-19} m/s
(C) 1.72×10^6 m/s (D) None of these

2-36 Two identical photocathodes receive light of frequencies f_1 and f_2. If the maximum velocities of the photoelectrons (of mass m) coming out are respectively v_1 and v_2, then :

(A) $v_1^2 - v_2^2 = \frac{2h}{m}(f_1 - f_2)$

(B) $v_1 + v_2 = \left[\frac{2h}{m}(f_1 + f_2)\right]^{1/2}$

(C) $v_1^2 + v_2^2 = \frac{2h}{m}(f_1 + f_2)$

(D) $v_1 - v_2 = \left[\frac{2h}{m}(f_1 - f_2)\right]^{1/2}$

2-37 A metal plate is exposed to light with wavelength λ. It is observed that electrons are ejected from the surface of the plate. When a retarding uniform electric field E is imposed, no electron can move away from the plate farther than a certain distance d. Then the threshold wavelength λ_0 for the material of plate is (e is the electronic charge, h is Planck's constant and c is the speed of light)

(A) $\lambda_0 = \left(\frac{1}{\lambda} - \frac{hc}{eEd}\right)^{-1}$ (B) $\lambda_0 = \left(\frac{1}{\lambda} - \frac{eEd}{hc}\right)^{-1}$

(C) $\lambda_0 = \lambda - \frac{hc}{eEd}$ (D) $\lambda_0 = \lambda - \frac{eEd}{hc}$

2-38 The energy of an α-particle, whose de-Broglie wavelength is 0.004 Å, will be :

(A) 1297 eV (B) 1245 KeV
(C) 1205 MeV (D) 1288 GeV

2-39 A small potassium foil is placed (perpendicular to the direciton of incidence of light) a distance r (= 0.5 m) from a point light source whose output power P_0 is 1.0W. Assuming wave nature of light how long would it take for the foil to soak up engouh energy (= 1.8 eV) from the beam to eject an electron? Assume that the ejected photoelectron collected its energy from a circular area of the foil whose radius equals the radius of a potassium atom (1.3×10^{-10} m).

(A) 11s (B) 14s
(C) 17s (D) 22s

2-40 A photon and an electron possess same de-Broglie wavelength. Given that c = speed of light and v = speed of electron, which of the following relations is correct ? Here E_e = KE of electron, E_{ph} = KE of photon, p_e = momentum of electron, p_{ph} = momentum of photon :

(A) $\frac{E_e}{E_{ph}} = \frac{2c}{v}$ (B) $\frac{E_e}{E_{ph}} = \frac{v}{2c}$

(C) $\frac{p_e}{p_{ph}} = \frac{2c}{v}$ (D) $\frac{p_e}{p_{ph}} = \frac{c}{2v}$

2-41 The maximum velocity of photoelectrons emitted by a photoemitter is 1.8×10^6 m/sec. Taking $e/m = 1.8 \times 10^{11}$ C/kg for electrons, the stopping potential of the emitter is :

(A) 1.82 V (B) 9.21 V
(C) 11.82 V (D) 23.64 V

2-42 A proton with KE equal to that a photon (E = 100 keV). λ_1 is the wavelength of proton and λ_2 is the wavelength of photon. Then $\frac{\lambda_1}{\lambda_2}$ is proportional to :

(A) $E^{1/2}$ (B) $E^{-1/2}$
(C) E (D) E^{-1}

2-43 How much potential is to be applied to accelerate an electron, so that its de-broglie wavelength should 0.4 Å ?

(A) 9434 V (B) 94.34 V
(C) 9.434 V (D) 943.4 V

2-44 A metallic surface is irradiated with monochromatic light of variable wavelength. Above a wavelength of 5000 Å, no photoelectrons are emitted from the surface. With an unknown wavelength, stopping potential of 3V is necessary to eliminate the photocurrent. Find the unknown wavelength :

(A) 2268 A (B) 1116A
(C) 3426 A (D) 4801 A

2-45 Illuminating the surface of a certain metal alternately with light of wavelengths λ_1 = 0.35 μm and λ_2 = 0.54 μm, it was found that the corresponding maximum velocities of photo electrons have a ratio η = 2. Find the work function of that metal :

(A) 3.22eV (B) 1.88eV
(C) 5.64eV (D) 6.28eV

2-46 The de-Broglie wavelength associated with a material particle when it is accelerated through a potential difference of 150 volt is 1 Å. The de-Broglie wavelength associated with the same particle when it is accelerated through a potential difference of 1350 V will be :

(A) $\frac{1}{4}$ Å (B) $\frac{1}{3}$ Å
(C) 1 Å (D) 0

2-47 An electron of mass m, when accelerated through a potential difference V, has de-Broglie wavelength λ. The de-Broglie wavelength associated with a proton of mass M accelerated through the same potential difference, will be :

(A) $\lambda\frac{M}{m}$ (B) $\lambda\frac{m}{M}$

(C) $\lambda\sqrt{\frac{M}{m}}$ (D) $\lambda\sqrt{\frac{m}{M}}$

2-48 In photoelectric experiment the plot between anode potential and photoelectric current is shown in figure-2.31. Which of the following is correct :

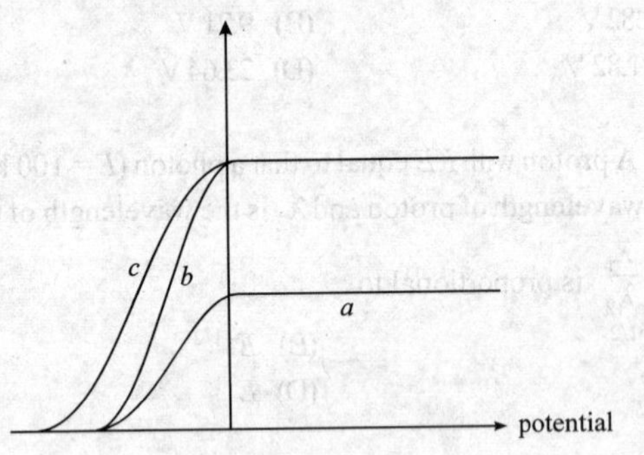

Figure 2.31

(A) Frequency of light corresponding to "a" is same as that of "b" and is different that corresponding to "c"

(B) Frequency of light corresponding to "a" is different from "b" & intensities are the same

(C) Frequency corresponding to "b" is same as that of "c", but intensities are different

(D) Frequency corresponding to "b" is different from that of "c", and intensities are different

2-49 If the momentum of electron is changed by P_m then the de-Broglie wavelength associated with it changes by 0.50%. The initial momentum of electron will be :

(A) $\frac{P_m}{200}$ (B) $\frac{P_m}{100}$

(C) $200P_m$ (D) $400P_m$

2-50 Light described at a place by the equation $E = (100 \text{ V/m}) [\sin(5 \times 10^{15} \text{ s}^{-1})t + \sin(8 \times 10^{15} \text{ s}^{-1})t]$ falls on a metal surface haivng work function 2.0 eV. Calculate the maximum kinetic energy of the photoelectrons :

(A) 3.27eV (B) 4.54eV

(C) 5.86eV (D) 6.54eV

2-51 A plate of mass 10 gm is in equilibrium in air due to the force exerted by light beam on plate. Calculate power of beam. Assume plate is perfectly absorbing.

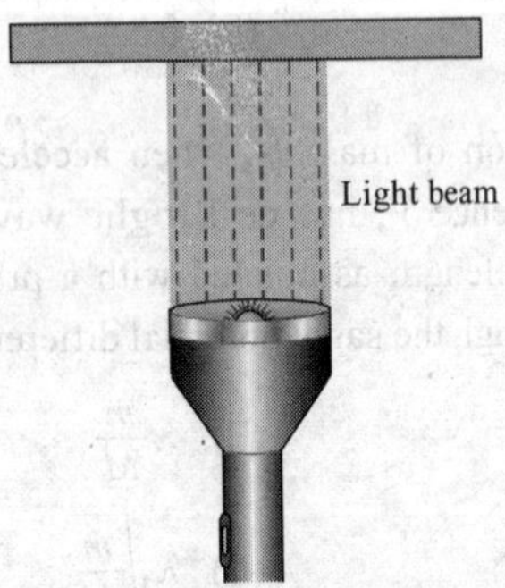

Figure 2.32

(A) 1.5×10^7 W (B) 3×10^7 W

(C) 4.5×10^7 W (D) 6×10^7 W

2-52 The energy that should be added to an electron, to reduce its debroglie wavelength from 2×10^{-9} m to 0.5×10^{-9} m will be:

(A) 1.1 MeV (B) 0.56 MeV

(C) 0.56 KeV (D) 5.67 eV

2-53 Light from a source of wavelength 5000 Å is incident on a photoelectric cell. It is known that only 1.6% of incident photons would produce photoelectrons. If the desired current in the cell is 3mA, find the source power (approximately)

(A) 1 W (B) 0.5 W

(C) 3 W (D) 2.5 W

2-54 Find the numerical value of de-Broglie wavelength of an electron in the 1st orbit of hydrogen atom assuming Bohr's atomic model. You can use standard values of the constants :

(A) 1.058π (B) 2.223π

(C) 2.116π (D) none of these

2-55 An enclosure filled with helium is heated to a temperature of 400 K. A beam of helium atom emerges out of the enclosure. The mean debroglie wavelength of this beam is :

(A) 0.44 Å (B) 0.63 Å

(C) 0.77 Å (D) none of these

2-56 If the short wavelength limit of the continuous spectrum coming out of a coolidge tube is 10 Å, then the debroglie wavelength of the electrons reaching the target metal in the coolidge tube is approximately :

(A) 0.3 Å (B) 3 Å

(C) 30 Å (D) 10 Å

2-57 A charge particle q_0 of mass m_0 is projected along the y-axis at $t = 0$ from origin with a velocity V_0. If a uniform electric field E_0 also exists along the x-axis, then the time at which debroglie wavelength of the particle becomes half of the initial value is :

(A) $\frac{m_0 v_0}{q_0 E_0}$ (B) $2\frac{m_0 v_0}{q_0 E_0}$

(C) $\sqrt{3}\,\frac{m_0 v_0}{q_0 E_0}$ (D) $3\frac{m_0 v_0}{q_0 E_0}$

2-58 Electrons in a sample of gas containing hydrogen like atom ($Z = 3$) are in fourth excited state. When photons emitted only due to transition from third excited state to second excited state are incident on a metal plate photoelectrons are ejected. The stopping potential for these photoelectrons is 3.95 eV. Now, if only photons emitted due to transition from fourth excited state to third excited state are incident on the same metal plate, the stopping potential for the emitted photoelectrons will be approximately equal to :

(A) 0.85 eV (B) 0.75 eV
(C) 0.65 eV (D) None of these

2-59 The threshold frequency for a certain metal is ν_0. When light of frequency $\nu = 2\nu_0$ is incident on it, the maximum velocity of photoelectrons is 4×10^6 m/s. If the frequency of incident radiation is increased to $5\nu_0$, then the maximum velocity of photoelectrons in m/s will be :

(A) $4/5 \times 10^6$ (B) 2×10^6
(C) 8×10^6 (D) 2×10^7

2-60 The ratio of de-Broglie wave length of a photon and an electron of mass '*m*' having the same kinetic energy *E* is : (Speed of light = *c*)

(A) $\sqrt{\dfrac{2mc^2}{E}}$ (B) $\sqrt{\dfrac{mc^2}{E}}$

(C) $\dfrac{2mc^2}{E}$ (D) $\dfrac{mc^2}{E}$

* * * * *

Advance MCQs with One or More Options Correct

2-1 A collimated beam of light of intensity 30 kWm^{-2} is incident normally on a 100 mm^2 completely absorbing screen. If P is the pressure exerted on the screen and Δp is the momentum transferred to the screen during a 1000 s interval then :

(A) $P = 10^{-3}\ Nm^{-2}$ (B) $P = 10^{-4}\ Nm^{-2}$

(C) $\Delta p = 10^{-4}\ kgms^{-1}$ (D) $\Delta p = 10^{-5}\ kgms^{-1}$

2-2 In a photo electric experiment, the collector plate is at 2.0 V with respect to the emitter plate made of copper ($\phi = 4.5$ eV). The emitter is illuminated by a source of monochromatic light of wavelength 2000 Å nm :

(A) the maximum kinetic energy of the photo electrons at collector is 1.7 eV

(B) the maximum kinetic energy of the photo electrons on the collector is 3.7 eV

(C) if the polarity of the battery is reversed then the minimum kinetic energy of the photo electrons on the collector is 0.

(D) if the polarity of the battery is reversed then the maximum kinetic energy of the photo electrons on the collector is 3.7 eV

2-3 The work function for aluminium surface is 4.2 eV and that for sodium surface is 2.0 eV. The two metals were illuminated with appropriate radiations so as to cause photo emission. Then :

(A) Both aluminium and sodium will have the same threshold frequency

(B) The threshold frequency of aluminium will be more than that of sodium

(C) The threshold frequency of aluminium will be less than that of sodium

(D) The threshold wavelength of aluminium will be more than that of sodium

2-4 The stopping potential for photo electron emitted from a metal surface of work function 1.7 eV is 10.4 V. Select correct choice

(A) The wavelength of light used is 1022 Å

(B) The wavelength of light used is 970.6 Å

(C) The light used is emitted by hydrogen gas sample which de-excites from $n = 3$ to $n = 1$

(D) The light used is emitted by hydrogen gas sample which de-excites from $n = 4$ to $n = 1$

2-5 H^+, He^+ and O^{++} all having the same kinetic energy pass through a region in which there is a uniform magnetic field perpendicular to their velocity. The masses of H^+, He^+ and O^{++} are $1u$, $4u$ and $16u$ respectively :

(A) H^+ will be deflected the most

(B) O^{++} will be deflected the most

(C) He^+ and O^{++} will be deflected equally

(D) All will be deflected equally

2-6 When an electron of hydrogen like atom jumps from a higher energy level to a lower energy level :

(A) angular momentum of the electron remains constant

(B) kinetic energy increases

(C) wavelength of de-Broglie wave, associated with motion of the electron, decreases

(D) none of these

2-7 Light rays are incident on an opaque sheet. Then they :

(A) exert a force on the sheet

(B) transfer an energy to the sheet

(C) transfer momentum to the sheet

(D) transfer impulse to the sheet

2-8 The angular momentum of an electron in an orbit is quantized because :

(A) Bohr's theory is based on this postulate

(B) It is a necessary condition for compatibility with the wave behavior of the electron

(C) it is a necessary condition for compatibility with the particle behavior of the electron

(D) it is a necessary condition for compatibility with Pauli's exclusion principle

2-9 The intensity of light falling on a phototube is increased while keeping the no of photons falling per seconds constant then for a given experiment

(A) Stopping potential will increase

(B) Saturation current will increase

(C) Saturation current will decrease

(D) Saturation current will remain unaffected

2-10 Two photocathodes are illuminated by the light emitted by a single source. The dependence of photocurrent versus voltages between cathode and anode is shown by curves 1 and 2 as shown in the figure. (I/I_{max} represents ratio of photocurrent to saturation current) :

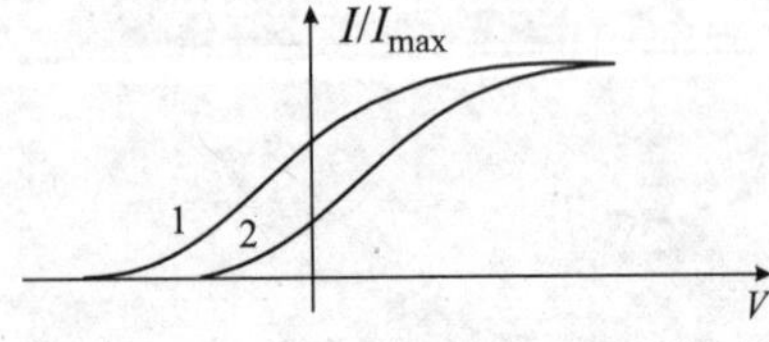

Figure 2.33

(A) Photocathode 1 has higher work function than 2

(B) Photocathode 2 has higher work function than 1

(C) Saturation current may be different for 1 and 2

(D) Saturation current must be same for 1 and 2

2-11 Photoelectric effect supports quantum nature of light because :

(A) There is a minimum frequency below which no photoelectrons are emitted

(B) The maximum kinetic energy of photoelectrons depends only on the frequency of light and not on its intensity

(C) Even when the metal surface is faintly illuminated the photoelectrons (if $\nu \geq \nu_{th}$) leave the surface immediately

(D) Electric charge of the photoelectrons is quantized

2-12 The momentum of a single photon of red light of frequency 400×10^{12} Hz moving through free space is given as :

(A) Zero (B) 8.8×10^{-28} kgms^{-2}

(C) 1.65×10^{-6} MeV/c (D) Data Insufficient

2-13 When a monochromatic point source of light is at a distance of 0.2 m from a photoelectric cell, the cutoff voltage and the saturation current are respectively 0.6 V and 18.0 mA. If the same source is placed 0.6 m away from the photoelectric cell, then :

(A) the stopping potential will be 0.2 V

(B) the stopping potential will be 0.6 V

(C) the saturation current will be 6.0 mA

(D) the saturation current will be 2.0 mA

2-14 In a photoelectric experiment, the collector plate is at 2.0 V with respect to the emitter plate made of copper ($\phi = 4.5$ eV). The emitter is illuminated by a source of monochromatic light of wavelength 200 nm.

(A) The minimum kinetic energy of the photoelectrons reaching the collector is 0.

(B) The maximum kinetic energy of the photoelectrons reaching the collector is 3.7 eV.

(C) If the polarity of the battery is reversed then answer to part A will be 0.

(D) If the polarity of the battery is reversed then answer to part B will be 1.7 eV

2-15 A small mirror of area A and mass m is suspended in a vertical plane by a light string. A beam of light of intensity I falls normally on the mirror and the string is deflected from the vertical by an angle θ in equilibrium. Assuming the mirror to be perfectly reflecting we have

(A) Radiation pressure equal to $\frac{2I}{c}$

(B) Radiation pressure equal to $\frac{I}{2c}$

(C) $\tan\theta = \frac{2IA}{mgc}$

(D) $\tan\theta = \frac{IA}{2mgc}$

2-16 When photons of energy 4.25 eV strike the surface of metal A, the ejected photoelectrons have maximum kinetic energy of photoelectrons liberated from another metal B by photons of energy 4.70 eV is $T_B = (T_A = 1.50)$ eV. If the de-Broglie wavelength of these photoelectrons is $\lambda_B = 2\lambda_A$ then

(A) the work function of A is 2.25 eV

(B) the work function of B is 4.20 eV

(C) $T_A = 2.00$ eV (D) $T_B = 2.75$ eV

2-17 In photoelectric effect, stopping potential depends on

(A) frequency of the incident light

(B) intensity of the incident light by varies source distance

(C) emitter's properties

(D) frequency and intensity of the incident light

2-18 The figure shows the results of an experiment involving photoelectric effect. The graphs A, B, C and D relate to a light beam having different wavelengths. Select the correct alternative

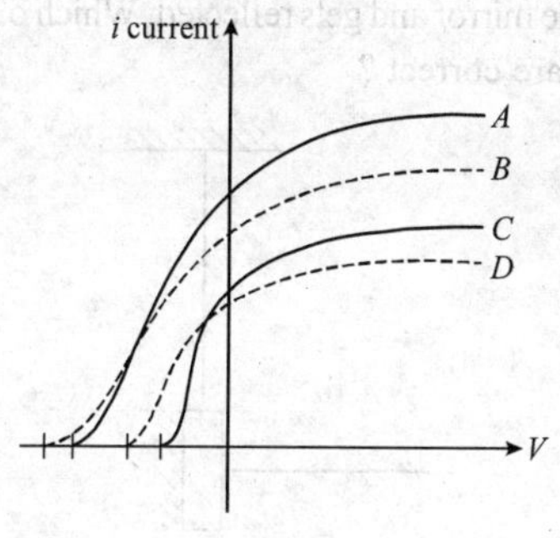

Figure 2.34

(A) Beam B has highest frequency

(B) Beam C has longest wavelength

(C) Beam A has highest rate of photoelectric emission

(D) Photoelectrons emitted by B have highest momentum

2-19 The photoelectric effect can not be explained by the wave theory of light because :

(A) the energy carried by the light waves is not given to a particular electron of the metal, rather it is distributed among all the electrons present on the surface of metal

(B) waves do not have energy

(C) energy of the waves becomes zero as it strikes the metal surface

(D) waves do not have sufficient energy which is required for electron emission

2-20 A non-monochromatic light is used in an experiment on photoelectric effect. The stopping potential :

(A) Is related to the mean wavelength

(B) Is related to the longest wavelength

(C) Is related to the shortest wavelength

(D) Is not related to the wavelength

2-21 In photoelectric effect energy of photon is directly proportional to the frequency and photons are totally absorbed by the electrons of metals then photoelectric current is :
(A) increased when the frequency of photon is increased
(B) decreased when the frequency of photon is increased
(C) independent of the frequency of photon but it only depends on the intensity of incident photons
(D) independent of the intensity of incident photons

2-22 Suppose frequency of emitted photon is f_0 when electron of stationary hydrogen atom jumps from a higher state m to a lower state n. If the atom is moving with a velocity v ($<< c$) and emits a photon of frequency f during the same transmission then which of the following statements are possible ?
(A) f may be equal to f_0 (B) f may be greater than f_0
(C) f may be less than f_0 (D) f cannot be equal to f_0

2-23 A small mirror is suspended by a thread as shown in figure-2.35. A short pulse of monochromatic light rays is incident normally on the mirror and gets reflected. Which of the following statements is/are correct ?

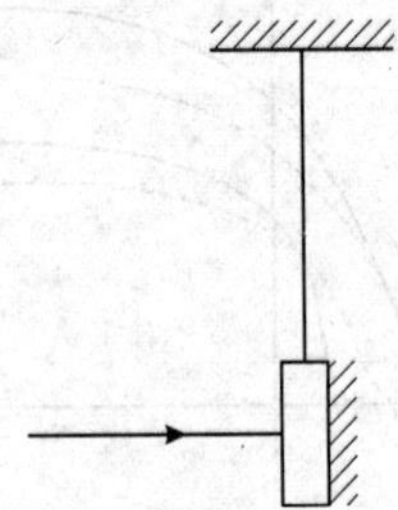

Figure 2.35

(A) mirror will start to oscillate
(B) wavelength of reflected rays will be greater than that of incident rays
(C) wavelength of reflected rays may be less than that of incident rays
(D) none of these

2-24 Light consisting of wavelength 400 nm to 800 nm falls on a metal plate A having work function 1.5 eV and saturation current 10 mA. Now the same light is incident on a metal plate B having work function 2.0 eV. Take spectral radiancy of light is uniform and take hc = 1240 eV-*nm*. Then choose the correct option(s) given below :
(A) Stopping potential for metal A is 3.1 volt
(B) Stopping potential for metal B is 1.1 volt
(C) Stopping potential for metal B is 1.6 volt
(D) Stopping potential for metal A is 1.6 volt

2-25 Mark the correct statement(s) related to the stopping potential difference :
(A) At the stopping potential, emitter plate is positive with respect to the collector
(B) At the stopping potential, emitter plate is negative with respect to the collector
(C) At the stopping potential, electrons does not come out of the plates
(D) At the stopping potential, electrons are able to reach the collector but return before being absorbed.

2-26 If the wavelength of light in an experiment on photo electric effect is doubled,
(A) The photoelectric emission will not take place
(B) The photoemission may or may not take place
(C) The stopping potential will increases
(D) The stopping potential will decrease under the condition that energy of photon of doubled. Wavelength is more than work function of metal.

2-27 Photo electric effect supports the quantum nature of light because :
(A) There is minimum frequency of light below which no photoelectrons are emitted
(B) The maximum kinetic energy of photoelectrons depends only on the frequency of light and not on intensity
(C) Even when a metal surface is faintly illuminated, the photoelectrons leave the surface immediately
(D) Electric charge of the photoelectrons is quantized

2-28 Photons of energy 5 eV are incident on cathode. Electrons reaching the anode have kinetic energies varying from 6 eV to 8 eV.

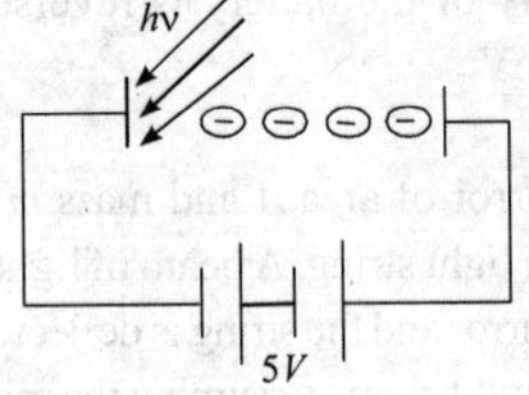

Figure 2.36

(A) Work function of the metal is 2 eV
(B) Work function of the metal is 3 eV
(C) Current in the circuit is equal to saturation value
(D) Current in the circuit is less than saturation value

* * * * *

Unsolved Numerical Problems for Preparation of NSEP, INPhO & IPhO

For detailed preparation of INPhO and IPhO students can refer advance study material on www.physicsgalaxy.com

2-1 Light from Balmer series of hydrogen is able to eject photoelectron from a metal. What can be the maximum work function of the metal?

Ans. [3.4 eV]

2-2 Monochromatic radiation of wavelength $\lambda_1 = 3000$ Å falls on a photocell operating in saturation mode. The corresponding spectral sensitivity of photocell is $J = 4.8$ mA/W. When another monochromatic radiation of wavelength $\lambda_2 = 1650$ Å and power $P = 5$ mW is incident, it is found that maximum velocity of photoelectrons increases to $n = 2$ times. Assuming efficiency of photoelectron generation per incident photon to be same for both the cases, calculate

(i) Threshold wavelength for the cell and

(ii) Saturation current in second case.

(Given, $h = 6.6 \times 10^{-34}$ Js, $c = 3 \times 10^8$ ms^{-1} and $e = 1.6 \times 10^{-19}$ coul.)

Ans. [(i) 4125 Å, (ii) 13.2 μA]

2-3 Photo electrons are liberated by ultraviolet light of wave length 3000 Å from a metallic surface for which the photoelectric threshold is a 4000 Å. Calculate the de-Broglie wave length of electrons emitted with maximum kinetic energy.

Ans. [12.08 Å]

2-4 A hydrogen atom emits a photons that has momentum with a magnitude of 5.452×10^{-27} kg-m/s. The photon is emitted because the electron in the atom makes a transition from a higher energy level to the $n = 1$ level. What is the quantum number of the initial energy level of the electron? Take Rydberg's constant 1.09×10^7 m^{-1}.

Ans. [2]

2-5 A parallel beam of monochromatic light of wavelength 663 nm is incident on a totally reflecting plane mirror. The angle of incidence is 60° and the number of photons striking the mirror per second is 10^{19}. Calculate the force exerted by the light beam on the mirror.

Ans. [10^{-8} N]

2-6 A perfectly reflecting ball of radius R and mass m is kept on a rough horizontal floor. A parallel light beam of intensity I is incident on the ball at an angle θ with the horizontal. Calculate initial acceleration of the ball.

Ans. [$\dfrac{5\pi IR^2 \cos\theta}{7mc}$]

2-7 A small piece of cesium metal ($\phi = 1.9$ eV) is kept at a distance of 20 cm from a large metal plate having a uniform surface charge density of 2×10^{-9} C/m^2 on surface facing the cesium piece. A monochromatic light of wavelength 400 nm is incident on the cesium piece. Calculate the maximum kinetic of the photoelectron reaching the large metal plate.

Ans. [23.8 eV]

2-8 The work function of Aluminium is 4.2 eV. Calculate the Kinetic energy of the fastest & the slowest photoelectrons, the stopping potential & the cut off wavelength when light of wavelength 2000 Å falls on a clean Aluminium surface.

Ans. [2 eV, 2 Volts, 3000 Å]

2-9 What potential difference must be applied to stop the fastest photoelectrons emitted by a nickel surface under the action of ultraviolet light of wavelength 2000 Å ? The work function of nickel is 5.01 eV.

Ans. [≅ + 1.2 V]

2-10 A sphere of radius 1 cm is placed in the path of a parallel beam of light of large aperture. The intensity of the light is 0.5 W/cm^2. If the sphere completely absorbs the radiation falling on it, find the force exerted by the light beam on the sphere.

Ans. [5.2×10^{-9} N]

2-11 Find the frequency of the light which ejects from a metal surface electrons fully stopped by a retarding potential of 3 V. The photo electric effect begins in this metal at a frequency 6×10^{14} s^{-1}. Find the work function for this metal.

Ans. [13.2398×10^{14} s^{-1}, 3.98×10^{-19} J]

2-12 State whether the following statements are TRUE or FALSE, giving reasons in brief to support your answer.

In a photo electric emission process the maximum energy of the photoelectrons increases with increasing intensity of the incident light.

Ans. [False]

2-13 A point isotropic light source of power $P = 12$ watt is located on the axis of a circular mirror plate of radius $R = 3$ cm. If distance of source from the plate is $\alpha = 39$ cm and reflection coefficient of mirror plate is $\alpha = 0.70$, calculate force exerted by light rays on the plate.

Ans. [1×10^{-10} N]

2-14 When a light of wavelength λ_1 is incident on the cathode of a photoelectric tube in an experiment, the maximum kinetic energy of the emitted photoelectrons is 1.75 eV. If the wavelength is reduced to half, the maximum kinetic energy of the emitted electrons is 5.5 eV. Find the work function of the cathode material.

Ans. [2 eV]

2-15 Light of wavelength 180 nm ejects photo electrons from a plate of a metal whose work function is 2 eV. If a uniform magnetic field of 5×10^{-5} tesla is applied parallel to the plate, what would be the radius of the path followed by electrons ejected normally from the plate with maximum energy.

Ans. [0.148 m]

2-16 Suppose the wavelength of the incident light is increased from 3000 Å to 3040 Å. Find the corresponding change in the stopping potential. (Take the product hc = 12.4×10^{-7} evm).

Ans. [$\Delta V_s = -5.5 \times 10^{-2}$ volt]

2-17 When a metal plate is exposed to monochromatic beam of light of wavelength 4000 Å, a negative potential of 1.1 volts is needed to stop the photocurrent. Find the threshold wavelength for the metal.

Ans. [6196 Å]

2-18 The ionisation energy of a hydrogen like Bohr atom is 4 Rydbergs.

(i) What is the wavelength of radiation emitted when the electron jumps from the first excited state to the ground state ?

(ii) What is the radius of the first orbit of this atom ?

(Bohr radius of hydrogen = 5×10^{-11} m; 1 Rydberg = 2.2×10^{-18} J)

Ans. [(i) 300 Å (ii) 2.5×10^{-11} m]

2-19 A stationary hydrogen atom emits a photon corresponding to first line of the Lyman series. What velocity does the atom acquire ?

Ans. [3.25 m/s]

2-20 From the condition of the foregoing problem, find how much (in %) the energy of the emitted photon differs from the energy of the corresponding transition in a hydrogen atom.

Ans. [$\frac{(E-E')}{E} = 0.55 \times 10^{-6}$ %]

2-21 From a polychromatic source of light, the emitted light is expressed by the equation

$$E = (100\ \text{V/m})\,[\sin(2\pi \times 10^{15}\ \text{s}^{-1})\,t + \sin(3\pi \times 10^{15}\ \text{s}^{-1})t]$$

This light falls on a metal surface having work function 2.1 eV. Calculate the maximum kinetic energy of the emitted photoelectrons.

Ans. [4.11 eV]

2-22 The peak emission from a black body at a certain temperature occurs at a wavelength of 6200 Å. On increasing its temperature, the total radiation emitted is increased 16 times. These radiations are allowed to fall on a metal surface. Photoelectrons emitted by the peak radiation at higher temperature can be bought to rest by applying a potential equivalent to the excitation potential corresponding to the transition for the level $n = 4$ to $n = 2$ from the Bohr's hydrogen atom. Calculate the work function of the metal.

Ans. [1.46 eV]

2-23 A proton is fired from very far away distance towards a fixed nucleus with charge 120 *e*, where *e* is the electronic charge. It makes a closest approach of 10 fm to the nucleus. The de Calculate the de-Broglie wavelength of the proton when it was fired. (Take the proton mass, $m_p = (5/3) \times 10^{-27}$ kg; 1 fm = 10^{-15} m; $h/e = 4.2 \times 10^{-15}$ J.s./C; $\frac{1}{4\pi\varepsilon_0} = 9 \times 10^9$ Nm²/C²]

Ans. [7×10^{-15} m]

2-24 The electric field associated with a monochromatic beam becomes zero 1.2×10^{15} times per second. Find the maximum kinetic energy of the photoelectrons when this light falls on a metal surface whose work function is 2.0 eV.

Ans. [0.48 eV]

2-25 In a radioactive chamber an α-emitter is used for energy production. One of the emitted α-particle is projected into a constant magnetic field normally. It is found that it moves in a circle with half the radius of an already moving electron in circular path in the same field. Calculate the ratio of de-Broglie wavelengths of the α-particle to that of the electron.

Ans. [1]

2-26 A toy truck has dimensions as shown in figure-2.37 and its width normal to the plane of this paper is *d*. Sun rays are incident on it as shown in figure. If intensity of sun rays is *I* and all surfaces of truck are perfectly black, calculate tension in thread used to keep truck stationary. Neglect fraction.

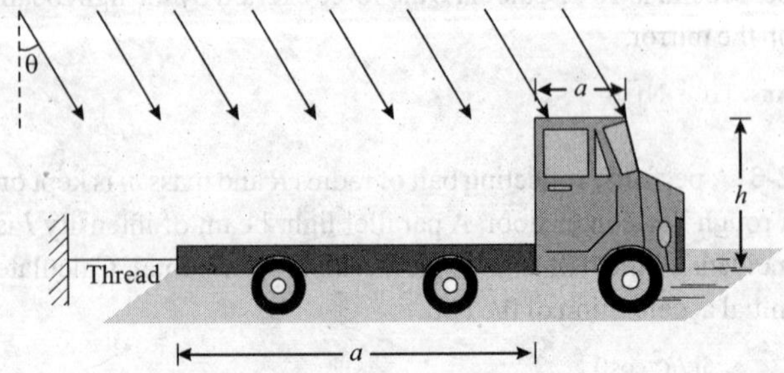

Figure 2.37

Ans. [$\frac{Id}{c}$ (b cos θ + a cos θ + h sin θ) sin θ]

2-27 A sphere of radius R is kept on smooth horizontal surface. It is connected with ideal spring of constant K as shown in figure-2.38. A parallel light beam having intensity I is falling at an angle $\theta = 30^\circ$ with vertical on the sphere, then find the compression in the spring in equilibrium position, assuming the at the sphere absorbs 100% of the light incident on it. [Take $\frac{IR^2}{Kc} = \frac{10}{\pi}$ SI unit, where c is speed of light in vacuum]

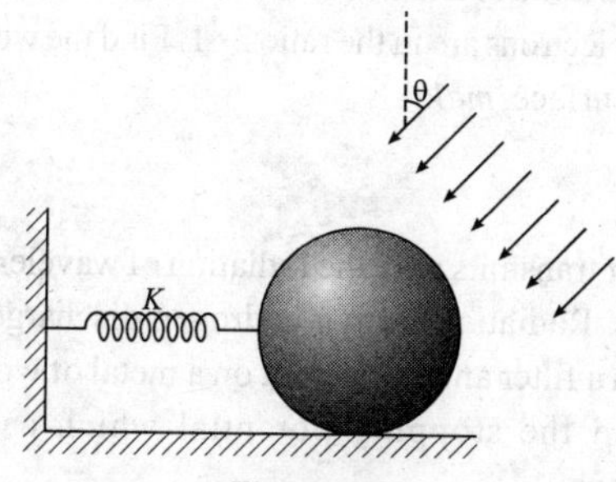

Figure 2.38

Ans. [5 m]

2-28 Electrons in hydrogen like atoms ($Z = 3$) make transition from the fifth to the fourth orbit and from the fourth to the third orbit. The resulting radiations are incident normally on a metal plate and eject photoelectrons. The stopping potential for the photoelectrons ejected by the shorter wavelength is 3.95 volt. Calculate the work function of the metal and the stopping potential for the photoelectrons ejected by the longer wavelength. [Rydberg constant = 1.094×10^7 m^{-1}]

Ans. [2.0 eV, 0.754 V]

2-29 An electron in a hydrogen like atom is in an excited state. It has a total energy of – 3.4 eV. Calculate :

(i) The kinetic energy, (ii) The de-Broglie wavelength of the electron.

Ans. [(i) $KE = 3.4$ eV (ii) $\lambda = 6.66$ Å]

2-30 When a light of wavelength 500 nm from a visible source of light is incident on a metal surface of work function 1.9 eV, photoelectrons are emitted. When the emitted photoelectrons are passed through a region containing He^{2+} atoms, a fastest photoelectron combines with He^{2+} atom to form He^{+} atom and a photon is emitted. The He^{+} atom thus formed is in its third excited state. Then find the energy of the photon emitted during the combination of He^{2+} with the fastest photoelectron. (Take $hc = 1240$ eV-nm)

Ans. [3.98 eV]

2-31 Light from a discharge tube containing hydrogen atoms falls on the surface of a piece of sodium. The kinetic energy of the fastest photoelectrons emitted from sodium is 0.73 eV. The work function for sodium is 1.82 eV. Find :

(a) the energy of the photons causing the photoelectric emission,

(b) the quantum numbers of the two levels involved in the emission of these photons,

(c) the change in the angular momentum of the electron in the hydrogen atom in the above transition, &

(d) the recoil speed of the emitting atom assuming it to be at rest before the transition (Ionisation potential of hydrogen is 13.6 eV).

Ans. [(a) 2.55 eV; (b) From 4 to 2; (c) $\frac{h}{\pi}$; (d) 0.847 m/s]

2-32 Find recoil speed when a hydrogen atom emits a photon during the transition from $n = 5$ to $n = 1$.

Ans. [4 m/s]

2-33 State whether the following statements are true or false. Give brief reasons in support of your answers.

(i) The dimension of (h/e) is the same as that of magnetic flux ϕ. Here h & e represents Planck's constant and electronic charge respectively.

(ii) Two metal plates of same surface area and work function are irradiated by a beam of light, incident normally. It is found that the photoelectric current from the two metals are different.

Ans. [(i) T, (ii) T]

2-34 A 40 W ultraviolet light source of wavelength 2480 Å illuminates a magnesium (Mg) surface placed 2 m away. Determine the number of photons emitted from the source per second & the number incident on unit area of the Mg surface per second. The photoelectric work function for Mg is 3.68 eV. Calculate the kinetic energy of the fastest electrons ejected from the surface. Determine the maximum wavelength for which the photoelectric effect can be observed with a Mg surface.

Ans. [5×10^{19}, $\frac{25 \times 10^{18}}{8\pi} \cong 1 \times 10^{18}$, 1.32 eV, 3370 Å]

2-35 Assuming a sphere is located at a distance r from the Sun as shown in figure-2.39 below and it absorbs all the light incident on it. Find the radius R of the sphere for which its gravitational attraction to the Sun is counterbalanced by the force that sunlight exerts on it. The power of light radiated by the Sun is equal to 4×10^{26} W and the density of the sphere is 1.0 g/cm^3. Use $G = \frac{20}{3} \times 10^{-11}$ Nm^2/kg^2, $\pi = \frac{25}{8}$ and mass of the Sun is $M_S = 2 \times 10^{30}$ kg.

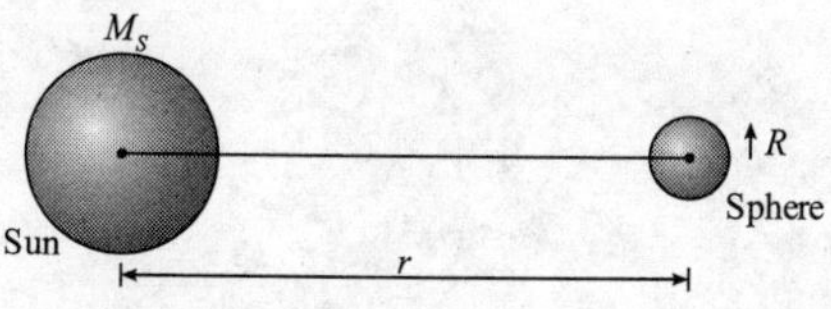

Figure 2.39

Ans. [6 m]

2-36 At a given instant there are 25% undecayed radioactive nuclei in a sample. After 10 second the number of undecayed nuclei reduces to 12.5%. Calculate :

(i) Mean life of the nuclei

(ii) The time in which the number of undecayed nuclei will further reduce to 6.25% of the reduced number.

Ans. [(i) 14.43 s, (ii) 40 s]

2-37 When a beam of 10.6 eV photons of intensity 2.0 W/m^2 falls on a platinum surface of area 1.0×10^{-4} m^2 and work function 5.6 eV, 0.53% of the incident photons eject photoelectrons. Find the number of photoelectrons emitted per second and their minimum energies (in *eV*). Take 1 eV = 1.6×10^{-19} J.

Ans. [6.25×10^{11}, 0]

2-38 In a photoelectric effect experiment, photons of energy 5 eV are incident on the photocathode of work function 3 eV. For photon intensity $I_A = 10^{15}$ m^{-2} s^{-1}, saturation current of 4.0 μA is obtained. Sketch the variation of photocurrent i_p against the anode voltage V_a in the figure below for photon intensity I_A (curve *A*) and $I_B = 2 \times 10^{15}$ m^{-2} s^{-1} (curve *B*).

Ans. [

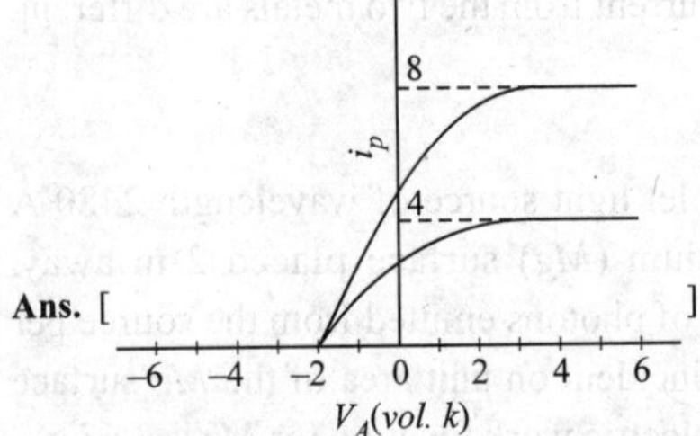

]

2-39 In a photoelectric setup, the radiations from the Balmer series of hydrogen atom are incident on a metal surface of work function 2 eV. The wavelength of incident radiations lies between 450 nm to 700 nm. Find the maximum kinetic energy of photoelectron emitted. (Given *hc*/*e* = 1242 eV-nm)

2-40 Monochromatic radiations of λ = 640.2 nm from a neon lamp irradiates photosensitive material made of cesium on tungsten. The stopping potential is measured as 0.54 V. The source is replaced by an iron source and its 427.2 nm line irradiates the same photocell. Predict the difference in stopping potential. (Round off to single digit)

Ans. [1 eV]

2-41 Irradiating the metal surface successively by radiations of wavelength 3000 Å and 5400 Å, it is found that the maximum velocities of electrons are in the ratio 2 : 1. Find the work function of the metal surface, *meV*.

Ans. [1690]

2-42 A filter transmits only the radiation of wavelength greater than 4400 Å. Radiation from a hydrogen discharge tube goes through such a filter and is incident on a metal of work function 2.0 eV. Find the stopping potential which can stop the photoelectrons.

Ans. [0.55 volts]

2-43 A parallel light beam of intensity 3000 W/m^2 and wavelength 100 nm having cross sectional area 100 cm^2 is incident normally on a glass slab, placed in air. The slab is made up of a material which reflects 40 % of light, transmits 40 % of light and absorbs 20 % of light incident on it. Calculate the force experienced by slab due to incident light beam.

Ans. [10^{-7} N]

2-44 If radiation from a black body are allowed to fall on a photosensitive material after passing it through a filter which selects the wavelength having maximum intensity to pass. The work-function of the material is 1.24 eV. Find the minimum temperature of the blackbody which will cause the emission of photoelectrons from this material.

(Given Weins constant b = 3×10^{-3} m-K & *hc* = 12400 eV-Å)

Ans. [3×10^3 K]

* * * * *

X-rays

3

FEW WORDS FOR STUDENTS

We have already discussed about the energy levels in atoms. In this chapter we will study about the utilization of the energy released from atomic transitions in heavy atoms in the form of X-rays. Now we will study from the discovery of X-rays to the fundamental utility along with the different production mechanism of X-rays.

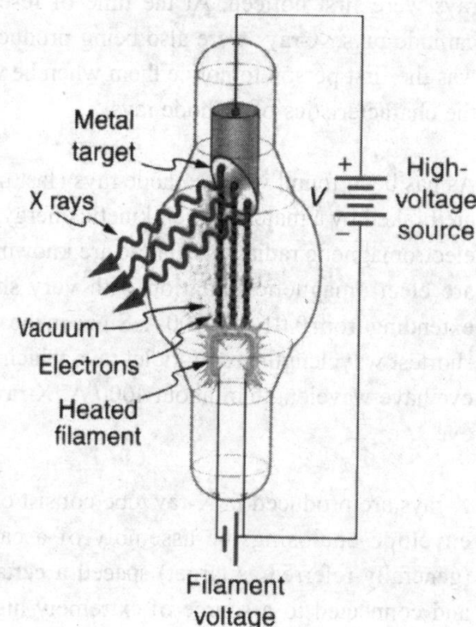

CHAPTER CONTENTS

COVER APPLICATION

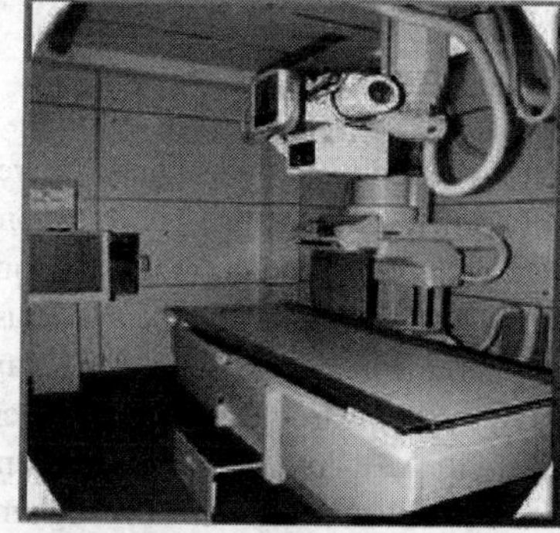

Figure (a)

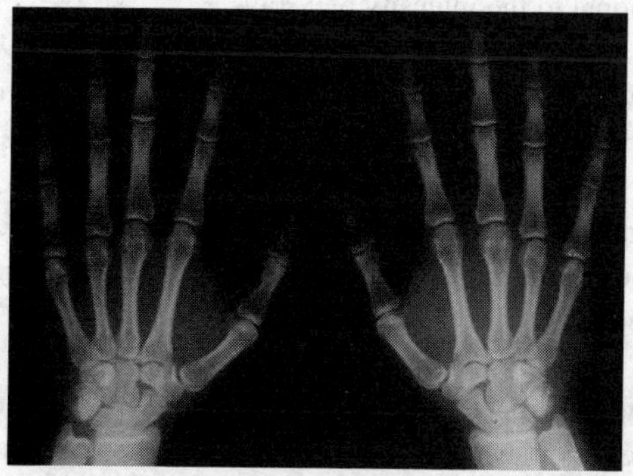

Figure (b)

Figure-(a) shows a commercial X-Ray machine used in various diagnostic labs in which X-rays are used to take photographs of various organs of human body. Figure-(b) is a typical X-Ray image of human hands taken on a commercial X-Ray machine.

3.1 Introduction to X-Rays

The discovery of X-rays was accidental by Wilhelm K. Roentgen in Germany. X-rays were discovered while investigating the discharge of electricity through rarefied gases, the same phenomenon and equipment through which cathode rays were first noticed. At the time of researches going on cathode rays, X-rays were also being produced but Roentgen was the first person to notice them when he was investigating the characteristics of cathode rays.

As has been found when cathode rays (fast moving electrons) are braked by a material, their kinetic energy is converted into electromagnetic radiations. These are known as X-rays. These are electromagnetic radiation with very short wavelengths extending from 0.01 Å to 100 Å. Since in the visible region, the shortest wavelength are of violet rays which are visible to the eye have wavelength of about 4000 Å, X-rays are invisible to eye.

X-rays are produced in X-ray tube consist of a glass or metal envelope enclosing the assembly of a cathode, an anode (generally referred as target) spaced a certain distance apart and connected to a source of extremely high tension (EHT) supply. The cathode acts as a source of electrons and the anode as a source of X-rays. The field setup between the cathode and the anode accelerates the electrons to energies of order 10^4 to 10^5 eV.

The invisible X-rays are detected by observing their effects. Among other things X-rays produce a strong photochemical action which blackens photographic plates. They are also capable of ionizing gases and causing fluorescence in phosphors. For measurement purposes, these are used in mainly for their applications of their photochemical and ionizing effects. In ionization chambers, the intensity of X-rays is determined by measuring the saturation current due to the ionization of the gas enclosed in the chamber, because the saturation current is proportional to the intensity of X-rays.

Roentgen discovered that the X-rays has following characteristics.

(a) X-rays are generated whenever high energy cathode rays strike solid materials. Generally the greater the density of impacted material the more X-rays are produced.

(b) Matter is more or less transparent to X-rays. Wood and flesh are very transparent bone and metals less so, which makes the use of X-rays in medicine so useful.

(c) X-rays are unaffected (undeviated) by electric and magnetic fields, hence these are uncharged.

(d) The wave nature of X-rays makes them useful tool for the study of the structure of crystals & molecules. This was later discovered.

3.1.1 Types of X-rays

According to the quality of X-rays, these can be divided in two groups, these are

(i) Soft X-rays : These are X-rays with low penetrating power. The wavelength range of these X-rays are from 10 Å and above hence their frequency is small and they have smaller energy. These are produced at comparatively low potential difference and high pressure.

(ii) Hard X-rays : These are X-rays having high penetrating power. The wavelength range of these X-rays are of the order of 1 Å so they have high frequencies and hence high energies. These are produced at comparatively low pressure and high potential difference.

3.2 Production Mechanism of X-rays

On the basis of production mechanism, X-rays are classified in two broad categories

1. Continuous X-Rays
2. Characteristic X-Rays

Now we'll discuss about the production mechanism of X-rays in detail.

3.2.1 Continuous X-rays

Continuous X-rays, as their name implies, have a continuous spectral distribution. They are produced when electrons accelerated in a vacuum strike a target and lose kinetic energy in passing through the strong electric field of the target nuclei, and resulting in a continuous X-ray spectrum. As according to the classical physics any accelerated charged particle emits electromagnetic radiation of continuous spectral distribution.

3.2.2 Production of Continuous X-rays

In the general X-ray production mechanism there is a discharge tube (generally called Coolidge tube) operated on high potential difference. The cathode used in the tube is the source of cathode rays i.e. fast moving electrons, and the anode used in the tube is the target material which is the source of X-rays. The X-rays are produced by the bombardment of anode material by cathode rays, so there will be a lot of heat generation in the anode material. The anode material should have high melting point as due to high energetic electrons, a high temperature is generated. For this purpose target is selected of high atomic mass. The coolidge tube assembly for the production of X-rays is shown in figure-3.1.

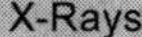

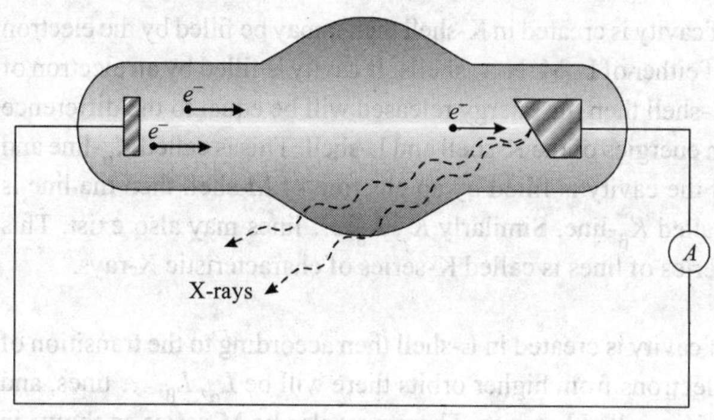

Figure 3.1

The mechanism for the production of continuous X-rays can be explained on the basis of figure-3.2. Figure shows an atom of the anode material of high atomic weight with its electron configuration. In the Coolidge tube an electron is projected towards the anode with an accelerating voltage V. So the kinetic energy of the projectile electron will be eV. As shown in the figure when the projectile electrons enters into the extremely high electric field of the nucleus of the atom of the anode material, it experiences a strong electric force towards the nucleus of the atom of the anode material, it experiences a strong electric force towards the nucleus of the atom and due to this strong attraction the velocity of this electron when it emerges from the atom will be highly reduced and negligibly compared with the initial velocity of the projectile electron. This electron in the influence of the highly positive nuclei experiences a very high acceleration and according to the classical theory every accelerated charged particle emits the electromagnetic radiations, so this electron will also emit electromagnetic radiations, these electromagnetic radiations are called X-rays. According to the law of conservation of energy, the energy of these electromagnetic radiation will be equal to the decrease in the kinetic energy of the projectile electron. This amount can be calculated.

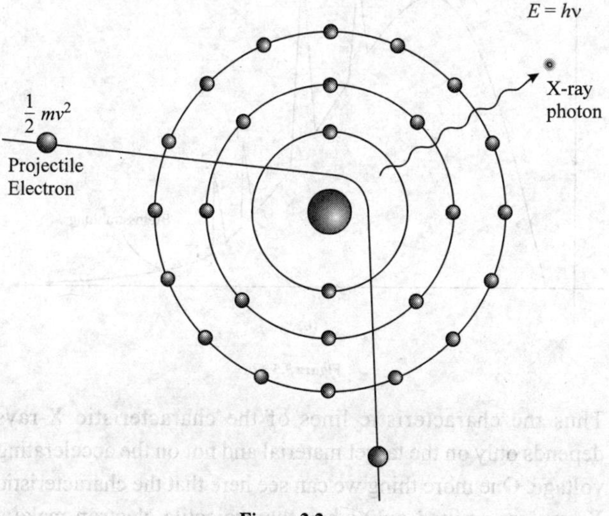

Figure 3.2

If the initial velocity of the projectile electron is v, then as the velocity is gained due to the accelerating voltage V, we have

$$eV = \frac{1}{2}mv^2 \qquad \ldots(3.1)$$

$$\Rightarrow \quad v = \sqrt{\frac{2eV}{m}} \qquad \ldots(3.2)$$

When this electron comes out from the atom of anode material the speed of this electron will be very less as compared to its initial speed. Thus the difference of kinetic energy of this electron is emitted in the form of an X-rays photon from the anode atom.

Those electrons which pass through the atom very close to the nucleus, will be more accelerated and the photon energy corresponding to these electrons will be more as compared to those electrons which pass through the atom at relatively large distance from nucleus. The maximum energy of X-photon will be corresponding to that electron which looses almost all of its energy during passing through the atom. The photon corresponding to this electron will have the shortest wavelength among all the photons radiated by other electrons. If this shortest wavelength is λ_c then we have

$$\Delta E = \frac{1}{2}mv^2 = eV = \frac{hc}{\lambda_c}$$

$$\Rightarrow \quad \lambda_c = \frac{hc}{eV} = \frac{12431}{V}\,\text{Å} \qquad \ldots(3.3)$$

This is the minimum wavelength of X-rays emitted from an X-ray tube which we call short wave cut off. Thus from equation-(3.3) we can see that the maximum energy or minimum wavelength of X-rays emitted depends only on the potential difference applied across the discharge tube.

Thus we can obtain X-rays in any range λ_c to ∞ by applying an appropriate voltage across discharge tube which will fix λ_c and other photons emitted from tube will have wavelength more than λ_c and ranging up to ∞. Thats why these X-rays are called continuous X-rays. The basic intensity per unit wavelength versus wavelength plot (wavelength spectrum) of continuous X-rays is shown in figure-3.3.

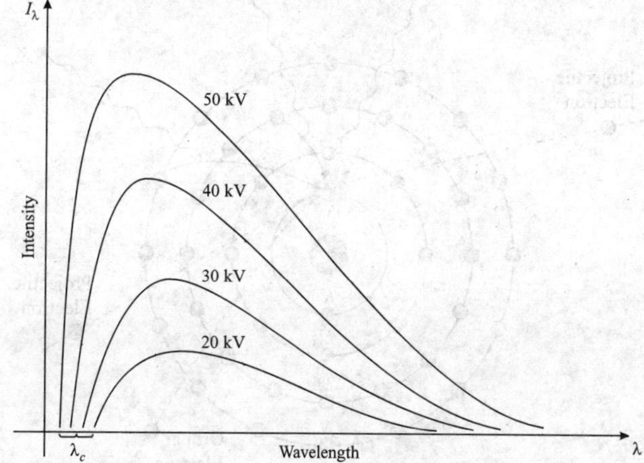

Figure 3.3

As we can see in the graph that the intensity of emitted X-rays will be maximum (maximum number of photons) for a particular value of wavelength at a particular accelerating voltage across the discharge tube. At a particular voltage the intensity of X-rays can be varied by changing the current in the circuit because the intensity of X-rays (number of photons) is proportional to the number of electrons attacking the anode. The broad continuous spectrum beyond the peak intensity is referred as "*Bremsstrahlung*".

3.2.3 Characteristic X-rays

These X-rays are called characteristic X-rays because they are characteristic of the element used as target anode. Characteristic X-rays has a line spectral distribution unlike to continuous X-rays. The wavelength spectrum of these X-rays is also a continuous spectrum but this spectrum is crossed over by distinct spectral lines. The frequencies corresponding to these lines are the characteristic of the material of the target i.e. anode material.

3.2.4 Production of Characteristic X-rays

Production of these X-rays can be explained with help of the figure-3.4. These X-rays are produced when the projectile electron towards the anode collides with an internal electron of the atom of the target material, and then secondary emission will happen. Now this will create a cavity in the inner shell of the target material, and then secondary emission will happen. Now this will create a cavity. There are so many ways in which the cavity may be filled. The cavity can be filled by an electron of higher orbit which make the transition from its orbit to the lower orbit in which cavity is created. When an electron make such a form of electromagnetic radiation, this energy is the characteristic line for the X-ray spectrum.

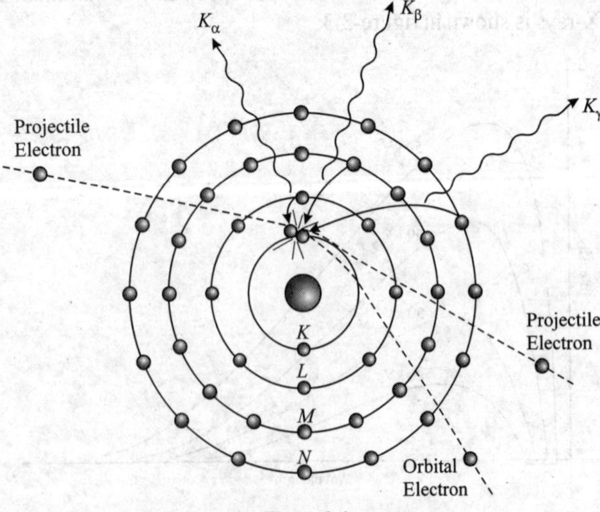

Figure 3.4

If cavity is created in K-shell then it may be filled by the electron of either of L, M, N ... shells. If cavity is filled by an electron of L-shell then the energy released will be equal to the difference in energies of the K-shell and L-shell. This is called K_α-line and if the cavity is filled by an electron of M-shell then the line is called K_β-line. Similarly K_γ, K_δ, ... lines may also exist. This series of lines is called K-series of characteristic X-rays.

If cavity is created in L-shell then according to the transition of electrons from higher orbits there will be L_α, L_β, ... lines, and this is called L-series. There may also be M-series as shown in figure-3.5(a). Figure-3.5(b) shows the wavelength spectrum for the characteristic X-rays when cavity is created in K-shell.

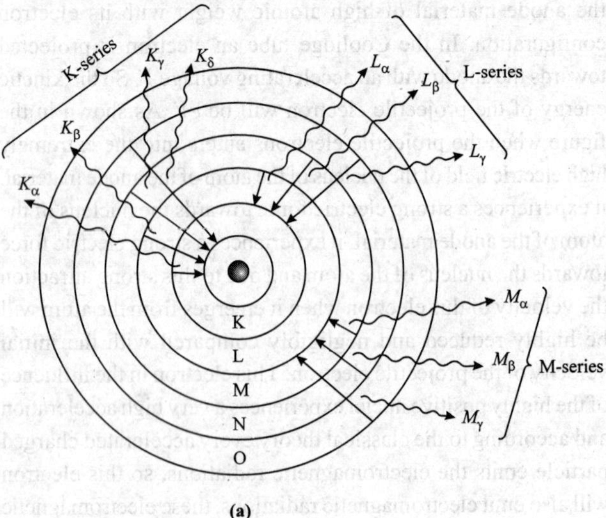

(a)

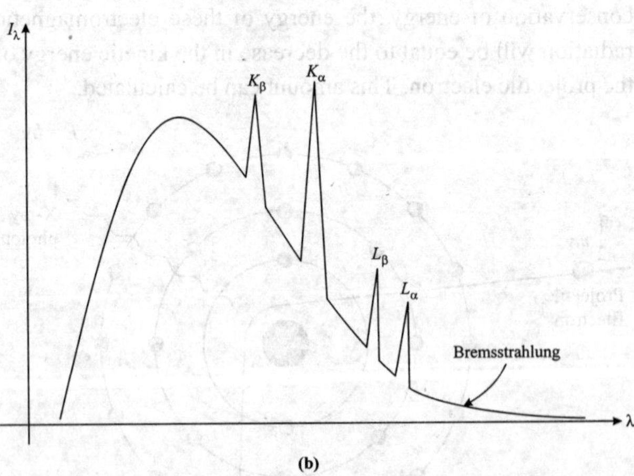

(b)

Figure 3.5

Thus the characteristic lines of the characteristic X-rays depends only on the target material and not on the accelerating voltage. One more thing we can see here that the characteristic X-rays are emitted only when the projectile electron make a collision with another bound electron of the atom of the target material. When cathode rays pass through the target then the probability of collision of a projectile electron to collide with the bound electron is very less. Majority of the projectile electron to collide with the bound electron is very less. Majority of the projectile electrons will pass through the anode without making the collision and they produce continuous X-rays. So always both type of X-rays, continuous and characteristic will be emitted. Only a single type can not be emitted.

3.3 Moseley's Law

Moseley found that the wavelengths of characteristic X-rays depend in a well defined manner on the atomic numbers of the element that emit X-rays (the target element). This dependence, is known as Moseley law, may be written as

$$\sqrt{\nu} = a(Z-\sigma) \qquad \ldots(3.4)$$

Where σ is known as screening constant so the term $(Z-\sigma)$ here is effective atomic number for the electron which takes part in the transition which results in characteristic X-rays and a is Moseley constant.

It can be seen that for K_α line the electron make a transition from L-shell to K-shell, and during this transition this electron move in the electric field of the nucleus and the one electron of the K-shell, so the screening on the transition electron is only due to the remaining one electron of the K-shell so we can take the effective atomic number for this transition as $(Z-1)$ so the frequency emitted for the K_α line can be given as

$$\sqrt{\nu} = a(Z-1)$$

The wavelength of the characteristic X-rays can be calculated by the relation

$$\frac{1}{\lambda} = R(Z-\sigma)^2\left[\frac{1}{n_1^2}-\frac{1}{n_2^2}\right] \qquad \ldots(3.5)$$

For K_α-line we use $\sigma = 1$ and $n_2 = 2$ and $n_1 = 1$, thus the wavelength of the K_α-line can be given as

$$\frac{1}{\lambda} = \frac{3}{4}R(Z-1)^2$$

$$\Rightarrow \qquad \nu = \frac{3}{4}Rc(Z-1)^2$$

Thus for K_α-line $a = \sqrt{\frac{3}{4}Rc}$, where R is the Rydberg constant.

3.4 Applications of X-rays

(1) Surgery : X-rays can pass through blood and not through bones. They are used to detect the fracture of bones, diseased organs and foreign bodies and growth in the human body. A person is allowed to stand between a fluorescent screen and the X-ray unit. The deep shadow of bones is formed on the fluorescent screen and the fracture of the bone can be detected. Instead of the fluorescent screen, a photograph known as radiograph can also be taken. X-rays are also used to diagnose diseases in the lungs, kidneys, intestines and other parts of the body.

(2) Radiotherapy : X-rays are used to destroy malignant tumors and to cure skin diseased. Long exposure of X-rays kills the germs in the body and hard X-rays are used to destroy tumors very deep inside the body.

(3) Industry : X-rays are used to detect defect in radio-valves, tennis balls, rubber tyres and the presence of pearls in oysters. They are also used to test the uniformity of the insulating materials and the quality of oil paintings.

(4) Engineering : X-rays are used to detect cracks in structures and blow holes in metals. They are used to test the quality of weldings, moulds and metal coatings. They also help in detecting any crack in the body of the aeroplane and motor cars.

(5) Detection departments : X-rays are commonly used to detect the smuggling of precious metals at the custom posts and to detect the explosives and other contraband goods like opium in sealed parcels and in leather cases. They are also used in mints, where coins are made and every person has to pass before an X-ray unit after the day's work is over.

(6) Research : X-rays are used in research to study the structure of crystals, arrangements of atoms and molecules in matter and their behaviour on different materials.

 # Illustrative Example 3.1

An X-rays tube operates at 20 kV. Find the maximum speed of the electrons striking the anticathode, given the charge of electron = 1.6×10^{-19} coulomb and mass of electron = 9×10^{-31} kg.

Solution

When an electron of charge e is accelerated through a potential difference V, it acquires energy eV. If m be the mass of the electron and v_{max} the maximum speed of electron, then

$$\frac{1}{2}mv_{max}^2 = eV$$

$$\Rightarrow \qquad v_{max} = \sqrt{\left(\frac{2eV}{m}\right)}$$

Substituting the given vales, we get

$$v_{max} = \sqrt{\left(\frac{2\times(1.6\times10^{-19})\times 20{,}000}{9\times10^{-31}}\right)}$$

$$v_{max} = 8.4\times10^{7}\text{ m/sec}$$

 # *Illustrative Example 3.2*

(a) An X-ray tube produces a continuous spectrum of radiation with its short-wavelength end at 0.45 Å. What is the maximum energy of a photon in the radiation ? (b) From your answer to (a), guess what order of accelerating voltage (for electrons) is required in such a tube ?

Solution

(a) Short wavelength is given as

$$\lambda_{min} = 0.45\text{ Å}$$

Maximum photo energy is given as

$$E_{max} = h\nu_{max} = \frac{hc}{\lambda_{min}}$$

$$\Rightarrow \quad E_{max} = \frac{12431}{0.45} = 27624.44\text{ eV}$$

$$\Rightarrow \quad E_{max} = 27.624\text{ keV}$$

(b) The minimum accelerating voltage for electrons is

$$\frac{27.6\text{ keV}}{e} = 27.6\text{ kV}$$

i.e. of the order of 30 kV

 # *Illustrative Example 3.3*

The wavelength of the characteristics X-ray K_α line emitted from zinc (Z = 30) is 1.415 Å. Find the wavelength of the K_α line emitted from molybdenum (Z = 42).

Solution

According to Moseley's law, the frequency for K series is given by

$$\nu \propto (Z-1)^2$$

$$\Rightarrow \quad \frac{c}{\lambda} \propto (Z-1)^2$$

$$\Rightarrow \quad \frac{1}{\lambda} = k(Z-1)^2 \qquad \ldots(3.6)$$

Where k is a constant. Let λ' be the wavelength of K_α line emitted from molybdenum, then

$$\frac{1}{\lambda'} = k(Z-1)^2 \qquad \ldots(3.7)$$

Dividing (3.6) and (3.7) we get

$$\lambda' = \left(\frac{Z-1}{Z'-1}\right)^2 \lambda$$

$$\Rightarrow \quad \lambda' = \left(\frac{30-1}{42-1}\right)^2 \times 1.415\text{ Å} = 0.708\text{ Å}$$

 # *Illustrative Example 3.4*

If the short series limit of the Balmer series for hydrogen is 3644 Å, find the atomic number of the element which give X-ray wavelengths down to 1 Å. Identify the element.

Solution

If the short series limit of the Balmer series is corresponding to transition $n = \infty$ to $n = 2$ which is given by

$$\frac{1}{\lambda} = R\left(\frac{1}{2^2} - \frac{1}{\infty^2}\right) = \frac{R}{4}$$

$$\Rightarrow \quad R = \frac{4}{\lambda} = \frac{4}{3644}\text{ (Å)}^{-1}$$

The shortest wavelength corresponds to $n = \infty$ to $n = 1$. Therefore λ_c is given as

$$\frac{1}{\lambda_c} = R(Z-1)^2\left[\frac{1}{1^2} - \frac{1}{\infty^2}\right]$$

$$\Rightarrow \quad (Z-1)^2 = \frac{1}{\lambda_c R} = \frac{1}{1\text{Å}\times\frac{4}{3644}\text{(Å)}^{-1}}$$

$$= \frac{3644}{4} = 911$$

$$\Rightarrow \quad Z-1 = 30.2$$

$$\Rightarrow \quad Z = 31.2 \simeq 31$$

Thus the atomic number of the element is 31 which is gallium.

 # *Illustrative Example 3.5*

A material whose K absorption edge is 0.2 Å is irradiated by X-rays of wavelength 0.15 Å. Find the maximum energy of the photoelectrons that are emitted from the K shell.

Solution

The binding energy for K shell in eV is

$$E_k = \frac{hc}{\lambda_k} = \frac{12431}{0.2}\text{ eV} = 62.155\text{ KeV}$$

The energy of the incident photon in eV is

$$E=\frac{hc}{\lambda}=\frac{12431}{0.15}=82.873 \text{ KeV}$$

Therefore, the maximum energy of the photoelectrons emitted from the K shell is

$$E_{max}=E-E_k=82.873-62.155 \text{ KeV}$$

$$\Rightarrow E_{max}=20.718 \text{ KeV}$$

 # Illustrative Example 3.6

Calculate the wavelength of the emitted characteristic X-ray from a tungsten ($Z=74$) target when an electron drops from a M shell to a vacancy in the K shell.

Solution

Tungsten is a multi-electron atom. Due to the shielding of the nuclear charge by the negative charge of the inner core electrons, each electron is subject to an effective nuclear charge Z_{eff}, which is different for different shells.

For an electron in the K shell ($\sigma = 1$) thus effective nuclear charge is given as

$$Z_{eff}=(Z-\sigma);$$

$$\Rightarrow Z_{eff}=Z-1$$

Here as electron drops from M shell ($n=3$) to K shell ($n=1$), the radiated emission we call K_β X-ray and from Mosley's law the wavelength emitted of K_β X-ray is given as

$$\frac{1}{\lambda_{K\beta}}=R(Z-1)^2\left[\frac{1}{1^2}-\frac{1}{3^2}\right]$$

$$\Rightarrow \frac{1}{\lambda_{K\beta}}=10967800\times(74-1)^2\left[\frac{8}{9}\right]$$

$$\Rightarrow \lambda_{K\beta}=0.192 \text{ Å}$$

 # Illustrative Example 3.7

A potential difference of 20 kV is applied a X-ray tube. Find the minimum wavelength of X-rays generated.

Solution

The X-rays produced under an accelerating potential V will have varying wavelengths with the minimum due to the entire energy of the accelerated electron being lost in a single collision with the target atoms. Here the shortest wavelength generated of X-rays can be given by

$$\lambda_c=\frac{12431}{V} \text{ Å}$$

$$=0.6215 \text{ Å}$$

 # Illustrative Example 3.8

The wavelength of K_α X-rays produced by a X-ray tube is 0.76 Å. What is the atomic number of the anode material of the tube ?

Solution

K_α X-rays are produced when an electron makes a transition from $n=2$ to $n=1$ to fill a vacancy in K-shell. The wavelength of X-ray lines is given by

$$\frac{1}{\lambda_{K\alpha}}=(Z-1)^2\left(\frac{1}{1^2}-\frac{1}{2^2}\right)$$

$$\Rightarrow \frac{1}{\lambda_{K\alpha}}=\frac{3}{4}R(Z-1)^2$$

$$\Rightarrow (Z-1)^2=\frac{4}{3R\lambda_{K\alpha}}$$

$$\Rightarrow (Z-1)^2=\frac{4}{3\times(1.097\times10^7)\times(0.76\times10^{-10})}$$

$$=1599.25$$

$$\Rightarrow (Z-1)^2\simeq 1600$$

$$\Rightarrow Z-1=40$$

$$\Rightarrow Z=41$$

 # Illustrative Example 3.9

The K-absorption edge of an unknown element is 0.171 Å :

(a) Identify the element.

(b) Find the average wavelengths of the K_α, K_β and K_γ lines.

(c) If a 100 eV electron strike the target of this element, what is the minimum wavelength of the X-ray emitted ?

Solution

From Moseley's law, the wavelength of K series of X-rays is given by taking $\sigma=1$ in modified in Rydberg's formula given as

$$\frac{1}{\lambda}=R(Z-1)^2\left(1-\frac{1}{n^2}\right) \text{ for } K \text{ lineswhere, } n=2,3,4,\ldots$$

(a) For K-absorption edge, we put $n=\infty$, in above expression gives

$$(Z-1)=\sqrt{\frac{1}{\lambda R}}$$

$$\Rightarrow Z=\sqrt{\frac{1}{(0.171\times10^{-10})(1.097\times10^7)}}+1$$

$$\Rightarrow Z=74.$$

The element is Tungsten

(b) For K_α line :

$$\frac{1}{\lambda_{K\alpha}} = R(74-1)^2\left[1-\frac{1}{2^2}\right]$$

$$\Rightarrow \qquad \lambda_{K\alpha} = 0.228\text{ Å}$$

For K_β line :

$$\frac{1}{\lambda_{K\beta}} = R(74-1)^2\left[1-\frac{1}{3^2}\right]$$

$$\Rightarrow \qquad \lambda_{K\beta} = 0.192\text{ Å}$$

For K_γ line :

$$\frac{1}{\lambda_{K\gamma}} = R(74-1)^2\left[1-\frac{1}{4^2}\right]$$

$$\Rightarrow \qquad \lambda_{K\gamma} = 0.182\text{ Å}$$

(c) The shortest wavelength corresponding to an electron with kinetic energy 100 eV is given by

$$\lambda_c = \frac{hc}{E} = \frac{12431}{100}\text{ Å}$$

$$\Rightarrow \qquad \lambda_c = 124.31\text{ Å}$$

Illustrative Example 3.10

The K_α X-ray emission line of tungsten occurs at $\lambda = 0.21$ Å. What is the energy difference between K and L levels in this atom ?

Solution

We know that K_α line is the radiation emitted when an electron from L-shell ($n = 2$) makes a transition to K-shell ($n = 1$) to fill a vacancy in it. Thus the released photon will have an energy equal to the energy difference of L-shell and K-shell, which is given by

$$\Delta E = \frac{hc}{\lambda_{K\alpha}} = \frac{12431}{0.21}\text{ eV}$$

$$\Delta E = 59.195\text{ KeV}$$

Web Reference at www.physicsgalaxy.com

Age Group - High School Physics | Age 17-19 Years
Section - MODERN PHYSICS
Topic - X-Rays
Module Number - 1 to 13

Practice Exercise 3.1

(i) Find the energy, the frequency and the momentum of an X-ray photon of wavelength 0.10 nm.

[12.431 keV, 3×10^{18} Hz, 6.63×10^{-24} kg-m/s]

(ii) What potential difference should be applied across an X-ray tube to get X-ray of wavelength not less than 0.10 nm ? What is the maximum energy of a photon of this X-ray in joule?

[12.431 kV, 1.99×10^{-15} J]

(iii) Find the maximum potential difference which may be applied across an X-ray tube with tungsten target without emitting any characteristic K or L X-ray. The energy levels of the tungsten atom with an electron knocked out are as follows.

Cell containing vacancy	K	L	M
Energy in keV	69.5	11.3	2.3

[Less than 11.3 kV]

(iv) A free atom of iron emits K_α X-rays of energy 6.4 keV. Calculate the recoil kinetic energy of the atom. Mass of an iron atom = 9.3×10^{-20} kg.

[3.9×10^{-10} eV]

(v) Iron emits K_α X-ray of energy 3.69 keV. Calculate the times taken by an iron K_α photon and a calcium K_α photon to cross through a distance of 3 km.

[10 μs by both]

(vi) The wavelength of K_α X-ray of tungsten is 21.3 pm. It takes 11.3 keV to knock out an electron from the L shell of a tungsten atom. What should be the minimum accelerating voltage across an X-ray tube having tungsten target which allows production of K_α X-ray ?

[69.5 kV]

(vii) The energy of a silver atom with a vacancy in K shell is 25.31 keV, in L shell is 3.56 keV and in M shell is 0.530 keV higher than the energy of the atom with no vacancy. Find the frequency of K_α, K_β and L_α X-rays of silver.

[5.25×10^{18} Hz, 5.98×10^{18} Hz, 7.32×10^{17} Hz]

Advance Illustrations Videos at www.physicsgalaxy.com

Age Group - Advance Illustrations
Section - Modern Physics
Topic - Atomic and Nuclear Physics
Illustrations - 54 In-depth Illustrations Videos

* * * * *

Discussion Questions

Q3-1 In a Coolidge tube, electrons strike the target and stop inside it. Does the target get more and more negatively charged as time passes?

Q3-2 Can X-rays be used for photoelectric effect?

Q3-3 X-ray and visible light travel at the same speed in vacuum. Do they travel at the same speed in glass?

Q3-4 Characteristic X-rays may be used to identify the element from which they are coming. Can continuous X-rays be used for this purpose?

Q3-5 Is it possible that in a Coolidge tube characteristic L_α X-rays are emitted but not K_α X-rays?

Q3-6 Can L_α X-ray of one material have shorter wavelength than K_α X-ray of another?

Q3-7 Can a hydrogen atom emit characteristic X-ray?

Q3-8 Why is exposure to X-ray injurious to health but exposure to visible light is not, when both are electromagnetic waves?

Q3-9 When a Coolidge tube is operated for some time it becomes hot. Where does the heat come from ?

Q3-10 Can X-rays be polarized ?

Q3-11 In terms of biological damage, ionization does more damage when you stand in front of a very weak (low power) beam of X-ray radiation than in front of a stronger beam of red light. How does the photon concept explain this paradoxical situation?

Q3-12 Why should a radiologist be extremely cautions about X-ray doses when treating pregnant women ?

Q3-13 Does the concept of photon energy shed any light (no pun intended) on the question of why X-rays are so much more penetrating than visible light ? Explain.

Q3-14 What is the basic distinction between x-ray energy levels and ordinary energy levels ?

Q3-15 Can x-rays be emitted by hydrogen ?

Q3-16 How are x-rays produced ? Explain the origin of the line spectra and the continuous spectra. What limits the minimum size of X-ray wavelengths ?

Q3-17 When a sufficient number of visible light photons strike a piece of photographic film, the film becomes exposed. An X-ray photon is more energetic than a visible light photon. Yet, most photographic films are not exposed by the X-ray machines used at airport security checkpoints. Explain what these observations imply about the number of photons emitted by the X-ray machines.

Q3-18 The drawing shows the X-ray spectra produced by an X-ray tube when the tube is operated at two different potential differences. Explain why the characteristic lines occur at the same wavelength in the two spectra, while the cutoff wavelength λ_0 shifts to the right when a smaller voltage is used to operate the tube.

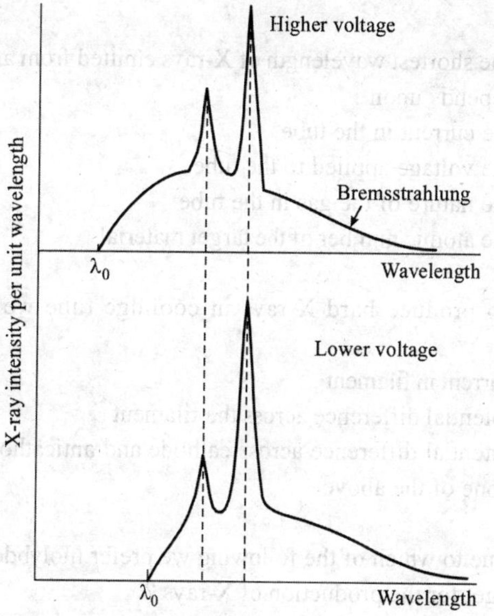

Figure 3.6

Q3-19 In the production of X-rays, it is possible to create Bremsstrahlung X-rays without producing the characteristic X-rays. Explain how this can be accomplished by adjusting the electric potential difference used to operate the X-ray tube.

Q3-20 The short wavelength side of X-ray spectra ends abruptly at a cutoff wavelength λ_0. Does this cutoff wavelength depend on the target material used in the X-ray tube > Give your reasoning.

* * * * *

Conceptual MCQs Single Option Correct

3-1 X-rays are produced when an element of high atomic weight is bombarded by high energy :
(A) Protons (B) Electrons
(C) Neutrons (D) Photons

3-2 Which of the following principle is involved in the generation of X-rays ?
(A) Conversion of kinetic energy into potential energy
(B) Conversion of mass into energy
(C) Conversion of electric energy into radiant energy
(D) Conversion of electric energy into electromagnetic waves

3-3 In X-ray tube when the accelerating voltage V is halved, the difference between the wavelengths of K_α line and minimum wavelength of continuous X-ray spectrum :
(A) Remains constant
(B) Becomes more than two times
(C) Becomes half
(D) Becomes less than two times

3-4 The shortest wavelength of X-rays emitted from an X-ray tube depends upon :
(A) The current in the tube
(B) The voltage applied to the tube
(C) The nature of the gas in the tube
(D) The atomic number of the target material

3-5 To produce hard X-rays in coolidge tube we should increase :
(A) Current in filament
(B) Potential difference across the filament
(C) Potential difference across cathode and anticathode
(D) None of the above

3-6 Due to which of the following we prefer molybdenum as the target for the production of X-rays ?
(A) Heavy element with high melting point
(B) Heavy element capable of deflecting electrons
(C) Possesses high melting point and can easily absorb the electrons
(D) High melting point and high thermal conductivity

3-7 X-rays from a given X-ray tube operating under specified conditions have a sharply defined minimum wavelength. The value of this minimum wavelength could be reduced by
(A) Increasing the temperature of the filament
(B) Increasing the potential difference between the cathode and the target
(C) Reducing the pressure in the tube
(D) Using a target material of higher relative atomic mass

3-8 With which characteristic of the target does the Mosley's law relates the frequency of X-rays ?
(A) Density (B) Atomic weight
(C) Atomic number (D) Interatomic space

3-9 X-rays are produced in an X-ray tube operating at a given accelerating voltage. The wavelength of the continuous X-rays has values from :
(A) 0 to ∞
(B) λ_{min} to ∞ where $\lambda_{min} > 0$
(C) 0 to λ_{max} where $\lambda_{max} < \infty$
(D) λ_{min} to λ_{max} where $0 < \lambda_{min} < \lambda_{max} < \infty$

3-10 The wavelength of K_α X-rays for lead isotopes Pb^{208}, Pb^{206}, Pb^{204} are λ_1, λ_2 are λ_3 respectively. Then :
(A) $\lambda_1 = \lambda_2 = \lambda_3$ (B) $\lambda_1 > \lambda_2 > \lambda_3$
(C) $\lambda_1 < \lambda_2 < \lambda_3$ (D) $\lambda_2 = \sqrt{\lambda_1 \lambda_3}$

3-11 X-rays of frequency ν are used to irradiate sodium and copper surface in two separate experiments and the stopping potential determined. Then :
(A) The stopping potential is more for copper than for sodium
(B) The stopping potential is more for sodium than for copper
(C) The stopping potential is the same for sodium and copper
(D) The stopping potential for both will vary as $1/\nu$

3-12 Increase in which of the following increases the penetrating power of the X-rays ?
(A) Intensity (B) Frequency
(C) Wavelength (D) Velocity

3-13 Which of the following are the characteristics required for the target to produce X-rays ?

	Melting point	Atomic number
(A)	High	Low
(B)	High	High
(C)	Low	Low
(D)	Low	High

3-14 The continuous X-ray spectrum is produced due to :
(A) Acceleration of electrons towards the nuclei of the target atoms
(B) Retardation of energetic electrons when they approach the nuclei of the target atoms
(C) Fall of the electrons of the target atoms from higher energy level to lower energy levels
(D) Knocking out of the electrons from the target atoms by the fast moving incident electrons

3-15 X-rays will not show the phenomenon of
(A) Diffraction
(B) Polarization
(C) Deflection by electric field
(D) Interference

3-16 An X-ray photon of wavelength λ and frequency ν collides with an electron and bounces off. If λ' and ν' are respectively the wavelength and frequency of the scattered photon, then :
(A) $\lambda' = \lambda;\ \nu' = \nu$
(B) $\lambda' < \lambda;\ \nu' > \nu$
(C) $\lambda' > \lambda;\ \nu' > \nu$
(D) $\lambda' > \lambda;\ \nu' < \nu$

3-17 Why do we not use X-rays in the RADAR ?
(A) They can damage the target
(B) They are absorbed by the air
(C) Their speed is low
(D) They are not reflected by the target

3-18 In an X-ray tube, electrons accelerated through a very high potential difference strike a metal target. If the potential difference is increased, the speed of the emitted X-rays :
(A) Increases
(B) Decreases
(C) Remains unchanged
(D) Is always equal to $3 \times 10^8\ \text{ms}^{-1}$ in space

3-19 In electromagnetic spectrum X-ray region lies between :
(A) Visible and short radio waves
(B) Ultraviolet and visible region
(C) Gamma rays and ultraviolet region
(D) Short radio waves and long radio waves

3-20 A direct X-ray photograph of the intestines is not generally taken by the radiologists because :
(A) Intestines would burst on exposure to X-rays
(B) The X-rays would not pass through the intestines
(C) The X-rays would pass through the intestines without casting a good shadow for any useful diagnosis
(D) A very small exposure of X-rays causes cancer in the intestines

3-21 Hydrogen atom does not emit X-rays because:
(A) Its energy levels are too close to each other
(B) Its energy levels are too far apart
(C) It is too small in size
(D) It has a single electrons

3-22 X-rays passing through a strong uniform magnetic field :
(A) Get deflected along the direction of field
(B) Get deflected opposite to the direction of field
(C) Get deflected perpendicular to the direction of field
(D) Do not get deflected at all

3-23 White X-rays are called '*white*' due to the fact that :
(A) they are electromagnetic radiations having nature same as that of white light
(B) they are produced most abundantly in X-ray tubes
(C) they have a continuous wavelength range
(D) they can be converted to visible light using coated screens and photographic plates are affected by them just like light

3-24 In the X-ray tube before striking the target we accelerate the electrons through a potential difference of V volt. For which of the following value of V, we will have X-rays of largest wavelength ?
(A) 10kV
(B) 20kV
(C) 30kV
(D) 40kV

3-25 In a characteristic X-ray spectra of some atom superimposed on continuous X-ray spectra :

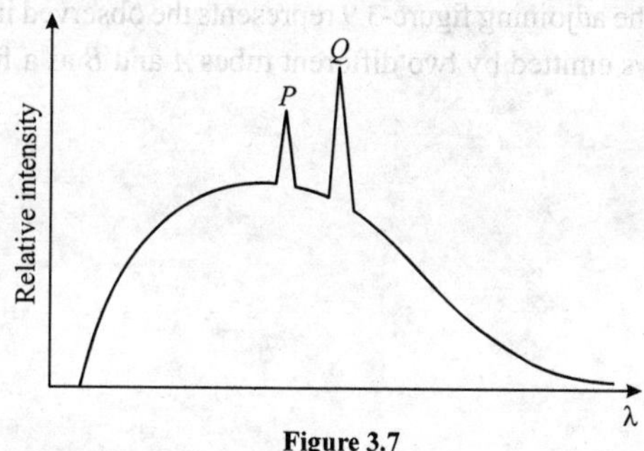

Figure 3.7

(A) P represents K_α line
(B) Q represents K_β line
(C) Q and P represent K_α and K_β lines respectively
(D) Position of K_α and K_β depend on the particular atom

3-26 Mosley's law for characteristic X-rays is

$$\frac{1}{\lambda} = R\,(Z-b)^2\left(\frac{1}{n_1^2}-\frac{1}{n_2^2}\right)$$

Which of the following statements is/are correct ?
(A) It is applicable to all those atoms to which Bohr's theory is not applicable
(B) It is applicable to all energy levels of some atoms only
(C) It can not be applied for higher values of n_1 and n_2
(D) It can not be applied for higher values of Z

3-27 For the structural analysis of various lattice, X-rays are used because :
(A) X-rays have wavelength of the order of the interatomic spacing
(B) X-rays are highly penetrating radiations
(C) Wavelength of X-rays is of the order of nuclear size
(D) X-rays are coherent radiations

3-28 The intensity of X-rays from a Coolidge tube is plotted against wavelength λ as shown in figure-3.8. The minimum wavelength as found is λ_C and the wavelength of the K_α-line is λ_K. As the accelerating voltage is increased :

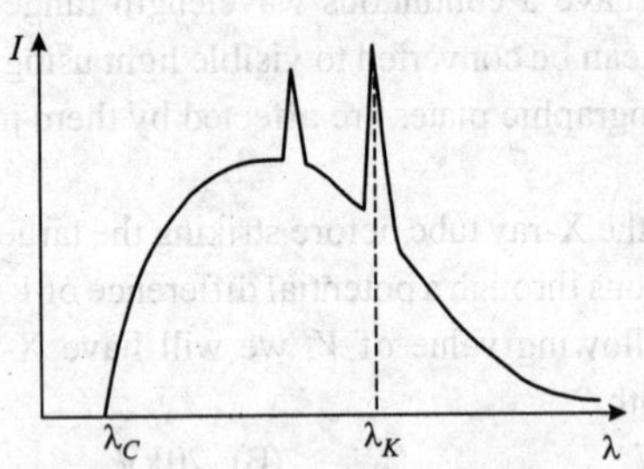

Figure 3.8

(A) $(\lambda_K - \lambda_C)$ increases (B) $(\lambda_K - \lambda_C)$ decreases
(C) λ_K increases (D) λ_K decreases

3-29 The adjoining figure-3.9 represents the observed intensity of X-rays emitted by two different tubes A and B as a function of wavelength λ. For the tube A, the potential difference between the filament and target is V_A and atomic number of target is Z_A. For the tube B, corresponding potential difference is V_B and the atomic number is Z_B. The solid curve is for tube A and dotted curve for tube B; then :

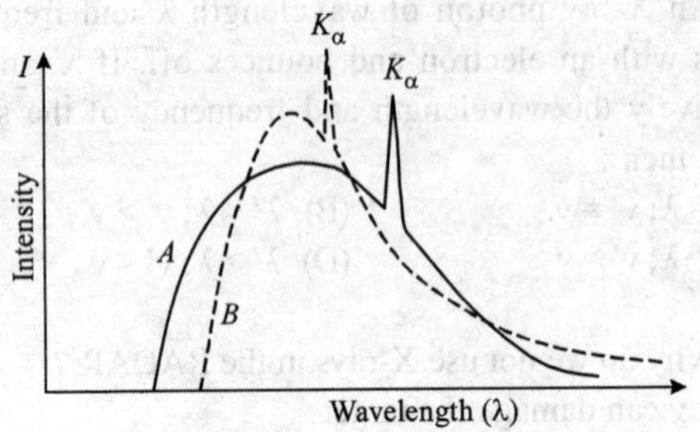

Figure 3.9

(A) $Z_A > Z_B$; $V_A > V_B$ (B) $Z_A = Z_B$; $V_A = V_B$
(C) $Z_A < Z_B$; $V_A < V_B$ (D) $Z_A < Z_B$; $V_A > V_B$

* * * * *

Numerical MCQs Single Option Correct

3-1 The binding energy of the innermost electron in tungsten is 40 keV. To produce K series characteristic X-rays using a tungsten target in an X-ray tube, the accelerating voltage should be greater than :
(A) 4kV (B) 40kV
(C) 400kV (D) 4000kV

3-2 When a beam of accelerated electrons hits a target, continuous X-ray spectrum is emitted from the target. Which one of the following wavelength is absent in the X-ray spectrum if the X-rays tube is operated at 40,000 V ?
(A) 1.5 Å (B) 0.5 Å
(C) 0.25 Å (D) 1.0 Å

3-3 Electrons with energy 80 keV are incident on the tungsten target of an X-ray tube. K shell electrons of tungsten have –71.5 keV energy. X-rays emitted by the tube contain :
(A) A continuous X-ray spectrum (Bremsstrahlung) with a minimum wavelength of about 0.155 Å
(B) A continuous X-ray spectrum (Bremsstrahlung) with all wavelengths
(C) The characteristic X-ray spectrum of tungsten
(D) A continuous X-ray spectrum (Bremsstrahlung) with a minimum wavelength of about 0.155 Å and the characteristics X-ray spectrum of tungsten

3-4 The wavelength of the K_α line for an element of atomic number 57 is λ. What is the wavelength of the K_α line for the element of atomic number 29 ?
(A) λ (B) 2λ
(C) 4λ (D) 8λ

3-5 An X-ray tube is working at potential of 20 kV. The potential difference is decreased to 10 kV. It is found that the difference of the wavelength of K_α X-ray and the most energetic continuous X-ray becomes 4 times the difference before the change of voltage. Find the atomic number of the target element.

[Take $b = 1$ and $\frac{1}{\sqrt{3.4}} = 0.54$]

(A) 28 (B) 55
(C) 56 (D) None of these

3-6 An X-ray tube operates at 50 kV. Consider that at each collision, an electron converts 50% of its energy into photons and 10% energy would be dissipated as thermal energy due to the collision, then the wavelength of emitted photons during 2nd collision is: [Take $hc = 1242$ eV-nm]
(A) 1.242 nm (B) 1.242 Å
(C) 4.968 nm (D) 4.968 Å

3-7 In a discharge tube when 200 V potential difference is applied 6.25×10^{18} electrons move from cathode to anode and 3.125×10^{18} singly charged positive ions move from anode to cathode in one second. Then the power of tube is :
(A) 100 watt (B) 200 watt
(C) 300 watt (D) 400 watt

3-8 Figure shows K_α & K_β X-rays along with continuous X-ray. Find the energy of L_α X-ray. (Use $hc = 12431$ eVÅ)

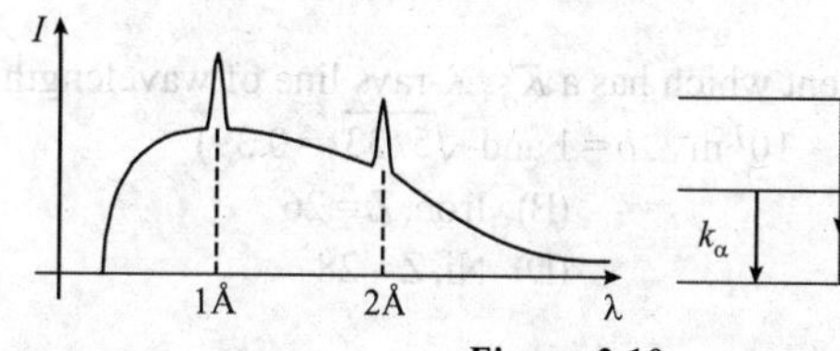

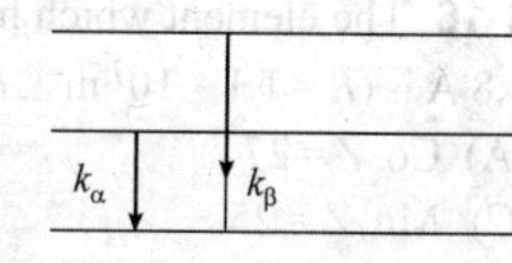

Figure 3.10

(A) 3.10 KeV (B) 4.63 KeV
(C) 6.21 KeV (D) 8.42 KeV

3-9 The wavelength of K_α line from an element of atomic number 51 is λ. From another element the wavelength of K_α line is 4λ. What is the atomic number of the second element ?
(A) 25 (B) 26
(C) 100 (D) 99

3-10 The minimum wavelength of X-rays produced in an X-ray tube is λ when the operating voltage is V. What is the minimum wavelength of the X-rays when the operating voltage is $V/2$?
(A) $\frac{\lambda}{2}$ (B) λ
(C) 2λ (D) 4λ

3-11 An X-ray tube with copper ($Z = 29$) being used as a target is found to be emitting lines other than those due to copper due to some mixed impurity in the metal. The K_α line of copper has a wavelength 1.5405 Å and other K_α line observed in spectrum has wavelength 0.7092Å. The impurity is likely :
(A) Molybdenum ($Z = 42$) (B) Nickel ($Z = 28$)
(C) Lead ($Z = 82$) (D) Zinc ($Z = 30$)

3-12 The voltage applied to an X-ray tube is 18 kV. The maximum mass of photon emitted by the X-ray tube will be :
(A) 2×10^{-13} kg (B) 3.2×10^{-36} kg
(C) 3.2×10^{-32} kg (D) 9.1×10^{-31} kg

3-13 The battery connected across a coolidge tube operates at a power level of 1W when the no. of electrons hitting the target in 1 second is 6.25×10^{13}. Find the minimum wavelength in the resulting X-rays spectrum :
(A) 0.06A (B) 0.12A
(C) 0.18A (D) 0.24A

3-14 The wavelength of characteristic X-ray K_α line emitted by hydrogen line atom is 0.32 Å. The wavelength of K_β line emitted by the same element is :
(A) 0.18 Å (B) 0.27 Å
(C) 0.38 Å (D) 0.48 Å

3-15 An X-ray tube produces a continuous spectrum of radiation with its short-wavelength end at 0.33 Å. What is the maximum energy of a photon in the radiation ?
(A) 35.3 keV (B) 37.6 keV
(C) 40.4 keV (D) 42.5 keV

3-16 The element which has a K_α X-rays line of wavelength 1.8 Å is ($R = 1.1 \times 10^7\ \text{m}^{-1}$, $b = 1$ and $\sqrt{5/33} = 0.39$)
(A) Co, Z = 27 (B) Iron, Z = 26
(C) Mn, Z = 25 (D) Ni, Z = 28

3-17 In a coolidge tube, the tungsten (Z = 74) target is bombarded by electrons. What is the minimum value of the accelerating potential to enable emission of characteristic K_α and K_β lines of tungsten. (The K, L & M levels of tungsten have Binding energies of 69.5, 11.3 & 2.30 keV respectively)
(A) 2.3 keV (B) 1.3 keV
(C) 69.5 keV (D) 72 keV

3-18 The potential difference across the Coolidge tube is 20 kV and 10 mA current flows through the voltage supply. Only 0.5% of the energy carried by the electrons striking the target is converted into X-rays. The power carried by X-ray beam is P.
(A) $P = 0.1$ W (B) $P = 1$ W
(C) $P = 2$ W (D) $P = 10$ W

3-19 When the accelerating voltage applied on the electrons, in an X-ray tube, is increased beyond a critical value :
(A) The spectrum of white radiation is unaffected
(B) Only the intensities of various wavelengths are increased
(C) Only the wavelength of characteristic radiation is affected
(D) The intensities of characteristic lines relative to the white spectrum are increased but there is no change in their wavelength

3-20 The wavelengths of K_α X-rays of two metals 'A' and 'B' are $\frac{4}{1875R}$ and $\frac{1}{675R}$ respectively, where 'R' is rydberg constant. The number of elements lying between 'A' and 'B' according to their atomic numbers is :
(A) 3 (B) 6
(C) 5 (D) 4

3-21 A cobalt (atomic no. = 27) target is bombarded with electrons, and the wavelengths of its characteristic X-ray spectrum are measured. A second weak characteristic spectrum is also found, due to an impurity in the target. The wavelengths of the K_α lines are 225.0 pm (cobalt) and 100.0 pm (impurity). Atomic number of the impurity is : (Take $b = 1$)
(A) 39 (B) 40
(C) 59 (D) 60

3-22 An X-ray tube is operated at 66 kV. Then, in the continuous spectrum of the emitted X-rays :
(A) Wavelengths 0.01 nm and 0.02 nm will both be present
(B) Wavelengths 0.01 nm and 0.02 nm will both be absent
(C) Wavelengths 0.01 nm will be present but wavelength 0.02 nm will be absent
(D) Wavelength 0.01 nm will be absent but wavelength 0.02 nm will be present

3-23 An X-ray tube is operating at 150 kV and 10 mA. If only 1% of the electric power supplied is converted into X-rays, the approximate rate at which the target is heated in calories per second is :
(A) 3.55 (B) 35.5
(C) 355 (D) 3550

3-24 The potential difference applied to an X-ray tube is 5 kV and the current through it is 3.2 mA. The number of electrons striking the target per second is :
(A) 2×10^{16} (B) 5×10^6
(C) 1×10^{17} (D) 4×10^{15}

3-25 A metal block is exposed to beam of X-rays of different wavelengths. X-rays of which wavelength penetrates most ?
(A) 2 Å (B) 4 Å
(C) 6 Å (D) 8 Å

3-26 The energy ratio of two K_α photons obtained in X-ray from two metal targets of atomic numbers Z_1 and Z_2 is :
(A) $\frac{Z_1}{Z_2}$ (B) $\left(\frac{Z_1}{Z_2}\right)^2$
(C) $\left(\frac{Z_1 - 1}{Z_2 - 1}\right)^2$ (D) $\sqrt{\frac{(Z_1 - 1)}{(Z_2 - 1)}}$

* * * * *

Advance MCQs with One or More Options Correct

3-1 Which of the following pairs constitute very similar radiations ?
(A) Hard ultraviolet rays and soft X-rays
(B) Soft ultraviolet rays and hard X-rays
(C) Very had X-rays and low-frequency γ-rays
(D) Soft X-rays and γ-rays

3-2 Let λ_α, λ_β and λ'_α denote the wavelengths of the X-rays of the K_α, K_β and L_α lines in the characteristic X-rays for a metal :
(A) $\lambda'_\alpha > \lambda_\alpha > \lambda_\beta$ (B) $\lambda'_\alpha > \lambda_\beta > \lambda_\alpha$
(C) $\frac{1}{\lambda_\beta} = \infty$ (D) $\frac{1}{\lambda_\alpha} + \frac{1}{\lambda_\beta} = \frac{1}{\lambda'_\alpha}$

3-3 Two electrons starting from rest are accelerated by equal potential difference :
(A) They will have same kinetic energy
(B) They will have same linear momentum
(C) They will have same de Broglie wave length
(D) They will produce X-rays of same minimum wave length when they strike different targets.

3-4 When an electron moving at a high speed strikes a metal surface, which of the following are possible ?
(A) The entire energy of the electron may be converted into an X-ray photon.
(B) Any fraction of the energy of the electron may be converted into an X-ray photon
(C) The entire energy of the electron may get converted to heat
(D) The electron may undergo elastic collision with the metal surface

3-5 Mark correct statement(s) :
(A) circumference of orbit of an electron in Bohr's model is equal to an integer multiple of de-Broglie wavelength of the electron
(B) Kinetic energy of electron increases with increase of principle quantum number
(C) when an X-ray photon is emitted, only energy conservation law is satisfied
(D) none of these

3-6 In an X-ray tube the voltage applied is 20 KV. The energy required to remove an electron from L shell is 19.9 KeV. In the X-rays emitted by the tube : (Take $hc = 12420$ eVÅ)
(A) Minimum wavelength will be 62.1 pm
(B) Energy of the characteristic X-rays will be equal to or less than 19.9 KeV
(C) L_α X-ray may be emitted
(D) L_α X-ray will have energy 19.9 KeV

3-7 Choose the correct statement :
(A) Energy of an atom with K shell electron knocked out is more than the energy of an atom with L shell electron knocked out.
(B) Energy of an atom with L shell electron knocked out is more than energy of an atom with K shell electron knocked out.
(C) Energy of K_β photon is the sum of the energies of an L_α and K_α photon.
(D) Total energy emitted in from of K_α photons is more than the total energy emitted in from of K_β photon from an X-ray setup.

3-8 In a Coolidge tube experiment, the minimum wavelength of the continuous X-ray spectrum is equal to 66.3 pm, then
(A) electrons accelerate through a potential difference of about 12.75 kV in the Coolidge tube
(B) electrons accelerate through a potential difference of about 18.75 kV in the Coolidge tube
(C) de-Broglie wavelength of the electrons reaching the anticathode is of the order of 10 mm
(D) de-Broglie wavelength of the electrons reaching the anticathode is 0.01 Å

3-9 The potential difference applied to an X-ray tube is increased. As a result, in the emitted radiation
(A) the intensity increases
(B) the minimum wavelength increases
(C) the intensity decreases
(D) the minimum wavelength decreases

3-10 A beam of electrons striking a copper target produces X-rays. Its spectrum is as shown. Keeping the voltage same if the copper target is replaced with a different metal, the cutoff wavelength and characteristic lines of the new spectrum will change in comparison with old as :

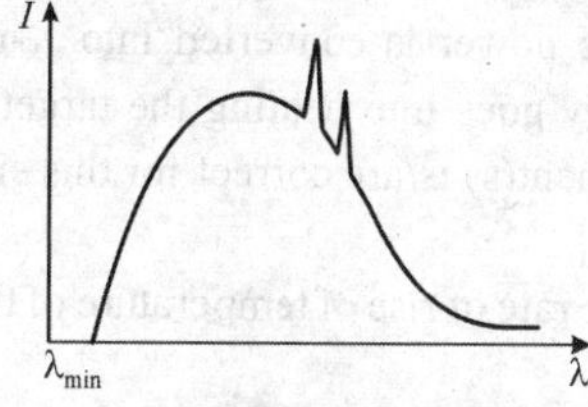

Figure 3.11

(A) Cutoff wavelength may remain unchanged while characteristic lines may be different.
(B) Both cutoff wavelength and characteristic lines may remain unchanged.
(C) Both cutoff wavelength and characteristic lines may be different.
(D) Cutoff wavelength will be different while characteristic lines may remain unchanged.

3-11 Which of the following statements is/are correct for an X-ray tube ?

(A) on increasing potential difference between filament and target, photon flux of X-rays increases

(B) on increasing potential difference between filament and target, frequency of X-rays increases

(C) on increasing filament current, cut off wavelength increases

(D) on increasing filament current, intensity of X-rays increases

3-12 The intensity of X-rays from a coolidge tube is plotted against wavelength λ as shown in the figure-3.12. Which of the following statements is/are correct :

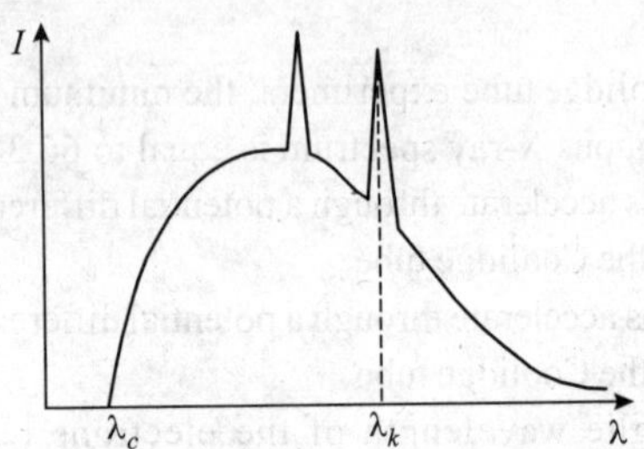

Figure 3.12

(A) On increasing the Z (atomic number) of target λ_k decreases

(B) On increasing the accelerating voltage of tube $\lambda_k - \lambda_c$ increases

(C) On increasing the power of cathode, I_0 increases

(D) On increasing the power of cathode, λ_k decreases

3-13 For a given material, the energy and wavelength of characteristic X-ray satisfy :

(A) $E(K_\alpha) > E(K_\beta) > E(K_\gamma)$ (B) $E(M_\alpha) > E(L_\alpha) > E(K_\alpha)$

(C) $\lambda(K_\alpha) > \lambda(K_\beta) > \lambda(K_\gamma)$ (D) $\lambda(M_\alpha) > \lambda(L_\alpha) > \lambda(K_\alpha)$

3-14 An X-ray tube is operating at 50 kV voltage and operating current 20 mA. The target material of the tube has a mass of 1.0 kg and specific heat 495 J kg^{-1} °C^{-1}. One percent of the supplied electric power is converted into X-rays and entire remaining energy goes into heating the target. Which of the following statement(s) is/are correct for this situation : [Take $hc = 12400$ eV-Å]

(A) The average rate of rise of temperature of the target would be 2°C/s

(B) The minimum wavelength of the X-rays emitted is about 0.25×10^{-10} m

(C) A suitable target material must have a low melting temperature

(D) A suitable target material must have low thermal conductivity

3-15 X-ray incident on a material :

(A) Exerts a force on it

(B) Transfer energy to it

(C) Transfers momentum to it

(D) Transfers impulse to it

3-16 Regarding X-ray spectrum, which of the following statements is are correct :

(A) The characteristic X-ray spectrum is emitted due to excitation of inner electrons of atom

(B) Wavelength of characteristic spectrum depend on potential difference across the tube

(C) Wavelength of continuous spectrum is dependent on the potential difference across tube

(D) None of these

3-17 Which of the following statements is/are false ?

(A) The energy of photo electrons emitted from a given metal by soft X-rays have less energy than those emitted by hard X-rays

(B) To increase the intensity of X-rays, the filament current should be increased

(C) The characteristic X-rays have continuous range of wavelengths

(D) X-rays were named so because of their mysterious nature at the time of discovery

3-18 Which of the following statements is/are true ?

(A) The wavelength of soft X-rays is less than that of hard X-rays

(B) X-rays are produced during acceleration of electrons

(C) The anticathode is a metal of low atomic weight

(D) The wavelength of the characteristic X-rays depends upon the nature of the metal of the target

* * * * *

Unsolved Numerical Problems for Preparation of NSEP, INPhO & IPhO

For detailed preparation of INPhO and IPhO students can refer advance study material on www.physicsgalaxy.com

3-1 The X-ray coming from a Coolidge tube has a cutoff wavelength of 80 pm. Find the kinetic energy of the electrons hitting the target.

Ans. [15.5 keV]

3-2 If the operating potential in an X-ray tube is increased by 1% by what percentage does the cutoff wavelength decrease ?

Ans. [Approximately 1%]

3-3 The distance between the cathode (filament) and the target in an X-ray tube is 1.5 m. If the cutoff wavelength is 30 pm, find the electric field between the cathode and the target.

Ans. [27.7 kV/m]

3-4 The short-wavelength limit shifts by 26 pm when the operating voltage in an X-ray tube is increased to 1.5 times the original value. What was the original approximate value of the operating voltage ?

Ans. [15.9 kV]

3-5 The electron beam in a colour TV is accelerated through 32 kV and then strikes the screen. What is the wavelength of the most energetic X-ray photon?

Ans. [38.8 pm]

3-6 When 40 kV is applied across an X-ray tube, X-ray is obtained with a maximum frequency of 9.7×10^{18} Hz. Calculate he value of Planck constant from these date.

Ans. [4.12×10^{-15} eV–s]

3-7 The K_β X-ray of argon has a wavelength of 0.36 nm. The minimum energy needed to ionize an argon atom is 16 eV. Find the energy needed to knock out an electron from the *K* shell of an argon atom.

Ans. [3.47 keV]

3-8 An X-ray tube operates at 40 kV. Suppose the electron converts 70% of its energy into a photon at each collision. Find the lowest three wavelength emitted from the tube. Neglect the energy imparted to the atom with which the electron collides.

Ans. [44.3 pm, 148 pm, 493 pm]

3-9 The K_α X-rays of molybdenum has wavelength 71 pm. If the energy of a molybdenum atom with a *K* electron knocked out is 23.32 keV, what will be the energy of this atom when an *L* electron is knock out ? In *eV*.

Ans. [5.82 keV]

3-10 The electric current in an X-ray tube (from the target to the filament) operating at 40 kV is 10 mA. Assume that on an average, 1% of the total kinetic energy of the electrons hitting the target are converted into X-ray. (a) What is the total power emitted as X-rays and (b) how much heat is produced in the target every second ?

Ans. [(a) 4 W (b) 396 J]

3-11 The K_α X-rays of aluminium ($Z = 13$) and zinc ($Z = 30$) have wavelengths 887 pm and 146 pm respectively. Use Moseley's law $\sqrt{v} = a(Z - b)$ to find the wavelength of the K_α X-ray of iron ($Z = 26$).

Ans. [198 pm]

3-12 A certain element emits K_α X-ray of energy 3.69 keV. Use the data from the previous problem to identify the element.

Ans. [Calcium]

3-13 The K_β X-ray from certain elements are given below. Draw a Moseley-type plot of $\sqrt{v}$ versus Z for K_β radiation.

Element	Ne	P	Ca	Mn	Zn	Br
Energy (keV)	0.858	2.14	4.02	6.51	9.57	13.3

3-14 Use Moseley's law with $b = 1$ to find the frequency of the K_α X-ray of La ($Z = 57$) if the frequency of the K_α X-ray of Cu ($Z = 57$) is known to be 1.88×10^{18} Hz.

Ans. [7.52×10^{18} Hz]

3-15 The K_α and K_β X-rays of molybdenum have wavelengths 0.71 Å and 0.63 Å respectively. Find the wavelength of L_α X-ray of molybdenum.

Ans. [5.64 Å]

3-16 The wavelengths of K_α and L_α X-rays of a material are 21.3 pm and 141 pm respectively. Find the wavelength of K_β X-ray of the material.

Ans. [18.5 pm]

3-17 Heat at the rate of 200 W is produced in an X-ray tube operating at 20 kV. Find the current in the circuit. Assume that only a small fraction of the kinetic energy of electrons is converted into X-rays.

Ans. [10 mA]

3-18 In a Coolidge tube, the potential difference used to accelerate the electron is increased from 12.4 kV to 24.8 kV. As a result, the difference between the wavelength of K_α line and minimum wavelength becomes thrice. Calculate the wavelength of the K_α line. [Take $hc = 12.4$ keV–Å)]

Ans. [1.25 Å]

3-19 Suppose a monochromatic X-ray beam of wavelength 10 pm is sent through a Young's double slit and the interference pattern is observed on a photographic plate placed 40 cm away from the slit. What should be the separation between the slits so that the successive maxima on the screen are separated by a distance of 0.1 mm ?

Ans. [4×10^{-7} m]

3-20 Moseley plot for K_α X-ray is shown in figure-3.13 below. The Moseley equation is given by $\sqrt{f} = a(Z-b)$. Calculate the constants a and b.

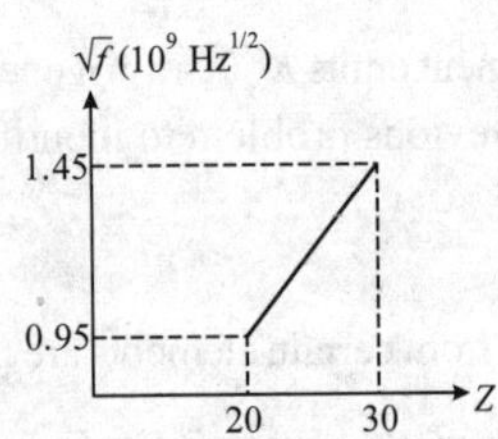

Figure 3.13

Ans. [$a = 5 \times 10^8$ Hz$^{1/2}$, $b = 1$]

3-21 A potential difference of 20 KV is applied across an X-ray tube. The minimum wave length of X-rays generated is ....

Ans. [41]

3-22 Characteristic X-rays of frequency 4.2×10^{18} Hz are emitted from a metal due to transition from L - to K-shell. Find the atomic number of the metal using Moseley's law. Take Rydberg constant $R = 1.1 \times 10^7$ m^{-1}.

Ans. [42]

3-23 An X-ray tube is operated at 20 kV and the current through the tube is 0.5 mA. Find the total energy falling on the target per second as the kinetic energy of the electrons in J.

Ans. [10]

* * * * *

Nuclear Physics and Radioactivity

4

FEW WORDS FOR STUDENTS

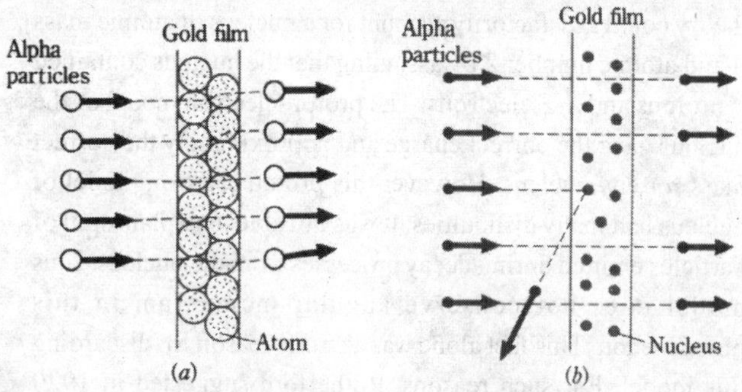

In preceding chapters we have discussed about structure of an atom and different experiments involving properties of atomic structure. Now we consider the composition and properties of the atomic nucleus. In this chapter we will discuss about the forces holding the nuclear matter within the nucleus, the nucleus and the nuclear structure. We next examine the condition of nuclear stability and the natural radioactive processes of alpha, beta and gamma decay. Finally we consider nuclear reactions and the energy involved in these reactions.

CHAPTER CONTENTS

COVER APPLICATION

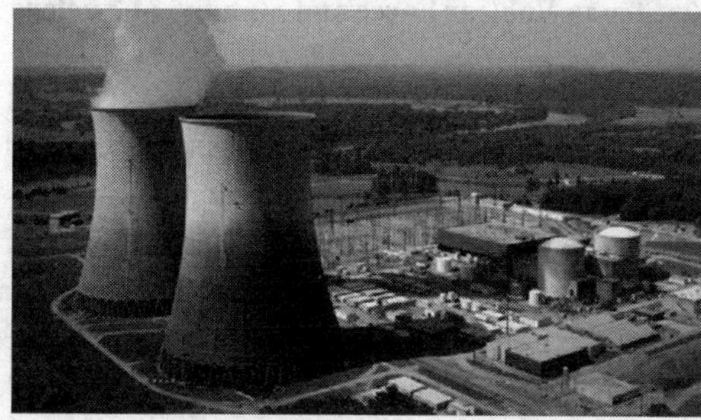

Figure (a)

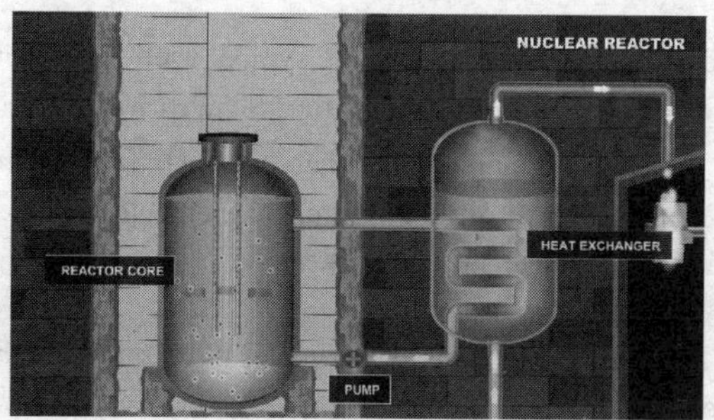

Figure (b)

Nuclear reactors are today major source of power across the globe. Figure-(a) shows a specific nuclear power plant in which power generation is done by nuclear reactors. Figure-(b) shows the internal block diagram of a nuclear reactor.

After Rutherford's discovery of the nucleus in 1911, scientists slowly realized that the nucleus must be made of smaller constituent parts. Earlier it was proposed that the nuclei of atoms heavier then hydrogen consisted of hydrogen nuclei, called protons, and electrons. The protons would provide the mass and positive charge and electrons which were presumed to be in the nucleus, would neutralize some of the charge. This theory could satisfactorily account for a nucleus of atomic mass A and atomic number Z by assuming that the nucleus contained A protons and A-Z electrons. The proton-electron model of the nucleus gave the correct charge and approximately the correct mass for any nucleus. However this proton electron model of nucleus had many difficulties. It was not able to explain spin of particles emitted during decay processes from the nucleus. This model does not conserve angular momentum in this phenomenon. This fact alone was a strong reason for discarding this model. For such reasons, Rutherford suggested in 1920 that the nucleus should contain a neutral particle of same mass as that of proton but not able to prove practically. Later in 1932 James Chadwick demonstrate the existence of such a neutral particle in his experiments. This particle was given the name neutron.

Now we'll discuss the fundamental properties of nucleus having protons and neutrons are the major constituents.

4.1 Composition and Structure of The Nucleus

Because protons and neutrons both appear in the nucleus, they are collectively called nucleons. According to today's accepted proton-neutron model of the nucleus, the number of protons in a nucleus is called atomic number of the element Z, and the number of protons plus the number of neutrons is called mass number of the element A. Some times A is also called nucleon number. A shorthand notation is often used to specify Z and A along with the chemical symbol for the element. It is generally written as

$${}_{Z}^{A}\mathrm{X} \quad \text{or} \quad {}_{Z}\mathrm{X}^{A}$$

Similarly in nuclear reactions the symbol used for a proton is ${}_{1}^{1}\mathrm{p}$ or ${}_{1}^{1}\mathrm{H}$. A neutron is denoted by ${}_{0}^{1}\mathrm{n}$. In case of electron we use ${}_{-1}^{0}\mathrm{e}$ (It has 0 mass and its charge is – 1). Some particular names are given to different group of elements having some similarity in nuclear structure. These are

(1) Isotopes : Elements those nuclei have same number of protons but different number of neutrons, are known as isotopes. Thus isotopes have same Z, but different A. Isotopes of same elements have same chemical properties because they have the same number and arrangement of electrons.

(2) Isobars : Elements having same mass numbers and different atomic numbers are called isobars. Thus isobars have same A, but different Z.

(3) Isotones : The elements which have same number of neutrons are called isotones. Thus isotones have same (A-Z).

(4) Isodiaphers : Those elements which have same difference in neutrons and protons are called Isodiaphers. Thus in isodiaphers (A-$2Z$) is same and this value (A-$2Z$) is called isotopic number of the element.

4.1.1 Size of a Nucleus

The Rutherford scattering experiment provided the first estimates of nuclear sizes. At that time a variety of experiments have been performed to calculate the nuclear dimensions. It was found that the volume of a nucleus is directly proportional to the number of nucleons in it. Thus it can be said that the density of nucleons is approximately same in the interiors of all nuclei.

If a nucleus is of radius R, its volume is $\frac{4}{3}\pi R^3$, thus here R^3 is directly proportional to the number of nucleons or mass member A of the element. Hence we have

$$R^3 \propto A$$

or $$R \propto A^{1/3}$$

or $$R = R_0 A^{1/3} \qquad \ldots(4.1)$$

Here R_0 is named fermi constant and its value is given as

$$R_0 \simeq 1.2 \times 10^{-15} \simeq 1.2 \text{ fm} \qquad \ldots(4.2)$$

As nuclei do not have sharp boundaries, the value of R_0 may also have slight deviations from its value given by equation-(4.2).

4.1.2 Strong Nuclear Force and Stability of Nucleus

We've discussed that inside a nucleus in a very small volume nucleons are bounded together. The positively charged protons inside the nucleus repel one another with a very strong electrostatic force. It is surprising that due to such a large repulsive force what keeps the nucleus from flying apart ? It is clear that there must be some kind of attractive force which hold the nucleons together as many atoms contain stable nuclei. The gravitational force of attraction between nucleons is two weak to counteract the repulsive electric force, so we can say that a different type of force must hold the nucleus together.

This force is strong nuclear force and is one of the four fundamental forces of nature.

The most important feature of the strong nuclear force is it is independent of electric charge. At a given separation between nucleons, approximately some nuclear force of attraction exist between two protons, two neutrons or between a proton and a neutron. The range of action of the strong nuclear force is extremely short. When two nucleons are very close at separation of the order of about 10^{-15} m, the nuclear force of attraction between the two is very large and almost zero for large separations. For electric force we already know that the range of action of electric force is very large. The electric force between two charges is very large at close separation and decreases to zero gradually as separation increases to very large values.

The very short range of strong nuclear force plays an important role in stability of nucleus. For a nucleus to be stable, the electrostatic repulsion between protons must be balanced by the attraction between nucleons due to strong nuclear force.

Inside a nucleus one protons repel all other protons. Since the electrostatic force has a long range of action. But a proton or a neutron due to strong nuclear force attracts only its nearest neighbours, thus in a large sized nucleus to counter balance the repulsive force more number of neutrons are required to maintain the stability of nucleus.

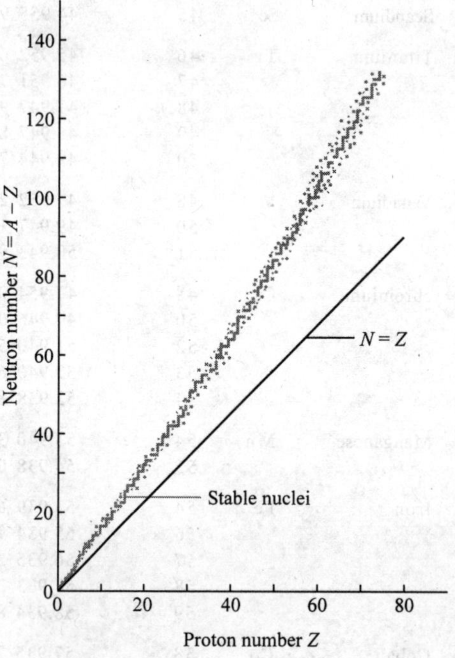

Figure 4.1

We can see that in the graph shown in figure-4.1 almost all points representing stable nuclei fall above the straight line $N = Z$, reflecting that the number of neutrons are greater then number of protons.

In very heavy nuclei as number of protons are large, there comes a point when balance of repulsive and attractive forces can not be achieved by an increased number of neutrons. For heavy nuclei, the size is also large and due to the limited range of strong nuclear force, extra neutrons in the nucleus cannot balance the long range electric repulsion of extra protons. In nature the stable nucleus with the largest number of protons is Bismuth $^{209}_{83}\text{Bi}$ which contains 83 protons and 126 neutrons. All nuclei above bismuth in nature are unstable due to unbalanced internal force and spontaneously break apart or rearrange the internal structure of nucleus. This phenomenon of spontaneous disintegration or rearrangement in internal structure of nucleus is called radioactivity. This phenomenon was first discovered by Henri Becquerel in 1896. In later part of this chapter we'll discuss radioactivity in detail.

4.2 Nuclear Binding Energy

We've discussed that in a stable nucleus, because of strong nuclear force of attraction, the nucleons are held tightly together in a small volume. As system is stable we can relatively say that the total potential energy of system is negative and to separate all the nucleons from each other some energy must be supplied to break the nucleus. The more stable the nucleus is, the greater is the energy needed to break it apart. This required energy, we call binding energy of the nucleus.

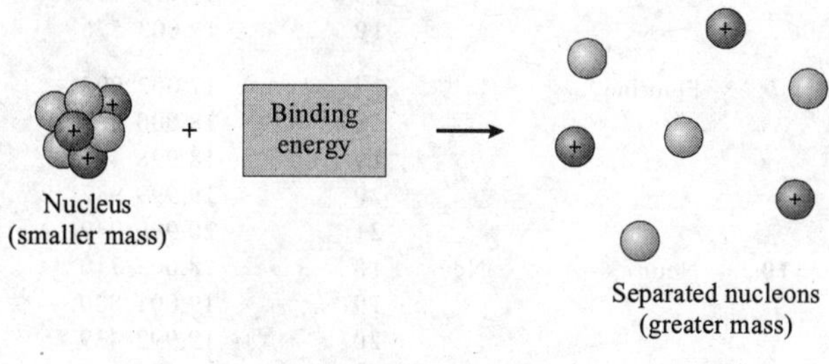

Figure 4.2

The origin of binding energy can be easily explained if we look into the masses of different elements in table-4.1. In nuclear physics, mass of atoms and nuclei are often measured in atomic mass unit (amu).

We can see clearly from the data given in table-4.1 that the mass of each element atom is less then the sum of masses of its constituent particles.

Table 4.1

Z	Element	Symbol	A	Atomic Mass, amu
0	Neutron	*n*	1	1.008 665
1	Hydrogen	H	1	1.007 825
			2	2.014 102
			3	3.016 050
2	Helium	He	3	3.016 029
			4	4.002 603
			6	6.018 891
3.	Lithium	Li	6	6.015 123
			7	7.016 004
			8	8.022 487
4.	Beryllium	Be	7	7.016 930
			9	9.012 182
			10	10.013 535
5.	Boron	B	10	10.012 938
			11	11.009 305
			12	12.014 353
6.	Carbon	C	10	10.016 858
			11	11.011 433
			12	12.000 000
			13	13.003 355
			14	14.003 242
			15	15.010 599
7.	Nitrogen	N	12	12.018 613
			13	13.005 739
			14	14.003 074
			15	15.000 109
			16	16.006 099
			17	17.008 449
8.	Oxygen	O	14	14.008 597
			15	15.003 065
			16	15.994 915
			17	16.999 131
			18	17.999 159
			19	19.003 576
9.	Fluorine	F	17	17.002 095
			18	18.000 937
			19	18.998 403
			20	19.999 982
			21	20.999 949
10.	Neon	Ne	18	18.005 710
			19	19.001 880
			20	19.992 439
			21	20.993 845
			22	21.991 384
			23	22.994 466
			24	23.993 613
11.	Sodium	Na	22	21.994 435
			23	22.989 770
			24	23.990 963
12.	Magnesium	Mg	23	22.994 127
			24	23.985 045
			25	24.985 839
			26	25.982 595
13.	Aluminum	Al	27	26.981 541

Z	Element	Symbol	A	Atomic Mass, amu
14.	Silicon	Si	28	27.976 928
			29	28.976 496
			30	29.973 772
15.	Phosphorus	P	30	29.978 310
			31	30.973 763
16.	Sulfur	S	32	31.972 072
			33	32.971 459
			34	33.967 868
			35	34.969 032
			36	35.967 079
17.	Chlorine	Cl	35	34.968 853
			36	35.968 307
			37	36.965 903
18.	Argon	Ar	36	35.967 546
			37	36.966 776
			38	37.962 732
			39	38.964 315
			40	39.962 383
19.	Potassium	K	39	38.963 708
			40	39.963 999
			41	40.961 825
20.	Calcium	Ca	40	39.962 591
			41	40.962 278
			42	41.958 622
			43	42.958 770
			44	43.955 485
			45	44.956 180
			46	45.953 689
			47	46.954 543
			48	47.952 532
21.	Scandium	Sc	45	44.955 914
22.	Titanium	Ti	46	45.952 633
			47	46.951 765
			48	47.947 947
			49	48.947 871
			50	49.944 786
23.	Vanadium	V	48	47.952 257
			50	49.947 161
			51	50.943 962
24.	chromium	Cr	48	47.954 033
			50	49.946 046
			52	51.940 510
			53	52.940 651
			54	53.938 882
25.	Manganese	Mn	54	53.940 360
			55	54.938 046
26.	Iron	Fe	54	53.939 612
			56	55.934 939
			57	56.935 396
			58	57.933 278
			59	58.934 878
27.	Cobalt	Co	58	57.935 755
			59	58.933 198
			60	59.933 820

Z	Element	Symbol	A	Atomic Mass, amu
28.	Nickel	Ni	58	57.935 347
			60	59.930 789
			61	60.931 059
			62	61.928 346
			64	63.927 968
29.	Copper	Cu	63	62.929 599
			64	63.929 766
			65	64.927 792
30.	Zinc	Zn	64	63.929 145
			65	64.929 244
			66	65.926 035
			67	66.927 129
			68	67.924 846
			70	69.925 325
31.	Gallium	Ga	69	68.925 581
			71	70.924 701
32.	Germanium	Ge	70	69.924 250
			72	71.922 080
			73	72.923 464
			74	73.921 179
			76	75.921 403
33.	Arsenic	As	74	73.923 930
			75	74.921 596
34.	Selenium	Se	74	73.922 477
			76	75.919 207
			77	76.919 908
			78	77.917 304
			80	79.916 520
			82	81.916 709
35.	Bromine	Br	79	78.918 336
			80	79.918 528
			81	80.916 290
36.	Krypton	Kr	78	77.920 397
			80	79.916 375
			81	80.916 578
			82	81.913 483
			83	82.914 134
			84	83.911 506
			86	85.910 614
37.	Rubidium	Rb	85	84.911 800
			87	86.909 184
38.	Strontium	Sr	84	83.913 428
			86	85.909 273
			87	86.908 890
			88	87.905 625
39.	Yttrium	Y	89	88.905 856
40.	Zirconium	Zr	90	89.904 708
			91	90.905 644
			92	91.905 039
			94	93.906 319
			96	95.908 272
41.	Niobium	Nb	93	92.906 378
42.	Molybdenum	Mo	92	91.906 809
			94	93.905 809
			95	94.905 838

Z	Element	Symbol	A	Atomic Mass, amu
			96	95.904 675
			97	96.906 018
			98	97.905 405
			100	99.907 473
43.	Technetium	Tc	99	98.906 252
44.	Ruthenium	Ru	96	95.907 596
			98	97.905 287
			99	98.905 937
			100	99.904 217
			101	100.905 581
			102	101.904 347
			104	103.905 422
45.	Rhodium	Rh	103	102.905 503
46.	Palladium	Pd	102	101.905 609
			104	103.904 026
			105	104.905 075
			106	105.903 475
			108	107.903 894
			110	109.905 169
47.	Silver	Ag	107	106.905 095
			108	107.905 956
			109	108.904 754
48.	Cadmium	Cd	106	105.906 461
			108	107.904 186
			110	109.903 007
			111	110.904 182
			112	111.902 761
			113	112.904 401
			114	113.903 361
			116	115.904 758
49.	Indium	In	113	112.904 056
			115	114.903 875
50.	Tin	Sn	112	111.904 823
			114	113.902 781
			115	114.903 344
			116	115.901 743
			117	116.902 954
			118	117.901 607
			119	118.903 310
			120	119.902 199
			122	121.903 440
			124	123.905 271
51.	Antimony	Sb	121	120.903 824
			123	122.904 222
52.	Tellerium	Te	120	119.904 021
			122	121.903 055
			123	122.904 278
			124	123.902 278
			125	124.904 435
			126	125.903 310
			127	126.905 222
			128	127.904 464
			130	129.906 229
53.	Iodine	I	127	126.904 477
			131	130.906 119

Z	Element	Symbol	A	Atomic Mass, amu
54.	Xenon	Xe	124	123.906 12
			126	125.904 281
			128	127.903 531
			129	128.904 780
			130	129.903 509
			131	130.905 076
			132	131.904 148
			134	133.905 395
			136	135.907 219
55.	Cesium	Cs	133	132.905 433
56.	Barium	Ba	130	129.906 277
			132	131.905 042
			134	133.904 490
			135	134.905 668
			136	135.904 556
			137	136.905 816
			138	137.905 236
57.	Lanthanum	La	138	137.907 114
			139	138.906 355
58.	Cerium	Ce	136	135.907 14
			138	137.905 996
			140	139.905 442
			142	141.909 249
59.	Praseodymium	Pr	141	140.907 657
60.	Neodymium	Nd	142	141.907 731
			143	142.909 823
			144	143.910 096
			145	144.912 582
			146	145.913 126
			148	147.916 901
			150	149.920 900
61.	Promethium	Pm	147	146.915 148
62.	Samarium	Sm	144	143.912 009
			147	146.914 907
			148	147.914 832
			149	148.917 193
			150	149.917 285
			152	151.919 741
			154	153.922 218
63.	Europium	Eu	151	150.919 860
			153	
64.	Gadolinium	Gd	152	151.919 803
			154	153.920 876
			155	154.922 629
			156	155.922 130
			157	156.923 967
			158	157.924 111
			160	159.927 061
65.	Terbium	Tb	159	158.925 350
66.	Dysprosium	Dy	156	155.924 287
			158	157.924 412
			160	159.925 203
			161	160.926 939
			162	161.926 805
			163	162.928 737
			164	163.929 183

Z	Element	Symbol	A	Atomic Mass, amu
67.	Holmium	Ho	165	164.930 332
68.	Erbium	Er	162	161.928 787
			164	163.929 211
			166	165.930 305
			167	166.932 061
			168	167.932 383
			170	169.935 476
69.	Thulium	Tm	169	168.934 225
70.	Ytterbium	Yb	168	167.933 908
			170	169.934 774
			171	170.936 338
			172	171.936 393
			173	172.938 222
			174	173.938 873
			176	175.942 576
71.	Lutetium	Lu	175	174.940 785
			176	175.942 694
72.	Hafnium	Hf	174	172.940 065
			176	175.941 420
			177	176.943 233
			178	177.943 710
			179	178.945 827
			180	179.946 561
73.	Tantalum	Ta	180	179.947 489
			181	180.948 014
74.	Tungsten	W	180	179.946 727
			182	181.948 225
			183	182.950 245
			184	183.950 953
			186	185.954 377
75.	Rhenium	Re	185	184.952 977
			187	186.955 765
76.	Osmium	Os	184	183.952 514
			186	185.953 852
			187	186.955 762
			188	187.955 850
			189	188.958 156
			190	189.958 455
			192	191.961 487
77.	Iridium	Ir	191	190.960 603
			193	192.962 942
78.	Platinum	Pt	190	189.959 937
			193	191.961 049
			194	193.962 679
			195	194.964 785
			196	195.964 947
			198	197.967 879
79.	Gold	Au	197	196.966 560
80.	Mercury	Hg	196	195.965 812
			198	197.966 760
			199	198.968 269
			200	199.968 316
			201	200.970 293
			202	201.970 632
			204	203.973 481

Z	Element	Symbol	A	Atomic Mass, amu
81.	Thallium	TI	203	202.972 336
			205	204.974 410
82.	Lead	Pb	204	203.973 037
			206	205.974 455
			207	206.975 885
			208	207.976 641
			210	209.984 178
			214	213.999 764
83.	Bismuth	Bi	209	209.980 388
			212	211.991 267
84.	Polonium	Po	210	209.982 876
			214	213.995 191
			216	216.001 790
			218	218.008 930
85.	Astatine	At	218	218.008 607
86.	Radon	Rn	220	220.001 401
			222	222.017 401
87.	Francium	Fr	223	223.019 73
88.	Radium	Ra	226	226.025 406
89.	Actinium	Ac	227	227.027 751
90.	Thorium	Th	228	228.028 750
			230	230.033 131
			232	232.038 054
			233	233.041 580
91.	Protactinium	Pa	233	233.040 244
92.	Uranium	U	232	232.037 168
			233	233.039 629
			234	234.040 947
			235	235.043 925
			238	238.050 786
93.	Neptunium	Np	237	237.048 169
			239	239.052 932
94.	Plutonium	Pu	239	239.052 158
			240	240.053 809
95.	Americium	Am	243	243.061 374
96.	Curium	Cm	247	247.070 349
97.	Berkelum	Bk	247	247.070 300
98.	Californium	Cf	251	251.079 581
99.	Einsteinium	Es	252	252.082 82
100.	Fermium	Fm	257	257.095 103
101.	Mendelevium	Md	258	258.098 57
102.	Nobelium	No	259	259.100 941
103.	Lawrencium	Lr	260	260.105 36
104.	Rutherfordium	Rf	261	261.108 69
105.	Hahnium	Ha	262	262.113 84

For example we discuss for ${}_{2}^{4}$He atom. We compare the mass of atom to that of its constituents. To calculate the masses of the components, we can either add the masses of two protons, two neutrons and two electrons or we can add the masses of two H-atoms and two neutrons. Using the values from table-4.1, we have

$$2m_H + 2m_n = 2(1.007825) + 2(1.008665)$$

$$= 4.0329804 \qquad \ldots(4.3)$$

Now we can see that in table mass ${}_{2}^{4}$He atom is 4.0026034 which is less then the value given in equation-(4.3), the sum of masses of constituent particles. Similar thing can be verified for all the elements, also the reason for this can be explained by equation-(4.4) which is a basic nuclear reaction for formation of a nuclei ${}_{Z}^{A}$X. In this reaction we can see that when *Z*-protons and *(A-Z)* neutrons fuse together to form a nucleus ${}_{Z}^{A}$X, some amount of energy must be released as nucleus is more stable form of nucleus

$$Zm_p + (A\text{-}Z)m_n \longrightarrow M_X + \text{Energy} \qquad \ldots(4.4)$$

If we think from where this energy come, we can simply say by Einstein mass energy relationship some amount of mass from independent nucleons is converted into energy and released when nucleons bounded with each other to form a stable nucleus. This is the energy what hold the nucleons together in a nucleus, we call '*Binding Energy*' of nucleus. So when this energy is supplied to a nucleus, it splits into its constituent particles.

For the above reaction given in equation-(4.4), if we calculate the difference in masses of nucleons and that of nucleons *X*, then it is given as

$$\Delta m = Zm_p + (A\text{-}Z)m_n - M_X \qquad \ldots(4.5)$$

This difference in masses of independent nucleons and mass of nucleus is called '*Mass Defect*' of the nuclear reaction. Using mass defect Δm we can find the energy released in a nuclear reaction, such as the binding energy of above nucleus *X* can be given as

$$\Delta E_{BE} = \Delta mc^2 \qquad \ldots(4.6)$$

In the similar way we can find the binding energy for any nucleus in nature for a known composition.

4.2.1 Mass Energy Equivalence

We've discussed in previous section that using mass defect of a nuclear reaction we can find the energy released in the nuclear process. We know generally nuclear masses are given in atomic mass unit where

$$1 \text{ amu} = 1.656 \times 10^{-27} \text{ kg}$$

If in a reaction 1 amu mass is converted into energy then using Einstein's mass energy relationship the amount of energy released is

$$\Delta E = \Delta mc^2$$

$$\Rightarrow \quad \Delta E = (1.656 \times 10^{-27})(3 \times 10^8)^2 \text{ joule}$$

$$\Rightarrow \quad \Delta E = \frac{(1.656\times10^{-27})\cdot(3\times10^8)^2}{1.6\times10^{-19}} \text{ eV}$$

$$\Rightarrow \quad \Delta E = 931.5 \times 10^6 \text{ eV}$$

$$\Rightarrow \quad \Delta E = 931.5 \text{ MeV}$$

Thus we can say that 1 amu mass is equivalent to 931.5 MeV energy.

4.2.2 Binding Energy Per Nucleon

If we wish to see how nuclear binding energy varies from nucleus to nucleus, it is necessary to compare the binding energy per nucleon basis. If we find binding energy per nucleon for a given element it can be given as binding energy divided by the nucleon number A as

$$(BE)_N = \frac{\Delta E}{A} = \frac{\Delta mc^2}{A} \qquad \ldots(4.7)$$

This value $(BE)_N$ in equation-(4.7) gives the criterion of stability among different elements. We can define binding energy per nucleon theoretically as the amount of energy needed to remove a nucleon from nucleus of an element. For example if we compare, say there are two elements X and Y with mass numbers A_X and A_Y $(A_X > A_Y)$ and binding energies ΔE_X and ΔE_Y such that $\Delta E_X > \Delta E_Y$. Here one can say that as for element X binding energy ΔE_X is more as compared to that for element Y, nucleus X is more stable then nucleus Y. But if we find the $(BE)_N$ values for both element it is given as

$$(BE_N)_X = \frac{\Delta E_X}{A_X}\,;\,(BE_N)_Y = \frac{\Delta E_Y}{A_Y}$$

and these values are such that $(BE_N)_X < (BE_N)_Y$ which implies that to remove a nucleon from element X requires less energy then from element Y. Which implies that for the nucleus of Y it is difficult to remove one nucleon from its nucleus, thus structure of Y is more stable then X.

To under this in a better way lets consider an example of ^{56}Fe and ^{209}Bi. Their binding energies are given as

$$\Delta E_{Fe} = 492.8 \text{ MeV}$$

and $$\Delta E_{Bi} = 1640 \text{ MeV}$$

From the above values it seems that to break the nucleus of Bi more energy is required hence it is more stable then that of Fe. But we should not ignore the bigger size of bismuth nuclei. If we find binding energy per nucleon for both of these nuclei, we get

$$(BE_N)_{Fe} = \frac{492.8}{56} = 8.8 \text{ MeV}$$

and $$(BE_N)_{Bi} = \frac{1640}{209} = 7.84 \text{ MeV}$$

Now we can see that removal of one electron from F_c nucleus is more difficult as compared to that from Bi nucleus. So Fe nuclei are more stable then Bi. Thus to judge or compare the stability of different nuclei we see binding energy per nucleon not the nuclear binding energy.

4.2.3 Variation of Binding Energy per Nucleon with Mass Number

The binding energy per nucleon is a characteristic property of elements. The graph in figure-4.3 shows the variation of binding energy per nucleon with mass number for all the elements of periodic table. In graph we can see that the binding energy per nucleon increases rapidly for nuclei with small masses and reaches a maximum of approximately 8.8 Mev/nucleon for Iron ($^{56}_{26}$Fe). For greater nucleon numbers, the binding energy per nucleon decreases gradually. Later, the binding energy per nucleon decreases enough so there is insufficient binding energy to hold the nucleons together in the nucleus. It is observed that nuclei with $A > 209$ are unstable and hence radioactive.

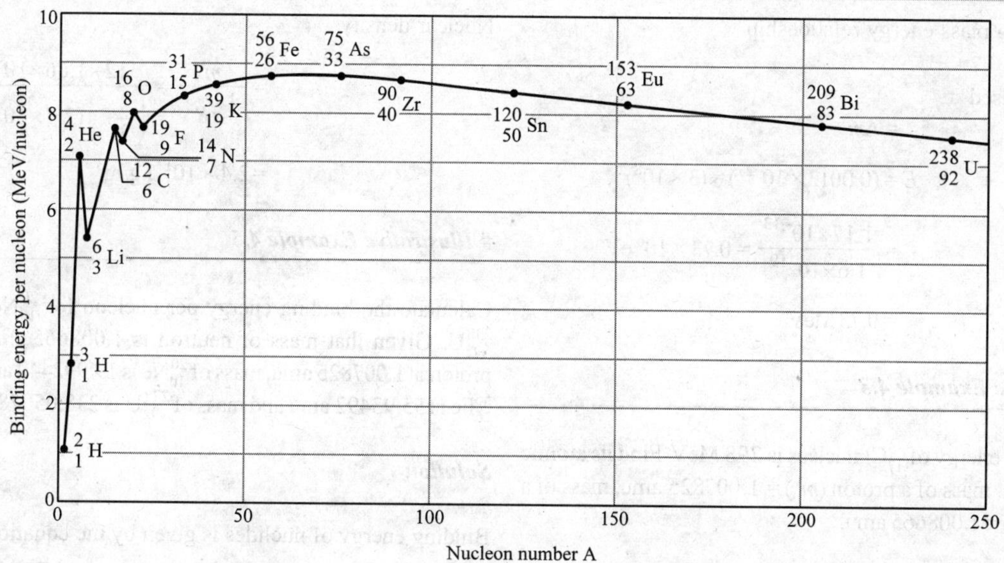

Figure 4.3

In the above figure in the beginning we can see that there are some fluctuations in the graph. We can see that binding energy per nucleon for ^4He, ^{12}C, ^{16}O are relatively higher as compared to their neighbouring elements or these elements have nuclei which are relatively more stable then their neighbours. This is because of the existence of nuclear energy levels in the nucleus. Each nuclear energy level can contain two neutrons of opposite spins or two protons of opposite spins. Energy level in nuclei are filled in sequence, just as energy levels in atoms to achieve configurations of minimum energy, and therefore maximum energy. Similar to the case of atomic orbitals here also the configuration of opposite spin in nucleons with pairs in nuclear energy level are more stable. This concept can be used to explain the reason of more stability of ^4He, ^{12}C and ^{16}O compared to their neighbouring elements.

 # Illustrative Example 4.1

Find the binding energy of an α-particle from the following data :

Mass of the helium nucleus = 4.001265 amu

Mass of proton = 1.007277 amu

Mass of neutron = 1.008665 amu

Take 1 amu = 931.5 MeV

Solution

Mass of two protons = 2 × 1.007277 = 2.014554 amu

Mass of two neutron = 2 × 1.008665 amu = 2.01733 amu

Total initial mass of two protons and neutrons

$$= 2.014554 + 2.01733 = 4.031884 \text{ amu}$$

Mass defect $\Delta m = 4.031814 - 4.001265$ amu

$$= 0.0306219 \text{ amu}$$

Now binding energy of α-particle in *MeV* is given as

$$\Delta E_B = \Delta m \times 931.2 \text{ MeV}$$

$$= 0.030619 \times 931.5 = 28.5216 \text{ MeV}$$

Binding energy per nucleon

$$= 28.5216/4 = 7.13039 \text{ MeV}$$

 # Illustrative Example 4.2

A neutron breaks into a proton and electron. Calculate the energy produced in this reaction in MeV. Mass of an electron = 9×10^{-31} kg. Mass of proton = 1.6725×10^{-27} kg, Mass of neutron = 1.6747×10^{-27} kg. Speed of light = 3×10^8 m/sec.

Solution

Mass defect of the process is given by

Δm = [Mass of neutron – (mass of proton + mass of electron)]

$$= [1.6747 \times 10^{-27} - (1.6725 \times 10^{-27} + 9 \times 10^{-31})]$$

$$= 0.0013 \times 10^{-27} \text{ kg}$$

According to mass energy relationship

Energy released

$$= \Delta m\, c^2$$

$$E = (0.0013 \times 10^{-27}) \times (3 \times 10^8)^2$$

$$= \frac{1.17 \times 10^{-13}}{1.6 \times 10^{-19}} = 0.73 \times 10^6 \text{ eV}$$

$$= 0.73 \text{ MeV}$$

Illustrative Example 4.3

The binding energy of $^{35}_{17}$Cl nucleus is 298 MeV. Find its atomic mass. Given, mass of a proton (m_p) = 1.007825 amu, mass of a neutron (m_n) = 1.008665 amu.

Solution

The $^{35}_{17}$Cl nucleus has 17 protons and 18 neutrons. Therefore, the mass of contents nucleus of $^{35}_{17}$Cl is

$$M = 17\, m_p + 18\, m_n$$

$$= 17 \times 1.007825 + 18 \times 1.008665$$

$$= 35.289 \text{ amu}$$

Now, mass defect for the nucleus is

$$\Delta m = \frac{298 \text{ MeV}}{9312 \text{ MeV/amu}} = 0.3200 \text{ amu}$$

Thus atomic mass of $^{35}_{17}$Cl = mass of contents the nucleus – mass of defect

$$= m - \Delta m = 35.289 \text{ amu}$$

$$- 0.3200 \text{ amu} = 34.969 \text{ amu}$$

Illustrative Example 4.4

Find the density of $^{12}_{6}$C nucleus. Take atomic mass of $^{12}_{6}$C is 12.0000 amu. Take $R_0 = 1.2 \times 10^{-15}$ m.

Solution

The radius of $^{12}_{6}$C nucleus can be given as

$$R = R_0\, A^{1/3}$$

or $$R = 1.2 \times 10^{-15} \times (2)^{1/3}$$

$$= 2.75 \times 10^{-15} \text{ m}$$

The atomic mass of $^{12}_{6}$C is 12 amu. Neglecting the masses and binding energies of the six electrons.

Nuclear density

$$= \frac{m}{\frac{4}{3}\pi R^3} = \frac{12 \times 1.66 \times 10^{-27}}{\left(\frac{4}{3}\pi\right)(2.7 \times 10^{-15})^3}$$

$$= 2.4 \times 10^{17} \text{ kg/m}^3$$

Illustrative Example 4.5

Calculate the binding energy per nucleon for $^{20}_{10}$Ne, $^{56}_{26}$Fe and $^{238}_{92}$U. Given that mass of neutron is 1.008665 amu, mass of proton is 1.007825 amu, mass of $^{20}_{10}$Ne is 19.992440 amu, mass of $^{56}_{26}$Fe is 55.93492 amu and mass of $^{238}_{92}$U is 238.050783 amu.

Solution

Binding energy of nuclides is given by the equation

$$B(^A_ZX) = [(A - Z)\, m_n + Zm_p - M(^A_ZX)]\, c^2$$

On dividing binding energy by the mass number, we obtain the binding energy per nucleon

$$B(^{20}_{10}\text{Ne}) = [10m_n + 10m_p - M(^{20}_{10}\text{Ne})]\, c^2$$

$$= [10 \times 1.008665 + 10 \times 1.007825$$

$$- 19.992440] \times 931.5 \text{ MeV}$$

$$= 160.6 \text{ MeV}$$

Hence binding energy per nucleon

$$= \frac{B(^{20}_{10}Ne)}{20} = 8.03 \text{ MeV/nucleon}$$

Similarly for ($^{56}_{26}$Fe),

$$B(^{56}_{26}\text{Fe}) = [30m_n + 26m_p - M(^{56}_{26}\text{Fe})]\, c^2$$

$$= [30 \times 1.008665 + 26 \times 1.007825$$

$$- 55.93492] \times 931.5 \text{ MeV}$$

$$= 492 \text{ MeV}$$

Hence binding energy per nucleon

$$= \frac{B(^{56}_{26}Fe)}{56} = 8.79 \text{ MeV/nucleon binding energy for } (^{238}_{92}\text{U})$$

$$= [146m_n + 92m_p - M(^{238}_{92}\text{U})]\, c^2$$

$$= [146 \times 1.008665 + 92 \times 1.007825$$

$$- 238.050783] \times 931.5 \text{ MeV}$$

$$= 1802 \text{ MeV}$$

Binding energy per nucleon is

$$= \frac{B(^{238}_{92}\text{Fe})}{238} = \frac{1802}{238} = 7.57 \text{ MeV}$$

Illustrative Example 4.6

Show that the nuclide ^{8}Be has a positive binding energy but is unstable with respect to decay into two alpha particles, where masses of neutron, ^{1}H and ^{8}Be are 1.008665 amu, 1.007825 amu and 8.005305 amu respectively.

Solution

The binding energy of ^{8}Be is determined by the equation

$$B(^8Be) = [4m_n + 4M(^1H) - M(^8Be)]\, c^2$$

The binding energy,

$$B(^8Be) = [4 \times 1.008665 + 4 \times 1.007825 - 8.005305] \times 931.5\ \text{MeV}$$

$$= 56.5\ \text{MeV}$$

Now we calculate the binding energy of the decay of ^{8}Be into two α-particles

$$^8Be \rightarrow 2\alpha + \Delta E$$

Here $\quad \Delta E = [2M(^4He) - (^8Be)]\, c^2$

$\Rightarrow \quad \Delta E = [2 \times 4.002603 - 8.005305] \times 931.5\ \text{MeV}$

$\Rightarrow \quad \Delta E = -0.092\ \text{MeV}$

Because B is negative for this reaction, hence ^{8}Be is unstable against decay to two alpha particles.

Web Reference at www.physicsgalaxy.com

Age Group - High School Physics | Age 17-19 Years
Section - MODERN PHYSICS
Topic - Nuclear Structure & Radioactivity
Module Number - 1 to 16

Practice Exercise 4.1

(i) In a thermonuclear reaction 1.00×10^{-3} kg hydrogen is converted into 0.993×10^{-3} kg helium.

(a) Calculate the energy released in joule.

(b) If the efficiency of the generator be 5%, calculate the energy in kilowatt hours.

[(a) 63.0×10^{10} J, (b) 8.75 kWh]

(ii) Find the binding energy and the binding energy per nucleon of the nucleus of $^{16}_{8}$O. Given, atomic mass of $^{16}_{8}$O (m) = 15.994915 amu, mass of proton (m_p) = 1.007825 amu, mass of a neutron (m_n) = 1.008665 amu and 1 amu = 931.5 MeV.

[127.62 MeV, 7.976 MeV]

(iii) Find : (a) An approximate expression for the mass of a nucleus of mass number A, if m is the mass of a nucleon (b) An expression for the volume of this nucleus in terms of the mass number, and (c) A numerical value for its density.

[(a) Am, (b) $\frac{4}{3}\pi r_0^3 A$, (c) 2.3×10^{17} kg/m^3]

(iv) Calculate the binding energy of the deuteron, which consists of a proton and a neutron, given that the atomic mass of the deuteron is 2.014102 amu. Take mass of proton (m_p) = 1.007825 amu, mass of a neutron (m_n) = 1.008665 amu and 1 amu = 931.5 MeV.

[2.224 MeV.]

(v) Find the binding energy of the nucleus of lithium isotope $^7_3$Li & hence find the binding energy per nucleon in it. (Given $^7_3$Li atom = 7.016005 amu; $_1$H^1 atom = 1.007825 amu ^1_0n = 1.008665 amu.)

[39.231 MeV , 5.604 MeV]

(vi) Calculate the electric potential energy due to the electric repulsion between two nuclei of ^{12}C when they 'touch' each other at the surface.

[9.435 MeV]

(vii) Find the binding energy of $^{56}_{20}$Fe. Atomic mass of ^{56}Fe is 55.934939 amu. Mass of a proton is 1.007825 amu and that of neutron = 1.008665 amu.

[496.95 MeV]

4.3 Radioactivity

As we've discussed that inside a nucleus electrostatic attraction is counterbalanced by short range strong nuclear forces and nucleus becomes stable. Despite the forces are balanced, many nuclides are unstable because of nuclear size or the limited range of nuclear forces or due to slight imbalance in small sized nuclides, these nuclides spontaneously disintegrate into other nuclide. This phenomenon of spontaneous disintegration we call radioactivity. In further section of the chapter we'll discuss the aspects of radioactivity by which unstable nuclide disintegrate to achieve stability.

4.3.1 Measurement of Radioactivity

Radioactivity of an element is measured in terms of "activity". The activity of a sample of any radioactive nuclide is the rate at which the nuclei of its constituent atoms disintegrate. If N are the number of nuclei present in a radioactive sample at an instant then activity of this sample is given as

$$A_C = -\frac{dN}{dt} \qquad \ldots(4.8)$$

Here $\frac{dN}{dt}$ is negative as with time always no. of elements decreases due to disintegration, due to negative sign, A_C is always taken positive. The activity of a substance is measured in terms of "dps" or disintegrations per second. The SI unit of activity is named after Becquerel, defined as

$$1 \text{ becquerel} = 1\ Bq = 1 \text{ disintegration/sec}$$

Generally activities of radioactive samples in nature are very high that's why becquerel is a very small unit for normal practice, more often MBq or GBq are used. For the same traditional units curie (Ci) and rutherford (Ru) are also used. These are defined as

$$1\ Ci = 3.7 \times 10^{10} \text{ dis/sec}$$

and $$1\ Ru = 10^6 \text{ dis/sec}$$

Roughly curie was originally defined as activity of 1 gm of $^{226}_{88}Ra$. Similarly it was observed that 1 kg of ordinary potassium has an activity of about 1 mCi (10^{-3} Ci) because in ordinary potassium small proportion of radioisotope $^{40}_{19}K$ is also present.

4.3.2 Fundamental Laws of Radioactivity

On the basis of experiments performed by Rutherford and Soddy some conclusions were made for behaviour of radioactive elements and the properties of Radioactivity, these conclusions we summarize as fundamental laws of radioactivity. These are

(1) Radioactivity is purely a nuclear process, it is not concerned in any manner with the extranuclear part of atom.

(2) As radioactivity is a nuclear process, it is independent from any chemical property of the element. As we've discussed that radioactive property of an element is only the process concerned with nucleus of the element. It does not effect the electronic configuration of the element. If this element takes part in a chemical reaction the product formed will also have the radioactive property in the same fraction by which the radioactive atom is present in the molecule of product.

(3) Radioactivity is a random process, its study is only possible by laws of probability mathematically. In a group of several radioactive atoms, which one will disintegrate first is just a matter of chance.

(4) As radioactivity is a random process, the disintegration density throughout the volume of a radioactive element remains constant. If an element X decays to a daughter nuclide Y then in a given volume of element, all portions of volume will have same ratio of number of atoms of Y to that of X.

Thus due to randomness, approximately the amount of disintegrations per unit volume per second (called disintegration density) remains constant in the whole volume of the substance.

4.3.3 Radioactive Decay Law

This law relates the activity of a substance with the number of active or undecayed atoms present in a group of radioactive atoms at an instant of time. This law is stated as

"The activity of a radioactive element at any instant is directly proportional to the number of undecayed active atoms (parent atoms) present at that instant."

Let us consider that at $t = 0$, there are N_0 parent atoms are there in a substance and after a time t, N-atoms are left undecayed. This implies that in the duration from $t = 0$ to $t = t$, $N_0 - N$ atoms are decayed to their daughter element. If in further time from $t = t$ to $t = t + dt$, dN more atoms will decay then at time $t = t$, we can say that the activity of the element is given as

$$A_c = \left|\frac{dN}{dt}\right| \qquad \ldots(4.9)$$

Now according to Radioactive Decay Law, we have

$$\left|\frac{dN}{dt}\right| \propto N$$

$$\Rightarrow \quad A_c = \left|\frac{dN}{dt}\right| = \lambda N \qquad \ldots(4.10)$$

Here λ is the proportionality constant, we call decay constant for the decay process. The value of decay constant differs for different elements. From equation-(4.10) we can see that if λ is high the element will have high value of activity and if λ is less, the activity will be relativity less. Thus we can say that the decay constant for a radioactive element gives a relative criteria of its stability if the value of λ for an element is more, it is more active or relatively less stable and if for an element λ is less, it is more stable. From equation-4.10, we can also write

$$\lambda = \frac{\left|\frac{dN}{dt}\right|}{N} \qquad \ldots(4.11)$$

Thus decay constant of a process can be given as "activity per atom" (as given in equation-(4.11)). This shows that for a given radioactive element the activity per atom always remains constant where as we've already discussed that with time the overall activity of a substance decreases with time as number of parent elements continuously decreases with time.

Now from equation-(4.10), we can write

$$\frac{dN}{dt} = -\lambda N \qquad \ldots(4.12)$$

Here negative sign shows that $\frac{dN}{dt}$, the rate at which the active elements are disintegrating is negative or number of active elements are decreasing with time. Now we have from equation-(4.12)

$$\frac{dN}{N} = -\lambda\, dt$$

Now we integrate this expression within time limits from $t = 0$, to $t = t$, we have

$$\int_{N_0}^{N} \frac{dN}{N} = -\int_{0}^{t} \lambda\, dt$$

$$\Rightarrow \quad [\ln N]_{N_0}^{N} = -\lambda t$$

$$\Rightarrow \quad \ln N - \ln N_0 = -\lambda t$$

$$\Rightarrow \quad \ln\left(\frac{N}{N_0}\right) = -\lambda t$$

$$\Rightarrow \quad N = N_0\, e^{-\lambda t} \qquad \ldots(4.13)$$

Here equation-(4.13) gives the number of active parent atoms N present at time t in the mixture. This equation, we call radioactive decay equation.

From equation-(4.13) we can have

$$\lambda N = \lambda N_0\, e^{-\lambda t}$$

$$\Rightarrow \quad A_c = A_{c0}\, e^{-\lambda t} \qquad \ldots(4.14)$$

Here $A_{c0} = \lambda N_0$ is the initial activity of substance at $t = 0$. equation-(4.14) is another form of radioactive decay equation. This equation can be used to find activity of a radioactive substance at any time instant.

4.3.4 Half Life Time

In previous section we've discussed that during decay of a radioactive sample, the amount of radionuclide fall off exponentially with time. Every radioactive sample has a characteristic half life. Half life time is defined as the time duration in which half of the total number of nuclei will decay or left undecayed. Say for example at any instant we look into the quantity of a sample of radioactive element, it is observed that after every 3 hour the number of undecayed parent element reduces to half thus accordingly the half life of the nuclide is 3 hour. Some half lives are only a millionth of a second for highly active elements and some less active elements have half life in billions of years.

In some nuclear power plants a major problem is disposal of the radioactive wastes since some of the nuclide present in waste have long half lives.

For a radioactive element in a sample if at $t = 0$, No nuclei are present of active parent element and during observation after $t = T$, $\frac{N_0}{2}$ are left then this duration T can be taken as half life of this element. From radioactive decay equation we have

$$N = N_0\, e^{-\lambda t} \qquad \ldots(4.15)$$

Here at $t = T$, $N = \frac{N_0}{2}$ thus we have in above equation

$$\frac{N_0}{2} = N_0 e^{-\lambda T}$$

$$\Rightarrow \quad \ln\left(\frac{1}{2}\right) = -\lambda T$$

$$\Rightarrow \quad \ln(2) = \lambda T$$

$$\Rightarrow \quad T = \frac{\ln(2)}{\lambda} = \frac{0.693}{\lambda} \qquad \ldots(4.16)$$

4.3.5 Alternate form of Decay Equation in terms of Half Life Time

If one radioactive element X decays to a daughter nucleus Y with a decay constant λ then for the process nuclear reaction, is written as

$$X \xrightarrow{\lambda} Y$$

If initially N_0 nuclei of element X are present then after time t, number of nuclei present in the sample are given by decay equation given as

$$N = N_0 e^{-\lambda t} \qquad \ldots(4.17)$$

If we rearrange the equation, we have

$$\ln\frac{N}{N_0} = -\lambda T \qquad \ldots(4.18)$$

We know that half life of substance is defined as

$$T = \frac{\ln(2)}{\lambda}$$

or we can write

$$\lambda = \frac{\ln(2)}{\lambda} \qquad \ldots(4.19)$$

Now from equation-(4.18) we have

$$\ln\left(\frac{N}{N_0}\right) = -\frac{\ln(2)}{T}t$$

$$\Rightarrow \qquad \ln\left(\frac{N}{N_0}\right) = \ln(2)^{-t/T}$$

Taking antilog on both sides, we get

$$\frac{N}{N_0} = (2)^{-t/T}$$

$$\Rightarrow \qquad N = N_0(2)^{-t/T} \qquad \ldots(4.20)$$

Equation-(4.20) is an alternate form of decay equation useful for numerical applications.

4.3.6 Mean Life Time

For a given radioactive substance, some nuclei disintegrate in the beginning and some will disintegrate after a long time. Thus we can say that some nuclei have very short life and some have very large life time for disintegration. For a radioactive element mean life is defined as

Mean life time

$$T_m = \frac{\text{Sum of lives of all nuclei in a sample}}{\text{Total number of nuclides in sample}}$$

$$T_m = \frac{1}{\lambda} \qquad \ldots(4.21)$$

The above numerical value is comes out to be reciprocal of decay constant of the element. This can not be directly calculated but we can calculate the value of mean life time for a radioactive element using basic probability laws as explained in the next section.

4.3.7 Calculation of Mean Life Time For a Radioactive Element

The half-life of a sample of radioactive nuclei is the time for half of the sample to disintegrate. The average or mean life of the sample is different. Some of the atoms in the sample exist much longer than others before decaying. To determine the mean life, consider an analogy. Imagine a collection of 10 people with the following death statistics; 3 die at age 60 y, 2 at age 70 y, 4 at 75 y, and 1 at a venerable 90 y. The average age is found by multiplying the number dying at each age, summing the results, and dividing the sum by the total sample size :

$$\text{Average age} = \frac{3(60y) + 2(70y) + 4(75y) + 1(90y)}{10}$$

$$= 71\,y$$

The average lifetime of an initial sample of N_0 radioactive atoms is found in a similar way. Let N be the number of atoms that still exit at time t. Between t and $t + dt$, we lose a few of these hearty atoms: dN of them decay. Thus the number of atoms that live a time t is dN. The sun in the number of the average is really an integration of the quantity $t\,dN$ between N_0 and 0 particles; the denominator is the sum of the particles, or the integration of dN over all the particles:

$$\text{Mean or average life} = \frac{\int_{N_0}^{0} t\,dN}{\int_{N_0}^{0} dN} \qquad \ldots(4.22)$$

For the integration in the numerator, we use the activity of the substance to find dN, given as

$$\frac{dN}{dt} = -\lambda N$$

$$dN = -\lambda N\,dt$$

We make the substitution for dN in the numerator of equation-(4.22). For the average life, we then have

$$\text{Mean or average life} = \frac{-\int_{0}^{\infty} t\lambda N\,dt}{-N_0} \qquad \ldots(4.23)$$

From radioactive decay equation we have

$$N = N_0 e^{-\lambda t}$$

Thus equation-(4.23) becomes

$$\text{Mean life} = \frac{\int_{0}^{\infty} t\lambda N_0 e^{-\lambda t}\,dt}{N_0} \qquad \ldots(4.24)$$

This integration is done by parts. The result comes out as

$$\text{Mean life} = \frac{1}{\lambda} \qquad \ldots(4.25)$$

Thus the numerical value of mean life is the reciprocal of the disintegration constant for the respective radioactive element.

 # *Illustrative Example 4.7*

The half life of radon is 3.8 days. After how many days will only one twentieth of radon sample be left over ?

Solution

We know that $\qquad \lambda = 0.693/T$

Here $\qquad T = 3.8$ day

$$\Rightarrow \qquad \lambda = \frac{0.693}{3.8} = 0.182 \text{ per day}$$

If initially at $t = 0$, the number of atoms present be N_0, then the number of atoms N left after a time t is given by

$$N = N_0 e^{-\lambda t}$$

$$\Rightarrow \quad \frac{N}{N_0} = e^{-\lambda t}$$

$$\Rightarrow \quad \frac{1}{20} = e^{-\lambda t}$$

$$\Rightarrow \quad e^{\lambda t} = 20$$

Taking log on both sides, we get

$$\lambda t = \ln(20) = 2.303 \log_{10} 20$$

$$t = \frac{2.303 \log_{10} 20}{\lambda}$$

$$= \frac{2.303 \log_{10} 20}{0.182} = 16.45 \text{ days}$$

Illustrative Example 4.8

One gm of a radioactive material having a half life period of 2 years is kept in store for a duration of 4 years. Calculate how much of the material remains unchanged ?

Solution

According to radioactive decay law we have

$$N = N_0 2^{-t/T}$$

Here we have $T = 2$ yrs. and $t = 4$ yrs

Thus we have $\quad N = N_0 2^{-U/2}$

$$\Rightarrow \quad N = \frac{N_0}{4} = \frac{1}{4} \text{ gm}$$

Thus after 4 years 0.25 gm of the material will be left.

Illustrative Example 4.9

1 gm of radioactive substance takes 50 sec to lose 1 centigram. Find its half life period.

Solution

Given that after 50 second the amount remaining is 0.99 gm as out of 1 gm, 1 centigram is lost. Now from radioactive decay equation, we have

$$N = N_0 2^{-t/T}$$

$$\Rightarrow \quad 0.99 = (1) 2^{-50/T}$$

$$\Rightarrow \quad \log_2\left(\frac{99}{100}\right) = -\frac{50}{T}$$

$$\Rightarrow \quad T = \frac{50}{\log_2\left(\frac{100}{99}\right)}$$

$$\Rightarrow \quad T = 50 \times \frac{\log_{10}(2)}{\log_{10}(100) - \log_2(99)}$$

$$\Rightarrow \quad T = 50\left[\frac{0.301}{2 - 1.9956}\right]$$

$$\Rightarrow \quad T = 3420 \text{ sec} = 57 \text{ min}$$

Illustrative Example 4.10

1 g of a radioactive substance disintegrates at the rate of 3.7×10^{10} disintegrations per second. The atomic mass of the substance is 226. Calculate its mean life.

Solution

Given that activity of substance is

$$A_c = 3.7 \times 10^{10} \text{ dps}$$

The number of atoms in 1 gm of substance are

$$N = \frac{1 \times 6.023 \times 10^{23}}{226}$$

$$\Rightarrow \quad N = 2.66 \times 10^{21} \text{ atoms}$$

If λ is the decay constant of the substance, we know that

Activity $\quad A_c = \lambda N$

$$\Rightarrow \quad \lambda = \frac{A_c}{N}$$

$$\Rightarrow \quad \lambda = \frac{3.7 \times 10^{10}}{2.66 \times 10^{21}} \text{ s}^{-1}$$

$$\Rightarrow \quad \lambda = 1.39 \times 10^{-11} \text{ s}^{-1}$$

Thus mean life of the radioactive substance is

$$T_m = \frac{1}{\lambda}$$

$$\Rightarrow \quad T_m = \frac{1}{1.39 \times 10^{-11}}$$

$$\Rightarrow \quad T_m = 7.194 \times 10^{10} \text{ s}$$

Illustrative Example 4.11

There is a stream of neutrons with a kinetic energy of 0.0327 eV. If the half life of neutron is 700 seconds, what fraction of neutrons will decay before they travel a distance of 10 km. (Mass of the neutrons = 1.6758×10^{-27} kg)

Solution

Given that kinetic energy of neutrons is

$$\frac{1}{2}mv^2 = 0.0327 \times (1.6 \times 10^{-19})\text{ J}$$

$$\Rightarrow \quad v^2 = \frac{2 \times 0.0327 \times (1.6 \times 10^{-19})}{1.675 \times 10^{-27}}$$

$$\Rightarrow \quad v^2 = 625 \times 10^4$$

$$\Rightarrow \quad v = 2500\text{ m/s}$$

Time to travel a distance of 10 km

$$t = \frac{10^4\text{ m}}{2500\text{ m/s}} = 4\text{ s}$$

After 4 second number of neutrons left can be given as

$$N = N_0 2^{-n}$$

When $n = \frac{t}{T}$ no. of half-lives. Here $n = \frac{4}{700} = \frac{1}{175}$

$$\Rightarrow \quad \frac{N}{N_0} = 2^{-1/175} = 0.996$$

$$\Rightarrow \quad N = 0.996\,\text{N}_0$$

Thus fraction of neutrons decayed is

$$f = \frac{N_0 - N}{N_0} = \frac{0.004N_0}{N_0} = 0.004$$

Illustrative Example 4.12

An experiment is done to determine that half life of a radioactive substance that emits one beta particle of each decay process. Measurements show that an average of 8.4 beta particles are emitted each second by 2.5 milligram of the substance. The atomic weight of the substance is 230. Find the half life of the substance.

Solution

Given that activity of the substance is

$$A_c = 8.4\text{ dps}$$

No. of atoms in 2.5 mg of substance are

$$N = \frac{2.5 \times 10^{-6} \times 6.023 \times 10^{23}}{230}$$

$$\Rightarrow \quad N = 6.54 \times 10^{18}\text{ atoms}$$

We know that activity is given as

$$A_c = \lambda N$$

or decay constant is

$$\lambda = \frac{A_c}{N}$$

$$\Rightarrow \quad \lambda = \frac{8.4}{6.54 \times 10^{18}}$$

$$\Rightarrow \quad \lambda = 1.28 \times 10^{-18}\text{ s}^{-1}$$

Thus half life of substance is

$$T = \frac{\ln(2)}{\lambda}$$

$$\Rightarrow \quad T = \frac{0.693}{1.28 \times 10^{-18}}\text{ s}$$

$$\Rightarrow \quad T = 5.41 \times 10^{17}\text{ s}$$

Illustrative Example 4.13

In an experiment on two radioactive isotopes of an element (which do not decay into each other), their mass ratio at a given instant was found to be 3. The rapidly decaying isotopes has larger mass and an activity of 1.0 μ curie initially. The half lives of the two isotopes are known to be 12 hours and 16 hours. What would be the activity of each isotope and their mass ratio after two days ?

Solution

Let the two isotopes are A and B such as their half lives are

$$T_A = 12\text{ hr}$$

and $$T_B = 16\text{ hr}$$

Initially their mass ratio is given $\frac{m_A}{m_B} = 3$ [As $m_A > m_B$]

Given that initially activity of isotope A is 1 μCi

$$A_{0A} = 1\ \mu Ci$$

Activity of isotope A after 2 days will be given as

$$A_A = A_{0A}(2)^{-48/12}$$

$$\Rightarrow \quad A_A = \frac{A_{0A}}{16}$$

$$\Rightarrow \quad = \frac{1\mu Ci}{16}$$

$$\Rightarrow \quad = 0.0625\ \mu Ci$$

For the second isotope B it atomic mass assumed to be same the initial activity can be given as

$$A_{0B} = \lambda_B N_B$$

$$\Rightarrow \quad = \frac{\ln(2)}{16} \times \frac{N_A}{3}$$

$$\Rightarrow \quad = \frac{\ln(2)}{16} \times \frac{A_{0A} \times 12}{3 \times \ln_2}$$

$$\Rightarrow \quad A_{0B} = \frac{A_{0A}}{4}$$

After two days activity of second isotope will be

$$A_B = A_{0B}\,(2)^{-48/16}$$

$$\Rightarrow \quad A_B = \frac{A_{0B}}{8} = \frac{A_{0A}}{32}$$

$$\Rightarrow \quad A_B = \frac{1\mu Ci}{32}$$

$$\Rightarrow \quad A_B = 0.03125\ \mu Ci$$

No. of atoms of isotopes A and B left after two days are

$$N'_A = N_A\,(2)^{-4}$$

$$N'_B = N_B\,(2)^{-3}$$

$$\Rightarrow \quad \frac{A'_A}{N'_B} = 3 \times \frac{1}{2} = \frac{3}{2}$$

Illustrative Example 4.14

A small quantity of solution containing Na^{24} radionuclide (half life 15 hours) of activity 1.0 microcurie is injected into the blood of a person. A sample of the blood of volume 1 cm^3 taken after 5 hours shows an activity of 296 disintegrations per minute. Determine the total volume of blood in the body of the person. Assume that the radioactive solution mixes uniformly in the blood of the person (1 curie = 3.7×10^{10} disintegration per second).

Solution

Given that initial activity is

$$A = 1\ \mu \text{Ci}$$

$$\Rightarrow \quad A = 3.7 \times 10^{10} \times 10^{-6} \text{ dps}$$

$$\Rightarrow \quad A = 3.7 \times 10^{4} \text{ dps}$$

After $t = 5$ hrs, the activity present in the solution is

$$A = A_0\,(2)^{-5/15}$$

$$\Rightarrow \quad A = 3.7 \times 10^4 \times 2^{-1/3} \text{ dps}$$

Given that in 1 cm^3 of blood sample is $\frac{296}{60}$ dps. If total value of blood is V then total activity is

$$\frac{296}{60}\,V = \frac{3.7 \times 10^4}{2^{1/3}}$$

$$\Rightarrow \quad V = \frac{3.7 \times 10^4 \times 60}{296 \times 2^{1/3}} \text{ cm}^3$$

$$\Rightarrow \quad V = 5952 \text{ cm}^3 = 5.952 \text{ ltr}$$

Illustrative Example 4.15

In an ore containing uranium, the ratio of ^{238}U to ^{206}Pb nuclei is 3. Calculate the age of the ore, assuming that all the lead present in the ore is the final stable product of ^{238}U. Take the half-life of ^{238}U to be 4.5×10^9 years.

Solution

Presently the ratio of ^{238}U to ^{206}Pb nuclei is 3

$$\frac{N_U}{N_{Pb}} = 3$$

If we consider no. of uranium atoms are

$$N_U = 3N_1$$

Then no. of lead atoms

$$N_{Pb} = N_1$$

Given that all lead atoms are the decay product of uranium thus in the beginning at $t = 0$, no. of uranium atoms can be taken as

$$N_{0U} = 4N_1$$

If are of ore is t then from radioactive decay equation, we have

$$N_U = N_{0U}\,(2)^{-t/T}$$

$$\Rightarrow \quad 3N_1 = 4N_1\,(2)^{-t/4.5 \times 10^9}$$

$$\Rightarrow \quad (2)^{-t/4.5 \times 10^9} = \frac{4}{3}$$

$$\Rightarrow \quad t = 4.5 \times 10^9\,\frac{\log_{10}(4/3)}{\log_{10}(2)} \text{ yrs}$$

$$\Rightarrow \quad t = \frac{4.5 \times 10^9 \times 0.125}{0.301} \text{ yrs}$$

$$\Rightarrow \quad t = 1.868 \times 10^9 \text{ yrs}$$

Illustrative Example 4.16

In the chemical analysis of a rock, the mass ratio of two radioactive isotopes is found to be 100 : 1. The mean lives of the two isotopes are 4×10^9 years and 2×10^9 years respectively. If it is assumed that, at the time of formation of the rock, the atoms of the two isotopes were in equal proportion, estimate the age of the rock. The ratio of the atomic weights of the two isotopes is 1.02 : 1.

Solution

Given that the present mass ratio of the two isotopes is

$$\frac{m_1}{m_2} = 100$$

The ratio of no. of atoms can be given as

$$\frac{N_1}{N_2} = \frac{m_1}{m_2} \times \frac{A_2}{A_1} = 100 \times \frac{1}{1.02} = \frac{100}{1.02}$$

From radioactive decay equation, we have

$$N_1 = N_{10}\, e^{-t/\tau_1} \qquad \ldots(4.26)$$

and

$$N_2 = N_{20}\, e^{-t/\tau_2} \qquad \ldots(4.27)$$

Dividing equation-(4.26) by equation-(4.27)

$$\frac{N_1}{N_2} = e^{-t\left(\frac{1}{\tau_1}-\frac{1}{\tau_2}\right)}$$

$$\Rightarrow \quad t = \frac{\ln\left(\frac{N_1}{N_2}\right)}{\left(\frac{1}{\tau_2}-\frac{1}{\tau_1}\right)}$$

$$\Rightarrow \quad t = \frac{2.303\log\left(\frac{100}{1.02}\right)}{\left(\frac{1}{2\times10^9}-\frac{1}{4\times10^9}\right)} \text{ yrs}$$

$$\Rightarrow \quad t = 1.833 \times 10^{10} \text{ yrs}$$

Illustrative Example 4.17

A bone suspected to have originated during the period of Ashoka the Great, was found in Bihar. Accelerator techniques gave its $\frac{^{14}C}{^{12}C}$ ratio as 1.1×10^{-12}. Is the bone old enough to have belonged to that period ? (Take initial ratio of ^{14}C with ^{12}C $= 1.2 \times 10^{-12}$ and half life of ^{14}C = 5730 years)

Solution

Given that initial ratio of ^{14}C to ^{12}C is

$$\frac{N_{014}}{N_{012}} = 1.2 \times 10^{-12}$$

After time t no. of atoms of ^{14}C can be calculated by decay equation as

$$N_{14} = N_{014}\,(2)^{-t/T}$$

$$\Rightarrow \quad \frac{N_{14}}{N_{012}} = \frac{N_{014}}{N_{012}}\,(2)^{-t/T}$$

[As N_{012} remain unchanged]

$$\Rightarrow \quad 1.1 \times 10^{-12} = 1.2 \times 10^{-12}\,(2)^{-t/T}$$

$$\Rightarrow \quad \frac{t}{T} = \log_2\left(\frac{1.2}{1.1}\right)$$

$$\Rightarrow \quad t = \frac{\log_{10}(12/11)}{\log_{10}(2)} \times 5730 \text{ yr}$$

$$\Rightarrow \quad t = \frac{0.0377}{0.301} \times 5730 \text{ yr}$$

$$\Rightarrow \quad t = 719.1 \text{ yr}$$

Web Reference at www.physicsgalaxy.com

Age Group - High School Physics | Age 17-19 Years

Section - MODERN PHYSICS

Topic - Nuclear Structure & Radioactivity

Module Number - 16 to 30

Practice Exercise 4.2

(i) The half life period of radium is 1590 years. After how many years will one gram of the pure element.

(a) be reduced to one centigram,

(b) lose one centigram.

[10564.78 years, 23.06 years]

(ii) The disintegration rate of a certain radioactive sample at any instant is 4750 disintegrations per minute. Five minutes later the rate becomes 2700 disintegrations per minute. Calculate the half life of the sample.

[6.135 minutes]

(iii) Calculate the activity of one gm sample of $^{90}_{38}$Sr whose half life period is 28.8 years.

[5.106×10^{12} dps]

(iv) The half life of a cobalt radioisotope is 5.3 years. What strength will a millicurie source of the isotope have after a period of one year.

[0.87 mCi]

(v) A sample contains 10^{-2} kg each of two substances A and B with half lives 4 seconds and 8 seconds respectively. Their atomic masses are in the ratio of 1 : 2. Find the amounts of A and B after an interval of 16 seconds.

[6.25×10^{-4} kg, 2.5×10^{-3} kg]

(vi) At a given instant there are 25% undecayed radioactive nuclei in a sample. After 10 seconds the number of undecayed nuclei reduces to 12.5%. Calculate (a) mean-life of the nuclei, and (b) the time in which the number of undecayed nuclei will further reduce to 6.25% of the reduced number.

[(a) 14.43 s, (b) 10 s]

(vii) 1 gram of cesium-137 ($^{137}_{55}$Cs) decays by β-emission with a half-life of 30 years. What is (a) the resulting isotope ? (b) the number of atoms left after 5 years? (c) If initial activity of sample is 1 mCi then what is the activity of cesium after 5 years ?

[(a) $^{137}_{56}$Ba, (b) 3.913×10^{21}, (c) 0.89 mCi.]

(viii) The normal activity of a living matter containing carbon is found to be 15 decays per minute per gram of carbon. An archaeological specimen gives 6 decays per minute per gram of carbon. If the half-life of carbon is 5730 years, estimate the approximate age of the specimen.

[7575.40 years]

(ix) A radioactive isotope X has a half life of 3 second. Initially a given sample of this isotope contains 8000 atoms. Calculate (a) its decay constant, (b) the time t_1 when 1000 atoms of the isotope X remain in the sample, and (c) the number of decay per second in he sample at $t = t_1$.

[(a) 0.231 s^{-1}, (b) 9 s, (c) 231 s^{-1}]

4.4 Radioactive Series

In the discovery of radioactivity we know it was formed that many of radioactive elements are relatively heavy. It was seen that sometime when one nucleus decays into another, the resulting daughter nucleus is also unstable or radioactive and it subsequently decays into another daughter nucleus until a stable element appears. This series of all daughter nuclides we call radioactive series and the end product of the series is a stable isotope.

There are four radioactive series discovered and majority of radioactive elements can be considered to be members of one of these radioactive series. Out of these four, three are naturally found radioactive series and one is artificial laboratory made series. The reason that there are exactly four series follows from the fact that when a radioactive element decays by α-decay, the mass number of nucleus reduces by 4. Due to this we can say that the heavy nuclides having mass number $A = 4n$, where n is an integer, can decay into one another in descending order of mass number constituting a radioactive series. Thus there can be four radioactive series having mass number specified by $4n$, $4n + 1$, $4n + 2$ and $4n + 3$. Table-4.2 lists the four radioactive series. Among all series, the half life of Neptunium is so short as compared to the age of solar system that the members of this series are not found on Earth. This series is produced in laboratory by bombarding other heavy nuclei with neutrons. From table we can see that all three natural radioactive series terminate with the end product lead (Pb) and the artificial series terminates in Bismuth (Bi)

Table 4.2

Mass Numbers	Series	Parent	Half - life, y	Stable End Product
$4n$	Thorium	$^{232}_{90}$Th	1.39×10^{10}	$^{208}_{82}$Pb
$4n+1$	Neptunium	$^{237}_{93}$Np	2.25×10^{6}	$^{209}_{83}$Bi
$4n+2$	Uranium	$^{238}_{92}$U	4.51×10^{9}	$^{206}_{82}$Pb
$4n+3$	Actinium	$^{235}_{92}$U	7.07×10^{8}	$^{207}_{82}$Pb

Figure-4.4 shows the uranium series ($A = 4n + 2$ series) which starts from the parent nucleus $^{238}_{92}$U and terminates in $^{206}_{82}$Pb. All the intermediate elements of the series are shown in figure. We can see here that some of the radioactive nuclei have alternate decay modes, decaying by either alpha emission or beta emission like ^{218}Po, ^{214}Bi, ^{210}Bi etc.

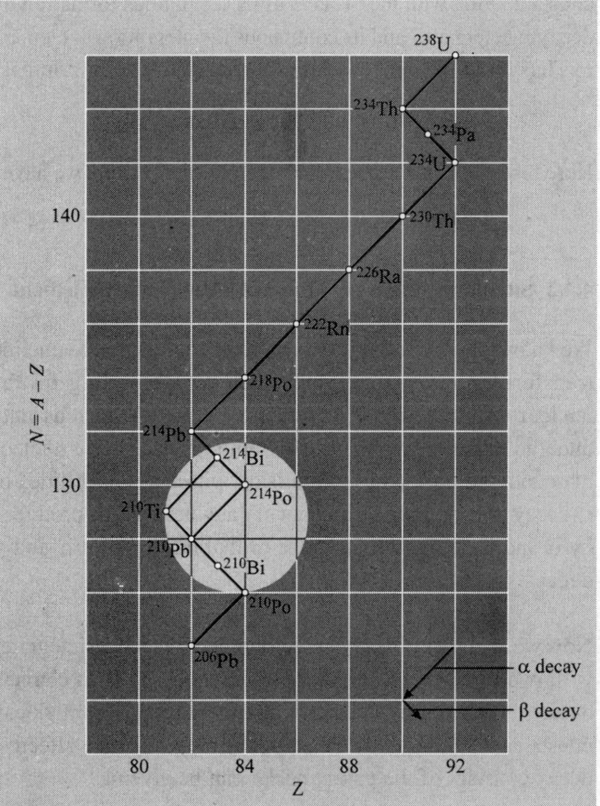

Figure 4.4

4.4.1 Radioactive Equilibrium

In a radioactive series if we talk about an intermediate element, it is produced due to the decay of its previous element and it decays to the next element of the series. In the equation-(4.28) shown an intermediate element J decays to K with a decay constant λ_1 & K decays to L with decay constant λ_2.

$$\longrightarrow \underset{N_1}{J} \xrightarrow{\lambda_1} \underset{N_2}{K} \xrightarrow{\lambda_2} L \qquad \ldots(4.28)$$

If at an instant, N_1 nuclei of J are present, its disintegration rate can be given as

$$R_1 = \lambda_1 N_1 \qquad \ldots(4.29)$$

As J decays to K, the above relation in equation-(4.29) also gives the formation rate of nuclei of K. If at this instant N_2 nuclei of K are present its decay rate can be given as

$$R_2 = \lambda_2 N_2 \qquad \ldots(4.30)$$

If at some instant the production rate and decay rate of the element K becomes equal then the amount of K appears to be a constant as the number of nuclei of K produced per second are equal to the number of nuclei of K disintegrating per second. This situation for the intermediate element K is called radioactive equilibrium. We can also state that this ėquilibrium is a dynamic equilibrium in which the amount of K element appears to be a constant along with the process of its continuous formation by decaying element J and its continuous disintegration to element L. Thus for an element condition of radioactive equilibrium is

$$\text{Rate of formation} = \text{Rate of disintegration}$$

Here fore element K to be in radioactive equilibrium, we have

$$\lambda_1 N_1 = \lambda_2 N_2 \qquad \ldots(4.31)$$

4.4.2 Simultaneous Decay Modes of a Radioactive Element

We know that due to radioactive disintegration a radio nuclide transformed into its daughter nucleus. Depending on the nuclear structure and its unstability a parent nucleus may undergo either α or β emission. Some times a parent nucleus may undergo both types of emission with the probabilities of α-decay or β-decay. The amount of daughter nuclide produced by α and β-decay will be in the probability ratio of α and β decays.

Now we analyze the decay of such elements which disintegrates with two or more decay modes simultaneously. If an element decays to different daughter nuclei with different decay constants $\lambda_1, \lambda_2, \lambda_3, \ldots$ for each decay mode then the effective decay constant of the parent nuclei can be given as

$$\lambda_{\text{eff}} = \lambda_1 + \lambda_2 + \ldots$$

Similarly for a radioactive element with decay constant λ which decays by both α and β-decay is given that the probability for an α emission is P_1 and that for β-emission is P_2 then the decay constant of the element can be split for individual decay modes, like in this case the decay constants for α and β decays separately can be given as

$$\lambda_\alpha = P_1 \lambda$$

and

$$\lambda_\beta = P_2 \lambda$$

4.4.3 Accumulation of a Radioactive Element in Radioactive Series

In a radioactive series, we've discussed that each element decays into its daughter nuclei until a stable element appears. Consider a radioactive series shown below

$$A_1 \xrightarrow{\lambda_1} A_2 \xrightarrow{\lambda_2} A_3 \xrightarrow{\lambda_3} \ldots$$

To analyze mathematically the above series, we assume initially at $t = 0$, N_0 atoms of parent element A_1 are present which decays to the element A_2 with a decay constant λ_1, thus after time t, number of undecayed nuclei of A_1 present at a time instant t can be given be decay law as

$$N_1 = N_0 e^{-\lambda_1 t} \qquad \ldots(4.32)$$

Due to disintegration of A_1, nuclei of A_2 are formed and these start decaying with a decay constant λ_2 to another element A_3. Let at an instant t, N_2 undecayed nuclei of A_2 are present then the decay rate of A_2 at this instant can be given as

$$\text{Decay rate of} \quad A_2 = \lambda_2 N_2 \qquad \ldots(4.33)$$

Due to disintegration of A_1, A_2 is produced thus the production rate of nuclei of A_2 will be the decay rate of nuclei of A_1, thus production rate of A_2 at this instant can be given as

$$\text{Production rate of} \quad A_2 = \lambda_1 N_1 \qquad \ldots(4.34)$$

Now in a further time dt, if dN_2 nuclei of element A_2 are accumulated then the accumulation rate of nuclei of element A_2 can be given as

$$\frac{dN_2}{dt} = \lambda_1 N_1 - \lambda_2 N_2$$

$$\Rightarrow \quad \frac{dN_2}{dt} + \lambda_2 N_2 = \lambda_1 N_0 e^{-\lambda_1 t} \qquad \ldots(4.35)$$

Equation-(4.35) is a simple linear differential equation which on solving gives the number of nuclei of element A_2 as a function of time t. On solving equation-(4.35) we get

$$N_2 = \frac{\lambda_1 N_0}{(\lambda_1 - \lambda_2)} (e^{-\lambda_2 t} - e^{-\lambda_1 t}) \qquad \ldots(4.36)$$

Here we can see that in the begging as $N_2 = 0$, due to disintegration of A_1, A_2 is being formed and as the amount of A_1 is decreased and that of A_2 is increased, decay rate of A_2 increases and that of A_1 decreases. After a time when both decay rate becomes equal, the element A_2 will be said to be in radioactive equilibrium and later the amount of A_2 start decreasing with time. Thus it is the state of radioactive equilibrium when the yield of the radionuclide A_2 is maximum.

Lets take some examples to understand the above phenomenon better.

Illustrative Example 4.18

A ^{32}P radionuclide with half life 14.3 days is produced in a reactor at a constant rate $q = 2.7 \times 10^9$ per second. How soon after the beginning of production of radionuclide will its activity be equal to $A = 1 \times 10^9$ disintegration/sec.

Solution

In the reactor just after production of radio nuclide, it starts decaying. The accumulation rate of the radio nuclide can be given as

$$\frac{dN}{dt} = q - \lambda N$$

$$\Rightarrow \quad \frac{dN}{q-\lambda N} = dt$$

$$\Rightarrow \quad \int_0^N \frac{dN}{q-\lambda N} = \int_0^t dt$$

$$\Rightarrow \quad -\frac{1}{\lambda}\ln\left(\frac{q-\lambda N}{q}\right) = t$$

$$\Rightarrow \quad q - \lambda N = q\,e^{-\lambda t}$$

$$\Rightarrow \quad t = \frac{1}{\lambda}\ln\left(\frac{q}{q-\lambda N}\right)$$

When activity $\lambda N = 1 \times 10^9$ dps then

$$\Rightarrow \quad t = \frac{14.3}{\ln(2)} \times \ln\left(\frac{2.7}{1.7}\right)$$

$$\Rightarrow \quad t = \frac{14.3}{\log_{10}(2)}\log_{10}\left(\frac{27}{17}\right)$$

$$\Rightarrow \quad t = \frac{14.3}{0.301} \times 0.201$$

$$\Rightarrow \quad t = 9.55 \text{ days}$$

Illustrative Example 4.19

The mean lives of a radioactive substance are 1620 years and 405 years for α-emission and β-emission respectively. Find out the time during which three fourth of a sample will decay if it is decaying both by α-emission and β-emission simultaneously.

Solution

The decay constants for α and β emissions are 1/1620 and 1/405 per year respectively.

In this case effective decay constant for both decays simultaneously is

$$\lambda = \lambda_\alpha + \lambda_\beta$$

$$\Rightarrow \quad \lambda = \frac{1}{1620} + \frac{1}{405} = \frac{1}{324}\ \text{year}^{-1}$$

Let t be time in which the given sample decays three fourth. Therefore, the fraction of sample undecayed in time t is 1/4. Hence

$$N = N_0/4$$

Now from decay equation

$$N = N_0\,e^{-\lambda t}$$

$$\Rightarrow \quad \frac{N_0}{4} = N_0\,e^{-\lambda t}$$

$$\Rightarrow \quad t = \frac{\ln(4)}{\lambda} = 1.386 \times 324 = 449 \text{ yr}$$

Illustrative Example 4.20

Lead ^{206}Pb is found in a certain uranium ore due to disintegration of uranium. What is the age of uranium ore if it now contains 0.8 gm of ^{206}Pb for each gram of ^{238}U given the half life of uranium $= 4.5 \times 10^9$ years.

Solution

206 grams of Pb is produced by 238 grams of ^{238}U

Hence 0.8 grams of Pb will produced by

$$\frac{238}{206} \times 0.8 = 0.92427 \text{ grams of } ^{238}U$$

Now from decay equation we use

$$m = m_0\,e^{-\lambda t}$$

$$\Rightarrow \quad 1 = 1.92427\,e^{-(0.693\,t/4.5 \times 10^9)}$$

Here $\qquad m_0 = 1 + 0.92427 = 1.92427$

$$\Rightarrow \quad \frac{1}{1.92427} = e^{-(0.693\,t/4.5\times10^9)}$$

$$\Rightarrow \quad \frac{0.693\,t}{4.5\times10^9} = \ln(1.92427)$$

$$= 2.303\log_{10}(1.92427)$$

$$\Rightarrow \quad t = \frac{4.5\times10^9}{0.693}[2.303\log_{10}(1.92427)]$$

$$= 4.25\times10^9\text{ yr}$$

Illustrative Example 4.21

Find the half-life of uranium, given that 3.32×10^{-7} gm of radium is found per gm of uranium in old minerals. The atomic weight of uranium and radium are 238 and 226 and half-life of radium is 1600 years. (Avogadro Number is 6.023×10^{23}/gm-atom)

Solution

In very old minerals, the amount of an element is constant this implies that the element exist in radioactive equilibrium thus here we can use

$$\lambda_U N_U = \lambda_R N_R$$

$$\Rightarrow \quad \frac{N_U}{T_U} = \frac{N_R}{T_R}$$

$$\Rightarrow \quad T_U = \frac{N_U}{N_R}\times T_R$$

$$\Rightarrow \quad T_U = \frac{m_U A_R}{m_R A_U}\times T_R$$

$$\Rightarrow \quad T_U = \frac{1\times226}{3.32\times10^{-7}\times238}\times1600\text{ yr}$$

$$\Rightarrow \quad T_U = 4.7\times10^9\text{ yr}$$

Illustrative Example 4.22

A sample of uranium is a mixture of three isotopes ${}^{234}_{92}U$, ${}^{235}_{92}U$ and ${}^{238}_{92}U$ present in the ratio of 0.006%, 0.71% and 99.284% respectively. The half-lives of these isotopes are 2.5×10^5 years, 7.1×10^8 years and 4.5×10^9 years respectively. Calculate the contribution to activity (in %) of each isotope in this sample.

Solution

Activity $\qquad R = \lambda N = \frac{0.693}{T}N$

Where T = half life period and N = number of molecules,

Further,

$$N = \frac{\text{mass of the sample}\times\text{Avogadro's number}}{\text{mass number}}$$

Let the total mass of uranium mixture be M

Then, mass of ${}^{234}_{92}U$,

$$M_1 = \frac{0.006}{100}M$$

mass of ${}^{235}_{92}U$,

$$M_2 = \frac{0.71}{100}M$$

and mass of ${}^{238}_{92}U$,

$$M_3 = \frac{99.284}{100}M$$

Again, $\quad N_1 = \frac{0.006}{100}M\times\frac{6.03\times10^{23}}{234}$

and $\quad R_1 = \frac{0.693}{2.5\times10^5}\times\frac{0.006M}{100}\times\frac{6.03\times10^{23}}{234}$

$$N_2 = \frac{0.71}{100}M\times\frac{6.03\times10^{23}}{235}$$

and $\quad R_2 = \frac{0.693}{7.1\times10^8}\times\frac{0.71M}{100}\times\frac{6.03\times10^{23}}{235}$

and $\quad N_3 = \frac{99.284}{100}M\times\frac{6.03\times10^{23}}{238}$

and $\quad R_3 = \frac{0.693}{4.5\times10^9}\times\frac{99.284\,M}{100}\times\frac{6.03\times10^{23}}{238}$

Thus activities are in the ratio

$$\frac{0.006}{234\times(2.5\times10^5)} : \frac{0.71}{235\times(7.1\times10^8)}$$

$$0.01026 : 0.000426$$

$$: \frac{99.284}{238\times(4.5\times10^9)}$$

$$: 0.00927$$

Total activity = 0.019956

%Activities, $\frac{0.01026}{0.019956}\times100 = 51.41\%$

$$\frac{0.000426}{0.019956}\times100 = 2.13\%$$

$$\frac{0.00927}{0.019956}\times100 = 46.45\%$$

Illustrative Example 4.23

A radionuclide with half life T is produced in a reactor at a constant rate p nuclei per second. During each decay, energy E_0 is released. If production of radionuclide is started at $t = 0$, calculate

(a) rate of release of energy as a function of time

(b) total energy released upto time t

Solution

As production rate of radionuclide is p, the accumulation rate of these nuclide in the reactor can be given as

$$\frac{dN}{dt} = p - \lambda N \qquad \left[\text{Where } \lambda = \frac{\ln_2}{T}\right]$$

$$\Rightarrow \quad \frac{dN}{p - \lambda N} = dt$$

$$\Rightarrow \quad \int_0^N \frac{dN}{p - \lambda N} = \int_0^t dt$$

$$\Rightarrow \quad -\frac{1}{\lambda} \ln\left(\frac{p - \lambda N}{p}\right) = t$$

$$\Rightarrow \quad \frac{p - \lambda N}{p} = e^{-\lambda t}$$

$$\Rightarrow \quad \lambda N = p(1 - e^{-\lambda t}) \qquad \ldots(4.37)$$

Thus after time t the activity of radionuclide in the reactor is

$$A_c = \lambda N = p(1 - e^{-\lambda t})$$

Given that during each decay an energy E_0 is released, thus rate of energy release or power of reactor P at time t is

$$P = A_c \times E_0$$

$$\Rightarrow \quad = p E_0 (1 - e^{-\lambda t}) \qquad \left[\text{Where } \lambda = \frac{\ln_2}{T}\right]$$

Upto time t, number of undecayed nuclei can be given by equation-(4.37) as

$$N = \frac{p}{\lambda}(1 - e^{-\lambda t})$$

In a time t, total number of nuclei produced are pt. Thus upto time t, number of nuclei decayed are

$$N_D = pt - N$$

Thus total energy released upto time t is

$$E_T = N_D \times E_0$$

$$\Rightarrow \quad = (pt - N) E_0$$

$$\Rightarrow \quad = pt E_0 - \frac{pE_0 T}{\ln_2}(1 - e^{-\lambda t})$$

Illustrative Example 4.24

Nuclei of a radioactive element A are being produced at a constant rate α. The element has a decay constant λ. At time $t = 0$, there are N_0 nuclei of the element.

(a) Calculate the number N of nuclei of A at time t

(b) If $\alpha = 2N_0\lambda$, calculate the number of nuclei of A after one half-life of A, and also the limiting value of N as $t \to \infty$

Solution

(a) At $t = 0$, $N = N_0$

Rate of decay $= -\lambda N$, and rate of formation $= \alpha$, thus accumulation rate of element is

$$\Rightarrow \quad \frac{dN}{dt} = \alpha - \lambda N$$

$$\Rightarrow \quad \frac{dN}{\alpha - \lambda N} = dt$$

Integrating this expression, we get

$$\Rightarrow \quad \ln\left[\frac{\alpha - \lambda N}{\alpha - \lambda N_0}\right] = -\lambda t$$

$$\Rightarrow \quad \frac{\alpha - \lambda N}{\alpha - \lambda N_0} = e^{-\lambda t}$$

$$\Rightarrow \quad \alpha - \lambda N = (\alpha - \lambda N_0) e^{-\lambda t}$$

$$\Rightarrow \quad N = \frac{1}{\lambda}[\alpha - (\alpha - \lambda N_0) e^{-\lambda t}]$$

(b) If $\alpha = 2N_0\lambda$

$$N = \frac{1}{\lambda}[2N_0\lambda - (2N_0\lambda - N_0\lambda)e^{-\lambda t}]$$

$$\Rightarrow \quad N = N_0[2 - e^{-\lambda t}]$$

At the time of half-life,

$$T = (0.693/\lambda)$$

So, $$N = N_0[2 - e^{-0.693}] = \frac{3N_0}{2}$$

Limiting value of N (as $t \to \infty$)

$$N = N_0[2 - e^{-\infty}] = 2N_0$$

Web Reference at www.physicsgalaxy.com

Age Group - High School Physics | Age 17-19 Years
Section - MODERN PHYSICS
Topic - Nuclear Structure & Radioactivity
Module Number - 31 to 37

Practice Exercise 4.3

(i) A radio nuclide A_1 with decay constant λ_1 transforms into a radio nuclide A_2 with decay constant λ_2. Assuming that at the initial moment the preparation contained only the radio nuclide A_1. Consider initially there were N_0 nuclei of A_1 were there at $t = 0$, find :

(a) The equation describing accumulation of radio nuclide A_2 with time.

(b) The time interval after which the activity of radio nuclide A_2 reaches its maximum value.

[(a) $N_2(t) = \frac{\lambda_1 N_0}{\lambda_2 - \lambda_1}(e^{-\lambda_1 t} - e^{-\lambda_2 t})$ (b) $\frac{\ln(\lambda_2/\lambda_1)}{\lambda_2 - \lambda_1}$]

(ii) $^{212}_{83}Bi$ can disintegrate either by emitting an α-particle or by emitting a β-particle.

(a) Write the two equations showing the products of the decays.

(b) The probabilities of disintegration by α- and β-decays are in the ratio 7/13. The overall half-life of ^{212}Bi is one hour. If 1 *g* of pure ^{212}Bi is taken at 12.00 noon, what will be the composition of this sample at 1 p.m. the same day ?

[(a) $^{212}_{83}Bi \rightarrow {}^{208}_{81}Tl + \alpha$, $^{212}_{83}Bi \rightarrow {}^{212}_{83}Bi \rightarrow {}^{212}_{84}Po + e^- + \bar{\nu}$, (b) 0.50 g – Bi, 0.175 g-Tl, 0.325 g – Po]

(iii) A ^{210}Bi radionuclide decays via the chain $^{210}Bi \xrightarrow[\lambda_1]{\beta^-} {}^{210}Po \xrightarrow[\lambda_2]{\alpha} {}^{206}Pb$ (stable), where the decay constants are $\lambda_1 = 1.6 \times 10^{-6}\ s^{-1}$, $\lambda_2 = 5.8 \times 10^{-8}\ s^{-1}$. Calculate α & β activities of the ^{210}Bi preparation of mass 1.00 mg a month after its manufacture.

[$N_p = N_0 \lambda_1 \exp.(-\lambda t) = 0.72 \times 10^{11}$ part/s, $A_\alpha = \frac{N_0 \lambda_1 \lambda_2}{\lambda_2 - \lambda_1}[e^{-\lambda_1 t} - e^{-\lambda_1 t}]$]

(iv) A human body excretes (removes by waste discharge, sweating etc.) certain materials by a law similar to radioactivity. If technetium is injected in some form in a human body, the body excretes half the amount in 24 hours. A patient is given an injection containing ^{99}Tc. This isotope is radioactive with a half-life of 6 hours. The activity from the body just after the injection is 6 μCi. How much time will elapse before the activity falls to 3 μCi ?

[4.8 hours]

(v) ^{57}Co decays to ^{57}Fe by β + emission. The resulting ^{57}Fe is in its excited state and comes to the ground state by emitting γ-rays. The half life of β^+ decay is 270 days and that of the γ-emission is 10^{-8} sec. A sample of ^{57}Co gives 5×10^9 gamma rays per second. How much time will elapse before the emission rate of gamma rays drops to 2.5×10^9 per second ?

[270 days]

(vi) A radionuclide A_1 goes through the transformation chain $A_1 \longrightarrow A_2 \longrightarrow A_3$ (stable) with respective decay constants λ_1 and λ_2. Assuming that at the initial moment the preparation contained only the radionuclide A_1 equal in quantity to N_{10} nuclei, find the equation describing accumulation of the stable isotope A_3.

[$\frac{N_{10}}{\lambda_2 - \lambda_1}\left(\lambda_2 - \lambda_1 + \left(\lambda_1 e^{-\lambda_2 t} - \lambda_2 e^{-\lambda_1 t}\right)\right)$]

4.5 Nuclear Reactions

When two nuclei came close to each other, nuclear reaction can occur that results in a new nuclei being formed. Generally it is very difficult to bring nuclei very close as they are positively charged and repulsion between them keeps them beyond the range where they can interact unless they are moving very fast toward each other to decrease the distance of their closest approach to start the nuclear reaction.

In Sun nuclear reactions are very frequent as the temperature is millions of kelvin, the nuclei have sufficient speed to bring then very close to each other and the energy released in reaction maintains the temperature there.

Most of the nuclear reactions occur in two stages or steps. In first step an incident particle strikes a target nucleus and the two combine to form a new nucleus called compound nucleus, which have atomic number and mass number equal to the sum of target nucleus and the striking particle. The compound nucleus is generally formed in excited state because of the initial kinetic energy of the striking particle. It is observed that the compound nuclei have very short life time of the order of 10^{-15} seconds. In second step these compound nuclei may decay in one or more different ways depending on their excitation energy.

Lets discuss an example when an α-particle incident on a $^{14}_{7}N$ nucleus with some kinetic energy. The corresponding nuclear reaction is given in equation-(4.38).

$$+ {}^{4}_{2}H \longrightarrow {}^{18}_{9}F \longrightarrow {}^{17}_{8}O + {}^{1}_{1}H \qquad \ldots(4.38)$$

Here fluorine nucleus $^{18}_{9}F$, formed in an excited state. This has some excess energy which automatically lead it to eject a particle like in this case, a proton ($^1_1$H). As the excited nucleus lasts only for a short time, it is commonly omitted from the equation of nuclear reaction thus above reaction can also be written as

$$^{14}_{7}\text{N} + ^{4}_{2}\text{H} \longrightarrow ^{17}_{8}\text{O} + ^{1}_{1}\text{H} \quad \ldots(4.39)$$

Nuclear reaction such as those written in above have a general form

$$\text{A} + \text{a} \longrightarrow \text{B} + \text{b} \quad \ldots(4.40)$$

Here uppercase letters represent the nuclei and the lowercase letter represent the particles. The shorthand form of above reaction is written as

$$\text{A (a, b) B} \quad \ldots(4.41)$$

For the example we've taken above equation-(4.39) can be written as

$$^{14}_{7}\text{N}(\alpha, \text{p})\, ^{17}_{8}\text{O} \quad \ldots(4.42)$$

4.5.1 Q-Value of Nuclear Reaction

Q-value of a nuclear reaction is defined as the difference in the rest mass energies of particle and nuclei before reaction and those of products formed after reaction. For example in a nuclear reaction.

$$\text{A} + \text{B} \longrightarrow \text{C} + \text{D} \quad \ldots(4.43)$$

The Q-value of above reaction is defined as

$$Q = (m_A + m_B - m_C - m_D)\, c^2 \quad \ldots(4.44)$$

If in a reaction energy is released, Q is a positive quantity. If in a reaction Q is a negative quantity then for reaction to take place energy must be supplied to the system.

There are two major categories of nuclear reactions, we'll discuss in detail. These are

(i) Nuclear fission

(ii) Nuclear fusion

lets discuss these in detail.

4.6 Nuclear Fission

Figure-4.5 shows the variation of Binding Energy per nucleon with mass number of different element. We have discussed that the middle weight elements are more stable then the heavy weight elements. Thus if we can break a large nucleus into smaller nuclei energy must be released. If the released energy is more then that required, to split the nucleus then the difference energy can be converted into useful forms.

The phenomenon of splitting a heavier nuclei into two or more lesser weight fragments is known as nuclear fission.

For example in the figure say ^{150}X is a heavy element with Binding energy per nucleon E_X then to break it into nucleons energy required is

$$U_1 = 150\, E_X \quad \ldots(4.45)$$

If nuclei splits into two fragments Y and Z according to reaction given in equation-(4.46)

$$^{150}X \longrightarrow {}^{60}Y + {}^{90}Z + \Delta E \quad \ldots(4.46)$$

Then the amount of energy released in formation of nuclei Y and Z is

$$U_2 = 60\, E_Y + 90\, E_Z \quad \ldots(4.47)$$

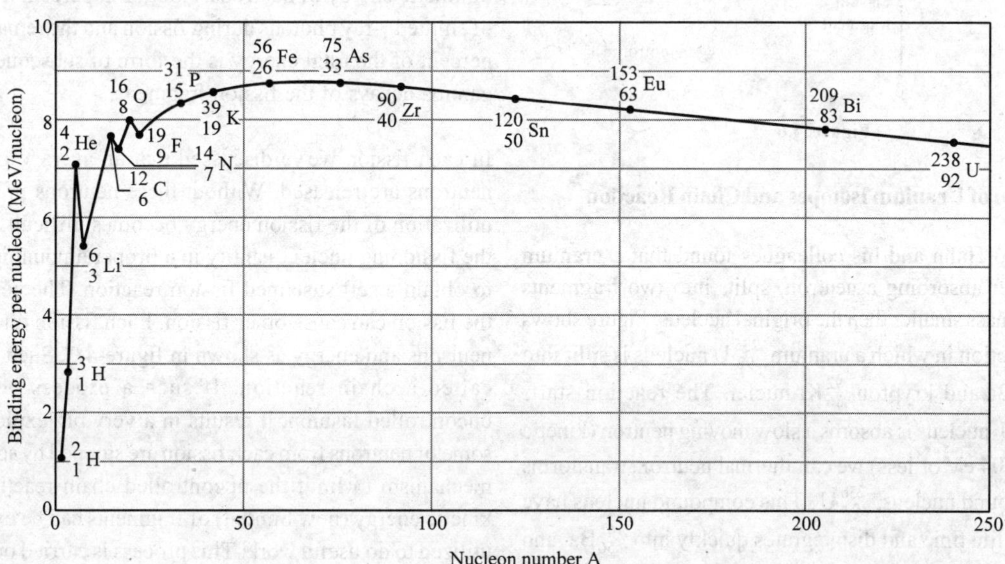

Figure 4.5

Where E_Y and E_Z are the binding energy per nucleon of nuclei Y and Z respectively. Thus the energy released in the fission of nucleus X per fission ΔE can be given as

$$\Delta E = U_2 - U_1$$

$$= 60\,E_Y + 90\,E_Z - 150\,E_X \quad \dots(4.48)$$

The above energy ΔE or Q-value of this reaction can also be calculated by mass defect Δm of this reaction as

$$\Delta E = \Delta mc^2$$

$$= (m_X - m_Y - m_Z)\,c^2 \quad \dots(4.49)$$

The fission fragments formed by fission of a heavy nuclei are of unequal size because the heavy nuclei have a greater neutron to proton ratio as compared to light nuclei, thus the fragments will have more neutrons. Hence to achieve stability generally out of two fission fragments, one is a middle weight fragment and other is a relatively heavy element because of excess neutrons in the heavy nucleus. To reduce this excess, two or three neutrons are emitted by the fragments as soon as they are formed and subsequent beta decays followed by γ-emission adjust their n/p ratio to stable values.

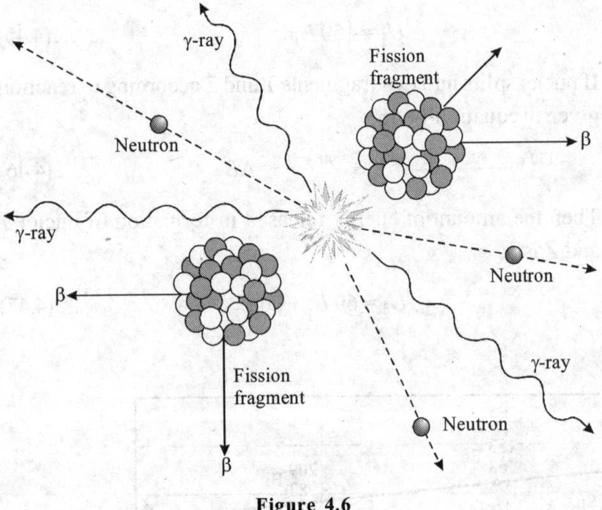

Figure 4.6

4.6.1 Fission of Uranium Isotopes and Chain Reaction

In 1939 Otto Hahn and his colleagues found that a uranium nucleus, after absorbing a neutron, splits into two fragments each with a mass smaller then the original nucleus. Figure shows a fission reaction in which a uranium $^{235}_{92}U$ nucleus is split into barium $^{141}_{56}Ba$ and krypton $^{92}_{36}Kr$ nuclei. The reaction starts when a $^{235}_{92}U$ nucleus is absorbs a slow moving neutron (kinetic energy $\simeq$ 0.04 eV or less) we call thermal neutron, transforms into a compound nucleus, $^{236}_{92}U$. This compound nucleus have a very short life time and disintegrates quickly into $^{141}_{56}Ba$ and $^{92}_{36}Kr$ and three neutrons. The reaction can be written as

$$^1_0n + {}^{235}_{92}U \rightarrow {}^{236}_{92}U^* \rightarrow {}^{141}_{56}Ba + {}^{92}_{36}Kr + 3\,{}^1_0n \quad \dots(4.50)$$

The above reaction is one out of many possible reactions like

$$^1_0n + {}^{235}_{92}U \rightarrow {}^{236}_{92}U^* \rightarrow {}^{140}_{54}Xe + {}^{94}_{38}Sr + 2\,{}^1_0n \quad \dots(4.51)$$

But it is observed that the maximum yield of the reaction is for equation-(4.50). Some reaction may produce as many as 5 neutrons but the average number of neutrons produced per fission is 2.5.

Fission processes have the possibility of some practical uses because we have positive Q-values of the reaction. The positive Q-value occurs because the heavy element break up into two fragments that are more tightly bound and therefore have less total mass energy.

A heavy nucleus undergo fission when it has enough excitation energy so that the compound nucleus oscillate violently. For example ^{238}U (which is about 99.3% in natural uranium) undergo fission reaction only by fast neutrons whose kinetic energy are more then 1 MeV. Whereas few nuclei like ^{235}U are able to split into two nuclei by just absorbing neutron. For such cases very slow neutrons are required to start fission reaction as in fast neutrons the contact time of neutron with the nuclei is very less to start fission with such nuclei.

Another important aspect of nuclear fission is the amount of large magnitude of energy released. For example during fission of each uranium nuclei about 200 MeV energy is released. In all fission reactions major fraction of the energy released is in the form of kinetic energy of the fragments. Roughly about 80 to 85 percent of the energy released is carried by the fragments of fission as their kinetic energy. About 2-3 percent is in the form of kinetic energy of neutrons. About 2-5 percent is in the form of emitted γ-ray photons during fission and the remaining 10-15 percent of the total energy is the form of subsequent beta and gamma decays of the fission fragments.

In each fission we've discussed that an average of about 2-5 neutrons are released. Without these neutrons practically the utilization of the fission energy becomes difficult. If we place the fissioning nuclei quantity in a proper amount it is possible to obtain a self sustained fission reaction. The neutrons from the fission can cause other fission. Each fission releasing more neutrons and energy as shown in figure-4.7. Such a process is called a chain reaction. If such a process occurs in an uncontrolled fashion, it results in a very big explosion. If the some of neutrons from each fission are stopped by some external mechanism to limit the uncontrolled chain reaction then the kinetic energy (now limited) of fragments can be extracted and utilized to do useful work. This process is carried out in nuclear fueled power plants.

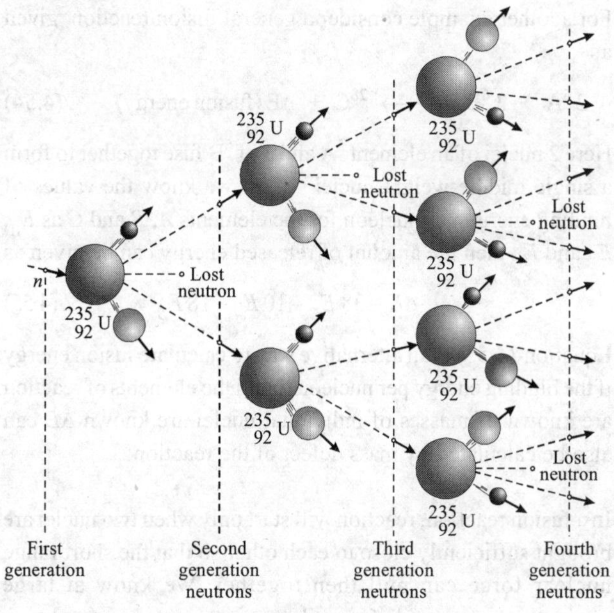

Figure 4.7

The major problem in above cases of energy production is, the products of the fission process are extremely radioactive. These are in majority γ-emitters with large lives, which is a wizard for health.

Most of the nuclear reactors use uranium as their nuclear fuel. As we've discussed that in natural uranium only 0.7% is ^{235}U rest is ^{238}U. In chain reaction ^{235}U plays an important role. Thus before using in nuclear reactor natural uranium is processed and enriched to about 3.5% of the isotope ^{235}U.

Some students may think why ^{238}U do not participate in a chain reaction. The answer is simple. As we've discussed that to start fission in ^{238}U we need very fast neutrons having kinetic energies more than about 1 MeV. Other wise ^{238}U when struck by a neutron, it captures the neutron to become ^{239}U and according to equation-(4.50) it decays to ^{239}Pu by emitting two β particles and ^{235}U immediately fissions when struck by a slow moving thermal neutron. The reactions

$$ {}^{1}_{0}n + {}^{238}_{92}U \longrightarrow {}^{239}_{92}U + \gamma \qquad \ldots(4.52a) $$

$$ {}^{239}_{92}U \longrightarrow {}^{239}_{93}Np + {}^{1}_{-0}e + \gamma \qquad \ldots(4.52b) $$

$$ {}^{239}_{93}Np \longrightarrow {}^{239}_{94}Pu + {}^{1}_{-0}e + \gamma \qquad \ldots(4.52c) $$

In a nuclear reactor, the probability that of a neutron will cause ^{235}U to fission is more for a slow moving neutrons. Thus there is less probability that the fast neutrons produced in fission will cause other fission to occur and chain reaction will start. To slow down these neutrons (to initiate more fission events) in a nuclear reactor moderator is used which may be ordinary water carbon or heavy water (D_2O).

The neutrons lose their kinetic energy by collisions with moderator and they slow down initial their kinetic energy is of the other of thermal neutrons to start further fission events. Detailed explanation of nuclear reactor is not given here as in earlier classes you have studied about a nuclear reactor in detail. We advise you to refer the same once again.

4.6.2 Liquid Drop Model

Nuclear fission of uranium can be understood on the basis of liquid drop model of nucleus. When a neutron strikes the ^{235}U nuclei, it is captured by the nucleus and it is transformed into the excited ^{236}U* which due to excess energy oscillates in a variety of ways. Figure-4.8(a) shows the stages of oscillations of the ^{236}U as a liquid drop. The drop in turn becomes a spheroid, a sphere, an oblate spheroid, a sphere and a prolate spheroid again and so on.

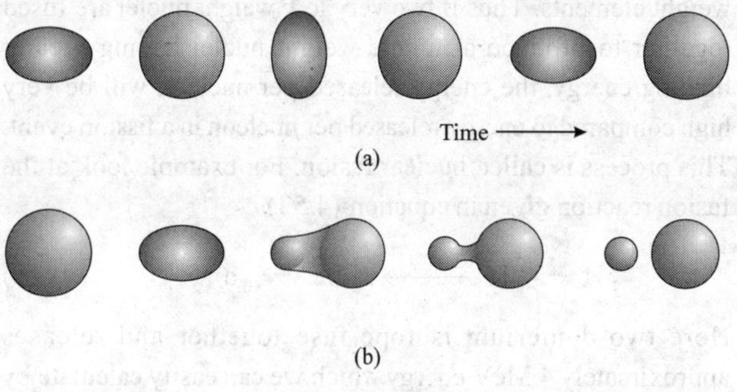

Figure 4.8

Oscillating stages of compound nucleus ^{236}U*

The inertia of the moving liquid molecules causes the drop to overshoot sphericity and go to the opposite extreme of distortion. It is observed the nuclei exhibit surface tension and these can vibrate like a liquid drop when in excited state. For small excitation it is possible to oscillate like this as distortion in nucleus is recovered back by its surface tension. But when excitation is large and distortion in nucleus is large, once the excitation energy of nucleus is given off in the form of γ-ray photon, the surface tension due to short range strong nuclear forces is not able to bring back the nucleus into its spheical shape and the nucleus splits into two parts as shown in figure-4.8(b).

4.7 Nuclear Fusion

If we again look at the figure-4.9 which shows variation of binding energy per nucleon of elements with mass number, we can see that for heavy weight elements average binding energy per nucleon is about 7.8 MeV and for middle weight stable elements it is about 8.6 MeV. Thus we can say that the average energy released per nucleon by fission is the difference between these two values about 0.9 MeV per nucleon.

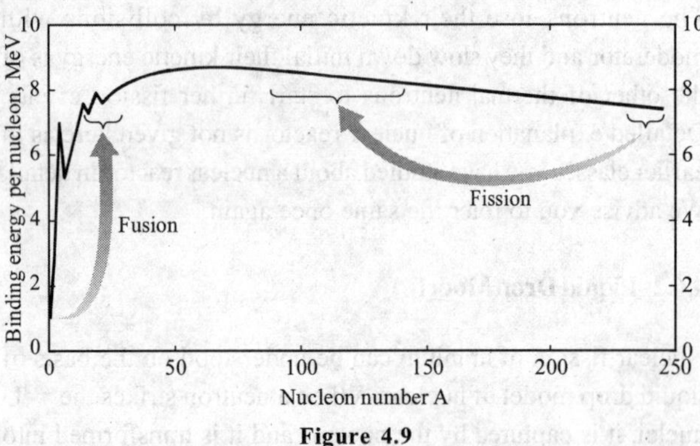

Figure 4.9

Now if we take a look on the left portion of this curves, the steepness is relatively high or we can say that the difference in binding energy per nucleon between very light nuclei and middle weight nuclei are much more compared to heavy and middle weight elements. Thus if two very low weight nuclei are fused together to produce a middle weight nuclei having greater binding energy, the energy released per nucleon will be very high compared to energy released per nucleon in a fission event. This process is called nuclear fusion. For example look at the fusion reaction given in equation-(4.53)

$$_1^2H + _1^2H \longrightarrow _2^3He + _0^1n \qquad \ldots(4.53)$$

Here two deuterium isotope fuse together and releases approximately 4 MeV energy which we can easily calculate by using mass defect of the reaction. This energy is about the same energy per nucleon released in a fission event. But the most important thing is most of the fusion reaction products such as $_2^3He$ here are stable and non radioactive.

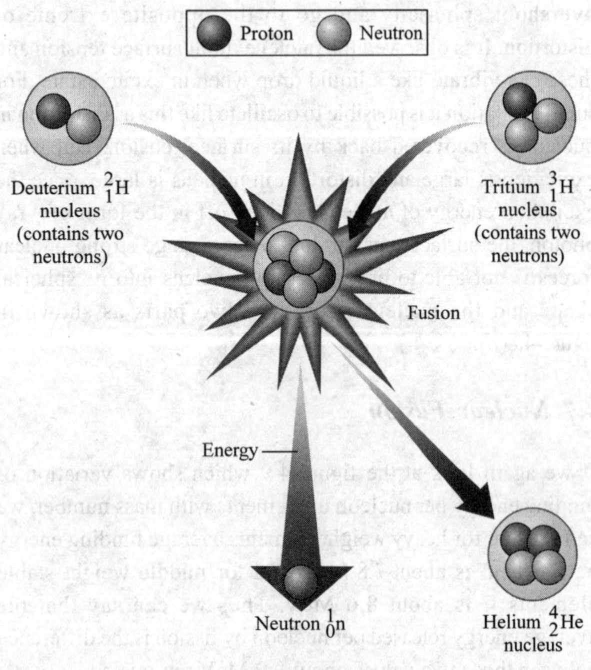

Figure 4.10

For another example consider a general fusion reaction, given as

$$2\,^5A + 3\,^6B \longrightarrow \,^{28}C + \Delta E\,(\text{fusion energy}) \quad \ldots(4.54)$$

Here 2 nuclei of an element ^5A and 3 of ^6B fuse together to form a single middle weight nuclei ^{28}C. If we know the values of binding energy per nucleon for the elements A, B and C as E_A, E_B and E_C then the amount of released energy can be given as

$$\Delta E = 38\,E_C - 10\,E_A - 18\,E_B \qquad \ldots(4.55)$$

Equation-(4.55) is an alternative way to calculate fusion energy if the binding energy per nucleon for all the elements of reaction are known. If masses of individual nuclei are known ΔE can also be calculated by mass defect of the reaction.

In a fusion reaction, reaction will start only when two nuclei are brought sufficiently close to each other so that the short range nuclear force can pull then together. We know at large separations coulomb force dominates and due to strong electrostatic repulsion between positive nuclei, it is very difficult to bring nuclei so close that strong nuclear force dominates and start the fusion reaction. This distance at which fusion starts is called coulomb potential energy barrier and it is of the order of 10^{-14} m. At such close distance nuclei will approach each other only when they have large kinetic energies which is possible only at high temperatures of the order of hundreds or thousands of million kelvin.

Such reactions which takes places only at such high temperatures are called thermonuclear reactions. Under such conditions all the atoms are completely ionized in gaseous form. Such a high temperature gas of positive and negative charged particles is called plasma.

The main problem in nuclear reactions is to confine plasma for a long enough time so that collisions among the ions can lead to fusion. There are three methods of confining the plasma named, magnetic confinement, inertial confinement and Z-pinch which is a slight modification of inertial confinement. Detailed analysis of these methods is beyond the scope of this book.

Illustrative Example 4.25

On disintegration of one atom of ^{235}U the amount of energy obtained is 200 MeV. The power obtained in a reactor is 1000 kW. How many atoms are disintegrated per second in the reactor ? What is the decay in mass per hour ?

Solution

Power produced in the reactor is

$$\Rightarrow \qquad P = 1000\,\text{kW} = 1000 \times 10^3\,\text{W}$$

$$\Rightarrow \quad P = 10^6 \text{ J/s}$$

$$\Rightarrow \quad P = \frac{10^6}{1.6 \times 10^{-19}} \text{ eV/s}$$

$$= 6.25 \times 10^{18} \text{ MeV/s}$$

As in each disintegration 200 MeV energy is released, number of atoms disintegrated per second are

$$N = \frac{6.25 \times 10^{18}}{200} = 3.125 \times 10^{16} \text{ s}^{-1}$$

Energy released per second is 10^6 J

Energy released per hour is

$$E = 10^6 \times 60 \times 60 \text{ J}$$

Thus mass decay per hour can be given as

$$\Delta m = \frac{\Delta E}{c^2} \text{ (Einstein's mass energy formula)}$$

$$\Rightarrow \quad \Delta m = \frac{10^6 \times 60 \times 60 \text{J}}{(3 \times 10^8 \text{ m/s})^2}$$

$$\Rightarrow \quad \Delta m = 4 \times 10^{-8} \text{ kg}$$

$$\Rightarrow \quad \Delta m = 4 \times 10^{-5} \text{ gm}$$

 # Illustrative Example 4.26

A reactor is developing nuclear energy at a rate of 32,000 kilowatts. How many kg of ^{235}U undergo fission per second ? How many kg of ^{235}U would be used up in 1000 hours of operation ? Assume an average energy of 200 MeV released per fission. Take Avogadro's number as 6×10^{23} and 1 MeV = 1.6×10^{-13} J.

Solution

Power developed by reactor

$$P = 32{,}000 \text{ kW}$$

$$\Rightarrow \quad P = 3.2 \times 10^7 \text{ watts}$$

Energy released by rector per sec in *eV* is

$$P = \frac{3.2 \times 10^7}{1.6 \times 10^{-13}} \text{ MeV/s}$$

$$P = 2 \times 10^{20} \text{ MeV/s}$$

As in each fission even 200 MeV energy is released, so number of fission events occurring in the reactor per second are

$$\dot{N} = \frac{2 \times 10^{20}}{200} = 10^{18} \text{ s}^{-1}$$

The number of atoms of ^{235}U consumed in 1000 hours are

$$N_1 = 10^{18} \times (1000 \times 3600) = 36 \times 10^{23}$$

Now 1 gm-atoms of ^{235}U has 6×10^{23} atoms. Therefore, the mass of ^{235}U consumed in 1000 hours of operation are

$$m = \frac{36 \times 10^{23}}{6 \times 10^{23}} \times 235 = 1410 \text{ gm}$$

$$\Rightarrow \quad m = 1.41 \text{ kg}$$

 # Illustrative Example 4.27

The fission type of war head of some guided missiles is estimated to be equivalent to 30000 tons of TNT. If 3.5×10^8 joules of energy are released by on tone of exploding TNT how may fissions occur and how much ^{235}U would be consumed in the explosion of war head ? An energy of 200 MeV is released by fission of one atom ^{235}U.

Solution

Energy released by war head = 3000 tons of TNT = $(3.5 \times 10^8)(30000) = 10.5 \times 10^{12}$ J

Number of fusions in war head

$$N = \frac{10.5 \times 10^{12}}{(200 \times 10^6)(1.6 \times 10^{-19})} \text{ gm}$$

$$\Rightarrow \quad N = 0.1279 \text{ kg}$$

 # Illustrative Example 4.28

Calculate the energy released by the fission of 2 gm of $^{235}_{92}$U in kWh. Given that the energy released per fission is 200 MeV.

Solution

The number of atoms in 2 gm of $^{235}_{92}$U are

$$N = \frac{2 \times 6.025 \times 10^{23}}{235} \text{ atoms}$$

Energy released per fission

$$N = 200 \text{ MeV}$$

$$\Rightarrow \quad N = 200 \times 1.6 \times 10^{-13} \text{ J}$$

$$\Rightarrow \quad N = 3.2 \times 10^{-11} \text{ J}$$

Energy released by 2 gm of $^{235}_{92}$U is

$$E = \frac{2 \times 6.025 \times 10^{23}}{235} \times (3.2 \times 10^{-11}) \text{ J}$$

$$\Rightarrow \quad = \frac{2\times 6.025\times 10^{23}}{235} \times \frac{(3.2\times 10^{-11})}{3600\times 10^{3}} \text{ kWh}$$

$$\Rightarrow \quad = 4.55 \times 10^{4} \text{ kWh}$$

Illustrative Example 4.29

In neutron-induced binary fission of $^{235}_{92}U$ (235.044 amu) two stable end products usually formed are $^{98}_{42}Mo$ (97.905 amu) and $^{136}_{54}Xe$ usually formed (135.917 amu). Assuming that these isotopes have come from the original fission process, find (i) what elementary particles are released (ii) mass defect of the reaction (iii) the equivalent energy released.

Solution

(i) The reaction is represented by

$$^{235}_{92}U + {}^{1}_{0}n \rightarrow {}^{98}_{42}Mo + {}^{136}_{54}X$$

From the reaction, it is obvious that the total Z value of two stable fission product is (42 + 54) = 96, which is 4 units more than Z value of left hand side.

This shows that the original unstable products must have emitted 4 β particles. Again mass number on right hand side is 2 units less than on left hand side i.e., two neutrons are also produced. Now the reaction can be represented as

$$^{235}_{92}U + {}^{1}_{0}n \rightarrow {}^{98}_{42}Mo + {}^{136}_{54}Xe + 4\,{}^{0}_{-1}e + 2\,{}^{1}_{0}n$$

(ii) Mass defect,

$$\Delta m = \text{mass of L.H.S.} - \text{mass of R.H.S.}$$

Mass of L.H.S. $= (235.044 + 1.009) = 236.053$ amu

Mass of R.H.S. $= (97.905 + 135.917) + 4\,(0.00055) + 2\,(1.009)$

$$= 235.842 \text{ amu}$$

Thus mass defect is

$$\Delta m = (236.053 - 235.842) \text{ amu}$$

$$= 0.211 \text{ amu}$$

The equivalent energy released is

$$\Delta E = \Delta m \times 931.5 \text{ MeV}$$

$$= 0.211 \times 931.5 \text{ MeV} = 196.54 \text{ MeV}$$

Illustrative Example 4.30

In a nuclear reactor, fission is produced in 1 gm of ^{235}U (235.0349 amu) in assuming that $^{92}_{53}Kr$ (91.8673 amu) and $^{141}_{36}Ba$ (140.9139 amu) are produced in all reactions and no energy is lost, write the complete reaction and calculate the total energy produced in kilowatt-hour. Given 1 amu = 931.5 MeV.

Solution

The nuclear fission reaction in the above process is

$$^{235}_{92}U + {}^{1}_{0}n \rightarrow {}^{141}_{56}Ba + {}^{92}_{36}Kr + 3\,{}^{1}_{0}n$$

The sum of the masses before reaction is

$$235.0439 + 1.0087 = 236.0526 \text{ amu}$$

The sum of the masses after reaction is

$$140.9139 + 91.8973 + (1.0087) = 235.8375 \text{ amu}$$

Mass defect, $\quad \Delta m = 236.0526 - 235.8373 = 0.2153$ amu

Energy released in the fission of ^{235}U nucleus is given by

$$\Delta E = \Delta m \times 931.5 \text{ MeV}$$

$$= 0.2153 \times 931.5 \cong 200 \text{ MeV}$$

Number of atoms in 1 gm of ^{235}U are

$$N = \frac{6.02\times 10^{23}}{235} = 2.56 \times 10^{21}$$

Energy released in fission of 1 gm of ^{235}U

$$E = 200 \times 2.56 \times 10^{21} \text{ MeV}$$

$$= 5.12 \times 10^{23} \text{ MeV}$$

$$= (5.12 \times 10^{23}) \times (1.6 \times 10^{-13})$$

$$= 8.2 \times 10^{10} \text{ joule}$$

$$= \frac{8.2\times 10^{10}}{3.6\times 10^{6}} \text{ kWh}$$

$$= 2.28 \times 10^{4} \text{ kWh}$$

Illustrative Example 4.31

A deuterium reaction that occurs in an experimental fusion reactor is in two stages :

(i) Two deuterium ($^{2}_{1}D$) nuclei fuse together to form a tritium nucleus, with a proton as a by-product written as $D\,(D, p)\,T$.

(ii) A tritium nucleus fuses with another deuterium nucleus to form a helium $^{4}_{2}He$ nucleus with neutron as a by-product, written as $T\,(D, n)\,{}^{4}_{2}He$.

Compute (a) the energy released in each of two stages (b) the energy released in the combined reaction per deuterium, and (c) what percentage of the mass energy of the initial deuterium is released.

Given

$${}_1^2D = 2.014102 \text{ amu}$$
$${}_1^3T = 3.016049 \text{ amu}$$
$${}_2^4He = 4.002603 \text{ amu}$$
$${}_1^1H = 1.007825 \text{ amu}$$
$${}_0^1n = 1.00665 \text{ amu}$$

Solution

(a) The reaction involved in the process is

$${}_1^2D + {}_1^2D \rightarrow {}_1^3T + {}_1^1p + E_1$$

Mass defect of the above reaction is

$$\Delta m = [2(2.014102) - (3.016049 + 1.007825)]$$
$$= 0.00433 \text{ amu}$$

Energy released in the process is

$$E_1 = 0.00433 \times 931.5 \text{ MeV} = 4.033 \text{ MeV}$$

The reaction involved in the process is

$${}_1^3T + {}_1^2D \rightarrow {}_2^4He + {}_0^1n + E_2$$

Mass defect of above reaction is

$$\Delta m = [(3.016049 + 2.014102) - (4.002603 + 1.008665)]$$
$$= 0.01888 \text{ amu}$$

Energy released in the process is

$$E_2 = 0.01888 \times 931.5 \text{ MeV} = 17.586 \text{ MeV}$$

Total energy released in both processes

$$= 17.586 + 4.033 = 21.619 \text{ MeV}$$

(b) Energy released per deuterium atom is

$$E_1 = \frac{21.619}{3} = 7.206 \text{ MeV}$$

(c) % of rest mass of ${}_1^2D$ released

$$f = \frac{7.206}{2.014102 \times 931} = 0.385\%$$

Illustrative Example 4.32

In the process of nuclear fission of 1 gram uranium, the mass lost is 0.92 milligram. The efficiency of power house run by the fission reactor is 10%. To obtain 400 megawatt power from the power house, how much uranium will be required per hour ? $(c = 3 \times 10^8 \text{ m/s})$

Solution

Power to be obtained from power house = 400 MW

In this case energy obtained per hour = 400 MW × 1 hour

$$= (400 \times 10^6 \text{ watt}) \times 3600 \text{ s}$$
$$= 144 \times 10^{10} \text{ J}$$

Here only 10% of output is utilized. In order to obtain 144×10^{10} joule of useful energy, the output energy from the power house is given by

$$E = \frac{(144 \times 10^{10}) \times 100}{10}$$
$$= 144 \times 10^{11} \text{ J}$$

Let, this energy is obtained from a mass-loss of Δm kg. Then

$$(\Delta m) c^2 = 144 \times 10^{11} \text{ J}$$

$$\Rightarrow \qquad \Delta m = \frac{144 \times 10^{11}}{(3 \times 10^8)^2} = 16 \times 10^{-5} \text{ kg}$$
$$= 0.16 \text{ gm.}$$

Since 0.92 milli gram (= 0.92×10^{-3} gm) mass is lost in 1 gm uranium, hence for a mass loss of 0.16 gm the uranium required is given by

$$\Delta m' = \frac{1 \times 0.16}{0.92 \times 10^{-3}} = 174 \text{ gm}$$

Thus to run the power house, 174 gm uranium is required per hour.

Illustrative Example 4.33

The energy received from the sun by earth and its surrounding atmosphere is 2 cals/cm^2/min on a surface normal to the rays of sun.

(a) What is the total energy received in joules by earth and its atmosphere.

(b) What is the total energy radiated in J/m by sun to the universe ? Distance of sun to earth is 1.49×10^8 km.

(c) At what rate in mega-grams per minute must hydrogen be consumed in the fusion reaction to provide the sun with the energy it radiates ?

Take mass of hydrogen atom = 1.008145 amu

Take mass of He atom = 4.003874 amu

Solution

(a) Let D be the diameter of earth. Then effective area of earth receiving radiation normally is given as

$$A = \pi R^2 = \frac{\pi D^2}{4}$$

$$= \frac{\pi(1.27\times10^4)^2}{4}\ \text{km}^2$$

$$= \frac{\pi}{4}(1.27)^2 \times 10^{18}\ \text{cm}^2$$

Energy received by earth per minute

$$= \left\{\frac{\pi}{4}(1.27)^2 \times 10^{18}\right\} \times (2\times 4.2)\ \text{J/m}$$

$$= 10.645 \times 10^{18}\ \text{J/m}$$

(b) The area of the surface surrounding sun at a distance equal to earth distance = $4\pi d^2$

$$= 4\pi\,(1.49 \times 10^8)^2 \times 10^6 \times 10^4\ \text{cm}^2$$

$$= 4p\,(1.49)^2 \times 10^{26}\ \text{cm}^2$$

The energy is received at the rate of 2 cal/cm^2/min on this surface. This amount of energy must be radiated by sun

The energy radiated by sun in J/min is

$$E = 2\times 4.2 \times [4\pi\,(1.49)^2 \times 10^{26}]\ \text{J/min}$$

$$= 2.3444 \times 10^{28}\ \text{J/min}$$

(c) We know that the fusion reaction in sum is

$$4\text{H} \rightarrow \text{He} + Q$$

The mass defect of this reaction is

$$\Delta m = 4\times 1.008145 - 4.003874$$

$$= 0.028706\ \text{amu}$$

The energy released in one reaction is

$$Q = 0.028706 \times 931.5\ \text{MeV}$$

Now mass of hydrogen required

$$= \frac{4.032580\times1.6598\times10^{-24}\times2.3444\times10^{28}}{0.028706\times931.5\times1.6\times10^{-19}}\ \text{gm/m}$$

$$= 3.6673 \times 10^{22}\ \text{gm/m}$$

$$= 3.6673 \times 10^{16}\ \text{mega gm/m}$$

Illustrative Example 4.34

A nuclear reactor generates power at 50% efficiency by fission of $^{235}_{92}$U into two equal fragments of $^{116}_{46}$Pd with the emission of two gamma rays of 5.2 MeV each and three neutrons. The average binding energies per particle of $^{235}_{92}$U and $^{116}_{46}$Pd are 7.2 MeV and 8.2 MeV respectively. Calculate the energy released in one fission event. Also estimate the amount to ^{235}U consumed per hour to produce 1600 megawatt power.

Solution

Energy released in one fission = Binding energy of two $^{116}_{46}$Pd nuclei – Binding energy of $^{235}_{92}$U nucleus – energy of two emitted gamma rays

Here binding energy of $^{235}_{92}$U nucleus is

$$(\Delta E)_U = 72 \times 235 = 1692\ \text{MeV}$$

Binding energy of two $^{116}_{46}$Pd nuclei

$$2(\Delta E)_{Pd} = 2\times 8.2\times 116 = 1902.4\ \text{MeV}$$

Energy of two emitted gamma rays is

$$2\,E_r = 2\times 5.2 = 10.4\ \text{MeV}$$

Total energy released is one event is

$$E = 1902.4 - 1692 - 10.4$$

$$\Rightarrow \quad E = 200\ \text{MeV}$$

$$\Rightarrow \quad E = 200 \times (1.6 \times 10^{-13})$$

$$\Rightarrow \quad E = 3.2 \times 10^{-11}\ \text{J}$$

Hence, the number of fission per second required to produce 1600×10^6 J of energy per second (1600 MW) is given as

$$N = \frac{1600\times10^6}{3.2\times10^{-11}} = 5 \times 10^{19}\ \text{s}^{-1}$$

So, we require 5×10^{19} nuclei of ^{235}U per second. The mass of these atoms will be

$$m = \frac{235}{6.02\times10^{23}} \times (5 \times 10^{19})$$

$$\Rightarrow \quad m = 195.2 \times 10^{-4}\ \text{gm/3}$$

Thus amount of ^{235}U consumed per hour is

$$m = (195.2 \times 10^{-4}) \times 3600$$

$$\Rightarrow \quad m = 70.27\ \text{gm/hr}$$

Since reactor efficiency is 50%, hence consumption of ^{235}U per hour is given by

$$m = 70.27 \times 2 = 140.5\ \text{gm}$$

 # Illustrative Example 4.35

In the fission of $^{239}_{94}Pu$, by a thermal neutron, two fission fragments of equal masses and sizes are produced and 4 neutrons are emitted. Find the force between the two fission fragments at the moment they are produced. Given $R_0 = 1.1$ fermi.

Solution

Total mass number of $^{239}_{94}Pu$ + neutron (thermal) = 239 + 1 = 240. Since 4 neutrons are produced, the mass number of each fragment $(A) = \dfrac{240-4}{2} = 118$. The atomic number of each fragment = 94/2 = 47. Therefore, charge of each fragment is

$$q = 47 \times 1.6 \times 10^{-19} = 7.52 \times 10^{-18}\,C$$

The radius of each nucleus of the fragment is

$$R = R_0(A)^{1/3}$$

$$\Rightarrow \quad R = 1.1 \times 10^{-15} \times (118)^{1/3} \quad (\text{As 1 fermi} = 10^{-15}\text{ cm})$$

$$\Rightarrow \quad R = 5.395 \times 10^{-15}\,m$$

Distance between the centres of the two fragments at the moment they are produced is

$$r = 2 \times 5.395 \times 10^{-15}$$

$$\Rightarrow \quad r = 10.79 \times 10^{-15}\,m$$

The electrostatic between them is,

$$F = \frac{1}{4\pi \in_0} \cdot \frac{Q^2}{r^2}$$

$$\Rightarrow \quad F = 9 \times 10^9 \frac{(7.52 \times 10^{-18})^2}{(10.79 \times 10^{-15})^2}$$

$$\Rightarrow \quad F = 4.37 \times 10^3\,N$$

 # Illustrative Example 4.36

A nuclear reactor using ^{235}U generates 250 MW of electrical power. The efficiency of the reactor (i.e. efficiency of conversion of thermal energy into electrical energy) is 25%. What is the amount of ^{235}U used in the reactor per year? The thermal energy released per fission of ^{235}U is 200 MeV.

Solution

Rate of electrical energy generation is 250 MW = 250×10^6 W (or Js^{-1}). therefore electrical energy generated in 1 year is

$$(250 \times 10^6\,Js^{-1}) \times (365 \times 24 \times 60 \times 60\,s) = 7.884 \times 10^{15}\,J$$

Thermal energy from fission of one ^{235}U nucleus is 200 MeV = $200 \times 1.6 \times 10^{-13} = 3.2 \times 10^{-11}$ J. Since the efficiency is 25%, the electrical energy obtained from the fission of one ^{235}U nucleus is

$$E_1 = 3.2 \times 10^{-11} \times \frac{25}{100} = 8.0 \times 10^{-12}\,J$$

Therefore, the number of fissions of ^{235}U required in one year will be

$$N = \frac{7.884 \times 10^{15}}{8.0 \times 10^{-12}} = 9.855 \times 10^{26}$$

Number of moles of ^{235}U required per year is

$$n = \frac{9.855 \times 10^{26}}{6.023 \times 10^{23}} = 1.636 \times 10^3$$

Therefore, mass of ^{235}U required per year is

$$m = 1.636 \times 10^3 \times 235 = 3.844 \times 10^5\,g$$

$$= 384.4\,kg$$

 # Illustrative Example 4.37

The deuterium-tritium fusion reaction (called the D-T reaction) is most likely to be the basic fusion reaction in a future thermonuclear fusion reactor is

$$^2_1H + {}^3_1H \rightarrow {}^4_2He + {}^1_0n + Q$$

(a) Calculate the amount of energy released in the reaction, given $m(^2_1H) = 2.014102$ amu, $m(^3_1H) = 3.016090$ amu, $m(^1_0n) =$ 1.008665 amu and $m(^4_2He) = 4.002603$ amu.

(b) Find the kinetic energy needed to overcome coulomb repulsion. Assume the radius of both deuterium and tritium to be approximately 1.5×10^{-15} m.

(c) To what temperature must the gases be heated to initiate the fusion reaction? Take Boltzmann constant $k = 1.38 \times 10^{-23}\,JK^{-1}$.

Solution

(a) The amount of energy released is given by

$$Q = [\{m(^2_1H) + m(^3_1H)\} - \{m(^4_2He) + m(^1_0n)\}] \times 931.2\,MeV$$

$$= [\{2.014102 + 3.016090\} - \{4.0092603 + 1.008665\}] \times 931.2\,MeV$$

$$= 0.018924 \times 931.5 = 17.62\,MeV$$

(b) In order to fuse, the two nuclei (D and T) must almost touch each other. Then the separation between them is equal to twice the radius of each which is given as

$$l = 2r = 2 \times 1.5 \times 10^{-15}$$

$$= 3.0 \times 10^{-15}\,m$$

In order to start the fusion reaction, deuterium and tritium have to be heated to a very high temperature. At such high temperature the two gases are ionized, i.e. the only electron in the atoms of each gas is removed, so that the two nuclei have a positive charge of 1.6×10^{-19} C, i.e. $q_1 = q_2 = 1.6 \times 10^{-19}$ C. The potential energy when they are almost touching is

$$U = \frac{Kq^2}{l}$$

$$\Rightarrow \quad U = \frac{9\times10^9 \times (1.6\times10^{-19})^2}{3.0\times10^{-15}}$$

$$\Rightarrow \quad U = 7.68 \times 10^{14}\ \text{J}$$

The kinetic energy must be just enough to overcome Coulomb repulsion between positively charged nuclei. Hence kinetic energy must be equal to potential energy calculated above. Thus we have

$$KE = 7.68 \times 10^{14}\ \text{J}$$

If this energy is supplied, the two nuclei will just overcome the repulsion and stay in touch.

(c) Let T be the required temperature of the nuclei to initiate the fusion reaction . Then the kinetic energy of the system at temperature T can be given as

$$KE = \frac{3}{2}kT$$

Where k is the Boltzmann constant. Hence to start fusion reaction this kinetic energy will be sufficient to fuse then together thus for this temperature is given as

$$T = \frac{2E_k}{3k} = \frac{2\times7.68\times10^{14}}{3\times1.38\times10^{-23}}$$

$$= 3.7 \times 10^9\ \text{K}$$

Illustrative Example 4.38

Calculate the excitation energy of the compound nuclei produced when ^{235}U and ^{238}U absorb thermal neutrons. Given masses are

$$M(^{235}\text{U}) = 235.0439\ \text{amu},$$
$$M(n) = 1.0087\ \text{amu},$$
$$M(^{238}\text{U}) = 238.0508\ \text{amu},$$
$$M(^{236}\text{U}) = 236.0456\ \text{amu},$$
$$M(^{239}\text{U}) = 239.0543\ \text{amu}$$

Solution

The two reactions are

$$n + {}^{235}\text{U} \rightarrow {}^{236}\text{U}^*$$
$$n + {}^{238}\text{U} \rightarrow {}^{239}\text{U}^*$$

We find the excitation energy from the atomic masses. A thermal neutron has a negligible kinetic energy (About 0.03 eV).

$$E(^{239}\text{U}^*) = [m(n) + M(^{235}\text{U}) - M(^{236}\text{U})]c^2$$

$$= [1.0087\ \text{amu} + 235.0439\ \text{amu} - 236.0456\ \text{amu}]c^2$$

$$= 0.0070 \times 931.5 = 6.5\ \text{MeV}$$

$$E(^{239}\text{U}^*) = [m(n) + M(^{238}\text{U}) - M(^{239}\text{U})]c^2$$

$$= [1.0087\ \text{amu} + 238.0508\ \text{amu} - 239.0543\ \text{amu}]\ c^2$$

$$= 0.0052 \times 931.5 = 4.8\ \text{MeV}$$

Thus ^{236}U* has more excitation energy than ^{239}U* when both are produced by thermal neutron absorption. This is why ^{235}U more easily undergoes thermal neutron fission.

Illustrative Example 4.39

Calculate the ground-state Q value of the induced fission reaction in the equation

$$n + {}^{235}_{92}\text{U} \rightarrow {}^{236}_{92}\text{U}^* \rightarrow {}^{99}_{40}\text{Zr} + {}^{134}_{52}\text{Te} + 3n$$

If the neutron is thermal. A thermal neutron is in thermal equilibrium with its environment; it has an average kinetic energy given by 3/2 kT.
Given masses are $m(n) = 1.0087$ amu; $M(^{235}\text{U}) = 235.0439$ amu; $M(^{99}\text{Zr}) = 98.916$ amu; $M(^{134}\text{Te}) = 133.9115$ amu.

Solution

Kinetic energy of a thermal neutron can be neglected; even for a temperature of 10^6 K, the thermal energy is only 130 eV. The Q value of the above reaction is given by the equation

$$Q = \Delta m \times 931.5\ \text{MeV}$$

Here Δm is the mass defect of the reaction, given as

$$\Delta m = [M(^{235}\text{U}) + m(n)] - [M(^{99}\text{Zr}) + M(^{134}\text{Te}) + 3\,m(n)]$$

$$= [235.0439 - 98.9165 - 133.9115 - 2(1.0087)]\ \text{amu}$$

$$= 0.1985\ \text{amu}$$

Thus energy released is

$$Q = 0.1985 \times 931.5 = 184.90\ \text{MeV}$$

Even with a thermal neutron of negligible kinetic energy a tremendous amount of energy is released.

 # Illustrative Example 4.40

Show that ${}^{230}_{92}U$ does not decay be emitting a neutron or proton. Given masses are
M (${}^{230}_{92}U$) = 230.033927 amu; M (${}^{229}_{92}U$) = 229.033496 amu; M (${}^{229}_{91}Pa$) = 229.032089 amu; $m(n)$ = 1.008665 amu, $m(p)$ = 1.007825 amu.

Solution

The corresponding decay equations would be

(i) $${}^{230}_{92}U \rightarrow n + {}^{229}_{92}U \text{ and}$$

(ii) $${}^{230}_{92}U \rightarrow p + {}^{229}_{91}Pa$$

In first equation the energy released can be given by

$$Q = [230.033927 - 229.033496 - 1.008665] \times 931.5 \text{ MeV}$$
$$= -7.7 \text{ MeV}$$

Because $Q < 0$, neutron decay is not possible spontaneously.

Similarly in second equation the energy released can be given as

$$Q = [230.033927 - 229.032089 - 1.007825] \times 931.5 \text{ MeV}$$
$$= -5.6 \text{ MeV}$$

As $Q < 0$, proton decay is also not possible spontaneously.

 # Illustrative Example 4.41

Compute the minimum kinetic energy of proton incident on ${}^{13}C$ nuclei at rest in the laboratory that will produce the endothermic reaction ${}^{13}C(p, n){}^{13}N$. Given masses are

$$M({}^{13}C) = 13.003355 \text{ amu},$$
$$M({}^{1}H) = 1.007825 \text{ amu}$$
$$m(n) = 1.008665 \text{ amu},$$
$$M({}^{13}N) = 13.005738 \text{ amu}$$

Solution

The threshold energy of the incident protons in the lab frame is given by

$$E_{th} = \frac{m+M}{M}|Q| \qquad \ldots(4.56)$$

The magnitude of the Q value of the reaction is

$$\frac{|Q|}{c^2} = m_{\text{final}} - m_{\text{initial}}$$
$$= [M({}^{13}N) + m_n] - [M({}^{13}C) + M({}^{1}H)]$$

Substituting given values of masses into the expression for $|Q|$ gives

$$|Q| = (14.014403 - 140.11180)\, u \,.\, c^2$$

$$\Rightarrow \quad |Q| = 0.003223 \times 931.5 \text{ MeV}$$

$$\Rightarrow \quad |Q| = 3.00 \text{ MeV}$$

Substituting this value

$$m = M({}^{1}H), M = M({}^{13}C)$$

into equation-(4.56), we get

$$E_{th} = \frac{1.007825 + 13.003355}{13.003355} \times 3.00$$
$$= 3.00 = 3.23 \text{ MeV}$$

 # Illustrative Example 4.42

The nuclear reaction,

$$n + {}^{10}_{5}B \rightarrow {}^{7}_{3}Li + {}^{4}_{2}He$$

is observed to occur even when very slow-moving neutrons (M_n = 1.0087 amu) strike a boron atom at rest. For a particular reaction in which K_n = 0, the helium (M_{He} = 4.0026 amu) is observed to have a speed of 9.30 × 10^6 m/s. Determine (a) the kinetic energy of the lithium (M_{Li} = 7.0160 amu), and (b) the Q-value of the reaction.

Solution

(a) Since the neutron and boron are both initially at rest, the total momentum before the reaction is zero and afterward is also zero. Therefore,

$$M_{Li}\, v_{Li} = M_{He}\, v_{He}$$

We solve this for v_{Li} and substitute it into the equation for kinetic energy. We can use classical kinetic energy with little error, rather than relativistic formulas, because v_{He} = 9.30 × 10^6 m/s is not close to the speed of light c and v_{Li} will be even less since $M_{Li} > M_{He}$. Thus we can write

$$K_{Li} = \frac{1}{2} M_{Li} v_{Li}^2 = \frac{1}{2} M_{Li} \left(\frac{M_{He} v_{He}}{M_{Li}}\right)^2$$

$$\Rightarrow \quad K_{Li} = \frac{M_{He}^2 v_{He}^2}{2M_{Li}}$$

We put in numbers, changing the mass in u to kg and recalling that 1.60 × 10^{-13} J = 1 MeV :

$$K_{Li} = \frac{(4.0026)^2 (1.66 \times 10^{-27})(9.30 \times 10^6)^2}{2(7.0160)(1.66 \times 10^{-27})}$$

$$\Rightarrow \quad K_{Li} = 1.64 \times 10^{-13} \text{ J} = 1.02 \text{ MeV}$$

(b) We are given the data

$$K_a = K_X = 0,$$

so $$Q = K_{Li} + K_{He},$$

where $$K_{He} = \frac{1}{2} M_{He} v_{He}^2$$

$$= \frac{1}{2}(4.0026)(1.66 \times 10^{-27})(9.30 \times 10^6)^2$$

$$= 2.87 \times 10^{-13}\ J = 1.80\ MeV$$

Hence, $$Q = 1.02\ MeV + 1.80\ MeV = 2.82\ MeV$$

Web Reference at www.physicsgalaxy.com

Age Group - High School Physics | Age 17-19 Years
Section - MODERN PHYSICS
Topic - Nuclear Reactions
Module Number - 1 to 9

Practice Exercise 4.4

(i) Find the amount of energy produced in joules due to fission of 1 gram of uranium assuming that 0.1 percent of mass is transformed into energy.

Take 1 amu = 1.66×10^{-27} kg = 931.5 MeV

Mass of uranium = 235 amu

Avogadro number = 6.02×10^{23}

[8.978×10^{10} J]

(ii) What is the power output of $^{235}_{92}$U reactor if it takes 30 days to use up 2 kg of fuel, and if each fission gives 185 MeV of usable energy ?

[58.52 MW]

(iii) Assuming that 200 MeV of energy is released per fission of uranium atom, find the number of fission per second required to release one kilowatt power.

[3.125×10^{13} fissions per second]

(iv) It is proposed to use the nuclear fusion reaction

$$^2_1H + ^2_1H \rightarrow ^4_2He$$

in a nuclear reactor of 200 MW rating. If the energy from the above reaction is used with a 25 % efficiency in the reactor, how many grams of deuterium fuel will be needed per day. (The masses of $^2_1$H and $^4_2$He are 2.0141 atomic mass units and 4.0026 atomic mass unit respectively and take 1 amu = 931.5 MeV).

[120.31 g]

(v) A fusion reaction of the type given below

$$^2_1D + ^2_1D \rightarrow ^3_1T + ^1_1p + \Delta E$$

is most promising for the production of power. Here D and T stand for deuterium and tritium, respectively. Calculate the mass of deuterium in gram required per day for a power output of 10^9 W. Assume that efficiency of the process to be 50%. Given

mass of ^2_1D = 2.014102 amu.

mass of ^3_1T = 3.01605 amu.

mass of ^1_1p = 1.007825 amu. and

1 amu = 931.5 MeV

[1778.51 gm]

(vi) The binding energies per nucleon for deuteron ($^2_1$H) and helium ($^4_2$He) are 1.1 MeV and 7.0 MeV respectively. Calculate the energy released when two deuterons fuse to form a helium nucleus ($^4_2$He).

[23.6 MeV]

(vii) Find the energy released when $^{235}_{92}$U nucleus undergoes fission by a thermal neutron into $^{92}_{36}$Kr and $^{141}_{56}$Ba. Given, mass of $^{235}_{92}$U = 235.043925 amu, mass of neutron = 1.008665 amu, mass of $^{92}_{36}$Kr = 91.8973 amu and mass of $^{141}_{56}$Ba = 140.9139 amu. Take 1 amu = 931.5 MeV.

[200.64 MeV]

(viii) How much energy is needed to remove a neutron from the nucleus of $^{41}_{20}$Ca ? Given m_n = 1.008665 amu, atomic mass of $^{41}_{20}$Ca = 40.962278 amu and atomic mass of $^{40}_{20}$Ca = 39.962591 amu. Take 1 amu = 931.5 MeV.

[8.363 MeV]

(ix) Find the Q value of the reaction $p + {}^7Li \rightarrow {}^4He + {}^4He$. Determine whether the reaction is exothermic or endothermic. The atomic mass of ^{1}H, ^{4}He and ^{7}Li are 1.007825 amu, 4.002603 amu and 7.016004 amu respectively.

[*Exothermic*, 17.347 MeV]

4.8 Properties of Radioactive Radiations

We know that an unstable nuclei achieves stability by radioactivity due to emission of α, β and γ-radiations. Now in this section we will discuss how these are emitted and the characteristics of these radiations one by one.

4.8.1 Alpha Decay

We've already discussed that the range of attractive nuclear forces among nucleons is very short and that of the electrostatic repulsive forces between protons is unlimited. This is the reason why nuclei with mass number above 210 are so large that the short range nuclear forces that hold the nucleon together are not sufficient to counterbalance the mutual repulsion between the protons. Alpha decay occurs in such nuclei as a means of increasing their stability by reducing their size.

In this case a question arises why only α-particles are emitted why not individual protons are emitted to decrease the repulsive force in the nucleus. The reason is very high binding energy of α-particles. To escape from nucleus, a particle should have sufficiently high kinetic energy and only α-particle mass is sufficiently smaller than the masses of its constituent nucleons for such energy to be available.

Whenever an α-particle is emitted, the mass number of the daughter element is less then 4 and atomic number less then 2. The equation of the nuclear reaction for α-decay can be written as

$$^{A}_{Z}X \longrightarrow\ ^{A-4}_{Z-2}Y +\ ^{4}_{2}\text{He} + \text{energy} \qquad \ldots(4.57)$$

In equation-(4.57) we can see that during α-decay some energy is released, this shows that the Q-value of the α-decay is positive and the total released energy is shared by both, the daughter nucleus and the emitted α-particle as shown in figure-4.11

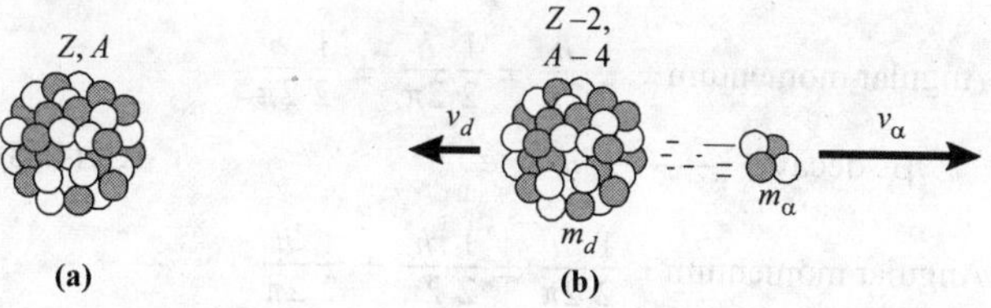

Figure 4.11

The energy released in the above process or the Q-value of the above nuclear reaction can be given as

$$Q = (m_X - m_Y - m_\alpha)\,c^2 \qquad \ldots(4.58)$$

Here $m_X \longrightarrow$ mass of parent nucleus X

$m_Y \longrightarrow$ mass of daughter nucleus Y

$m_\alpha \longrightarrow$ mass of α-particle ($^4_2$He)

During α-emission linear momentum of system must be conserved, hence if the speeds attained by α-particle and the daughter nuclide Y in the above process are v_α and v_y then we must have

$$m_y v_y = m_\alpha v_\alpha \qquad \ldots(4.59)$$

and from energy conservation we can say that the released energy Q is distributed in both, hence we have

$$Q = \frac{1}{2} m_y v_y^2 + \frac{1}{2} m_\alpha v_\alpha^2 \qquad \ldots(4.60)$$

$$\Rightarrow \quad Q = \frac{1}{2} m_y \left(\frac{m_\alpha v_\alpha}{m_y}\right)^2 \frac{1}{2} m_\alpha v_\alpha^2$$

$$\Rightarrow \quad Q = \frac{1}{2} m_\alpha v_\alpha^2 \left(1 + \frac{m_\alpha}{m_y}\right)$$

$$\Rightarrow \quad Q = E_\alpha \left(\frac{m_y + m_\alpha}{m_y}\right)$$

$$\Rightarrow \quad E_\alpha \simeq Q\left(\frac{m_y}{m_x}\right)$$

$$\Rightarrow \quad E_\alpha \simeq \left(\frac{A-4}{A}\right) Q \qquad \ldots(4.61)$$

Equation-(4.61) shows that the kinetic energy of ejected α-particle in the decay process is $\left(\frac{A-4}{A}\right)$ times the Q-value of the nuclear reaction in the process.

It is seen that all the α-emitter radioactive element have mass number $A > 210$ so we can say that most of the energy produced during decay appears as the kinetic energy of the emitted α-particle.

4.8.2 Beta Decay

Similar to emission of α-decay, β-decay also makes the composition of nucleus more stable. There are three fundamental beta decay processes are observed. There are

(1) Beta Minus Emission (β^-) : β^- are the electrons, which are emitted from the nucleus when inside a neutron decays to a proton and an electron, this electron is emitted from the nucleus with some kinetic energy and it is called β^- decay, the process involved inside the nucleus in β^- decay is

$$n \longrightarrow p +\ ^{0}_{-1}e + \bar{\nu}\ (\beta^- \text{ emission}) \qquad \ldots(4.62)$$

In reaction represented by equation-(4.62) also includes a particle with β^- emission it is $\bar{\nu}$ (nu-bar), denotes an antineutrino. About this we'll discuss in next section.

(2) Beta Plus Emission (β^+) : β^+ are the positions, which are emitted from the nucleus when inside a nucleus a proton transforms to a neutron and position. The position emitted from the nucleus, is called β^+ decay. The process involved inside the nucleus in β^+-decay is

$$p \longrightarrow n +\ ^{0}_{+1}e + \nu\ (\beta^+ \text{ emission}) \qquad \ldots(4.63)$$

In the above equation-(4.63) the reaction involves another particle ν (nu) with β^+ emission, called neutrino. About this also we'll discuss in next section.

When a proton inside a β^+ decay inside a nucleus, the parent radionuclide X transforms to a daughter nuclide according to the reaction

$$ {}_Z^A X \longrightarrow {}_{Z-1}^{A}Y + {}_{+1}^{0}\beta + \nu \qquad \ldots(4.64)$$

Here position emission leads to a daughter nucleus of lower atomic number Z by 1 and leaving the mass number A unchanged. Also remember that a proton can not decay into a neutron outside a nucleus because of its smaller mass. This is possible only inside a nucleus.

(3) Electron Capture or K-capture : This is a third kind of β-decay it properties are similar to β^+ emission in which a nucleus pulls in or captures one of the orbital electrons from outside the nucleus and inside the nucleus a proton absorbs this electron and transforms into a neutron. This process is called electron capture, or K-capture, since the electron is normally captured from the innermost or K-shell. The process of electron capture inside a nucleus can be given as

$$ {}_1^1 p + {}_{-1}^{0}e \longrightarrow n + \nu \qquad \ldots(4.65)$$

As in this process also a proton transforms into a neutron, neutrino is also emitted and we can say that basically this process resembles with β^+ emission but no particle ${}_{-1}^{0}e$ or ${}_{+1}^{0}e$ are emitted from the nucleus. For a radioactive element X decays to a daughter element Y, by electron capture, the reaction can be given as

$$ {}_Z^A X \longrightarrow {}_{Z-1}^{A}Y + \nu \qquad \ldots(4.66)$$

Here also similar to β^+ decay the atomic number of daughter nuclei decreases by one and mass number remain unchanged.

4.8.3 Apparent Violation of Conservation Laws in β-decay

As we've discussed that by beta decay also the nucleus becomes more stable. During beta decay it is observed that the basic conservation laws of energy, linear momentum and angular momentum are all apparently violated as discussed now.

(1) Law of Conservation of Energy

We know when a radionuclide X-decays to a daughter nuclide Y with β-decay the amount of energy released or Q-value of the nuclear reaction can be calculated by using mass defect of the reaction. But when the emitted β-particles are observed they do not have enough energy to account for the total energy released. If β-particle carries away only a part of the energy, where the remaining energy is going. This was a serious puzzle among physicists in late 1920 s. It was very difficult to accept that law of energy conservation is not valid in this case.

(2) Law of Conservation of Linear Momentum

During β-decay when the directions of emitted β-particles (e^- or e^+) and that of recoiling nuclei are observed, they are almost never exactly opposite as required for linear momentum to be conserved as shown in figure-4.12. It seems that one more particle is to be emitted in other direction to conserve linear momentum but no other particle was detected during beta emission.

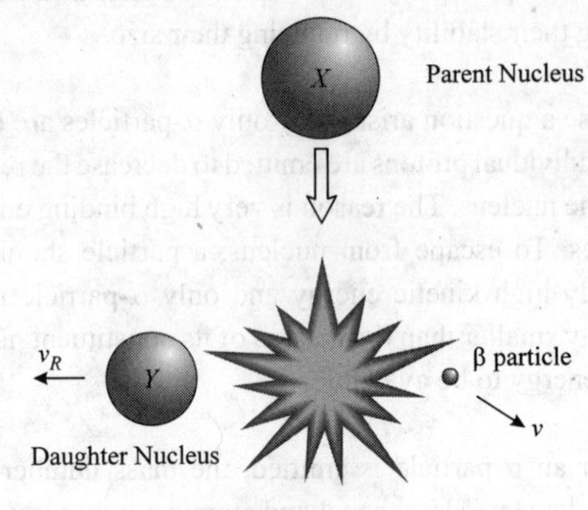

Figure 4.12

(3) Law of Conservation of Angular Momentum

Inside a nucleus, every nucleon-neutrons protons, electrons or positions each have a spin angular momentum $\pm \frac{1}{2}\frac{h}{2\pi}$. If we once again look into the equations of β-decay processes, these are

$$\beta^- \text{decay } n \longrightarrow p + e^- \qquad \ldots(4.67)$$

$$\text{Angular momentum} \pm \frac{1}{2}\frac{h}{2\pi} \quad \pm \frac{1}{2}\frac{h}{2\pi} \quad \pm \frac{1}{2}\frac{h}{2\pi}$$

$$\beta^+ \text{decay } p \longrightarrow n + e^+ \qquad \ldots(4.68)$$

$$\text{Angular momentum} \pm \frac{1}{2}\frac{h}{2\pi} \quad \pm \frac{1}{2}\frac{h}{2\pi} \quad \pm \frac{1}{2}\frac{h}{2\pi}$$

In both of above equations we can see that when a nucleon decays in the two on left hand side of equation before decay its angular momentum is either $+\frac{1}{2}\frac{h}{2\pi}$ or $-\frac{1}{2}\frac{h}{2\pi}$ but after decay on right hand side of equation the total angular momentum will be $\pm \frac{h}{2\pi}$ or 0.

Thus here we can see that on the two sides of the equation-(4.67) and (4.68), angular momentum are not equal. For an isolated system like nucleus, we can not expect this to happen. But again this one can not accept that the law of conservation of angular momentum is not applicable here.

The above three conservation laws apparently violet in the process of β-decay. This remain a series problem among physicists until 1930 when Pauli proposed that during β-decay one more particle is emitted, called neutrino. Existence of neutrino was verified experimentally in 1956. Lets discuss Pauli's Neutrino Hypothesis in detail.

4.8.4 Pauli's Neutrino Hypothesis

As discussed above Pauli suggested that during emission of a β-particle an additional particle is also emitted, named neutrino and this hypothesis made all the above conservation laws working finely for the process of β-decay. According to Pauli the particle neutrino has the following characteristics :

(i) Its charge is zero

(ii) It is an energy particle like a photon.

(iii) Its rest mass is zero like a photon.

(iv) It carries linear momentum like a photon.

(v) It carries angular momentum like other nucleons $\pm \frac{1}{2}\frac{h}{2\pi}$.

(vi) During β-decay, β^+ emission is accomplished by emission of a neutrino (ν) where as β^--emission is accomplished by emission of an antineutrino ($\bar{\nu}$)

(vii) It is extremely difficult to detect a neutrino because it interacts very weakly with matter. It can be concluded on basis of experiments that an average neutrino can penetrate about 10^{12} km distance in the most dense material lead without interacting with it. Even though more then 10^9 neutrinos pass through our body every second without any effect. It is difficult but in Japan Super Kamiokande neutrino detector was made to detect neutrino.

Thus the new reactions for β-decay processes can be rewritten as

$$\beta^- \text{ decay } n \longrightarrow p + e^- + \bar{\nu} \qquad \ldots(4.69)$$

$$\beta^+ \text{ decay } p \longrightarrow n + e^+ + \nu \qquad \ldots(4.70)$$

Now using the above two equations if we again look into the energy, momentum and angular momentum of the nucleons involved in the decay process all conservation laws now seems to appear valid due to the presence of this additional particle in the reaction.

Here we've discussed that the emitted β-particles carries energy less then that evolved in the process. The remaining energy is carried by the neutrino. Thus we can say that for every emission the sum of energies of β-particle and neutrino (or antineutrino) remains constant in the decay. Similarly the direction of emitted neutrino will account for the conservation of linear momentum and in the equations for decay processes, if we account for the angular momentum of neutrino (or antineutrino) then on both side of equality angular momentum will get conserved.

4.8.5 Mass Defect Calculation For β-decay

We've discussed that there are three fundamental β-decay processes. Here mass defect involved in the nuclear reaction are very small as mass of β-particle (e^- or e^+) is very small. Generally the masses we use for calculation of mass defect in a nuclear reaction are the masses of atoms where we neglect the masses of electrons which is included in the mass of atom.

Here for the β-decay process the mass of β-particle itself is same as that of an electron, we can not neglect the weight of all the orbital electrons present in an atom thus for an atom ${}^A_ZX - Z$ (mass of electron) thus for calculation of mass defect for a β-decay process, we first find the mass of nuclein involved in the reaction then we find mass defect. Lets discuss this one by one for each type of β-decay.

(i) Mass Defect for β^--decay :

For an element ${}^A_ZX$ when undergoes β^- emission, the decay equation is written as

$${}^A_ZX \longrightarrow {}^{A}_{Z+1}Y + {}^{0}_{-1}e + \bar{\nu}$$

Here the mass defect of the above reaction can be written as

$$\Delta m = (M_X - Zm_e) - \{(M_Y - (Z+1)\,m_e) + m_e\}$$

or $\Delta m = M_X - M_Y$

Thus Q-value of this reaction can be given as

$$\Delta E = (M_X - M_Y)\,C^2$$

(ii) Mass Defect of β^+-decay :

For an element ${}^A_ZX$ when undergoes β^+ decay, the decay equation can be written as

$${}^A_ZX \longrightarrow {}^{A}_{Z-1}Y + {}^{0}_{+1}e + \bar{\nu}$$

Here the mass defect of the above reaction can be written as

$$\Delta m = (M_X - Zm_e) - \{(M_Y - (Z-1)\,m_e) + m_e\}$$

or $\Delta m = M_X - M_Y - 2\,m_e$

Thus Q-value of this reaction can be given as

$$\Delta E = (M_X - M_Y - 2\,m_e)\,C^2$$

(iii) K-Capture :

For an element ${}^A_ZX$ undergoes K-capture, the decay equation can be written as

$${}^{A}_{Z+e^-}X \longrightarrow {}^{A}_{Z-1}Y + \bar{\nu}$$

Here the mass defect of the reaction can be given as

$$\Delta m = (M_X - Zm_e + m_e) - (M_Y - (Z-1)\,m_e)$$

or $$\Delta m = M_X - M_Y$$

Thus Q-value of the above reaction is given as

$$\Delta E = (M_X - M_Y)\, C^2$$

4.8.6 Gamma Decay

Just like an atom, nucleus can also exist in different energy states higher then its ground state. An excited nucleus is denoted by an asterisk after its symbol like X^*. Such excited nuclei return to their ground state by emitting photons of energy equal to the energy difference between the final and initial states in the transitions involved. These photons have range of energies upto several MeV are traditionally known as gamma rays (γ-rays).

Whenever a radionuclide undergoes α or β-emission, the daughter nuclide may remain in excited state just after decay which after some time (its life time) transit to ground state with release of γ-ray photon.

Lets consider an example β-active Mg which decays to Al. Look at the following reactions :

$$\text{Mg} \longrightarrow \text{Al}^* + \beta^- + \bar{\nu} \qquad \ldots(4.71)$$

$$\text{Al}^* \longrightarrow \text{Al} + \gamma \qquad \ldots(4.72)$$

In the above reaction we can see when β^- is emitted from Mg nucleus some part of the released energy is absorbed by the daughter nucleus & gets in excited state Al* and remaining energy is carried by β^- & $\bar{\nu}$. After a short duration Al* releases the excess energy in form of γ-ray photon and transit to its ground state Al as shown in equation-(4.72). Some times due to more excitation energy one or may be two gamma decays takes place for daughter nucleus to reach the ground state.

Some times the energy of γ-ray photon from the nucleus which it releases at the time of transition from higher state to ground state, is absorbed by the atomic electrons around it. This process is similar to photo electric process in which this atomic electron is emitted with a kinetic energy equal to the nuclear excitation energy minus the binding energy of electron in the atom. This phenomenon we call internal conservation.

 # Illustrative Example 4.43

How many alpha and beta particles are emitted when uranium ($^{238}_{92}$U) decays to lead $^{206}_{82}$Pb ?

Solution

Let a and b, the number of α and β particles are emitted when $^{238}_{92}$U decays to $^{206}_{82}$Pb.

We know that

(i) The emission of α-particle ($^4_2$He) decreases the charge number by two and mass number by four.

Thus emission of a, α-particles reduce the charge number by $2a$ and mass number by $4a$.

(ii) The emission of β-particle increase the charge number by one and leaving the mass number unchanged.

Thus emission of b, β-particles increase the charge number by $b \times 1 = b$.

Thus $$^{238}_{92}\text{U} \rightarrow {}^{206}_{82}\text{Pb} + a\,(^4_2\text{He}) + b\,(^{\;0}_{-1}\beta)$$

Applying the law of conservation of charge number and mass number before and after the decay, we have

$$92 = 82 + 2a - b \qquad \ldots(4.73)$$

and $$238 = 206 + 4a \qquad \ldots(4.74)$$

From equation-(4.74),

$$a = 8$$

From equation-(4.73),

$$b = 1$$

 # Illustrative Example 4.44

The nucleus ^{23}Ne decays by β-emission into the nucleus ^{23}Na. Write down the β-decay equation and determine the maximum kinetic energy of the electrons emitted. Given m ($^{23}_{10}$Ne) = 22.994466 amu and m ($^{23}_{11}$Na) = 22.989770 amu Ignore the mass of antineutrino ($\bar{\nu}$).

Solution

The β-decay of ^{23}Ne is represented by the equation

$$^{23}_{10}\text{Ne} \rightarrow {}^{23}_{11}\text{Na} + e^- + \bar{\nu} + Q$$

Mass defect for the above reaction is

$$\Delta m = [(^{23}_{10}\text{Ne}) - \text{M}\,(^{23}_{11}\text{Na})]$$

$$= [22.994466 - 22.989770]\ \text{amu}$$

$$= 0.004696\ \text{amu}$$

Now Q-value of the above reaction is given as

$$Q = \Delta m \times 931.5\ \text{MeV}$$

$$= 0.004696 \times 931.5\ \text{MeV}$$

$$= 4.374\ \text{MeV}$$

The energy Q released is shared by ^{23}Na nucleus and the electron-antineutrino pair. Since ^{23}Na is massive, most of the kinetic energy is carried by the $e - \bar{\nu}$ pair. The electron will carry the maximum energy if the antineutrino carries zero energy. Thus the maximum energy of the electrons emitted is 4.374 MeV.

 # Illustrative Example 4.45

A radioactive source in the form of metal sphere of diameter 10^{-3} m emits beta particle at a constant rate of 6.25×10^{10} particle per second. If the source is electrically insulated how long will it take for its potential to rise by 1.0 volt, assuming that 80% of the emitted beta particles escape from the source ?

Solution

Let t be the time for the potential of metal sphere to rise by one volt. Then upto this time β-particles emitted from sphere are

$$N = (6.25 \times 10^{10}) \times t$$

Number of β-particles escaped in this time are

$$N_e = (80/100) \times (6.25 \times 10^{10})\, t$$

$$= 5 \times 10^{10}\, t$$

Thus charge acquired by the sphere in t sec

$$Q = (5 \times 10^{10}\, t) \times (1.6 \times 10^{-19})$$

$$= 8 \times 10^{-9}\, t \text{ coulomb} \qquad \ldots(4.75)$$

(Q emission of β-particle leads to a charge e on metal sphere)

The capacitance C of a metal sphere is given by

$$C = 4\pi\epsilon_0 \times r$$

$$= \left(\frac{1}{9\times10^9}\right)\times\left(\frac{10^{-3}}{2}\right)$$

$$= \frac{10^{-12}}{18} \text{ farad} \qquad \ldots(4.76)$$

We know that, $Q = C \times V$ (Here $V = 1$ volt)

$$\Rightarrow \quad (8 \times 10^{-9})\, t = \left(\frac{10^{-12}}{18}\right) \times 1$$

Solving it for t, we get

$$t = 6.95\ \mu \text{ sec}$$

 # Illustrative Example 4.46

A nucleus X, initially at rest, undergoes alpha-decay according to the equation.

$${}^{A}_{92}\text{X} \rightarrow {}^{228}_{Z}\text{Y} + \alpha$$

(a) Find the values of A and Z in the above process.

(b) The alpha particle produced in the above process is found to move in a circular track of radius 0.11 m in a uniform magnetic field of 3 Tesla. Find the energy (in MeV) released during the process and the binding energy of the parent nucleus X.

Given that :

$$m(\text{Y}) = 228.03 \text{ amu};$$

$$m({}^{1}_{0}\text{n}) = 1.009 \text{ amu}$$

$$m({}^{4}_{2}\text{He}) = 4.003 \text{ amu};$$

$$m({}^{1}_{1}\text{H}) = 1.008 \text{ amu}$$

Solution

Given nuclear reaction is

$${}^{A}_{92}\text{X} \rightarrow {}^{228}_{Z}\text{Y} + \alpha$$

$$\Rightarrow \quad {}^{A}_{92}\text{X} \rightarrow {}^{228}_{Z}\text{Y} + {}^{4}_{2}\text{He}$$

(a) According to principle of conservation of charge number, we have for above equation

$$92 = Z + 2$$

$$\Rightarrow \quad Z = 90$$

And according to principle to conservation of mass number, we have for above equation

$$A = 228 + 4 = 232$$

$$\Rightarrow \quad A = 232$$

(b) For circular track of a charge particle in uniform magnetic field, we have

$$\frac{mv^2}{r} = qvB$$

$$\Rightarrow \quad mv = qBr$$

Here momentum of α-particle is given as

$$p = mv = 2e \times B \times r$$

$$p = 2 \times (1.6 \times 10^{-19})\,(3)\,(0.11) \text{ kg-m/sec}$$

$$\Rightarrow \quad p = 1.056 \times 10^{-19} \text{ kg-m/sec}$$

K.E. of α-particle is given by

$$E_\alpha = \frac{p^2}{2m_\alpha} = \frac{(1.056\times10^{-19})^9}{2\times4.003\times1.66\times10^{-27}}$$

$$= 0.0839 \times 10^{-11} \text{ joule}$$

$$= \frac{0.0839\times10^{-11}}{1.6\times10^{-13}} \text{ MeV}$$

$$= 5.244 \text{ MeV}$$

The parent nucleus is at rest and hence its momentum is zero. Now the sum of momenta of daughter nucleus Y and α-particle must be zero i.e., the momentum of daughter nucleus Y is equal and opposite to momentum of α-particle.

Thus K.E. of daughter nucleus Y is

$$Y = E_Y = \frac{p^2}{2M_Y} = \frac{(1.056\times10^{-19})^2}{2\times228.03\times1.66\times10^{-27}}$$

$$= 0.001473\times10^{-11}\text{ joule} = 0.092\text{ MeV}$$

In above reaction, the total energy released is in the form of kinetic energy of particles hence we have

Total energy $\quad E_T = E_\alpha + E_\gamma = 5.336\text{ meV}$

Mass defect of the reaction is

$$\Delta m = \text{Mass of } X - (\text{Mass of } Y + \text{Mass of α-particle})$$

$$\frac{5.336}{931.5}\text{ amu} = M_X - (228.03 + 4.003)$$

$$M_X = (232.0387)\text{ amu}$$

Now mass defect of parent nucleus ${}^{232}_{92}X$ is given as

$$= 92\,m_p + (232-92)m_n - M_X$$

$$= (92\times1.008 + 140\times1.009 - 232.0387)$$

$$= 1.9573\text{ amu}$$

$\Rightarrow$ Binding energy of parent nucleus X is

$$(\Delta E)_X = 1.9573\times931.5\text{ MeV}$$

$$= 1823.225\text{ MeV}$$

 # Illustrative Example 4.47

Polonium (${}^{210}_{81}$Po) emits ${}^{4}_{2}$He particles and is converted into lead (${}^{206}_{82}$Pb). This reaction is used for producing electric power in a space mission ^{210}Po has half life of 138.6 days. Assuming an efficiency of 10% for the thermoelectric machine, how much ^{210}Po is required to produce 1.2×10^7 J of electric energy per day at the end of 693 days. Also find the initial activity of the material.

[Given: masses of nuclei $M({}^{210}\text{Po}) = 209.98264$ amu, $M({}^{206}\text{Pb}) = 205.97440$ amu, $M({}^{4}_{2}\text{He}) = 4.00260$ amu)]

Solution

The nuclear reaction for the above process can be expressed as

$${}^{210}_{84}\text{Po} \to {}^{206}_{82}\text{Pb} + {}^{4}_{2}\text{He}$$

Mass defect of this reaction can be given as

$$\Delta m = [\text{M}({}^{210}_{84}\text{Po}) - \text{M}({}^{206}_{82}\text{Pb}) - \text{M}({}^{4}_{2}\text{He})]$$

$$\Delta m = 209.98264 - 205.97440 - 4.00260$$

$$= 0.00564\text{ amu}$$

Thus Q-value of the nuclear reaction is

$$Q = 0.00564\times931\text{ MeV} = 5.25\text{ MeV}$$

$$\Rightarrow \quad = 5.25\times(1.6\times10^{-13})$$

$$\Rightarrow \quad = 8.4\times10^{-13}\text{ joule}$$

The decay constant λ is given by for ^{210}Po is given by

$$\lambda = \frac{0.693}{T} = \frac{0.693}{138.6\text{ days}} = 0.005\text{ day}^{-1}$$

Let M gm be required to produce 1.2×10^7 joule per day

Number of nuclei in M gm

$$N = \frac{(6\times10^{23})\,M}{210}$$

Now decay rate by N nuclei per day or the activity of N nuclei are

$$-\frac{dN}{dt} = \lambda N$$

$$= 0.005\times\frac{(6\times10^{23})M}{210}\text{ per day} \qquad \ldots(4.77)$$

Thus energy produced per day

$$= 0.005\times\frac{(6\times10^{23})M}{210}\times(8.4\times10^{-13})\text{ J} \qquad \ldots(4.78)$$

This should be equal to 1.2×10^7 joule

$$\text{Hence}\quad 0.005\times\frac{(6\times10^{23})M}{210}\times(8.4\times10^{-13}) = 1.2\times10^7$$

$$\Rightarrow \quad M = 1\text{ gm} \qquad \ldots(4.79)$$

The efficiency is 10%. Hence the quantity required will be 10 gm.

From equation-(4.77), activity is

$$A = 0.005\times\frac{(6\times10^{23})10}{210}$$

$$\Rightarrow \quad A = \frac{1}{7}\times10^{21}\text{ per day}$$

Let A_0 be the activity before 693 days, then from decay equation we have

$$A_c = A_0\,(2)^{-\frac{693}{138.6}}$$

$$\Rightarrow \quad A_{c0} = A_c(2)^5$$

$$\Rightarrow \quad A_0 = \left(\frac{1}{7}\times10^{21}\right)\times32 = 4.57\times10^{21}\text{ per day}$$

Illustrative Example 4.48

Find whether alpha decay or any of the beta decay are allowed for $^{226}_{89}$Ac. Given masses are

$M(^{226}_{89}Ac) = 226.028356$ amu, $M(^{222}_{87}Fr) = 222.017415$ amu, $M(^{226}_{90}Th) = 226.017388$ amu,

$M(^{226}_{88}Ra) = 226.025406$ amu, $M(^{4}_{2}He) = 4.002603$ amu.

Solution

Our first step will be to write the reaction, then to find the disintegration energy Q. If $Q > 0$, the decay is allowed.

Alpha decay : $^{226}_{89}Ac \rightarrow {}^{222}_{87}Fr + \alpha$

$$Q = [M(^{226}_{89}Ac) - M(^{222}_{87}Fr) - M(^{4}He)]c^2$$

$$= 5.50 \text{ MeV (Alpha decay is allowed)}$$

β^- decay : $^{226}_{89}Ac = {}^{226}_{90}Th + \beta^- + \bar{\nu}$

$$Q = [M(^{226}_{89}Ac) - M(^{226}_{90}Th)]\,c^2$$

$$= 1.12 \text{ MeV} \quad (\beta^- \text{ decay is allowed})$$

β^+ decay : $^{226}_{89}Ac \rightarrow {}^{226}_{88}Ra + \beta^+ + \nu$

$$Q = [M(^{226}_{89}Ac) - M(^{226}_{88}Ra) - 2m_e]\,c^2$$

$$= -0.38 \text{ MeV} \quad (\beta^+ \text{ decay is not allowed})$$

Electron capture : $^{226}_{89}Ac + e^- \rightarrow {}^{226}_{88}Ra + \nu$

$$Q = [M(^{226}_{89}Ac) - M(^{226}_{88}Ra)]c^2$$

$$= 0.64 \text{ MeV} \quad (\text{Electron capture is allowed})$$

In above analysis it is clear that during α-decay, Q-value is maximum thus chances of α-decay are maximum.

Illustrative Example 4.49

Show that $^{55}_{26}$Fe may electron capture, but not β^+ decay. Masses given are

$M(^{55}_{26}Fe) = 54.938298$ amu; $M(^{55}_{25}Mn) = 54.938050$ amu; $m(e) = 0.000549$ amu.

Solution

The two possible reactions for electron capture and β^+ decay by $^{55}_{26}$Fe are

$$^{55}_{26}Fe + e \rightarrow {}^{55}_{25}Mn + n \quad \text{Electron capture} \quad \ldots(4.80)$$

$$^{55}_{26}Fe \rightarrow {}^{55}_{25}Mn + \beta^+ + \nu \;\; \beta^+ \text{ decay} \quad \ldots(4.81)$$

First we will determine the disintegration energy Q of equations-(4.80) and (4.81) :

$$M(^{55}_{26}Fe) = 54.938298 \text{ amu},$$

$$M(^{55}_{25}Mn) = 54.938050 \text{ amu and } m_e = 0.000549 \text{ amu}$$

For β^+ decay the Q-value of reaction is

$$Q = [54.938298 - 54.938050 - 2 \times 0.000549] \times 931.5 \text{ MeV}$$

$$= -0.79 \text{ MeV}$$

Negative value of Q implies that positron decay is not possible spontaneously

For electron capture the Q-value of reaction is

$$Q = [54.938298 - 54.938050] \times 931.5 \text{ MeV}$$

$$= 0.23 \text{ MeV}$$

Positive value of Q implies that electron capture is possible in this case.

Illustrative Example 4.50

A sample of ^{18}F is used internally as a medical diagnostic tool to look for the effects of the positron decay ($T_{1/2} = 110$ min). How long does it take for 99% of the ^{18}F to decay ?

Solution

Radioactive decay equation is

$$N = N_0 e^{-\lambda t} = N_0 e^{-\ln(2)t/T} \quad [\text{As } \lambda = \frac{\ln_2}{T}]$$

After decay of 99% of the initial sample only 1% will be left, and $N/N_0 = 1\%$. We then have

$$\frac{N}{N_0} = \frac{1}{100} = e^{-\ln(2)t/T}$$

If we take the natural logarithm, we have

$$-\ln 100 = -\frac{\ln 2 \times t}{T}$$

Which on solving for t yields

$$t = \frac{\ln 100}{\ln 2} \times T$$

$$= \frac{\log 100}{\log 2} \times T$$

$$= \frac{2}{0.3010} \times 110$$

$$= 731 \text{ min} = 12.2 \text{ h}$$

Web Reference at www.physicsgalaxy.com

Age Group - High School Physics | Age 17-19 Years
Section - MODERN PHYSICS
Topic - Nuclear Reactions
Module Number - 10 to 22

Practice Exercise 4.5

(i) A radioactive source, in the form of a metallic sphere of radius 10^{-2} m emits β-particles at the rate of 5×10^{10} particles per second. The source is electrically insulated. How long will it take for its potential to be raised by 2 volt, assuming that 40% of the emitted β-particle escape the source.

[6.94×10^{-4} s]

(ii) The nucleus of ${}^{230}_{90}\text{Th}$ is unstable against α-decay with a half-life of 7.6×10^3 years. Write down the equation of the decay and estimate the kinetic energy of the emitted α-particle from the following data : $m({}^{230}_{90}\text{Th}) = 230.033131$ amu, $m({}^{226}_{88}\text{Ra}) = 226.025406$ amu and $m({}^{4}_{2}\text{He}) = 4.002603$ amu. Take 1 amu = 931.5 MeV

[3.267 MeV]

(iii) ${}^{239}_{94}\text{Pu}$ is undergoing α-decay according to the equation

$${}^{239}_{94}\text{Pu} \rightarrow {}^{235}_{92}\text{U} + {}^{4}_{2}\text{He}$$

The process is accompanied by an emission of γ-rays of wavelength 0.125 Å. Find the speed of the emitted α-particle. Given, mass of ${}^{239}_{94}\text{Pu}$ = 239.052158 amu, mass of ${}^{235}_{92}\text{U}$ = 235.043925 amu, mass of ${}^{4}_{2}\text{He}$ = 4.002603 amu and 1 amu = 931.5 MeV.

[1.56×10^7 m/s]

(iv) Calculate the maximum kinetic energy of the beta particle emitted in the following decay process:

$${}^{12}\text{N} \longrightarrow {}^{12}\text{C}^* + e^+ + \nu;$$

$${}^{12}\text{C}^* \longrightarrow {}^{12}\text{C} + \gamma\,(4.43\text{ MeV})$$

Atomic mass of ${}^{12}\text{N}$ = 12.018613 amu and mass of $e^+ = 0.00055$ amu. Take 1 amu = 931.5 MeV

[11.88 MeV]

(v) The α-decay of ${}^{210}\text{Po}$ nuclei (in the ground state) is accompanied by emission of two groups of α-particles with kinetic energies 5.30 & 4.50 MeV. Following the emission of these particles the daughter nuclei are found in the ground & excited states. Find the energy of gamma–quanta emitted by the excited nuclei.

[0.81 MeV]

(vi) Proton with kinetic energy $T = 1.0$ MeV striking a lithium target induces a nuclear reaction ${}^{1}_{1}\text{p} + {}^{7}_{3}\text{Li} \rightarrow 2\,{}^{4}_{2}\text{He}$. Find the kinetic energy of each α–particle and the angle of their divergence provided their motion directions are symmetrical with respect to that of incoming protons. Take 1 amu = 931.5 amu.

[$m_p = 1.007825$ amu, $m_{Li} = 7.016004$ amu, $m_{He} = 4.002603$ amu]

[9.1735 MeV, 170.5°]

(vii) ${}^{228}\text{Th}$ emits an alpha particle to reduce to ${}^{224}\text{Ra}$. Calculate the kinetic energy of the alpha particle emitted in the following decay :

$${}^{228}\text{Th} \longrightarrow {}^{224}\text{Ra}^* + \alpha;$$

$${}^{224}\text{Ra}^* \longrightarrow {}^{224}\text{Ra} + \gamma\,(217\text{ keV})$$

Atomic masses are : $\text{Th}^{228} = 228.028726$ amu; ${}^{224}\text{Ra} = 224.020196$ amu; ${}^{4}\text{He} = 4.00260$ amu. Take 1 amu = 931.5 MeV

[5.214 MeV]

(viii) When thermal neutrons (energy = 0.04 eV) are used to induce the reaction;

${}^{10}_{5}\text{B} + {}^{1}_{0}\text{n} \longrightarrow {}^{7}_{3}\text{Li} + {}^{4}_{2}\text{He}$. α-particles are emitted with an energy of 1.83 MeV.

Given the masses of boron neutron & ${}^{4}\text{He}$ as 10.01167, 1.00894 & 4.00260 amu respectively. What is the mass of ${}^{7}_{3}\text{Li}$?

[7.013662 amu]

Advance Illustrations Videos at www.physicsgalaxy.com

Age Group - Advance Illustrations
Section - Modern Physics
Topic - Atomic and Nuclear Physics
Illustrations - 54 In-depth Illustrations Videos

* * * * *

Discussion Questions

Q4-1 Is the mass excess of an alpha particle greater than or less than the particle's total binding energy ?

Q4-2 We have stimulated emission and spontaneous emission. Do we also have stimulated absorption and spontaneous absorption?

Q4-3 Tritium is the ^{3}H isotope of hydrogen. Its atomic mass is 3.016 amu; the atomic mass of ^{1}H is 1.0078 amu, and that for the neutron is 1.00867 amu. What do you predict about the stability of tritium? Repeat for ^{2}H, deuterium, which has an atomic mass of 2.0141 amu.

Q4-4 If neutron exert only attractive force, why don't we have a nucleus containing neutrons alone ?

Q4-5 Consider two pairs of neutrons. In each pair, the separation between the neutrons is the same. Can the force between the neutrons have different magnitudes for the two pairs ?

Q4-6 A molecule of hydrogen contains two protons and two electrons. The nuclear force between these two protons is always neglected while discussing the behaviour of a hydrogen molecule. Why ?

Q4-7 Is it easier to take out a nucleon from carbon or from iron? From iron or from lead ?

Q4-8 Suppose we have 12 protons and 12 neutrons. We can assemble them to from either a ^{24}Mg Nucleus or two ^{12}C nuclei. In which of the two cases more energy will be liberated ?

Q4-9 What is the difference between cathode rays and beta rays? When the two are travelling in space, can you make out which is the cathode ray and which is the beta ray ?

Q4-10 At $t = 0$, a sample of radionuclide A has the same decay rate as a sample of radionuclide B has at t = 30 min. The disintegration constants are λ_A and λ_B, with $\lambda_A < \lambda_B$. Will the two samples ever have (simultaneously) the same decay rate ?

Q4-11 At $t = 0$ we begin to observe two identical radioactive nuclei with a half life of 5 min. At t = 1 min one of the nuclei decays. Does that event increase or decrease the chance of the second nucleus decaying in the next 4 min. or is there no effect on the second nucleus ?

Q4-12 If the nucleus of a nucleus are separated from each other, the total mass is increased. Where does this mass come from ?

Q4-13 The radionuclide ^{49}Sc has a half life of 57.0 min. The counting rate of sample of this nuclide at $t = 0$ is 6000 counts/min above the general background activity, which is 30 counts/min. Without actual computation, determine whether the counting rate of the sample will be about equal to the background rate in about 3 h, 7 h, 10 h, or a time much longer than 10 h.

Q4-14 The radionuclides ^{209}At and ^{209}Po emit alpha particles with energies of 5.65 and 4.88 MeV, respectively. Which nuclide has the longer half life ?

Q4-15 In beta decay, an electron (or a positron) is emitted by a nucleus. Does the remaining atom get oppositely charged ?

Q4-16 When a boron nucleus ($^{10}_{5}$B) is bombarded by a neutron, an α-particle is emitted. Which nucleus will be formed as a result ?

Q4-17 Does a result lose mass when it suffers gamma decay ?

Q4-18 In a typical fission reaction, the nucleus is split into two middle weight nuclei of unequal masses. Which of the two (heavier or lighter) has greater kinetic energy? Greater linear momentum ?

Q4-19 Consider the fission reaction

$$^{235}\text{U} + \text{n} \longrightarrow \text{X} + \text{Y} + 2\text{n}$$

Rank the following possible nuclides for representation by X (or Y), most likely first :

(a) ^{152}Nd, (b) ^{140}I, (c) ^{128}In,

(d) ^{115}Pd, (e) ^{105}Mo

Q4-20 If three helium nuclei combine to form a carbon nucleus, energy is liberated. Why can't helium nuclei combine on their own and minimize the energy ?

Q4-21 Estimate the atomic mass of $^{64}_{30}$Zn from the fact that the binding energy per nucleon for it is about 8.7 MeV.

Q4-22 Why do chemists consider different isotopes to be the same element even through their nuclei are not the same ?

Q4-23 Suppose that a ^{238}U nucleus "swallows" a neutron and then decays not by fission but by beta decay, emitting an electron and a neutrino. Which nuclide remains after this decay:

(a) ^{239}Pu, (b) ^{238}Np, (c) ^{239}Np,

or (d) ^{238}Pa ?

Q4-24 The neutron number is not conserved in a beta decay. Is this a violation of the conservation of nucleons ? Explain.

Q4-25 Which physical or chemical properties affect the decay rate or half-life of a radioactive isotope ?

Q4-26 One radioactive nuclide has a decay constant that is half that of another. If the two nuclides start with the same number of undecayed nuclei, will twice as many of its nuclei decay in a given time ? Explain.

Q4-27 A basic assumption of radiocarbon dating is that the cosmic ray intensity has been generally constant for the last 40 000 y or so. Suppose it were found that the intensity was much less 10 000 y ago than it is today. How would this affect ^{14}C dating ?

Q4-28 A patient receives a dose of radiation of 1.0 rad from X-rays and a dose of 1.0 rad from an alpha source. (a) Which has the greater biological (damage) effectiveness ? (b) What are the doses in rems ?

Q4-29 The energy produced in fission reactions is carried off as kinetic energies of the products. How is this energy converted to heat in a nuclear reactor ?

Q4-30 Why is it so difficult to detect neutrinos experimentally ?

Q4-31 Why are heavy nuclei unstable ?

Q4-32 Why do nearly all the naturally occurring isotopes lie above the $N = Z$ line in figure 4.1 ?

Q4-33 If a nucleus has a half-life of 1 year, does this mean it will be completely decayed after 2 years ? Explain.

Q4-34 What fraction of a radioactive sample has decayed after two half-lives have elapsed ?

Q4-35 Two samples of the same radioactive nuclide are prepared. Sample A has twice the initial activity of sample B. How does the half-life of A compare with the half-life of B ? After each has passed through five half-lives, what is the ratio of their activities ?

Q4-36 Explain why the half-lives for radioactive nuclei are essentially independent of temperature.

Q4-37 If a nucleus such as ^{226}Ra initially at rest undergoes alpha decay, which has more kinetic energy after the decay, the alpha particle or the daughter nucleus ?

Q4-38 Can a nucleus emit alpha particles that have different energies ? Explain.

Q4-39 Explain why many heavy nuclei undergo alpha decay but do not spontaneously emit neutrons or protons.

Q4-40 If an alpha particle and an electron have the same kinetic energy, which undergoes the greater deflection when passed through a magnetic field ?

Q4-41 If film is kept in a wooden box, alpha particles from a radioactive source outside the box cannot expose the film but beta particles can. Explain.

Q4-42 Why would a fusion reactor produce less radioactive waste than a fission reactor ?

Q4-43 What factors make a fusion reaction difficult to achieve ?

Q4-44 Discuss the advantages and disadvantages of fusion power from the point of safety, pollution, and resources.

Q4-45 Discuss three major problems associated with the development of a controlled fusion reactor.

Q4-46 If two radioactive samples have the same activity measured in curies, will they necessarily create the same damage to a medium ? Explain.

Q4-47 How can you be sure that nuclei are not made of protons and electrons rather than protons and neutrons ?

Q4-48 Why aren't the masses of all nuclei exact integer multiples of the mass of a single nucleon ?

Q4-49 Compared to α particles with the same energy, β-particles can much more easily penetrate through matter Why is this ?

Q4-50 Some decays that are not possible from a nucleus in its ground state are possible if the nucleus is in an excited state. Explain why.

Q4-51 What are the properties of a nucleus that is likely to undergo (a) alpha decay, (b) beta decay, and (c) gamma decay ?

Q4-52 What would the distribution of electron kinetic energies be like if no neutrinos were emitted in beta decay ? What would it look like if a very massive neutral particle wave always emitted ?

Q4-53 Why is the decay rate of radioactive nuclei not changed by chemical environment, heating, or pressure ?

Q4-54 Why is radium still found in nature ? Its half-life is 1600 years, and the estimated age of the universe is five billion years.

Q4-55 How can isotopes of an element be separated, since they have the same chemical properties ?

Q4-56 Can you suggest any reasons why natural radioactivity contains helium nuclei but neither hydrogen nor lithium nuclei ?

Q4-57 What could be some of the reasons why stable nuclei have about the same number of protons and neutrons, with an excess number of neutrons as A increases ?

* * * * *

Conceptual MCQs Single Option Correct

4-1 A radioactive element $^{238}_{90}X$ decays into $^{222}_{83}Y$. The number of β-particles emitted are : (Consider only β^- emission)
(A) 4 (B) 6
(C) 2 (D) 1

4-2 Three specimens *A*, *B*, *C* of same radioactive element have activities, 1 curie, 1 rutherford and 1 becquerel respectively. Which specimen has maximum mass :
(A) *A* (B) *B*
(C) *C* (D) All have equal mass

4-3 Which of the following radiations has the least wavelength ?
(A) γ-rays (B) β-rays
(C) α-rays (D) X-rays

4-4 A nucleus with $Z = 92$ emits the following in a sequence:

$$\alpha, \alpha, \beta^-, \beta^-, \alpha, \alpha, \alpha, \alpha; \ \beta^-, \beta^-, \alpha, \beta^+, \beta^+, \alpha$$

The *Z* of the resulting nucleus is :
(A) 76 (B) 78
(C) 82 (D) 74

4-5 When aluminium is bombarded with fast neutrons, it changes into sodium with emission of particle according to the equation

$$^{27}_{13}Al + ^{1}_{0}n \rightarrow ^{24}_{11}Na + x$$

What is the name of *x* ?
(A) Electron (B) Proton
(C) Neutron (D) Alpha-particle

4-6 The mean density of the nuclei is proportional to :
(A) Mass number (B) Atomic number
(C) The number of nucleons (D) None of the above

4-7 In the equation

$$^{27}_{13}Al + ^{4}_{2}He \rightarrow ^{30}_{15}P + X,$$

The correct symbol for *X* is :
(A) $^{0}_{-1}e$ (B) $^{1}_{1}H$
(C) $^{4}_{2}He$ (D) $^{1}_{0}n$

4-8 Choose the WRONG statement. A thermonuclear fusion reactor is better than a fission reactor for the following reasons:
(A) For the same mass of substances involved, a fusion reaction releases much more energy than a fission reaction
(B) A fusion reaction can be much more easily controlled than a fission reaction
(C) A fusion reaction produces almost no radioactive waste
(D) The fuel required for fusion is readily available in abundance from sea-water

4-9 The chemical behaviour of an atom depends upon :
(A) The number of electrons orbiting around its nucleus
(B) The number of protons in its nucleus
(C) The number of neutrons in its nucleus
(D) The number of nucleons in its nucleus

4-10 The critical mass of a fissionable material can be reduced by :
(A) Heating it
(B) Cooling it
(C) Adding impurities to it
(D) Surrounding it with a shield that will reflect neutrons

4-11 Cadmium rods are used in a nuclear reactor for :
(A) Slowing down fast neutrons
(B) Speeding up slow neutrons
(C) Absorbing neutrons
(D) Regulating the power level of the reactor

4-12 A β^--particle is emitted by a radioactive nucleus at the time of conversion of a :
(A) Neutron into a proton (B) Proton into a neutron
(C) Nucleon into energy (D) Positron into energy

4-13 Why does the fusion occur at high temperature ?
(A) Atoms are ionised at high temperature
(B) Molecules break up at high temperature
(C) Nuclei break up at high temperature
(D) Kinetic energy is high enough to overcome repulsion between nuclei

4-14 Mass defect of an atom refers to :
(A) Inaccurate measurement of mass of nucleons
(B) Mass annihilated to produce energy to bind the nucleus
(C) Packing fraction
(D) Difference in number of neutrons and protons in the nucleus

4-15 If *M* is the mass of a nucleus and *A* its atomic mass, then the packing fraction is :
(A) $\frac{M-A}{M+A}$ (B) $\frac{M-A}{M}$
(C) $\frac{M-A}{A}$ (D) $\frac{M+A}{M-A}$

4-16 The fusion of hydrogen into helium is more likely to take place :
(A) At high temperature and high pressure
(B) At high temperature and low pressure
(C) At low temperature and low pressure
(D) At low temperature and high pressure

4-17 The average number of neutrons released by the fission of one uranium atom is :

(A) 1 (B) 2

(C) 2.5 (D) 3

4-18 A beam of fast-moving alpha particles was directed towards a thin gold film. The parts *A'*, *B'* and *C'* of the transmitted and reflected beams corresponding to the incident parts *A*, *B* and *C* of the beam are shown in the following figure-4.13. The number of alpha particles in :

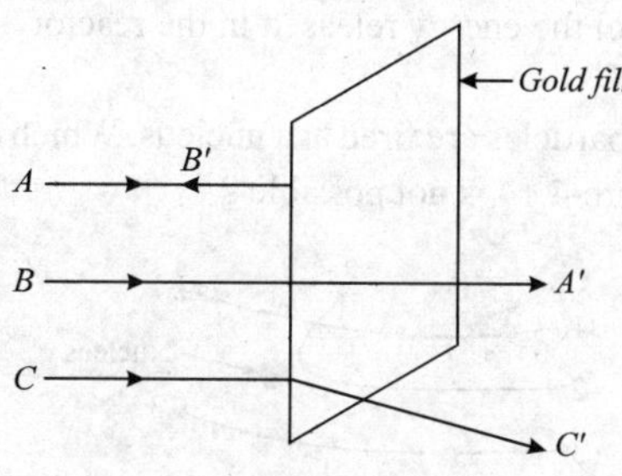

Figure 4.13

(A) *B'* will be minimum and in *C'* maximum

(B) *A'* will be maximum and in *B'* minimum

(C) *A'* will be minimum and in *B'* maximum

(D) *C'* will be minimum and in *B'* maximum

4-19 From the following equations pick out the possible nuclear fusion reaction :

(A) ${}^{13}_{6}C + {}^{1}_{1}H \rightarrow {}^{14}_{6}C + 4.3\text{ MeV}$

(B) ${}^{12}_{6}C + {}^{1}_{1}H \rightarrow {}^{13}_{7}C + 2\text{ MeV}$

(C) ${}^{14}_{7}C + {}^{1}_{1}H \rightarrow {}^{16}_{8}O + 7.3\text{ MeV}$

(D) ${}^{235}_{92}U + {}^{1}_{0}n \rightarrow {}^{140}_{54}Xe + {}^{94}_{38}Sr + 2\,({}^{1}_{0}n) + \gamma + 200\text{ MeV}$

4-20 Radio carbon dating is done by estimating in the specimen :

(A) The amount of ordinary carbon still present

(B) The amount of radio carbon still present

(C) The ratio of the amounts of ${}^{14}_{6}C$ to ${}^{12}_{6}C$ still present

(D) None of the above

4-21 Which of the following cannot be emitted by radioactive substances during their decay ?

(A) Protons (B) Neutrinos

(C) Helium nuclei (D) Electrons

4-22 The electron emitted in beta radiation originates from :

(A) Inner orbits of atoms

(B) Free electrons existing in nuclei

(C) Decay of neutron in a nucleus

(D) Photon escaping from the nucleus

4-23 In the nuclear reaction, given by ${}_{2}He^{4} + {}_{7}N^{14} \rightarrow {}_{q}X^{p} + {}_{1}H^{1}$
The nucleus X is :

(A) Nitrogen of mass 16 (B) Nitrogen of mass 17

(C) Oxygen of mass 16 (D) Oxygen of mass 17

4-24 What is the number of α and β particles emitted in the following radioactive decay (Consider only beta minus decay)?

$${}^{200}_{90}X \rightarrow {}^{168}_{80}Y$$

(A) 8 and 6 (B) 6 and 8

(C) 8 and 8 (D) 6 and 6

4-25 The radioactive nucleus of an element *X* decays to a stable nucleus of element *Y*. A graph of the rate of formation of *Y* against time would look like :

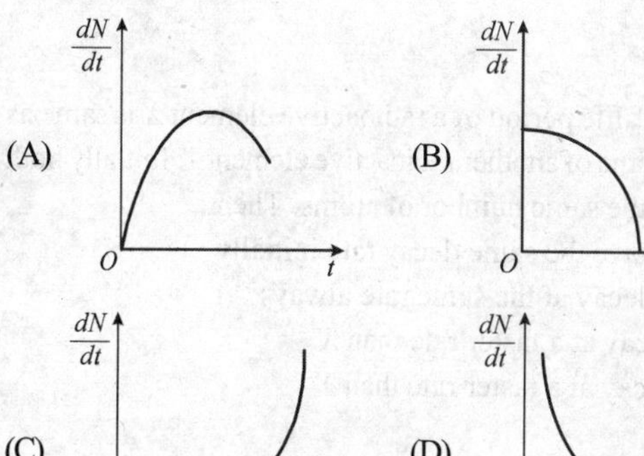

4-26 The radioactive decay of uranium into thorium is represented by the equation :

$${}^{238}_{92}U \rightarrow {}^{234}_{90}Th + x$$

What is *x* ?

(A) An electron (B) A proton

(C) An alpha particle (D) A neutron

4-27 As a result of radioactive decay a ${}^{238}_{92}U$ nucleus is changed to a ${}^{234}_{91}P$ nucleus. Which particles are emitted in the decay?

(A) One proton and two neutrons

(B) One α-particle and one β-particle

(C) Two β-particles and one neutron

(D) Two β-particles and one proton

4-28 A free neutron decays into a proton, an electron and :

(A) A neutrino (B) An antineutrino

(C) An α-particle (D) A β-particle

4-29 A carbon nucleus emits a particle *x* and changes into nitrogen according to the equation :

$${}^{14}_{6}C \rightarrow {}^{14}_{7}N + x$$

What is *x* ?

(A) An electron (B) A proton

(C) An alpha particle (D) A photon

4-30 $^{239}_{92}U$ decays emitting a β-particle producing neptunium nucleus, which further decays emitting a β-particle and the daughter product is plutonium (Pu). The grand daughter product can be expressed as :

(A) $^{239}_{90}Pu$ (B) $^{241}_{90}Pu$
(C) $^{239}_{94}Pu$ (D) $^{241}_{94}Pu$

4-31 The half-life of a radioactive substance depends upon :
(A) Its temperature
(B) The external pressure on it
(C) The mass of the substance
(D) The strength of the nuclear force between the nucleons of its atom

4-32 The half-life period of a radioactive element X is same as the mean-life time of another radioactive element Y. Initially both of them have the same number of atoms. Then :
(A) X and Y have the same decay rate initially
(B) X and Y decay at the same rate always
(C) Y will decay at a faster rate than X
(D) X will decay at a faster rate than Y

4-33 The radioactive decay of an element X to elements Y and K is represented by the equation

$$^{A}_{Z}X \rightarrow {}^{A}_{Z+1}Y \rightarrow {}^{A+4}_{Z-1}K \rightarrow {}^{A-4}_{Z-1}K$$

The sequence of the emitted radiations is :
(A) α, β, γ (B) β, α, γ
(C) γ, α, β (D) β, γ, α

4-34 The nuclear reaction $^{107}_{48}Cd \rightarrow {}^{107}_{47}Ag$ can occur with the :
(A) Electron capture (B) Positron capture
(C) Proton emission (D) α-particle emission

4-35 Two radioactive elements X and Y have half-life times of 50 minutes and 100 minutes, respectively. Samples X and Y initially contain equal numbers of atoms. After 200 minutes, the ratio

$$\frac{\text{number of undecayed atoms of } X}{\text{number of undecayed atoms of } Y} \text{ is}$$

(A) 4 (B) 2
(C) 1/2 (D) 1/4

4-36 When a β^--particle is emitted from a nucleus, the neutron-proton ratio :
(A) Is decreased (B) Is increased
(C) Remains the same (D) First (A) then (B)

4-37 In the given reaction :

$$^{A}_{Z}X \xrightarrow{p} {}^{A}_{Z+1}Y \xrightarrow{q} {}^{A-4}_{Z-1}K \xrightarrow{r} {}^{A-4}_{Z-1}K$$

radioactive radiations, p, q, r are emitted. The radiations p, q, r are respectively :
(A) α, β, γ (B) β, α, γ
(C) γ, α, β (D) α, γ, β,

4-38 Graphite and heavy water are two common moderators used in a nuclear reactor. The function of the moderator is :
(A) To slow down the neutrons to thermal energies
(B) To absorb the neutrons and stop the chain reaction
(C) To cool the reactor
(D) To control the energy released in the reactor

4-39 Alpha particles are fired at a nucleus. Which of the paths shown in figure-4.14 is not possible ?

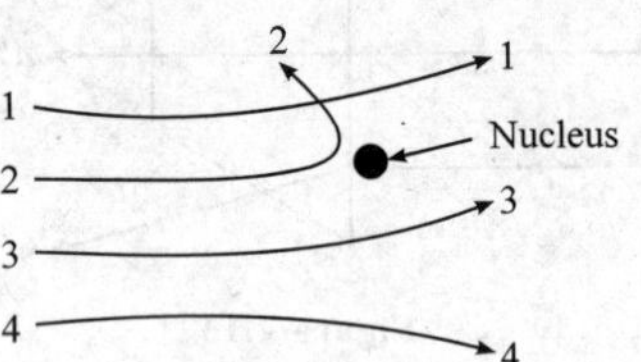

Figure 4.14

(A) 1 (B) 2
(C) 3 (D) 4

4-40 The decay constant λ of a radioactive sample:
(A) Decreases with increase of external pressure and temperature
(B) Increases with increase of external pressure and temperature
(C) Decreases with increase of temperature and increase of pressure
(D) Is independent of temperature and pressure

4-41 When high energy alpha particles ($^{4}_{2}He$) pass through nitrogen gas, an isotope of oxygen is formed with the emission of particles named x. The nuclear reaction is

$$^{14}_{7}N + {}^{4}_{2}He \rightarrow {}^{17}_{8}O + x$$

What is the name of x ?
(A) Electron (B) Proton
(C) Neutron (D) Positron

4-42 When boron ($^{10}_{5}B$) is bombarded by neutron, α-particle is emitted. The resulting nucleus has a mass number :
(A) 11 (B) 7
(C) 6 (D) 15

4-43 Consider α-particles, β-particles and γ-rays, each having an energy of 0.5 MeV. In increasing order of penetrating powers, the radiations are :
(A) α, β, γ (B) α, γ, β
(C) β, γ, α (D) γ, β, α

4-44 A radioactive nucleus emits a beta particle. The parent and daughter nuclei are :

(A) Isotopes (B) Isobars
(C) Isomers (D) Isotones

4-45 Fast neutrons can easily be slowed down by :

(A) The use of lead shielding
(B) Passing them through water
(C) Elastic collisions with heavy nuclei
(D) Applying a strong electric field

4-46 A nucleus ruptures into two nuclear parts, which have their velocity ratio equal to 2 : 1. What will be the ratio of their nuclear size (nuclear radius)?

(A) $3^{1/2} : 1$ (B) $1 : 3^{1/2}$
(C) $2^{1/3} : 1$ (D) $1 : 2^{1/3}$

4-47 For nuclei with $A > 100$, mark the INCORRECT statement :

(A) The binding energy per nucleon decreases on the average as A increases
(B) If the nucleus breaks into two roughly equal parts, energy is released
(C) If two nuclei fuse to form a bigger nucleus energy is released
(D) The nucleus with $Z > 83$ are generally unstable

4-48 Figure 4.15 shows a roughly approximated curve of binding energy per nucleon with mass number. W, X, Y and Z are four nuclei indicated on the curve. According to this curve, the process that would release energy is :

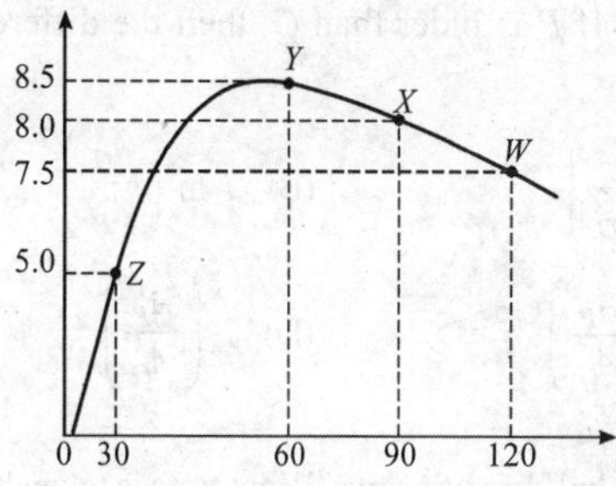

Figure 4.15

(A) $Y \rightarrow 2Z$ (B) $W \rightarrow X + Z$
(C) $W \rightarrow 2Y$ (D) $X \rightarrow Y + Z$

* * * * *

Numerical MCQs Single Option Correct

4-1 Two identical samples (same material and same amount) P and Q of a radioactive substance having mean life T are observed to have activities A_P & A_Q respectively at the time of observation. If P is older than Q, then the difference in their ages is :

(A) $T\ln\left(\frac{A_P}{A_Q}\right)$ (B) $T\ln\left(\frac{A_Q}{A_P}\right)$

(C) $\frac{1}{T}\ln\left(\frac{A_P}{A_Q}\right)$ (D) $T\left(\frac{A_P}{A_Q}\right)$

4-2 Bi has a half life of 5 days. What time is taken by $(7/8)^{th}$ part of the sample to decay ?

(A) 3.4 days (B) 10 days
(C) 15 days (D) 20 days

4-3 A certain radioactive substance has a half life of 5 years. Thus for a nucleus in a sample of the element, probability of decay in 10 years is :

(A) 50% (B) 75%
(C) 60% (D) 100%

4-4

$$A \xrightarrow{\lambda_1} B \xrightarrow{\lambda_2} C$$

	A	B	C
$t=0$	N_0	0	0
t	N_1	N_2	N_3

In the above radioactive decay C is stable nucleus. Then :

(A) rate of decay of A will first increase and then decrease

(B) number of nuclei of B will first increase and then decrease

(C) if $\lambda_2 > \lambda_1$, then activity of B will always be higher than activity of A

(D) if $\lambda_1 >> \lambda_2$, then number of nucleus of C will always be less than number of nucleus of B.

4-5 The half-life of a radioactive substance is 10 days. This means that :

(A) The substance completely disintegrates in 20 days

(B) The substance completely disintegrates in 40 days

(C) 1/8 part of the mass of the substance will be left intact at the end of 40 days

(D) 7/8 part of the mass of the substance disintegrates in 30 days

4-6 90% of the active nuclei present in a radioactive sample are found to remain undecayed after 1 day. The percentage of undecayed nuclei left two days will be :

(A) 85% (B) 81%
(C) 80% (D) 79%

4-7 The atomic weight of boron is 10.81 and it has two isotopes $^{10}_{5}B$ and $^{11}_{5}B$. The ratio of $^{10}_{5}B$: $^{11}_{5}B$ in nature would be :

(A) 19:81 (B) 10:11
(C) 15:16 (D) 81:19

4-8 Half-lives of two radioactive substances A and B are 20 minutes and 40 minutes respectively. Initially samples A and B have equal number of nuclei. After 80 minutes, the ratio of the remaining number of A and B nuclei is :

(A) 1:16 (B) 4:1
(C) 1:4 (D) 1:1

4-9 A 100 ml solution having activity 50 dps is kept in a beaker. It is now constantly diluted by adding water at a constant rate of 10 ml/sec and 2 ml/sec of solution is constantly being taken out. Find the activity of 10 ml solution which is taken out, assuming half life to be effectively very large :

(A) $10\left[1-\left(\frac{2}{7}\right)^{1/4}\right]$ (B) $10\left[1-\left(\frac{5}{7}\right)^{1/2}\right]$

(C) $50\left[1-\left(\frac{5}{7}\right)^{1/4}\right]$ (B) $50\left[1-\left(\frac{2}{7}\right)^{1/2}\right]$

4-10 A radioactive source has a half life of 3 hours. A freshly prepared sample of the same emits radiation 16 times the permissible safe value. The minimum time after which it would be possible to work safely with the source is :

(A) 6 hours (B) 12 hours
(C) 18 hours (D) 24 hours

4-11 The half life period of a sample is 100 second. If we take 40 gram of the radioactive sample, then after 400 second how much substance will be left undecayed ?

(A) 10 gram (B) 5 gram
(C) 2.5 gram (D) 1.25 gram

4-12 The kinetic energy of a 300 K thermal neutron is :

(A) 300 eV (B) 300 eV
(C) 0.026 eV (D) 0.026 MeV

4-13 A sample has two isotopes ^{150}A and ^{xx}B having masses 50 g and 30 g respectively. A is radioactive and B is stable. A decays to A' by emitting α particles. The half life of A is 2 hrs. Find the mass of the sample after 4 hour :

(A) 43 gm (B) 58 gm
(C) 61 gm (D) 79 gm

4-14 In previous question find the approximate number of alpha particles emitted :

(A) 1.2×10^{23} (B) 1.5×10^{23}
(C) 2.3×10^{23} (D) 3.4×10^{23}

4-15 What is the energy released in the fission reaction

$$^{236}_{92}U \rightarrow \, ^{117}_{46}X + \, ^{117}_{46}Y + 2\, ^{1}_{0}n$$

given that the binding energy per nucleon of X and Y is 8.5 MeV and that of $^{236}_{92}U$ is 7.6 MeV ?

(A) 176.2 MeV (B) 183.7 MeV
(C) 195.4 MeV (D) 208.6 MeV

4-16 The count rate from 100 cm^3 of a radioactive liquid is c. Some of this liquid is now discarded. The count rate of the remaining liquid is found to be $c/10$ after three half-lives. The volume of the remaining liquid, in cm^3, is :

(A) 20 (B) 40
(C) 60 (D) 80

5-17 A sample of radioactive material decays simultaneously by two processes A and B with half lives $\frac{1}{2}$ and $\frac{1}{4}$ hr respectively. For first half hr it decays with the process A, next one hr with the process B and for further half an hour with both A and B. If originally there were N_0 nuclei, find the number of nuclei after 2 hr of such decay :

(A) $\frac{N_0}{(2)^8}$ (B) $\frac{N_0}{(2)^4}$

(C) $\frac{N_0}{(2)^6}$ (D) $\frac{N_0}{(2)^5}$

4-18 The binding energy of deuteron (^2_1H) is 1.15 MeV per nucleon and an alpha particle (^4_2He) has a binding energy of 7.1 MeV per nucleon. Then in the reaction

$$^2_1H + ^2_1H \rightarrow \, ^4_2He + Q$$

the energy Q released is :

(A) 1 MeV (B) 11.9 MeV
(C) 23.8 MeV (D) 931 MeV

4-19 A radioactive substance is being produced at a constant rate of 200 nuclei/s. The decay constant of the substance is 1 s^{-1}. After what time the number of radioactive nuclei will become 100. Initially there are no nuclei present :

(A) 1 sec (B) $\frac{1}{\ln(2)}$ sec

(C) ln (2) sec (D) 2 sec

4-20 What is the rest mass energy of an electron ?

(A) 1 eV (B) 0.51 MeV
(C) 931 MeV (D) None of these

4-21 Figure below shows initial steps of a radioactive series

	A $\xrightarrow{\lambda}$	B $\xrightarrow{2\lambda}$	C
$t = 0$	N_0	0	0
t	N_1	N_2	N_3

The ratio of N_1 to N_2 when N_2 is maximum is :

(A) at no time this is possible
(B) 2
(C) 1/2
(D) $\frac{ln2}{2}$

4-22 After two hours 1/6th of the initial amount of a certain radioactive isotope remains undecayed. The half life of the isotope is :

(A) 17.3 min (B) 34.7 min
(C) 46.4 min (D) 1 hour

4-23 The half life of ^{218}Pa is 3 minutes. What mass of a 16 g sample of ^{218}Pa will remain after 15 minutes ?

(A) 3.2 g (B) 2.0 g
(C) 1.6 g (D) 0.5 g

4-24 N atoms of a radioactive element emit n alpha particles per second at an instant. Then the half-life of the element is :

(A) $\frac{n}{N}$ sec (B) 1.44 $\frac{n}{N}$ sec

(C) 0.69 $\frac{n}{N}$ sec (D) 0.69 $\frac{N}{n}$ sec

4-25 Consider a nuclear decay process

$$A \longrightarrow B \longrightarrow C \text{ (stable)}$$

At a certain time, the activity of nuclei A is 'x' and the net rate of increase of number of nuclei B is 'y'. The activity of nuclei B at this instant is :

(A) y (B) $x - y$
(C) $y - x$ (D) x

4-26 The activity of a radioactive sample A_0 decreases to one third of the original value in 9 years. What will be its activity after further 9 years ?

(A) $A_0/3$ (B) $A_0/6$
(C) $A_0/9$ (D) $A_0/18$

4-27 The radioactivity of a sample is X at a time t_1 and Y at a time t_2. If the mean life of the specimen is τ, the number of atoms that have disintegrated in the time interval $(t_2 - t_1)$ is :

(A) $Xt_1 - Yt_2$ (B) $X - Y$
(C) $(X - Y)/\tau$ (D) $(X - Y)\tau$

4-28 A radioactive nucleus can decay by either emitting an α particle or by emitting a β particle. Probability of α decay is 75% while that of β decay is 25%. The decayconstant of α decay is λ_1 and that of β decay is λ_2. $\frac{\lambda_1}{\lambda_2}$ is :

(A) 3 (B) $\frac{1}{3}$

(C) 1 (D) cannot be said

4-29 Part of the uranium decay series is shown

$_{92}U^{238} \longrightarrow {_{90}Th^{234}} \longrightarrow {_{91}Pa^{234}} \longrightarrow {_{92}U^{234}} \longrightarrow$

$_{90}Th^{230} \longrightarrow {_{88}Ra^{226}}$

How many pairs of isotopes are there in the above series

(A) 1 (B) 2

(C) 3 (D) 0

4-30 A radioactive element X with half life of 2 hours decays giving a stable element Y? After how many hours the ratio of X to Y will be 1 : 7 ?

(A) 6 hours (B) 8 hours

(C) 10 hours (D) 12 hours

4-31 The energy released by the fission of one uranium atom is 200 MeV. The number of fissions per second required to produce 3.2 MW of power is :

(A) 10^7 (B) 10^{10}

(C) 10^{15} (D) 10^{17}

4-32 Nuclei X decay into nuclei Y by emitting α particles. Energies of α particle are found to be only 1 MeV & 1.4 MeV. Disregarding the recoil of nuclei Y. The energy of γ photon emitted will be :

(A) 0.8 MeV (B) 1.4 MeV

(C) 1 MeV (D) 0.4 MeV

4-33 An element X decays, first by positron emission and then two α-particles are emitted in successive radioactive decay. If the product nuclei has a mass number 229 and atomic number 89, the mass number and atomic number of element X are :

(A) 237, 93 (B) 237, 94

(C) 221, 84 (D) 237, 92

4-34 The decay constant of a radioactive substance is 1 per month. The percentage of radioactive substance left undecayed after two months will be :

(A) 25% (B) 50%

(C) 66% (D) 87%

4-35 The rate of disintegration of a radioactive substance falls from 800 decay/min to 100 decay/min in 6 hours. The half-life of the radioactive substance is :

(A) 6/7 hour (B) 2 hrs

(C) 3 hrs (D) 1 hr

4-36 The activity of a radioactive sample decreases to one-tenth of the original activity A_0 in a period of one year further. After further 9 years, its activity will be :

(A) $\frac{A_0}{100}$ (B) $\frac{A_0}{90}$

(C) $\frac{A_0}{10^{10}}$ (D) None of these

4-37 Half life of a radioactive elements is 12.5 hour and its quantity is 256 gm. After how much time its quantity will remain 1 gm?

(A) 50 hrs (B) 100 hrs

(C) 150 hrs (D) 200 hrs

4-38 An unknown stable nuclide after absorbing a neutron emits an electron, and the new nuclide splits spontaneously into two alpha particles. The unknown nuclide is :

(A) $_4Be^9$ (B) $_3Li^7$

(C) $_2He^4$ (D) $_5B^{10}$

4-39 A radioactive material is made at the constant rate of 10^4 nuclei per second and the material is getting decayed with decay constant 0.0123 month^{-1}. Activity of material after a very long time (if initially there was no radioactive material) is :

(A) $\frac{10^4}{0.0123}$ dps (B) 1.6×10^8 dps

(C) 10^4 dps (D) None of these

4-40 The half life of a certain radio isotope is 10 minutes. The number of radioactive nuclei at a given instant of time is 10^8. Then the number of radioactive nuclei left 5 minutes later would be :

(A) $\frac{10^8}{2}$ (B) 10^4

(C) $\sqrt{2} \times 10^7$ (D) $\frac{10^8}{\sqrt{2}}$

4-41 A uranium nucleus (atomic number 92, mass number 238) emits an alpha particle and the resultant nucleus emits a β-particle. The atomic and mass numbers respectively of the final nucleus are :

(A) 90, 240 (B) 90, 236

(C) 91, 234 (D) 92, 232

4-42 A radioactive nuclide having decay constant λ is produced at the constant rate of n per second (say, by bombarding a target with neutrons). The expected number N of nuclei in existence t seconds after the number is N_0 is given by :

(A) $N = N_0 e^{-\lambda t}$
(B) $N = \frac{n}{\lambda} + N_0 e^{-\lambda t}$
(C) $N = \frac{n}{\lambda} + \left(N_0 - \frac{n}{\lambda}\right) e^{-\lambda t}$
(D) $N = \frac{n}{\lambda} + \left(N_0 + \frac{n}{\lambda}\right) e^{-\lambda t}$

4-43 The equation

$$4\,{}_1^1H^+ \rightarrow {}_2^4He^+ + 2e^+ + 26 \text{ MeV represents}$$

(A) β-decay
(B) ϕ-decay
(C) Fusion
(D) Fission

4-44 At time $t = 0$, N_1 nuclei of decay constant λ_1 & N_2 nuclei of decay constant λ_2 are mixed. The decay rate of the mixture at time 't' is:

(A) $N_1 N_2 e^{-(\lambda_1+\lambda_2)t}$
(B) $\left(\frac{N_1}{N_2}\right) e^{-(\lambda_1-\lambda_2)t}$
(C) $(N_1\lambda_1 e^{-\lambda_1 t} + N_2\lambda_2 e^{-\lambda_2 t})$
(D) $N_1\lambda_1\, N_2\lambda_2\, e^{-(\lambda_1+\lambda_2)t}$

4-45 The number of α and β^- emitted during the radioactive decay chain starting from ${}^{226}_{88}Ra$ and ending at ${}^{206}_{82}Pb$ is :

(A) 3α & $6\beta^-$
(B) 4α & $5\beta^-$
(C) 5α & $4\beta^-$
(D) 6α & $6\beta^-$

4-46 Two identical nuclei A and B of the same radioactive element undergo β decay. A emits a β-particle and changes to A'. B emits a β-particle and then a γ-ray photon immediately afterwards, and changes to B' :

(A) A' and B' have the same atomic number and mass number.
(B) A' and B' have the same atomic number but different mass numbers.
(C) A' and B' have different atomic numbers but the same mass number.
(D) A' and B' are isotopes.

4-47 In nuclear fission 0.1% mass is converted into energy. How much electrical energy can be generated by the fission of 1 kg of fuel ?

(A) 1 kWh
(B) 10^7 kWh
(C) 2.5 kWh
(D) 2.5×10^7 kWh

4-48 If the binding energy per nucleon in ${}_3^7Li$ and ${}_2^4He$ nuclei is respectively 5.60 MeV and 7.06 MeV, then the energy of the reaction

$${}_3^7Li + {}_1^1p \longrightarrow 2\,{}_2^4He \text{ is}$$

(A) 19.60 MeV
(B) 12.26 MeV
(C) 8.46 MeV
(D) 17.28 MeV

4-49 In which of the following process the number of protons in the nucleus increases.

(A) α – decay
(B) β^- – decay
(C) β^+ – decay
(D) k – capture

4-50 A radioactive nucleus 'X' decays to a stable nucleus 'Y'. Then the graph of rate of formation of 'Y' against time 't' will be :

(A)
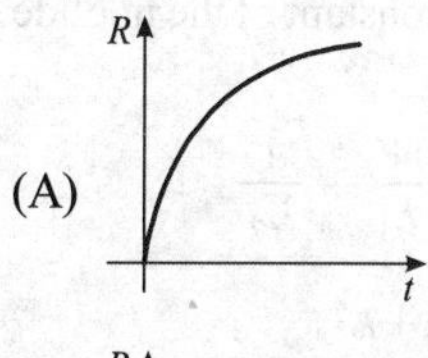

(B)
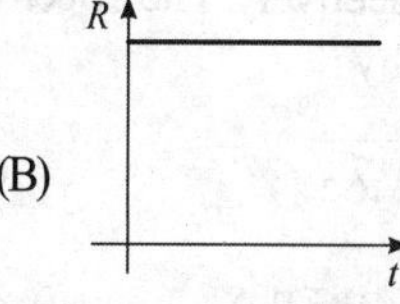

(C)
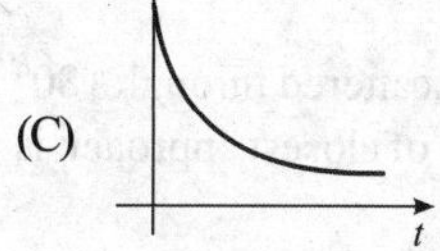

(D)
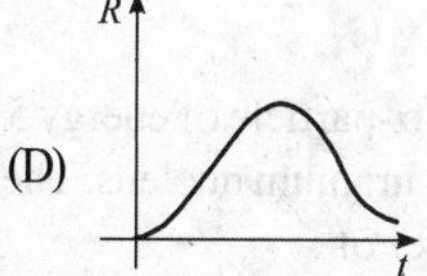

4-51 Suppose the speed of light were half of the present value, the amount of energy released in the atomic bomb explosion will be decreased by a fraction :

(A) $\frac{1}{4}$
(B) $\frac{1}{2}$
(C) $\frac{3}{4}$
(D) $\frac{3}{8}$

4-52 The graph shows how the count-rate A of a radioactive source varies with time t. A and t are related as : (assume ln (12) = 2.5)

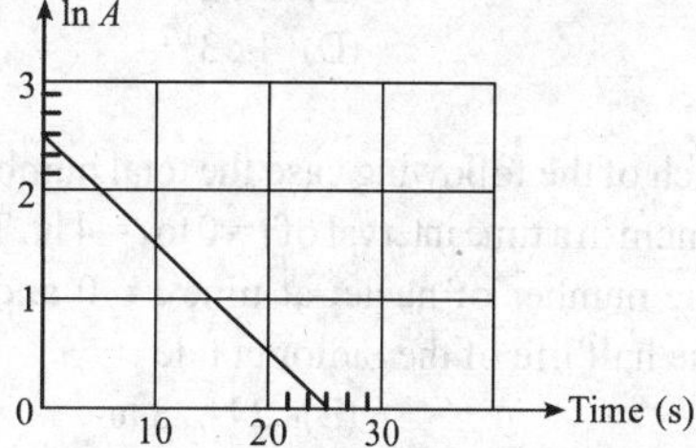

Figure 4.16

(A) $A = 2.5\, e^{-10t}$
(B) $A = 12\, e^{10t}$
(C) $A = 2.5\, e^{-0.1t}$
(D) $A = 12\, e^{-0.1t}$

4-53 The ratio of molecular mass of two radioactive substance is $\frac{3}{2}$ and the ratio of their decay constant is $\frac{4}{3}$. Then the ratio of their initial activity per mole will be :

(A) 2
(B) $\frac{8}{9}$
(C) $\frac{4}{3}$
(D) $\frac{9}{8}$

4-54 The count rate of a Geiger Muller counter for the radiation of the a radioactive material of half-life of 30 minutes decreases to 5 dps after 2 hours. The initial count rate was :

(A) 80 $second^{-1}$ (B) 625 $second^{-1}$
(C) 20 $second^{-1}$ (D) 25 $second^{-1}$

4-55 A radioactive nuclide can decay simultaneously by two different processes which have individual decay constants λ_1 and λ_2 respectively. The effective decay constant of the nuclide is λ given by :

(A) $\lambda = \sqrt{\lambda_1\lambda_2}$ (B) $\frac{1}{\lambda} = \frac{1}{\lambda_1} + \frac{1}{\lambda_2}$
(C) $\lambda = \frac{1}{2}(\lambda_1 + \lambda_2)$ (D) $\lambda = \lambda_1 + \lambda_2$

4-56 An α-particle of energy 5 MeV is scattered through 180° by a fixed uranium nucleus. The distance of closest approach is of the order of :

(A) 1 Å (B) 10^{-10} cm
(C) 10^{-12} cm (D) 10^{-15} cm

4-57 Half lives of two isotopes *X* and *Y* of a material are known to be 2×10^9 years and 4×10^9 years respectively. If a planet was formed with equal number of these isotopes, then the current age of planet, given that currently the material has 20% of *X* and 80% of *Y* by number, will be :

(A) 2×10^9 years (B) 4×10^9 years
(C) 6×10^9 years (D) 8×10^9 years

4-58 A nucleus raptures into two nuclear parts which have their velocities in the ratio of 2 : 1. What will be the ratio of their nuclear sizes (radii) ?

(A) $2^{1/3} : 1$ (B) $1 : 2^{1/3}$
(C) $3^{1/2} : 1$ (D) $1 : 3^{1/2}$

4-59 In which of the following case the total number of decays will be maximum in a time interval of $t = 0$ to $t = 4$ hr. The first term represents the number of nuclei at time $t = 0$ and the second represents the half life of the radionuclide :

(A) N_0, 4 hr (B) 2 N_0, 3 hr
(C) 3 N_0, 2hr (D) 4 N_0, 1 hr

4-60 There are two radioactive substances *A* and *B*. Decay constant of *B* is two times that of *A*. Initially both have equal number of nuclei. After *n* half lives of *A* rate of disintegration of both are equal. The value of *n* is :

(A) 1 (B) 2
(C) 4 (D) All of these

4-61 An atom of mass number 15 and atomic number 7 captures an alpha particle and then emits a proton. The mass number and atomic number of the resulting atom will be :

(A) 14 and 2 respectively (B) 16 and 4 respectively
(C) 17 and 6 respectively (D) 18 and 8 respectively

4-62 A radioactive element *X* converts into another stable element *Y*. Half life of *X* is 2 hrs. Initially only *X* is present. After time *t*, the ratio of atoms of *X* and *Y* is found to be 1 : 4, then *t* in hours is :

(A) 2 (B) 4
(C) between 4 and 6 (D) 6

4-63 Two radioactive materials X_1 and X_2 have decay constants 10 λ and λ respectively. If initially they have the same number of nuclei, then the ratio of the number of nuclei of X_1 to that of X_2 will be $1/e$ after a time :

(A) $\frac{1}{10\lambda}$ (B) $\frac{1}{11\lambda}$
(C) $\frac{11}{10\lambda}$ (D) $\frac{1}{9\lambda}$

4-64 A radioactive material decays by simultaneous emission of two particles with respective half lives 1620 and 810 years. The time in years after which one-fourth of the material remains is :

(A) 1080 (B) 2430
(C) 3240 (D) 4860

4-65 A star initially has 10^{40} deuterons. It produces energy via the processes

$$^2_1H + ^2_1H \rightarrow ^3_1H + p$$

and

$$^2_1H + ^3_1H \rightarrow ^4_2He + n$$

where the masses of the nuclei are : m (^{2}H) = 2.014102 amu, $m(p)$ = 1.007825 amu, $m(n)$ = 1.008665 amu and m (^{4}He) = 4.002603 amu. If the average power radiated by the star is 10^{16} W, the deuteron supply of the star is exhausted in a time of the order of :

(A) 10^6 s (B) 10^8 s
(C) 10^{12} s (D) 10^{16} s

4-66 Masses of two isobars $^{64}_{29}$Cu and $^{64}_{30}$Zn are 63.929766 amu and 93.929145 amu respectively. It can be concluded from these data that :

(A) Both the isobars are stable
(B) ^{64}Zn is radioactive, decaying to ^{64}Cu through β-decay
(C) ^{64}Cu is radioactive, decaying to ^{64}Zn through γ-decay
(D) ^{64}Cu is radioactive, decaying to ^{64}Zn through β-decay

4-67 A radioactive substance *X* decays into another radioactive substance *Y*. Initially only *X* was present λ_x and λ_y are the disintegration constants of *X* and *Y*. N_x and N_y are the number of nuclei of *X* and *Y* at any time *t*. Number of nuclei N_y will be maximum when :

(A) $\frac{N_y}{N_x - N_y} = \frac{\lambda_y}{\lambda_x - \lambda_y}$ (B) $\frac{N_y}{N_x - N_y} = \frac{\lambda_x}{\lambda_x - \lambda_y}$
(C) $\lambda_y N_y = \lambda_x N_x$ (D) $\lambda_y N_x = \lambda_x N_y$

4-68 A particle of mass M at rest decays into two particles of masses m_1 and m_2, having nonzero velocities. The ratio of the de-Broglie wavelengths of the particles, λ_1/λ_2, is :

(A) m_1/m_2 (B) m_2/m_1

(C) 1.0 (D) $\sqrt{m_2/m_1}$

4-69 A radioactive nucleus is being produced at a constant rate α per second. Its decay constant is λ. If N_0 are the number of nuclei at time $t = 0$, then maximum number of nuclei possible are :

(A) $\frac{\alpha}{\lambda}$ (B) $N_0 + \frac{\alpha}{\lambda}$

(C) N_0 (D) $\frac{\lambda}{\alpha} + N_0$

4-70 A radioactive isotope X with half-life of 1.37×10^9 years decays to Y which is stable. A sample of rocks from the moon was found to contain both the elements X and Y which were in the ratio 1 : 7. The age of the rocks is :

(A) 1.96×10^8 years (B) 3.85×10^9 years

(C) 4.11×10^9 years (D) 9.59×10^9 years

4-71 N_1 atoms of a radioactive element emit N_2 beta particles per second. The decay constant of the element is (in s^{-1})

(A) $\frac{N_1}{N_2}$ (B) $\frac{N_2}{N_1}$

(C) $N_1 \ln(2)$ (D) $N_2 \ln(2)$

4-72 Sun radiates energy in all direction. The average energy received at earth is 1.4 KW/m^2. The average distance between the earth and the sun is 1.5×10^{11} m. If this energy is released by conservation of mass into energy, then the mass lost per day by the sun is approximately (Use 1 day = 86400 sec)

(A) 4.4×10^9 kg (B) 7.6×10^{14} kg

(C) 3.8×10^{12} kg (D) 3.8×10^{14} kg

4-73 Power output of $^{235}_{92}U$ reactor if it takes 30 days to use up 2 kg of fuel, and if each fission gives 185 MeV of usable energy, is :

(A) 5.85 MW (B) 58.5 KW

(C) .585 MW (D) None of these

4-74 A radioactive material of half-life T was produced in a nuclear reactor at different instants, the quantity produced second time was twice of that produced first time. If now their present activities are A_1 and A_2 respectively, then their age difference equals :

(A) $\frac{T}{\ln 2}\left|\ln \frac{2A_1}{A_2}\right|$ (B) $T\left|\ln \frac{A_1}{A_2}\right|$

(C) $\frac{T}{\ln 2}\left|\ln \frac{A_2}{2A_1}\right|$ (D) $T \ln\left|\frac{A_2}{2A_1}\right|$

4-75 The half life of a radioactive material is 12.7 hr. What fraction of the original active material would become inactive in 63.5 hr.

(A) 1/32 (B) 1/23

(C) 31/32 (D) 23/32

4-76 In the nuclear fusion reaction,

$$^2_1H + ^3_1H \rightarrow ^4_2He + n$$

given that the repulsive potential energy between the two nuclei is ~ 7.7×10^{-14} J, the temperature at which the gases must be heated to initiate the reaction is nearly [Boltzmann's constant $k = 1.38 \times 10^{-23}$ J/K]

(A) 10^7 K (B) 10^5 K

(C) 10^3 K (D) 10^9 K

4-77 The activity of a radioactive sample is A_1 at time t_1 and A_2 at time t_2. If the mean life of the sample is τ, then the number of nuclei decayed in time $(t_2 - t_1)$ is proportional to :

(A) $A_1t_1 - A_2t_2$ (B) $\frac{A_1 - A_2}{\tau}$

(C) $(A_1 - A_2)(t_2 - t_1)$ (D) $(A_1 - A_2)\,\tau$

5-78 Nuclei of radioactive element A are produced at rate 't^2' at any time t. The element A has decay constant λ. Let N be the number of nuclei of element A at any time t. At time $t = t_0$, $\frac{dN}{dt}$ is minimum. Then the number of nuclei of element A at time $t = t_0$ is :

(A) $\frac{2t_0 - \lambda t_0^2}{\lambda^2}$ (B) $\frac{t_0 - \lambda t_0^2}{\lambda^2}$

(C) $\frac{2t_0 - \lambda t_0^2}{\lambda}$ (D) $\frac{t_0 - \lambda t_0^2}{\lambda}$

4-79 Suppose a radioactive substance disintegrates completely in 10 days. Each day it disintegrates at a constant rate which is twice the rate of the previous day. The percentage of the material left to be disintegrated after passing of 9 days is :

(A) 10 (B) 20

(C) 25 (D) 50

* * * * *

Advance MCQs with One or More Options Correct

4-1 When a nucleus with atomic number Z and mass number A undergoes a radioactive decay process :

(A) Both Z and A will decrease, if the process is α decay

(B) Z will decrease but A will not change, if the process is β^+ decay

(C) Z will increase but A will not change, if the process is β^- decay

(D) Z and A will remain unchanged, if the process is γ decay

4-2 When the nucleus of an electrically neutral atom undergoes a radioactive decay process, it will remain neutral after the decay if the process is :

(A) An α decay (B) A β^- decay

(C) A γ decay (D) A K-capture process

4-3 Which of the following assertions are correct ?

(A) A neutron can decay to a proton only inside a nucleus

(B) A proton can change to a neutron only inside a nucleus

(C) An isolated neutron can change into a proton

(D) An isolated proton can change into a neutron

4-4 Disintegration constant of a radioactive material is λ :

(A) Its half life equal to $\frac{\log_e 2}{\lambda}$

(B) Its mean life equals to $\frac{1}{\lambda}$

(C) At time equal to mean life, 63% of the initial radioactive material is left undecayed

(D) After 3-half lives, $\frac{1}{3}$rd of the initial radioactive material is left undecayed.

4-5 A nucleus undergoes a series of decay according to the scheme $A \xrightarrow{\alpha} B \xrightarrow{\beta} C \xrightarrow{\alpha} D \xrightarrow{\gamma} E$

Atomic number and mass numbers of E are 69 and 172

(A) Atomic number of A is 72

(B) Mass number of B is 176

(C) Atomic number of D is 69

(D) Atomic number of C is 69

4-6 The half life of a radioactive substance is T_0. At $t = 0$, the number of active nuclei are N_0. Select the correct alternative.

(A) The number of nuclei decayed in time internal $0 - t$ is $N_0 e^{-\lambda t}$

(B) The number of nuclei decayed in time interval $0 - t$ is $N_0(1 - e^{-\lambda t})$

(C) The probability that a radioactive nuclei does not decay in interval $0 - t$ is $e^{-\lambda t}$

(D) The probability that a radioactive nuclei does not decay in interval $1 - e^{-\lambda t}$

4-7 Two identical nuclei A and B of the same radioactive element undergo similar β decay. A emits a β-particle and changes to A'. B emits a β-particle and then a γ-ray photon immediately afterwards, and changes to B' :

(A) A' and B' may have the same atomic number and mass number

(B) A' and B' may have the same atomic number but different mass numbers

(C) A' and B' may have different atomic numbers but the same mass number

(D) A' and B' may are isotopes

4-8 A and B are isotopes, B and C are isobars. All three are radioactive :

(A) A, B and C must belong to the same element

(B) A, B and C may belong to the same element

(C) It is possible that A will change to B through a radioactive decay process

(D) It is possible that B will change to C through a radioactive decay process

4-9 A nuclide A undergoes α-decay and another nuclide B undergoes β-decay :

(A) All the α-particles emitted by A will have almost the same speed

(B) The α-particles emitted by A may have widely different speeds

(C) All the β-particles emitted by B will have almost the same speed

(D) The β-particles emitted by B will have different speeds

4-10 Which of the following is correct for a nuclear reaction?

(A) A typical fission represented by ${}_{92}U^{235} + {}_0n^1 \rightarrow {}_{56}Ba^{143} + {}_{36}Kr^{93} + \text{Energy}$

(B) Heavy water is used as moderator in preference to ordinary water

(C) Cadmium rods increase the reactor power when they go in, decrease when they go outward

(D) Slower neutrons are more effective in causing fission than faster neutrons in case of U^{235}

4-11 The decay constant of a radioactive substance is 0.173 (years)$^{-1}$. Therefore

(A) Nearly 63% of the radioactive substance will decay in (1/0.173) year

(B) Half life of the radio active substance is (1/0.173) years.

(C) One-fourth of the radioactive substance will be left after nearly 8 years

(D) All the above statements are true

4-12 Which of the following statement(s) is (are) correct ?

(A) The rest mass of a stable nucleus is less than the sum of the rest masses of its separated nucleons.

(B) The rest mass of a stable nucleus is greater than the sum of the rest masses of its separated nucleons.

(C) In nuclear fission, energy is released by fusing two nuclei of medium mass (approximately 100 u)

(D) In nuclear fission, energy is released by fragmentation of a very heavy nucleus.

4-13 A radioactive sample has initial concentration N_0 of nuclei :

(A) The number of undecayed nuclei present in the sample decays exponentially with time

(B) The activity (R) of the sample at any instant is directly proportional to the number of undecayed nuclei present in the sample at that time

(C) The number of decayed nuclei grows linearly with time

(D) The number of decayed nuclei grows exponentially with time

4-14 For the graph shown in figure-4.17, which of the following statements is/are possible ?

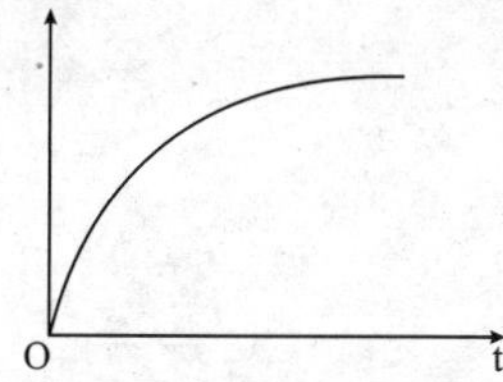

Figure 4.17

(A) y-axis shows number of nuclei of a radioactive element which is produced at a constant rate

(B) y-axis represents number of nuclei decayed in a radio nuclide

(C) y-axis represents activity of a radio nuclide

(D) none of these

4-15 ${}_{92}U^{235}$ is α (alpha) active. Then in a large quantity of the element :

(A) the probability of nucleus disintegrating during one second is lower in the first half life and greater in the fifth half life

(B) the probability of a nucleus disintegrating during one second remains constant for all time

(C) quite an appreciable quantity of U^{235} will remain, even after the average life

(D) the energy of the emitted 'α' particle is less than the disintegration energy of the U^{235} nucleus

4-16 Let m_p be the mass of proton, m_n the mass of neutron. M_1 the mass of ${}^{20}_{10}$Ne nucleus and M_2 the mass of ${}^{40}_{20}$Ca nucleus. Then :

(A) $M_2 = 2M_1$ (B) $M_2 > 2M_1$

(C) $M_2 < 2M_1$ (D) $M_1 < 10\,(m_n + m_p)$

4-17 Assume that the nuclear binding energy per nucleon (B/A) versus mass number (A) is as shown in the figure-4.18. Use this plot to choose the correct choice(s) given below.

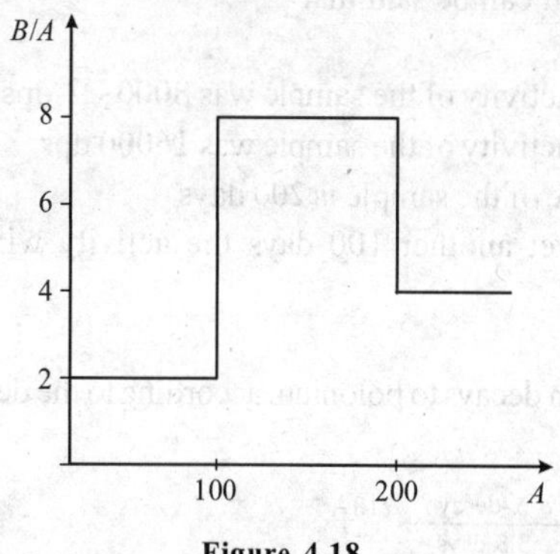

Figure 4.18

(A) Fusion of two nuclei with mass numbers lying in the range of $1 < A < 50$ will release energy

(B) Fusion of two nuclei with mass numbers lying in the range of $51 < A < 100$ will release energy

(C) Fission of a nucleus lying in the mass range of $100 < A < 200$ will release energy when broken into two equal fragments

(D) Fission of a nucleus lying in the mass range of $200 < A < 260$ will release energy when broken into two equal fragments

4-18 During radioactive decay :

(A) atomic mass number cannot increases

(B) atomic number may increase

(C) atomic number may decrease

(D) atomic number may remain unchanged

4-19 A large population of radioactive nucleus starts disintegrating at $t = 0$. At time t, if N = number of parent nuclei present, D = the number of daughter nuclei present and R = rate at which the daughter nuclei are produced , then the correct representation will be :

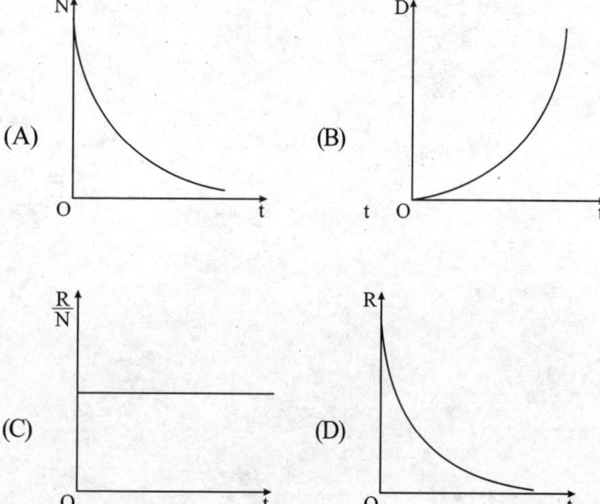

4-20 After 200 days the activity of a radioactive sample reduces to 8000 dps. After another 100 days the activity reduces to $\frac{8000}{\sqrt{2}}$ dps. It can be said that :

(A) Initial activity of the sample was $8000\sqrt{2}$ dps
(B) Initial activity of the sample was 16000 dps
(C) Half life of the sample is 200 days
(D) After yet another 100 days the activity will reduce to 4000 dps

4-21 Radon decays to polonium according to the decay reaction given as

$$^{222}_{88}\text{Rn} \xrightarrow[3.8 \text{ days}]{\alpha\text{-decay}} {}^{218}_{84}\text{Po}$$

Which of the following statement(s) is/are true for this decay process: [Take $\ln 2 = 0.693$]

(A) If the original mass of radon in a closed container was 1 mg, the amount of radon left after 11.4 days will be 0.125 mg
(B) Activity of radon after 7.6 days will be $\frac{A_0}{4}$ where A_0 is original activity of sample at $t = 0$
(C) If the original number of radon in a closed container was 8 atoms, the number of radon left after 7.6 day will be 2 atoms
(D) Po is more stable than Rn

4-22 In the α-decay process occurring in different types of nuclei at rest :

(A) The kinetic energy of the daughter nucleus is always greater than the kinetic energy of the α-particle
(B) The kinetic energy of the daughter nucleus is always less than the kinetic energy of the α-particle
(C) The magnitudes of the linear momenta of the α-particle and the daughter nucleus are always equal
(D) The daughter nucleus is always in a stable state

4-23 At $t = 0$, a sample of radionuclide A has the same decay rate as a sample of radionuclide B has at $t = 60$ min. The disintegration constants of A and B are λ_A and λ_B respectively, with $\lambda_A < \lambda_B$.

(A) The half life of radionuclide A is greater than that of B.
(B) At $t = 60$ min, number of atoms in sample of material A is greater than that of sample B.
(C) The two samples will never have the same decay rate simultaneously.
(D) After some time, the two samples will have the same decay rate simultaneously for an instant.

* * * * *

Unsolved Numerical Problems for Preparation of NSEP, INPhO & IPhO

For detailed preparation of INPhO and IPhO students can refer advance study material on www.physicsgalaxy.com

4-1 When charcoal is prepared form a living tree it shows a disintegration rate of 15.3 disintegration of ^{14}C per gram per minute. A sample from an ancient piece of charcoal shows ^{14}C activity to be 12.3 disintegration per gram per minute. How old is this sample ? Half life of ^{14}C is 5730 yrs.

Ans. [1804.6 years]

4-2 The half life of ^{226}Ra is 1602 yrs. Calculate the activity of 0.1 gm of $RaCl_2$ in which all the radium is in the form of ^{226}Ra. Taken atomic weight of Ra to be 226 gm/mole and that of Cl to be 35.5 gm/mole.

Ans. [2.8×10^9 dps]

4-3 A vessel of volume 125 cm^3 contains tritium (T = 12.3 yrs) at 500 kPa and 300 K. Calculate the activity of the gas.

Ans. [724 Ci]

4-4 A piece of ancient wood shows an activity of 3.9 disintegration per sec per gram of ^{14}C. Calculate the age of the wood. $T_{1/2}$ of ^{14}C = 5570 years. Activity of fresh ^{14}C = 15.6 disintegration per second per gram.

Ans. [11140 yrs]

4-5 Consider the β-decay

$$^{198}Au \rightarrow {}^{198}Hg + \beta^- + \nu^-$$

where ^{198}Hg represents a mercury nucleus in an excited state of energy 1.088 MeV above the ground state. What can be the maximum kinetic energy of the electron emitted. The atomic mass of ^{198}Au is 197.968233 amu and that of ^{198}Hg is 197.966760 amu. 1 u = 931 MeV/c^2.

Ans. [0.2834 MeV]

4-6 Determine the age of ancient wooden items if it is known that the specific activity of ^{14}C nuclide in them amounts to 3/5 of that in lately felled trees. The half life of ^{14}C nuclei is 5570 years. [Take ln 0.6 = – 0.51]

Ans. [4.1×10^3 years]

4-7 A sample of Uranium is a mixture of two isotopes $^{234}_{92}U$ and $^{238}_{92}U$ present in the ratio 10% and 90% by weight. The half lives of these isotopes are 2.5×10^5 years and 4.5×10^5 years respectively. Calculate the contribution to activity in percentage of each isotope in this sample.

Ans. [16.67% and 83.33%]

4-8 In a uranium ore the ratio of ^{238}U nuclei to ^{206}Pb nuclei is $h = 2.8$. Evaluate the age of the ore assuming all the lead ^{206}Pb to be a final decay product of the uranium series. The half – life of ^{238}U nuclei is 4.5×10^9 years. [ln (14/19) = 0.3054]

Ans. [About 2×10^9 years]

4-9 4×10^{23} tritium atoms are contained in a vessel. The half life of decay of tritium nuclei is 12.3 yrs. Find :

(a) the activity of the sample.

(b) the number of decays in the next 10 hours. (c) the number of decays in the next 6.15 yrs.

Ans. [7.146×10^{14} dps, 2.57×10^{19}, 1.17×10^{23}]

4-10 (a) The half life period of radium is 1590 yrs. After how many years will one gram of the pure element,

(i) be reduced to one centigram. (ii) lose one centigram.

(b) The half life of radon is 3.8 days. After how many days will only one twentieth of radon sample be left over ?

(c) 1 gm of radioactive substance takes 50 sec to lose 1 centigram. Find its half life period ?

Ans. [(a) 10560 yrs, 23.25 yrs. (b) 16.45 days (c) 57.75 min.]

4-11 A nucleus of rest undergoes α-decay according to the equation.

$$^{255}_{92}X \rightarrow Y + \alpha$$

At time $t = 0$, the emitted α-particle enters in a region of space where a uniform magnetic field $\vec{B} = B_0\hat{i}$ and electric field $\vec{E} = E_0\hat{i}$ exist. The α-particle enters in the region with velocity $\vec{v} = v_0\hat{j}$ from $x = 0$. At time $t = \sqrt{3} \times 10 \dfrac{m_\alpha}{q_\alpha E_0}$ sec, the particle was observed to have speed twice the initial velocity v_0 then find

(a) the velocity of α-particle at time t

(b) the initial velocity v_0 of the α-particle

(c) the binding energy per nucleon of α-particle

Given that :

$m(Y) = 221.03$ amu, $m(\alpha) = 4.003$ amu

$m(n) = 1.009$ amu, $m(p) = 1.0084$ amu

charge on α-particle $q_\alpha = 6.4 \times 10^{-19}$ C

and 1 amu = 1.67×10^{-27} kg = 931 MeV/c^2

Ans. [(a) $\left(\dfrac{q_\alpha E_0}{m_\alpha}t\right)\hat{i} + v_0 \cos\theta\,\hat{j} - v_0 \sin\theta\,\hat{k}$ where $\theta = \omega t$ and $\omega = \dfrac{q_\alpha B}{m_\alpha}$, (b) 10^7 m/s, (c) 8.00 MeV]

4-12 Some amount of radio active substance (half life = 30 days) is spread inside a room & consequently the level of radiation becomes 50 times permissible level for normal occupancy of the room. After how many days would the room be safe for occupation.

Ans. [169.35 days]

4-13 Protons and singly ionized atoms of ^{235}U & ^{238}U are passed in turn through a velocity selector (where a magnetic field causes them to describe semicircular path). The protons describe semicircles of radius 10 mm. What is the separation between the ions of ^{235}U and ^{238}U after describing semicircle?

Ans. [60 mm]

4-14 Calculate the final energy of a neutron of mass m_1 when it collides elastically and head on with a stationary nucleus of mass m_2 in the *L*-frame (Laboratory frame). Consider zero *Q* value of the interaction between the two particles and initial kinetic energy of neutron E_k.

Ans. [$\left(\frac{m_1 - m_2}{m_1 + m_2}\right)^2 E_k$]

4-15 The specific activity of a preparation consisting of radioactive ^{58}Co and non radioactive ^{59}Co is equal to 2.2×10^{12} dis/sec. The half life of ^{58}Co is 71.3 days. Find the ratio of the mass of radioactive cobalt in that preparation to the total mass of the preparation (in percent).

Ans. [0.19%]

4-16 A solution contains a mixture of two isotopes *A* (half life = 10 days) and *B* (half life = 5 days). Total activity of the mixture is 10^{10} disintegrations per second at time $t = 0$, the activity reduces to 20% in 20 days. Find

(a) the initial activities of *A* and *B*

(b) the ratio of initial number of their nuclei

Ans. [(a) 0.73×10^{10} dps, 0.27×10^{10} dps, (b) 5.4]

4-17 Find the quantity of polonium $^{210}_{80}$Po whose activity is 3.7×10^{10} dps. Find also the number of atoms of polonium disintegrated during its mean life. (Half life of Polonium is 138 days)

Ans. [0.22 mg, 4.03×10^{17}]

4-18 The nuclei involved in the nuclear reaction $A_1 + A_2 \rightarrow A_3 + A_4$ have the binding energies E_1, E_2, E_3 and E_4. Find the energy of this reaction.

Ans. [$Q = (E_3 + E_4) - (E_1 + E_2)$]

4-19 Complete the following nuclear reactions :

(a) $^{14}_{7}N + ^{4}_{2}He \rightarrow ^{17}_{8}O +$ ______ .

(b) $^{30}_{15}P \rightarrow ^{30}_{14}Si +$ ______ .

(c) $^{9}_{4}Be + ^{4}_{2}He \rightarrow ^{12}_{6}C +$ ______ .

(d) $^{3}_{1}H + ^{2}_{1}H \rightarrow ^{4}_{2}He +$ ______ .

(e) $^{9}_{4}Be(p, \alpha)$ ______ .

(f) $^{43}_{20}Ca\ (\alpha,$ ______ $)\ ^{46}_{21}Sc$

Ans. [(a) $^1_1$H (b) ^0_1e (c) $^1_0$n (d) $^1_0$n (e) $^6_3$Li (f) $^1_1$p]

4-20 On an average neutron loses half of its energy per collision with a free proton. How many collisions, on the average are required to reduce a 2 MeV neutron to a thermal energy of 0.04 eV?

Ans. [N ≅ 26]

4-21 A radio nuclide with half life *T* = 14.3 days is produced in a reactor at a constant rate $q = 10^9$ nuclei per second. How soon after the beginning of production of that radionuclide will, its activity be equal to $A = 10^8$ disintegrations per second. Plot a rough graph of its activity with time.

Ans. [2.167 days,]

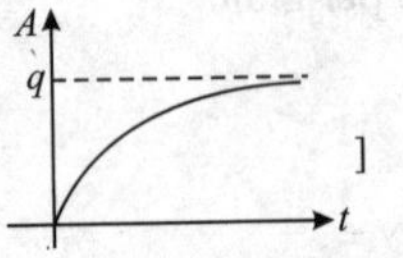

4-21 (a) Calculate the energy released if ^{238}U emits an α particle. (b) Calculate the energy to be supplied to ^{238}U if two protons and two neutrons are to be emitted one by one. The atomic masses are :

^{238}U = 238.0508 amu ^{234}Th = 234.04363 amu $_2^4$He = 4.0026 amu

$_0^1$n = 1.008665 amu $_1^1$p = 1.007276 amu

Ans. [(a) 4.25 MeV; (b) 23 MeV]

4-22 The radius of a nucleus of a mass number *A* is given by $R = R_0 A^{1/3}$, where $R_0 = 1.3 \times 10^{-15}$ m. Calculate the electrostatic potential energy between two equal nuclei produced in the fission of $^{238}_{92}$U at the moment of their fission.

Ans. [238.3 MeV]

4-23 Consider the case of bombardment of ^{235}U nucleus with a thermal neutron. The fission products are ^{95}Mo & ^{139}La and two neutrons. Calculate the energy released. (Rest masses of the nuclides ^{235}U = 235.0439 amu, $_0^1$n = 1.0087 amu, ^{95}Mo = 94.9058 amu, ^{139}La = 138.9061 amu) [Use 1 amu = 931 MeV]

Ans. [207.9 MeV]

4-24 A radionuclide with disintegration constant λ is produced in a reactor at a constant rate α nuclei per second. During each decay energy E_0 is released. 20% of this energy is utilized in increasing the temperature of water. Find the increase in temperature of m mass of water in time t. Specific heat of water is s. Assume that there is no loss of energy through water surface.

Ans. [$\dfrac{0.2E_0\left[\alpha t-\frac{\alpha}{\lambda}(1-e^{-\lambda t})\right]}{ms}$]

4-25 ^{238}U & ^{235}U occur in nature in an atomic ratio 140 : 1. Assuming that at the time of earth's formation the two isotopes were present in equal amounts. Calculate the age of the earth. [$T_{1/2}$ of $^{238}U = 4.5 \times 10^9$ year & that of $^{235}U = 7.13 \times 10^8$ year) [ln (140) = 4.94]

Ans. [6.04×10^9 years]

4-26 Consider a nuclear power plant to be put up to deliver 4×10^3 MW power.

(a) What will be the rate of consumption of ^{235}U to operate this plant for 1 year ?

(b) Typically 3% of the ^{235}U mass is converted into $^{90}_{38}Sr$, which is a beta emitter, with half life 29 yrs. What is the beta activity in the Sr produced in curies, just after the end of 1 yr. Assume 200 MeV is the average yield per fission of ^{235}U.

Ans. [1541 kg per year, 6.324×10^6 Ci]

4-27 An isotopic species of lithium hydride LiH is a potential fuel in a reactor on the basis of reaction $^6_3Li + ^2_1H \rightarrow 2^4_2He$.

Find the possible power production in kW associated with the consumption of 1 g of $^6Li^2H$ per day, if the efficiency of the process is 100 %.

[M($^6_3$Li) = 6.01702 amu; M($^2_1$H) = 2.01474 amu; M($^4_2$He) = 4.00388 amu]

Ans. [3129 KW]

4-28 Find the number of neutrons generated per unit time in a uranium reactor whose thermal power is P = 100 MW, if the average number of neutrons liberated in each nuclear splitting is ν = 2.5. Each splitting is assumed to release an energy E = 200 MeV.

Ans. [$N = \dfrac{\nu P}{E} = 0.8 \times 10^{19}\ s^{-1}$]

4-29 (a) The half life of ^{198}Au is 2.7 days.

(i) Find the activity of a sample containing 1 gm of ^{198}Au.

(ii) What will be the activity after 7 days ?

(b) If 3×10^{-9} kg of radioactive $^{200}_{79}Au$ has an activity of 58.9 Ci, what is its half – life ?

Ans. [(a) (i) 0.244 MCi, (ii) 0.04 MCi (b) $T_{1/2}$ = 48 min]

4-30 In a nuclear reactor ^{235}U undergoes fission liberating 200 MeV of energy. The reactor has a 10% efficiency and produces 1000 MW power. If the reactor is to function for 10 years, find the total mass of uranium required.

Ans. [3.847×10^4 kg]

4-31 The $^{235}_{92}U$ absorbs a slow neutron (thermal neutron) & undergoes a fission represented by

$^{235}_{92}U + ^1_0n \longrightarrow ^{236}_{92}U \longrightarrow ^{141}_{56}Ba + ^{92}_{36}Kr + 3\,^1_0n + E$. Calculate :

(i) The energy release E per fission.

(ii) The energy release when 1 g of $^{236}_{92}U$ undergoes complete fission.

Given : $^{235}_{92}U$ = 235.1175 amu (atom); $^{141}_{56}Ba$ = 140.9577 amu (atom); $^{92}_{36}Kr$ = 91.9264 amu (atom); ^1_0n = 1.00898 amu.

Ans. [(i) 200.68 MeV (ii) 22.86 MWh]

4-32 The kinetic energy of an α-particle which flies out of the nucleus of a ^{226}Ra atom in radioactive disintegration is 4.78 MeV. Find the total energy evolved during the escape of the α-particle.

Ans. [4.87 MeV]

4-33 A town has a population of 1 million. The average electric power needed per person is 300 W. A reactor is to be designed to supply power to this town. The efficiency with which thermal power is converted into electric power is aimed at 25%.

(a) Assuming 200 MeV of thermal energy to come from each fission event on an average, find the number of events that should take place every day.

(b) Assuming the fission to take place largely through ^{238}U, at what rate will the amount of ^{238}U decrease ? Express your answer in kg/day.

(c) Assuming that uranium enriched to 3% in ^{238}U will be used. How much uranium is needed per month (30 days) ?

Ans. [3.24×10^{24}, 1.264 kg/day, 1263 kg]

4-34 A radionuclide with half life T = 693.1 days emits β-particles of average kinetic energy $E = 8.4 \times 10^{-14}$ joule. This radionuclide is used as source in a machine which generates electrical energy with efficiency η = 12.6%. Calculate number of moles of the nuclide required to generate electrical energy at an initial rate P = 441 KW. [Take Avogadro number, $N = 6 \times 10^{23}$], [$\log_e 2 = 0.6931$]

Ans. [6000]

4-35 (a) What isotope is produced from the α-radioactive $^{226}_{88}Ra$ as a result of five α disintegrations & four β disintegrations ?

(b) How many α & β decays does $^{238}_{92}U$ experience before turning finally into the stable $^{206}_{82}Pb$ isotope ?

Ans. [(a) $^{206}_{82}Pb$ (b) 8α decays & 6 β decays]

4-36 A radio nuclide with half life $T = 69.31$ second emits β-particles of average kinetic energy $E = 11.25$ eV. At an instant concentration of β-particles at distance, $r = 2$ m from nuclide is $n = 3 \times 10^{13}$ per m^3.

(i) Calculate number of nuclei in the nuclide at that instant.

(ii) If a small circular plate is placed at distance r from nuclide such that β-particles strike the plate normally and come to rest, calculate pressure experienced by the plate due to collision of β-particles. [Mass of β-particle $= 9 \times 10^{-31}$ kg]

Ans. [(i) $9.6\,\pi \times 10^{22}$, (ii) 1.08×10^{-4} Nm^{-2}]

4-37 The half-life of ^{238}U is about 4.5×10^9 years & its end product is ^{206}Pb. We find that the oldest uranium bearing rocks on earth contain about 50 – 50 mixture by mass of ^{238}U and ^{206}Pb. What is the age of those rocks. [$\ln(222/103) = 0.768$]

Ans. [4.9 billion years]

4-38 Carbon with mass number 11 decays to boron.

(a) Is it a β^+ decay ?

(b) The half life of the decay scheme is 20.3 minutes. How much time will elapsed before a mixture of 90% carbon – 11 and 10% boron – 11 (by the number of atoms) converts itself into a mixture of 10% carbon – 11 and 90% boron – 11 ?

Ans. [β^+, 64 min]

4-39 A radio nuclide consists of two isotopes. One of the isotopes decays by α-emission and the other by β-emission with half lives $T_1 = 405$ second and $T_2 = 1620$ second, respectively. At $t = 0$, probabilities of getting α and β particles from the radionuclide are equal. Calculate their respective probabilities at $t = 1620$ second. If at $t = 0$, total number of nuclei in the radionuclide are N_0, calculate time t when total number of nuclei remained undecayed becomes equal to $\frac{N_0}{2}$.

Given, $\log_{10} 2 = 0.30103$, $\log_{10} 5.94 = 0.7742275$

$x^4 + 4x - 2.5 = 0 \Rightarrow x = 0.594$

Ans. [$\frac{1}{9}, \frac{8}{9}, 1215s$]

4-40 A small amount of solution containing ^{24}Na radionuclide with activity $A = 2 \times 10^3$ dis/sec was injected in the blood stream of a man. The activity of 1 cm^3 of blood sample taken $t = 5$ hrs later turned out to be $A' = 16$ dis/min/cm^3. The half life of radionuclide is $T = 15$ hrs. Find the volume of the man's blood.

Ans. [6 litre]

4-41 Radio active phosphorus 32 has a half life of 14 days. A source containing this isotope has an initial activity of 10 m Ci.

(i) What is the activity of the source after 42 days ?

(ii) What time elapses before the activity of the source falls to 2.5 mCi ?

Ans. [(i) 1.25 mCi (ii) 28 days]

4-42 A radioactive element X decays to Y. In the radionuclide, the ratio of mass of element X to that of Y is n at $t = 0$. It is observed that at time $t = t_0$, this ratio becomes equal to $1/n$. Assuming that all the decay products (except γ-photons) remain in the sample, calculate half life of X.

Ans. [$\frac{\log_2}{\log_n} \cdot t_0$]

4-43 The half life of ^{40}K is 1.3×10^9 yrs. A sample of 1 gm of pure KCl gives 160 counts per seconds. Calculate the relative abundance of ^{40}K (fraction of K present) in natural potassium.

Ans. [0.12 %]

4-44 In a reactor, an element X decays to a radioactive element Y, at a constant rate r atoms per second. Each decay reaction releases energy E_1. Half life of element Y is equal to T and decays to a stable element. During each decay of Y, energy E_2 is released. If at $t = 0$, there was no atom of element Y and all the energy released is used in the reactor for generation of electrical power with efficiency η, calculate electrical power generated in the reactor

(i) at time t and (ii) in steady state.

Ans. [(i) $\eta r\left[E_1 + E_2\left(1 - e^{-\frac{t\log 2}{T}}\right)\right]$, (ii) $\eta r\,(E_1 + E_2)$]

4-45 Find the kinetic energy of the α-particle emitted in the decay $^{238}Pu \rightarrow {}^{234}U + \alpha$. The atomic masses needed are as follows:

^{238}Pu	^{234}U	^{4}He
238.04955 amu	234.04095 amu	4.002603 amu

Neglect any recoil of the residual nucleus.

Ans. [5.58 MeV]

4-46 Calculate the Q-volume in the following decays:

(a) $^{19}O \rightarrow {}^{19}F + e + \bar{\nu}$

(b) $^{25}Al \rightarrow {}^{25}Mg + e^+ + \nu$

The atomic masses needed are as follows :

^{19}O	^{19}F
19.003576 amu	18.998403 amu
^{25}Al	^{25}Mg
24.990432 amu	24.985839 amu

Ans. [(a) 4.816 MeV, (b) 3.254 MeV]

4-47 Find the maximum energy that a beta particle can have in the following decay

$$^{176}Lu \rightarrow {}^{176}Hf + e + \bar{\nu}$$

Atomic mass of ^{176}Lu is 175.942694 amu and that of ^{176}Hf is 175.941420 amu.

Ans. [1.182 MeV]

4-48 A radioactive sample has 6.0×10^{18} active nuclei at a certain instant. How many of these nuclei will still be in the same active state after two half-lives ?

Ans. [1.5×10^{18}]

4-49 The number of ^{238}U atoms in an ancient rock equals the number of ^{206}Pb atoms. The half-life of decay of ^{238}U is 4.5×10^9 y. Estimate the age of the rock assuming that all the ^{206}Pb atoms are formed from the decay of ^{238}U.

Ans. [4.5×10^9 *y* old]

4-50 Find the energy liberated in the reaction

$$^{223}Ra \rightarrow {}^{209}Pb + {}^{14}C$$

^{223}Ra	^{209}Pb	^{14}C
223.018 amu	208.981 amu	14.003 amu

Ans. [31.65 MeV]

4-51 ^{32}P beta-decays to ^{32}S. Find the sum of the energy of the antineutrino and the kinetic energy of the β-particle. Neglect the recoil of the daughter nucleus. Atomic mass of $^{32}P = 31.974$ amu and that of $^{32}S = 31.972$ amu.

Ans. [1.86 MeV]

4-52 The selling rate of a radioactive isotope is decided by its activity. What will be the secondhand rate of a one month old $^{32}P(t_{1/2} = 14.3$ days) source if it was originally purchased for 800 rupees?

Ans. [187 rupees]

4-53 In an agricultural experiment, a solution containing 1 mole of a radioactive material ($t_{1/2} = 14.3$ days) was injected into the roots of a plant. The plant was allowed 70 hours to settle down and then activity was measured in its fruit. If the activity measured was 1 μCi, what percent of activity is transmitted from the root to the fruit in steady state ?

Ans. [1.26×10^{-11} %]

4-54 Calculate the energy released by 1 g of natural uranium assuming 200 MeV is released in each fission event and that the fissionable isotope ^{235}U has an abundance of 0.7% by weight in natural uranium.

Ans. [5.7×10^8 J]

4-55 A radioactive nucleus *X* decays to a nucleus *Y* with a decay constant $\lambda_X = 0.1$ sec^{-1}. *Y* further decays to a stable nucleus *Z* with a decay constant $\lambda_Y = 1/30$ sec^{-1}. Initially, there are only *X* nuclei and their number is $N_0 = 10^{20}$. Setup the rate equations for the populations of *X*, *Y* and *Z*. The population of the *Y* nucleus as a function of time is given by $N_Y(t) = \{N_0\lambda_X/(\lambda_X - \lambda_Y)\}\{\exp(-\lambda_Y t) - \exp(-\lambda_X t)\}$. Find the time at which N_Y is maximum and determine the population of *X* and *Z* at that instant.

Ans. [(i) $\frac{dN_x}{dt} = -\lambda_x N_x$, $\frac{dN_y}{dt} = \lambda_x N_x - \lambda_y N_y$, $\frac{dN_z}{dt} = \lambda_y N_y$, (ii) 16.48 s, (iii) $N_x = 1.92 \times 10^{19}$, $N_y = 5.76 \times 10^{19}$, $N_z = 2.32 \times 10^{19}$]

4-56 Calculate the *Q*-value of the fusion reaction

$$^4He + {}^4He = {}^8Be$$

Is such a fusion energetically favourable ? Atomic mass of ^8Be is 8.0053 amu and that of ^4He is 4.0026 amu.

Ans. [– 93.1 keV, no]

4-57 Calculate the energy that can be obtained from 1 kg of water through the fusion reaction

$$^2H + {}^2H \rightarrow {}^3H + p$$

Assume that 1.5×10^{-2} % of natural water is heavy water D_2O (by number of molecules) and all the deuterium is used for fusion.

Ans. [3200 MJ]

4-58 What minimum kinetic energy must a proton possess to split a deuteron ^2H whose binding energy is $E_b = 2.2$ MeV ?

Ans. [$T \geq E_b \frac{m_p + m_d}{m_d} = 3.3$ MeV]

4-59 An α–particle with kinetic energy $T = 5.3$ MeV initiates a nuclear reaction $^9Be(\alpha, n)\,^{12}C$ with energy yield $Q = +5.7$ MeV. Find the kinetic energy of the neutron outgoing at right angles to the motion direction of the α-particle.

Ans. [$T_n = \frac{Q + (1 - m_\alpha/m_c)T}{1 + m_n/m_c} = 8.5$ MeV]

4-60 Assuming the radius of nucleus to be equal to $R = 0.13\sqrt[3]{A}$ pcm, where A is its mass number evaluate the density of nuclei and the number of nucleons per unit volume of the nucleus.

Ans. [2×10^{11} kg/cm^3, 1×10^{38} nuclie/cm^3]

4-61 A radioactive nucleus can decay by two different processes. The half-life for the first process is t_1 and that for the second process is t_2. Show that the effective half-life t of the nucleus is given by

$$\frac{1}{t} = \frac{1}{t_1} + \frac{1}{t_2}$$

4-62 In the decay $^{64}Cu \rightarrow {}^{64}Ni + e^+ + \nu$, the maximum kinetic energy carried by the positron is found to be 0.650 MeV.

(a) What is the energy of the neutrino which was emitted together with a positron of kinetic energy 0.150 MeV ?

(b) What is the momentum of this neutrino in kg-m/s ? Use the formula applicable to a photon.

Ans. [(a) 500 keV, (b) 2.67×10^{-22} kg-m/s]

4-63 Over what distance in free space will the intensity of a 5 eV neutron beam reduced by a factor one – half ?
[$T_{1/2}$ = 12.8 min]

Ans. [23808 km]

4-64 About 185 MeV of usable energy is released in the neutron induced fissioning of a $^{235}_{92}U$ nucleus. If the reactor using $^{235}_{92}U$ as fuel continuously generates 100 MW of power how long will it take for 1 kg of the uranium to be used up ?

Ans. [8.781 days]

4-65 Assuming 1 metric ton of coal gives heat of combustion equal to 8 kcal and a single fission of ^{235}U releases 200 MeV. Calculate the minimum consumption in kg of ^{235}U to be heat equivalent to 100 ton of coal.

Ans. [M = 4.077×10^{-8} kg]

4-66 $^{235}_{92}U$ undergoes a fission giving 0.1% of its original mass released as energy.

(a) How much energy is released by an atomic bomb that contains 10 kg of ^{235}U.

(b) If 1 ton TNT releases 4×10^9 joule. What is the TNT equivalent of the bomb ?

Ans. [9×10^{14}, 2.25×10^5 ton]

4-67 A point source emitting alpha particles is placed at a distance of 1 m from a counter which records any alpha particle falling on its 1 cm^2 window. If the source contains 6×10^{16} active nuclei and the counter records a rate of 50000 counts/sec. Find the decay constant. Assume that the source emits alpha particles uniformly in all directions and the alpha particles fall nearly normally on the window.

Ans. [1.05×10^{-7} sec^{-1}]

4-68 In a fusion reactor the reaction occurs in two stages :

(i) Two deuterium (^2_1D) nuclei fuse to form a tritium (^3_1T) nucleus with a proton as product. The reaction may be represented as $D(D, p)\,T$.

(ii) A tritium nucleus fuses with another deuterium nucleus to form a helium (^4_2He) nucleus with neutron as another product. The reaction is represented as $T(D, n)\,\alpha$. Find :

(a) The energy release in each stage.

(b) The energy release in the combined reaction per deuterium &

(c) What % of the mass energy of the initial deuterium is released.

Given : (^2_1D) = 2.014102 amu; (^3_1T) = 3.016049 amu; (^4_2He) = 4.002603 amu; (^1_1P) = 1.00785 amu; (^1_0n) = 1.008665 amu

Ans. [(a) 4 MeV, 17.6 (b) 7.2 MeV, (c) 0.384 %]

4-69 If the nucleus of hydrogen fuses with a nucleus of lithium to form two helium nuclei,

(a) write down the nuclear reaction equation

(b) find the release of energy in joule per fusion

(c) find the number of hydrogen atoms required to generate 9.8 J

Mass of hydrogen, lithium and helium atoms are 1.0078 amu, 7.017 amu and 4.0036 amu respectively.

Ans. [0.263×10^{-11} J, 37.26×10^{11}]

4-70 Find the energy required for separation of a ^{20}Ne nucleus into two α-particles and a ^{12}C nucleus if it is known that the binding energies per one nucleon in ^{20}Ne, ^4He & ^{12}C nuclei are equal to 8.03, 7.07 & 7.68 MeV respectively.

Ans. [$E = 20\,E_{Ne} - 2.4\,E_\alpha - 12\,E_c$ = 11.9 MeV, where E is the B.E. per nucleon in the corresponding nucleus]

4-71 A radioactive sample contains two radio nucleoids A and B having decay constant λ hr^{-1} and 2λ hr^{-1}. Initially 25% of total decay comes from A. How long (in hr) will it take before 75% of total decay comes from A. [Take λ = ln 3]

Ans. [2]

4-72 Assuming that the splitting of a ^{235}U nucleus liberates the energy of 200 MeV. Find :

(a) The energy liberated in the fission of one Kg of ^{235}U isotope, the mass of coal with calorific value of 30 kJ/g, which is equivalent to that for one kg of ^{235}U &

(b) The mass of ^{235}U isotope required to produce same amount of energy as produced during the explosion of the atomic bomb with 30×10^3 kg of trotyl, if the calorific value of trotyl is 4.1 kJ/g.

Ans. [(a) 8.2×10^{10} kJ, 2.7×10^6 kg (b) 1.5 g]

4-73 Calculate the energy (in joule) that can be obtained from 1 kg of water through the fusion reaction $^2H + ^2H \rightarrow ^3H + p$. It is analyzed that 0.015% of natural water is heavy water D_2O by number of molecules and all the deuterium is used for in above fusion reaction. Atomic masses used are given as

$$m(^2_1H) = 2.0141202u,\ m(^3_1H) = 3.016049u$$

$$m_p = 1.007276u \text{ and } 1u = 931\frac{\text{MeV}}{c^2}$$

Ans. [3.67×10^9 J]

4-74 A count rate-meter is used to measure the activity of a given sample. At one instant the meter shows 4750 counts per minute. Five minutes later is shows 2700 counts per minute. Find the half life of the sample. Also find the decay constant. Given, $\log_{10}(1.760) = 0.2455$.

Ans. [0.113 min^{-1}, 6.1 min]

4-75 A radioactive nucleus undergoes a series of decay according to the scheme

$$A \xrightarrow{\alpha} A_1 \xrightarrow{\beta^-} A_2 \xrightarrow{\alpha} A_3 \xrightarrow{\gamma} A_4$$

If the mass number and atomic number of A are 180 and 72 respectively, what are these numbers for A_4?

Ans. [172 and 69]

4-76 There is a stream of neutrons with a kinetic energy of 0.0327 eV. If the half life of neutrons is 70 seconds, what fraction of neutrons will decay before they travel a distance of 0 km? Given, mass of a neutron = 1.676×10^{-27} kg.

Ans. [4×10^{-3}]

4-77 A radioactive element decays by β^- emission. If mass of parent and daughter atoms are m_1 and m_2 respectively, calculate energy liberated during the emission. Mass of an electron = m.

Ans. [$(m_1 - m_2 - 2m)\,c^2$]

4-78 The half lives of two longest lived radioactive isotopes of phosphorus P^{32} and P^{33} are 14 days and 28 days respectively. A sample has been prepared by mixing the two isotopes in the ratio of 4 : 1 of their atoms. Initial activity of the mixed sample is 90 mCi. Find the activity (in mCi) of the sample after 80 days. [Take ln2 = 0.7 and $e^{-2} = 0.14$]

Ans. [3]

4-79 Neon-23 undergoes beta decay in the following way:

$$_{10}Ne^{23} \rightarrow {}_{11}Na^{23} + {}_{-1}e^0 + \bar{\nu}$$

Atomic masses of ^{23}Ne and ^{23}Na are 22.9945u and 22.9898u respectively. Determine the minimum and maximum kinetic energy of β-particle in MeV. ($1u = 931.5$ MeV/c^2)

Ans. [0, 4.4 MeV]

4-80 Two radioactive materials A and B have initial activity A_0 and $2A_0$. After 1 half life of A, the total combined activity of A and B is $\frac{1}{4}$ times of their initial total activity. Their half lives are T_A and T_B then calculate $\frac{T_A}{T_B}$.

Ans. [8]

4-81 A nuclear reactor generates $P = 20$ MW power at efficiency $\eta = 60\%$ by nuclear fission of a radionuclide whose half life is $T = 2.2$ years. If each fission releases energy $E = 200$ MeV, calculate time during which $\mu = 10$ mole of the radionuclide will be consumed completely.

(Avogadro number, $N = 6 \times 10^{23}$, $\log_e 2 = 0.693$, 1 year = 3.15×10^7 s)

Ans. [$\frac{T}{\ln 2}\ln\left(1 + \frac{\mu N \eta E \ln 2}{PT}\right)$ = 10^8 ln (1.0576) s]

4-82 It is proposed to use the nuclear fusion reaction $^2_1H + ^2_1H \rightarrow ^4_2He$ in a nuclear reactor of 200 MW rating. If the energy from the above reaction is used with a 25% efficiency in the reactor, how many grams of deuterium fuel will be needed per day ? (The masses of ^2_1H and ^4_2He are 2.0141 atomic mass unit and 4.0026 atomic mass unit respectively)

Ans. [121.3 g]

4-83 Consider the following fusion reaction

$$_1H^2 + {}_1H^3 \rightarrow 2He^4$$

If 20 MeV of energy is released in above reaction per fusion. Mass of $_1H^2$ consumed per day is 0.1 gm. What is the power output of the reaction?

Ans. [1 MV]

4-84 A sample of ^{18}F is used internally as a medical diagnostic tool to look for the effects of the positron decay ($T_{1/2}$ = 110 min). How long does it take for 99% of the ^{18}F to decay ?

Ans. [12.2 hr]

4-85 A proton with invariant mass of 938272.0 keV and kinetic energy of 1 MeV hits a nucleus of the isotope $^{7}_{3}Li$ with mass of 7 m_1 and induces a decay to two non-excited α particles with invariant mass of 3.727379 GeV·c^{-2}. What will be the total kinetic energy of these two particles? Consider m_1 = 931.2720 MeV·c^{-2} and c = 299792458 m/s.

Ans. [3.418 MeV]

4-86 In nature, a decay chain series starts with $_{90}Th^{232}$ and finally terminates at $_{82}Pb^{208}$. A thorium ore sample was found to contain 8 × 10^{-5} ml of helium at STP and 5 × 10^{-7} g of Th^{232}. Find the age of the ore sample assuming the source of helium to be only to the decay of Th^{232}. Also assume complete retention of helium within the ore. (Half life of Th^{232} = 1.39 × 10^{10} year)

Ans. [154.26 years]

4-87 A nuclear explosion is designed to deliver 1 MW of heat energy. How many fission events must be required in a second to attain this power level ? If this explosion is designed with a nuclear fuel consisting of uranium-235 to run a reactor at this power level for one year, then calculate the amount of fuel needed. You can assume that the amount of energy released per fission event is 200 MeV.

Ans. [3.125 × 10^{16}, 384.5 g]

4-88 The element Curium $_{96}Cm^{248}$ has a mean life of 10^{13} s. Its primary decay modes are spontaneous fission and α decay, the former with a probability of 8% and the latter with a probability of 92%. Each fission releases 200 MeV of energy. The masses involved in α decay are

$m(_{96}Cm^{248})$ = 248.072220u;

$m(_{94}Pu^{244})$ = 244.064100u;

and $m(_2He^4)$ = 4.002603u

Calculate the power output from a sample of 10^{20} Cm atoms [Take 1u = 931 MeV/c^2]

Ans. [3.3 × 10^{-5} W]

4-89 A nucleus at rest undergoes a decay emitting an α-particle of de-Broglie wavelength, λ = 5.76 × 10^{-15} m. If the mass of the daughter nucleus is 223.610 amu and that of the α-particle is 4.002 amu, determine the total kinetic energy in the final state. Hence, obtain the mass of the parent nucleus in amu. [1 amu = 931.470 MeV/c^2]

Ans. [6.25 MeV, 227.62 amu]

4-90 Suppose, the daughter nucleus in a nuclear decay is itself radioactive. Let λ_p and λ_d be the decay constants of the parent and the daughter nuclei. Also, let N_p and N_d be the number of parent and daughter nuclei at time t. Find the condition for which the number of daughter nuclei becomes constant.

Ans. [$\lambda_p N_p = \lambda_d N_d$]

4-91 Potassium-40 can decay in three modes. It can decay by β$^-$ emission, β$^+$ emission or electron capture.

(a) Write the equations showing the end products.

(b) Find the Q-values in each of the three cases. Atomic masses of $^{40}_{18}Ar$, $^{40}_{19}K$ and $^{40}_{20}Ca$ are 39.9624 U, 39.9624 amu and 39.9640 amu and 39.9626 amu respectively.

Ans. [(a) $^{40}_{19}K \rightarrow ^{40}_{20}Ca + e^- + \bar{\nu}$, $^{40}_{19}K \rightarrow ^{40}_{18}Ar + e^+ + \nu$, $^{40}_{19}K + e^{-1} \rightarrow ^{40}_{18}Ar + \nu$, (b) 1.3034 MeV, 0.4676 MeV, 1.490 MeV]

4-92 Natural water contains a small amount of tritium (^3_1H). This isotope beta-decays with a half-life of 12.5 years. A mountaineer while climbing towards a difficult peak finds debris of some earlier unsuccessful attempt. Among other things he finds a sealed bottle of whisky. On return he analyses the whisky and finds that it contains only 1.5 per cent of the ^3_1H radioactivity as compared to a recently purchased bottle marked '8 years old'. Estimate the time of that unsuccessful attempt.

Ans. [About 83 years ago]

4-93 $^{197}_{80}Hg$ decays to $^{197}_{79}Au$ through electron capture with a decay constant of 0.257 per day.

(a) What other particle or particles are emitted in the decay ?

(b) Assume that the electron is captured from the K shell. Use Moseley's law $\sqrt{\nu} = \alpha(Z - b)$ with α = 4.95 × 10^7 s$^{-1/2}$ and b = 1 to find the wavelength of the $K\alpha$ X-ray emitted following the electron capture.

Ans. [(a) Neutrino, (b) 20 pm]

4-94 A radioactive isotope is being produced at a constant rate $dN/dt = R$ in an experiment. The isotope has a half-life $t_{1/2}$. Show that after a time $t >> t_{1/2}$, the number of active nuclei will become constant. Find the value of this constant.

Ans. [$\frac{Rt_{1/2}}{0.693}$]

4-95 Consider the situation of the previous problem. Suppose the production of the radioactive isotope starts at t = 0. Find the number of active nuclei at time t.

Ans. [$\frac{R}{\lambda}(1 - e^{-\lambda t})$]

4-96 A body of mass m_0 is placed on a smooth horizontal surface. The mass of the body is decreasing exponentially with disintegration constant λ. Assuming that the mass is ejected backward with a relative velocity u. Initially the body was at rest. Find the velocity of it after time t.

Ans. [$u\lambda t$]

4-97 Radioactive isotopes are produced in a nuclear physics experiment at a constant rate $dN/dt = R$. An inductor of inductance 100 mH, a resistor of resistance 100 Ω and a battery are connected to form a series circuit. The circuit is switched on at the instant the production of radioactive isotope. It is found that i/N remains constant in time where i is the current in the circuit at time t and N is the number of active nuclei at time t. Find the half-life of the isotope.

Ans. [6.93×10^{-4} s]

4-98 A charged capacitor of capacitance C is discharged through a resistance R. A radioactive sample decays with an average life τ. Find the value of R for which the ratio of the electrostatic field energy stored in the capacitor to the activity of the radioactive sample remains constant in time.

Ans. [$2\tau/C$]

4-99 A small bottle contains powdered beryllium Be & gaseous radon which is used as a source of α-particles. Neutrons are produced when α-particles of the radon react with beryllium. The yield of this reaction is (1/4000) i.e. only one α-particle out of 4000 induces the reaction. Find the amount of radon (^{222}Rn) originally introduced into the source, if it produces 1.2×10^6 neutrons per second after five days. [$T_{1/2}$ of R_n = 3.8 days]

Ans. [2.1×10^{-6} g]

4-100 The energy of alpha particles emitted by ^{210}Po is 5.3 MeV. The half life of this alpha emitter is 138 days.

(a) What mass of ^{210}Po is needed to power a thermoelectric cell of 1 W output if the efficiency of energy conservation is 8 percent?

(b) What would be the power output after 1 year?

Ans. [88.4 mg, 0.16 watt]

4-101 ^{238}U decays with a half life of 4.51×10^9 yrs, the decay series eventually ending at ^{206}Pb, which is stable. A rock sample analysis shoes that the ratio of the numbers of atoms of ^{206}Pb to ^{238}U is 0.0058. Assuming that all the ^{206}Pb has been produced by the decay of ^{238}U and that all other half lives in the chain are negligible. Calculate the age of the rock sample.

Ans. [38×10^6 yrs]

4-102 A number N_0 of atoms of a radio active element are placed inside a closed volume. The radioactive decay constant for the nucleus of this element is λ_1. The daughter nucleus that form as a result of the decay process are assumed to be radioactive too with a radioactive decay constant λ_2. Determine the time variation of the number of such nucleus. Consider two limiting cases $\lambda_1 >> \lambda_2$ and $\lambda_1 << \lambda_2$.

Ans. [$N_0 e^{-\lambda_2 t}, \frac{\lambda_1 N_0}{\lambda_2}(1-e^{-\lambda_2 t})$]

4-103 A sample of 100 millicurie of krypton gas consists of a mixture of the active isotope ^{85}Kr & the stable isotope ^{84}Kr. If the volume of the mixture is 10 cm^3 at STP & half-life of ^{85}Kr is 10 years. Calculate the % by weight of ^{85}Kr present in the mixture.

Ans. [0.632 %]

4-104 A stationary $^{200}_{82}$Pb nucleus emits an α – particle with kinetic energy T_α = 5.77 MeV. Find the recoil velocity of a daughter nucleus. What fraction of the total energy liberated in this decay is accounted for by the recoil energy of daughter nucleus ?

Ans. [3.4×10^5 m/s, 0.020]

4-105 Energy evolved from the fusion reaction is to be $2\,^2_1\text{H} = {}^4_2\text{He} + Q$ used for the production of power. Assuming the efficiency of the process to be 30 %. Find the mass of deuterium that will be consumed in a second for an output of 50 MW.
[Mass of $^4_2$He = 4.002603 amu; $^2_1$H = 2.014102 amu]

Ans. [2.9×10^{-7} kg]

4-106 Find the amount of heat generated by 1.00 mg of a ^{210}Po preparation during the mean life time period of these nuclei, if the emitted α – particles are known to possess the kinetic energy 5.3 MeV & practically all daughter nuclei are formed directly in the ground state.

Ans. [≅ 1.6 MJ]

4-107 To investigate the β-decay of ^{23}Mg radionuclide a counter was activated at moment $t = 0$. It registered N_1 β-particles by a moment t_1 = 2.0 s and a moment $t_2 = 3t_1$, the number of registered β-particles was 2.66 time greater. Find the mean life time of the given nuclei. [Take ln (0.88) = – 0.125]

Ans. [τ = 16 s]

4-108 Find the decay constant and the mean life time of ^{55}Co radionuclide if its activity is known to decrease 4% per hour. The decay product is nonradioactive.

Ans. [$\lambda \simeq 1.1 \times 10^{-5}$ s^{-1}]

4-109 A radioactive decay is illustrated as

$$A \xrightarrow[t_{1/2}=8 \text{ yrs}]{} B$$

At $t = 0$ only A is present. Find the time at which if we are able to pick one atom out of the sample, then probability of getting B is 15 times that of getting A.

Ans. [32 years]

4-110 An α – particle with kinetic energy $T_\alpha = 7.0$ MeV is scattered elastically by an initially stationary ^{6}Li nucleus. Find the kinetic energy of the recoil nucleus if the angle of divergence of the two particles is $\theta = 60°$. Take masses of α particle and lithium as m and M respectively.

Ans. [$T = \dfrac{T_\alpha}{[1+(M-m)^2/4mM\cos^2\theta]} = 6.0$ MeV]

4-111 A neutron collides elastically with an initially stationary deuteron. Find the fraction of the kinetic energy lost by the neutron. Take masses of neutron and deuteron as m and M respectively.

(i) in a head–on–collision.

(ii) in scattering at right angles.

Ans. [(a) $\eta = 4$ Mm $(m + M)^2 = 0.89$, (b) $\eta = \dfrac{2m}{(m+M)} = \dfrac{2}{3}$]

4-112 Find the energy of the reaction ^{14}N (α, p) ^{17}O, if the kinetic energy of the incoming α–particle is $T_\alpha = 4.0$ MeV & the proton outgoing at an angle $\theta = 60°$ to the motion direction of the α-particle has a kinetic energy $T_p = 2.09$ MeV.

Ans. [$Q = (1 + \eta_p)\, T_p - (1 - \eta_\alpha)\, T_\alpha - 2\sqrt{\eta_p \eta_\alpha T_p T_\alpha}\, \cos\theta = -1.2$ MeV,

where $n_p = m_p/m_o$, $n_\alpha = \dfrac{m_\alpha}{m_0}$]

4-113 Find the greatest possible angle through which a deuteron is scattered as result of elastic collision with an initially stationary proton ? Take m_1 & m_2 as masses of a proton & a deuterium.

Ans. [$\beta_{max} = \sin^{-1}\dfrac{m_1}{m_2} = 30°$]

4-114 The element Curium $^{248}_{96}$Cm has a mean life of 10^{13} seconds. Its primary decay modes are spontaneous fission and α-decay modes are spontaneous fission and α-decay, the former with a probability of 8% and the latter with a probability of 92%. Each fission releases 200 MeV of energy. The masses involved in α-decay are as follows. ($1\,u = 931$ MeV/c^2). Calculate the power output from a sample of 10^{20} Cm atoms.

Ans. [3.32×10^{-5} Js^{-1}]

4-115 The nuclear reaction,

$$n + {}^{10}_{5}\text{B} \rightarrow {}^{7}_{3}\text{Li} + {}^{4}_{2}\text{He}$$

is observed to occur even when very slow-moving neutrons ($m_n = 1.0087$ u) strike a boron atom at rest. For a particular reaction in which initial kinetic energy of neutrons is considered almost negligible, the helium ($M_{He} = 4.0026$ u) is observed to have a speed of 9.30×10^6 m/s. Determine (a) the kinetic energy of the lithium ($M_{Li} = 7.0160$ u), and (b) the Q-value of the reaction.

Ans. [(a) 1.02 MeV; (b) 2.82 MeV]

4-116 The mean path length of α-particles in air under standard conditions is defined by the formula $R = 0.98 \times 10^{-27}\, V_0^3$ cm, where V_0 (cm/s) is the initial velocity of an α-particle. Using this formula, find for an α-particle with initial kinetic energy 7.0 MeV.

(a) Its mean path length.

(b) The average number of ion pairs formed by the given α-particle over the whole path R as well as over its first half. Assuming the ion pair formation energy to be equal to 34 eV.

Ans. [(a) 6.1 cm; (b) 2.1×10^5 and 0.77×10^5]

* * * * *

Geometrical Optics

5

FEW WORDS FOR STUDENTS

The topic of ray optics or geometrical optics is concerned with the analysis of propagation of light in a medium by considering it as the propagation of a 'Ray'. A ray defines the path, along with light propagates and it can be assumed as an infinitesimally thin pencil of light moving in a specific direction at a given point in space. In this topic of ray optics we do not bother about the nature of light and we ignore the wave and photon character of light. Here we focus on how light behaves on a large scale.

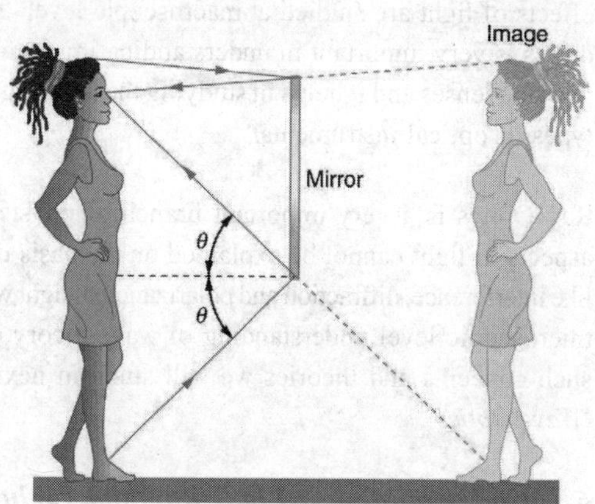

CHAPTER CONTENTS

COVER APPLICATION

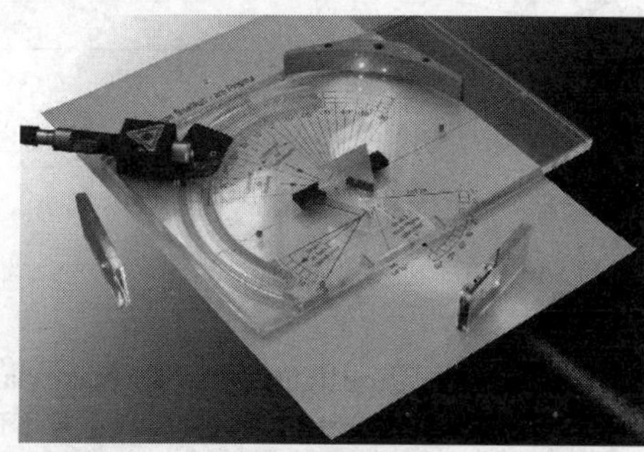

Figure (a)

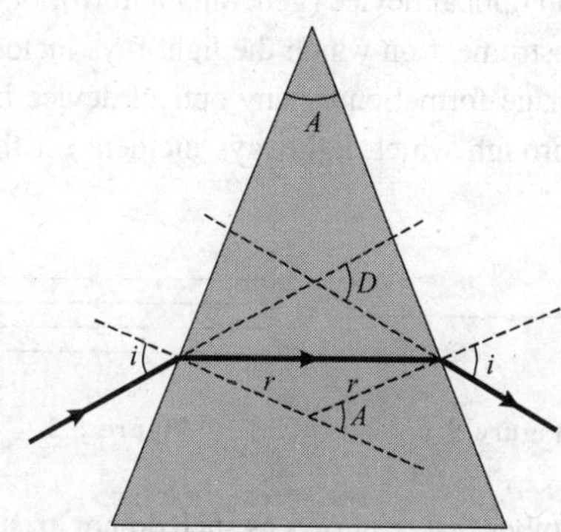

Figure (b)

Figure-(a) shows the experimental setup of refraction of light through a trihedral prism and understanding of minimum deviation of light and figure-(b) shows the ray diagram of light refraction through the prism.

In this chapter of light, we will involve only geometric considerations for light propagation and all laws are formulated using the concepts of geometry thats why, ray optics is also called '*Geometrical Optics*'. The basic concept we use is that a light ray travels along a well-defined path. Ray optics in reality is an approximation but it is very important when character and effects of light are studied at macroscopic level. Topic of ray optics is very important in understanding image formation by mirrors, lenses and it helps in studying the working of different types of optical instruments.

Ray Optics is a very important branch of physics but many aspects of light cannot be explained on the basis of ray optics like interference, diffraction and polarization of light which require microscopic level understanding of wave theory of light and such concepts and theories we will study in next chapter of '*Wave Optics*'.

5.1 Understanding a Light Ray and Light Beams

In previous grades you have studied that light travels in a straight line that's what we call '*Law of Rectilinear Propagation of Light*'. This is the concept based on which we say that an object placed in the path of light coming from a source produces a sharp shadow on a flat surface or a screen. This law of rectilinear propagation is considered valid only at macroscopic level or large scale. Light does not travel in a straight line when the size of object or obstacle is of the order of wavelength of light. Such concepts we will study in microscopic analysis of light under wave optics and not considered here.

As already explained that a light ray can be imagined as a very thin pencil of light travelling in a specific direction. It is represented by drawing a straight line with an arrow in the direction of light propagation as shown in figure-5.1. A bundle of several light rays is called a light beam which is shown in figure-5.2. For analysis of ray optics it is very important to understand different types of light rays and light beams in reference to an optical device (generally a mirror or a lens) or any optical instrument on which the light rays incident as the concept of image formation by any optical device involves a light beam through which light rays incident on the optical device.

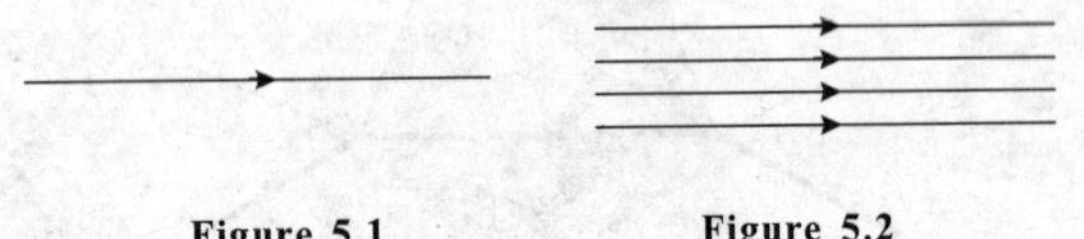

Figure 5.1 **Figure 5.2**

Always remember that light rays as such do not exist in reality and by any method light rays cannot be isolated experimentally from a light beam, these exist only in theoretical understanding.

5.1.1 Different Types of Light Rays

When light rays incident on an optical device like a spherical mirror, a spherical surface, a lens or an optical instrument then in reference to the optical device light rays are categorized in two ways paraxial rays and marginal rays. Lets discuss these in detail.

Paraxial Rays : These are the light rays which incident on an optical device very close to its principal axis and make very small angle with it or which are nearly parallel to principal axis of the device. In case of some lenses and mirrors paraxial rays are shown in figure-5.3. Most of the analysis of image formation in geometrical optics, we will study in this chapter are restricted to paraxial rays only.

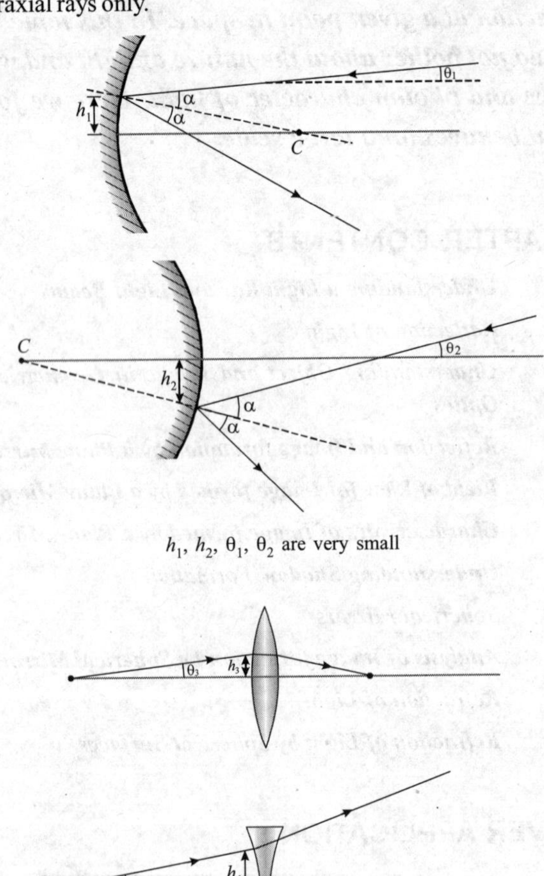

Figure 5.3

Marginal Rays : These are light rays which makes large angles to the principal axis of the optical device falling on it. Figure-5.4 shows some marginal rays in different cases of optical devices. Images formed by marginal rays are blurred and distorted so these rays are not generally used in image formation while analyzing the cases under geometrical optics.

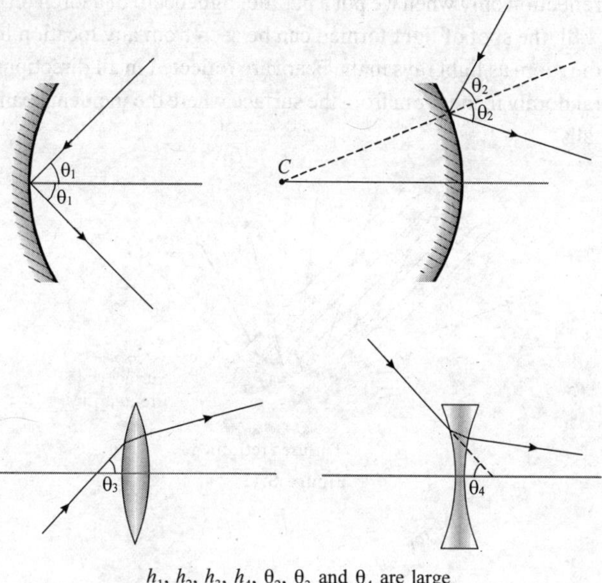

h_1, h_2, h_3, h_4, θ_2, θ_3 and θ_4 are large

Figure 5.4

5.1.2 Different Types of Light Beams

From a source of light always several rays are emitted in form of a beam. A single light ray cannot be considered as only ray emitted from a light source. Depending upon the behaviour of light propagation, light beam is categorized in three ways - Convergent Beam, Divergent Beam and Parallel Beam of light. Lets discuss these in detail.

Divergent Beam of Light : This is a light beam in which the diameter of light beam increases in the direction of light propagation and all light rays appear to be coming from a point opposite to the direction of propagation of light. A general divergent beam of light is shown in figure-5.5(a). From a luminous point source of light diverging beam of light is emitted in its surrounding in all direction as shown in figure-5.5(b)

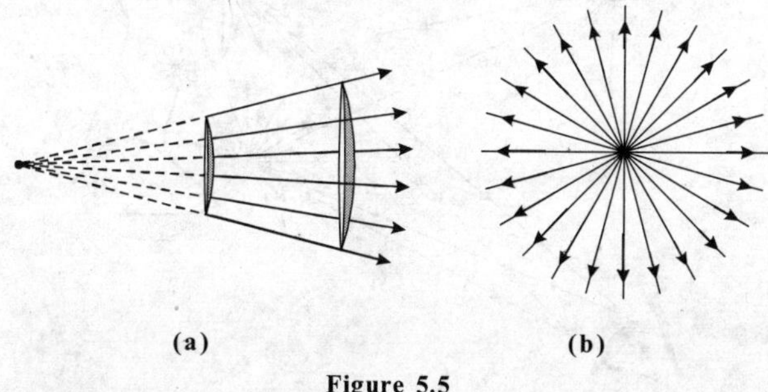

(a) (b)

Figure 5.5

Convergent Beam of Light : This is a light beam in which the diameter of light beam decreases in the direction of light propagation and all light rays appear to converge at a point in space which is called the point of convergence of the light beam. A general convergent beam of light is shown in figure-5.6.

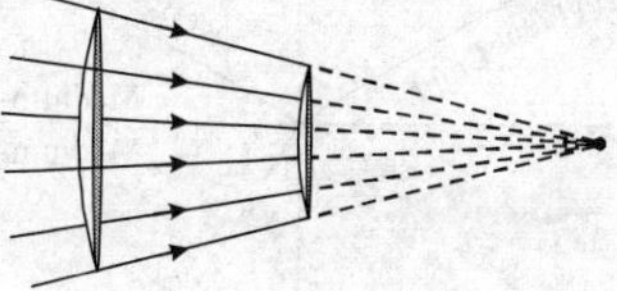

Figure 5.6

Generally such a beam is incident on an object (or optical device) which is placed between the light beam and its point of convergence as shown in figure-5.7(a). If the object (or optical device) is placed beyond the point of convergence then the incident beam will be diverging not converging as shown in figure-5.7(b)

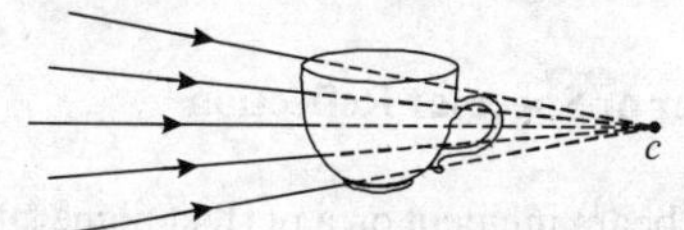

Converging incident rays falling on object

(a)

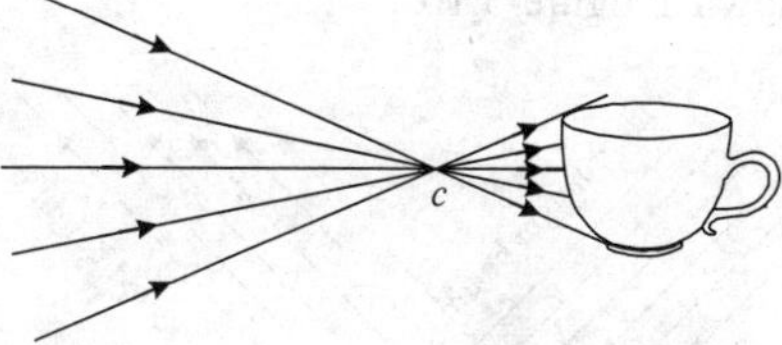

Diverging incident rays falling on object

(b)

Figure 5.7

Parallel Beam of Light : This is a light beam in which all rays constituting the beam move parallel to each other and the diameter of the beam remains same throughout the propagation of light. A parallel beam of light is shown in figure-5.8.

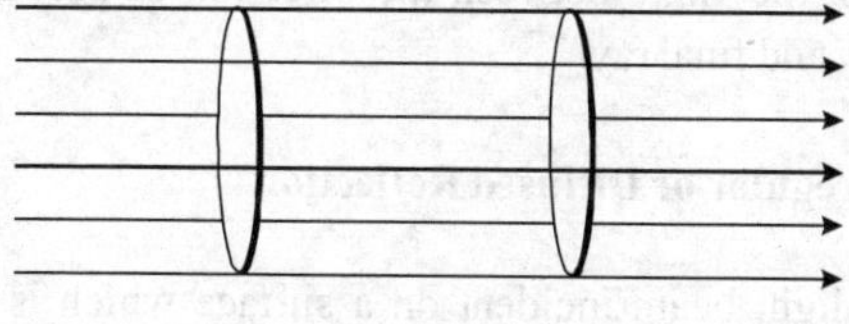

Figure 5.8

5.2 *Reflection of Light*

Whenever a light ray incident on a boundary of two media then a part of light is bounced back into the same medium and a part goes into the other medium as shown in figure-5.9. This phenomenon of bouncing of light energy into the medium from which light incident on the boundary is called '*Reflection of Light*'.

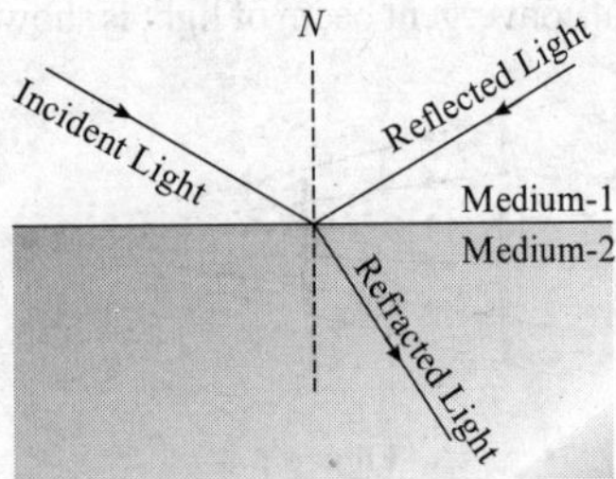

Figure 5.9

Transmission of light energy into the other medium is called '*Refraction of Light*'. In this section we will study reflection of light in detail then later we will cover refraction of light. Reflection of light from a surface or a medium boundary is classified in two ways. These are '*Regular Reflection*' or '*Specular Reflection*' and '*Diffused Reflection*'.

5.2.1 Regular or Specular Reflection

When a light beam incident on a perfect plane surface then the reflection is called Regular or Specular Reflection. In such a case the reflected light beam has high intensity only in one direction which is the direction of propagation of the reflected beam as shown in figure-5.10.

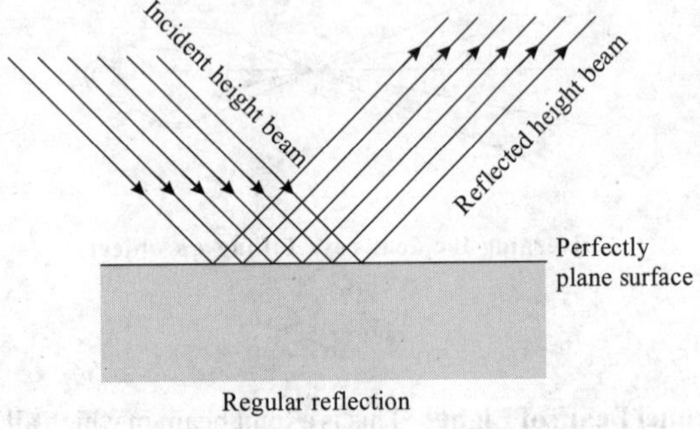

Figure 5.10

Angle of Deviation : In figure-5.10 the total angle by which the light ray is rotated which is shown as δ is called angle of deviation, the angle between the direction of propagation of initial ray and final ray.

5.2.2 Irregular or Diffused Reflection

When a light beam incident on a surface which is rough or having irregularities then the light rays in the incident beam of light will be reflected in irregular behaviour as shown in figure-5.11. Each light ray of the beam is reflected from the local point on the surface on which it incidents and different light rays are reflected in random directions depending upon the irregularities on the surface. The figure-5.11 is a highly enlarged view of a rough surface, if we look onto it normally it looks like figure-5.12 where on a point if a narrow light beam incident, it gets reflected in all directions from the point so the light spot on the surface can be seen from all directions. Due to diffused reflection only when we put a parallel light beam of a torch on a wall, the spot of light formed can be seen from any location in the room as light rays in the beam are reflected in all directions randomly in the room from the surface where the incident beam falls.

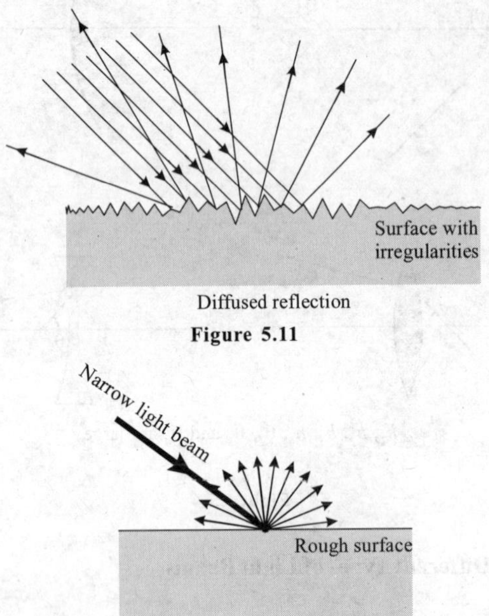

Figure 5.11

Figure 5.12

5.2.3 How we see an object in our surrounding

When from any luminous source of light, light rays incident on an object, due to the roughness of the surface of object these rays are reflected from the object surface in diffused manner in all directions so wherever an observer is situated, she will be able to see the face of object in front of her eye as shown in figure-5.13

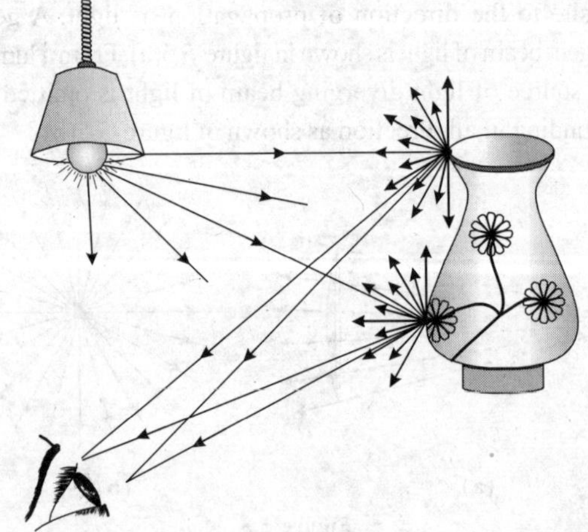

Figure 5.13

For understanding of observer's view it is very important to understand how our eyes perceive the shape, size and colour of an object. Every object in our surrounding which is not point sized (these are called extended objects) can be considered as a combination of several points on its surface and from each point on the surface of object, light rays falling on it will be irregularly (diffused) reflected in all directions so from any side of object on which any light is falling, it is visible to observer's eyes in which irregularly (diffused) reflected light rays from the surface are incident as shown in figure-5.13.

The light rays which are irregularly reflected from the surface of object carry information of color and its brightness and from all points of surface and boundaries of the object these rays fall into observer's eye simultaneously due to which observer is able to see the whole object, its specific size, shape and colour.

5.2.4 Laws of Reflection

Laws of Reflection governs the way light is reflected from the surface of a boundary of two different media. There are two reflection laws which explains how light is reflected from a surface.

When a light ray is incident on a surface then the angle it makes with the normal to the surface is called '*angle of incidence*' and after reflection, the angle which the reflected ray makes with the normal is called '*angle of reflection*'. In the figure-5.14 these angles are represented by angle *i* and angle *r* respectively.

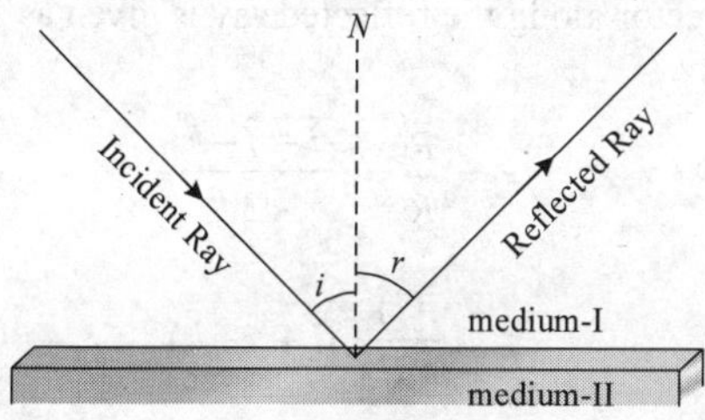

Figure 5.14

First Law of Reflection : In the reflection process the incident ray, the reflected ray and the normal at the point of incidence lie in same plane. This plane is called '*Plane of Incidence*' as shown in figure-5.15.

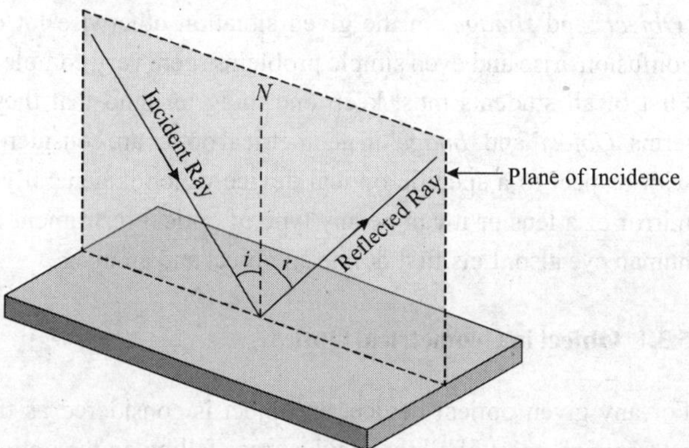

Figure 5.15

Second Law of Reflection : The angle of reflection is equal to the angle of incidence so according to this law we have

$$i = r \quad \dots(5.1)$$

5.2.5 Vector Analysis of Laws of Reflection

Laws of reflection can be analyzed with the help of vector algebra also by considering unit vectors in the direction of incident rays, reflected rays and normal to the boundary. Keeping above two laws of reflection we relate these unit vectors with the angles of incidence and angle of reflection.

In the figure-5.16, reflection of a light ray incident on a plane surface is shown. If we consider $\hat{i}$, $\hat{r}$ and $\hat{n}$ as unit vectors along the direction of incident ray, reflected ray and normal to the surface as shown then first we can write components of $\hat{i}$ and $\hat{r}$ in terms of the unit vectors along the normal and along the surface. Here we are considering $\hat{t}$ as a unit vector along the surface so these are given as

$$\hat{i} = (\sin\theta)\,\hat{t} - (\cos\theta)\,\hat{n} \quad \dots(5.2)$$

$$\hat{r} = (\sin\theta)\,\hat{t} + (\cos\theta)\,\hat{n} \quad \dots(5.3)$$

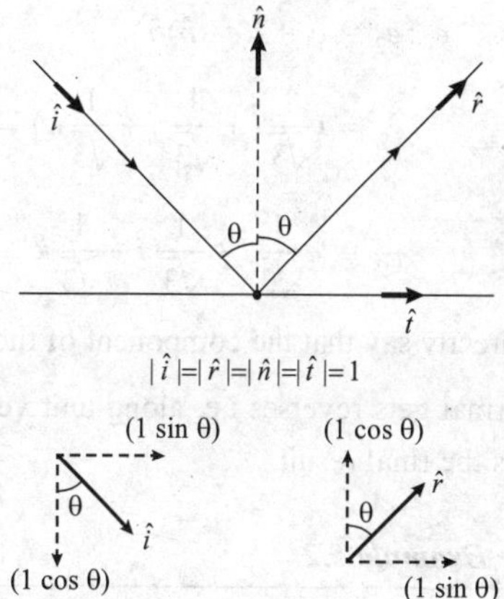

Figure 5.16

Now from equations-(5.2) and (5.3), subtracting these we get

$$\hat{r} = \hat{i} + (2\cos\theta)\,\hat{n} \quad \dots(5.4)$$

From the dot product of $\hat{i}$ and $\hat{n}$ we have

$$\hat{i} \cdot \hat{n} = -\cos\theta \quad \dots(5.5)$$

From above equations we get

$$\hat{r} = \hat{i} - 2(\hat{i} \cdot \hat{n})\,\hat{n} \quad \dots(5.6)$$

Above equation-(5.6) is called the equation of laws of reflection which account for both the laws as vector form includes the plane of incidence as well as equal angle of incidence and angle of reflection as shown in figure-5.16.

Illustrative Example 5.1

A ray of light is incident on the $(y-z)$ plane mirror along a unit vector $\hat{e}_1 = \frac{1}{\sqrt{3}}\hat{i} + \frac{1}{\sqrt{3}}\hat{j} + \frac{1}{\sqrt{3}}\hat{k}$. Find the unit vector along the reflected ray.

Solution

The normal unit vector to the $(y-z)$ plane mirror is along x direction so we have

$$\hat{n} = \hat{i}$$

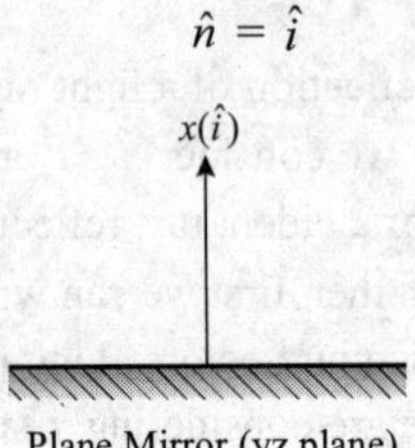

Figure 5.17

Then the unit vector along reflected ray is given as $\hat{e}_2$ and the relation between $\hat{e}_2$ and $\hat{e}_1$ is given as

$$\hat{e}_1 : \hat{e}_2 = \hat{e}_1 - 2(\hat{e}_1 \cdot \hat{n})\hat{n}$$

$$\hat{e}_2 = (\frac{1}{\sqrt{3}}\hat{i} + \frac{1}{\sqrt{3}}\hat{j} + \frac{1}{\sqrt{3}}\hat{k}) - 2(\frac{1}{\sqrt{3}})\hat{i}$$

$$\Rightarrow \quad \hat{e}_2 = -\frac{1}{\sqrt{3}}\hat{i} + \frac{1}{\sqrt{3}}\hat{j} + \frac{1}{\sqrt{3}}\hat{k}$$

Or we can directly say that the component of the incident ray along the normal gets reverses i.e. along unit vector $\hat{i}$ which directly gives the final result.

Illustrative Example 5.2

Two plane mirrors are combined to each other as such one is in $(y-z)$ plane and other is in $(x-z)$ plane. A ray of light along vector $\frac{1}{\sqrt{3}}\hat{i} + \frac{1}{\sqrt{3}}\hat{j} + \frac{1}{\sqrt{3}}\hat{k}$ is incident on the first mirror. Find the unit vector in the direction of emergence ray after successive reflections through these mirrors.

Solution

Just like the case of previous problem here we can see that after reflection from the mirror along yz plane the component of the incident ray along x direction gets reverses so the unit vector of the ray after reflection from first mirror is given as

$$\hat{e}_2 = -\frac{1}{\sqrt{3}}\hat{i} + \frac{1}{\sqrt{3}}\hat{j} + \frac{1}{\sqrt{3}}\hat{k}$$

and finally after reflection through the second plane mirror placed along xz plane the unit vector of the ray is given as

$$\hat{e}_3 = -\frac{1}{\sqrt{3}}\hat{i} - \frac{1}{\sqrt{3}}\hat{j} + \frac{1}{\sqrt{3}}\hat{k}$$

Illustrative Example 5.3

A ray of light is incident on a plane mirror along a vector $\hat{i} + \hat{j} - \hat{k}$. The normal on incidence point is along $\hat{i} + \hat{j}$. Find a unit vector along the reflected ray.

Solution

As component of incident ray along the normal gets reversed while the component along the surface remains unchanged. Thus the component of incident ray vector $\vec{A} = \hat{i} + \hat{j} - \hat{k}$ parallel to normal, i.e., $\hat{i} + \hat{j}$ gets reversed while perpendicular to it, i.e. along the surface, $-\hat{k}$ remains unchanged. Thus, the reflected ray can be written as

$$\vec{R} = -\hat{i} - \hat{j} - \hat{k}$$

The unit vector along the reflected ray is given as

$$\hat{r} = \frac{\vec{R}}{R} = \frac{-\hat{i} - \hat{j} - \hat{k}}{\sqrt{3}}$$

$$\Rightarrow \quad \hat{r} = -\frac{1}{\sqrt{3}}(\hat{i} + \hat{j} + \hat{k})$$

5.3 *Understanding Object and Image in Geometrical Optics*

In analysis of various situations and cases of geometrical optics, it is very important to have a clear understanding of the terms '*Object*' and '*Image*' in the given situation otherwise lot of confusion arise and even simple problems seem very complex. First of all students must keep one thing in mind that these terms '*Object*' and '*Image*' in geometrical optics are considered with respect to a specific optical device which is generally a mirror or a lens or it can be any type of optical instrument or human eye also. Lets first define an object and an image.

5.3.1 Object in Geometrical Optics

For any given optical device, an object is considered as the intersection point of all the incident rays falling on the optical device. For existence of object for a device it is not necessary that these incident rays really intersect. Objects can be point sized or extended, as shown in figure-5.12 and 5.13 if object is extended then every point on surface of object is considered as a point object and combination of all these point object is taken as the extended object.

There are three ways in which object is classified in geometrical optics depending on the type of light rays incident on the optical device. Lets understand these cases of various incident rays on a device for a point object.

Case-I : Diverging Incident Rays on an Optical Device

When light rays incident on an optical device are in diverging manner then their intersection point will be in the direction opposite to the direction of propagation of light as shown in figure-5.18. This point is always regarded as a '*Real Object*' for the optical device irrespective of whether light rays are really intersecting on this point (actually coming from this point) or not. The type of object (in this case a real object) is defined only by the type of light rays in the vicinity of the optical device and not from the actual source from where light rays are coming.

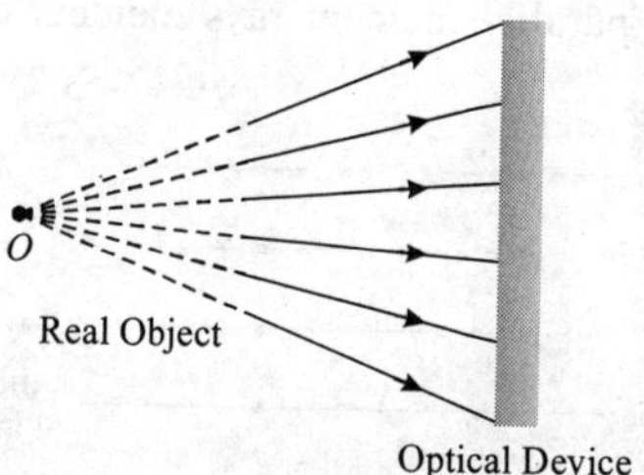

Figure 5.18

Note : Most of the irregularly reflected light rays from objects in our surrounding fall in our eye in diverging manner as shown in figure-5.12 so for our eye (or for an observer's eye) what we see in our surrounding can be taken as a '*Real Object*'.

Case-II : Converging Incident Rays on an Optical Device

When light rays incident on an optical device are in converging manner then their intersection point will lie in the direction of propagation of light behind the optical device as shown in figure-5.19. These light rays cannot intersect really in such a case and in this case this point O is regarded as a '*Virtual Object*' for the optical device. In this case also the type of object (virtual object in this case) is defined only by the type of light rays in the vicinity of the optical device and not from the actual source from where light rays are coming.

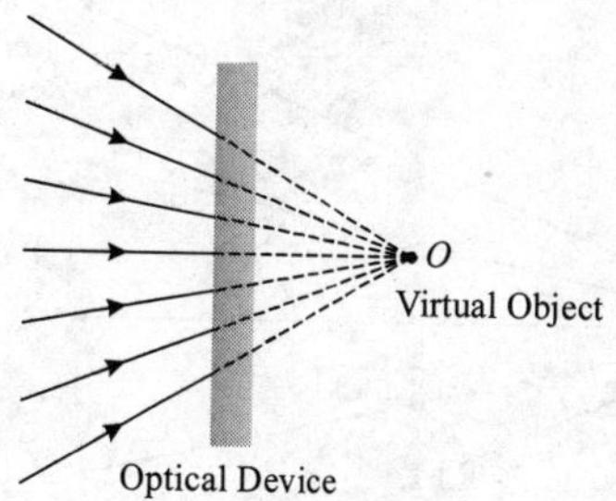

Figure 5.19

Case-III : Parallel Incident Rays on an Optical Device

When light rays incident on an optical device are parallel then in this case we consider object is located at infinity as parallel rays can only be considered intersecting at infinity. So when object is located at infinity, we do not talk about its nature whether real or virtual. Figure-5.20 below shows the case when parallel incident rays incident on an optical device.

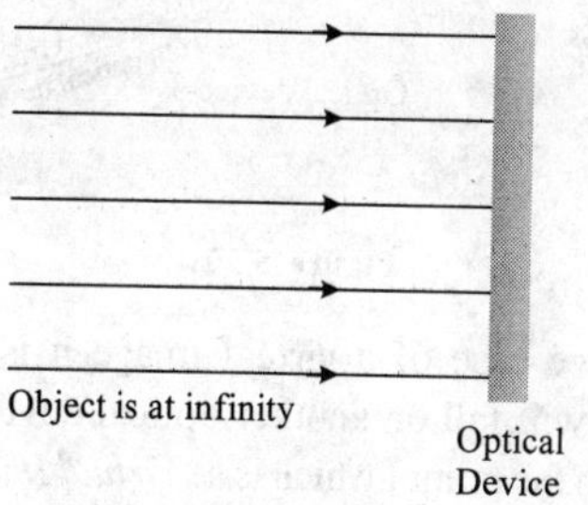

Figure 5.20

5.3.2 Image in Geometrical Optics

For any given optical device, an image is considered as the intersection point of all the reflected or refracted rays from the device depending whether the device is a reflecting or refracting one. Based on the type of reflected or refracted rays coming from the device, image can also be classified in three ways in geometrical optics in reference to the device producing the image.

Case-I : Diverging Reflected or Refracted Rays from the Optical Device

When light rays coming from the optical device are in diverging manner then their intersection point will lie behind the device opposite to the direction of propagation of light as shown in figure-5.21. This point is always regarded as a '*Virtual Image*' for this optical device. Always remember that for diverging light rays it is not possible to really meet or intersect in the direction of light propagation so such reflected or refracted rays are considered to produce a virtual image.

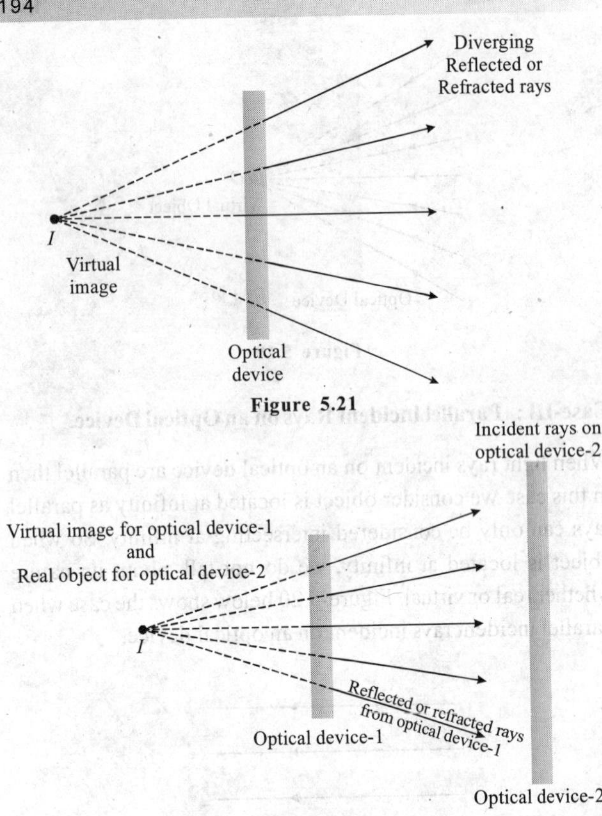

Figure 5.21

Figure 5.22

Note : In above case of a virtual image it is clear if these diverging rays will fall on another optical device as shown in figure-5.22 then the point I which is a '*Virtual Image*' for optical device-1 will act like a '*Real Object*' for optical device-2 as explained above in figure-5.22.

Case-II : Converging Reflected or Refracted Rays from the Optical Device

When light rays coming from an optical device are in converging manner then their intersection point will lie in the direction of propagation of light as shown in figure-5.23. These light rays can intersect really in such a case and in this case this point I is regarded as a '*Real Image*' for the optical device. In this case the type of image (real image in this case) is defined only by the type of reflected or refracted light rays in the vicinity of the optical device, it is not necessary whether these rays will really intersect or not.

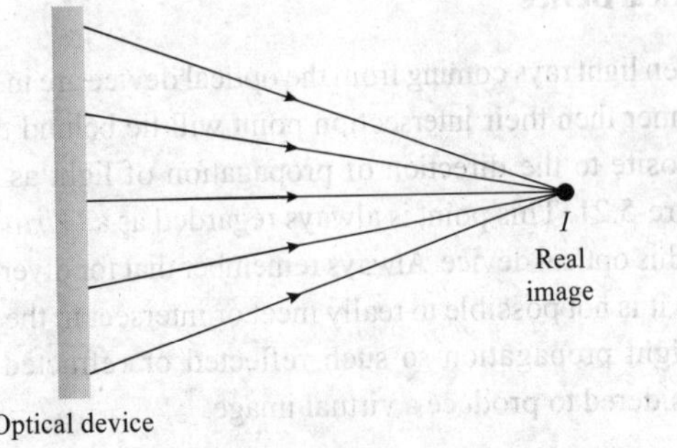

Figure 5.23

If we look at the figure-5.24, here for optical device-1, I is a '*Real Image*' as reflected or refracted rays from this device are converging but before actually intersecting at I light rays incident on another optical device-2 so for this second device-1 will act like a '*Virtual Object*', as shown in figure-5.24.

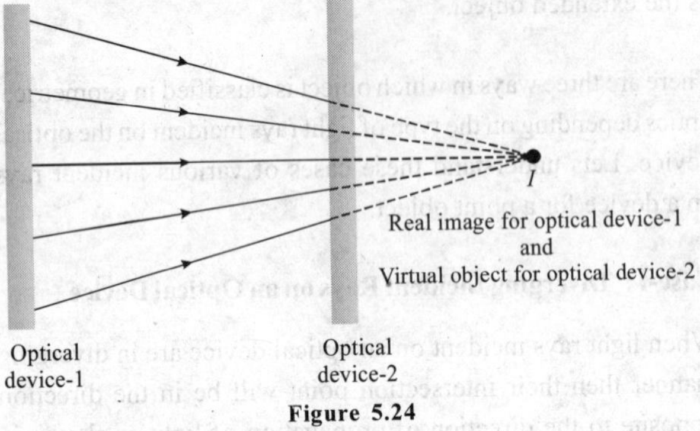

Figure 5.24

Case-III : Parallel Reflected or Refracted Rays from the Optical Device

When light rays are reflected or refracted from an optical device are parallel then in this case we consider image is located at infinity as parallel rays can only be considered intersecting at infinity and when image is located at infinity, we do not talk about its nature whether real or virtual. Figure-5.25 below shows the case when parallel incident rays incident on an optical device.

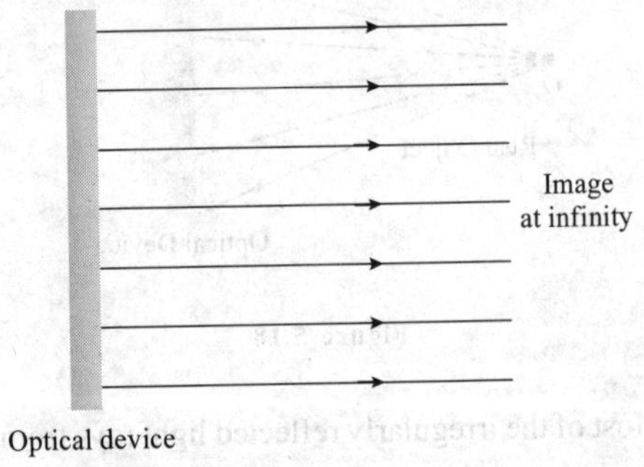

Figure 5.25

5.4 *Reflection and Image formation by a Plane Mirror*

A plane mirror is a piece of glass which is polished on one side of it which makes its other side reflecting. Glass is considered as a smooth plane surface so we consider regular reflection from every point of the reflecting surface of the plane mirror. Figure-5.26 shows the way how we represents cross section of a plane mirror on paper by a straight line with hatching on the side of polished surface.

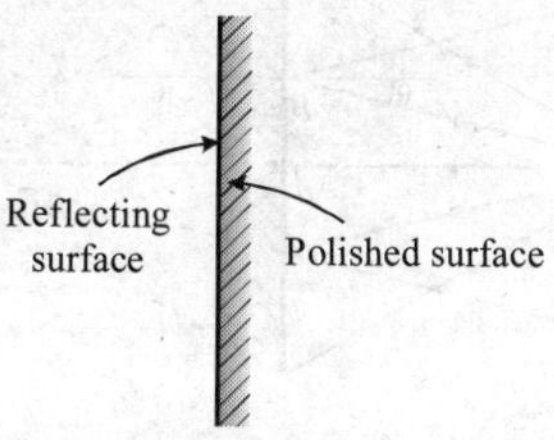

Figure 5.26

Figure-5.27(a) shows the '*Ray Diagram*' of formation of image by a plane mirror for a point object O and the image I produced by intersection of reflected rays from the mirror by extending these behind the mirror. If these rays fall into an observer's eye then observer will feel and see these light rays are coming from the point I behind the mirror. As the reflected rays from the mirror are diverging so the image produced here will be a '*Virtual Image*' as discussed in case-I of article-1.3.2. And the light rays which are incident on observer's eye are diverging (same rays which are reflected by mirror) so the observer will see point I as a '*Real Object*' as discussed in Case-I of article-1.3.1. Here figure-5.27(b) shows a realistic view of image produced and observed by an observer of a point source of light.

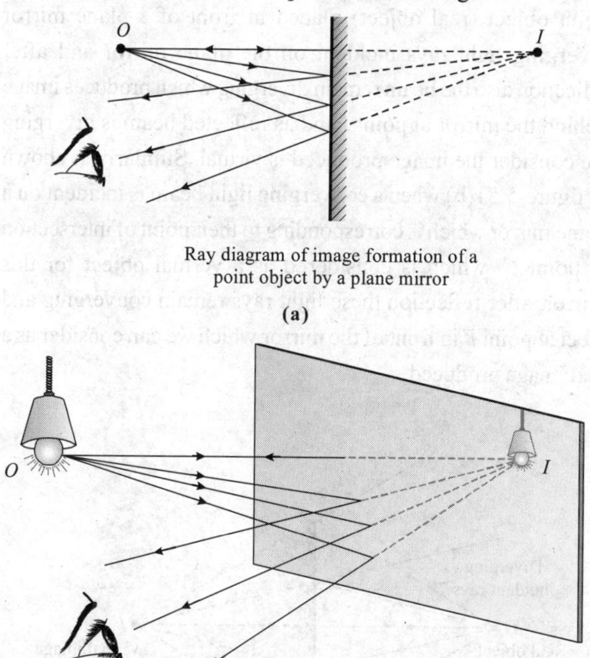

Figure 5.27

In geometrical optics we will mainly focus on ray diagrams of image formation by different devices but it is also important to imagine realistic situation corresponding to each ray diagram because the feeling of actual understanding always helps in solving variety of questions in geometrical optics.

Note : The region in front of a mirror is called '*Real Space*' as light rays actually exist in this region only and the region behind the mirror is called '*Virtual Space*' as light rays actually never exist in this region but in this region light rays can be back extended to a point from where we can consider light rays appear to be coming.

5.5 *Field of View for Image formed by a Plane Mirror*

Field of View is a region of space in surrounding of a mirror in which any image located at a position can be seen by an observer. Field of view can be defined in two ways - one for a specific image and for a specific observer. Lets discuss both in detail.

5.5.1 Field of View of an image

It is the region of space from which the image can be seen. Figure-5.28 shows the field of view of the image I of an object O placed in front of a small plane mirror. The field of view of image is shown by the grey shaded region which is bounded by the lines joining the image and the edges of the mirror.

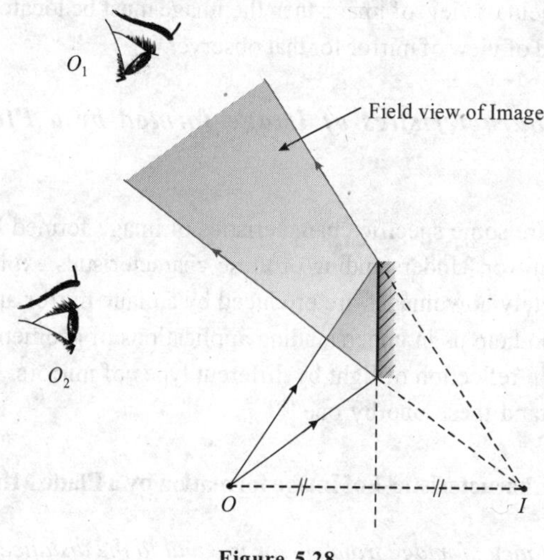

Figure 5.28

In above figure we can feel that the observer O_1 which lies in the field of view of image will be able to see the image because the reflected rays from mirror are falling into eye of this observer but there is no reflected ray falling into the eye of observer O_2 which will not be able to see the image I.

5.5.2 Field of View of a Mirror for an observer

It is the region behind the mirror which is bounded by the lines joining the observer's eye to the edges of mirror. It is shown in figure-5.29 by the grey shaded region for observer O_1 and dark grey shaded region for observer O_2. Any image located in this region can be seen by the respective observer.

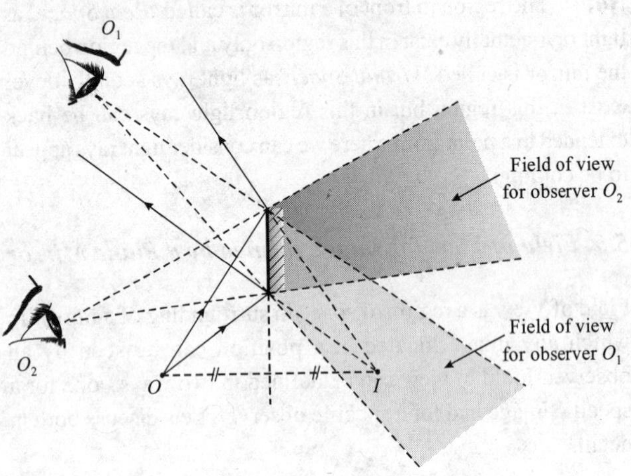

Figure 5.29

In above figure, as we can see that image I lies in the field of view of mirror for observer O_1 but not in the field of view of mirror for observer O_2 so it can be seen by observer O_1 and not by O_2. In other words we can say that if an observer is situated in the field of view of image then the image must be located in the field of view of mirror for that observer.

5.6 *Characteristics of Image formed by a Plane Mirror*

There are some specific characteristics of image formed by a plane mirror. Understanding of these characteristics explains completely how images are produced by a plane mirror and it will also help us in understanding applications of geometrical optics in reflection of light by different types of mirrors. Lets understand these one by one.

5.6.1 Characteristic-1 of Image formation by a Plane Mirror

"Distance of image from mirror is equal to the distance of object from mirror"

Whenever an image is produced by a plane mirror, distance of image produced from the line of mirror is always equal to the distance of object from the line of mirror. Figure-5.30 shows the ray diagram of image formed for a point object O. In this diagram we can see by geometry that ΔOAB and ΔIAB are similar hence we get $OA = IA$. Thus always the image produced which is the line of intersection of reflected rays from the mirror is situated at the same distance from mirror at which object is situated from the mirror.

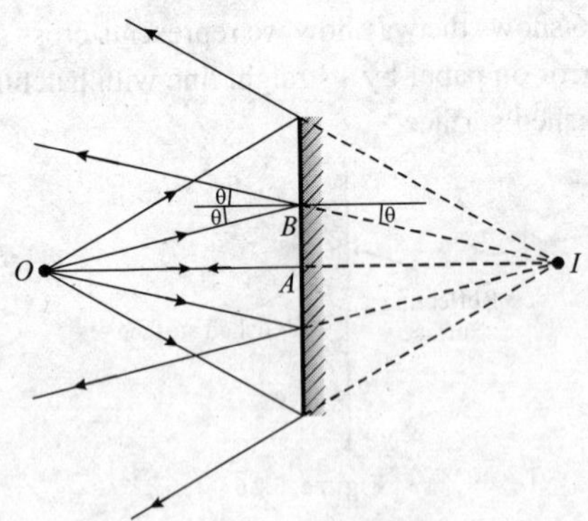

Figure 5.30

5.6.2 Characteristic-2 of Image formation by a Plane Mirror

"Nature of image produced by a plane mirror is opposite to that of the object."

Whenever a light beam incidents on a plane mirror, it reflects the beam keeping its behaviour same. A diverging incident beam on a plane mirror is reflected as a diverging beam and a converging incident beam on a plane mirror is reflected as a converging beam. So we can see from figure-5.31(a) that from a point object (real object) placed in front of a plane mirror diverging light rays incident on the plane mirror and after reflection also the beam remain diverging which produces image behind the mirror at point I and as reflected beam is diverging we consider the image produced is virtual. Similarly as shown in figure-5.31(b) when a converging light beam is incident on a plane mirror which is corresponding to their point of intersection at point O' which is considered as a vertual object for this mirror, after reflection these light rays remain converging and meet at point I' in front of the mirror which we can consider as a real image produced.

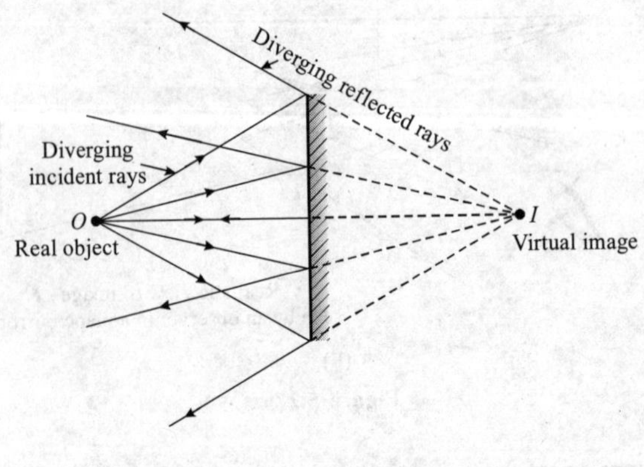

(a)

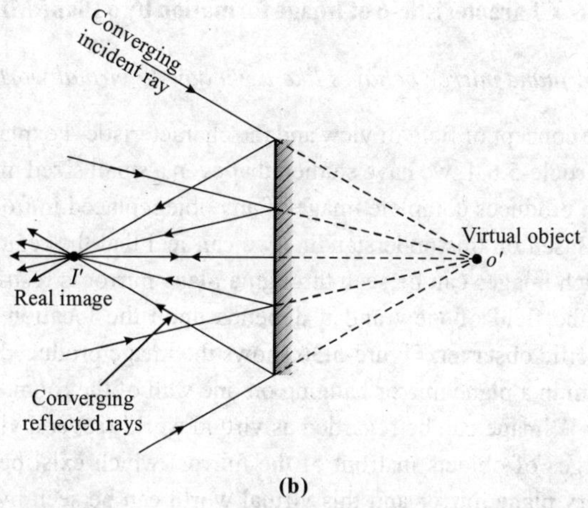

(b)
Figure 5.31

Above analysis shows that a plane mirror always produces image of opposite nature then its object. If object is real, image produced will be virtual and if object is virtual, image produced will be real. Understanding of real and virtual object and image for any optical device (in this case for a plane mirror) we have already discussed in articles-1.3.1 and article-1.3.2.

5.6.3 Characteristic-3 of Image formation by a Plane Mirror

"Image produced by a plane mirror is erect and laterally inverted"

We have discussed for an extended object that every point on the body of object behaves like a point object and the extended object can be considered as combination of all such point objects on the surface of the body. Figure-5.32 shows the image formation of an extended object by a plane mirror. Here if we consider two points A, B and C on the body of the object then their corresponding images are produced at the same distance behind the mirror at points A', B' and C' respectively and similarly all points on the body of object images are produced and combination of all such point images will produce the image of the extended object as shown in this figure.

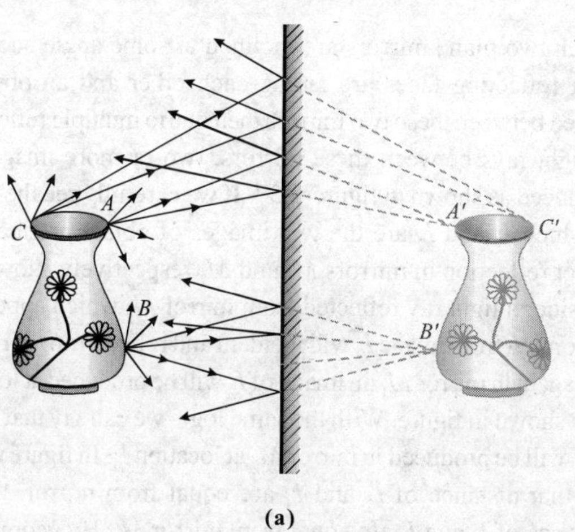

(a)

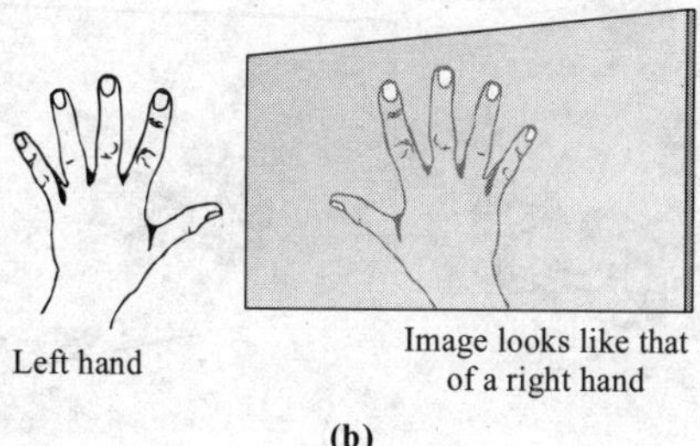

(b)
Figure 5.32

As image of all points on object are produced at the same distance behind the mirror, the image produced will be erect and laterally inverted because the points which are close to mirror will have their images close to mirror behind it (like point A and its image at A') and those which are relatively far from mirror will have their images far from mirror behind it (like point C and its image at C'). If we see the points A which is vertically above point B on object and in image also its image A' is vertically above image B' so the vertical orientation of image will be same as that of object or we can say that image produced is erected for the given object. Figures-5.33 and 5.34 show more examples of lateral inversion of images produced by a plane mirror, most common is what we see usually that in a plane mirror image of a left hand appears that like a right hand.

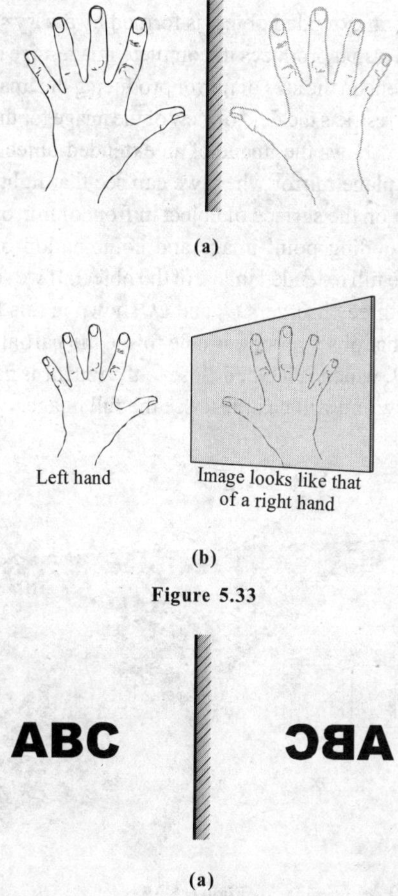

(b)
Figure 5.33

ABC | ABC (mirrored)

(a)

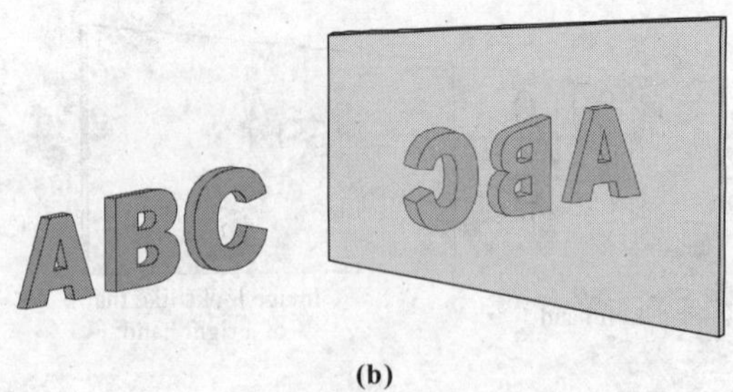

(b)

Figure 5.34

5.6.4 Characteristic-4 of Image formation by a Plane Mirror

"Image produced by a plane mirror is always of same size as that of object"

From the figure-5.32 and 5.33 we can see that in vertical direction orientation of image particle does not change and every point image is produce at the same distance of its corresponding point object on the surface of extended object hence we can say that the height and width of image of the extended object will always be equal to that of the object.

5.6.5 Characteristic-5 of Image formation by a Plane Mirror

"A small part of a mirror also produces full sized image of object"

If image of an extended object is formed by a very small sized mirror then also it produces its complete image, size of image is not dependent on the size of mirror producing the image. Size of mirror only restricts the field of view of the image for the observer. Figure-5.35 shows the image of an extended object produced by a small plane mirror where we can see that light rays from every point on the surface of object in front of mirror produces its corresponding point image and combination of all these points is the full extended image of the object. If we see the field of view of three observers O_1 and O_2 shown in this figure then it is clear that observers O_1 is able to see the partial image but observer O_2 which is located close to the mirror is having wide field of view and will be able to see the full image.

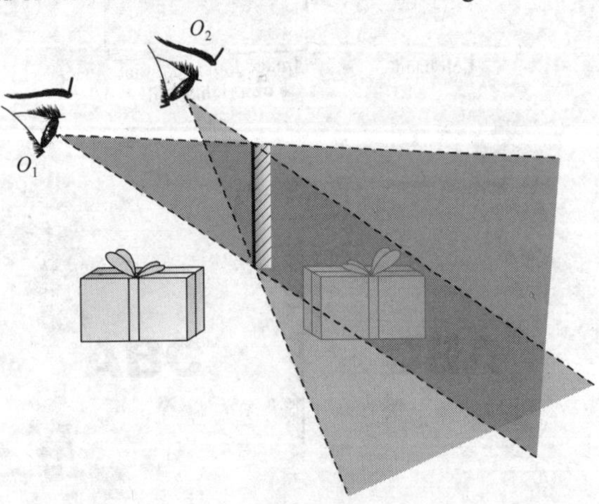

Figure 5.35

5.6.6 Characteristic-6 of Image formation by a Plane Mirror

"A plane mirror behaves like a window to virtual world"

The concept of field of view and the characteristic-4 explained in article-5.6.4, we have studied that even a small sized mirror also produces complete image of any object placed in front of it. Based on this understanding we can feel that the region in which images can be seen through a plane mirror is restricted by the field of view and it depends upon the location of a specific observer. Figure-5.36 shows the image produced of a room in a plane mirror hanging on one wall of the room. This whole image can be regarded as virtual world (several virtual images of objects in front of the mirror) which exist behind every plane mirror and this virtual world can be seen by any observer who looks into the mirror.

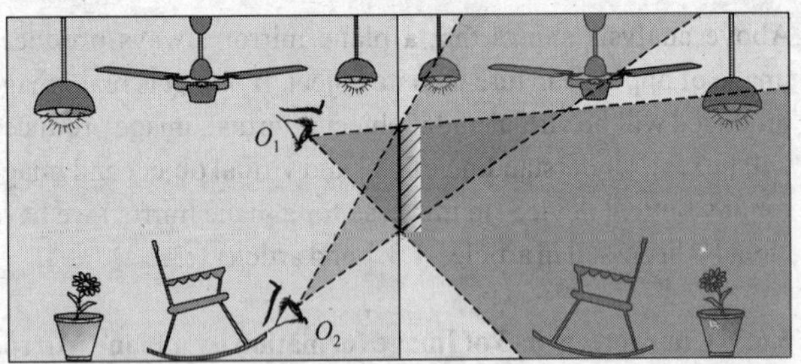

Figure 5.36

From above figure it is clear that the vision of virtual world will be different for different observers depending upon their location which will decide the field of view. We can also consider this situation as mirror behaving as a window through which this virtual world can be seen.

5.6.7 Characteristic-7 of Image formation by a Plane Mirror

"If an object is placed between two inclined mirrors then several images are produced, all of which lie on a circle with center of circle located at the point of intersection of the two mirrors."

When two plane mirrors are inclined at some angle such that their reflecting faces are facing each other and an object is placed between these two mirrors then due to multiple reflections of light rays between these mirrors, two or more images are produced as shown in figure-5.37. If we carefully see the figure in which I_1 and I_2 are the two images of object produced by direct reflection in mirrors M_1 and M_2 respectively. Now if we consider a light ray reflected from mirror M_2 which appears to be coming from image I_2 will incident and reflect from mirror M_1 and again in mirror M_1 an image of I_2 will be produced at location I_3 as shown in figure. With the same logic we can say that image of I_1 will be produced in mirror M_2 at location I_4. In figure we can see that distance of I_2 and I_3 are equal from mirror M_1 and distance of I_1 and I_4 are equal from mirror M_2. By geometrical symmetry we can see that all these images will be located at the same distance from the point C so all will lie on a circle of which center will coincide with the intersection point of the two mirrors.

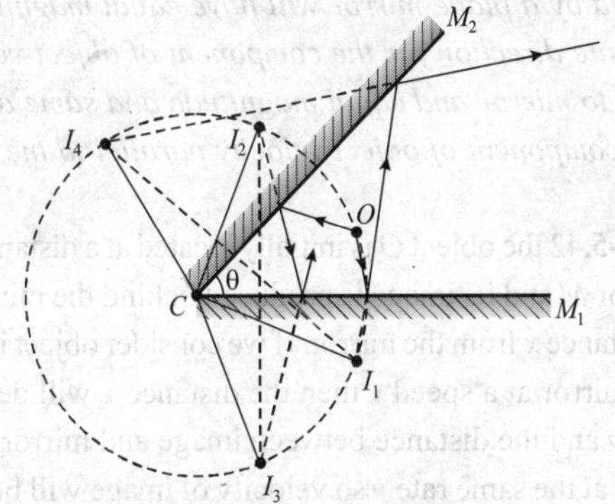

Figure 5.37

Total number of images produced by a setup of inclined mirrors

Total number of images can be counted by the concept explained in the figure-5.38. Here if we consider an object is placed at a point between the two mirrors M_1 and M_2 inclined at an angle θ such that the angle between object line and mirror M_1 is α and that between object line and mirror M_2 is ϕ. If we consider I_1 and I_2 are the images produced by mirrors M_1 and M_2 for the reflection of light from object then these are at angular separation α and ϕ from mirrors M_1 and M_2 as shown in figure. Now these images will act as object for other mirrors as discussed above and images I_3 and I_4 are thus obtained and their angular separation from these mirrors M_1 and M_2 are $(\alpha + \theta)$ and $(\phi + \theta)$ respectively. Again these images can again act as object for these mirrors and produce further images at locations I_5 and I_6 at angular separation from mirrors M_2 and M_1 at $(\alpha + 2\theta)$ and $(\phi + 2\theta)$ respectively. You can easily verify these angles by drawing these image on your own carefully at same separation from the mirrors for their respective object positions. These multiple reflections will continue to produce successive images until the angular separation of an image from a mirror increases beyond 180° as after this no more reflection from the other mirror will take place. So total images you can count by the table given below

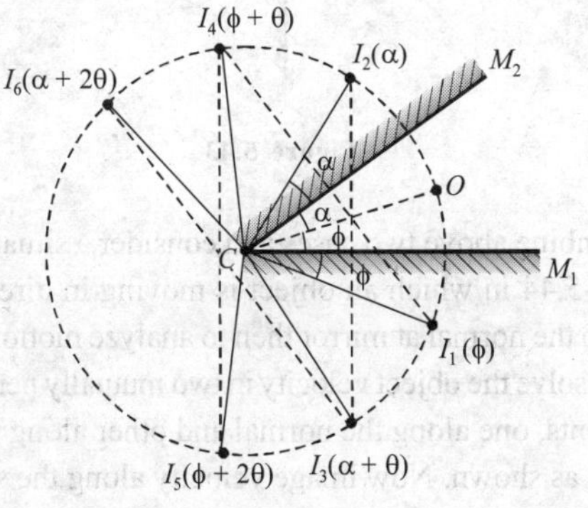

Figure 5.38

Table 5.1

Image formed by mirror M_1	Image formed by mirror M_2
α	ϕ
$\phi + \theta$	$\phi + \theta$
$\alpha + 2\theta$	$\phi + 2\theta$
$\phi + 3\theta$	$\alpha + 3\theta$
upto the limit till this angle is less than 180°	upto the limit till this angle is less than 180°

In case the object is placed at angle bisector of the two mirrors and the angle θ between mirrors is such that $\frac{360°}{\theta}$ is an even number then the total number of images can be directly given as

$$N = \frac{360°}{\theta} - 1 \qquad \ldots(5.7)$$

In above equation-(5.7), 1 is subtracted from the ratio of 360° and θ because if $\frac{360°}{\theta}$ is an even number than $\frac{180°}{\theta}$ is an integer and in that case last two images produced by the two mirrors will overlap as a single image.

5.6.8 Characteristic-8 of Image formation by a Plane Mirror

"If an object is rotated by an angle θ then image will also rotate by the same angle θ but in opposite direction."

In figure-5.39 if I is the image of object produced by the shown plane mirror M and we shift the object to a new position which is shifted by angular displacement θ with respect to its initial position about a center C in clockwise direction then by geometrical symmetry we can see that image will also get shifted to the position I' as shown which is at the same angular displacement θ but in anticlockwise direction (opposite direction to movement of object).

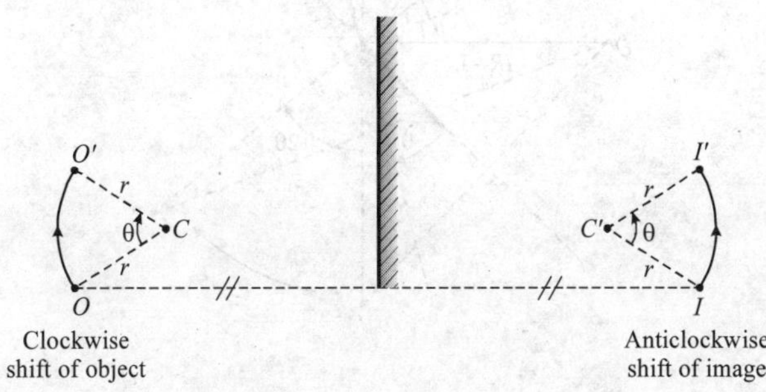

Figure 5.39

If there is an extended object of which image is produced in a plane mirror as shown in figure-5.40 then on rotating this object by an angular speed ω, image will also rotate by the same angular speed ω but in opposite direction.

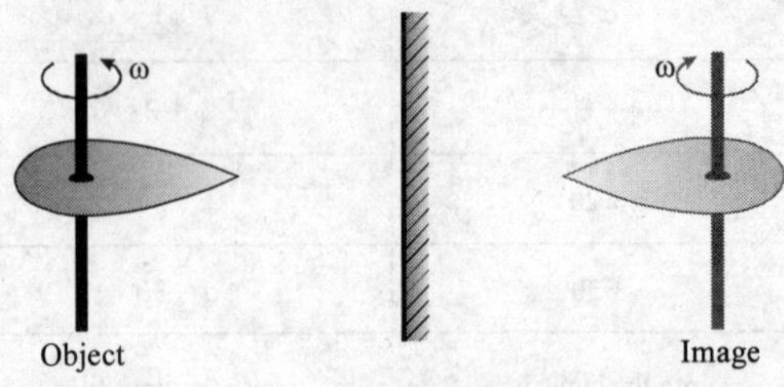

Figure 5.40

5.6.9 Characteristic-9 of Image formation by a Plane Mirror

"If object is kept fixed and mirror is rotated by an angle θ then image produced by this mirror will rotate by twice the angle of rotation of mirror in same direction mirror is rotated."

Figure-5.41 shows an object O of which image I is produced in the mirror M. Here we consider an incident light ray IR-1 falling on the mirror at an angle of incidence i which is reflected as reflected ray RR-1 at same angle and appear to be coming from the image I. Now we rotate the mirror by an angle θ to a new position M' as shown. Due to mirror rotation, the normal to the surface is also rotated by same angle to a new position mentioned as N' and the angle of incidence of IR-1 for this new position of normal will now be $(i-\theta)$ so the angle between this incident ray IR-1 and new reflected ray RR-2 is $2(i-\theta)$ which appears to be coming from the new position of the image I' after mirror rotation as shown in figure. If we calculate the angle between the two reflected rays (initial and final) then it is $(2i-2\theta)-2i=2\theta$.

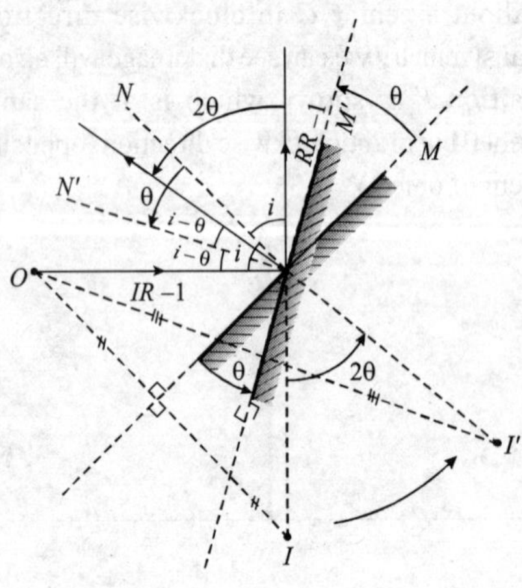

Figure 5.41

5.6.10 Characteristic-10 of Image formation by a Plane Mirror

"If an object is in motion then the velocity of its image produced by a plane mirror will have equal magnitude and opposite direction for the component of object velocity normal to mirror and equal magnitude and same direction for the component of object velocity parallel to the mirror."

In figure-5.42 the object O is initially located at a distance x from the mirror M and its image is produced behind the mirror at the same distance x from the mirror. If we consider object is moving toward mirror at a speed v then the distance x will decrease at the rate v and the distance between image and mirror will also decrease at the same rate v so velocity of image will be same as that of object but in opposite direction. Thus in case if object is moving in direction normal to mirror, always image will also move with same speed but in opposite direction.

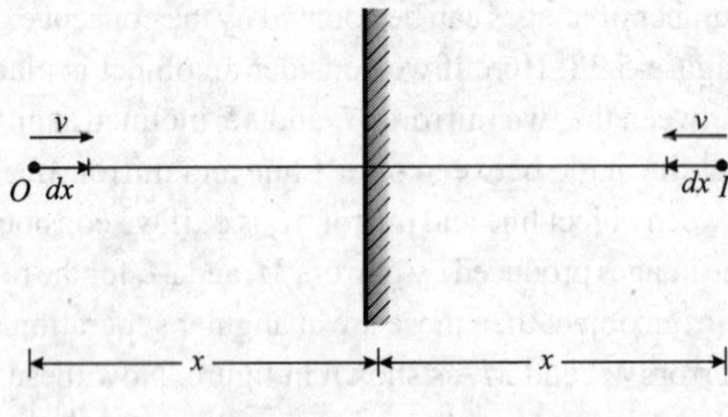

Figure 5.42

Figure-5.43 shows an object moving in direction parallel to mirror surface with a speed v, as image is produced at the same distance behind the mirror, it will always be located at the same distance as that of object, it will also be moving in the same direction parallel to mirror surface as shown.

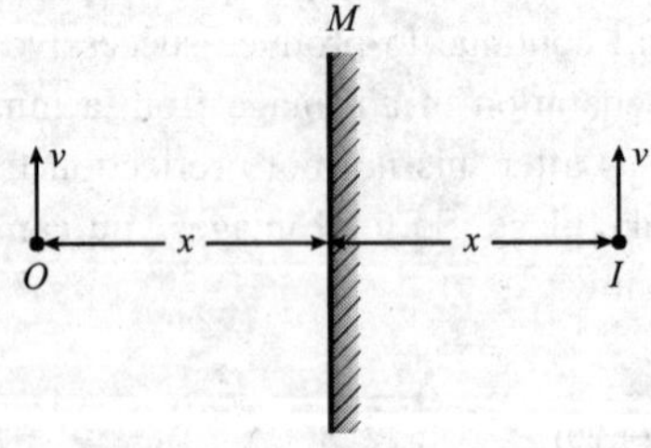

Figure 5.43

If we combine above two cases and consider a situation shown in figure-5.44 in which an object is moving in direction at an angle θ to the normal at mirror then to analyze motion of image, we can resolve the object velocity in two mutually perpendicular components, one along the normal and other along the surface of mirror as shown. Now image velocity along the surface can be taken as same as that of object velocity component v (||) and image velocity along normal to mirror will be equal in magnitude as that of object velocity component $v(\perp)$ but in opposite direction.

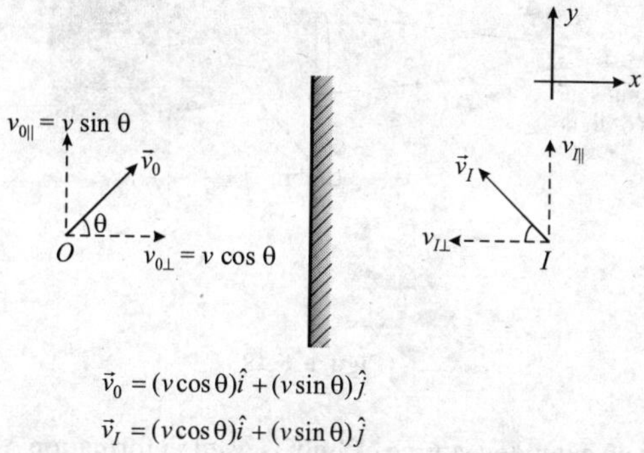

$$\vec{v}_0 = (v\cos\theta)\hat{i} + (v\sin\theta)\hat{j}$$
$$\vec{v}_I = (v\cos\theta)\hat{i} + (v\sin\theta)\hat{j}$$

Figure 5.44

5.6.11 Characteristic-11 of Image formation by a Plane Mirror

"If object is kept fixed and a plane mirror is in motion then its motion along its surface does not affect the motion of image but motion of mirror along its normal affects the image motion. Along the normal image moves with twice the speed in same direction as that of mirror."

Figure-5.45 shows a situation in which at an instant an object and its image are at a distance x from the mirror and keeping object fixed, mirror starts moving along its surface. We can see that it does not affect the image position, image will still remain at rest as observer is not moving. It will be maintained at position which is at same distance behind the mirror at which object is situated in front of it.

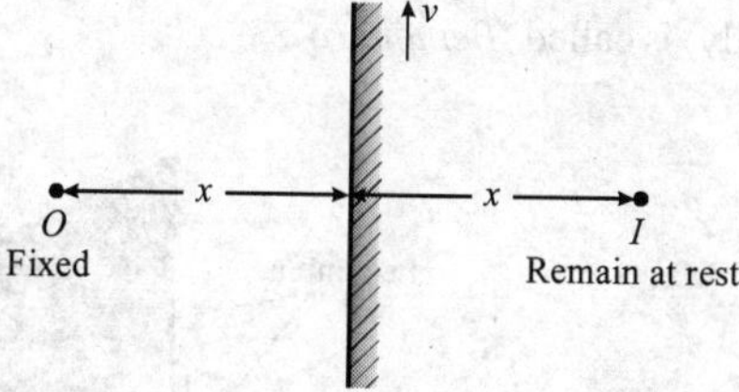

Figure 5.45

Figure-5.46 shows a situation in which at an instant an object and its image are at a distance x from the mirror. If object is kept fixed and mirror moves by a distance dx then distance between mirror and object decreases by dx so distance between image and mirror will also become $(x - dx)$. As object is kept fixed mirror displaces by $2dx$ in the direction of mirror motion in same duration hence the image speed is twice that of the mirror in direction normal to the surface of mirror.

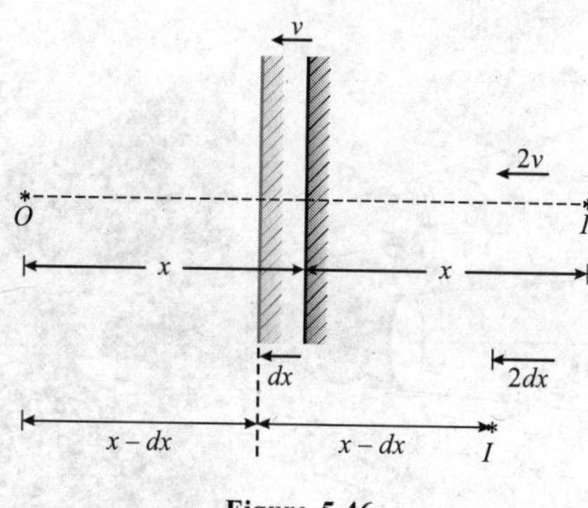

Figure 5.46

5.7 Understanding Shadow Formation

Shadow formation of any object in light is explained by the law of rectilinear propagation of light according to which in a homogeneous medium light travels along a straight line path. When an opaque object is placed in the path of a light beam then the boundaries of the object cast a shadow behind the object which can be obtained on a screen placed in the path of light beam after object as shown in figure-5.47 for three different light beams - parallel, diverging and converging.

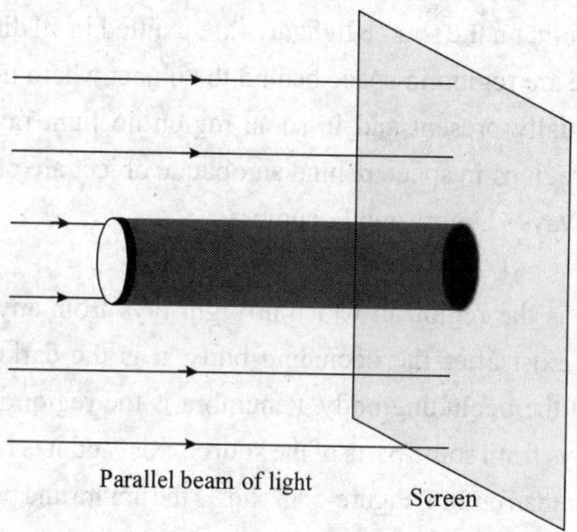

(a)

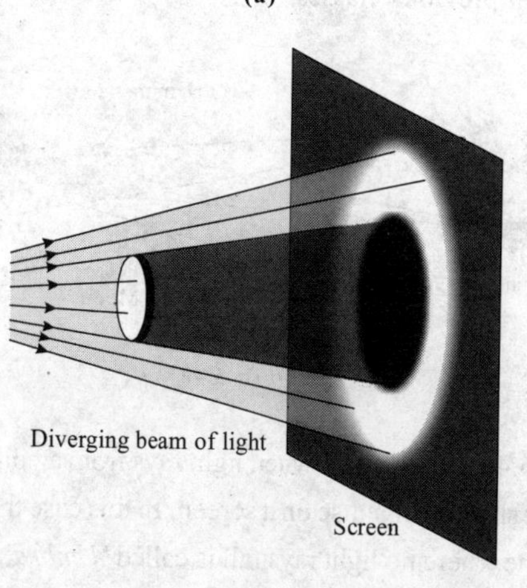

(b)

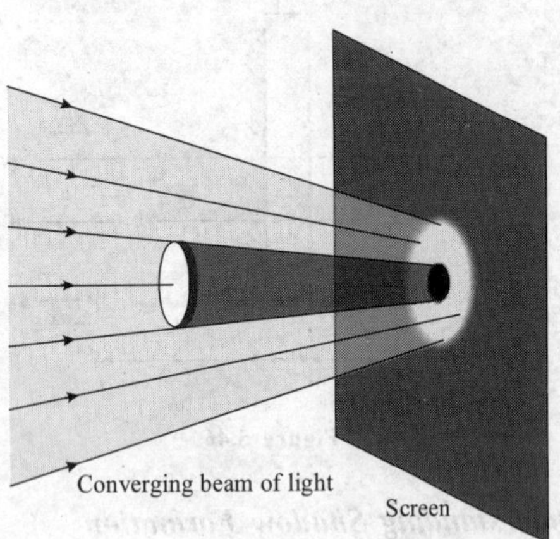

(c)

Figure 5.47

5.7.1 Umbra and Penumbra Regions

These are regions of space which are useful in analysis of shadow formation if the source of light used is not a point source because in case of an extended source of light from every point on the source light rays are emitted in all directions so there are region in space behind the object where light rays are partially present and in some region no light rays exist. These regions in space behind an opaque object are classified in two ways - Umbra and Penumbra.

Umbra is the region in which no light rays from any part of source exist after the occluding body, it is the darkest zone beyond the occluding body. Penumbra is the region in which light rays from some parts of the source exist and it is relatively brighter than umbra. Figure-5.48 shows the umbra and penumbra regions at the situation of solar eclipse which you might have studied in previous classes.

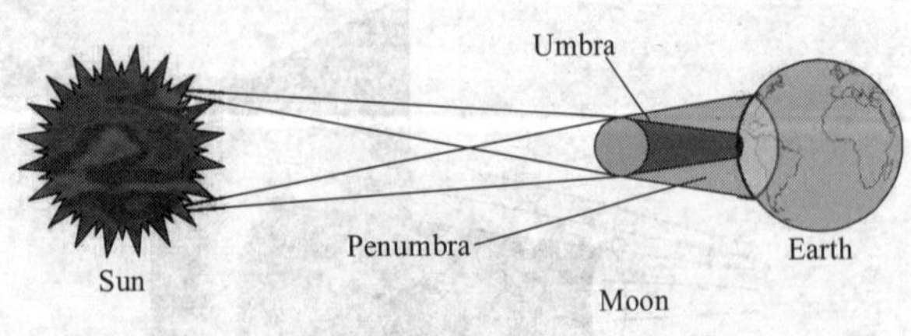

Figure 5.48

Figure-5.49 shows a case when light rays from a point source is forming shadow of a disc on a screen. In this case the complete dark zone where no light rays fall is called '*Umbra*'.

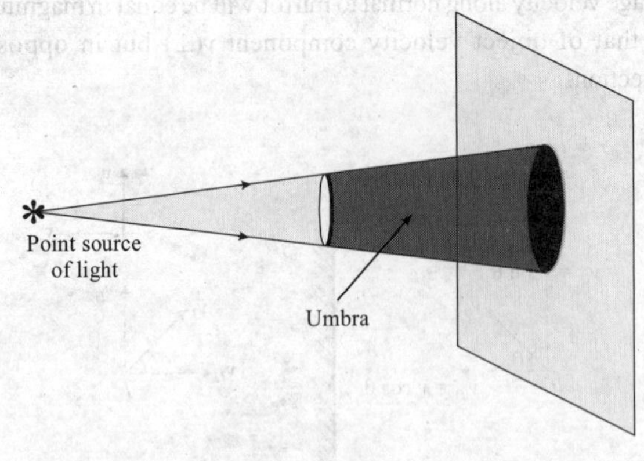

Figure 5.49

When an extended source of light is used in formation of image then we can see that there are two regions in space behind the occluding body which are different in respect of shadow formation. Figure-5.50 shows a torch as an extended source of light forming the shadow of a disc placed in front of it. If we consider two points A and B on torch face which will act as two separate point sources of light. Here from point A consider two light rays A_1 and A_2 which are grazing the two edges (top and bottom) of the disc and then falling on the screen and all the light rays between these two rays A_1 and A_2 will be blocked by the disc and all the rays outside of A_1 and A_2 will fall on screen directly. Similarly from point B consider two rays B_1 and B_2 grazing from the two edges of the disc and falling on the screen. All such points on the outer edge of the light source such light rays will fall on screen and produce shadow on the screen which is shown in this figure-5.50. The central circular shadow spot will be darkest as no light ray from any point of the face of torch are falling onto it, this the region we are calling '*Umbra*'. The annular shadow outside of umbra where light rays are falling on screen from some points of the torch face (not all points, see this carefully) is called '*Penumbra*'.

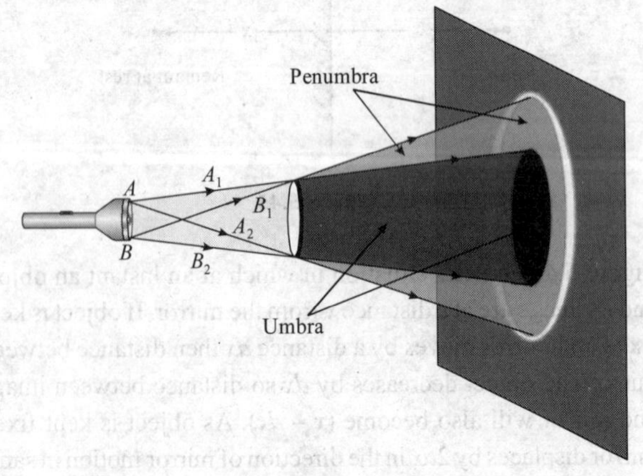

Figure 5.50

Figure-5.51 shows a situation when size of light source is bigger than that of the occluding body. In this case umbra is smaller region and penumbra may be even bigger than umbra. Even in case of solar eclipse shown in figure-5.48 also the situation is similar to this.

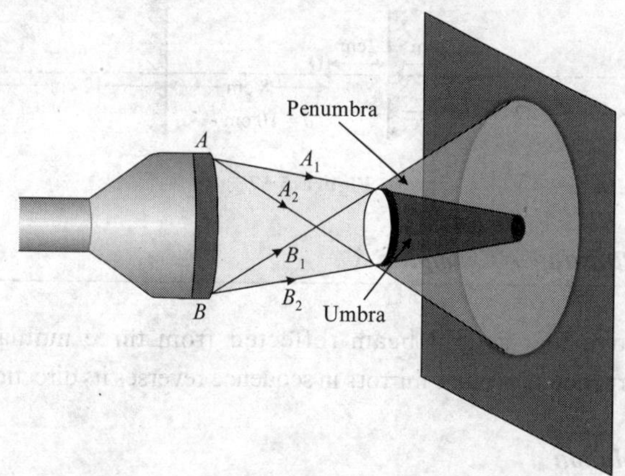

Figure 5.51

5.7.2 Antumbra Region

It is a region from which the whole occluding body appears within the disc of the light source. In figure-5.52(a) if we try to feel the view from the observer's eye shown, then it will look like as shown in figure-5.52(b) where the whole sphere appears to be within the disc of the light source. This region shown in figure-5.52(a) is called *'Antumbra'*.

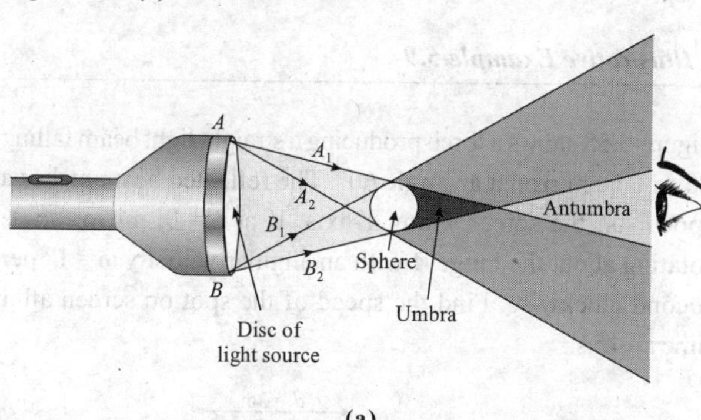

(a)

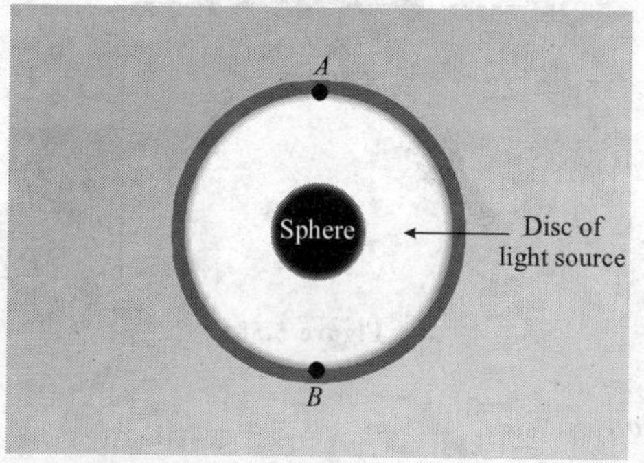

(b)

Figure 5.52

Illustrative Example 5.4

Figure shows a mirror M on which a light ray incident at an angle 40° from normal. If the ray is rotated by 10° clockwise find the change in angle of deviation of light after reflection.

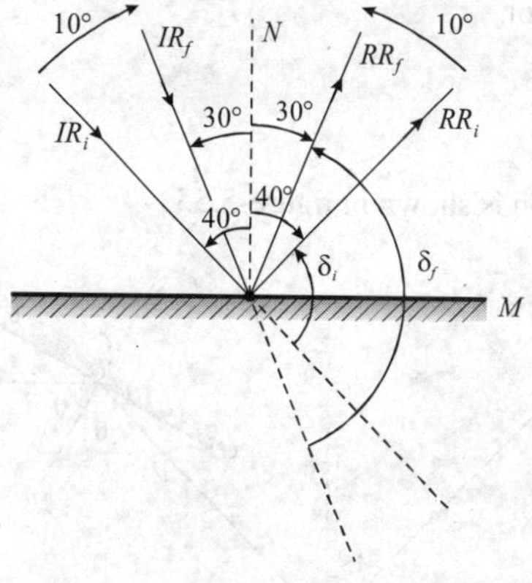

Figure 5.53

Solution

Initial deviation angle

$$\delta_i = 180 - 80 = 100°$$

Find deviation angle

$$\delta_f = 180 - 60 = 120°$$

Change in deviation angle

$$\Delta\delta = \delta_f - \delta_i = 20°$$

Illustrative Example 5.5

A man is standing in a room of length 20 m and height 3 m at a distance 5 m from one wall. On the facing wall a mirror is hanging. Find the minimum size of mirror required in which man will be able to see complete height of wall behind him.

Solution

By similarly we use

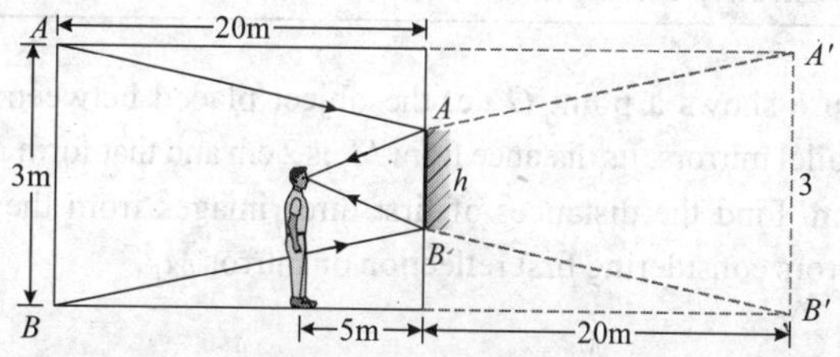

Figure 5.54

$$\frac{h}{5} = \frac{3}{25}$$

$$\Rightarrow \quad h = \frac{3}{5}\ m = 0.6\ m$$

Illustrative Example 5.6

Rays of light strike a horizontal plane mirror at an angle of 45°. At what angle should a second plane mirror be placed in order that the reflected ray finally be reflected horizontally from the second mirror.

Solution

The situation is shown in figure-5.55

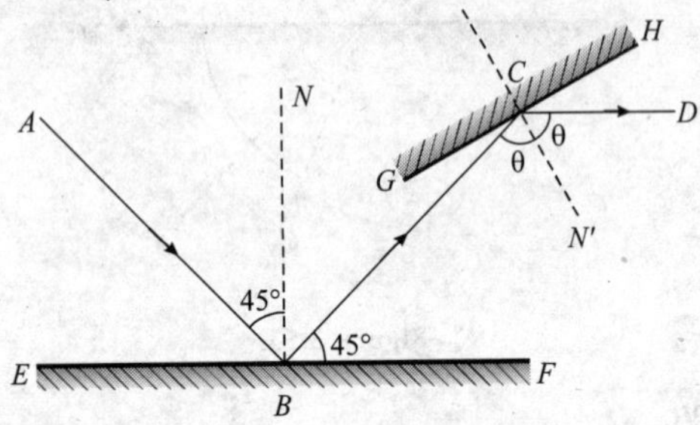

Figure 5.55

The ray AB strikes the first plane mirror EF at an angle of 45°. Now, the second mirror GH is arranged such that the ray BC after reflection from this mirror becomes horizontal.

From the figure we see that emergent ray CD is parallel to mirror EF and BC is a line intersecting these parallel lines, thus we use

$$\angle DCB + \angle CBF = 180°$$

$$\angle DCN' + \angle N'CB + \angle CBF = 180°$$

$$\theta + \theta + 45° = 180°$$

$$\Rightarrow \quad \theta = 67.5°$$

So the second mirror should be placed in such a way that it is inclined to the horizontal at an angle 22.5°.

Illustrative Example 5.7

Figure shows a point O i.e. the object placed between two parallel mirrors. Its distance from M_1 is 2 cm and that form M_2 is 8 cm. Find the distances of first three images from the two mirrors considering first reflection on mirror M_1.

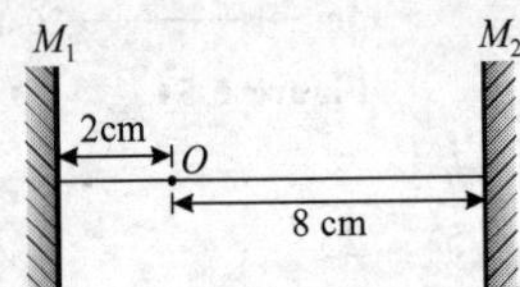

Figure 5.56

Solution

Since given that reflection on mirror M_1 first than in figure below first three images produced in succession are shown.

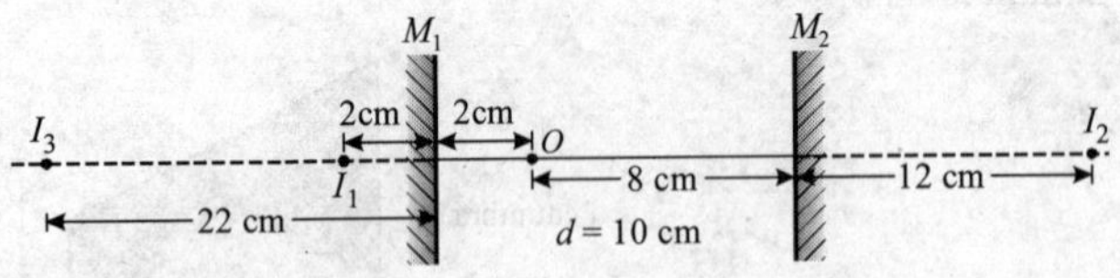

Figure 5.57

Illustrative Example 5.8

Prove that a light beam reflected from three mutually perpendicular plane mirrors in sequence reverses its direction.

Solution

If the three mutually perpendicular plane mirror have their planes along XY, YZ and ZX planes respectively and if a light ray along a unit vector $\hat{m} = a\hat{i} + b\hat{j} + c\hat{k}$ incident on these mirrors in sequence then after each reflection are component of ray reverses which is along the normal to that specific mirror so after three successive reflections at the three mirrors, unit vector along reflected ray becomes $\hat{n} = -a\hat{i} - b\hat{j} - c\hat{k}$ which is indirection opposite to incident ray.

Illustrative Example 5.9

Figure-5.58 shows a torch producing a straight light beam falling on a plane mirror at an angle 60°. The reflected beam makes a spot P on the screen along Y-axis. If at $t = 0$, mirror starts rotating about the hinge A with an angular velocity $\omega = 1°$ per second clockwise. Find the speed of the spot on screen after time $t = 15$ s.

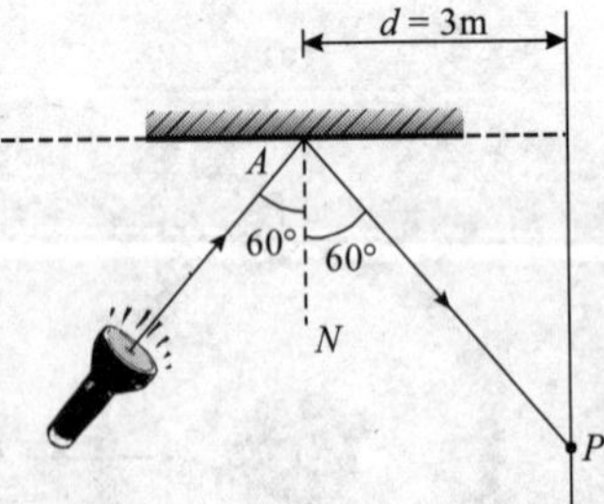

Figure 5.58

Solution

In 15 seconds mirror will rotate 15° in clockwise direction and due to this the reflected ray will rotate 30° in clockwise direction

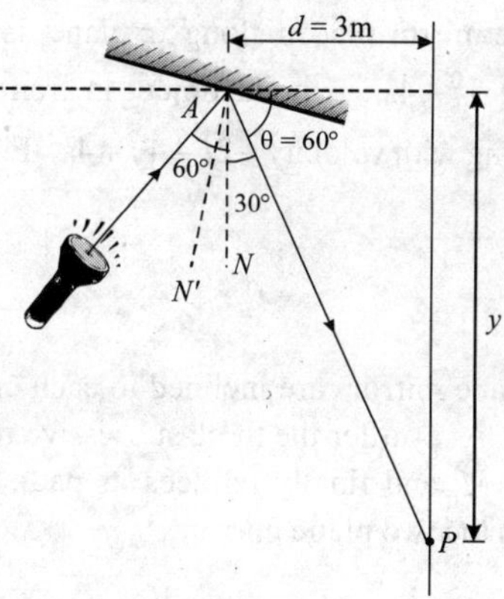

Figure 5.59

$$y = 3\tan\theta$$

$$\Rightarrow \quad \frac{dy}{dt} = (3\sec^2\theta).\frac{d\theta}{dt} \quad \ldots(5.8)$$

Here $\frac{dy}{dt} = v_P, \quad \frac{d\theta}{dt} = 2°\ \text{sec}^{-1}$

$$\Rightarrow \quad \frac{dy}{dt} = \frac{2\times\pi}{180} = \frac{\pi}{90}\ \text{rad per second.}$$

At $t = 15$ s and $\theta = 30° + 30° = 60°$

Substituting the values in equation-(5.8) we have,

$$v_P = (3\sec^2 60°)\left(\frac{\pi}{90°}\right)$$

$$\Rightarrow \quad v_P = 3\times4\times\frac{\pi}{90}\ \text{m/s}$$

$$\Rightarrow \quad v_P = \frac{2\pi}{15}\ \text{m/s}$$

Illustrative Example 5.10

Figure-5.60 shows a plane mirror onto which a light ray is incident. If the incident light ray is rotated by 10° and the mirror by 20°, as shown in figure below, find the angle by which the reflected ray is rotated.

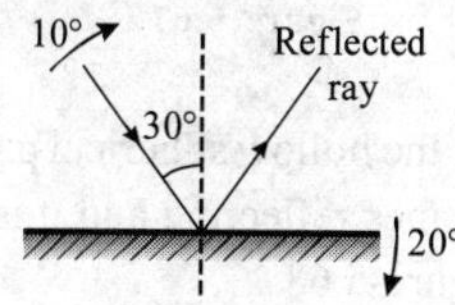

Figure 5.60

Solution

As we studied when Incident ray is rotated by some angle the reflected ray rotates by same angle in opposite direction and when mirror is rotated by some angle the reflected ray rotates by twice the angle in same direction hence total angle turned by the reflected ray in above case is

$$= 40° \circlearrowright + 10° \circlearrowleft \Rightarrow 30° \circlearrowright \Rightarrow 30°\ \text{(clockwise)}$$

Web Reference at www.physicsgalaxy.com
Age Group - High School Physics | Age 17-19 Years
Section - OPTICS
Topic - Geometrical Optics I - Reflection of Light
Module Number - 8 to 23

Practice Exercise 5.1

(i) A person's eye is at a height of 1.5 m. He stands in front of a 0.3 m length plane mirror bottom of which is 0.8 m above ground. Find the length of his image he will be able to see in this mirror.

[0.6 m]

(ii) How far must an object be placed in front of a convex mirror of focal length 20 cm to form an image $(1/4)^{th}$ of the size of the object.

[60 cm]

(iii) In figure-5.61 shown a light ray 1 after getting reflected from mirror M_1 strikes another mirror M_2 and reflected as ray 2. If angle between M_1 and M_2 is 60° find angle θ.

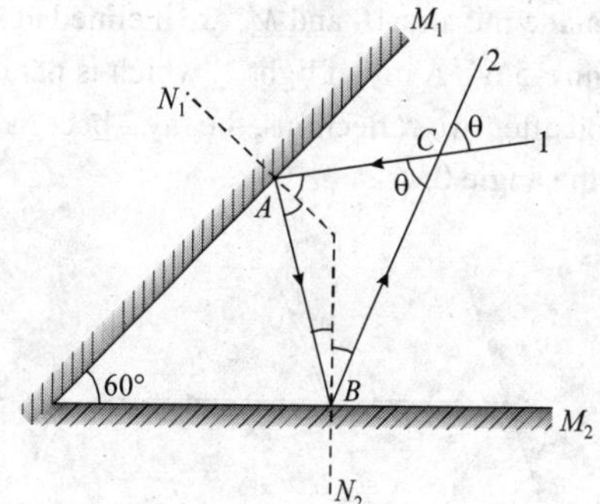

Figure 5.61

[60°]

(iv) Find the number of images formed by three mirrors AB, BC and AC arranged in form of an equilateral triangle in situation as shown in figure-5.62. The object is at the centre of triangle.

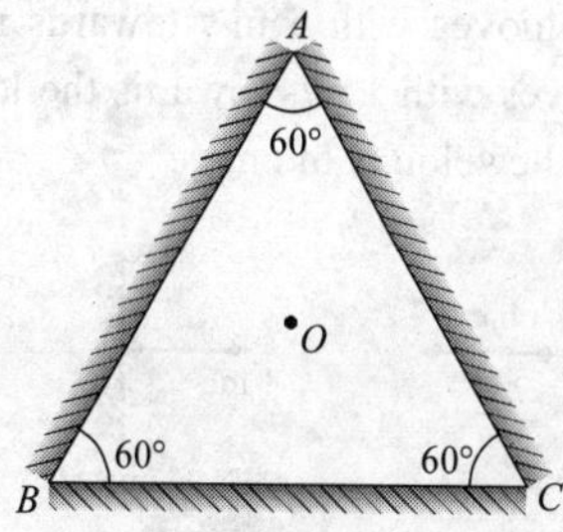

Figure 5.62

[12]

(v) A point source of light B is placed at a distance L in front of the centre of a mirror of width d hung vertically on a wall. A man walks in front of the mirror along a line parallel to the mirror at a distance $2L$ from it as shown in figure-5.63. The greatest distance over which he can see the image of the light source in the mirror is :

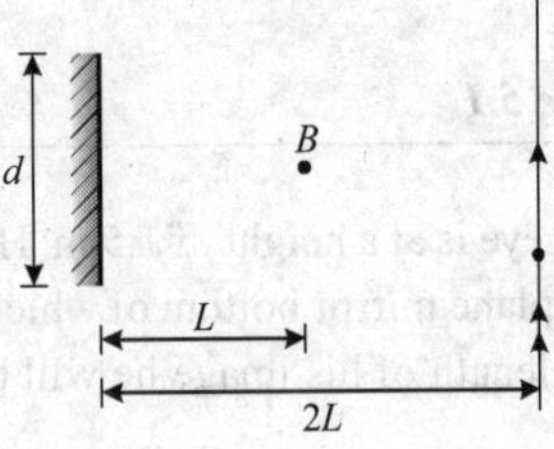

Figure 5.63

[$3d$]

(vi) In a 3D coordinate system a plane mirror is placed parallel to XY plane and above the mirror a point object is moving at velocity $\vec{v}_0 = 5\hat{i} - 3\hat{j} - 11\hat{k}$ m/s. If mirror is also moving parallel to itself at velocity $\vec{v}_m = 2\hat{i} + \hat{j} - 3\hat{k}$, find the velocity of image produced in mirror.

[$5\hat{i} - 3\hat{j} + 5\hat{k}$ m/s]

(vii) Two plane mirrors M_1 and M_2 are inclined at angle θ as shown in figure-5.64. A ray of light 1, which is parallel to M_1 strikes M_2 and after two reflections, the ray 2 becomes parallel to M_2. Find the angle θ.

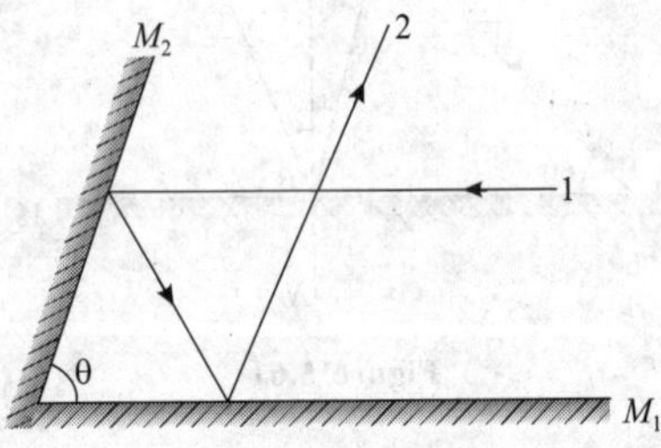

Figure 5.64

[60°]

(viii) An object moves with 5 m/s towards right while the mirror shown moves with 1 m/s towards the left as shown in figure-5.65. Find the velocity of image.

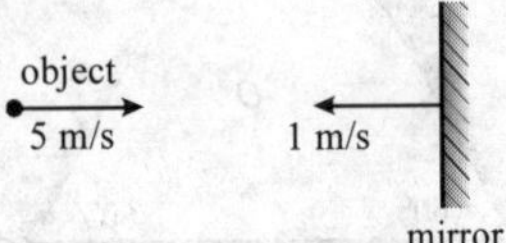

Figure 5.65

[7 m/s]

(ix) A plane mirror placed along xz plane is moving with velocity $-3\hat{i} + 5\hat{j} - 4\hat{k}$. A point object in front of the plane mirror is moving with velocity $-2\hat{i} - 4\hat{j} + 4\hat{k}$. Find velocity of image.

[$-2\hat{i} + 14\hat{j} + 4\hat{k}$]

(x) Two plane mirrors are inclined to each other as shown in figure-5.66. A ray after the three successive reflection falls on the mirror M_1 and finally retraces its path. Calculate the angle between the two plane mirror.

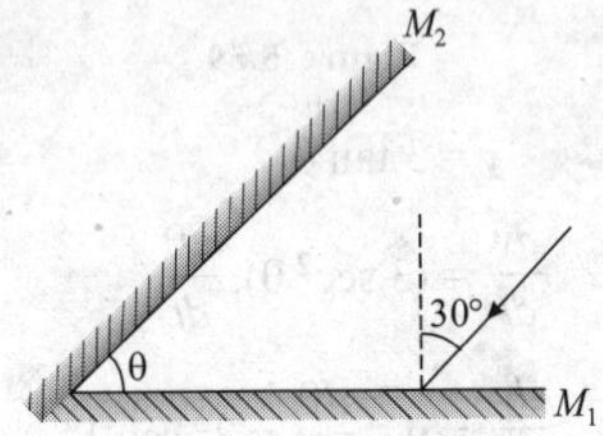

Figure 5.66

[15°]

5.8 Spherical Mirrors

A spherical mirror is a part of hollow glass sphere polished on one of its surface. If inner surface of sphere is polished then its outer surface becomes reflecting and it is called a convex mirror as shown in figure-5.67.

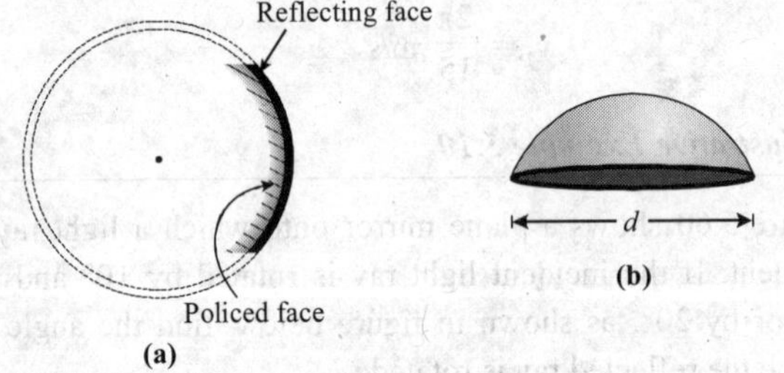

Figure 5.67

If the outer surface of the hollow spherical part is polished then its inner surface becomes reflecting and it is called a concave mirror as shown in figure-5.68.

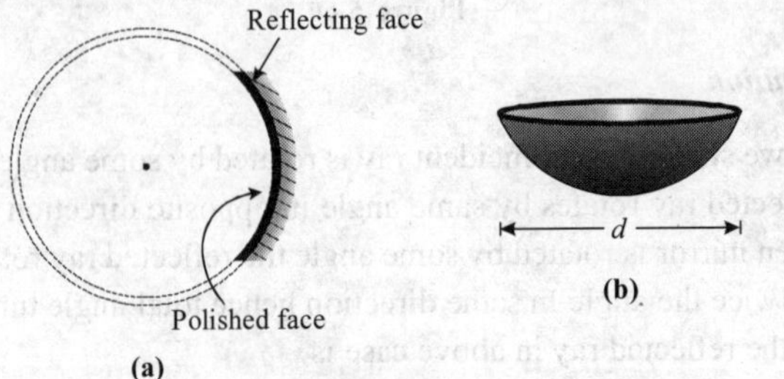

Figure 5.68

5.8.1 Standard terms related to Spherical Mirrors

For concave or convex mirrors there are some specific terms and their definition associated which are useful in analyzing image formation by these mirrors so first we will discuss all these terms one by one.

(i) Pole or Optic Center of Mirror : It is the center of the physical spherical mirror as denoted by point P in figure-5.69.

(ii) Center of Curvature of Mirror : It is the center of the spherical shell of which mirror is a part. It is denoted by point C in figure-5.69 and 5.70

(iii) Principal Axis of Mirror : It is the line joining the optic center of mirror and its center of curvature as shown in figure-5.69.

(iv) Radius of Curvature of Mirror : It is the radius of the spherical shell of which the mirror is a part which is the distance OC and it is also denoted by 'R' as shown in figure-5.69.

(v) Focal point of Mirror : It is the mid point of line joining the optic center and center of curvature and denoted by 'F'. This is a point where it is considered that all paraxial light rays falling on the mirror which are parallel to principal axis will converge in case of concave mirror as shown in figure-5.70(a) and appear to diverge from this point in case of convex mirror as shown in figure-5.70(b). It is also called '*Principal Focus*' of the spherical mirror.

(vi) Aperture of the Mirror : It is the diameter of the actual mirror cross section through which light rays incident will fall on the mirror surface. This is shown as 'd' in figure-5.67(b) and 5.68(b) and as AB in figure-5.69(a) and 5.69(b)

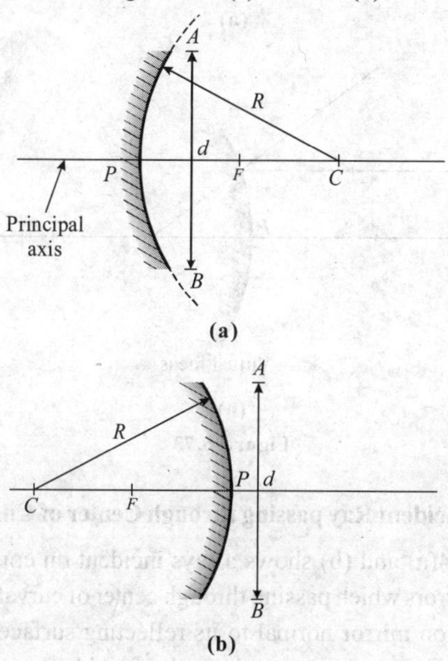

Figure 5.69

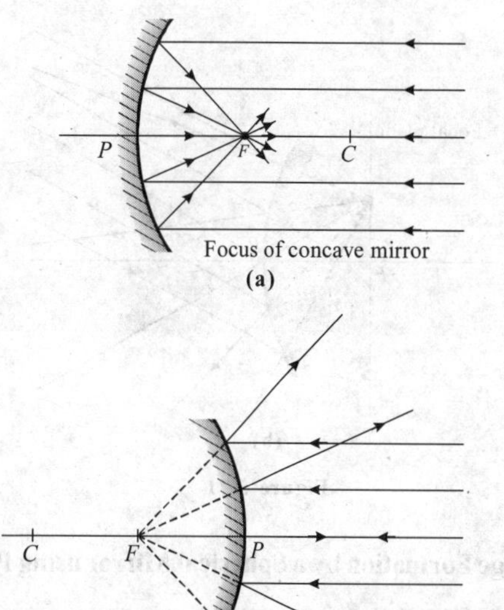

Figure 5.70

5.8.2 Focal Length of a Spherical Mirror

It is the distance of Principal focus of mirror to the Optics Center of the Mirror. Generally concave mirrors are also referred as '*Converging Mirrors*' because these converge all parallel rays incident on it. This convergence occurs at focal point if incident rays are parallel to the principal axis of mirror as shown in figure-5.70(a). In this manner all convex mirrors are also referred as '*Diverging Mirrors*' because these diverge all parallel rays incident on it. If incident rays fall on a convex mirror parallel to the principal axis then all these rays diverge in such a manner that these appear to be diverging from the focal point of the mirror as shown in figure-5.70(b).

The situation slightly differs when incident rays are not parallel to principal axis. In this case also concave mirror converges these rays and convex mirror diverges these rays but the point of convergence and divergence like in a plane normal to principal axis passing through the focus of mirror as shown in figure-5.71(a) and 5.71(b).

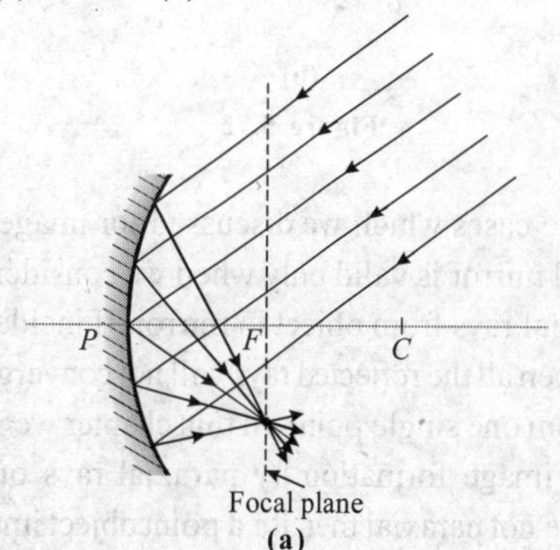

(a)

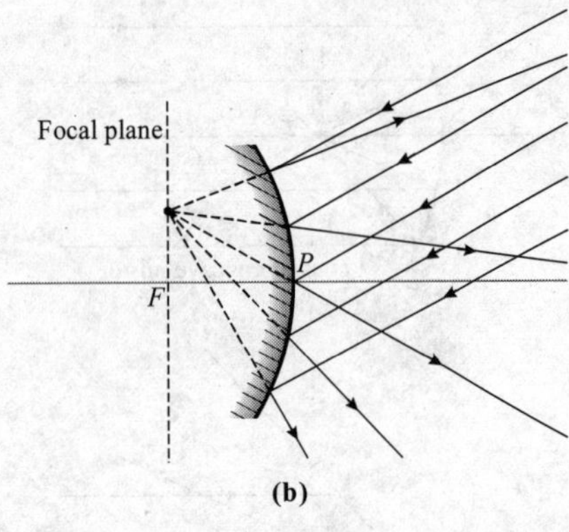

(b)

Figure 5.71

5.8.3 Image Formation by a Spherical Mirror using Paraxial Rays

It is observed that for a specific point object placed in front of a spherical mirror all the light rays incident on the mirror are reflected such that these all reflected rays converge or appear to diverge only from one point which is considered as '*Image*' of the '*Object*' produced by the mirror. Figure-5.72(a) and (b) shows images I_1 and I_2 formed by the mirrors M_1 and M_2. Here we can see that image I_1 is produced is a '*Real Image*' because reflected ray are converging and image I_2 produced is a '*Virtual Image*' because reflected rays are diverging.

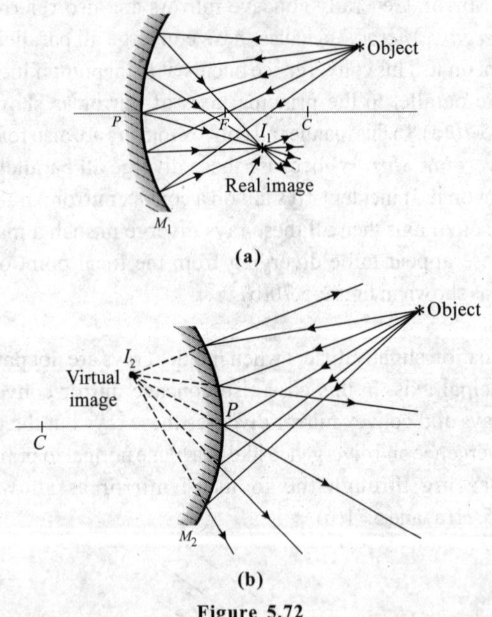

(b)

Figure 5.72

Note : Above cases which we discussed for image formation by a spherical mirror is valid only when we consider incidence of only paraxial rays from object to mirror. If incident rays are not paraxial then all the reflected rays will not converge or appear to diverge from one single point. In this chapter we will mainly consider the image formation by paraxial rays only. If rays considered are not paraxial then for a point object image formed will not be a sharp point, it will get blurred. At the end of chapter we will discuss on the defect in image formation if rays are not paraxial under the topic of spherical aberration.

5.8.4 Standard Reflected Light Rays for Image Formation by Spherical Mirrors

For understanding of image formation by a spherical mirror, we need to consider some standard light rays incident on the mirror and their corresponding reflected rays. If any two of these rays incident on a spherical mirror and their corresponding reflected rays are used then image can be obtained by finding the intersection point of the these two reflected rays as we have already discussed that all the reflected rays intersect at the same point (image) if all incident rays are paraxial. Lets discuss four standard rays used in image formation by ray diagram for spherical mirrors.

Ray-1 : Incident Ray parallel to Principal Axis

Figure-5.73(a) and (b) shows a rays incident on concave and convex mirrors which is parallel to principal axis. Such a ray after reflection passes through the principal focus of the mirror as shown. In case of concave mirror it actually passes through the focus and in convex mirror it gets reflected such that it appear to pass through its focal point in virtual space behind the mirror.

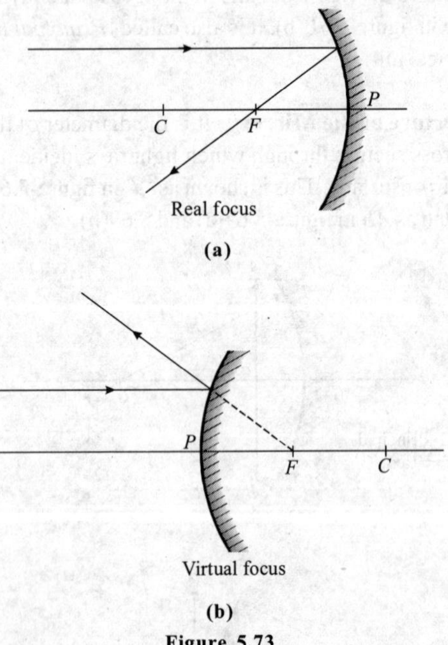

(b)

Figure 5.73

Ray-2 : Incident Ray passing through Center of Curvature

Figure-5.74(a) and (b) shows a rays incident on concave and convex mirrors which passing through center of curvature. Such a ray falls on mirror normal to its reflecting surface and gets reflected as it is and retraces the path of incident ray.

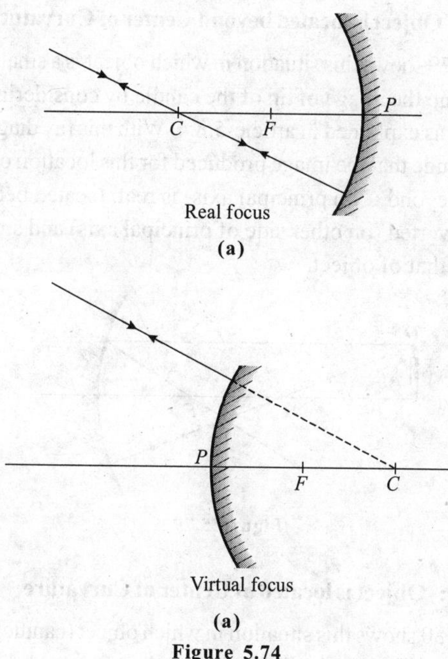

(a)

(a)

Figure 5.74

Ray-3 : Incident Ray passing through Focus

Figure-5.75(a) and (b) shows a rays incident on concave and convex mirrors which passing through focus of the mirror. Such a ray after reflection gets parallel to the principal axis of mirror as shown. In case of concave mirror light actually passes through focus and then after reflection becomes parallel to the principal axis but in case of convex mirror it incident on the mirror in such a way that it appear to pass through virtual focus of the mirror and after reflection it becomes parallel to the principal axis as shown in figure.

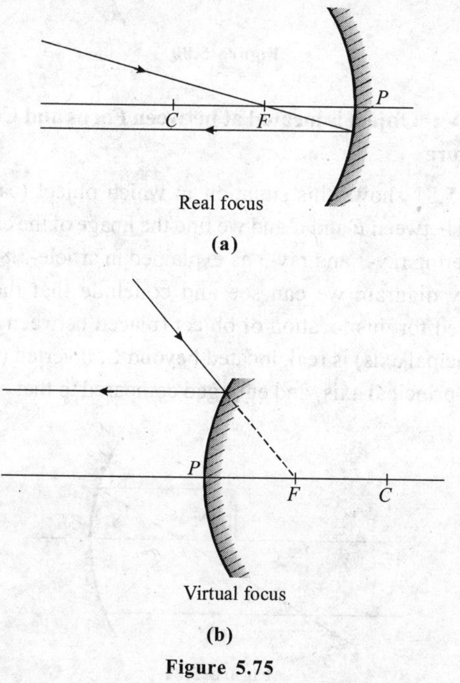

(a)

(b)

Figure 5.75

Ray-4 : Incident Ray Incident on Pole of the Mirror

Figure-5.76(a) and (b) shows a ray incident on concave and convex mirrors on its pole. At this point the mirror normal is the principal axis only so the light ray is reflected as if it is reflected from a plane mirror at the same angle from principal axis at which it incidents as shown in figure.

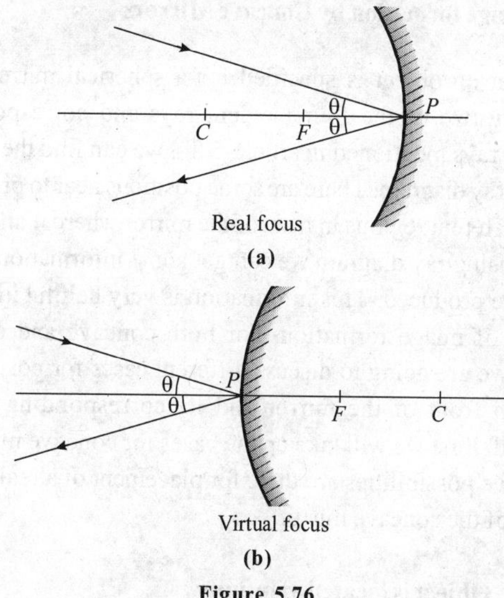

(a)

(b)

Figure 5.76

5.8.5 Relation in focal length and Radius of Curvature of a Spherical Mirror

Figure-5.77 shows a light ray which is parallel to principal axis of the mirror shown and it incident at a point A of the mirror at an angle θ to the normal (dotted line AC) at this point which passes through the center of curvature of the mirror. According to laws of reflection it will get reflected at the same angle θ and pass through a point B on principal axis as shown in figure. Now in Δ ABC we can use

$$AC = R = 2BC\cos\theta$$

$$\Rightarrow \qquad BC = \frac{R}{2\cos\theta}$$

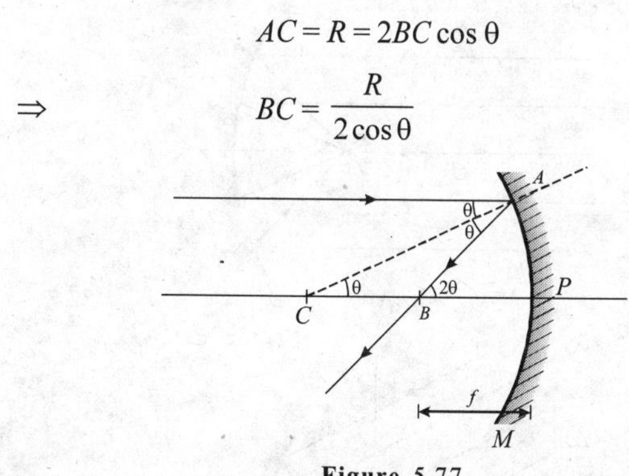

Figure 5.77

Thus focal length of mirror can be given here as distance PB so we have

$$PB = R - BC$$

$$\Rightarrow \qquad PB = R - \frac{R}{2\cos\theta} \qquad \ldots(5.9)$$

If the incident light ray is paraxial then θ will be small so we can use $\cos\theta \sim 1$ so $PB = f = R/2$. Equation-(5.9) is gives the distance PB where parallel marginal rays after reflection will intersect on principal axis. Distance PB can be considered as focal length only when incident rays are paraxial.

5.8.6 Image formation by Concave Mirrors

Whenever an object is specified for a spherical mirror then using any two of the four incident rays and corresponding reflected rays mentioned in article-5.8.4 we can find the image by using ray diagram. There are some positions near to principal axis in different regions in front of the mirror where if an object is kept, using ray diagram we can get some information about the image produced. This information is very helpful in rough analysis of image formation. For both concave and convex mirrors we are going to discuss different cases for position of object in front of the mirror and its corresponding image produced. First we will take up the cases for concave mirror in which five possibilities are there for placement of a real object in front of the concave mirror.

Case-I : Object is located at infinity

We have already discussed the case when object is located at infinity, incident rays falling on the mirror will be parallel and for parallel incident rays there are two possibilities. One is when all incident rays are parallel to principal axis when image produced is real and located at focus of the mirror as shown in figure-5.78(a) and other possibility is when these are at some angle to principal axis when image produced is real and located in focal plane as shown in figure-5.78(b). In both of these cases we have considered the image produced is highly diminished in size, real and inverted (produced on the other side of principal axis as that of object).

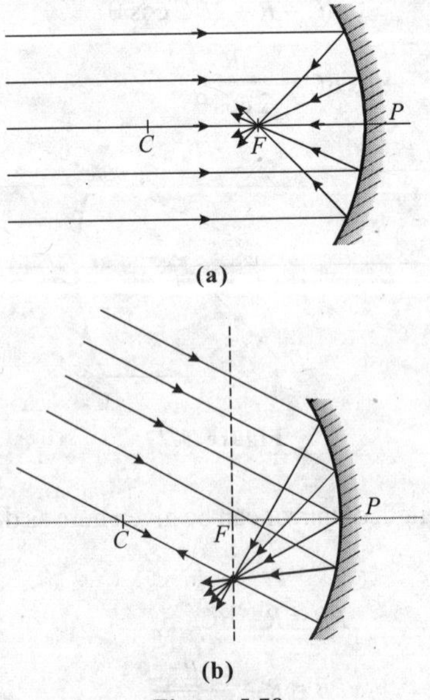

Figure 5.78

Case-II : Object is located beyond Center of Curvature

Figure-5.79 shows this situation in which object is a small candle and we find the image of tip of the candle by considering ray-1 and ray-2 as explained in article-5.8.4. With this ray diagram we can conclude that the image produced for this location of object (placed beyond C on principal axis) is real, located between F and C, inverted (on other side of principal axis) and smaller in size than that of object.

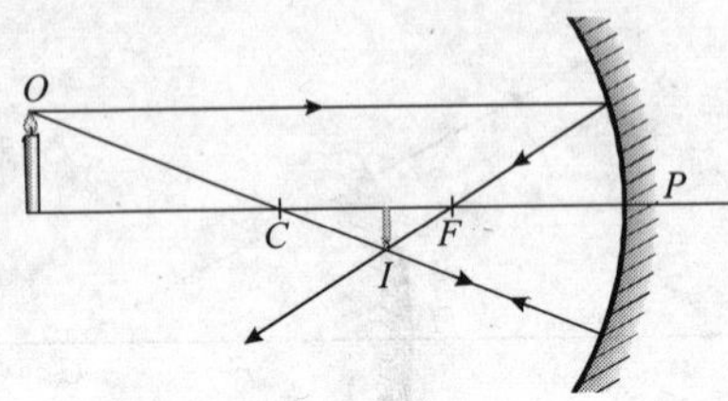

Figure 5.79

Case-III : Object is located at Center of Curvature

Figure-5.80 shows this situation in which object (candle) located at C and we find the image of the candle by considering ray-1 and ray-4 as explained in article-5.8.4. With this ray diagram we can see and conclude that the image produced for this location of object (placed at C on principal axis) is real, located at C, inverted (on other side of principal axis) and of same size as that of object.

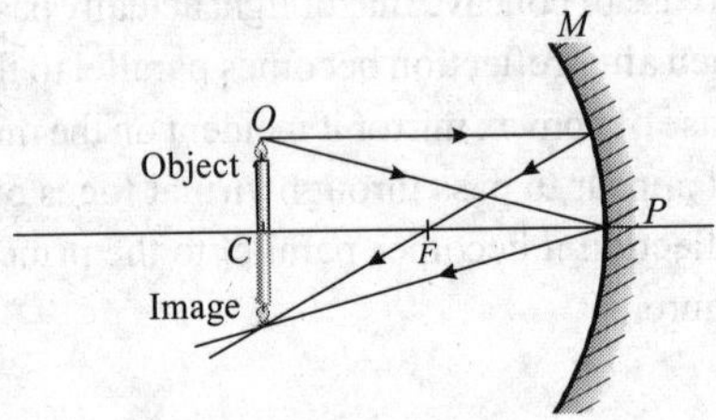

Figure 5.80

Case-IV : Object is located at between Focus and Center of Curvature

Figure-5.81 shows this situation in which object (candle) is located between F and C and we find the image of the candle by considering ray-1 and ray-3 as explained in article-5.8.4. With this ray diagram we can see and conclude that the image produced for this location of object (placed between F and C on principal axis) is real, located beyond C, inverted (on other side of principal axis) and enlarged compared to that of object.

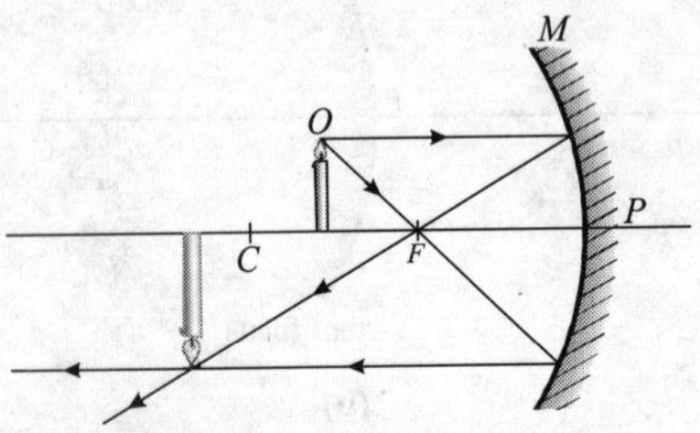

Figure 5.81

Case-V : Object is located at Focus

Figure-5.82 shows this situation in which object (candle) is located at focal point of the mirror and we find the image of the candle by considering ray-1 and ray-4 as explained in article-5.8.4. With this ray diagram we can see that the reflected rays are parallel and will produce image at infinity. So we can conclude with this diagram that image produced will be at infinity, inverted (on the other side of principal axis) and highly enlarged.

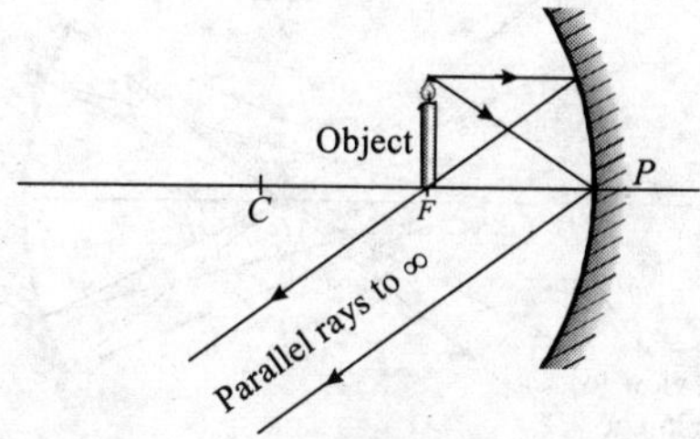

Figure-5.82

Case-VI : Object is located between Focus and Pole

Figure-5.83 shows this situation in which object (candle) is located between O and F and we find the image of the candle by considering ray-1, ray-2 and ray-4 as explained in article-5.8.4. With this ray diagram we can see that all the three reflected rays from mirror are diverging in a way that these appear to be coming from the point I behind the mirror from a virtual image. So for this location of object (placed at F on principal axis) image is produced behind the mirror, virtual, erected (on the same side of principal axis) and enlarged.

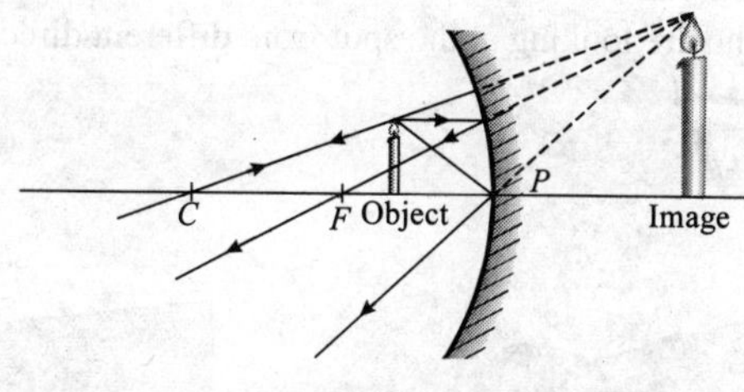

Figure 5.83

Above five cases are general cases which explains the relative position, nature and orientation of image produced by a concave mirror for a real object placed close to its principal axis using paraxial rays. While solving different questions above cases gives an idea about the estimation of image produced upto some extent before going for the exact process of image formation.

5.8.7 Image formation by Convex Mirrors

Unlike to the different cases of image formation by a concave mirror for different positions of object in front of it, in case of convex mirror there are only two possibilities of image formation for a real object placed in front of it.

Case-I : Object is located at infinity

When light rays from distant object fall on a convex mirror, these rays diverge after reflection in such a way that for incident rays parallel to principal axis image is obtained at focal point of mirror as shown in figure-5.84(a) and for incident rays non parallel to principal axis image is obtained in focal plane as shown in figure-5.84(b). The image produced will be virtual, diminished and erected (produced on the same side of principal axis where object is located).

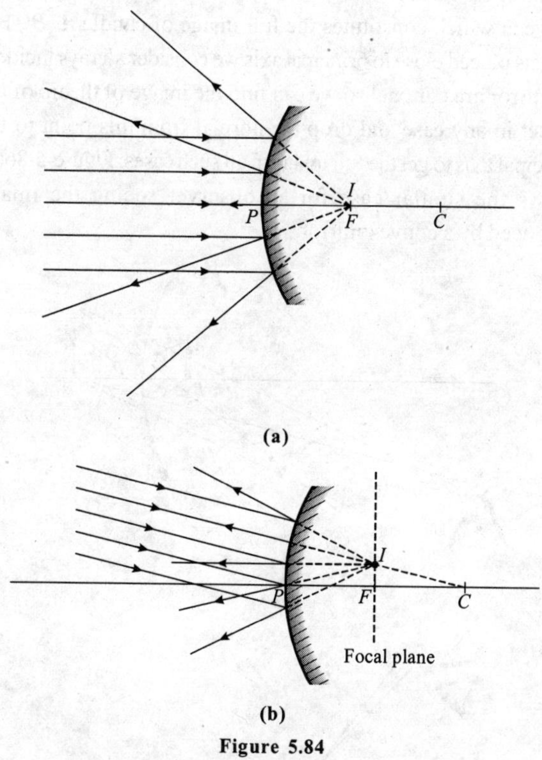

Figure 5.84

Case-II : Object is placed anywhere in front of mirror

Figure-5.85 shows a situation in which the object (candle) is placed in front of the convex mirror and to find image using ray diagram we consider ray-1, ray-2 and ray-4 as mentioned in article-5.8.4. We can see in this figure that the image is formed by back extension of the reflected rays corresponding to these incident rays from the object and the image is produced behind the mirror between F and O, virtual, diminished and erected (on the same side of principal axis as that of object).

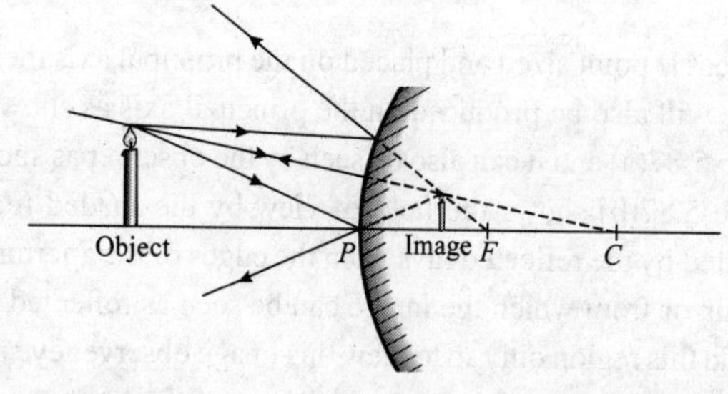

Figure 5.85

5.8.8 How an observer sees image of an extended object in a spherical mirror

Figure-5.86(a) shows an object (candle) placed in front of a concave mirror placed between its pole and focus. This we have already discussed in case-V of article-5.8.6. From the tip and bottom points of the objects AB the light rays are incident on the mirror gets reflected and falls into the eye of observer. Here observer simultaneously sees the image of top and bottom points of object as A' and B' and simultaneously for all points in between which constitutes the full image of candle $A'B'$. For objects placed close to principal axis we consider all rays incident on mirror are paraxial so we can find the image of the tip of the object in any case and drop the normal from this point to the principal axis to get the full image in all such cases. Figure-5.86(b) shows the similar case for an observer seeing the image produced by a convex mirror.

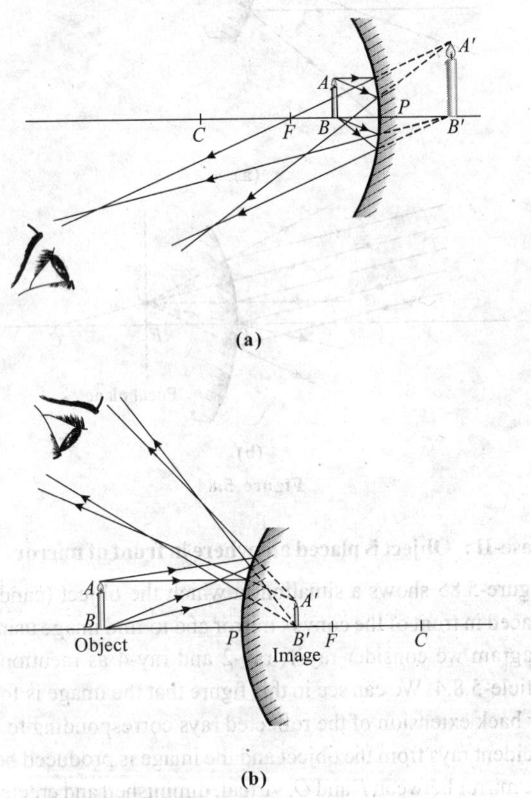

Figure 5.86

If object is point sized and placed on the principal axis then its image will also be produced on the principal axis as shown in figure-5.87(a) and it can also be seen by the observer as shown. Figure-5.87(b) shows the field of view by the shaded region bounded by the reflected rays from the edges of the aperture of the mirror from which the image can be seen as reflected rays exist in this region only so to view this image observer eye must lie in this region.

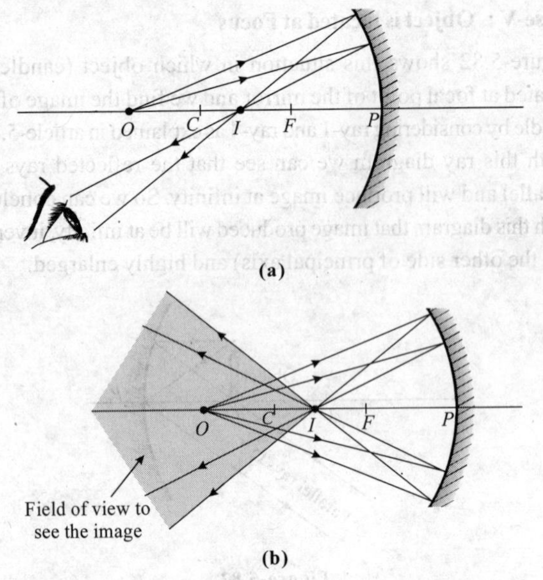

Figure 5.87

5.8.9 How image produced by a spherical mirror can be obtained on a screen

A screen is generally an opaque and rough white surface. Any point of which if light rays fall are diffused reflected in all direction from the point of screen. If a light beam falls on the screen than it makes a light spot on screen which can be seen from any direction in front of it as every point in the spot light rays are diffused reflected by screen in all directions as shown in figure-5.88. In this figure the light spot formed due to the light beam can be seen by all the observers O_1, O_2 and O_3 shown who are looking at the spot from different directions.

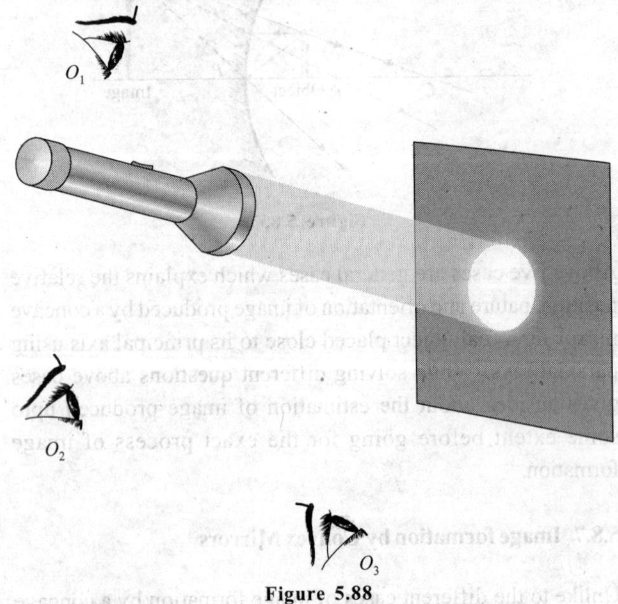

Figure 5.88

Figure-5.89 shows a case when image formed by a concave mirror for an object (point light source) is obtained on a screen.

We can see in figure-5.89(a) when screen is placed exactly at the location of image produced then all the light rays reflected from the mirror will be meeting at point I on screen and a bright and sharp image can be obtained on the screen. If we displace the screen slightly toward the mirror, sharp image will not be obtained on screen and a blurred spot is produced due to light rays falling on the screen before meeting at point I as shown in figure-5.89(b). If we displace the screen slightly behind the image then also we can see that a blurred spot will be formed on screen rather than sharp image as shown in figure-5.89(b).

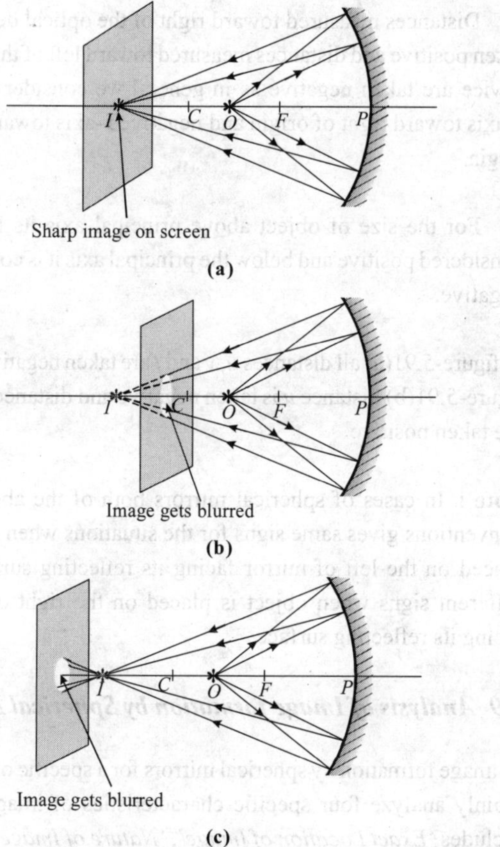

Figure 5.89

Figure-5.90 shows the formation of image of an extended object (candle) on a screen. Here in figure-5.90(a) the screen is placed exactly at the location of image in which the sharp image of candle is obtained on screen which can be seen from any direction if we look at screen. But if screen is slightly displaced along principal axis in any direction, the image will get blurred as shown in figure-5.90(b) and 5.90(c).

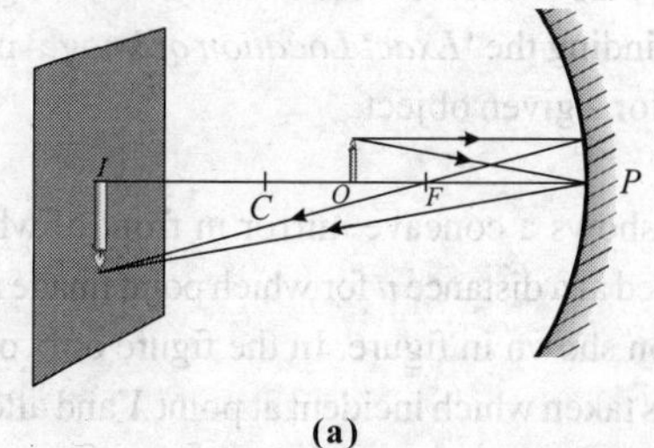

(a)

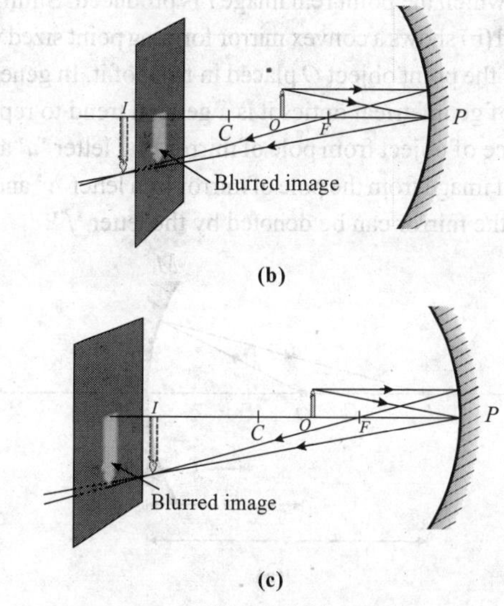

(c)

Figure 5.90

With the above analysis it is clear that sharp image can be obtained on a screen only if screen is placed exactly at the location of image. Anther fact about images obtained on screen is that only real images can be obtained on screen because real images are produced by converging rays. Diverging rays falling on a screen can only produce brightness on screen as no sharp boundaries can be made by diverging rays on any surface.

5.8.10 Sign Convention

For a given spherical mirror, object and its corresponding image may lie anywhere either in front of the mirror if image is real or behind the mirror if image is virtual. For mathematical analysis of image formation by a spherical mirror, we associate a sign convention with the given situation of mirror and in analysis of image formation all the distances of object, image, focal length or radius of curvature of mirror, we measure, will be considered with proper '+' or '–' signs according to the sign convention used.

There are several sign conventions invented in past to be used in geometrical optics for different cases of reflection and refraction. We are discussing here two sign conventions both of which are very popular for analyzing image formation in different cases of reflection and refraction. In this book we will be using the first convention however if students wish then for each case studied they can use second convention and verify that the results obtained are same. It is most important to understand and follow a sign convention properly.

First Convention : Incident Ray Reference Sign Convention

This sign convention is also called '*New Cartesian Sign Convention*'. If we look at the situation shown in figure-5.91(a). It shows a concave mirror and in front of it a point object O is placed of which the point real image I is produced. Similarly in figure-5.91(b) shows a convex mirror forming point sized virtual image I of the point object O placed in front of it. In general for any case of geometrical optics it is a general trend to represent the distance of object from pole of mirror by a letter 'u' and the distance of image from the pole of mirror by a letter 'v' and focal length of the mirror can be denoted by the letter 'f'.

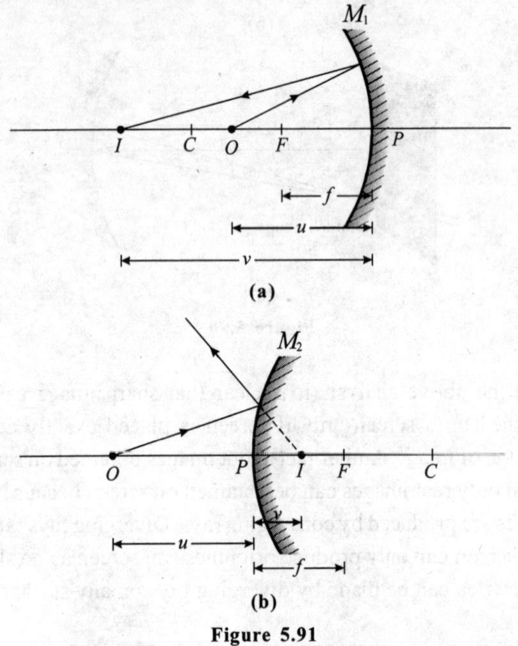

Figure 5.91

Important points of measurements about this sign convention are -

- All distances are measured from the pole of spherical mirrors.

- Distances measured in the direction (or along) of incident ray are taken positive and those measured opposite to the direction of incident ray are taken negative.

- For the size of object above principal axis its height is considered positive and below the principal axis it is considered negative.

In figure-5.91(a) all distances u, v and f are taken negative because these are measured from pole of mirror in direction opposite to the incident ray and in figure-5.91(b) distance u is taken negative and distances f and v are taken positive.

Second Convention : Cartesian Coordinate System Sign Convention

For the same situation shown in figure-5.91(a) and 5.91(b) in this sign convention we consider a simple two dimensional coordinate system associated with the given spherical mirror for all measurements of distances.

Important points of measurements about this sign convention are -

- All distances are measured from the pole of spherical mirrors.

- The origin of the Cartesian coordinate system is considered at the centre of the optical device (pole of spherical mirror in this case).

- Distances measured toward right of the optical device are taken positive and distances measured toward left of the optical device are taken negative as in general we consider positive x-axis toward right of origin and negative x-axis toward left of origin.

- For the size of object above principal axis its height is considered positive and below the principal axis it is considered negative.

In figure-5.91(a) all distances u, v and f are taken negative and in figure-5.91(b) distance u is taken negative and distances f and v are taken positive.

Note : In cases of spherical mirrors both of the above sign conventions gives same signs for the situations when object is placed on the left of mirror facing its reflecting surface and different signs when object is placed on the right of mirror facing its reflecting surface.

5.9 *Analysis of Image formation by Spherical Mirrors*

In image formation by spherical mirrors for a specific object, we mainly analyze four specific characteristics of image which includes '*Exact Location of Image*', '*Nature of Image*' (real or virtual), '*Orientation of Image*' (erected or inverted) and '*Magnification of Image*' (enlarged or diminished with exact size of image). Lets discuss all these characteristics one by one.

5.9.1 Mirror Formula for Location of Image

Mirror Formula is a mathematical relation between object distance, image distance and focal length of a spherical mirror from its pole. This formula is used in analysis of image formation and used in finding the '*Exact Location of Image*' produced by a the mirror for a given object.

Figure-5.92 shows a concave mirror in front of which a point object is placed at a distance u for which point image I is obtained at the location shown in figure. In the figure only one light ray from object is taken which incident at point X and after reflection it passes through I. The line joining point X and center of curvature of mirror C is the normal to the mirror at point X at which angle of incidence and angle of reflection is same.

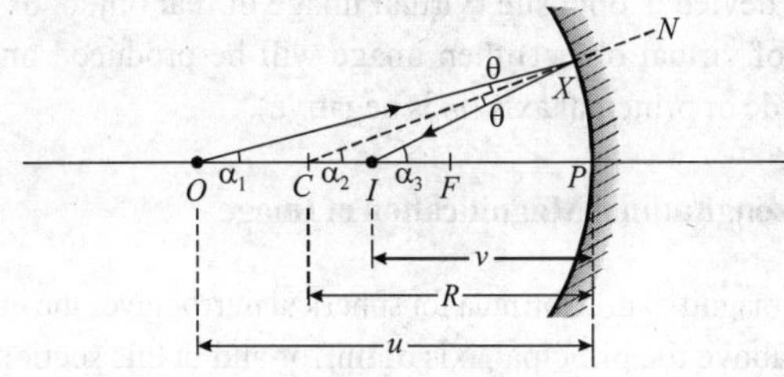

Figure 5.92

For paraxial rays in the given figure we can consider angles θ_1, θ_2 and θ_3 are very small so we can use

$$\alpha_1 = \frac{h}{u};\ \alpha_2 = \frac{h}{R} \text{ and } \alpha_3 = \frac{h}{v}$$

Now from ΔCXO we have $\alpha_2 = \alpha_1 + \theta$ and in ΔCXI we have $\alpha_3 = \alpha_2 + \theta$ and from these relations we have

$$2\alpha_2 = \alpha_1 + \alpha_3$$

Now substituting the values of α_1, α_2 and α_3 in terms of h we get

$$\frac{2}{R} = \frac{1}{u} + \frac{1}{v}$$

As $R = f/2$ we can write

$$\frac{1}{f} = \frac{1}{u} + \frac{1}{v} \qquad \ldots(5.10)$$

Above equation-(5.10) is called '*Mirror Formula*' which is valid for both concave and convex mirrors and in this relation values of u, v and f are substituted with proper signs according to any of the sign conventions stated in article-5.8.8. In this book we will use Cartesian Coordinate System Sign Convention whereas in many books New Cartesian Sign Convention is used but it hardly makes any difference from student point of view. For all the questions we are going to take up in this book, students can also try solving these questions by the first sign convention also for getting a clear picture of analysis.

Equation-(5.10) can be rearranged in three forms and used as per requirement for calculation of u, v or f as given below.

$$f = \frac{uv}{u+v} \qquad \ldots(5.11)$$

$$v = \frac{uf}{u-f} \qquad \ldots(5.12)$$

$$u = \frac{vf}{v-f} \qquad \ldots(5.13)$$

Note : It is advisable to always draw ray diagram while solving a question of reflection by a spherical mirror to get the proper understanding of the given situation and image formation by reflected light rays. Also students must note that above relations of Mirror formula is only valid for paraxial rays. Also students must note that above relations of mirror formula is only valid for paraxial rays.

5.9.2 Analyzing Nature of Image Produced by a Spherical Mirror

By mirror formula when we analyze the location of image then with the location we get a clear idea whether reflected rays are converging or diverging. If image is produced in front of the mirror then reflected rays will be converging and image produced is real and if image is produced behind the mirror then reflected rays will be diverging and image produced is virtual. Figure-5.93 shows the situation of real and virtual image formation by converging and diverging rays.

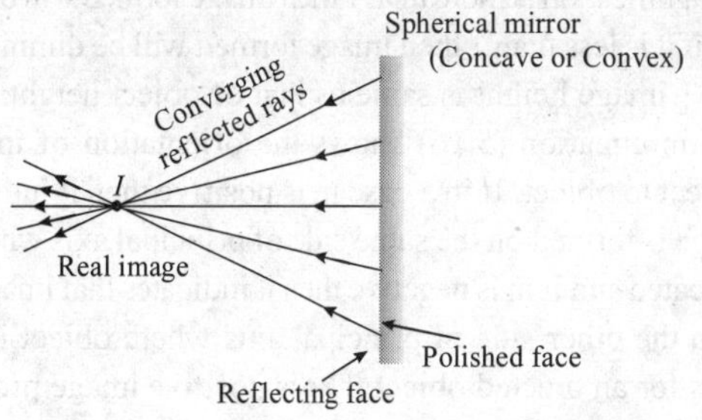

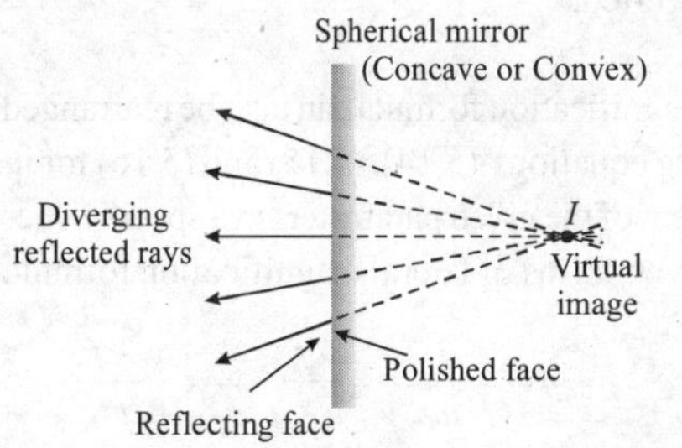

Figure 5.93

5.9.3 Magnification Formula for Size and Orientation of Image

Figure-5.94 shows the image produced for an extended object (candle) by a concave mirror. In this case we are using ray-1, ray-2 and ray-4 as mentioned in article-5.8.4 for image formation. Now in this figure if we analyze in ΔAPB and $\Delta A'PB'$ for paraxial rays we can get the relation in height of object $h_0(AB)$ and height of image $h_i(A'B')$ perpendicular to principal axis.

$$\frac{h_0}{u} = \frac{-h_i}{v} \qquad \ldots(5.14)$$

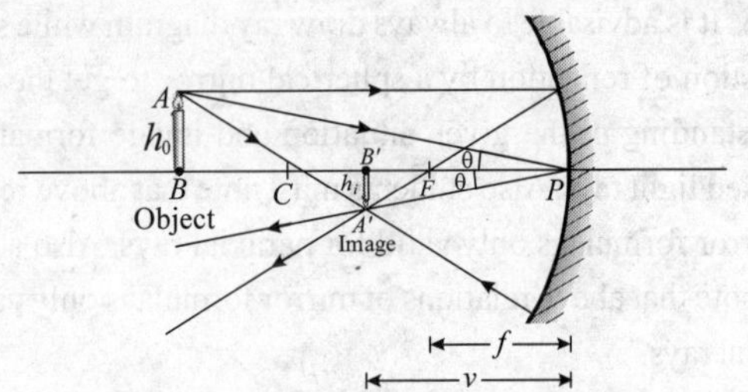

Figure 5.94

Magnification of image is given as

$$m = \frac{\text{Height of Image}}{\text{Height of Ojbect}} \quad \text{...(5.15)}$$

from equation-(5.14) we have

$$m = \frac{h_i}{h_0} = -\frac{v}{u} \quad \text{...(5.16)}$$

Equation-(5.16) is called '*Lateral Magnification*' of the image which relates the object and image height with their locations. If magnification is more than 1 then image formed will be enlarged and if it is less than 1 then image formed will be diminished. For $m = 1$ image height is same as that of object height. Negative sign in equation-(5.16) shows the orientation of image with respect to object. If in a case m is positive then it indicates that image is formed on the same side of principal axis where object is located and if m is negative then it indicates that image formed is on the other side of principal axis where object is located. Thus for an erected object if m is positive image produced by the mirror will be erected and if m is negative then image produced will be inverted.

Lateral magnification formula can also be rearranged in different ways using equations-(5.14), (5.15) and (5.16) for its uses as per requirement of the given parameters in a specific question. Below are the given forms of lateral magnification formula.

$$m = -\frac{v}{u} = -\frac{f}{u-f} = -\frac{v-f}{f} \quad \text{...(5.17)}$$

Note : As already discussed about the mirror formula that it is applicable only when paraxial rays are forming the image so the magnification formula as explained above will also be valid only when paraxial rays are in consideration.

5.9.4 Relation in Nature and Orientation of Image

For all the optical devices in geometrical optics we can find the orientation of image produced using the method explained here. This method is only using the basic geometry in finding the image orientation on principal axis.

Always remember if nature of an object and its corresponding image produced by any optical device are same (real image of real object or virtual image of virtual object) then image will be produced on other side of principal axis (m is negative) and if nature of object and its corresponding image produced by any optical device is opposite (virtual image of real object or real image of virtual object) then image will be produced on the same side of principal axis (m is negative).

5.9.5 Longitudinal Magnification of Image

Lateral magnification formula for spherical mirror gives the image height above the principal axis of mirror and in this section we will discuss on how to calculate the image width along the principal axis of mirror. The relation in object and image width along the principal axis of mirror is called '*Longitudinal Magnification*' as given below.

Longitudinal magnification of image is given as

$$m_L = \frac{\text{Width of Image along Principal Axis}}{\text{Width of Object along Principal Axis}}$$

Figure-5.95 shows image formation of an object located at a distance x from the concave mirror of focal length f which produces an image of this object at a distance y which is real inverted and enlarged because object was placed between F and C. Here we can see that object edge A was close to C so corresponding image edge A' is also closer to C. If we consider object is of very small width dx and image produced is having a width dy then from mirror formula we have

$$\frac{1}{f} = \frac{1}{x} + \frac{1}{y}$$

Differentiating this expression we get

$$0 = -\frac{1}{x^2}dx - \frac{1}{y^2}dy$$

From this relation we can get the '*Longitudinal Magnification*' as

$$m_L = \frac{dy}{dx} = -\frac{y^2}{x^2} = -m^2 \quad \text{...(5.18)}$$

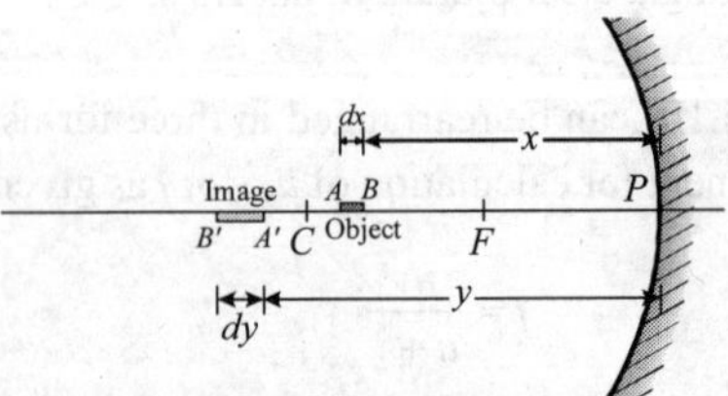

Figure 5.95

For small width object if image is produced by a spherical mirror (concave or convex) then image width can be calculated by use of the equation-(5.18). But if object size is large then this relation cannot be used and in that case we need to calculate the image of both edges of the object along principal axis and take the difference as explained in figure-5.96. Here we first need to consider the distance of edge B of the object as x_1 and find the corresponding image of this edge at B' located at a distance y_1 using mirror formula then we consider the distance of edge A of the object as $x_2 = x_1 + w_0$ and find the corresponding image A' at location y_2 using mirror formula. Now the width of image $A'B'$ can be obtained as

$$w_i = y_2 - y_1$$

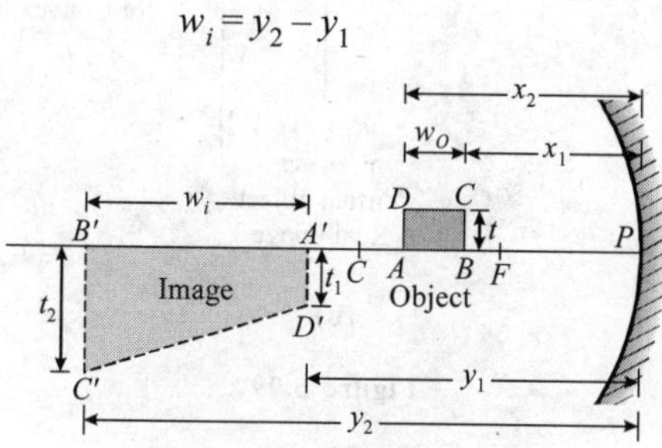

Figure 5.96

In the same manner we can find the height of the image at the edges $A'D'(t_1)$ and $B'C'(t_2)$ by separately using the lateral magnification at both the edges.

5.9.6 Superficial Magnification by a Spherical Mirror

As we have studied the lateral and longitudinal magnification, we can easily find out the magnification in area for the image produced by a spherical mirror. There are two cases in which area of image is calculated which are given here one by one. In both of these cases we are considering object size very small compared to the distance of object from the mirror.

Case-I : Object is placed normal to principal axis

Figure-5.97(a) shows a square object $ABCD$ which is placed at a point between F and C of a concave mirror at a distance u from the mirror. The image is produced as $A'B'C'D'$ at a distance v from the mirror as shown and the image will also be of square shape as both edges of the object are perpendicular to principal axis of mirror so in both we use lateral magnification and size of both will be same. Similar situation for a convex mirror is shown in figure-5.97(b)

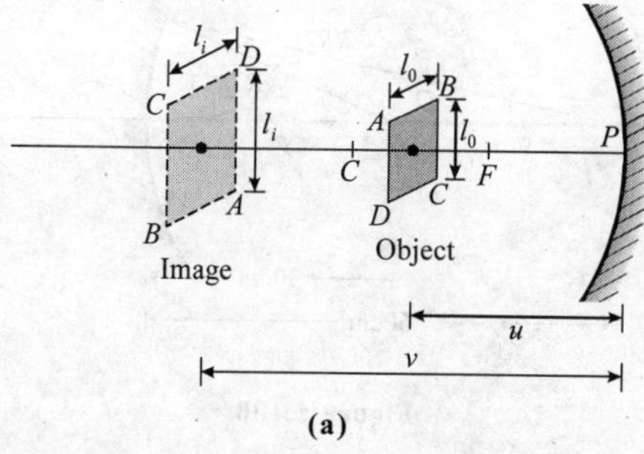

(a)

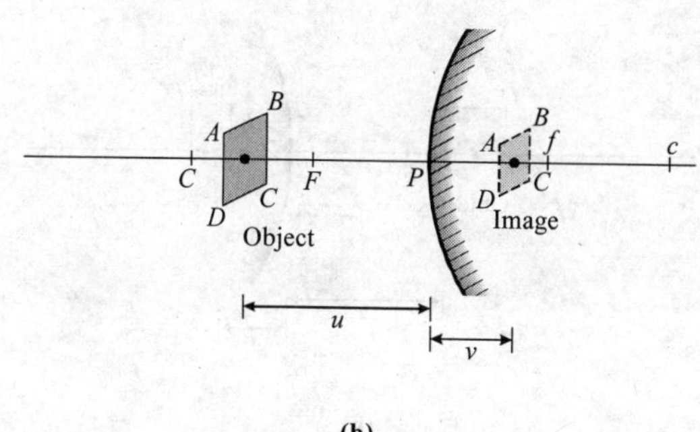

(b)

Figure 5.97

In figure-5.97(a) image edge l_i can be obtained by lateral magnification as $l_i = m\,l_0$ (where $m = -v/u$) in both sides of the square edges same l_i will be there so final image produced is a magnified square real image and similar to this in figure-5.97(b) for convex mirror image will be a diminished square virtual image.

The area of image produced is given as $A_i = l_i^2 = m^2 l_0^2 = m^2 A_0$ ($A_0 = l_0^2$ is the area of object surface)

Case-II : Object is placed in the plane of principal axis

Figure-5.98(a) shows a small square object $ABCD$ of edge l_0 ($l_0 << f$) which is placed at a point between F and C of a concave mirror at a distance u from the mirror. The image is produced $A'B'C'D'$ at a distance v from the mirror as shown and in this case the image produced will be in shape of a rectangle because for the edges BC and AD of the object which are perpendicular to the principal axis, we use lateral magnification and for the edges AB and CD which are along the principal axis, we use longitudinal magnification.

So in this case the image height and width are given as

$$h_i = m l_0$$

$$w_i = m^2 l_0$$

where lateral magnification is given as $m = -v/u$

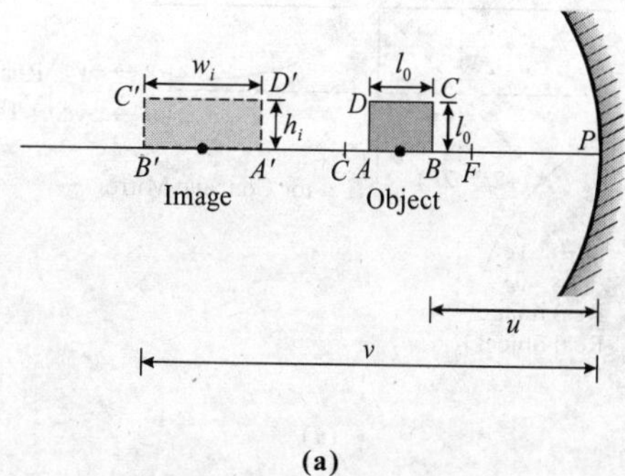

(a)

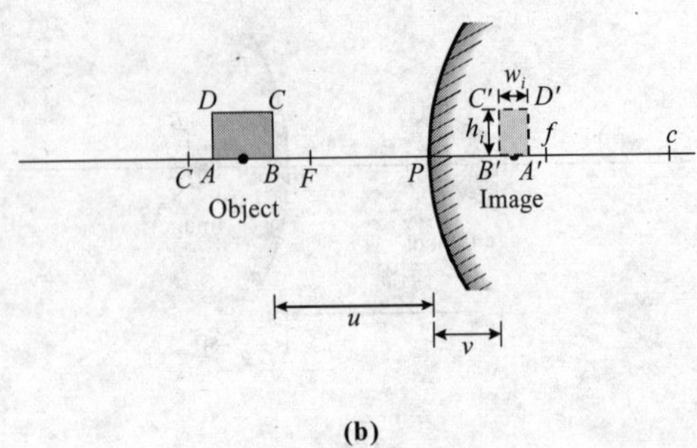

(b)

Figure 5.98

As l_0 and w_i are small we consider almost same height for image edges $A'D'$ and $B'C'$ and similar case for a convex mirror is shown in figure-5.98(b)

5.9.7 Variation Curves of Image Distance vs Object Distance

We have discussed the mirror formula which relates the image distance from pole of mirror for a given object distance. The mirror formula is given as

$$\frac{1}{f} = \frac{1}{u} + \frac{1}{v}$$

$$\Rightarrow \quad v = \frac{u}{\frac{u}{f} - 1}$$

As focal length of a given mirror is constant and it can be positive or negative depending upon the sign convention and type of mirror. The above function can be plotted as shown in figure-5.99(a) or (b) for a concave and convex mirror facing toward left along negative x direction which we generally consider.

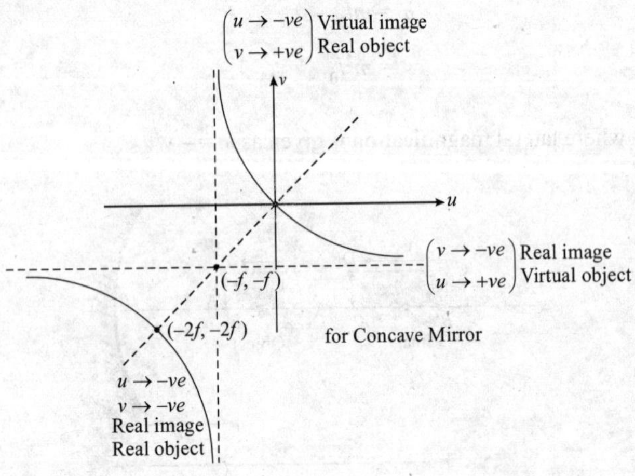

(a)

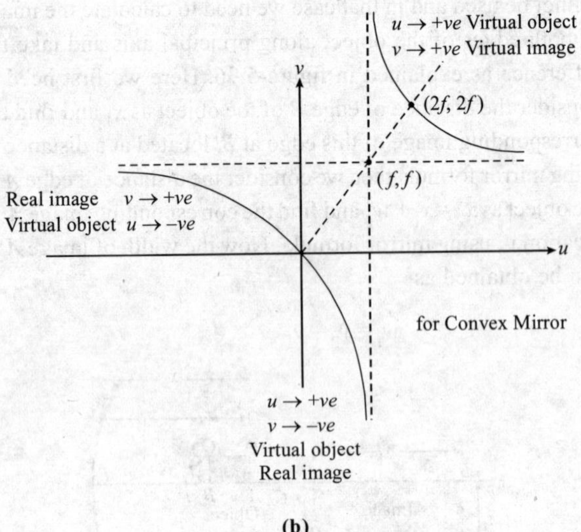

(b)

Figure 5.99

Illustrative Example 5.11

A point object is placed at a distance 30 cm in front of a concave mirror of focal length 20 cm. Find the nature and location of image obtained.

Solution

In this case for mirror formula we use

$$u = -30 \text{ cm}$$

$$f = -20 \text{ cm}$$

Using mirror formula

$$v = \frac{uf}{u-f} = \frac{+30 \times +20}{-30-(-20)}$$

$$\Rightarrow \quad v = \frac{30 \times 20}{-10} = -60 \text{ cm}$$

The image formation is shown in ray diagram and we can see that image produced is real and located at a distance of 60 cm from the pole of mirror in front of it.

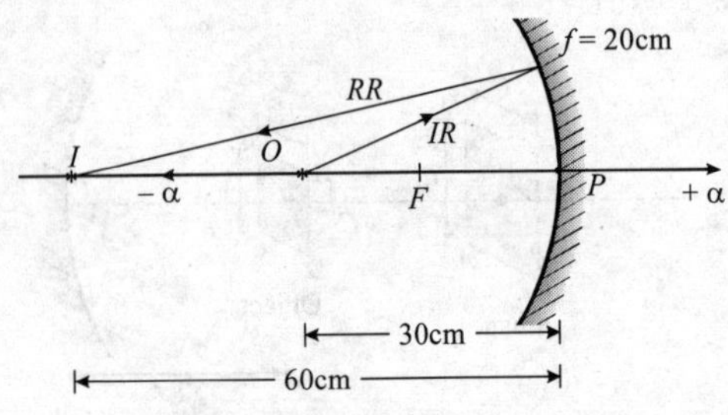

Figure 5.100

Illustrative Example 5.12

A thin rod of length $d/3$ is placed along the principal axis of a concave mirror of focal length = d such that its image, which is real and elongated, just touches the rod. Find the length of the image ?

Solution

Given that image is touching the object that means this point must be at the center of curvature of the mirror as shown in figure-5.101. The image of A is formed at the same position (since is at Center of curvature). For image of B we will use mirror formula.

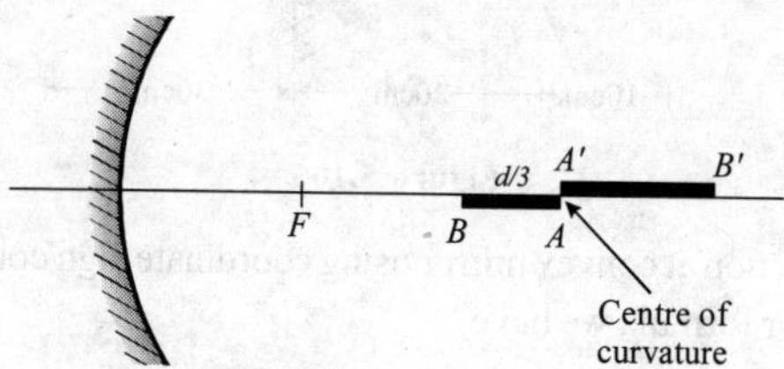

Figure 5.101

Applying mirror formula for image of B, according to cartesian coordinate sign convention, we use $u = +5d/3$ and $f = +d$

$$\frac{1}{v}+\frac{1}{u}=\frac{1}{f}$$

$$\Rightarrow \quad \frac{1}{v}+\frac{1}{\frac{5d}{3}}=\frac{1}{d}$$

$$\Rightarrow \quad v=\frac{5d}{2}$$

Hence length of image obtained is

$$A'B'=\frac{5d}{2}-2d=\frac{d}{2}$$

Illustrative Example 5.13

In figure shown find the distance from pole P of the concave mirror shown in figure-5.102, at which when a plane mirror is placed, image produced by both mirror for the object O will coincide.

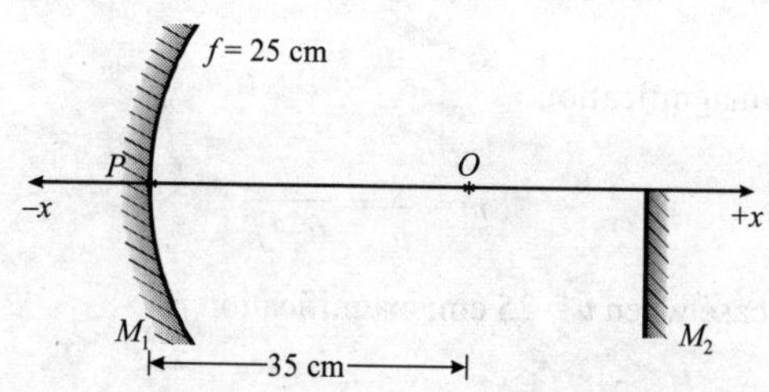

Figure 5.102

Solution

For image produced by concave mirror, by coordinate sign convention for mirror formula, we use

$$u = +35 \text{ cm}, f = +25 \text{ cm}$$

Now by mirror formula we have

$$v=\frac{uf}{u-f}=\frac{35\times 25}{10}=+87.5 \text{ cm}$$

Thus image produced by concave mirror I is located at a distance 87.5 cm from P which is at $87.5-35=52.5$ cm from the object O.

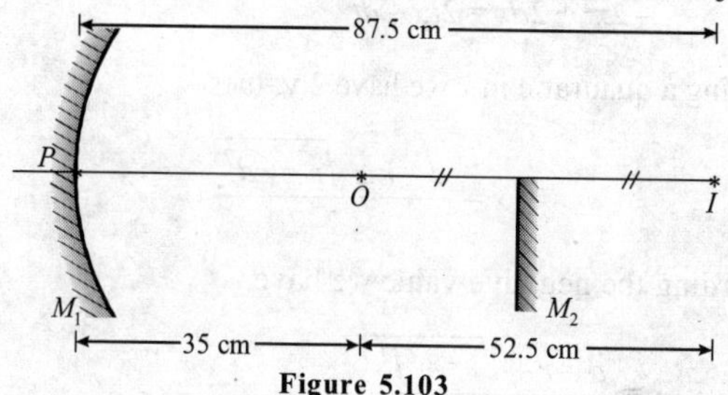

Figure 5.103

Separation between O & I is

$$= 87.5 - 35 = 52.5 \text{ cm}$$

Position of M_2 from object is at O distance

$$=\frac{52.5}{2}=26.25 \text{ cm}$$

Distance of M_2 from pole of mirror is

$$P = 35 + 26.25 = 61.25 \text{ cm.}$$

Illustrative Example 5.14

An observer whose least distance of distinct vision is 'd', views his own face in a convex mirror of radius of curvature 'r'. Prove that the magnification produced can not exceed $\frac{r}{d+\sqrt{d^2+r^2}}$.

Solution

For clear vision, the distance between object and image OI must be more than d. If in the figure shown distance OP be x then by mirror formula, we have

$$\frac{1}{v}+\frac{1}{u}=\frac{1}{f}$$

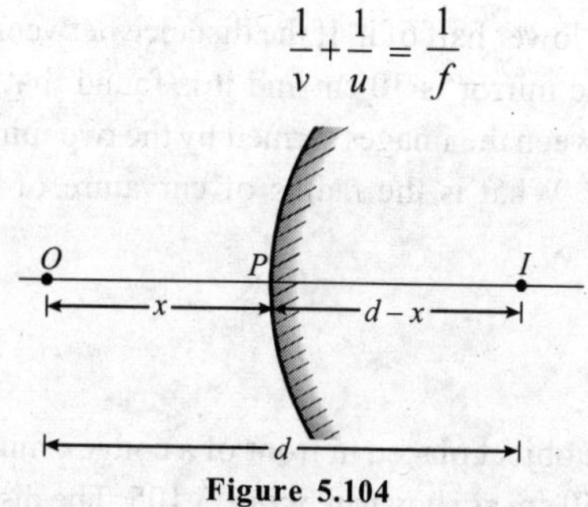

Figure 5.104

Here by coordinate sign convention, for maximum magnification we use $OI = d$, so we use

$$v = +(d-x)\,;\, u = -x;\; f = +\frac{r}{2}\ (\text{for } x > 0)$$

$$\frac{1}{d-x} - \frac{1}{x} = \frac{2}{r}$$

$$\Rightarrow \quad \frac{x-d+x}{(d-x)(x)} = \frac{2}{r}$$

$$\Rightarrow \quad -2x^2 + 2dx = 2rx - dr$$

Forming a quadratic in x we have 2 values

$$x = \frac{d-r \pm \sqrt{r^2+d^2}}{2}$$

discarding the negative value we have

$$x = \frac{d-r+\sqrt{r^2+d^2}}{2},$$

Magnification produced by the mirror is

$$m = -\frac{d-x}{x} = \frac{d+r-\sqrt{r^2+d^2}}{d-r+\sqrt{r^2+d^2}}$$

Rationalising the above equation, we get

$$m = \frac{(d+r)-(\sqrt{r^2+d^2})^2}{(d-r+\sqrt{r^2+d^2})(d+r+\sqrt{r^2+d^2})}$$

$$= \frac{2rd}{2d^2+2d(\sqrt{r^2+d^2})}$$

Thus the maximum magnification produced by the mirror can be given as

$$m_{\max} = \frac{r}{d+\sqrt{r^2+d^2}}$$

Illustrative Example 5.15

An object is placed in front of a convex mirror at a distance of 50 cm a plane mirror is introduced in front of the convex mirror covering the lower half of it. If the distance between the object and the plane mirror is 30 cm and it is found that there is no parallax between the images formed by the two mirrors for the same object. What is the radius of curvature of the convex mirror?

Solution

Let O be the object placed in front of a convex mirror M_1 at a distance of 50 cm as shown in figure-5.105. The distance of the plane mirror M_2 from the object is 30 cm. We know that in a plane mirror the image is formed behind the mirror at the same distance as the object in front of it. It is also given that there is no parallax between the images formed by the two mirrors, thus the image produced by the convex mirror is formed at a distance of 10 cm behind the convex mirror which will coincide with the image produced by plane mirror at a distance 30 cm behind at position Q as shown in figure below.

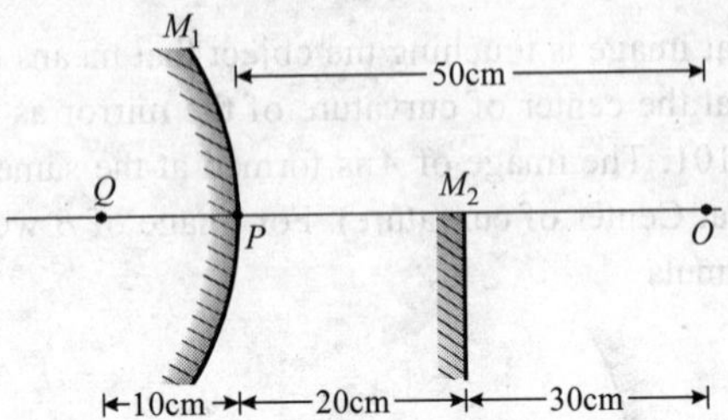

Figure 5.105

For reflection at convex mirror using coordinate sign convention for mirror formula we have

$$u = 50 \text{ cm},\ v = -10 \text{ cm}$$

Using mirror formula, we have

$$\frac{1}{f} = \frac{1}{u} + \frac{1}{v}$$

$$\frac{1}{f} = \frac{1}{50} - \frac{1}{10} = -\frac{4}{50}$$

$$f = -\frac{50}{4}$$

So radius of curvature of the mirror is

$$R = 2f = -\frac{50 \times 2}{4} = -25 \text{ cm}$$

the radius of curvature of convex mirror is 25 cm.

Illustrative Example 5.16

Using a certain concave mirror, the magnification is found to be 4 times as great when the object was 25 cm from the mirror as it was with the object at 40 cm from the mirror, the image being real in each case. Find the focal length of the mirror.

Solution

We use magnification

$$m = \frac{v}{u} = \frac{f}{u-f}$$

In first case when $u = 25$ cm, magnification is

$$m_1 = \frac{f}{25-f} \quad \ldots(5.19)$$

In second case when $u = 40$ cm, magnification is

$$m_2 = \frac{f}{40-f} \qquad \ldots(5.20)$$

As it is given that $m_1 = 4m_2$ we use

$$\frac{f}{25-f} = 4\left(\frac{f}{40-f}\right)$$

Solving we get $f = 20$ cm.

 # Illustrative Example 5.17

A concave and a convex mirror each 30 cm in radius are placed opposite to each other 60 cm apart on the same axis. An object 5 cm in height is placed midway between them. Find the position and size of the image formed by two successive reflections, consider first reflection at convex and then at the concave mirror.

Solution

The ray diagram of image formation is shown in the below figure-5.106.

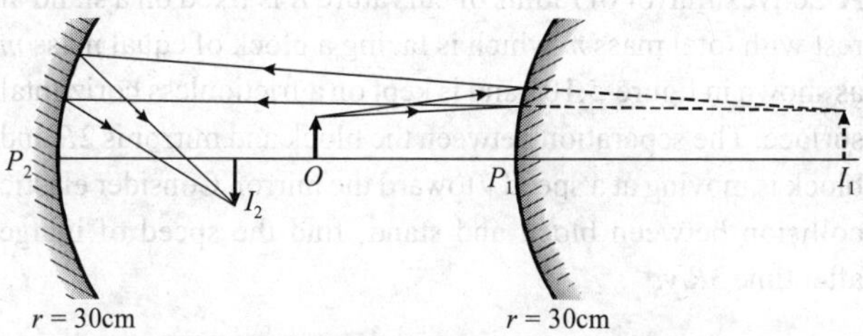

Figure 5.106

For first reflection at convex mirror, using coordinate sign convention we have for mirror formula

$$u_1 = -30 \text{ cm}, \; f_1 = +15 \text{ cm}$$

Now using mirror formula we have

$$\frac{1}{15} = \frac{1}{-30} + \frac{1}{v_1}$$

or $\quad v_1 = +10$ cm

Thus image produced will be virtual. This is formed at I_1 behind the convex mirror at a distance of 10 cm. The image I_1 acts as a real object for concave mirror because its diverging light rays fall on the concave mirror.

Now for second reflection at concave mirror, using coordinate sign convention for mirror formula, we have

$$u_2 = P_2I_1 = 60 + 10 = +70 \text{ cm}, \quad f_2 = +15 \text{ cm}$$

Now using mirror formula we have

$$\frac{1}{15} = \frac{1}{70} + \frac{1}{v_2}$$

Solving we get $\quad v_2 = \dfrac{210}{11}$ cm

Thus final image I_2 is formed in front of concave mirror at a distance of (210/11) cm and it is real.

Magnification m_1 for first reflection is

$$= \frac{v_1}{u_1} = \frac{10}{30} = \frac{1}{3}$$

Magnification m_2 for second reflection is

$$= \frac{v_2}{u_2} = \frac{(210/11)}{70} = \frac{3}{11}$$

$$\text{Final magnification} = m_1 \times m_2 = \frac{1}{3} \times \frac{3}{11} = \frac{1}{11}$$

Thus size of the final image $= 5 \times \dfrac{1}{11} = \dfrac{5}{11}$ cm.

5.9.8 Effect of Moving Object and Spherical Mirror on Image

When object or mirror is in motion the distance between object and mirror changes which affects the position and size of image. To find the image velocity and for analysis of image's motion we can differentiate the mirror formula and find the rate at which distances between object or image and mirror is changing. If we consider x and y as object and image distance from pole of mirror of focal length f then by mirror formula we have

$$\frac{1}{f} = \frac{1}{x} + \frac{1}{y}$$

Differentiating the above relation with respect to time, we get

$$0 = -\frac{1}{x^2} \cdot \frac{dx}{dt} - \frac{1}{y^2} \cdot \frac{dy}{dt}$$

Where $\dfrac{dx}{dt}$ is the relative velocity of object with respect to the mirror and $\dfrac{dy}{dt}$ is the velocity of image with respect to mirror.

$$\Rightarrow \qquad 0 = -\frac{1}{x^2} \cdot v_0 - \frac{1}{y^2} \cdot v_i$$

$$\Rightarrow \qquad v_i = -\frac{y^2}{x^2} v_0 = -m^2 v_0 \qquad \ldots(5.21)$$

Where m is the lateral magnification produced by the mirror. The expression of image speed as given in equation-(5.21) is valid only for the velocity component of the image and object along the principal axis. If the object and mirror is in motion along the direction normal to principal axis we can directly differentiate the height of object and image above principal axis which are related as

$$h_i = mh_0$$

Differentiating this with respect to time we get

$$\frac{dh_i}{dt} = m\frac{dh_o}{dt}$$

$$\Rightarrow \qquad v_{iN} = mv_{ON}$$

Here we can use $\frac{dh_i}{dt} = v_{iN}$ and $\frac{dh_0}{dt} = v_{ON}$ which are the velocity components of image and object respectively in direction normal to the principal axis.

Illustrative Example 5.18

A thief is driving away on a road in a car with velocity of 20 m/s. A police jeep is chasing him, which is sighted by thief in his rear view mirror, which is a convex mirror of focal length 10 m. He observes that the image of the jeep is moving towards him with a velocity of 1 cm/s. If the magnification of the mirror for the jeep at that time is 1/10. Find :

(a) The actual speed of the jeep.

(b) The rate at which magnification is changing.

Assume that police jeep is on axis of the mirror.

Solution

(a) The velocity of image with respect to mirror is related to velocity of object with respect to mirror is given as

$$(V_{I/m})_{\perp} = -m^2 (V_{O/m})$$

$$\Rightarrow \qquad -1 \times 10^{-2} = \frac{-1}{10^2}(V_{O/m})$$

$$\Rightarrow \qquad (V_{O/m}) = +1 \text{ m/s} = +1\hat{i}$$

Velocity of object with respect to ground is given as

$$\vec{V}_{O/G} = \vec{V}_{O/m} + \vec{V}_{m/G}$$

$$\Rightarrow \qquad \vec{V}_{O/G} = 1 + 20 = (+21 \text{ m/s})\,\hat{i}$$

(b) The magnification produced by the mirror is

$$m = \frac{f}{f-u} = \frac{1}{10}$$

If police jeep is at a distance d behind the thief's car then we can use $u = -d$ so we have

$$\frac{10}{10-(-d)} = \frac{1}{10}$$

$$\Rightarrow \qquad d = 90 \text{ m}$$

Thus distance of image from mirror is

$$v = -mu = \frac{-1}{10} \times -90 = 9 \text{ m}$$

Now rate at which magnification is changing is given as

$$\frac{dm}{dt} = \frac{u\frac{dv}{dt} - v\frac{du}{dt}}{u^2}$$

$$\Rightarrow \qquad \frac{dm}{dt} = \left[\frac{(-90)(-1\times10^{-2}) - 9(1)}{90^2}\right] \text{s}^{-1}$$

$$\Rightarrow \qquad \frac{dm}{dt} = \left[\frac{-81}{10\times8100}\right] = +1 \times 10^{-3} \text{ s}^{-1}$$

Illustrative Example 5.19

A Convex mirror of radius of curvature R is fixed on a stand at rest with total mass m which is facing a block of equal mass m as shown in figure-5.107 and is kept on a frictionless horizontal surface. The separation between the block and mirror is $2R$ and block is moving at a speed v toward the mirror. Consider elastic collision between block and stand, find the speed of image after time $3R/v$.

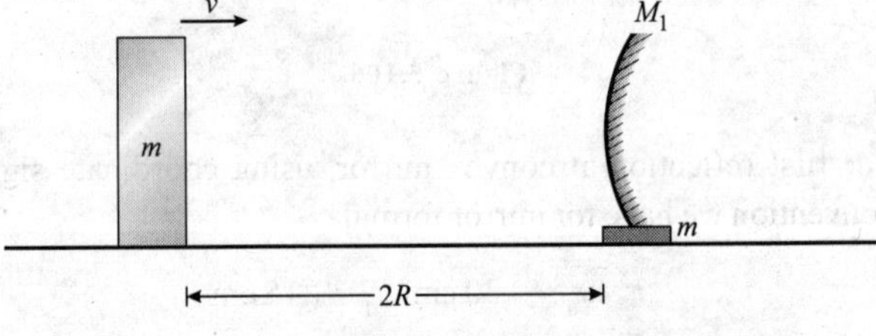

Figure 5.107

Solution

After elastic collision block will come to rest and mirror with stand starts moving at the same speed v and the collision occur at time $2R/v$ and after a further time R/v when total time elapsed is $3R/v$ the separation between block and mirror will be R and at this instant the position of image will be given by mirror formula with

$$u = -R, f = +R/2$$

Now using mirror formula we get

$$v = \frac{uf}{u-f} = \frac{-R\times(R/2)}{-R-R/2} = \frac{R}{3}$$

At this instant magnification is

$$m = -\frac{v}{u} = -\frac{R/3}{-R} = \frac{1}{3}$$

Speed of image with respect to mirror is given as

$$v_{iM} = m^2 . v_{oM}$$

$$\Rightarrow \qquad v_{iM} = \left(\frac{1}{3}\right)^2 v = \frac{v}{9}$$

Speed of image with respect to ground is $v + \frac{v}{9} = \frac{10}{9}v$

5.9.9 Effect of shifting Principal Axis of a Mirror

Figure-5.84 shows a point object and its corresponding point image produced by a concave mirror. If in this situation the mirror is displaced upward by a small distance Δx in upward direction then with mirror its principal axis will also shift as shown in figure-5.108 and in final state object will be located at a distance Δx below the principal axis of mirror. Due to this image will be displaced up and finally obtained above the principal axis at a distance $\Delta x + \Delta y$ from its initial position. Here Δy can be directly given as

$$\Delta y = m\, \Delta x$$

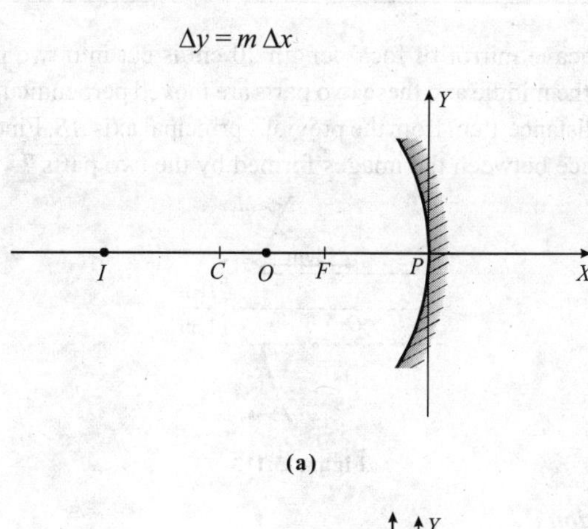

(a)

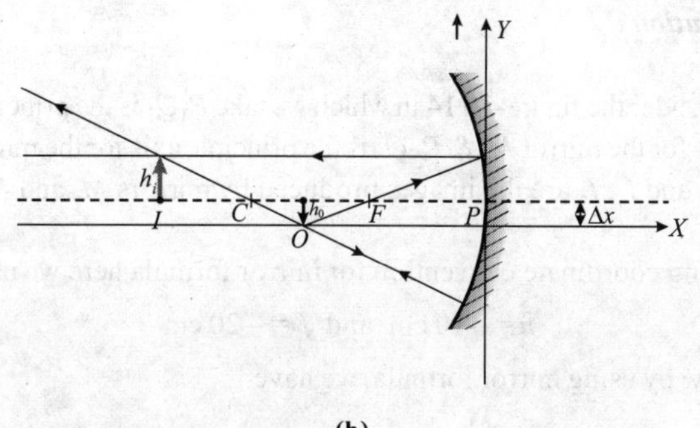

(b)

Figure 5.108

Same effect can be there on image if a spherical mirror is cut and displaced. In figure-5.109(a) a concave mirror is forming image I of an object O. If it is cut at center and the two parts M_1 and M_2 are displaced in direction normal to principal axis by a distance x as shown in figure-5.109(b) then each part of the mirror will behave like a separate mirror and produces its own separate image of the given object. Due to this cutting and displacement of mirror parts, object distance from each of principal axis of these parts has become $x/2$ and by these two mirror parts two images are produced at a distance y above and below the two principal axis in the same plane of previous image as shown in figure-5.109(b) where y is given as

$$y = \left|\frac{v}{u}\right| . x$$

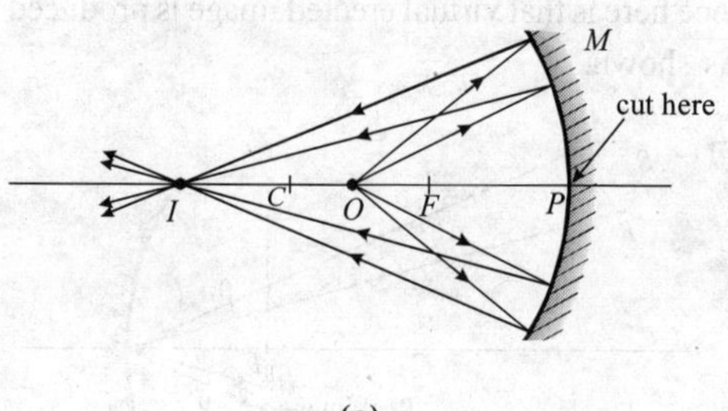

(a)

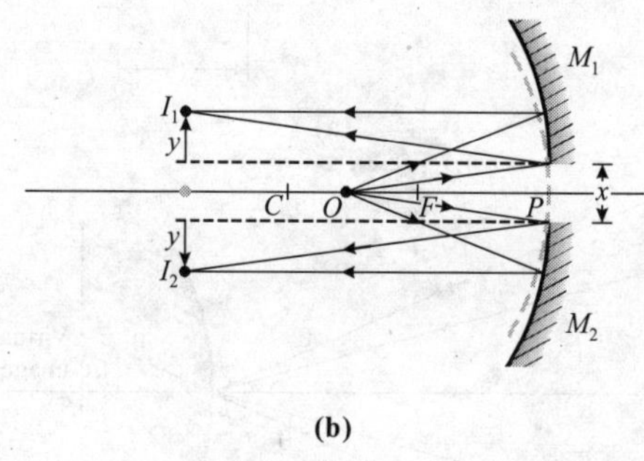

(b)

Figure 5.109

Note : If in figure-5.109(a), a small section at its center of width x is cut and removed as shown in figure-5.110 then image will remain at the same position where it was because now the two parts of mirror will behave as a single mirror with same principal axis.

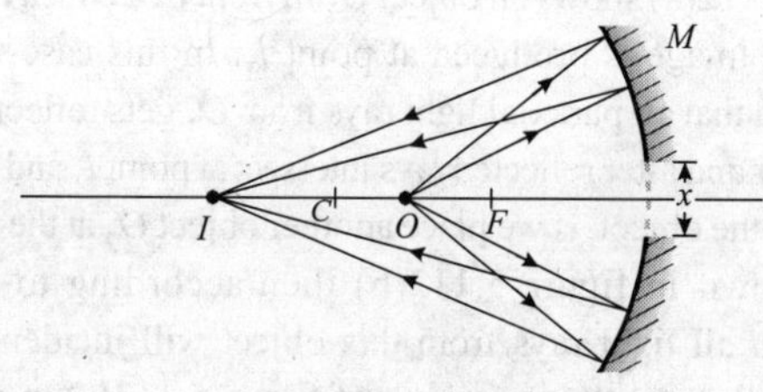

Figure 5.110

5.9.10 Image formation of distant Objects by Spherical Mirrors

For distant object, we know that a spherical mirror produces its image in focal plane. The size of image can be calculated by analyzing its angular width with respect to the pole of mirror. Figure-5.111(a) shows the formation of image of Sun by a concave mirror. S is the solar disc and here θ is the angle subtended by solar disc at any point on earth surface which will be same at the pole of mirror as shown. Here we consider two light rays from the edges of the solar disc which incident at pole of mirror at angle θ and these get reflected at the same angle and produce the real image of Sun on focal plane. Here we can see that the image produced is inverted and its diameter can be given as $d = f\theta$ as θ is a very small angle and image is obtained at a distance f from the pole. Figure-5.111(b) shows the formation of image of the Sun by a convex mirror. The only difference here is that virtual erected image is produced at focal plane as shown.

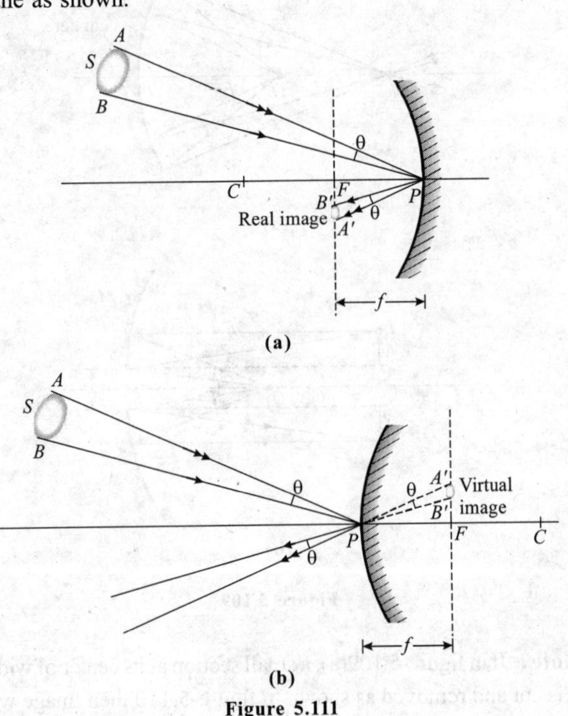

Figure 5.111

5.9.11 Concept of Reversibility of Light

Figure-5.112(a) shows an object O_1 in front of a concave mirror of which image is produced at point I_1. In this case we have discussed that all paraxial light rays from O_1 gets reflected from the mirror and after reflected rays intersect at point I_1 and produce image of the object. If we place another object O_2 at the position I_1 as shown in figure-5.112(b) then according to laws of reflection all light rays from this object will incident on the mirror following the same path of figure-5.112(a) in opposite direction and gets reflected from mirror and follow the path of incident rays of figure-5.112(a) and meet at point O_1 and produce the image I_2 at this location as shown.

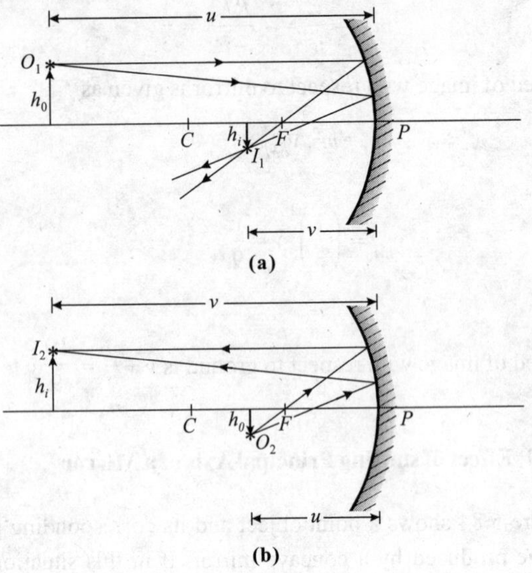

Figure 5.112

Here we can state if an object is placed at the location of image produced by a spherical mirror then for this position of object, image is produced at the location of initial object. This concept is called '*Reversibility of Light*' for image formation by mirrors.

Illustrative Example 5.20

A concave mirror of focal length 20 cm is cut into two parts from the middle and these two parts are moved perpendicularly by a distance 1 cm from the previous principal axis AB. Find the distance between the images formed by the two parts ?

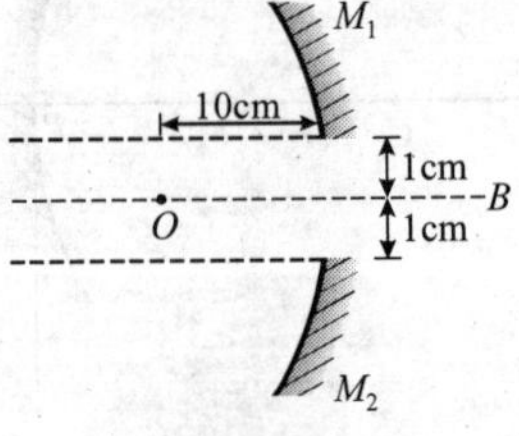

Figure 5.113

Solution

Consider the figure-5.114 in which we take P_1Q_1 is the principal axis for the mirror M_1 & P_2Q_2 is the principle axis for the mirror M_2 and I_1, I_2 are the images produced by mirrors M_1 and M_2.

Using coordinate convention for mirror formula here we use

$$u = -10 \text{ cm and } f = -20 \text{ cm}$$

Now by using mirror formula, we have

$$\frac{1}{-10} + \frac{1}{v} = \frac{1}{-20}$$

$$\Rightarrow \qquad v = +20 \text{ cm}$$

Thus image will be produced by both mirrors at a distance 20 cm behind the mirrors as v is '+ ve'. Now the magnification produced is $m = -20/(-10) = +2$ thus image will be produced on the same side of principal axis at a height 2(1 cm) = 2 cm from the principal axis.

Figure-5.114 below shows the two images I_1 and I_2 produced by the two mirrors.

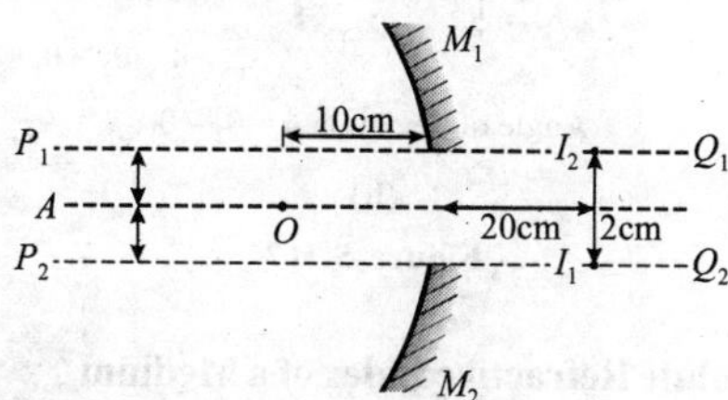

Figure 5.114

The heights of the two images are given as

h_{I_1} = 2 cm below the principal axis P_1Q_1

and h_{I_2} = 2 cm above the principal axis P_2Q_2

Thus the separation between the images is given as

$I_1I_2 = 2$ cm

Illustrative Example 5.21

An object is located at a distance 30 cm on principal axis from the pole of a concave mirror of focal length 20 cm. Suddenly the mirror is displaced by a distance 1.5 cm in the direction normal to its principal axis. Calculate the displacement of image produced by the mirror due to this.

Solution

By using coordinate convention if we consider the object to be located to the left of the mirror, we have

$$u = -30 \text{ cm and } f = -20 \text{ cm}$$

By mirror formula we use

$$u = \frac{vf}{v-f} = \frac{-30\times-20}{-10} = -60 \text{ cm}$$

$$\text{Magnification is } m = -\frac{v}{u} = -\frac{-60}{-30} = -2$$

If mirror is displaced up by a distance 1.5 cm then object distance from principal axis of the mirror becomes 1.5 cm and the new position of image will be at a height –2 (1.5) = – 3 cm from the principal axis which was earlier produced on principal axis.

Thus displacement of image is 3 cm.

<u>Web Reference at www.physicsgalaxy.com</u>

Age Group - High School Physics | Age 17-19 Years
Section - OPTICS
Topic - Geometrical Optics I - Reflection of Light
Module Number - 24 to 40

Practice Exercise 5.2

(i) Find the distance from a convex mirror, of focal length 60 cm where an object of height 12 cm should be placed so that its image is produced at 35 cm from mirror. Also find the height of image.

[– 84 cm, 5 cm]

(ii) A 2cm high object is placed on the principal axis of a concave mirror at a distance 12 cm from the pole of mirror. Find the location of the image and focal length of mirror if the image height is 5 cm and it is inverted.

[30 cm, 8.6 cm]

(iii) A point object on the principal axis of a concave mirror of focal length 20 cm, is moving at a speed of 5 cm/s at an angle 45° to the principal axis as shown in figure-5.115. Initially object is located at a distance of 25 cm from the pole of mirror. Find the velocity components of image along and normal to principal axis at this instant.

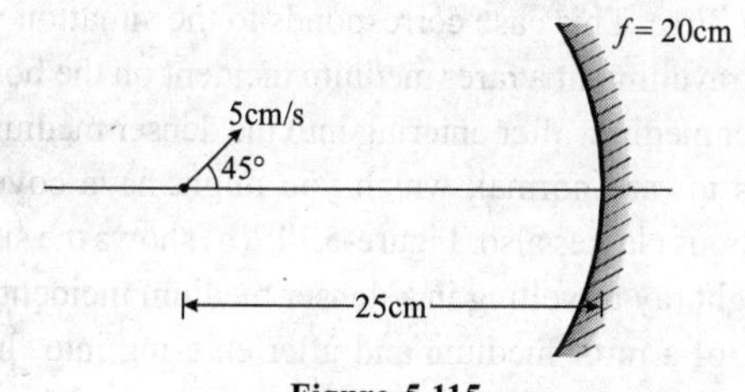

Figure 5.115

[$40\sqrt{2}$ cm/s, $10\sqrt{2}$ cm/s]

(iv) A man uses a concave mirror for shaving and sees his 2 times enlarged image in mirror when his face is at a distance 40 cm from mirror. Find focal length of mirror.

[80 cm]

(v) A 2 cm high object is placed on the principal axis of a concave mirror at a distance of 12 cm from the pole. If the image is inverted, real and 5 cm high, find the focal length of mirror. If the object starts moving at a speed of 1.2 cm/s toward the mirror find the speed of image and its direction of motion.

[7.5 cm/s]

(vi) Figure-5.116 shows two spherical mirrors M_1 and M_2 on same optical axis at a separation of 50 cm. A point object O is placed midway between mirrors on optical axis. Find location & nature of its image after two successive reflections first at M_1 then at M_2.

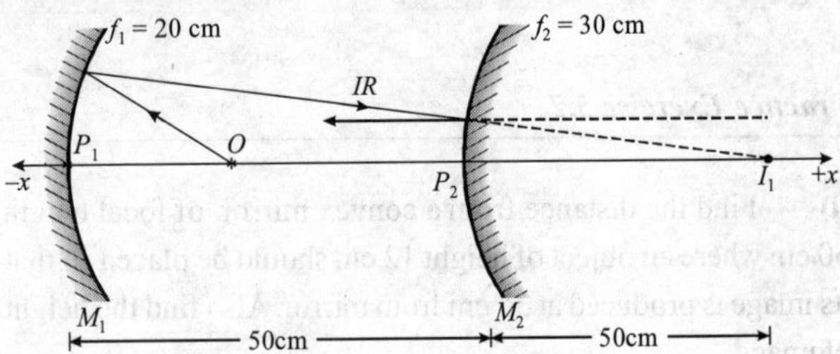

Figure 5.116

[75 cm]

5.10 Refraction of Light

Whenever a light ray is incident on the boundary of two different media, a part of it is transmitted into the second medium and whenever a light enters in a transparent medium, it suffers a sudden change in velocity of light which we call refraction of light. In the process of refraction the direction of propagation of light ray changes if it incidents on the surface at some angle of incidence to the normal to boundary as shown in figure-5.117(a). This case corresponds to the situation when a light ray travelling in a rarer medium incident on the boundary of a denser medium after entering into the denser medium light ray bends toward normal, which you might have covered in your previous classes also. Figure-5.117(b) shows the situation when a light ray travelling in a denser medium incident on the boundary of a rarer medium and after entering into the rarer medium light ray bends away from the normal as shown.

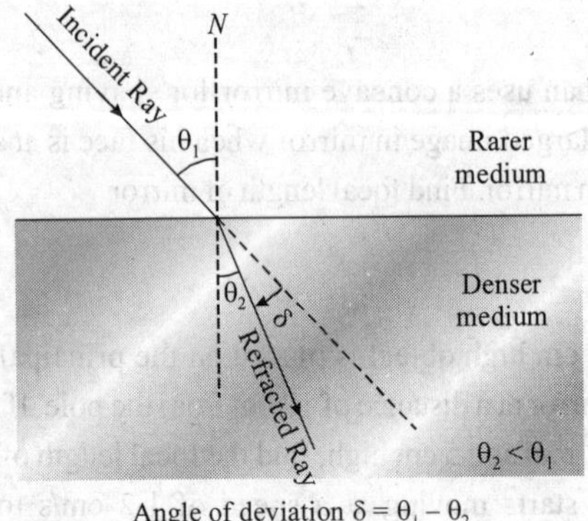

Angle of deviation $\delta = \theta_1 - \theta_2$

(a)

Angle of deviation $\delta = \theta_2 - \theta_1$

(b)

Figure 5.117

5.10.1 Absolute Refractive Index of a Medium

When a light ray enters a medium then how its speed changes is measured by '*Refractive Index*' of the medium. It is defined as the ratio of speed of light in the medium to the speed of light in free space and this is also called absolute refractive index of the medium.

Absolute Refractive Index of a Medium

$$= \frac{\text{Speed of Light in free Space}}{\text{Speed of Light in the Medium}}$$

$$\mu = \frac{c}{v} \qquad \ldots(5.22)$$

Where c is the speed of light in free space and v is the speed of light in the given medium. Thus the medium in which light travels faster has lower refractive index and is called '*Rarer Medium*' compared to another medium in which light travels slower and has higher refractive index which is called '*Denser Medium*'.

5.10.2 Relative Refractive Index of a Medium

Many time refractive index of a medium is specified as relative refractive index with respect to another medium. This can be defined by the relation similar to equation-(5.22). Relative refractive index of a medium-1 with respect to another medium-2 is given as

Relative R. I of medium-1 with respect to medium-2

$$= \frac{\text{Speed of Light in Medium-2}}{\text{Speed of Light in Medium-1}}$$

$$_2\mu_1 = \frac{v_2}{v_1} \qquad \ldots(5.23)$$

Here $_2\mu_1$ is the way how we denote refractive index of medium-1 with respect to medium-2. So if we define refractive index of medium-2 with respect to medium-1, we write

$$_1\mu_2 = \frac{1}{_2\mu_1} = \frac{v_1}{v_2} = \frac{\mu_2}{\mu_1}$$

Here for the two media if their absolute refractive indices are taken as μ_1 and μ_2 we can write $\mu_1 = \frac{c}{v_1}$ and $\mu_2 = \frac{c}{v_2}$.

5.10.3 Laws of Refraction

When a light ray propagates through an interface of two different media then its behaviour is governed by certain laws called laws of refraction which are also known as '*Snell's Laws*'. There are two laws of refraction which are described here.

First Law of Refraction : In the refraction of a light ray at a medium interface the incident ray, refracted ray and normal to the interface lie in same plane called '*Plane of Incidence*' on the medium interface. Figure-5.118(a) shows the incident ray, refracted ray and normal and in this figure the plane of paper is considered as plane of incidence. Figure-5.118(b) shows a perspective view of the refraction of the same light ray in which plane of incidence is shown by the grey shaded plane which makes the understanding better.

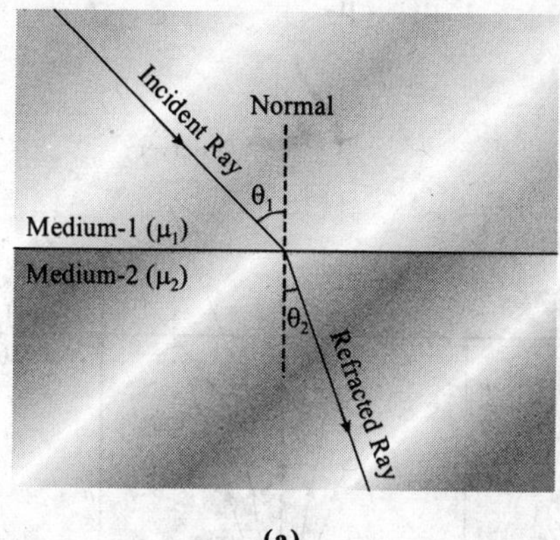

(a)

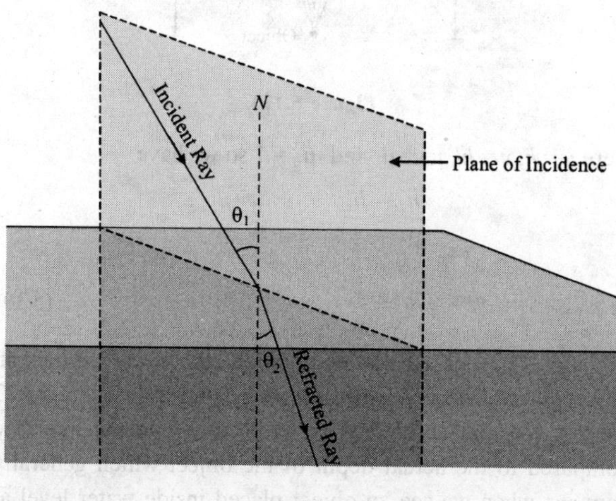

(b)

Figure-5.118

Second Law of Refraction : For the situation shown in figure-5.118(a) for the refraction of light ray going from medium-1 to medium-2 the product of refractive index of the medium and the sine of the angle made by the light ray with normal in that medium remain constant. In this case we have

$$\mu_1 \sin\theta_1 = \mu_2 \sin\theta_2 = \text{Constant} \qquad \ldots(5.24)$$

Even for several media separated by parallel interfaces as shown in figure-5.119, the same relation holds valid.

(1) $\sin\theta_0 = \mu_1 \sin\theta_1 = \mu_2 \sin\theta_2 = \mu_3 \sin\theta_3 = \mu_4 \sin\theta_4 = \ldots$ = constant

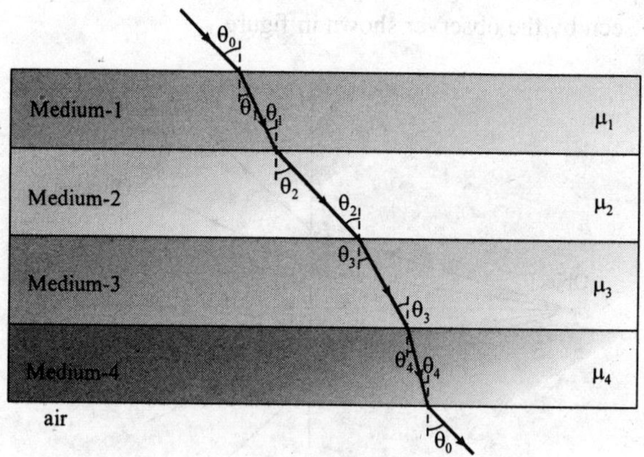

Figure-5.119

As shown in above figure we can see that for parallel interfaces when light comes out in air again it comes out at the same angle θ_0 and emerges out parallel to the incident ray.

5.10.4 Vector form of Snell's Law of Refraction

The second law of refraction relates the refractive index and the angle light ray makes with the normal in that medium. The angle can be expressed by using unit vectors in the direction of incident ray, refracted ray and normal to the boundary. If in figure-5.120 we consider unit vectors $\hat{i}$, $\hat{r}$ and $\hat{n}$ along the direction of incident ray, refracted ray and normal as shown then the equation-(5.25) can be written as

$$\mu_1(\hat{i} \times \hat{n}) = \mu_2(\hat{r} \times \hat{n}) \qquad \ldots(5.25)$$

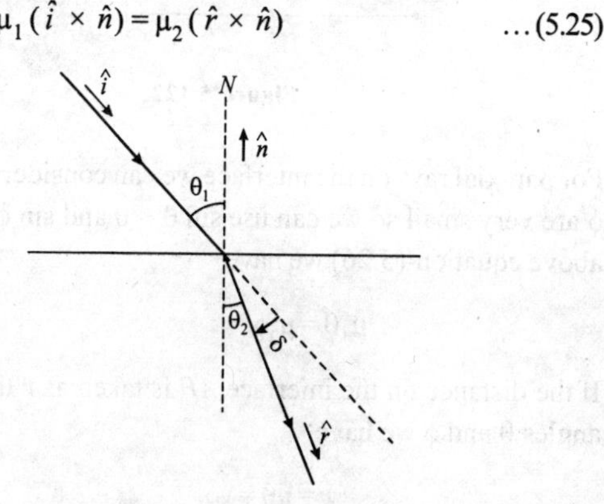

Figure 5.120

Above equation-(5.25) is used for analyzing law of refraction in vector analysis whenever in different questions light rays are specified in vector form or vectors are given along the direction of incident and reflected rays.

5.10.5 Image Formation due to Refraction at a Plane Surface

When all light rays from an object falling on the plane interface of two different media as shown in figure-5.121 these all rays are refracted in such a way that after refracting these rays will appear to be coming from a point *I* which is the image of object as seen by the observer shown in figure.

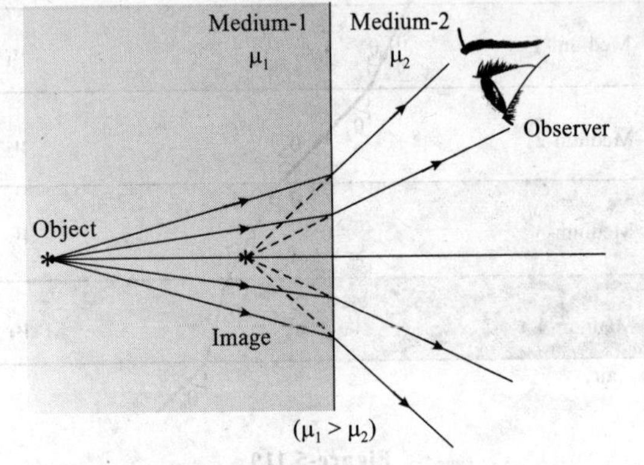

Figure 5.121

If we consider a specific paraxial ray from object incident as shown in figure-5.122 which incident on the interface at an angle θ and gets refracted at angle ϕ then by Snell's law we can write

$$\mu_1 \sin\theta = \mu_2 \sin\phi \quad \text{...(5.26)}$$

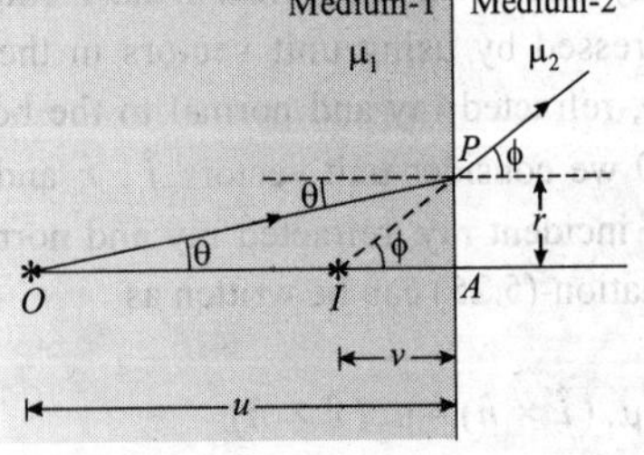

Figure 5.122

For paraxial rays on the interface we can consider angles θ and ϕ are very small so we can use $\sin\theta \sim \theta$ and $\sin\phi \sim \phi$ so from above equation-(5.26) we have

$$\mu_1\theta = \mu_2\phi \quad \text{...(5.27)}$$

If the distance on the interface *AP* is taken as *r* then for small angles θ and ϕ we have

$$r = u\theta = v\phi \quad \text{...(5.28)}$$

Dividing equation-(5.28) by equation-(5.27) we get

$$\frac{u}{\mu_1} = \frac{v}{\mu_2} \quad \text{...(5.29)}$$

Equation-(5.29) is called as refraction formula for image formation by refraction of light at plane surfaces. Whenever an object is placed at a distance *u* from a plane interface of two transparent media then the image of object as seen from the other media will appear at a distance *v* as shown in figure-5.121 which can be obtained by using this formula given in equation-(5.29) and this image distance is also called '*Apparent Depth*' of the object.

5.10.6 An Object placed in a Denser Medium is seen from Air

Figure-5.123 shows an object placed in water (denser medium) having refractive index μ and it is seen by an observer from air. If object is placed at a depth *h* below the air-water interface then the image of the object is seen by the observer at a depth *h'* (apparent depth) given by refraction formula as

$$\frac{u}{\mu_1} = \frac{v}{\mu_2}$$

Figure 5.123

Here $u = h$, $v = h'$, $\mu_1 = \mu$ and $\mu_2 = 1$ so we have

$$\frac{h}{\mu} = \frac{h'}{1}$$

$$\Rightarrow \qquad h' = \frac{h}{\mu} \quad \text{...(5.30)}$$

Equation-(5.30) is the relation used for '*Apparent Depth*' of an object placed in a denser medium seen from air. In figure-5.123 we can see that object appear to be closer to the interface compared to the actual depth of the object which generally happens when we see an object placed inside water level at some depth. The shift of object due to refraction can also be calculated and given as

$$\text{Shift} \qquad \Delta S = h - \frac{h}{\mu} = h\left(1 - \frac{1}{\mu}\right) \quad \text{...(5.31)}$$

Above equation-(5.30) and equation-(5.31) are valid only for paraxial rays. In case of plane surface we consider it only for observation of object along the normal or with the light rays at near normal incidence.

5.10.7 An Object placed in Air and seen from a Denser Medium

Figure-5.124 shows an object placed in air having refractive and it is seen by an observer from water (denser medium) with refractive index μ. If object is placed at a depth h above the air-water interface then the image of the object is seen by the observer at a depth h' (apparent depth) given by refraction formula as

$$\frac{u}{\mu_1} = \frac{v}{\mu_2}$$

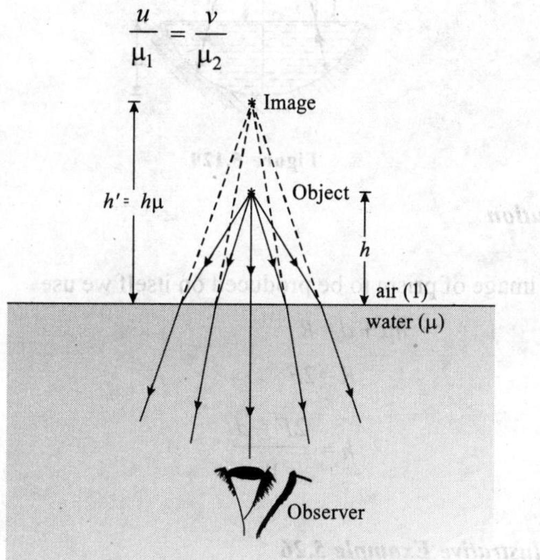

Figure 5.124

Here $u = h$, $v = h'$, $\mu_1 = 1$ and $\mu_2 = \mu$ so we have

$$\frac{h}{1} = \frac{h'}{\mu}$$

$$\Rightarrow \quad h' = \mu h \quad \dots (5.32)$$

Equation-(5.32) is the relation used for '*Apparent Depth*' of an object placed in air as seen from a denser medium. In figure-5.95 we can see that object appear to be displaced farther away from the interface compared to the actual depth of the object this generally happens when an underwater diver sees an object placed outside in air level at some height above the water level, the object appear to be further away from water level compared to its actual height. The shift of object due to refraction can also be calculated and given as

$$\text{Shift} \quad \Delta S = \mu h - h = h(\mu - 1) \quad \dots (5.33)$$

In this case also above equation-(5.32) and equation-(5.33) are also valid only for paraxial rays as these are obtained by the refraction formula which we derived using light rays with small angle of incidence or near normal incidence.

Illustrative Example 5.22

A converging beam of light rays incident on a glass-air interface as shown in figure-5.125. Find where these rays will meet after refraction.

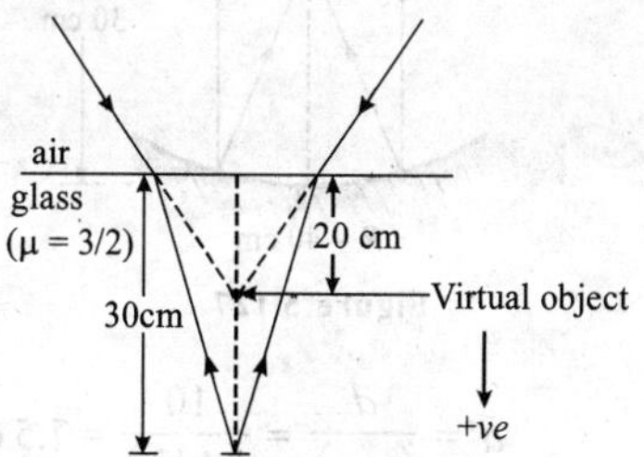

Figure 5.125

Solution

For plane surface we can use refraction formula as

$$\mu_1 = 1$$

$$\mu_2 = \frac{5}{2}$$

$$u = +20$$

$$\frac{\mu_1}{u} = \frac{\mu_2}{v}$$

$$\Rightarrow \quad \frac{1}{20} = \frac{3/2}{v}$$

$$\Rightarrow \quad v = +30\text{ cm}$$

Illustrative Example 5.23

A concave mirror is placed inside water with its shining surface upwards and principal axis vertical as shown in figure-5.126. Rays are incident parallel to the principal axis of the concave mirror. Find the position of the final image.

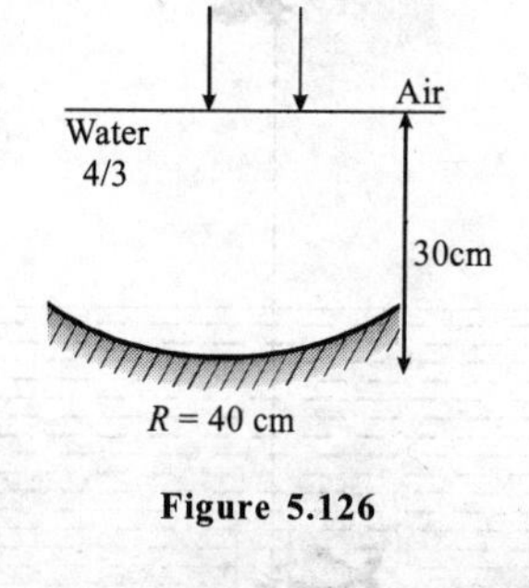

Figure 5.126

Solution

The incident rays will pass undeviated through the water surface and strike the mirror parallel to its principal axis. Therefore for the mirror, object is at ∞ its image A (in figure-5.127) will be formed at focus which is 20 cm from the mirror. Now for the interface between water and air, $d = 10$ cm

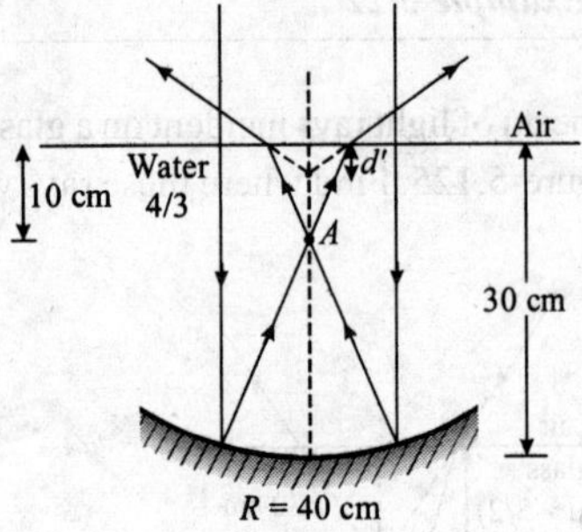

Figure 5.127

$$\Rightarrow \qquad d' = \frac{d}{\left(\frac{n_w}{n_a}\right)} = \frac{10}{\left(\frac{4/3}{1}\right)} = 7.5 \text{ cm}$$

Illustrative Example 5.24

A bird in air is diving vertically over a tank with speed 6 cm/s. The base of the tank is silvered. The fish in the tank is rising upward along the same line with speed 4 cm/s. (Take: $\mu_{water} = 4/3$). Find :

(a) The speed of the image of the fish as seen directly by the bird.

(b) The speed of the image of the bird relative to the fish looking upwards.

Solution

(a) Velocity of fish in air $= 4 \times \frac{3}{4} = 3 \uparrow$

Velocity of fish w.r.t. bird $= 3 + 6 = 9 \uparrow$

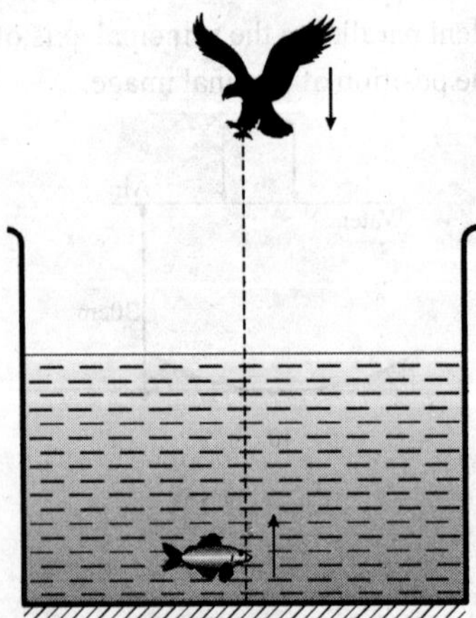
Figure 5.128

(b) Velocity of bird in water $= 6 \times \frac{4}{3} = 8 \downarrow$

w.r.t. fish $= 8 + 4 = 12 \downarrow$

Illustrative Example 5.25

Figure-5.129 shows a concave mirror of focal length F with its principal axis vertical. In mirror a transparent liquid of refractive index μ is filled upto height d. Find where on axis of mirror a pin should be placed so that its image will be formed on itself.

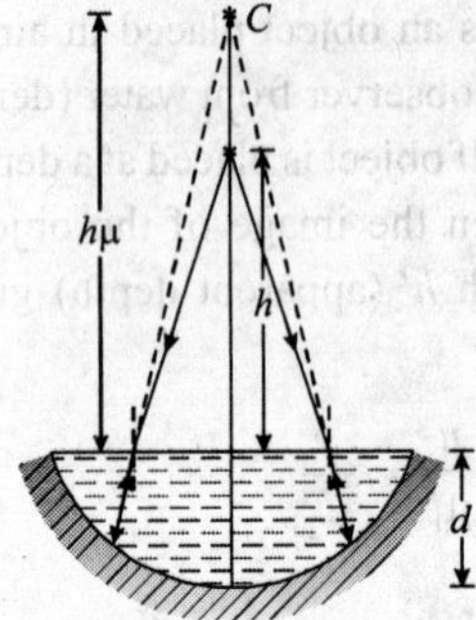

Figure 5.129

Solution

For image of prism to be produced on itself we use

$$h\mu + d = R$$

$$R = 2F$$

$$h = \frac{2F - d}{\mu}$$

Illustrative Example 5.26

The X-Y plane is the boundary between two transparent media. Medium-1 with $z \geq 0$ has a refractive index $\sqrt{2}$ and medium-2 with $z \leq 0$ has a refractive index $\sqrt{3}$. A ray of light in medium-1 given by the vector $\vec{A} = 6\sqrt{3} + 8\sqrt{3}\,\hat{j} - 10k$ is incident on the plane of separation. Find the unit vector in the direction of the refracted ray in medium-2.

Solution

See figure-5.130

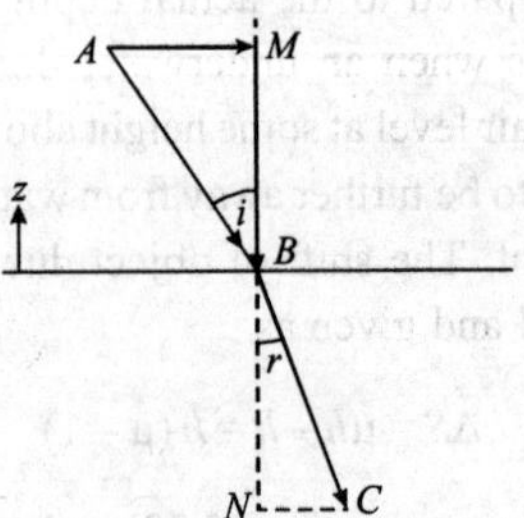

Figure 5.130

Given that $\qquad \overrightarrow{AB} = 6\sqrt{3}\,\hat{i} + 8\sqrt{3}\,\hat{j} - 10\,\hat{k}$

From figure $\overrightarrow{AB} = \overrightarrow{AM} + \overrightarrow{MB}$

Thus we have $\overrightarrow{AM} = 6\sqrt{3}\,\hat{i} + 8\sqrt{3}\,\hat{j}$ and $\overrightarrow{MB} = -10\,\hat{k}$

The angle between the two vectors can be obtained by using the following formula

$$\cos i = \frac{\overrightarrow{AB}\cdot\overrightarrow{MB}}{|\overrightarrow{AB}||\overrightarrow{MB}|}$$

Hence $(\overrightarrow{AB})\cdot(-\hat{k}) = |\overrightarrow{AB}||-\hat{k}|\cos i$

$$\cos i = \frac{10}{\sqrt{36\times3+64\times3+100}} = \frac{1}{2}$$

$$\Rightarrow \quad \cos i = \frac{1}{2} \text{ and } \sin i = \sqrt{3}/2 \qquad \ldots(5.34)$$

By using Snell's law, we have

$$\mu_1 \sin i = \mu_2 \sin r$$

$$\Rightarrow \quad \sqrt{2}\sin i = \sqrt{3}\sin r$$

$$\Rightarrow \quad \sqrt{2}\times(\sqrt{3}/2) = \sqrt{3}\sin r$$

$$\Rightarrow \quad \sin r = \frac{1}{\sqrt{2}} \text{ and } \cos r = \frac{1}{\sqrt{2}} \Rightarrow r = 45^\circ$$

consider vector BN.

$$\overrightarrow{BN} = BN\cos r\,(-\hat{k}) + BN\sin r\,\hat{e}$$

where $\hat{e}$ is unit vector along CD

$$\hat{e} = \widehat{AM} = \frac{6\sqrt{3}\hat{i}+8\sqrt{3}\hat{j}}{10\sqrt{3}} = \frac{6}{10}\hat{i}+\frac{8}{10}\hat{j}$$

unit vector along reflected rays is

$$\Rightarrow \quad \widehat{BC} = \frac{\overrightarrow{BD}}{|\overrightarrow{BD}|} = \frac{1}{\sqrt{2}}(-\hat{k}) + \frac{1}{\sqrt{2}}\left(\frac{6}{10}\hat{i}+\frac{8}{10}\hat{j}\right)$$

$$= \frac{1}{10\sqrt{2}}(-10\boldsymbol{k}) + \frac{1}{10\sqrt{2}}(6\boldsymbol{i}+8\boldsymbol{j})$$

$$= \frac{1}{10\sqrt{2}}[6\hat{i} + 8\hat{j} - 10\hat{k}]$$

$$= \frac{\sqrt{2}}{10}[3\hat{i} + 4\hat{j} - 5\hat{k}]$$

5.10.8 Shift of image due to Refraction of Light by a Glass Slab

When a light ray from an object O is incident on a glass slab at some angle i it gets refracted inside the slab at angle r and from its other face it emerges out in air at the same angle i as shown in figure-5.131(a). In the whole process light ray suffers two refractions at the two parallel surfaces of the glass slab. If we consider object is placed at a distance h from the front face of the slab, first image I_1 due to first refraction will be produced at a distance μh from the surface as shown which is given by equation-(5.32). If glass slab thickness is t then for the second refraction image I_1 will act like an object located at a distance $(t + \mu h)$ and final image I_2 is produced at a distance $(t + \mu h)/\mu$ at a distance from this face of glass slab which is given by equation-(5.33). So for the observer looking at the object from the other side of glass slab the shift of object observed will be given as

$$\text{Shift} \qquad \Delta S_{slab} = h + t - \left(\frac{t+\mu h}{\mu}\right)$$

$$\Rightarrow \qquad \Delta S_{slab} = t\left(1-\frac{1}{\mu}\right) \qquad \ldots(5.35)$$

Equation-(5.35) is the expression used for calculation of shift of object due to refraction by a parallel sided glass slab.

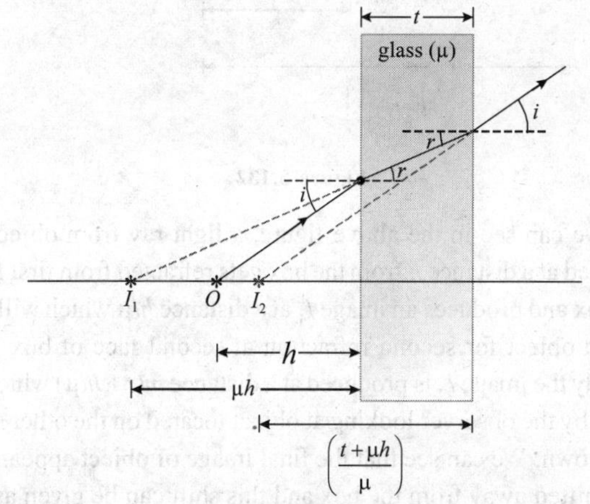

(a)

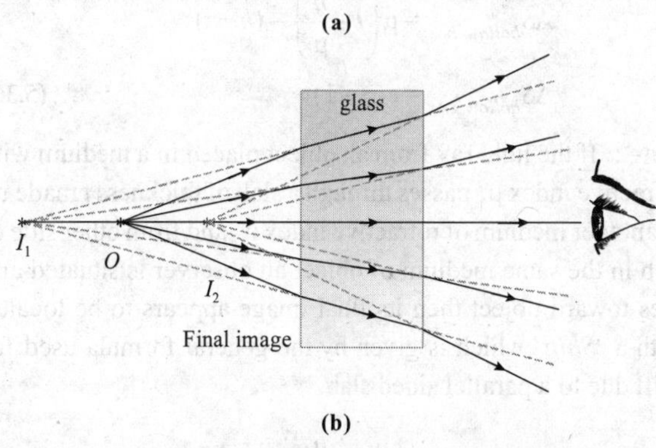

(b)

Figure 5.131

Figure-5.131(b) shows the ray diagram of formation of image which is seen by an observer from the other side of glass slab. The expression of shift of object as given in equation-(5.35) is also valid only for near normal viewing as the result is obtained for paraxial rays only.

5.10.9 Shift due to Refraction of Light by a Hollow thin walled Glass Box placed inside a Denser Medium

Figure-5.132 shows a hollow box made up of thin walls of glass is placed in water and a light ray from an object O falls on the first interface of the box in which the light enters into air from water as very thin walls of glass can be neglected because these thin walls of glass will not produce any shift or lateral displacement in path of light ray.

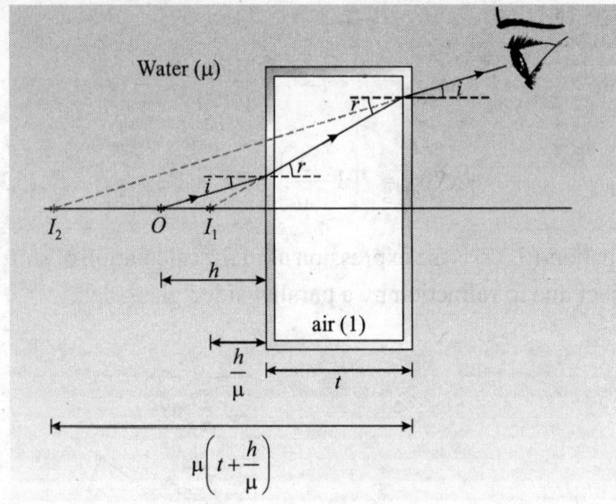

Figure 5.132

As we can see in the above figure, a light ray from object O located at a distance h from the box gets refracted from first face of box and produces an image I_1 at a distance h/μ which will act as an object for second refraction at second face of box and finally the image I_2 is produced at a distance $m(t + h/\mu)$ which is seen by the observer looking at object located on the other side as shown. We can see that the final image of object appears to be shifted away from the box and this shift can be given as

$$\Delta S_{hollow\ box} = \mu\left(t + \frac{h}{\mu}\right) - (h + t)$$

$$\Rightarrow \quad \Delta S_{hollow\ box} = t(\mu - 1) \qquad \ldots(5.36)$$

Note : If the light ray from an object placed in a medium with refractive index μ_1 passes through a slab of thickness t made up of another medium of refractive index μ_2 and from other side of slab in the same medium of object an observer is situated and sees toward object then its final image appears to be located with a *'Shift'* which is given by the general formula used for shift due to a parallel sided slab

$$\Delta S = t\left(1 - \frac{\mu_1}{\mu_2}\right) \qquad \ldots(5.37)$$

In equation-(5.37) if ΔS is positive then shift is taken toward the slab and if it comes negative then it is taken away from the slab. With a careful analysis of this formula you can get equation-(5.35) and equation-(5.36) by properly substituting the values of μ_1 and μ_2 in it.

5.10.10 Lateral Displacement of Light Ray by a Glass Slab

Figure-5.133 shows the refraction of a light ray through a parallel sided glass slab which incidents on the slab at an angle of incidence i and enters into the slab at angle of refraction r finally emerges out in direction parallel to the initial ray. If refractive index of the glass used is μ then at the point A in figure we can apply Snell's law as

$$\sin i = \mu \sin r \qquad \ldots(5.38)$$

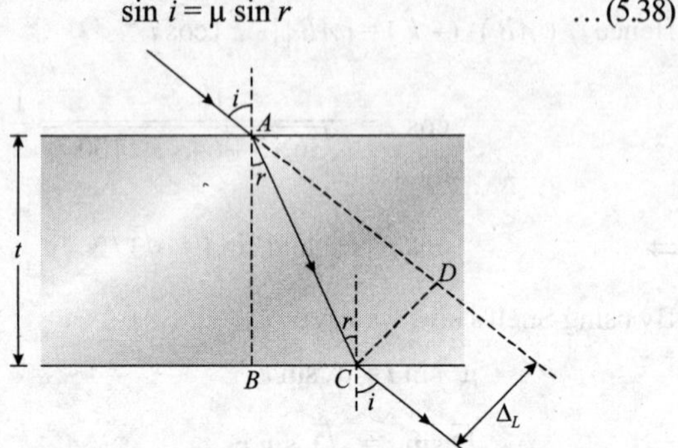

Figure 5.133

In the above figure in right angled triangle ΔACD we can use

$$\sin(i - r) = \frac{CD}{AC}$$

Lateral Displacement of light ray

$$\Delta_L = CD = AC \sin(i - r) \qquad \ldots(5.39)$$

in ΔABC we have $\cos r = \frac{t}{AC}$

$$\Rightarrow \quad AC = \frac{t}{\cos r} \qquad \ldots(5.40)$$

From equation-(5.39) and equation-(5.40) we get lateral displacement of light ray is given as

$$\Delta = \frac{t.\sin(i - r)}{\cos r} \qquad \ldots(5.41)$$

If incidence angle i is very small (for near normal incidence), then we can use

$$\sin(i - r) \simeq i - r$$

$$\cos r = 1$$

$$\Delta = t(i - r)$$

For very small i, from equation-(5.38) we can use

$$i = \mu r \qquad \text{(as for small } \theta, \sin\theta \simeq \theta)$$

$$r = \frac{i}{\mu}$$

Thus in equation-(5.41) for small angles we can write $\sin(i - r) \simeq (i - r)$ and $\cos r \simeq 1$, we get

$$\Delta = ti\left(1 - \frac{1}{\mu}\right)$$

5.10.11 Lateral Displacement of a Light Ray due to Refraction by Multiple Glass Slabs

When several parallel sided glass slabs are placed adjoining to each other then due to refraction while passing through these slabs the light ray is displaced laterally which can be calculated by summing up the individual displacement of the light which occurs when the ray passes through the slabs independently as shown in figure-5.134.

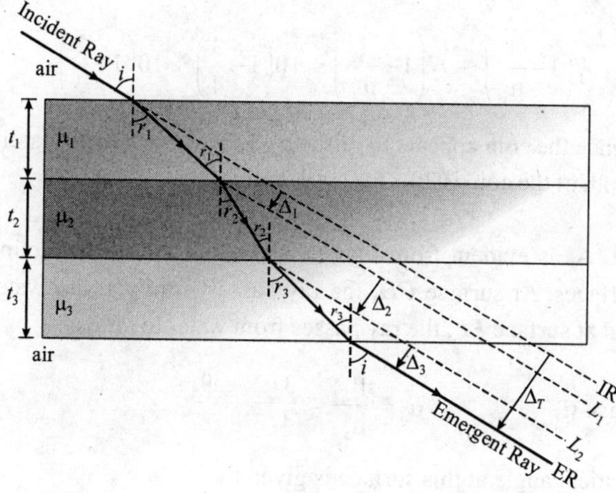

Figure 5.134

As shown in figure-5.134 when a light ray is incident from air on the surface of the first slab and if only this slab is present in air, the light will come out in air along the dotted line L_1 as shown in figure and the displacement of the light would have been Δ_1 and if adjoining next slab is placed at a negligible separation with first slab then it enters into it and comes out along the dotted line L_2 and the lateral displacement of the light ray would have been $\Delta_1 + \Delta_2$. In the same manner if third or more slabs are placed all the lateral displacements produced by each slab independently for the angle of incidence i are added together. If r_1, r_2, r_3 are the angles which light ray is making with the normal in each of these slabs then the total lateral displacement of light ray is given by

$$\Delta_T = \Delta_1 + \Delta_2 + \Delta_3 + \ldots$$

$$\Rightarrow \Delta_T = \frac{t.\sin(i - r_1)}{\cos r_1} + \frac{t.\sin(i - r_2)}{\cos r_2} + \frac{t.\sin(i - r_3)}{\cos r_3} + \ldots \quad \ldots(5.42)$$

For near normal incidence of light this equation-(5.42) will reduce to the equation given below

$$\Delta_T = t_1 i\left(1 - \frac{1}{\mu_1}\right) + t_2 i\left(1 - \frac{1}{\mu_2}\right) + t_3 i\left(1 - \frac{1}{\mu_3}\right) + \ldots \quad \ldots(5.43)$$

5.10.12 Concept of Reflection by a Thick Mirror

A plane mirror is a thin glass slab polished at one of its surfaces due to which the other side becomes reflecting. If the glass used in making mirror is thick then it also shifts the image before reflection from the rear polished surface as well as after reflection and before coming out in air. Light passes through the glass of mirror twice as shown in figure-5.135(a). Figure-5.135(b) shows a thick plane mirror of glass thickness t placed in front of a point object O. A light ray from O first gets refracted from the front glass face S_1 then gets reflected from mirror M (polished face) and after reflection again gets refracted from the front face S_1 before coming out in air and finally produces the image I_3. Here I_1 and I_2 are the intermediate images produced by the light ray.

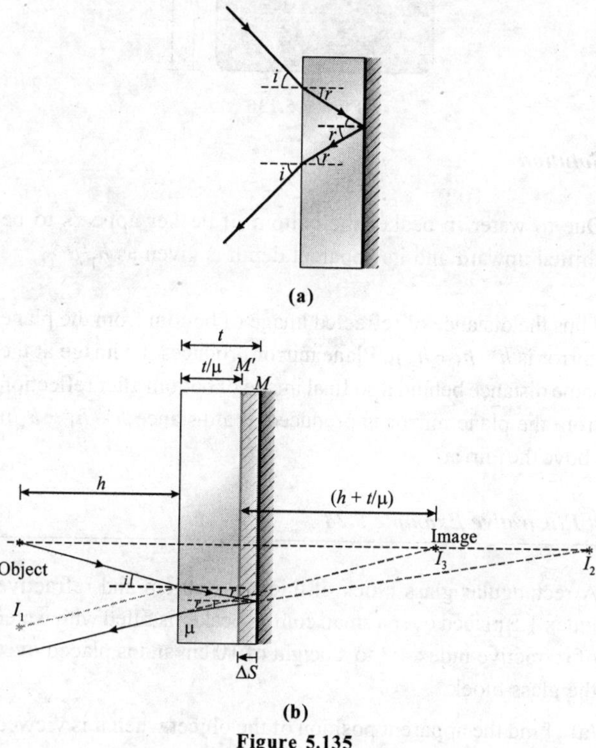

Figure 5.135

Final position of image produced can be directly calculated by considering the shift in rear surface as observed by the observer. Due to thickness of glass the polished face appear to be at an apparent depth t/μ as shown in figure due to which the distance between object and this new position M' of the mirror will be $(h + t/\mu)$ and now the image will be produced exactly at the same distance behind the mirror. So the separation between object and image can be given as

$$L_{OI} = 2\left(h + \frac{t}{\mu}\right) \quad \ldots(5.44)$$

Students are advised to verify the separation given in equation-(5.44) using calculations in stepped manner by finding the locations of images I_1 and I_2 then I_3 step by step.

Illustrative Example 5.27

Consider the situation shown in figure-5.136. A plane mirror is fixed at a height h above the bottom of a beaker containing water of refractive index m up to a height h_1. Find the position of the image of the bottom formed by the mirror.

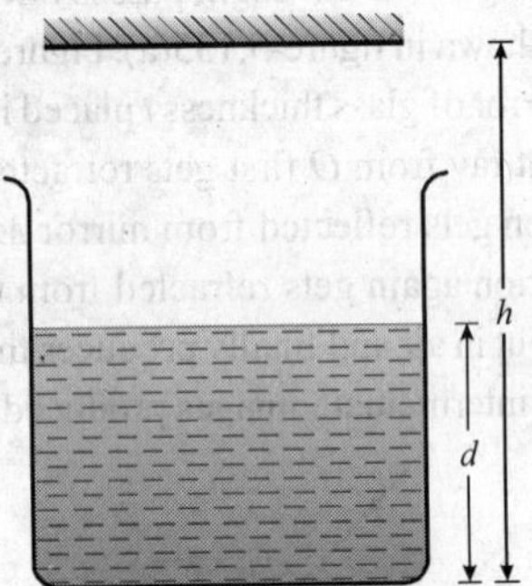

Figure 5.136

Solution

Due to water in beaker the bottom of beaker appears to be shifted upward and its apparent depth is given as h_1/μ.

Thus the distance of refracted image of bottom from the plane mirror is $h - h_1 + h_1/\mu$. Plane mirror produces the image at the same distance behind it so final image of bottom after reflection from the plane mirror is produced at a distance $h - h_1 + h_1/\mu$ above the mirror.

Illustrative Example 5.28

A rectangular glass block of thickness 10 cm and refractive index 1.5 placed over a small coin. A beaker is filled with water of refractive index 4/3 to a height of 10 cm and is placed over the glass block.

(a) Find the apparent position of the object when it is viewed at near normal incidence.

(b) if the eye is slowly moved away from the normal at a certain position, the object is found to disappear, due to total internal reflection. At what surface does this happen and why?

Solution

Let $ABCD$ be a glass block (μ = 1.5) placed over a coin as shown in figure-5.137. Let a beaker containing water upto a height 10 cm placed over glass slab.

(a) As the ray from coin passes from glass slab to water it moves away from the normal as it enters a rarer medium from a denser medium. Similarly at surface EF, the ray again moves away from the normal. When viewed from N, the coin appears to be at I_2. Apparent shift in multiple slabs is given by

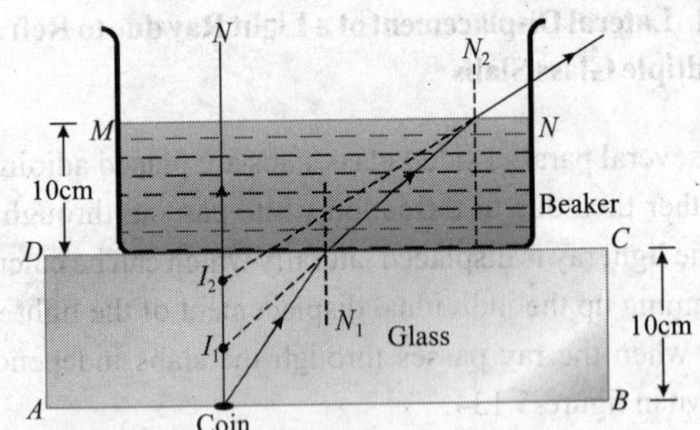

Figure 5.137

$$t_1\left(1-\frac{1}{\mu_1}\right)+t_2\left(1-\frac{1}{\mu_2}\right)=10\left(1-\frac{3}{4}\right)+10\left(1-\frac{2}{3}\right)$$

Hence the coin appears to raised by 5.8 cm. Now the apparent depth of the coin is 20 – 5.8 = 14.2 cm.

(b) As is evident from figure CD and EF are the refracting surfaces. At surface CD, the ray passes from glass to water and at surface EF, the ray passes from water to air.

Case-(i) $${}_w\mu_g=\frac{\mu_g}{\mu_w}=\frac{3/2}{4/3}=\frac{9}{8}$$

Critical angle at this surface is given by

$$C_1=\sin^{-1}(8/9) \text{ or } C_1=62°\,45'$$

Case-(ii) Similarly,

$${}_a\mu_w=\frac{\mu_w}{\mu_a}=\frac{4}{3}$$

$$\therefore \quad C_2=\sin^{-1}(3/4) \text{ or } C_2=48°\,36'.$$

As we see that critical angle is smaller in case (ii), total internal reflection occurs at the upper surface EF earlier as the eye is moved away from the normal.

Illustrative Example 5.29

A glass slab of thickness 3 cm and refractive index 1.5 is placed in front of a concave mirror of focal length 20 cm. Where should a point object be placed if it is to image on to itself ?

Solution

The glass slab and the concave mirror are shown in figure-5.138. Let the distance of the object from the mirror be x. The slab causes a shift in position of object which is given as

$$s=t\left[1-\frac{1}{\mu}\right]=1\text{ cm}$$

The direction of shift is towards the concave mirror so the apparent distance of the object from the mirror is $(x - 1)$ cm.

To produce the image on itself the reflected rays must retrace the path of incident rays so the object should appear at the centre of curvature of the mirror.

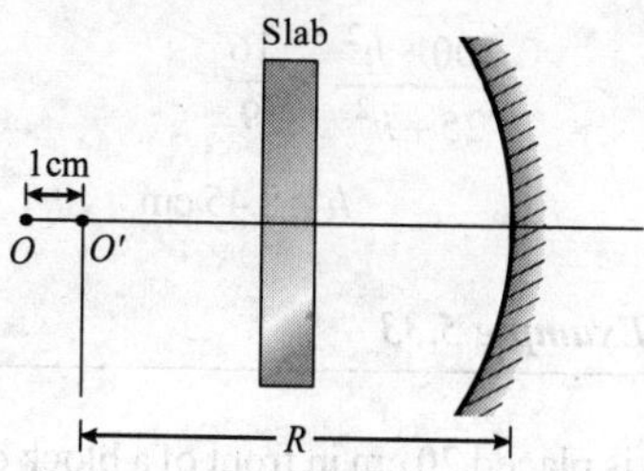

Figure 5.138

Thus we use $\quad x - 1 = 2f = 40$ cm

$\Rightarrow \quad x = 41$ cm from the mirror

Illustrative Example 5.30

A concave mirror has the form of a hemisphere with a radius of $R = 60$ cm. A thin layer of an unknown transparent liquid is poured into the mirror. The mirror-liquid system forms one real image and another real image is formed by mirror alone of the source in a certain position. Image produced by combination coincides with the source and that produced by mirror alone is located at a distance of $l = 30$ cm from the source away from mirror. Find the refractive index μ of the liquid.

Solution

For concave mirror with unknown liquid, equivalent focal length of the combined mirror is given as

$$\frac{1}{f_{eq}} = \frac{2}{f_L} + \frac{1}{f_M}$$

Where $$\frac{1}{f_L} = (\mu - 1)\left(\frac{1}{\infty} - \frac{1}{-60}\right)$$

$$\Rightarrow \quad \frac{1}{f_L} = \left(\frac{\mu - 1}{60}\right)$$

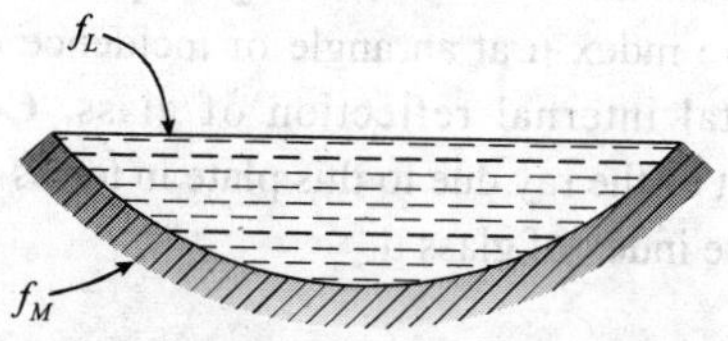

Figure 5.139

and focal length of mirror is

$$f_m = \frac{60}{2} = 30 \text{ cm}$$

Thus equivalent focal length of the combination mirror is given as

$$\Rightarrow \quad \frac{1}{f_{eq}} = 2\left(\frac{\mu - 1}{60}\right) + \frac{2}{60} = \frac{2\mu}{60}$$

$$\Rightarrow \quad f_e = \frac{30}{\mu}$$

As image formed by the mirror liquid system coincides with the source, the location of object is at $2f_e$

$$\Rightarrow \quad u = 2f_e = \frac{60}{\mu}$$

According to the given condition, $\frac{60}{\mu} + 30$ is the distance of the image formed by the mirror itself, thus using mirror formula we have

$$\frac{1}{v} + \frac{1}{u} = \frac{1}{f}$$

$$\Rightarrow \quad \frac{1}{v} + \frac{1 \times \mu}{-60} = -\frac{1}{30}$$

$$\Rightarrow \quad v = \frac{60}{\mu - 2} = -\left(\frac{60}{2 - \mu}\right)$$

Image distance from the mirror is $\frac{60}{2 - \mu}$, thus form the already obtained condition we use

$$\frac{60}{\mu} + 30 = \frac{60}{2 - \mu}$$

$$\Rightarrow \quad \mu^2 + 2\mu - 4 = 0$$

$$\Rightarrow \quad \mu = -1 \pm \sqrt{5}$$

$$\Rightarrow \quad \mu = -1 + \sqrt{5} \text{ (as } \mu \text{ cannot be negative)}$$

Illustrative Example 5.31

In previous illustrations if image formed by the mirror coincides with the source and that produced by the combination is produced at a distance 30 cm from the source away from mirror then find the refractive index of the liquid.

Solution

Mirror produces its image on source when the source is located at the center of curvature thus source position must be at 60 cm from the pole of mirror.

Now we use mirror formula for calculation of image distance for mirror liquid combination

$$\frac{1}{v} + \frac{1}{u} = \frac{1}{f_e}$$

$$\Rightarrow \quad \frac{1}{v} + \frac{1}{-60} = -\frac{\mu}{30}$$

$$\Rightarrow \qquad v = \frac{60}{1-2\mu} = -\left(\frac{60}{2\mu-1}\right)$$

According to the given condition we use

$$\frac{60}{2\mu-1} + 30 = 60$$

$$\Rightarrow \qquad \mu = 1.5$$

Illustrative Example 5.32

A person looking through a telescope T just sees the point A on the rim at the bottom of a cylindrical vessel when the vessel is empty. When the vessel is completely filled with a liquid (μ = 1.5), he observes a mark at the centre B, of the bottom without moving the telescope or the vessel. What is the height of the vessel if the diameter of its cross section is 10 cm.

Solution

In the figure-5.140 shown if we consider the position of telescope is at T when the point A is visible on the rim. Now when the vessel is filled with a liquid, point B is observed at the same arrangement and position of telescope due to refraction of the ray at point D on water surface.

Here in figure we use

$$\sin i = \frac{BC}{BD} = \frac{BC}{\sqrt{[(BC)^2 + (CD)^2]}}$$

$$\Rightarrow \qquad \sin i = \frac{5}{\sqrt{(5^2 + h^2)}}$$

Again $\qquad \angle NDT = \angle ADC = \angle r$

$$\Rightarrow \qquad \sin r = \frac{AC}{AD} = \frac{AC}{\sqrt{[(AC)^2 + (CD)^2]}}$$

$$\Rightarrow \qquad \sin r = \frac{10}{\sqrt{(10^2 + h^2)}}$$

Now using Snell's law, we have

$$\mu_L \sin i = \mu_a \sin r$$

Figure 5.140

$$\Rightarrow \qquad \frac{5}{\sqrt{(5^2 + h^2)}} \times \frac{\sqrt{(10^2 + h^2)}}{10} = \frac{1}{1.5}$$

$$\Rightarrow \qquad \frac{100 + h^2}{25 + h^2} = \frac{16}{9}$$

$$\Rightarrow \qquad h = 8.45 \text{ cm}$$

Illustrative Example 5.33

A small object is placed 20 cm in front of a block of glass 10 cm thick and its farther side silvered. The image is formed 23.2 cm behind the silvered face. Find the refractive index of glass.

Solution

In figure-5.141 $ABCD$ be the block of glass whose side BC is silvered as shown.

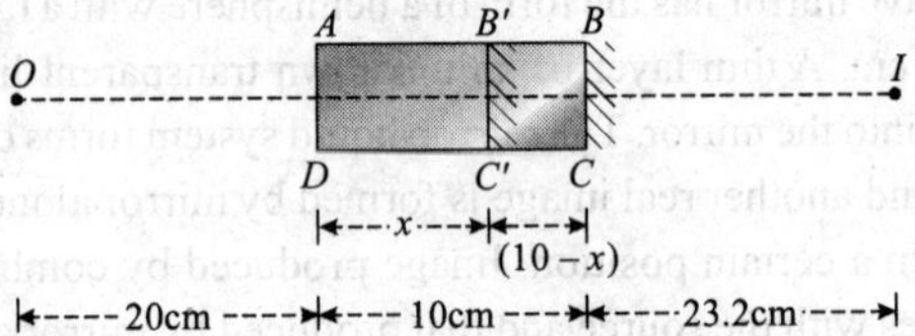

Figure 5.141

Suppose it appears that the image is formed due to the reflection at image of silvered face $B'C'$ and if the apparent depth of glass block is x cm then we use

$$20 + x = 23.2 + (10 - x)$$

$$\Rightarrow \qquad x = 5.6 \text{ cm}$$

As we know the refractive index is the ratio of real depth and apparent depth, we have

$$\mu = \frac{\text{real depth}}{\text{apparent depth}} = \frac{10}{6.6} = 1.51$$

Illustrative Example 5.34

A light ray from air is incident on a glass plate of thickness t and refractive index μ at an angle of incidence equal to the angle of total internal reflection of glass. Compute the displacement of the ray due to this plate in terms of thickness and refractive index of glass μ.

Solution

Figure-5.142 shows the ray diagram of the light ray passing through the slab. Here the angle of incidence is given as

$$\sin i = \frac{1}{\mu} \qquad \text{(As } i \text{ is equal to critical angle)}$$

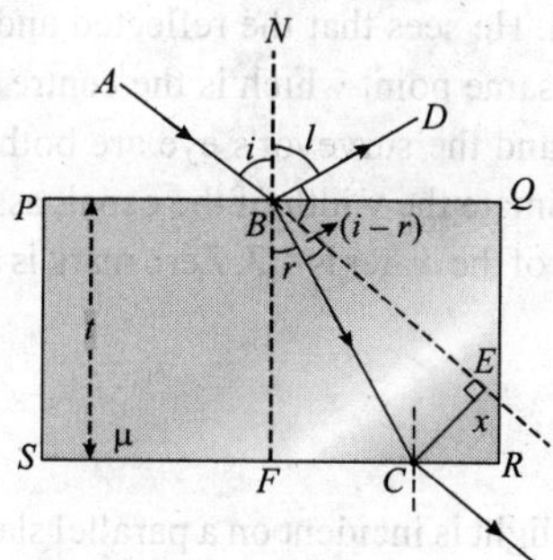

Figure 5.142

By Snell's law, $\frac{\sin i}{\sin r} = \mu$

$$\Rightarrow \qquad \sin r = \frac{\sin i}{\mu} = \frac{1}{\mu^2}$$

In figure we can see that displacement of the light ray is given as

$$CE = x = BC \sin (i - r)$$

In figure we also have

$$\cos r = \frac{BF}{BC}$$

$$\Rightarrow \qquad BC = \frac{t}{\cos r}$$

$$\Rightarrow \qquad x = \frac{t}{\cos r} \sin (C - r)$$

$$\Rightarrow \qquad x = \frac{t}{\cos r} [\sin C \cos r - \cos C \sin r]$$

$$\Rightarrow \qquad x = t \sin C \left[1 - \frac{\sin r}{\sin C} \times \frac{\cos C}{\cos r}\right]$$

$$\Rightarrow \qquad x = \frac{t}{\mu}\left[1 - \frac{1}{\mu} \times \frac{\mu}{\sqrt{(\mu^2 + 1)}}\right]$$

$$\Rightarrow \qquad x = \frac{1}{\mu}\left[1 - \frac{1}{\sqrt{(\mu^2 + 1)}}\right]$$

 # Illustrative Example 5.35

A concave mirror of radius 40 cm lies on a horizontal table and water in filled in it upto a height of 5.0 cm as shown in figure-5.143. A small dust particle floats on the water surface at a point P vertically above the point of contact of the mirror with the table. Locate the image of the dust particle as seen from a point directly above it. The refractive index of water is 1.33.

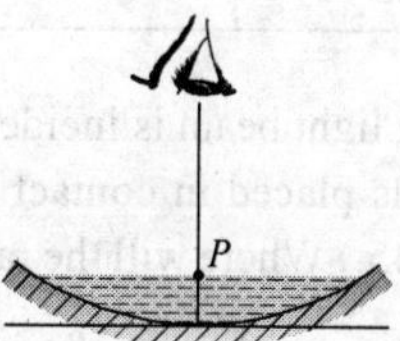

Figure 5.143

Solution

The image formation of the dust particle is shown in figure-5.144

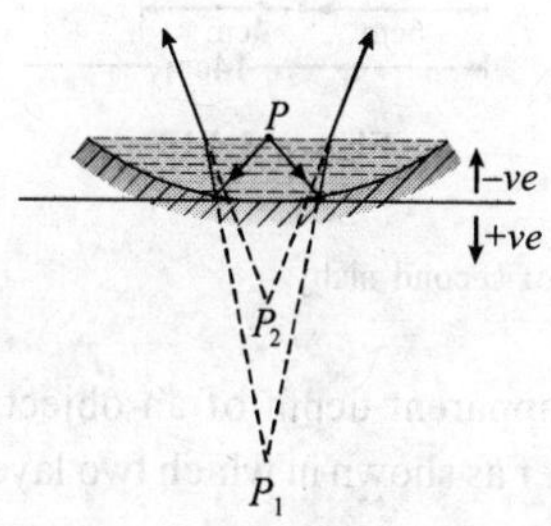

Figure 5.144

Here we first consider the image formed by concave mirror.

For which we use $R = -40$ cm and $u = -5$ cm for using in the mirror formula, which gives

$$\frac{1}{u} + \frac{1}{v} = \frac{2}{R}$$

$$\Rightarrow \qquad \frac{1}{v} = \frac{2}{-40} - \frac{1}{-5} = \frac{6}{40}$$

$$\Rightarrow \qquad v = \frac{40}{6} \text{ cm} = 6.67 \text{ cm}$$

As v is positive, the image P_1 is formed below the mirror (virtual). The reflected rays are refracted at water surface. The depth of point P_1 from the water surface is 6.67 + 5.00 = 11.67. Due to presence of water, the image P_1 will be shifted up and the final position of image is given by its apparent depth given as

$$\text{Image position} = \frac{h}{\mu} = \frac{11.67}{1.33} = 8.77 \text{ cm}$$

Thus final image is formed 8.77 cm below the water surface.

Web Reference at www.physicsgalaxy.com

Age Group - High School Physics | Age 17-19 Years

Section - OPTICS

Topic - Geometrical Optics II - Refraction of Light

Module Number - 1 to 8 and 25 to 32

Practice Exercise 5.3

(i) A converging light beam is incident on two glass slabs of different materials placed in contact with each others (as shown in figure-5.145.) Where will the rays finally converge ?

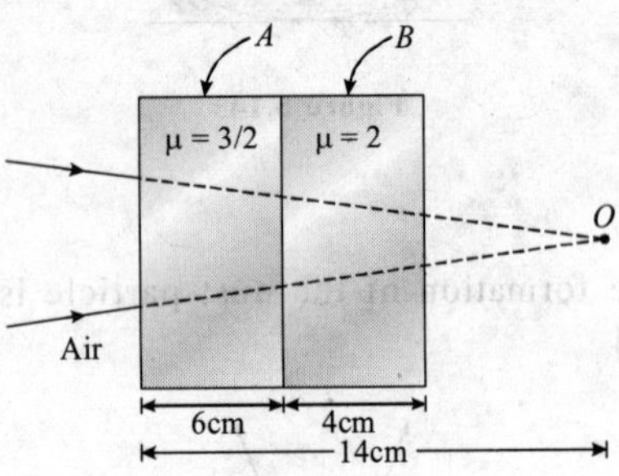

Figure 5.145

[8 cm to the right of second slab]

(ii) Find the apparent depth of an object O placed at the bottom of a beaker as shown in which two layers of transparent liquids are filled :

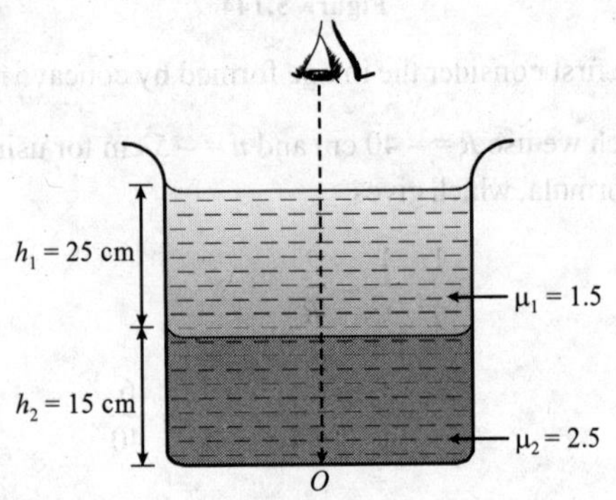

Figure 5.146

[22.67 cm]

(iii) A point object is placed 33 cm from a convex mirror of curvature radius 40 cm. A glass plate of thickness 6 cm and index 2.0 is placed between the object and the mirror, closer to the mirror. Find the distance of final image from the object ?

[42 cm]

(iv) A light ray falling at 60° angle with the surface of a glass slab of thickness 1 m and is refracted at angle 75° with the surface. Calculate the time taken by the light to cross the slab.

[$\frac{2}{3}\times 10^{-8}$ s]

(v) A surveyor on one bank of a canal observes the image of the 4 inch mark and 17 ft mark on a vertical staff, which is partially immersed in the water and held against the bank directly opposite to him. He sees that the reflected and refracted rays come from the same point which is the centre of the canal. If the 17 ft mark and the surveyor's eye are both 6 ft above the water level, estimate the width of the canal, assuming that the refractive index of the water is 4/3. Zero mark is at the bottom of the canal.

[16 feet]

(vi) A ray of light is incident on a parallel slab of thickness t and refractive index μ. If the angle of incidence is θ then for small θ show that the lateral displacement of light ray will be

$$\Delta = \frac{t\theta(\mu - 1)}{\mu}$$

(vii) How much water should be filled in a container of height 21 cm so that it will appear half filled when viewed along normal to water surface. Take refractive index of water $\mu_w = 4/3$.

[12 cm]

(viii) A glass plate has a thickness t and refractive index μ. A light ray is allowed to incident on the plate from air. Find at what angle of incidence will the rays refracted and reflected by the plate be perpendicular to each other ? For this angle of incidence, calculate the lateral displacement of the ray.

[$\frac{t(\mu^2 - 1)}{\mu\sqrt{1+\mu^2}}$]

(ix) A man standing on the edge of a swimming pool looks at a stone lying on the bottom. The depth of the swimming pool is equal to h. At what distance from the surface of water is the image of the stone formed if the line of vision makes an angle θ with the normal to the surface ?

[$\frac{\mu^2 h\cos^3\theta}{(\mu^2 - \sin^2\theta)^{3/2}}$]

(x) In a river 2 m deep, a water level measuring post embedded into the river stands vertically with 1 m of it above the water surface. If the angle of inclination of sun above the horizon is 30°, calculate the length of the post on the bottom surface of the river. (μ for water = 4/3)

[3.44 m]

(xi) A concave mirror of radius of curvature one metre is placed at the bottom of a tank of water. The mirror forms an image of the sun when it is directly overhead. Calculate, the distance of the images from the mirror for different depths, 80 cm and 40 cm of the water in the tank.

[47.5 cm, 57.5 cm]

(xii) A small object is kept at the centre of bottom of a cylindrical beaker of diameter 6 cm and height 4 cm filled completely with water ($\mu = 4/3$). Consider the light ray from an object leaving the beaker through a corner. If this ray and the ray along the axis of beaker is used to locate the image, find the apparent depth in this case.

[2.25 cm]

5.11 Refraction of Light by Spherical Surfaces

Figure-5.147(a) shows a spherical interface separating two different media 1 and 2 with refractive indices μ_1 and μ_2. Here C is the center of curvature of the spherical surface, R is the radius of curvature of the surface, P is the central point on the surface called optic center of the surface and line XX' is considered as the '*Optical Axis*' for the given setup. In general the optical axis for the refraction surface can also be called as principal axis, the term which we generally use for spherical mirrors and lenses.

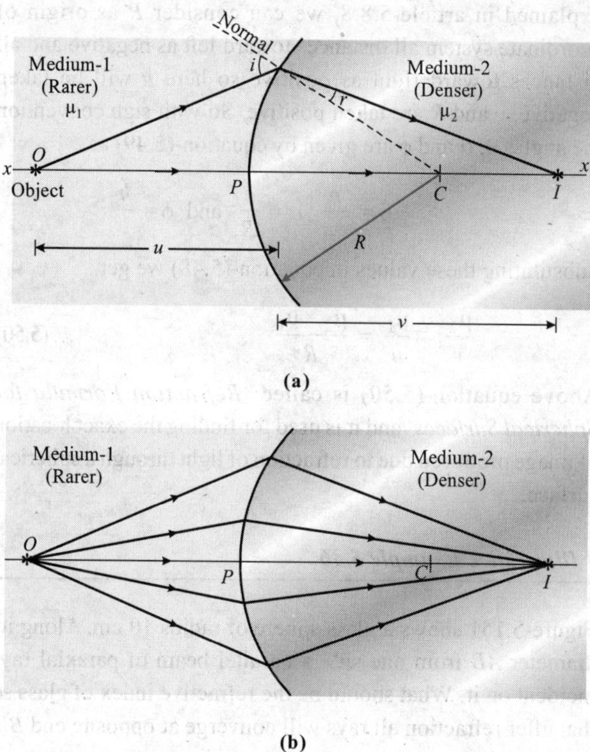

Figure 5.147

If we consider a light ray from an object placed in medium-1 incident on the spherical interface at an angle of incidence i gets refracted at an angle r and the refracted ray in other medium meets the optical axis at point I. We can also consider a ray of light from the object along the optical axis which passes undeviated at the interface. Always for image formation we can consider one ray along the optical axis and one other ray in surrounding to produce image. In figure-5.147(b) we can see all paraxial rays from object after refraction meet at the point I which is the image produced due to refraction of light at the spherical surface.

In above situation explained in figure-5.147, image produced is real image as refracted rays are converging. Depending upon the refractive indices of the two media refracted rays may be diverging as shown in figure-5.148(a) and (b) in which the final image produced is virtual.

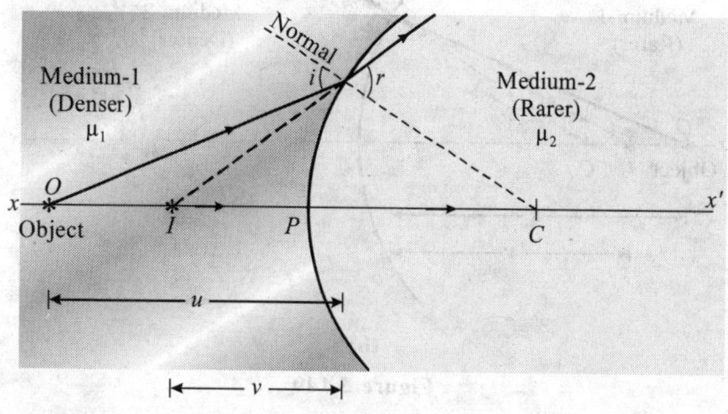

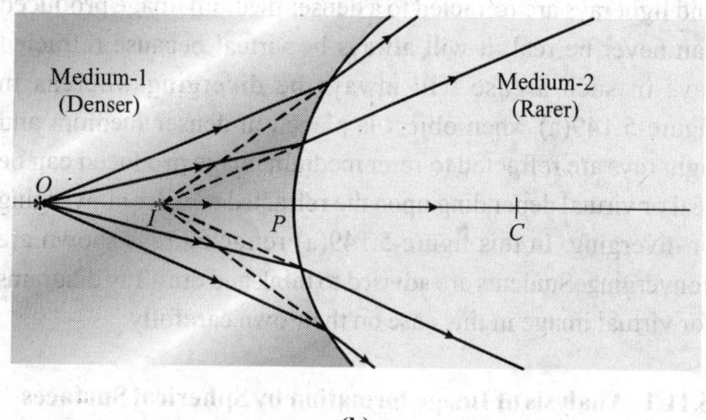

Figure 5.148

Note : In figure-5.148 when object is placed in denser medium and light rays are refracted to a rarer medium the image produced can never be real, it will always be virtual because refracted rays in such a case will always be diverging but when object is placed in rarer medium as shown in figure-5.147 and light rays are refracted to denser medium image produced can be real or virtual depending upon the refracted rays are converging or diverging. In figure-5.147 refracted rays shown are converging. Students are advised to think and draw ray diagrams for the situation for virtual image formation in this case on their own carefully.

Similar situation can also be analysed by students for a concave surface facing the object as shown in figure-5.149.

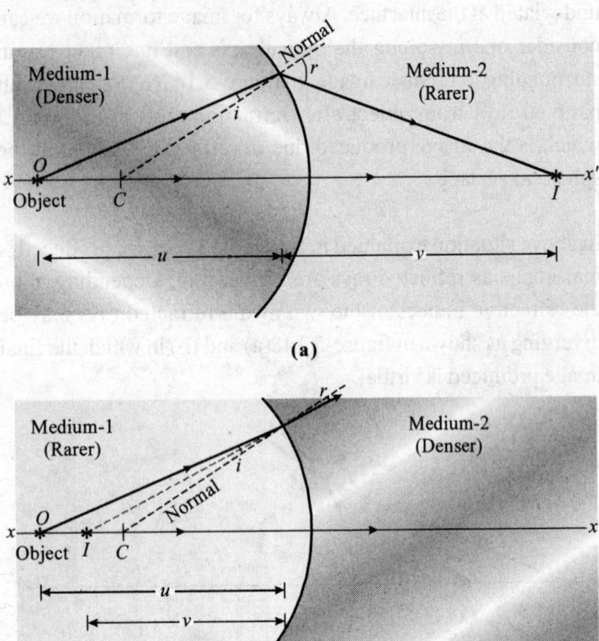

Figure 5.149

Note : In figure-5.149(b) when object is placed in rarer medium and light rays are refracted to a denser medium image produced can never be real, it will always be virtual because refracted rays in such a case will always be diverging whereas in figure-5.149(a) when object is placed in denser medium and light rays are refracted to rarer medium image produced can be real or virtual depending upon the refracted rays are converging or diverging. In this figure-5.149(a) refracted rays shown are converging. Students are advised to think and draw ray diagrams for virtual image in this case on their own carefully.

5.11.1 Analysis of Image formation by Spherical Surfaces

Figure-5.150 shows an object placed on the left of a spherical surface from which a light ray is considered which incidents on the surface at point A and after refraction meet at point I on the optical axis as shown.

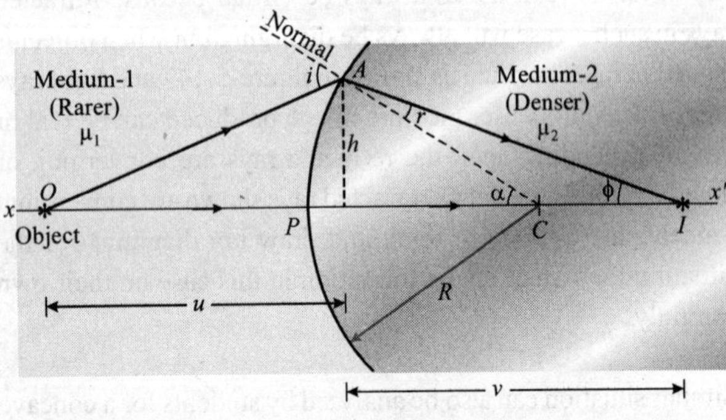

Figure 5.150

Using Snell's law at point A we have

$$\mu_1 \sin i = \mu_2 \sin r$$

For paraxial rays we can use small angles so we have

$$\mu_1 i = \mu_2 r \quad \ldots(5.45)$$

In the geometry of figure shown we can relate different angles from properties of triangles as

$$\alpha = r + \phi \quad \ldots(5.46)$$

and

$$i = \theta + \alpha \quad \ldots(5.47)$$

Combining above three equations we get

$$\mu_1(\theta + \alpha) = \mu_2(\alpha - \phi)$$

$$\Rightarrow \quad \mu_1\theta + \mu_2\phi = (\mu_2 - \mu_1)\,\alpha \quad \ldots(5.48)$$

From figure-5.148 for small angles we can use the length of normal AM on optical axis as

$$AM = h = u\theta = R\alpha = v\phi \quad \ldots(5.49)$$

If we use coordinate sign convention for this situation as explained in article-5.8.8, we can consider P as origin of coordinate system all distances toward left as negative and all distances toward right as positive so here u will be taken negative, v and R are taken positive. So with sign convention the angles θ, α and ϕ are given by equation-(5.49) as

$$\Rightarrow \quad \theta = \frac{h}{-u};\ \alpha = \frac{h}{R} \text{ and } \phi = \frac{h}{v}$$

Substituting these values in equation-(5.48) we get

$$\frac{\mu_2}{v} - \frac{\mu_1}{u} = \frac{\mu_2 - \mu_1}{R} \quad \ldots(5.50)$$

Above equation-(5.50) is called '*Refraction Formula for Spherical Surfaces*' and it is used for finding the exact location of image produced due to refraction of light through a spherical surface.

 # Illustrative Example 5.36

Figure-5.151 shows a glass sphere of radius 10 cm. Along its diameter AB from one side a parallel beam of paraxial rays incident on it. What should be the refractive index of glass so that after refraction all rays will converge at opposite end B.

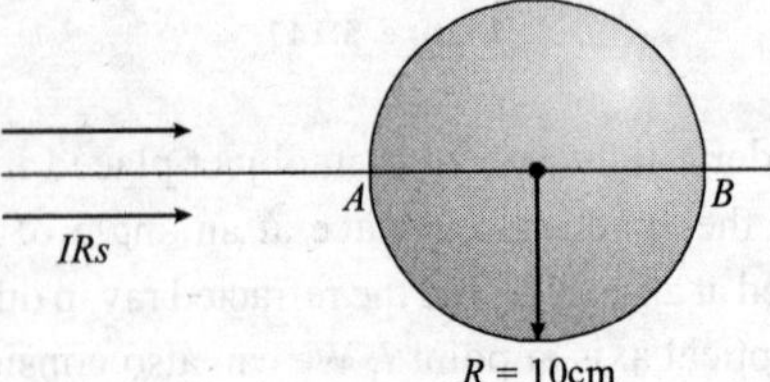

Figure 5.151

Solution

For refraction formula, we use

$$u = \infty$$

$$v = 2R = +20 \text{ cm}$$

$$R = +10 \text{ cm}$$

$$\mu_1 = 1$$

$$\mu_2 = \mu$$

Using refraction formula, we have

$$\frac{\mu_2}{v} - \frac{\mu_1}{u} = \frac{\mu_2 - \mu_1}{R}$$

$$\Rightarrow \quad \frac{\mu}{20} = \frac{\mu - 1}{10}$$

$$\Rightarrow \quad \mu = 2\mu - 2$$

$$\Rightarrow \quad \mu = 2$$

Illustrative Example 5.37

Figure-5.152 shows a glass hemisphere M of $\mu = \frac{3}{2}$ and radius 10 cm. A point object O is placed at a distance 20 cm behind the flat face which is viewed by an observer from the curved side. Find location of final image after two refractions as seen by observer.

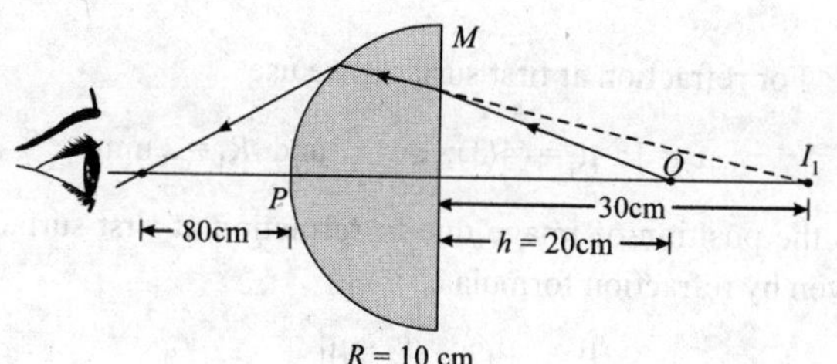

Figure 5.152

Solution

After first refraction at flat surface image is produced at a distance given as

$$\mu h = \frac{3}{2} \times 20 = 30 \text{ cm}$$

For second refraction at spherical surface, for refraction formula we use

$$u = +40 \text{ cm}; \; R = +10 \text{ cm}; \; \mu_1 = \frac{3}{2}; \; \mu_2 = 1$$

Substituting values in refraction formula, we get

$$\frac{\mu_2}{v} - \frac{\mu_1}{u} = \frac{\mu_2 - \mu_1}{R}$$

$$\frac{1}{v} - \frac{3}{2 \times 40} = \frac{1 - \frac{3}{2}}{10}$$

$$\Rightarrow \quad \frac{1}{v} = \frac{3}{90} - \frac{1}{20} = -\frac{1}{80}$$

$$\Rightarrow \quad v = -80 \text{ cm}$$

Thus final image is seen by observer at a distance 80 cm from the pole of curved surface and it is a real image.

Illustrative Example 5.38

A glass rod has spherical ends as shown in figure-5.153. The refractive index of glass is μ. The object O is at a distance $2R$ from the surface of larger radius of curvature. The distance between apexes of ends is $3R$. Find the distance of image formed of the point object from right hand vertex. What is the condition to be satisfied if the final image obtained is to be real?

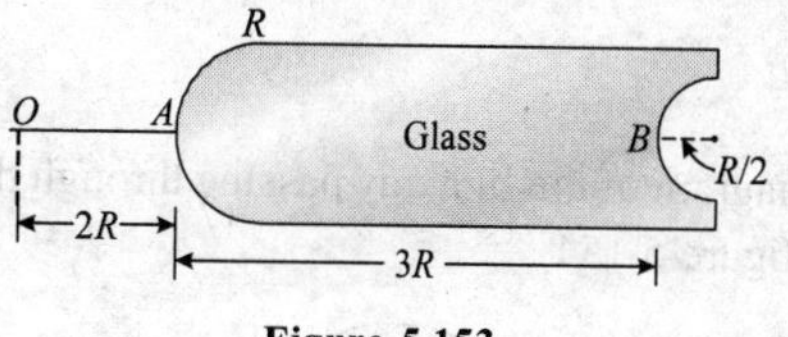

Figure 5.153

Solution

For first refraction at surface A, we use $u = -2R$ in refraction formula as

$$\frac{\mu_2}{v'} - \frac{\mu_1}{u} = \frac{\mu_2 - \mu_1}{R_1}$$

$$\Rightarrow \quad \frac{\mu}{v'} + \frac{1}{2R} = \frac{(\mu - 1)}{R} \qquad \ldots(5.51)$$

Solving for v', we get

$$v' = \frac{2\mu R}{(2\mu - 3)} \qquad \ldots(5.52)$$

For refraction at surface B, we use $u = -\left(3R - \frac{2\mu R}{(2\mu - 3)}\right)$ in refraction formula as

$$\frac{\mu_2}{v} - \frac{\mu_1}{u} = \frac{\mu_2 - \mu_1}{R_2}$$

$$\Rightarrow \quad \frac{1}{v} + \frac{\mu}{\left[3R - \frac{2\mu R}{2\mu - 3}\right]} = \frac{1 - \mu}{(R/2)} \qquad \ldots(5.53)$$

$$\Rightarrow \quad \mu = -\left[3R - \frac{2\mu R}{2\mu - 3}\right]$$

Solving equation-(5.53) for v, we get

$$v = \frac{(9 - 4\mu)R}{(10\mu - 9)(\mu - 2)}$$

The image will be real if above value of v is positive for which finally refracted rays will be converging, so condition for real image is

$$\frac{(9-4\mu)R}{(10\mu-9)(\mu-2)}>0$$

On simplifying we get that it happens when refractive index of glass is between 2 and 9/4.

Illustrative Example 5.39

A ray of light passes through a transparent sphere of refractive index μ and radius R. If b is the distance between the incident ray and a parallel diameter of the sphere, show that the angle of deviation θ is given by the expression

$$\sin\frac{\theta}{2}=(b/\mu R^2)\,[(\mu^2R^2-b^2)^{1/2}-(R^2-b^2)^{1/2}]$$

Solution

The ray diagram of the light ray passing through the sphere is shown in figure-5.154

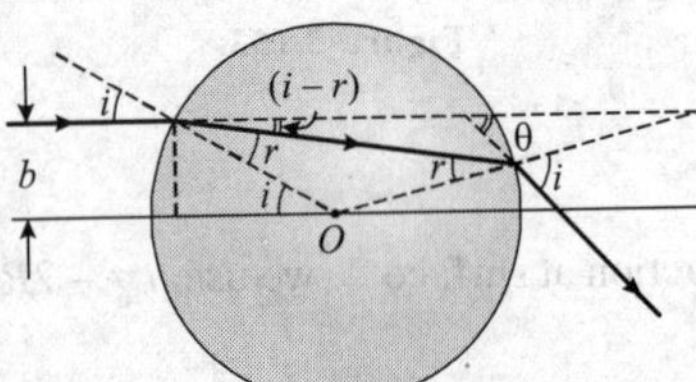

Figure 5.154

From above figure, the angle of deviation is given as

$$\theta=(i-r)+(i-r)=2i-2r=2(i-r)$$

$$\Rightarrow\quad \frac{\theta}{2}=(i-r)$$

Taking sine on both sides of above equation, we get

$$\sin\frac{\theta}{2}=\sin(i-r)$$

$$\Rightarrow\quad \sin\frac{\theta}{2}=\sin i\cos r-\cos i\sin r \qquad \dots(5.54)$$

Also from the figure we have

$$\sin i=\frac{b}{R}$$

$$\Rightarrow\quad \cos i=\sqrt{\left(1-\frac{b^2}{R^2}\right)}$$

By Snell's law we have

$$\sin r=\frac{\sin i}{\mu}=\frac{b}{\mu R}$$

and

$$\cos r=\sqrt{\left(1-\frac{b^2}{\mu^2R^2}\right)}$$

Substituting these values in equation-(5.54), we get

$$\sin\frac{\theta}{2}=\frac{b}{R}\sqrt{\left(1-\frac{b^2}{\mu^2R^2}\right)}-\sqrt{\left(1-\frac{b^2}{R^2}\right)}\frac{b}{\mu R}$$

$$\Rightarrow\quad \sin\frac{\theta}{2}=\frac{b}{R}\sqrt{\left(\frac{\mu^2R^2-b^2}{\mu^2R^2}\right)}-\sqrt{\left(\frac{R^2-b^2}{R^2}\right)}\frac{b}{\mu R}$$

$$\Rightarrow\quad \sin\frac{\theta}{2}=\frac{b}{\mu R^2}\sqrt{(\mu^2R^2-b^2)}-\sqrt{(R^2-b^2)}\frac{b}{\mu R^2}$$

$$\Rightarrow\quad \sin\frac{\theta}{2}=\frac{b}{\mu R^2}[(\mu^2R^2-b^2)^{1/2}-(R^2-b^2)^{1/2}]$$

Illustrative Example 5.40

A parallel beam of light travelling in water (refractive index = 4/3) is refracted by a spherical air bubble of radius 2 mm, situated in water. Assuming the light rays to be parallel

(a) Find the position of the image due to refraction at the first surface and the position of the final image.

(b) Draw a ray diagram showing the positions of both the images.

Solution

(a) For refraction at first surface, we use

$$\mu_2=1;\ \mu_1=(4/3);\ u=\infty \text{ and } R_1=2\text{ mm}$$

So the position of image due to refraction at first surface is given by refraction formula as

$$\frac{\mu_2}{v}-\frac{\mu_1}{u}=\frac{\mu_2-\mu_1}{R}$$

$$\Rightarrow\quad \frac{1}{v_1}-\frac{(4/3)}{\infty}=\frac{1-(4/3)}{2}$$

Solving we get $\quad v_1=-6$ mm

Hence the image is formed at a distance of 6 mm to the left of first surface. The ray diagram is shown in figure-5.155.

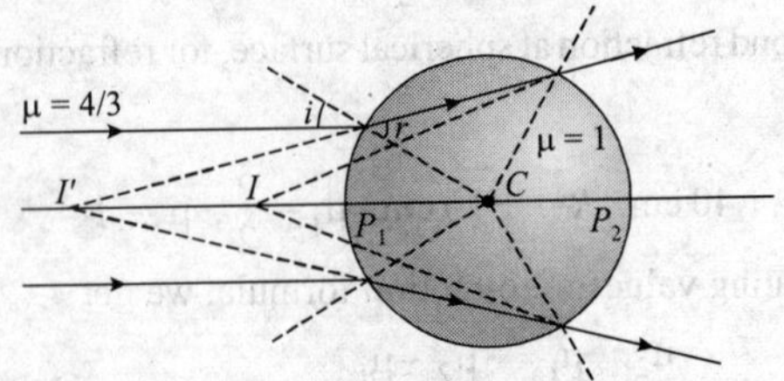

Figure 5.155

(b) For refraction at second surface we use

$u_1 = -(6+4) = -10$ mm,

$\mu_1 = 1$; $\mu_2 = (4/3)$ and $R_2 = -2$ mm

$$\Rightarrow \quad \frac{(4/3)}{v} - \frac{1}{(-10)} = \frac{(4/3)-1}{(-2)}$$

Solving we get $v = -5$ mm

So the final image is produced at a distance of 5 mm to the left of the second surface.

5.11.2 Lateral Magnification of Image by Refraction

Figure-5.156 shows an object of height h above the optical axis of which image produced is of height h'. As we have already studied that for a real object if image produced is real, it will be inverted or on the other side of principal axis. In the figure we have produced image by two paraxial light rays, one which is passing through center of curvature of the interface which will get refracted undeviated and other which is incident on the optic center of the surface at an angle of incidence i which gets refracted at an angle r.

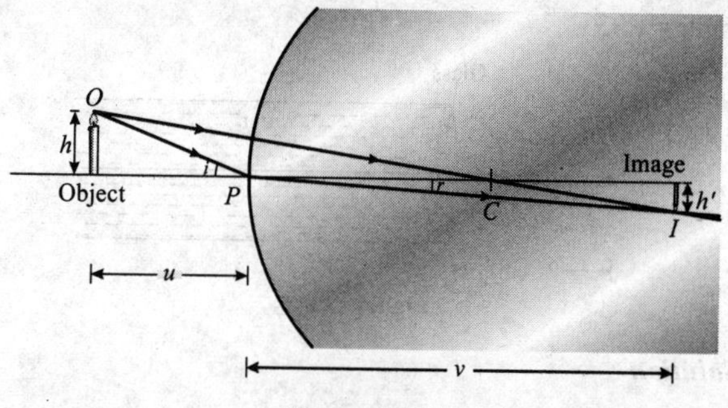

Figure 5.156

The angles i and r are very small angles as light rays are paraxial so these are related by Snell's law as

$$\mu_1 i = \mu_2 r \qquad \ldots(5.55)$$

By geometry in this figure we can use $i = \frac{h}{-u}$ and $r = \frac{-h'}{v}$ so we get

$$\frac{\mu_1 h}{u} = \frac{\mu_2 h'}{v}$$

Here we used image height h' and object distance u negative according to the sign convention.

Thus lateral magnification of image can be given as

$$m = \frac{h'}{h} = \frac{\mu_1 v}{\mu_2 u} \qquad \ldots(5.56)$$

As already discussed that above relation given by equation-(5.56) is only valid for paraxial rays. The sign of lateral magnification gives the orientation of image whether image formed is on the same side of optical axis as that of object or erected (positive) or it is on the other side of object or inverted (negative)

5.11.3 Longitudinal Magnification of Image

Figure-5.157 shows an object of width dx which is placed on optical axis of the refracting surface S at a distance x from the optic center P. After refraction its image I is produced at a distance y from the optic center which is of width dy as shown in figure.

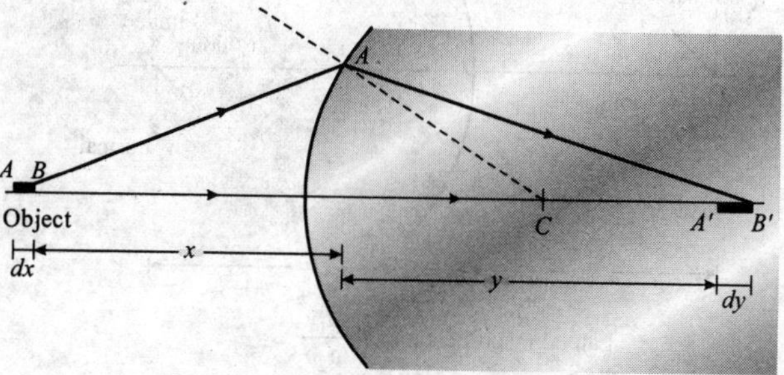

Figure 5.157

In above figure the distances of object and image from the optic center of the surface are related by the refraction formula given as

$$\frac{\mu_2}{v} - \frac{\mu_1}{u} = \frac{\mu_2 - \mu_1}{R}$$

Here we use $u = -x$, $R = +R$ and $v = +y$ which gives

$$\frac{\mu_2}{y} + \frac{\mu_1}{x} = \frac{\mu_2 - \mu_1}{R} \qquad \ldots(5.57)$$

Differentiating the above equation we get

$$-\frac{\mu_2}{y^2} - dy - \frac{\mu_1}{x^2} dx = 0 \qquad \ldots(5.58)$$

From above equation-(5.58), we get longitudinal magnification as

$$m_L = \frac{dy}{dx} = -\frac{\mu_1 y^2}{\mu_2 x^2} \qquad \ldots(5.59)$$

As already discussed that above relation given by equation-(5.59) is only valid for paraxial rays. Here negative sign shows lateral inversion of the image.

5.11.4 Effect of motion of Object or Refracting Surface on Image

Similar to the case we've discussed in case of spherical mirrors, here also for small velocities of the object or refracting surfaces, the velocity magnification along and perpendicular to the optical axis can be given by the expressions of lateral and longitudinal magnifications. Figure-5.158 shows an object moving with some velocity at a direction shown in such a way that its velocity component along the optical axis with respect to the refracting surface is $v_{o\text{-}along}$ and in direction normal to the optical axis is $v_{o\text{-}normal}$ then the image velocity components can be directly given as

$$v_{i\text{-}normal} = m \cdot v_{o\text{-}normal}$$

$$v_{i\text{-}along} = m_L \cdot v_{o\text{-}along}$$

v_0-normal, Image, v_i-along I, O v_0-along, Object, v_i-normal, u, v

Lateral magnification $m = \frac{\mu_1 v}{\mu_2 u}$

Longitudinal magnification $m_L = -\frac{\mu_1 v^2}{\mu_2 u^2}$

Figure 5.158

Illustrative Example 5.41

Figure-5.159 shows a small object M of length 1 mm which lies along a diametrical line of a glass sphere of radius 10 cm and $\mu = \frac{3}{2}$ which is viewed by an observer as shown. Find the size of object as seen by the observer.

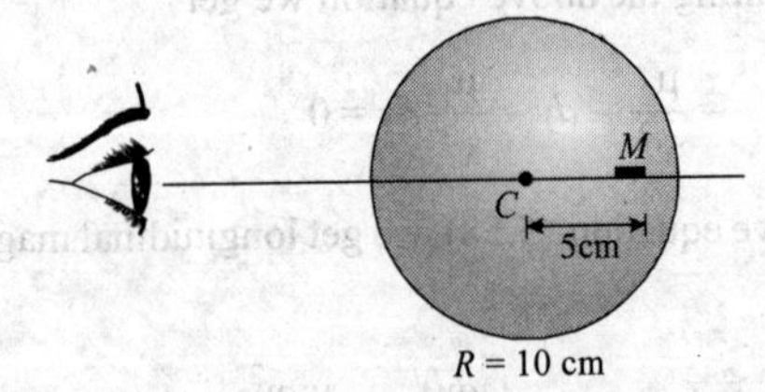

Figure 5.159

Solution

For refraction at glass-air interface, we use

$$u = +15 \text{ cm}; \; R = +10 \text{ cm}; \; \mu_1 = 3/2 \text{ and } \mu_2 = 1$$

Substituting values in refraction formula, we get

$$\frac{\mu_2}{v} - \frac{\mu_1}{u} = \frac{\mu_2 - \mu_1}{R}$$

$$\Rightarrow \quad \frac{1}{v} - \frac{3/2}{15} = \frac{1 - 3/2}{10}$$

$$\Rightarrow \quad \frac{1}{v} = \frac{1}{10} - \frac{1}{20} = \frac{1}{20}$$

$$\Rightarrow \quad v = +20 \text{ cm}$$

Longitudinal magnification for refraction is given as

$$m = \frac{\mu_1 v^2}{\mu_2 u^2} = \frac{3/2 \times (20)^2}{1 \times (15)^2}$$

$$m = \frac{1.5 \times 400}{225} = \frac{8}{3}$$

Image size $\quad \frac{8}{3} \times 1 = \frac{8}{3}$ mm

Illustrative Example 5.42

A long cylindrical tube containing water is closed by an equiconvex lens of focal length 10 cm in air. A point source is placed along the axis of the tube outside it at a distance of 21 cm from the lens. Locate the final image of the source. Refractive index of the material of the lens = 1.5 and that of water = 1.33

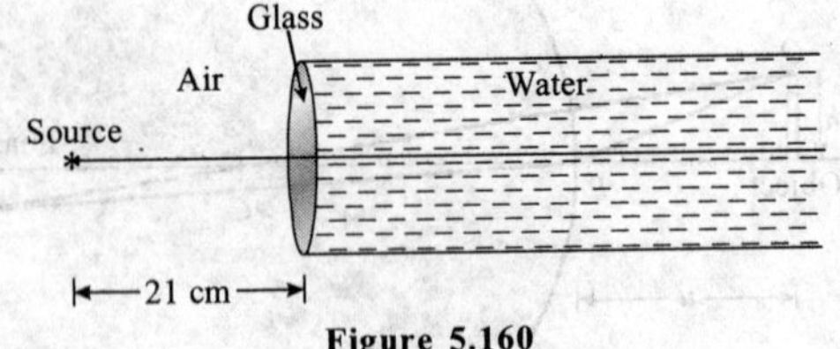

Figure 5.160

Solution

We consider first refraction at air-glass interface, using refraction formula we get

$$\frac{\mu_2}{v_1} - \frac{\mu_1}{u} = \frac{\mu_2 - \mu_1}{R}$$

Substituting $u = -21$ cm; $m_1 = 1$; $m_2 = 1.5$ and $R = +R$, we get

$$\Rightarrow \quad \frac{1.5}{v_1} + \frac{1}{21} = \frac{0.5}{R} \qquad \ldots(5.60)$$

The image formed by the first surface will act as the object for the second surface and the radius of curvature of the second surface will be taken as $-R$ for second refraction as the lens is equiconvex. For glass-water interface, we use refraction formula with $m_1 = 1.5$ and $m_2 = 1.33$ we get

$$\frac{1.33}{v} - \frac{1.5}{v_1} = \frac{1.33 - 1.5}{-R} = \frac{0.17}{R} \qquad \ldots(5.61)$$

Adding equations-(5.60) and (5.61), we get

$$\frac{1.33}{v} + \frac{1}{21} = \frac{0.67}{R} \qquad \ldots(5.62)$$

The focal length of the lens in air is 10 cm. So by using lens maker's formula we have

$$\frac{1}{f}=(\mu-1)\left(\frac{1}{R_1}-\frac{1}{R_2}\right)$$

$$\Rightarrow \quad \frac{1}{10}=(1.5-1)\left(\frac{1}{R}+\frac{1}{R}\right)=\frac{0.5}{2R}=\frac{1}{4R}$$

or $\quad R=2.5\text{ cm} \quad \ldots(5.63)$

Substituting the value of R in equation-(5.62) and solving it, we get

$$v=70\text{ cm}$$

Thus final image is formed 70 cm inside the tube and it is real.

Illustrative Example 5.43

A cylindrical glass rod of radius 0.1 m and refractive index $\sqrt{3}$ lies on horizontal plane mirror. A horizontal ray of light moving perpendicular to the axis of the rod is incident on it. At what height from the mirror should the ray be incident so that it leaves the rod at a height of 0.1 m above the plane mirror? At what distance a second similar rod, parallel to the first, be placed on the mirror, such that the emergent ray from the second rod is in line with the incident ray on the first rod ?

Solution

The situation and ray diagram is shown in figure-5.161.

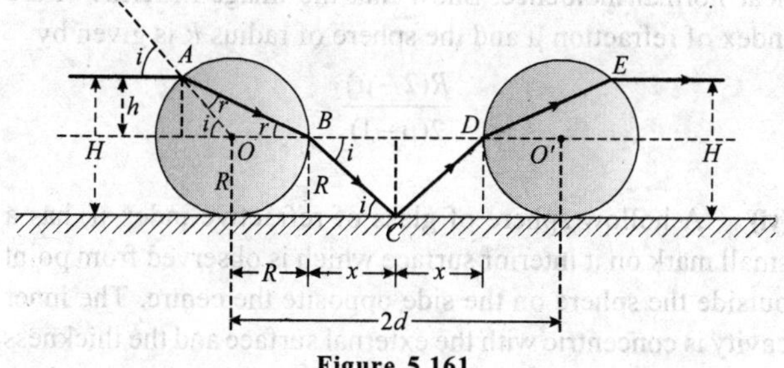

Figure 5.161

From figure we have $i=2r$

and we have $\quad h=AO\sin i$

$$=R\sin i$$

$$=R\sin 2r=2R\sin r\cos r \quad \ldots(5.64)$$

By Snell's law we have

$$\mu=\frac{\sin i}{\sin r}=\frac{\sin 2r}{r}=2\cos r$$

From equation-(5.64) we have

$$h=2R\sin r\cos r$$

$$\Rightarrow \quad h=\mu R\sin r=\mu R\sqrt{(1-\cos^2 r)}$$

$$\Rightarrow \quad h=\mu R\left[1-\frac{\mu^2}{2}\right]^{1/2}=\frac{\mu R}{2}\sqrt{(4-\mu^2)}$$

$$\Rightarrow \quad h=\frac{\sqrt{3}\times 0.1}{2}\sqrt{(4-3)}=0.086\text{ metre}$$

Total height of light ray above the plane mirror is

$$H=R+h=0.1+0.086=0.186\text{ metre}$$

From figure we have

$$x=R\cot i$$

also we use $\quad d=R+x=R(1+\cot i)$

$$\Rightarrow \quad d=R(1+\cot 2r)=R\left(1+\frac{\cos 2r}{\sin 2r}\right)$$

$$\Rightarrow \quad d=R\left(1+\frac{2\cos^2 r-1}{2\sin r\cos r}\right)$$

$$\Rightarrow \quad d=R\left[1+\frac{(2\mu^2/4)-1}{\mu\sqrt{(1-\mu^2/4)}}\right]$$

$$\Rightarrow \quad d=R\left[1+\frac{1/2}{\sqrt{3}/2}\right]=0.1\left[1+\frac{1}{\sqrt{3}}\right]$$

Distance of the second rod from the first rod is

$$2d=\left[1+\frac{1}{\sqrt{3}}\right]=0.3155\text{ m}$$

Illustrative Example 5.44

A quarter cylinder of radius R and refractive index 1.5 is placed on a table. A point object P is kept at a distance $m\,R$ from it. Find the value of m for which a ray from P will emerge parallel to the table as shown in figure-5.162.

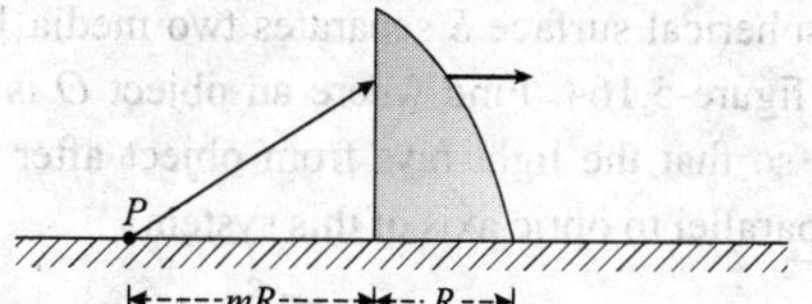

Figure 5.162

Solution

To solve this problem, we use the principle of reversibility of light.

To analyze the situation we consider that the light is incident from the right parallel to the horizontal surface of table as shown and we find where it converges on the table after emerging from the plane surface. This must be point P if path of light ray is reversed as specified in the question.

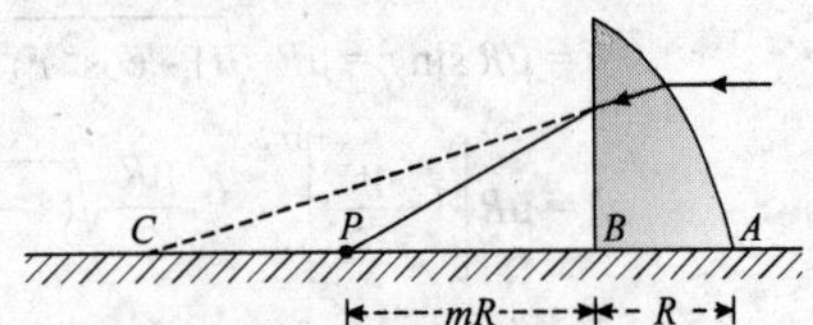

Figure 5.163

Using refraction formula for curved surface, we have

$$\frac{\mu_2}{v} - \frac{\mu_1}{u} = \frac{\mu_2 - \mu_1}{R}$$

According to the given problem we use

$$u = \infty;\ \mu_2 = 1.5;\ \mu_1 = 1 \text{ and } R = +R$$

Substituting the values in refraction formula, we get

$$\frac{1.5}{v} - \frac{1}{\infty} = \frac{1.5-1}{R}$$

$$\Rightarrow \quad v = 3R$$

When the light ray incident on the plane surface, it gets refracted and produces an image at a distance $2R/\mu = 2R/1.5 = 4R/3$.

From the given condition of we can use

$$mR = \frac{4R}{3}$$

$$\Rightarrow \quad m = \frac{4}{3}$$

Web Reference at www.physicsgalaxy.com

Age Group - High School Physics | Age 17-19 Years

Section - OPTICS

Topic - Geometrical Optics II - Refraction of Light

Module Number - 16 to 24 and 33

Practice Exercise 5.4

(i) A spherical surface S separates two media 1 and 2 as shown in figure-5.164. Find where an object O is placed in medium-I so that the light rays from object after refraction becomes parallel to optic axis of this system.

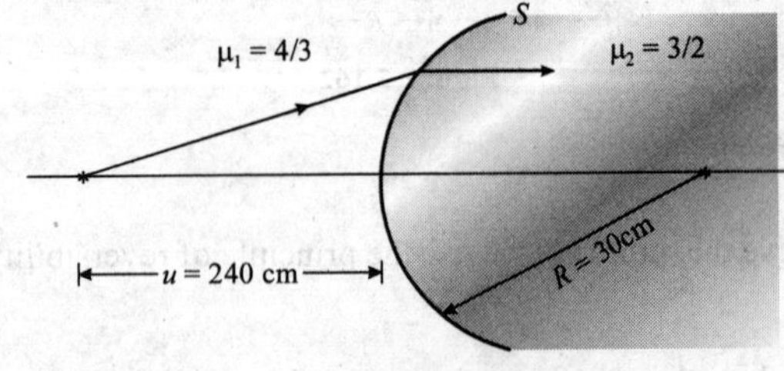

Figure 5.164

[240 cm]

(ii) A glass sphere of radius 5 cm has a small bubble at a distance 2 cm from its centre. The bubble is viewed along a diameter of the sphere from the side on which it lies. How far from the surface will it appear. Refractive index of glass is 1.5.

[2.5 cm behind the surface]

(iii) A ray of light refracted through a sphere, whose material has a refractive index μ in such a way that it passes through the extremities of two radii which make an angle θ with each other. Prove that if α is the deviation of the ray caused by its passage through sphere

$$\cos\frac{1}{2}(\theta - \alpha) = \mu \cos \theta/2$$

(iv) A ray is incident on a glass sphere as shown in figure-5.165. The opposite surface of the sphere is partially silvered. If the net deviation of the ray transmitted at the partially silvered surface is 1/3rd of the net deviation suffered by the ray reflected at the partially silvered surface (after emerging out of the sphere), find the refractive index of the sphere.

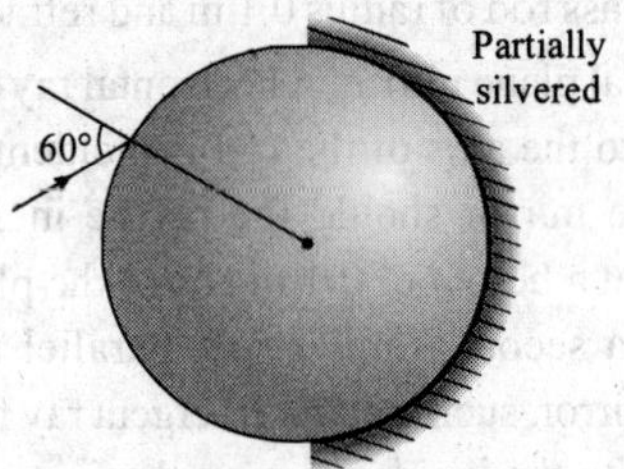

Figure 5.165

[$\sqrt{3}$]

(v) A parallel incident beam falls on a solid glass sphere at near normal incidence. Show that the image in terms of the index of refraction μ and the sphere of radius R is given by

$$\frac{R(2-\mu)}{2(\mu-1)}$$

(vi) A hollow sphere of glass of refractive index μ, has a small mark on it interior surface which is observed from point outside the sphere on the side opposite the centre. The inner cavity is concentric with the external surface and the thickness of glass is everywhere equal to the radius of the inner surface. Prove that the mark will appear nearer than it really is by a distance $(\mu - 1)\, R/(3\mu - 1)$, where R is the radius of the inner surface.

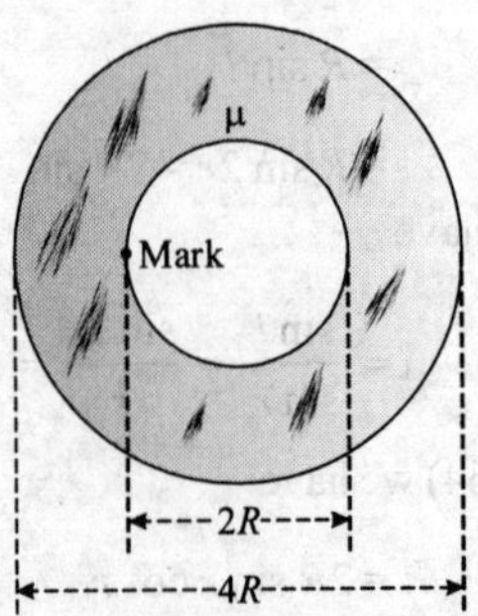

Figure 5.166

(vii) A transparent sphere of radius R has a cavity of radius $\frac{R}{2}$ as shown in figure-5.167. Find the refractive index of the sphere if a parallel beam of light falling on left surface focuses at point P.

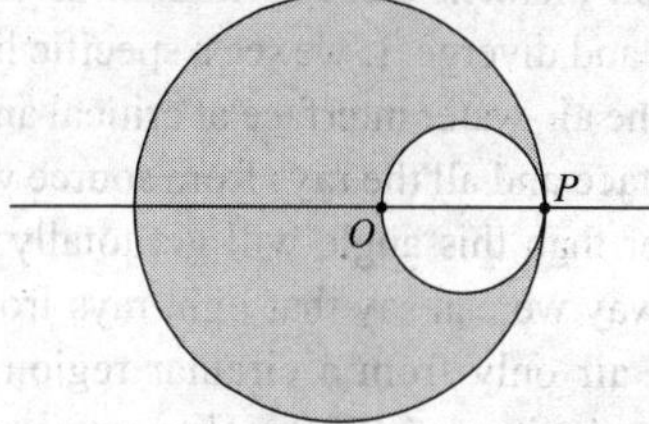

Figure 5.167

[$\frac{3+\sqrt{5}}{2}$]

(viii) A light ray incident at a point on the surface of a glass sphere of $\mu = \sqrt{3}$ at an angle of incidence 60°. It is reflected and refracted at the farther surface of sphere. Find the angle between reflected and refracted ray at this surface.

[90°]

(ix) A glass sphere ($\mu = 1.5$) with a radius of 15.0 cm has a tiny air bubble 5 cm above its centre. The sphere is viewed looking down along the extended radius containing the bubble. What is the apparent depth of the bubble below the surface of the sphere ?

[8.57 cm from top]

(x) Figure-5.168 shows a glass hemisphere placed on a white horizontal sheet. A vertical paraxial light beam of diameter d incident on the curved surface of hemisphere as shown. Find the diameter of the light spot formed on sheet after refraction.

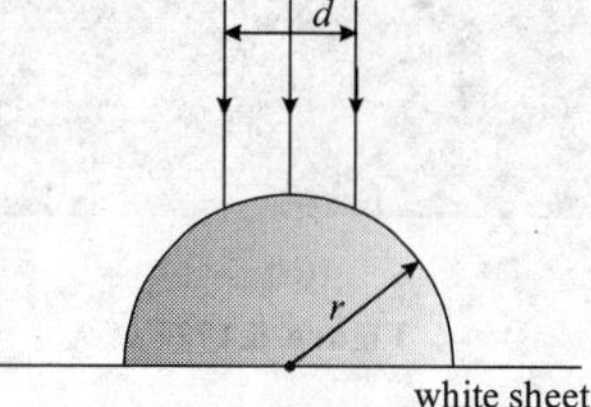

Figure 5.168

[$\frac{2d}{3}$]

(xi) Figure shows a fish bowl of radius 10 cm in which along a diametrical line a fish F is moving at speed 2 mm/sec. Find the speed of fish as observed by an observer from outside along same line when fish is at a distance 5 cm from the centre of bowl to right of it as shown in figure-5.169.

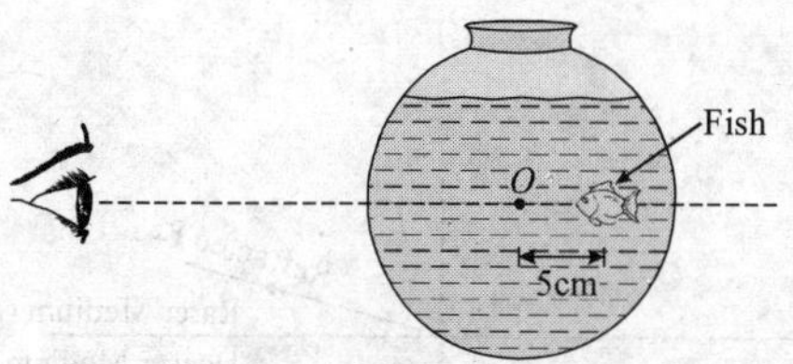

Figure 5.169

[3.84 mm/s]

(xii) Figure-5.170 shows an irregular block of material of refractive index $\sqrt{2}$. A ray of light strikes the face AB as shown in figure. After refraction it is incident on a spherical surface CD of radius of curvature 0.4 m and enter a medium of refractive index 1.514 to meet PQ at E. Find the distance OE upto two places of decimal.

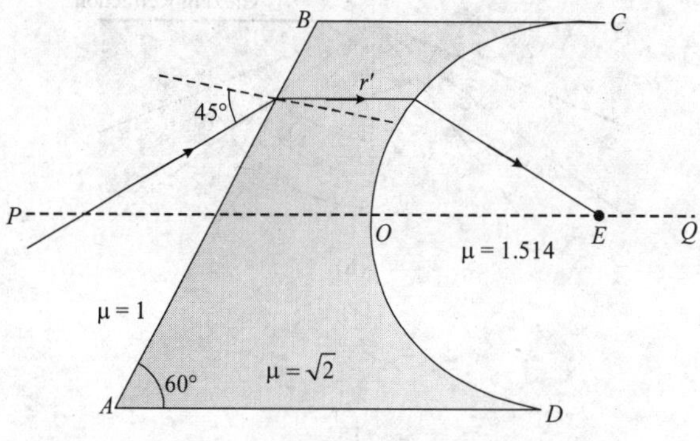

Figure 5.170

[6.06 m]

5.12 *Total Internal Reflection*

Figure-5.171(a) shows a light ray refracting through an interface of two media. The incident light ray is travelling in denser medium and after refraction it bends away from normal as we know and this figure also shows the reflected ray which is always present in all cases of incidence and it is reflected at the same angle of incidence. If we increase the angle of incidence as shown in figure-5.171(b), the angle of refraction also increases. As the angle of refraction is more than the angle of incidence it will approach to 90° at some specific value of i as shown. This angle of incidence at which the refracted ray grazes along the interface of the two media is called *'Critical Angle'* for this pair of two media. Figure-5.171(c) shows a light ray incident on the medium boundary at an angle slightly greater than critical angle at which no refracted ray exist and only reflected ray exist. This is called *'Total Internal Reflection'* and it occurs when a light ray travelling in a denser medium incident on a boundary of a rarer medium at an angle greater than the critical angle.

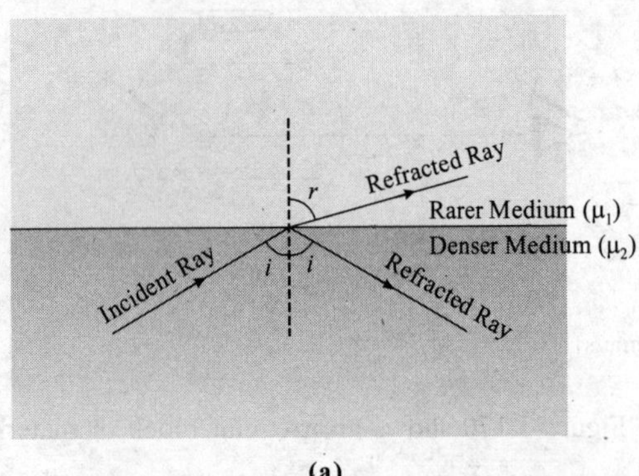

(a)

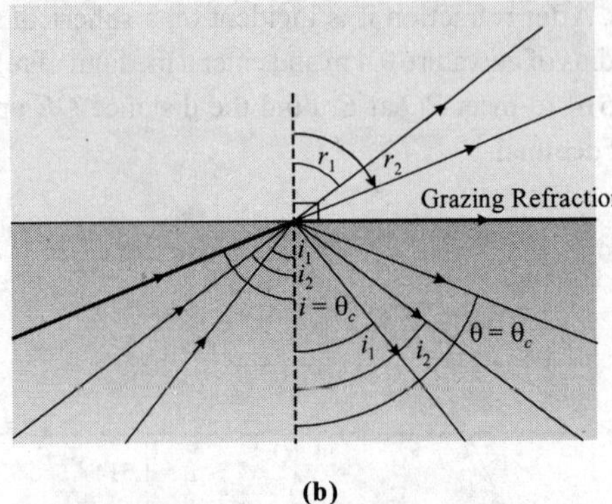

(b)

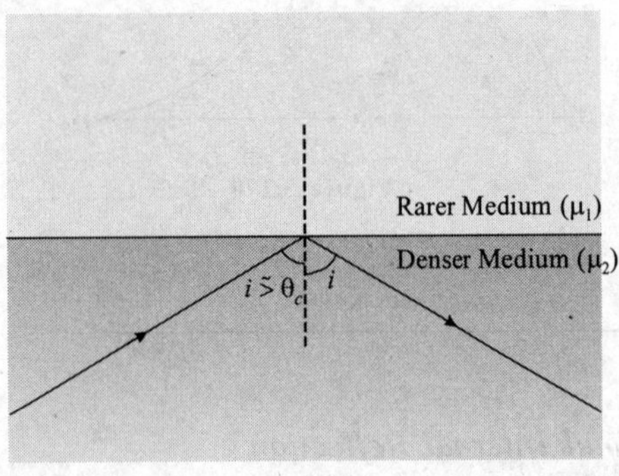

(c)

Figure 5.171

The critical angle can be given by Snell's law at the boundary as

$$\mu_2 \sin \theta_c = \mu_1 \sin 90^\circ$$

$$\Rightarrow \qquad \sin \theta_c = \frac{\mu_1}{\mu_2}$$

$$\Rightarrow \qquad \theta_c = \sin^{-1}\left(\frac{\mu_1}{\mu_2}\right)$$

For a light ray passing through a denser medium having refractive index μ incident on the boundary of air ($\mu_{air} = 1$) in the surrounding of the medium then critical angle for this medium can be given as

$$\theta_c = \sin^{-1}\left(\frac{1}{\mu}\right)$$

5.12.1 Refraction of Light Rays from a Source in a Denser Medium to Air

Figure-5.172(a) shows a point isotropic source of light placed inside water at a depth h below the air-water boundary. The light rays which incident close to normal as shown will get refracted to air and diverge. If we see a specific light ray which is incident on the air-water interface at critical angle will graze along the interface and all the rays from source which incident at angle greater than this angle will get totally reflected into water. In this way we can say that light rays from source will emerge out in air only from a circular region as shown by perspective view in figure-5.172(b). Here we can see that all the light rays from the source on the surface of a conical region of half angle θ_c will graze radially along the air-water interface and all light rays from source falling on interface within this conical region will escape to air and all the light rays falling on interface outside this conical region will get totally internally reflected and will not come out in air.

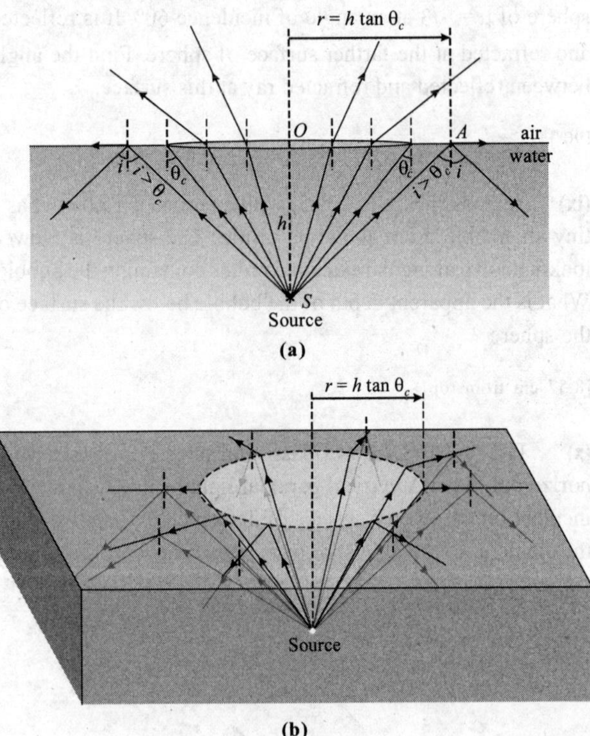

Figure 5.172

In figure-5.172(a) in *DSOA* we can write

$$\tan \theta_c = \frac{r}{h}$$

$$\Rightarrow \qquad r = h \tan \theta_c \qquad \ldots(5.65)$$

Equation-(5.65) gives the radius of the circle on the interface just above the point source of light from which light rays escape to air. By using the concept of solid angle of this cone we can also find the fraction of total light power of the source which gets refracted to air in this case. The solid angle of the cone shown in figure-5.172(b) with half angle θ_c is given as

$$\Omega = 2\pi(1-\cos\theta_c)$$

$$\Rightarrow \quad \Omega = 2\pi(1-\sqrt{1-\sin^2\theta_c})$$

$$\Rightarrow \quad \Omega = 2\pi\left(1-\sqrt{1-\frac{1}{\mu^2}}\right) \text{(As } \sin\cos\theta_c = \frac{1}{\mu}\text{)}$$

At the source all light rays are emitted isotropically in total solid angle 4π steradian in which total power of light source is distributed uniformly. If we consider the source power is P watt then the light power which is escaping out from water to air is the power within the shaded conical region as shown in figure-5.172(b) which is given as

$$P_{\text{to air}} = \frac{P}{4\pi} \times \Omega$$

$$\Rightarrow \quad P_{\text{to air}} = \frac{P}{4\pi} \times 2\pi\left(1-\sqrt{1-\frac{1}{\mu^2}}\right) = \frac{P}{2}\left(1-\sqrt{1-\frac{1}{\mu^2}}\right)$$

The fraction of light power of source which escapes from water is given as

$$f = \frac{P_{to\ air}}{P} = \frac{1}{2}\left(1-\sqrt{1-\frac{1}{\mu^2}}\right)$$

5.12.2 Cases of Grazing Incidence of Light on a Media Interface

We know that path of a light ray in cases of reflection and refraction is retractable and we have studied that a light ray travelling in denser medium when incident on a boundary of rarer medium at critical angle will graze along the boundary as shown in figure-5.173(a). So by the concept of reversibility of light we can state that a light ray travelling in a rarer medium when incident on the boundary of a denser medium at angle of incidence approximately 90° which is called grazing incidence of light as shown in figure-5.173(b), the light will enter in the denser medium at critical angle θ_c.

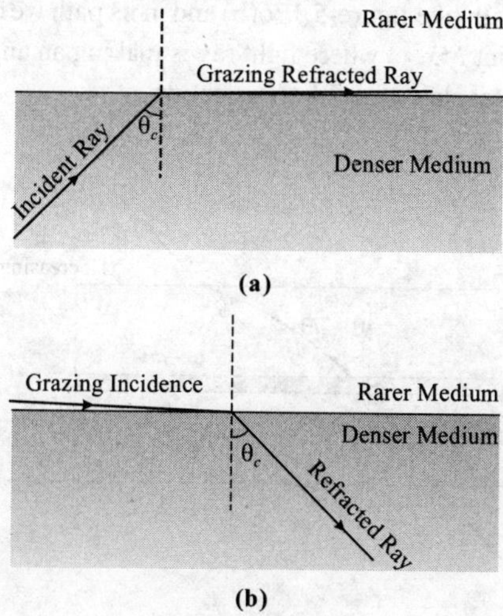

Figure 5.173

When a light ray incident on the boundary of two media from the side of denser medium in a grazing manner at incidence angle 90° as shown in figure-5.174 then the light ray passes as it is incident on the boundary as the incidence angle is more than critical angle so it gets internally reflected.

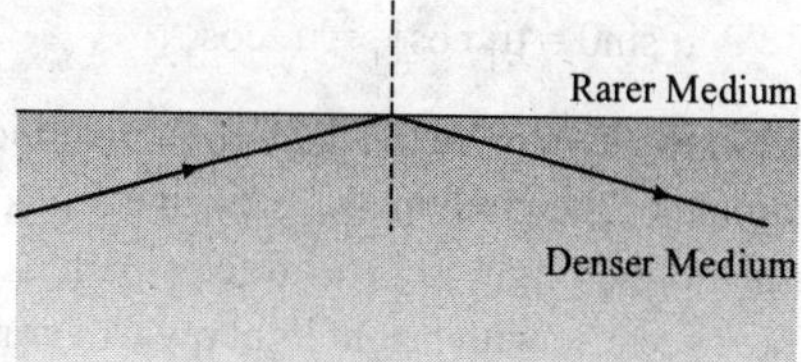

Figure 5.174

5.12.3 Refraction by a Transparent Medium of varying Refractive Index

When a light ray incident on the surface of a medium having continuously varying refractive index with distance then the path of light ray is not a straight line. Figure-5.175 shows a medium in which we consider that its refractive index increases with x-coordinate of the position. To understand the path of light shown in this figure we consider an elemental slab of medium at a position x and having thickness dx which is shown in figure by a shaded region. When a light ray incident on this slab at an angle θ then it will slightly bent toward normal as refractive index of the medium slightly increases on the right side of slab. In the same sense as continuously refractive index of the medium is increasing to the right, the light will continuously bend toward normal to each elemental slab which is resulting in a curved path as shown in the figure.

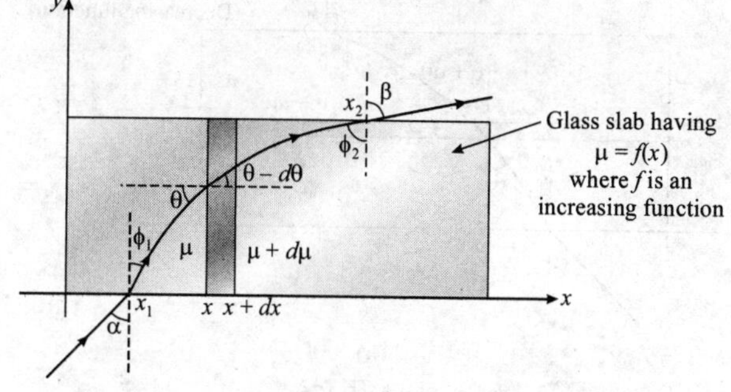

Figure 5.175

In above figure, inside the medium for all parallel normals, we can relate the angles ϕ_1 and ϕ_2 by Snell's law at points A and B where refractive indices are μ_1 and μ_2 as given below.

$$\mu_1 \sin(90° - \phi_1) = \mu_2 \sin(90° - \phi_2)$$

$$\Rightarrow \quad \mu_1 \cos\phi_1 = \mu_2 \cos\phi_2 \quad \ldots(5.66)$$

At points A and B we can also apply Snell's law to relate incidence and emergence angle α and β as

$$\sin\alpha = \mu_1 \sin\phi_1 \quad \ldots(5.67)$$

and

$$\sin\beta = \mu_2 \sin\phi_2 \quad \ldots(5.68)$$

Above equations-(5.66), (5.67) and (5.68) are used to relate the refractive indices and the angle made by the light ray with the medium boundaries. At a general point inside the slab also the refractive index m and the angle θ can be related with terminal angles as

$$\mu \sin\theta = \mu_1 \cos\phi_1 = \mu_2 \cos\phi_2 \quad \ldots(5.69)$$

Figure-5.176 shows a medium in which refractive index varies with y-coordinate of the medium. If refractive index increases with y-coordinate then light ray will trace a path as shown in figure-5.176(a) because with height light ray will continuously bend toward the normal to all elemental slabs considered parallel to x-axis. If refractive index decreases with y-coordinate then light ray will trace a path as shown in figure-5.176(b) because in this case light ray will continuously bend away from the normal to all elemental slabs.

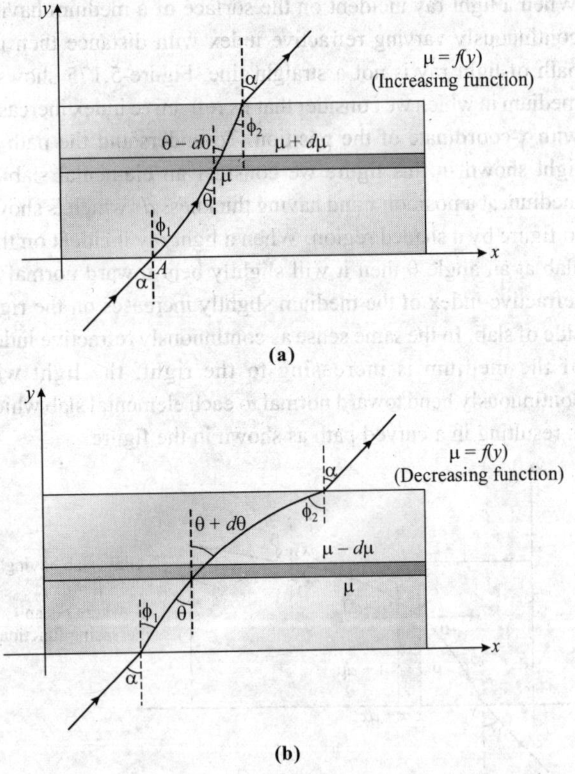

Figure 5.176

In both of the above cases light will emerge out in air at the same angle α at which light ray incident on the slab. This is because all the elemental slabs are considered horizontally and all the normals in between the slabs at intermediate refraction as well as at medium boundaries are parallel.

5.12.4 Total Internal Reflection in a Medium of varying Refractive Index

Figure-5.177 shows a medium in which its refractive index varies with height(y-coordinate) so light after entering into the medium follows a path like the one shown in figure-5.176(b). In this process light ray will continuously bend away from normal and at some height y_m the value of refractive index approaches to such a value that the angle of incidence of light ray on elemental slab becomes 90°. After this point light ray will start bending inward and follows a path which is mirror image of the initial curved path during refraction upto this point after incidence and from point B light ray will come out in air at the same angle α at which it was incident.

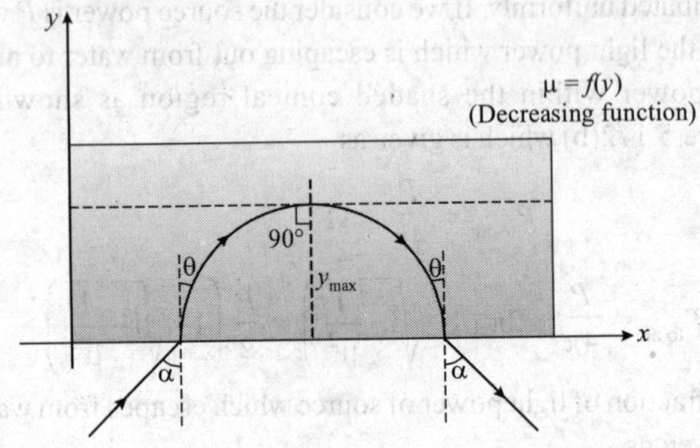

Figure 5.177

In above figure maximum height to which light ray can ascend can be obtained by using Snell's law at the point of incidence and at the topmost point as given below.

$$\sin\alpha = \mu_{ym} \sin(90°)$$

$$\Rightarrow \quad \sin\alpha = f(y_m)$$

Solving the above equation we can get the value of y_m.

5.12.5 Equation of Trajectory of a Light Ray in a Medium of varying Refractive Index

Figure-5.178 shows a medium in which its refractive index varies with y-coordinate according to the function $\mu = f(y)$ which is a decreasing function. The light ray after entering in the medium follows a path like figure-5.176(b) and in its path we consider a general point $P(x, y)$ where light ray is making an angle θ with the elemental slab of width dx as shown.

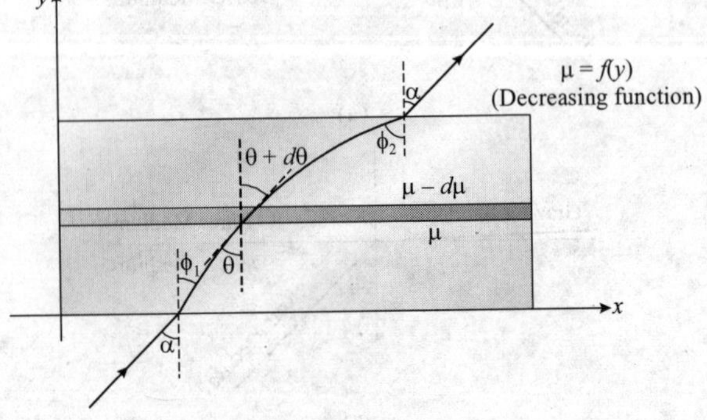

Figure 5.178

In above figure, at point P the angle θ can be related with incident angle α by Snell's law as given below.

$$\sin\alpha = \mu_y \sin\theta \qquad \text{...(5.70)}$$

At point $P(x, y)$ the slope of light ray can be written as

$$\frac{dy}{dx} = \cot\theta = \frac{\sqrt{1-\sin^2\theta}}{\sin\theta} \qquad \text{...(5.71)}$$

Substituting the value of $\sin\theta$ from equation-(5.70) into equation-(5.71), we get

$$\frac{dy}{dx} = \frac{\sqrt{1-\left[\dfrac{\sin\alpha}{f(y)}\right]^2}}{\left[\dfrac{\sin\alpha}{f(y)}\right]} \qquad [\text{As } \mu_y = f(y)] \text{ ...(5.72)}$$

In above equation-(5.72) we can separate the variables and integrate the equation on both sides for x and y which will give us a relation in x and y as equation of trajectory of the light ray in the medium. The expression in equation-(5.72) seems complex for integration but generally the function $f(y)$ is given in such a way that the overall integration term is not very lengthy in calculations.

Illustrative Example 5.45

Find at what angle a fish inside a lake will see a rising sun. (Take $\mu_\omega = 4/3$)

Solution

Figure-5.179 shows the situation of a fish looking at a rising sun. The light rays from the rising sun incident on the water surface of the lake in grazing incidence manner which enters in side water at critical angle which is seen by the fish as shown. The sun in this situation will appear at critical angle from the normal to the water surface.

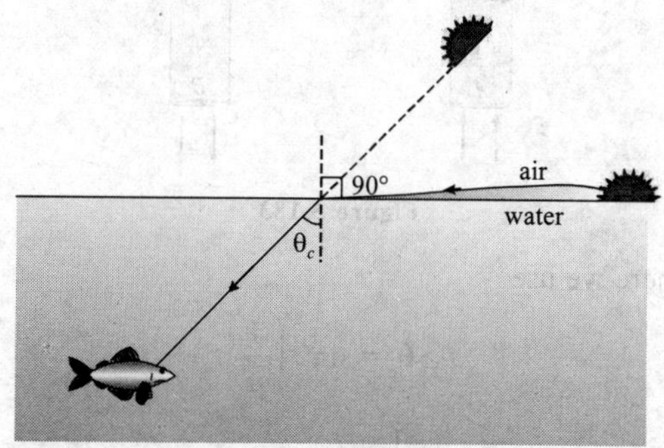

Figure 5.179

Critical angle for air-water interface is given as

$$\theta_c = \sin^{-1}\left(\frac{1}{\mu}\right)$$

$$\Rightarrow \qquad \theta_c = \sin^{-1}\left(\frac{3}{4}\right)$$

Illustrative Example 5.46

A light ray incident from glass $\left(\mu = \dfrac{3}{2}\right)$ to air interface. Find the angle of incidence at which deviation angle of light will becomes 90°.

Solution

For deviation angle to be 90° light must reflect internally as for glass critical angle is less than 45° so for all refracted rays deviation angle will be smaller. This is shown in figure-5.180.

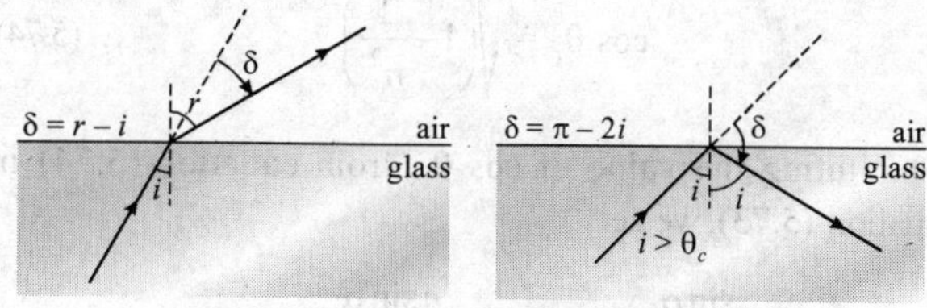

Figure 5.180

Deviation angle δ will be 90° in figure shown when

$$\delta = \pi - 2i = 90°$$

$$\Rightarrow \qquad i = \frac{\pi - \dfrac{\pi}{2}}{2} = \frac{\pi}{4}$$

$$\Rightarrow \qquad i = 45°$$

Illustrative Example 5.47

Light is incident at an angle α on one planar end of a transparent cylindrical rod of refractive index n. Determine the least value of n so that the light entering the rod does not emerge from the curved surface of the rod irrespective of the value of α.

Solution

The situation is shown in figure-5.181. From the figure we can see that the light entering the rod will not emerge from the curved surface if the angle $(90 - r)$ is greater than the critical angle i.e., $(90 - r) > \theta_C$ or $r < (90 - \theta_C)$.

According to Snell's law we have

$$\frac{\sin\alpha}{\sin r} = n$$

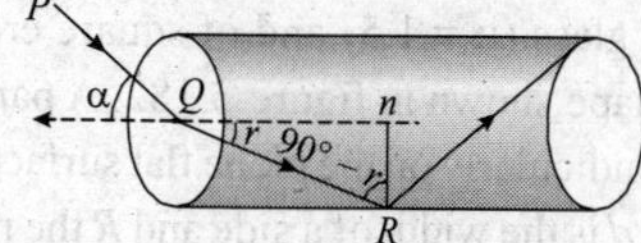

Figure 5.181

For the given condition

$$\sin\alpha = n\sin r < n\sin(90 - \theta_C)$$

$$\Rightarrow \quad \frac{\sin\alpha}{\sin(90-\theta_C)} < n$$

$$\Rightarrow \quad \frac{\sin\alpha}{\cos\theta_C} < n \quad \ldots(5.73)$$

As $\quad n = \dfrac{1}{\sin\theta_C}$

$$\Rightarrow \quad \sin\theta_C = \frac{1}{n}$$

$$\Rightarrow \quad \cos\theta_C = \sqrt{\left(1-\frac{1}{n^2}\right)} \quad \ldots(5.74)$$

Substituting the value of $\cos\theta_C$ from equation-(5.74) in equation-(5.73), we get

$$\frac{\sin\alpha}{\sqrt{\left(1-\frac{1}{n^2}\right)}} < n \text{ or } \frac{n\sin\alpha}{\sqrt{(n^2-1)}} < n$$

The maximum value of $\sin\alpha = 1$

$$\Rightarrow \quad \frac{1}{\sqrt{(n^2-1)}} < 1 \text{ or } (n^2-1) > 1 \text{ or } n^2 > 2$$

$$\Rightarrow \quad n > \sqrt{2}$$

So the least value of n is $\sqrt{2}$

Alternative Direct Method : In the figure-5.181 shown the light ray will be internally reflected when the angle $(90° - r)$ is more than or equal to θ_C and maximum value of the angle $(90° - r)$ will occur when r is maximum and maximum possible value of r is also θ_C thus for internal reflection at inner surface we use

$$90° - \theta_C > \theta_C$$

$$\Rightarrow \quad \theta_C < 45°$$

Thus refractive index of the material is given as

$$n > \frac{1}{\sin\theta_C}$$

$$\Rightarrow \quad n > \sqrt{2}$$

 # Illustrative Example 5.48

A rod made of glass ($\mu = 1.5$) and of square cross-section is bent into the shape shown in figure-5.182. A parallel beam of light falls perpendicularly on the plane flat surface A. Referring to the diagram, d is the width of a side and R the radius of inner semicircle. Find the maximum value of ratio (d/R) so that all light entering the glass through surface A emerge from the glass through B.

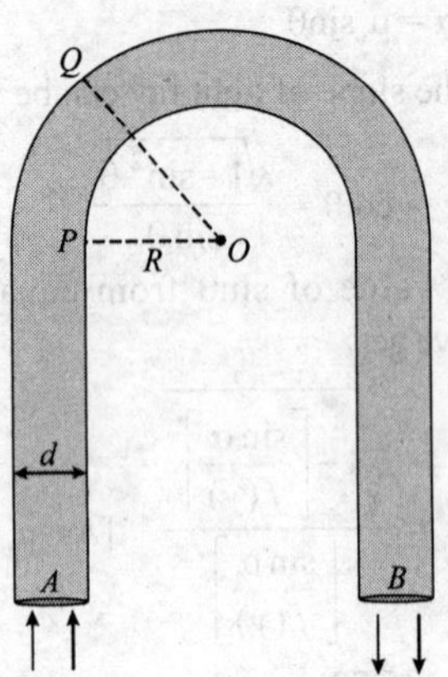

Figure 5.182

Solution

In order that all the light rays entering at end A emerge out from end B, the minimum angle of incident i for the light ray (say PQ as shown in figure-5.183), should be equal to or greater than critical angle θ_c for air glass interface. If it happens for ray PQ then for all the light rays total internal reflection occurs at inner surface of rod and all these rays will emerge out only from end B.

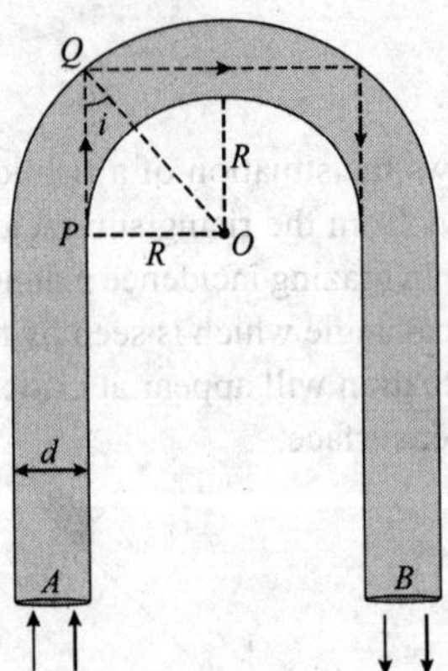

Figure 5.183

Thus here we use

$$i \geq \theta_c = \sin^{-1}\left(\frac{1}{\mu}\right)$$

$$\Rightarrow \quad \sin i \geq \frac{1}{\mu}$$

From figure, we have

$$\sin i = \frac{PO}{OQ} = \frac{R}{(R+d)}$$

$$\Rightarrow \quad \frac{R}{(R+d)} \geq \frac{1}{1.5}$$

$$\Rightarrow \quad 1.5R \geq (R+d)$$

$$\Rightarrow \quad 0.5R \geq d \quad \text{or} \quad d/R \leq 0.5$$

$$\Rightarrow \quad \left(\frac{d}{R}\right)_{max} = 0.5$$

Illustrative Example 5.49

Due to a vertical temperature gradient in the atmosphere, the index of refraction varies. Suppose index of refraction varies as $n = n_0\sqrt{1+ay}$, where n_0 is the index of refraction at the surface and $a = 2.0 \times 10^{-6}\ m^{-1}$. A person of height $h = 2.0$ m stands on a level surface. Beyond what distance will he not see the runway ?

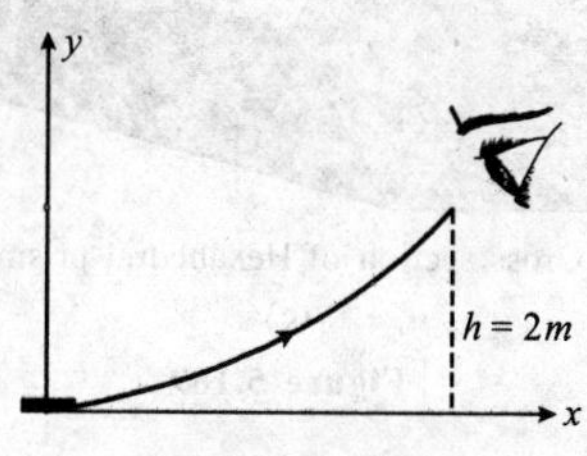

Figure 5.184

Solution

We draw a tangent on the trajectory of light at any point (x, y) which makes an angle θ with optical normal as shown in figure-5.185.

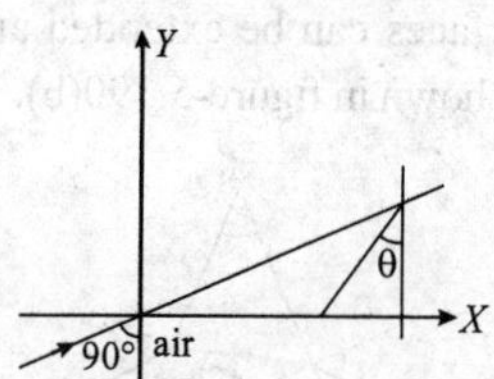

Figure 5.185

From the Snell's law, we use

$$n_0 \sin 90 = n_0\sqrt{1+ay}\ \sin\theta$$

$$\Rightarrow \quad \sin\theta = \frac{1}{\sqrt{1+ay}} \quad \ldots(5.75)$$

Slope of the tangent, we have

$$\frac{dy}{dx} = \tan(90-\theta) \quad \ldots(5.76)$$

From equation-(5.75) and (5.76) we use

$$\frac{dy}{dx} = \sqrt{ay}$$

$$\Rightarrow \quad \int_0^y \frac{dy}{\sqrt{ay}} = \int_0^x dx$$

$$\Rightarrow \quad x = 2\sqrt{\frac{y}{a}}$$

Substituting the values of a and y, we get

$$x_{max} = 2000\text{ m}$$

Illustrative Example 5.50

A prism has refracting angle 30° and μ = 2. One of the mat surfaces of the prism is polished to make it reflecting. Find the incidence angle of a light ray on other mat surface of prism so that after reflection the ray will retrace the path of incident ray.

Solution

For retracing the path of light it should incident normally on face AC as shown in figure-5.186.

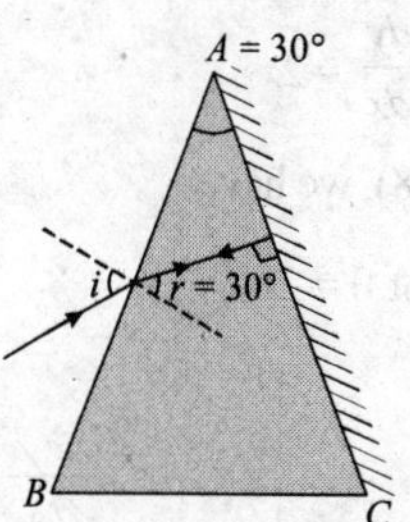

Figure 5.186

By Snell's law, we use

$$\sin i = \mu \sin r$$

$$\sin i = 2 \times \frac{1}{2} = 1$$

$$i = 90°$$

This happens for grazing incidence of light.

Illustrative Example 5.51

Find the variation of Refractive index assuming it to be a function of y such that a ray entering origin at grazing incident follows a parabolic path $y = x^2$ as shown in figure-5.187.

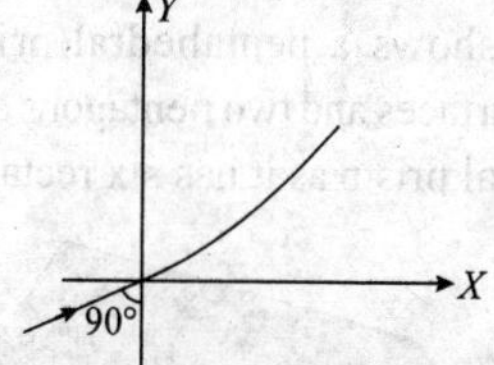

Figure 5.187

Solution

We draw a tangent at any point (x, y) which makes an angle θ with optical normal parallel to y axis.

From the Snell's law, we have

$$1.\sin 90 = \mu \sin\theta$$

$$\Rightarrow \quad \sin\theta = \frac{1}{\mu} \quad \text{... (5.77)}$$

Slope of tangent is

$$\frac{dy}{dx} = \tan(90-\theta)$$

$$\Rightarrow \quad \frac{dy}{dx} = \cot\theta \quad \text{... (5.78)}$$

The trajectory of the light ray is

$$y = x^2$$

$$\Rightarrow \quad \frac{dy}{dx} = 2x$$

From equation-(5.78), we have

$$\cot\theta = 2x$$

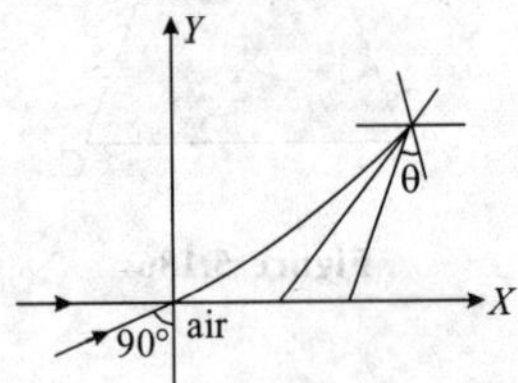

Figure 5.188

This gives $\mu = \frac{1}{\sin\theta} = \operatorname{cosec}\theta$

$$\Rightarrow \quad \mu = \sqrt{1+\cot^2\theta} = \sqrt{1+4x^2}$$

5.13 Prism

Prism is a transparent region bounded by three or more rectangular side faces and two identical polygon surfaces. Figure-5.189(a) shows the basic prism having three rectangular surfaces and two triangles bounding a transparent region. As this consist of three surfaces it is called trihedral prism. Similarly Figure-5.189(b) shows a pentahedral prism as it has five rectangular side surfaces and two pentagons and figure-5.189(c) shows a hexahedral prism as it has six rectangular surfaces.

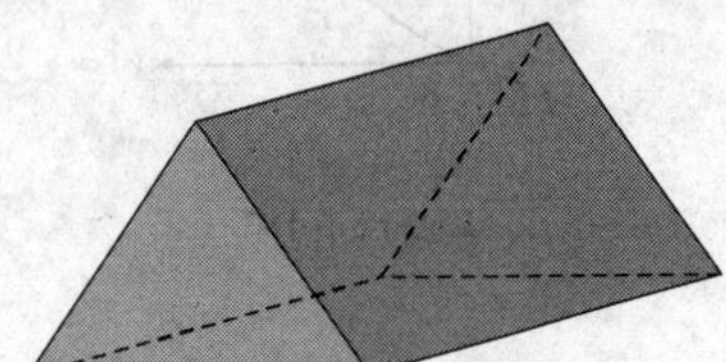
Trihedral prism
(a)

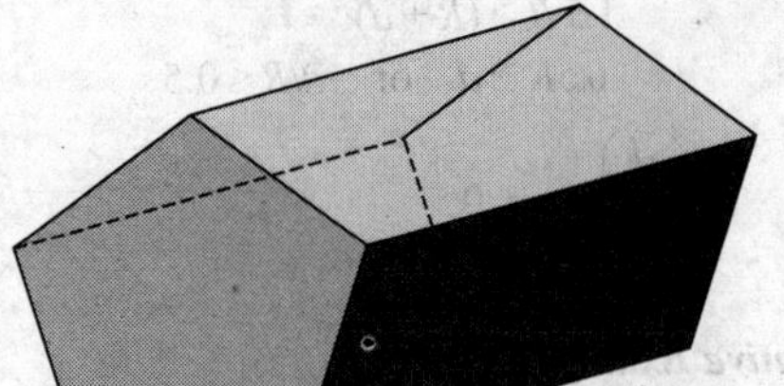
Pentahedral prism
(b)

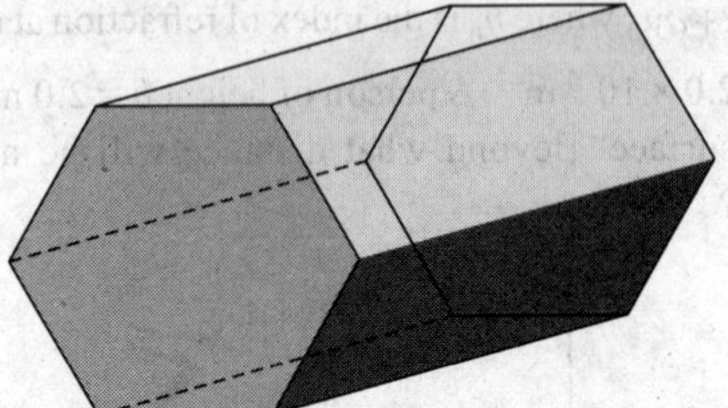
Cross section of Hexahedral prism
(c)

Figure 5.189

In this chapter mainly we will discuss about light refraction from a trihedral prism as shown in figure-5.190(a) in which we can see that a light ray falling on one surface of the prism gets refracted and then again it suffers refraction at the other side surface of prism and light ray emerge out in air. Similar to this for any-hedral prism when light is refracted from any two of its surfaces, these surfaces can be extended and considered as a trihedral prism as shown in figure-5.190(b).

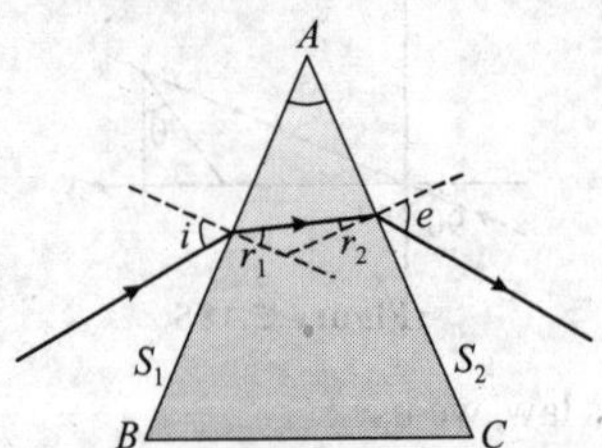

Light refraction by a trihedral prism (cross-sectional view)
(a)

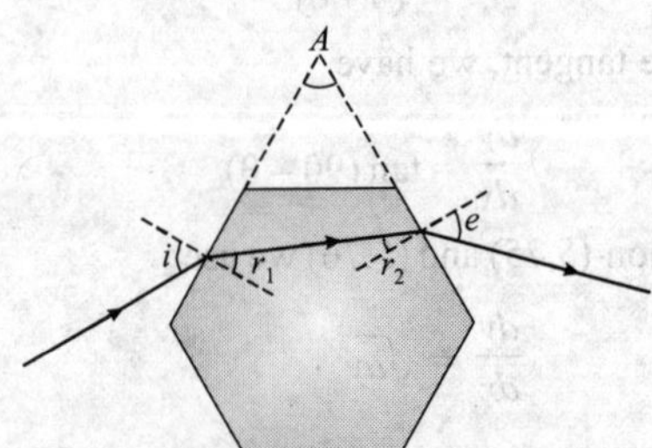

Light refraction by hexahedral prism (cross-sectional view)
(b)

Figure 5.190

5.13.1 Refraction of Light through a Trihedral Prism

As discussed in previous section, understanding of light refraction through a trihedral prism will be useful for analysis of refraction of any light ray passing through any two surfaces of a prism. Figure-5.191 shows a light ray incident on the face AB of the prism, gets refracted and emerges out after second refraction at face AC. Here AB and AC are called '*mat*' surfaces of the prism through which a light ray passes and the bottom face BC is called '*base*' of prism. The angle A which is the angle between the mat (refracting) surfaces of the prism is called '*Prism Angle*' or '*Refracting Angle of Prism*'.

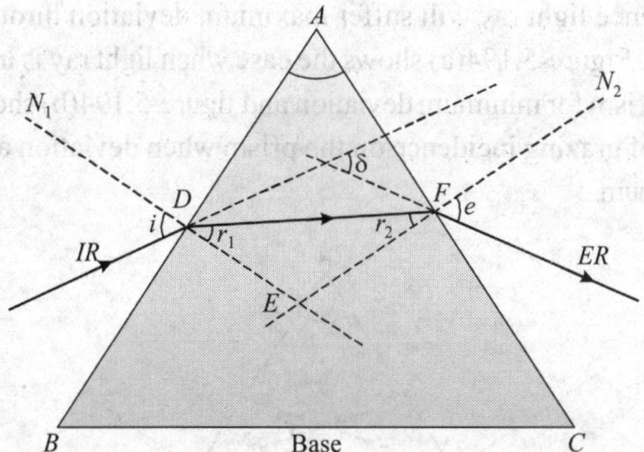

Figure 5.191

In the above figure, i is the incidence angle, r_1 and r_2 are the angle of refractions of light ray which it makes with the normal to the two refracting surfaces, e is the angle of emergence and δ is the angle of deviation of the light ray by which incident ray is totally deviated while passing through the prism.
If we use Snell's law at the points D and F, we get

$$\sin i = \mu \sin r_1 \qquad \ldots(5.79)$$

and

$$\sin e = \mu \sin r_2 \qquad \ldots(5.80)$$

In quadrilateral $ADEF$ we can see that angles ADE and AFE are right angles so we have

$$A + E = 180°$$

$$\Rightarrow \quad A + (180° - r_1 - r_2) = 180°$$

$$\Rightarrow \quad A = r_1 + r_2 \qquad \ldots(5.81)$$

From ΔDFG, we can calculate the angle of deviation as

$$\delta = (i - r_1) + (e - r_2)$$

$$\Rightarrow \quad \delta = i + e - (r_1 + r_2)$$

$$\Rightarrow \quad \delta = i + e - A \qquad \ldots(5.82)$$

In equation-(5.82) we can see that angle of deviation depends upon the incidence angle i as angle of emergence also depends upon i. To analyze the variation of deviation angle we use equations-(5.80) and (5.81) and eliminate i and e from equation-(5.82) and find deviation angle in terms of r_1.

$$\delta = \sin^{-1}(\mu \sin r_1) + \sin^{-1}[\mu \sin (A - r_1)] - A \qquad \ldots(5.83)$$

In equation-(5.83) δ depends upon r_1 and with first two terms it is clear that at $r_1 = 0$ or $r_1 = A$ the value of δ approaches to same value which signifies a minimum value of δ at some specific angle r_1 which can be obtained by the concept of maxima and minima, so we find the derivative of δ with respect to r_1 and equate to zero.

$$\frac{d\delta}{dr_1} = 0$$

$$\Rightarrow \quad \frac{d\delta}{dr_1} = \frac{\mu \cos r_1}{\sqrt{1-\mu^2 \sin^2 r_1}} - \frac{\mu \cos(A - r_1)}{\sqrt{1-\mu^2 \sin^2(A - r_1)}} = 0$$

$$\Rightarrow \quad \frac{\mu\sqrt{1-\sin^2 r_1}}{\sqrt{1-\mu^2 \sin^2 r_1}} - \frac{\mu\sqrt{1-\sin^2(A-r_1)}}{\sqrt{1-\mu^2 \sin^2(A-r_1)}} = 0$$

Taking terms on both sides of equality and squaring the terms, we get

$$(\mu^2 - 1)\sin^2 r_1 = (\mu^2 - 1)\sin^2 (A - r_1) \qquad \ldots(5.84)$$

As $r_1 < 90°$, from equation-(5.84) we get

$$r_1 = (A - r_1)$$

$$\Rightarrow \quad r_1 = \frac{A}{2} = r_2$$

So we can state that angle of deviation for a light passing through a trihedral prism will be minimum when $r_1 = r_2 = A/2$ which is the case when light passes through the prism symmetrically as shown in figure-5.192. In this case angle of incidence and angle of emergence will also be equal and given as

$$i = e = \sin^{-1}\left(\mu \sin \frac{A}{2}\right) \qquad \ldots(5.85)$$

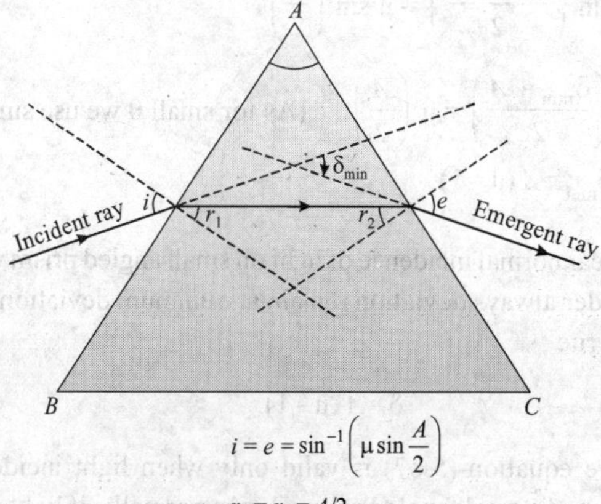

Figure 5.192

The minimum value of deviation angle is given from equation-(5.82) as

$$d_{min} = 2i - A$$

$$\Rightarrow \quad \frac{\delta_{min} + A}{2} = i = \sin^{-1}\left(\mu \sin\left(\frac{A}{2}\right)\right)$$

$$\Rightarrow \quad \sin\left(\frac{\delta_{min} + A}{2}\right) = \mu \sin\left(\frac{A}{2}\right) \qquad \ldots(5.86)$$

Above expression as given in equation-(5.86) gives the value of minimum deviation angle for a light by any prism having refracting angle A and refractive index of its material μ. A prism of which A and μ are given, it cannot deviate a light at an angle less then the deviation angle given by equation-(5.86).

5.13.2 Deviation Produced by a Small Angled Prism

Figure-5.193 shows a very small angled prism on which a light ray is incident with a very small angle to the normal on its surface, we call near normal incidence. In such a case the light will emerge almost parallel to the initial ray and we can consider that the light ray is passing symmetrically through the prism and deviation angle of light will be very small and can be given by equation-(5.86).

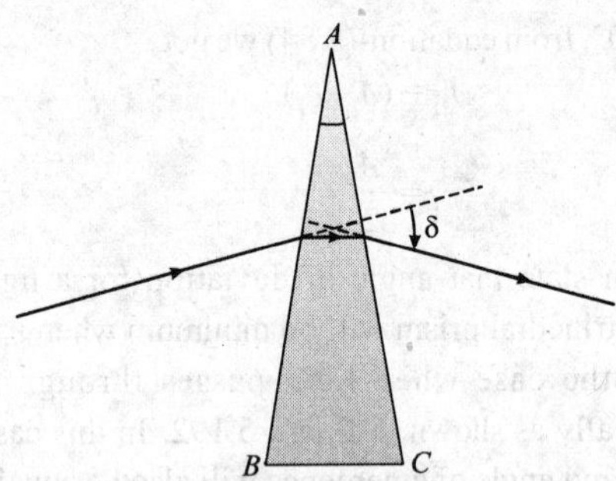

Figure 5.193

Equation-(5.86) can be rewritten for small angles δ_{min} and A as

$$\sin\left(\frac{\delta_{min} + A}{2}\right) = \mu \sin\left(\frac{A}{2}\right)$$

$$\Rightarrow \quad \left(\frac{\delta_{min} + A}{2}\right) = \mu\left(\frac{A}{2}\right) \qquad \text{(As for small } \theta \text{ we use } \sin\theta \sim \theta)$$

$$\Rightarrow \quad \delta_{min} = A(\mu - 1)$$

For near normal incidence of light on small angled prism we can consider always deviation remain at minimum deviation so we can write

$$\delta = A(\mu - 1) \qquad \ldots(5.87)$$

Above equation-(5.87) is valid only when light incident on surface of a small angled prism almost normally, if light falls at higher angle of incidence then this relation will not be valid and in that case we find deviation by using refraction at both surfaces by Snell's law.

5.13.3 Maximum Deviation of Light Ray by a Prism

As already discussed that equation-(5.86) gives the minimum deviation angle for a light ray which passes through a prism of refractive index μ and prism angle A. This happens when light ray incident on the prism surface at a specific angle of incidence when light ray passes through it symmetrically. If angle of incidence is increased or decreased, the value of angle of deviation increases. If we increase the angle of incidence to its maximum possible value of 90° then for this case of grazing incidence light ray will suffer maximum deviation through the prism. Figure-5.194(a) shows the case when light ray is incident on a prism for minimum deviation and figure-5.194(b) shows the case of grazing incidence on the prism when deviation angle is maximum.

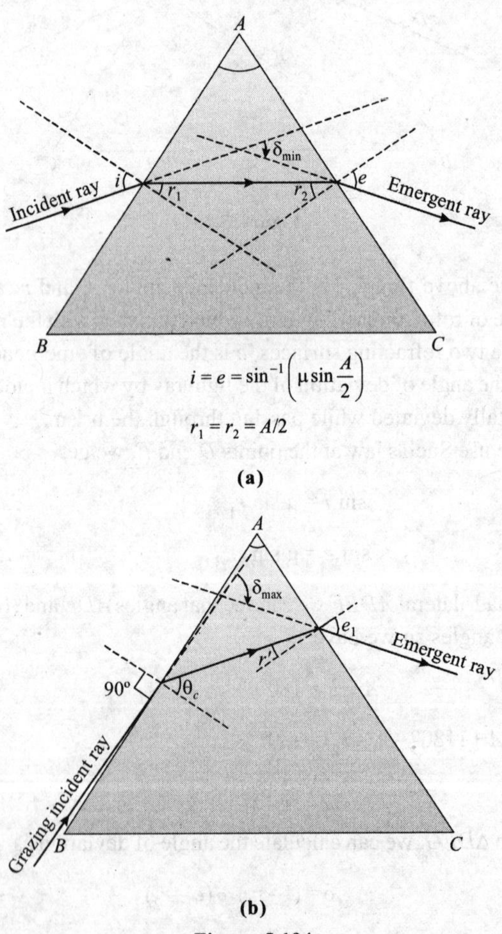

Figure 5.194

As we know that path of a light ray is re-traceable so if a light ray incident on a prism surface at such an angle of incidence at which light ray after refraction from first surface incident on the second surface at critical angle then the emergent ray will graze along the surface as shown in figure-5.195. This situation is similar to the reverse path of light ray shown in figure-5.194(b) and the angle of incidence in figure-5.195 will be equal to the angle of emergence shown in figure-5.194(b).

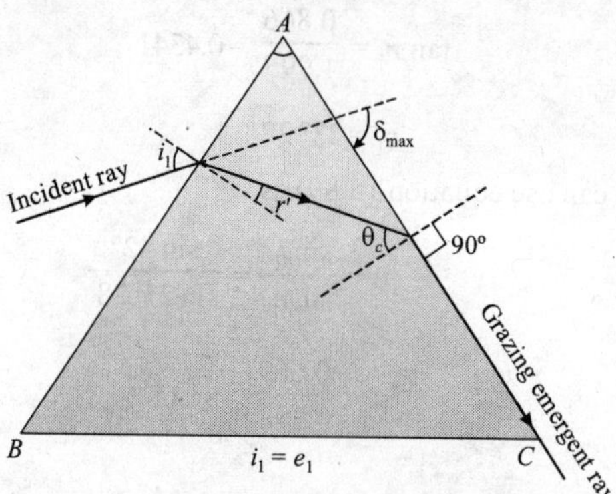

Figure 5.195

With the above analysis we can state that for a given prism there are two incidence angles at which deviation produced by the prism will be maximum. One angle is certainly 90° (case of grazing incidence) and other angle of incidence at which deviation will be maximum would be equal to the angle of emergence in case of grazing incidence. If we plot the variation of deviation angle with angle of incidence then it will look like the curve shown in figure-5.196.

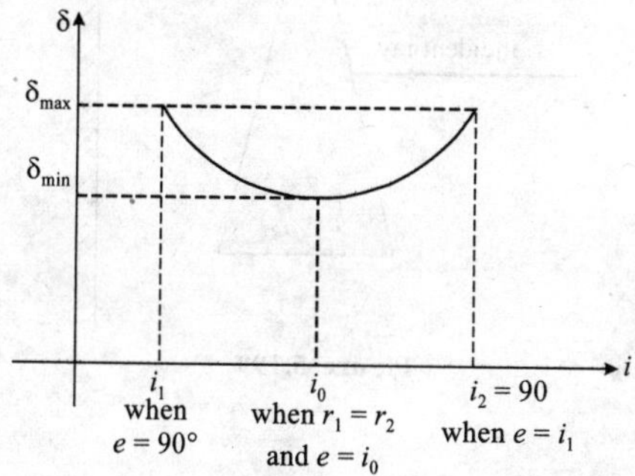

Figure 5.196

5.13.4 Condition of a Light Ray to pass through a Prism

When a light ray incident on a prism surface at some angle i and it gets refracted at an angle r as shown in figure-5.197(a). The refracted ray inside the prism incident on the second surface of the prism at an angle $(A - r)$ as by equation-(5.81) we have already know $r_1 + r_2 = A$.

If this angle $(A - r)$ is more than critical angle for the glass-air interface for this prism then this light will get totally internally reflected at this face of prism and will not come out of the prism as shown in figure-5.197(b). If incidence angle i increases, r also increases and $(A - r)$ decreases. At maximum incidence angle $i = 90°$ we know r will be equal to critical angle θ_c and the other angle becomes $(A - \theta_c)$ which is the minimum possible value of r_2 for any prism as r_1 can never exceed θ_c for the case of grazing incidence. If this angle $(A - \theta_c)$ somehow becomes more than θ_c then light cannot come out of prism for any value of i as at all other values r_1 will be less than critical angle and r_2 will be certainly more than critical angle.

So for any light ray to come out of prism after two refractions at one or more values of incidence angles, we must have

$$A - \theta_c < \theta_c$$

$$\Rightarrow \quad A < 2\theta_c \quad \ldots(5.88)$$

Equation-(5.88) is a necessary condition for a light ray to pass through a prism after two refractions for multiple values of incidence angle. We can also state that for $A = 2\theta_c$ there is only one value $i = 90°$ at which light can pass through the prism. On the other way we can also state that for a given prism if its prism angle is more than twice the critical angle for its material and surrounding then no light ray can pass through the prism after two refractions from its surfaces.

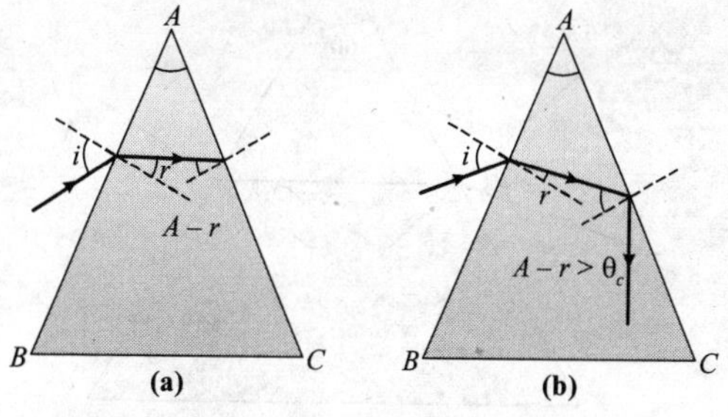

Figure 5.197

Illustrative Example 5.52

Find the angle of incidence of a light ray on an equilateral prism of refractive index $\mu = \sqrt{2}$ for which light will suffer minimum deviation also find this minimum deviation angle.

Solution

Minimum deviation produced by a prism can be calculated by using the relation

$$\sin\left(\frac{A+\delta_m}{2}\right) = \mu \sin\left(\frac{A}{2}\right)$$

$$\Rightarrow \quad \sin\left(\frac{60° + \delta_m}{2}\right) = \sqrt{2}.\sin 30° = \frac{1}{\sqrt{2}}$$

$$\Rightarrow \quad \frac{60 + \delta_m}{2} = 45°$$

$$\Rightarrow \quad \delta_m = 30°$$

At minimum deviation, we know that angle of incidence and angle of emergence are equal thus we use

$$i = e$$

$$\Rightarrow \quad \delta_m = 2i - A$$

$$\Rightarrow \quad i = \frac{\delta_m + A}{2} = \frac{30+60}{2} = 45°$$

Illustrative Example 5.53

The angle of incidence of a ray of light entering a 60° prism is 42°. If the ray is just totally reflected at the second face of the prism, determine the refractive index of the prism material for the light.

Solution

The ray diagram is shown in the figure-5.198 for the given situation.

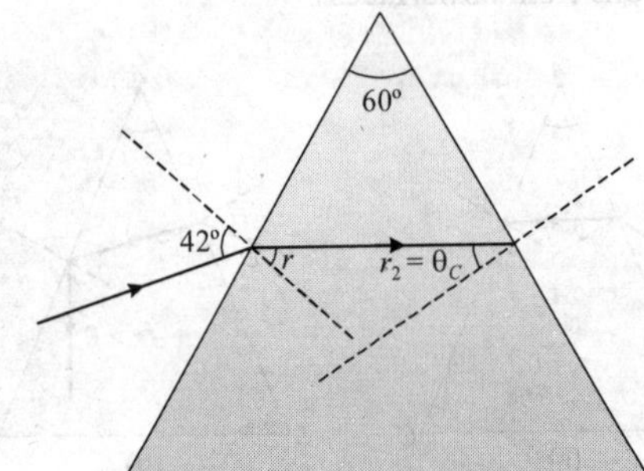

Figure 5.198

As the ray is totally reflected at the second face, light must incident on this face at critical angle by Snell's law we have

$$\frac{\sin 42°}{\sin r_1} = \mu \quad \ldots(5.89)$$

$$\Rightarrow \quad \sin r_1 = \frac{0.6691}{\mu} \quad \ldots(5.90)$$

and
$$\sin \theta_C = \frac{1}{\mu} \quad \ldots(5.91)$$

From equations-(5.90) and (5.91) we have

$$\frac{\sin r_1}{\sin r_2} = 0.6691 \quad \ldots(5.92)$$

We also know that $r_1 + r_2 = A$

$$\Rightarrow \quad r_2 = 60° - r_1$$

$$\Rightarrow \quad \sin r_2 = \sin (60 - r_1)$$

$$\Rightarrow \quad \sin r_2 = \sin 60 \cos r_1 - \cos 60° \sin r_1$$

$$\Rightarrow \quad \frac{\sin r_1}{0.6691} = 0.866 \cos r_1 - 0.5 \sin r_1$$

$$\Rightarrow \quad \sin r_1 \left(\frac{1}{0.6691} + 0.5\right) = 0.866 \cos r_1$$

$$\Rightarrow \quad 1.995 \sin r_1 = 0.866 \cos r_1$$

$$\Rightarrow \quad \tan r_1 = \frac{0.866}{1.995} = 0.4341$$

$$\Rightarrow \quad r_1 = 23° 28'$$

Now we can use equation-(5.89) as

$$\mu = \frac{\sin i_1}{\sin r_1} = \frac{\sin 42°}{\sin 23°28'}$$

$$\Rightarrow \quad \mu = \frac{0.6691}{0.3982} = 1.68$$

Illustrative Example 5.54

Figure-5.199 shows a small angled prism of prism angle 4° and $\mu = \frac{3}{2}$. A light ray almost normally incident on the prism is refracted and falls on a vertical mirror as shown. Find the total deviation of the ray after reflection from the mirror.

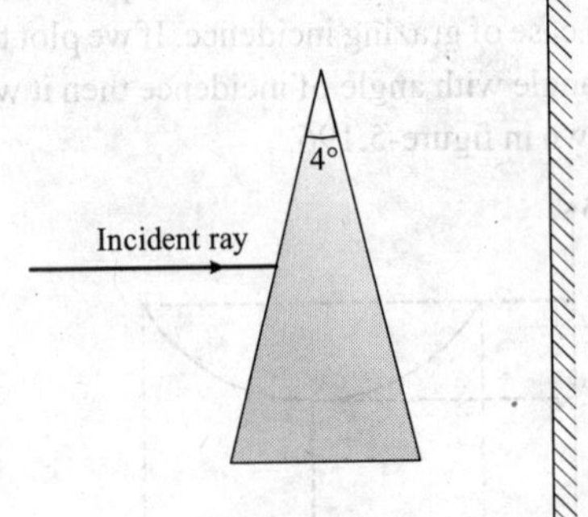

Figure 5.199

Solution

Figure-5.200 below shows the ray diagram of the light ray refracting from the prism and then reflecting from the plane mirror.

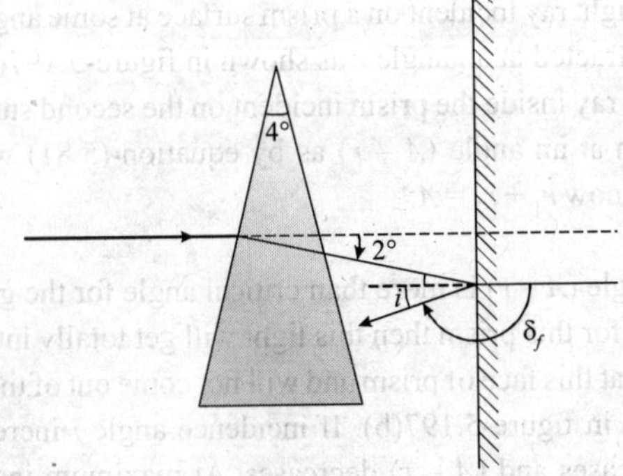

Figure 5.200

Deviation produced by the small angled prism is given as

$$\delta = A(\mu - 1) = 4\left(\frac{3}{2} - 1\right) = 2°$$

Total deviation of light ray after reflection from mirror can be calculated from figure as

$$\delta_f = 180° - 2°$$

$$\Rightarrow \quad \delta_f = 178° \text{ clockwise}$$

Illustrative Example 5.55

A right angle prism (45° – 90° – 45°) of refractive index n has a plate of refractive index $n_1 (n_1 < n)$ cemented to its diagonal face. The assembly is in air. A ray is incident on AB (figure-5.201)

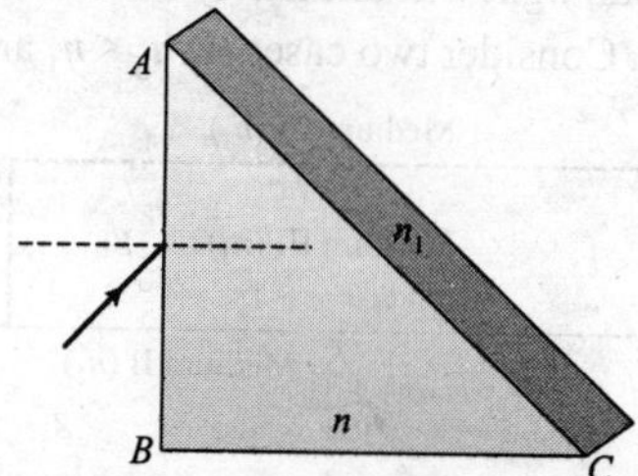

Figure 5.201

(i) Calculate the angle of incidence at AB for which the ray strikes the diagonal face at the critical angle.

(ii) Assuming $n = 1.352$, calculate the angle of incidence at AB for which the refracted ray passes through the diagonal face undeviated.

Solution

(i) In the given situation we consider the critical angle for face AC be θ_C. Then by Snell's law we have

$$\sin \theta_C = (n_1/n) \quad \ldots(5.93)$$

Let the required angle of incidence be i and angle of refraction at face AB is r as shown in figure-5.202.

From figure, $\quad r + \theta_C = 45°$

$$\Rightarrow \quad r = (45° - \theta_C) \quad \ldots(5.94)$$

For refraction at P (using Snell's law), we have

$$\sin i = n \sin r \quad \ldots(5.95)$$

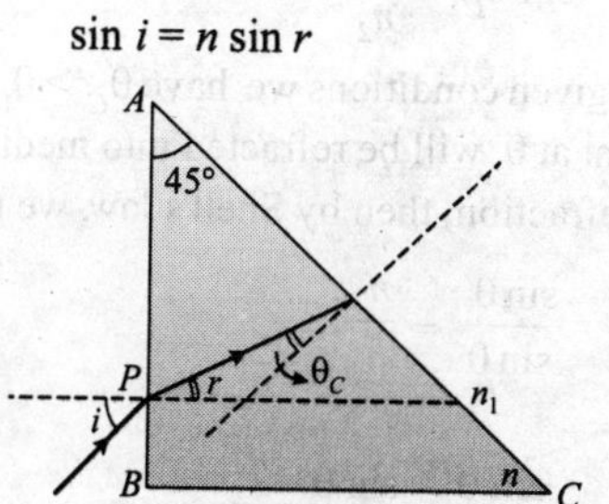

Figure 5.202

Substituting the value of r from equation-(5.94) in equation-(5.95), we get

$$\sin i = n \sin (45° - \theta_C)$$

$$\Rightarrow \quad \sin i = n \sin [45° - \sin^{-1} (n_1/n)]$$

$$\Rightarrow \quad i = \sin^{-1} [n \sin \{45° - \sin^{-1} (n_1/n)\}]$$

(ii) For the ray to pass through the diagonal face undeviated, the ray must strike normally on the face, i.e.,

$$\frac{\sin i}{\sin 45°} = 1.352$$

$$\Rightarrow \quad \sin i = \sin 45° \times (1.352)$$

$$\Rightarrow \quad \sin i = \frac{1.352}{\sqrt{2}} = 0.9562$$

$$i = \sin^{-1} (0.9562) = 72.9°$$

Illustrative Example 5.56

In figure-5.203, light refracts from material 1 into a thin layer of material 2, crosses that layer, and then is incident at the critical angle on the interface between materials 2 and 3.

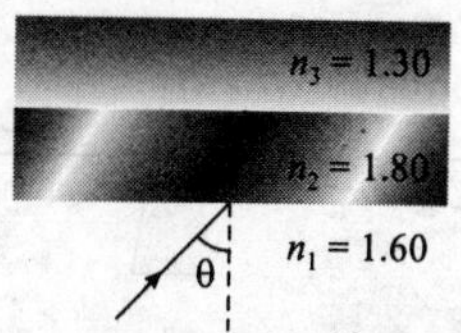

Figure 5.203

(a) What is the angle θ ?

(b) If θ is decreased, is there refraction of light into material 3?

Solution

(a) By Snell's law we have for the two interfaces

$$\mu_1 \sin i_1 = \mu_2 \sin i_2 = \mu_2 \sin \theta_c$$

For interface of medium 1 and 2, we use

$$(1.6) \sin \theta = (1.80)\left(\frac{1.30}{1.80}\right)$$

$$\Rightarrow \quad \theta = \sin^{-1}\left(\frac{13}{16}\right)$$

(b) If θ is decreased, then angle of incidence on the second interface will decrease from the critical angle. So light refraction will occur into medium-3.

Illustrative Example 5.57

Find the co-ordinates of image of the point object '*O*' formed after reflection from concave mirror as shown in figure-5.204 assuming prism to be thin and small in size and of prism angle 2°. Refractive index of the prism material is 3/2.

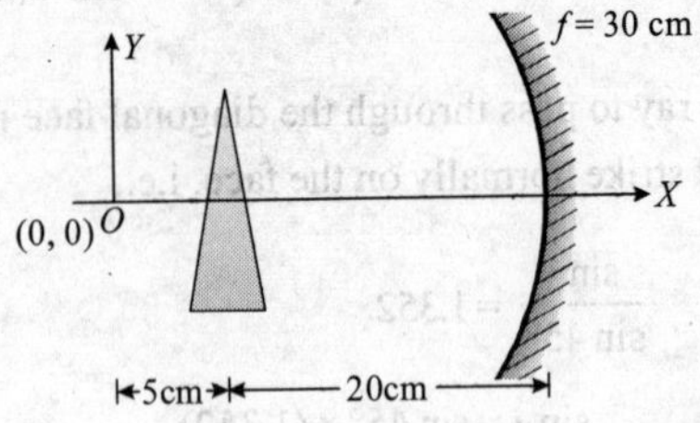

Figure 5.204

Solution

When light rays passes through prism, all incident rays will be deviated by the deviation angle given as

$$\delta = (\mu - 1)A = \left(\frac{3}{2} - 1\right)2° = 1° = \frac{\pi}{180}\text{ rad}$$

As prism is thin, object and image will be in the same plane as shown in figure-5.205 below

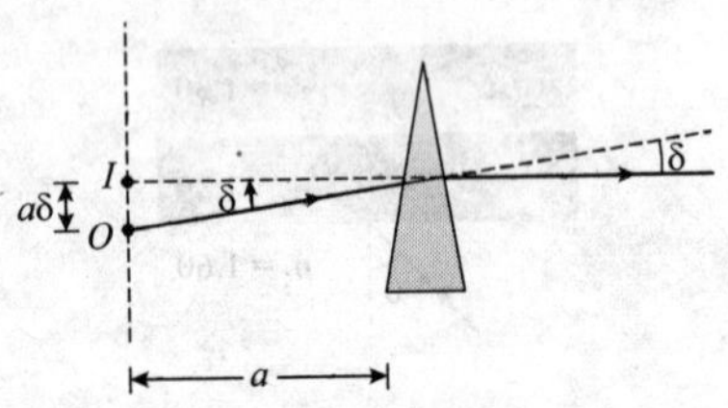

Figure 5.205

Thus in this case the shift of image due to prism in y-direction is given as

$$\text{Shift } d = a\delta = 5\left(\frac{\pi}{180}\right)$$

$$\Rightarrow \quad d = \frac{\pi}{36}\text{ cm}$$

Now this image will act as an object for concave mirror. So for mirror formula we use

$$u = -25\text{ cm and } f = -30\text{ cm}$$

$$\Rightarrow \quad v = \frac{uf}{u - f} = 150\text{ cm}$$

$$\text{Also,} \quad m = -\frac{v}{u} = +6$$

Thus distance of image from principal axis is given as

$$\Rightarrow \quad = \frac{\pi}{36} \times 6 = \frac{\pi}{6}\text{ cm}$$

So co-ordinates of image formed after reflection from concave mirror are $\left(175\text{cm}, \frac{\pi}{6}\text{cm}\right)$.

Illustrative Example 5.58

Monochromatic light is incident on a plane interface *AB* between two media of refractive indices n_1 and n_2 ($n_2 > n_1$) at an angle of incidence θ as shown in figure-5.206. The angle θ is infinitesimally greater than the critical angle for the two media so that total internal reflection takes place. Now if a transparent slab *DEFG* of uniform thickness and refractive index n_3 is introduced on the interface (as shown in figure), show that for any value of n_3 all light will ultimately be reflected back again into medium II. Consider two cases (i) $n_3 < n_1$ and (ii) $n_2 > n_1$.

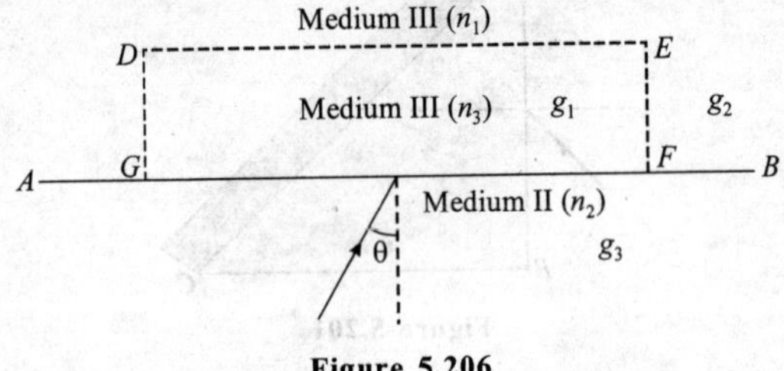

Figure 5.206

Solution

(i) In this case as $n_3 < n_1$, we can see that for $n_2 > n_1$ we have $n_3 << n_2$. If we consider θ_C be the critical angle for medium n_1 and n_2 then we have

$$\sin\theta_C = \frac{n_1}{n_2}$$

It is given that θ is infinitesimally greater than θ_C. Here we consider refraction from n_2 to n_3 where $n_3 < n_2$ and if θ_C' be the critical angle for this interface, then we have

$$\sin\theta_C' = \frac{n_3}{n_2}$$

With the given conditions we have $\theta_C' < \theta_C$ and so $\theta > \theta_C'$. Thus the ray will be totally reflected back into the medium n_2.

(ii) In this case when $n_2 > n_1$. In this case we have

$$\sin\theta_C' = \frac{n_3}{n_2}$$

But as per the given conditions we have $\theta_C' > \theta_C$ and $\theta < \theta_C'$ so the ray incident at θ, will be refracted into medium n_3. If θ′ be the angle of refraction, then by Snell's law, we use

$$\frac{\sin\theta'}{\sin\theta} = \frac{n_2}{n_3}$$

$$\Rightarrow \quad \sin\theta' = \sin\theta \times \frac{n_2}{n_3} \quad \ldots(5.96)$$

As θ is slightly greater than θ_C we can use

$$\sin\theta = \frac{n_1}{n_2}$$

Thus from equation-(5.96), we have

$$\Rightarrow \quad \sin\theta' = \frac{n_1}{n_2} \times \frac{n_2}{n_3} = \frac{n_1}{n_3}$$

Thus the light ray refracted into n_3 will be incident at the interface DE at an angle θ' which is slightly greater than the corresponding critical angle. Thus the ray will be totally reflected back into n_3 and finally transmitted to n_2.

Illustrative Example 5.59

A prism with prism angle 60° and refractive index $\sqrt{7/3}$ is given. Find the minimum possible angle of incidence, so that the light ray is refracted from the second surface. Also find δ_{max}.

Solution

As we know that minimum and maximum incidence angles are corresponding to the maximum deviation of light ray through the prism. Figure-5.207 shows the ray diagram for the case of minimum incidence angle.

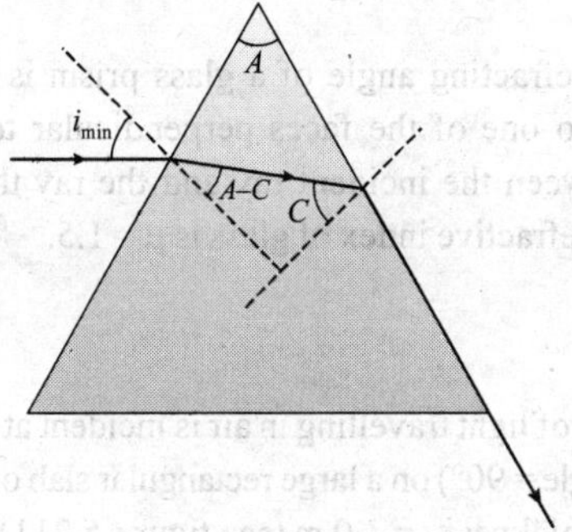

Figure 5.207

According to Snell's law, we have

$$1 \times \sin i_{min} = \sqrt{\frac{7}{3}} \sin(A - C)$$

$$\Rightarrow \quad \sin i_{min} = \sqrt{\frac{7}{3}} (\sin A \cos C - \cos A \sin C)$$

$$\Rightarrow \quad \sin i_{min} = \sqrt{\frac{7}{3}} \left(\sin 60\sqrt{1 - \frac{3}{7}} - \cos 60\sqrt{\frac{3}{7}}\right) = \frac{1}{2}$$

$$\Rightarrow \quad i_{min} = 30°$$

$$\Rightarrow \quad \delta_{max} = i_{min} + 90° - A = 30° + 90° - 60° = 60°$$

Web Reference at www.physicsgalaxy.com
Age Group - High School Physics | Age 17-19 Years
Section - OPTICS
Topic - Geometrical Optics II - Refraction of Light
Module Number - 9 to 15 and 34 to 44

Practice Exercise 5.5

(i) A glass prism of angle 72° and index of refraction 1.66 is immersed in a liquid of refractive index 1.33. Find the angle of minimum deviation for a parallel beam in light passing through the prism.

[22° 22′]

(ii) In figure-5.208 shown find the angle of incidence of the light ray on face AB of the prism for which light will reach face AC at incidence angle 60°.

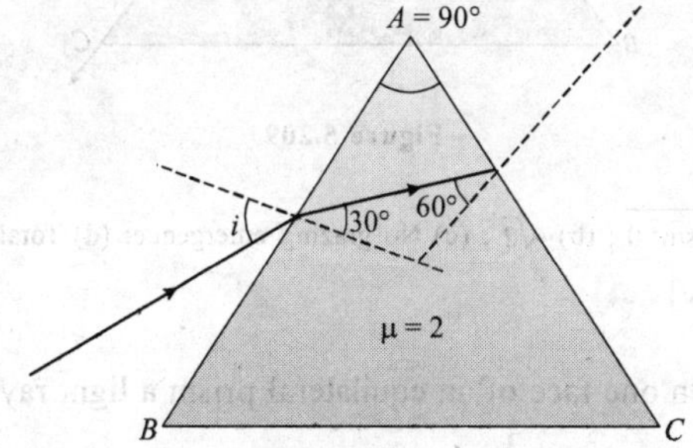

Figure 5.208

[90°]

(iii) A ray of light is incident on a glass slab at grazing incidence. The refractive index of the material of the slab is given by $\mu = \sqrt{(1+y)}$. If the thickness of the slab is d, determine the equation of the trajectory of the ray inside the slab and the coordinates of the point where the ray exits from the slab. Take the origin to be at the point of entry of the ray.

[$y = \frac{x^2}{4}$]

(iv) A point source of light is placed directly below the surface of a lake at a distance h from the surface. Find the area on water from which the light will come out from water.

[$\frac{\pi h^2}{(\mu^2 - 1)}$]

(v) A ray of light incident normally on one face of the faces of a right angled isosceles prism is found to be totally reflected. What is the minimum value of the refractive index of the material of the prism? When the prism is immersed in water, trace the path of the emergent rays for the same incident ray, indicating values of emergence angle. ($\mu_w = 4/3$)

[1.414, 48°35']

(vi) Figure-5.209 shows a triangular prism of refracting angle 90°. A ray of light incident at face AB at an angle θ refracts at point Q with an angle of refraction 90°. (a) What is the refractive index of the prism in terms of θ ? (b) What is the maximum value that the refractive index can have ? What happens to the light at Q if the incident angle at P is (c) increased slightly and (d) decreased slightly ?

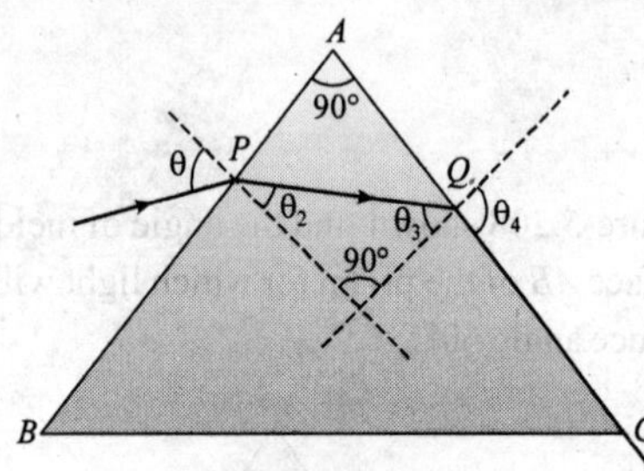

Figure 5.209

[(a) $\sqrt{1+\sin^2\theta}$; (b) $\sqrt{2}$; (c) No grazing emergence; (d) Total Internal Reflection]

(vii) On one face of an equilateral prism a light ray strikes normally. If its $\mu = \dfrac{3}{2}$, find the angle between incident ray and the ray that leaves the prism.

[60°]

(viii) A long rectangular slab of transparent medium of thickness d is placed on a table with length parallel to x-axis and width parallel to the y-axis. A ray of light is traveling along y-axis at origin. The refractive index μ of the medium varies as $\mu = \sqrt{1+e^{x/d}}$. The refractive index of the air is 1.

(a) Determine the x-coordinate of the point A, where the ray intersects the upper surface of the slab-air boundary.

(b) Write down the refractive index of the medium at A.

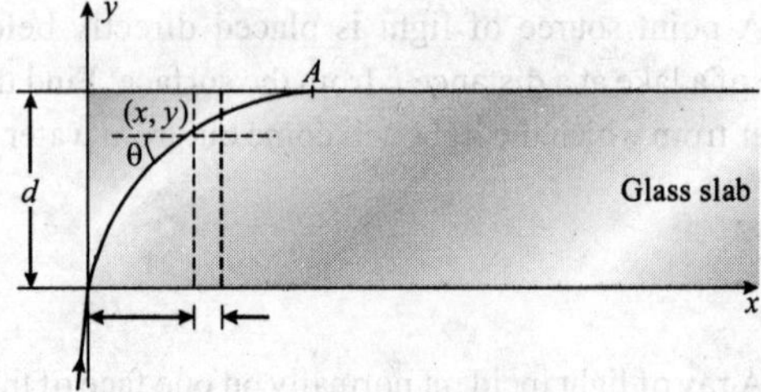

Figure 5.210

[$2d$ ln (2), $\sqrt{5}$]

(ix) A light ray composed of two monochromatic components passes through a trihedral prism with refracting angle $A = 60°$. Find the angle $\Delta\delta$ between the components of the ray after it passes through the prism if their respective indices of refraction are equal to 1.515 and 1.520. The prism is oriented to provide the least deflection angle.

[0.5° approx]

(x) A parallel beam of light falls normally on the first face of a prism of small angle. At the second face, it is partly transmitted and partly reflected. The reflected beam strikes at the first face again, and emerges from it in a direction making an angle 6°30' with the reversed direction of the incident beam. The refracted beam is found to have undergone a deviation of 1°15' from the original direction. Find the refractive index of the glass and the angle of the prism.

[$\frac{13}{8}$]

(xi) A ray of light is incident at an angle of 60° on one face of a prism which has an angle of 30°. The ray emerging out of the prism makes an angle of 30° with the incident ray. Show that the emergent ray is perpendicular to the face through which it emerges and calculate the refractive index of the material of prism.

[$\sqrt{3}$]

(xii) The refracting angle of a glass prism is 30°. A ray is incident onto one of the faces perpendicular to it. Find the angle δ between the incident ray and the ray that leaves the prism. The refractive index of glass is $\mu = 1.5$.

[18.6°]

(xiii) A ray of light travelling in air is incident at grazing angle (incident angle = 90°) on a large rectangular slab of a transparent medium of thickness $t = 1.0$ m (see figure-5.211). The point of incident is the origin $A(0, 0)$.

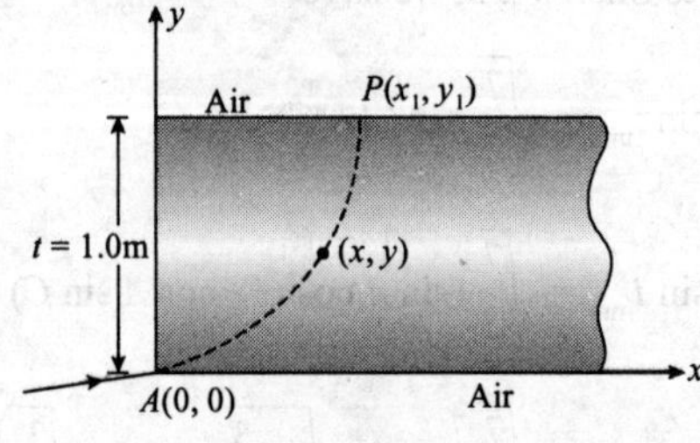

Figure 5.211

The medium has a variable index of refraction $\mu(y)$ given by

$$\mu(y) = (ky^{3/2} + 1)^{1/2}$$

where $k = 1.0\ m^{-3/2}$. The refractive index of air is 1.0.

(a) Obtain a relation between the slope of the trajectory of the ray at point $B(x, y)$ in the medium and the incident angle at that point.

(b) Obtain an equation for the trajectory $y(x)$ of the ray in the medium.

(c) Determine the coordinates (x_1, y_1) of the point P, where the ray intersects the upper surface of the slab-air boundary.

(d) Indicate the path of the ray subsequently.

[(a) $\theta = \cot^{-1}\sqrt{\mu^2 - 1}$; (b) $x\sqrt{k} = 4y^{1/4}$; (c) 4, 1; (d)]

5.14 Thin Lenses

Lenses are the transparent medium bounded by two spherical surfaces. There are two types of lenses in general based on thickness of the lens at its center, thin and thick. Both lenses differ in context of image formation and analysis of image characteristics. One by one we will discuss upon both but more important is to understand '*Thin Lenses*' which are most commonly used lenses in practice.

Figure-5.212 shows the way how lenses are made by using two spherical surfaces. Figure-5.212(a) shows a case when the two surfaces bounding a region in between intersect at the edges and figure-5.212(b) shows the case when the two surfaces bounding a region in between do not intersect at the edges. First one is called '*Convex Lens*' and second one is called '*Concave Lens*'.

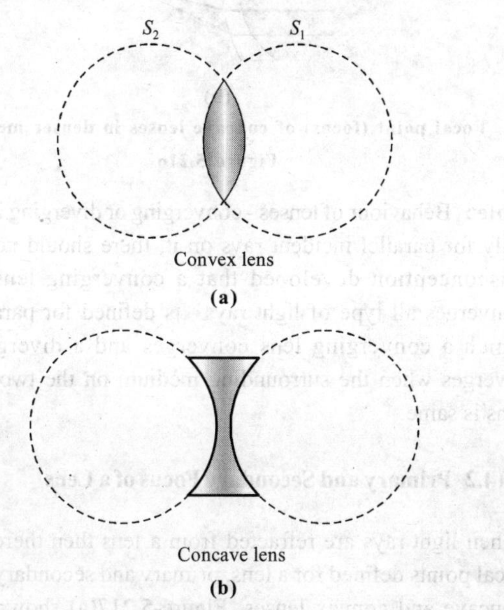

Figure 5.212

Convex and Concave lenses shown in figure-5.212 are basically lens families and these are further categorized in three ways. Convex lenses are of three types as given below

1. **Biconvex Lenses :** These are the lenses bounded by two intersecting spherical surfaces having their center of curvature on different sides of the lens as shown in figure-5.213.

2. **Plane Convex Lenses :** These are the lenses bounded by one spherical surface intersecting with one plane surface as shown in figure-5.213.

3. **Concavo Convex Lenses :** These are the lenses bounded by two intersecting spherical surfaces having their center of curvature on same side of the lens as shown in figure-5.213.

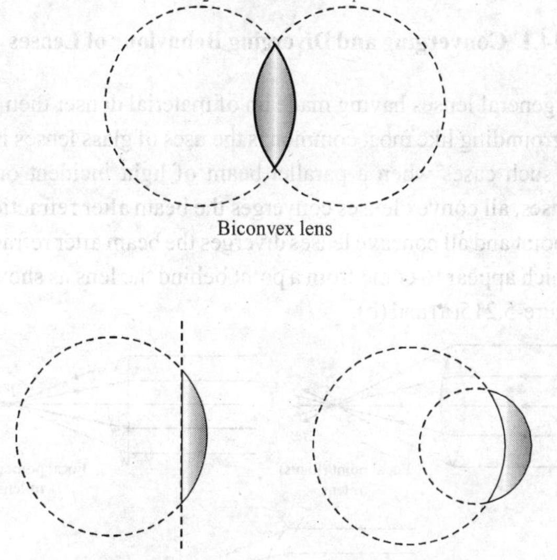

Figure 5.213

In the manner described above for convex lenses, concave lenses are of three types as given below

1. **Biconcave Lenses :** These are the lenses bounded by two non-intersecting spherical surfaces having their center of curvature on different sides of the lens as shown in figure-5.214.

2. **Plane Convex Lenses :** These are the lenses bounded by one spherical surface not intersecting with one plane surface as shown in figure-5.214.

3. **Concavo Convex Lenses :** These are the lenses bounded by two non-intersecting spherical surfaces having their center of curvature on same side of the lens as shown in figure-5.214.

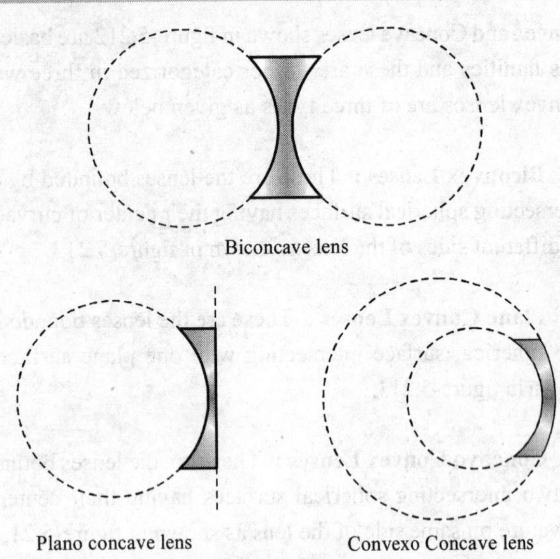

Figure 5.214

5.14.1 Converging and Diverging Behaviour of Lenses

In general lenses having made up of material denser then their surrounding like most common is the uses of glass lenses in air. In such cases when a parallel beam of light incident on the lenses, all convex lenses converges the beam after refraction to a point and all concave lenses diverges the beam after refraction which appear to come from a point behind the lens as shown in figure-5.215(a) and (b).

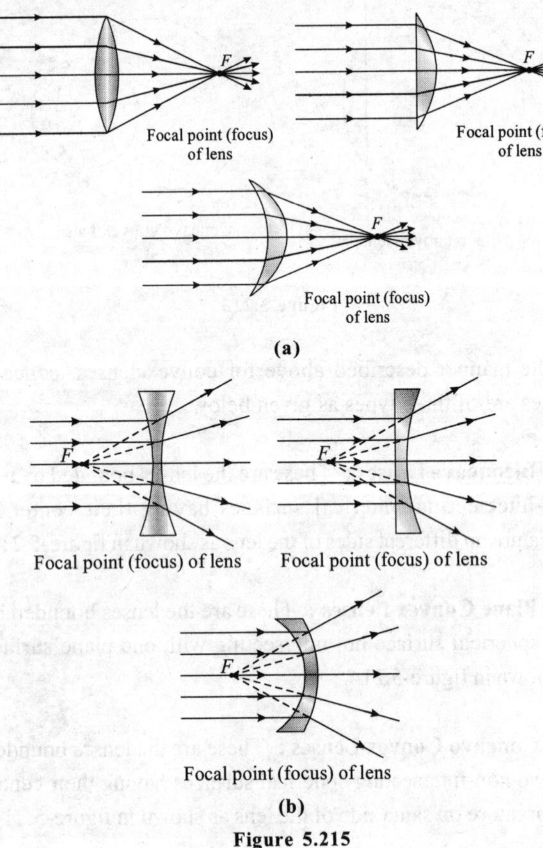

Figure 5.215

Due to the above behaviour all convex lenses placed in rarer surrounding medium are called '*Converging Lenses*' and all concave lenses placed in rarer surrounding medium are called '*Diverging Lenses*'. As shown in figure-5.215 we can see that the converging lenses have a '*Real Focus*' on the side of lens where refracting rays exist and diverging lenses have a '*Virtual Focus*' on the side of the lens where incident rays exist.

The behaviour of both type of lens families get interchanged when the surrounding is denser than lens material. This is explained in figure-5.216(a) and (b)

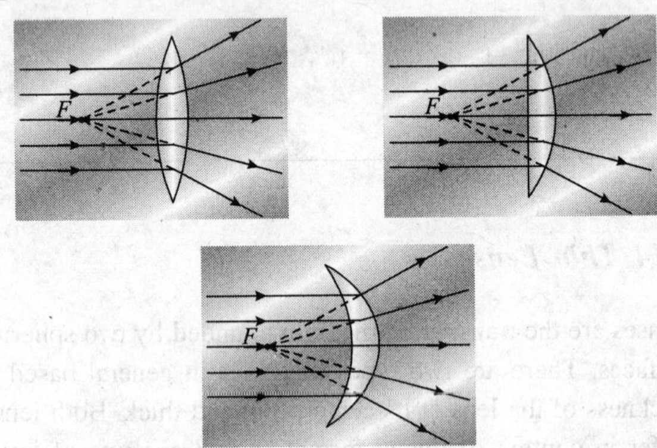

Focal point (focus) of convex lenses in denser medium

(a)

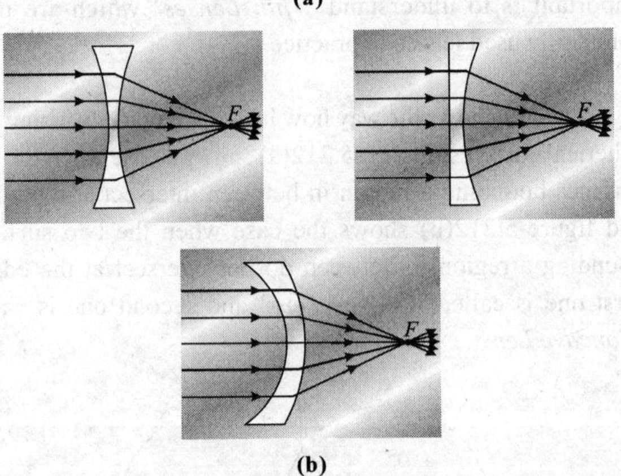

(b)

Focal point (focus) of concave lenses in denser medium

Figure 5.216

Note : Behaviour of lenses - converging or diverging is defined only for parallel incident rays on it, there should not be any misconception developed that a converging lens always converges all type of light rays. Its defined for parallel rays which a converging lens converges and a diverging lens diverges when the surrounding medium on the two sides of lens is same.

5.14.2 Primary and Secondary Focus of a Lens

When light rays are refracted from a lens then there are two focal points defined for a lens, primary and secondary for both concave and convex lenses. Figure-5.217(a) shows primary focus of a convex lens. This is the point on one side of lens where if an object is placed then after refraction all light rays will become parallel to the principal axis of the lens. Figure-5.217(b) shows the primary focus of a concave lens. This is the point toward which if a converging beam of light is incident on lens then after refraction these light rays become parallel to principal axis of the lens.

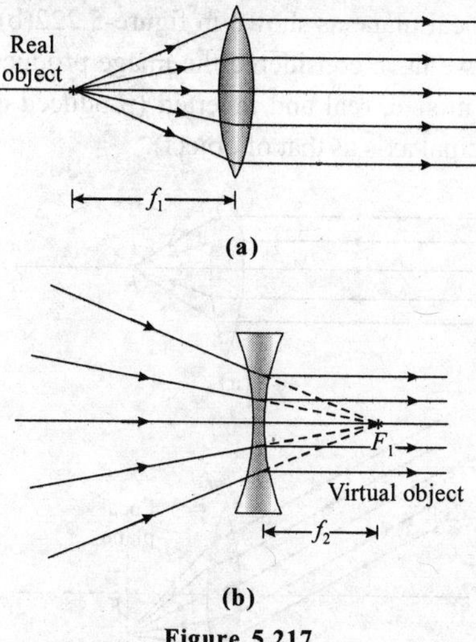

Figure 5.217

Figure-5.218(a) shows parallel light rays incident on a convex lens which after refraction through the lens meet at the focus on the other side of lens, this is called secondary focus of the convex lens. Similarly when parallel rays incident on a concave lens as shown in figure-5.218(b), after refraction light rays diverge in such a way that these appear to come from the focal point located behind the lens, this is called secondary focus of the concave lens.

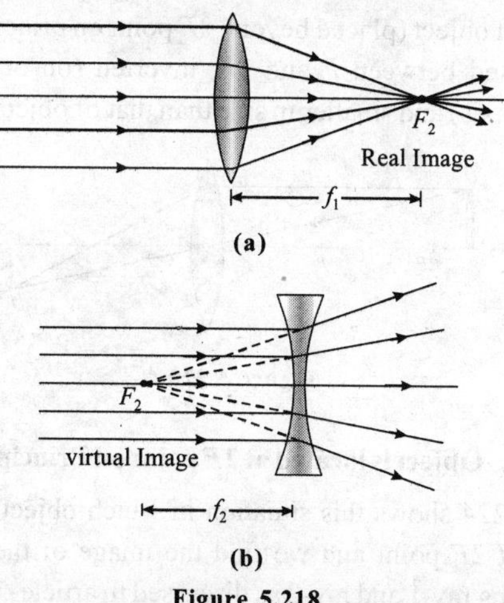

Figure 5.218

Note : For thin lenses the focal length of the lens for both primary and secondary focus is same. This we can also prove after understanding the calculation of focal length of the lens in coming sections.

5.14.3 Standard Reflected Light Rays for Image Formation by Thin Lenses

There are three standard incident paraxial rays and their corresponding refracted rays after double refraction through a thin lens, using which we can roughly analyze the location of image on the principal axis of the lens. Any two of the three standard rays we can use for finding the relative position of image produced and understanding of these rays also helps in analyzing the ray diagram for image formation by a lens in different situations. We will discuss these rays one by one.

Ray-1 : Incident on the lens parallel to the principal axis

Figure-5.219(a) and (b) shows a paraxial light ray incident on the convex and concave lens which is parallel to principal axis which after refraction from the two surfaces of the lens passes through the primary secondary focus of the lens. In case of convex lens it actually passes through the focal point whereas in case of concave lens it appears to pass through the focal point as shown.

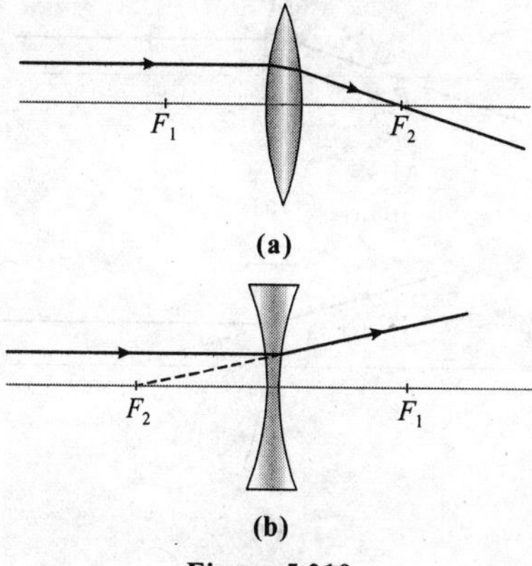

Figure 5.219

Ray-2 : Incident on the lens directly at the optic center of the lens

Figure-5.220(a) and (b) shows a paraxial light ray incident on the convex and concave lens at the optic center of the lens. As lens is thin at the center it behaves like a glass slab as shown in inset view so the light ray passes undeviated with small lateral displacement which can be ignored and considered the ray passing straight if incident on the optic center of the lens.

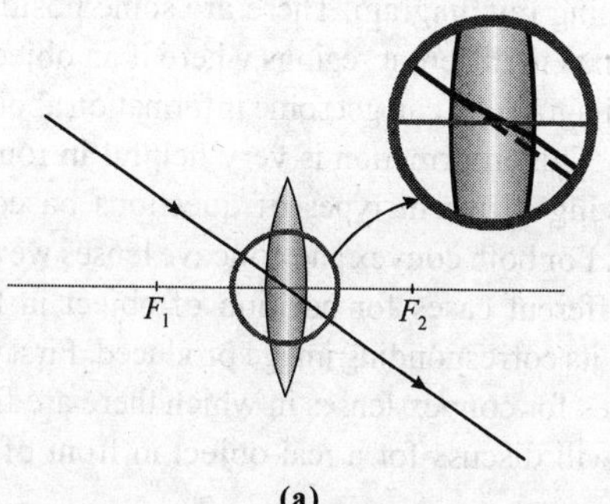

(a)

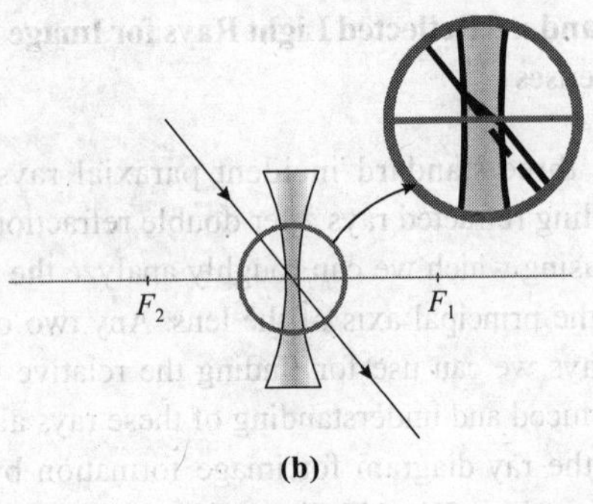

(b)

Figure 5.220

Ray-3 : Incident on the lens along the direction of primary focus

Figure-5.221(a) shows a paraxial ray passing through the primary focus of the convex lens and then incident on the lens, this ray after refraction becomes parallel to the principal axis of the lens. Similarly for a concave lens, a light ray which is incident on the lens along the line passing through its primary focus as shown in figure-5.221(b) becomes parallel after refraction.

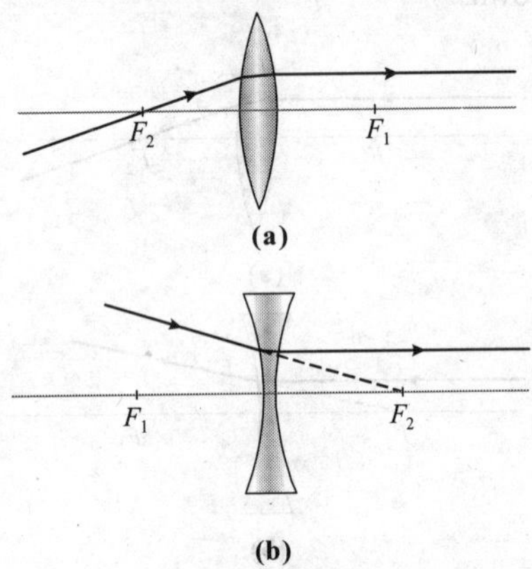

Figure 5.221

Now using these cases of paraxial incident and refracted rays we can discuss various cases of image formation by convex and concave mirrors for different positions of object.

5.14.4 Image Formation by Convex Lenses

Whenever an object location is given for a convex lens then using any two of the three incident rays and corresponding refracted rays discussed in article-5.12.3 we can find the image location using ray diagram. There are some positions near to principal axis in different regions where if an object is placed, using ray diagram we can get some information about the image formation. This information is very helpful in rough analysis while solving different types of questions based on image formation. For both convex and concave lenses we are going to discuss different cases for position of object in front of the lenses and its corresponding image produced. First we will take up the cases for convex lenses in which there are five possible cases we will discuss for a real object in front of the convex lens.

Case-I : Object is located at infinity

As already discussed while analyzing reflection cases that there are two possibilities of an object at infinity. One is when all incident rays are parallel to principal axis when image produced is real and located at focus of the mirror as shown in figure-5.222(a) and other possibility is when incident rays are at some angle to principal axis when image produced is real and located in focal plane as shown in figure-5.222(b). In both of these cases we have considered the image produced is highly diminished in size, real and inverted (produced on the other side of principal axis as that of object).

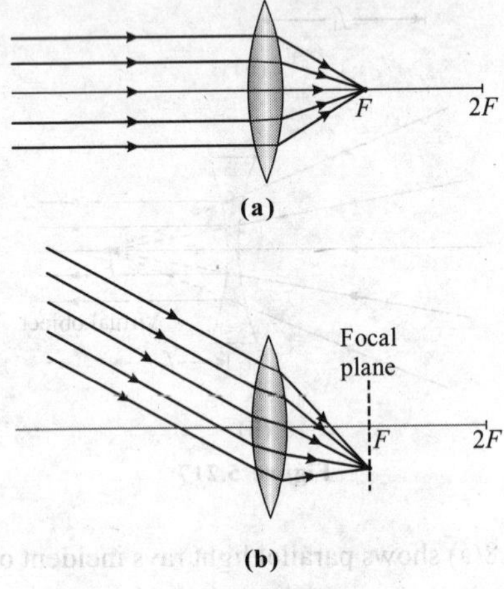

Figure 5.222

Case-II : Object is located beyond 2F point

Figure-5.223 shows this situation in which object is a small candle and we find the image of tip of the candle by considering ray-1 and ray-2 as discussed in article-5.12.3. With this ray diagram we can conclude that the image produced for this location of object (placed beyond $2F$ point on principal axis) is real, located between F and $2F$, inverted (on other side of principal axis) and smaller in size than that of object.

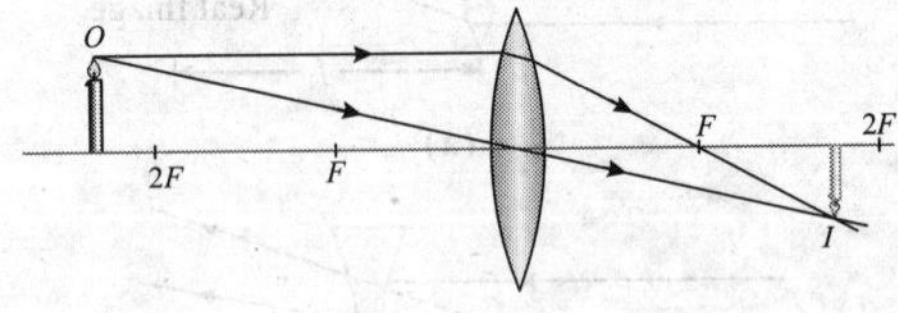

Figure 5.223

Case-III : Object is located at $2F$ point on Principal Axis

Figure-5.224 shows this situation in which object (candle) is located at $2F$ point and we find the image of the candle by considering ray-1 and ray-2 as discussed in article-5.12.3. With this ray diagram we can see and conclude that the image produced for this location of object (placed at $2F$ point on principal axis) is real, located at $2F$ point on other side of lens, inverted (on other side of principal axis) and of same size as that of object.

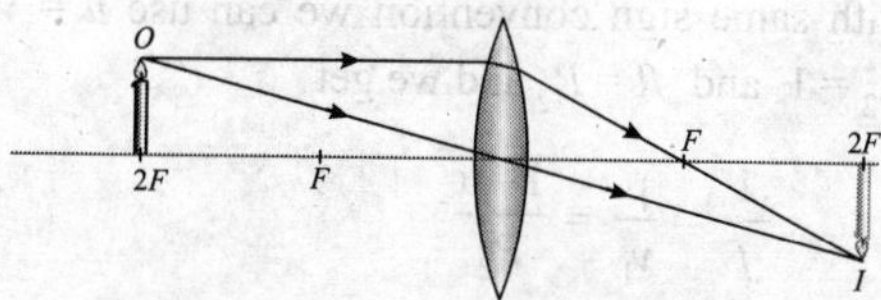

Figure 5.224

Case-IV : Object is located between F and 2F points on, Principal Axis

Figure-5.225 shows this situation in which object (candle) is located between F and $2F$ points and we find the image of the candle by considering ray-1 and ray-2 as discussed in article-5.12.3. With this ray diagram we can see and conclude that the image produced for this location of object (placed between F and $2F$ points on principal axis) is real, located beyond $2F$ point, inverted (on other side of principal axis) and enlarged compared to that of object.

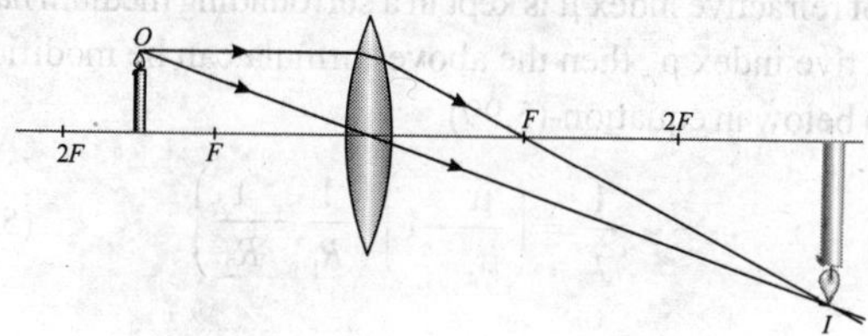

Figure 5.225

Case-V : Object is located at Focus

Figure-5.226 shows this situation in which object (candle) is located at focal point of the lens and we find the image of the candle by considering ray-1 and ray-2 as discussed in article-5.12.3. With this ray diagram we can see that the refracted rays are parallel and will produce image at infinity. So we can conclude with this diagram that image produced will be at infinity, inverted (on the other side of principal axis) and highly enlarged.

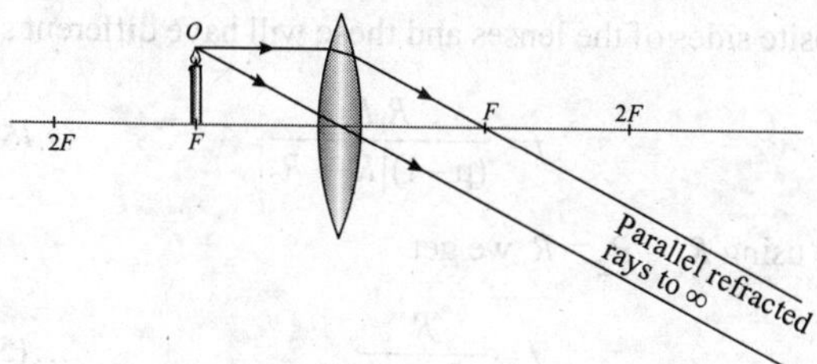

Figure 5.226

Case-VI : Object is located between Focus and Optic Center

Figure-5.227 shows this situation in which object (candle) is located between O and F and we find the image of the candle by considering ray-1 and ray-2 as discussed in article-5.12.3. With this ray diagram we can see that these refracted rays from lens are diverging in a way that these appear to be coming from the point I behind the lens from a virtual image. So for this location of object (placed between O and F on principal axis) image produced is located behind the lens, virtual, erected (on the same side of principal axis) and enlarged.

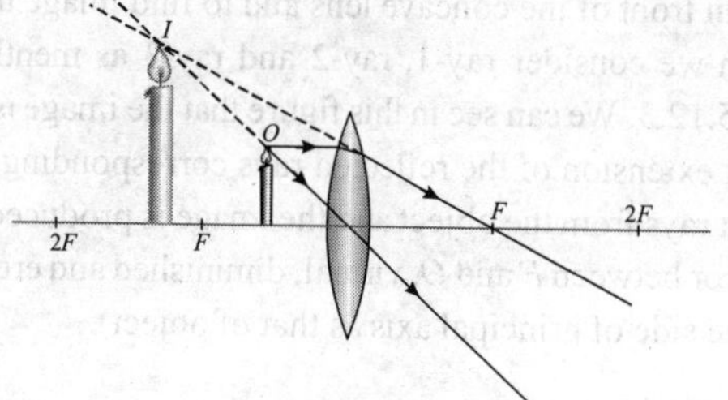

Figure 5.227

Above six cases are general cases which explains the relative position, nature and orientation of image produced by a convex lens for a real object placed close to its principal axis using paraxial rays. While solving different questions above cases give an idea about the estimation of image produced upto some extent before going for the exact process of image formation.

5.14.5 Image formation by Concave Lenses

Unlike to the different cases of image formation by a convex lens for different positions of object in front of it, in case of a concave lens there are only two possibilities of image formation for a real object placed in front of it.

Case-I : Object is located at infinity

When light rays from distant object fall on a concave lens, these rays diverge after refraction in such a way that for incident rays parallel to principal axis a image is obtained at focal point of mirror as shown in figure-5.228(a) and for incident rays non parallel to principal axis image is obtained in focal plane as shown in figure-5.228(b). The image produced will be virtual, diminished and erected (produced on the same side of principal axis where object is located).

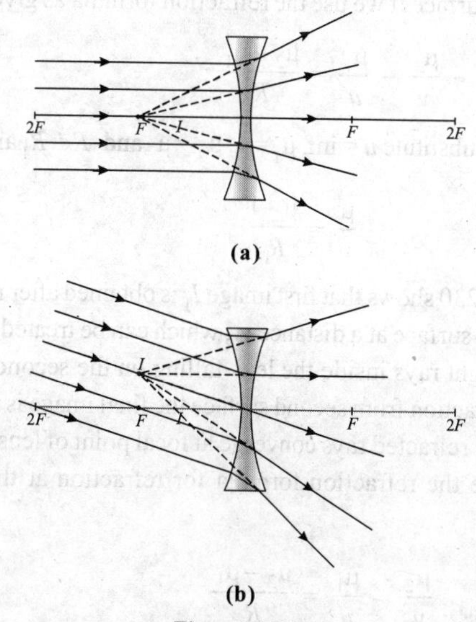

Figure 5.228

Case-II : Object is placed anywhere in front of the lens

Figure-5.229 shows a situation in which the object (candle) is placed in front of the concave lens and to find image using ray diagram we consider ray-1, ray-2 and ray-3 as mentioned in article-5.12.3. We can see in this figure that the image is formed by back extension of the reflected rays corresponding to these incident rays from the object and the image is produced behind the mirror between F and O, virtual, diminished and erected (on the same side of principal axis as that of object).

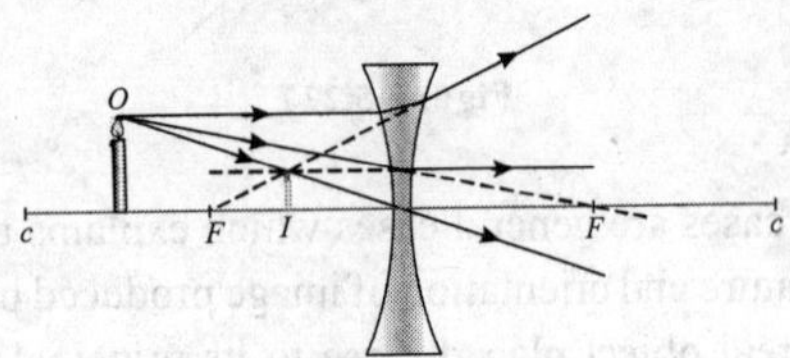

Figure 5.229

5.14.6 Focal length of a thin lens

Figure-5.230 shows a thin convex lens on which parallel light rays incident from left and after two refractions at its spherical surfaces of radius R_1 and R_2 light rays converge to its focal point at a distance called the '*Focal Length*' of the lens and it is denoted by 'f'. We will find out this focal length f by using the analysis of refraction of light at the two surface.

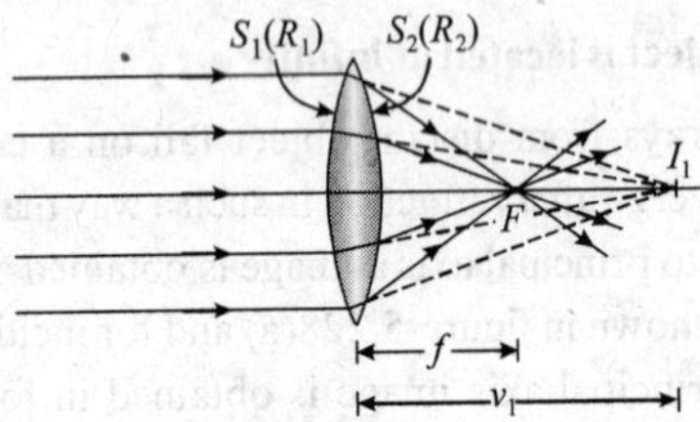

Figure 5.230

For first surface if we use the refraction formula as given below

$$\frac{\mu_2}{v} - \frac{\mu_1}{u} = \frac{\mu_2 - \mu_1}{R}$$

Here we substitute $u = \text{inf}$, $\mu_1 = 1$, $\mu_2 = \mu$ and $R = R_1$ and we get

$$\frac{\mu}{v} = \frac{\mu - 1}{R_1} \qquad \ldots(5.97)$$

Figure-5.230 shows that first image I_1 is obtained after refraction from first surface at a distance v_1, which can be treated as object for the light rays inside the lens falling on the second surface. After refraction from second surface the final image is produced at F as all refracted rays converge at focal point of lens. So if we again use the refraction formula for refraction at the second surface

$$\frac{\mu_2}{v_1} - \frac{\mu_1}{u} = \frac{\mu_2 - \mu_1}{R}$$

Again with same sign convention we can use $u = v_1$, $v = f$, $\mu_1 = \mu$, $\mu_2 = 1$ and $R = R_2$ and we get

$$\frac{1}{f} - \frac{\mu}{v_1} = \frac{1 - \mu}{R_2} \qquad \ldots(5.98)$$

Note : In above equations-(5.97) and (5.98) we have not considered the signs of u, R_1 and R_2 as the lens can be of different types among the six types as explained in article-5.12. Adding the two equations, we get

$$\frac{1}{f} = (\mu - 1)\left(\frac{1}{R_1} - \frac{1}{R_2}\right) \qquad \ldots(5.99)$$

Above equation-(5.99) is called '*Lens Makers Formula*' used to calculate the focal length of a thin lens. With this expression we can see that focal lens of thin lens for both primary and secondary focus remain same on the two sides of the lens. The above formula is used when a thin lens is kept in air and if a thin lens of refractive index μ is kept in a surrounding medium having refractive index μ_a then the above formula can be modified as given below in equation-(5.99).

$$\frac{1}{f} = \left(\frac{\mu}{\mu_s} - 1\right)\left(\frac{1}{R_1} - \frac{1}{R_2}\right) \qquad \ldots(5.100)$$

5.14.7 Focal length of different types of standard thin lenses

By using Lens Makers Formula we can find the focal length of any thin lens but for quick reference we are giving here the direct relations for magnitude of focal length of some standard shaped lenses.

1. Equiconvex or Equiconcave Lenses : These lenses have same radii of curvature of the two surfaces so we use $R_1 = R_2 = R$ and for this equation-(5.99) will reduce to the form given below because the two center of curvatures of the surfaces are on the opposite sides of the lenses and these will have different signs.

$$f = \frac{R_1 R_2}{(\mu - 1)|R_1 + R_2|} \qquad \ldots(5.101)$$

Now using $R_1 = R_2 = R$, we get

$$f = \frac{R}{2(\mu - 1)} \qquad \ldots(5.102)$$

Equation-(5.102) gives only the magnitude of the lens. When we use this focal length in image formation by a lens then it is substituted with appropriate sign.

2. Plano-Convex or Plano-Concave Lenses : These lenses have one plane surface so we can take $R_1 = \text{inf}$ and $R_2 = R$ and for this equation-(5.99) will reduce to the form given below.

$$f = \frac{R}{(\mu - 1)} \qquad \ldots(5.103)$$

3. Concavo-Convex or Convexo-Concave Lenses : Such lenses have different radii of curvature and their centers of curvature lie on the same side of lens so the signs of the two radii R_1 and R_2 will be same and the equation-(5.99) will reduce to the form given below

$$f = \frac{R_1 R_2}{(\mu - 1)|R_1 - R_2|} \quad \ldots (5.104)$$

Above equations-(5.101) to (5.104) students can keep on tips for quick reference for calculation of focal length magnitude of any thin lens while solving a problem of image formation.

5.15 Analysis of Image Formation by Thin Lenses

For finding the exact location of image produced by a thin lens made up of a medium of refractive index μ, we can start by using refraction formula twice for refraction at the two surfaces of the lens. Figure-5.231 shows a biconvex lens and a point object is placed at a distance u from the optic center of the lens on its principal axis. If we analyze the image produced due to refraction at its first surface S_1 which is at location I_1 as shown in figure, we will use the refraction formula for this.

$$\frac{\mu_2}{v} - \frac{\mu_1}{u} = \frac{\mu_2 - \mu_1}{R} \quad \ldots (5.105)$$

Here we use $u = u$, $v = v_1$, $\mu_1 = 1$, $\mu_2 = \mu$ and $R = R_1$ (for first surface) and we are not using signs as in general case lenses can be of different types and object can also be at different locations. This gives

$$\frac{\mu}{v_1} - \frac{1}{u} = \frac{\mu - 1}{R_1} \quad \ldots (5.106)$$

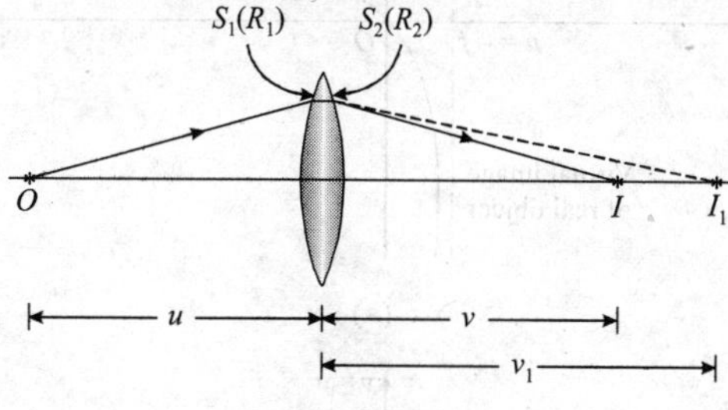

Figure 5.231

Now for the light ray inside the lens which falls on the second surface S_2 will again suffer refraction for which again we use the refraction formula as given in equation-(5.105) with $u = v_1$, $v = v$, $\mu_1 = \mu$, $\mu_2 = 1$ and $R = R_2$. This gives

$$\frac{1}{v} - \frac{\mu}{v_1} = \frac{1 - \mu}{R_2} \quad \ldots (5.107)$$

Adding equations-(5.106) and (5.107), we get

$$\frac{1}{v} - \frac{1}{u} = (\mu - 1)\left(\frac{1}{R_1} - \frac{1}{R_2}\right) = \frac{1}{f}$$

As we have $\quad \frac{1}{f} = (\mu - 1)\left(\frac{1}{R_1} - \frac{1}{R_2}\right)$

$$\Rightarrow \quad \frac{1}{v} - \frac{1}{u} = \frac{1}{f} \quad \ldots (5.108)$$

Equation-(5.108) is called '*Lens Formula*' used to find the location of image produced by a thin lens for a specific object for paraxial rays incident on the lens.

As we have already discussed that for thin lenses magnitude of primary and secondary focal lengths of lenses are equal but their signs are different as these exist on two different sides of the lens. For thin lenses when a light ray incident on it then in above lens formula we always use its secondary focal length. If we use incident ray reference sign convention then always the focal length of a converging lens is positive and that of a diverging lens is negative whereas in cartesian coordinate system sign convention it depends upon the direction from which light ray incident on the lens. As already discussed that in this chapter we are using cartesian coordinate sign convention in solving different questions of geometrical optics. If students wish then they can also solve each problem using the other convention also.

5.15.1 Lateral Magnification in Image Formation by a Thin Lens

Figure-5.232 shows a small object (candle) placed on the principal axis of the lens at a distance u from the optic center of the lens and it produces an image I which is real and inverted. If the heights of the object and image above the principal axis are h and h' respectively then from the figure we can see that the angular sizes of both the object and image are same on the two sides of lens and it is equal to θ.

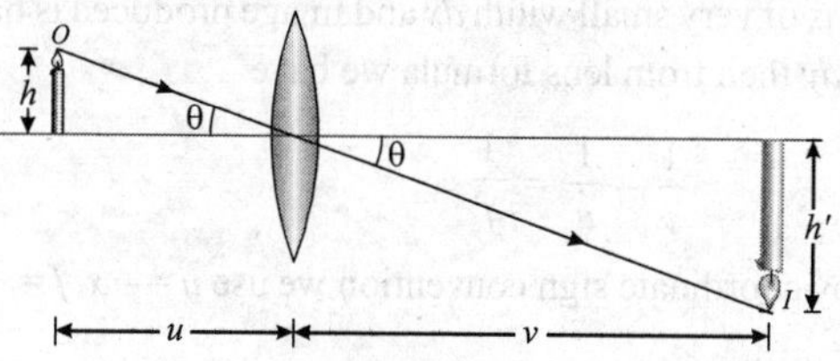

Figure 5.232

From the two triangles formed by object height and image height on principal axis we have

$$\frac{h}{u} = \frac{h'}{v}$$

$$\Rightarrow \quad h' = \left(\frac{v}{u}\right)h = mh$$

Where $\quad m = \frac{\text{Height of Image } (h')}{\text{Height of Ojbect } (h)} = \frac{v}{u}$

Here $m = (v/u)$ is called '*Lateral Magnification*' by a thin lens used to find the size of image and its orientation. In this relation of lateral magnification u and v are substituted with proper signs according to sign convention which can result in positive and negative values of m. Positive value of m denotes that image is erected or on the same side of principal axis and negative value of m denotes that image is inverted or on the opposite side of the principal axis of the lens.

5.15.2 Longitudinal Magnification by a Thin Lens

Lateral magnification formula for thin lenses gives the image height above the principal axis of mirror and in this section we will discuss about the image width along the principal axis of a thin lens. The relation in object and image width along the principal axis of mirror is called '*Longitudinal Magnification*' as given below.

Longitudinal magnification of image is given as

$$m_L = \frac{\text{Width of Image along Principal Axis}}{\text{Width of Object along Principal Axis}}$$

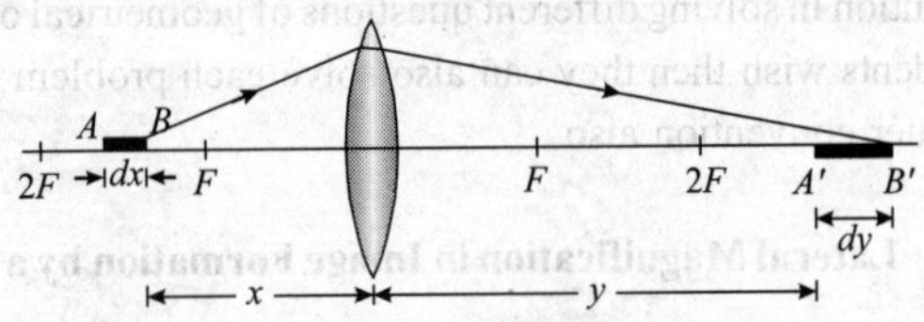

Figure 5.233

Figure-5.233 shows image formation of an object located at a distance x from the convex lens of focal length f which produces an image of this object at a distance y which is real inverted and enlarged because object was placed between F and $2F$ points. Here we can see that object edge A was close to C so corresponding image edge A' is also closer to C. If we consider object is of very small width dx and image produced is having a width dy then from lens formula we have

$$\frac{1}{v} - \frac{1}{u} = \frac{1}{f}$$

Here by coordinate sign convention we use $u = -x, f = +f$ and $v = +y$

$$\frac{1}{f} = \frac{1}{y} - \frac{1}{-x}$$

Differentiating this expression we get

$$0 = -\frac{1}{x^2}dx - \frac{1}{y^2}dy$$

From this relation we can get the '*Longitudinal Magnification*' as

$$m_L = \frac{dy}{dx} = -\frac{y^2}{x^2} = -m^2 \qquad \ldots(5.109)$$

For small width object if image is produced by a thin lens (converging or diverging) then image width can be calculated by using the equation-(5.109). But if object size is large then this relation cannot be used and in that case we need to calculate the image of both edges of the object along principal axis and take the difference as explained in figure-5.80 in aricle-5.9.5 for spherical mirrors.

5.15.3 Variation Curves of Image Distance vs Object Distance for a Thin Lens

We have discussed the lens formula which relates the image distance from pole of mirror for a given object distance. The lens formula is given as

$$\frac{1}{f} = \frac{1}{v} - \frac{1}{u}$$

$$\Rightarrow \quad v = \frac{u}{\frac{u}{f}+1} \qquad \ldots(5.110)$$

As focal length of a given lens is constant and it can be positive or negative depending upon the sign convention and type of lens used. The above function given in equation-(5.110) can be plotted as shown in figure-5.234(a) and (b) for a converging and diverging lens with negative x direction on left and positive x-direction on right which we generally consider.

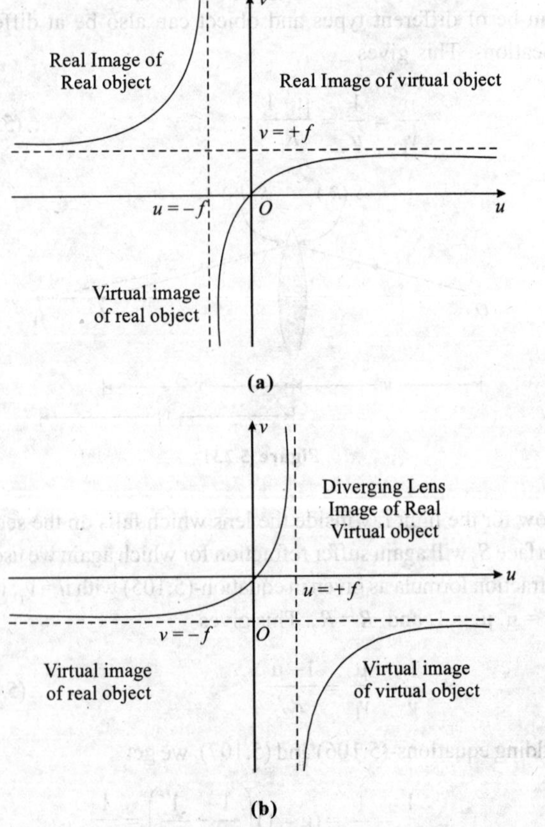

Figure 5.234

5.15.4 Effect of motion of Object and Lens on Image

When object or lens is in motion the distance between object and lens changes which affects the position and size of image. To find the image velocity and for analysis of image's motion we can differentiate the lens formula and find the rate at which distances between image and lens is changing. If we consider x and y as object and image distance from pole of mirror of focal length f then by lens formula we have

$$\frac{1}{f}=\frac{1}{y}-\frac{1}{x}$$

Differentiating the above relation with respect to time, we get

$$0=-\frac{1}{x^2}\cdot\frac{dx}{dt}-\frac{1}{y^2}\cdot\frac{dy}{dt}$$

Where $\frac{dx}{dt}$ is the relative velocity of object with respect to the lens and $\frac{dy}{dt}$ is the velocity of image with respect to lens.

$$\Rightarrow \quad 0=-\frac{1}{x^2}\cdot v_0-\frac{1}{y^2}\cdot v_i \text{ (using } \frac{dx}{dt}=v_0 \text{ and } \frac{dy}{dt}=v_i\text{)}$$

$$\Rightarrow \quad v_i=-\frac{y^2}{x^2}v_0=-m^2v_0 \qquad \ldots(5.111)$$

Where m is the lateral magnification produced by the mirror. The expression of image speed as given in equation-(5.111) is valid only for the velocity component of the image and object along the principal axis of the lens. If the object and mirror is in motion along the direction normal to principal axis we can directly differentiate the height of object and image above principal axis which are related as

$$h_i=mh_0$$

Differentiating this with respect to time we get

$$\frac{dh_i}{dt}=m\frac{dh_0}{dt}$$

$$\Rightarrow \quad v_{iN}=m\,v_{0N}$$

Here we can use $\frac{dh_i}{dt}=v_{iN}$ and $\frac{dh_0}{dt}=v_{oN}$ which are the velocity components of image and object respectively in direction normal to the principal axis.

Illustrative Example 5.60

Focal length of a thin lens in air, is 10 cm. Now medium on one side of the lens is replaced by a medium of refractive index $\mu=2$. The radius of curvature of surface of lens, in contact with the medium, is 20 cm. Find the point on principal axis where parallel rays incident on lens from air parallel to axis will converge.

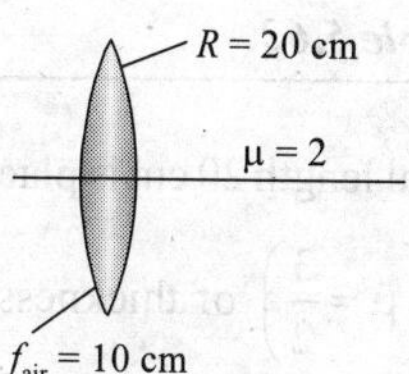

Figure 5.235

Solution

Let the radius of first surface be R_1 and refractive index of lens be μ and parallel rays be incident on the lens. Applying refraction formula at first surface

$$\frac{\mu}{v_1}-\frac{1}{\infty}=\frac{\mu-1}{R_1} \qquad \ldots(5.112)$$

Refraction formula at second surface

$$\frac{2}{v}-\frac{\mu}{v_1}=\frac{2-\mu}{-20} \qquad \ldots(5.113)$$

Adding equation-(5.112) and (5.113), we get

$$\Rightarrow \quad \frac{\mu}{v_1}-\frac{1}{\infty}+\frac{2}{v}-\frac{\mu}{v_1}=\frac{\mu-1}{R_1}+\frac{2-\mu}{-20}$$

$$\Rightarrow \quad \frac{2}{v}=(\mu-1)\left(\frac{1}{R_1}-\frac{1}{-20}\right)-\frac{\mu-1}{20}-\frac{2-\mu}{20}$$

$$\Rightarrow \quad \frac{2}{v}=\frac{1}{f}\text{ (in air)}+\frac{1}{20}-\frac{2}{20}=\frac{1}{10}-\frac{1}{20}=\frac{1}{20}$$

$$\Rightarrow \quad v=40\text{ cm}$$

Thus all parallel rays incident on the lens will focus at a point 40 cm from the lens in the medium with refractive index 2.

Illustrative Example 5.61

A biconvex lens has focal length 50 cm and the radius of curvature of one surface is double that of other. Find the radii of curvature if refractive index of lens material is 2.

Solution

For biconvex lens focal length of lens is given as

$$f=\frac{R_1R_2}{(\mu-1)(R_1+R_2)}$$

And we are given with $R_2=2R_1$

$$\Rightarrow \quad f=\frac{2R_1}{(\mu-1)(3R_1)}=\frac{2R_1}{3(\mu-1)}$$

$$\Rightarrow \quad 50=\frac{2R_1}{3(2-1)}$$

$$\Rightarrow \quad R_1=75\text{ cm}$$

$$\Rightarrow \quad R_2=150\text{ cm}$$

Illustrative Example 5.62

A convex lens of focal length 20 cm is placed at a distance 5 cm from a glass plate $\left(\mu = \frac{3}{2}\right)$ of thickness 3 cm. An object is placed at a distance 30 cm from lens on the other side of glass plate. Locate the final image produced by this optical setup.

Solution

Figure-5.236 shows the optical setup described in question and the ray diagram for image formation.

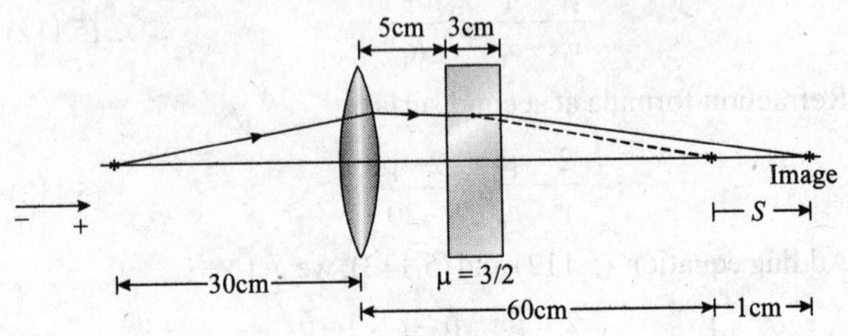

Figure 5.236

For lens formula to be used in refraction by lens, we use

$$u = -30 \text{ cm}$$

$$f = +20 \text{ cm}$$

$$\Rightarrow \quad \frac{1}{v} - \frac{1}{u} = \frac{1}{f}$$

$$\Rightarrow \quad \frac{1}{v} + \frac{1}{30} = \frac{1}{20}$$

$$\Rightarrow \quad v = \frac{20 \times 30}{10} = 60 \text{ cm}$$

Shift of image due to refraction by the glass slab is given as

$$S = t\left(1 - \frac{1}{\mu}\right)$$

$$\Rightarrow \quad S = 3\left(1 - \frac{2}{3}\right) = 1 \text{ cm}$$

Thus position of final image = 60+ 1 = 61 cm

Illustrative Example 5.63

A diverging lens of focal length 20 cm is placed coaxially 5 cm toward left of a converging mirror of focal length 10 cm. Where would an object be placed toward left of the lens so that a real image is formed on object itself.

Solution

Due to reflection by a mirror, image of object is formed on itself when reflected rays falls normally on the mirror and retrace the path of incident rays. For this the image produced by the lens must be formed at the center of curvature of the mirror as shown in ray diagram-5.237.

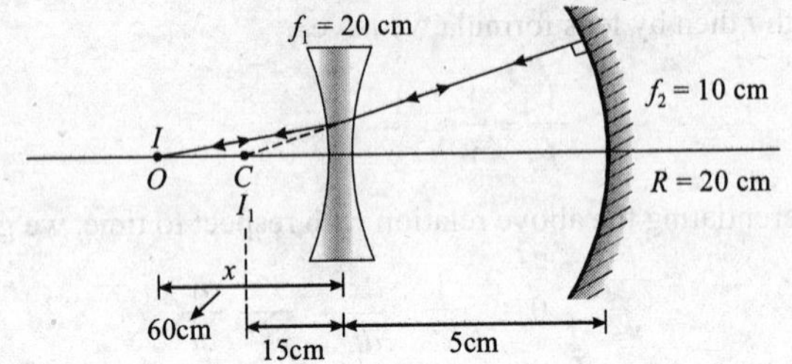

Figure 5.237

For lens formula, we use

$$u = -x$$

$$f = -20 \text{ cm}$$

$$v = -15 \text{ cm}$$

$$\Rightarrow \quad \frac{1}{v} - \frac{1}{u} = \frac{1}{f}$$

$$\Rightarrow \quad -\frac{1}{15} + \frac{1}{x} = \frac{-1}{20}$$

$$\Rightarrow \quad \frac{1}{x} = \frac{1}{15} - \frac{1}{20} = \frac{4-3}{60} = \frac{1}{60}$$

$$\Rightarrow \quad x = 60 \text{ cm}$$

Illustrative Example 5.64

A convex lens is held 45 cm above the bottom of an empty tank. The image of a point on the bottom of a tank is formed 36 cm above the lens. Now a liquid is poured into the tank to a depth of 40 cm. It is found that the distance of the image of the same point on the bottom of the tank is 48 cm above the lens. Find the refractive index of the liquid.

Solution

When the tank in empty and point object O is placed at the bottom of the tank, then for lens formula we use

$$u = -45 \text{ cm and } v = +36 \text{ cm}$$

Using lens formula, we have

$$\frac{1}{v} - \frac{1}{u} = \frac{1}{f}$$

$$\Rightarrow \quad f = \frac{uv}{u - v} = \frac{-45 \times 36}{-45 - 36} = \frac{1620}{81} = 20 \text{ cm}$$

When the liquid is poured in the tank to a depth 40 cm, then image is produced at 48 cm above the lens so again for lens formula we use

$$v' = +48 \text{ cm}$$

If u' be the distance of the object O' for image to be produced at 48 cm from lens then we use

$$\frac{1}{u'} = \frac{1}{v'} - \frac{1}{f} = \frac{1}{48} - \frac{1}{20}$$

Solving we get

$$u' = -34.29 \text{ cm}$$

The distance between liquid surface and lens is 5 cm

Distance of O' from the surface is $34.29 - 5 = 29.29$ cm which is the apparent depth of object below water surface at which when it is placed, image is produced at the specified location.

The refractive index of liquid is given as

$$\mu = \frac{\text{Real depth}}{\text{Apparent depth}} = \frac{40}{29.29} = 1.37$$

Illustrative Example 5.65

An object of height 4 cm is kept to the left of and on the axis of a converging lens of focal length 10 cm at a distance of 15 cm from the lens. A plane mirror is placed inclined at 45° to the lens axis, 10 cm to the right of the lens. Find the position and size of the image formed by the lens and mirror combination. Trace the path of the rays forming the image.

Solution

Let AB be the object placed at a distance of 15 cm from the lens as shown in figure-5.238. We shall calculate the position of image formed by this lens in absence of plane mirror.

For lens formula we use $u_1 = -15$ cm, and $f = +10$ cm

$$\Rightarrow \quad \frac{1}{v_1} = \frac{1}{10} - \frac{1}{15} = \frac{3-2}{30} = \frac{1}{30}$$

or $\quad v_1 = +30$ cm

So the image would be formed at 30 cm from the lens to the right of it

Magnification by lens is $m_1 = \frac{v_1}{u_1} = \frac{30}{15} = 2$

$\Rightarrow$ Size of the image $= 2 \times 4 = 8$ cm

The image produced by lens is I_1 which is shown by A_1B_1 in figure-5.238.

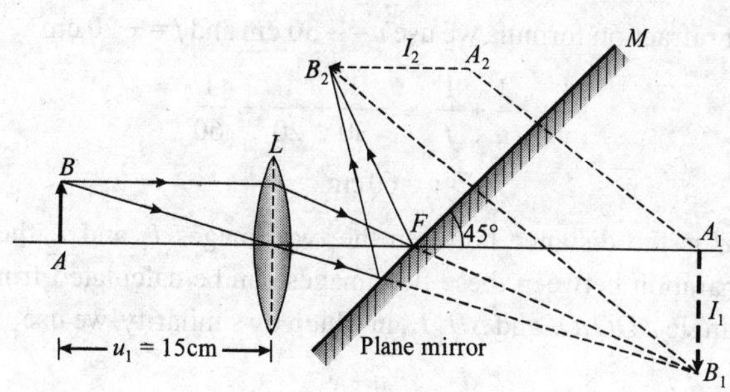

Figure 5.238

The image I_1 acts as the object for the plane mirror and after reflection of light rays from the plane mirror final image produced is A_2B_2. In a plane mirror, the image formed is at same distance at which object is kept from it and size remain same. So the final image is produced at a distance $30 - 10 = 20$ cm as shown in figure-5.238 at an angle 90° to the principal axis as mirror rotates the reflected rays by twice the angle at which mirror is rotated.

Illustrative Example 5.66

A point object is placed at a distance of 0.3 m from a convex lens of focal length 20 cm which is cut into two halves each of which is displaced by 0.5 mm as shown in figure-5.239. Find the position of the image. If more than one image is formed, find their number and the distance between them.

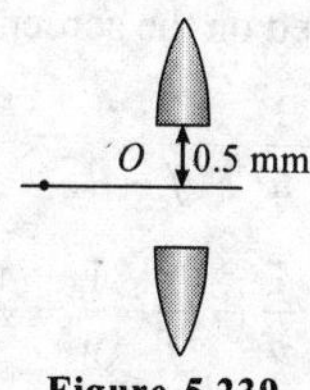

Figure 5.239

Solution

We have studied that every part of a lens behaves like complete lens and produces a separate image so in this case two images are obtained. The image formation is shown in figure-5.240.

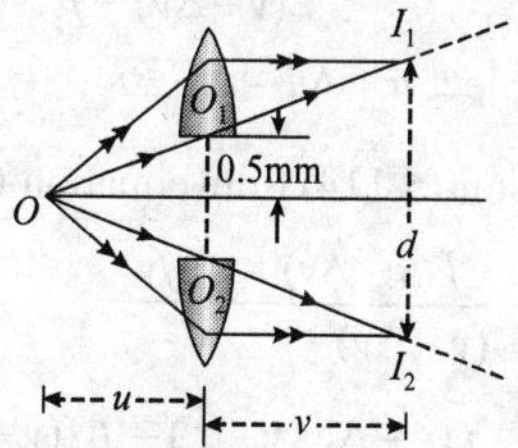

Figure 5.240

The light rays from object passes through optical centres O_1 and O_2 undeflected. The images of O are produced at I_1 and I_2 due to upper and lower part of lenses. To find the location of images we use refraction formula as

$$\frac{1}{v} - \frac{1}{u} = \frac{1}{f}$$

For refraction formula we use $u = -30$ cm and $f = +20$ cm

$$\Rightarrow \quad \frac{1}{v} = \frac{1}{u} + \frac{1}{f} = -\frac{1}{30} + \frac{1}{20} = \frac{1}{60}$$

$$\Rightarrow \quad v = 60 \text{ cm}$$

If d is the distance between the two images I_1 and I_2 then separation between these two images can be calculated from triangle ΔOO_1O_2 and ΔII_1I_2, in which by similarity, we use

$$\frac{d}{O_1O_2} = \frac{u+v}{u}$$

$$\Rightarrow \quad \frac{d}{0.05+0.05} = \frac{30+60}{30}$$

Solving we get $\quad d = 3$ mm

Illustrative Example 5.67

A thin converging lens of focal length $f = 25.0$ cm forms the image of an object, on the screen, at a distance 5 cm from the lens. The screen is then drawn closer by a distance 18 cm. By what distance should the object be shifted so that its image on the screen is sharp again?

Solution

Since the image is formed on the screen, it is real

Now $\quad \frac{1}{v} + \frac{1}{u} = \frac{1}{f}$

or $\quad \frac{1}{u} = \frac{1}{f} - \frac{1}{v} = \frac{v-f}{fv}$

$$\Rightarrow \quad u = \frac{fv}{v-f} \quad \text{...(5.114)}$$

In the second case, let the image is formed at $v - \Delta v$. Let the corresponding position of object be $u - \Delta u$. Now

$$u + \Delta u = \frac{f(v-\Delta v)}{(v-\Delta v)-f} \quad \text{...(5.115)}$$

The shift of the object $u + \Delta u - u = \Delta u$

Subtracting equation-(5.114) from equation-(5.115), we get

$$\Delta u = \frac{f(v-\Delta v)}{(v-\Delta v)-f} - \frac{fv}{v-f}$$

$$\Rightarrow \quad \Delta u = \frac{f(v-\Delta v)(v-f) - fv((v-\Delta v)f)}{\{(v-\Delta v)-f\}(v-f)}$$

$$\Rightarrow \quad \Delta u = \frac{f^2\Delta v}{(v-\Delta v-f)(v-f)}$$

$$\Rightarrow \quad \Delta u = \frac{f^2\Delta v}{(v-f)^2\left[1-\frac{\Delta v}{(v-f)}\right]}$$

$$\Rightarrow \quad \Delta u = \frac{f^2\Delta v}{(v-f)^2}\left[1-\frac{\Delta v}{(v-f)}\right]^{-1}$$

$$\Rightarrow \quad \Delta u \approx \frac{f^2\Delta v}{(v-f)^2} \quad \text{(neglecting higher terms)}$$

Substituting the given values, we have

$$\Rightarrow \quad \Delta u \approx \frac{(25)^2\times 18}{(500-25)^2} \approx \frac{(25)^2\times 18}{(475)^2} \approx 0.5 \text{ mm}$$

Illustrative Example 5.68

Determine the position of the image produced by an optical system consisting of a concave mirror with a focal length of 10 cm and a convergent lens with a focal length of 20 cm. The distance from the mirror to the lens is 30 cm and from the lens to the object is 40 cm. Find the image produced after one refraction from lens and one reflection from mirror.

Solution

Object is placed at distance $2f$ from the lens so its image is also formed at distance $2f$ on other side. For mirror this image acts as an object which is located at a distance of 10 cm and we apply mirror formula in this case for which we use $u = +10$ cm and $f = -10$ cm

$$\Rightarrow \quad \frac{1}{u} + \frac{1}{v} = \frac{1}{f}$$

$$\Rightarrow \quad \frac{1}{v} + \frac{1}{+10} = \frac{1}{-10}$$

$$\Rightarrow \quad v = -5 \text{ cm}$$

Ray diagram for image formation is shown in figure-5.241 below

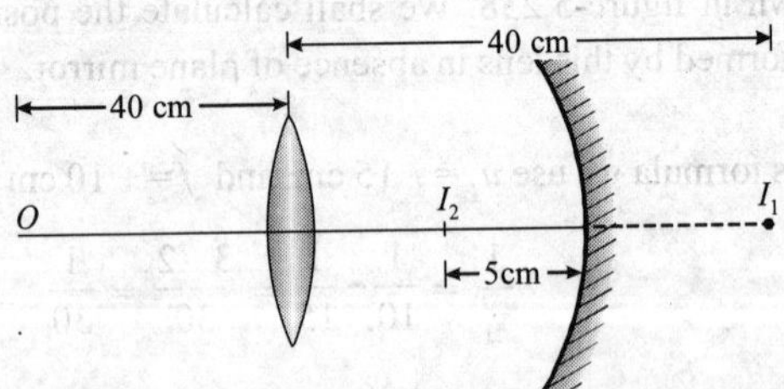

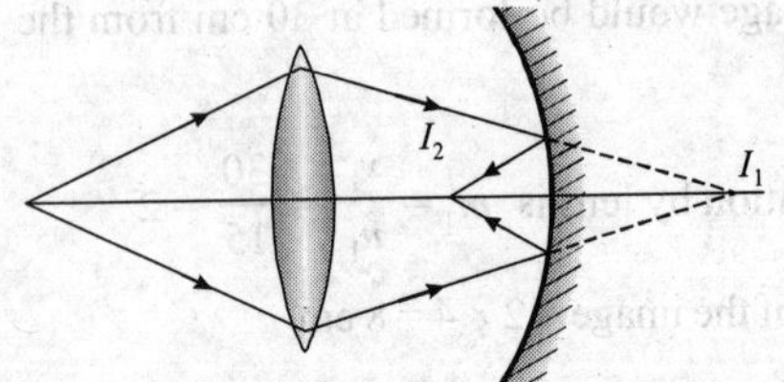

Figure 5.241

Illustrative Example 5.69

A small angled prism (refractive index μ and angle α) and a convex lens are arranged as shown in figure. A point object O is placed as shown.

(a) Calculate the angle of deviation of the rays hitting the prism at nearly normal incidence

(b) If the distance between object, prism and the lens are shown in the figure, locate the position of the image both along and transverse to the axis.

Solution

The optical setup described in question is shown in figure-5.242 below.

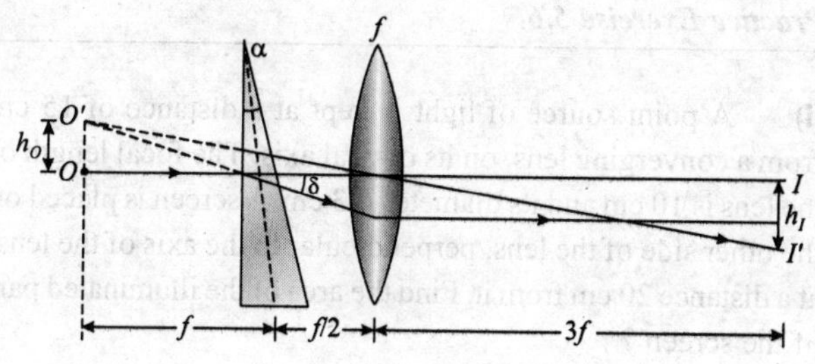

Figure 5.242

Figure change from printouts...

(a) The deviation produced by the prism

$$\delta=(\mu-1)\alpha$$

(b) The prism forms image of the object at O'.

$$\Rightarrow \quad OO'=\delta f=(\mu-1)\alpha f$$

The image O' becomes object for lens.

Now using lens formula, we have $u=-\dfrac{3f}{2}$ so we use

$$\frac{1}{v}-\frac{1}{u}=\frac{1}{f}$$

$$\Rightarrow \quad \frac{1}{v}-\frac{1}{\frac{3f}{2}}=\frac{1}{f}$$

$$\Rightarrow \quad \frac{1}{v}=\frac{1}{3f}$$

$$\Rightarrow \quad v=3f$$

Also $\quad \dfrac{II'}{OO'}=\dfrac{v}{u}$

$$=\frac{3f}{\left(\frac{3f}{2}\right)}=2$$

Which gives $\quad II'=2(OO')$

$$\Rightarrow \quad II'=2(\mu-1)\alpha f$$

Thus image position is $3f$ on the right side of the lens along the axis, and $2(\mu-1)\alpha f$ transverse to axis.

Illustrative Example 5.70

A strong source of light when used with a convex lens produces a number of images of the source owing to feeble internal reflections and refraction called flare spots as shown in figure-5.243. These extra images are $F_1, F_2, \ldots$. If F_n is the position of nth flare spot, then show that

$$\frac{1}{f_n}=\frac{(n+1)\mu-1}{f(\mu-1)}$$

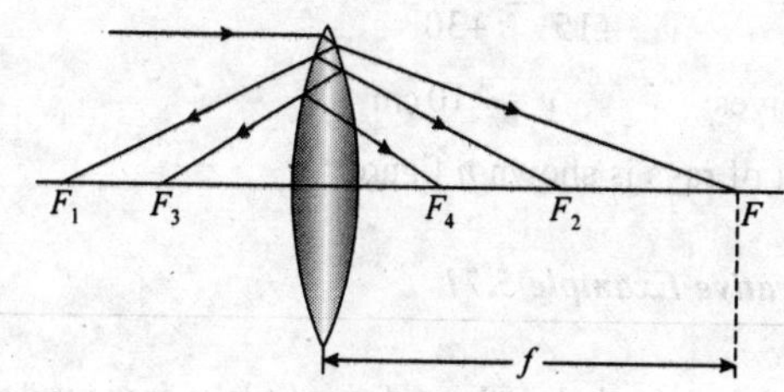

Figure 5.243

Solution

Light converges at F_1 after two refractions and one reflection from the lens. So we use

$$\frac{1}{F_1}=\frac{2}{f_e}+\frac{1}{f_m}$$

Where focal length of equivalent independent lens is given do

$$\frac{1}{f_e}=(\mu-1)\left(\frac{1}{R_1}-\frac{1}{R_2}\right)$$

$$\Rightarrow \quad \frac{1}{f}=(\mu-1)\left(\frac{1}{+R}-\frac{1}{-R}\right)=(\mu-1)\frac{2}{R}$$

$$\Rightarrow \quad R=2(\mu-1)f$$

$$\Rightarrow \quad \frac{1}{F_1}=\frac{2}{f}+\frac{2}{2(\mu-1)f}$$

$$\Rightarrow \quad \frac{1}{F_1}=\frac{2\mu-1}{(\mu-1)f}$$

For F_2, there are three refractions and two reflections

$$\frac{1}{F_2}=\frac{3}{f_1}+\frac{2}{f_m}$$

$$\Rightarrow \quad =\frac{3}{f}+\frac{2}{R/2}=\frac{3}{f}+\frac{4}{R}$$

$$\Rightarrow \quad = \frac{3}{f} + \frac{4}{2(\mu-1)f}$$

$$\Rightarrow \quad = \frac{3}{f} + \frac{2}{(\mu-1)f}$$

$$\Rightarrow \quad = \frac{3(\mu-1)+2}{(\mu-1)f} = \frac{3\mu-1}{(\mu-1)f}$$

$$\Rightarrow \quad \frac{1}{F_n} = \frac{(n+1)\mu-1}{(\mu-1)f}$$

By using lens formula

$$\frac{1}{v} - \frac{1}{u} = \frac{1}{f},$$

where $u = +15$ cm, $f = +30$ cm

we have $\frac{1}{v} - \frac{1}{+15} = \frac{1}{+30}$

which gives $v = +10$ cm

The plot of rays is shown *n* figure.

Illustrative Example 5.71

A small fish, 0.4 m below the surface of a lake, is viewed through a simple converging lens of focal length 3 m. The lens is kept at 0.2 m above the water surface such that the fish lies on the optical axis of the lens. Find the image of the fish seen by the observer. The refractive index of water is 4/3.

Solution

The apparent position of the object O from the surface of water is

$$h' = \frac{h}{\mu} = \frac{0.4}{4/3}$$

$$\Rightarrow \quad h' = 0.3$$

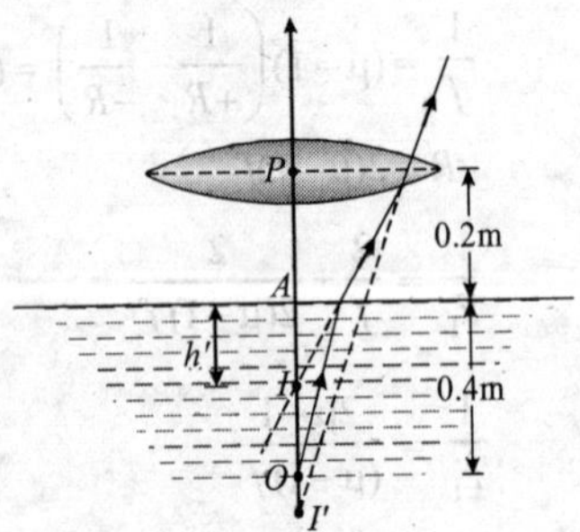

Figure 5.244

The distance $PI = 0.3 + 0.2 = 0.5$ m

For convex lens, we use

$$u = -0.5 \text{ m}, f = +3 \text{ m}$$

By lens formula,

$$\frac{1}{v} - \frac{1}{u} = \frac{1}{f}, \text{ we have}$$

$$\Rightarrow \quad \frac{1}{v} - \frac{1}{-0.5} = \frac{1}{3}$$

$$\Rightarrow \quad v = -0.6 \text{ m}$$

Practice Exercise 5.6

(i) A point source of light is kept at a distance of 15 cm from a converging lens, on its optical axis. The focal length of the lens is 10 cm and its diameter is 3 cm. A screen is placed on the other side of the lens, perpendicular to the axis of the lens, at a distance 20 cm from it. Find the area of the illuminated part of the screen ?

[(π/4) cm^2]

(ii) A 5.0 diopter lens forms a virtual image which is 4 times the object placed perpendicularly on the principal axis of lens, find the distance of object from lens.

[15 cm]

(iii) A point object is placed at a distance of 25 cm from a convex lens of focal length 20 cm. If a glass slab of thickness t and refractive index 1.5 is inserted between the lens and the object, the image is formed at infinity. Find the thickness t ?

[15 cm]

(iv) A convex lens of focal length 20 cm and a concave lens of focal length 10 cm are placed 10 cm apart with their principle axis coinciding. A parallel beam of light of diameter 5 mm is incident on convex lens symmetrically. Prove that emerging beam will also be parallel & find its diameter.

[2.5 mm]

(v) A convex lens of focal length 20 cm is placed 10 cm in front of a convex mirror of radius of curvature 15 cm. Where should a point object be placed in front of the lens so that it produces image on itself ?

[100 cm]

(vi) A converging lens of focal length 20 cm is separated 8 cm from a diverging lens of focal length 30 cm. A parallel beam of light falls on converging lens and after passing through diverging lens focussed at point *P*. Find the location of point P. Repeat the calculation for the case when the parallel beam first falls on diverging lens.

[42.2 cm from convex lens]

(vii) Two symmetric double convex lenses *A* and *B* have same focal length but the radii of curvature differ so that $R_A = 0.9\,R_B$. If refractive index of *A* is 1.63 find the refractive index of *B*.

[1.7]

(viii) An object is placed at 20 cm left of the convex lens of focal length 10 cm. If a concave mirror of focal length 5 cm is placed at 30 cm to the right of the lens, find the magnification and the nature of the final image. Draw the ray diagram and locate the position of the final image.

[At the object and of same size]

(ix) In the figure-5.245 it is shown, the focal length *f* of the two thin convex lenses is the same. They are separated by a horizontal distance 3*f* and their optical axes are displaced by a vertical separation '*d*' ($d << f$), as shown. Taking the origin of coordinates *O* at the centre of the first lens, find the *x* and *y* coordinates of the point where a parallel beam of rays coming from the left finally gets focussed ?

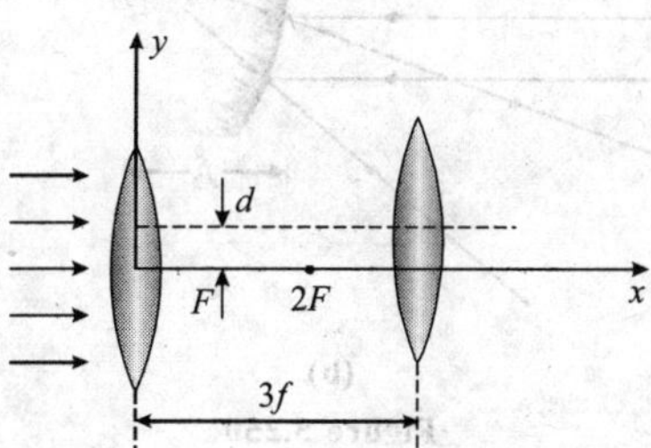

Figure 5.245

[(5*f*, 2*d*)]

(x) A convex lens of focal length 10 cm is placed 30 cm in front of a second convex lens also of the same focal length. A plane mirror is placed behind the two lenses. Where should a point object be placed in front of the first lens so that its image is produced on itself ?

[20 cm]

(xi) A small pin of size 5 mm is placed along principal axis of a convex lens of focal length 6 cm at a distance 11 cm from the lens. Find the size of image of pin.

[7.2 mm]

(xii) An object is kept at a distance of 16 cm from a thin lens and the image formed is real. If the object is kept at a distance of 6 cm from the same lens, the image formed is virtual. If the size of the images formed in above two cases are same, find the focal length of the lens?

[11 cm]

(xiii) An object is placed midway between the lens and the mirror as shown in figure-5.246. The mirror's radius of curvature is 20.0 cm and the lens has a focal length of – 16.7 cm. Considering only the rays that leaves the object and travels first toward the mirror, locate the final image formed by this system. Is this image real or virtual? Is it upright or inverted ? What is the overall magnification ?

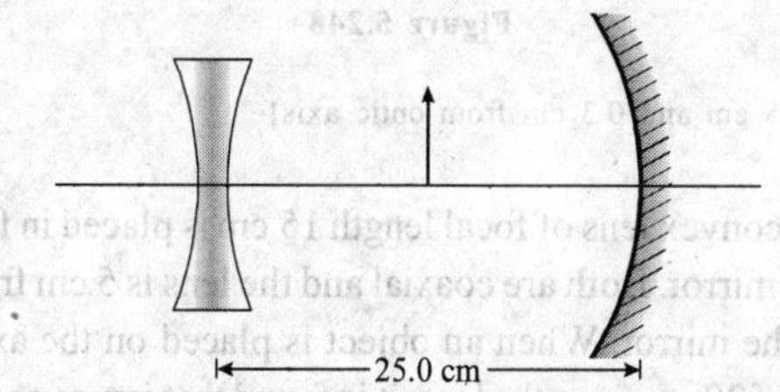

Figure 5.246

[25.3 cm from mirror, virtual, erected, 8.048]

(xiv) Two thin convex lenses of focal lengths f_1 and f_2 are separated by a horizontal distance d ($d < f_1$ and $d < f_2$) and their centres are displaced by a vertical separation Δ as shown in figure-5.247. Taking the origin of coordinates *O* as the centre of first lens, what would be the *x* and *y* coordinate of the focal point of this lens system for a parallel beam of rays coming from left?

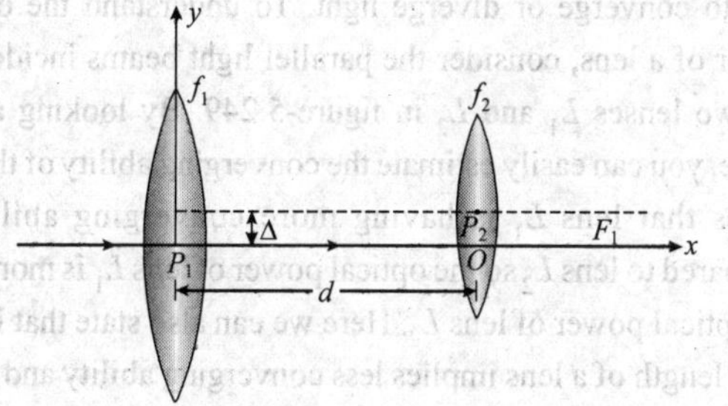

Figure 5.247

$$\left[\frac{f_1 f_2 + d(f_1 - d)}{(f_1 + f_2 - d)}, \frac{\Delta(f_1 - d)}{(f_1 + f_2 - d)}\right]$$

(xv) A convex lens of focal length 15 cm and a concave mirror of focal length 30 cm are kept with their optic axis *PQ* and *RS* parallel but separated in vertical direction by 0.6 m as shown. The distance between lens and mirror is 30 cm. An upright object AB of height 1.2 m is placed on the optic axis PQ of the lens at a distance of 20 cm from the lens. If $A'B'$ is the image after refraction from the lens and reflection from the mirror, find the distance of $A'B'$ from the pole of the mirror and obtain magnification. Also locate position of A' and B' with respect to the optic axis RS.

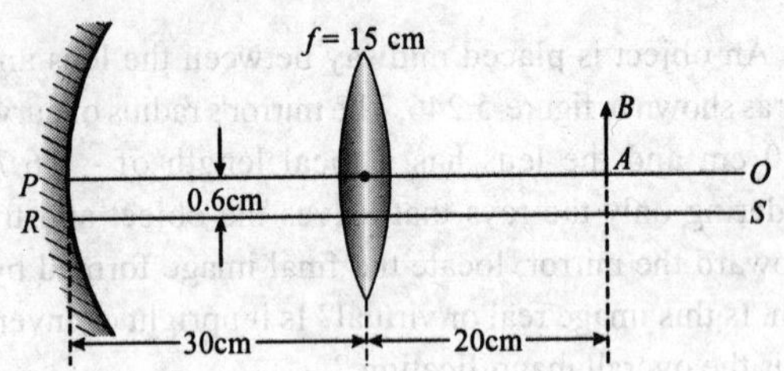

Figure 5.248

[15 cm, 1.5 cm and 0.3 cm from optic axis]

(xvi) A convex lens of focal length 15 cm is placed in front of a convex mirror. Both are coaxial and the lens is 5 cm from the apex of the mirror. When an object is placed on the axis at a distance of 20 cm from the lens, it is found that image coincides with the object. Calculate the radius of curvature of mirror.

[55 cm]

5.16 Optical Power of a Thin Lens or a Spherical Mirror

Optical Power of a thin lens or a spherical mirror or any optical system is defined as the degree to which that optical device is able to converge or diverge light. To understand the optical power of a lens, consider the parallel light beams incident on the two lenses L_1 and L_2 in figure-5.249. By looking at this figure, you can easily estimate the converging ability of the two lenses that lens L_1 is having more converging ability as compared to lens L_2 so the optical power of lens L_1 is more than the optical power of lens L_2. Here we can also state that higher focal length of a lens implies less converging ability and lesser optical power of the lens. Same is the case we can define for diverging lenses as well as spherical mirrors.

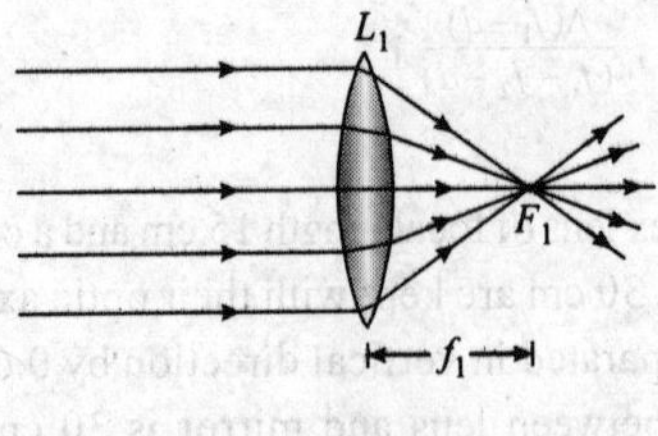

(a)

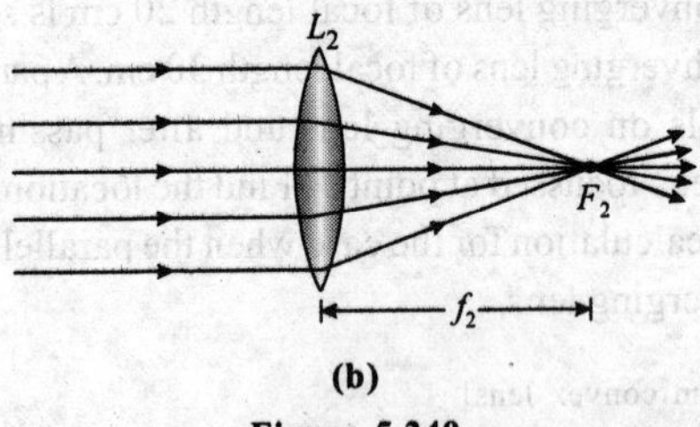

(b)

Figure 5.249

Figure-5.250 shows that the optical power of mirror M_1 is less than optical power of mirror M_2.

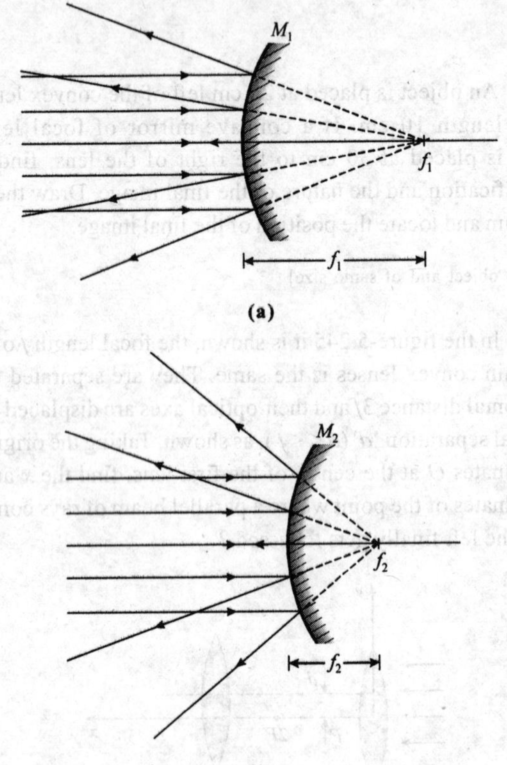

Figure 5.250

Mathematically the magnitude of optical power of a lens or mirror is given by reciprocal of the focal length. The SI unit for measurement of optical power is m^{-1} and is also called '*dioptre*' and denoted by '*D*'. Thus optical power of a thin lens or spherical mirror is given as

$$P = \frac{1}{f}$$

Conventionally for converging optical devices optical power is taken positive and for diverging optical devices optical power is taken negative. In this chapter also we will be using the same convention for optical power but this conventions is limited to assess whether the optical device is converging or diverging. This convention should not be applied directly in lens or mirror formula if coordinate convention is being followed.

5.16.1 Combination of Thin Lenses

When two thin lenses L_1 and L_2 are placed in contact as shown in figure-5.251(a) then for image formation there are two ways. One by one we can use lens formula for refraction of light at the two lenses and consider image produced by first lens as object for the second lens and find the final image. Other method is to find an equivalent lens which can replace the combination of the two lenses which can produce the same image for the given object. Figure-5.251(b) shows a single lens which is producing the image at the same position at a distance v_2 which is produced by the lens system shown in figure-5.251(a) for the object located at a distance u from it. As lenses are thin, we ignore their thickness as well as separation as we are considering them in contact.

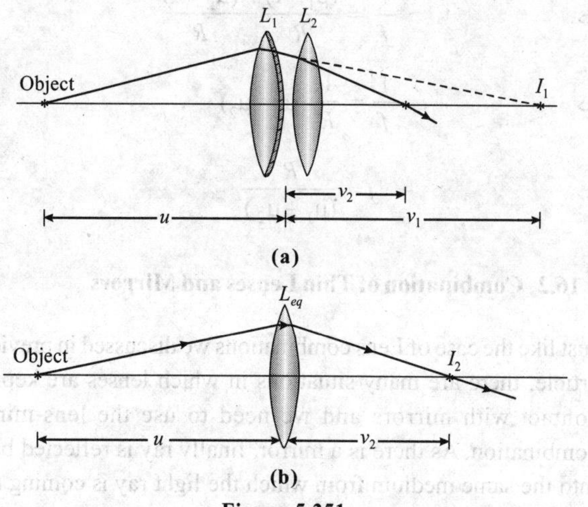

Figure 5.251

In figure-5.251(a) we use lens formula to find the image I_1 produced by first lens L_1 of focal length f_1 by which we find the position of this first image at a distance v_1 given as

$$\frac{1}{f_1}=\frac{1}{v_1}-\frac{1}{u} \qquad ...(5.116)$$

Now the refracted light rays from first lens going toward I_1 fall on second lens L_2 having focal length f_2 and this image I_1 will act as an object for the second lens and final image I_2 is obtained at a distance v_2 from this lens system as shown which can be obtained by using lens formula again for the second lens as

$$\frac{1}{f_2}=\frac{1}{v_2}-\frac{1}{v_1} \qquad ...(5.117)$$

Adding the equation-(5.116) and (5.117) we get

$$\frac{1}{f_1}+\frac{1}{f_2}=\frac{1}{v_2}-\frac{1}{u}$$

$$\Rightarrow \quad \frac{1}{f_{eq}}=\frac{1}{v_2}-\frac{1}{u} \quad \left(\text{Here we are using } \frac{1}{f_{eq}}=\frac{1}{f_1}+\frac{1}{f_2}\right)$$

Here we used f_{eq} as the equivalent focal length of the lens replacing the combination of lenses L_1 and L_2 in contact. As v_2 is the final image obtained by this lens combination for an object placed at a distance u, we can use the lens formula for any combination as

$$\frac{1}{f_{eq}}=\frac{1}{v}-\frac{1}{u} \qquad ...(5.118)$$

where equivalent focal length of the combination of two or more lenses can be given as

$$\frac{1}{f_{eq}}=\frac{1}{f_1}+\frac{1}{f_2}+\frac{1}{f_3}+... \qquad ...(5.119)$$

For analysis of different situation of image formation by combination of lenses we can use equation-(5.119) for finding the equivalent focal length of the lens system and use it in equation-(5.118) for finding the location of the final image. All values of focal lengths, object and image distances we use with proper signs according to sign convention being used.

Note : For equation-(5.119) it is advisable to use positive sign for focal length of converging lenses and negative sign for focal length of diverging lenses and find the equivalent focal length of lens system. If the equivalent focal length is coming positive then it is behaving like a converging lens and if it comes negative then we treat equivalent lens as a diverging lens.

So here equation-(5.119) we can also be written in terms of optical power as

$$P_{eq}=P_1+P_2+P_3+...$$

Above analysis shows that in case of two or more lenses kept in contact as a single optical system then due to their converging or diverging behaviour, for the combination its equivalent optical power can be given as sum of all the individual optical power of lenses kept in contact. Be careful of taking positive sign for converging powers and negative sign for diverging powers before summing up.

 # Illustrative Example 5.72

A point object is placed at a distance of 15 cm from a convex lens. The image is formed on the other side of lens at a distance 30 cm from lens. When a concave lens is placed in contact with convex lens, image is shifted away further by 30 cm. Calculate the focal lengths of the two lenses.

Solution

For convex lens, we use

$$u=-15\text{ cm}$$

$$v=+30\text{ cm}$$

By lens formula, we have

$$\frac{1}{v}-\frac{1}{u}=\frac{1}{f_1}$$

$$\Rightarrow \quad \frac{1}{f_1}=\frac{1}{30}+\frac{1}{15}=\frac{3}{30}$$

$$\Rightarrow \quad f_1=10\,\text{cm}$$

For combination of lenses

$$u=-15\,\text{cm}$$

$$v=+60\,\text{cm}$$

By lens formula, we have

$$\frac{1}{v}-\frac{1}{u}=\frac{1}{f_{eq}}$$

$$\Rightarrow \quad \frac{1}{f_{eq}}=\frac{1}{60}+\frac{1}{15}=\frac{5}{60}=\frac{1}{12}$$

$$f_{eq}=12\,\text{cm}$$

For combination of the two lenses in contact

$$f_1=+10\,\text{cm}$$

$$f_{eq}=+12\,\text{cm}$$

$$\Rightarrow \quad \frac{1}{f_{eq}}=\frac{1}{f_1}+\frac{1}{f_2}$$

$$\Rightarrow \quad \frac{1}{12}=\frac{1}{10}+\frac{1}{f_2}$$

$$\Rightarrow \quad f_2=-60\,\text{cm}$$

 # Illustrative Example 5.73

The figure-5.252 below shows a thin plano-convex lens of refractive index μ_1 and a thin plano-concave lens of refractive index μ_2, both having same radius of curvature R of their curved surfaces. Another thin lens of refractive index μ_3 has same radius of curvature R on the two surfaces between the plano-convex and plano-concave lenses that the plane surfaces are parallel to each other. Find the focal length of the combination.

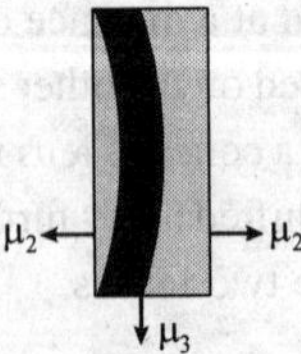

Figure 5.252

Solution

By lens makers formula, focal length of plane convex lens is given as

$$\frac{1}{f_1}=(\mu_1-1)\left(\frac{1}{\infty}+\frac{1}{R}\right)=\frac{\mu_1-1}{R}$$

For the middle lens the focal length is given as

$$\frac{1}{f_3}=(\mu_3-1)\left(-\frac{1}{R}+\frac{1}{R}\right)=0$$

For the plano-concave lens, the focal length is given as

$$\frac{1}{f_3}=(\mu_2-1)\left(-\frac{1}{R}+\frac{1}{\infty}\right)=-\frac{(\mu_2-1)}{R}$$

Equivalent focal length of the combination is given as

$$\frac{1}{f}=\frac{1}{f_1}+\frac{1}{f_2}+\frac{1}{f_3}$$

$$\Rightarrow \quad \frac{1}{f}=\frac{(\mu_1-1)}{R}-\frac{(\mu_2-1)}{R}$$

$$\Rightarrow \quad \frac{1}{f}=\frac{1}{R}(\mu_1-\mu_2)$$

$$\Rightarrow \quad f=\frac{R}{(\mu_1-\mu_2)}$$

5.16.2 Combination of Thin Lenses and Mirrors

Just like the case of Lens combinations we discussed in previous article, there are many situations in which lenses are kept in contact with mirrors and we need to use the lens-mirror combination. As there is a mirror, finally ray is reflected back into the same medium from which the light ray is coming and incident on the lens-mirror system. Figure-5.253(a) shows a convex lens kept in contact with a concave mirror, this combination will overall behave like a concave (converging) mirror for the incident ray as both convex lens L and concave mirror M are converging in nature and their converging powers will get added up and overall lens-mirror system will be more converging then individual lens or mirror and having lesser equivalent focal length. If focal lengths of the lens and mirror used in this case are f_1 and f_2 then the equivalent power of this lens-mirror combination can be given as

$$P_{eq}=P_1+P_2+P_1=2P_1+P_2 \qquad \ldots(5.120)$$

or in terms of focal lengths we can use

$$\frac{1}{f_{eq}}=\frac{2}{f_1}+\frac{1}{f_2} \qquad \ldots(5.121)$$

In equation-(5.121) we have used the power of lens twice because in overall reflection of the light ray from this lens-mirror combination, light ray is passing through the lens twice, first just after incidence and then after getting reflected from the mirror before coming out in air. So the lens is effecting the light ray twice due to its converging behaviour in sequence. As both lens and mirror are of converging behaviour, their focal lengths in equation-(5.121) we take positive and that gives equivalent focal length also positive, thus we can say that this system of lens-mirror combination is behaving like a converging mirror. Figure-5.136(b) shows that we can replace this lens-mirror system by a single concave (converging) mirror with equivalent focal length given by equation-(5.121) and it produces the same image of the given object which was produced by the combination which can be calculated by use of f_{eq} in mirror formula applied for the equivalent mirror.

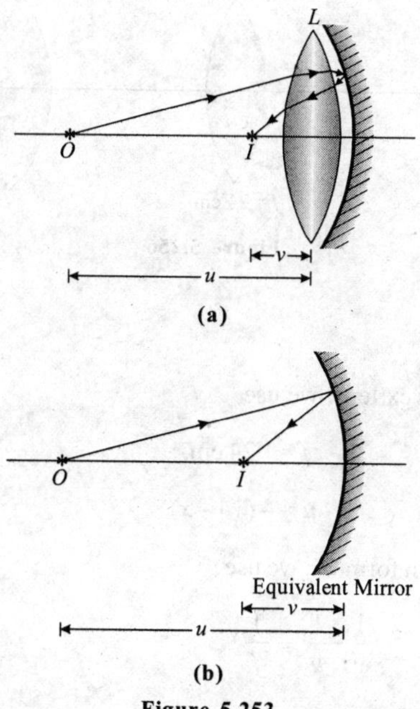

Figure 5.253

A similar case is shown in figure-5.254 in which two lenses L_1 (converging) and L_2 (diverging) are kept in contact and right-most surface of the lens L_2 is silvered so that it starts behaving like a convex mirror M. As per the analysis we have done above we can give the equivalent power and focal length of the equivalent mirror as

$$P_{eq} = P_1 + P_2 + P_M + P_2 + P_1 = 2P_1 + 2P_2 + P_M \quad \ldots(5.122)$$

$$\Rightarrow \quad \frac{1}{f_{eq}} = \frac{2}{f_1} + \frac{2}{f_2} + \frac{1}{f_M} \quad \ldots(5.123)$$

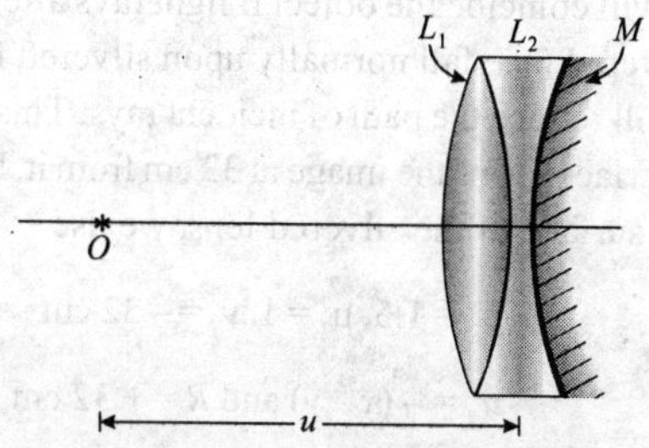

Figure 5.254

Like the first case discussed here also we are taking the powers of both lenses twice as light ray passes through these two lenses twice and reflected once at the mirror. Overall behaviour of the equivalent lens for this lens-mirror combination depends upon the magnitudes of the individual lenses and mirror. In above equation-(5.123) we use f_1 positive, f_2 negative and f_M also negative due to their converging or diverging behaviour. Here students must remember that for finding the equivalent focal length the signs used in equations-(5.121) or (5.123) are based on the behaviour of lenses or mirrors and after finding the equivalent focal length of the combination and its behaviour by the sign of f_{eq} use it in lens or mirror formula as per the coordinate sign convention we already studied.

Note : If some students are using Incident Ray Reference Sign Convention then they can use same sign convention for equation-(5.121) but in equation-(5.123) they need to modify this relation by replacing '+' sign with '–' the term of power of mirror. In many cases this becomes confusing for students who do not have lot of practice so in this chapter we are using coordinate convention as used till now.

 # Illustrative Example 5.74

The convex surface of a thin concavo-convex lens of glass of refractive index 1.5 has a radius of curvature 20 cm. The concave surface has a radius of curvature 60 cm. The convex side is silvered and placed at horizontal surface as shown in figure-5.255.

(i) Where should a pin be placed on the optic axis such that its image is formed at the same place?

(ii) If the concave part is filled with water of refractive index 4/3, find the distance through which the pin should be moved so that the image of the pin again coincide with pin.

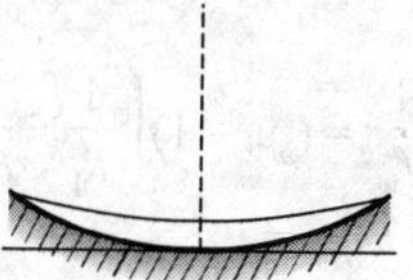
Figure 5.255

Solution

(i) First we calculate the combined focal length of this given combination. The refraction takes place from concavo-convex lens, and then reflection from lower surface which is acting as a mirror and finally again refraction from the lens. Thus equivalent focal length of the combination is given as

$$\frac{1}{F_1} = \frac{1}{f_g} + \frac{1}{f_m} + \frac{1}{f_g} = \frac{2}{f_g} + \frac{1}{f_m} \quad \ldots(5.124)$$

Here $\qquad f_m = R_2/2 = 20/2 = 10 \text{ cm}$

The value of f_g can be obtained by using the formula

$$\frac{1}{f_g}=({}_a\mu_g-1)\left(\frac{1}{R_1}-\frac{1}{R_2}\right)$$

$$\Rightarrow \quad \frac{1}{f_g}=(1.5-1)\left(\frac{1}{20}-\frac{1}{60}\right)$$

$$\Rightarrow \quad f_g=60\text{ cm}$$

Substituting these values in equation-(5.124), we have

$$\frac{1}{F_1}=\frac{20}{60}+\frac{1}{10}=\frac{2+6}{60}=\frac{8}{60}=\frac{2}{15}$$

$$\Rightarrow \quad F_1=\frac{15}{2}=7.5\text{ cm}$$

For the image to be formed at the same point of object

$$u=2F_1=2\times 7.5=15\text{ cm}$$

Hence the object should be placed as 15 cm from the lens on the optic axis.

(ii) In this case, the focal length F_2 of the combination is given as

$$\frac{1}{F_2}=\frac{1}{f_w}+\frac{1}{f_g}+\frac{1}{f_m}+\frac{1}{f_g}+\frac{1}{f_w}$$

$$\Rightarrow \quad \frac{1}{F_2}=\frac{2}{f_w}+\frac{2}{f_g}+\frac{1}{f_m} \quad \ldots(5.125)$$

Here $f_g=60$ cm and $f_m=10$ cm

The value of f_w can be calculated by using the formula

$$\frac{1}{f_w}=({}_a\mu_w-1)\left(\frac{1}{R_1}-\frac{1}{R_2}\right)$$

$$\Rightarrow \quad \frac{1}{f_w}=\left(\frac{4}{3}-1\right)\left(\frac{1}{60}\right)=\frac{1}{180}$$

$$\Rightarrow \quad f_w=180\text{ cm}$$

Substituting these values in equation-(5.125), we have

$$\frac{1}{F_2}=\frac{2}{180}+\frac{2}{60}+\frac{1}{10} \text{ or } F'=\frac{90}{13}$$

Now $u'=2F_2=\dfrac{2\times 90}{13}=\dfrac{180}{13}$ cm

Displacement of the pin

$$x=u-u'=15-\frac{180}{13}=\frac{15}{13}=1.14\text{ cm}$$

 # *Illustrative Example 5.75*

The radius of curvature of the curved surfaces of an equiconvex lens is 32 cm and its refractive index is μ= 1.5. One of its side is slivered and placed 14 cm away from an object as shown in figure-5.256. At what distance *x* should a second convex lens of focal length 24 cm be placed so that the image coincides with the object.

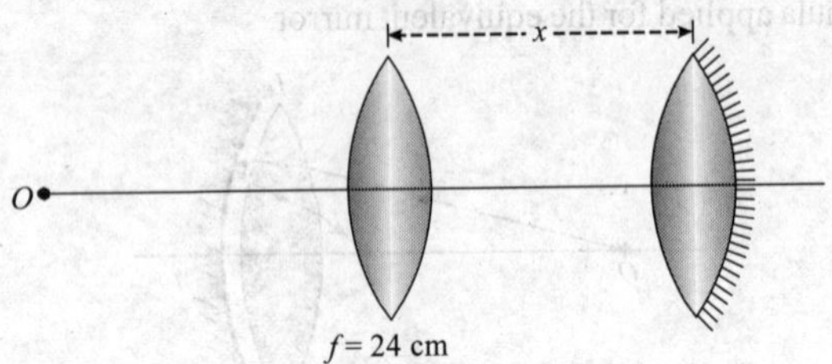

Figure 5.256

Solution

For the convex lens, we use

$$f=+24\text{ cm},$$

and $u=-(14-x)$

By refraction formula, we use

$$\frac{1}{v}-\frac{1}{u}=\frac{1}{f}$$

$$\Rightarrow \quad \frac{1}{v}=\frac{1}{u}+\frac{1}{f}$$

$$\Rightarrow \quad \frac{1}{v}=\frac{1}{24}-\frac{1}{(14-x)}=\frac{14-x-24}{24(14-x)}$$

$$\Rightarrow \quad \frac{1}{v}=\frac{-(x+10)}{24(14-x)}$$

$$\Rightarrow \quad v=-\left[\frac{(336-24x)}{(x+10)}\right]$$

The image will coincide the object if light rays after refraction from un-silvered face fall normally upon silvered face so that these rays will retrace the path of incident rays. This is possible when first surface forms the image at 32 cm from it. Now for the un-silvered surface of the silvered lens, we use

$$\mu_2=1.5, \mu_1=1, v_1=-32\text{ cm},$$

$$u_1=-(x-v)\text{ and }R=+32\text{ cm}$$

By using refraction formula, we have

$$\frac{\mu}{v_1}-\frac{1}{u_1}=\frac{\mu-1}{R}$$

$$\Rightarrow \frac{1.5}{-32}+\frac{1}{\left[x-\left\{-\frac{336-24x}{(x+10)}\right\}\right]}=\frac{1.5-1}{32}$$

$$\Rightarrow \frac{(x+10)}{x(x+10)+(336-24x)}=\frac{0.5}{32}+\frac{1.5}{32}=\frac{1}{16}$$

$$\Rightarrow x^2+10x+336-24x=16x+160$$

$$\Rightarrow x^2-30x+176=0$$

$$\Rightarrow x=8 \text{ or } x=22$$

Hence the lens should be placed 8 cm from silvered surface.

5.16.3 Deviation in a Light Ray due to Refraction through a Thin Lens

Figure-5.257(a) shows a paraxial light ray parallel to the principal axis of a lens at a distance h incident on a convex lens. After refraction from the lens light ray gets deviated by an angle δ which we can calculate by considering the refraction points of light ray on the two surfaces of a small angled prism of prism angle A as shown in figure-5.257(b). Thus all paraxial rays (near normal) incident on the lens at this section $ABCD$ of the lens will get deviated by angle δ. Here the deviation angle δ is given as

$$\delta=\frac{h}{f} \quad \ldots(5.126)$$

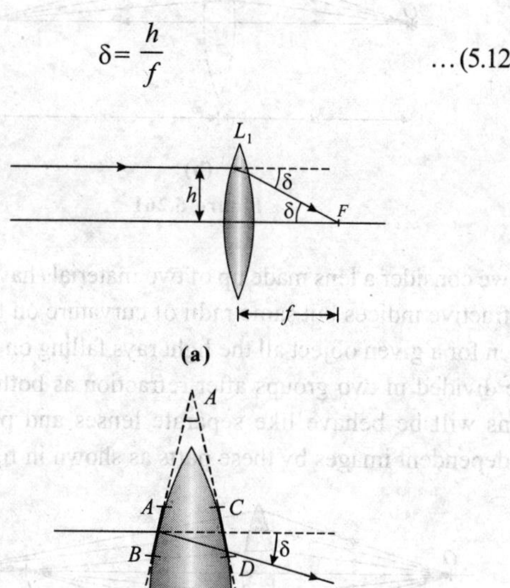

Figure 5.257

If we look at the figure-5.258 in which for an object O, after refraction image I is produced by the same lens then a specific light ray from O which falls on this section $ABCD$ of the lens after deviation by same angle δ the refracted light ray will meet at point I on principal axis as shown. In this case we can say that any paraxial light ray which incident on the lens at a height h above (or below) the principal axis, will suffer a deviation by an angle δ given by equation-(5.126).

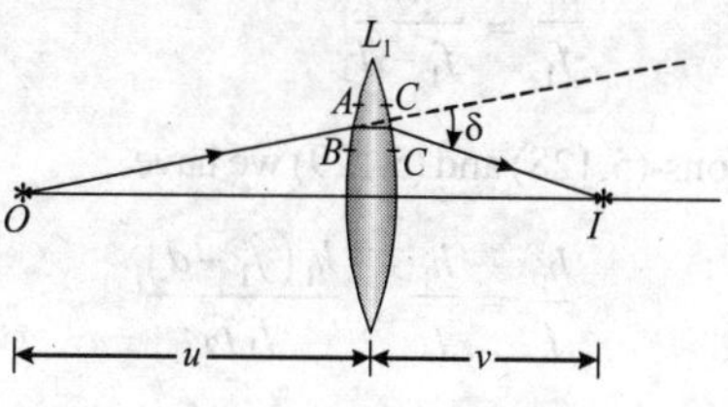

Figure 5.258

5.16.4 Combination of Two Thin Lenses at some Separation

Figure-5.259 shows two convex lenses L_1 and L_2 with focal lengths f_1 and f_2 placed at a separation d. We consider a paraxial light ray in the parallel beam of light which incident on the lens L_1 at a height h_1 above the principal axis which gets deviated by angle δ_1 and it incidents on the second lens L_2 at a height h_2 as shown and again it gets deviated by an angle δ_2 due to the refraction at this second lens and finally meet the principal axis at point I. This point I can be considered as the point where all the incident rays in the beam will converge and meet after refraction through the two lenses. This point can also be regarded as the focal point of the two lens system.

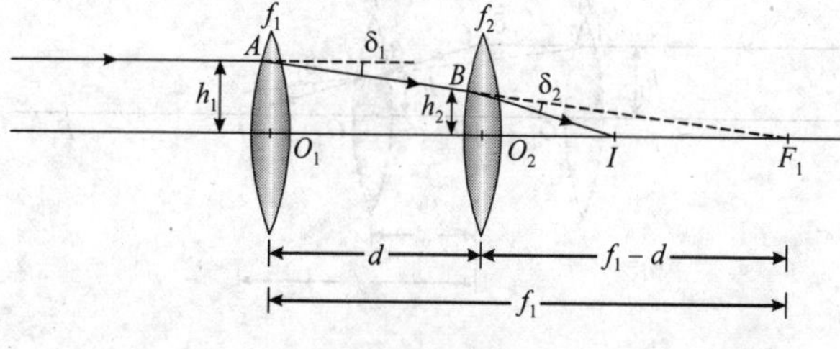

Figure 5.259

In above situation total deviation produced by the lens system in light ray is given as

$$\delta=\delta_1+\delta_2 \quad \ldots(5.127)$$

In above case we can use the values of δ_2 and δ_1 as $\delta_1=\frac{h_1}{f_1}$ and

$\delta_2=\frac{h_2}{f_2}$ and total deviation can be given as

$$\delta_2=\frac{h_1}{f}$$

Where f is the equivalent focal length of this lens system on which a light ray incident on height h_1 above the principal axis. Now using these values of deviation angles in equation-(5.127) we get

$$\frac{h_1}{f}=\frac{h_1}{f_1}+\frac{h_2}{f_2} \quad \ldots(5.128)$$

From the above figure in ΔAO_1F_1 and ΔBO_2F_1 we use by similarity

$$\frac{h_1}{f_1} = \frac{h_2}{f_1 - d} \quad \dots(5.129)$$

From equations-(5.128) and (5.129) we have

$$\frac{h_1}{f} = \frac{h_1}{f_1} + \frac{h_1(f_1 - d)}{f_1 f_2}$$

$$\Rightarrow \quad \frac{1}{f} = \frac{1}{f_1} + \frac{1}{f_2} - \frac{d}{f_1 f_2} \quad \dots(5.130)$$

Equation-(5.130) gives the equivalent focal length of a lens system of two lenses separated by a distance d. One important thing to be considered here is the position of equivalent lens for application purpose. In the figure-5.259 we can see that on principal axis lenses L_1 and L_2 are placed at locations O_1 and O_2. If this system is to be replaced by a single lens of focal length given by equation-(5.130) it is essential for us to find the position of this equivalent lens. In figure-5.260 the position of equivalent lens is shown by the dotted line which is located at a distance f from the point I where all parallel rays will converge.

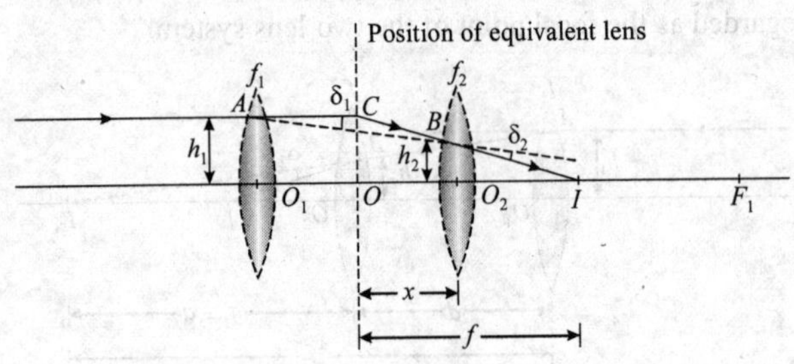

Figure 5.260

If we consider the light ray falling on the equivalent lens at a height h_1 then also it will meet the principal axis at point I. In above figure in ΔCOI and ΔBO_2I we have

$$\frac{h_1}{f} = \frac{h_2}{f_1 - x}$$

$$\Rightarrow \quad \frac{h_1}{h_2} = \frac{f}{f - x}$$

From equation-(5.129) we use $\frac{h_1}{h_2} = \frac{f_1}{f_1 - d}$ and from above equation we get

$$\frac{f}{f - x} = \frac{f_1}{f_1 - d}$$

$$\Rightarrow \quad x = \frac{fd}{f_1} \quad \dots(5.131)$$

Equation-(5.131) gives the distance of equivalent lens from the second lens L_2 of the system.

5.16.5 Multiple images produced by a Lens made up of different materials

Focal length of a lens depends upon the radii of curvature of two of its surfaces and refractive index of its material. Figure-5.261(a) shows the image produced by a convex lens. All the light rays (considered paraxial) from object falling on the lens gets refracted twice from its two surfaces and converges at a point on principal axis and forming the image I. In this case if we remove a part of lens as shown in figure-5.261(b) then also the image will be produced at the same point but number of rays producing the image will be less.

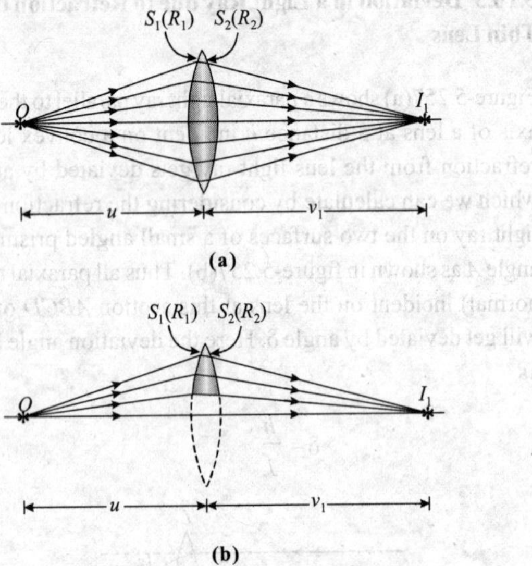

Figure 5.261

If we consider a lens made up of two materials having different refractive indices but same radii of curvature on the two sides then for a given object all the light rays falling on this lens will be divided in two groups after refraction as both the parts of lens will be behave like separate lenses and produce their independent images by these parts as shown in figure-5.262.

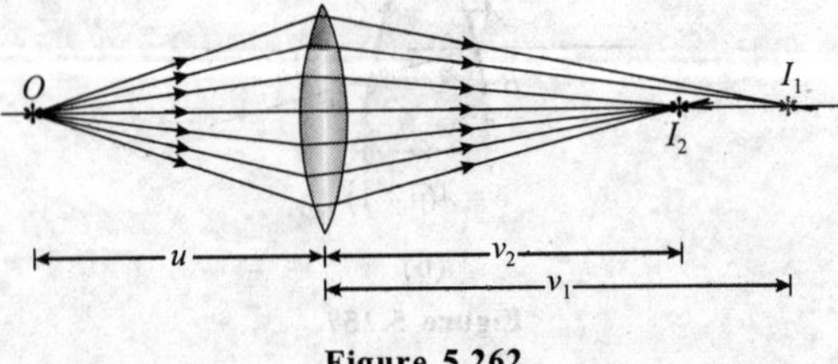

Figure 5.262

Similar to this if a lens is made by two materials having several parts but same radius of curvature as shown in figure-5.263 then also there will be only two images obtained as all the parts of same material will behave like one lens system only. Now if a lens has parts which are made up of three or more materials then number of images obtained will be same as number of materials used in making the lens.

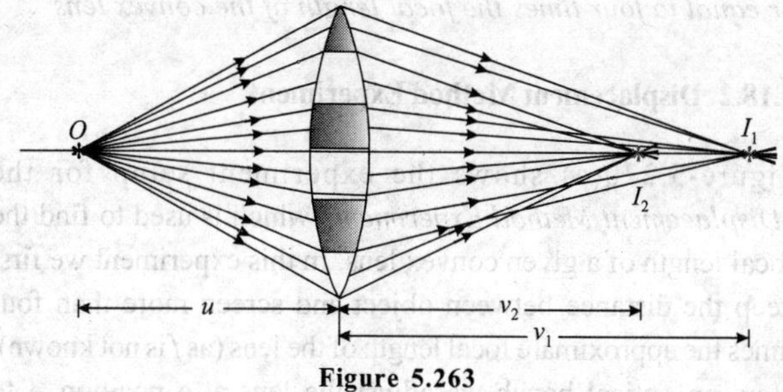

Figure 5.263

Above cases we discussed for parts of lens are valid only when these parts are joined with horizontal cuts as shown in all above figures. If a lens is vertically cut in two parts as shown in figure and the two parts are made up of different materials then we consider this as a case of combination of two thin lenses and we can find the equivalent focal length of this combination and use this as a single equivalent lens. In such a case single image is formed by this lens system as shown in figure-5.264.

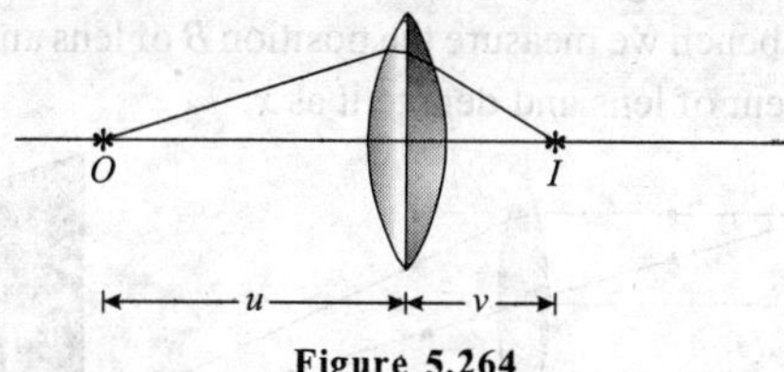

Figure 5.264

5.17 Lens and Mirrors submerged in a Transparent Medium

Figure-5.265(a) shows a spherical mirror producing image of a given object by reflection of light and we have already studied that analysis of image formation for relation in u, v and f is done by using mirror formula for paraxial rays. If the whole setup shown in figure-5.265(a) is submerged in a transparent medium (like water) as shown in figure-5.265(b) then the position of image remain unchanged because within water also the light rays incident on mirror will be reflected according to laws of reflection and the reflected rays will remain unaffected by presence of water. We can also state that inside a transparent medium also the focal length of mirror remain unchanged.

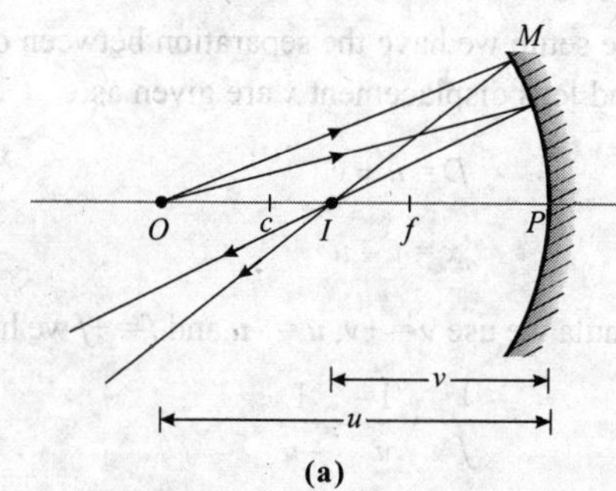

(a)

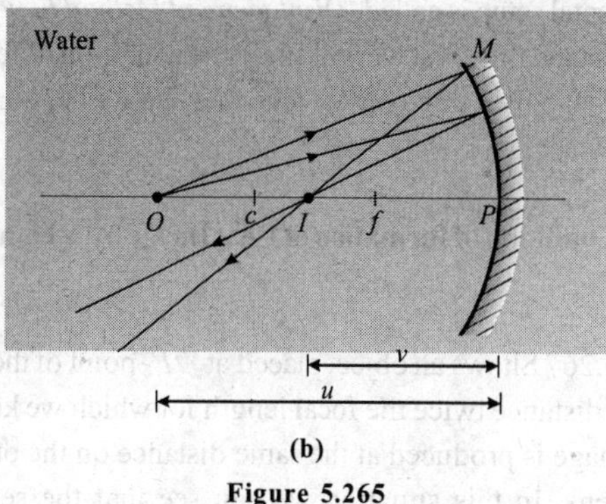

(b)

Figure 5.265

If we look at the situation shown in figure-5.266(a) in which a converging lens is producing image of a point object. Here the distances u, v and f are related by lens formula if only paraxial rays are considered. If this setup is submerged in a transparent medium (like water) then we know by Lens Maker's formula that inside a transparent medium (with $\mu_{surrounding} < \mu_{lens}$) then the focal length of a lens increases due to which the image will get shifted to a distance v' as shown in figure-5.266(b).

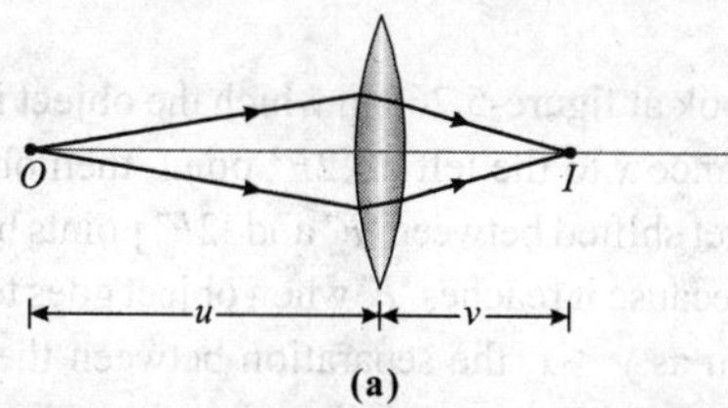

(a)

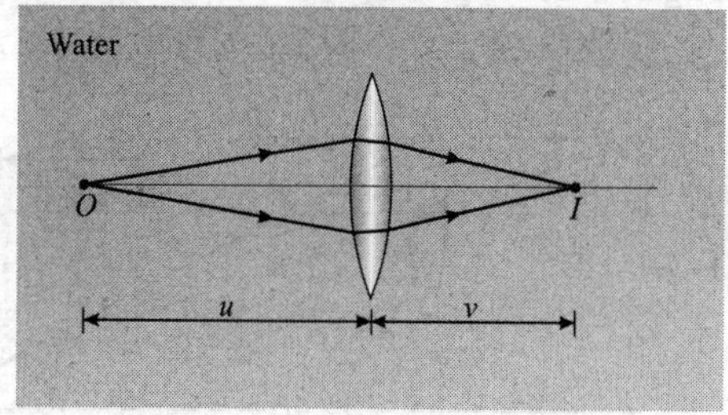

(b)

Figure 5.266

Note : When a mirror is submerged in a transparent medium, its focal length remain same but when a lens is submerged in a transparent medium, its focal length changes.

5.18 Displacement Method Experiment to measure focal length of a Convex Lens

Using the concept of image formation by a convex lens there is a an experimental setup in which we obtain real image of a light source on screen and then we displace the lens by some distance and again obtain the image for the same position of object and screen. With the distances and size of image produced in this experiment we analyze and calculate the focal length of the convex lens used and actual size of object and this whole experimental setup is called '*Displacement Method Experiment*'. To understand this, first we will study the condition of formation of real image by a thin convex lens then we will continue with the experiment.

5.18.1 Condition of formation of Real Image by a Thin Convex Lens

Figure-5.267 Shows an object placed at '$2F$' point of the convex lens at a distance twice the focal length for which we know that a real image is produced at the same distance on the other side of the lens. In this situation we can see that the separation between the object and its real image is four times the focal length.

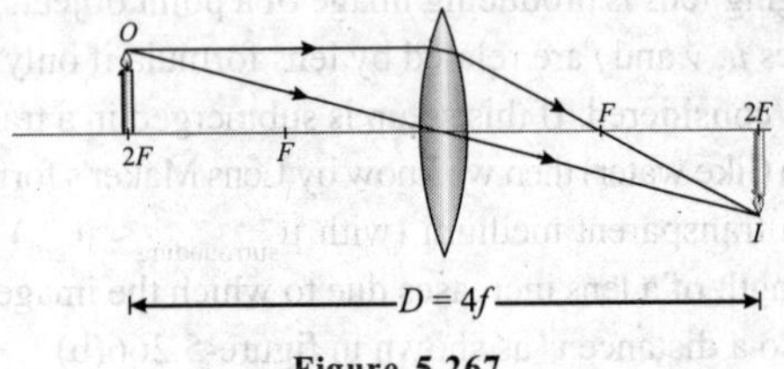

Figure 5.267

If we now look at figure-5.268 in which the object is shifted by a small distance x to the left of '$2F$' point, then obviously the image will get shifted between 'F' and '$2F$' points by a distance y but $y < x$ because it reaches 'F' when object goes to infinity. In this situation as $y < x$, the separation between the object and image in figure-5.154 is greater than four times the focal length of lens.

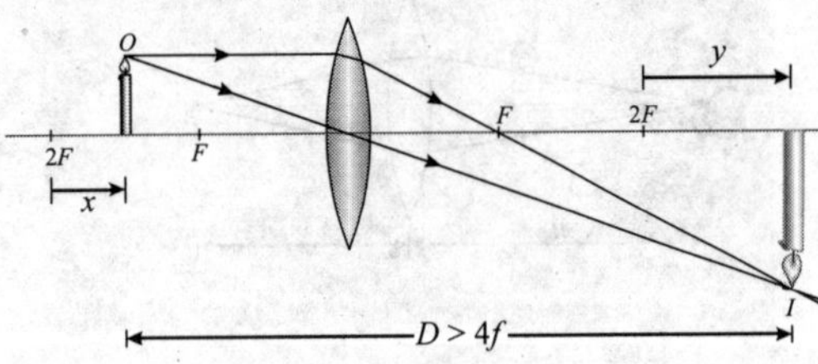

Figure 5.268

Similar to above case if object is shifted by a small distance x to the right of '$2F$' point as shown in figure-5.269, then the image will get shifted beyond '$2F$' point by a distance y with $y > x$ because it goes to infinity when object reaches 'F'. In this case also as $y > x$, the separation between the object and image in figure-5.269 is greater then four times the focal length of the lens.

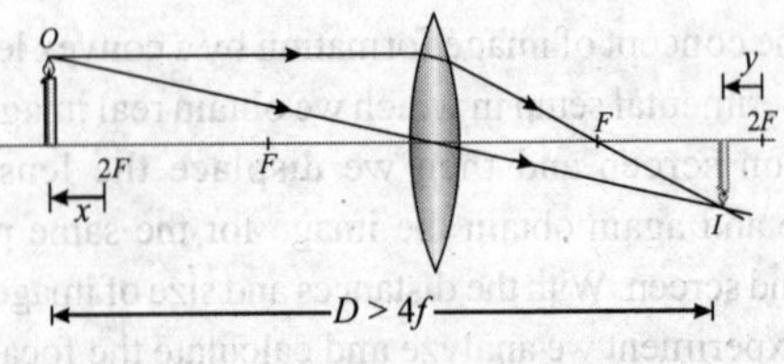

Figure 5.269

Withe the above qualitative analysis we can state that "*In case of a convex lens producing real image of a given real object, always the separation between object and image will be greater than or equal to four times the focal length of the convex lens*".

5.18.2 Displacement Method Experiment

Figure-5.270(a) shows the experiment setup for the "*Displacement Method Experiment*" which is used to find the focal length of a given convex lens. In this experiment we first keep the distance between object and screen more than four times the approximate focal length of the lens (as f is not known). Now on optical bench we adjust the lens at a position A to obtain the sharp image of the object on screen. As lens position A is close to object than screen, image size will be smaller then object. At this position we measure the lens position on the bench.

According to reversibility of light if lens is shifted to a position B at a distance v from object than image will be produced at a distance u (on same screen). This is shown in figure-5.270(b) in which size of image produced will be more than object. Again on optical bench we measure the position B of lens and find the displacement of lens and denote it as x.

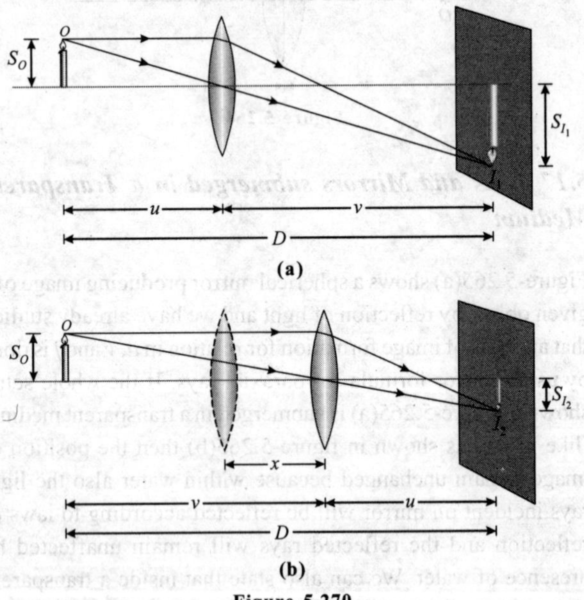

Figure 5.270

In the above setup we have the separation between object and screen D and lens displacement x are given as

$$D = u + v \qquad \text{...(5.132)}$$

$$x = v - u \qquad \text{...(5.133)}$$

In lens formula we use $v = +v$; $u = -u$ and $f = +f$ we have

$$\frac{1}{f} = \frac{1}{v} - \frac{1}{-u}$$

$$\Rightarrow \qquad f = \frac{uv}{u+v} \qquad \ldots(5.134)$$

Substituting the values of D and x in equation-(5.134) we get

$$f = \frac{(u+v)^2-(u-v)^2}{4(u+v)}$$

$$\Rightarrow \qquad f = \frac{D^2-x^2}{4D} \qquad \ldots(5.135)$$

Using equation-(5.135) we can calculate the focal length of the convex lens and same experiment can be repeated for different values of D ($>4f$) and every time we calculate the corresponding values of x and from this equation-(5.135) focal length can be calculated then find the average of all such values to get the experimental focal length of the convex lens used in the setup.

In above setup shown in figure-5.270(a) the magnification for the image obtained can be given as $m_1 = v/u$ and in figure-5.270(b) the magnification will be $m_2 = u/v$ so the image sizes S_{I1} and S_{I2} obtained in the two situations can be related to object size S_O with the relations given below.

Size of image in position A of the lens is $S_{I1} = m_1.S_O$ ...(5.136)
Size of image in position B of the lens is $S_{I2} = m_2.\,S_O$...(5.137)

As $m_1 \,.\, m_2 = 1$, from equations-(5.136) and (5.137) size of object is given as

$$S_O = \sqrt{S_{I1}\cdot S_{I2}} \qquad \ldots(5.138)$$

Equation-(5.138) shows that the object size is geometric mean of the two image sizes obtained in the displacement method experiment corresponding to the two positions of the convex lens and this equation is also used to find object size measurement with a good level of accuracy.

 # Illustrative Example 5.76

A point source of light is placed inside water and a thin converging lens of refractive index μ_2 is placed just outside the plane surface of water. The image of the source is formed at a distance x from the surface of water. If the lens is now placed just inside water and the image is now formed at a distance x' from the surface of water, show that

$$\frac{1}{x}-\frac{1}{x_1} = \frac{\mu_1-1}{\mu_2-1}\times\frac{1}{f},$$

Where f is the focal length of the lens and μ_1 is the refractive index of water.

Solution

Let f and f_w be the focal lengths of the lens when it is outside and inside the water respectively, then

$$\frac{1}{f} = (\mu_2-1)\left(\frac{1}{R_1}-\frac{1}{R_2}\right) \qquad \ldots(5.139)$$

and

$$\frac{1}{f_w} = \left(\frac{\mu_2}{\mu_1}-1\right)\left(\frac{1}{R_1}-\frac{1}{R_2}\right) \qquad \ldots(5.140)$$

Consider when lens is in air and u be the distance of the object from the surface, then we use apparent depth of object to be u/μ_1 so we use in lens formula

$$\frac{1}{x}-\frac{\mu_1}{u} = \frac{1}{f} \qquad \ldots(5.141)$$

When lens is in water then if image is produced at a distance x' from lens then due to refraction from water surface final image is produced at a distance $\mu_1 x$, so we use

$$\frac{1}{\mu_1 x'}-\frac{1}{u} = \frac{1}{f_w} \qquad \ldots(5.142)$$

Multiplying equation-(5.142) by μ_1, we get

$$\frac{1}{x'}-\frac{\mu_1}{u} = \frac{\mu_1}{f_w} \qquad \ldots(5.143)$$

Subtracting equations-(5.143) and (5.141), we get

$$\frac{1}{x}-\frac{1}{x'} = \frac{1}{f}-\frac{\mu_1}{f_w} \qquad \ldots(5.144)$$

from equation-(5.140), we have

$$\frac{1}{f_w} = \left(\frac{\mu_2-\mu_1}{\mu_1}\right)\left(\frac{1}{R_1}-\frac{1}{R_2}\right)$$

$$\Rightarrow \qquad \frac{1}{f_w} = \left(\frac{\mu_2-\mu_1}{\mu_1}\right)\frac{1}{f(\mu_2-1)}$$

Substituting this value in equation-(5.144), we get

$$\frac{1}{x}-\frac{1}{x'} = \frac{1}{f}-\frac{(\mu_2-\mu_1)}{\mu_1 f(\mu_2-1)}$$

$$\Rightarrow \qquad \frac{1}{x}-\frac{1}{x'} = \frac{1}{f}\left[1-\frac{(\mu_2-\mu_1)}{(\mu_2-1)}\right]$$

$$\Rightarrow \qquad \frac{1}{x}-\frac{1}{x'} = \frac{1}{f}\left(\frac{\mu_1-1}{\mu_2-1}\right)$$

 # Illustrative Example 5.77

A thin plano-convex lens of focal length f is split into two halves. One of the halves is shifted along the optical axis as shown in figure-5.271. The separation between object and image planes is 1.8 m. The magnification of the image, formed by one of the half lens is 2. Find the focal length of the lens and separation between the two halves. Draw the ray diagram for image formation.

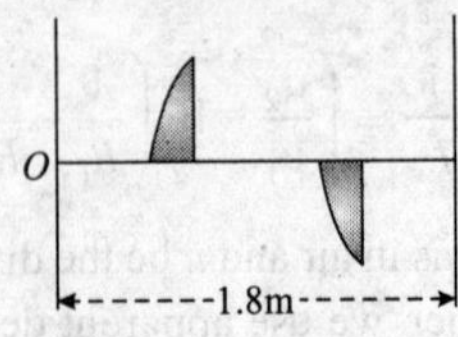

Figure 5.271

Solution

For both the halves, position of object and image is same. The case is same as experiment of displacement method for measurement of focal length of a convex lens as covered in article 5.18 in detail.

Now for the first half lens we use

$$|v/u| = 2 \text{ or } |v| = 2|u|$$

We use $u = -x$ and $v = +2x$

and $|u| + |v| = 1.8\,\text{m}$

Solving, we get

$$3x = 1.8\,\text{m}$$

or $x = 0.6\,\text{m}$

$\Rightarrow$ $u = -0.6\,\text{m}$ and $v = +1.2\,\text{m}$

Using lens formula, we have

$$\frac{1}{f} = \frac{1}{v} - \frac{1}{u} = \frac{1}{1.2} - \frac{1}{-0.6} = \frac{1}{0.4}$$

$$\Rightarrow \quad f = 0.4\,\text{m}$$

For the second half lens we use

$$\frac{1}{f} = \frac{1}{1.2-d} - \frac{1}{-(0.6+d)}$$

$$\Rightarrow \quad \frac{1}{0.4} = \frac{1}{1.2-d} + \frac{1}{(0.6+d)}$$

Solving this, we get $d = 0.6\,\text{m}$

 # *Illustrative Example 5.78*

A thin converging lens is placed between an object and a screen whose position are fixed. There are two positions of the lens at which the sharp image of the object is formed on the screen. Find the transverse dimension of the object if at one position of the lens the image dimension equals $h' = 2.0$ mm and at the other, $h'' = 4.5$ mm.

Solution

Here we consider if l be the distance between object and screen and a lens of focal length f is placed at a distance u from the source such that the image is formed on the screen. Then by lens formula, we have

$$\frac{1}{(l-u)} - \frac{1}{-u} = \frac{1}{f}$$

$$\Rightarrow \quad \frac{l-u+u}{u(l-u)} = \frac{1}{f}$$

$$\Rightarrow \quad u^2 - lu + lf = 0$$

The two roots of the quadratic equations are

$$u = \frac{l}{2}[1 \pm \sqrt{(1-(4f/l))}]$$

Here, both source and image are real and thus we use u and $v = (l-u)$ are real positive so $u < l$.

Here, we consider the following possible cases :

Case-I : If $f = l/4$ then $u = l/2$

Only one position of lens is possible in this case. The lens should be placed half way between source and screen.

Case-II : If $f < l/4$ and $u = \frac{l}{2}\left[1 \pm \sqrt{\left(1-\frac{4f}{l}\right)}\right]$

In this case two positions of lens are possible. These are given as

$$u_1 = \frac{l}{2}\left[1 + \sqrt{\left(1-\frac{4f}{l}\right)}\right],$$

$$v_1 = \frac{l}{2}\left[1 - \sqrt{\left(1-\frac{4f}{l}\right)}\right]$$

and

$$u_2 = \frac{l}{2}\left[1 - \sqrt{\left(1-\frac{4f}{l}\right)}\right],$$

$$v_2 = \frac{l}{2}\left[1 + \sqrt{\left(1-\frac{4f}{l}\right)}\right]$$

These positions are conjugate to each other.

Case-III : If $f > l/4$ then u is non real so no physical position for the lens is possible in this case.

If m_1 and m_2 be the lateral magnifications in the above cases then, we have

$$m_1 = \frac{I_1}{O} = \frac{v_1}{u_1} \text{ and } m_2 = \frac{I_2}{O} = \frac{v_2}{u_2}$$

$$\Rightarrow \quad \frac{I_1 I_2}{O^2} = \frac{v_1}{u_1} \times \frac{v_2}{u_2} = 1$$

Hence $O = \sqrt{(I_1 I_2)} = \sqrt{(2 \times 4.5)} = 3\,\text{mm}$

Illustrative Example 5.79

A thin equiconvex lens of glass of refractive index $\mu = 3/2$ and of focal length 0.3 m in air is sealed into an opening at one end of tank filled with water ($\mu = 4/3$). On the opposite side of the lens, a mirror is placed inside the tank on the tank wall perpendicular to the lens axis as shown in figure-5.272.

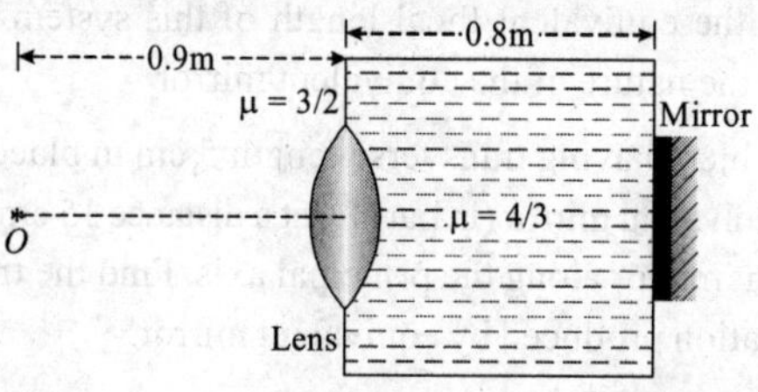

Figure 5.272

The separation between the lens and the mirror is 0.8 m. A small object is placed outside the tank in front of the lens at a distance of 0.9 m from the lens along its axis. Find the position (relative to the lens) of image formed by the system.

Solution

For equiconvex lens, we know the focal length is given by lens makers formula as

$$\frac{1}{f} = (\mu - 1)\left[\frac{1}{R} - \left(-\frac{1}{R}\right)\right]$$

$$\Rightarrow \quad f = \frac{R}{2(\mu - 1)}$$

$$\Rightarrow \quad R = 0.3 \qquad \ldots(5.145)$$

For refraction at the first surface of the lens, we use refraction formula as

$$\frac{\mu_2}{v_1} - \frac{\mu_1}{u} = \frac{\mu_2 - \mu_1}{R}$$

$$\Rightarrow \quad \frac{3}{2v_1} + \frac{1}{0.9} = \frac{(3/2) - 1}{R}$$

$$v_1 = 2.7\text{ m}$$

For refraction at the second surface of the lens, we again use refraction formula

$$\frac{\mu_2}{v_2} - \frac{\mu_1}{u} = \frac{\mu_2 - \mu_1}{R}$$

$$\Rightarrow \quad \frac{4}{3v_2} - \frac{3}{2 \times 2.7} = \frac{(4/3) - (3/2)}{-0.3}$$

$$\Rightarrow \quad \frac{4}{3v_2} = \frac{1}{1.8} + \frac{1}{1.8} = \frac{1}{0.9}$$

$$\Rightarrow \quad v_2 = \frac{4 \times 0.9}{3} = 1.2\text{ m}$$

So, the image formed by the lens will be behind the mirror at a distance 40 cm. Now, the image formed by the mirror will be at a distance of 40 cm in front of the mirror.

After this again the light rays will pass through the lens so for refraction at water glass surface, by refraction formula, we use

$$\frac{\frac{3}{2}}{v_3} - \frac{4/3}{0.4} = \frac{3/2 - 4/3}{-0.3}$$

$$\Rightarrow \quad v_3 = \left(\frac{2.7}{5}\right)\text{ m}$$

Now, for refraction at glass air surface, we use refraction formula again as

$$\frac{1}{v_4} - \frac{3/2}{2.7/5} = \frac{1 - (3/2)}{0.3}$$

$$\Rightarrow \quad v_4 = -0.9\text{ m}$$

Thus the final image is formed on the source.

NOTE : Students must carefully study above illustration as in this case image is produced on source but light rays are not falling on mirror normally and not retracing the path of incident rays.

Illustrative Example 5.80

Bottom of a glass beaker is made of a thin equiconvex lens having bottom side silver polished as shown in the figure-5.273. Water is filled in the beaker upto a height 4 m. The image of point object, floating at middle point of beaker at the surface of water coincides with it. Find out the radius of curvature of the lens. Given that refractive index of glass is 3/2 and that of water is 4/3.

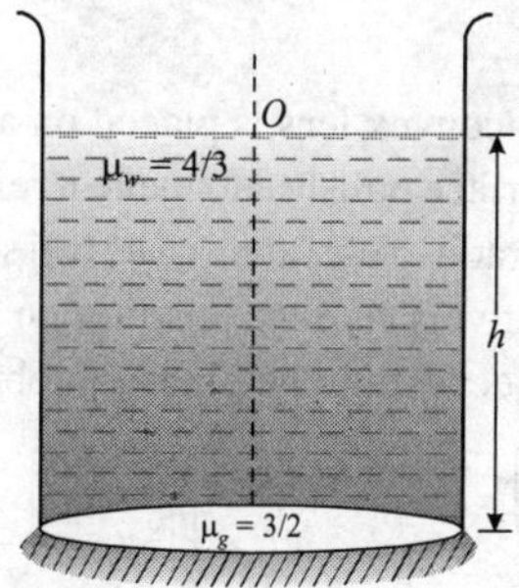

Figure 5.273

Solution

The slivered lens placed at the bottom of tank behaves like an equivalent mirror and if object is placed at the center of curvature of the mirror then its image is produced on itself. Here the focal length of the glass lens with respect to water in surrounding is given as

$$\frac{1}{f_L}=\left(\frac{3/2}{4/3}-1\right)\left(\frac{1}{R}+\frac{1}{R}\right)$$

$$\Rightarrow \quad \frac{1}{f_L}=\frac{1}{8}\times\frac{2}{R}=\frac{1}{4R}$$

$$\Rightarrow \quad f_2=4R$$

Focal length of mirror is $R/2$, so the equivalent focal length of combination is given as

$$\frac{1}{f_{eq}}=\frac{2}{f_L}+\frac{1}{f_M}=\frac{2}{4R}+\frac{2}{R}=\frac{5}{2R}$$

$$\Rightarrow \quad f_{eq}=-\frac{2}{5}R,$$

Thus object is to be placed at $2f_{eq}$ so that its image is produced on itself, thus we have object height given as

$$h=2\times\frac{2}{5}R=4\text{ m}$$

$$\Rightarrow \quad R=5\text{ m}$$

Web Reference at www.physicsgalaxy.com

Age Group - High School Physics | Age 17-19 Years

Section - OPTICS

Topic - Geometrical Optics III - Thin Lenses

Module Number - 15 to 32

Practice Exercise 5.7

(i) A thin lens of focal length + 10.0 cm lies on a horizontal plane mirror. How far above the lens should an object be held if its image is to coincide with the object ?

[10 cm]

(ii) A concavo-convex lens is placed on a horizontal table with its convex surface polished to make it reflecting as shown in figure-5.274. If radii of curvature of its two surfaces are 30 cm and 60 cm respectively find the position on its principal axis where a point object should be placed to obtain its image on itself. $\left(\mu_{lens}=\frac{3}{2}\right)$

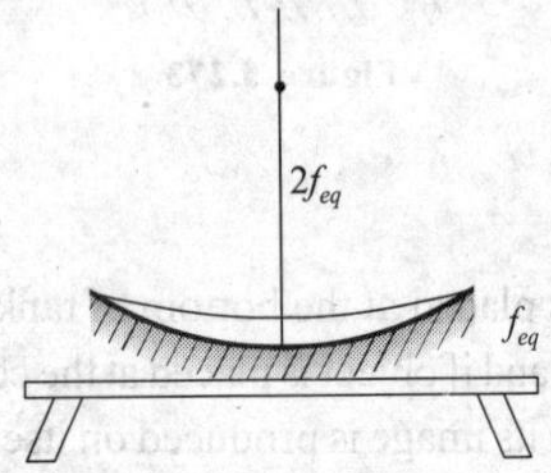

Figure 5.274

[24]

(iii) A thin plano-convex lens fits exactly into a plano-concave lens with their plane surfaces parallel to each other as shown in the figure-5.275. The radius of curvature of the curved surface R = 30 cm. The lenses are made of different materials having refractive indices $\mu_1 = 3/2$ and $\mu_2 = 5/4$ as shown in the figure.

(a) If plane surface of the plano-convex lens is slivered, then calculate the equivalent focal length of this system and also calculate the nature of the equivalent mirror.

(b) An object having transverse length 5 cm in placed on the axis of equivalent mirror (in part 1), at a distance 15 cm from the equivalent mirror along the principal axis. Find the transverse magnification produced by equivalent mirror.

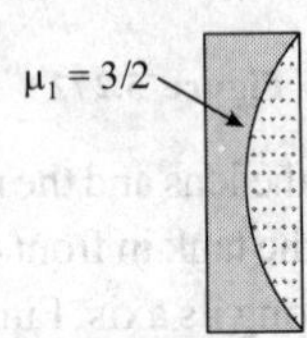

Figure 5.275

[+ 60, + 4/5]

(iv) Two identical thin converging lenses are kept in contact at a distance 12.5 cm from an object. If image produced is 4 times enlarged then what is the optical power of each lens.

[5D]

(v) An object is placed at a distance of 20 cm to the left of and on the axis of a convex lens L_1 of focal length 25 cm. A second convex lens L_2 of focal length 20 cm is placed coaxially to the right of the lens L_1 at a distance of 10 cm from L_1. Find the position of the image and its magnification.

[24.4 cm, $\frac{10}{9}$]

(vi) When a lens is inserted between an object and a screen which are a fixed distance apart the size of the image is either 6 cm or $\frac{2}{3}$ cm. Find size of the object.

[2 cm]

(vii) A point source of light S is placed at the bottom of a vessel containing a liquid of refractive index 5/3. A person is viewing the source from above the surface. There is an opaque disc of radius 1 cm floating on the surface. The centre of the disc lies vertically above the source S. The liquid from the vessel is gradually drained out through a tap. What is the maximum height of the liquid for which the source can not at all be seen from above.

[1.33 cm]

(viii) An equiconvex lens $\mu = 1.5$ with radii 4 cms is located at a distance of 4 cms from an equiconcave lens of $\mu = 1.6$ with radii 8 cms. The lenses are thin and the medium between them is water of $\mu = 4/3$, while on both sides of lenses the medium is air. Find the equivalent focal-length of the system.

[8.9 cm]

(ix) In figure L is half part of an equiconvex lens of refractive index 1.5 whose surfaces have radius of curvature 40 cm and its right surface is silvered as shown in figure-5.276. Normal to its principal axis, a plane mirror M is placed on right of lens. Distance between lens L and mirror M is b. A small object O is placed on left of the lens such that there is no parallax between final images formed by the lens and mirror. If transverse length of final image formed by the lens is twice that of image formed by the mirror, calculate distance a between lens and object and distance b.

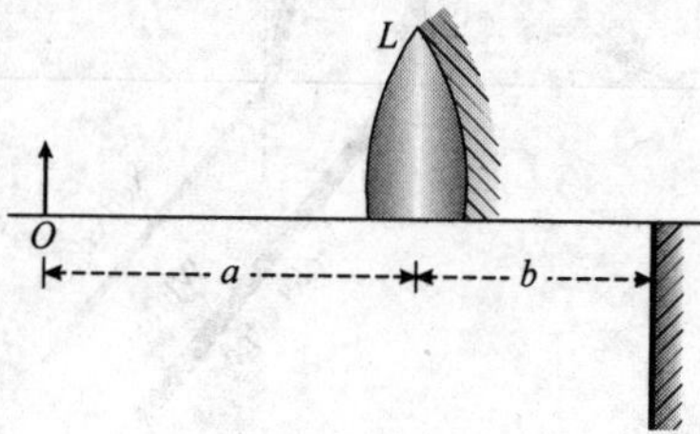

Figure 5.276

[5 cm, 2.5 cm]

(x) Convex surface of a plano convex lens of focal length 30 cm is silvered to make it reflecting. If lens material has refractive index $\frac{3}{2}$, find the image location for an object placed 40 cm from the lens on its principal axis.

[$\frac{40}{7}$ cm]

(xi) There are two thin symmetrical lenses : one is converging with $\mu_1 = 1.70$ and other diverging with $\mu_2 = 1.51$. Both lenses have same curvature radius of their surfaces is equal to 10 cm. The lenses were put close together and submerged into water. What is the focal length of this system in water.

[33.3 cm]

(xii) A point object is located at a distance of 100 cm from a screen. A lens of focal length 23 cm mounted on a movable frictionless stand is kept between the source and the screen. The stand is attached to a spring of natural length 50 cm and spring constant 800 N/m as shown in figure-5.277. Mass of the stand with lens is 2 kg. How much impulse P should be imparted to the stand so that a real image of the object is formed on the screen after a fixed time gap. Also find this time gap also. (Neglect the width of the stand)

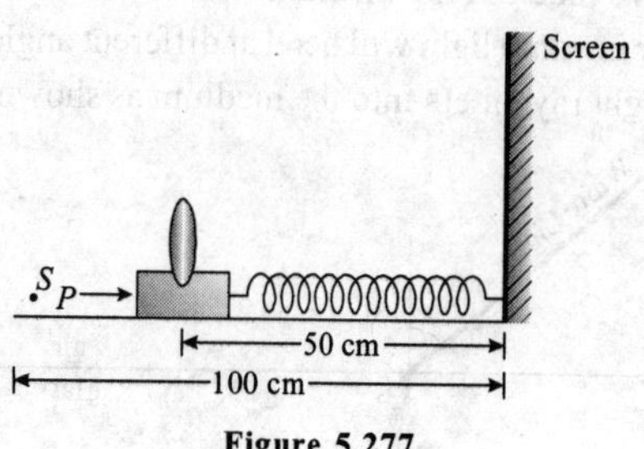

Figure 5.277

[8 kg - m/s]

5.19 Dispersion of Light

In your previous grades we've studied about dispersion as splitting of white light into colours when it passes through a prism. In this section we'll discuss dispersion of light in more details and in analytical way. To understand the concept of dispersion its better to first understand how the refractive index of a transparent medium varies with light wavelength.

It is experimentally analyzed and researched that the refractive index of a transparent medium depends on the wavelength of light and empirically a relation was obtained between the two called '*Cauchy's Equation*' given as

$$\mu = A + \frac{B}{\lambda^2} + \frac{C}{\lambda^4} + \qquad \ldots(5.146)$$

In above equation the coefficients C and other coefficients used with higher powers of wavelength are not much significant as their values are so small that for general analysis we can ignore such coefficients and most commonly we use the two term form of Cauchy's Equation given as

$$\mu = A + \frac{B}{\lambda^2} \qquad \ldots(5.147)$$

With the above equation-(5.147) we can see that light with lower wavelength has higher refractive index in a medium and hence travels slower. So if we compare violet and red light in same medium then we can see that violet light travel slower than red light in the medium.

This difference in speed causes light rays of different wavelength to refract differently when these travel from one medium to another and that is the cause of the phenomenon called '*Dispersion of Light*'.

Figure-5.278 shows a light ray of white light which incident on a transparent medium. As we know white light consist of all colours so we can consider this light ray as overlapping of light rays of all colours making the white light and for each colour the refractive index of the medium will be different and ray of each colour in white light will bend at different angles and split when the light ray enters into the medium as shown in figure.

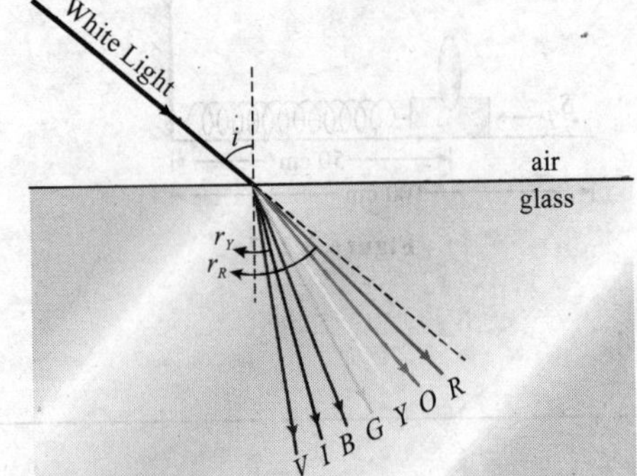

Figure 5.278

The situation shown in figure-5.278 is an ideal situation which doesn't happen in general practice because of the dimensions of the light ray. Actually a light ray is a theoretical concept which does not have any dimensional thickness but in practice we consider a very thin light beam as a light ray. Look at the figure-5.279 which is a magnified view of the figure-5.278 in which a light beam (enlarged view of light ray) incident on the medium. In this beam we can consider several light rays incident on the medium boundary at the same angle of incidence. Due to dispersion each light ray will split into its colours and you can see that except the light rays at the boundaries of the beam all the colours in between will merge into each other and produce white light again. Only the edges of light beam will have violet colour at the left edge in the medium and red colour at the right edge in the medium. This is the reason why at the time of refraction, colours are not seen in the refracted light beam.

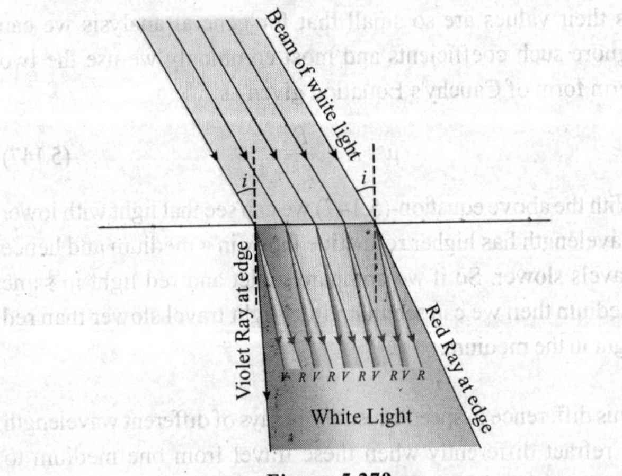

Figure 5.279

5.19.1 Dispersion of White Light through a Glass Slab

Figure-5.280 shows a light beam incident on a parallel sided glass slab at some angle of incidence. Due to the concept explained in previous section we can see that the edges of the refracted beam (slightly divergent) are having violet and red colours but when this refracted beam emerges out of the slab in air then all the light rays inside the refracted beam will come out at same angle of emergence which is equal to angle of incidence so all the rays become parallel after coming out and form a parallel white light beam with edges of violet and red colour only. We can also see that due to dispersion the emergent beam of light is slightly thicker than the incident light beam.

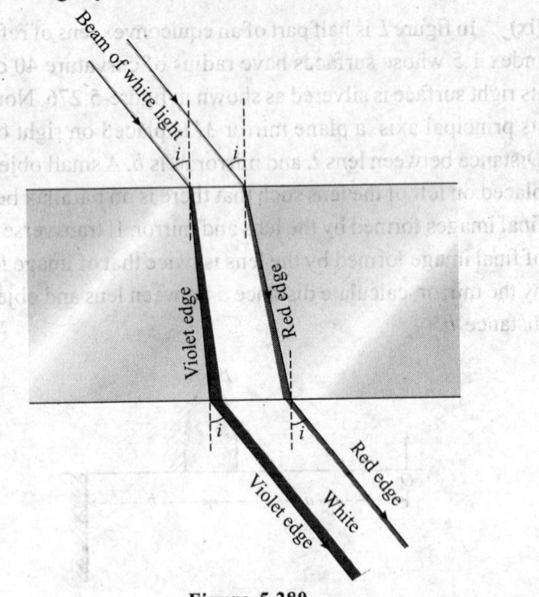

Figure 5.280

5.19.2 Dispersion of White Light through a Glass Prism

When a beam of white light passes through a glass prism then due to two refractions of beam of white light the colours in beam gets separated from each other and at some distance from the prism after refraction if we place a screen, coloured spectrum is obtained as shown in figure-5.281(b).

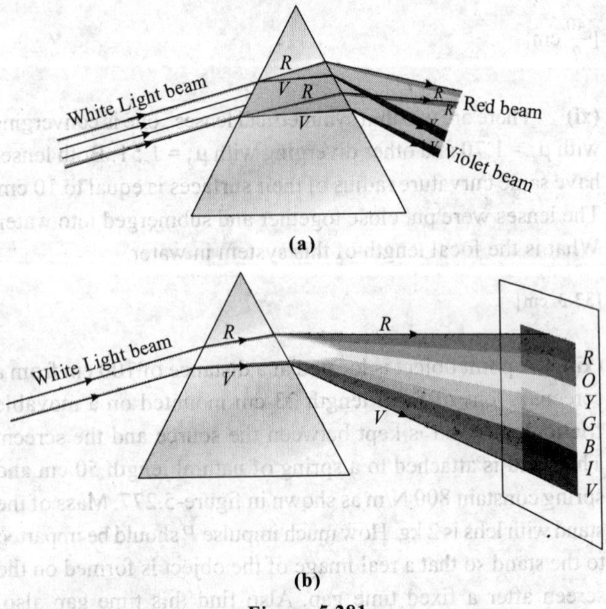

Figure 5.281

Figure-5.281(a) shows how the coloured beams get separated after second refraction. We can see in this figure that at first refraction at surface AB of the prism, white light gets refracted into the prism and the middle region between the violet and red edges will be white because of mixing of all the coloured light rays in this region as explained in figure-5.280 but at the second refraction when all these rays incident on the face AC of the prism then each colour at the incident region '*mn*' of beam on face AC will emerge out at the same angle like all violet rays in this region '*mn*' will emerge out at same angle as a parallel beam and all red rays of this region emerge out as separate parallel beam because both colours will have different emergent angles. This situation is unlike to the case discussed in figure-5.280 when all coloured light rays emerge from the glass slab at same angle and produce an emerging white light beam due to overlapping of all colours in same direction.

Figure-5.281(b) shows practical situation in which all the colours get separated after some distance and produce a spectrum on a screen.

5.19.3 Dispersive Power of a Prism Material

Dispersive power of a substance is its ability to disperse light passing through it. Dispersive Power of a material is defined as relative deviation of light beam from its mean path as a function of refractive index of the material. For a given material it is given as

$$\omega = \frac{d\theta}{\theta} \qquad \ldots(5.148)$$

In equation-(5.148) angle θ is the mean deviation of light for all the wavelengths present in it and $d\theta$ is the change in deviation due to variation of refractive index $d\mu$ which is corresponding to the wavelength change $d\lambda$ in the beam. The dispersive power for a prism material can be calculated by passing a light through a small angled prism as shown in figure-5.282. If we consider a light consist of very small wavelength range l to $l + dl$ and it is passed through the small angled prism of prism angle A as shown, the mean deviation of light for the wavelength l is given as

$$\theta = A(\mu - 1)$$

$$\Rightarrow \qquad d\theta = Ad\mu = \left(\frac{\theta}{\mu - 1}\right) d\mu$$

Now from equation-(5.148) the dispersive power of material is given as

$$\omega = \frac{d\theta}{\theta} = \frac{d\mu}{\mu - 1} \qquad \ldots(5.149)$$

Above equation-(5.149) gives the dispersive power of a prism material which is having the wavelength range $d\lambda$ in the light beam. If the range of wavelength is large then we take the difference of refractive indices corresponding to the wavelength limits in the light beam.

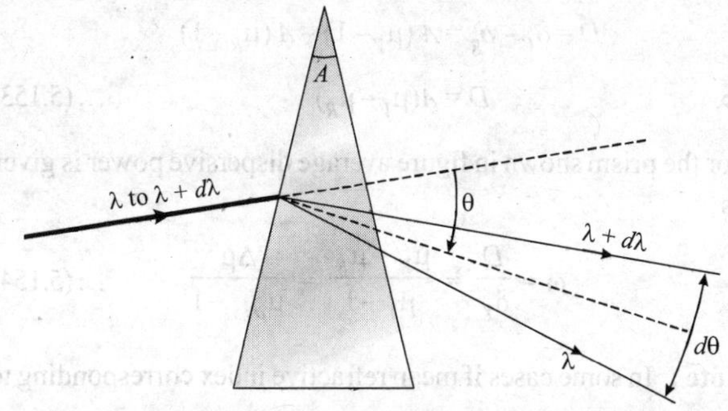

Figure 5.282

The concept of dispersive power is used in taking corrective measures in image formation by refracting devices due to dispersion. We'll discuss it later in the topic of '*Chromatic Aberration*'.

5.19.4 Dispersion Analysis for a Small Angled Prism

Figure-5.283 shows a white light incident on a small angled prism with prism angle A. In general for a white light we consider its wavelength limits are bounded by violet and red rays and mean wavelength is considered as yellow light. If the refractive indices of the prism material for these colours are given as μ_V, μ_R and μ_Y respectively and δ_V, δ_R and δ_Y are the corresponding deviation angles when these colours pass through the prism then the relation among these are given below.

$$\delta_V = A(\mu_V - 1) \qquad \ldots(5.150)$$

$$\delta_R = A(\mu_R - 1) \qquad \ldots(5.151)$$

$$\delta_Y = A(\mu_Y - 1) \qquad \ldots(5.152)$$

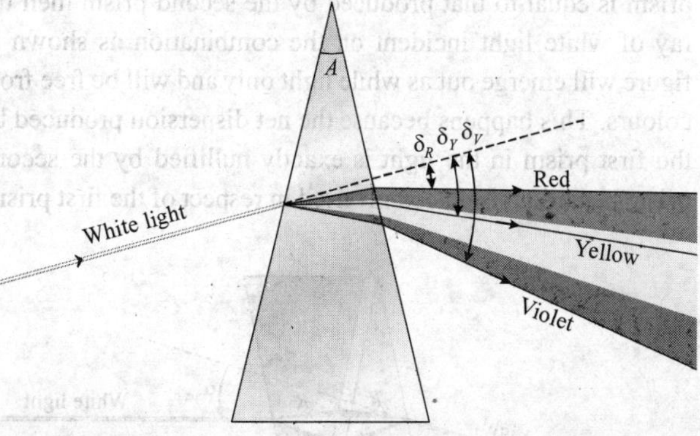

Figure 5.283

In above figure mean deviation of the incident light ray is considered corresponding to the mean wavelength present in the light so here mean deviation of incident light is taken as δ_Y.

The '*Angular Dispersion*' for the light passing through the prism is defined as the angle by which light will totally disperse. Here angular dispersion is given as

$$D = \delta_V - \delta_R = A(\mu_V - 1) - A(\mu_R - 1)$$

$$\Rightarrow \qquad D = A(\mu_V - \mu_R) \qquad \ldots(5.153)$$

For the prism shown in figure average dispersive power is given as

$$\omega = \frac{D}{\delta_Y} = \frac{\mu_V - \mu_R}{\mu_Y - 1} = \frac{\Delta\mu}{\mu_{avg} - 1} \qquad \ldots(5.154)$$

Note : In some cases if mean refractive index corresponding to yellow light is not given then students can use $\mu_Y = \frac{\mu_V + \mu_R}{2}$.

5.19.5 Achromatic Prism Combination

When two prisms of materials having different dispersive powers are placed in relative inverted positions with their prism angles are chosen in such a way that dispersion produced by one prism gets compensated by the other one then a ray of white light passing through this combination gets refracted and deviated but in emergent beam no colors are seen or no overall dispersion of light beam take place then such a combination of prisms is called '*Achromatic Prism Combination*'.

Figure-5.284 shows combination of two prisms placed in contact with opposite positions of their prism angles. The prism angles of these prisms are A and A'. These prisms materials have their refractive indices μ_R and μ_V for first prism and μ_R' and μ_V' for the second prism corresponding to red and violet light respectively. If the values of prism angles and refractive indices are adjusted such that the angular dispersion produced by first prism is equal to that produced by the second prism then the ray of white light incident on the combination as shown in figure will emerge out as while light only and will be free from colours. This happens because the net dispersion produced by the first prism in the light is exactly nullified by the second prism because it is placed inverted in respect of the first prism.

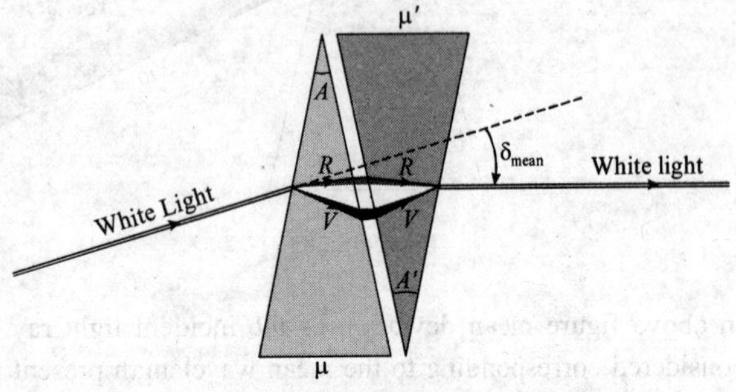

Figure 5.284

For the above case which we call the setup of prism combination for '*Deviation without Dispersion*' or '*Achromatic Prism Combination*'. In above case the total dispersion is zero hence the angular dispersion by the two prisms must be equal. If D and D' are the angular dispersion by the first and second prism then the condition of deviation without dispersion is given as

$$D = D'$$

$$\Rightarrow \qquad A(\mu_V - \mu_R) = A'(\mu_V' - \mu_R') \qquad \ldots(5.155)$$

In above case the total mean deviation of the white light can be given as

$$\delta_{mean} = \delta_Y - \delta_Y'$$

$$\Rightarrow \qquad \delta_{mean} = A(\mu_Y - 1) - A'(\mu_Y' - 1) \qquad \ldots(5.156)$$

5.19.6 Direct Vision Prism Combination

When two prisms of different materials are placed in contact with relative inverted positions and their refractive indices and prism angles are chosen in such a way that emerging light beam will not suffer any mean deviation but having dispersion in same direction then such a prism combination is called '*Direct Vision Prism Combination*'.

Figure-5.285 shows combination of two prisms with inverted relative positions. The prism angles of these prisms are A and A' and having refractive indices for red and violet lights μ_R, μ_V and μ_R', μ_V' respectively. If these values of prism angles and refractive indices are adjusted such that the mean deviation for yellow colour by first prism is exactly equal to that by second prism then the total deviation of the white light incident on this combination will be zero and the dispersed light beam will emerge out in the same direction of incidence as shown in the figure.

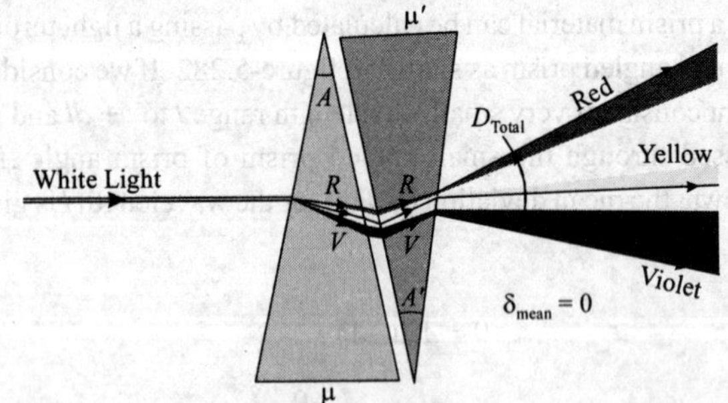

Figure 5.285

In above case of direct vision prism combination if δ_Y and δ_Y' are the mean deviation of light by the two prisms then the condition for this top happen is given as

$$\delta_Y = \delta_Y'$$

$$\Rightarrow \qquad A(\mu_Y - 1) = A'(\mu_Y' - 1) \qquad \ldots(5.157)$$

In this case if D and D' are the angular dispersions produced by the two prisms then the net angular dispersion of the emerging light beam from the prism combination is given as

$$D_{Total} = D - D'$$

$$\Rightarrow \quad D_{Total} = A(\mu_V - \mu_R) - A'(\mu_V' - \mu_R') \quad \ldots(5.158)$$

5.20 *Optical Aberrations in Lenses and Mirrors*

Optical aberrations are the defects in image formation by optical devices due to deviation in performance of the device because of non-paraxial rays or polychromatic light used in optical systems. Aberrations occur because all light rays from one point object do not converge (or diverge) at a single point after undergoing reflection or refraction through the optical device in use. In optical systems the image produced gets blurred due to aberrations which causes unclear image formation by different optical instruments. While designing optical instruments corrective measures must be taken to avoid or minimize aberrations.

Optical aberrations are classified in two broad categories in general. These are '*Spherical Aberrations*' and '*Chromatic Aberrations*'. Spherical aberrations are due to the curvature of optical devices which causes marginal rays not to meet at the point of image formation by paraxial rays and chromatic aberrations are due to the presence of several wavelengths of light in the incident beam which causes different wavelength rays to refract differently from the optical device. Chromatic aberrations are considered only in refracting optical devices as reflecting devices are free from chromatic aberrations.

5.20.1 Spherical Aberrations

Due to large aperture of mirrors and lenses when marginal rays incident on the outer part of the mirrors or lenses, these do not converge at the point where paraxial rays are meeting and forming the image. Figure-5.286(a) and (b) shows the parallel light rays incident on a convex lens and a concave mirror. All paraxial rays in these cases will converge at focal point but the rays which are incident on outer edge of the mirror or lens converge before focal point and causes image to get blurred. Due to this reason a mirror or a lens having large aperture fails to produce sharp image of an object or point image of a point object.

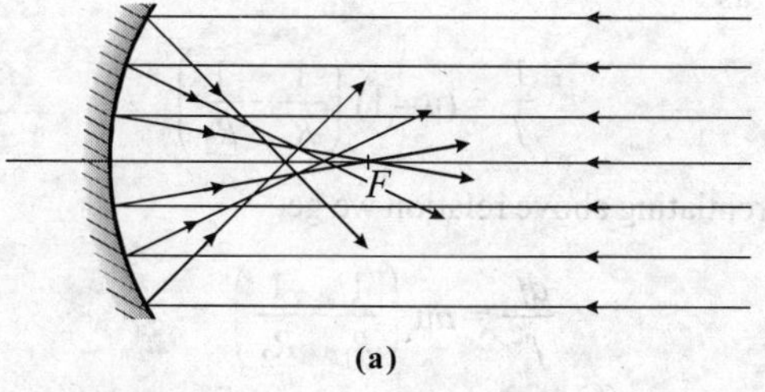

(a)

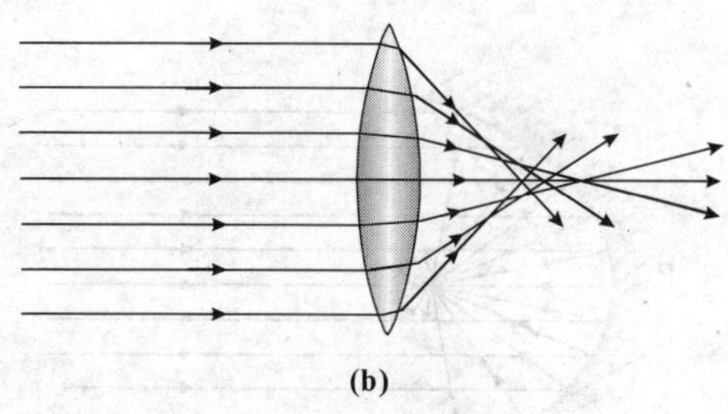

(b)

Figure 5.286

5.20.2 Methods to Reduce Spherical Aberrations

There are different ways by which corrective measures can be taken to reduce the spherical aberrations in image formation. Some specific methods are given here for basic understanding, detailed analysis is not covered here.

(i) Use of Stops : Stops are the opaque planes having a small aperture used to cutoff marginal rays to incident on the optical device as shown in figure-5.287(a) and (b).

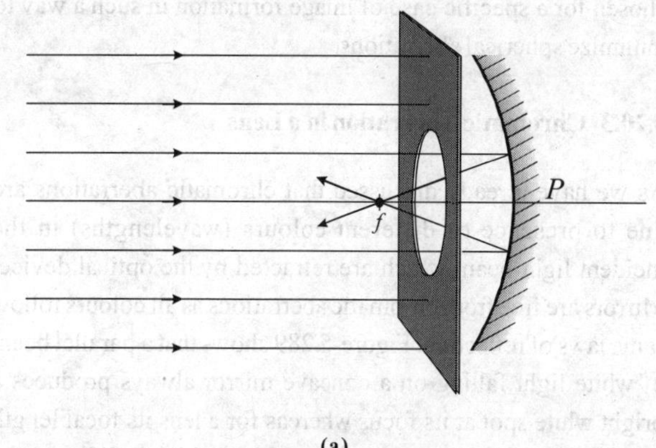

(a)

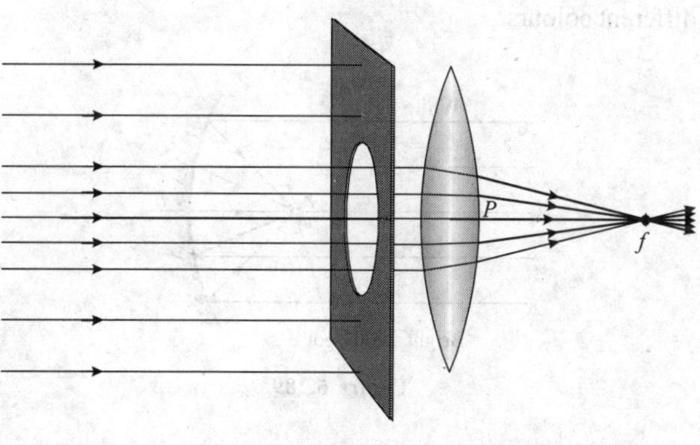

(b)

Figure 5.287

(ii) Using Parabolic Mirrors : For focussing parallel rays, spherical mirrors can be replaced by parabolic mirrors as parabolic mirrors focuses all parallel light rays falling on it parallel to principal axis at a single focal point as shown in figure-5.288.

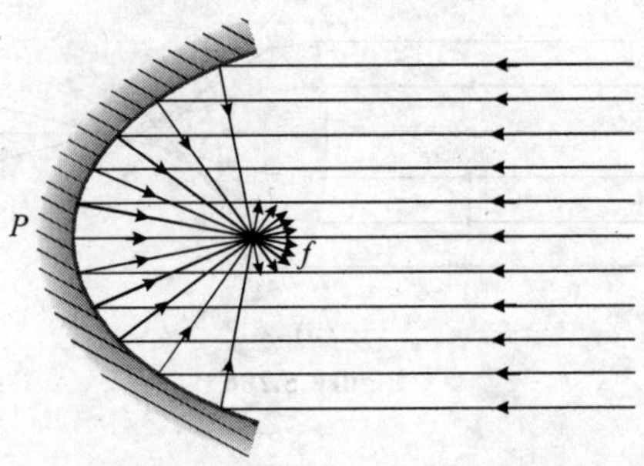

Figure 5.288

(iii) Using Convex Lenses at some separation : When two convex lenses are separated by a distance equal to the difference in their focal lengths ($d = |f_1 - f_2|$) then by using this combination for image formation, spherical aberrations are minimized.

(iv) Using Crossed Lenses : Crossed lenses are specially designed lenses with their radii of curvature of the two surfaces chosen for a specific case of image formation in such a way to minimize spherical aberrations.

5.20.3 Chromatic Aberration in a Lens

As we have already discussed that chromatic aberrations are due to presence of different colours (wavelengths) in the incident light beam which are refracted by the optical device. Mirrors are free from chromatic aberrations as all colours follow same laws of reflection. Figure-5.289 shows that a parallel beam of white light falling on a concave mirror always produces a bright white spot at its focus whereas for a lens its focal length depends upon the refractive index of lens which is different for different colours.

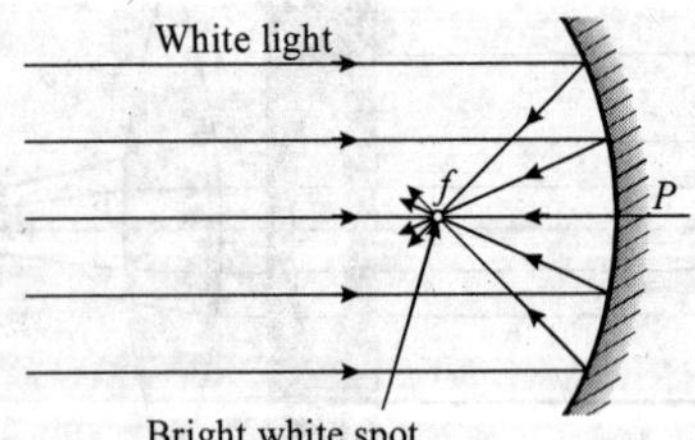

Figure 5.289

Below figure-5.290 shows the situation when a parallel beam of white light incident on the convex lens, due to dispersion it splits into colours and produces several coloured images because focal length of all colours of this lens given by lens maker's formula will be different. As $\mu_V > \mu_R$ by lens maker's formula we get $f_V < f_R$ because of which the focal point will spread in the region from F_V to F_R as shown in figure.

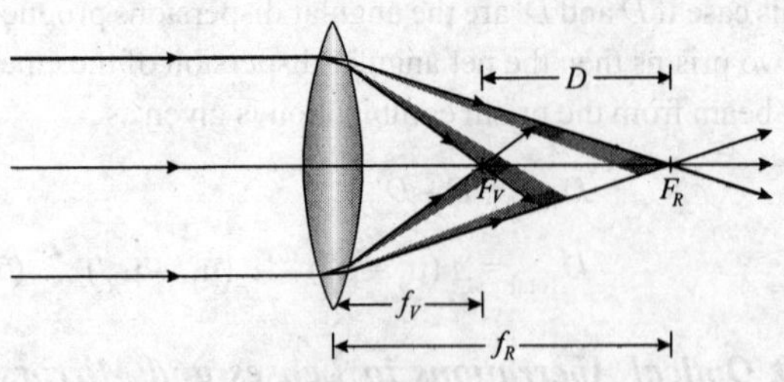

Figure 5.290

In above figure, the focal lengths f_V and f_R are given as

$$\frac{1}{f_V} = (\mu_V - 1)\left(\frac{1}{R_1} - \frac{1}{R_2}\right) \qquad \ldots(5.159)$$

and
$$\frac{1}{f_R} = (\mu_R - 1)\left(\frac{1}{R_1} - \frac{1}{R_2}\right) \qquad \ldots(5.160)$$

From above equations-(5.159) and (5.160) we get

$$\frac{1}{f_V} - \frac{1}{f_R} = (\mu_V - \mu_R)\left(\frac{1}{R_1} - \frac{1}{R_2}\right)$$

We can multiply the RHS numerator and denominator by the term $(\mu_Y - 1)$ where μ_Y is the refractive index for yellow (mean) colour in white light

$$\frac{1}{f_V} - \frac{1}{f_R} = (\mu_V - \mu_R)\left(\frac{1}{R_1} - \frac{1}{R_2}\right) \times \frac{(\mu_Y - 1)}{(\mu_Y - 1)}$$

$$\Rightarrow \frac{1}{f_V} - \frac{1}{f_R} = \frac{(\mu_V - \mu_R)}{(\mu_Y - 1)} \times (\mu_Y - 1)\left(\frac{1}{R_1} - \frac{1}{R_2}\right)$$

As $\frac{1}{f_Y} = (\mu_Y - 1)\left(\frac{1}{R_1} - \frac{1}{R_2}\right)$

$$\Rightarrow \frac{f_R - f_V}{f_V f_R} = \frac{(\mu_V - \mu_R)}{(\mu_Y - 1)} \times \frac{1}{f_Y}$$

$$\Rightarrow f_R - f_V = \omega f_Y \qquad \ldots(5.161)$$

As for mean colour we can use $f_V f_R = f_Y^2$

Equation-(5.161) is called '*Longitudinal Chromatic Aberration*' by a lens for white light. In general when a light consist of wavelengths of small range from λ to $\lambda + d\lambda$ then corresponding variation in refractive index of the material of lens will be from μ to $d\mu$. In this case the focal length of the lens for the light can be given as

$$\frac{1}{f} = (\mu - 1)\left(\frac{1}{R_1} - \frac{1}{R_2}\right) \qquad \ldots(5.162)$$

Differentiating above relation we get

$$-\frac{df}{f^2} = d\mu\left(\frac{1}{R_1} - \frac{1}{R_2}\right) \qquad \ldots(5.163)$$

Dividing equation-(5.163) by (5.162) we get

$$-\frac{df}{f}=\frac{d\mu}{(\mu-1)}=\omega$$

$$\Rightarrow \qquad -df=\omega f \qquad \ldots(5.164)$$

Above equation-(5.164) gives the spread of focal point df due to the wavelength spread $d\lambda$ in the light beam and is the '*Longitudinal Chromatic Aberration*' for the given light beam.

5.20.4 Achromatic Combination of Lenses

Due to chromatic aberrations in a lens always the image produced by the lens for any light consisting more than one wavelength, overlapped images are produced due to spread in focal point of the lens. To avoid or minimize the chromatic aberration we combine a lens with another lens of opposite nature to compensate the chromatic aberrations. Such combination of lenses are called achromatic combinations and the condition is called '*Achromatism*'.

From equation-(5.164) in previous article we have studied that spread in focus due to aberration is given as

$$-df=\omega f$$

For a lens combination of focal lengths f_1 and f_2 we use

$$\frac{1}{f_{eq}}=\frac{1}{f_1}+\frac{1}{f_2}$$

Differentiating above relation we get

$$-\frac{1}{f_{eq}^2}df_{eq}=-\frac{1}{f_1^2}df_1-\frac{1}{f_2^2}df_2$$

If the combination is free from chromatic aberration then we can use $df_{eq}=0$ hence we get

$$-\frac{1}{f_{eq}^2}df_{eq}=-\frac{1}{f_1^2}df_1-\frac{1}{f_2^2}df_2$$

$$\Rightarrow \qquad 0=-\frac{1}{f_1}\cdot\frac{df_1}{f_1}-\frac{1}{f_2}\cdot\frac{df_2}{f_2}$$

$$\Rightarrow \qquad \frac{\omega_1}{f_1}+\frac{\omega_2}{f_2}=0 \qquad \ldots(5.165)$$

where ω_1 and ω_2 are the dispersive powers of the material of the two lenses used in above combination. This equation-(5.165) is the condition of achromatic combination of two lenses which shows that a lens combination is free from achromatic aberrations if f_1 and f_2 are of opposite signs or the two lenses must be of opposite nature.

Illustrative Example 5.81

An achromatic convergent lens of focal length 150 cm is made by combining flint and crown glass lenses. Calculate the focal lengths of both the lenses and point out which one is divergent, if the ratio of the dispersive powers of flint and crown glasses are 3 : 2.

Solution

For the given combination, we have

$$\frac{1}{150}=\frac{1}{f_1}+\frac{1}{f_2} \qquad \ldots(5.166)$$

Condition of achromatism is

$$\frac{f_1}{f_2}=-\frac{\omega_1}{\omega_2}=-\frac{2}{3} \qquad \ldots(5.167)$$

Solving the equations-(5.166) and (5.167) we get

$$f_1=+50\text{ cm}$$

and $$f_2=-75\text{ cm}$$

Illustrative Example 5.82

Find the angle of a prism of dispersive power 0.021 and refractive index 1.52 to form an achromatic combination with a prism of angle 4.2° and dispersive power 0.045 having refractive index 1.65. Find the resulting deviation.

Solution

The dispersive power of prism material is given as

$$\omega=\frac{\mu_V-\mu_R}{(\mu-1)}$$

Dispersion and for the combination is given as

$$\theta=(\mu_V-\mu_R)A=\omega(\mu-1)A$$

Dispersion for first prism

$$\theta_1=0.045(1.65-1)4.2$$

for achromatic combination $\theta_1=\theta_2$

$$\Rightarrow \qquad 0.021(1.52-1)A_1=0.045\times 0.65\times 4.2$$

$$\Rightarrow \qquad A_1=11.25°$$

Deviation by the first prism is

$$\delta_1=(\mu_1-1)A_1=(1.52-1)(11.25)=5.85°$$

Deviation from the second prism is

$$\delta_2=(1.65-1)4.2=2.73°$$

Net deviation produced by the combination is

$$\delta_T=5.85-2.73=3.12°$$

Illustrative Example 5.83

A ray of white light falls into the side surface of an isosceles prism at such an angle that the refracted ray leaves the prism perpendicular to the second face. Find the deviation of the red and violet rays from the initial direction if refraction angle of the prism is 45°. The refractive indices of the prism material for red and violet rays are 1.37 and 1.42 respectively.

Solution

According to the situation shown in figure we have

$$r_2 = 0, r_1 = 45°$$

For prism refraction we have

$$r_1 + r_2 = A$$

By Snell's law, we have

$$\mu_r = \frac{\sin i}{\sin r}$$

$$\Rightarrow \quad 1.37 = \frac{\sin i}{\sin 45°}$$

$$\Rightarrow \quad \sin i = 1.37 \times 1/\sqrt{2} = 0.9687$$

$$\Rightarrow \quad i = 75°37'$$

Angle of deviation for the red ray is given as

$$i + e = A + \delta_r$$

$$\Rightarrow \quad 75°37' + 0 = 45 + \delta_r$$

$$\Rightarrow \quad \delta_r = 30°37'$$

$$\Rightarrow \quad \mu_V = \frac{\sin 75°37'}{\sin r_1}$$

$$\Rightarrow \quad \sin r_1 = \frac{0.9687}{1.42} = 0.6822$$

$$\Rightarrow \quad r_1 = 43°1' \text{ and } r_2 = 45 - 43°1' = 1°59'$$

By Snell's law we have

$$\frac{\sin e_2}{\sin r_2} = \mu_V$$

$$\Rightarrow \quad \frac{\sin e_2}{0.0346} = 1.42$$

$$\Rightarrow \quad \sin e_2 = 1.42 \times 0.0346 = 0.04913$$

$$\Rightarrow \quad e_2 = 2°49'$$

Angle of deviation for violet ray is given as

$$i + e = A + \delta_V$$

$$\Rightarrow \quad 75°375' + 2°49' = 45 + \delta_V$$

$$\Rightarrow \quad \delta_V = 33°26'$$

Illustrative Example 5.84

A prism of angle 60° is made of glass of refractive index 1.50 for red and 1.56 for violet. Find the angular separation of these rays when a narrow pencil of composite light is incident at minimum deviation.

Solution

The minimum deviation produced by a prism for a light ray refracted through it is given by the relation

$$\mu = \frac{\sin \frac{A + \delta_m}{2}}{\sin \frac{A}{2}}$$

For red light the minimum deviation δ_R is given as

$$\Rightarrow \quad 1.5 = \frac{\sin \frac{60° + \delta_R}{2}}{\sin 30°}$$

$$\Rightarrow \quad \sin \frac{60° + \delta_R}{2} = 1.5 \times \frac{1}{2} = 0.75 = \sin 48°35'$$

$$\Rightarrow \quad 60° + \delta_R = 97°10'$$

$$\Rightarrow \quad \delta_R = 37°10'$$

Similarly for violet light, minimum deviation of light is given as

$$\sin \frac{60° + \delta_v}{2} = 1.56 \times 0.5 = 0.78 = \sin 51°16'$$

$$\Rightarrow \quad 60 + \delta_v = 102°32'$$

$$\Rightarrow \quad \delta_v = 42°32'$$

The angular separation between the red and violet rays is given as

$$\theta = 42°32' - 37°10' = 5°22'$$

Illustrative Example 5.85

A thin biconvex lens is placed with its principal axis first along a beam of parallel red light and then along a beam of parallel blue light. If the refractive indices of the lens for red and blue light are respectively 1.514 and 1.524 and if the radius of curvature of the faces are 30 cm and 20 cm, calculate the separation of foci for red and blue light. If the focal length for the mean colour (yellow) is 23.1 cm, find the dispersive power of the material of the lens.

Solution

By lens makers formula, we have

$$\frac{1}{f} = (\mu - 1)\left(\frac{1}{R_1} - \frac{1}{R_2}\right)$$

Here for red light, we use

$$\frac{1}{f_r} = (1.514 - 1)\left(\frac{1}{20} + \frac{1}{30}\right)$$

$$\Rightarrow \quad = 0.514 \times (1/12)$$

$$\Rightarrow \quad f_r = 23.33$$

For blue light, we use

$$\frac{1}{f_b} = (1.524 - 1)\left(\frac{1}{20} + \frac{1}{30}\right)$$

$$\Rightarrow \quad f_b = \frac{12}{0.524} = 22.9 \text{ cm}$$

Separation between the focal points is

$$\Delta f = f_r - f_b = 23.33 - 22.9 = 0.43 \text{ cm}$$

We use $\frac{1}{f_b} - \frac{1}{f_r} = \left(\frac{\mu_b - \mu_r}{\mu - 1}\right)\frac{1}{f} = \frac{\omega}{f}$

where dispersive power of the lens material is given as

$$\omega = \left(\frac{\mu_b - \mu_r}{\mu - 1}\right)$$

$$\Rightarrow \quad f_r - f_b = \frac{\omega}{f} \times (f_b \times f_r) = \frac{\omega f^2}{f} = \omega f$$

$$\Rightarrow \quad \omega = \frac{\text{separation}}{\text{mean focal length}} = \frac{0.43}{23.1}$$

$$\Rightarrow \quad \omega = 0.019$$

Illustrative Example 5.86

Two parallel beams of light P and Q (separation d) containing radiations of wavelengths 4000 Å and 5000 Å (which are mutually coherent in each wavelength separately) are incident normally on a prism as shown in figure-5.291.

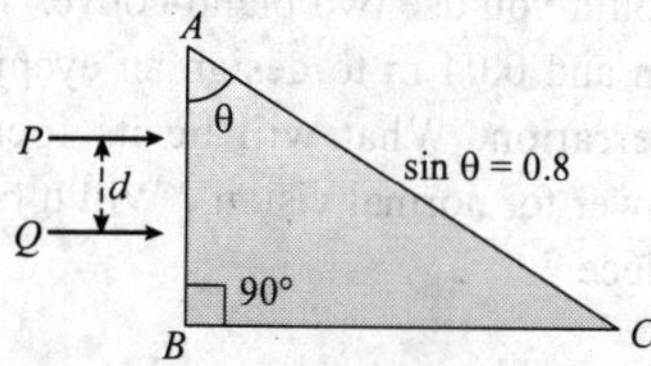

Figure 5.291

The refractive index of the prism as a function of wavelength is given by the relation

$$\mu(\lambda) = 1.20 + \frac{b}{\lambda^2}$$

where λ is in Å and b is a positive constant. The value of b is such that the condition for total reflection at the face AC is just satisfied for one wavelength and is not satisfied for the other.

(a) Find the value of b.

(b) Find the deviation of the beams transmitted through the face AC.

(c) A convergent lens is used to bring these transmitted beams into focus. If the intensities of the upper and the lower beams, immediately after transmission from the face AC, are $4I$ and I respectively, find the resultant intensity at the focus.

Solution

(a) We are given with the wavelengths of light beams as

$$\lambda_P = 4000 \text{ Å and } \lambda_Q = 5000 \text{ Å}$$

$$\sin\theta = 0.8$$

$$\Rightarrow \quad \theta = 53° \text{ and } \mu(\lambda) = 1.20 + (b/\lambda^2)$$

If θ_C be the critical angle for total internal reflection, then we have

$$\mu = \frac{1}{\sin\theta_C}$$

This shows that grater is the value of μ, smaller is the critical angle θ_C.

As $\quad \lambda_P < \lambda_Q$

$$\Rightarrow \quad \mu_P > \mu_Q$$

According to the given situation, the angle of incidence for both beams P and Q at face AC are same ($\theta = 53°$). Thus the beam P satisfies the condition of just total internal reflection while the beam Q gets transmitted thus we use

$$\mu_P = \frac{1}{\sin\theta_C} = \frac{1}{0.8} = 1.25$$

Substituting λ_P and μ_P is the given equation, we get

$$1.25 = 1.20 + \frac{1}{(4000)^2}$$

Solving we get $b = 0.8 \times 10^6$ Å^2

(b) Deviation of light beam P at grazing emergence of light is given as

$$\delta_P = 90° - \theta_C$$

where θ_C is the angle of incidence of P at face AC.

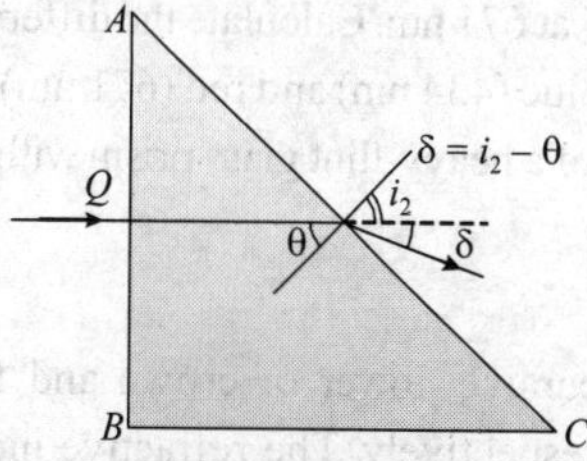

Figure 5.292

$$\Rightarrow \quad \delta_P = 90° - 53° 8' = 36°52'$$

For light beam Q, by Snell's law, we use

$$\mu_Q = \frac{\sin i_2}{\sin\theta}$$

$$\Rightarrow \quad \sin i_2 = \mu_Q = \sin\theta$$

$$\Rightarrow \quad \mu_Q = 1.20 + \frac{b}{\lambda_Q^2}$$

$$\Rightarrow \quad \mu_Q = 1.20 + \frac{0.8\times10^6}{(5000)^2} = 1.232$$

$$\Rightarrow \quad \sin i_2 = 1.232\times0.8 = 0.9856$$

$$\Rightarrow \quad i_2 = 80°16'$$

Deviation of beam Q is given as

$$\delta_Q = i_2 - \theta = 80°16' - 53° = 27°16'$$

(c) As the two beams have light wave of different wavelengths, these are non coherent light waves. When two or more non coherent light waves superpose each other on a point, the average resulting intensity is the sum of individual intensities of the component waves. Thus here the resulting intensity of the light at focus is $4I + I = 5I$.

Web Reference at www.physicsgalaxy.com
Age Group - High School Physics | Age 17-19 Years
Section - OPTICS
Topic - Dispersion of Light
Module Number - 1 to 12

Practice Exercise 5.8

(i) Two thin prisms are combined to form an achromatic combination. For first prism $A = 4°$, $\mu_R = 1.35$, $\mu_Y = 1.40$, $\mu_v = 1.42$. For second prism $\mu'_R = 1.7$, $\mu'_Y = 1.8$ and $\mu'_R = 1.9$ find the prism angle of second prism and the net mean derivation.

[1.4°, 0.48°]

(ii) The index of refraction of heavy flint glass is 1.68 at 434 nm and 1.65 at 671 nm. Calculate the difference in the angle of deviation of blue (434 nm) and red (671 nm) light incident at 65° on one side of a heavy-flint glass prism with apex angle 60°.

[2.8°]

(iii) The dispersive power of crown and flint glasses are 0.03 and 0.05 respectively. The refractive indices for yellow light for these glasses are 1.517 and 1.621 respectively. It is desired to form an achromatic combination of prisms of crown and flint glasses which can produce a deviation of 1° in the yellow ray. Find the refracting angles of the two prisms needed.

[4.8°, 2.4°]

(iv) A crown glass prism of angle 5° is to be combined with a flint prism in such a way that the mean ray passes undeviated. Find (a) the angle of the flint glass prism needed and (b) the angular dispersion produced by the combination when white light goes through it. Refractive indices for red, yellow and violet light are 1.514, 1.517 and 1.523 respectively for crown glass and 1.613, 1.620 and 1.632 for flint glass.

[(a) 4.169°, (b) 0.0348°]

(v) For a crown and flint glass for C and F lines $\mu_C = 1.515$ and $\mu_F = 1.523$ and $\mu_C = 1.644$, $\mu_F = 1.664$ respectively. Calculate the angle of flint glass prism which may be combined with crown glass prism having refracting angle 20 μ such that the combination is achromatic for C and F rays.

[8°]

(vi) The prism of a spectrometer has a refracting angle 60° and is made of glass whose refractive indices for red and violet are respectively 1.514 and 1.530. A while source is used and the instrument is set to give minimum deviation for red. Determine (a) angle of incidence, (b) the angle of the emergence for violet light and (c) the angular width of spectrum.

[(a) 49°12′, (b) 50°38′, (c) 1°26′]

(vii) An equiconvex lens of crown glass and an equiconvex lens of flint glass make an achromatic system. The radius of curvature of convex lens is 0.54 m. If the focal length of the combination for the mean colour is 1.54 m and the refractive indices for the crown glass are $\mu_R = 1.53$ and $\mu_V = 1.55$, find the dispersive power of the flint glass.

[0.055]

(viii) How would you use two plano-convex lenses of focal lengths 0.06 m and 0.04 m to design an eyepiece free from chromatic aberration. What will be its focal length and magnifying power for normal vision ? Will it be a positive or negative eyepiece ?

[0.048 m, 5.2, Negative]

(ix) An achromatic lens-double is formed by placing in contact a convex lens of focal length 20 cm and a concave lens of focal length 30 cm. The dispersive power of the material of the convex lens is 0.18.

(a) Determine the dispersive power of the material of the concave lens.

(b) Calculate the focal length of the lens-doublet.

[(a) 0.27, (b) 60 cm]

5.21 Optical Instruments

Optical Instruments are the devices which utilize the phenomenon of reflection and refraction for image formation of various objects for their study in detail. All optical instruments are generally categorized in two groups. One group of devices are those which produce real images of an object which is projected on a screen or a photographic plate and such images can be viewed simultaneously by many observers. Many different types of Projectors and Spectroscopes belong to this category which we will not discuss in details as their construction and working is not in scope of this book. The other group of devices are those which forms virtual image of an object and only one observer can see the image. The virtual image formed by the instrument is transformed by observer's eye into a real image on its retina. Some such optical instruments are also called as '*Optical Aids*' and such instruments are also used to correct defects in human eye. Most commonly used optical instruments in this group are spectacles, microscopes and telescopes which we study in detail.

5.21.1 The Human Eye

In all types of optical instruments the observer's eye is an essential part as the optical instruments we are going to study in coming sections, the analysis is based on observation of final image by observer's eye so a good knowledge of human eye is very important however in previous grades you might have studied it. Still for a quick reference we are discussing the same here again. Figure-5.293(a) shows a sectional view of the human eye which is nearly spherical in shape having an average diameter of 2.5 cm for an adult and figure-5.293(b) shows the front view of a normal human eye. The rough outer protective and stiff skin of eye ball is called '*Sclera*'. At the front portion of eye, the sclera extends into a thin transparent membrane which is called '*Cornea*' in front of the eye lens. Just at the back of cornea is the '*Iris*', which is a textured pattern muscular ring. Iris can be of different colours which causes different color of eye in different people. At the center of iris there is an aperture through which light incident on the eye lens. This aperture is called '*Pupil*' and its diameter is variable and it gets broader or shrink to adapt to changing light intensity falling on eye. Behind the iris there is a crystalline '*Eye Lens*' which is biconvex and made up of fibrous jelly. The eye lens is soft at the edges and hard at the center. This eye lens is held by circular ring shaped '*Ciliary Muscles*' at the outer edge in front of the eye ball. The region between the eye lens and cornea contains a liquid called '*Aqueous Humor*' and behind the lens eye is filled with a water based jelly type liquid called '*Vitreous Humor*'.

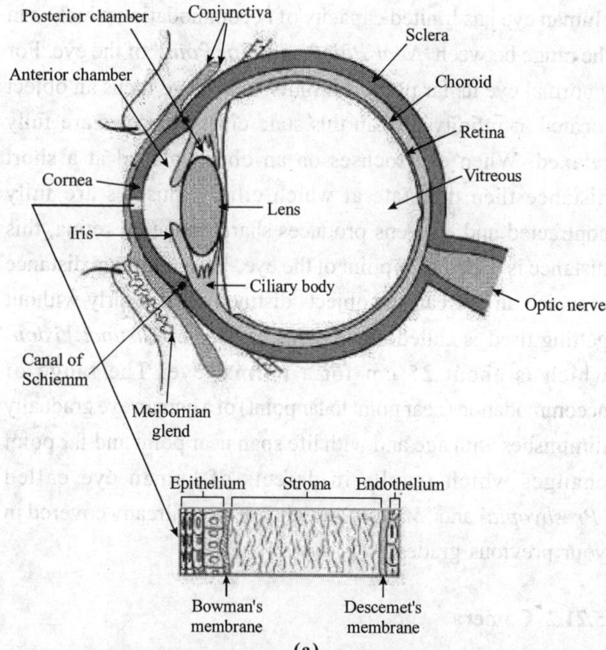

(a)

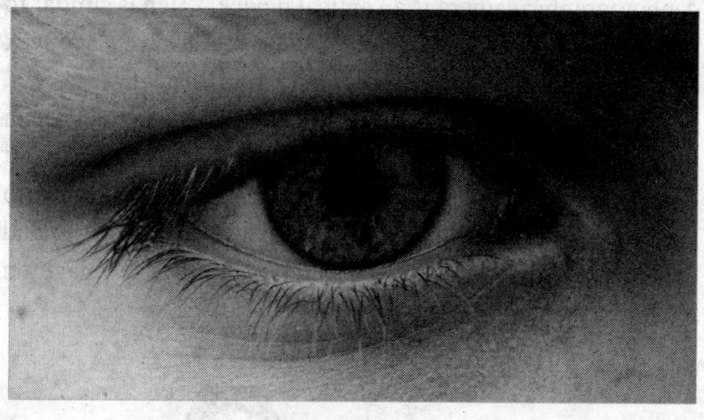

(b)

Figure 5.293

When light rays enters into the eye through the cornea and gets refracted from the eye lens and produces the image on a thin layer of sensory cells inside the sclera. This thin lining is called '*Retina*' which acts as a screen for image formation. The surface of retina is hemispherical in shape and it contains light receptor cells called '*Rods*' and '*Cones*'. These cells sense the image produced on retina and transmit it to human brain via the '*Optic Nerve*' shown in figure-5.293(a).

For an object to be seen sharply, the image must be formed exactly at retina. For different positions of object, eye adjusts to different object distances by changing the focal length of its lens, the distance between lens and retina does not change. The focal length of eye is adjusted by varying the radius of curvature of the lens by the ciliary muscles. This process by which ciliary muscles changes the curvature of eye lens to obtain sharp image of different object is called '*Accommodation*'.

Human eye has limited capacity of accommodation which is in the range between '*Near Point*' and '*Far Point*' of the eye. For a normal eye its far point is infinity. When eye focus an object located at infinity then in this state ciliary muscles are fully relaxed. When eye focuses on an object placed at a short distance then the state at which ciliary muscles are fully contracted and eye lens produces sharp image on retina, this distance is called near point of the eye. This minimum distance at which an eye can see objects distinctly and clearly without getting tired is called the '*Least Distance of Distinct Vision*' which is about 25 cm for a normal eye. The range of accommodation (near point to far point) of a human eye gradually diminishes with age and with life span near point and far point changes which results in defects of human eye called '*Presbyopia*' and '*Myopia*' which you have already covered in your previous grades.

5.21.2 Camera

A photographic camera is an optical device which is similar to human eye in which image of an object is produced by a convex lens (camera lens) on photographic film instead of retina. Figure-5.294 shows the structural diagram of a camera in which through the aperture light passes into the camera for short duration and produces a diminished real image on the photo sensitive film. The duration for which aperture opens and captures the image decides the illumination of the image on film.

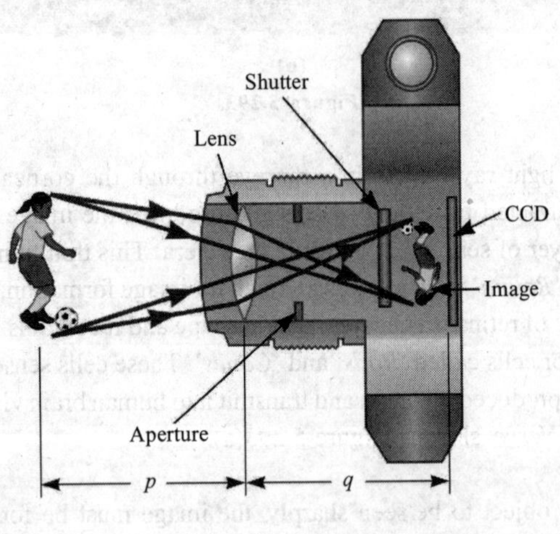

Figure 5.294

5.21.3 Angular Size of Objects and Images

When the observer sees an object directly or by using an optical instrument then the size of image appears to observer's eye is analyzed by angular size of image which also depends upon the distance where the image is located. For an object located close to eye it appears large and if it is displaced away its size appear small due to decrease in angular size of the object which it is subtending on eye. Figure-5.295(a) and (b) shows an object of size 'h' which is located at distances x_1 and x_2 from an observer's eye. The angular size of the object as seen by eye in the two situations is given as

$$\theta_1 = \frac{h}{x_1} \quad \text{and} \quad \theta_2 = \frac{h}{x_2}$$

(a)

(b)

Figure 5.295

Here angle θ_2 is less than θ_1 in the two positions of the same object and as we know the object which is located far away from us appear smaller thats why here angle θ_2 is less than angle θ_1.

5.21.4 Simple Microscope

A '*Simple Microscope*' or a '*Magnifying Glass*' is a converging lens of small focal length. When a magnifying glass is held close to the object and observer's eye is placed on the other side then in this situation the size of virtual image produced is larger then object and its distance is also farther from the object as shown in figure-5.296(b). In this figure the angular size of image is same as that of object which is θ as shown.

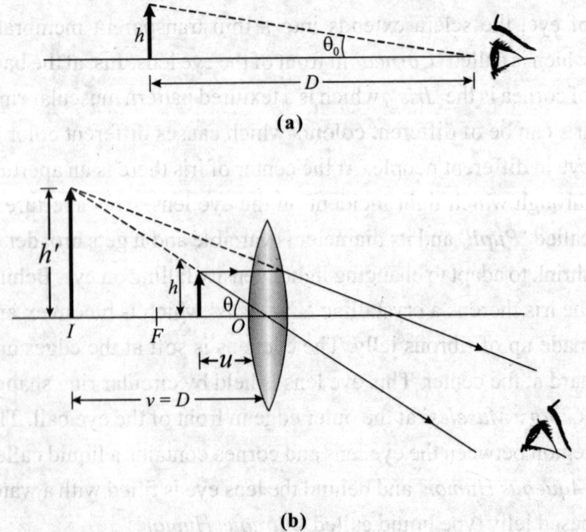

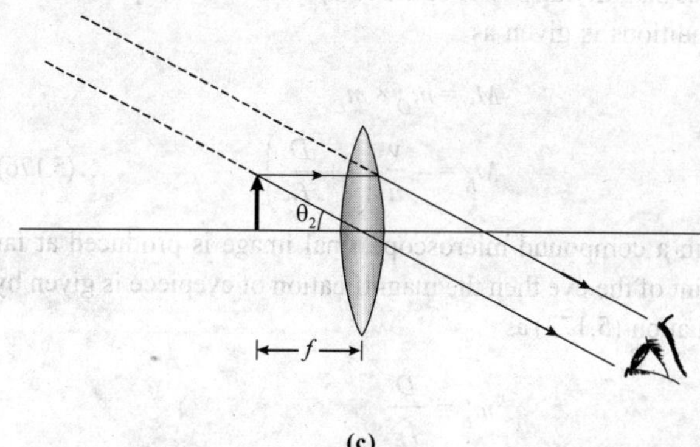

Figure 5.296

Here if the same object is kept a distance of near point of the eye as shown in figure-5.296(a) and compare it with the case shown above when image is produced at a distance of near point then in presence of converging lens the angular size observed is large and by using the lens we can see the magnified image of the same object at near point.

In figure-5.296(c) the object is kept at focal point of the lens so that its image is seen by the observer's eye at infinity with the angular size θ_2. In this case the image is obtained at far point of eye so the eye is in fully relaxed state.

From figure-5.296(a) the angular size of object located at near point is given as

$$\theta_0 = \frac{h}{D} \quad \ldots(5.168)$$

The angular size of image produced at near point as shown in figure-5.296(b) is given as

$$\theta_1 = \frac{h}{u} \quad \ldots(5.169)$$

Where u is the object distance which produces the image at near point distance and it can be obtained by lens formula as

$$u = \frac{Df}{D+f} \quad \ldots(5.170)$$

Substituting value of u from equation-(5.170) to equation-(5.169), we get

$$\theta_1 = \frac{h}{\left(\frac{Df}{D+f}\right)} = \frac{h(D+f)}{Df} \quad \ldots(5.171)$$

The angular size of image produced at far point (infinity) as shown in figure-5.296(c) is given as

$$\theta_2 = \frac{h}{f} \quad \ldots(5.172)$$

5.21.5 Magnification of Simple Microscope

In case of optical instruments the magnification is given as '*Angular Magnification*' which is not same as lateral magnification. Angular magnification is the ratio of angular size of ana image to the angular size of corresponding object which is generally considered to be located at near point of the eye. Students must understand the difference between the two like for the case shown in figure-5.296(c) angular magnification is $\frac{\theta_2}{\theta_0}$ whereas lateral magnification is infinite. Here if $\frac{\theta_2}{\theta_0} = 2$ (say) then the size of image will appear twice as large as that of the object to the observer's eye but actual size of image will be infinite.

For a simple microscope, the angular magnification for image produced at 'Near Point' of eye is given as

$$m_N = \frac{\theta_1}{\theta_0} = \frac{\left(\frac{h(D+f)}{Df}\right)}{\frac{h}{D}} = \frac{D+f}{D}$$

$$\Rightarrow \quad m_N = 1 + \frac{D}{f} \quad \ldots(5.173)$$

For the simple microscope, the angular magnification for image produced at '*Far Point*' of eye is given as

$$m_F = \frac{\theta_2}{\theta_0} = \frac{\left(\frac{h}{f}\right)}{\left(\frac{h}{D}\right)}$$

$$\Rightarrow \quad m_F = \frac{D}{f} \quad \ldots(5.174)$$

Above equations-(5.173) and equations-(5.174) give the angular magnification produced by the simple microscope for the two situations of image produced. Above given angular magnifications are also called '*Magnifying Power*' of a simple microscope.

5.21.6 Compound Microscope

A simple microscope has limitations on its magnifying power so in case when large magnification is needed we use compound microscope which uses two stage magnification and produces highly magnified image of a given object.

A compound microscope uses two lenses called '*Objective*' and '*Eyepiece*' placed on a common principal axis. The working of a compound microscope is shown in figure-5.297. Here an object AB is placed at a distance u which is slightly greater than the focal length of the objective so that it produces a real magnified inverted image $A'B'$ at a distance v as shown. This image $A'B'$ is obtained at a distance u_e from the eyepiece which is less than focal length of the eyepiece so that it produces a virtual magnified image CD at a distance equal to near point of the observer's eye which is kept close to the eyepiece on the other side for viewing the image.

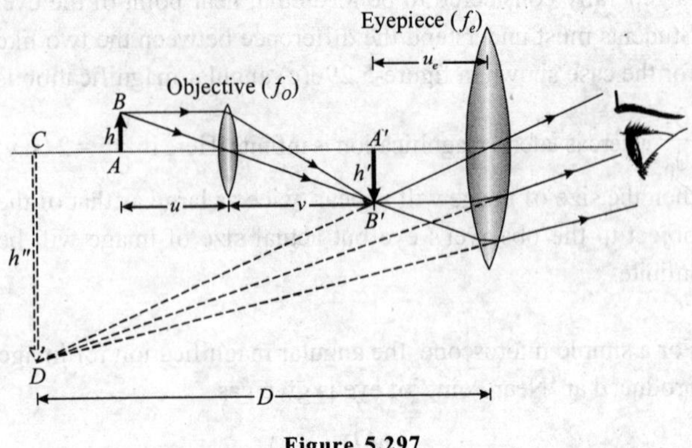

Figure 5.297

Figure-5.298 shows the situation when the image produced by the objective $A'B'$ is at the focal point of eyepiece due to which the final image seen by the observer is at its far point (infinity).

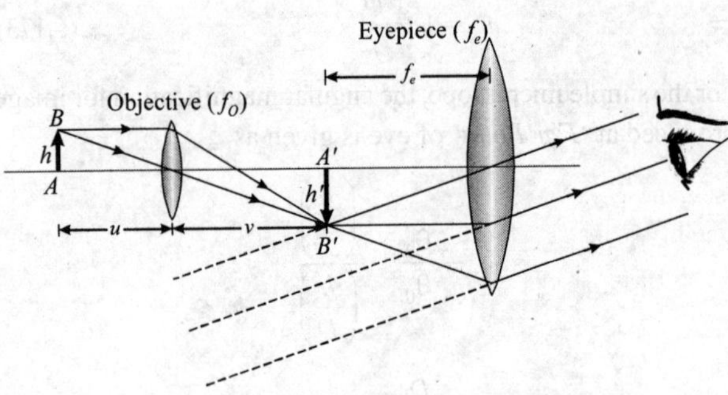

Figure 5.298

5.21.7 Magnifying Power of Compound Microscope

Overall angular magnification of the compound microscope is the product of two factors. First is the lateral magnification of the objective, which gives the linear size of its image $A'B'$ and second factor is the angular magnification of the eyepiece which is given by equation-(5.173) and equation-(5.174) in the two cases of image formation at near point and far point of the eye.

The lateral magnification of the objective is given as

$$m_O = -\frac{v}{u} = -\left(\frac{f_O}{u - f_O}\right) \quad \ldots(5.175)$$

For a compound microscope in normal conditions when image is produced at near point then magnification of eyepiece is given by equation-(5.173)

$$m_E = 1 + \frac{D}{f}$$

Thus magnifying power of the compound microscope in normal conditions is given as

$$M_N = m_O \times m_E$$

$$\Rightarrow \quad M_N = -\frac{v}{u}\left(1 + \frac{D}{f_E}\right) \quad \ldots(5.176)$$

If in a compound microscope final image is produced at far point of the eye then the magnification of eyepiece is given by equation-(5.173) as

$$m'_E = \frac{D}{f_E}$$

Thus magnifying power of the compound microscope for final image at far point of eye is given as

$$M_F = m_O \times m'_E$$

$$\Rightarrow \quad M_F = -\frac{v}{u}\left(\frac{D}{f_E}\right) \quad \ldots(5.177)$$

5.21.8 Tube Length of a Compound Microscope

The distance between two lenses, objective and eyepiece of the compound microscope is called Tube Length. We can calculate tube length of a compound microscope in two cases when it produces final image at the near point and at far point of the observer's eye.

Case-I : When Image is produced at Near Point

This situation is shown in figure-5.174 in which the tube length can be given as

$$L_N = v + u_e$$

$$\Rightarrow \quad L_N = \frac{uf_O}{u - f_O} + \frac{Df_E}{D + f_E} \quad \ldots(5.178)$$

In equation-(5.178) all values are substituted in magnitude as signs are already considered with symbols.

Case-II : When Image is produced at Far Point

This situation is shown in figure-5.175 in which the tube length can be given as

$$L_F = v + f_e$$

$$\Rightarrow \quad L_F = \frac{uf_O}{u - f_O} + f_E \quad \ldots(5.179)$$

In equation-(5.179) all values are substituted in magnitude as signs are already considered with symbols.

5.21.9 Refracting Astronomical Telescope

A telescope is used to view heavenly bodies. As heavenly bodies are very far away from earth, they subtend very small angular size on the observer's eye looking at these so these bodies appear very small in size. A telescope produces a magnified image of such bodies which is having large angular size so that eye can see more details of these bodies in enlarged view of image. A telescope which uses a lens as an objective is called a '*Refracting Telescope*'.

A simple astronomical telescope consists of two lenses- objective and eyepiece. The objective is a convex lens of long focal length and it forms the real image of distant object in focal plane of the objective. Figure-5.299 shows the optical system of a simple refracting telescope. The image *AB* formed by objective acts as an object for eyepiece and based on distance of eyepiece from the focal plane of objective it produces a virtual and enlarged image of *AB* either at near point of observer's eye or at far point (infinity).

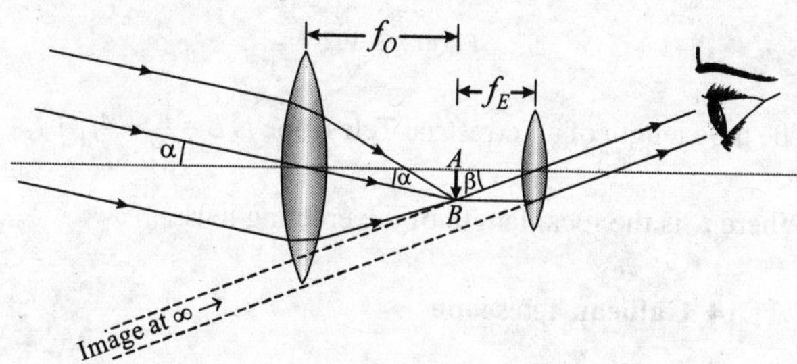

Figure 5.299

Above figure-5.299 shows the normal adjustment of lenses in telescope in which the final image is produced at infinity and observer's eye is in relaxed state which is the most common adjustment for a telescope used in general and figure-5.300 shows the situation when final image is produced by eyepiece at near point of the eye.

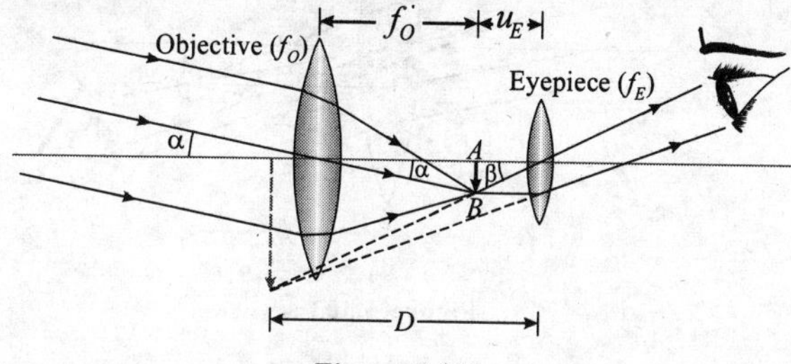

Figure 5.300

5.21.10 Magnifying Power of a Refracting Telescope

In all cases of telescopes always object is considered located far away from the device so we only discuss in terms of the angular size of object and image. As shown in figure-5.299 or figure-5.300 the angular size of object can be taken as α and first image *AB* is produced in the focal plane of objective, if $AB = h$ then we can use

$$\alpha = \frac{h}{f_O} \qquad \text{...(5.180)}$$

For the normal adjustment of telescope for final image obtained at infinity as shown in figure-5.299 the angular size of image can be taken as β which is given as

$$\beta = \frac{h}{f_E} \qquad \text{...(5.181)}$$

From equations-(5.180) and (5.181), the magnifying power of telescope for normal adjustment is given as

$$M_F = \frac{\beta}{\alpha}$$

$$\Rightarrow \quad M_F = -\frac{f_O}{f_E} \qquad \text{...(5.182)}$$

In equation-(5.182) a negative sign is inserted as the image produced by objective is inverted. For the situation when telescope produces final image at near point of observer's eye as shown in figure-5.300 the image size β' is given as

$$\beta = \frac{h}{u_E} \qquad \text{...(5.183)}$$

From equation-(5.180) and (5.183), the magnifying power of telescope for image at near point of observer's eye is given as

$$M_N = \frac{\beta'}{\alpha} = \frac{f_O}{u_E} \qquad \text{...(5.184)}$$

In figure-5.300, the distance u_E is such that image by eyepiece is obtained at a near point *D* from eyepiece of focal length f_E so by lens formula u_E is given as

$$u_E = \frac{Df_E}{D + f_E} \qquad \text{...(5.185)}$$

Substituting the value of u_E from equation-(5.185) in equation-(5.184) we get

$$M_N = -\frac{f_O}{\left(\frac{Df_E}{D + f_E}\right)}$$

$$\Rightarrow \quad M_N = -\frac{f_O}{f_E}\left(1 + \frac{f_E}{D}\right) \qquad \text{...(5.186)}$$

In equation-(5.186) a negative sign is inserted as the image produced by objective is inverted.

5.21.11 Tube Length of a Refracting Telescope

The distance between two lenses, objective and eyepiece of the telescope is called its '*Tube Length*'. We can calculate tube length of a refracting telescope in two cases when it produces final image at the near point and at far point of the observer's eye.

Case-I : When Image is produced at Near Point

This situation is shown in figure-5.300 in which the tube length can be given as

$$L_N = f_O + u_e$$

$$\Rightarrow \quad L_N = f_O + \frac{Df_E}{D+f_E} \quad \ldots(5.187)$$

In equation-(5.187) all values are substituted in magnitude as signs are already considered with symbols.

Case-II : When Image is produced at Far Point

This situation is shown in figure-5.299 in which the tube length can be given as

$$L_N = f_O + f_E \quad \ldots(5.188)$$

5.21.12 Reflecting Telescope

In a reflecting telescope the objective is replaced with a large concave mirror. This is an '*Astronomical Telescope*' which is used for astronomical observations. To study the details of distant astronomical bodies large aperture of objective has many advantages. Large aperture causes brighter image with fine details in the image produced and mounting of large sized mirror is much easier compared to mounting of a large lens. Figure-5.301 shows the working of a reflecting telescope in normal adjustment for obtaining the final image at infinity. We can see that the final image in a reflecting telescope is formed in the region where incoming rays are traveling in tube of telescope by placing a small mirror at an angle 45° to the axis of tube and placing eyepiece at the side of the tube.

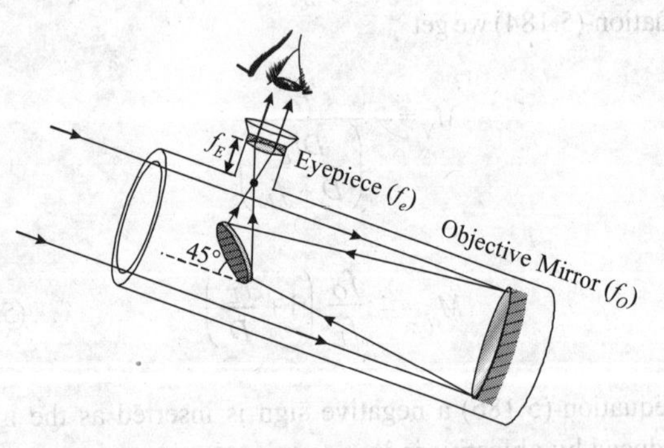

Figure 5.301

Refracting telescope uses a thin lens as objective and lenses of large aperture cannot be properly manufactured. If made then due to chromatic and spherical aberrations distorted images are formed. Due to use of parabolic mirrors as objective in reflecting telescope these are almost free from chromatic and spherical aberrations.

5.21.13 Terrestrial Telescope

This is also an '*Astronomical Telescope*' which produces erected images. This is similar to a normal refracting telescope but it uses an erecting lens between objective and eyepiece as shown in figure-5.302. The disadvantage of this telescope is its large tube length due to which it is rarely used.

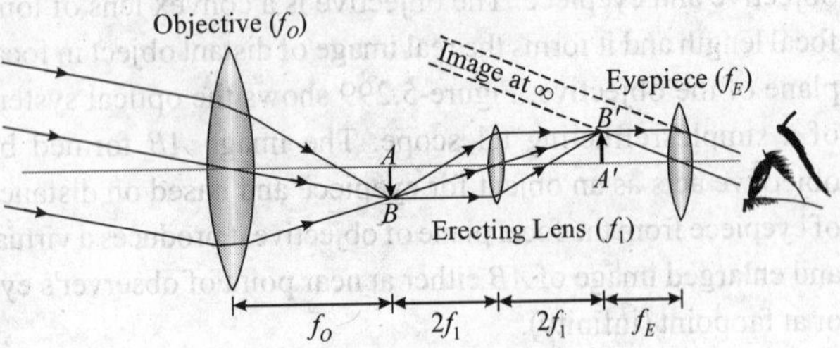

Figure 5.302

The tube length of a Terrestrial Telescope is $L = f_O + 4f_1 + f_E$

Where f_1 is the focal length of the erecting lens.

5.21.14 Galilean Telescope

This is one among the oldest known telescopes made by Galileo Galilei in 1609. This uses a concave lens as eyepiece as shown in figure-5.303 which shows the normal adjustment of the telescope. The advantage of this telescope is shorter tube length and it gives erected image without using the erecting lens.

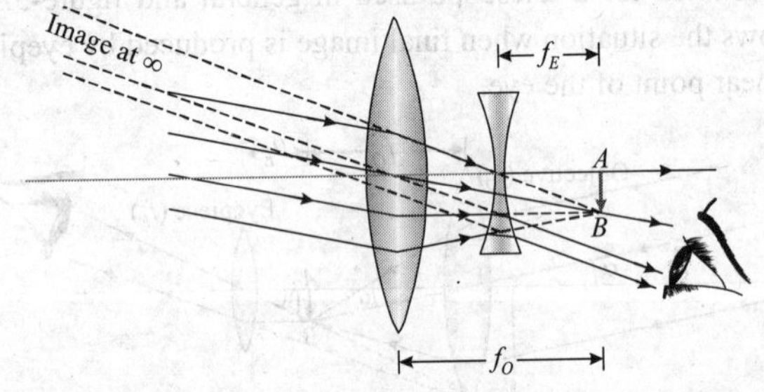

Figure 5.303

 # Illustrative Example 5.87

A shortsighted man, the accommodation of whose eye is between 12 cm and 60 cm wears spectacles through which he can see remote objects distinctly. Determine the minimum distance at which the man can read a book through his spectacles.

Solution

As per the given situation, a man can manage to see objects clearly if placed between 12 cm and 60 cm (accommodation of eye). If v is the distance between eye lens and retina then the focal length of eye lens when an object is placed at 60 cm distance is given by lens formula, used as

$$\frac{1}{v}-\frac{1}{-60}=\frac{1}{f_e} \quad \ldots(5.189)$$

If he uses spectacles with focal length of its lens f then he can see far objects clearly, that means for far objects the combination of eye lens and spectacles lens produces the image at retina at distance v from eye lens then for the combination of the lenses, we use lens formula as

$$\frac{1}{v}-\frac{1}{\infty}=\frac{1}{f_e}+\frac{1}{f} \quad \ldots(5.190)$$

From equation-(5.189) and (5.190), we get

$$f=-60 \text{ cm}$$

For the near point of the eye at 12 cm if the focal length of the eye lens is f_e' then by lens formula we use

$$\frac{1}{v}-\frac{1}{-12}=\frac{1}{f_e'} \quad \ldots(5.191)$$

If the minimum distance at which the person can read a book clearly is placed at a distance D from eye then with spectacles lenses, we use lens formula as

$$\frac{1}{v}-\frac{1}{-D}=\frac{1}{f_e'}+\frac{1}{-60} \quad \ldots(5.192)$$

From equation-(5.191) and (5.192), we get

$$D=15 \text{ cm.}$$

Illustrative Example 5.88

The focal lengths of the objective and eyepiece of a microscope are 4 mm and 25 mm respectively, and the length of the tube is 16 cm. If the final image is formed at infinity and the least distance of distinct vision is 25 cm, then calculate the magnifying power of the microscope.

Solution

Magnification of microscope is given as

$$M=\frac{v_0}{u_0}\left(\frac{D}{f_e}\right)$$

Here $\quad v_0=16-2.5=13.5 \text{ cm}$

and $\quad f_0=+4 \text{ mm}=+0.4 \text{ cm}$

Using the lens formula, we have

$$\frac{1}{v_0}-\frac{1}{u_0}=\frac{1}{f_0}$$

$$\Rightarrow \quad u_0=-\left(\frac{54}{131}\right) \text{ cm}$$

$$\Rightarrow \quad M=-\frac{13.5}{(54/131)}\times\frac{25}{2.5}=-327.5$$

Illustrative Example 5.89

A telescope has an objective of focal length 50 cm and eyepiece of focal length 5 cm. The distance of distinct vision is 25 cm. The telescope is focussed for distinct vision on a scale 200 cm away from the objective. Calculate

(i) The separation between the objective and eyepiece,

(ii) The magnification produced.

Solution

The situation is shown in figure-5.304 with ray diagram.

(i) If the separation between the two lenses be x then for lens formula for refraction at objective lens we use

$$u_0=-200 \text{ cm and } f_0=+50 \text{ cm}$$

From lens formula, we have

$$\frac{1}{v_0}-\frac{1}{u_0}=\frac{1}{f_0}$$

$$\Rightarrow \quad \frac{1}{v_0}=\frac{1}{f_0}+\frac{1}{u_0}=\frac{1}{50}-\frac{1}{200}$$

$$\Rightarrow \quad \frac{1}{v_0}=\frac{4-1}{200}=\frac{3}{200}$$

$$\Rightarrow \quad v_0=+\frac{200}{3} \text{ cm}$$

Thus a real image is formed at a distance of 200/3 from the objective. This image acts as object for the eyepiece. For refraction through eyepiece, we use

$$u_e=-\left(x-\frac{200}{3}\right)$$

$$v_e=-25 \text{ cm and } f_e=+5 \text{ cm}$$

$$\Rightarrow \quad -\frac{1}{25}+\frac{1}{\left(x-\dfrac{200}{3}\right)}=\frac{1}{5}$$

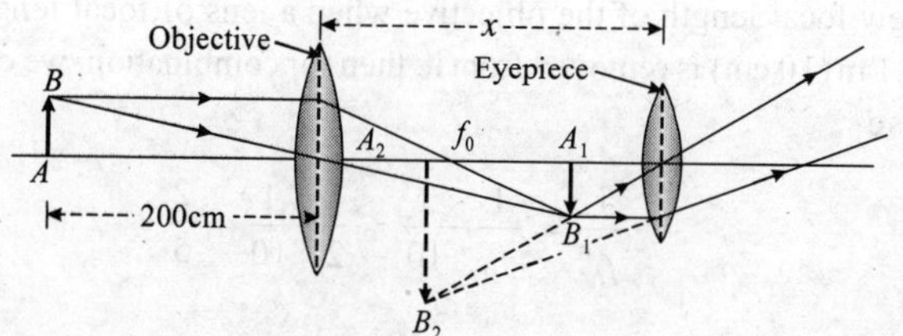

Figure 5.304

$$\Rightarrow \quad \frac{1}{\left(x-\frac{200}{2}\right)}=\frac{1}{5}+\frac{1}{25}=\frac{6}{25}$$

$$\Rightarrow \quad 6x-400=25$$

$$\Rightarrow \quad 6x=425$$

$$\Rightarrow \quad x=\frac{425}{6}=70.80 \text{ cm}$$

(ii) Magnification of Objective $=\frac{v_0}{u_0}=\frac{200}{3\times 200}=\frac{1}{3}$

Magnification of Eyepiece $=\frac{v_e}{u_e}=\frac{25\times 6}{25}=6$

Total magnification $=\frac{1}{3}\times 6=2$

Illustrative Example 5.90

A compound microscope is used to enlarge an object kept at a distance of 0.03 m from its objective which consists of several convex lenses in contact and has focal length 0.02 m. If a lens of focal length 0.1 m is removed from the objective, find out the distance by which the eyepiece of the microscope must moved to refocus the image.

Solution

Sol. Let v_0 be the distance of the image formed by the objective alone so by lens formula for objective, we use

$$\frac{1}{v_0}-\frac{1}{u_0}=\frac{1}{f_0}$$

$$\Rightarrow \quad \frac{1}{v_0}=\frac{1}{u_0}+\frac{1}{f_0}$$

$$\Rightarrow \quad \frac{1}{v_0}=-\frac{1}{3}+\frac{1}{2}=\frac{1}{6}$$

$$\Rightarrow \quad v_0=+6 \text{ cm}$$

The image is formed at 6 cm behind the objective. If f_0' be the new focal length of the objective when a lens of focal length 0.1 m (10 cm) is removed from it, then for combination, we can use

$$\frac{1}{f_0'}=\frac{1}{f_0}-\frac{1}{10}=\frac{1}{2}-\frac{1}{10}=\frac{2}{5}$$

$$\Rightarrow \quad f_0'=+(5/2) \text{ cm}$$

Let v_0' be the new distance of the image formed by the objective then by using lens formula again, we have

$$\frac{1}{v_0'}=\frac{1}{u_0}+\frac{1}{f_0'}=-\frac{1}{3}+\frac{2}{5}=\frac{1}{15}$$

$$\Rightarrow \quad v_0'=+15 \text{ cm}$$

Thus the image is shifted from the objective through a distance 15 cm – 6 cm = 9 cm. So the eyepiece should be moved away from the objective by 9 cm to refocus the image at same position.

Illustrative Example 5.91

In a compound microscope the objective and eyepiece have focal lengths of 0.95 cm and 5 cm respectively, and are kept at a distance of 20 cm. The final image is formed at a distance of 25 cm from eyepiece. Calculate the position of the object and the total magnification.

Solution

From the lens formula for eyepiece, we use

$$v_e=-25 \text{ cm and } f_e=+5 \text{ cm}$$

$$\Rightarrow \quad \frac{1}{u_e}=\frac{1}{v_e}-\frac{1}{f_e}=-\frac{1}{25}-\frac{1}{5}=-\frac{6}{25}$$

$$\Rightarrow \quad u_e=-(25/6) \text{ cm}$$

For the objective, we use

$$f_0=0.95 \text{ cm and } v_0=20-(25/6)=95/6 \text{ cm}$$

Using lens formula, we have

$$\frac{1}{v_0}-\frac{1}{u_0}=\frac{1}{f_0}$$

$$\frac{1}{v_0}-\frac{1}{f_0}=\frac{1}{u_0}$$

$$\Rightarrow \quad \frac{1}{u_0}=\frac{6}{5}-\frac{1}{0.96}=\frac{6-100}{95}$$

$$\Rightarrow \quad \frac{1}{u_0}=-\frac{94}{95}$$

$$\Rightarrow \quad u_0=\frac{95}{94} \text{ cm}$$

Total Magnification $\quad M=\frac{v_0}{u_0}\left(1+\frac{D}{f_e}\right)$

$$\Rightarrow \quad M=\frac{(95/6)}{-(95/94)}\left(1+\frac{25}{5}\right)=-94$$

Illustrative Example 5.92

The focal lengths of the objective and the eyepiece of an astronomical telescope are 0.25 m and 0.02 m, respectively. The telescope is adjusted to view an object at a distance of 1.5 m from the objective, the final image being 0.25 m from the eye of the observer. Calculate the tube length of the telescope and the magnification produced by it.

Solution

For objective, by lens formula, we have

$$\frac{1}{v_0} - \frac{1}{-1.5} = \frac{1}{+0.25}$$

$$\Rightarrow \quad \frac{1}{v_0} = \frac{1}{0.25} - \frac{1}{1.5} = 4 - 0.6667 = 3.3333$$

$$\Rightarrow \quad v_0 = +0.3 \text{ m}$$

For eyepiece, by lens formula we have

$$\frac{1}{-0.25} - \frac{1}{-u_e} = \frac{1}{+0.02}$$

$$\Rightarrow \quad \frac{1}{u_e} = \frac{1}{0.25} + \frac{1}{0.02} = 4 + 50 = 54$$

$$\Rightarrow \quad u_e = +0.01852 \text{ m}$$

The tube length of the telescope is given as

$$L = 0.3 + 0.01852 = 0.31852 \text{ m}$$

Magnificationby objective is

$$m_o = \frac{v_o}{u_o} = \frac{0.3}{1.5} = 0.2$$

Magnification by eyepiece is

$$m_e = \frac{v_e}{u_e} = \frac{0.25}{0.001852} = 136.98$$

Total Magnification $m_T = m_1 \times m_2 = 27.39$

Illustrative Example 5.93

A shortsighted person cannot see objects situated beyond 2 m from him distinctly. What should be the power of the lens which he should use for seeing distant objects clearly?

Solution

If f_e be the accommodate focal length of the eye-lenses for 2 m, then by lens formula, we have

$$\frac{1}{v} - \frac{1}{-2} = \frac{1}{f_e} \quad \dots(5.193)$$

Where v is the distance between eye lens and retina.

If f be the focal length of the correcting lens for seeing distant objects then by lens formula for combination, we have

$$\frac{1}{v} - \frac{1}{\infty} = \frac{1}{f_e} + \frac{1}{f} \quad \dots(5.194)$$

Subtracting equation-(5.193) from equation-(5.194), we get

$$f = -2 \text{ m}$$

Thus power of the lens required is

$$P = \frac{1}{f} = \frac{1}{-2} = -0.5 \text{ dioptre}$$

Web Reference at www.physicsgalaxy.com

Age Group - High School Physics | Age 17-19 Years
Section - OPTICS
Topic - Optical Instruments
Module Number - 1 to 20

Practice Exercise 5.9

(i) A projector lens has a focal length 10 cm. It throws an image of a 2 cm × 2 cm slide on a screen 5 metre from the lens. Find (i) the size of the picture on the screen and (ii) the ratio of illumination of the slide and of the picture on the screen.

[2401]

(ii) The focal length of the objective of a microscope is $f_o = 3$ mm and of the eyepiece $f_e = 5$ cm. An object is placed at a distance of 3.1 mm from the objective. Find the magnification of the microscope for a normal eye, if the final image is produced at a distance 25 cm from the eye (or eyepiece). Also final the separation between the lenses of microscope.

[180, 13.46 cm]

(iii) The optical powers of the objective and eyepiece of a microscope are equal to 100 *D* and 20 *D* respectively. The microscope magnification is equal to 50 when image is produced at near point of eye. What will be magnification of the microscope be when the distance between the objective and eyepiece is increased by 2 cm ?

[62]

(iv) The focal lengths of the objective and the eyepiece of an astronomical telescope are 0.25 m and 0.025 m, respectively. The telescope is focussed on an object 5 m from the objective, the final image being formed 0.25 m from the eye of the observer. Calculate the tube length of the telescope and its magnifying power.

[0.2859 m, 11.6]

(v) An astronomical telescope consisting of two convex lenses of focal length 50 cm and 5 cm is focussed on the moon. What is the distance between the two lenses in this position ? If the telescope is then turned towards an object 10 m away, how much would the eyepiece have to be moved to focus on the object without altering the accommodation of the eye? Calculate the magnification (angular) produced by the telescope in the two adjustments.

[10]

(vi) The eyepiece and objective of a microscope, of focal lengths 0.3 m and 0.4 m respectively, are separated by a distance of 0.2 m. The eyepiece and the objective are to be interchanged such that the angular magnification of the instrument remains same. What is the new separation between the lenses ?

[0.2575 m]

(vii) An astronomical telescope in normal adjustment has a tube length of 93 cm and magnification (angular) of 30. If the eyepiece is to be drawn out by 3 cm to focus a near object, with the final image at infinity, find how far away is the object and the magnification (angular) is this case.

[27.9 m, 31]

---

* * * * *

Discussion Questions

Q5-1 What is the function of the circular stop at the focal plane of the objective of a telescope? Give reasons.

Q5-2 A beam of white light passing through a hollow prism gives no spectrum. Is this true or false? Give reasons.

Q5-3 The magnifying power of a telescope in normal adjustment is greater than that when it is focussed for least distance of distinct vision. Is this true or false? Give reasons.

Q5-4 Can you think of a specific optical setup with a trihedral prism (no other device) in which a light ray passes undeviated through the prism. Think and draw the ray diagram.

Q5-5 Can a real image be photographed by a camera ?

Q5-6 Can you obtain image produced by a convex lens on a screen without using any other device.

Q5-7 It is difficult to thread a needle with one eye closed. Why?

Q5-8 If a single lens is used to form an image, it is better to use a lens of large diameter, in which the outer parts near the rim are blocked off. Explain.

Q5-9 What is the best position of the eye for viewing an object through a microscope?

Q5-10 Can the optical length between two points ever be less than the geometrical path between these points?

Q5-11 Can two lenses of the same material produce achromatism when placed in contact ? Explain.

Q5-12 Why is the objective of a telescope of large focal length and large aperture?

Q5-13 A diver inside the sea observes a ship on the water surface. Does he finds the ship taller or smaller then its actual height above the water surface. Give reason and draw ray diagram to support your logic.

Q5-14 A plane projector is projecting a sharp still image on a screen, the image consists of objects of several colours. Can you comment on sharpness of all these coloured objects in image.

Q5-15 Why does the moon, purely white during the day, have a yellowish hue after sunset?

Q5-16 How focal length of a spherical mirror changes when placed in different media.

Q5-17 An air bubble inside water broadly behaves as a concave lens. Is this true or false.

Q5-18 Why does an aeroplane flying at a great altitude not cast a shadow on the earth ?

Q5-19 The magnifying power of a telescope in normal adjustment is greater than that when it is focussed for least distance of distinct vision. Is this true or false?

Q5-20 When sun rays pass through a small hole in the foliage at the top of a high tree, they produce an elliptical spot of light on the ground. Explain why. When will the spot be a circle?

Q5-21 If a mirror reverses right and left, why doesn't it reverse up and down?

Q5-22 Is it possible to photograph a virtual image ?

Q5-23 Is it possible for a given lens to act as a converging lens in one medium, and as a diverging lens in another?

Q5-24 A camera lens is marked *f*/1.8. What is the meaning of this mark?

Q5-25 Some motor cars have additional yellow headlights. Why?

Q5-26 Why are lenses often coated with thin films of transparent material ?

Q5-27 If there are scratches on the lens of a camera, they do not appear on a photograph taken with the camera. Explain. Do the scratches affect the photograph at all?

Q5-28 The sun seems to rise before it actually rises and it seems to set long after it actually sets. Explain why.

Q5-29 Does the focal length of a lens depend on the medium in which the lens is immersed? Is it possible for a lens to act as a converging lens in one medium and a diverging lens in another medium?

Q5-30 Explain why the use of goggles enables an underwater swimmer to see clearly under the surface of a lake.

Q5-31 Why does an aeroplane flying at a great altitude not case a shadow on the earth ?

* * * * *

Conceptual MCQs Single Option Correct

5-1 A beaker containing liquid is placed on the table underneath a microscope which can be moved along a vertical scale. The microscope is focussed, through the liquid onto a mark on the table when the reading on the scale is a. It is next focussed on the upper surface of liquid and the reading is b. More liquid is added and the observations are repeated. The corresponding readings are c and d. The refractive index of liquid is :

(A) $\dfrac{d-b}{d-c-b+a}$ (B) $\dfrac{d-c-b+a}{d-b}$

(C) $\dfrac{b-d}{d-c-b+a}$ (D) $\dfrac{d-c-b+a}{b-d}$

5-2 An insect of negligible mass is sitting on a block of mass M, tied with a spring of force constant k. The block performs simple harmonic motion with amplitude A in front of a plane mirror placed as shown in figure-5.305. The maximum speed of insect relative to its image will be :

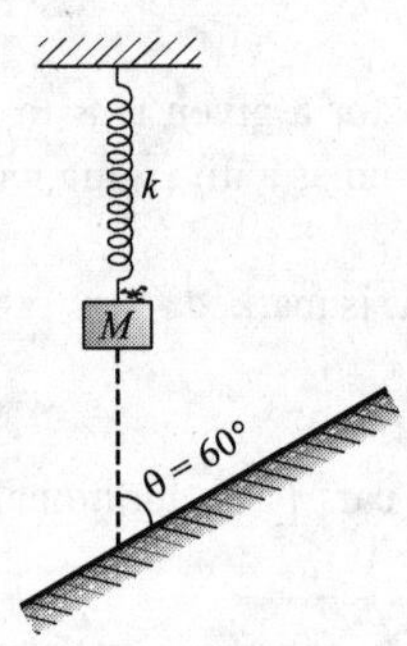

Figure 5.305

(A) $A\sqrt{\dfrac{k}{M}}$ (B) $\dfrac{A\sqrt{3}}{2}\sqrt{\dfrac{k}{M}}$

(C) $A\sqrt{3}\sqrt{\dfrac{k}{M}}$ (D) $2A\sqrt{\dfrac{M}{k}}$

5-3 Inside a solid glass sphere of radius R, a point source of light is embedded at a distance $x(x < R)$ from centre of the sphere. The solid sphere is surrounded by air of refractive index 1.0. The maximum angle of incidence for rays incident on the spherical glass-air interface directly from the point source is :

(A) $\cos^{-1}\dfrac{x}{R}$ (B) $\sin^{-1}\dfrac{x}{R}$

(C) $\cos^{-1}\sqrt{\dfrac{x}{R}}$ (D) $\sin^{-1}\sqrt{\dfrac{x}{R}}$

5-4 Two plane mirrors of length L are separated by distance L and a man M_2 is standing at distance L from the connecting line of mirrors as shown in figure-5.306. A man M_1 is walking in a straight line at distance $2L$ parallel to mirrors at speed u, then man M_2 at O will be able to see image of M_1 for total time :

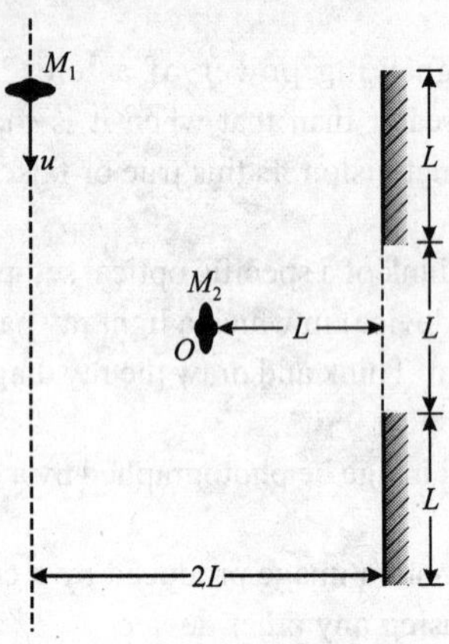

Figure 5.306

(A) $\dfrac{4L}{u}$ (B) $\dfrac{3L}{u}$

(C) $\dfrac{6L}{u}$ (D) $\dfrac{9L}{u}$

5-5 A point source has been placed as shown in the figure-5.307. What is the length on the screen that will receive reflected light from the mirror ?

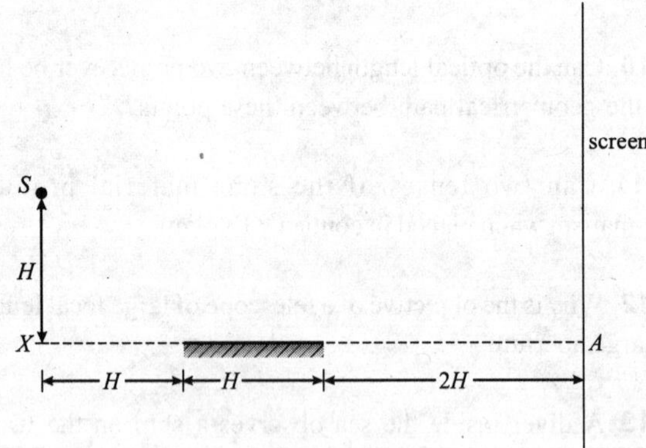

Figure 5.307

(A) $2H$ (B) $3H$

(C) H (D) None of these

5-6 A thin lens of focal length f and its aperture has a diameter d. It forms an image of intensity I. Now the central part of the aperture upto diameter $(d/2)$ is blocked by an opaque paper. The focal length and image intensity would change to

(A) $f/2, I/2$ (B) $f, I/4$

(C) $3f/4, I/2$ (D) $f, 3I/4$

5-7 A ray of light falls on a plane mirror. When the mirror is turned, about an axis which is at right angle to the plane of the mirror through 20°, the angle between the incident ray and new reflected ray is 45°. The angle between the incident ray and original reflected ray was :

(A) 65°
(B) 25°
(C) 25° or 65°
(D) 45°

5-8 In the figure shown-5.308, light is incident on the interface between media 1 (refractive index μ_1) and 2 (refractive index μ_2) at angle slightly greater than the critical angle, and is totally reflected. The light is then also totally reflected at the interface between media 1 and 3 (refractive index μ_3), after which it travels in a direction opposite to its initial direction. The media must have a refractive indices such that :

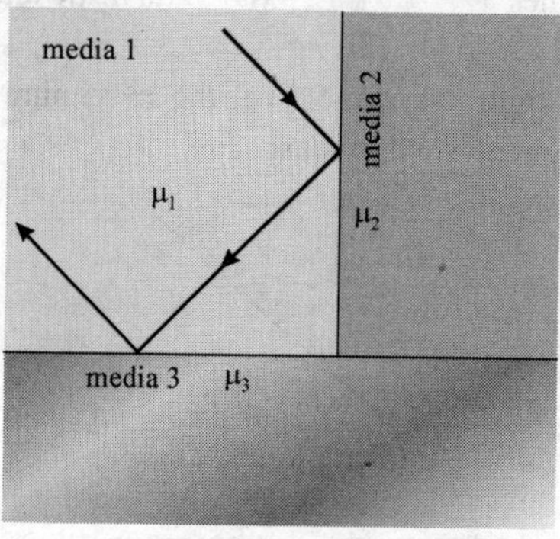

Figure 5.308

(A) $\mu_1 < \mu_2 < \mu_3$
(B) $\mu_1^2 - \mu_3^2 > \mu_2^2$
(C) $\mu_1^2 - \mu_2^2 < \mu_3^2$
(D) $\mu_1^2 + \mu_2^2 > \mu_3^2$

5-9 Figure-5.309 shows a spherical cavity in a solid glass block. The cavity is filled with a liquid and from outside an observer sees the distance AB which is the diameter of the cavity and it appear as infinitely large to the observer. If refractive index of liquid is μ_1 and that of glass is μ_2, then $\frac{\mu_1}{\mu_2}$ is :

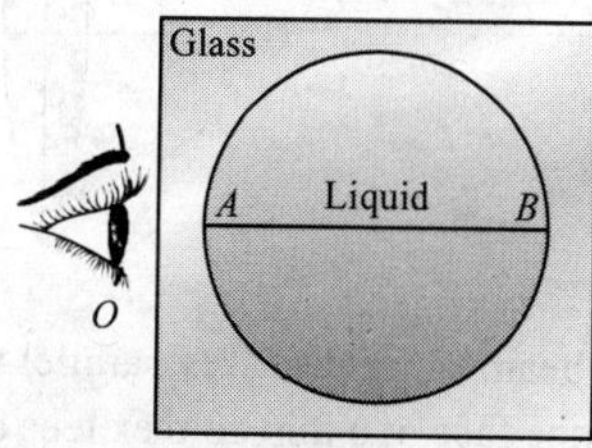

Figure 5.309

(A) 2
(B) 1/2
(C) 4
(D) None of these

5-10 An infinitely long rectangular strip is placed on principal axis of a concave mirror as shown in figure-5.310. One end of the strip coincides with centre of curvature as shown. The height of rectangular strip is very small in comparison to focal length of the mirror. Then the shape of image of strip formed by concave mirror is similar to a :

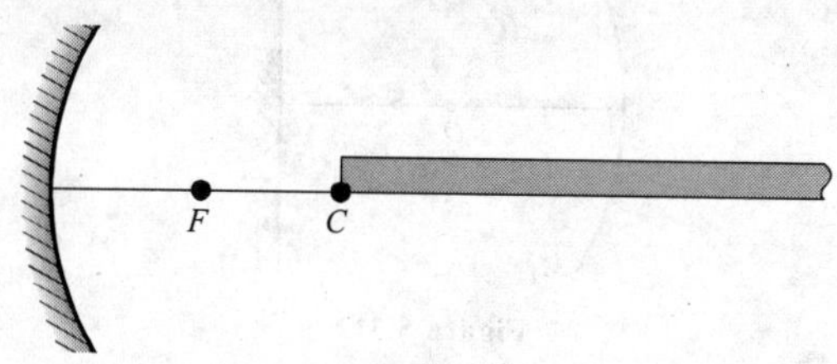

Figure 5.310

(A) Rectangle
(B) Trapezium
(C) Triangle
(D) Square

5-11 A concave spherical surface of radius of curvature 10 cm separates two mediums X and Y of refractive indices 4/3 and 3/2 respectively. Centre of curvature of the surface lies in the medium X. An object is placed in medium X:

(A) Image is always real
(B) Image is real if the object distance is greater than 90 cm
(C) Image is always virtual
(D) Image is virtual only if the object distance is less than 90 cm

5-12 In the figure shown-5.311 a slab of refractive index $\frac{3}{2}$ is moved at speed 1 m/s towards a stationary observer. A point 'P' is observed by the observer with the help of paraxial rays through the slab. Both 'O' and observer lie in air. The velocity with which the image will move is :

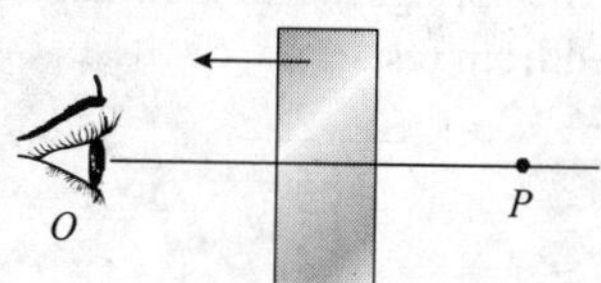

Figure 5.311

(A) 2 m/s towards left
(B) $\frac{4}{3}$ m/s towards left
(C) 3 m/s towards left
(D) Zero

5-13 Light passes from air into flint glass with index of refraction n. The angle of incidence must the light have for the component of its velocity perpendicular to the interface to remain same in both mediums is :

(A) $\sin^{-1} n$
(B) $\sin^{-1} (1/n)$
(C) $\cos^{-1} n$
(D) $\tan^{-1} n$

5-14 In the figure-5.312 M_1 and M_2 are two fixed mirrors shown. If the object 'O' located between the two mirrors moves towards the plane mirror, then the image I which is formed after two successive reflections first from M_1 & then from M_2 respectively will move :

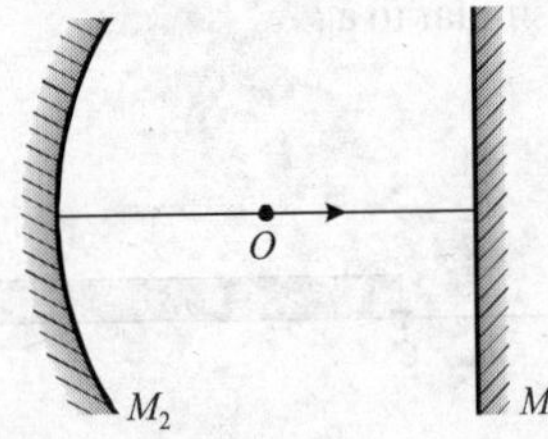

Figure 5.312

(A) Always towards right (B) Always towards left
(C) Depends on position of O (D) Cannot be determined

5-15 A person AB of height 170 cm is standing in front of a plane mirror. His eyes are at height 164 cm. At what distance from P should a hole be made in the mirror so that he cannot see the top of his head :

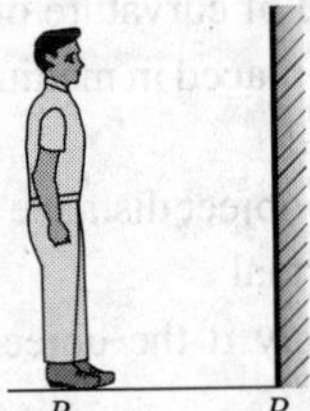

Figure 5.313

(A) 167 cm (B) 161 cm
(C) 163 cm (D) None of these

5-16 In the figure shown-5.314, blocks P and Q are in contact but do not stick to each other. The lower face of P behaves as a plane mirror. The springs are in their natural lengths. The system is released from rest.

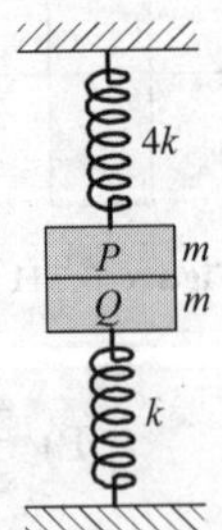

Figure 5.314

Then the distance between Q and its image when Q is at the lowest point first time will be :

(A) $\frac{2mg}{K}$ (B) $\frac{4mg}{K}$

(C) $\frac{3mg}{K}$ (D) 0

5-17 A point object is moving along principal axis of a concave mirror with uniform velocity towards pole. Initially the object is at infinite distance from pole on right side of the mirror as shown in the figure-5.315. Before the object collides with mirror, the number of times at which the distance between object and its image is 40 cm are.

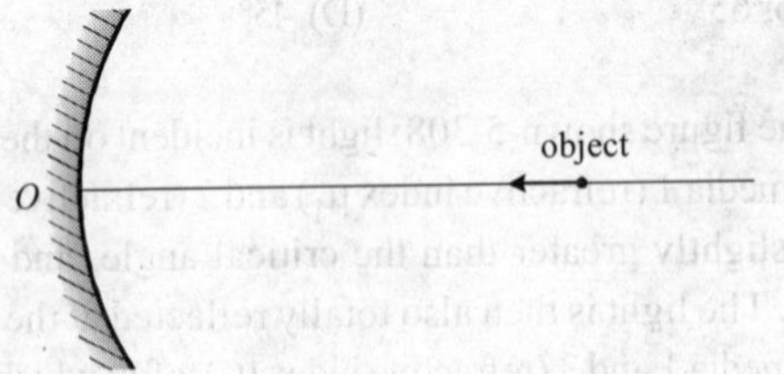

Figure 5.315

(A) One time (B) Two times
(C) Three times (D) Data insufficient

5-18 In the figure shown-5.316, the maximum number of reflections light rays will undergo are :

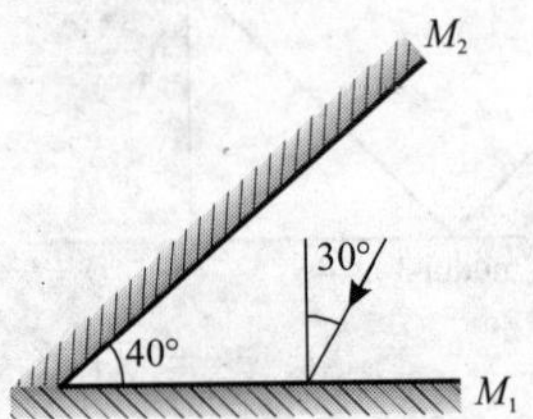

Figure 5.316

(A) 2 (B) 3
(C) 4 (D) 1

5-19 A convex lens is cut into two parts in different ways that are arranged in four manners, as shown. Which arrangement will give maximum optical power ?

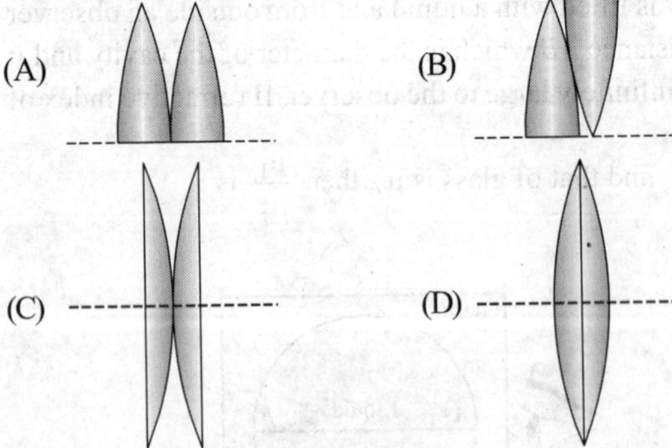

5-20 A parallel beam of light passes parallel to the principal axis and falls on one face of a thin convex lens of focal length f and after two internal reflections from the second face forms a real image. The distance of image from lens if the refractive index of material of lens is 1.5 :

(A) $f/7$ (B) $f/2$
(C) $7f$ (D) None of these

5-21 An object and a plane mirror are shown in figure-5.317. Mirror is moved with velocity V as shown. The velocity of image is :

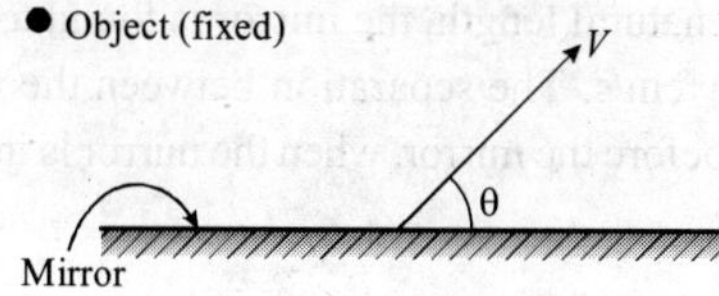

Figure 5.317

(A) $2V\sin\theta$ (B) $2V$
(C) $2V\cos\theta$ (D) None of these

5-22 A prism of angle A and refractive index 2 is surrounded by medium of refractive index $\sqrt{3}$. A ray is incident on side PQ at an angle of incidence i ($0 \le i \le 90°$) as shown in the figure-5.318. The refracted ray is then incident on side PR of prism. The minimum angle A of prism for which ray incident on side PQ does not emerge out of prism from side PR (for any value of i) is :

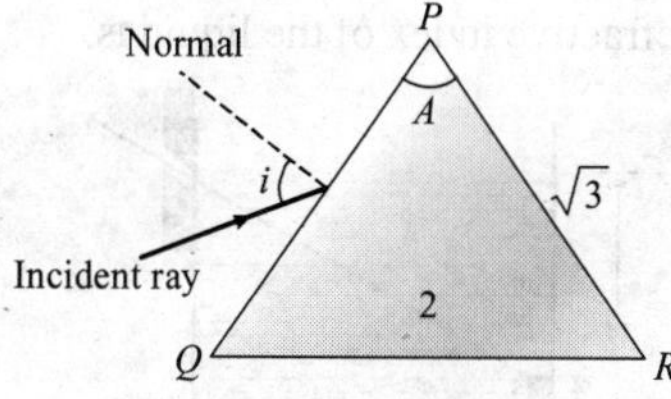

Figure 5.318

(A) 30° (B) 45°
(C) 60° (D) 120°

5-23 Two plane mirrors are joined together as shown in figure-5.319. Two point objects O_1 and O_2 are placed symmetrically such that $AO_1 = AO_2$. The image of the two objects is common if :

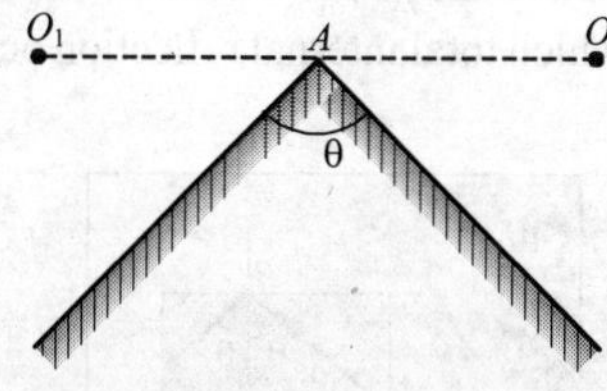

Figure 5.319

(A) $\theta = 60°$ (B) $\theta = 90°$
(C) $\theta = 30°$ (D) $\theta = 45°$

5-24 The position of a real point object and its point image are as shown in the figure-5.320. AB is the principal axis. This can be achieved by using :

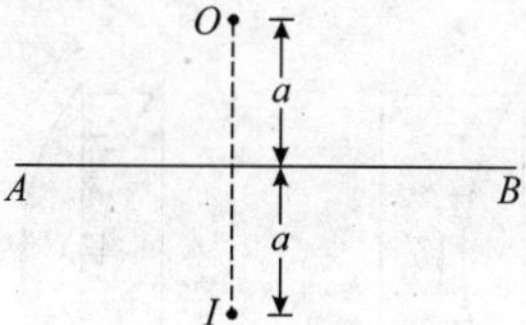

Figure 5.320

(A) Convex mirror (B) Concave mirror
(C) Plane mirror only (D) Convex mirror only

5-25 The image of the moon is produced by a convex lens of focal length f. The area of image is directly proportional to :

(A) f (B) f^2
(C) $1/f$ (D) $1/f^2$

5-26 A converging lens of focal length 20 cm and diameter 5 cm is cut along the line AB. The part of the lens shown shaded in the diagram is now used to form an image of a point P placed 30 cm away from it on the line XY, which is perpendicular to the plane of the lens. The image of P will be formed :

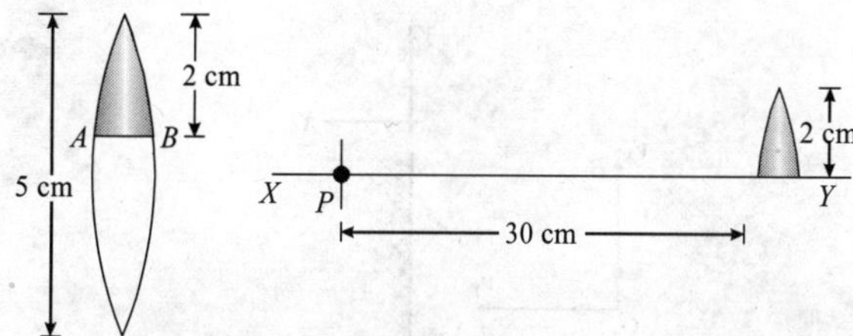

Figure 5.321

(A) 0.5 cm above XY (B) 1 cm below XY
(C) on XY (D) 1.5 cm below XY

5-27 A man stands on a glass slab of height h and inside an elevator accelerated upwards with 'a'. If μ_g is refractive index of glass then the bottom of the slab appears to have shifted with respect to the man by a distance :

(A) less than h/μ_g (B) greater than h/μ_g
(C) equal to h/μ_g (D) can't be said

5-28 When an object is at a distance u_1 and u_2 from the optical centre of a lens, a real and virtual image are formed respectively, with the same magnification. The focal length of lens is :

(A) $(u_1 + u_2)$ (B) $u_1 + \frac{u_2}{2}$

(C) $\frac{u_1 + u_2}{2}$ (D) $\frac{u_1 - u_2}{2}$

5-29 A liquid of refractive index 1.33 is placed between two identical plano-convex lenses, with refractive index 1.50. Two possible arrangement P and Q are shown in figure-5.322. The system is :

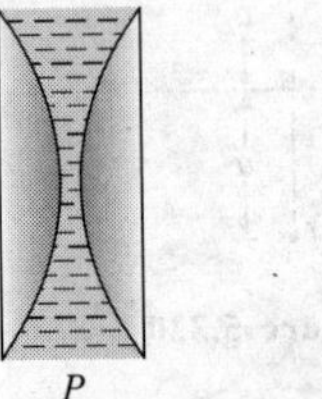

Figure 5.322

(A) Divergent in P, convergent in Q
(B) Convergent in P, divergent in Q
(C) Convergent in both
(D) Divergent in both

5-30 Two particles A & B of mass m_1 and m_2 respectively start moving from O with speeds v_1 and v_2. A moves towards the plane mirror and B moves parallel to mirror horizontally. The mirror is in y-z plane. The absolute-speed of image of centre of mass of the system (image of A + image of B) is :

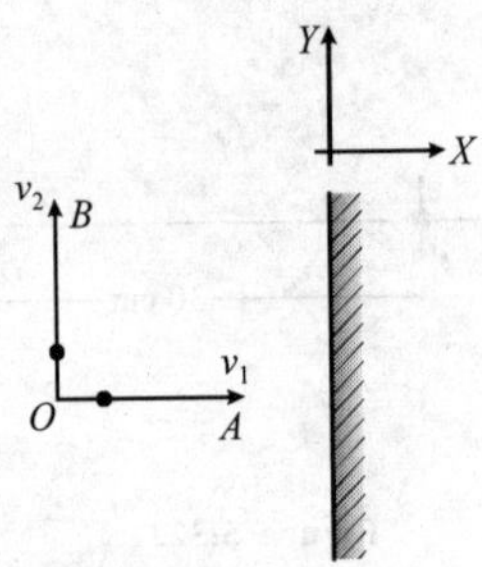

Figure 5.323

(A) Zero
(B) $\frac{m_1 v_1}{m_2}$
(C) $\frac{m_2 v_2}{m_1}$
(D) None of these

5-31 A mango tree is at the bank of a river and one of the branch of tree extends over the river. A tortoise lives in river. A mango falls just above the tortoise. The acceleration of the mango falling from tree appearing to the tortoise is (Refractive index of water is 4/3 and the tortoise is stationary):

(A) g
(B) $\frac{3g}{4}$
(C) $\frac{4g}{3}$
(D) None of these

5-32 A plane mirror having a mass m is tied to the free end of a massless spring of spring constant k. The other end of the spring is attached to a wall. The spring with the mirror held vertically to the floor on which it can slide smoothly. When the spring is at its natural length, the mirror is found to be moving at a speed of v cm/s. The separation between the images of a man standing before the mirror, when the mirror is in its extreme positions :

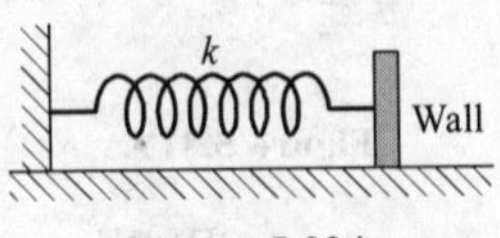

Figure 5.324

(A) $v\sqrt{\frac{m}{k}}$
(B) $\frac{v}{2}\sqrt{\frac{m}{k}}$
(C) $2v\sqrt{\frac{m}{k}}$
(D) $4v\sqrt{\frac{m}{k}}$

5-33 An observer can see, through a pinhole, the top end of a thin rod of height h, placed as shown in the figure-5.325. The beaker height is $3h$ and its radius is h. When the beaker is filled with a liquid up to a height $2h$, he can see the lower end of the rod. Then the refractive index of the liquid is:

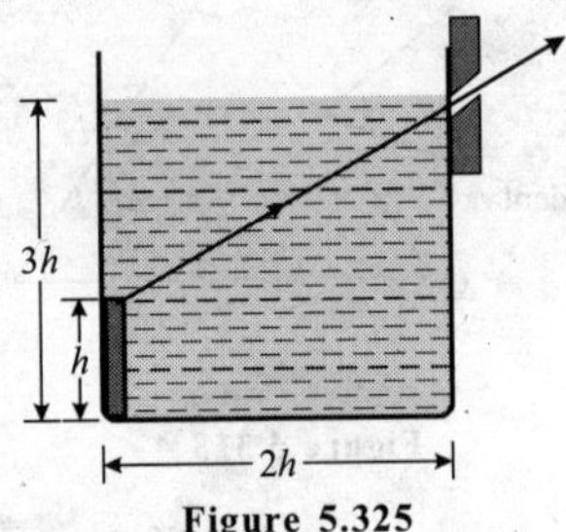

Figure 5.325

(A) 5/2
(B) $\sqrt{5/2}$
(C) $\sqrt{3/2}$
(D) 3/2

5-34 A ray of light is incident on the left vertical face of a glass cube of refractive index μ_2, as shown in figure-5.326. The plane of incident is the plane of the page, and the cube is surrounded by liquid of refractive index μ_1. What is the largest angle of incidence θ_1 for which total internal reflection occurs at the top surface?

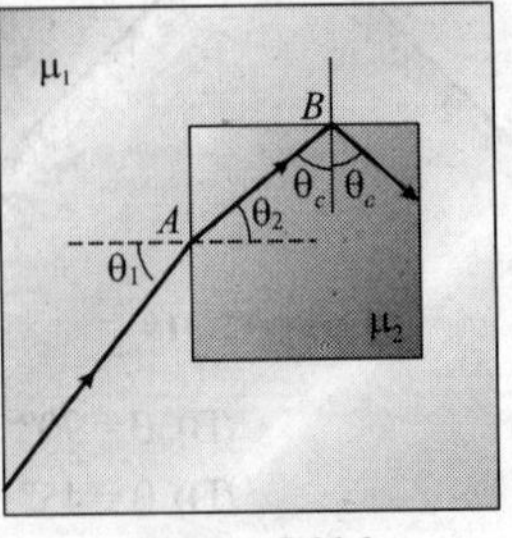

Figure 5.326

(A) $\sin 1 = \sqrt{\left(\frac{\mu_2}{\mu_1}\right)^2 - 1}$ (B) $\sin 1 = \sqrt{\left(\frac{\mu_2}{\mu_1}\right)^2 + 1}$

(C) $\sin 1 = \sqrt{\left(\frac{\mu_1}{\mu_2}\right)^2 + 1}$ (D) $\sin 1 = \sqrt{\left(\frac{\mu_1}{\mu_2}\right)^2 + 1}$

5-35 Two plane mirrors are inclined to each other at angle θ. A ray of light is reflected first at one mirror and then at the other. Find the total deviation of the ray :

(A) $360° - 2\theta$ (B) $360° + 2\theta$
(C) $180° - 2\theta$ (D) $180° + 2\theta$

5-36 Two plane mirrors are inclined to each other such that a ray of light incident on the first mirror and parallel to the second is reflected from the second mirror parallel to the first mirror. Determine the angle between the two mirrors:

(A) 60° (B) 30°
(C) 90° (D) 180°

5-37 A slab of high quality flat glass, with parallel faces, is placed in the path of a parallel light beam before it is focussed to a spot by a lens. The glass is rotated slightly back and forth from the dotted centre about an axis coming out of the page, as shown in the diagram. According to ray optics the effect on the focussed spot is:

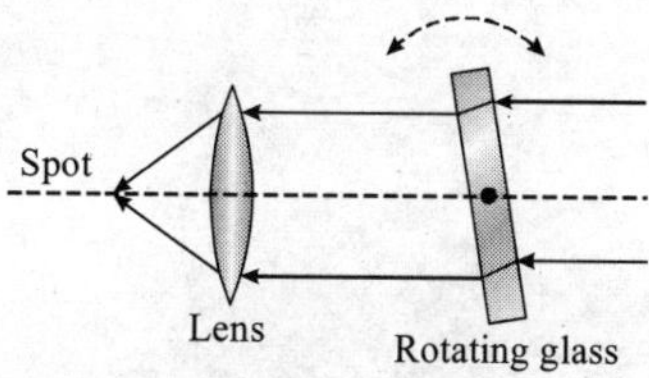

Figure 5.327

(A) There is no movement of the spot
(B) The spot moves towards then away from the lens
(C) The spot moves up and down parallel to the lens
(D) The spot moves along a line making an angle a (neither zero nor 90°) with axis of lens

5-38 A parallel glass slab of refractive index $\sqrt{3}$ is placed in contact with an equilateral prism of refractive index $\sqrt{2}$. A ray is incident on left surface of slab as shown. The slab and prism combination is surrounded by air. The magnitude of minimum possible deviation of this ray by slab-prism combination is:

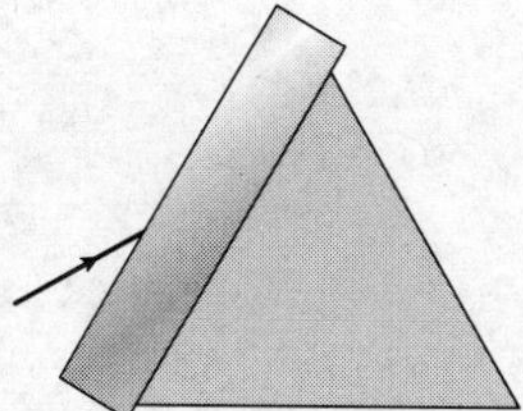
Figure 5.328

(A) 30° (B) 45°
(C) 60° (D) $60° - \sin^{-1}\sqrt{\frac{2}{3}}$

5-39 The mirror of length L moves horizontally as shown in the figure-5.329 with a velocity v. The mirror is illuminated by a point source of light 'P' placed on the ground. The rate at which the length of the light spot on the ground increases is :

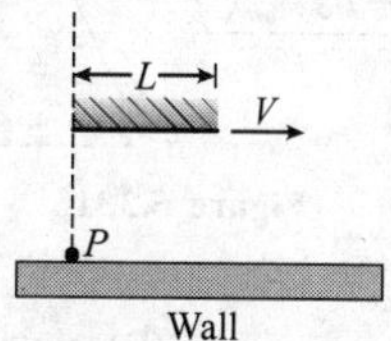

Figure 5.329

(A) v (B) Zero
(C) $2v$ (D) $3v$

5-40 Monochromatic light rays parallel to x-axis strike a convex lens AB of refractive index 0.5. If the lens oscillates such that AB tilts upto a small angle θ (in radian) on either side of y-axis, then find the distance between extreme positions of oscillating image :

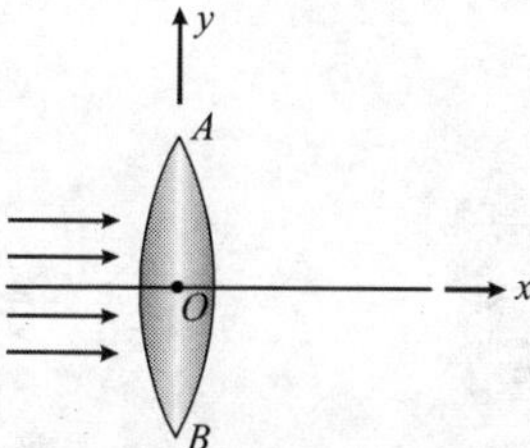

Figure 5.330

(A) $f\sec\theta$ (B) $f\sec^2\theta$
(C) $f(\sec\theta - 1)$ (D) The image will not move

5-41 The focal length of a concave mirror is f and the distance from the object to the principal focus is x. Then the ratio of the size of the image to the size of the object is:

(A) $\frac{(f+x)}{f}$ (B) $\frac{f}{x}$

(C) $\sqrt{\frac{f}{x}}$ (D) $\frac{f^2}{x^2}$

5-42 A light ray gets reflected from a pair of mutually $\perp$ mirrors, not necessarily along axes. The intersection point of mirrors is at origin. The incident light ray is along $y = x + 2$. If the light ray strikes both mirrors in succession, then it may get reflected finally along the line:

(A) $y = 2x - 2$ (B) $y = -x + 2$
(C) $y = -x - 2$ (D) $y = x - 4$

5-43 A ray is incident on the first prism at an angle of incidence 53° as shown in the figure-5.331. The angle between side *CA* and *B′A′* for the net deviation by both the prisms to be double of the deviation produced by the first prism, will be :

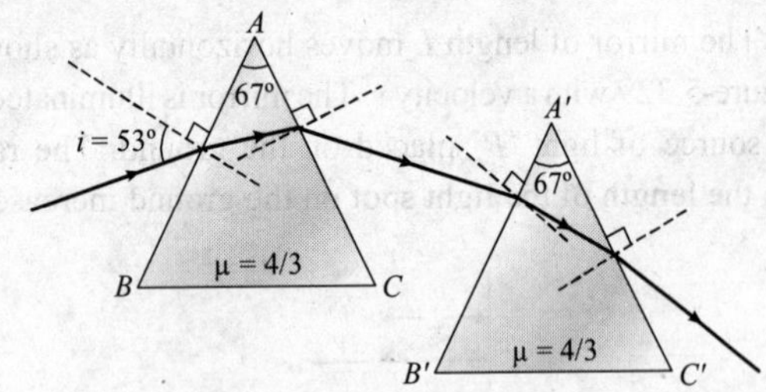

Figure 5.331

(A) $\sin^{-1}\dfrac{2}{3}+53°$ (B) $\sin^{-1}\dfrac{2}{3}+37°$

(C) $\cos^{-1}\dfrac{2}{3}+53°$ (D) $2\sin^{-1}\dfrac{2}{3}$

* * * * *

Numerical MCQs Single Option Correct

5-1 An equilateral prism deviates a ray through 45° for two angles of incidence differing by 20°. The refractive index of the prism is :

(A) 1.567 (B) 1.467
(C) 1.5 (D) 1.65

5-2 Two plane mirrors L_1 and L_2 are parallel to each other and 3 m part. A person standing x m from the right mirror L_2 looks into this mirror and sees a series of images. The distance between the first and second image is 4 m. Then the value of x is :

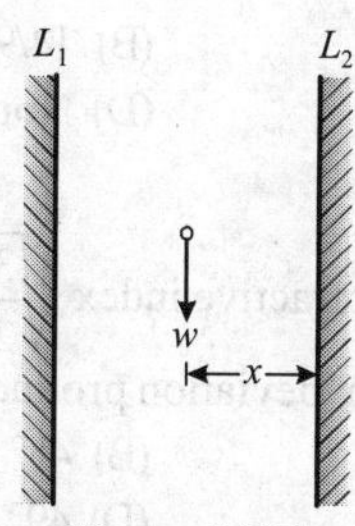

Figure 5.332

(A) 2 m (B) 1.5 m
(C) 1 m (D) 2.5 m

5-3 An elevator at rest which is at 10th floor of a building is having a plane mirror fixed to its floor. A particle is projected with a speed $\sqrt{2}$ m/s and at 45° with the horizontal as shown in the figure-5.333. At the very instant of projection, the cable of the elevator breaks and the elevator starts falling freely. What will be the separation between the particle and is image 0.5 s after the instant of projection ?

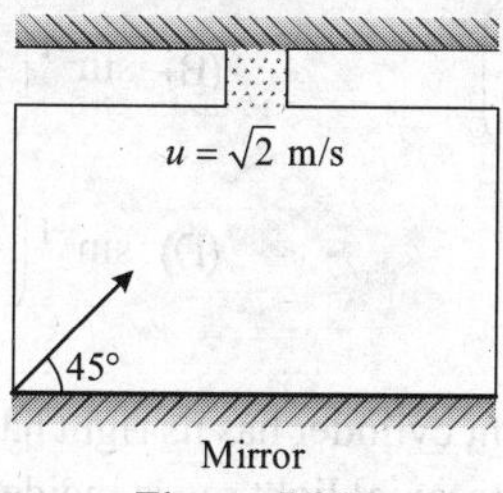

Figure 5.333

(A) 0.5 m (B) 1 m
(C) 2 m (D) 1.5 m

5-4 A plane mirror is moving with velocity $4\hat{i}+4\hat{j}+8\hat{k}$. A point object in front of the mirror moves with a velocity $3\hat{i}+4\hat{j}+5\hat{k}$. Here $\hat{k}$ is along the normal to the plane mirror and facing towards the object. The velocity of the image is :

(A) $-3\hat{i}-4\hat{j}+5\hat{k}$ (B) $3\hat{i}+4\hat{j}+11\hat{k}$
(C) $-4\hat{i}+5\hat{j}+11\hat{k}$ (D) $7\hat{i}+9\hat{j}+3\hat{k}$

5-5 Two plane mirrors AB and AC are inclined at an angle $\theta = 20°$. A ray of light starting from point P is incident at point Q on the mirror AB, then at R on mirror AC and again on S on AB. Finally the ray ST goes parallel to mirror AC. The angle which the ray makes with the normal at point Q on mirror AB is:

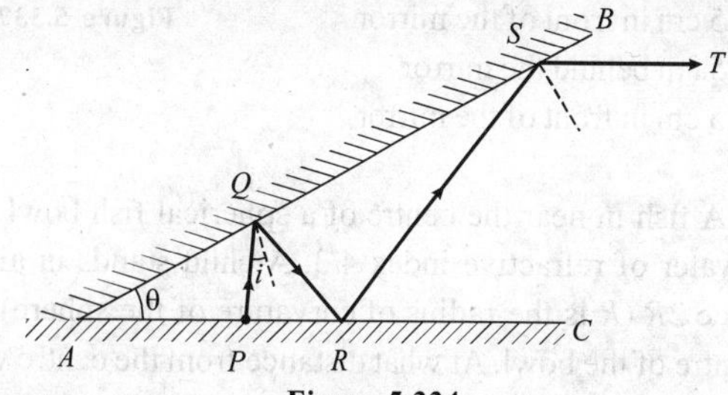

Figure 5.334

(A) 20° (B) 30°
(C) 40° (D) 60°

5-6 A person's eye level is 1.5 m. He stands in front of a 0.3 m long plane mirror which is 0.8 m above the ground. The length of the image he sees of himself is :

(A) 1.5 m (B) 1.0 m
(C) 0.8 m (D) 0.6 m

5-7 A plane mirror of length 8 cm is present near a wall in situation as shown in figure-5.335. Then the length of spot formed on the wall is :

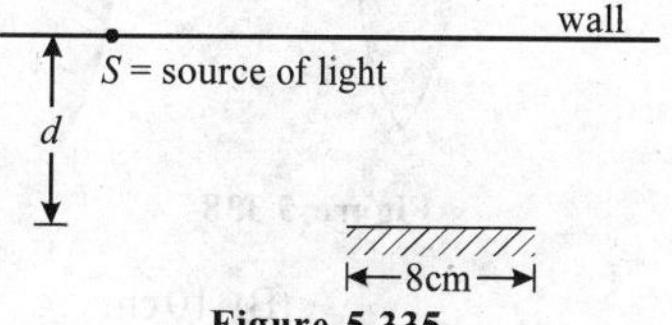

Figure 5.335

(A) 8 cm (B) 4 cm
(C) 16 cm (D) None of these

5-8 An object 'O' is kept in air in front of a thin plano-convex lens of radius of curvature 10 cm. It's refractive index is 3/2 and the medium towards right of plane surface is water of refractive index 4/3. What should be the distance 'x' of the object so that the rays become parallel finally.

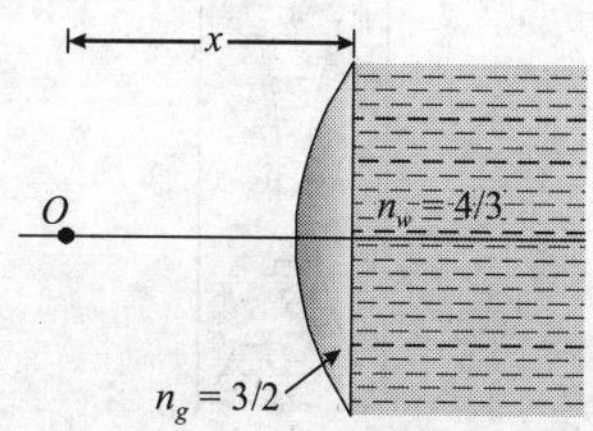

Figure 5.336

(A) 5 cm (B) 10 cm
(C) 20 cm (D) None of these

5-9 A diverging lens of focal length 10 cm is placed 10 cm in front of a plane mirror as shown in the figure-5.337. Light from a very far away source falls on the lens. The final image is at a distance :

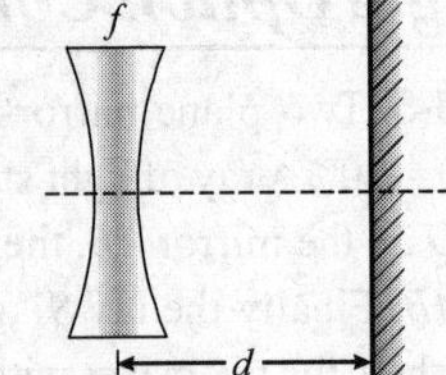

Figure 5.337

(A) 20 cm behind the mirror
(B) 7.5 cm in front of the mirror
(C) 7.5 cm behind the mirror
(D) 2.5 cm in front of the mirror

5-10 A fish in near the centre of a spherical fish bowl filled with water of refractive index 4/3. A child stands in air at a distance $2R$ (R is the radius of curvature of the sphere) from the centre of the bowl. At what distance from the centre would the child's nose appear to the fish situated at the centre :

(A) $4R$ (B) $2R$
(C) $3R$ (D) $4R$

5-11 An object is placed at a distance of 15 cm from a convex lens of focal length 10 cm. On the other side of the lens, a convex mirror is placed at its focus such that the image formed by the combination coincides with the object itself. The focal length of the convex mirror is :

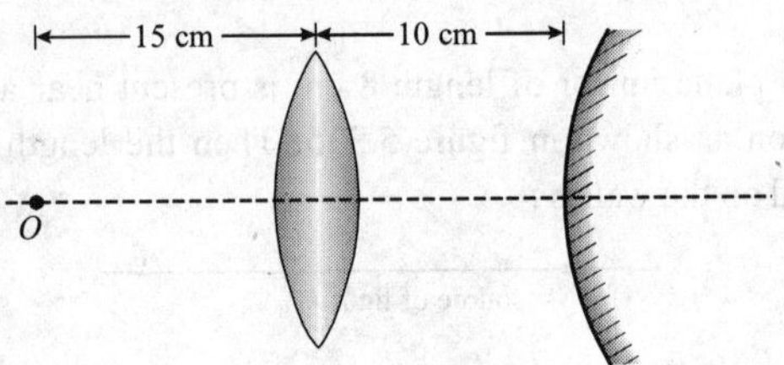

Figure 5.338

(A) 20 cm (B) 10 cm
(C) 15 cm (D) 30 cm

5-12 Two plano-convex lenses each of focal length 10 cm & refractive index 3/2 are placed as shown-5.339. Water ($\mu = 4/3$) is filled in the space between the two lenses. The whole arrangement is in air. The optical power of the system in diopters is :

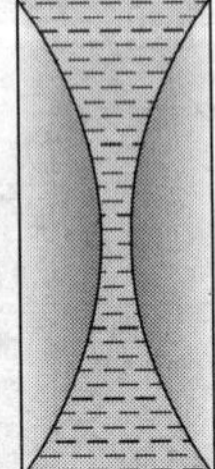
Figure 5.339

(A) 6.67 (B) –6.67
(C) 33.3 (D) 20

5-13 The curvature radii of a concavo-convex glass lens are 20 cm and 60 cm. The convex surface of the lens is silvered. With the lens horizontal, the concave surface is filled with water. The focal length of the effective mirror is (μ of glass = 1.5, μ of water = 4/3) :

(A) 90/13 cm (B) 80/13 cm
(C) 20/3 cm (D) 45/8 cm

5-14 A plano-convex lens, when silvered at its plane surface is equivalent to a concave mirror of focal length 28 cm. When its curved surface is silvered and the plane surface not silvered, it is equivalent to a concave mirror of focal length 10 cm, then the refractive index of the material of the lens is :

(A) 9/14 (B) 14/9
(C) 17/9 (D) None

5-15 A prism has a refractive index $\sqrt{\frac{3}{2}}$ and refracting angle 90°. Find the minimum deviation produced by the prism.

(A) 40° (B) 45°
(C) 30° (D) 49°

5-16 A certain prism is found to produce a minimum deviation of 38°. It produces a deviation of 44° when the angle of incidence is either 42° or 62°. What will be the angle of incidence when it undergoes minimum deviation ?

(A) 45° (B) 49°
(C) 40° (D) 55°

5-17 A light ray is incident on a prism of angle $A = 60°$ and refractive index $\mu = \sqrt{2}$. The angle of incidence at which the emergent ray grazes the surface is given by :

(A) $\sin^{-1}\left(\frac{\sqrt{3}-1}{2}\right)$ (B) $\sin^{-1}\left(\frac{1-\sqrt{3}}{2}\right)$
(C) $\sin^{-1}\left(\frac{\sqrt{3}}{2}\right)$ (D) $\sin^{-1}\left(\frac{2}{\sqrt{3}}\right)$

5-18 A transparent cylinder has its right half polished so as to act as a mirror. A paraxial light ray is incident from left, that is parallel to principal axis, exits parallel to the incident ray as shown. The refractive index n of the material of the cylinder is :

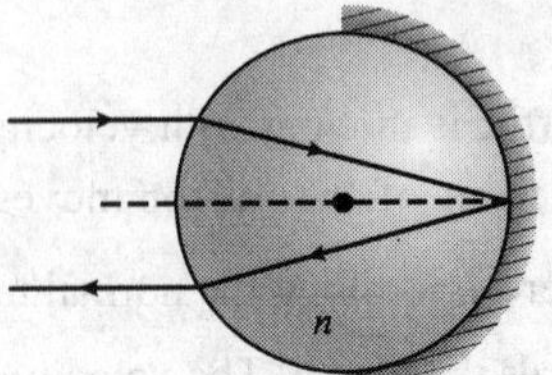

Figure 5.340

(A) 1.2 (B) 1.5
(C) 1.8 (D) 2.0

5-19 A composite slab consisting of different media is placed in front of a concave mirror of radius of curvature 150 cm. The whole arrangement is placed in water. An object O is placed at a distance 20 cm from the slab. The refractive indices of different media are given in the diagram shown in figure-5.341. Find the position of the final image formed by the system :

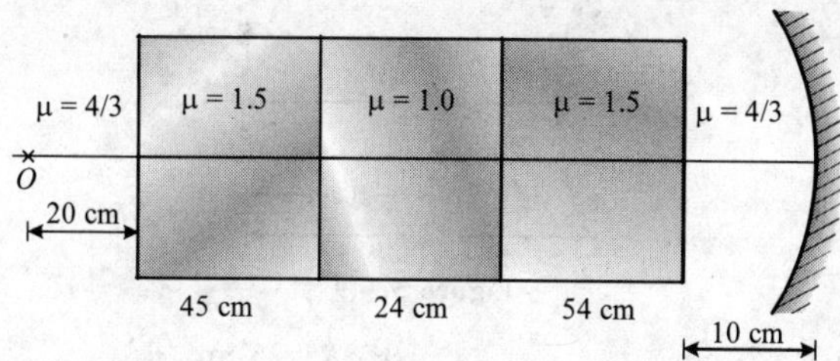

Figure 5.341

(A) To the left of Object
(B) On the Object
(C) To the right of Object
(C) Data insufficient to calculate the image position

5-20 A luminous point object is moving along the principal axis of a concave mirror of focal length 12 cm towards it. When its distance from the mirror is 20 cm its velocity is 4 cm/s. The velocity of the image in cm/s at that instant is :

(A) 6, towards the mirror (B) 6, away from the mirror
(C) 9, away from the mirror (D) 9, towards the mirror

5-21 Two blocks each of mass m lie on a smooth table. They are attached to two other masses as shown in the figure-5.342. The pulleys and strings are light. An object O is kept at rest on the table. The sides AB & CD of the two blocks are made reflecting. The acceleration of two images formed in those two reflecting surfaces w.r.t. each other is :

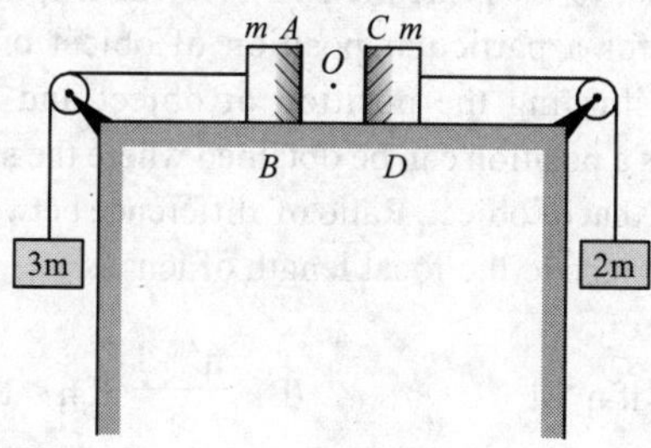

Figure 5.342

(A) $5g/6$ (B) $5g/3$
(C) $g/3$ (D) $17g/6$

5-22 An opaque sphere of radius a is just immersed in a transparent liquid as shown in figure-5.343. A point source is placed on the vertical diameter of the sphere at a distance $a/2$ from the top of the sphere. One ray originating from the point source after refraction from the air liquid interface forms tangent to the sphere. The angle of refraction for that particular ray is 30°. The refractive index of the liquid is :

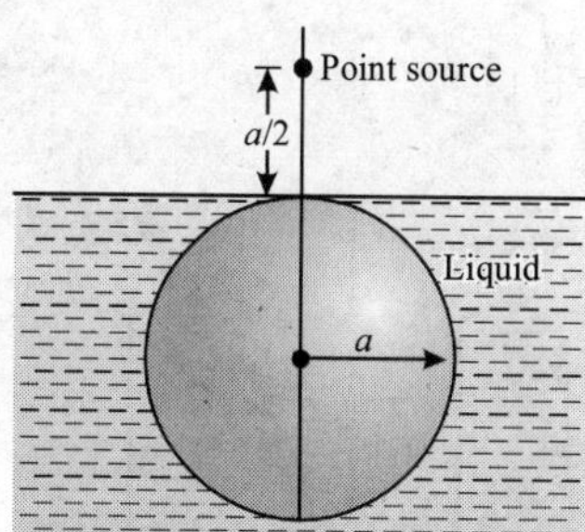

Figure 5.343

(A) $\frac{2}{\sqrt{3}}$ (B) $\frac{3}{\sqrt{5}}$

(C) $\frac{4}{\sqrt{5}}$ (D) $\frac{4}{\sqrt{7}}$

5-23 In the figure-5.344 ABC is the cross section of a right angled prism and $BCDE$ is the cross section of a glass slab. The value of θ so that light incident normally on the face AB does not cross the face BC is (given $\sin^{-1}(3/5) = 37°$) :

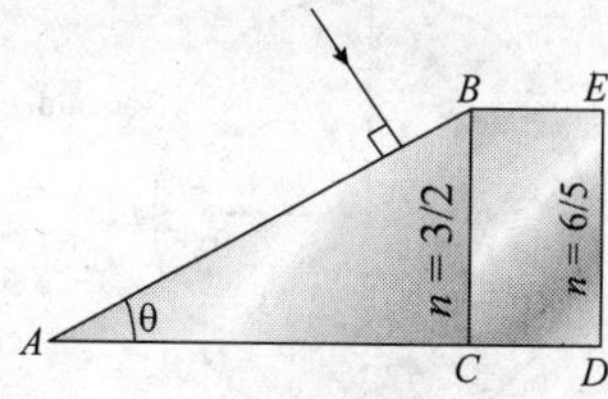

Figure 5.344

(A) $\theta \le 37°$ (B) $\theta < 37°$
(C) $\theta \le 53°$ (D) $\theta < 53°$

5-24 A linear object AB is placed along the axis of a concave mirror. The object is moving towards the mirror with speed V. The speed of the image of the point A is $4V$ and the speed of the image of B is also $4V$. If centre of the line AB is at a distance L from the mirror then length of the object AB will be :

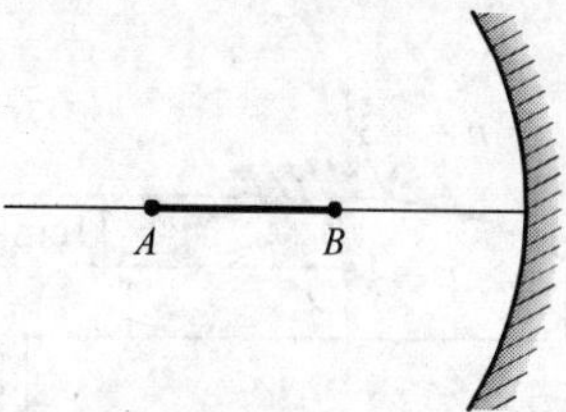

Figure 5.345

(A) $\frac{3L}{2}$ (B) $\frac{5L}{3}$

(C) L (D) $\frac{4L}{3}$

5-25 A small rod ABC is put in water making an angle 6° with vertical. If it is viewed paraxially from above, it will look like bent shaped ABC'. The angle of bending ($\angle CBC'$) will be in degree is $\left(n_w = \frac{4}{3}\right)$.

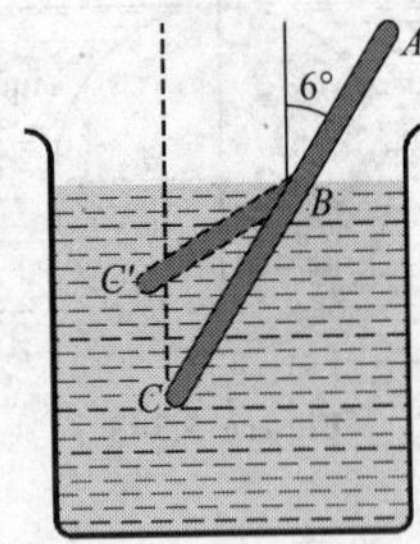

Figure 5.346

(A) 2°
(B) 3°
(C) 4°
(D) 4.5°

5-26 It is found that all electromagnetic signals sent from A towards B reach point C. The speed of electromagnetic signals in glass can not be :

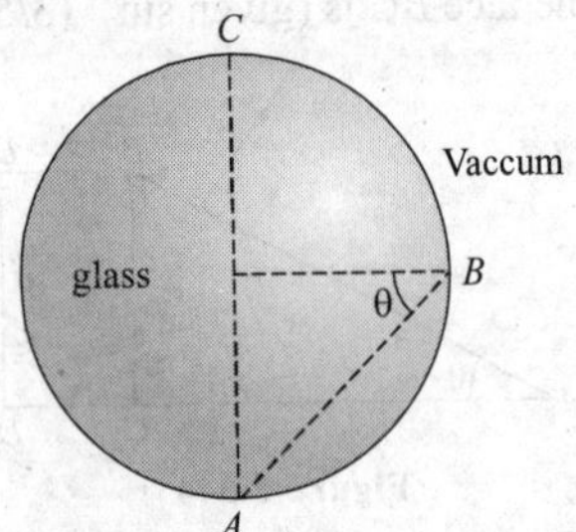

Figure 5.347

(A) 1.0×10^8 m/s
(B) 2.4×10^8 m/s
(C) 2×10^7 m/s
(D) 4×10^7 m/s

5-27 A concave mirror of focal length 2 cm is placed on a glass slab as shown in the figure-5.348. Then the image of object O formed due to reflection at mirror and then refraction by the slab is :

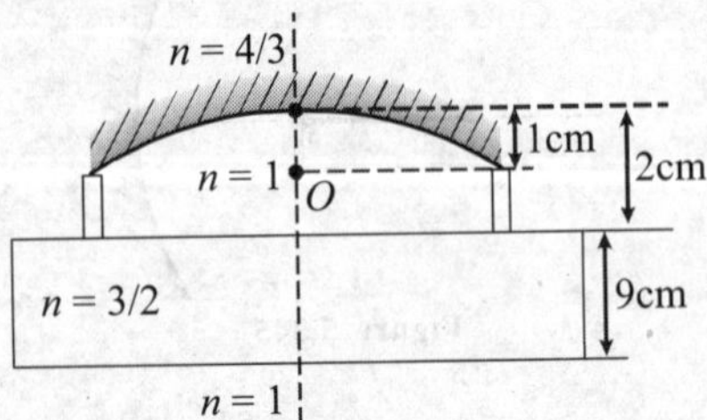

Figure 5.348

(A) Will be virtual and will be at 2 cm from the pole of the concave mirror
(B) Will be virtual and formed on the pole of the mirror
(C) Will be real and on the object itself
(D) None of these

5-28 In the figure-5.349, an object is placed 25 cm from the surface of a convex mirror, and a plane mirror is set so that the image formed by the two mirrors lie adjacent to each other in the same plane. The plane mirror is placed at 20 cm from the object. What is the radius of curvature of the convex mirror?

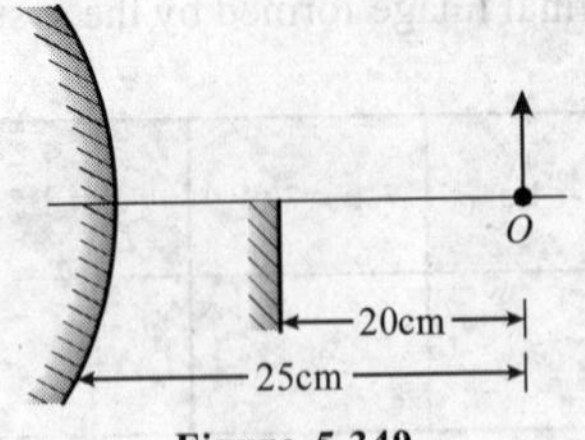

Figure 5.349

(A) $R = 80$ cm
(B) $R = 25$ cm
(C) $R = 75$ cm
(D) None of these

5-29 A uniform, horizontal parallel beam of light is incident upon a prism as shown-5.350. The prism is in the shape of a quarter cylinder, of radius 5 cm, and has refractive index 5/3. The width of the region at which the incident rays after normal incidence on plane surface and subsequent refraction at curved surface intersect on x axis is (Neglect the ray which travels along x-axis)

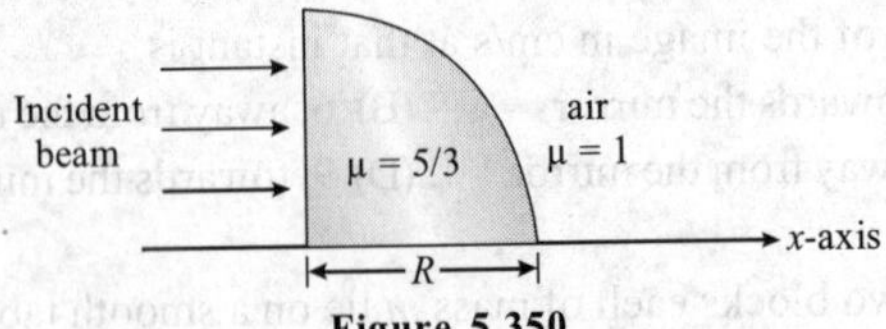

Figure 5.350

(A) 4 cm
(B) 5/4 cm
(C) 9/4 cm
(D) 25/4 cm

5-30 Sharp image of extended object which is placed perpendicular to the principle axis of a lens is η times that of the object for a particular position of object on a screen. Without disturbing the position of object and screen, by shifting lens a position can be obtained where the sharp image is 1/η times that of object. Ratio of difference between the two positions of lens to the focal length of lens is:

(A) $\frac{\eta^2 - 1}{\eta}$ if $\eta > 1$
(B) $\frac{\eta^2 - 1}{\eta}$ if $\eta < 1$

(C) $\frac{\eta^2 - 1}{\eta}$ for all values of η
(D) η

5-31 A beaker is filled with water as shown in figure-5.351(a). The bottom surface of the beaker is a concave mirror of large radius of curvature and small aperture. The height of water is $h = 40$ cm. It is found that when an object is placed 4 cm above the water surface, the image coincides with the object. Now the water level h is reduced to zero but there will still be some water left in the concave part of the mirror as shown in figure-5.351(b). The new height of the object h' above the new water surface so that the image again coincides with the object, will be: (Refractive index of water = 4/3)

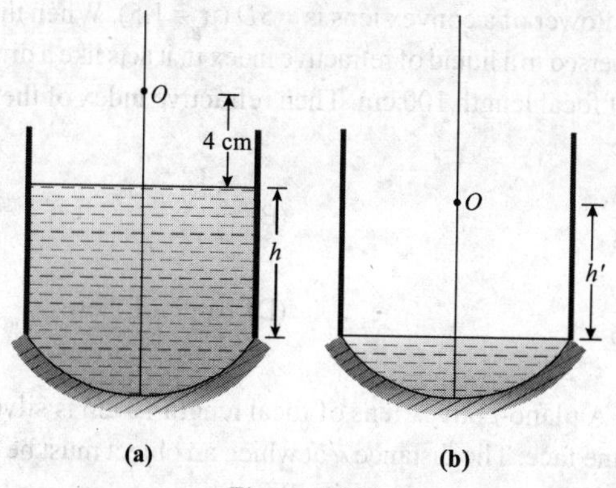

Figure 5.351

(A) 34 cm (B) 10 cm
(C) 74 cm (D) Zero

5-32 Which of the following relations is correct for a spherical mirror if a point object is kept on the principal axis. Here 'P' is the pole, 'C' is centre of curvature of mirror, 'O' is the location where object is placed, and image is produced at point 'I'.

(A) $\frac{OP}{OC}=\frac{IP}{IC}$ (B) $\frac{OP}{IC}=\frac{IP}{OC}$

(C) $\frac{PC}{PO}=\frac{PI}{PC}$ (D) $\frac{IO}{CP}=\frac{IP}{CO}$

5-33 A plane mirror is placed with its plane at an angle 30° with the y-axis. Plane of the mirror is perpendicular to the xy-plane and the length of the mirror is 3 m. An insect moves along x-axis starting from a distant point, with speed 2 cm/s. The duration of the time for which the insect can see its shown image in the mirror is :

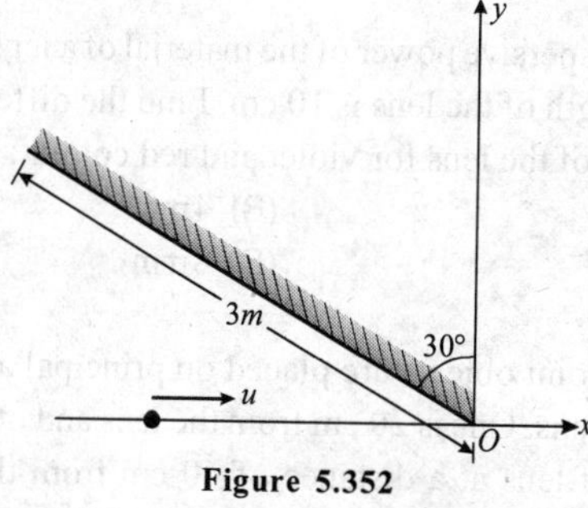

Figure 5.352

(A) 300 s (B) 200 s
(C) 150 s (D) 100 s

5-34 A particle revolves in clockwise direction (as seen from point A) in a circle C of radius 1 cm and completes one revolution in 2 sec. The axis of the circle and the principal axis of the mirror M coincide. The radius of curvature of the mirror is 20 cm. Then the direction of revolution (as seen from A) of the image of the particle and its speed is :

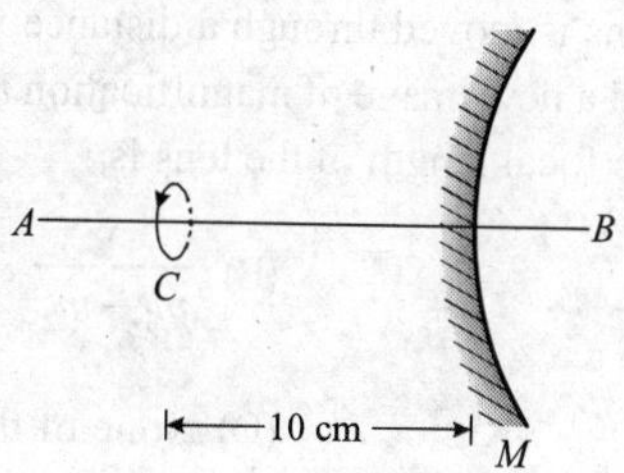

Figure 5.353

(A) Clockwise, 1.57 cm/s (B) Clockwise, 3.14 cm/s
(C) Anticlockwise, 1.57 cm/s (D) Anticlockwise, 3.14 cm/s

5-35 An elevator at rest which is at 10th floor of a building is having a plane mirror fixed to its floor. A particle is projected with a speed $\sqrt{2}$ m/s and at 45° with the horizontal as shown in the figure. At the very instant of projection, the cable of the elevator breaks and the elevator starts falling freely. What will be the separation between the particle and its image 0.5 second after the instant of projection?

(A) 0.5 m (B) 1 m
(C) 2 m (D) 1.5 m

5-36 A beam of light converges towards a point 10 cm behind the concave mirror of focal length 20 cm. The distance of image from pole of the mirror is :

(A) 10 cm in front of mirror (B) 20 cm in front of mirror
(C) 10/3 cm behind the mirror (D) 20/3 cm in front of mirror

5-37 Two thin slabs of refractive indices μ_1 and μ_2 are placed parallel to each other in the x-z plane. If the direction of propagation of a ray in the two media are along the vectors $\vec{r}_1 = a\hat{i} + b\hat{j}$ and $\vec{r}_2 = c\hat{i} + d\hat{j}$ then we have :

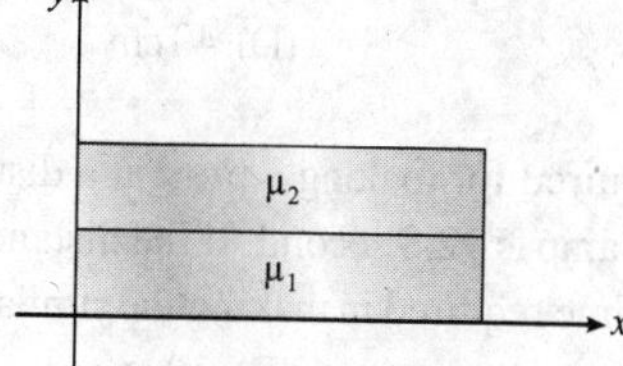

Figure 5.354

(A) $\mu_1 a = \mu_2 b$ (B) $\frac{\mu_1 a}{\sqrt{a^2+b^2}} = \frac{\mu_2 a}{\sqrt{c^2+d^2}}$

(C) $\mu_1(a^2+b^2) = \mu_2(c^2+d^2)$ (D) None of these

5-38 A particle moves towards a concave mirror of focal length 30 cm along its axis and with a constant speed of 4 cm/sec. What is the speed of its image when the particle is at 90 cm from the mirror?

(A) 2 cm/sec (B) 8 cm/sec
(C) 1 cm/sec (D) 4 cm/sec

5-39 A screen beaming a real image of magnification m_1 formed by a convex lens is moved through a distance x. The object is the moved until a new image of magnification m_2 is formed on the screen. The focal length of the lens is :

(A) $\frac{x}{m_2 - m_1}$ (B) $\frac{x}{m_1 - m_2}$

(C) $\frac{x}{\sqrt{m_1 m_2}}$ (D) None of these

5-40 A ray incident at a point at an angle of incidence of 60° enters a glass sphere with refractive index $\sqrt{3}$ and it is reflected and refracted at the farther surface of the sphere. The angle between the reflected and refracted rays at this surface is:

(A) 50° (B) 60°

(C) 90° (D) 40°

5-41 A layer of oil 3 cm thick is floating on a layer of coloured water 5 cm thick. Refractive index of coloured water is 5/3 and the apparent depth of the two liquids appears to be 36/7 cm. Find the refractive index of oil :

(A) 1.6 (B) 1.4

(C) 1.9 (D) 0.9

5-42 A small filament is at the centre of a hollow glass sphere of inner and outer radii 8 cm and 9 cm respectively. The refractive index of glass is 1.50. Calculate the position of the image of the filament when viewed from outside the sphere.

(A) 9 cm (B) – 9 cm

(C) – 19 cm (D) +19 cm

5-43 Both radii of curvature of a convex lens are 20 cm and refractive index of the material of the lens is 1.5. Rays parallel to the axis of the lens will converge at:

(A) 10 cm (B) 20 cm

(C) 30 cm (D) 40 cm

5-44 Time required for making a print at a distance of 40 cm from a 60 watt lamp is 12.8 second. If the distance is decreased to 25 cm, then time required in making the similar print will be :

(A) 15 sec (B) 10 sec

(C) 5 sec (D) Remains some

5-45 Find the maximum angle of deviation for a prism with angle $A = 60°$ and $\mu = 1.5$:

(A) 50° (B) 58°

(C) 64° (D) 60°

5-46 A glass sphere ($\mu = 1.5$) of radius 8 cm is placed in sunlight. Where is the image of the sun formed by the light passing through the sphere after refraction by second surface of sphere?

(A) 4 cm (B) 6 cm

(C) 15 cm (D) 50 cm

5-47 Power of a convex lens is $+5D$ ($\mu_g = 1.5$). When this lens is immersed in a liquid of refractive index μ, it acts like a divergent lens of focal length 100 cm. Then refractive index of the liquid will be:

(A) $\frac{5}{3}$ (B) $\frac{5}{4}$

(C) $\frac{6}{5}$ (D) None of these

5-48 A plano-convex lens of focal length 10 cm is silvered at its plane face. The distance d at which an object must be placed in order to get its image on itself is :

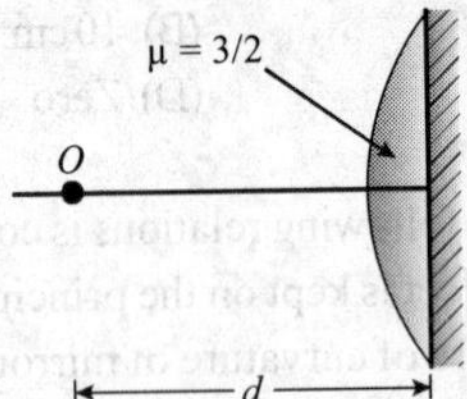

Figure 5.355

(A) 5 cm (B) 20 cm

(C) 10 cm (D) 2.5 cm

5-49 A lens of focal length 20.0 cm and aperture radius 2.0 cm is placed at a distance 30.0 cm from a point source of light. On the other side a screen is placed at a distance 50.0 cm from the lens. The radius of spot of light formed on screen is. (Neglect spherical aberration through lens):

(A) 0.5 cm (B) 0.3 cm

(C) 0.2 cm (D) 1.0 cm

5-50 The dispersive power of the material of a lens is 0.04 and the focal length of the lens is 10 cm. Find the difference in the focal length of the lens for violet and red colour :

(A) 2 mm (B) 4 mm

(C) 6 mm (D) 8 mm

5-51 Two point objects are placed on principal axis of a thin converging lens. One is 20 cm from the lens and other is on the other side of lens at a distance of 40 cm from the lens. The images of both objects coincide. The magnitude of focal length of lens is :

(A) $\frac{80}{3}$ cm (B) $\frac{40}{3}$ cm

(C) 40 cm (D) $\frac{20}{3}$ cm

* * * * *

Advance MCQs with One or More Options Correct

5-1 A point source of light S is placed on the axis of a lens of focal length 20 cm as shown in figure-5.356. A screen is placed normal to the axis of lens at a distance x from it. Treat all rays as paraxial.

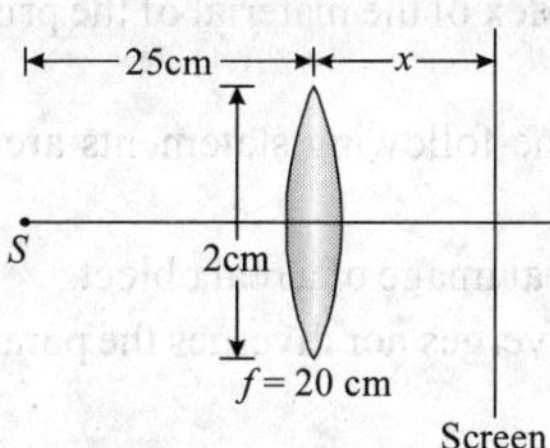

Figure 5.356

(A) As x is increased from zero, intensity continuously decreases

(B) As x is increased from zero, intensity first increases and then decreases

(C) Intensity at centre of screen for $x = 90$ cm and $x = 110$ cm is same

(D) radius of bright circle obtained on screen is equal to 1 cm for $x = 200$ cm

5-2 A point object is placed at 30 cm from a convex glass lens $\left(\mu_g = \frac{3}{2}\right)$ of focal length 20 cm. The final image of object will be formed at infinity if :

(A) Another concave lens of focal length 60 cm is placed in contact with the previous lens

(B) Another convex lens of focal length 60 cm is placed at a distance of 30 cm from the first lens

(C) The whole system is immersed in a liquid of refractive index 4/3

(D) The whole system is immersed in liquid of refractive index 9/8

5-3 A converging lens of focal length f_1 is placed in front of and coaxial with a convex mirror of focal length f_2. Their separation is d. A parallel beam of light incident on the lens returns as a parallel beam from the arrangement :

(A) The beam diameters of the incident and reflected beams must be the same

(B) $d = |f_1| - 2|f_2|$

(C) $d = |f_1| - |f_2|$

(D) If the entire arrangement is immersed in water, the conditions will remain unaltered

5-4 Two plane mirrors M_1 and M_2 are placed parallel to each other 20 cm apart. A luminous point object 'O' is placed between them at 5 cm from M_1 as shown in figure-5.357 :

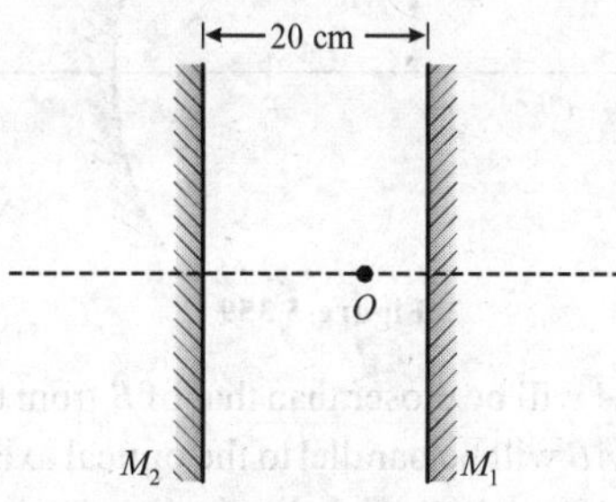

Figure 5.357

(A) The distances (in cm) of three nearest images from mirror M_1 are 5, 35 and 45 respectively

(B) The distances (in cm) of three nearest images from mirror M_2 are 5, 35 and 45 respectively

(C) The distances (in cm) of three neatest images from mirror M_1 are 15, 25 and 55 respectively

(D) The distances (in cm) of three nearest images from mirror M_2 are 15, 25 and 55 respectively

5-5 A ray of light is incident normally on one face of 30° – 60° – 90° prism of refractive index $\frac{5}{3}$, immersed in water of refractive index $\frac{4}{3}$ as shown in the figure-5.358:

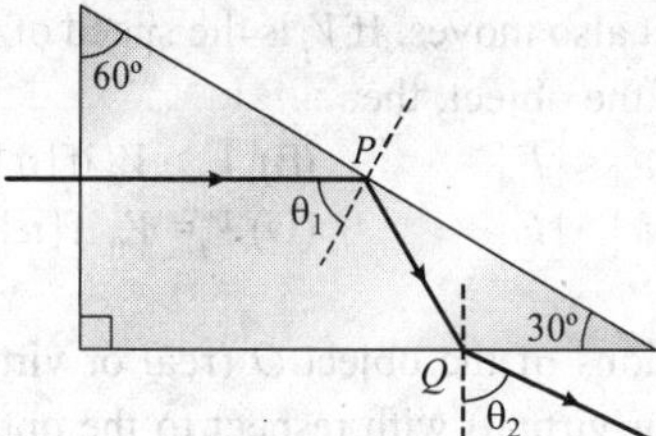

Figure 5.358

(A) The exit angle θ_2 of the ray is $\sin^{-1}\left(\frac{5}{8}\right)$

(B) The exit angle θ_2 of the ray is $\sin^{-1}\left(\frac{5}{4\sqrt{3}}\right)$

(C) Total internal reflection at point ceases if the refractive index of water in increased to $\frac{5}{2\sqrt{3}}$ by dissolving some substance

(D) Total internal reflection at point P ceases if the refractive index of water is increased to $\frac{5}{6}$ by dissolving some substance

5-6 An object AB is placed parallel and close to the optical axis between focus F and centre of curvature C of a converging mirror of focal length f as shown in figure-5.359:

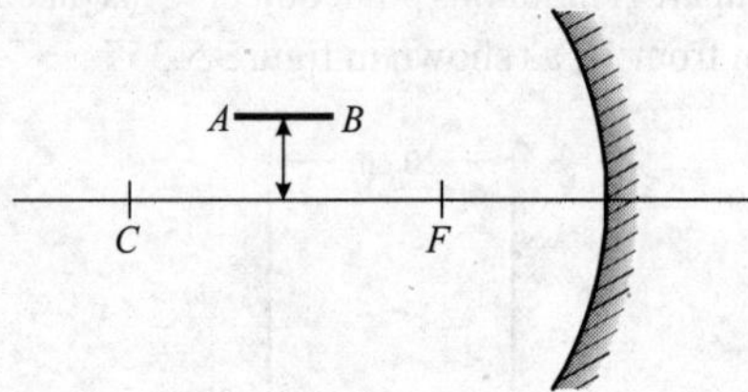

Figure 5.359

(A) Image of A will be closer than that of B from the mirror
(B) Image of AB will be parallel to the optical axis
(C) Image of AB will be straight line inclined to the optical axis
(D) Image of AB will not be straight line

5-7 Which of the following statements is/are correct about the refraction of light from a plane surface when light ray is incident in denser medium. [θ_C is critical angle]

(A) The maximum angle of deviation during refraction is $\frac{\pi}{2} - \theta_C$, it will be at angle of incidence is θ_C
(B) The maximum angle of deviation for all angle of incidences is $\pi - 2\theta_C$, when angle of incidence is slightly greater than θ_C
(C) If angle of incidence is less than θ_C then deviation increases if angle of incidence is also increased
(D) If angle of incidence is greater than θ_C then angle of deviation decreases if angle of incidence is increased

5-8 A particle is moving towards a fixed convex mirror. The image of object also moves. If V_i is the speed of image and V_0 is the speed of the object, then :

(A) $V_i \le V_0$ if $|u| < |F|$ (B) $V_i > V_0$ if $|u| > |F|$
(C) $V_i < V_0$ if $|u| > |F|$ (D) $V_i = V_0$ if $|u| = |F|$

5-9 The positions of the object O (real or virtual) and the image I (real or virtual) with respect to the optical axis of a spherical mirror is shown in figure-5.360. Then select the possible mirror and its position to realise it :

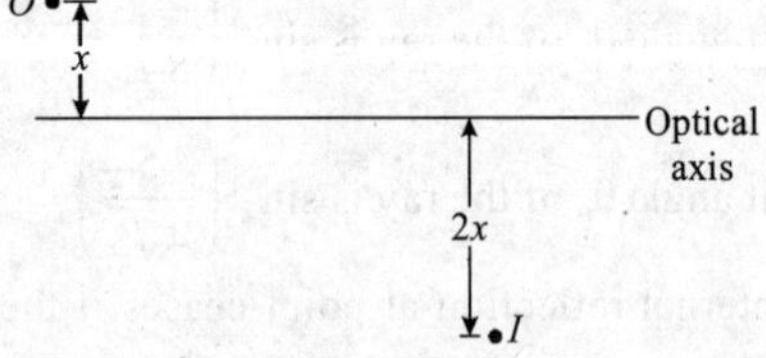

Figure 5.360

(A) Concave mirror closer to object
(B) Concave mirror closer to image
(C) Convex mirror closer to object
(D) Convex mirror closer to image

5-10 A small air bubble is trapped inside a transparent cube of size 12 cm. When viewed from one of the vertical faces, the bubble appears to be at 5 cm from it. When viewed from opposite face, it appears at 3 cm from it :

(A) The distance of the air bubble from the first face is 7.5 cm
(B) The distance of the air bubble from the first face is 9 cm
(C) Refractive index of the material of the prism is 2.0
(D) Refractive index of the material of the prism is 1.5

5-11 Which of the following statements are true for a plane mirror :

(A) It can form real image of a real object
(B) It neither converges nor diverges the parallel rays incident on it
(C) It cannot form real image of a real object
(D) None of these

5-12 A convex lens forms an image of an object on a screen. The height of the image is 9 cm. The lens is now displaced until an image is again obtained on the screen. The height of this image is 4 cm. The distance between the object and the screen is 90 cm :

(A) The distance between the two positions of the lens is 30 cm
(B) The distance of the object from the lens in its first position is 36 cm
(C) The height of the object is 6 cm
(D) The focal length of the lens is 21.6 cm

5-13 A ray of light is incident on an equilateral triangular prism parallel to its base as shown in the figure-5.361. The ray just fails to emerge from the face AC. If μ be the refractive index of the prism then the incorrect relation (s) is/are :

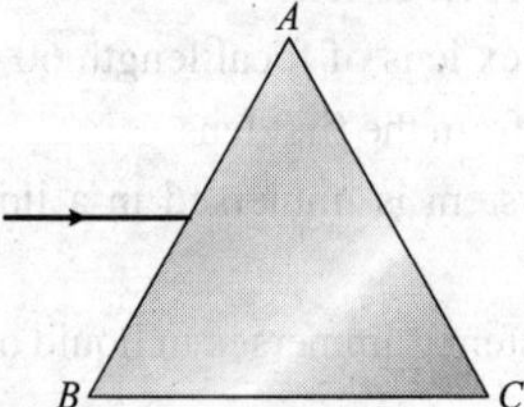

Figure 5.361

(A) $2\sin^{-1}\left(\frac{1}{\mu}\right) = \pi/3$

(B) $\sin^{-1}\left(\frac{1}{\mu}\right) + \sin^{-1}\left(\frac{1}{2\mu}\right) = \frac{\pi}{6}$

(C) $\sin^{-1}\left(\frac{1}{\mu}\right) + \sin^{-1}\left(\frac{1}{2\mu}\right) = \frac{\pi}{3}$

(D) $\sin^{-1}\left(\frac{1}{\mu}\right) + \sin^{-1}\left(\frac{\mu}{4}\right) = \frac{\pi}{3}$

5-14 A convex lens forms a real image of an object with magnification 0.5. If the object is displaced by 20 cm along the principal axis, a real image equal to the size of the object is formed :
(A) the focal length of lens is 20 cm
(B) the distance of the image from the lens initially is 25 cm
(C) the distance of the object from the lens initially is 60 cm
(D) the distance of the image finally from the lens is 30 cm

5-15 Sun ray are incident at an angle of 24° with the horizon. They be directed parallel to the horizon using a plane mirror for this plane mirror should be placed at an angle :
(A) 12° to the horizontal (B) 48° to the horizontal
(C) 72° to the horizontal (D) 78° to the horizontal

5-16 At what values of the refractive index of a rectangular prism can a ray travel as shown in figure-362. The section of the prism is an isosceles triangle & the ray is normally incident onto the face *AC*.

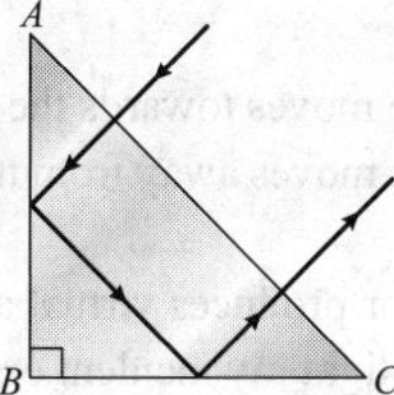

Figure 5.362

(A) $\mu>1.2$ (B) $\mu>1.3$
(C) $\mu>1.5$ (D) $\mu>1.7$

5-17 Two plane mirrors are inclined to each other with their reflecting faces making acute angle. A light ray is incident on one plane mirror. The total deviation after two successive reflections is:
(A) Independent of the initial angle of incidence
(B) Independent of the angle between the mirrors
(C) Dependent on the initial angle of incidence
(D) Dependent on the angle between the mirrors

5-18 An equiconvex lens of refractive index μ_2 is placed such that the refractive :

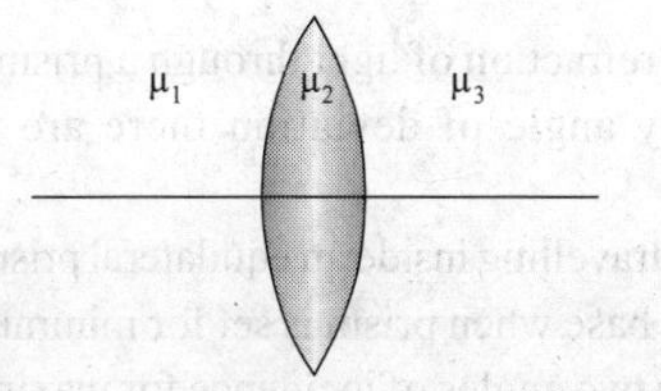

Figure 5.363

(A) Must be diverging if μ_2 is less than the arithmetic mean of μ_1 and μ_3
(B) Must be converging if μ_2 is greater than the arithmetic mean of μ_1 and μ_3
(C) May be diverging if μ_2 is less than the arithmetic mean of μ_1 and μ_3
(D) Will neither be diverging nor converging if μ_2 is equal to arithmetic mean of μ_1 and μ_3

5-19 A ray of light is incident on a prism of refracting angle *A*. If θ_C is the critical angle for the material of the prism with respect to the surrounding air, then :
(A) An emergent ray will be there for all values of θ_C
(B) An emergent ray will be there only for $A<2\theta_C$
(C) A ray incident at an angle *i* can pass through the prism if $\sin i > \dfrac{\sin(A-\theta_C)}{\sin\theta_C}$ for $\theta_C<A<2\theta_C$
(D) None of above is correct

5-20 A point source of light is placed at a distance *h* below the surface of a large and deep lake. If *f* is the fraction of light energy that escapes directly from water surface and μ is refractive index of water then :
(A) *f* varies as a function of *h*
(B) *f* is independent of value of *h*
(C) *f* depends only on the refractive index of water
(D) *f* is independent of refractive index of water

5-21 In the figure shown-5.364 a point object *O* is placed in air on the principal axis. The radius of curvature of the spherical surface is 60 cm. I_f is the final image formed after all the refractions and reflections:

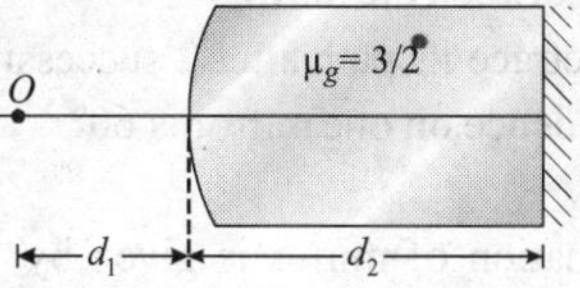

Figure 5.364

(A) If $d_1 = 120$ cm, then the 'I_f' is formed on '*O*' for any value of d_2
(B) If $d_1 = 240$ cm, then the 'I_f' is formed on '*O*' only if $d_2 = 360$ cm
(C) If $d_1 = 240$ cm, then the 'I_f' is formed on '*O*' for all value of d_2
(D) If $d_1 = 240$ cm, then the 'I_f' cannot be formed on '*O*'

5-22 A fish, *F* in the pond is at a depth of 0.8 m from water surface and is moving vertically upwards with velocity 2 ms^{-1}. At the same instant a bird *B* is at a height of 6 m from water surface and is moving downwards with velocity 3 ms^{-1}. At this instant both are on the same vertical line as shown in figure-5.365. Which of the following statements is/are correct ?

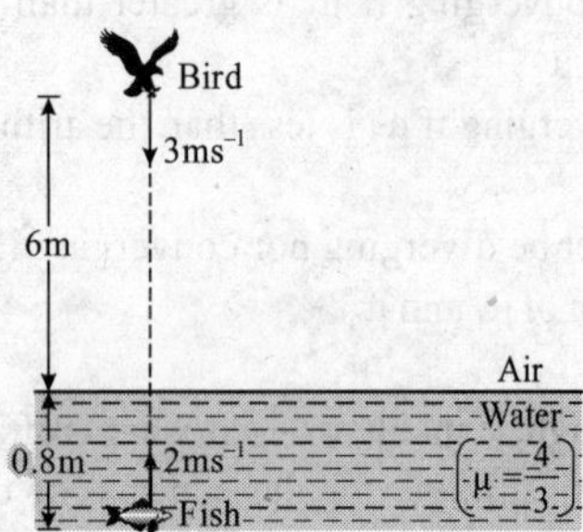

Figure 5.365

(A) height of B, observed by F (from itself)
(B) depth of F, observed by B (from itself) is equal to 6.60 m
(C) height of B, observed by F (from itself) is equal to 8.80 m
(D) none of these

5-23 A man of height 170 cm wants to see his complete image in a plane mirror (while standing). His eyes are at a height of 160 cm from the ground, then to see his complete image :
(A) Minimum length of the mirror = 80 cm
(B) Minimum length of the mirror = 85 cm
(C) Bottom of the mirror should be at a height 80 cm
(D) Bottom of the mirror should be at a height 85 cm

5-24 Two plane mirrors at an angle such that a ray incident on a mirror undergoes a total deviation of 240° after two reflections :
(A) the angle between the mirrors is 60°
(B) the number of images formed by this system will be 5, if an object is placed symmetrically between the mirrors
(C) the number of images will be 5 if an object is kept unsymmetrical between the mirrors
(D) a ray will retrace its path after 2 successive reflections, if the angle of incidence on one mirror is 60°

5-25 If the equation of mirror is given by $y = (2/\pi)\sin\pi x$ $(y > 0, 0 \le x \le 1)$ then find the point on which horizontal ray should be incident so that the reflected ray become perpendicular to the incident ray :

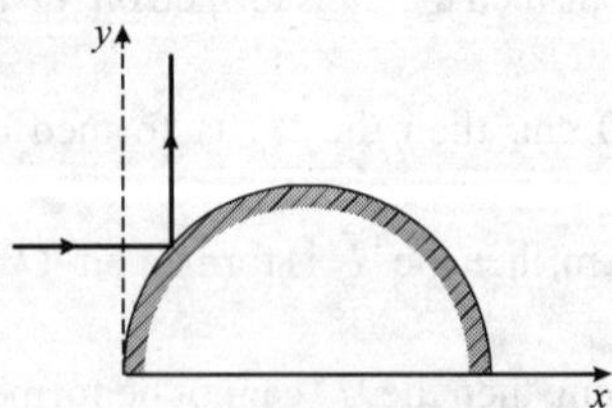

Figure 5.366

(A) $\left(\frac{1}{3}, \frac{\sqrt{3}}{\pi}\right)$ (B) $\left(\frac{\sqrt{3}}{\pi}, \frac{1}{3}\right)$

(C) $\left(\frac{2}{3}, \frac{\sqrt{3}}{\pi}\right)$ (D) (1,0)

5-26 AB is a straight rod kept along the principal axis of a convex mirror in front of it as shown in figure-5.367. Another plane mirror is placed in front of the convex mirror and facing it. In the figure shown consider the first reflection at the plane mirror and second at the convex mirror then which is of the following is correct.

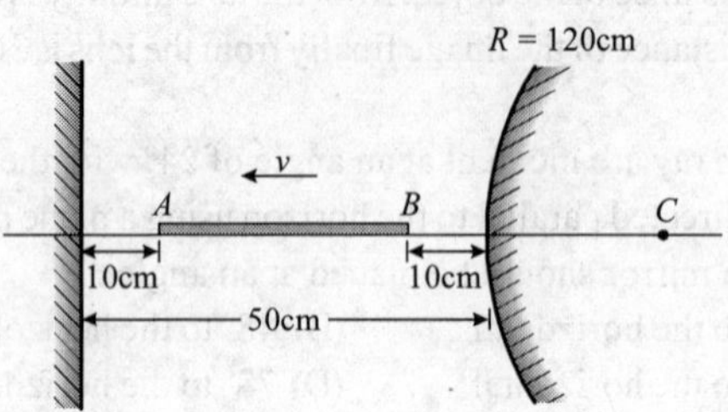

Figure 5.367

(A) the second image is real and inverted with magnification 1/5
(B) the second image is virtual and erect with magnification 1/5
(C) the second image moves towards the convex mirror
(D) the second image moves away from the convex mirror

5-27 A convex mirror produces virtual and erect image. The figure-5.368 shows a light ray incident on a plane boundary at an angle $i = 60°$. The angle of refraction in other medium is r. The graph shows the variation of deviation angle of light $\theta = |r - i|$ versus $\frac{\mu_1}{\mu_2} = k$. Choose the correct alternative.

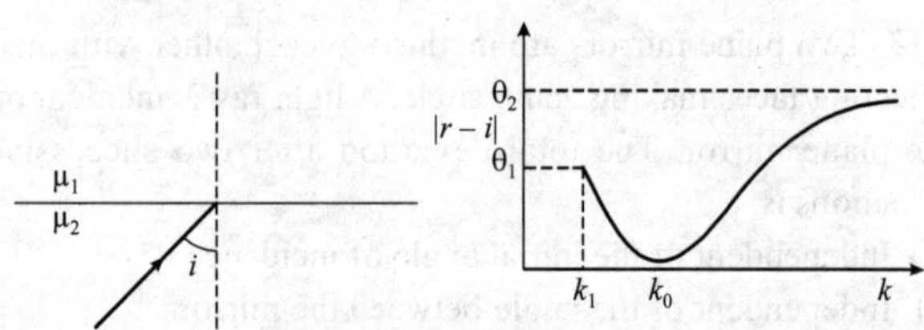

Figure 5.368

(A) The value of k_1 is $\frac{2}{\sqrt{3}}$ (B) The value of θ_1 is $\pi/6$
(C) The value of θ_2 is $\pi/3$ (D) The value of k_0 is 1

5-28 For the refraction of light through a prism
(A) For every angle of deviation there are two angles of incidences
(B) The light travelling inside an equilateral prism is necessarily parallel to the base when prism is set for minimum deviation
(C) There are two angles of incidence for maximum deviation
(D) Angle of minimum deviation will increase if refractive index of prism (μ_P) is increased keeping the refractive index of the outside medium (μ_S) unchanged if $\mu_P > \mu_S$.

5-29 An object O is kept infront of a converging lens of focal length 30 cm behind which there is a plane mirror placed at a distance 15 cm from the lens. Then which of the following statements is/are correct.

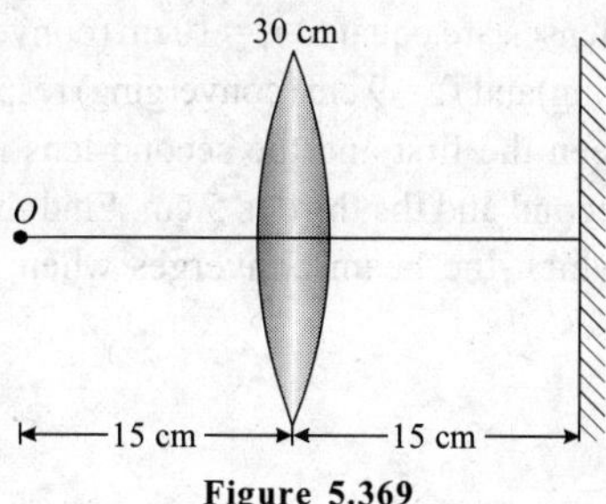

Figure 5.369

(A) The final image is formed at 60 cm from the lens towards right of it
(B) The final image is at 60 cm from lens towards left of it
(C) The final image is real
(D) The final image is virtual

5-30 Choose the correct alternative corresponding to the object distance 'u', image distance 'v' and the focal length 'F' of a converging lens from the following.

(i) The average speed of the image as the object moves with uniform speed from distance $\frac{3F}{4}$ to $\frac{F}{2}$ is greater than the average speed of the image as the object moves with same speed from distance $\frac{F}{2}$ to $\frac{F}{4}$

(ii) The minimum distance between a real object and its real image in case of a converging lens is $4F$ where F is its focal length.

(A) both are correct
(B) both are incorrect
(C) (i) is correct, (ii) is incorrect
(D) (i) is incorrect, (ii) is correct

5-31 An object and a screen are fixed at a distance d apart. When a lens of focal length f is moved between the object and the screen, sharp images of the object are formed on the screen for two positions of the lens. The magnifications produced at these two positions are M_1 and M_2:

(A) $d > 2f$
(B) $d > 4f$
(C) $M_1 M_2 = 1$
(D) $|M_1| - |M_2| = 1$

* * * * *

Unsolved Numerical Problems for Preparation of NSEP, INPhO & IPhO

For detailed preparation of INPhO and IPhO students can refer advance study material on www.physicsgalaxy.com

5-1 The left end of a long glass rod of index 1.6350 is grounded and polished to a convex spherical surface of radius 2.50 cm. A small object is located in the air and on the axis 9.0 cm from the vertex. Find the lateral magnification.

Ans. [– 0.0777]

5-2 Focal length of a convex lens in air is 10 cm. Find its focal length in water. Given that $\mu_g = 3/2$ and $\mu_w = 4/3$.

Ans. [40 cm]

5-3 Find the distance of an object from a convex lens if image is two times magnified. Focal length of the lens is 10 cm.

Ans. [5 cm, 15 cm from lens]

5-4 A pole 4 m high driven into the bottom of a lake is 1 m above the water. Determine the length of the shadow of the pole on the bottom of the lake if the sun rays make an angle of 45° with the water surface. The refractive index of water is 4/3.

Ans. [2.88 m]

5-5 An object is placed 12 cm to the left of a diverging lens of focal length 6.0 cm. A converging lens with a focal length of 12.0 cm is placed at a distance d to the right of the diverging lens. Find the distance d such that the final image is produced at infinity.

Ans. [8 cm]

5-6 A solid glass sphere with radius R and an index of refraction 1.5 is silvered over one hemisphere. A small object is located on the axis of the sphere at a distance $2R$ to the left of the vertex of the unsilvered hemisphere. Find the position of final image after all refractions and reflections have taken place.

Ans. [On the pole of mirror]

5-7 A glass sphere with 10 cm radius has a 5 cm radius spherical hole at its centre. A narrow beam of parallel light is directed into the sphere. Find the location of final image produced ? The index of refraction of the glass is 1.50.

Ans. [5 cm to the left of the surface of sphere]

5-8 A source of light is located at double focal length from a convergent lens. The focal length of the lens is f = 30 cm. At what distance from the lens should a flat mirror be placed so that the rays reflected from the mirror are parallel after passing through the lens for the second time ?

Ans. [45 cm]

5-9 A parallel beam of light is incident on a system consisting of three thin lenses with a common optical axis. The focal lengths of the lenses are equal to f_1 = 10cm (converging) and f_2 = 20cm (divering)and f_3 = 9 cm (converging) respectively. The distance between the first and the second lens is 15 cm and between the second and the third is 5 cm. Find the position of the point at which the beam converges when it leaves the system of lenses.

Ans. [Infinity]

5-10 A composite mirror is formed by arranging the upper half of a concave mirror above the lower half of a convex mirror as shown in figure below. A linear object AB is placed on the common principal axis as shown and it is found that images formed by the two halves of the composite mirror are equidistant from the point O on the two sides of the mirror. If the radii of curvature of the concave mirror and convex mirror halves are 20 cm and 30 cm respectively. Calculate the distance of the object AB from O.

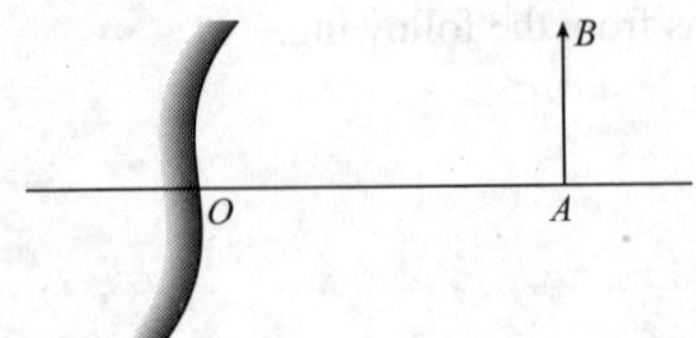

Figure 5.370

Ans. [60 cm]

5-11 One face of a prism with prism angle 30° is coated with silver to make it reflecting. A ray incident on another face at an angle of 45° is refracted and reflected from the silver coated face and retraces its path. What is the refractive index of the prism ?

Ans. [$\sqrt{2}$]

5-12 In an isosceles prism of prism angle 45°, it is found that when the angle of incidence is same as the prism angle, the emergent ray grazes the emergent surface. Find the refractive index of the material of the prism. For what angle of incidence the angle of deviation will be minimum ?

Ans. [$\sqrt{3}$, 41.51°]

5-13 An astronomical telescope with objective of focal length 100 cm and eyepiece of focal length 10 cm is used by a shortsighted man whose far point is 33 cm from his eye, to form an image of an infinitely distant object at his far point. Find the separation of the lenses, and magnification obtained.

Ans. [107.5 cm, 13.3]

5-14 Figure-5.371 shows a right angled prism ABC having refractive index $\mu_g = \frac{3}{2}$ lowered into water $\left(\mu_\omega \frac{4}{3}\right)$. Find angle α so that the incident ray normal to face AB will be reflected at face BC completely.

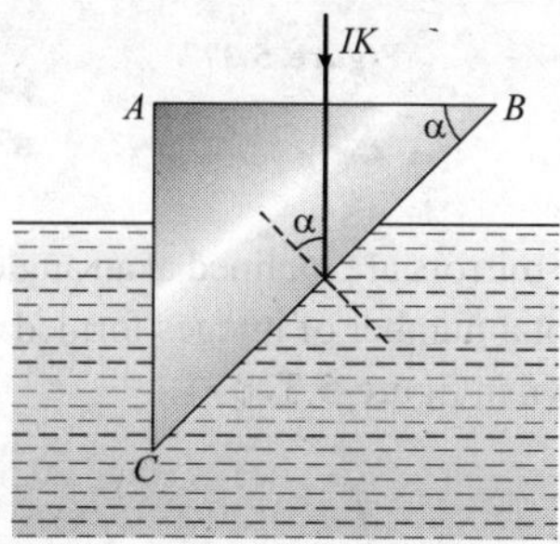

Figure 5.371

Ans. [$\alpha > \sin^{-1}\left(\frac{8}{9}\right)$]

5-15 An equilateral prism deviates a ray through 40° for two incidence angle which differ by 20°. Find the two incidence angles.

Ans. [60° and 40°]

5-16 A ray of light strikes a glass slab of thickness t.

(i) Prove that it emerges on the opposite face, parallel to the initial ray.

(ii) Prove that the value of deflection of beam which passed through the plate is

$$t \sin i_1 \left[1 - \sqrt{\left(\frac{1-\sin^2 i_1}{{}_a\mu_g{}^2 - \sin^2 i_1}\right)}\right]$$

(iii) Prove that for a small angle of incidence i_1, the internal shift x is given by

$$x = t\, i_1\left(1 - \frac{1}{{}_a\mu_g}\right)$$

where ${}_a\mu_g$ is the refractive index of glass with respect to air.

5-17 A plano-convex lens has a thickness of 4 cm. When placed on a horizontal table with the curved surface in contact with it, the apparent depth of the bottommost point of the lens is found to be 3 cm. If the lens is inverted such that the plane face is in contact with the table, the apparent depth of the centre of the plane face of the lens is found to be 25/8 cm. Find the focal length of the lens.

Ans. [75 cm]

5-18 An image Y is formed of a point object X by a lens whose optic axis is AB as shown in figure-5.372. Draw a ray diagram to locate the lens and its focus. If the image Y of the object X is formed by a concave mirror (having the same optic axis AB) instead of lens, draw another ay diagram to locate the mirror and focus. Write down the steps of construction of the ray diagrams.

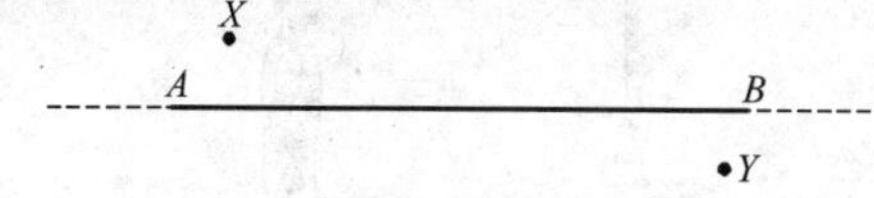

Figure 5.372

Ans. [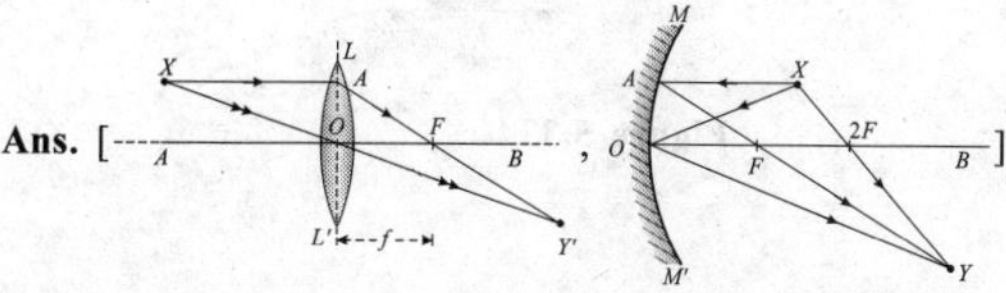]

5-19 A thin plano-convex lens of focal length f is split into two halves : One of the halves is shifted along the optical axis (figure-5.373) The separation between object and image planes is 1.8 m. The magnification of the image formed by one of the half lens is 2. Find the focal length of the lens and separation between the two halves. Draw the ray diagram for image formation.

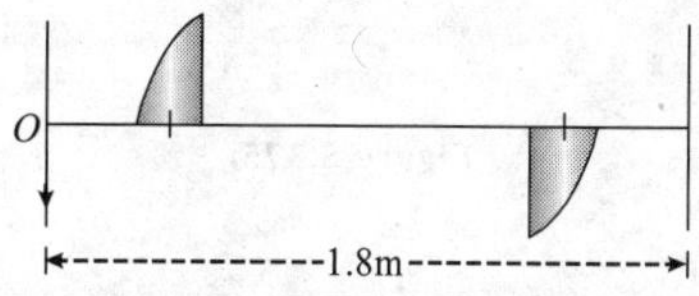

Figure 5.373

Ans. [40 cm, 60 cm]

5-20 The focal lengths of the objective and the eyepiece of a compound microscope are 1 cm and 5 cm respectively. An object placed at a distance of 1.1 cm from the objective has its final image formed at (i) infinity (ii) least distance of distinct vision. Find the magnifying power and the distance between the lenses. Least distance of distinct vision is 25 cm.

Ans. [(i) 16 cm, – 50; (ii) 15.17 cm, – 60]

5-21 Find the minimum size of mirror required to see the full image of a wall behind a man standing at the centre of room, where H is the height of wall.

Ans. [H/3]

5-22 Two mirrors are inclined by an angle 30°. An object is placed making 10° with the mirror M_1. Find the positions of the first two images formed by each mirror. Find the total number of images.

Ans. [10° and 50° from M_1 and 20° and 40° from M_2, 11]

5-23 AB is a man of height 2 m and M is a mirror of length 0.5 m and mass 0.1 kg. Initially top of mirror M and A are at the same level and the M starts falling freely always remaining vertical. If the level of the eyes of the man is 1.5 cm below his head A, find the time after which the man sees the reflection of his feet.

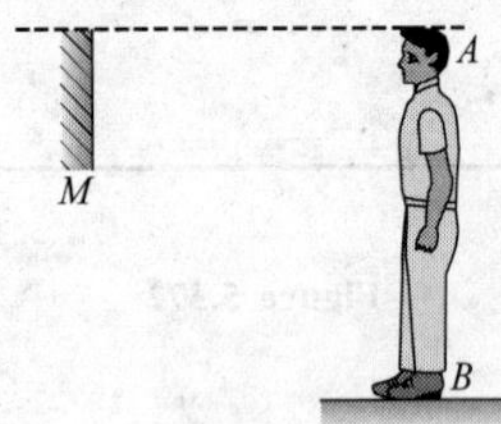

Figure 5.374

Ans. [0.318 s]

5-24 Figure-5.375 shows a point object A and a plane mirror MN. Find the position of image of object A, in mirror MN, by drawing a ray diagram. Indicate the region in which observer's eye must be present in order to view the image.

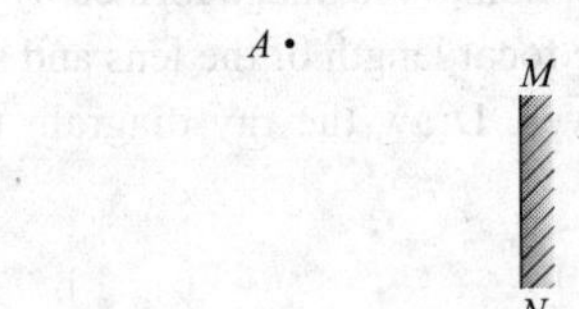

Figure 5.375

Ans. [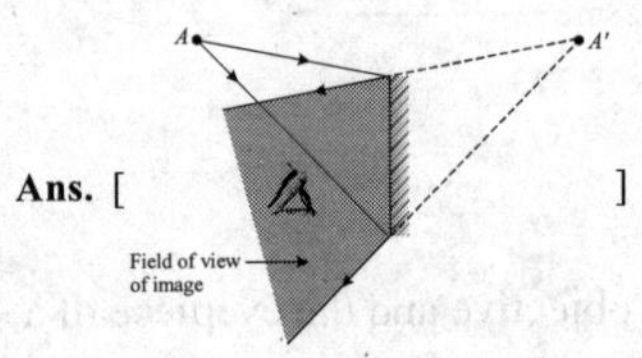]

5-25 An object is placed at $A(2, 0)$ and MN is a plane mirror, as shown in figure-5.376. Find the region on Y-axis in which reflected rays are present.

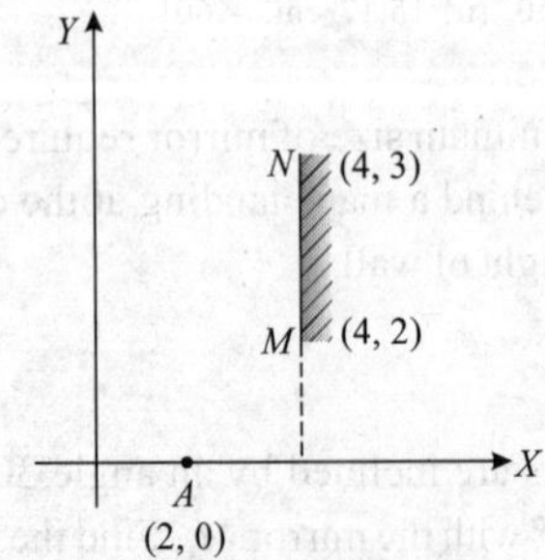

Figure 5.376

Ans. [Reflected rays exist on Y-axis between (0,6) and (0,9)]

5-26 See the following figure-5.377. Which of the object(s) shown in figure will not form its image in the mirror.

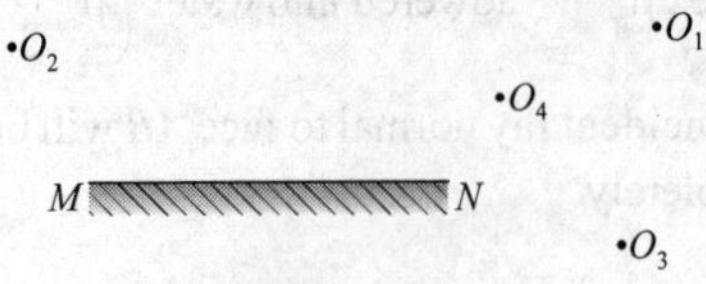

Figure 5.377

Ans. [O_3]

5-27 Two plane mirrors are inclined at an angle of 75° to each other. Find the total number of images formed when an object is placed as shown in figure-5.378.

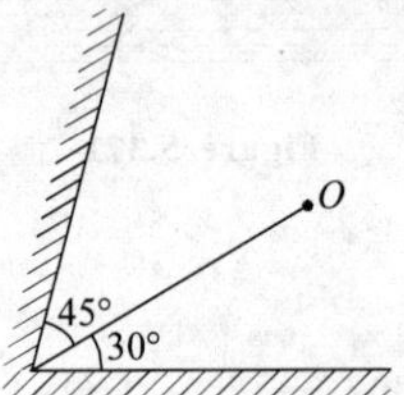

Figure 5.378

Ans. [4]

5-28 Two plane mirrors are inclined at an angle of 70° to each other. Find the total number of images formed when object is placed as shown in figure-5.379. Total images = 5

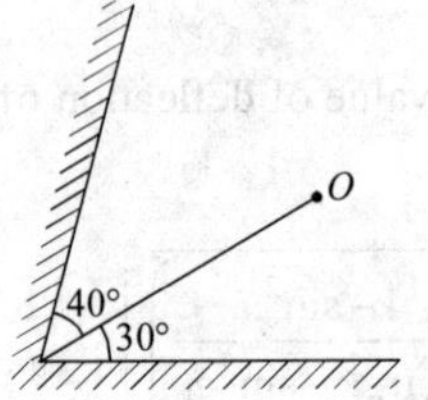

Figure 5.379

Ans. [5]

5-29 There is a point object placed in front of a plane mirror. If the mirror is displaced 10 cm away from the object, find the distance by which its image will get displaced.

Ans. [20 cm]

5-30 A crown glass prism of refracting angle 8° is combined with a flint glass prism to obtain deviation without dispersion. If the refractive indices for red and violet rays for the crown glass are 1.514 and 1.524 and for the flint glass are 1.645 and 1.665 respectively, find the angle of flint glass prism and net deviation.

Ans. [1.53°]

5-31 An opaque cylindrical tank with an open top has a diameter of 3.00 m and is completely filled with water. When the setting sun reaches an angle of 37° above the horizontal, sunlight ceases to illuminate any part of the bottom of the tank. How deep is the tank ?

Ans. [4 m]

5-32 In the situation shown in figure-5.380, find the velocity vector of image in the coordinate system shown in figure.

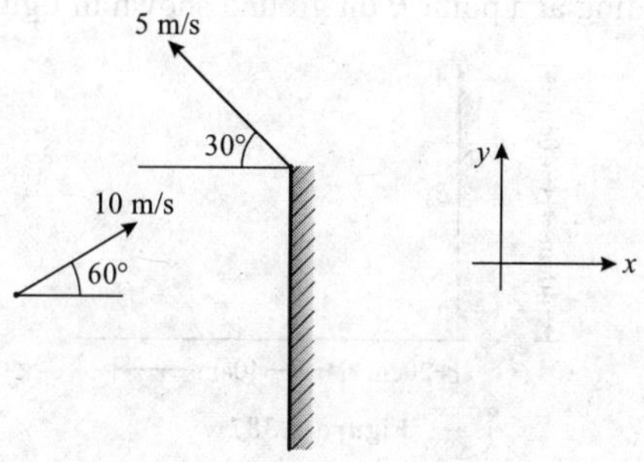

Figure 5.380

Ans. [$-5(1+\sqrt{3})\hat{i}+5\hat{j}$ m/s]

5-33 Find the velocity of the image of a moving object in situation shown in figure-5.381 in which object and mirror velocities in horizontal and vertical directions are shown.

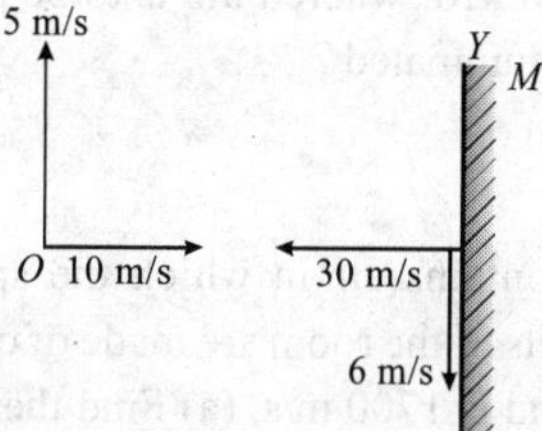

Figure 5.381

Ans. [70.178 m/s]

5-34 Two plane mirrors are inclined to each other at an angle 30° to each other. A ray of light is incident at an angle of 40° to the mirror (M_1). Find the total angle of deviation of the ray after the third successive reflection due to mirrors.

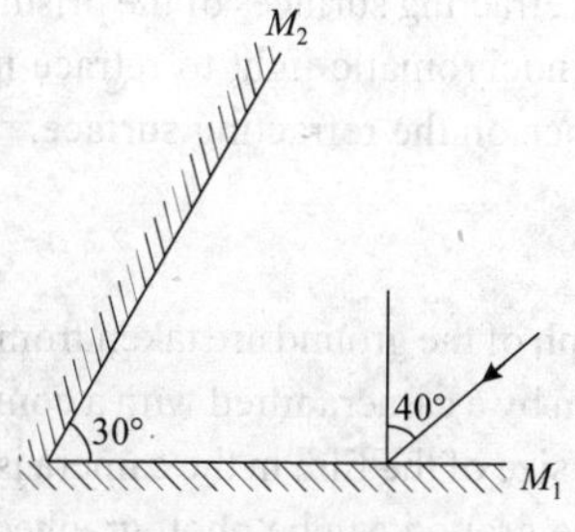

Figure 5.382

Ans. [160° Clockwise]

5-35 Figure shows a torch producing a straight light beam falling on a plane mirror at an angle of 60° as shown in figure-5.383. The reflected beam makes a spot P on the vertical screen as shown. If at $t = 0$, mirror starts rotating clockwise about the hinge A with an angular velocity $\Omega = 1°$ per second. Find the speed of the spot on screen after time $t = 15$ s.

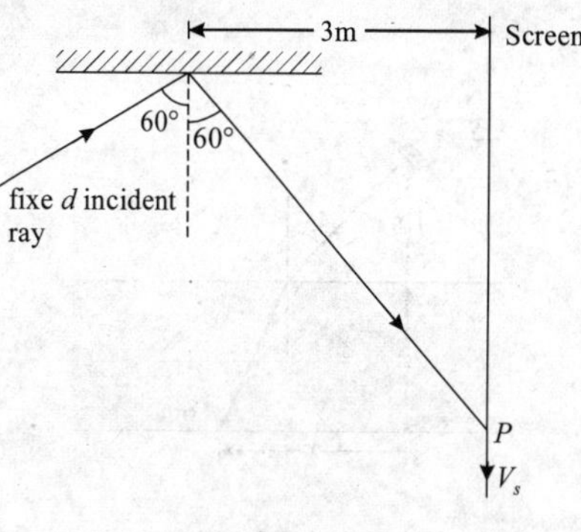

Figure 5.383

Ans. [$\frac{2\pi}{15}$ m/s]

5-36 A light ray I is incident on a plane mirror M. The mirror is rotated in the direction as shown in the figure-5.384 by an arrow at the frequency ($9/\pi$) rev/sec. The light reflected by the mirror is received on the wall W which is at a distance 10 m from the axis of rotation. When the angle of incidence becomes 37°, find the speed of the light spot on the wall.

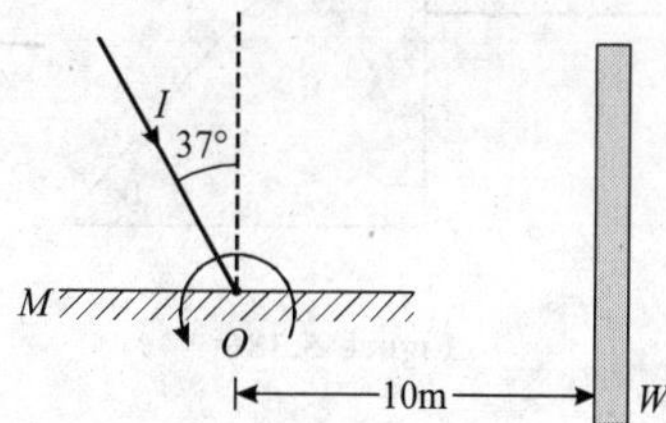

Figure 5.384

Ans. [1000 m/s]

5-37 A spherical light bulb with a diameter of 3.0 cm radiates light equally in all directions, with a power of 4.5π W. (a) Find the light intensity at the surface of the bulb. (b) Find the light intensity 7.50 m from the centre of the bulb. (c) At 7.50 m, a convex lens is set up with its axis pointing toward the bulb. The lens has a circular face with a diameter of 15.0 cm and a focal length of 30.0 cm. Find the diameter of the image of the bulb formed on a screen kept at the location of the image. (d) Find the light intensity at the image.

Ans. [(a) 5000 W/m^2; (b) 0.02 W/m^2; (c) 0.125 W/m^2; (d) 288 W/m^2]

5-38 A coin lies on the bottom of a lake 2 m deep at a horizontal distance x from the spotlight S which is a source of thin parallel beam of light situated 1 m above the surface of the liquid of refractive index $\mu = \sqrt{2}$ as shown in figure. The liquid height is 2 m. Find x so that a narrow beam of light from S when incident on the liquid surface at incidence angle 45° falls directly on the coin.

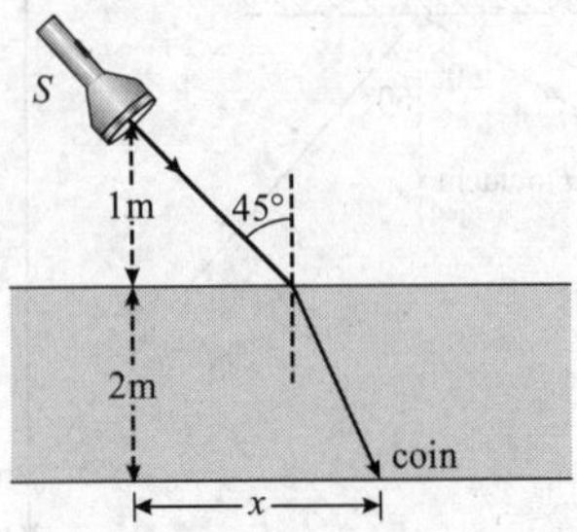

Figure 5.385

Ans. $\left[\left(1+\frac{2}{\sqrt{3}}\right) \text{m}\right]$

5-39 What should be the value of angle θ such that light entering normally through the surface AC of a prism ($n = 3/2$) does not cross the second refracting surface AB.

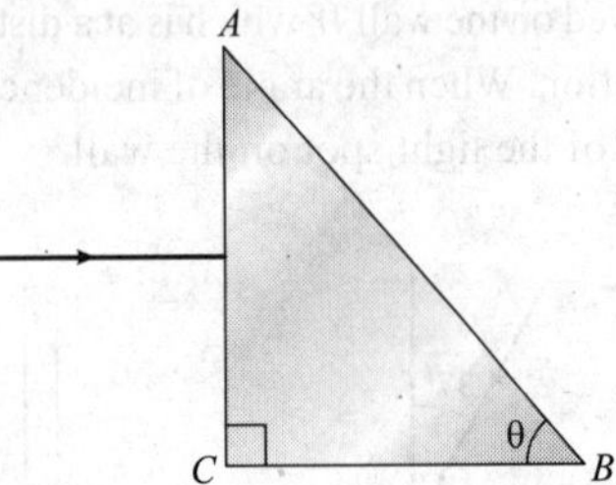

Figure 5.386

Ans. $\left[\theta < \cos^{-1}\left(\frac{2}{3}\right)\right]$

5-40 Refracting angle of a prism $A = 60°$ and its refractive index is, $n = 3/2$, what is the angle of incidence i to get minimum deviation. Also find the minimum deviation. Assume the surrounding medium to be air ($n = 1$).

Ans. $\left[\sin^{-1}\left(\frac{3}{4}\right), 2\sin^{-1}\left(\frac{3}{4}\right) - \frac{\pi}{3}\right]$

5-41 The refractive indices of flint glass for red and violet light are 1.613 and 1.632 respectively. Find the angular dispersion produced by a thin prism of flint glass with refracting angle 5°.

Ans. [0.095°]

5-42 A small object of height 0.5 cm is placed in front of a convex surface of glass ($\mu = 1.5$) of radius of curvature 10 cm. Find the height of the image formed in glass.

Ans. [1 cm]

5-43 In figure-5.387 shown AB is a plane mirror of length 40 cm placed at a height 40 cm from ground. There is a light source S at a point on the ground. Find the minimum and maximum height of a man (eye height) required to see the image of the source if he is standing at a point P on ground shown in figure.

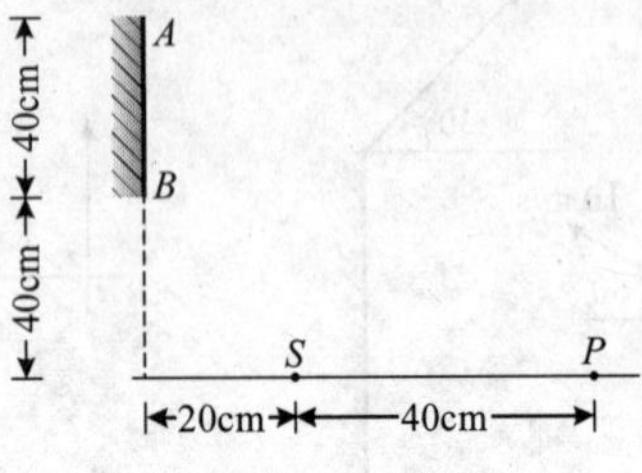

Figure 5.387

Ans. [320 cm]

5-44 A plane mirror of circular shape with radius $r = 20$ cm is fixed to the ceiling. A bulb is to be placed on the axis of the mirror. A circular area of radius $R = 1$ m on the floor is to be illuminated after reflection of light from the mirror. The height of the room is 3 m. What should be the maximum distance from the centre of the mirror where bulb is to be placed so that the required area is illuminated ?

Ans. [75 cm]

5-45 A room contains air in which the speed of sound is 340 m/s. The walls of the room are made of concrete, in which the speed of sound is 1700 m/s. (a) Find the critical angle for total internal reflection of sound at the concrete-air boundary, (b) In which medium should the sound be travel to undergo total internal reflection ?

Ans. [(a) $\sin^{-1}\left(\frac{1}{5}\right)$; (b) air]

5-46 A prism of refractive index $\sqrt{2}$ has a refracting angle of 30°. One of the refracting surfaces of the prism is polished. For the beam of monochromatic light to retrace its path, find the angle of incidence on the refracting surface.

Ans. [45°]

5-47 Photograph of the ground are taken from an aircraft at an altitude of 10 km by a camera fitted with a convex lens of focal length 1 m. The size of the film in the camera is 10 cm × 10 cm. What area of the ground can be photographed by this camera at any time ?

Ans. [1 km^2]

5-48 An equilateral prism deviates a ray through 23° for two angles of incidence differing by 23°. Find μ of the prism ?

Ans. [$\frac{\sqrt{43}}{5}$]

5-49 A plano-convex lens ($\mu = 1.5$) has a maximum thickness of 1 mm. If the diameter of its aperture is 4 cm. Find (a) Radius of the curvature of the curved surface; (b) its focal length in air.

Ans. [(a) 20 cm; (b) 40 cm]

5-50 A convex lens of focal length 1.5 m is placed in a system of coordinate axis such that its optical centre is at the origin and principal axis coinciding with the x-axis. An object and a plane mirror are arranged on the principal axis as shown in the figure-5.388. Find the value of d (in m) so that y-coordinate of image (after refraction and reflection) is 0.3 m. (take $\tan\theta = 0.3$)

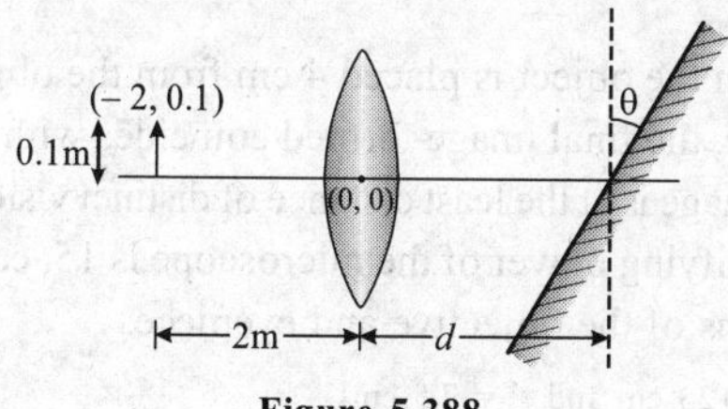

Figure 5.388

Ans. [5 m]

5-51 A ray in incident normally on a right angle prism whose refractive index is $\sqrt{3}$ and prism angle $\alpha = 30°$. After crossing the prism, ray passes through a glass sphere. It strikes the glass sphere at $\frac{R}{\sqrt{3}}$ distance from principal axis, as shown in the figure-5.389. The sphere is half polished. Find the total angle of deviation of the incident ray after all reflections and refractions from this optical setup.

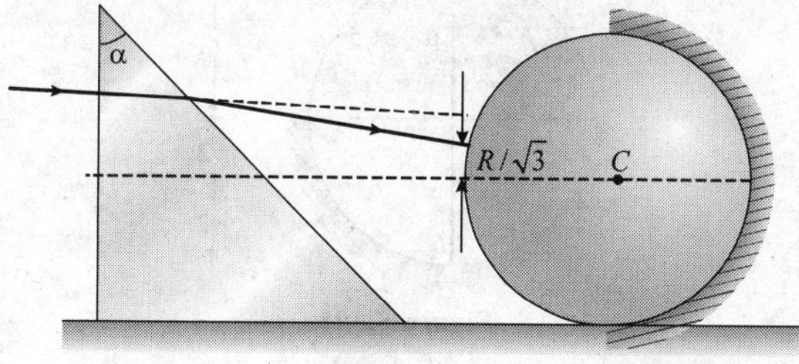

Figure 5.389

Ans. [180°]

5-52 A shortsighted man, the accommodation of whose eye is between 12 cm and 60 cm wears spectacles through which he can see remote objects distinctly. Determine the minimum distance at which the man can read a book through his spectacles.

Ans. [15 cm]

5-53 A stationary observer O looking at a fish F in water ($\mu_w = 4/3$) through a converging lens of focal length 90.0 cm. The lens is allowed to fall freely from a height 62.0 cm with its axis vertical. The fish and the observer are on the principal axis of the lens. The fish moves up with constant velocity 100 cm/s. Initially it was at a depth of 44.0 cm. Find the velocity (in cm/s) with which the fish appears to move with respect to lens, to the observer at $t = 0.2$ sec. (Take $g = 10$ m/s^2)

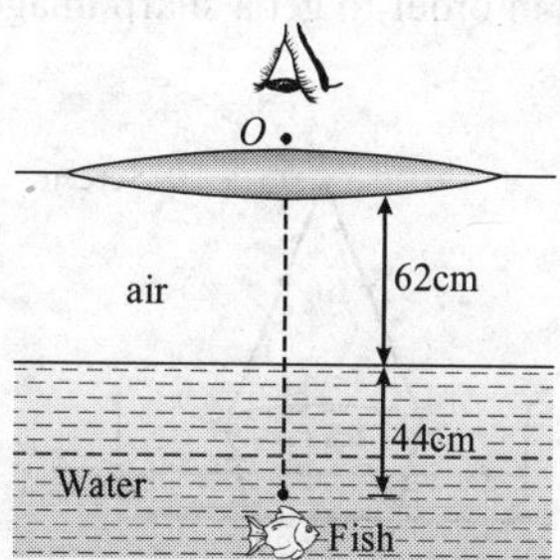

Figure 5.390

Ans. [2475 cm/s]

5-54 An equilateral prism ABC is placed in air with its base side BC lying horizontally along x-axis as shown in the figure-5.391. A ray given by $\sqrt{3}z + x = 10$ is incident at a point P on the face AB of the prism.

(a) Find the value of μ for which the ray grazes the face AC.

(b) Find the direction of the finally refracted ray if $\mu = \frac{3}{2}$.

(c) Find the equation of ray coming out of the prism if bottom BC is silvered.

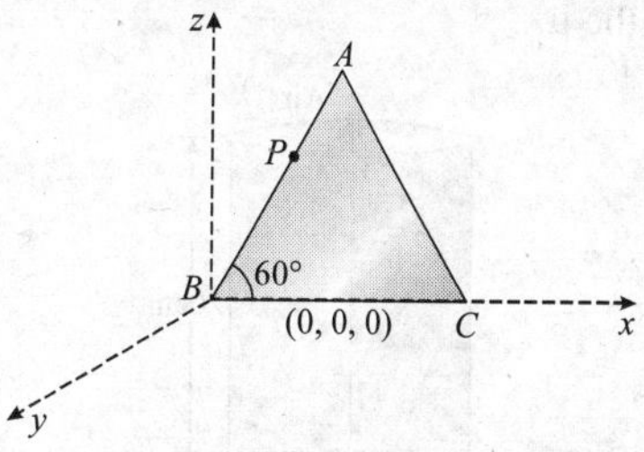

Figure 5.391

Ans. [(a) $\frac{2}{\sqrt{3}}$; (b) Along $-z$ axis; (c) $\sqrt{3}z + x = 10$]

5-55 A convex lens of focal length 20 cm and a concave lens of focal length 10 cm are placed 10 cm apart on the same optic axis. A beam of light travelling parallel to the optic axis and having a beam diameter 5.0 mm, is incident on the convex lens. Show that the emergent beam is parallel to the incident one. Find the beam diameter of the emergent beam.

Ans. [2.5 mm]

5-56 A thin convex lens of refractive index $\mu = 1.5$ is placed between a point source of light S and a screen A, as shown in the figure. Light rays from the source S are brought to focus on the screen A, forming a point image P. The distance SP is equal to 50 cm. Water $\left(\mu = \frac{4}{3}\right)$ is now poured into a vessel interposed between the object and the lens, and it is observed that when the water level is 8 cm the screen has to be moved up by a distance of 6 cm in order to get a sharp image. Find the focal length of the lens.

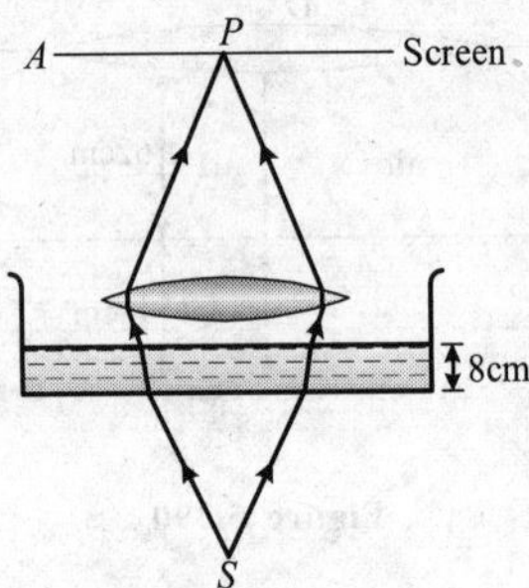

Figure 5.392

Ans. [12 cm]

5-57 A thin equiconvex glass lens ($\mu_g = 1.5$) is being placed on the top of a vessel of height $h = 20$ cm as shown in the figure-5.393. A luminous point source is being placed at the bottom of the vessel on the principal axis of the lens. When the air is on both the sides of the lens, the image of luminous source is formed at a distance of 20 cm from the lens out side the vessel. When the air inside the vessel is being replaced by a liquid of refractive index μ_1, the image of the same source is being formed at a distance 30 cm from the lens outside the vessel. Find the μ_1.

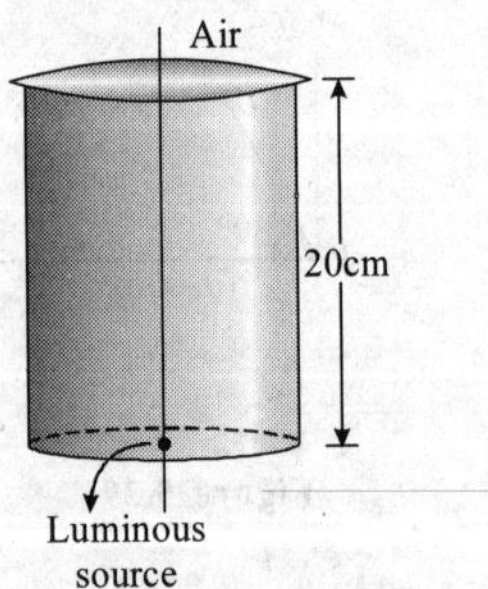

Figure 5.393

Ans. [1.11]

5-58 Light passes symmetrically through a 60° prism of refractive index 1.54. After emergence out from the prism the light ray is incident on a plane mirror fixed to the base of the prism extending beyond it. Find the total deviation of the light ray after reflection from the mirror.

Ans. [0°]

5-59 A glass rod has ends as shown in figure-5.394. The refractive index of glass is μ. The object O is at a distance $2R$ from the surface of larger radius of curvature. The distance between apexes of ends is $3R$. Find the distance of image formed of the point object from right hand vertex. What is the condition on μ for formation of a real image.

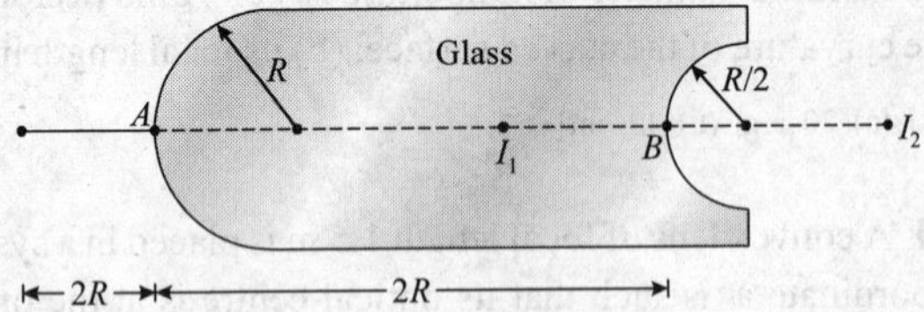

Figure 5.394

Ans. $\left[\frac{(9-4\mu)R}{(10\mu-9)(\mu-2)}, 2 < \mu < 9/4\right]$

5-60 When the object is placed 4 cm from the objective of a microscope, the final image formed coincides with the object. The final image is at the least distance of distinct vision (24 cm). If the magnifying power of the microscope is 15, calculate the focal lengths of the objective and eyepiece.

Ans. [$f_0 = 3.125$ cm and $f_e = 7.5$ cm]

5-61 A hemispherical portion of the surface of a solid glass sphere ($\mu = 1.5$) of radius r is silvered to make the inner side reflecting. An object is placed on the axis of the hemisphere at a distance $3r$ from the centre of the sphere. The light from the object is refracted at the unsilvered part, then reflected from the slivered part and again refracted at the unsilvered part. Locate the final image formed.

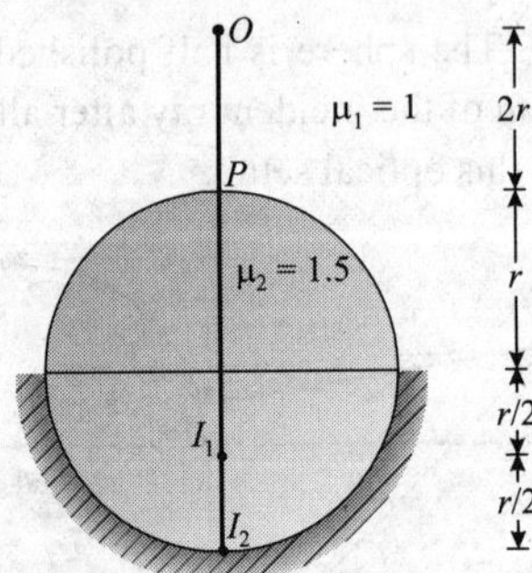

Figure 5.395

Ans. [At the pole of silvered face]

5-62 The focal lengths of the objective and the eyepiece of an astronomical telescope are 0.25 m and 0.02 m, respectively. The telescope is adjusted to view an object at a distance of 1.5 m from the objective, the final image being 0.25 m from the eye of the observer. Calculate the length of the telescope and the magnification produced by it.

Ans. [31.85×10^{-2} m, 16.2]

5-63 A thin converging lens of focal length $f = 1.5$ m is placed along y-axis such that its optical centre coincides with the origin. A small light source S is placed at (– 2.0 m, 0.1 m) as shown in figure-5.396. Where should a plane mirror inclined at an angle θ with $\tan\theta = 0.3$, be placed such that y-coordinates of final image is 0.3 m. Also find x coordinate of final image.

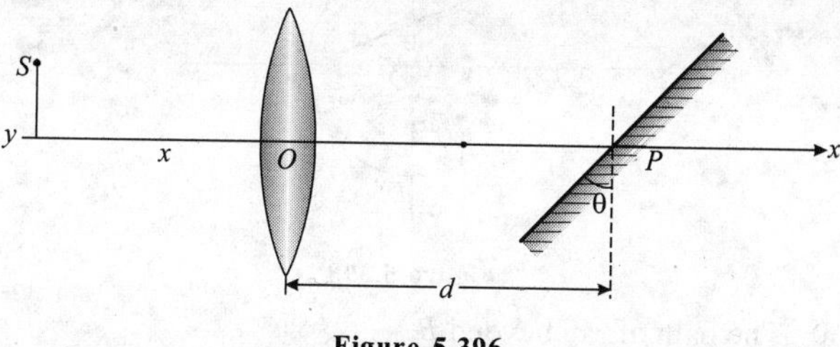

Figure 5.396

Ans. [5 m, 4 m]

5-64 A ball is kept at a height y_0 above the surface of a transparent sphere of radius R, made of material of refractive index μ. At $t = 0$, the ball is dropped to fall normally on the sphere. Find the speed of the image formed as a function of time for $t < \sqrt{\frac{2y_0}{g}}$. Consider the image by a single refraction.

Ans. [$\frac{\mu R^2 gt}{[(\mu-1)(y_0 - \frac{1}{2}gt^2) - R]^2}$]

5-65 A prism of angle 60° is made of glass of refractive index 1.50 for red and 1.56 for violet. Find the angular separation of these rays when a narrow pencil of composite light is incident at minimum deviation.

Ans. [5°22′]

5-66 An chromatic telescope objective of focal length 1.5 m consists of two thin lenses of dispersive powers 0.050 and 0.075, respectively, placed in contact. Find the focal length of each lens.

Ans. [For convex lens : $f = 50$ cm, $\omega = 0.050$, for concave lens: $f = 75$ cm, $\omega = 0.075$]

5-67 Calculate the focal lengths of a convex lens of crown glass of dispersive power 0.012 and concave lens of dispersive power 0.020 that from an achromatic converging combination of focal length 0.3 m when placed in contact.

Ans. [12 cm for convex lens, 20 cm for concave lens]

5-68 Show that in the achromatic combination of two thin lenses of the same material and nature the first principal plane lies at the first principal focus of the first lens and the second principal plane at the second principal focus of the second lens.

5-69 In a simple astronomical telescope the focal length of the object glass is 0.75 m and that of the eyepiece is 0.05 m. Calculate the magnifying power when the final image of a distant object is seen (a) a long way off, (b) at a distance of 0.25 m. Find the distance between the two lenses in each case.

Ans. [(a) 0.0417 m (b) 0.7917 m]

5-70 An astronomical telescope consisting of two convex lenses of focal length 50 cm and 5 cm is focussed on the moon. What is the distance between the two lenses in this position? If the telescope is then turned towards an object 10 m away, how much would the eyepiece have to be moved to focus on the object without altering the accommodation of the eye? Calculate the angular magnification produced by the telescope in the two adjustments.

Ans. [10]

5-71 How would you use two plano-convex lenses of focal lengths 6 cm and 4 cm to design an eyepiece free from chromatic aberration. What will be its focal length and magnifying power for normal vision? Will it be a positive or negative eyepiece?

Ans. [4.8 cm, 5.2, negative]

5-72 A shortsighted person cannot see objects situated beyond 2 m from him distinctly. What should be the power of the lens which he should use for seeing distant objects clearly?

Ans. [– 0.5D]

5-73 An astronomical telescope in normal adjustment has a tube length of 93 cm and magnification (angular) of 30. If the eyepiece is to be drawn out by 3 cm to focus a near object, with the final image at infinity, find how far away is the object and the magnification (angular) is this case.

Ans. [27.9 m, 31]

5-74 The focal lengths of the objective and the eyepiece of an astronomical telescope are 0.25 m and 0.025 m, respectively. The telescope is focussed on an object 5 m from the objective, the final image being formed 0.25 m from the eye of the observer. Calculate the length of the telescope and its magnifying power.

Ans. [0.2859 m, 11.6]

5-75 A telescope with magnification $M = 15$ was submerged in water so that the inside of the telescope is filled up with water. To make the system work as a telescope within the former dimensions, the objective was removed. What was the magnification of the telescope after the change? μ of the material of the eyepiece = 1.5 and μ of water = $\frac{4}{3}$.

Ans. [3]

5-76 A man stands on a vertical tower of height 20 m. Calculate the distance up to which he will be able to see on the surface of the earth. Neglect the height of the man. Take the radius of the earth = 6400 km.

Ans. [16 km]

5-77 The radius of curvature of the face of a plano-convex lens is 12 cm and its refractive index is 1.5.

(a) Find the focal length of the lens. The plane surface of the lens is now silvered

(b) At what distance from the lens will parallel rays incident on the convex face converge ?

(c) Sketch the ray diagram to locate the image, when a point object is placed on the axis, 20 cm from the lens.

(d) Calculate the image distance when the object is placed as in part (c).

Ans. [(a) +24 cm; (b) – 36 cm; (c) 12 cm; (d) – 180 cm]

5-78 An object A is at a distance of $a = 36$ cm from a lens with a focal length of $f = 30$ cm. A flat mirror turned through 45° with respect to the optic axis of the lens is placed behind at a distance of $l = 1$ m. At what distance h from the optic axis should the bottom of a tray filled with water up to depth $d = 20$ cm be placed to obtain a sharp image of the object at the bottom ?

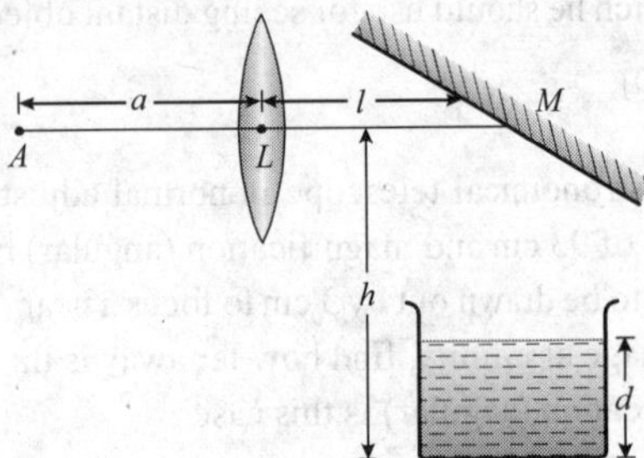

Figure 5.397

Ans. [0.85 m]

5-79 The focal length of a thin biconvex lens is 20 cm. When an object is moved from a distance of 25 cm in front of it to 50 cm, the magnification of its image changes from m_{25} to m_{50}.

The ratio $\frac{m_{25}}{m_{50}}$ is.

Ans. [6]

5-80 An object is placed 20 cm to the left of a convex lens of focal length 10 cm. If a concave mirror of focal length 5 cm is placed 30 cm to the right of the lens, find the magnification and the nature of the final image. Draw the ray diagram and locate the position of the image.

Ans. [The image coincides with the object]

5-81 A glass sphere with centre O is shown in the figure-5.398. AOB and COD are two diameters at right angles to each other. A ray parallel to AOB strikes the sphere at P, a point midway between A and C. After refraction, it proceeds along PB. Find.

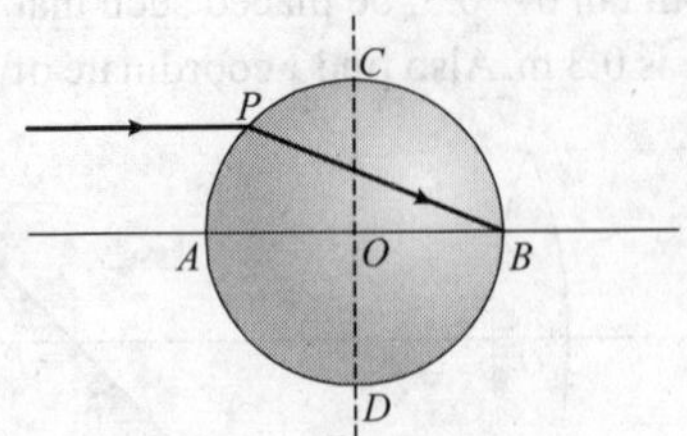

Figure 5.398

(a) The path of ray beyond B,

(b) The refractive index of glass, and

(c) The deviation of the ray as it emerges out of the sphere.

Ans. [1.85, 45°]

5-82 A hollow sphere of glass of refractive index μ has a small mark on its interior surface which is observed from a point outside the sphere on the side opposite the centre. The inner cavity is concentric with the external surface and the thickness of the glass is uniform and equal to the radius of the inner surface. Prove that the mark will appear nearer than it really is by a distance $\frac{(\mu-1)R}{(3\mu-1)}$ where R is the radius of the inner surface.

5-83 Two thin similar watch glass pieces are joined together, front to front, with rear portion silvered and the combination of glass pieces is placed at a distance $a = 60$ cm from a screen. A point object is placed on optical axis of the combination such that its two times magnified image is formed on the screen. If air between the glass pieces is replaced by water ($\mu = 4/3$), calculate the distance through which the object must be displaced so that a sharp image is again formed on the screen.

Ans. [15 cm towards the combination]

5-84 Two convex lenses of focal lengths f_1 and f_2 are placed coaxially, a distance d apart. If the axis of one of the lenses is lifted parallel to itself by Δ, find the distance by which the focal point is shifted and the distance of the focal point from the first lens.

Ans. [$\frac{\Delta(f_1-d)}{f_1+f_2-d}$; $\frac{f_1 f_2 + d(f_1-d)}{f_1+f_2-d}$]

5-85 A prism of angle 60° deviates a ray of light through 31° for two angles of incidence, which differ by 17°. What is the refractive index of the glass of the prism?

Ans. [1.40]

5-86 Two large plane mirrors OM and ON are arranged as shown in figure-5.399. Find the length of the part of large screen SS' in which two images of the object placed at P can be seen ?

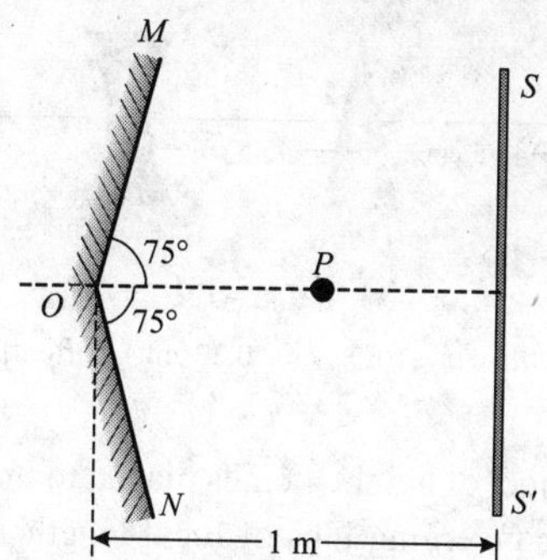

Figure 5.399

Ans. [$\frac{2}{\sqrt{3}}$ m]

5-87 A concave lens of focal length 20 cm is placed 15 cm in front of a concave mirror of radius of curvature 26 cm and another 10 cm away from the lens is placed an object. The principal axis of the lens and the mirror are coincident and the object is on the axis. Find the position and the nature of the image.

Ans. [140 cm in front of the lens]

5-88 A double convex lens is placed on a horizontal plane mirror. A pin held horizontally above the lens coincides with its own image when it is 18 cm from the lens. The space between the lens and the mirror is filled with glycerine and water, turn by turn, and the positions of coincidence of the pin with the image are 28 cm and 24 cm from the lens, respectively. Calculate the refractive index of glycerine, given that the refractive index of water is 4/3.

Ans. [1.48]

5-89 A prism has a refractive index $\sqrt{3/2}$ and refracting angle 90°. Calculate the minimum deviation produced by the prism and the corresponding angle of incidence. Show that the minimum value of the angle of incidence for which an emergent ray exists is 45°.

5-90 Image of an object approaching a convex mirror of radius of curvature 20 m along its optical axis is observed to move from $\frac{25}{3}$ m to $\frac{50}{7}$ m in 30 s. What is the speed of the object in km per hour?

Ans. [3]

5-91 A concave mirror of focal length 20 cm and a convex lens of focal length 10 cm are kept with their optic axis parallel but separated by 0.5 mm as shown in figure. The distance between lens and mirror is 10 cm. An object of height 3 mm is placed on the optic axis of lens at distance 15 cm from the lens. Find height of image formed after reflection of light rays by mirror.

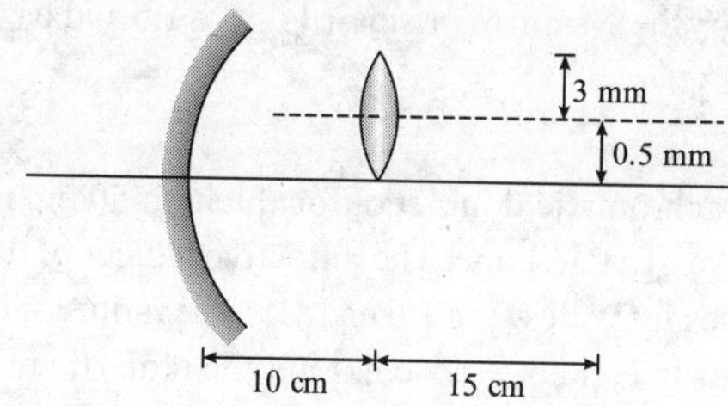

Figure 5.400

Ans. [3 mm]

5-92 Light is incident on the side of a 30°-60°-90° prism, as shown in the figure. A thin layer of a liquid is spread over the hypotenuse of the prism. If the refractive index of the prism is 1.5, find the maximum refractive index of the liquid in order that a ray passing normally through the 60°-base may be totally reflected.

Ans. [1.299]

5-93 A convex lens of crown glass is perfectly cemented to a plano-concave lens of flint glass to form an achromatic combination of power + 5D. Calculate the radii of curvature of the convex lens from the following data.

	Refractive index	Dispersive power
Crown glass	1.50	0.01
Flint glass	1.60	0.02

Ans. [8.6 cm, 12 cm]

5-94 A converging system of convex lenses free from chromatic aberration and of focal length 2.5 cm is to be constructed by using a convex lens of focal length 2 cm and dispersive power 0.04 and another convex lens of dispersive power 0.03. What should be the focal length of the second lens and at what distance from the first lens should it be placed ?

Ans. [3 cm]

5-95 For a ray of light refracted through a prism of angle 60°, the angle of incidence is equal to the angle of emergence, each equal to 45°. Find the refractive index of the material of the prism.

Ans. [1.414]

5-96 In a biprism experiment, 21 fringes are seen distinctly on a screen at a distance 1 m, when the sources are 0.5 mm apart. What is the coherent length and coherent time of the setup. ($\lambda = 6000$ Å)

Ans. [2×10^{-4} s]

5-97 In a direct vision spectroscope there are two flint glass prisms each of angle 5° and dispersive power 0.36 and two crown glass prisms of dispersive power 0.24. Calculate the angle of each crown glass prism and the net dispersion produced by the system of prisms. (μ_{crown} = 1.5 and μ_{flint} = 1.68)

Ans. [6.8°, 49′]

5-98 An achromatic doublet of focal length 50 cm is used as an objective of a telescope. The refractive indices of the glasses of the lenses for yellow are 1.6 and 1.5. The radius of curvature of the sides in contact is 15 cm. Find the radii of curvature of the other surfaces. The dispersive powers of the glasses are 0.33 and 0.24.

Ans. [45 cm and 12.5 cm]

5-99 A ray of light incident normally on one of the faces of a right-angled isosceles glass prism is found to be totally reflected. What is the minimum value of the refractive index of the material of the prism? When the prism is immersed in water, trace the path of the emergent ray for the same incident ray, indicating the values of all angles. (μ = 4/3)

Ans. [1.414, 48.6°]

5-100 The focal lengths of the objective and eyepiece of a compound microscope are 1 cm and 5 cm, respectively. An object is placed 11 mm from the objective and the final image is 25 cm from the eye. Find :

(a) magnification produced and

(b) the separation of the lenses.

Ans. [66, 15.1 cm]

5-101 Two lenses in contact, made of materials with dispersive powers in the ratio 2 : 1, behave as an achromatic lens of focal length 10 cm. What are the individual focal lengths of the two lenses ?

Ans. [10 cm for concave and 5 cm for convex]

5-102 A compound microscope has an objective of focal length 2 cm and eyepiece of focal length 5 cm. The distance between the two lenses is 25 cm. If the final image is at a distance of 25 cm from the eyepiece, find the magnifying power of the microscope. What would be the magnifying power if the microscope were reversed?

Ans. [56.5]

5-103 A point source of light is placed on optical axis of a concave lens having focal length 30 cm at a distance of 90 cm from the lens. A thin prism having prism angle 5° and made of two materials having refractive indices n_1 = 3/2 and n_2 = 4/3 respectively, is placed at a distance of 44.5 cm from the lens. Find the co-ordinates of images formed assuming position of source as origin and optical axis of lens as x-axis, also state whether the images are real or virtual.

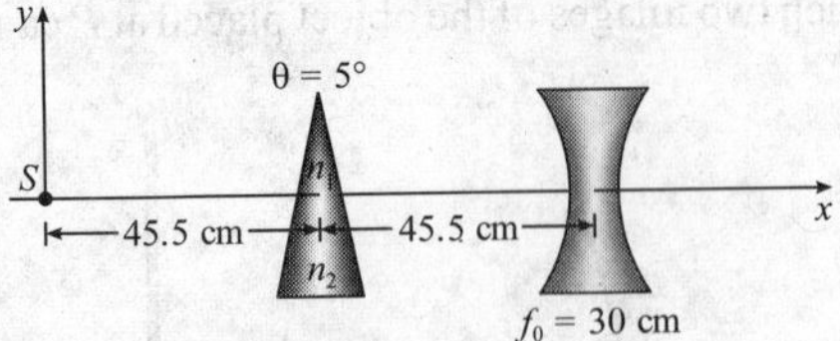

Figure 5.401

Ans. [(67.5 cm, 0.5 cm), (67.5 cm, 0.33 cm), virtual]

5-104 An object of height 4 cm is placed to the left of and on the axis of a converging lens of focal length 10 cm. A plane mirror is placed inclined at 45° to the axis, 10 cm to the right of the lens. Find the position and size of the image formed by the lens and mirror. Trace the path of the rays forming the image. The distance of the object is 15 cm to the left of the lens.

Ans. [20 cm from the mirror, 8 cm]

5-105 The refractive index of the material of a prism of refracting angle 45° is 1.6 for a certain monochromatic ray. What should be the minimum angle of incidence of this ray on this prism so that no internal reflection takes place as the ray comes out of the prism ?

Ans. [10.1°]

5-106 A point source of light S is placed at the bottom of a vessel containing a liquid of refractive index 5/3. A person is viewing the source from above the surface. There is an opaque disc of radius 1 cm floating on the surface. The centre of the disc lies vertically above the source S. The liquid from the vessel is gradually drained out. What is the maximum height of the liquid for which the source cannot be seen from above ?

Ans. [1.33 cm]

5-107 of refractive index $\sqrt{3}$ as shown in figure-5.402.

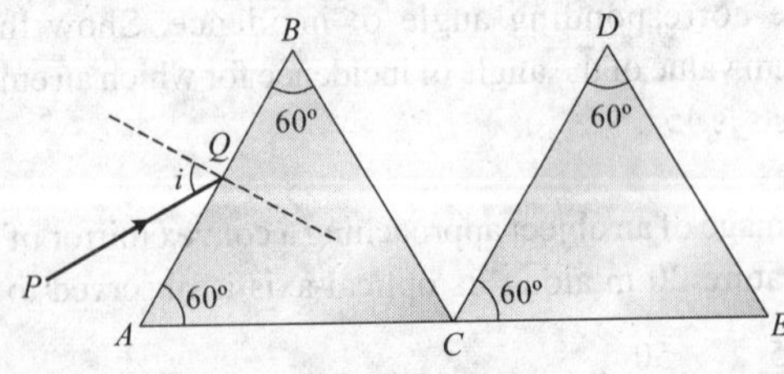

Figure 5.402

(a) Find the angle of incidence for which the deviation of light ray by the prism ABC is minimum.

(b) By what angle the second prism must be rotated, so that the final ray suffer net minimum deviation.

Ans. [(a) 60°; (b) 60°]

* * * * *

6

Wave Optics

FEW WORDS FOR STUDENTS

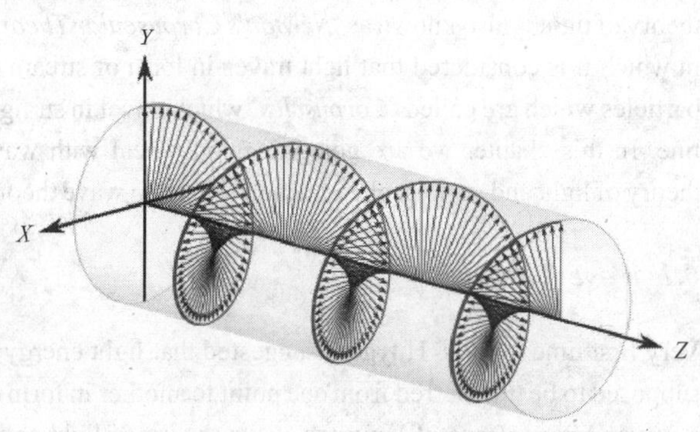

In geometrical optics we studied the rectilinear propagation of light and its behaviour as a 'Light Ray'. All the phenomenon we studied in geometrical optics are considered valid at macroscopic level which is an environment in which all the obstacles, apertures and devices used in geometrical optics are considered of size much larger than wavelength of light. When behaviour of light is analyzed for the obstacles, apertures and devices which are of size comparable to wavelength of light then to study the behaviour of light we need to go beyond the concepts of geometrical optics. Wave Optics is the branch of physics in which we analyze the behaviour of light as a wave and the effects its wave character produces in different situations.

CHAPTER CONTENTS

COVER APPLICATION

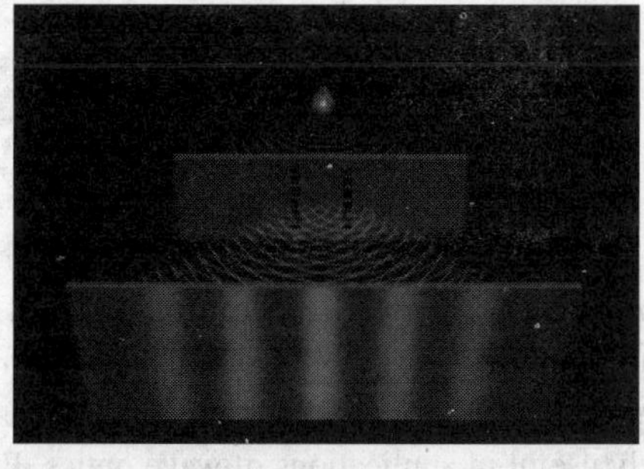

Figure (a)

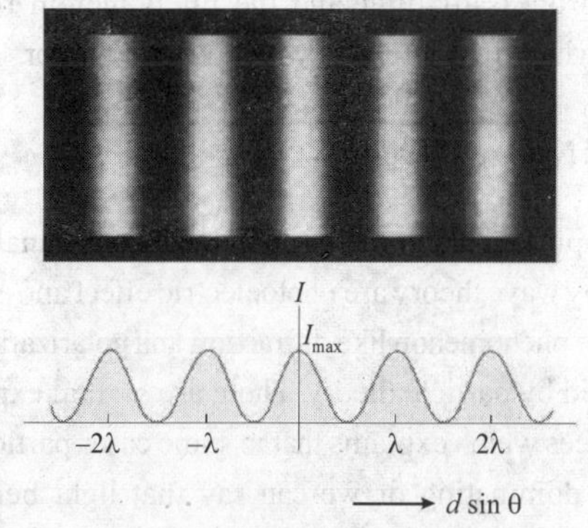

Figure (b)

Figure-(a) shows the Young's Double Slit Experiment setup in which light from one source splits into two and produces interference fringes on the screen and figure-(b) shows the intensity curve of the YDSE fringes at the center and near neighborhood of the screen.

Light is a form of energy which gives sensation of vision to an eye. There are several phenomenon associated with light, some of these are - Rectilinear propagation of light, Reflection, Refraction, Dispersion, Interference, Diffraction, Polarization, Scattering, Photoelectric Effect etc. To understand these and many more such phenomenon various theories were given to understand the nature of light. There were two most general such theories '*Particle Theory*' and '*Wave Theory*'. Particle theory of light is also known as '*Newton's Corpuscular Theory*' in which it is considered that light traves in form of stream of particles which are called '*Corpuscles*' which travel in straight line. In this chapter we are going to mainly deal with wave theory of light and various phenomenon related to wave theory.

6.1 Wave Theory

Very first time in 1678 Huygens suggested that light energy is supposed to be transferred from one point to another in form of a wave. After release of Huygens' wave theory of light some objections were raised by contemporaries due to which this theory was not globally accepted but over a period of time various experiments done by physicist in support of wave theory. Thomas Young analyzed and explained the colors seen in thin films like soap bubbles which was based on concept of superposition of waves. Fresnel framed a mathematical analysis of wave theory which removed the defects of Huygens' principle but also it explained the concept of diffraction of light and rectilinear propagation of light at macroscopic level. In 1873 Maxwell has given his electromagnetic theory of light. It describes that light propagates in the form of two mutually coupled vector waves, an electric field wave and a magnetic field wave like all other electromagnetic radiations. The electromagnetic theory was highly successful in explaining the propagation of light waves and most of related phenomenon. However electromagnetic wave theory accepted all over but still it could not explain the phenomenon of absorption and the emission process of light and the phenomenon related to situations when light interacts with physical matter.

6.1.1 Dual Nature of Light

The two important phenomenon which cannot be analyzed and explained by wave theory are photoelectric effect and scattering similarly the phenomenon like diffraction and polarization cannot be explained by particle theory. There are several experiments and evidences which explains that in some cases particle nature of light is dominating or we can say that light behave like particles and in some cases wave nature of light is dominating or light behave like a wave. Now both the natures of light is accepted by physicists.

6.1.2 Wavefront of a Light Wave

To understand the phenomenon concerned to wave theory it is essential to first understand the concept of wavefront. A wavefront is defined as a cross sectional surface of constant phase in a light beam. Being a cross sectional plane of light beam, it is considered that light energy travels in direction perpendicular to the wavefront. Figure-6.1(a) shows a plane light beam. Perpendicular to light beam the cross sectional planes are flat wavefronts in which it is considered that oscillation of the wave are all in same phase. In the whole topic of wave optics whenever we use the terms of oscillations and phase of light then it is to be kept in mind that we are discussing about oscillations of electric and magnetic field in space at a point. Figure-6.1(b) shows a diverging beam of light in which we consider wavefronts are convex in shape and for a converging beam shown in figure-6.1(c) the wavefronts are concave in shape.

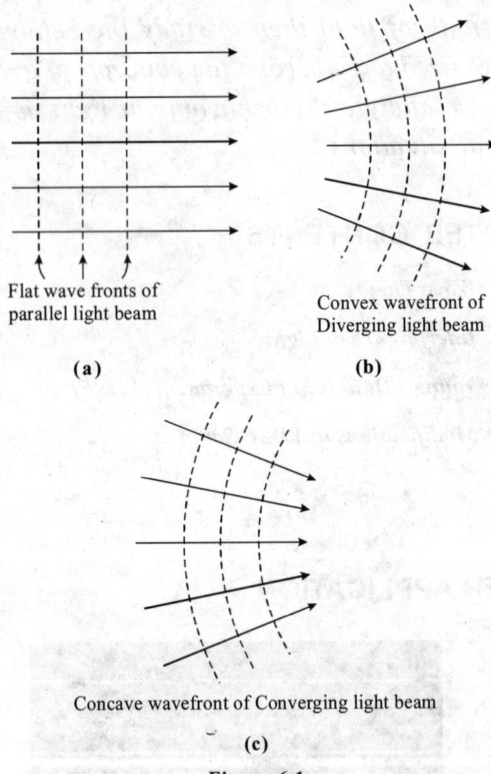

Figure 6.1

A wavefront is a surface in a light beam on which all same phase points are lying which are emitted at the same time from the light source. There are two important assumptions which are extremely useful in applications of wave optics. First is "*The lines perpendicular to the wavefront in any light beam are considered as light rays*" and second is "*The time taken by light to travel from one wavefront to another is same for all the light rays connecting these wavefronts*".

A point source of light emits light isotropically in all directions so we can consider that the wavefront emitted by a point light source is spherical in shape. Figure-6.2(a) shows the spherical wavefronts emitted from a point source of light which propagates away from the source and the radius of these wavefronts increases at speed of light. Similarly figure-6.2(b) shows the cylindrical wavefronts emitted by a line source of light in its surrounding.

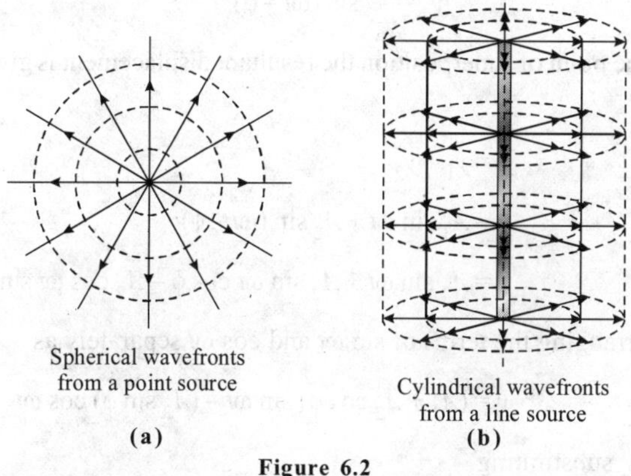

Figure 6.2

6.1.3 Huygen's Wave Theory

Huygen's Wave Theory explains that every light source produces some disturbances in surrounding space which propagate at speed of light. The theory of wave propagation in a medium is summarized in below two points which are called Huygen's Principal of Wavefront propagation.

1. Every point on a wavefront of light beam acts as a source of new disturbances in surrounding which travel in all directions and these sources in wavefront of beam are called secondary wave sources. These secondary sources produce their own spherical wavefronts which are called secondary wavelets.

2. Wavefronts move in space with the velocity of wave in that medium and in propagation of light the common tangential plane of secondary wavelets is considered as the new wavefront in the direction of light propagation as shown in figure-6.3(a), (b) and (c)

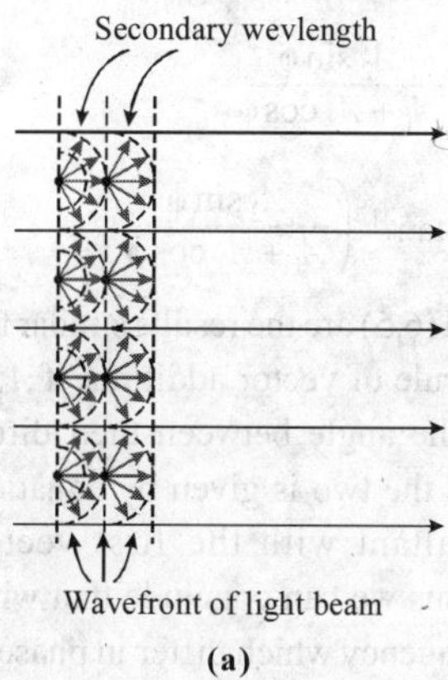

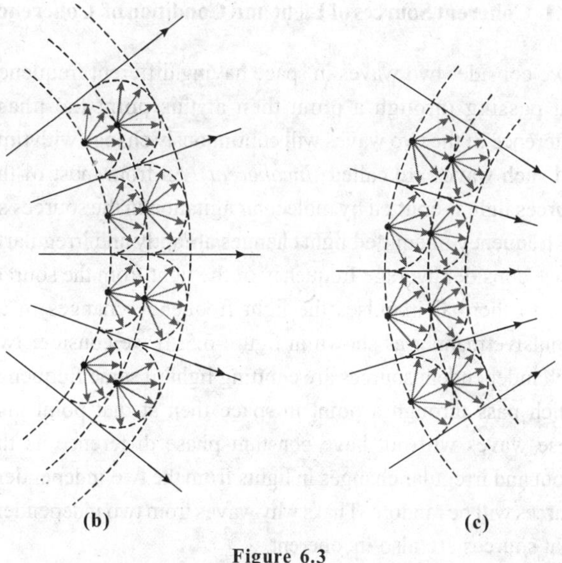

Figure 6.3

6.2 Interference of Light

Phenomenon of interferences we've already studied in section of sound and string waves and it is analyzed almost in the same way for light also. When two ore more light waves from coherent sources superpose at a point then the resultant intensity at the point is different from the sum of the intensities of these independent waves. This modification in light intensity at the point of superposition of coherent waves is called '*Interference of Light*'. Figure-6.4 shows two coherent sources S_1 and S_2 from which light waves superpose at point P. Due to superposition, the wave disturbance at point P gets modified according to principal of superposition which we studied in the section of '*Interference*' for mechanical waves.

In mechanical waves we consider displacements of particles which varies with position and time and in light waves we consider electric field magnitude which varies with position and time in a specific plane of oscillations as light waves are transverse waves. We specifically consider electric field and not magnetic field because electric field is mainly responsible for sensation of vision due to light in human eye.

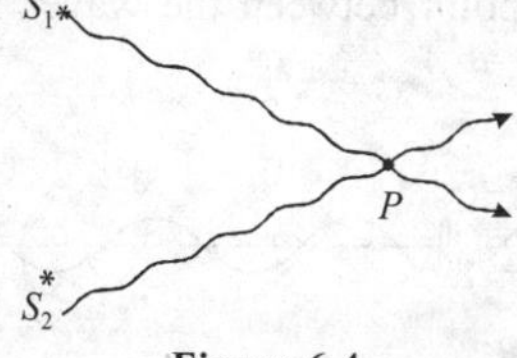

Figure 6.4

In general mechanical wave equations are given as $y = A \sin(\omega t \pm kx + \alpha)$ where y is the displacement of a medium particle located at a distance x from origin and A is the amplitude of the wave. Equation of a light wave can also be expressed in the same way where y represent corresponding magnitudes of the oscillating electric field at a point and A is its amplitude.

6.2.1 Coherent Sources of Light and Condition of Coherence

If we consider two waves in space having different frequency and passing through a point then at this point the phase difference of the two waves will continuously change with time and such waves are called '*Incoherent*'. As from most of the sources light is emitted by molecular agitation in the sources so the frequency of emitted light changes abruptly and irregularly so we consider average frequency of the light from the source. Due to thermal impulses the light frequency changes in an impulsive manner as shown in figure-6.5. If we consider two such independent sources are emitting light of same frequency which pass through a point in space then at that point also these waves will not have constant phase difference as the about and irregular changes in lights from the two independent sources will be random. That's why waves from two independent light sources are also incoherent.

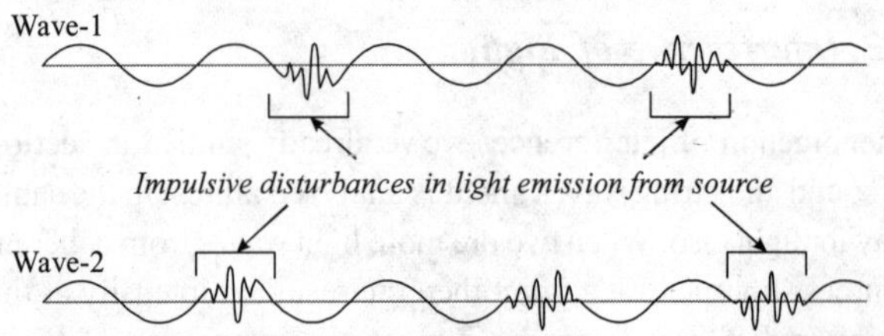

Waves from two independent sources of same frequency

Figure 6.5

If we consider two waves from one single source of light and one wave is somehow changed in direction by reflection or some means and these two waves meet at a point in space then at this point both the waves will have a constant phase difference as all the time the frequency of the two waves will be exactly same and if any sudden and irregular changes occur in source due to thermal agitation of its molecules then also both the waves will have same variation in their displacement curve and will maintain the phase relationship. Such waves are called '*Coherent Waves*'. Figure-6.6 shows two waves from same source in which due to synchronized impulsive changes phase difference at any point between the waves remain constant with time.

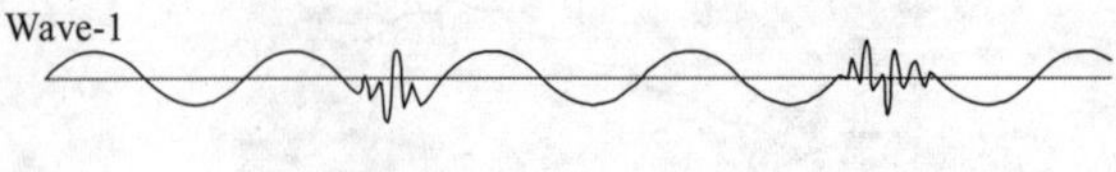

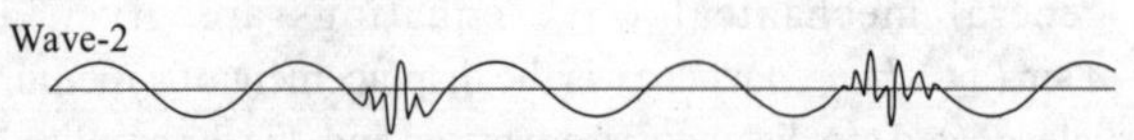

Waves from a single light source

Figure 6.6

6.2.2 Theory of Interference of Two Waves

When two coherent waves of angular frequency ω and amplitude A_1 and A_2 superpose at a point with phase difference ϕ then the independent oscillation displacements of the two waves at the point of superposition are taken as

$$y_1 = A_1 \sin \omega t$$

and $$y_2 = A_2 \sin (\omega t - \phi)$$

At the point of superposition the resultant displacement is given as

$$y = y_1 + y_2$$

$$\Rightarrow \quad y = A_1 \sin \omega t + A_2 \sin (\omega t - \phi)$$

$$\Rightarrow \quad y = A_1 \sin \omega t + A_2 \sin \omega t \cos \phi - A_2 \cos \omega t \sin \phi$$

Rearranging the terms of $\sin \omega t$ and $\cos \omega t$ separately as

$$y = (A_1 + A_2 \cos \phi) \sin \omega t - (A_2 \sin \phi) \cos \omega t$$

Now substituting

$$R \cos \theta = A_1 + A_2 \cos \phi \quad \ldots(6.1)$$

and $$R \sin \theta = A_2 \sin \phi \quad \ldots(6.2)$$

We get $$y = R \cos \theta \sin \omega t - R \sin \theta \cos \omega t$$

$$\Rightarrow \quad y = R \sin (\omega t - \theta) \quad \ldots(6.3)$$

Equation-(6.3) is an equation of Simple Harmonic Motion, thus we can state that after superposition of the two waves, the displacement at the point of superposition P executes SHM with amplitude R and initial phase lag θ with respect to the oscillations produced at the point P by the first wave.

Here R and θ can be given by equation-(6.1) and (6.2). Squaring and adding the two equations, we get

$$R = \sqrt{(A_1 + A_2 \cos \phi)^2 + (A_2 \sin \phi)^2}$$

$$\Rightarrow \quad R = \sqrt{A_1^2 + A_2^2 + 2A_1A_2 \cos \phi} \quad \ldots(6.4)$$

Dividing equation-(6.2) and (6.1) gives

$$\tan \theta = \frac{A_2 \sin \phi}{A_1 + A_2 \cos \phi}$$

$$\Rightarrow \quad \theta = \tan^{-1}\left(\frac{A_2 \sin \phi}{A_1 + A_2 \cos \phi}\right) \quad \ldots(6.5)$$

Equation-(6.4) and (6.5) are the results similar to those obtained by parallelogram rule of vector addition. If A_1 and A_2 are two vectors and ϕ is the angle between their directions then the resultant vector of the two is given by equation-(6.3) and the direction of resultant with the first vector is given by equation-(6.4). Thus we can conclude that when two or more waves of same frequency which differ in phase, superpose on a medium particle then the resulting motion of that medium particle is also SHM with same frequency. Its amplitude can be given by treating the individual amplitudes as vectors with their phase differences as the angles between them and finding the resultant of these vectors.

6.2.3 Interference of two Coherent Waves of Same Amplitude

If the two waves are of equal amplitude $A_1 = A_2 = A$, then resulting amplitude R at the point of superposition is given by equation-(6.4) as

$$R = \sqrt{A^2 + A^2 + 2A^2 \cos\phi}$$

$$\Rightarrow \quad R = \sqrt{2A^2(1+\cos\phi)}$$

$$\Rightarrow \quad R = 2A\cos\left(\frac{\phi}{2}\right) \quad \ldots(6.6)$$

Here we can see that the resultants amplitude R after superposition, depends on the amplitudes of component waves and on the phase difference ϕ between the two component waves. Thus if the phase difference between the two waves changes at the point of superposition, the resulting amplitude of at that point also changes. From equation-(6.4), we can see that the amplitude at the point of interference is maximum when

$$\cos\phi = +1$$

$$\Rightarrow \quad \phi = 2N\pi \quad [N \in I] \quad \ldots(6.7)$$

Then the maximum value of R is given as

$$R_{max} = \sqrt{A_1^2 + A_2^2 + 2A_1A_2}$$

$$\Rightarrow \quad R_{max} = A_1 + A_2 \quad \ldots(6.8)$$

If $A_1 = A_2 = A$ then $R_{max} = 2A$

Thus when the phase difference between two superposition waves is an integral multiple of 2π i.e. when the two waves superpose on a medium particle in same phase then the resultant amplitude of that medium particle will be maximum given by equation-(6.8) and this situation is called '*Constructive Interference*' of waves at the medium particle.

Similarly from equation-(6.4) we can see that the amplitude at the point of superposition is minimum when

$$\cos\phi = -1$$

$$\Rightarrow \quad \phi = (2N+1)\pi \quad [N \in I] \quad \ldots(6.9)$$

Then the minimum amplitude is given as

$$R_{min} = \sqrt{A_1^2 + A_2^2 - 2A_1A_2}$$

$$\Rightarrow \quad R_{min} = A_1 - A_2 \quad \ldots(6.10)$$

If $A_1 = A_2 = A$ then $R_{min} = 0$

Thus when the phase difference between two superposing waves is an odd multiple of π i.e. when the two waves superpose at a point in opposite phase, then the resultant amplitude will be minimum and is given by equation-(6.10) and this situation is called '*Destructive Interference*' of the waves at the point of superposition.

6.2.4 Intensity of Light at the Point of Interference

We've seen when two coherent waves superpose each other at a point, interference takes place. The resultant amplitude at the point of interference depends on the phase difference of the two waves. If R is the resulting amplitude given by equation-(6.4) and I_R be the resulting intensity at the point of interference then it can be given as

$$I_R = kR^2$$

$$\Rightarrow \quad I_R = k(A_1^2 + A_2^2 + 2A_1A_2\cos\phi)$$

$$\Rightarrow \quad I_R = kA_1^2 + kA_2^2 + 2kA_1A_2\cos\phi$$

$$\Rightarrow \quad I_R = I_1 + I_2 + 2\sqrt{I_1 I_2}\cos\phi \quad \ldots(6.11)$$

Here $I_1 = kA_1^2$ and $I_2 = kA_2^2$ are the intensities of first and second wave respectively. The expression in equation-(6.11) gives the resultant intensity at the point of interference due to superposition of two coherent waves having independent intensities I_1 and I_2 respectively. Equation-(6.7) shows that the resultant intensity at the point of interference depends on the individual intensities I_1, I_2 and the phase difference ϕ between the two waves at that point. If the waves are of equal intensities $I_1 = I_2 = I_0$ then after interference the intensity at the point of interference is given by equation-(6.11) as

$$I_R = I_0 + I_0 + 2I_0\cos\phi$$

$$\Rightarrow \quad I_R = 2I_0(1+\cos\phi)$$

$$\Rightarrow \quad I_R = 4I_0\cos^2\left(\frac{\phi}{2}\right) \quad \ldots(6.12)$$

We know when two coherent waves interfere constructively, phase difference between the two is zero or multiple of 2π. Thus from equation-(6.11) for $\cos\phi = +1$ and maximum intensity at the point of constructive interference can be given as

$$I_{max} = I_1 + I_2 + 2\sqrt{I_1 I_2} \quad \ldots(6.13)$$

$$\Rightarrow \quad I_{max} = (\sqrt{I_1} + \sqrt{I_2})^2 \quad \ldots(6.14)$$

For waves of equal intensities if $I_1 = I_2 = I_0$ then we have

$$I_{max} = 4I_0 \quad \ldots(6.15)$$

Similarly for destructive interference as the phase difference between waves should be an odd multiple of π so in equation-(6.11) we use $\cos\phi = -1$ and the minimum intensity at the point of destructive interference can be given as

$$I_{min} = I_1 + I_2 - 2\sqrt{I_1 I_2} \quad \dots(6.16)$$

$$\Rightarrow \quad I_{min} = (\sqrt{I_1} - \sqrt{I_2})^2 \quad \dots(6.17)$$

For waves of equal intensities of $I_1 = I_2 = I_0$, then we have

$$I_{min} = 0 \quad \dots(6.18)$$

From equation-(6.14) and (6.17) we can see that in constructive interference the resultant intensity is more than the sum of individual intensities of the component waves and in destructive interference the resultant intensity is less than the sum of individual intensities of the component waves.

By dividing equations-(6.14) and (6.17) we get

$$\gamma = \left(\frac{\sqrt{I_1} + \sqrt{I_2}}{\sqrt{I_1} - \sqrt{I_2}}\right)^2 = \left(\frac{A_1 + A_2}{A_1 - A_2}\right)^2 \quad \dots(6.19)$$

The ratio g in above equation-(6.19) is called contrast ratio of light in the region of interference where at some points constructive and at some points destructive interference take place.

6.2.5 Condition of Path Difference for Interference

We have already studied in section of mechanical waves that for two waves superposing at a point if their phase difference is ϕ then at that point the path difference in the two waves is given as

$$\Delta = \frac{\lambda}{2\pi} \times \phi \quad \dots(6.20)$$

For the case of constructive interference of two waves we know that the phase difference between the waves is given as $2N\pi$. Thus for constructive interference condition on path difference between the two waves is given as

$$\Delta = \frac{\lambda}{2\pi} \times 2N\pi = N\lambda \quad \dots(6.21)$$

From above equation-(6.21) we can state that two waves interfere constructively when their path difference at the point of superposition is $\Delta = \lambda, 2\lambda, 3\lambda, \dots N\lambda$.

Similarly for the case of destructive interference of two waves we know that the phase difference between two waves is given as $(2N \pm 1)\pi/2$. Thus for constructive interference condition on path difference between the two waves is given as

$$\Delta = \frac{\lambda}{2\pi} \times (2N-1)\pi = (2N-1)\frac{\lambda}{2} \quad \dots(6.22)$$

From above equation-(6.22) we can state that two waves interfere destructively when their path difference at the point of superposition is $\Delta = \lambda/2, 3\lambda/2, 5\lambda/2, \dots (2N-1)\lambda/2$.

In case of destructive interference the path difference between waves should be an odd multiple of $\lambda/2$. For odd multiple, here we've chosen multiplier $(2N-1)$ in equation-(6.21) however it can also be taken as $(2N+1)$.

 # Illustrative Example 6.1

Determine the resulting intensity due to interference of the two waves at a point given below :

$$y_1 = 3\sin(100\pi t)$$

$$y_2 = 4\sin\left(100\pi t + \frac{\pi}{3}\right)$$

Given that intensity due to first wave is I_0.

Solution

If intensity at point due to second wave is I', we use

$$\frac{I'}{I_0} = \left(\frac{A_L}{A_L}\right)^2 = \left(\frac{4}{3}\right)^2$$

$$\Rightarrow \quad I' = \frac{16I_0}{9}$$

Resulting intensity at the point of interference is

$$I_R = I_1 + I_2 + 2\sqrt{I_1 I_2}\cos\phi$$

$$\Rightarrow \quad I_R = I_0 + \frac{16I_0}{9} + 2\sqrt{I_0 \cdot \frac{16I_0}{9}} \cdot \cos\left(\frac{\pi}{3}\right)$$

$$\Rightarrow \quad I_R = I_0 + \frac{16}{9}I_0 + \frac{8}{3}I_0 \times \frac{1}{2}$$

$$\Rightarrow \quad I_R = \frac{37}{9}I_0$$

 # Illustrative Example 6.2

Radio waves coming vertically at an angle α are received by a radar after reflection from a nearby water surface & directly. What should be the height of antenna from water surface so that is records a maximum intensity. (wavelength $= \lambda$).

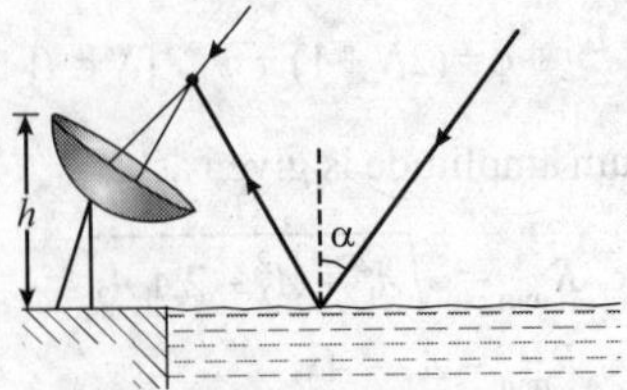

Figure 6.7

Solution

For the maximum intensity path difference, $\Delta x = n\lambda$

At the point C, two rays interfere, one is mc and other is ABC.

Then, path difference,

$$\Delta x = \left(ABC + \frac{\lambda}{2}\right) - (A'C)$$

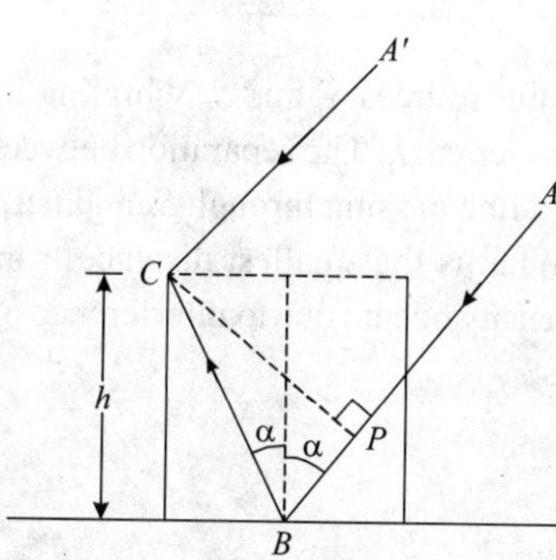

Figure 6.8

As the light ray AB is reflected at the boundary of denser medium at point D, there is an extra path difference added which is equal to $\frac{\lambda}{2}$.

$$\Rightarrow \quad \Delta x = (ABC - A'C) + \frac{\lambda}{2}$$

$$\Rightarrow \quad \Delta x = (BC + PB) + \frac{\lambda}{2} \qquad (\text{As } AP = A'C)$$

$$\Rightarrow \quad \Delta x = \left[\frac{h}{\cos\alpha} + \frac{h(\cos 2\alpha)}{\cos\alpha}\right] + \frac{\lambda}{2}$$

$$\Rightarrow \quad \Delta x = \frac{h}{\cos\alpha}(1 + \cos 2\alpha) + \frac{\lambda}{2}$$

$$\Rightarrow \quad \Delta x = \frac{2h\cos^2\alpha}{\cos\alpha} + \frac{\lambda}{2}$$

$$\Rightarrow \quad \Delta x = 2h\cos\alpha + \frac{\lambda}{2}$$

For the maximum intensity at reception point, we have

$$\Delta x = n\lambda$$

$$\Rightarrow \quad 2h\cos\alpha + \frac{\lambda}{2} = n\lambda$$

For $n = 1$, we have

$$\Rightarrow \quad h = \frac{\lambda}{4\cos\alpha}$$

Illustrative Example 6.3

Two coherent light beams of intensities I and $4I$ superpose in a region. Find the maximum and minimum possible intensities due to superposition in this region.

Solution

Due to interference of light beams at the point of interference maximum intensity is

$$I_{max} = (\sqrt{I_1} + \sqrt{I_2})^2$$

$$\Rightarrow \quad I_{max} = (\sqrt{I_0} + \sqrt{4I})^2$$

$$\Rightarrow \quad I_{max} = 9I$$

Minimum intensity is

$$I_{min} = (\sqrt{I_2} - \sqrt{I_1})^2$$

$$\Rightarrow \quad I_{min} = (\sqrt{4I} - \sqrt{I_1})^2$$

$$\Rightarrow \quad I_{min} = I$$

Illustrative Example 6.4

Two coherent waves are described by the expressions.

$$E_1 = E_{0\sin}\left(\frac{2\pi x_1}{\lambda} - 2\pi ft + \frac{\pi}{6}\right)$$

$$\text{and } E_2 = E_{0\sin}\left(\frac{2\pi x_2}{\lambda} - 2\pi ft + \frac{\pi}{8}\right)$$

Determine the relationship between x_1 and x_2 that produces constructive interference when the two waves are superposed?

Solution

At the point of interference, we use resulting displacement is given as

$$E_R = E_1 + E_2$$

Phase difference at $t = 0$, is given as $\Delta\phi = \phi_1 - \phi_2$ where

$$\phi_1 = \frac{2\pi x_1}{\lambda} - 2\pi ft + \frac{\pi}{6}$$

and

$$\phi_2 = \frac{2\pi x_2}{\lambda} - 2\pi ft + \frac{\pi}{8}$$

$$\Rightarrow \quad \Delta\phi = \left(\frac{2\pi x_1}{\lambda} + \frac{\pi}{6}\right) - \left(\frac{2\pi x_2}{\lambda} + \frac{\pi}{8}\right)$$

For constructive interference, we use

$$\Delta\phi = \pm 2n\pi \qquad (\text{where } n = 0, 1, 2, 3, \ldots)$$

$$\Rightarrow \quad \pm 2n\pi = \frac{2\pi}{\lambda}(x_1 - x_2) + \frac{\pi}{24}$$

$$\Rightarrow \quad \pm\left(n - \frac{1}{48}\right)\lambda = (x_1 - x_2)$$

Illustrative Example 6.5

In figure-6.9, a microwave transmitter a height a above the water level of a wide lake transmits microwaves of wavelength λ towards a receiver on the opposite shore, a distance x above the water level. The microwaves reflecting from the water interfere with the microwaves arriving directly from the transmitter. Assuming that the lake width D is much greater than a and x, and that $\lambda >> a$, at what values of x is the signal at the receiver maximum?

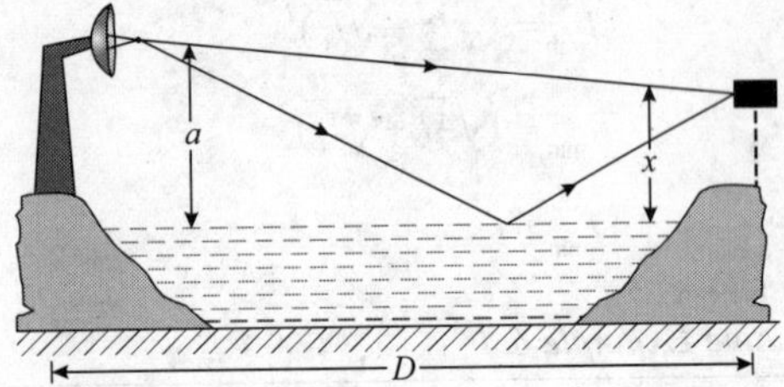

Figure 6.9

Solution

The wave which gets reflected from the water surface suffers a phase changes of π rad or path difference of $\frac{\lambda}{2}$. The reflected wave appear to be coming from the image of the transmitter in the water level. The situation is shown in below figure-6.10.

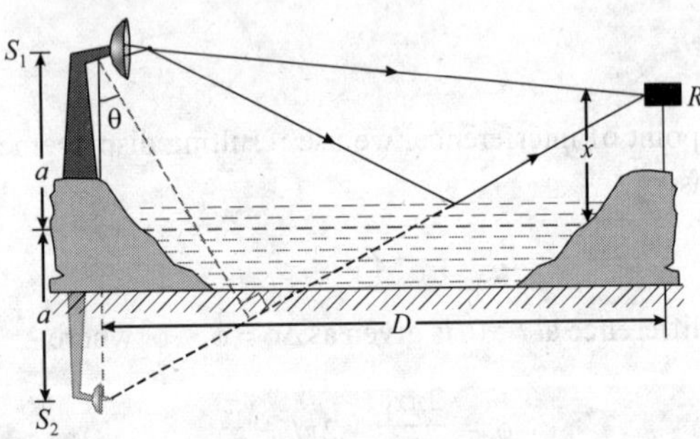

Figure 6.10

The path difference between the waves receiving at R is,

$$\Delta x = 2a \sin\theta$$

As lake width is much greater than the transmitter and receiver heights, we can take θ to be very small. So we can use

$$\Delta x \simeq 2a\theta$$

$$\Rightarrow \quad \Delta x = 2a\frac{x}{D}$$

The effective path difference including the reflection from water surface will be given as

$$\Delta x_e = 2a\frac{x}{D} \pm \frac{\lambda}{2}$$

For interference maxima, we use

$$\Delta x_e = n\lambda$$

$$\Rightarrow \quad 2a\frac{x}{D} + \frac{\lambda}{2} = n\lambda$$

$$\Rightarrow \quad x = \frac{D}{2a}\left(\frac{2n+1}{2}\right)\lambda \text{ where } n = 0, 1, 2$$

Illustrative Example 6.6

The coherent point sources S_1 and S_2 vibrating in same phase emit light of wavelength λ. The separation between the sources is 2λ. Consider a line passing through S_2 and perpendicular to the line $S_1 S_2$. What is the smallest distance from S_2 where a minimum of intensity occurs due to interference of waves from the two sources?

Solution

Path difference at a general point P is given as

$$\Delta x = \sqrt{d^2 + x^2} - x$$

$\Delta x_{min} = 0$, when $x \to \infty$, and maxima will occur.

$\Delta x_{max} = 2\lambda$, when $x = 0$, again maxima will occur.

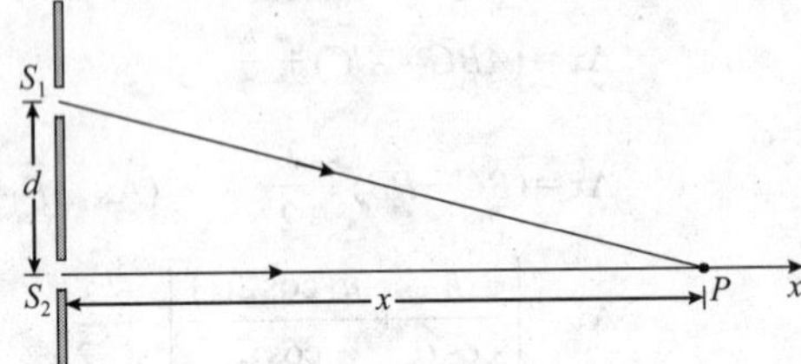

Figure 6.11

For nearest minima from source S_2 we have

$$\Delta x = \frac{3\lambda}{2}$$

$$\Rightarrow \quad \sqrt{d^2 + x^2} - x = \frac{3\lambda}{2}$$

$$\Rightarrow \quad d^2 + x^2 = \left(\frac{3\lambda}{2} + x\right)^2$$

$$\Rightarrow \quad d^2 + x^2 = \frac{9\lambda^2}{4} + x^2 + 3\lambda x$$

$$\Rightarrow \quad x = \frac{\left[d^2 - \frac{9\lambda^2}{4}\right]}{3\lambda}$$

$$\Rightarrow \quad x = \frac{(2\lambda)^2 - \frac{9\lambda^2}{4}}{3\lambda}$$

$$\Rightarrow \quad x = \frac{7\lambda}{12}$$

6.3 Young's Double Slit Experiment (YDSE)

This was one of the most successful and first experimental demonstration of interference of light waves, executed by Thomas Young in 1801. In this experiment stable and stationary interference pattern of light can be seen on a screen and analysis of this experiment is a good learning for interference of light waves.

The *YDSE* setup is shown in figure-6.12(a) in which a plane parallel beam of light is allowed to incident on a single slit of a cardboard from which cylindrical wavefronts are produced by the secondary wave sources in the slit as shown in the cross sectional view in figure-6.12(b). From the slit plane-1 when parallel light beam incident on it then by the card board all the secondary sources of wavefront are blocked except those which are located in the region of rectangular slit in the cardboard. Only those secondary wavelets will pass in the region between slit planes which are passing through the slit *S*. The common tangential plane of all these secondary wavelets will be cylindrical wavefront in the diverging beam from slit *S* and it falls on slit plane-2. This beam illuminates simultaneously two slits S_1 and S_2 in slit plane-2 which are closely separated ($d << D$) and located equidistant from slit *S*. As slits S_1 and S_2 are illuminated by same light beam so these are considered as coherent light sources having same phase as these are illuminated at the same instant.

Light waves from S_1 and S_2 further propagate in diverging beams with their cylindrical wavefronts as shown in figure-6.12(b) and superpose on the screen with different path difference at different points of the screen. The points on screen where the light interfere constructively, a bright fringe is produced and at those points where light interfere destructively, a dark fringe is produced as shown in figure-6.12(a). On the screen these bright and dark fringes alternatively produced and this interference pattern on screen is called fringe pattern. In next session we will analyze this interference pattern and see how light intensity varies on screen with distance.

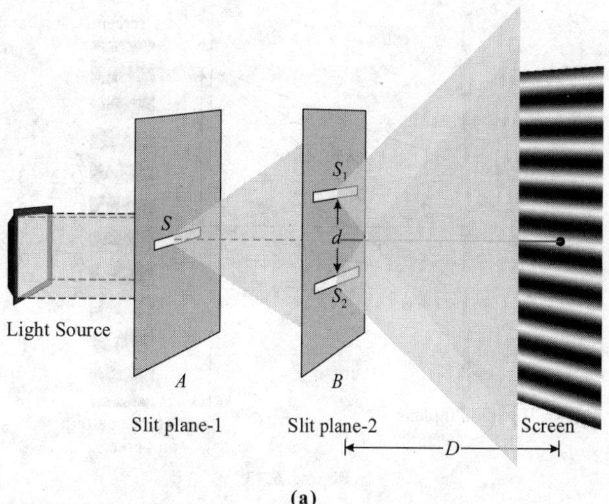

(a)

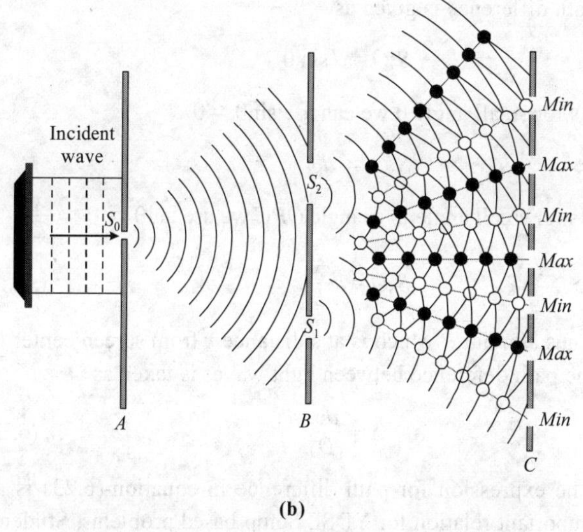

(b)

Figure-6.12

6.3.1 Analysis of Interference Pattern in YDSE

The interference pattern is obtained in YDSE due to the different path difference in component waves from slits S_1 and S_2 at different points on screen. Figure-6.13 shows two light waves travelling along paths S_1P and S_2P and interfering at point *P* on screen which is located at a distance *x* from screen center *C*. As both the slits are illuminated at the same time by the light beam falling on this slit plane, we consider zero phase difference between the light waves from these two slit sources. In the figure we drop a perpendicular from S_1 to line S_2P at point *Q*. As $d << D$ and θ is the angle between line *OP* and *OC*, we can consider $S_1P \approx QP$ so the path difference in the light waves from S_1 and S_2 at point *P* is given as

$$\Delta = S_2P - S_1P \approx S_2Q$$

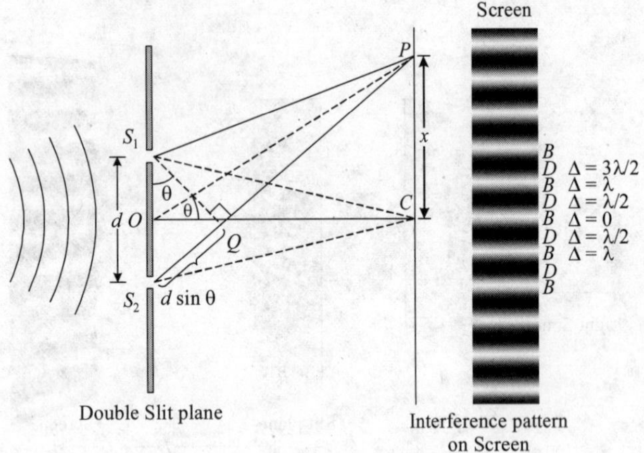

Figure 6.13

Here as $D >> d$, we can see that angle S_2S_1Q is also θ so the path difference is given as

$$S_2Q = d\sin\theta$$

As for small angle θ we can use $\sin\theta \simeq \theta$

$$\Rightarrow \quad S_2Q \simeq d\theta$$

As for small angle in triangle OPC we use $\tan\theta \simeq \theta \simeq \frac{x}{D}$

$$\Rightarrow \quad S_2Q = d\frac{x}{D}$$

Thus at point P which is at a distance x from screen center C, the path deference between light waves is taken as

$$\Delta = \frac{dx}{D} \qquad \dots(6.23)$$

The expression for path difference in equation-(6.23) is an important relation for YDSE Setup based problems. Students are advised to keep this formula in mind for future use.

If we consider screen center C where path difference is zero and at this point the two waves will interfere constructively and a bright fringe is produced and as we move away from C (say upward on screen) then the path of wave from S_2 increases and that from S_1 decreases so path difference increases. Due to variation in path difference intensity of light also decreases as we move away from central bright fringe. At the location of first dark fringe the path difference becomes $l/2$ and waves interfere destructively then l at first bright fringe as shown in figure-6.13 which is resulting in a sustained interference pattern on the screen.

6.3.2 Position of Bright and Dark Fringes in YDSE Interference Pattern

As shown in figure-6.14, if point P is located at n^{th} bright fringe of pattern then the path difference at point P can be given as

$$\Delta = n\lambda$$

$$\Rightarrow \quad \frac{dx}{D} = n\lambda$$

$$\Rightarrow \quad x = \frac{n\lambda D}{d} \qquad \dots(6.24)$$

Equation-(6.24) gives the distance of nth bright fringe from screen center if the slit sources S_1 and S_2 are in same phase.

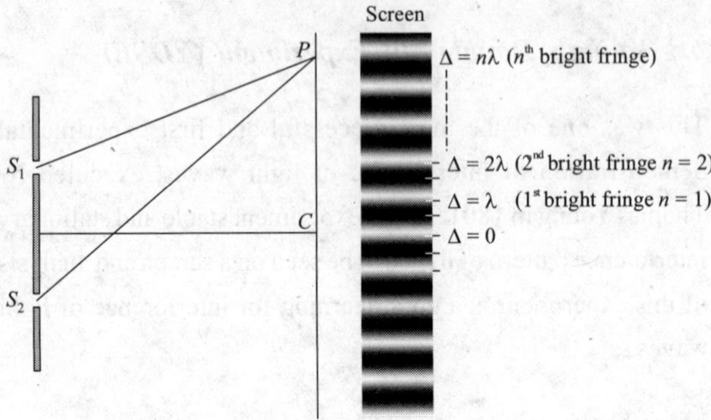

Figure 6.14

Similarly as shown in figure-6.15, if point P is located at n^{th} dark fringe of pattern then the path difference between at point P can be given as

$$\Delta = (2n-1)\frac{\lambda}{2} \qquad \text{where } n = 1, 2, 3\dots N$$

$$\Rightarrow \quad \frac{dx}{D} = (2n-1)\frac{\lambda}{2}$$

$$\Rightarrow \quad x = \frac{(2n-1)\lambda D}{2d} \qquad \dots(6.25)$$

Equation-(6.25) gives the distance of nth dark fringe from screen center if the slit sources S_1 and S_2 are in same phase.

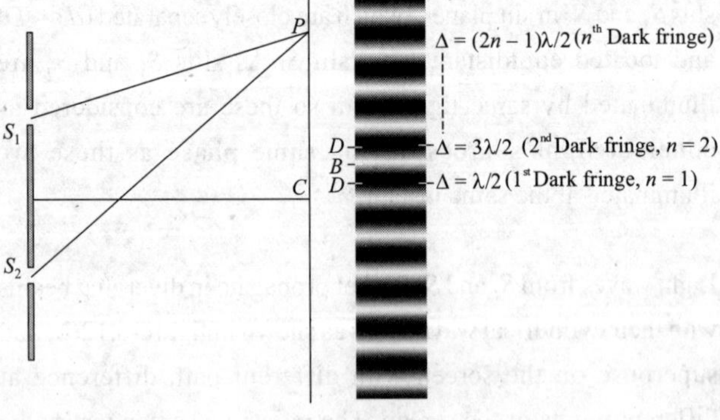

Figure 6.15

6.3.3 Light Intensity on Screen in YDSE Setup

At a general point P on screen in YDSE interference pattern shown in figure-6.16, we have obtained that path difference in the two light waves is given as

$$\Delta = \frac{dx}{D}$$

The phase difference at point P in the two waves is given as

$$\phi = \frac{2\pi}{\lambda} \times \Delta = \frac{2\pi}{\lambda} \times \frac{dx}{D} = \frac{2\pi dx}{\lambda D} \quad \dots (6.26)$$

If intensity of light due to both the slits individually at screen is I_0 then resulting intensity at point P can be given by equation-(6.26) as

$$I_R = 4I_0 \cos^2 \frac{\phi}{2}$$

$$\Rightarrow \quad I_R = 4I_0 \cos^2 \frac{\pi dx}{\lambda D} \quad \dots (6.27)$$

From equation-(6.27) we can see that bright fringes where $x = N\lambda D/d$, intensity is $4I_0$ and at the location of dark fringes where $x = (2N-1)\lambda D/2d$, intensity is zero. Figure-6.16 shows the variation of light intensity in the interference pattern of YDSE.

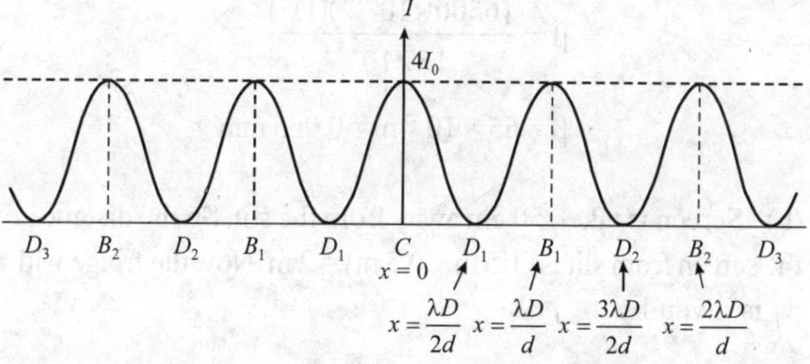

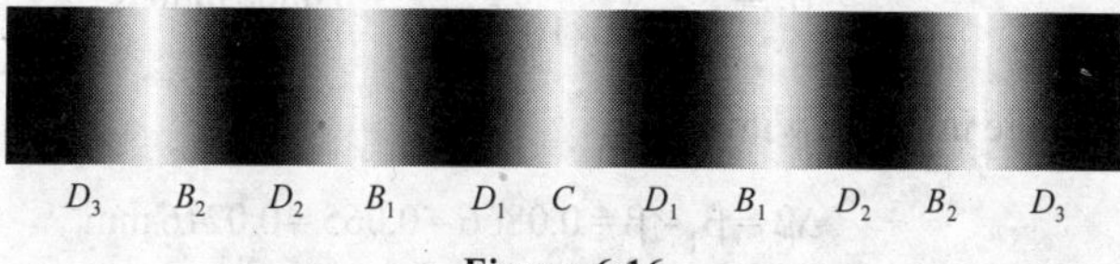

Figure 6.16

6.3.4 Fringe Width in YDSE Interference Pattern

Figure-6.17 shows the YDSE interference pattern which we have analyzed that due to continuous variation in path difference on different points of screen alternative bright and dark fringes are obtained on the two sides of screen center where path difference is zero.

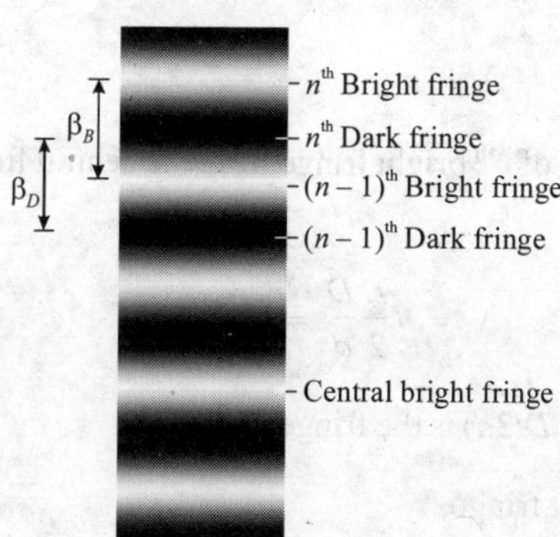

Figure 6.17

The intensity of light gradually changes when we move from a bright fringe to a dark fringe and the separation between two bright or two dark fringes is called '*Fringe Width*' as shown in figure. The fringe width can be calculated by separation between two successive bright or dark fringes as given below.

For Bright fringes we use fringe width β is given as

$$\beta = x_n - x_{n-1} = \frac{n\lambda D}{d} - \frac{(n-1)\lambda D}{d}$$

$$\Rightarrow \quad \beta = \frac{\lambda D}{d} \quad \dots (6.28)$$

For Dark fringes we use fringe width β is given as

$$\beta = x_n - x_{n-1} = \frac{(2n-1)\lambda D}{2d} - \frac{(2n-3)\lambda D}{d}$$

$$\Rightarrow \quad \beta = \frac{\lambda D}{d} \quad \dots (6.29)$$

From equation-(6.28) and (6.29) we can see that the separation between two successive bright or dark fringes remain same and this is termed as fringe width of the interference pattern in YDSE.

Some times fringe width is also accounted as '*Angular Fringe Width*'. It is the angular separation between two successive bright or dark fringes as measured from center of double slit plane. Figure-6.18 shows the angular fringe width θ_β in YDSE Setup. If β is the fringe width on screen in interference pattern and D is the separation between double slit plane and screen, the angular fringe width can be given as

$$\theta_\beta = \frac{\beta}{D} = \frac{\left(\frac{\lambda D}{d}\right)}{D} = \frac{\lambda}{d} \quad \dots (6.30)$$

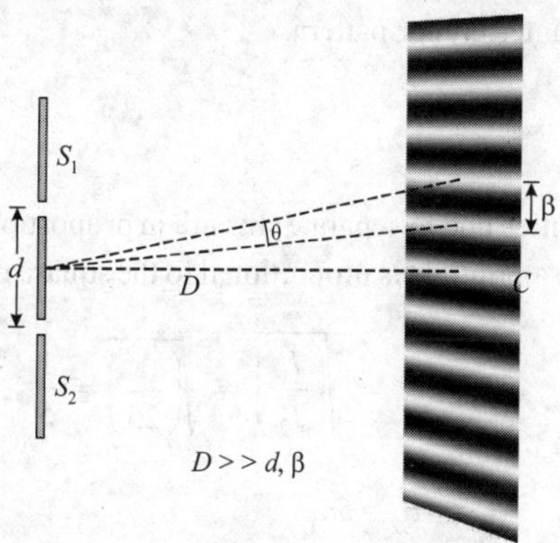

Figure 6.18

Illustrative Example 6.7

A double-slit arrangement produces interference fringes for sodium light ($\lambda = 589$ nm) that have an angular separation of 3.50×10^{-3} rad. For what wavelength would the angular separation be 10% greater ?

Solution

The angular of fringes is given by, $\alpha = \frac{\lambda}{d}$. Thus for 10% greater value of α, there need the wavelength 1.1 λ. Therefore required wavelength = $1.1 \times 589 = 648$ nm.

 # Illustrative Example 6.8

In a YDSE setup sodium light of wavelength 5893Å is being used. The interference pattern is obtained on a screen which is located at a distance 1 m from the slit plane. In the interference pattern it is observed that 10th bright fringe is located at a distance of 12 mm from the central maximum. Find the slit separation.

Solution

In a YDSE setup the distance of nth bright fringe from central maximum is given as

$$x_{nB} = \frac{n\lambda D}{d}$$

$$\Rightarrow \quad x_{nB} = \frac{10 \times 5893 \times 10^{-10} \times 1}{d} = 12 \times 10^{-3}$$

$$\Rightarrow \quad d = 4.9 \times 10^{-4}\ \text{m} = 0.49\ \text{mm}$$

 # Illustrative Example 6.9

Two slits in Young's interference experiment have width in the ratio 1 : 25. Deduce the ratio of intensity at the maxima and minima in interference pattern.

Solution

The intensities due to separate slits are in proportion to the slit width. The amplitude is proportional to the square of intensity.

$$\frac{a_1}{a_2} = \sqrt{\left(\frac{I_1}{I_2}\right)} = \sqrt{\left(\frac{1}{25}\right)} = \frac{1}{5}$$

$$\Rightarrow \quad a_2 = 5a_1$$

$$\text{Now} \quad \frac{I_{max}}{I_{min}} = \frac{(a_1 + a_2)^2}{(a_1 - a_2)^2} = \frac{(a_1 + 5a_1)^2}{(a_1 - 5a_1)^2}$$

$$\Rightarrow \quad \frac{I_{max}}{I_{min}} = \frac{36a_1^2}{16a_1^2} = \frac{36}{16} = \frac{9}{4}$$

$$\Rightarrow \quad I_{max} : I_{min} = 9 : 4$$

 # Illustrative Example 6.10

In Young's experiment, interference bands are produced on the screen placed at 1.5 m from the two slits 0.15 mm apart and illuminated by light of wavelength 6500 Å. Find (a) the fringe width and (b) the change in the fringe width if the screen is taken away from the slit by 50 cm.

Solution

(a) The fringe width β is given by

$$\beta = \frac{\lambda D}{2d}$$

Here we use $\lambda = 6500\ \text{Å} = 6500 \times 10^{-10}$ m

$D = 1.5$ m and $2d = 0.15$ mm $= 15 \times 10^{-5}$ m

$$\Rightarrow \quad \beta = \frac{(6500 \times 10^{-10})(1.5)}{15 \times 10^{-5}}$$

$$\Rightarrow \quad \beta = 65 \times 10^{-4}\ \text{m} = 0.065\ \text{mm}$$

(b) Screen is taken 50 cm away from the slit. So the distance of the screen from slit is (1.5 m + 0.5 m) = 2 m. Now the fringe width β_1 is given by

$$\beta_1 = \frac{(6500 \times 10^{-10})(2)}{15 \times 10^{-5}} = 0.0866\ \text{mm}$$

Change in fringe width

$$\Delta\beta = \beta_1 - \beta = 0.0866 - 0.065 = 0.0216\ \text{mm}$$

 # Illustrative Example 6.11

In Young's double slit experiment the slits are 0.5 mm apart and interference is observed on a screen placed at a distance of 100 cm from the slits. It is found that the 9th bright fringe is at a distance of 8.835 mm from the second dark fringe from the centre of the fringe pattern. Find the wavelength of light used.

Solution

The distance of nth bright fringe from the central fringe is given by

$$x_n = n\frac{\lambda D}{2d} = n\beta$$

where $\beta = (\lambda D/2d)$ is the fringe width.

For 9th bright fringe,

$$x_9 = 9\beta \quad \ldots(6.31)$$

The distance of nth dark fringe from the central fringe is given by

$$x_n' = n\frac{(2n-1)\lambda D}{4d}$$

$$\Rightarrow \quad x_n' = \left(n-\frac{1}{2}\right)\frac{\lambda D}{2d} = \left(n-\frac{1}{2}\right)\beta$$

For 2nd dark fringe,

$$x_2' = \frac{3}{2}\beta \qquad \ldots(6.32)$$

From equations-(6.31) and (6.32), we get

$$x_9 - x_2' = 9\beta - \frac{3}{2}\beta = \frac{15}{2}\beta$$

Given that $x_9 - x_2' = 8.835\,\text{mm}$

$$\Rightarrow \quad \frac{15}{2}\beta = 8.835$$

$$\Rightarrow \quad \beta = 1.178\,\text{mm} = 1.178\times10^{-3}\,\text{m}$$

Further $\quad \lambda = \beta\frac{2d}{D}$

$$\Rightarrow \quad \lambda = (1.178\times10^{-3})\frac{(0.5\times10^{-3})}{1}$$

$$\Rightarrow \quad \lambda = 5.89\times10^{-7}\,\text{m} = 5890\,\text{Å}$$

6.4 Modifications in YDSE Setup

In previous article we've studied the Young's Double Slit Experiment for demonstration of interference of light waves. There are various modifications which are done to the YDSE setup and with modification the interference pattern is observed and studied. In this section we'll study some modifications and alternative setups to produces interference patterns similar to YDSE.

6.4.1 Effect of Changing the direction of Incident Light in *YDSE*

Figure-6.19 shows a YDSE setup in which on the double slit plane a coherent parallel light beam is allowed to incident which is at an angle of incidence θ to the slit plane as shown. Due to the inclined incidence of beam we can see that slit S_2 will be illuminated earlier than S_1 so waves from S_2 will lead in phase over the waves from S_1 because of the extra path $d\sin\theta$ which the wavefront illuminating slit S_2 will travel till it reaches slit S_1. If we analyze the path difference in the two waves interfering at screen center C then the two waves travel equal path after slit plane upto this point but due to initial path difference before slit plane, the total path difference in waves at point C will be $d\sin\theta$.

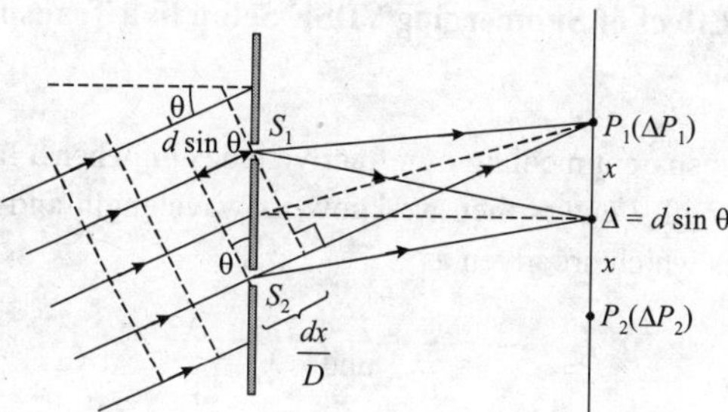

Figure 6.19

In above situation the phase difference between waves from slits S_1 and S_2 at screen center C is given as

$$\phi = \frac{2\pi}{\lambda}\times d\sin\theta$$

If I_0 is the light intensity on screen due to each of the slit S_1 and S_2 then using above phase difference we can find the intensity of light at center of screen at point C, given as

$$I_C = 4I_0\cos^2\left(\frac{\phi}{2}\right) = 4I_0\cos^2\left(\frac{\pi d\sin\theta}{\lambda}\right) \qquad \ldots(6.33)$$

If we analyze the interference of the two waves at a point P_1 located at a distance x above screen center as shown then at this point after slit plane the path difference in waves is dx/D which we have already studied. As after slit plane at point P_1 wave from S_2 is travelling longer path and before slit plane wave to S_1 is longer then the total path difference in the two waves at point P_1 is given as

$$\Delta_{P_1} = \frac{dx}{D} - d\sin\theta \qquad \ldots(6.34)$$

Similarly if we find the total path difference between waves at point P_2 which is located at a distance x below the screen center as shown then at point P_2 the total path difference is given as

$$\Delta_{P_2} = \frac{dx}{D} + d\sin\theta \qquad \ldots(6.35)$$

From equation-(6.34) we can see somewhere at a point above the screen center this path difference Δ_{P_1} can be zero at a distance x_0 from screen center where

$$\frac{dx_0}{D} = d\sin\theta$$

$$\Rightarrow \quad x_0 = D\sin\theta \qquad \ldots(6.36)$$

Above equation-(6.36) gives the position where path difference is zero or the position of central bright fringe after changing the direction of incident light beam on double slit plane. If the parallel light beam incident on the double slit plane normally then both the slits will get illuminated simultaneously and the point of zero path difference (central maxima) would be located at point C and if the incident beam is rotated downward upto the situation shown in figure-6.19 then with above analysis we can state that during rotation of the beam the interference pattern will shift upward by a distance given by equation-(6.35).

6.4.2 Effect of Submerging YDSE Setup in a Transparent Medium

In a transparent medium of refractive index *m*, when a light of wavelength *l* enters then we know its wavelength and speed reduces which are given as

$$v_m = \frac{c}{\mu} \quad \text{and} \quad \lambda_m = \frac{\lambda}{\mu}$$

If a YDSE setup is submerged in a transparent liquid as shown in figure-6.20 then in the submerged part due to decreased wavelength fringe width of the interference pattern also decreases which is given as

$$\beta_m = \frac{\lambda_m D}{d} = \frac{\lambda D}{\mu d} \qquad \ldots(6.37)$$

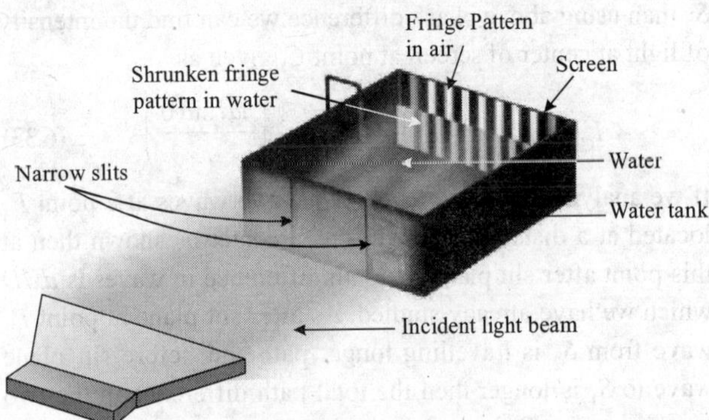

Figure 6.20

Here $\beta_m < \beta$, so we can say that on submerging a given YDSE setup in a transparent medium, the interference pattern shrinks.

6.4.3 Path difference between two parallel waves due to a denser medium in path of one beam

Figure-6.21 shows two coherent light rays (thin beams) from a single source of light travelling in same direction parallel to each other. If in path of first beam a glass slab of refractive index μ is placed which is of width w then the light ray-1 will slow down after it enters in slab at point A and its speed will reduce to c/m. When the ray-1 which enters in slab comes out at point B then in this duration the ray-2 which was travelling in space would have travelled a longer path as it was travelling at speed c.

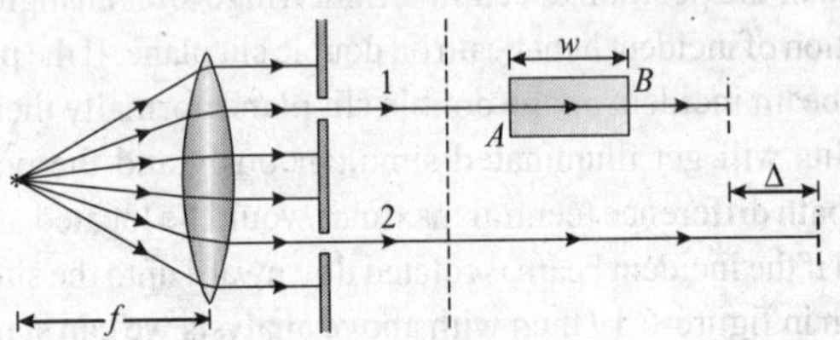

Figure 6.21

The time taken by ray-1 in travelling through the glass slab is

$$\delta t = \left(\frac{w}{c/\mu}\right) = \frac{\mu w}{c}$$

Path length covered by ray-2 in space while ray-1 was travelling in slab is

$$l = c \times \frac{\mu w}{c} = \mu w \qquad \ldots(6.38)$$

Thus path difference between the two rays after the glass slab is given as

$$\Delta = \mu w - w = w(\mu - 1) \qquad \ldots(6.39)$$

If these two light waves (rays) are brought to focus of a converging lens as shown then the two waves will interfere with a phase difference given as

$$\phi = \frac{2\pi}{\lambda} \times w(\mu - 1) \qquad \ldots(6.40)$$

If each of the light wave in the two thin light beams (rays) have intensity I_0 then at the focal point of the lens the resulting intensity of light is given as

$$I_R = 4I_0 \cos^2\left(\frac{\phi}{2}\right) = 4I_0 \cos^2\left(\frac{\pi w(\mu - 1)}{\lambda}\right) \qquad \ldots(6.41)$$

6.4.4 Effect of Placing a Thin Transparent Film in front of one of the slits in YDSE Setup

Figure-6.22 shows a YDSE setup and in front of slit S_1 a thin transparent film of thickness t and refractive index μ is placed. Due to this film the light coming out from slit S_1 will get delayed by some path as it gets slower in the film medium. At the screen center where the physical path difference is zero in the two light waves coming from slit S_1 and S_2, due to thin film an optical path difference is introduced in the path of light waves which is given by equation-(6.39).

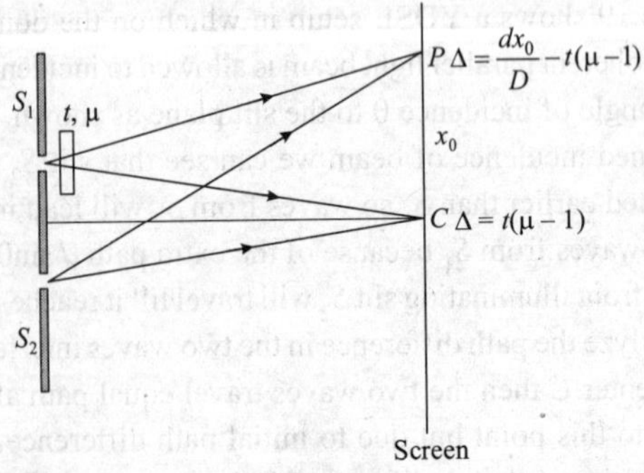

Figure 6.22

Optical path difference in the two light waves from the slits at screen center C is given as

$$\Delta = t(\mu - 1) \quad \dots(6.42)$$

At screen center the extra path given by above equation-(a) is introduced in the light coming from slit S_1 as it got delayed while travelling inside the film. If we try to locate a point on screen where optical path difference is zero then we can clearly state that it will be located above point C on screen where the extra optical path introduced in first wave is compensated by the extra physical path travelled by the second wave which is given by equation-(6.42). If P is the point of net zero path difference located at a distance x_0 from the screen center C in figure-6.13 then at point P we can use

$$\frac{dx_0}{D} = t(\mu - 1)$$

$$\Rightarrow \quad x_0 = \frac{t(\mu - 1)D}{d} \quad \dots(6.43)$$

Above equation-(6.43) gives the shift of interference pattern on screen due to insertion of thin film in front of one of the slits because the fringe of zero path difference was located at screen center in YDSE before the film was inserted in front of S_1. At a general point P on screen located in upper half of screen at a distance x from C, the path difference is given as

$$\Delta_P = \frac{dx}{D} - t(\mu - 1) \quad \dots(6.44)$$

And at a general point P' located in lower half of screen at a distance x from C, the path difference is given as

$$\Delta_P = \frac{dx}{D} + t(\mu - 1) \quad \dots(6.45)$$

6.4.5 Concept of z-value in Interference Pattern of YDSE

At any point in interference pattern on YDSE screen, we can define a numeric parameter 'z' for relating path difference in the two light waves and wavelength of light as

$$\Delta_P = z_P\lambda$$

$$\Rightarrow \quad z_P = \frac{\Delta_P}{\lambda} \quad \dots(6.46)$$

Above numerical parameter z_P is a constant which gives the multiplier of light wavelength at any point on screen that gives the path difference at a the specific point on screen. This '*z-value*' helps in quickly determining the number of bright and dark fringes in any length of interference pattern of YDSE.

For example if we look at the YDSE Setup shown in figure-6.14 in which a thin film is placed in front of slit S_1 due to which the overall fringe pattern is shifted upward by some distance. In this case obviously it is not necessary that at screen center there is a bright fringe because the path difference at point C is now given as $\Delta_C = t(\mu - 1)$. If we find the '*z-value*' at screen center then it is given by equation-(i) as

$$z_C = \frac{\Delta_C}{\lambda} = \frac{t(\mu - 1)}{\lambda} \quad \dots(6.47)$$

Say the expression obtained in equation-(6.47) gives a numerical value 6.23 after substituting the numerical values of all constants in it. That means at point C on screen the path difference in the two waves is 6.23λ or it shows that the original center bright fringe is located about 6 fringes above the point C where path difference will be zero.

Thus at any point on screen if you calculate the '*z-value*' then it directly gives you an idea about the path difference of bright or dark fringes above or below this point which helps us in calculating the total number of fringes in any region of interference pattern.

 # Illustrative Example 6.12

A double slit arrangement produces interference fringes for sodium light (λ = 5890 Å) that are 0.40° apart. What is the angular fringe separation if the entire arrangement is immersed in water ?

Solution

In double slit arrangement, the angular separation is given by

$$\beta = \frac{\lambda D}{2d}$$

Let angular separation in air and water be β_A and β_W respectively

Now $$\beta_A = \frac{\lambda_A D}{2d} \text{ and } \beta_W = \frac{\lambda_W D}{2d}$$

$$\Rightarrow \quad \frac{\beta_W}{\beta_A} = \frac{\lambda_W}{\lambda_A} \quad \dots(6.48)$$

We know that $$\mu = \frac{\text{Velocity of light in air}}{\text{Velocity of light in water}}$$

$$\Rightarrow \quad \frac{4}{3} = \frac{V_A}{V_W} = \frac{f\lambda_A}{f\lambda_W} = \frac{\lambda_A}{\lambda_W}$$

where f is the frequency of light

Now $$\frac{\lambda_W}{\lambda_A} = \frac{3}{4} \quad \dots(6.49)$$

From equation-(6.48) and (6.49), we have

$$\frac{\beta_W}{\beta_A} = \frac{\lambda_W}{\lambda_A} = \frac{3}{4}$$

$$\Rightarrow \quad \beta_W = \beta_A \times \frac{3}{4} = 0.40° \times \frac{3}{4} = 0.30°$$

Illustrative Example 6.13

A *YDSE* setup is immersed in water (μ = 1.33). If has slit separation 1 mm and distance between slits and screen is 1.33 m. Incident light on slits have wavelength 6300Å. Find the fringe width on screen.

Solution

W/L of light in water

$$\lambda_\omega = \frac{\lambda}{\mu} = \frac{6300}{1.33} \text{Å}$$

In *YDSE* fringe width is given as

$$A = \frac{\lambda_\omega D}{d} = \frac{6300 \times 10^{-10} \times 1.53}{1.33 \times 10^{-3}}$$

$$\Rightarrow \quad A = 6.3 \times 10^{-4} \text{ m}$$

$$\Rightarrow \quad A = 0.63 \text{ mm}$$

Illustrative Example 6.14

There are two coherent sources S_1 and S_2 which produce waves in same phase placed on *Y* axis at points (0, 2*d*) and (0, *d*) as shown in figure-6.23. A detector *D* is placed at origin which moves along *X* direction, find the number of maxima recorded by detector excluding points *x* = 0 and *x* = ∞. Given that wavelength of light produced is 6200 *A* and separation between sources is 0.34 mm.

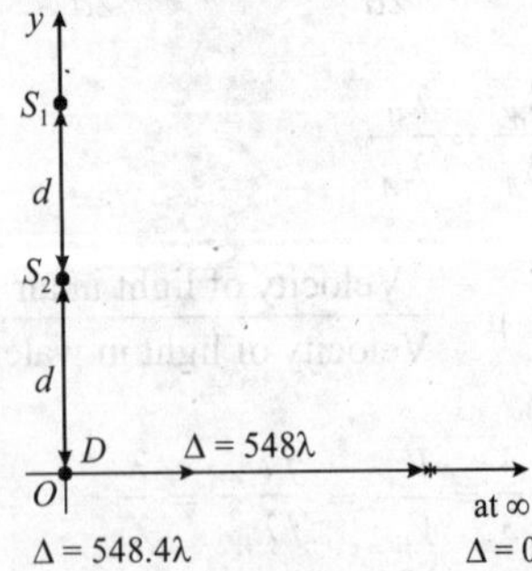

Figure 6.23

Solution

Path different between waves from S_1 and S_2 at origin

$$\Delta = d = 3.4 \times 10^{-4} m \times \frac{\lambda}{\lambda}$$

$$\Rightarrow \quad \Delta = \frac{3.4 \times 10^{-4}}{6.2 \times 10^{-7}} \lambda = 548.4\lambda$$

Total no of maxima on *x* axis ___ by *D* are = 548

Illustrative Example 6.15

In *YDSE* setup slits are illuminated by a light of wavelength 4000 Å and a light of unknown wavelength. It is observed that fourth dark fringe of known wavelength coincide with second bright fringe of unknown wavelength. Find the unknown wavelength.

Solution

For n^{th} dark fringe from centre

$$x_{ND} = \frac{(N-1)\lambda D}{2d}$$

for $N = 4, \lambda = 4000\text{Å}$

$$\Rightarrow \quad x_{4D} = \frac{7 \times 4 \times 10^{-7} \times D}{2d}$$

For n^{th} bright fringe from centre

$$x_{ND} = \frac{N\lambda D}{d}$$

for $N = 2, \lambda = ?$

$$\Rightarrow \quad x_{2B} = \frac{2\lambda D}{d}$$

Given that $x_{4D} = x_{2B}$

$$\Rightarrow \quad \frac{7 \times 4 \times 10^{-7} D}{2d} = \frac{2\lambda D}{d}$$

$$\Rightarrow \quad \lambda = 7 \times 10^{-7} \text{ m} = 7000\text{Å}$$

Illustrative Example 6.16

In a *YDSE* setup, light of wavelength 5000 Å is used and slit separation is 3 × 10^{-7} m. When a transparent sheet of thickness 1.5 × 10^{-7} m is placed over one of the slits which has μ = 1.17, find the shift of fringe pattern. Take separation between slits and screen is 1 m.

Solution

At *C* path different

$$\Delta = t(\mu - 1)$$

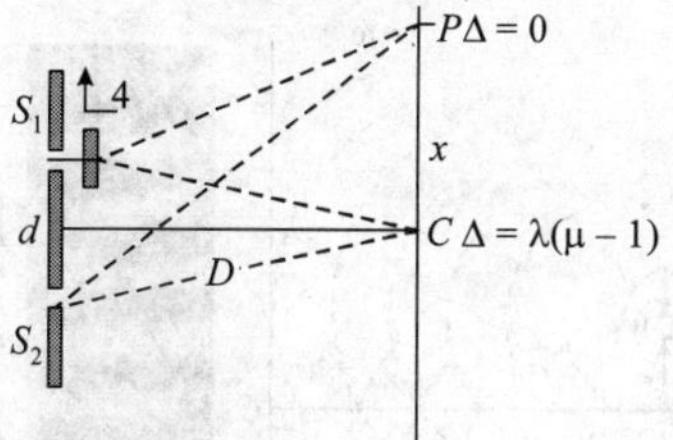

Figure 6.24

At point P we have

$$\frac{dx}{D} = t(\mu - 1)$$

$$\Rightarrow \qquad x = \frac{Dt(\mu - 1)}{\alpha} = \frac{1 \times 1.5 \times 10^{-7} \times 0.17}{3 \times 10^{-7}}$$

$$\Rightarrow \qquad x = 0.055\text{ m} = 8.5\text{ cm}$$

Illustrative Example 6.17

In *YDSE* setup find the distance between two slits that result in the third minimum for 4200 Å violet light at an angle 30°. Take $d \ll D$.

Solution

At point P on screen path different between waves from S_1 and S_2 is

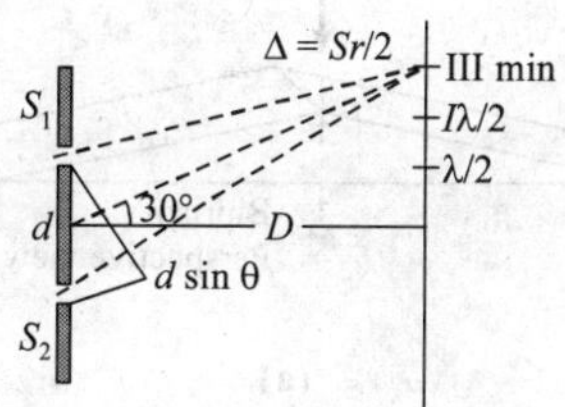

Figure 6.25

$$\Delta = d \sin 30° = \frac{d}{x} = \frac{5\lambda}{2} \text{ (for II min)}$$

$$\Rightarrow \qquad d = 5\lambda = 5 \times 4200 \times 10^{-10}\text{ m}$$

$$\Rightarrow \qquad d = 2.1 \times 10^{-6}\text{ m}$$

6.4.6 Use of White Light in YDSE

When white light is used in YDSE setup, all the component waves of white light will have zero path difference at screen center C and all colors in white light will interfere constructively and a bright white fringe is produced. But as we move away from the center then closest to screen center first the destructive interference of violet color will take place as violet color has minimum wavelength in white light at a point V_D shown in figure-6.26 where path difference will become $\lambda_V/2$ on both sides of C. At these points violet colour will be missing from white light due to destructive interference and the colour seen on screen will be reddish white (not red as it is white - violet) because other then violet all other colours will be present at this point as only violet will be completely absent.

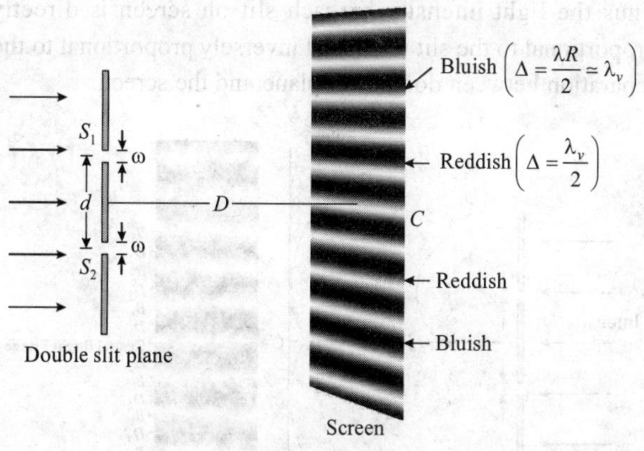

Figure 6.26

Similarly if we move further away from point C on screen next point will be the point of destructive interference of red light which is having the maximum wavelength in white light where red colour will be absent and path difference at this point will be $\lambda_R/2$. As the wavelength of red colour is approximately double that of violet colour so at this point violet color light will also have higher intensity and the colour of fringe here will appear '*Bluish*' (Not blue as other colours are also present here). Beyond this point on screen all colours will mix and no specific colour will be seen on screen and screen looks '*Mixed White*' or '*Off White*' in colour.

6.4.7 Effect of Changing Slit Width in YDSE Setup

In a YDSE setup if each slit is producing light intensity I_0 on screen then this intensity is directly proportional to the width of the slits in double slit plane. Figure-6.27 show that a plane parallel beam of light of intensity I_1 illuminates the double slit plane. If each slit is of width w and length l then the light power which pass through these slits will be given as

$$P_{Slit} = I_1 \,.\, lw \qquad \ldots(6.50)$$

Thus the power of light from each slit will be proportional to the slit area given by equation-(6.50) and as we have already studied in section of spherical and cylindrical waves that intensity due to any light source is given by the ratio of source power and the surface area of wavefront at any point. We know that a slit produces half cylindrical wavefronts after double slit plane and the wavefront W_1 so at a distance x from a slit the light intensity can be given as

$$I_{Slit} = \frac{P_{Slit}}{\pi xl} = \frac{I_1 lw}{\pi xl} = \frac{I_1 w}{\pi x} \qquad \ldots(6.51)$$

Thus the light intensity I_0 on screen at a distance D from double slit plane due to each slit is given as

$$I_{\text{Slit}} = \frac{I_1 w}{\pi D} \quad \ldots(6.52)$$

Thus the light intensity by each slit on screen is directly proportional to the slit width and inversely proportional to the separation between double slit plane and the screen.

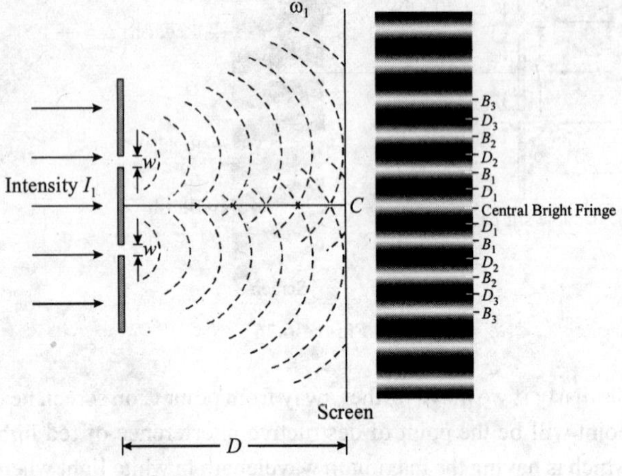

Figure 6.27

If both slits S_1 and S_2 are of equal width then intensity by both slits will be same I_0 on screen and the resulting intensity of bright and dark fringes will be

$$I_{Bright} = (\sqrt{I_0} + \sqrt{I_0})^2 = 4I_0 \quad \ldots(6.53)$$

and
$$I_{Dark} = (\sqrt{I_0} - \sqrt{I_0})^2 = 0 \quad \ldots(6.54)$$

From equation-(6.54) we can see that dark fringes will be perfectly black and separating the bright fringes and in such a case proper interference pattern can be seen in which we can clearly distinguish bright and dark fringes as shown in figure-6.27.

If the width of the slits are unequal as shown in figure-6.28 then the intensities of the two slits on screen will be different, say I_{01} and I_{02} respective then the light intensity of bright and dark fringes on screen will be

$$I_{Bright} = (\sqrt{I_{02}} + \sqrt{I_{02}})^2 = I_{01} + I_{02} + 2\sqrt{I_{01} I_{02}} \quad \ldots(6.55)$$

and
$$I_{Dark} = (\sqrt{I_{02}} - \sqrt{I_{02}})^2 = I_{01} + I_{02} - 2\sqrt{I_{01} I_{02}} \quad \ldots(6.56)$$

From above equation-(6.56) we can see that the intensity of dark fringe is not zero due to which in the interference patter we cannot clearly distinguish bright and dark fringes as shown in figure-6.28.

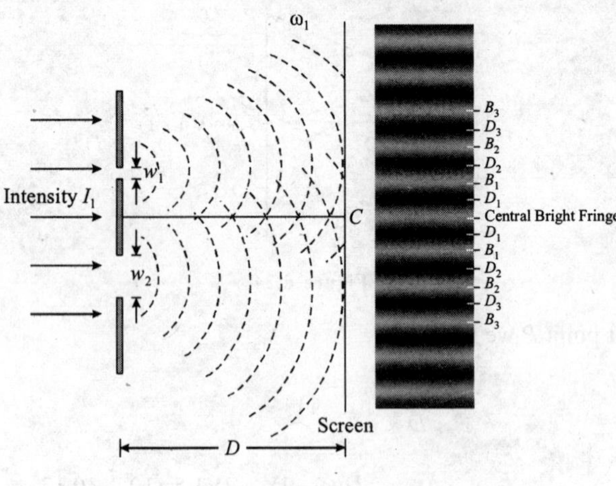

Figure 6.28

6.4.8 Fresnel's Biprism as a Limiting case of YDSE

Fresnel demonstrated interference pattern similar to YDSE by using a biprism. The biprism consists of two prisms of very small refracting angles joined base to base. It is made by grinding a thin glass plate with opposite inclination on the two halves of the plate on one side as shown in figure-6.29.

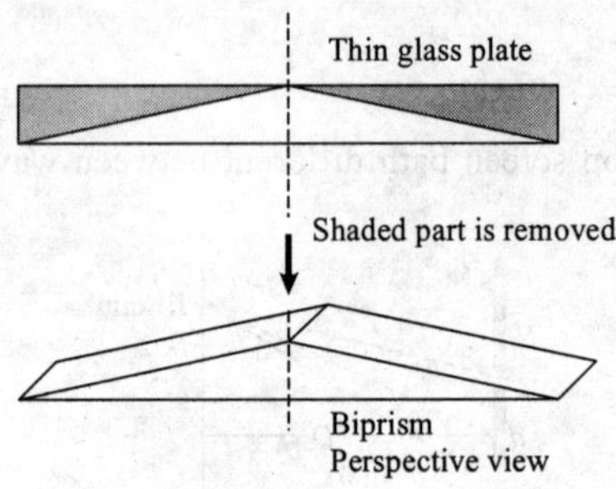

(a)

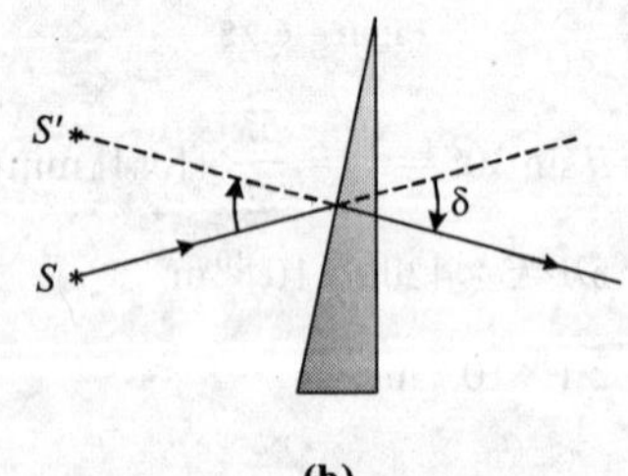

(b)

Figure 6.29

We've already studied that a light ray from a source S when incident on a small angled prism at near normal incident as shown in figure-6.29(b), it gets deviated by angle of deviation δ, and from the other side it appears to be coming from the image of the light source S'. The angle of deviation δ is given as

$$\delta = A(\mu - 1) \quad \ldots(6.57)$$

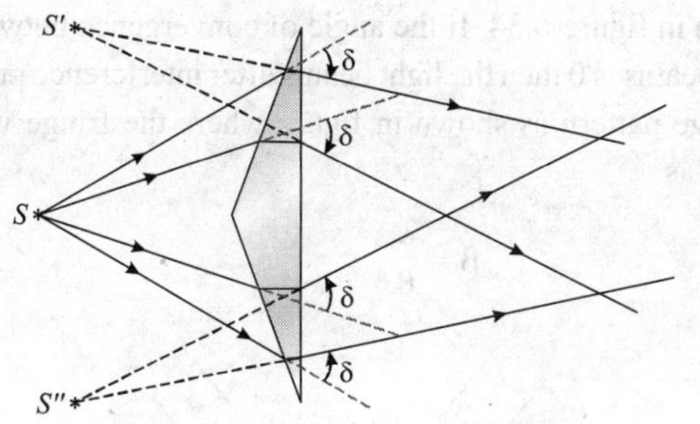

Figure 6.30

Now if we look at figure-6.30 in which two light rays from a source S incident on a biprism then these bends after refraction through biprism by same angle of deviation toward base of prisms such that the refracted beams appear to be coming from the two images of the source S' and S''.

Figure-6.31 shows the interference setup of '*Fresnel's Biprism Experiment*' in which there is only one slit kept at a distance '*a*' from the biprism and at a distance '*b*' from the biprism screen is kept. Due to refraction, biprism splits the incident light in two beams and from the other side the light beams appear to be coming from the two images S' and S'' of the slit and these beams interfere and produces the interference pattern similar to YDSE on screen.

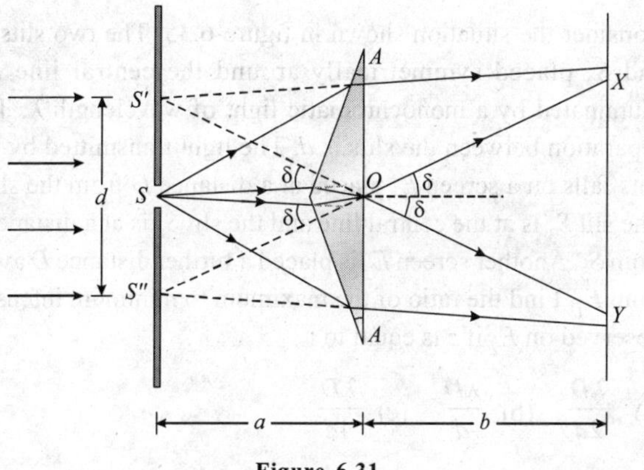

Figure 6.31

In above figure we can see that each light from slit S falling on biprism gets deviated by the deviation angle given by equation-(6.57). For the region between slit plane and biprism for the $\Delta SOS'$ we can use for small value of δ, we have

$$\frac{d}{2} = a\tan\delta \approx a\delta$$

$$\Rightarrow \qquad \frac{d}{2} = aA(\mu - 1)$$

$$\Rightarrow \qquad d = 2aA(\mu - 1) \qquad \ldots(6.58)$$

Equation-(6.58) gives the separation between the two coherent sources S' and S'' from which the interference pattern is being produced and the separation between the plane of images of the slit and screen is taken as $D = a + b$ so the fringe width on the screen can be given in the same wave we use for YDSE setup.

Fringe width in Fresnel Biprism setup is $\beta = \dfrac{\lambda D}{d}$

Substituting the values of D and d in above expression we get

$$\beta = \frac{\lambda(a+b)}{2aA(\mu-1)} \qquad \ldots(6.59)$$

6.4.9 Lloyd's Mirror as a limiting case of YDSE

In 1834 Lloyd made a setup to demonstrate interference using a single mirror and a slit of light at almost grazing incidence of light. Figure-6.32 shows the Lloyd's Mirror setup of interference in which light from the slit S_1 falls on the mirror and the reflected light interfere with the direct light on the screen. The reflected light appears to be coming from the image S_2 of the slit as shown. For the region of screen in which the two lights interfere, interference pattern is obtained which is similar to YDSE setup.

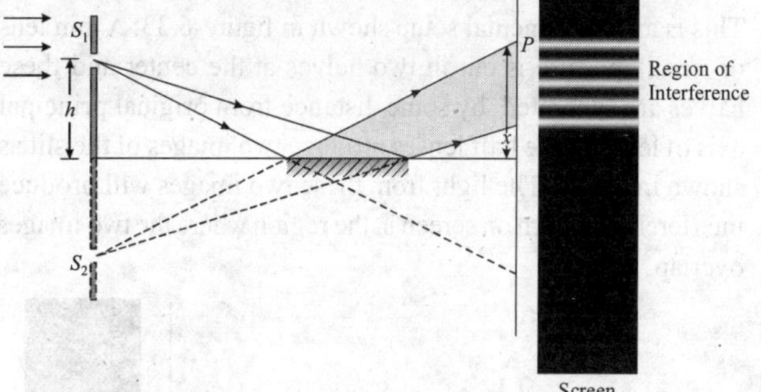

Figure 6.32

In the above setup the separation between the two slits is taken as $d = 2h$ and the separation between slit plane and screen is given as D. If we consider a general point P on the screen in the region of interference then the path difference at point P between the lights from the two sources is given as

$$\Delta = \frac{dx}{D} + \frac{\lambda}{2} \qquad \ldots(6.60)$$

In above equation-(6.60), the first term is the physical path difference in the path travelled by the two light waves reaching at point P and the second term is the extra path introduced in the reflected light due to its reflection from a denser medium at mirror.

In this setup at point P, a bright fringe will be obtained if the path difference is an integral multiple of the light wavelength so we use

$$\Delta = \frac{dx}{D} + \frac{\lambda}{2} = N\lambda \qquad \ldots(6.61)$$

$$\Rightarrow \qquad x_{NB} = (2N-1)\frac{\lambda D}{2d} \qquad \ldots(6.62)$$

Similarly we can say that at point P there will be dark fringe if the path difference in the two waves at P is an odd multiple of half of the light wavelength so we use

$$\Delta = \frac{dx}{D} + \frac{\lambda}{2} = (2N+1)\frac{\lambda}{2} \quad \dots(6.63)$$

$$\Rightarrow \quad x_{ND} = \frac{N\lambda D}{d} \quad \dots(6.64)$$

From equations-(6.62) and (6.64) we can analyze that the interference pattern obtained in this setup is inverse to that of the YDSE setup. At the location of bright fringes in YDSE, here we are getting dark fringes and vice verse. But we can see that the distance between two successive bright or dark fringes which is the fringe width remain same. Fringe Width in interference pattern obtained in Lloyd's Mirror setup is given as

$$\beta = \frac{\lambda D}{d} = \frac{\lambda D}{2h}$$

6.4.10 Billet Split Lens as a limiting case of YDSE

This is an experimental setup shown in figure-6.33. A thin lens of small aperture is cut in two halves at the center and these halves are separated by some distance from original principal axis of lens. These half lenses produce two images of the slit as shown in figure. The light from these two images will produce interference pattern on screen in the region where the two images overlap.

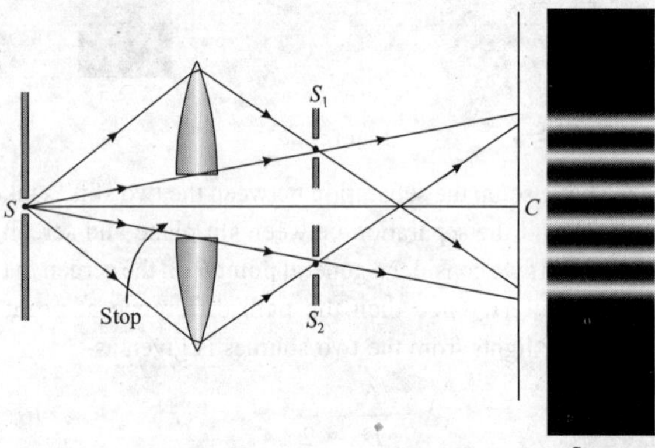

Figure 6.33

This setup is similar to YDSE setup if we look at the plane of two images of the slit producing interference pattern on the screen. By using lens formula and magnification we can find out the location of these images and their separation by which using the formula of fringe width in YDSE setup we can find the fringe width in this setup.

6.4.11 Interference of Two Converging Coherent Parallel Beams of Light

When two monochromatic and coherent parallel light beams incident on a surface (or screen) in a converging manner as shown in figure-6.34. If the angle of convergence between the light beams is θ then the light beams after interference produces a fringe pattern as shown in figure where the fringe width is given as

$$\beta = \frac{\lambda}{\theta} \quad \dots(6.65)$$

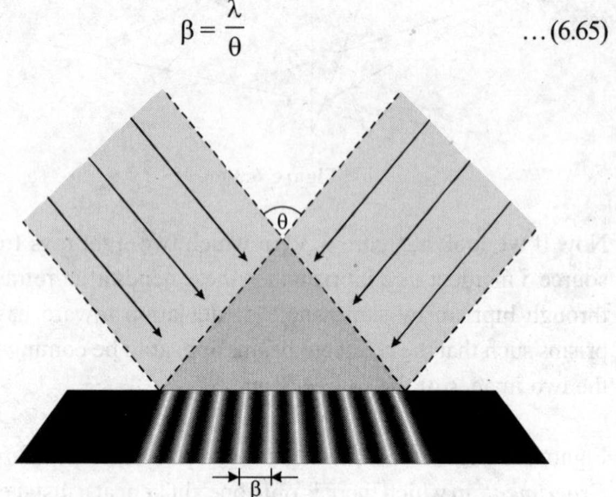

Figure 6.34

The derivation of above equation-(6.65) is left for students as an exercise.

Illustrative Example 6.18

Consider the situation shown in figure-6.35. The two slits S_1 and S_2 placed symmetrically around the central line are illuminated by a monochromatic light of wavelength λ. The separation between the slits is d. The light transmitted by the slits falls on a screen E_1 placed at a distance D from the slits. The slit S_3 is at the central line and the slit S_4 is at a distance z from S_3. Another screen E_2 is placed a further distance D away from E_1. Find the ratio of the maximum to minimum intensity observed on E_2 if z is equal to :

(a) $\frac{\lambda D}{2d}$ (b) $\frac{\lambda D}{d}$ (c) $\frac{\lambda D}{4d}$

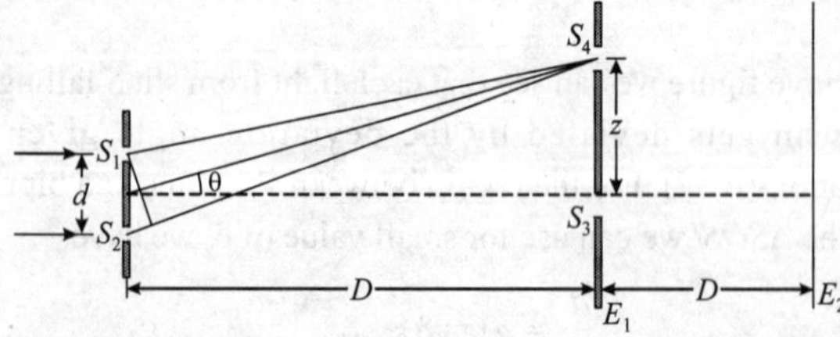

Figure 6.35

Solution

Light from sources S_1 and S_2 get interfered and thereafter S_3 and S_4 becomes new sources. At S_3 the path difference between the lights coming from S_1 and S_2 is zero. Therefore they interfere constructively and so $a_3 = (a + a) = 2a$

(a) At S_4 the path difference

$$\Delta x = d\sin\theta \simeq d\tan\theta$$

$$\Rightarrow \quad \Delta x = d\frac{z}{D} = \frac{d\times\frac{\lambda D}{2d}}{D}$$

$$\Rightarrow \quad \Delta x = \frac{\lambda}{2}$$

Corresponding phase difference = π radian

$$\Rightarrow \quad a_4 = 0$$

The ratio $\dfrac{I_{max}}{I_{min}} = \dfrac{(a_3+a_4)^2}{(a_3-a_4)^2} = \dfrac{(2a+0)^2}{2a-0} = 1$

(b) $$\Delta x = \frac{dz}{D} = \frac{d\left(\frac{\lambda D}{d}\right)}{D} = \lambda$$

Corresponding phase difference = 2π radian.

Now $a_4 = a + a = 2a$

and $\dfrac{I_{max}}{I_{min}} = \dfrac{(2a+2a)^2}{(2a-2a)^2} = \infty$

(c) $$\Delta x = \frac{dz}{D} = \frac{d\left(\frac{\lambda D}{4d}\right)}{D} = \frac{\lambda}{4}$$

Corresponding phase difference = $\dfrac{\lambda}{2}$ radian

$$a_4^2 = a^2 + a^2 + 2aa\cos\frac{\pi}{2} = 2a^2$$

$$\Rightarrow \quad a_4 = \sqrt{2}a$$

So we have $\dfrac{I_{max}}{I_{min}} = \dfrac{(2a+\sqrt{2}a)^2}{(2a-\sqrt{2}a)^2} = \dfrac{(3.414)^2}{(0.586)^2}$

$$\Rightarrow \quad \frac{I_{max}}{I_{min}} = 34$$

Illustrative Example 6.19

The two coherent sources of monochromatic light of wavelength λ are located at a separation λ. The two sources are placed on a horizontal line and screen is placed perpendicular to the line joining the sources. Find position of the farthest minima from the centre of the sources.

Solution

Suppose at P the farthest minima will occur. Let it subtends an angle θ at the centre of the sources.

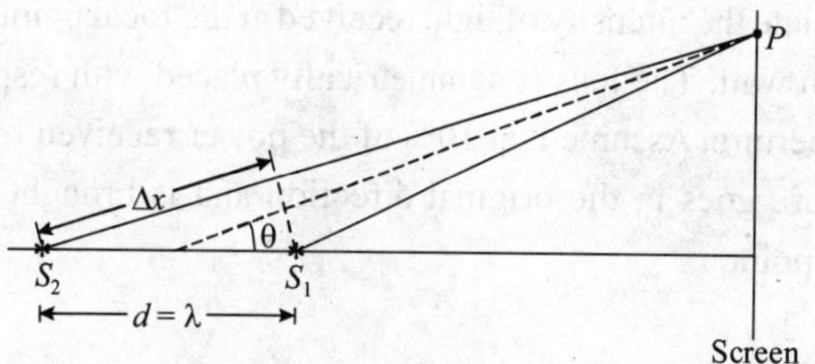

Figure 6.36

The path difference

$$\Delta x = S_2P - S_1P$$

$$\Rightarrow \quad \Delta x = d\cos\theta$$

$$\Rightarrow \quad \Delta x = \lambda\cos\theta$$

The maximum path difference can be

$$\Delta x_{max} = \lambda;\ \text{when } \cos\theta = 1 \text{ or } \theta = 0°$$

and minimum path difference

$$\Delta x_{min} = 0;\ \text{when } \cos\theta = 0 \text{ or } \theta = 90°$$

Thus in between these two positions there is only one minima for which

$$\Delta x = \frac{\lambda}{2}$$

$$\Rightarrow \quad \frac{\lambda}{2} = \lambda\cos\theta$$

$$\Rightarrow \quad \cos\theta = \frac{1}{2}$$

$$\Rightarrow \quad \theta = 60°$$

Illustrative Example 6.20

In a modified Young's double slit experiment, a monochromatic uniform and parallel beam of light of wavelength 6000Å and intensity $\frac{10}{\pi}$ W/m² is incident normally on two circular aperture A and B of radii 0.001 m and 0.002 m respectively. A perfect transparent film of thickness 2000 Å and refractive index 1.5 for the wavelength of 6000 Å is placed infront of aperture A as shown in figure-6.37.

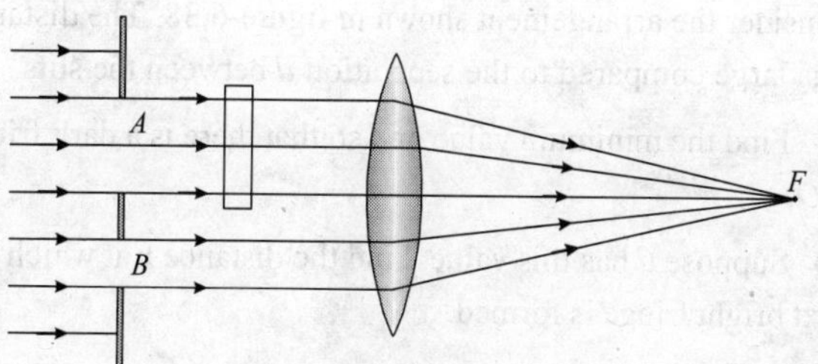

Figure 6.37

Calculate the intensity of light received at the focal point of the lens in watt. The lens is symmetrically placed with respect to the aperture. Assume that 10% of the power received by each aperture goes in the original direction and is brought to the focal point.

Solution

The intensities of light from the sources S_1 and S_2 are given as

$$I_1 = \left(\frac{10}{\pi}\right) \times \pi(0.01)^2 = 10^{-5}\,W$$

$$I_2 = \left(\frac{10}{\pi}\right) \times \pi(0.02)^2 = 4\times 10^{-5}\,W$$

The intensities of sources after emerging from the lenses are

$$I_A = 0.10\times 10^{-5}\,W = 10^{-6}\,W$$

$$I_B = 0.10\times 4\times 10^{-5}\,W = 4\times 10^{-6}\,W$$

The path difference produced due to film

$$\Delta x = (\mu - 1)t = (1.5 - 1)\times 2000\times 10^{-10} = 10^{-7}\,\text{m}$$

$$\Rightarrow \quad \phi = \frac{2\pi}{\lambda}\times\Delta x = \frac{2\pi}{6000\times 10^{-10}}\times 10^{-7}$$

$$\Rightarrow \quad \phi = \frac{\pi}{3}\ \text{radian}$$

As refraction through lens do not introduce any path difference so above will be the net phase difference in the two light beams superposing at focal point of the lens. So net intensity received at F is given as

$$I = I_A + I_B + 2\sqrt{I_A I_B}\cos\phi$$

$$\Rightarrow \quad I = 10^{-6} + 4\times 10^{-6} + 2\sqrt{10^{-6}\times 4\times 10^{6}}\ \cos\frac{\pi}{3}$$

$$\Rightarrow \quad I = 7\times 10^{-6}\,W$$

Illustrative Example 6.21

Consider the arrangement shown in figure-6.38. The distance D is large compared to the separation d between the slits.

(a) Find the minimum value of d so that there is a dark fringe at O.

(b) Suppose d has this value. Find the distance x at which the next bright fringe is formed.

(c) Find the fringe width.

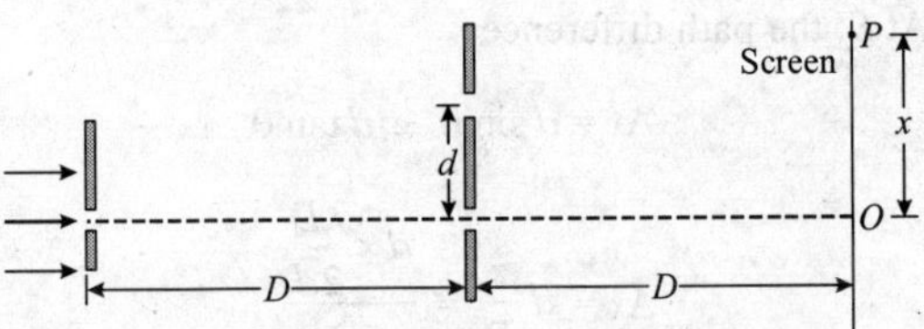

Figure 6.38

Solution

(a) The path difference at O is given as

$$\Delta x = 2\sqrt{D^2 + d^2} - 2D$$

For the dark fringe at O, this path difference should be

$$\Delta x = \frac{\lambda}{2}, \frac{3\lambda}{2}, \ldots$$

For minimum value of d, we use

$$2\sqrt{D^2 + d^2} - 2D = \frac{\lambda}{2}$$

$$\Rightarrow \quad (D^2 + d^2)^{1/2} - D = \frac{\lambda}{4}$$

$$\Rightarrow \quad D\left(1 + \frac{d^2}{D^2}\right)^{1/2} - D = \frac{\lambda}{4}$$

$$\Rightarrow \quad D\left(1 + \frac{d^2}{2D^2}\right) - D = \frac{\lambda}{4}$$

$$\Rightarrow \quad D + \frac{d^2}{2D} - D = \frac{\lambda}{4}$$

$$\Rightarrow \quad d = \sqrt{\frac{D\lambda}{2}}$$

(b) At the above calculated value of d, first bright fringe will be obtained at a position where the path difference between the two waves will be λ.

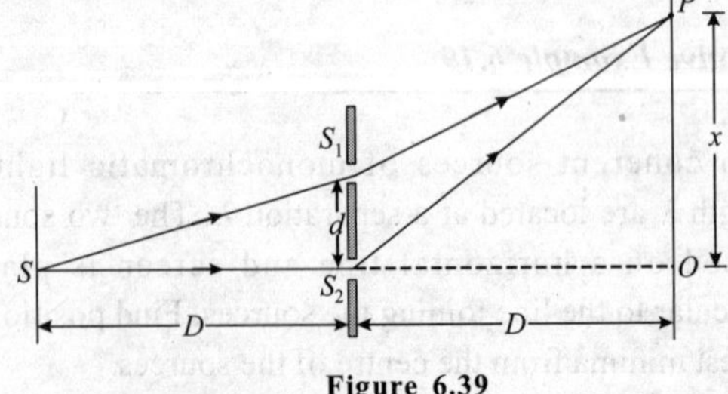

Figure 6.39

For the situation shown in figure-6.39, the path difference in waves from S_1 and S_2 at point P is given as

$$\Delta x = (SS_1 + S_1P) - (SS_2 + S_2P)$$

$$= \left[\sqrt{(D^2+d^2)}+\sqrt{(x-d)^2+D^2}\right]-\left[D+\sqrt{D^2+x^2}\right]$$

For the next bright fringe after first dark fringe, $\Delta x = \lambda$

$$\Rightarrow \left[\sqrt{D^2+d^2}+\sqrt{(x-d)^2+D^2}\right]-\left[D+\sqrt{D^2+x^2}\right]=\lambda$$

$$\Rightarrow D\left(1+\frac{d^2}{D^2}\right)^{1/2}+D\left(1+\frac{(x-d)^2}{D^2}\right)^{1/2}$$

$$-\left[D+D\left(1+\frac{x^2}{D^2}\right)^{1/2}\right]=\lambda$$

$$\Rightarrow \left(D+\frac{d^2}{2D}\right)+D+D+\frac{(x-d)^2}{2D}-\left(D+D+\frac{x^2}{2D}\right)=\lambda$$

$$\Rightarrow \frac{d^2+(x-d)^2-x^2}{2D}=\lambda$$

$$\Rightarrow d^2+x^2+d^2-2xd-x^2=2\lambda D$$

$$\Rightarrow 2d^2-2xd=2\lambda D$$

For $d=\sqrt{\frac{D\lambda}{2}}$, we get

$$2\left(\sqrt{\frac{D\lambda}{2}}\right)^2-2x\sqrt{\frac{D\lambda}{2}}=2\lambda D$$

$$\Rightarrow 2\frac{D\lambda}{2}-2x\sqrt{\frac{D\lambda}{2}}=2\lambda D$$

$$\Rightarrow 2x\sqrt{\frac{D\lambda}{2}}=-D\lambda$$

$$\Rightarrow \left(2x\sqrt{\frac{D\lambda}{2}}\right)^2=(-D\lambda)^2$$

Solving, we get $x=\sqrt{\frac{D\lambda}{2}}=d$

(c) Fringe width on screen can be given by the relation we studied in YDSE, given as

$$\beta=\frac{D\lambda}{d}.$$

Illustrative Example 6.22

In Billet's Lens Arrangement, a convex lens of focal length 50 cm is cut along the diameter into two identical halves *A* and *B* and in the process a layer *C* of the lens thickness 1 mm is lost. Then the two halves *A* and *B* are put together to form a composite lens. Now, infront of this composite lens a source of light emitting wavelength $\lambda = 6000$ Å is placed at a distance of 25 cm as shown in the figure. Behind the lens there is a screen at a distance 50 cm from it. Find the fringe width of the interference pattern obtained on the screen.

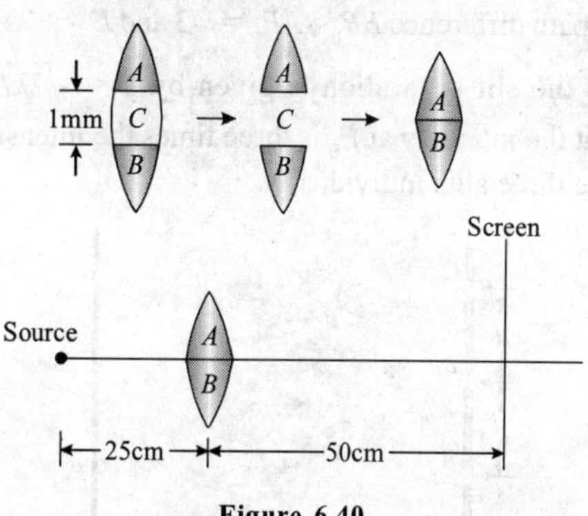

Figure 6.40

Solution

From the given condition, we have

$$u=-25 \text{ cm}$$

$$\Rightarrow \frac{1}{v}-\frac{1}{-25}=\frac{1}{50}$$

$$\Rightarrow \frac{1}{v}=-\frac{1}{50}$$

$$\Rightarrow v=-50 \text{ cm}$$

The two parts *A* and *B* of the lenses produce two virtual images of the source at I_1 and I_2 at a distance 50 cm behind the lens. Figure-6.41 shows the locations of I_1 and I_2 which are obtained by joining the source with the optic centers of the two lenses.

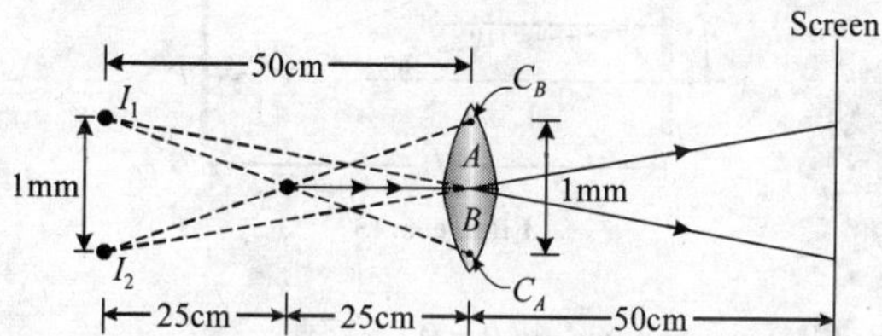

Figure 6.41

Now on the screen, interference pattern is obtained due to interference of light waves from the sources I_1 and I_2 which are separated by a distance 1 mm and at a distance 1 m from the screen. Thus fringe width of the fringes obtained on screen is given as

$$\beta=\frac{\lambda D}{d}$$

$$\Rightarrow \beta=\frac{6\times10^{-7}\times1}{10^{-3}}=6\times10^{-4}=0.6\text{ mm}$$

Illustrative Example 6.23

Figure-6.42 shows three equidistant slits of equal width being illuminated by a monochromatic parallel beam of light. If in this situation path difference $BP_0 - AP_0 = \lambda/3$ and $D >> \lambda$. (a) Show that case the slit separation is given by $d = \sqrt{2\lambda D/3}$. (b) Show that the intensity at P_0 is three times the intensity due to any of the three slits individually.

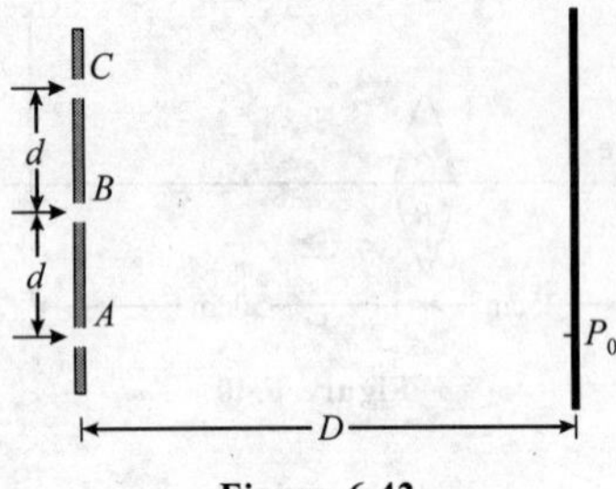

Figure 6.42

Solution

Figure-6.43 shows the calculation of path difference in the given situation. As we are given the path difference in the waves reaching from slit A and B to point P_0 as

$$BP_0 - AP_0 = \frac{\lambda}{3}$$

$$\Rightarrow \quad d\sin\theta = \frac{\lambda}{3}$$

Figure 6.43

For small θ, we can use $\sin\theta = \theta$

$$d\theta = \frac{\lambda}{3} \quad \ldots(6.66)$$

From figure-6.43, for $D >> d$, θ is given as

$$\theta = \frac{d/2}{D}$$

From equation-(6.66), we have

$$\Rightarrow \quad d\left(\frac{d}{2D}\right) = \frac{\lambda}{3}$$

$$\Rightarrow \quad d = \sqrt{\frac{2\lambda D}{3}}$$

(b) If we consider Δx_{AB} as the path difference between waves coming from A and B which is given as $\lambda/3$. If ϕ_{AB} is the corresponding phase difference then it is given as

$$\phi_{AB} = \frac{2\pi}{\lambda}\Delta x_{AB} = \frac{2\pi}{3}$$

Similarly, for waves coming from slits B and C to point P_0, we use

$$\Delta x_{BC} = d\sin\phi,$$

$$\Rightarrow \quad \Delta x_{BC} = d\left(\frac{3d/2}{D}\right) = \frac{3d^2}{2D} = \lambda$$

$$\Rightarrow \quad \phi_{BC} = 2\pi$$

Thus the waves from slits B and C will reach point P_0 in same phase so the resulting amplitude due to superposition of the waves from slits B and C will become 2A and this is at a phase difference of $2\pi/3$ with the waves coming from slit A having amplitude A. Thus amplitude of resultant wave at point P_0 is given by

$$A_P = \sqrt{A^2 + (2A)^2 + 2(A)(2A)\cos 120^\circ} = \sqrt{3}A$$

As intensity of light is directly proportional to the square of amplitude, we can see that intensity at point P_0 will be three times the intensity due to any of the three slits individually.

Web Reference at www.physicsgalaxy.com

Age Group - High School Physics | Age 17-19 Years

Section - OPTICS

Topic - Nature of Light and Interference

Module Number - 15 to 38

Practice Exercise-6.1

(i) Two slits in Young's interference experiment have width in the ratio 1 : 4. Find the ratio of intensity at the maxima and minima in their interference.

[9]

(ii) In *YDSE* setup a light of wavelength 6000 Å is used. What should be the separation between the slits so that on screen in front of one of the slit there will be third bright fringe. Take $D = 1$ m.

[$0.6\sqrt{10}$ mm]

(iii) A narrow slit S is transmitting light of wavelength λ and it is placed at a distance d above a large plane mirror as shown in figure-6.44. The light coming directly from the slit and that coming after reflection interfere at a screen Σ placed at a distance D ($D >> d$) from the slit.

(a) What will be the intensity at a point just above the mirror at point O ?

(b) At what distance from O does the first maximum will occur?

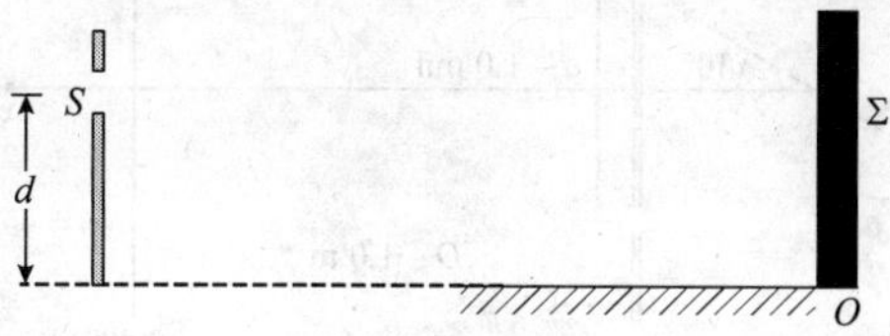

Figure 6.44

[(a) Zero; (b) $\frac{D\lambda}{4d}$]

(iv) In *YDSE* experiment a uniform intensity light beam is incident on slit plane which has two slits having width ratio 9 : 4. Find the ratio of intensities of bright and dark fringes on screen.

[25]

(v) A vessel *ABCD* of 10 cm width has two small slits S_1 and S_2 sealed with identical glass plates of equal thickness. The distance between the slits is 0.8 mm, *POQ* is the line perpendicular to the plane *AB* and passing through *O*, the mid point of S_1 and S_2. A monochromatic light source is kept at *S*, 40 cm below *P* and 2 m from the vessel, to illuminate the slits as shown in the figure below. (a) Calculate the position of the central bright fringe on the other wall *CD* with respect to the line *OQ*. (b) Now, a liquid is poured into the vessel and filled up to *OQ*. The central bright fringe is found to be at *Q*. Calculate the refractive index of the liquid.

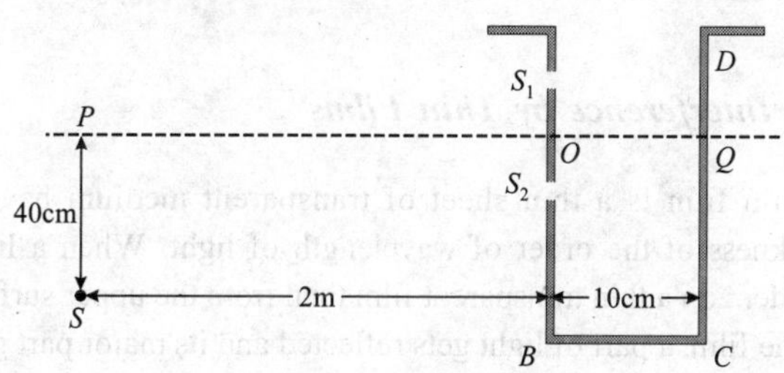

Figure 6.45

[(a) 2.04 cm; (b) 1.0016]

(vi) In a YDSE setup a parallel light beam containing two wavelength 4000 Å and 5600 Å is allowed to incident at an angle 30° on a diaphragm having two narrow slits at a separation 2 mm as shown in figure-6.46. The screen is placed at a distance 40 cm from the slits. A mica film of thickness 5 mm is placed in front of one of the slits and the whole apparatus is submerged in water. If the central bright fringe is observed at point *C*, which is equidistant from both the slits. Calculate

(a) The refractive index of the slab.

(b) The distance of the first black line from *C*.

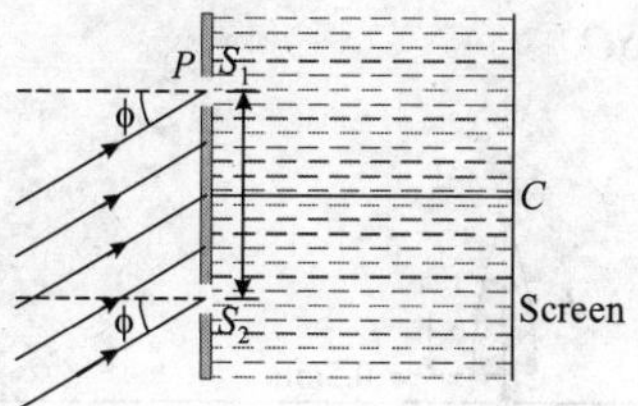

Figure 6.46

[(a) 1.6; (b) 210 μm]

(vii) A monochromatic light of wavelength 5000 Å incident normally on slit plane of *YDSE* setup. If $d = 5 \times 10^{-4}$ m and $D = 1$ m and a thin film of thickness 1.5×10^{-6} m and $\mu = 1.5$ is place in front of one of the slits, find intensity of light at the centre of screen if each slit produces an intensity I_0 on screen.

[0]

(viii) Two transparent sheets of thickness t_1 and t_2 and refractive indexes μ_1 and μ_2 are placed infront of the slits in *YDSE* setup as shown in figure-6.47. If *D* is the distance of the screen from the slits, then find the distance of zero order maxima from the centre of the screen. What is the condition that zero order maxima is formed at the centre *O* ?

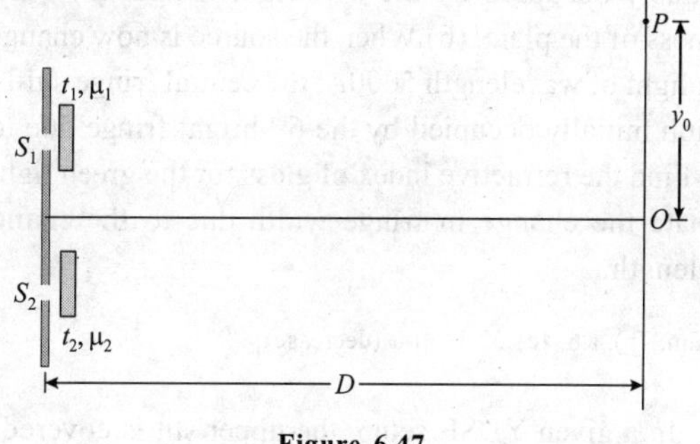

Figure 6.47

[$\frac{D[(\mu_1-1)t_1-(\mu_2-1)t_2]}{d}$; $(\mu_2-1)t_2$]

(ix) A Lloyd's mirror of length 5 cm is illuminated with monochromatic light of wavelength 6000 Å from a narrow slit 1 mm above the plane of mirror and 5 cm from one edge of mirror. Find fringe width on a screen at a distance 120 cm from slit and also find the width of interference pattern on screen.

[0.36 mm; 1.2 cm]

(x) In the given figure-6.48 *S* is a monochromatic point source emitting light of wavelength 5000Å. A thin lens of circular shape and focal length 0.10 m is cut into two identical halves L_1 and L_2 by a plane passing through a diameter. The two halves are placed symmetrically about the central axis SO with a gap of 0.5 mm. The distance along the axis from S to L_1 and L_2 is 0.15 m, while that from L_1 & L_2 to O is 1.30 m. The screen at O is normal to SO.

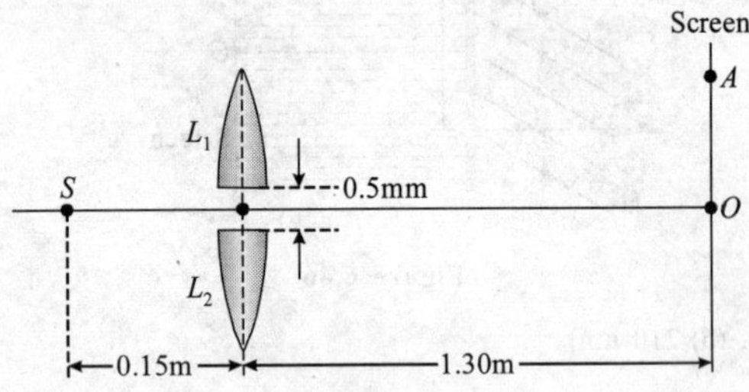

Figure 6.48

(a) If the third intensity maximum occurs at a point A on the screen, find the distance OA.

(b) If the gap between L_1 & L_2 is reduced from its original value of 0.5 mm, will the distance OA increase, decrease or remain the same ?

[(a) 1 mm; (b) Increase]

(xi) In a given *YDSE* setup, the source is red light of wavelength 7000Å. When a thin glass plate of refractive index 1.5 at this wavelength is put in the path of one of the interfering beams, the central bright fringe shifts by 10^{-3} m to the position previously occupied by the 5th bright fringe. (a) Find the thickness of the plate. (b) When the source is now changed to green light of wavelength 5000Å, the central fringe shifts to a position initially occupied by the 6th bright fringe due to red light. Find the refractive index of glass for the green light. (c) Estimate the change in fringe width due to the change in wavelength.

[(a) 7μm; (b) 1.6, (c) 57.14 μm (decrease)]

(xii) In a given YDSE setup, the upper slit is covered by a thin glass plate of refractive index 1.4 while the lower slit is covered by another glass plate having the same thickness as the first one but having refractive index 1.7. Interference pattern is observed using light of wavelength 5400 Å. It is found that the point P on the screen where the central maximum ($n = 0$) fell before the glass plates were inserted now has 3/4 the original intensity. It is further observed that what used to be the 5th maximum earlier, lies below the point P while the 6th minimum lies above P. Calculate the thickness of the glass plate. (Absorption of light by glass plate may be neglected).

[9.3 μm]

(xiii) A coherent parallel beam of microwaves of wavelength $\lambda = 0.5$ mm falls on a YDSE apparatus. The separation between the slits is 1.0 mm. The intensity of microwaves is measured on the screen placed parallel to the plane of the slits at a distance of 1.0 m from it, as shown in the figure-6.49.

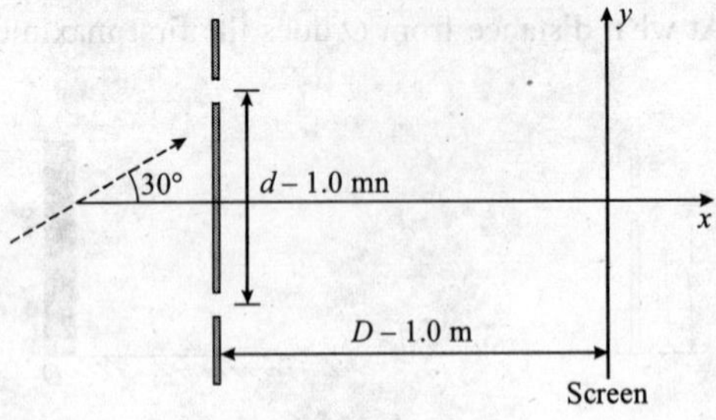

Figure 6.49

(a) If the incident beam falls normally on the double slit apparatus, find the y-coordinates of all the interference minima on the screen

(b) If the incident beam makes an angle of 30° with the x-axis (as in the dotted arrow shown in the figure-6.49), find the y-coordinates of the first minima on either side of central maximum.

[(a) $\pm\frac{1}{\sqrt{15}}$ m, $\pm\frac{3}{\sqrt{7}}$; (b) $+\frac{1}{\sqrt{15}}$ m, $+\frac{3}{\sqrt{7}}$ m]

(xiv) A slit of width d is illuminated by white light (which consists of all the wavelengths in the visible range).

(a) For what value of d will the first minimum for red light of wavelength $\lambda = 6500$Å appear at $\theta = 15°$?

(b) What is the wavelength λ' of the light whose first side diffraction maximum is at 15°, thus coinciding with the first minimum for the red light ?

[(a) 2.5μ m; (b) 4300Å]

6.5 Interference by Thin Films

A thin film is a thin sheet of transparent medium having thickness of the order of wavelength of light. When a light incident on a thin transparent film then from the upper surface of the film, a part of light gets reflected and its major part gets transmitted into the film. Now again when the part of light which enters into the film is reflected back into the film by the bottom surface and rest of it emerges out of the film. The light inside the film gets reflected partially several times in succession within the film as shown in figure-6.50.

The top and bottom surfaces of the transparent film are very weakly reflecting the light, most of the light is transmitted. If we ignore the absorption of light then a thin film having refractive index 1.5 in air reflects only about 4.2% of light at first reflection at the top surface and at its bottom surface only about 3.8% light is reflected out of which about 3.6% emerges out from the top surface and about 0.2% is reflected back out of which 0.15% emerges out from the bottom surface. But after this the light intensity drops to a significant level and we can ignore subsequent reflection and transmission from the film due to back and forth internal reflection of the light inside the film.

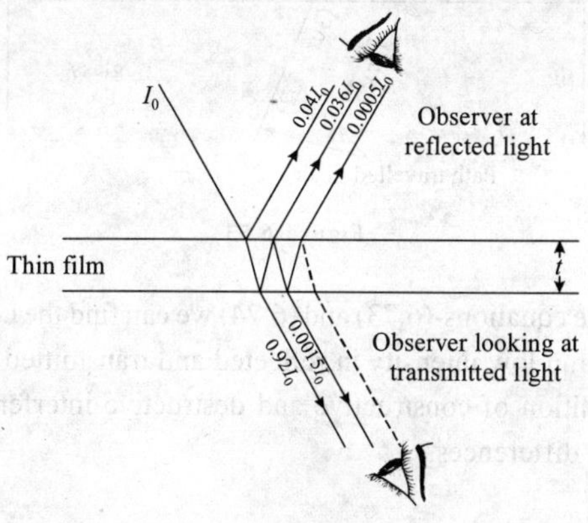

Figure 6.50

The first two reflected and transmitted waves forms the reflected and transmitted light from the thin film. When we look at the film from top, both the reflected light rays (low intensity) are observed and their resulting interference gives the light perception of reflected light. Similarly when we look at the film from the bottom, first two emerging lights (one high intensity and one low intensity) goes into the observer's eye and their interference gives the light perception of transmitted light.

One important fact is also required to be kept in mind while studying interference due to thin films. That is a restriction on thickness of the film. We know well that different colours are observed when we look at thin film in white light like a soap bubble or a thin layer of oil on surface of water. It is due to interference of waves of different colours in reflected light from surface of film but such colours are not seen when we look at a window glass or thick glass plates. So the phenomenon of interference is observed only in very thin films which have thickness in the range of wavelength of light as if film is thick then the reflected waves do not satisfy the conditions of '*Spatial Coherence*' and '*Temporal Coherence*'. Spatial coherence is concerned with the correlation between waves at different points in space and temporal coherence is concerned to the correlation between waves observed at different moments in time. Detailed analysis of spatial and temporal coherence is not in scope of this book.

6.5.1 Interference due to Thin Film in Reflected Light at Near Normal Incidence

Figure-6.51 shows a transparent thin film of refractive index μ and thickness t which is bounded by the two parallel surfaces B_1 and B_2 by air (or free space) on both sides. We consider a light wave incident almost normally on the film which is shown as 'Ray-1' in the figure. This ray splits in 'Ray-2' and 'Ray-3' at the boundary B_1 and further 'Ray-3' again splits in 'Ray-4' and 'Ray-5' at the boundary B_2. The 'Ray-5' which is reflected at the bottom of film again splits at boundary B_1 in 'Ray-6' and 'Ray-7' as shown. When the film is seen in reflected light then interference of 'Ray-2' and 'Ray-6' will occur in eye and will produce the perception of resulting intensity for the observer looking at it.

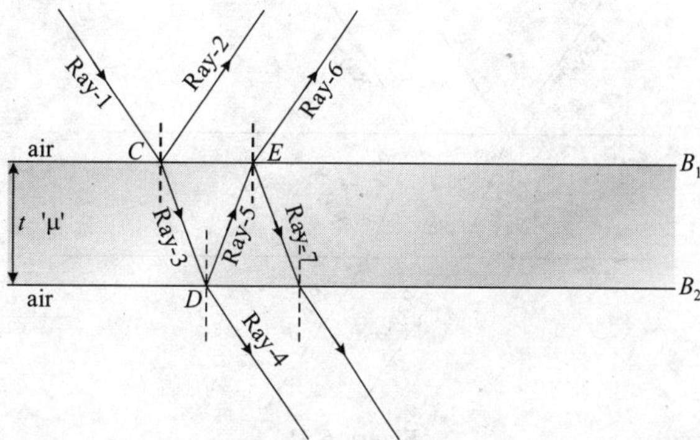

Figure 6.51

At point C where 'Ray-1' gets reflected then due to reflection from the denser medium 'Ray-2' will suffer a phase leg of '*π-radians*' or an equivalent additional path difference of $\lambda/2$. 'Ray-3' which will get transmitted will again gets reflected from the bottom of film and emerge out as 'Ray-6' at top of the film. This 'Ray-6' will travel an extra path of length $2t$ in the film of refractive index μ so the equivalent path length of 'Ray-6' in air will be $2\mu t$. 'Ray-3' is reflected at the bottom from the air boundary so it will be reflected in same phase and will not get and extra path of $\lambda/2$ added to it at point D. Thus the path difference in the light rays 2 and 6 when these will interfere in observer's eye will be given as

$$\Delta_{6-2} = 2\mu t - \frac{\lambda}{2} \quad \text{...(6.67)}$$

If the path difference given in equation-(6.67) is an integral multiple of wavelength of light, then reflected waves will interfere constructively and high intensity is seen in reflected light. So we can write the condition of path difference for bright reflection of light from a thin film as given below.

$$\Delta_{6-2} = 2\mu t - \frac{\lambda}{2} = N\lambda \quad \text{...(6.68)}$$

Similarly the condition of low intensity in the reflected light is destructive interference of the two reflected waves which will occur when their path difference is an odd multiple of half wavelength.

$$\Delta_{6-2} = 2\mu t - \frac{\lambda}{2} = (2N+1)\frac{\lambda}{2} \quad \text{...(6.69)}$$

6.5.2 Interference due to Thin Film in Transmitted Light a Near Normal Incidence

Figure-6.52 shows a transparent thin film of refractive index μ and thickness t which is bounded by the two parallel surfaces B_1 and B_2 by air (or free space) on both sides. This figure is similar to figure-6.51 but here we analyze the interference of light rays 'Ray-4' and 'Ray-8' emerging out at the bottom boundary B_2 of the film.

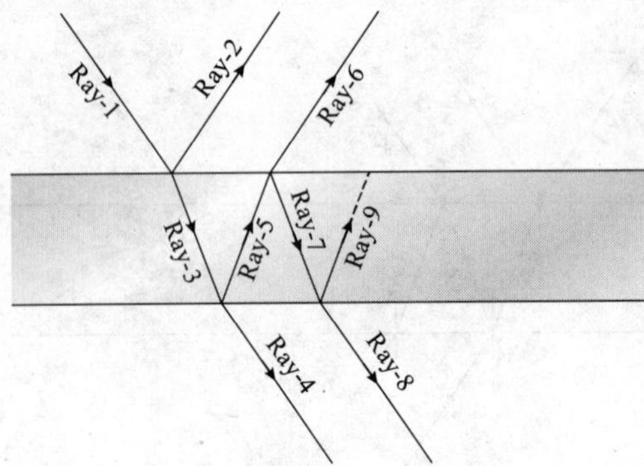

Figure 6.52

The total path travelled by 'Ray-4' in air is μt and that by 'Ray-8' is 3 μt as none of these is reflected by a boundary of denser medium so the path difference in the two emerging waves in 'Ray-4' and 'Ray-8' can be given as

$$\Delta_{8-4} = 3\mu t - \mu t = 2\mu t \qquad \ldots(6.70)$$

For the high intensity in transmitted light, this path difference given in equation-(6.70) will be an integral multiple of wavelength and the condition for bright transmission of light through the film is given as

$$\Delta_{8-4} = 2\mu t = N\lambda \qquad \ldots(6.71)$$

For low intensity transmission of light through the film, the two rays should interfere destructively and the condition for this will be

$$\Delta_{8-4} = 2\mu t = (2N+1)\frac{\lambda}{2} \qquad \ldots(6.72)$$

6.5.3 Interference due to a Thin Liquid Film on Glass

Figure-6.53 shows a glass slab of refractive index μ_g at the top surface of which a thin coating of a transparent liquid having refractive index μ_L ($\mu_L < \mu_g$) is done which is forming a thin liquid film on glass surface. When a light incident on this coating of thin film, the reflected ray at the bottom boundary B_2 will also suffer a phase leg of π-raidans or an additional path λ/2. So the path difference in reflected and transmitted light waves can be given as

$$\Delta_{reflection} = 2\mu t \qquad \ldots(6.73)$$

$$\Delta_{transmission} = 2\mu t + \frac{\lambda}{2} \qquad \ldots(6.74)$$

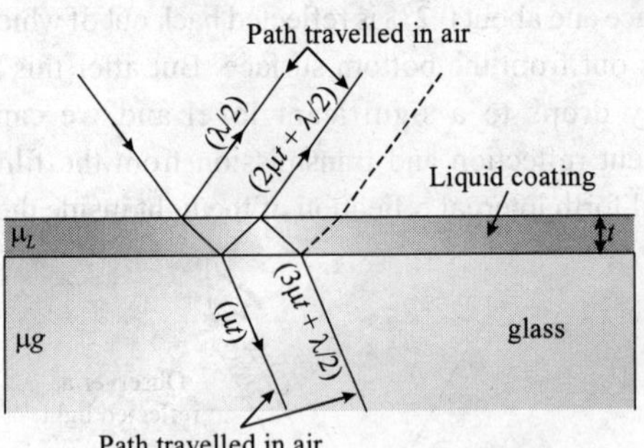

Figure 6.53

Using the equations-(6.73) and (6.74) we can find the condition of high and low intensity in reflected and transmitted light by the condition of constructive and destructive interference on the path differences.

6.5.4 Interference in Reflected Light by a Very Thin Film in Air

In figure-6.51 if the film thickness is very small then the path difference in the two reflected waves in 'Ray-2' and 'Ray-6' as given by equation-(6.67) is λ/2 only. Thus the two light waves will interfere destructively in reflected light and have low intensity. Such a film of very small thickness is considered to reflect almost no light from it of any wavelength.

6.5.5 Interference in Reflected Light from a Thin Film for Oblique Incidence

All the above cases we studied were for near normal incidence of the light on a thin film. Figure-6.54 shows a thin film on which a light is incident at an angle of incidence i and gets refracted into the film at angle of refraction r. Due to oblique incidence of light the two light rays which are coming out of the boundary B_1 in air will get refracted at points C and E as shown in figure.

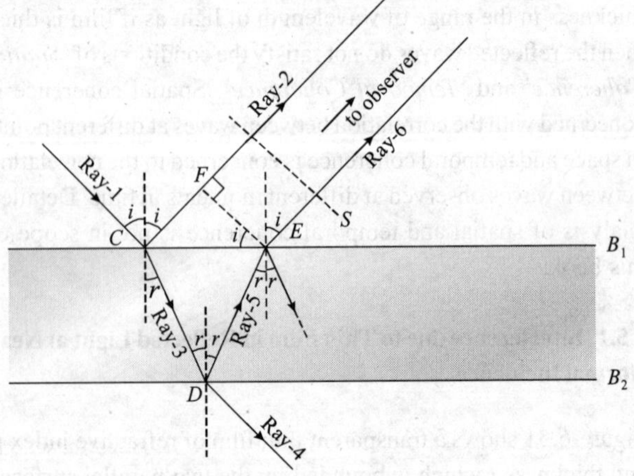

Figure 6.54

When Ray-2 and Ray-6 are in air as reflected light beam, the physical path difference at any section of reflected beam (say section S shown by dotted line in figure) can be taken as $CD + DE - CF$ where CD and DE are the path travelled by wave inside the film which will be multiplied with its refractive index to get the equivalent optical path in air and with path length CF we will add an additional path $\lambda/2$ due to reflection of this light by the boundary of denser medium.

Thus in Reflected light waves the optical path difference can be given as

$$\Delta_{reflection} = \mu(CD+DE) - (CF + \frac{\lambda}{2}) \qquad \ldots(6.75)$$

In ΔCDE we use

$$CD = DE = \frac{t}{\cos r} \qquad \ldots(6.76)$$

and $\quad CE = 2t \tan r$

$$\Rightarrow \quad CF = CE \sin i$$

$$\Rightarrow \quad CF = (2t \tan r) \sin i$$

$$\Rightarrow \quad CF = 2t\left(\frac{\sin r}{\cos r}\right)\cdot(\mu \sin r) = \frac{2\mu t \sin^2 r}{\cos r} \qquad \ldots(6.77)$$

Substituting the values from equations-(6.76) and (6.77) in equation-(6.75), the path difference in reflected light waves is given as

$$\Delta_{reflection} = \mu\left(\frac{2t}{\cos r}\right) - \left(\frac{2\mu t \sin^2 r}{\cos r} + \frac{\lambda}{2}\right)$$

$$\Rightarrow \quad \Delta_{reflection} = \frac{2\mu t}{\cos r}(1-\sin^2 r) - \frac{\lambda}{2}$$

$$\Rightarrow \quad \Delta_{reflection} = \frac{2\mu t}{\cos r}\cos^2 r - \frac{\lambda}{2}$$

$$\Rightarrow \quad \Delta_{reflection} = 2\mu t \cos^2 r - \frac{\lambda}{2} \qquad \ldots(6.78)$$

Using the expression for path difference in equation-(6.78) we can find the condition of maxima and minima in reflection based on the condition of constructive and destructive interference in reflected waves.

Reflected light will have high intensity if these will interfere constructively then the condition on path difference will be

$$2\mu t \cos r - \frac{\lambda}{2} = N\lambda \qquad \ldots(6.79)$$

$$\Rightarrow \quad 2\mu t \cos r = (2N+1)\frac{\lambda}{2} \qquad \ldots(6.80)$$

Similarly the condition on path difference for low intensity in reflected light can be given for destructive interference as

$$2\mu t \cos r - \frac{\lambda}{2} = (2N-1)\frac{\lambda}{2} \qquad \ldots(6.81)$$

$$\Rightarrow \quad 2\mu t \cos r = N\lambda \qquad \ldots(6.82)$$

6.5.6 Interference in Transmitted Light from a Thin Film for Oblique Incidence

Figure-6.55 shows the multiple reflections inside a thin film of a light wave incident obliquely on the film. When Ray-4 and Ray-8 are in air as transmitted light beam, the physical path difference at any section of transmitted beam (say section S shown by dotted line in figure) can be taken as $DE + EG - DH$ where DE and EG are the path travelled by wave inside the film after reflection at bottom surface of film at point D which will be multiplied with its refractive index to get the equivalent optical path in air and the path length DH is the path travelled by 'Ray-4' after it emerges out from point D. Before point D both rays 4 and 8 travelled same path so we do not consider any path before point D. In this case any ray do not get reflected from the boundary of denser medium so we do not include the additional path of $\lambda/2$ which we included in previous case.

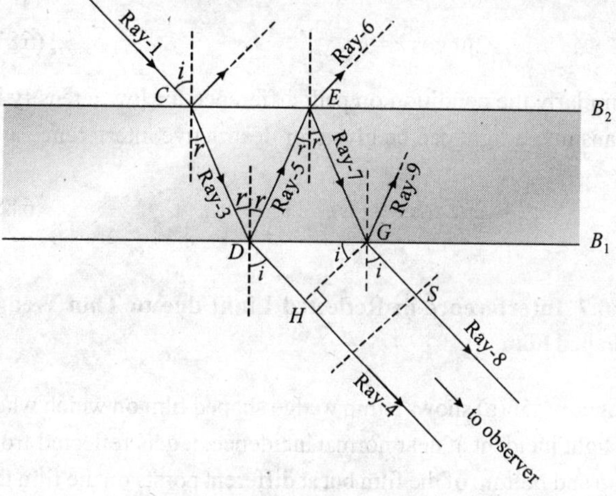

Figure 6.55

Thus in Reflected light waves the optical path difference can be given as

$$\Delta_{reflection} = \mu(DE+EG) - DH \qquad \ldots(6.83)$$

In ΔDEG we use

$$DE = EG = \frac{t}{\cos r} \qquad \ldots(6.84)$$

and $\quad DG = 2t \tan r$

$$\Rightarrow \quad DH = DG \sin i$$

$$\Rightarrow \quad DH = (2t \tan r) \sin i$$

$$\Rightarrow \quad DH = 2t\left(\frac{\sin r}{\cos r}\right)\cdot(\mu \sin r) = \frac{2\mu t \sin^2 r}{\cos r} \qquad \ldots(6.85)$$

Substituting the values from equations-(6.84) and (6.85) in equation-(6.83), the path difference in reflected light waves is given as

$$\Delta_{tansmission} = \mu\left(\frac{2t}{\cos r}\right) - \frac{2\mu t \sin^2 r}{\cos r}$$

$$\Rightarrow \quad \Delta_{reflection} = \frac{2\mu t}{\cos r}(1 - \sin^2 r)$$

$$\Rightarrow \quad \Delta_{reflection} = \frac{2\mu t}{\cos r}\cos^2 r$$

$$\Rightarrow \quad \Delta_{reflection} = 2\mu t \cos r \qquad \ldots(6.86)$$

Using the expression for path difference in equation-(6.86) we can find the condition of maxima and minima in reflection based on the condition of constructive and destructive interference in reflected waves.

Transmitted light from the film will have high intensity if these will interfere constructively then the condition on path difference will be

$$2\mu t \cos r = N\lambda \qquad \ldots(6.87)$$

Similarly the condition on path difference for low intensity in transmitted light can be given for destructive interference as

$$2\mu t \cos r = (2N-1)\frac{\lambda}{2} \qquad \ldots(6.88)$$

6.5.7 Interference in Reflected Light due to Thin Wedge shaped Film

Figure-6.56(a) shows a thin wedge shaped film on which when a light incident at near normal incidence, it gets reflected from top and bottom of the film but at different points on the film the reflected waves will have different path differences due to varying thickness of wedge film. Due to continuous variation in path difference for reflected light, fringes are observed in reflected beam of light as shown in figure-6.56(b)

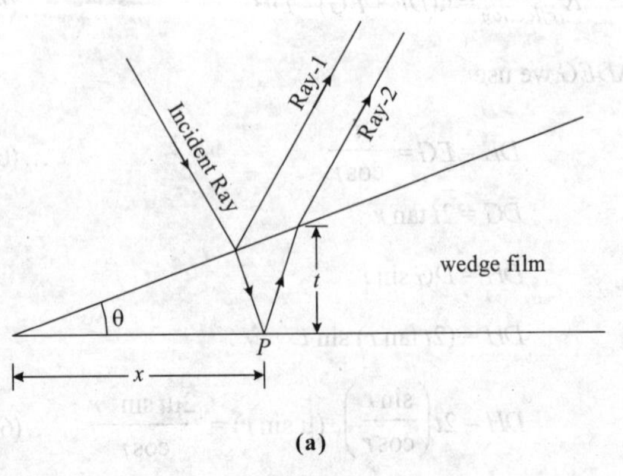

(a)

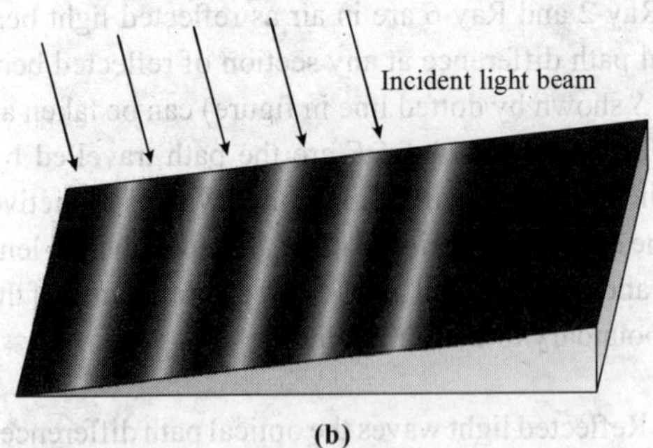

(b)

Figure 6.56

If we consider a point P at a distance x from the edge of the wedge film as shown in figure, the thickness of the wedge at this point is can be taken as $t = x\theta$ where θ is the wedge angle. The optical path difference between reflected waves 1 and 2 from point P can be calculated in the same way we did for thin films as

$$\Delta_{12} = 2\mu t - \frac{\lambda}{2} \qquad \ldots(6.89)$$

If we carefully look at the edge of the wedge where thickness is almost zero the path difference in reflected light will be $\lambda/2$ and the two waves will destructively interfere in the same way which we discussed for a very thin film in article-2.5.4 and a dark fringe is seen here. At some distance x_1 from the edge where $2\mu t = \lambda/2$ the path difference in reflected waves will be zero and due to constructive interference a bright fringe is obtained then alternate dark and bright fringes are seen as shown in figure-6.56(b).

At the point P a bright fringe is located if

$$\Delta_P = 2\mu t - \frac{\lambda}{2} = N\lambda$$

$$\Rightarrow \quad 2\mu x\theta = (2N+1)\frac{\lambda}{2}$$

$$\Rightarrow \quad x = (2N+1)\frac{(2N+1)\lambda}{4\mu} \qquad \ldots(6.90)$$

Equation-(6.90) gives the distance of a bright fringe from the edge of the wedge film. Here students must be careful that for first bright fringe we need to consider $N = 0$, for second bright fringe we will consider $N = 1$ and so on. So expression in equation-(6.90) gives the distance of $(N+1)^{th}$ bright fringe from the edge of the wedge film.

Similarly for a dark fringe located at point P, we can use

$$\Delta_P = 2\mu t - \frac{\lambda}{2} = (2N-1)\frac{\lambda}{2}$$

$$\Rightarrow \quad 2\mu x\theta = N\lambda$$

$$\Rightarrow \quad x = \frac{N\lambda}{2\mu\theta} \qquad \ldots(6.91)$$

Equation-(6.91) gives the distance of a dark fringe from the edge of the wedge film. Here $N = 0$ for the dark fringe at the edge and $N = 1, 2, 3...$ is used for further dark fringes. So expression in equation-(6.91) gives the distance of Nth dark fringe from the edge of the wedge film.

In case of transmitted light from a thin wedge shaped film, students can themselves derive the expression of fringe positions in the same way we did above and for the analysis done for thin films earlier.

6.5.8 Interference by an Air Wedge

Figure-6.57 shows an air wedge between two glass plates separated at one end by a small pin or a paper due to which at one end O, the plates are touching each other and thickness of air wedge is zero. When a light beam incident on this system of plates the interference take place in reflected waves from the bottom surface of upper plate and top surface of lower plate. The path difference in the reflected rays 1 and 2 shown in figure is given as

$$\Delta_P = 2t - \frac{\lambda}{2} \qquad ...(6.92)$$

Now we can find the condition of reflection for high or low intensity for bright and dark fringes seen in reflected light by equating the path difference given in equation-(6.92) to multiple of wavelength or odd multiple of half wavelength. If the air wedge is filled with a transparent medium of refractive index m between the plates then the path difference will be given as

$$\Delta_P = 2\mu t - \frac{\lambda}{2} \qquad ...(6.93)$$

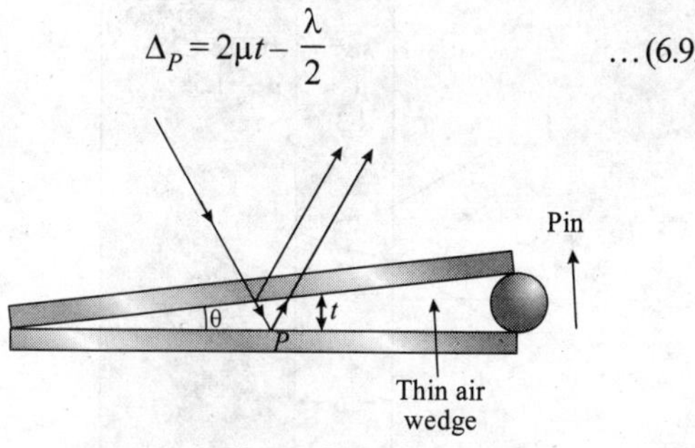

Figure 6.57

6.5.9 Shape of Interference Fringes in Reflected Light from different Air Wedges

In previous article-2.5.8 we analyzed how by variation in path difference fringes are obtained by a triangular flat air wedge. Consider figure-6.58(a) which shows a plano convex lens placed on a glass plate on which from the top a parallel light beam incident normally. The lower curved surface of plano convex lens and the top surface of the glass plate forms a thin air film of which thickness is varying from the point of contact of lens and plate. Due to continuous variation in path difference in reflected light as we move away from point of contact, alternate bright and dark circular fringes are obtained as shown in figure-6.58(b). These circular ring shaped fringes are called '*Newton's Rings*'. As due to the curvature of the lens surface, the thickness of air film is not linearly varying unlike to the case of triangular air wedge already discussed, the fringe width keep on decreasing as the radius of fringes increase.

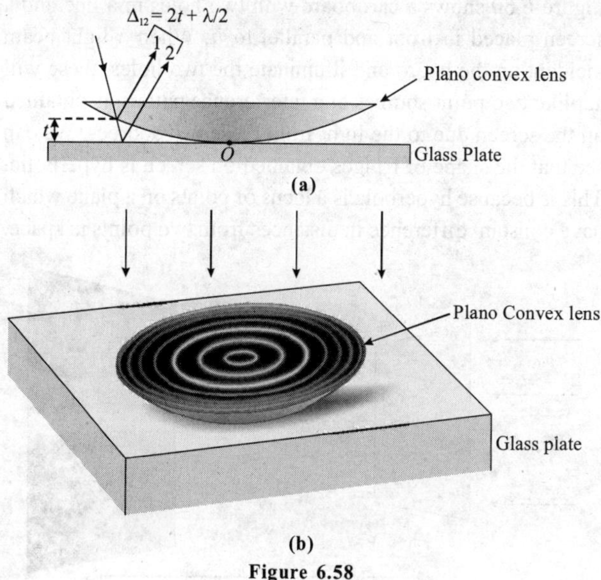

Figure 6.58

Similar to above case if we consider a cylindrical plano convex lens as shown in figure-6.59(a) then the interference fringes in reflected light beam will be straight but their width will decrease as we move away from the contact line of the lens with the glass plate.

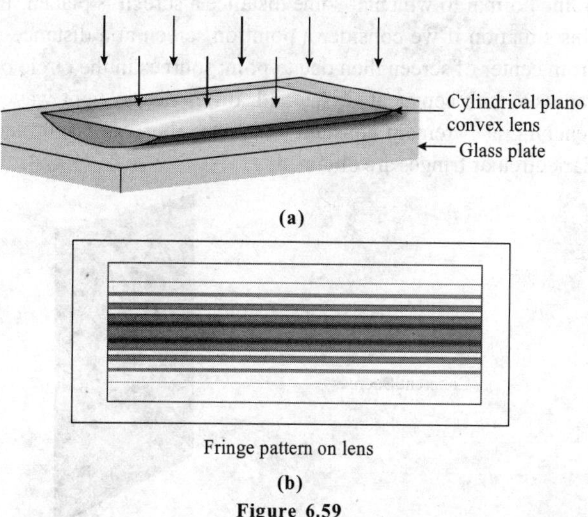

Figure 6.59

6.5.10 Shape of Interference Fringes due to different types of Sources

In YDSE setup we've seen that fringes are straight and parallel to the slits because all the points on screen where the path difference of the light waves from the two sources is same will have same intensity and forms a fringe of same intensity. Now we will discuss different cases of two light sources which produce interference pattern on a screen and analyze the shape of fringes obtained in the resulting interference pattern.

Case-I : Two Point Sources in a Line placed parallel to Screen

Figure-6.60 shows a cardboard with two holes in a line and a screen placed in front and parallel to it. When a light beam incident on the board and illuminate the two holes, these will act like two point sources and interference pattern is obtained on the screen due to the light from these two sources. We can see that the shape of fringes obtained on screen is hyperbolic. This is because hyperbola is a locus of points on a plane which have constant difference in distances from two points in space.

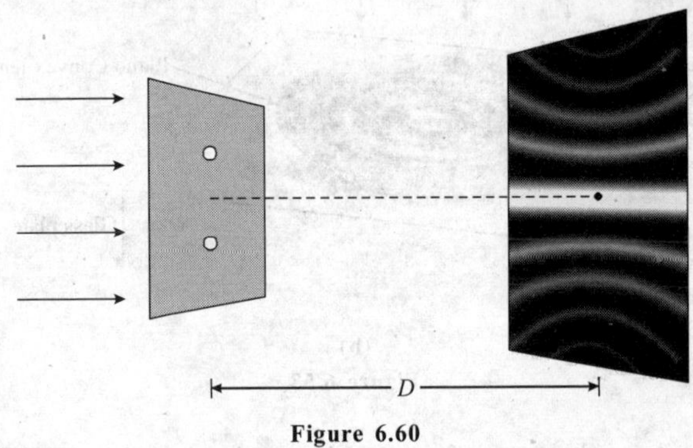

Figure 6.60

Case-II : Two Point Sources in a Line placed normal to the Screen

Figure-6.61 shows two point coherent sources S_1 and S_2 along a line normal to which at some distance a screen is placed. In this situation if we consider a point on screen at a distance x from center of screen then due to point sources in the circle of radius x with center at C, the path difference in light waves reaching at P remain constant thats why alternate bright and dark circular fringes are obtained.

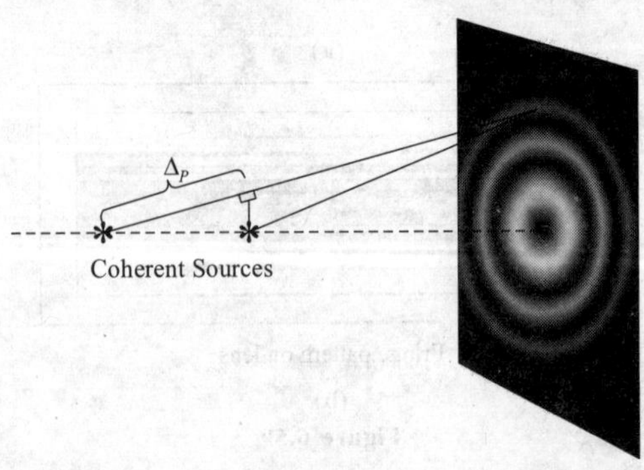

Figure 6.61

Case-III : Two rectangular Slit Sources in plane parallel to Screen (YDSE Setup)

Figure-6.62 shows the fringe pattern obtained in YDSE setup in which the light waves from two slit sources S_1 and S_2 interfere on screen. Due to length l of the slits at the middle region of screen fringes are straight and parallel but after a distance from screen center along the length of slits the shape of fringes will be approximately hyperbolic due to the reason mentioned in 'Case-I' above.

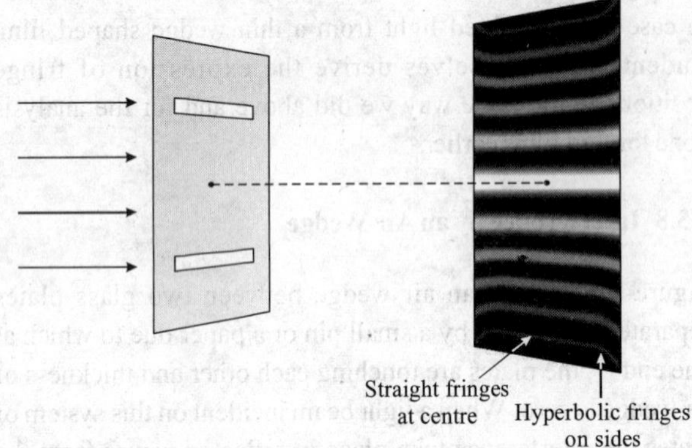

Figure 6.62

 # Illustrative Example 6.24

Figure-6.63 shows a glass lens is coated on one side with a thin film of magnesium fluoride (KgF_2) to reduce reflection from the lens surface. The refractive index of MgF_2 is 1.38 and that of glass is 1.50. What is the least coating thickness that eliminates (via interference) the reflections at the middle of the visible spectrum (λ = 5500Å) ? Assume that the light is approximately perpendicular to the coating surface.

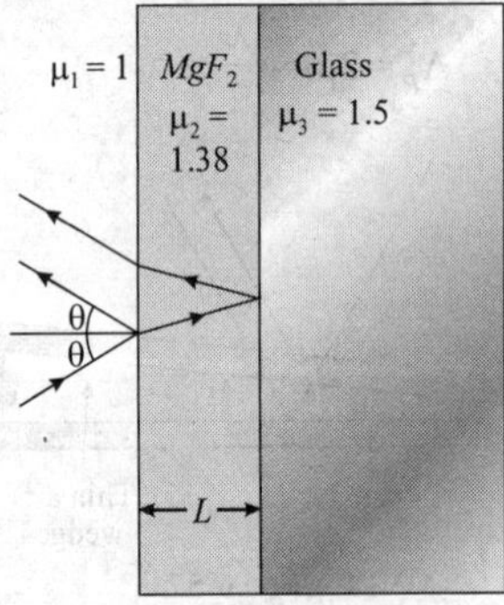

Figure 6.63

Solution

In the situation given the air-MgF_2 and MgF_2-glass both act as boundary of denser medium, so for destructive interference in reflected light, we use

$$2\mu_2 t = (2n-1)\frac{\lambda}{2}$$

$$\Rightarrow \quad t = (2n-1)\frac{\lambda}{4\mu_2}$$

For least value of thickness, $n = 1$ and $\mu_2 = 1.38$.

$$\Rightarrow \quad \lambda = (2 \times 1 - 1) \times \frac{(550 \times 10^{-9})}{4 \times 1.38}$$

$$\Rightarrow \quad \lambda = 996\text{Å}$$

Illustrative Example 6.25

Find the minimum thickness of an oil film in air that gives an interference maxima in reflected light for wavelength 5360Å at normal incidence. Take $\mu_{oil} = 1.34$.

Solution

Path different of two waves in reflected beam for normal incidence is

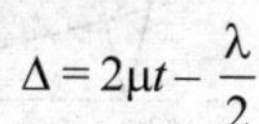

$$\Delta = 2\mu t - \frac{\lambda}{2}$$

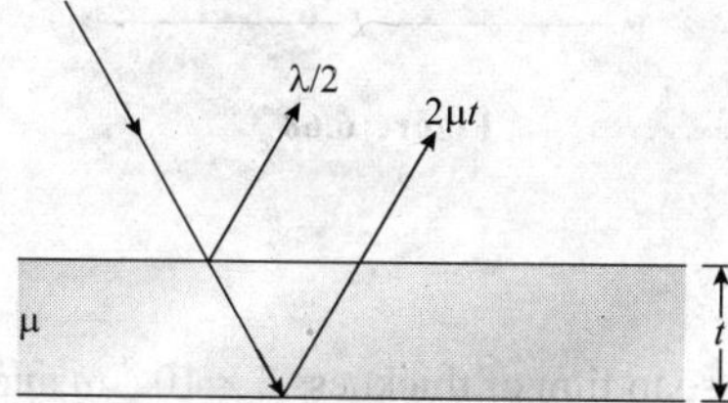

Figure 6.64

For maximum reflection, reflected beams should interfere constructively so for minimum thickness of film, we use

$$2\mu t - \frac{\lambda}{2} = 0$$

$$\Rightarrow \quad t = \frac{\lambda}{4\mu} = \frac{5360 \times 10^{-10}}{4 \times 1.34} = 10^{-7}\text{m}$$

Illustrative Example 6.26

A wedge of angle 0.5° is illuminated with sodium light whose two lines corresponds to the wavelengths 5890Å and 5896Å. Find the distance from the apex at which the maxima due to the two wavelengths first coincide when observed in the reflected light. (The wedge contains air).

Solution

If the thickness of the wedge at the point where the maximums of both coincides be t then for constructive interference in reflected light, we have

$$2\mu t = (2n + 1)\frac{\lambda}{2}$$

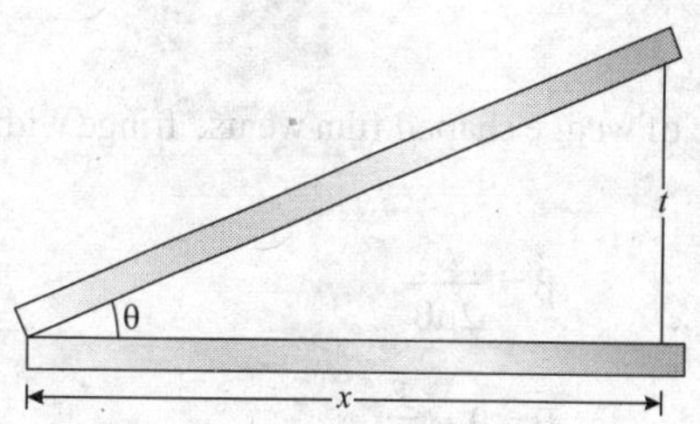

Figure 6.65

As $\mu_{air} = 1$, we consider one maxima of one wavelength will coincide with the next order maxima of the lower wavelength so we use

$$2t = (2n + 1)\frac{\lambda_1}{2}$$

and

$$2t = (2n + 3)\frac{\lambda_2}{2}$$

According to given condition, we can write

$$\frac{(2n+1)\lambda_1}{2} = \frac{(2n+3)\lambda_2}{2}$$

$$\Rightarrow \quad (2n + 1)(5896) = (2n + 3)(5890)$$

$$\Rightarrow \quad n = 1499 \quad \text{(whole number)}$$

and

$$t = (2n + 1)\frac{\lambda_1}{4}$$

$$\Rightarrow \quad t = \frac{(2 \times 1499 + 1)}{4} \times 5896 \times 10^{-10}$$

$$\Rightarrow \quad t = 0.004 \text{ cm}$$

Let x be the required distance from the apex, then we use

$$\frac{t}{x} = \tan\theta = \theta$$

$$\Rightarrow \quad x = \frac{t}{\theta}$$

$$\Rightarrow \quad x = \frac{0.004}{0.5 \times \dfrac{\pi}{180}} = 4.58 \text{ cm}$$

Illustrative Example 6.27

A broad source of light of wavelength 6800Å illuminates two glass plates 120 mm long normally. These glass plates meet at one end and are separated by a wire 0.048 mm in diameter at the other end as shown in figure-6.66. Find the number of bright fringes formed over the distance of 120 mm.

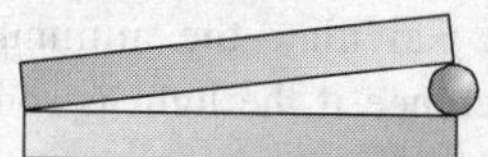

Figure 6.66

Solution

In this case of wedge shaped film we use fringe width is given as

$$\beta = \frac{\lambda}{2\mu\theta}$$

Here $\quad \tan\theta = \theta = \frac{y}{l}$

Let N be the number of fringes formed over a given length l then we use

$$l = N\beta$$

$$\Rightarrow \quad l = N\left(\frac{\lambda}{2\mu\theta}\right)$$

$$\Rightarrow \quad N = \frac{2\mu l\theta}{\lambda}$$

Figure 6.67

$$\Rightarrow \quad N = \frac{2\mu y}{\lambda} \qquad \left(\text{As } \theta = \frac{y}{l}\right)$$

For air we use $\mu = 1$

$$\Rightarrow \quad N = \frac{2\times1\times0.048\times10^{-3}}{680\times10^{-9}} = 141$$

Web Reference at www.physicsgalaxy.com

Age Group - High School Physics | Age 17-19 Years
Section - OPTICS
Topic - Nature of Light and Interference
Module Number - 39 to 47

Practice Exercise-6.2

(i) A glass plate of refractive index 1.5 is coated with a thin layer of thickness t and refractive index 1.8. Light of wavelength λ travelling in air is incident normally on the layer. It is partly reflected at the upper and the lower surfaces of the layer and the two reflected rays interfere. Write the condition for their constructive interference. If λ = 6480Å , obtain the least value of t for which the rays interfere constructively.

[$t = \frac{\lambda}{7.2}, \frac{3\lambda}{7.2}, \ldots\ t_{\text{minium}}$ = 900Å]

(ii) Most of our discussion of the techniques for determining constructive and destructive interference by reflection from a thin film in air has been confined to rays striking the film at nearly normal incidence. Assume that a ray is incident at an angle of 45° (relative to the normal) on a film with an index of refraction of $\sqrt{2}$. Calculate the minimum thickness for constructive interference if the light is sodium light with a wavelength of 6000Å.

[1224Å]

(iii) A soap film of thickness 0.0011 mm appears dark when seen by reflected light of wavelength 5800 Å. What is the refractive index of soap solution if it is between 1.2 and 1.5.

[μ = 1.318]

(iv) A wedge-shaped film of air is produced by placing a fine wire of diameter D between the ends of two flat glass plates of length L = 20 cm, as shown in the figure-6.68. When the air film is illuminated with light of wavelength λ = 5500Å, there are 12 dark fringes found per centimeter on the wedge. Find the wire diameter D.

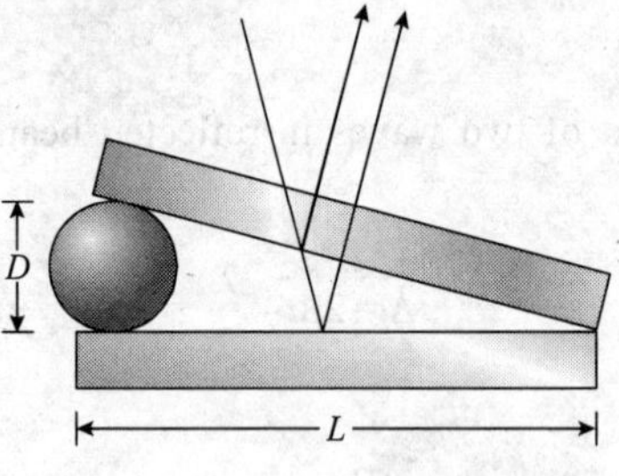

Figure 6.68

[6.6×10^{-5} m]

(v) A thin soap film of thickness 3×10^{-7} m and μ = 1.5 is spreaded on a glass surface. When white light is normally incident on this sheet, find the colour which will be reflected strongly by the film.

[4500Å]

(vi) A ray of light of intensity I is incident on a parallel glass-slab at a point A as shown in the figure-6.69. It undergoes partial reflection and refraction. At each reflection 20% of incident energy is reflected. The rays AB and $A'B'$ undergo interference. Find the ratio I_{max}/I_{min}.

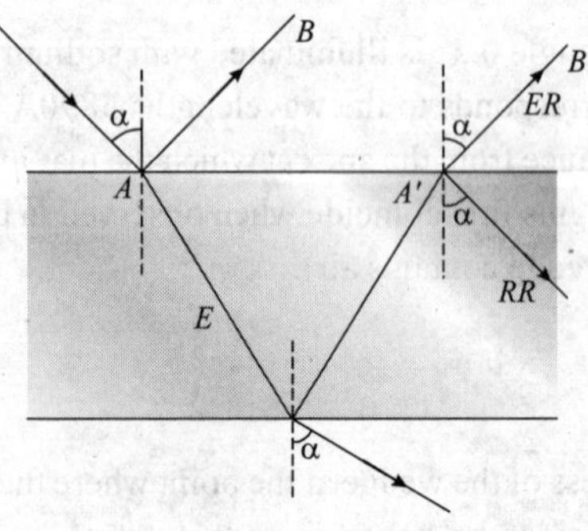

Figure 6.69

[81 : 1]

(vii) A point source S emitting light of wavelength 6000Å is placed at a very small height h above the flat reflecting surface AB as shown in figure-6.70. The intensity of the reflected light is 36% of the incident intensity. Interference fringes are observed on a screen placed parallel to the reflecting surface at a very large distance D from it.

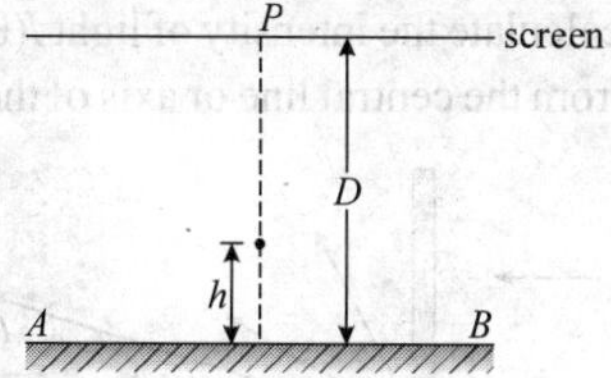

Figure 6.70

(a) What is the shape of the interference fringes on the screen?

(b) Calculate the ratio of the minimum to the maximum intensities in the interference fringes formed near the point P shown in the figure-6.70.

(c) If the intensities at point P corresponds to a maximum, calculate the minimum distance through which the reflecting surface AB should be shifted so that the intensity at P again becomes maximum.

[(a) Circular; (b) 1/16; (c) 3000Å]

6.6 Diffraction of Light

When the light passes through edges of an obstacle, it flares out in the shadow zone after the obstacle. This bending/flaring of light around the edges of obstacle is called '*Diffraction*'. The diffraction effects are significantly observed when the dimensions of obstacles is of the order of wavelength of light. We will also analyze and study that for large sized objects diffraction effects are negligible and light follows almost rectilinear propagation of light and its analysis is done by phenomena studied in geometrical optics.

Figure-6.71 shows a light passing through a narrow slit of width 'b'. If width of slit is large it almost passes undeviated and follows rectilinear propagation. If the width of slit is reduced to an extent that it is in the range of wavelength of light, the light flares out in the side regions as shown in figure-6.71(b) and if slit width is decreased to a value even lesser than light wavelength then the flaring is maximum in side zones as shown in figure-6.71(c). In later sections we will mathematically analyze this behaviour of light.

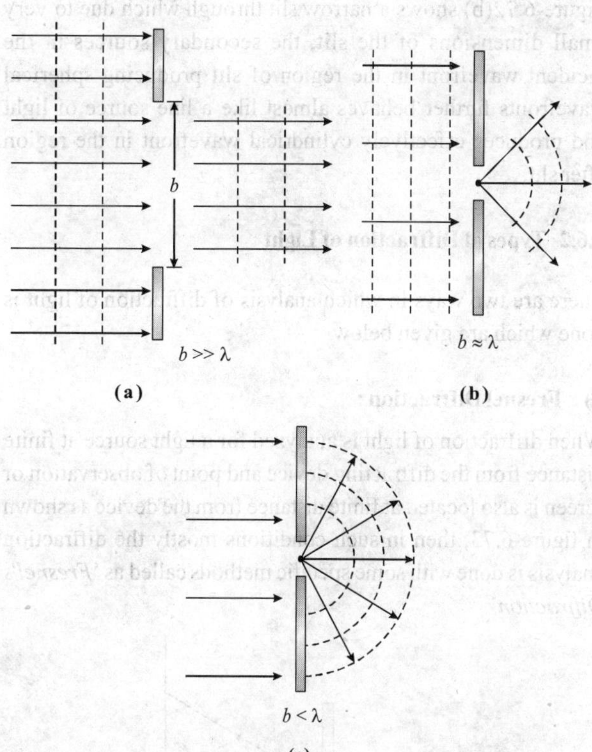

Figure 6.71

6.6.1 Explanation of Diffraction by Huygen's Wave Theory

Figure-6.72(a) shows a plane light beam incident on a broad slit in a plane. As already discussed according to theory wavefront propagation the secondary point sources of wavefront which are in the region of slit produce their spherical secondary wavefronts and new common tangential plane of these secondary wavefronts is considered as next position of the travelling wavefront. If the slit width is large then the light flaring in side region of the slit will be negligible compared to the light propagating straight so the diffraction effects are not significantly perceptible.

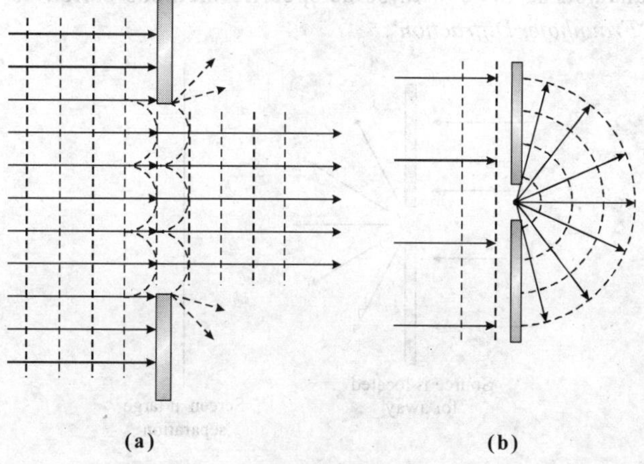

Figure 6.72

Figure-6.72(b) shows a narrow slit through which due to very small dimensions of the slit, the secondary sources in the incident wavefront in the region of slit producing spherical wavefronts further behaves almost like a line source of light and produces effectively cylindrical wavefront in the region after slit.

6.6.2 Types of Diffraction of Light

There are two ways in which analysis of diffraction of light is done which are given below.

(i) Fresnel Diffraction :

When diffraction of light is analyzed for a light source at finite distance from the diffracting device and point of observation or screen is also located at finite distance from the device as shown in figure-6.73, then in such conditions mostly the diffraction analysis is done with some specific methods called as '*Fresnel's Diffraction*'.

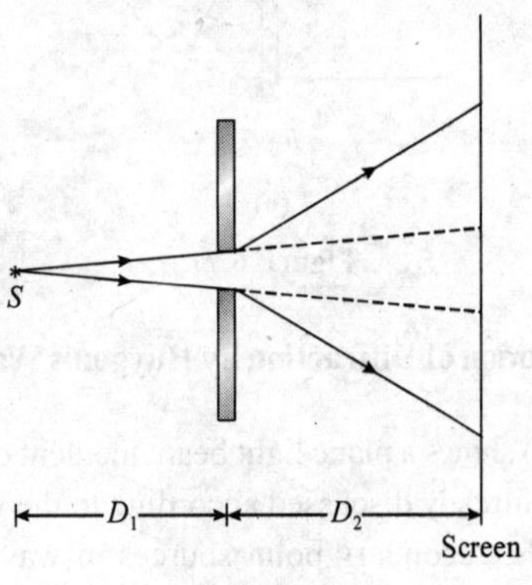

Figure 6.73

(ii) Fraunhofer Diffraction :

When diffraction is analyzed for a source at very large distance from the diffracting device and point of observation or screen is also at very large distance from the device as shown in figure-6.74, then in such conditions mostly the diffraction analysis is done with some specific methods called as '*Fraunhofer Diffraction*'.

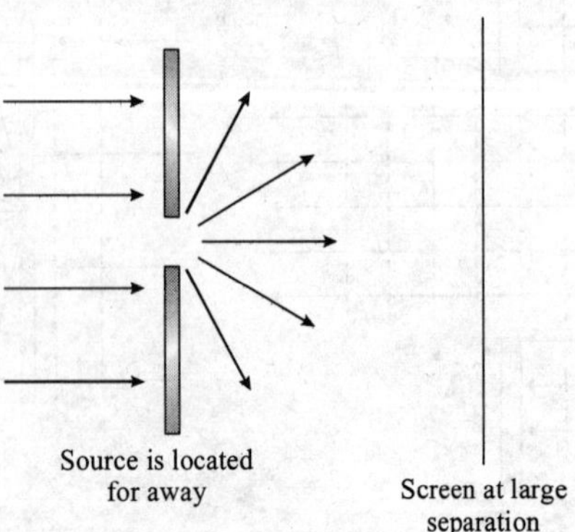

Figure 6.74

In this book we will cover mainly some specific cases of Fraunhofer Diffraction in detail.

6.6.3 Diffraction of Light by a Single Slit

In figure-6.75 a parallel beam of light is incident on a narrow slit through which light gets diffracted and at distance far away from the slit we calculate the intensity of light $I(\theta)$ at an angular displacement θ from the central line or axis of the slit as shown.

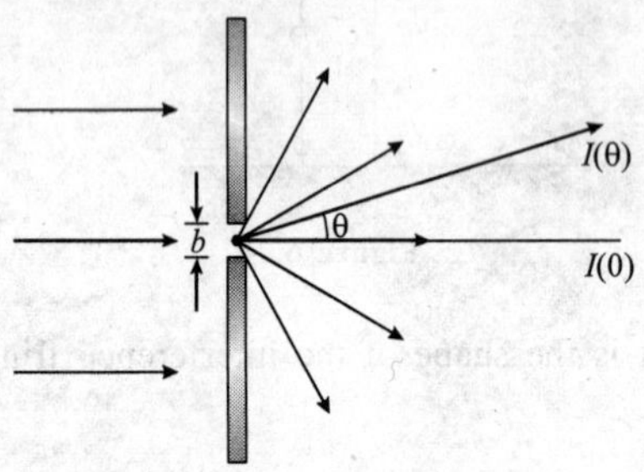

Figure 6.75

To analyze the light intensity $I(\theta)$ at an angular position θ from the center line, look at the figure-6.76 which shows the magnified view of the slit in figure-6.75. This figure shows the secondary sources of the incident light in the slit zone and we consider light waves due to all these secondary sources in the direction θ and find the resulting intensity $I(\theta)$ due to the interference of all these waves from the secondary sources in this direction.

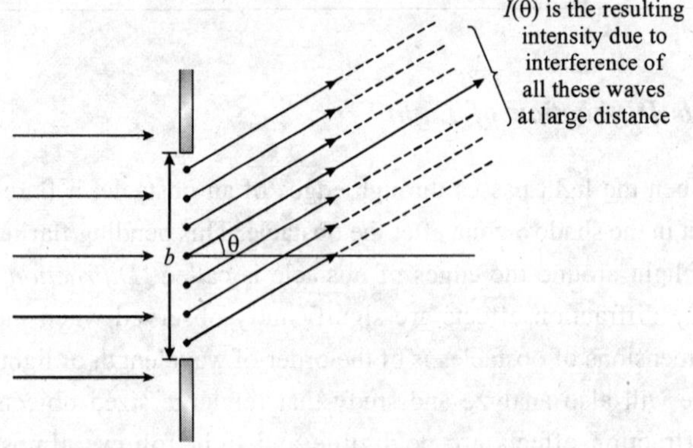

Figure 6.76

In this analysis of Fraunhofer diffraction as the distances are large, it becomes practically very difficult to see the light intensity on a screen placed far away from slit as intensity decreases with square of distance from slit. In laboratory experimental setups practically distances are also finite due to limitation of space so we use convex lenses for analysis of diffraction and to overcome above problems in practical conditions as shown in figure-6.77. A source is kept at the focal point of a convex lens by which refracted rays becomes parallel and used as incident light on the slit. After the slit also we use a convex lens to focus the parallel light rays from all secondary sources of wavefront on screen to obtain the diffraction pattern on screen at far away point.

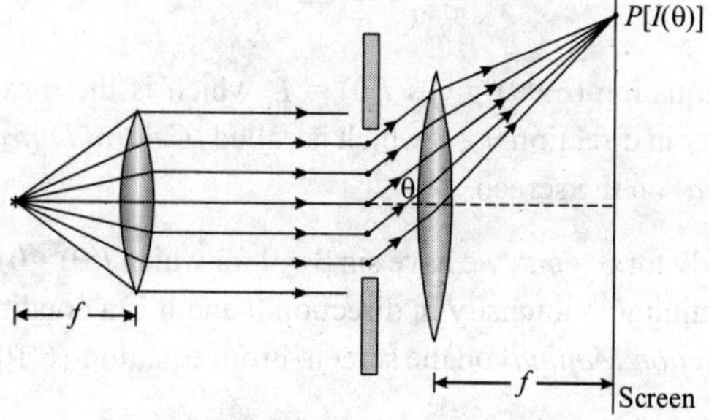

Figure 6.77

6.6.4 Analysis of Diffraction of Light by a Single Slit

The analysis of diffraction of light by a single slit is done in the way explained in article-6.6.3 by considering the interference of all the light waves by secondary sources in slit zone in a specific direction. To analyze the same we number these secondary sources 1, 2, 3...N in the slit as shown in figure-6.78(a) such that the separation between the two adjacent sources is d and we can use $(N-1)d = b$ and for $N \to \infty$ we use $Nd = b$. At an angular direction θ, we consider the oscillating displacements due to these sources are taken as $y_1, y_2, y_3 \ldots y_N$.

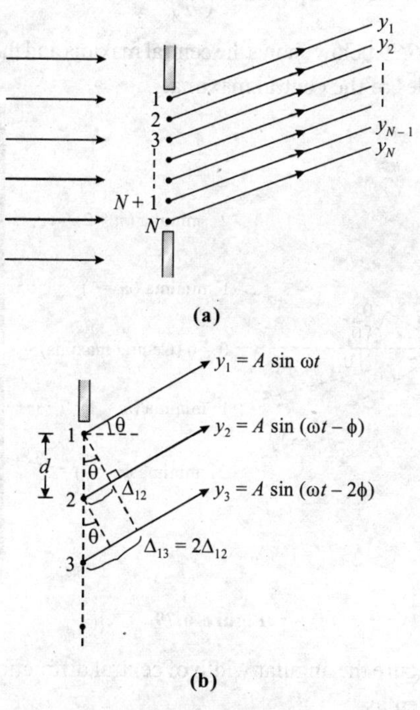

Figure 6.78

Figure-6.78(b) shows the magnified view of a portion of slit with secondary sources in which we can see that in the direction θ, wave from secondary source 2 is travelling an extra path D given as

$$\Delta_{12} = d \sin \theta \qquad \ldots(6.94)$$

Similarly the path difference in the light waves from sources 1,3 and 1,4 and so on can be given as

$$\Delta_{13} = 2d \sin \theta \qquad \ldots(6.95)$$

$$\Delta_{14} = 3d \sin \theta \qquad \ldots(6.96)$$

Using the above relations we can find the phase difference in the waves from sources 2, 3, 4... from the wave from source 1 as

$$\phi_{12} = \frac{2\pi}{\lambda} d \sin \theta = \phi$$

$$\phi_{13} = \frac{2\pi}{\lambda}(2d \sin \theta) = 2\phi$$

$$\phi_{14} = \frac{2\pi}{\lambda}(3d \sin \theta) = 3\phi$$

With the above phase differences with can write the equation for displacements due to the waves from secondary sources. If A is taken as the amplitude due to each secondary source at a point on screen then these displacement equations can be written as

$$y_1 = A \sin \omega t$$

$$y_2 = A \sin (\omega t - \phi)$$

$$y_2 = A \sin (\omega t - 2\phi)$$

$$\ldots$$

$$y_N = A \sin(\omega t - (N-1)\phi)$$

By the superposition principal, the resulting displacement at point P on screen shown in figure-6.42 can be given as

$$y_R = y_1 + y_2 + y_3 + \ldots + y_N$$

$\Rightarrow$ $y_R = A \sin \omega t + A \sin (\omega t - \phi) + A \sin (\omega t - 2\phi) + \ldots + A \sin(\omega t - (N-1)\phi)$

$$\Rightarrow \qquad y_R = \left(\frac{A \sin\left(\frac{N\phi}{2}\right)}{\sin\left(\frac{\phi}{2}\right)}\right) \cdot \sin\left(\omega t - \frac{(N-1)\phi}{2}\right)$$

Above equation-(6.94) can be written as

$$y_R = R \,.\, \sin(\omega t - \theta)$$

[at a large distance from slit or at a point P on screen with convex lens]

where the amplitude of wave in angular direction θ is given as

$$R = \frac{A \sin\left(\frac{N\phi}{2}\right)}{\sin\left(\frac{\phi}{2}\right)} \qquad \ldots(6.97)$$

The intensity in angular direction θ is given as $I(\theta) = kR^2$ where R is the resulting amplitude given by equation-(6.97) which gives

$$I(\theta) = k\left(\frac{A\sin\left(\frac{N\phi}{2}\right)}{\sin\left(\frac{\phi}{2}\right)}\right)^2$$

In above expression we multiply numerator and denominator both by N^2 gives

$$I(\theta) = k\left(\frac{A\sin\left(\frac{N\phi}{2}\right)}{\sin\left(\frac{\phi}{2}\right)}\right)^2 \times \frac{N^2}{N^2}$$

As for small angle ϕ we use $\sin\left(\frac{\phi}{2}\right) \approx \frac{\phi}{2}$, thus we have

$$\Rightarrow \quad I(\theta) = k\left(\frac{(NA)\sin\left(\frac{N\phi}{2}\right)}{\left(\frac{N\phi}{2}\right)}\right)^2 \quad \ldots(6.98)$$

As in the slit the secondary sources are considered in same wavefront of incident light, we consider the amplitude of the wave is equally divided among all sources so if A_0 is the amplitude of incident light on slit then we can use $A_0 = NA$ so if I_0 is the light intensity due to slit in front of it then we can use

$$I_0 = kA_0^2 = kN^2A^2$$

Thus from above equation-(6.98) we have

$$I(\theta) = I_0 \frac{\sin^2\left(\frac{N\phi}{2}\right)}{\left(\frac{N\phi}{2}\right)^2}$$

$$\Rightarrow \quad I(\theta) = I_0 \frac{\sin^2\beta}{\beta^2} \quad \ldots(6.99)$$

Where $\beta = \frac{N\phi}{2} = \frac{N}{2}\left(\frac{2\pi}{\lambda} d\sin\theta\right)$

For $N \to \infty$ we can use $Nd \approx b$ thus we have

$$\beta = \frac{\pi b\sin\theta}{\lambda} \quad \ldots(6.100)$$

With the value of b given by equation-(6.100), equation-(6.99) gives the value of intensity $I(\theta)$ in the angular direction θ from the slit.

6.6.5 Diffraction Minima due to Single Slit

As we analyzed in the previous article then intensity in angular direction θ is given by equation-(6.99), in this equation we can see that at θ = 0, β = 0 and we get

$$\lim_{\beta\to 0} \frac{\sin\beta}{\beta} = 1$$

Thus equation-(6.99) gives $I(0) = I_0$ which is the maximum intensity in direction θ = 0 which is called '*Central Diffraction Maxima*' on the screen.

Similarly for $\beta = m\pi$, we have $\sin\beta = 0$ for which $I(\theta) = 0$ which is the minimum intensity in direction θ and it is a condition of '*Diffraction Minima*' on the screen. From equation-(6.100) we use

$$m\pi = \frac{\pi b\sin\theta}{\lambda}$$

$$\Rightarrow \quad b\sin\theta = m\lambda \quad \ldots(6.101)$$

Thus the above expression in equation-(6.101) with $m = 1, 2, 3\ldots$ gives the values of θ at which intensity is zero or the points corresponds to diffraction minima on the screen.

Here we can see for $m = 1$ (First Minima) from equation-(6.101), angular position of first minima is given as

$$\sin\theta_1 = \frac{\lambda}{b}$$

$$\Rightarrow \quad \theta_1 = \sin^{-1}\left(\frac{\lambda}{b}\right)$$

The figure-6.79 below shows the central maxima and the minima's on both sides of the central maxima.

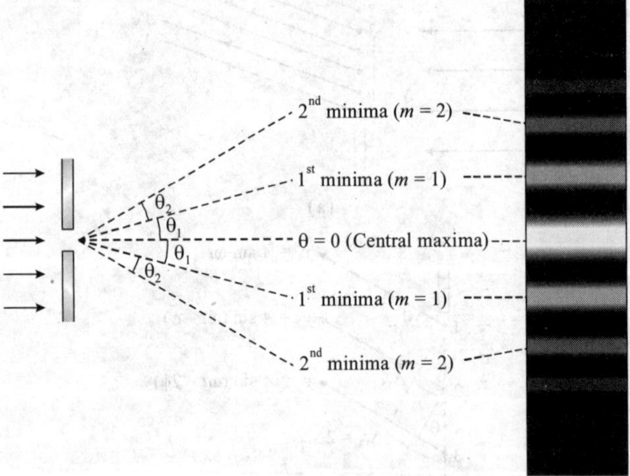

Figure 6.79

In above figure the angular width of central diffraction maxima can be given as

$$\Delta\theta_C = 2\theta_1 = 2\sin^{-1}\left(\frac{\lambda}{b}\right)$$

6.6.6 Diffraction Maxima due to Single Slit

In above figure-6.79 the angular positions of diffraction minima can be given by the condition of equation-(6.101) and to find the angular positions of diffraction maxima other than central maxima we differentiate equation-(6.99) and equate it to zero.

$$\frac{dI(\theta)}{d\beta} = \frac{\beta^2(2\sin\beta\cos\beta)-(\sin^2\beta)(2\beta)}{\beta^4} = 0$$

$$\Rightarrow \quad \tan\beta = \beta \qquad \ldots(102)$$

In equation-(102), $\beta = 0$ corresponds to central maxima and for all values of b satisfying this equation will correspond to higher order diffraction maxima in the diffraction pattern which can be calculated graphically by finding the intersection point of curves $y = \tan\beta$ and $y = \beta$ as shown in figure-6.80 below.

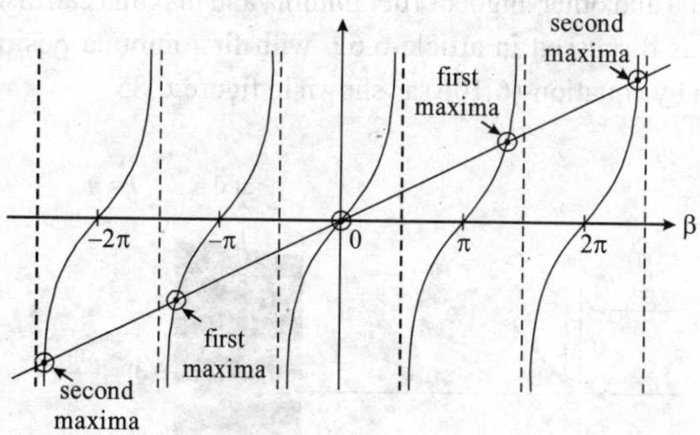

Figure 6.80

In above figure we can see that successive higher order maxima are not located at the mid points of all the minima's.

6.6.7 Observing Single Slit Diffraction Pattern on a Screen

Figure-6.81 shows an experimental setup with highly magnified view of the slit. In this setup the screen is placed at a distance equal to the focal length of the lens placed in front of the slit and lens focuses all light waves from secondary sources from slit onto the screen and diffraction pattern is obtained on the screen.

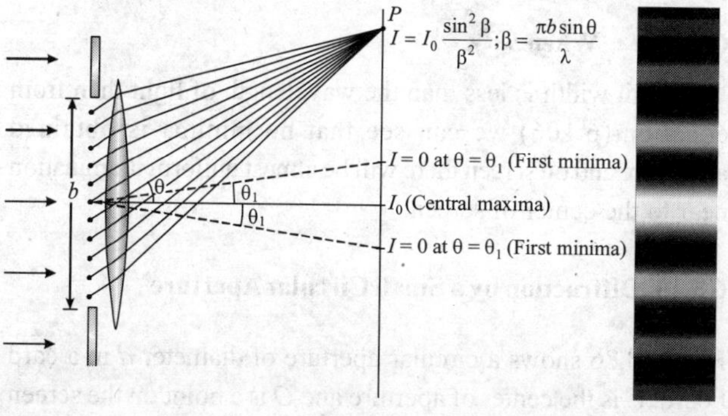

Figure 6.81

In above pattern the width of central bright fringe formed due to diffraction can be given as

$$w_C = f(2\theta_1) = 2f\sin^{-1}\left(\frac{\lambda}{b}\right) \qquad \ldots(6.103)$$

For higher values of b we can use the width of central maxima as

$$w_C = \frac{2f\lambda}{b} \qquad \ldots(6.104)$$

The angular positions of dark fringes in the diffraction pattern are given by the angles given by equation-(6.101) as

$$\theta_{min} = \sin^{-1}\left(\frac{m\lambda}{b}\right) \qquad \ldots(6.105)$$

If we find out the intensities at different diffraction maxima then for higher order maxima using the values of β obtained graphically in equation-(6.99), we will see that it decreases by a large extent as shown in figure-6.82.

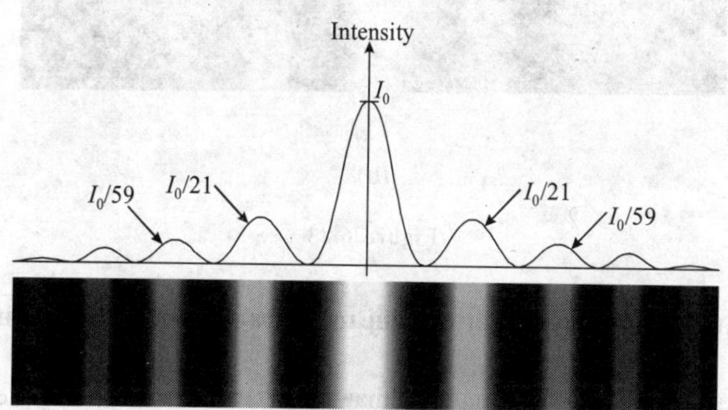

Figure 6.82

6.6.8 Difference between Double Slit Interference and Single Slit Diffraction Patterns

Figure-6.83(a) and (b) shows the intensity distribution curves of double slit interference pattern and single slit diffraction patterns and with these patterns we can distinguish main differences in the two patterns.

1. In interference pattern all fringes are of same width but in diffraction pattern fringe width decreases as we move away from center.

2. In interference pattern all fringes are having same brightness whereas in diffraction pattern brightness decreases as we move away from center.

3. Double slit interference is produced by interference of two monochromatic coherent light sources (slits) whereas diffraction pattern is produced by interference of several monochromatic coherent secondary light sources in the slit.

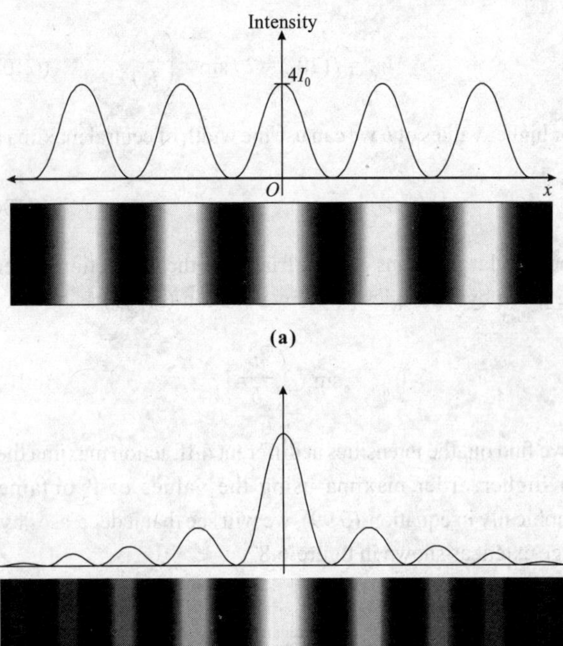

Figure 6.83

6.6.9 Illumination Pattern due to Diffraction by a Single Slit

As we have already analyzed that the first minima in the single slit diffraction pattern is obtained at an angle given as

$$\theta_1 = \sin^{-1}\left(\frac{\lambda}{b}\right) \quad \ldots (6.106)$$

On the above angle given in equation-(6.106) which gives the edges of central diffraction maxima which is most prominent in the illumination pattern of single slit diffraction. Now for different wavelengths and slit widths we can see different cases and the resulting illumination pattern as given below.

Case-I : When $b >> \lambda$

When slit width is very large compared to wavelength of light then in equation-(6.106) we can use

$$\theta_1 = \sin^{-1}\left(\frac{\lambda}{b}\right) \to 0$$

Which results in rectilinear propagation of light as light does not flare out of the region beyond $\theta = 0$. This is shown in figure-6.84 below in which the central maxima will just be the projection of light on screen which is of width equal to that of the slit.

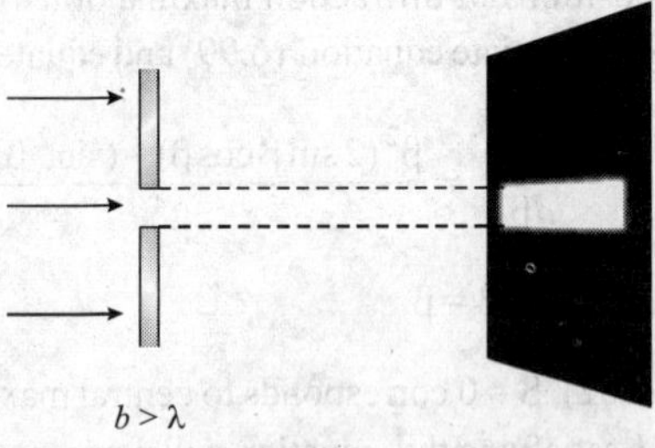

Figure 6.84

Case-II : When $b > \lambda$

When slit width b is more than the wavelength of light then first minima and other higher order minima and maxima can also be seen as discussed in article-6.6.6 with first minima positions given by equation-(6.106) as shown in figure-6.85

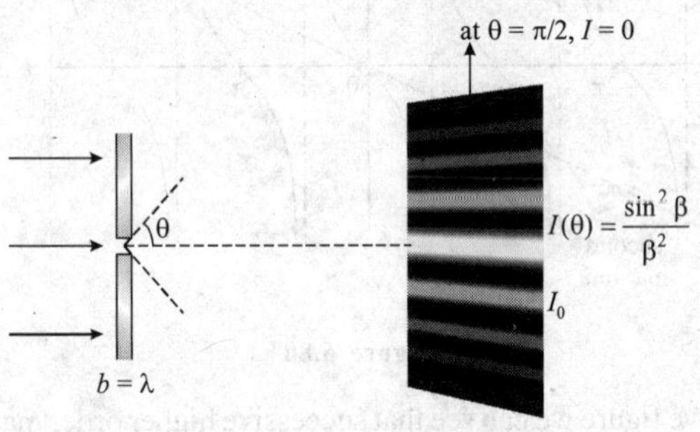

Figure 6.85

Case-III : When $b = \lambda$

In this case we can see from equation-(p) we get

$$\theta_1 = \sin^{-1}(1) = \frac{\pi}{2}$$

Thus the central maxima will spread on the whole screen and as we move away from center of screen the intensity of light gradually decreases with the function given by equation-(6.99)

Case-IV : When $b < \lambda$

When slit width is less than the wavelength of light then from equation-(6.106) we can see that no minima is obtained anywhere and on screen there will be almost uniform illumination near to the center of screen.

6.6.10 Diffraction by a Small Circular Aperture

Figure-6.86 shows a circular aperture of diameter d in a card board. C is the center of aperture and O is a point on the screen in front of point C. Due to diffraction of light through the circular aperture, alternative bright and dark circular fringes are obtained on screen as shown in figure. Similar to the case of diffraction by a single slit, in this case also the central bright disc is having maximum intensity and the intensities of higher order fringes is very less.

In the diffraction pattern due to a circular aperture consists of a bright circular disc as central maxima which is called Airy's disc. The angular position of first dark fringe at the outer edge of the Airy's disc is given as

$$\theta_1 = \frac{1.22\lambda}{d} \quad \ldots(6.107)$$

If r_0 is the radius of the Airy's disc then we use

$$r_0 = f\theta_1 = \frac{1.22\lambda f}{d} \quad \ldots(6.108)$$

Similar to the case of diffraction due to a rectangular slit, if here we increase the aperture diameter then the radius of the central bright disc decreases and at large aperture, central disc size approaches to the size of aperture by rectilinear propagation of light.

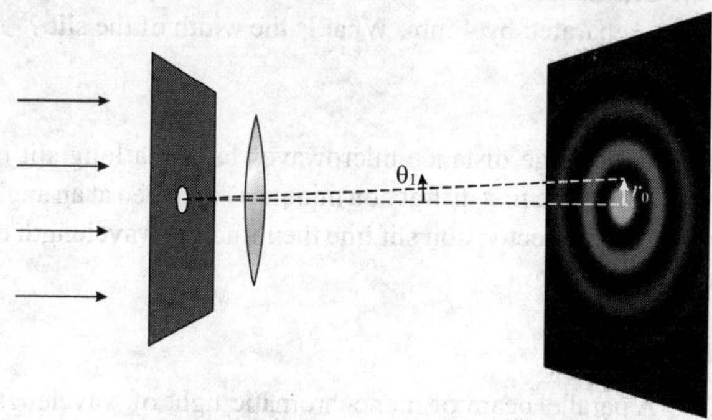

Figure 6.86

Illustrative Example 6.28

A parallel beam of monochromatic light of wavelength 4500Å is allowed to incident on a long slit of width 0.2 mm. Find the angular divergence in which most of the light is diffracted.

Solution

As we've studied that in diffraction through a single slit, most of the light is diffracted in central maxima, i.e. between the two first minima. The angular spread of first order minima is given by the relation

$$b \sin\theta = \lambda$$

$$\Rightarrow \quad \sin\theta = \pm\frac{\lambda}{b}$$

$$\Rightarrow \sin\theta = \pm\frac{4500\times10^{-10}}{0.2\times10^{-3}} = \pm2.25\times10^{-3} \text{ rad}$$

For small angles we can use $\sin\theta = \theta$

$$\Rightarrow \quad \theta = \pm 2.25\times10^{-3} \text{ rad}$$

Thus angular spread is $2\theta = \pm4.5\times10^{-3}$ rad

Illustrative Example 6.29

Angular width of central maximum in the Fraunhofer diffraction pattern of a slit is measured. The slit is illuminated by another wavelength, the angular width decreases by 30%. Calculate the wavelength of this light. The same decrease in angular width of central maximum is obtained when the original apparatus is immersed in a liquid. Find the refractive index of the liquid.

Solution

For diffraction minima on screen, we use

$$b\sin\theta = n\lambda \text{ where } n = 1, 2, 3, \ldots$$

Angular width of central maxima is 2θ for $n = 1$

$$\Rightarrow \quad b\sin\theta = \lambda$$

For small θ, we use

$$\Rightarrow \quad b\,\theta = \lambda$$

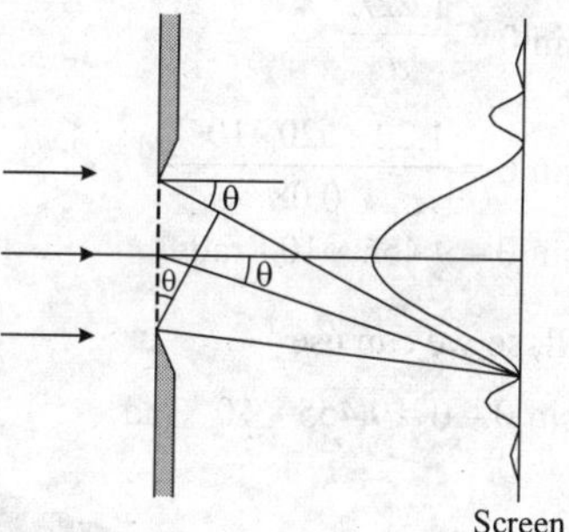

Figure 6.87

$\Rightarrow$ Angular width of central maxima is given as

$$\beta = 2\theta = \frac{2\lambda}{b}$$

$$\Rightarrow \quad = \frac{2\times6000\times10^{-10}}{b}$$

When the wavelength is changed the angular width of central maxima is reduced by 30%. Thus new angular width is given as

$$\text{Angular width after reduction} = \beta - 0.3\,\beta = 0.7\,\beta$$

$$\Rightarrow \quad 0.7\beta = \frac{2\lambda'}{b}$$

$$\Rightarrow \quad \lambda' = 0.7\beta\times\frac{b}{2} = 0.7\left(\frac{2\times6000\times10^{-10}}{b}\right)\times\frac{b}{2}$$

$\Rightarrow \quad \lambda' = 0.7 \times 6000 \times 10^{-10} = 4200 \times 10^{-10} \text{m}$

$\Rightarrow \quad \lambda' = 4200\text{Å}$

When the setup is submerged in a liquid then also the angular width of central maxima decreases by 30% which indicates that the wavelength of light decreases by 30%. Which gives

$$\lambda' = \frac{\lambda}{\mu}$$

$$\Rightarrow 0.7\lambda = \frac{6000\text{Å}}{\mu} = \frac{6000 \times 10^{-10}}{\mu}\text{Å}$$

$$\Rightarrow 0.7 \times 6000 \times 10^{-10} = \frac{6000 \times 10^{-10}}{\mu}$$

$$\Rightarrow \quad \mu = \frac{1}{0.7} = 1.43$$

Illustrative Example 6.30

A convex lens of diameter 8.0 cm is used to focus a parallel beam of light of wavelength 6200Å. If the light be focused at a distance of 20 cm from the lens, what would be the radius of the central bright spot formed ?

Solution

The angular spread of central bright spot is given as

$$\sin\theta = \frac{1.22\lambda}{d}$$

$$\Rightarrow \quad \sin\theta = \frac{1.22 \times 620 \times 10^{-9}}{0.08}$$

$$\Rightarrow \quad \sin\theta = 9.455 \times 10^{-6} \text{ rad}$$

Since θ is small, so we can use

$$\sin\theta = \theta = 9.455 \times 10^{-6} \text{ rad}$$

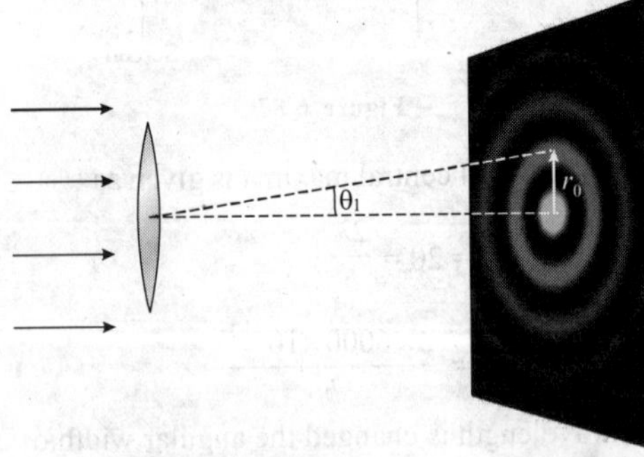

Figure 6.88

From the figure-6.88, we use

$$\theta = \frac{R}{D}$$

$$\Rightarrow \quad \frac{R}{D} = 9.45 \times 10^{-6}$$

$$\Rightarrow \quad R = 9.45 \times 10^{-6} \times 0.20$$

$$\Rightarrow \quad R = 1.89 \times 10^{-6} \text{ m}$$

Web Reference at www.physicsgalaxy.com

Age Group - High School Physics | Age 17-19 Years

Section - OPTICS

Topic - Diffraction of Light

Module Number - 1 to 12

Practice Exercise-6.3

(i) A narrow slit of width 0.025 mm is illuminated by a parallel beam of light. The diffraction pattern is observed through a telescope. It is found that to reach the first minimum, the telescope has to be rotated through 1°24' from the direction of the direct ray. Calculate the wavelength of light used.

[6100 Å]

(ii) A slit is located '*at infinity*' in front of a lens of focal length 1 m and is illuminated normally with light of wavelength 6000Å. The first minima on either side of the central maximum of the diffraction pattern observed in the focal plane of the lens are separated by 4 mm. What is the width of the slit ?

[0.3 mm]

(iii) From large distance microwaves fall on a long slit of width 5 cm. If the first diffraction minima is obtained at an angle 30° from the direct vision slit line then find the wavelength of the microwaves.

[2.5 cm]

(iv) A parallel beam of monochromatic light of wavelength 5900Å falls normally on a convex lens of diameter 10 cm which focuses the light on a flat normal screen located at a distance of 20 cm from the lens. What would be the radius of the central bright spot formed on the screen ?

[1.44×10^{-6} m]

6.7 Polarization of Light

Light is an electromagnetic wave in which electric and magnetic fields vibrate perpendicular to each other and to the direction of propagation. As already discussed earlier that in light wave, the sensation of visibility due to light is considered to be produced by the electric field component of the wave. Thus the oscillations of electric field are mainly considered in understanding of polarization of light. Figure-6.89(a) shows a general electromagnetic wave with oscillating electric field oscillating in *xz* plane and magnetic field oscillating in *yz* plane and the wave is propagating in *z* direction. In figure-6.89(b) shows only the oscillations of electric field in the same electromagnetic wave for which we define the plane *xz* as plane of oscillations of the wave.

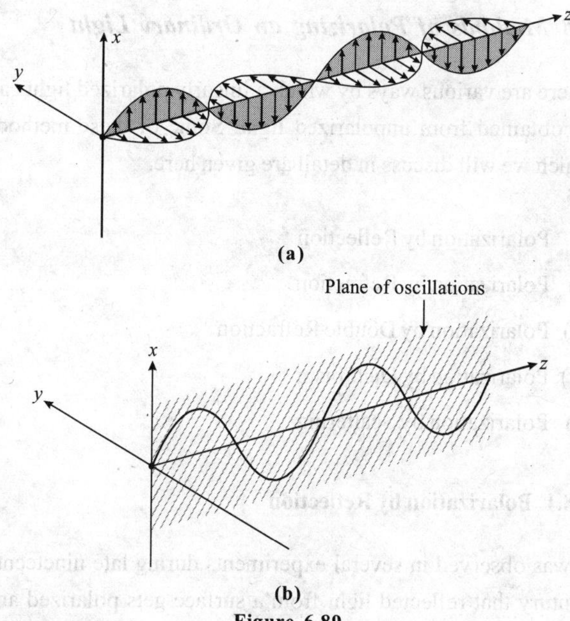

Figure 6.89

An ordinary light source consists of a very large number of particles which emit light and every particle emits light in different oscillation planes. An electromagnetic wave as shown in figure-6.89 can have many different oscillations plane when it propagates. Figure-6.90 shows different waves which have different oscillation planes.

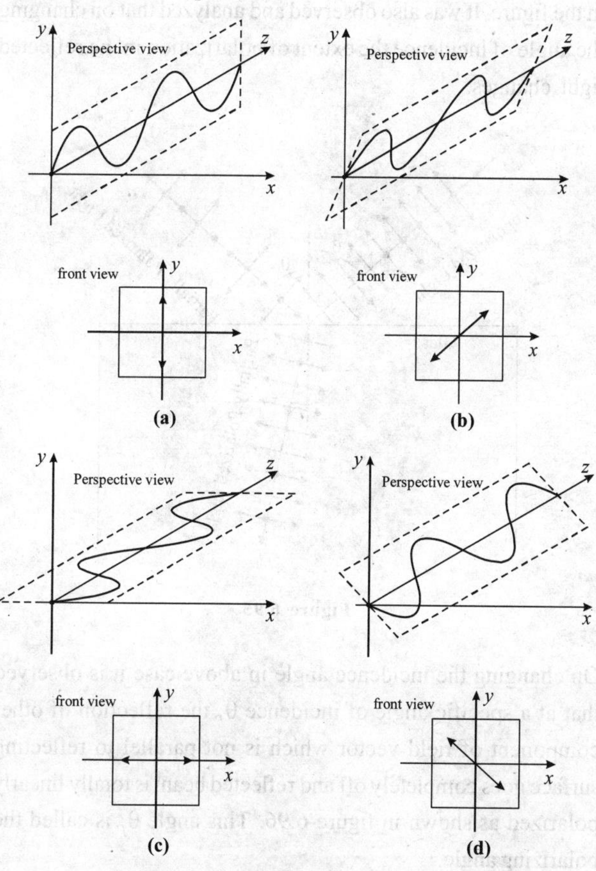

Figure 6.90

As shown in figure-6.90 a light wave can have infinite different oscillation planes and from an ordinary light source when light is emitted, it has electric field vectors oscillating in all possible planes as wave propagates and ordinary light wave is represented by figure-6.91 in its cross section which shows that in ordinary light field vectors oscillates in all planes and such a light is called '*Unpolarized Light*'. If we consider a light wave which consist of only one plane of oscillation and no field vector exist in any other planes as shown in figure-6.89(b) or figure-6.90(a), (b), (c) and (d) then such a light wave is called '*Polarized Light*' or '*Linearly Polarized Light*'.

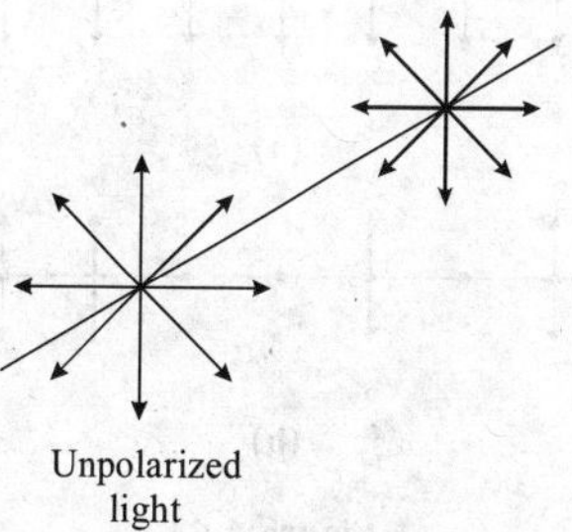

Figure 6.91

The optical phenomenon by which an unpolarized light is transformed to polarized light is called '*Polarization of Light*'. In other words we can also state "*Restricting the oscillations of field vectors in a light only in one plane is called Polarization of Light and the plane of oscillations in polarized light is called Plane of Polarization*".

6.7.1 Representation of Unpolarized and Polarized Light

As discussed in previous article polarized light consist of only one plane in which field vector oscillate as wave propagate and in unpolarized light field vectors oscillate in all possible planes of polarizations as ordinary light is emitted by lot of atomic emitters in a light source and waves are emitted with different planes of oscillations. Figure-6.92(a) shows the representation of unpolarized light on paper. In this diagram we represent all oscillation planes of field vectors having two mutually perpendicular components, one along the plane of paper which is represented by vertical arrow and other in the direction normal to the plane of paper which is represented by dots at the center.

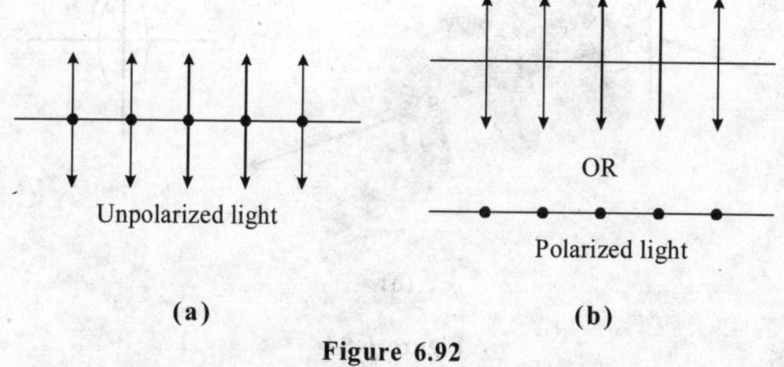

Figure 6.92

Figure-6.92(b) above shows the representation of polarized light which consist of field vectors oscillating only in one plane either in the plane of paper or normal to the plane of paper. Figure-6.93(a) shows a light which is partially polarized which mainly consists of oscillations of field vectors in the plane of paper but also having some oscillations in normal direction. Similarly figure-6.93(b) also shows a partially polarized light which is having oscillations of field vectors in the direction normal to the paper and having some oscillations in the plane of paper also.

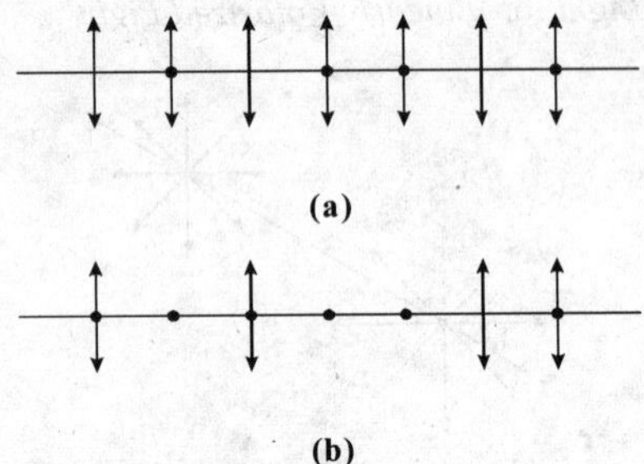

Figure 6.93

6.7.2 Circularly and Elliptically Polarized Light

In a circularly or elliptically polarized light its electric field vector continuously rotates in a plane normal to the direction of propagation either clockwise or anticlockwise. Figure-6.94(a) shows a circularly polarized light in which the tip of electric field vector revolves at any point in space in a circle in a plane normal to direction of propagation of light. Figure-6.94(b) shows an elliptically polarized light in which the tip of electric field vector revolves in elliptical path.

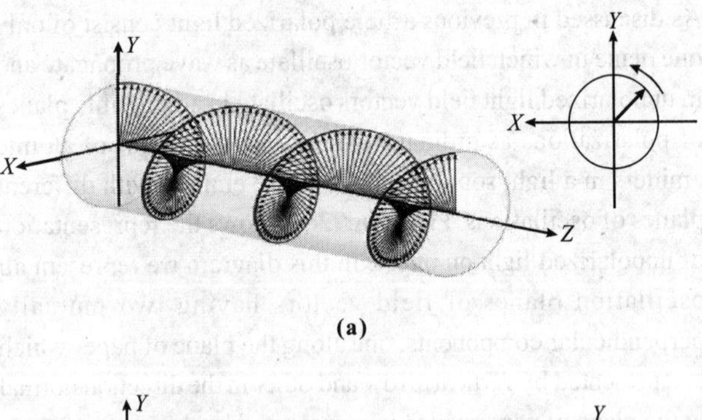

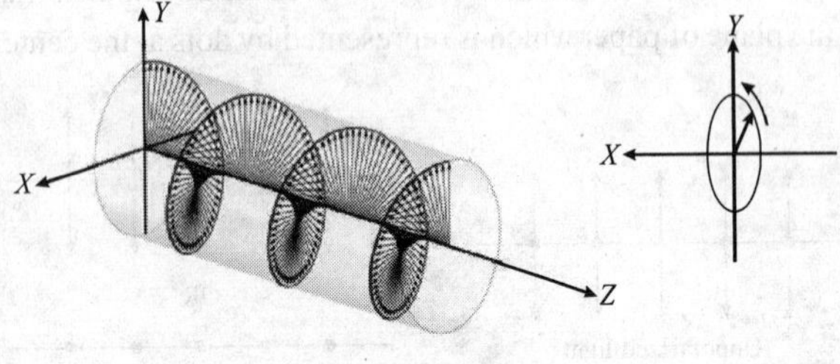

Figure 6.94

6.8 Methods of Polarizing an Ordinary Light

There are various ways by which a linearly polarized light can be obtained from unpolarized light. Some of these methods which we will discuss in detail are given here.

(i) Polarization by Reflection

(ii) Polarization by Refraction

(iii) Polarization by Double Refraction

(iv) Polarization by Dichroism

(v) Polarization by Scattering

6.8.1 Polarization by Reflection

It was observed in several experiments during late nineteenth century that reflected light from a surface gets polarized and polarization of light depends upon the angle of incidence of light and the refractive index of the medium. Figure-6.95 shows an unpolarized light incident on the surface of a glass slab. On analysis of reflected light it was observed to have more of the component of field vector which is parallel to the reflecting surface and the reflected light gets partially polarized as shown in the figure. It was also observed and analyzed that on changing the angle of incidence the extent of polarization in the reflected light changes.

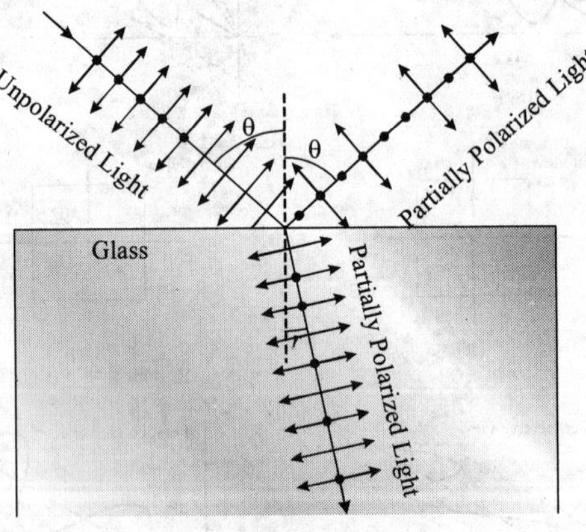

Figure 6.95

On changing the incidence angle in above case it is observed that at a specific angle of incidence θ_P the reflection of other component of field vector which is not parallel to reflecting surface goes completely off and reflected beam is totally linearly polarized as shown in figure-6.96. This angle θ_P is called the polarizing angle.

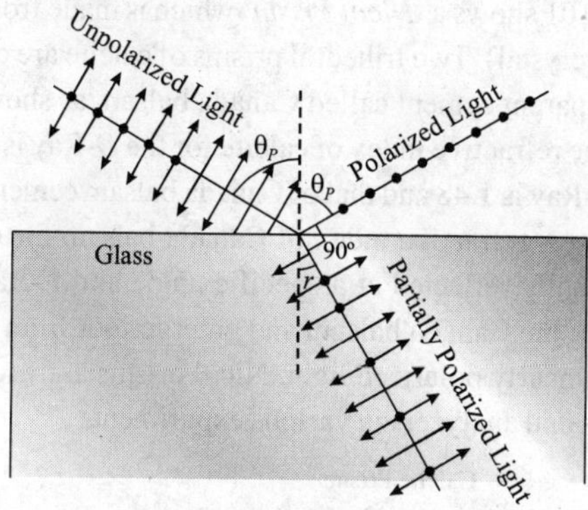

Figure 6.96

This method of polarization by reflection is not popularly used as the portion of light reflected is very small and most of light is transmitted into the medium.

6.8.2 Brewster's Law

Based on several experiments on polarization of light by reflection, Sir David Brewster found that the polarizing angle depends upon the refractive index of the medium. These series of experiments revealed that the reflected light gets completely polarized when the reflected and refracted light rays from the point of incidence are mutually perpendicular as shown in figure-6.96. By Snell's law we can relate these angles as

$$\sin \theta_P = \mu \sin r \quad \ldots(6.109)$$

If the reflected and refracted light rays are mutually perpendicular then we can use $\theta_P + r = 90°$. Thus from above equation-(i) we get

$$\sin \theta_P = \mu \sin (90° - \theta_P)$$

$$\Rightarrow \quad \sin \theta_P = \mu \cos \theta_P$$

$$\Rightarrow \quad \mu = \tan \theta_P \quad \ldots(6.110)$$

With above relation we can state "*The tangent of the angle at which polarization is obtained by reflection is numerically equal to the refractive index of the medium*" and this is called '*Brewster's Law*'. After this the polarizing angle θ_P is also known as '*Brewster Angle*'. Light reflected from any angle other than Brewster angle is partially polarized and light reflected at Brewster angle is polarized in direction normal to the plane of incidence.

6.8.3 Polarization by Refraction

As studied in the previous article-6.8.2 when unpolarized light is reflected at Brewster angle gets linearly polarized with field vector oscillations normal to the plane of incidence and refracted light partially polarized with more oscillations in the plane of incidence and less in the plane normal to that of incidence plane. If an unpolarized light is passed through a stack of glass plates as shown in figure-6.97 placed at Brewster angle then at each plate the reflected light will be containing the field vector components normal to the plane of incidence and due to these successive reflections the field vector components normal to plane of incidence get filtered and ultimately the transmitted ray consists of the oscillation in the plane of incidence.

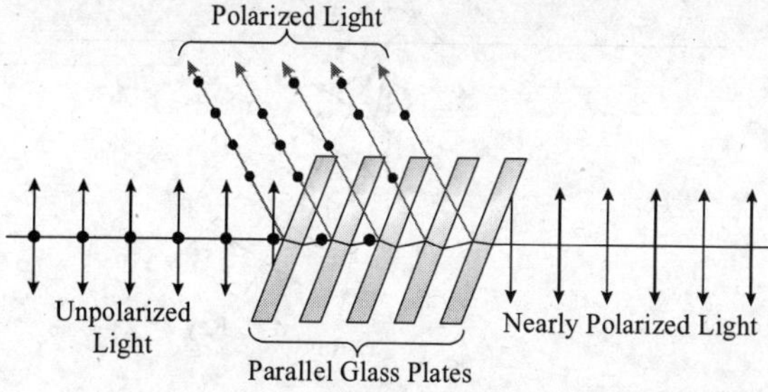

Figure 6.97

With the above method the polarized light obtained in transmitted light beam after several refractions, the degree of polarization increases as we increase the number of glass plates. However this method of obtaining polarized light is also not very effective as a large portion of the light is lost in so many reflections.

6.8.4 Polarization by Double Refraction

There are some specific crystals like Calcite, Quartz, Tourmaline etc. on which when natural light is incident then after refraction the light splits into two refracted rays which have different properties. This phenomenon of splitting of refracted rays by a crystal is called '*Birefringence*' or '*Double Refraction*' and such crystals are called '*Birefringent*'.

The two rays produced in double refraction are observed to be linearly polarized having field components oscillating in perpendicular directions. Out of the two rays one ray is observed to follow the laws of refraction and this is called 'O-Ray' or '*Ordinary Ray*' and the other ray does not follow the laws of refraction and it is called 'E-Ray' or '*Extraordinary Ray*'. The ordinary ray obeys the Snell's law and gets refracted into the crystal medium at an angle given by the refractive index of the medium but the extraordinary ray refracts into the medium for which we cannot define a specific refractive index according to Snell's law.

There are two types of Birefringent crystals which behave differently for the E-Ray and O-Ray when a light gets refracted into these. Figure-6.98 shows a case when a light splits into the two rays with E-Ray has a lesser value of refractive index then O-ray thats why O-Ray is closer to the normal to the boundary. Such crystals are called '*Negative Birefringent Crystals*' and figure-6.99 shows a case when after refraction E-Ray is closer to the normal to boundary and having higher refractive index of medium than O-Ray, such crystals are called '*Positive Birefringent Crystals*'.

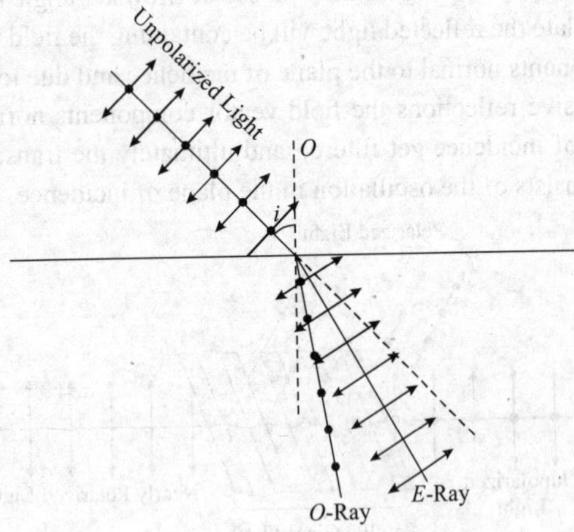

Figure 6.98

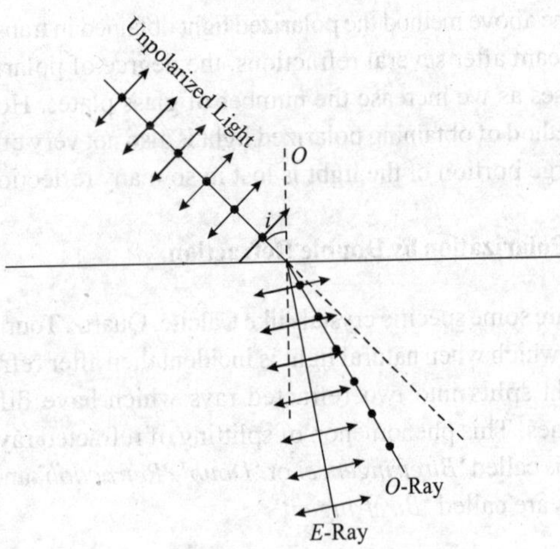

Figure 6.99

Figure-6.100 shows a calcite crystal which is a negative crystal. If an observer sees a source of light through this crystal as shown in figure then he will see two images of the object, one due to the *E*-Ray and other due to *O*-Ray. If we rotate the crystal about an axis along the direction of light propagation then as shown in figure the observer will see that the image produced by the *O*-Ray will move in a circle around the image produced by the *E*-Ray. If the crystal is replaced by a positive crystal like quartz then image produced by *E*-Ray will rotate around the image produced by *O*-Ray on rotating the crystal.

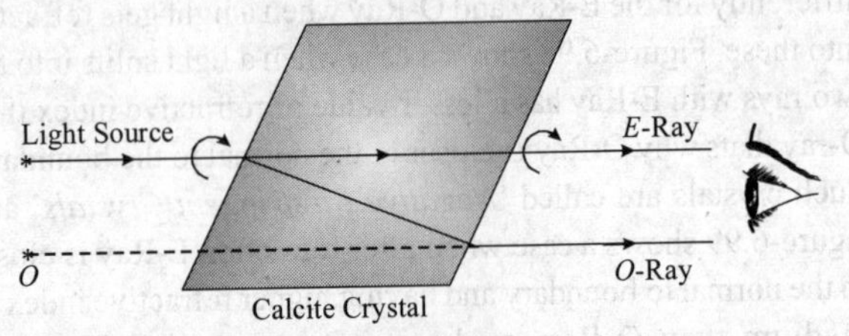

Figure 6.100

Figure-6.101 shows a '*Nicol Prism*' which is made from calcite (negative crystal). Two trihedral prisms of calcite are cemented by a transparent cement called Canada balsam as shown in the figure. The refractive index of calcite for the *O*-Ray is 1.66 and that for *E*-Ray is 1.48 and that of Canada balsam cement is 1.55. Due to lower refractive index of Canada balsam for *O*-Ray, it gets internally reflected at a specific angle and *E*-Ray passes on through the Canada balsam and emerges out from the nicol prism as linearly polarized light. Nicol prisms are widely used polarizers and analyzers in various experiments.

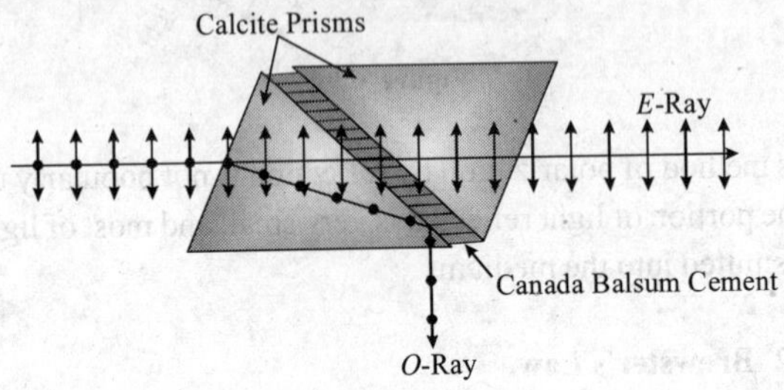

Figure 6.101

6.8.5 Polarization by Dichroism

In early Nineteenth century it was discovered that some mineral crystals absorb oscillations of field vector of light in a specific direction as light penetrates through such crystals and allow the field vector in direction normal to the absorbed components. In such crystals after some distance of penetration one direction component of field vector is completely absorbed and the light will contain only the perpendicular component and will get linearly polarized as shown in figure-6.102. This property of crystals of absorbing field vector oscillations only in one direction is called '*Selective Absorption*' or '*Dichroism*' and such crystals are called '*Dichroic Crystals*'. Commonly used polaroid glasses are made of such dichroic crystals.

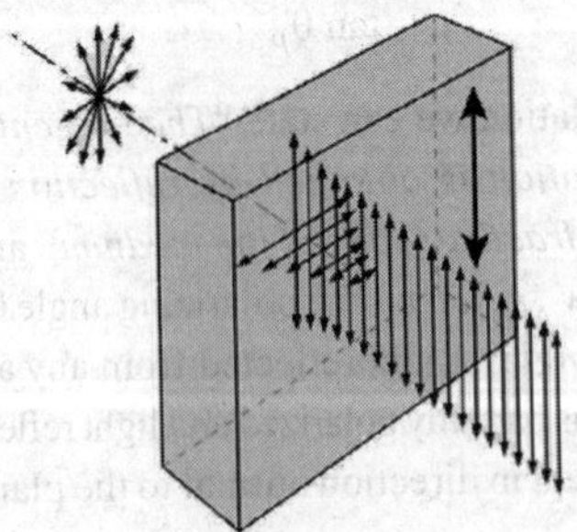

Figure 6.102

6.8.6 Polarization by Scattering

When unpolarized light incident on a medium containing microscopic suspended particles then the incident light on these particles is scattered in different direction which is partially polarized. The degree of polarization in scattered light depends upon the angle of scattering. It is observed that the beam of light scattered at 90° with respect to the incident direction is linearly polarized and the light in the direction of incident direction and other directions is partially polarized as shown in figure-6.103. In three dimensional space the actual directions in which the linearly polarized lights will scatter will depend upon the orientation of the suspension particles in space.

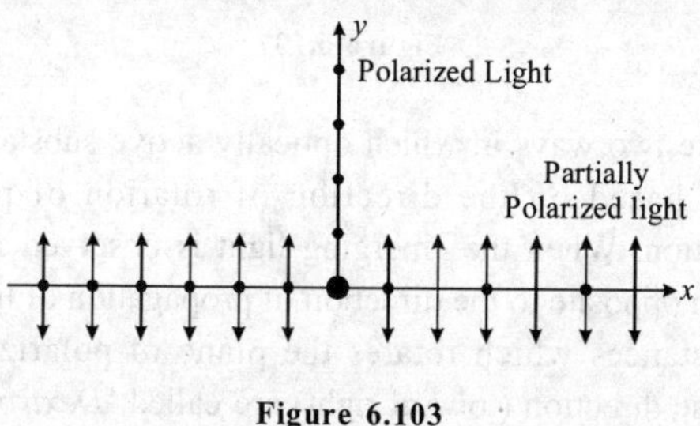

Figure 6.103

6.8.7 Malus' Law

When an unpolarized light incident on a polarizer, the light transmitted through the polarizer is linearly polarized and if this polarized light again incident on an analyzer (another polarizer) the transmitted intensity varies with the angle between the transmission axes of the polarizer and analyzer.

Figure-6.104 shows that the angle between the transmission axis of polarizer and analyzer is θ and when the polarized light incident on the analyzer, only that component of the electric field vector passes through the analyzer which is along the transmission axis of analyzer. If A is the amplitude of the field vector then in figure we can see that $A\cos\theta$ is the component along the transmission axis of analyzer which passes through it and other perpendicular component $A\sin\theta$ is blocked by it.

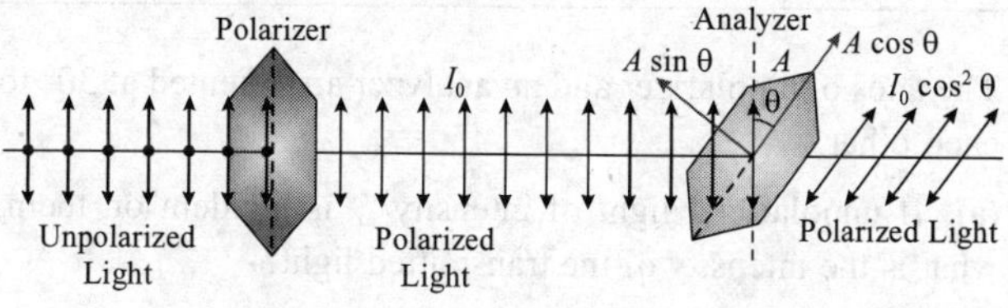

Figure 6.104

If I_0 is the intensity of polarized light after first polarizer then we can use

$$I_0 = kA^2$$

then the intensity of the light after analyzer can be given as

$$I_P = k(A\cos\theta)^2$$

$$\Rightarrow \quad I_P = I_0\cos^2\theta \quad \ldots(6.111)$$

From the above equation-(6.111) we can state "*When a polarized light is passed through an analyzer then the intensity of light transmitted through it is proportional to the square of the cosine of angle between the plane of transmission of the analyzer and the plane of transmission of the polarizer*", this is called Malus' law. So if an analyzer is kept after a polarizer with its transmission axis perpendicular to the transmission axis of polarizer then no light will pass through it as shown in figure-6.105(a) and if both the polarizer and analyzer are kept with their transmission axis parallel then full intensity of polarized light will pass through the analyzer as shown in figure-6.105(b).

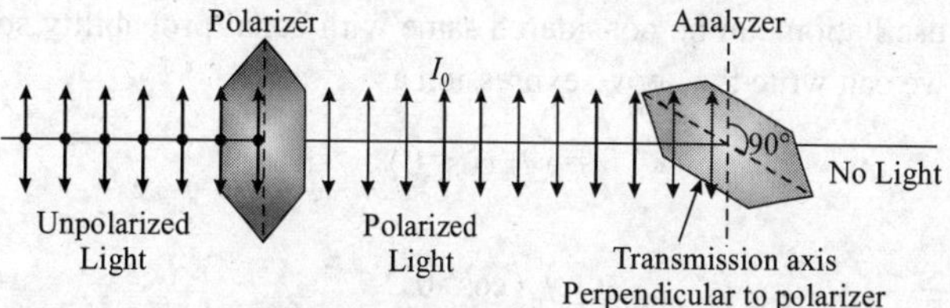

(a)

(b)

Figure 6.105

6.8.8 Intensity of Polarized light through a Polaroid (Polarizer)

As already discussed, an unpolarized light has field vector oscillations in all directions perpendicular to the direction of propagation of light as shown in a cross sectional plane in figure-6.106. When this unpolarized light is passed through a polaroid then components of all oscillating field vectors in the direction along the transmission axis of polaroid will pass through it and components perpendicular to transmission axis are blocked.

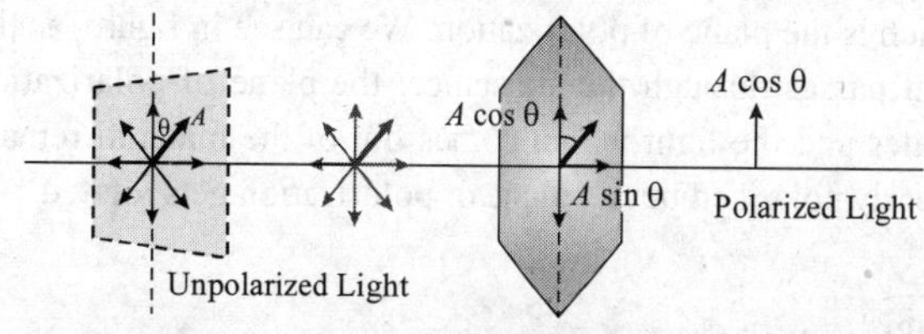

Figure 6.106

If we consider an oscillation amplitude A shown by a bold arrow in above figure which is at an angle θ to the transmission axis of the polaroid then its component $A\cos\theta$ will pass and its component $A\sin\theta$ will be blocked. The resulting amplitude of the polarized light after transmission through the polaroid will be sum of all $A\cos\theta$ for all the oscillations of the field vector in unpolarized light with value of θ varying from 0 to 2π. If intensity of unpolarized light is I_0 then the intensity of the transmitted light can be given as

$$I_T = k\left(\sum_{\theta=0}^{\theta=2\pi} A\cos\theta\right)^2$$

As at all angles θ in unpolarized light, the amplitude of oscillation can be considered same with equal probability so we can write the above expression as

$$I_T = \left\langle I_0 \cos^2\theta \right\rangle_{average\ from\ \theta=0\ to\ 2\pi}$$

$$\Rightarrow \qquad I_T = I_0 \left\langle \cos^2\theta \right\rangle_{average\ from\ \theta=0\ to\ 2\pi}$$

As average value of square of cosine of an angle varying from 0 to 2π is given as $\left\langle \cos^2\theta \right\rangle = \frac{1}{2}$

$$\Rightarrow \qquad I_T = I_0\left(\frac{1}{2}\right) = \frac{I_0}{2} \qquad \ldots(6.112)$$

With the result obtained in above equation-(6.112) we can state *"The intensity of unpolarized light after passing through a polarizer reduces to half in polarized light"*.

6.8.9 Optical Activity of Substances

Some specific transparent substances have property to rotate the plane of polarization of a polarized light when the light is passed through it, such substances are called '*Optically Active*' substances and this ability of substances to rotate the plane of polarization of light is called '*Optical Activity*'. Quartz and Cinnabar are common examples of optically active crystals and substances which are optically active in both solid and liquid state are Sugar and Camphor. Figure-6.107 shows an optically active substance on which a polarized light is incident with the field vector oscillations in a plane which is in the plane of paper which is the plane of polarization. We can see in figure, as the light passes through the substance, the plane of polarization rotates and the light which comes out of the material remain linearly polarized but its plane of polarization gets rotated.

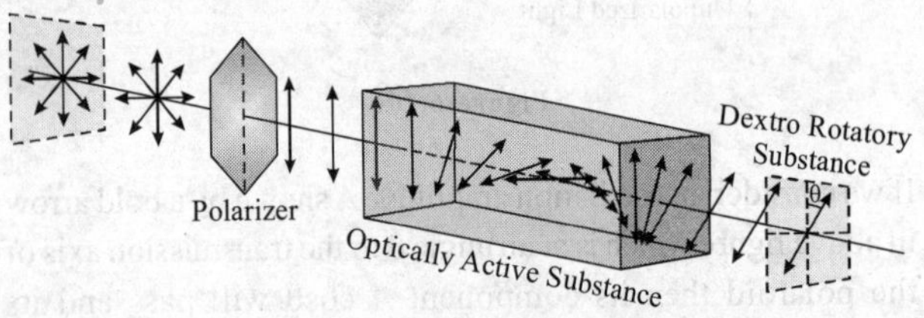

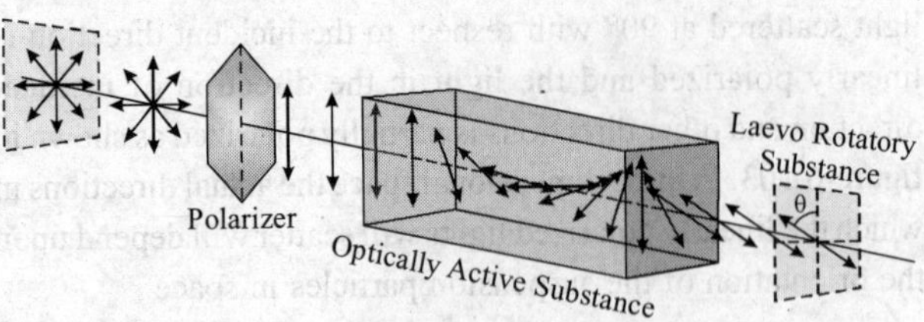

Figure 6.107

There are two ways in which optically active substances are divided based on the direction of rotation of plane of polarization. When the emerging light is observed from the direction opposite to the direction of propagation of light then the substances which rotates the plane of polarization in clockwise direction (toward right) are called '*Dextrorotatory Substances*' and those which rotate the plane of polarization of light in anticlockwise direction (toward left) are called '*Levorotatory Substances*'.

The optical activity of a substance is analytically measured in terms of '*Specific Rotation*' of a substance which is defined for a given wavelength of light as the rotation produced by one decimeter long column of the solution containing unit concentration (1 gm/cm^3) of the substance. If a polarized light passes through a solution of optically active substance having concentration C (in gm/cm^3) and of length l (in decimeter) and the angle by which plane of polarization of light gets rotated by θ then specific rotation of the substance is given as

$$S_\lambda^t = \frac{\theta}{lC}$$

Illustrative Example 6.31

The axes of a polarizer and an analyzer are oriented at 30° to each other.

(a) If unpolarized light of intensity I_0 is incident on them, what is the intensity of the transmitted light?

(b) Polarized light of intensity I_0 is incident on this polarizer-analyzer system. If the amplitude of the light makes an angle of 30° with the axis of the polarizer, what is the intensity of the transmitted light ?

Solution

(a) Half the light passes through the polarizer, so the intensity of the polarized light incident on the analyser is $I = \frac{1}{2} I_0$, and the intensity I' of the light passing through the analyzer is $I' = I\cos^2\theta = \frac{1}{2} I_0 \cos^2 30° = 0.375\, I_0$.

(b) After passing through the polarizer the intensity is $I = I_0 \cos^2\theta = I_0 \cos^2 30° = 0.75\, I_0$. This light is now polarized at 30° to the axis of the analyzer, so the intensity of the light passing through the analyzer is

$$I' = I\cos^2\theta = 0.75\, I_0 \cos^2 30° = 0.563 I_0$$

Illustrative Example 6.32

A beam of plane polarised light falls normally on a polariser (cross-sectional area 3×10^{-4} m^2) which rotates about the axis of the ray with an angular velocity of 31.4 rad/s. Find the energy of light passing through the polariser per revolution and the intensity of the emergent beam if flux of energy of the incident ray is 10^{-3} *W*.

Solution

If I_0 is the intensity of plane polarised light incident on the polariser, then intensity of emerging light is given by

$$I = I_0 \cos^2\theta$$

The average value of I over one revolution can be calculated as :

$$I_{av} = \frac{1}{2\pi}\int_0^{2\pi} I d\theta$$

$$\Rightarrow \quad I_{av} = \frac{1}{2\pi}\int_0^{2\pi} I_0 \cos^2\theta d\theta$$

$$\Rightarrow \quad I_{av} = \frac{I_0}{2}$$

Intensity is given by

$$I_0 = \frac{\text{Power}}{\text{area}}$$

$$\Rightarrow \quad I_0 = \frac{10^{-3}}{3\times10^{-4}} = \frac{10}{3}\ \text{W/m}^2$$

$$\text{and} \quad I_{av} = \frac{I_0}{2} = \frac{5}{3}\ \text{W/m}^2$$

The energy of light passing through the polariser per revolution

$$E = I_{av} \times A \times T = I_{av} \times A \times \frac{2\pi}{\omega}$$

$$= \frac{5}{3} \times (3\times10^{-4}) \times \frac{2\pi}{31.4}$$

$$= 10^{-4}\ \text{J}$$

Illustrative Example 6.33

The axes of a polarizer and an analyzer are oriented at right angles to each other. A third Polaroid sheet is placed between them with its axis at 45° to the axes of the polarizer and analyzer.

(a) If unpolarized light of intensity I_0 is incident on this system, what is the intensity of the transmitted light ?

(b) What is the intensity of the transmitted light when the middle Polaroid sheet is removed ?

Solution

(a) The light that passes through the polarizer has an intensity of $\frac{1}{2}I_0$ and is polarized at 45° to the middle sheet. Thus the light that passes through the middle sheet has the intensity $I = \frac{1}{2}I_0 \cos^2 45° = 0.25 I_0$ and is polarized 45° to the axis of the analyzer. Thus the intensity of the light passing through the analyzer is $I' = I\cos^2 45° = 0.125 I_0$.

(b) If the middle Polaroid sheet is removed, we have a crossed polarizer-analyzer and no light gets through.

> Web Reference at www.physicsgalaxy.com
>
> **Age Group** - High School Physics | Age 17-19 Years
>
> **Section** - OPTICS
>
> **Topic** - Polarization of Light
>
> **Module Number** - 1 to 13

Practice Exercise-6.4

(i) (a) Ordinary light incident on one Polaroid sheet falls on a second Polaroid whose plane of vibration makes an angle of 30° with that of the first Polaroid. If the Polaroids are assumed to be ideal, what is the fraction of the original light transmitted through both Polaroids?

(b) If the second Polaroid is rotted until the transmitted intensity is 10 percent of the incident intensity, what is the new angle ?

[(a) 3/8; (b) 63.4°]

(ii) Three nicols prisms are placed such that, first and third are mutually perpendicular. Unpolarised light is incident on first nicol's prism, the intensity of light emerges from third nicol's prism is 1/16 the intensity of incident light. Find the angle between first and second nicol's prisms.

[22.5°]

(iii) Polarized light of intensity I_0 is incident on a pair of Polaroid sheets. Let θ_1 and θ_2 be the angles between the incident amplitude and the axes of the first and second sheet, respectively. Show that the intensity of the transmitted light is $I = I_0 \cos^2 \theta_1 \cos^2 (\theta_1 - \theta_2)$.

(iv) A mixture of plane polarised and unpolarised light falls normally on a polarising sheet. On rotating the polarising sheet about the direction of the incident beam, the transmitted intensity varies by a factor 4. Find the ratio of the intensities I_p and I_0 respectively of the polarised and unpolarised components in the incident beam. Next the axis of polarising sheet is fixed at an angle of 45° with the direction when the transmitted intensity is maximum. Then obtain the total intensity of the transmitted beam in terms of I_0.

[$\frac{3}{2}$, $\frac{5I_0}{4}$]

---

* * * * *

Discussion Questions

Q6-1 When sun rays pass through a small hole in the foliage at the top of a high tree, they produce an elliptical spot of light on the ground. Explain why. When will the spot be a circle?

Q6-2 If a mirror reverses right and left, why doesn't it reverse up and down?

Q6-3 Is it possible to photograph a virtual image?

Q6-4 Is is possible for a given lens to act as a converging lens in one medium, and as a diverging lens in another?

Q6-5 A camera lens is marked $f/1.8$. What is the meaning of this mark?

Q6-6 If these are scratches on the lens of a camera, they do not appear on a photograph taken with the camera. Explain. Do the scratches affect the photograph at all ?

Q6-7 The sun seems to rise before it actually rises and it seems to set long after it actually sets. Explain why.

Q6-8 Does the focal length of a lens depend on the medium in which the lens is immersed? Is it possible for a lens to act as a conversing lens in one medium and a diverging lens in another medium?

Q6-9 Explain why the use of goggles enables an underwater swimmer to see clearly under the surface of a lake.

Q6-10 Some motor cars have additional yellow headlights. Why?

Q6-12 Why does a column of smoke rising above the roof of houses seem blue against the dark background of the surrounding objects, and yellow or even reddish against the background of a bright sky?

Q6-13 What are primary colours ? Why are they so called ?

Q6-14 A beam of white light passing through a hollow prism gives no spectrum. Is this true of false ?

Q6-15 Ordinary paper becomes transparent when it is oiled. Explain why.

Q6-16 Whey does the moon, purely white during the day, have a yellowish hue after sunset ?

Q6-17 What is the best position of the eye for viewing an object through a microscope?

Q6-18 What is the function of the circular stop at the focal plane of the objective of a telescope?

Q6-19 Why is the objective of a telescope of large focal length and large aperture ?

Q6-20 Can the optical length between two points even be less than the geometrical path between these points ?

* * * * *

Conceptual MCQs Single Option Correct

6-1 A parallel monochromatic beam of light is incident normally on a narrow slit. A diffraction pattern is formed on a screen placed perpendicular to the direction of incident beam. At the first minima of the diffraction pattern, the phase difference between the rays coming from the edges of the slit is :

(A) 0 (B) $\frac{\pi}{2}$

(C) π (D) 2π

6-2 In Fraunhofer diffraction experiment, L is the distance between screen and the obstacle, b is the size of obstacle and λ is wavelength of incident light. The general condition for the applicability of Fraunhofer diffraction is :

(A) $\frac{b^2}{L\lambda} >> 1$ (B) $\frac{b^2}{L\lambda} = 1$

(C) $\frac{b^2}{L\lambda} << 1$ (D) $\frac{b^2}{L\lambda} \neq 1$

6-3 In a Fraunhofer diffraction experiment at a single slit using a light of wavelength 400 nm, the first minimum is formed at an angle of 30°. The direction θ of the first secondary maximum is given by :

(A) $\sin^{-1}\left(\frac{2}{3}\right)$ (B) $\sin^{-1}\left(\frac{3}{4}\right)$

(C) $\sin^{-1}\left(\frac{1}{4}\right)$ (D) $\sin^{-1}\left(\frac{2}{3}\right)$

6-4 If we observe the single slit Fraunhofer diffraction with wavelength λ and slit width b, the width of the central maxima is 2θ. On decreasing the slit width for the same λ :

(A) θ increases
(B) θ remains unchanged
(C) θ decreases
(D) θ increases or decreases depending on the intensity of light

6-5 In diffraction from a single slit, the angular width of the central maxima does not depend on :

(A) λ of light used
(B) Width of slit
(C) Distance of slits from screen
(D) Ratio of λ and slit width

6-6 The critical angle of a certain medium is $\sin^{-1}\left(\frac{3}{5}\right)$. The polarizing angle of the medium is :

(A) $\tan^{-1}\left(\frac{4}{3}\right)$ (B) $\tan^{-1}\left(\frac{3}{4}\right)$

(C) $\tan^{-1}\left(\frac{5}{3}\right)$ (D) $\tan^{-1}\left(\frac{4}{5}\right)$

6-7 Which of the following cannot be polarized ?

(A) Ultraviolet rays (B) Ultrasonic waves
(C) X-rays (D) Radiowaves

6-8 An unpolarised beam of intensity I_0 falls on a polaroid. The intensity of the emergent light is :

(A) $\frac{I_0}{2}$ (B) I_0

(C) $\frac{I_0}{4}$ (D) Zero

6-9 Which of the following is a dichroic crystal ?

(A) Quartz (B) Tourmaline
(C) Mica (D) Selenite

6-10 An unpolarised beam of intensity I_0 is incident on a pair of Nicol's prisms making an angle of 60° with each other. The intensity of light emerging from the pair is :

(A) I_0 (B) $I_0/2$
(C) $I_0/4$ (D) $I_0/8$

6-11 When an unpolarized light of intensity I_0 is incident on a polarizing sheet, the intensity of the light which does not get transmitted is :

(A) $\frac{1}{2}I_0$ (B) $\frac{1}{4}I_0$

(C) Zero (D) I_0

6-12 An optically active compound :

(A) Rotates the plane polarised light
(B) Changing the direction of polarised light
(C) Do not allow plane polarised light to pass through
(D) None of the above

6-13 A 20 cm length of a certain solution causes right handed rotation of 38°. A 30 cm length of another solution causes left handed rotation of 24°. The optical rotation caused by 30 cm length of a mixture of the above solutions in the volume ratio 1 : 2 is :

(A) Left handed rotation of 14°
(B) Right handed rotation of 14°
(C) Left handed rotation of 3°
(D) Right handed rotation of 3°

6-14 Specific rotation of sugar solution is 0.5 deg m^2/kg. 200 kgm^{-3} of impure sugar solution is taken in a simple polarimeter tube of length 20 cm and optical rotation is found to be 19°. The percentage of purity of sugar is :
(A) 20% (B) 80%
(C) 95% (D) 89%

6-15 Two polaroids are placed in the path of unpolarized beam of intensity I_0 such that no light is emitted from the second polaroid. If a third polaroid whose polarization axis makes an angle θ with the polarization axis of first polaroid, is placed between these polaroids, then the intensity of light emerging from the last polaroid will be :

(A) $\left(\frac{I_0}{8}\right)\sin^2 2\theta$ (B) $\left(\frac{I_0}{4}\right)\sin^2 2\theta$

(C) $\left(\frac{I_0}{2}\right)\cos^4\theta$ (D) $I_0\cos^4\theta$

6-16 Two light waves arrives at a certain point on a screen. The waves have the same wavelength. At the arrival point, their amplitudes and phase differences are :
(I) $2a_0$, $6a_0$ and π rad (II) $3a_0$, $5a_0$ and π and
(III) $9a_0$, $7a_0$, and 3π rad (IV) $2a_0$, $2a_0$ and 0.
The pair/s which has greatest intensity is/are:
(A) I (B) II
(C) II, III (D) I, IV

6-17 Two beams of light having intensities I and $4I$ interfere to produce a fringe pattern on the screen. Phase difference between the beams is $\frac{\pi}{2}$ at point A and π at point B. The difference in intensities of resulting light at points A and B is :
(A) $3I$ (B) $4I$
(C) $5I$ (D) $6I$

6-18 A plane electromagnetic wave of frequency w_0 falls normally on the surface of a mirror approaching with a relativistic velocity v. Then frequency of the reflected wave will be :

$\left(\text{given } \beta = \frac{v}{c}\right)$

(A) $\left(\frac{1-\beta}{1+\beta}\right)w_0$ (B) $\frac{1+\beta}{(1-\beta)w_0}$

(C) $\frac{(1+\beta)w_0}{(1-\beta)}$ (D) $\frac{(1-\beta)}{(1+\beta)w_0}$

6-19 White light is used to illuminate two slits in Young's double slit experiment. Separation between the slits is b and the screen is at a distance d (>> b) from the slits. Then wavelengths missing at a point on the screen directly in front of one of the slit are :

(A) $\frac{b^2}{d}, \frac{b^2}{bd}$ (B) $\frac{b^2}{d}, \frac{b^2}{4d}$

(C) $\frac{b^2}{2d}, \frac{b^2}{3d}$ (D) $\frac{b^2}{2d}, \frac{b^2}{4d}$

6-20 Ratio of intensities between a point A and that of central fringe is 0.853. If we consider slits are of equal width then path difference between two waves at point A will be :

(A) $\frac{\lambda}{2}$ (B) $\frac{\lambda}{4}$

(C) $\frac{\lambda}{8}$ (D) λ

6-21 Two waves of same intensity produce interference. If intensity at maximum is $4I$, then intensity at the minimum will be:
(A) 0 (B) $2I$
(C) $3I$ (D) $4I$

6-22 Intensity of central bright fringe due to interference of two identical coherent monochromatic sources is I. If one of the source is switched off, then intensity of central bright fringe becomes :

(A) $\frac{I}{2}$ (B) $\frac{I}{3}$

(C) $\frac{I}{4}$ (D) I

6-23 In an experiment to demonstrate interference of flight using Young's slits, separation of two slits is doubled. In order to maintain same spacing of fringes, distance D of screen from slits must be changed to :

(A) D (B) $\frac{D}{2}$

(C) $2D$ (D) $\frac{3D}{4}$

6-24 In Young's double slit experiment, 12 fringes are obtained to be formed in a certain segment of the screen when light of wavelength 6000Å is used. If wavelength of light is changed to 4000Å, number of fringes observed in the same segment of the screen is given by :
(A) 18 (B) 24
(C) 30 (D) 36

6-25 In Young's double slit experiment, interference pattern is found to have an intensity ratio between bright and dark fringes as 9. Then amplitude ratio will be :
(A) 1 (B) 2
(C) 9 (D) 3

6-26 If A is the amplitude of the waves coming from a point source at distance r then which of the following is correct :

(A) $A \propto r^{-2}$ (B) $A \propto r^{-1}$
(C) $A \propto r^{2}$ (D) $A \propto r^{1}$

6-27 If A is the amplitude of the wave coming from a line source at a distance r, then :

(A) $A \propto r$ (B) $A \propto r^{-1/2}$
(C) $A \propto r^{-2}$ (D) $A \propto r^{1/2}$

6-28 Phase difference between two coherent light waves having same amplitude A is $2\pi/3$. If these waves superpose each other at a point, then resultant amplitude at the point of superposition will be :

(A) $2A$ (B) 0
(C) A (D) A^2

6-29 Ratio of amplitudes of the waves coming from two slits having widths in the ratio 4 : 1 will be

(A) 1 : 2 (B) 2 : 1
(C) 1 : 4 (D) 4 : 1

6-30 Two slits S_1 and S_2 illuminated by a white light source give a white central maxima. A transparent sheet of refractive index 1.25 and thickness t_1 is placed in front of S_1. Another transparent sheet of refractive index 1.50 and thickness t_2 is placed in front of S_2. If central maxima is not effected, then ratio of the thickness of the two sheets will be :

(A) 1 : 2 (B) 2 : 1
(C) 1 : 4 (D) 4 : 1

6-31 If a thin film of thickness t and refractive index μ is placed in the path of light coming from a source S, then increase in length of optical path is :

(A) μt (B) μ/t
(C) $(\mu - 1)\,t$ (D) None of these

6-32 In the adjacent diagram, CP represents a wavefront and AO and BP, the corresponding two rays. Find the condition on θ for constructive interference at P between the ray BP and reflected ray OP :

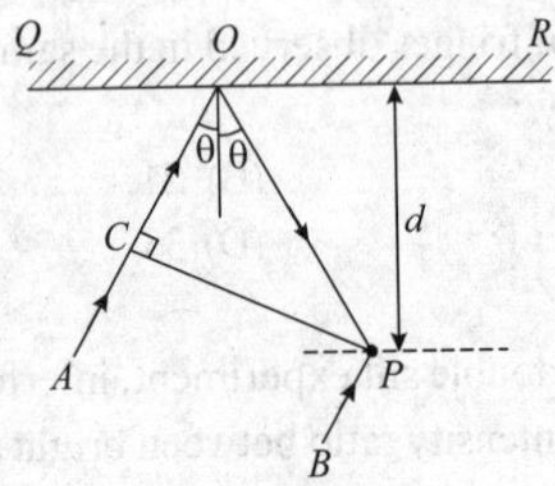

Figure 6.108

(A) $\cos\theta = \dfrac{2\lambda}{2d}$ (B) $\cos\theta = \dfrac{\lambda}{4d}$

(C) $\sec\theta - \cos\theta = \dfrac{\lambda}{d}$ (D) $\sec\theta - \cos\theta = \dfrac{4\lambda}{d}$

6-33 In a young double slit experiment, D equals the distance of screen and d is the separation between the slit. The distance of the nearest point to the central maximum where the intensity is same as that due to a single slit, is equal to :

(A) $\dfrac{D\lambda}{d}$ (B) $\dfrac{D\lambda}{2d}$

(C) $\dfrac{D\lambda}{3d}$ (D) $\dfrac{2D\lambda}{d}$

6-34 In the given figure-6.109, if a parallel beam of white light is incident on the plane of the slits then the distance of the white spot on the screen from O is [Assume $d << D$, $\lambda << d$] :

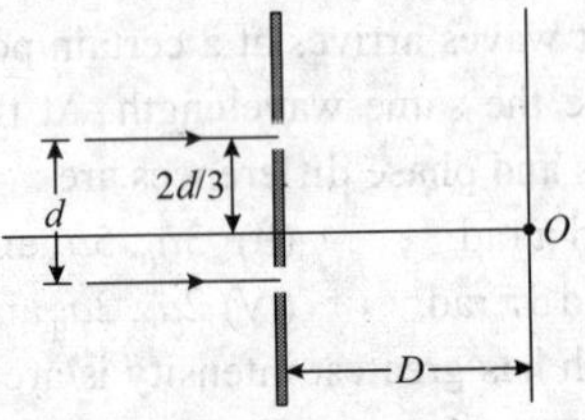

Figure 6.109

(A) 0 (B) $d/2$
(C) $d/3$ (D) $d/6$

6-35 In YDSE (as shown in the figure-6.110), a parallel beam of light is incident on the slit from a medium of refractive index n_1. The wavelength of light in this medium is λ_1. A transparent slab of thickness 't' and refractive index n_3 is put infront of one slit. The medium between the screen and the plane of the slits in n_2. The phase difference between the light waves reaching point 'O' (symmetrical, relative to the slits) is :

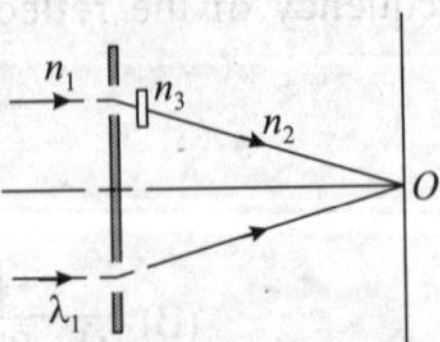

Figure 6.110

(A) $\dfrac{2\pi}{n_1\lambda_1}(n_3 - n_2)t$ (B) $\dfrac{2\pi}{\lambda_1}(n_3 - n_2)t$

(C) $\dfrac{2\pi n_1}{n_2\lambda_1}\left(\dfrac{n_3}{n_2} - 1\right)t$ (D) $\dfrac{2\pi n_1}{\lambda_1}(n_3 - n_1)t$

* * * * *

Numerical MCQs Single Option Correct

6-1 In a Young's double slit experiment, angular width of a fringe formed on a distant screen is 0.1°. If wavelength of light used is 6000 Å, then distance between the slits will be :
(A) 0.241 mm (B) 0.344 mm
(C) 0.519 mm (D) 0.413 mm

6-2 In a Young's double slit experiment two narrow slit 0.8 mm apart are illuminated by the same source of yellow light of wavelength 5893 Å. If distance between slits and screen is 2 m then separation between adjacent bright lines will be :
(A) 14.73 mm (B) 14.73 cm
(C) 1.473 mm (D) 147.3 mm

6-3 Two stars are situated at a distance of 8 light year from the earth. These are to be just resolved by a telescope of diameter 0.25 m. If the wavelength of light used is 5000 Å, then the distance between the stars must be :
(A) 3×10^{10} m (B) 3.35×10^{11} m
(C) 1.95×10^{11} m (D) 4.32×10^{10} m

6-4 A beam of light of wavelength 6000Å from a distant source falls on a single slit 1 mm wide and the resulting diffraction pattern is observed on a screen 2 m away. The distance between the first dark fringes on either side of the central bright fringe is:
(A) 1.2 cm (B) 1.2 mm
(C) 2.4 cm (D) 2.4 mm

6-5 A single slit of width d is illuminated by violet light of wavelength 4000Å and the width of the central maxima is measured as y. When half of the slit width is covered and illuminated by yellow light of wavelength 6000Å., the width of the central maxima is :
(A) The pattern vanishes
(B) $y/3$
(C) $3y$
(D) None of the above

6-6 A beam of natural light falls on a system of 5 polaroids, which are arranged in succession such that the pass axis of each polaroid is turned through 60° with respect to the preceding one. The fraction of the incident light intensity that passes through the system is :
(A) $\frac{1}{64}$ (B) $\frac{1}{32}$
(C) $\frac{1}{512}$ (D) $\frac{1}{128}$

6-7 When the angle of incidence on a material is 60°, the reflected light is completely polarized. The velocity of the refracted ray inside the material is (in ms^{-1}) :
(A) 3×10^8 (B) $\left[\frac{3}{\sqrt{2}}\right] \times 10^8$
(C) $\sqrt{3} \times 10^8$ (D) 0.5×10^8

6-8 A double slit experiment is done with monochromatic light of wavelength 6000 Å. Slits are 2 mm apart and fringes are observed on a screen placed 10 cm away from the slits. If a transparent plate of thickness 0.5 mm is placed in front of one of the slit, interference pattern shifts by 5 mm. Then refractive index of transparent plate should be :
(A) 1.1 (B) 1.2
(C) 1.3 (D) 1.5

6-9 A ray of light is incident on a medium boundary at polarising angle such that its deviation is 24°, then angle of incidence is :
(A) 24° (B) 57°
(C) 66° (D) 90°

6-10 If the polarizing angle of a piece of glass for green light is 54.74°, then the angle of minimum deviation for an equilateral prism made of same glass is :
[Given : $\tan 54.74^\circ = 1.414$]
(A) 45° (B) 54.74°
(C) 60° (D) 30°

6-11 In Young's double slit experiment the light emitted from source has $\lambda = 6500$Å and the distance between the two slits is 1 mm. Distance between the screen and slit is 1 metre. Distance between third dark and fifth birth fringe will be :
(A) 3.2 mm (B) 1.63 mm
(C) 0.585 mm (D) 2.31 mm

6-12 In Young's double slit experiment, if the widths of the slit are in the ratio 4 : 9, ratio of intensity of maxima to intensity of minima will be :
(A) 25 : 1 (B) 9 : 4
(C) 3 : 2 (D) 81 : 16

6-13 A light source approaches the observer with velocity 0.5 cm. Doppler shift for light of wavelength 550 Å is :
(A) 616 Å (B) 1833 Å
(C) 5500 Å (D) 6160 Å

6-14 A plane monochromatic light falls normally on a diaphragm with two narrow slits separated by a distance $d = 2.5$ mm. A fringe pattern is formed on the screen placed at $D = 100$ cm behind the diaphragm. If one of the slits is covered by a glass plate of thickness 10 μm, then distance by which these fringes will be shifted will be :

(A) 2mm (B) 3mm

(C) 4mm (D) 5mm

6-15 In a single slit diffraction pattern the angular width of a central maxima is 30° when the slit is illuminated by light of wavelength 6000 Å. Then width of the slit will be approximately given as :

(A) 12×10^{-6} m (B) 12×10^{-7} m

(C) 12×10^{-8} m (D) 12×10^{-9} m

6-16 Light of wavelength 6000Å is incident on a single slit. First minimum is obtained at a distance of 0.4 cm from the centre. If width of the slit is 0.3 mm, then distance between slit and screen will be :

(A) 1.0 m (B) 1.5 m

(C) 2.0 m (D) 2.3 m

6-17 If velocity of a galaxy relative to earth is 1.2×10^6 ms^{-2} then percentage increase in wavelength of light from galaxy as compared to the similar source on earth will be :

(A) 0.3% (B) 0.4%

(C) 0.5% (D) 0.6%

6-18 Light of wavelength 5000 Å is incident normally on a slit. First minimum of diffraction pattern is formed at a distance of 5 mm from the central maximum. If slit width is 0.2 mm, then distance between slit and screen will be :

(A) 1 m (B) 1.5 m

(C) 2.0 m (D) 2.5 m

6-19 Doppler shift for the light of wavelength 6000 Å emitted from the sun is 0.04 Å. If radius of the sun is 7×10^8 m then time period of rotation of the sun will be :

(A) 30 days (B) 365 days

(C) 24 hours (D) 25 days

6-20 On introducing a thin mica sheet of thickness 2×10^{-6} m and refractive index 1.5 in the path of one of the waves, central bright maxima shifts by n fringes. Wavelength of the wave used is 5000 Å, then n is :

(A) 1 (B) 2

(C) 5 (D) 10

6-21 A radar operates at wavelength 50.0 cm. If the beat frequency between the transmitted signal and the signal reflected from aircraft ($\Delta\nu$) is 1 kHz, then velocity of the aircraft will be :

(A) 800 km/hr (B) 900 km/hr

(C) 1000 km/hr (D) 1032 km/hr

6-22 A parallel beam of light of wavelength 6000 Å gets diffracted by a single slit of width 0.3 mm. The angular position of the first minima of diffracted light is :

(A) 6×10^{-3} rad (B) 1.8×10^{-3} rad

(C) 3×10^{-3} rad (D) 2×10^{-3} rad

6-23 A spectral line of wavelength 0.59 mm is observed in the directions along the opposite edges of the solar disc along its equator. A difference in wavelength equal $\Delta\lambda = 8$ pm is observed. Period of Sun's revolution around its own axis will be about : (Radius of sun = 6.95×10^8 m)

(A) 30 days (B) 24 hours

(C) 25 days (D) 365 days

6-24 If light with wavelength 0.50 mm falls on a slit of width 10 mm and at an angle $\theta = 30°$ to its normal. Then angular position of first minima located on any sides of the central Fraunhofer's diffraction will be at :

(A) 33.4° (B) 26.8°

(C) 39.8° (D) None of these

6-25 Angular width of central maximum in the Fraunhofer's diffraction pattern is measured. Slit is illuminated by the light of another wavelength, angular width decreases by 30%. Wavelength of light used is :

(A) 3500 Å (B) 4200 Å

(C) 4700 Å (D) 6000 Å

6-26 A parallel beam of white light falls on a thin film whose refractive index is 1.33. If angle of incidence is 52° then thickness of the film for the reflected light to be coloured yellow ($\lambda = 6000$ Å) most intensively must be :

(A) $14(2n+1)$ m (B) $1.4(2n+1)$ m

(C) $0.14(2n+1)$ m (D) $142(2n+1)$ m

6-27 Light of wavelength 6000 Å is normally incident on a slit. Angular position of second minimum from central maximum us 30°. Width of the slit should be :

(A) 12×10^{-5} cm (B) 18×10^{-5} cm

(C) 24×10^{-5} cm (D) 36×10^{-5} cm

6-28 Interference fringes from sodium light of wavelength 5890 Å in a double slit experiment have an angular width 0.20°. To increase the fringe width by 10%, wavelength of light used should be :

(A) 5892 Å (B) 4000 Å

(C) 8000 Å (D) 6479 Å

6-29 In Young's double slit experiment, using monochromatic light, fringe pattern shifts by a certain distance on the screen when a mica sheet of refractive index 1.6 and thickness 1.964 mm is introduced in the path of one of the two waves. If now mica sheet is removed and distance between slit and screen is doubled, distance between successive maximum or minimum remains unchanged. The wavelength of the monochromatic light used in the experiment is :

(A) 4000 Å (B) 5500 Å
(C) 5892 Å (D) 6071 Å

6-30 In a YDSE setup with monochromatic light, fringes are obtained on a screen placed at some distance from the slits. If screen is moved by 5×10^{-2} m towards the slits, then change in fringe width is 3×10^{-5} m. If the distance between slits is 10^{-3} m then wavelength of the light used will be :
(A) 4000 Å (B) 6000 Å
(C) 5890 Å (D) 8000 Å

6-31 Monochromatic light of wavelength 5000 Å is incident on two slits separated by a distance of 5×10^{-4} m. Interference pattern is seen on the screen placed at a distance of 1 m from the slits. A thin glass plate of thickness 1.5×10^{-6} m and refractive index 1.5 is placed between one of the slits and the screen. If intensity in the absence of plate at center of screen was I_0 then new intensity at the centre of the screen will be :
(A) 0 (B) I_0
(C) $\frac{I_0}{2}$ (D) $\frac{3I_0}{4}$

6-32 In Young's double slit experiment, separation between the slits is 2×10^{-3} m and distance of the screen from the slit is 2.5 m. Light in the range of 2000 – 8000 Å is allowed o fall on the slits. Wavelength in the visible region that will be present on the screen at 10^{-3} m from the central maxima will be :
(A) 4000 Å (B) 5000 Å
(C) 6000 Å (D) 8000 Å

6-33 A double slit experiment is immersed in a liquid of refractive index 1.33. Separation between the slits is 1.0 mm and the distance between slit and screen is 1.33 m. If slits are illuminated by a parallel beam of light whose wavelength is 6300 Å, then fringe width will be :
(A) 6.3 mm (B) 63 mm
(C) 0.63 mm (D) None of these

6-34 In a YDSE arrangement, incident yellow light is composed of two wavelength 5890 Å and 5895 Å. Distance between the slits is 1 mm and the screen is placed 1 m away. Order upto which fringes can be seen on the screen will be :
(A) 384 (B) 486
(C) 512 (D) 589

6-35 When light is incident on a soap film of thickness 5×10^{-5} cm, wavelength which is maximum reflected in the visible region is 5320 Å. The refractive index of the film will be :
(A) 1.22 (B) 1.33
(C) 1.51 (D) 1.83

6-36 A ray of unpolarised light is incident on a glass plate of refractive index 1.54 at polarising angle, then angle of refraction is :
(A) 33° (B) 44°
(C) 57° (D) 90°

6-37 First diffraction minima due to a single slit of width 1.0×10^{-5} cm is at 30°. Then wavelength of light used is :
(A) 400 Å (B) 500 Å
(C) 600 Å (D) 700 Å

6-38 Light of wavelength 6328 Å is incident normally on a slit of width 0.2 mm. Angular width of the central maximum on the screen will be :
(A) 0.9° (B) 0.18°
(C) 0.54° (D) 0.36°

6-39 Light of wavelength λ is incident on a slit. First minima of the diffraction pattern is found to lie at a distance of 6 mm from the central maximum on a screen placed at a distance of 2 m from the slit. If slit width is 0.2 mm, then wavelength of the light used will be :
(A) 4000 Å (B) 6000 Å
(C) 7000 Å (D) 7400 Å

6-40 A slit 5 cm wide when irradiated by waves of wavelength 10 mm results in the angular spread of the central maxima on either side of incident light by about :
(A) 1/2 radian (B) 1/4 radian
(C) 3 radian (D) 1/5 radian

6-41 In Young's double slit experiment, ten slits separated by a distance of 1 mm are illuminated by a monochromatic light source of wavelength 5×10^{-7} m. If the distance between slit and screen is 2 metre, then separation of bright lines in the interference pattern will be :
(A) 0.5 mm (B) 1.0 mm
(C) 1.5 mm (D) 1.75 mm

6-42 A star is moving away from earth and shift in spectral line of wavelength 5700 Å is 1.90 Å. Velocity of the star is :
(A) 50 km s^{-1} (B) 70 km s^{-1}
(C) 80 km s^{-1} (D) 100 km s^{-1}

6-43 In two separate set ups of Young's double slit experiment, fringes of equal width are observed when lights of wavelengths in the ratio 1 : 2 are used. If the ratio of slit separation in two cases is 2 : 1, then ratio of distances between the plane of slits and the screen in the two set ups is :
(A) 1 : 2 (B) 2 : 1
(C) 1 : 4 (D) 4 : 1

6-44 In a young's double slit experiment, two slits are illuminated by a mixture of two wavelengths 12000Å and 10000Å. At 6.0 mm from the common central bright fringe on a screen 2 m away from the slits, a bright fringe of one interference pattern coincides with the bright fringe of other. Distance between the slits should be :

(A) 1.0 mm (B) 1.5 mm
(C) 2.0 mm (D) 2.5 mm

6-45 In a young's double slit experiment, slits are illuminated by a monochromatic source of wavelength 6000Å and fringes are obtained. If screen is moved by a distance of 5 cm towards slits, change in fringe width is 3×10^{-5} m. Then separation between the slits will be :

(A) 1 mm (B) 1.2 mm
(C) 1.5 mm (D) 1.63 mm

6-46 An unpolarized beam of light is incident on a group of three polarizing sheets which are arranged in such a way that plane of rotation of one make an angle of 60º with the adjacent one. The percentage of incident light transmitted by first polarizer will be :

(A) 6.25% (B) 12.5%
(C) 50% (D) None of these

6-47 80 gm of impure sugar when dissolved in a litre of water gives an optical rotation of 9.9º when placed in a tube of length 20 cm. If concentration of sugar solution is 75 gm/litre then specific rotation of sugar is :

(A) 44º (B) 55º
(C) 66º (D) 73º

6-48 In a YDSE setup interference fringes are obtained by sodium light of wavelength 5890Å. On screen the fringes have an angular width 0.20º. Now the wavelength of light is changed and it is found that fringe width increases by 10%, the new wavelength of incident light is:

(A) 5896Å (B) 7321Å
(C) 6300Å (D) 6479Å

6-49 In a Young Double Slit Experiment, 12 fringes are observed to be formed in a certain segment of the screen when light of wavelength 600 nm is used. If the wavelength of light is changed to 400 nm, number of fringes observed in the same segment of the screen in given by :

(A) 12 (B) 18
(C) 24 (D) 30

* * * * *

Advance MCQs with One or More Options Correct

6-1 If one of the slits of a standard Young's double slit experiment is covered by a thin parallel sided glass slab so that it transmits only one half the light intensity of the other, then :
(A) The fringe pattern will get shifted towards the covered slit
(B) The fringe pattern will get shifted away from the covered slit
(C) The bright fringes will become less bright and the dark ones will becomes more bright
(D) The fringe width will remain unchanged

6-2 To observe a stationary interference pattern formed by two light waves, which of the following is not a necessary condition :
(A) Same frequency (B) Same amplitude
(C) Constant phase difference (D) Same intensity

6-3 In YDSE setup when white light is used then which of the following statements are correct for the interference pattern obtained.
(A) The fringe next to the central maxima will be Reddish white
(B) Central maxima will be white in colour
(C) The fringe next to the central maxima will be Bluish white
(D) There will be no fringe which is perfectly dark

6-4 In an interference arrangement similar to Young's double-slit experiment, the slits S_1 and S_2 are illuminated with coherent microwave sources, each of frequency 10^6 Hz. The sources are synchronized to have zero phase difference. The slits are separated by a distance $d = 150.0$ m. The intensity $I(\theta)$ is measured as a function of θ, where θ is defined as shown. If I_0 is the maximum intensity, then $I(\theta)$ for $0 \le \theta \le 90°$ is given by :

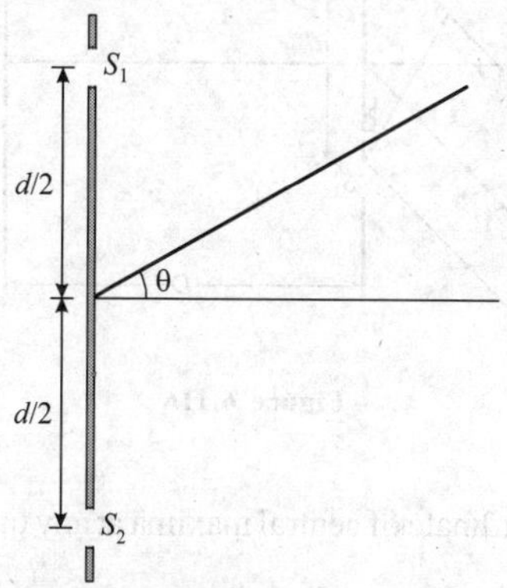

Figure 6.111

(A) $I(\theta) = I_0/2$ for $\theta = 30°$
(B) $I(\theta) = I_0/4$ for $\theta = 90°$
(C) $I(\theta) = I_0$ for $\theta = 0°$
(D) $I(\theta)$ is constant for all values of θ

6-5 In a given YDSE setup if the wavelength of light beam incident on slit plane is decreased then which of the following statements is/are correct :
(A) The intensity of bright fringes will decrease
(B) Fringe pattern will shrink
(C) Total number of bright fringes appearing on screen will increase
(D) Only central fringe intensity will increase

6-6 Figure-6.112 shows plane waves refracted from air to water using Huygen's principle a, b, c, d, e are lengths on the diagram. The refractive index of water w.r.t air is the ratio :

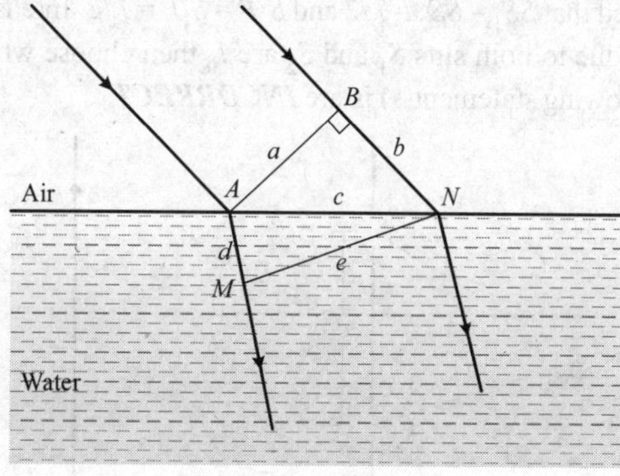

Figure 6.112

(A) a/e (B) b/e
(C) b/d (D) d/b

6-7 Figure shows a thin film on which a monochromatic light falls normally. The thickness of film is equal to the wavelength of light in the medium of film. Which of the following statements is/are correct :
(A) Reflected light will be maximum if $\mu_1 < \mu_2 < \mu_3$
(B) Reflected light will be maximum if $\mu_1 < \mu_2 > \mu_3$
(C) Transmitted light will be maximum if $\mu_1 < \mu_2 < \mu_3$
(D) Transmitted light will be maximum if $\mu_1 < \mu_2 > \mu_3$

6-8 A light wave is travelling along -Y direction. For this light wave, which of the following equations of planes may represent its wavefront.
(A) $x = 6$ (B) $x + y + 2z = 8$
(C) $y = 9$ (D) $z = 2$

6-9 In a single slit diffraction pattern obtained on a screen, if the slit width is gradually decreased, which of the following statements is/are correct :
(A) Fringe pattern will expand (B) Fringe pattern will shrink
(C) Fringes may disappear (D) No effect on fringe pattern

6-10 Two coherent light waves each having intensities I_0 interfering at a point in space where resulting intensity observed is $I_0/2$, the phase difference between the two waves at the point of interference can be :

(A) $\pi/3$ (B) $2\pi/3$

(C) $4\pi/3$ (D) $5\pi/3$

6-11 In a series of polaroids placed in such a way that optical axis of each polaroid makes same angle with the next one. When unpolarized light falls on first and if no light is coming out from the last polaroid then by using how many number of polaroids in series this can be achieved :

(A) 3 (B) 4

(C) 5 (D) 6

6-12 In the *YDSE* setup shown in figure-6.113 below, it is specified that $SS_1 - SS_2 = \lambda/2$ and $S_2P - S_1P = \lambda/2$. Intensity on screen due to both slits S_1 and S_2 are I_0 then choose which of the following statement(s) is/are ***INCORRECT***.

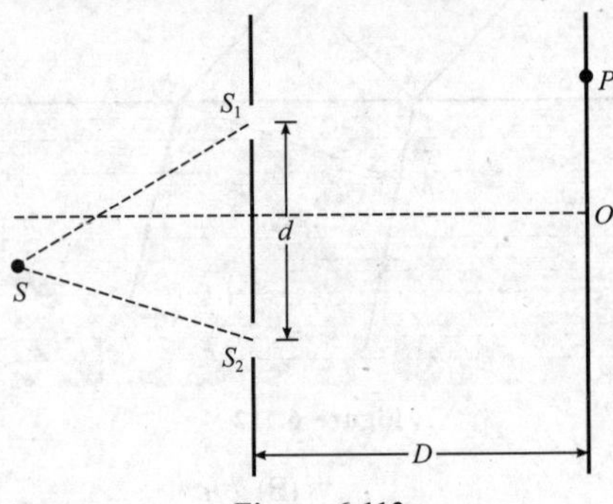

Figure 6.113

(A) Central maxima will form at point *P*

(B) Central maxima will form at point *O*

(C) Resultant intensity at *P* is 0

(D) Resultant intensity at *P* is $4I_0$

6-13 Two point monochromatic and coherent sources of light of wavelength λ are placed on the dotted line in front of a large screen. The source emit waves in phase with each other. The distance between S_1 and S_2 is *d* while their distance form the screen is much larger. Then :

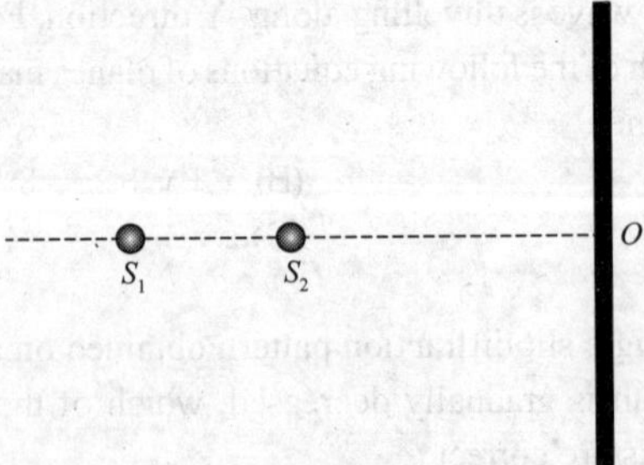

Figure 6.114

(A) If $d = 7\lambda/2$, *O* will be a minima

(B) If $d = 4.3\lambda$, there will be a total of 8 minima on screen

(C) If $d = 7\lambda$, *O* will be a maxima

(D) If $d = \lambda$ there will be only one maxima on the screen

6-14 In an interference experiment as shown in the figure-6.115, the source plane and screen are separated by a distance 1 m. At a certain position of source, fringe width is 1/4 mm and by moving the source away from mirror along the line *AB* by 0.6 mm, the fringe width changed to 1/6 mm. Which of the following statement(s) is/are correct :

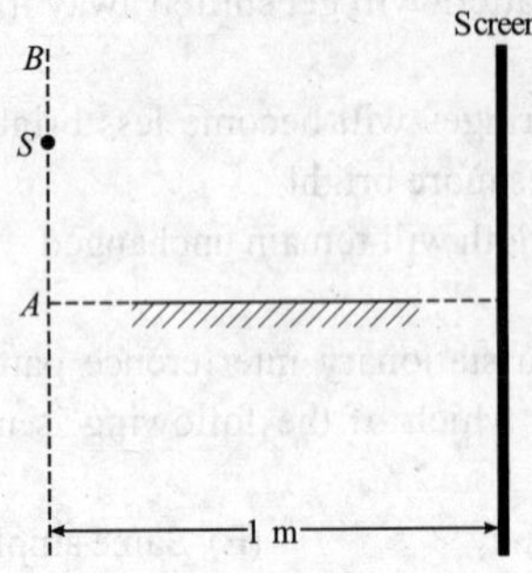

Figure 6.115

(A) Wavelength of light used is 5000 Å

(B) Wavelength of light used is 6000Å

(C) Initial distance of source from *A* is 1.2 mm

(D) Initial distance of source from *A* is 0.6 mm

6-15 For a *YDSE* setup, a monochromatic source of light of wavelength is λ is used, the slits are separated by distance *d*. Incident light falling on slit plane in the direction shown in figure-6.116 below. Now the refractive index of the medium between slit plane and screen starts changing with time as $\mu = \mu_0 + kt$ due to this the fringe pattern starts shifting on screen. Which of the following statement(s) is/are correct for this setup :

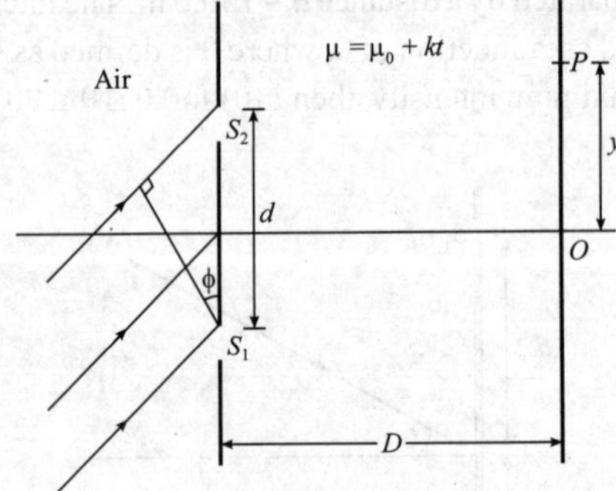

Figure 6.116

(A) The *y* coordinate of central maxima at any time *t* is $\dfrac{D\sin\phi}{\mu_0 + kt}$

(B) The *y* coordinate of central maxima at any time *t* is $\dfrac{D\cos\phi}{\mu_0 + kt}$

(C) Velocity of central maxima at any time *t* is $-\dfrac{kD\sin\phi}{(\mu_0 + kt)^2}$

(D) Velocity of central maxima at any time *t* is $-\dfrac{kD\cos\phi}{(\mu_0 + kt)^2}$

* * * * *

Unsolved Numerical Problems for Preparation of NSEP, INPhO & IPhO

For detailed preparation of INPhO and IPhO students can refer advance study material on www.physicsgalaxy.com

6-1 A prism having angle $A°$ (which is very small) is placed in front of a point source S at a small distance d. A screen is placed at a large distance D as shown in the figure-6.117. Find the fringe width of interference pattern given that source is emitting light of wavelength λ and refractive index of prism is μ.

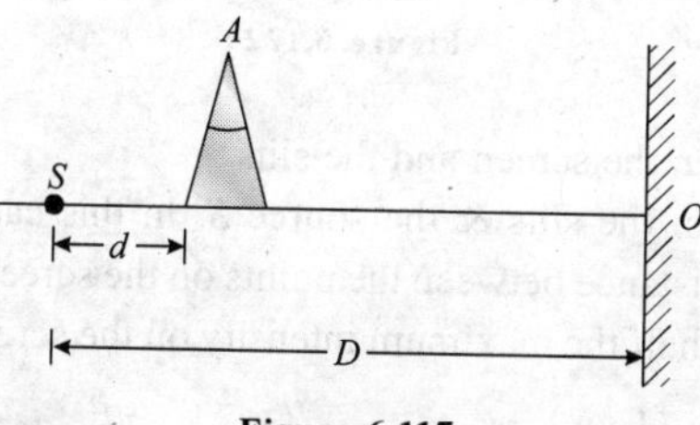

Figure 6.117

Ans. [$\frac{D\lambda}{(\mu-1)Ad}$]

6-2 A thin glass plate of thickness t and refractive index μ is inserted between screen & one of the slits in a Young's experiment. If the intensity at the center of the screen is I, what was the intensity at the same point prior to the introduction of the sheet.

Ans. [$I_0 = I \sec^2\left[\frac{\pi(\mu-1)t}{\lambda}\right]$]

6-3 A young's double-slit arrangement produces interference fringes for sodium light ($\lambda = 5890Å$) that are 0.20° apart. What is the angular fringe separation if the entire arrangement is immersed in water (refractive index of water is 4/3).

Ans. [0.15°]

6-4 Two coherent narrow slits emitting light of wavelength λ in the same phase are placed parallel to each other at a small separation of 2λ. The light is calculated on a screen S which is placed a distance ($D >> \lambda$) from the slit S_1 as shown in figure-6.118. Find the distance x such that the intensity at P is equal to the intensity at point O.

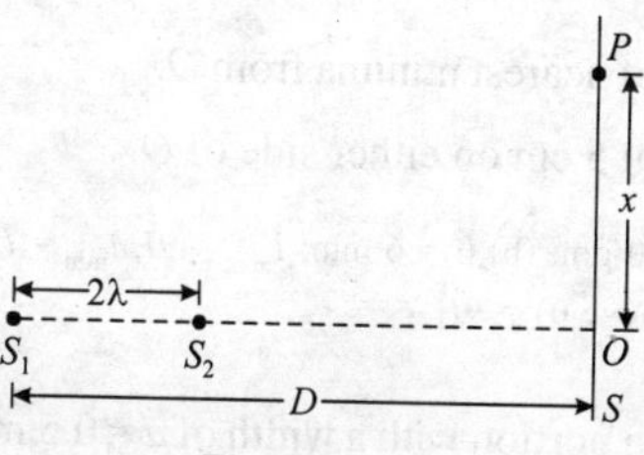

Figure 6.118

Ans. [$\sqrt{3}D$]

6-5 In Young's doubled slit experiment the slits are 0.5 mm apart and the interference is observed on a screen at a distance of 100 cm from the slit. It is found that the 9th bright fringe is at a distance of 7.5 mm from the second dark fringe from the center of the fringe pattern on same side. Find the wavelength of the light used.

Ans. [5000 Å]

6-6 Light of wavelength 520 nm passing through a double slit, produces interference pattern of relative intensity versus deflection angle θ as shown in the figure-6.119. Find the separation d between the slits.

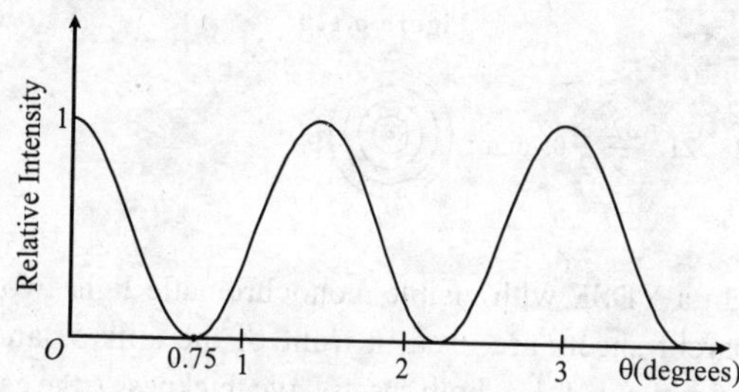

Figure 6.119

Ans. [1.99×10^{-2} mm]

6-7 The distance between two slits in a *YDSE* apparatus is 3 mm. The distance of the screen from the slits is 1 m. Microwaves of wavelength 1 mm are incident on the plane of the slits normally. Find the distance of the first maxima on the screen from the central maxima.

Ans. [35.35 cm app., 5]

6-8 One radio transmitter A operating at 60.0 MHz is 10.0 m from another similar transmitter B that is 180° out of phase with transmitter A. How far must an observer move from transmitter A towards transmitter B along the line connecting A and B to reach the nearest point where the two beams are in phase ?

Ans. [1.25 m]

6-9 The central fringe of the interference pattern produced by the light of wavelength 6000 Å is found to shift to the position of 4th bright fringe after a glass sheet of refractive index 1.5 is introduced. Find the thickness of the glass sheet.

Ans. [4.8 μm]

6-10 A board source of light of wavelength 680 nm illuminates normally two glass plates 120 mm long that meet at one end and are separated by a wire 0.048 mm in diameter at the other end. Find the number of bright fringes formed over the 120 mm distance.

Ans. [141]

6-11 Two microwave coherent point sources emitting waves of wavelength λ are placed at 5λ distance apart. The interference is being observed on a flat non-reflecting surface along a line passing through one source, in a direction perpendicular to the line joining the second source (refer figure-6.120) Considering λ as 4 mm, calculate the positions of maxima and draw shape of interference pattern. Take initial phase difference between the two sources to be zero.

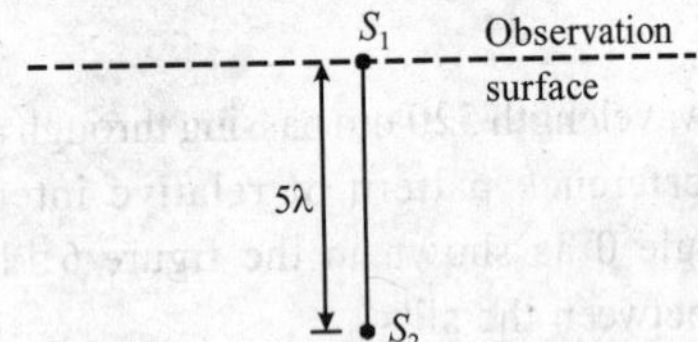

Figure 6.120

Ans. [48, 21, $\frac{32}{3}$, $\frac{9}{2}$, 0, m.m;]

6-12 In a YDSE with visible monochromatic light two thin transparent sheets are used in front of the slits S_1 and S_2. $\mu_1 = 1.6$ and $\mu_2 = 1.4$. If both sheets have thickness t, the central maximum is observed at a distance of 5 mm from center O. Now the sheets are replaced by two sheets of same material of refractive index $\frac{\mu_1 + \mu_2}{2}$ but having thickness t_1 & t_2 such that $t = \frac{t_1 + t_2}{2}$. Now central maximum is observed at a distance of 8 mm from center O on the same side as before. Find the thickness t_1 (in μm) [Given: $d = 1$ mm. $D = 1$ m]

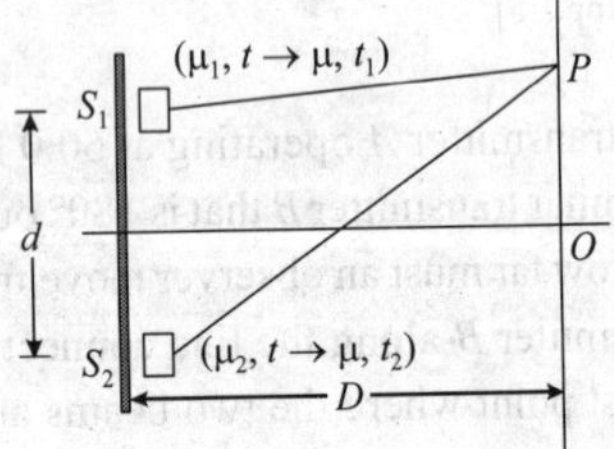

Figure 6.121

Ans. [33]

6-13 Orange light of wavelength 6000×10^{-10} m in illuminates a single slit of width 0.6×10^{-4} m. Calculate the maximum possible number of diffraction minima produced on both sides of the central maximum.

Ans. [198]

6-14 A source S is kept directly behind the slit S_1 in a double slit apparatus. What will be the phase difference at P, if a liquid of refraction index μ is filled : (wavelength of light in air is λ due to the source, assume $l >> d$, $D >> d$)

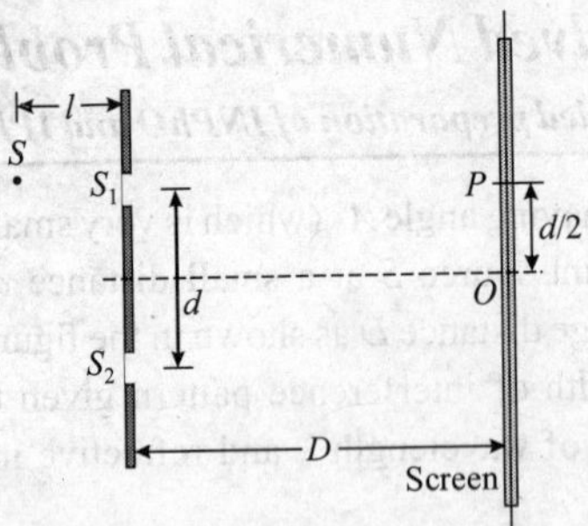

Figure 6.122

(a) Between the screen and the slits.

(b) Between the slits & the source S. In this case, find the minimum distance between the points on the screen where the intensity is half the maximum intensity on the screen.

Ans. [(a) $\Delta\phi = \left(\frac{1}{l} + \frac{\mu}{D}\right)\frac{\pi d^2}{\lambda}$; (b) $\Delta\phi = \left(\frac{\mu}{l} + \frac{1}{D}\right)\frac{\pi d^2}{\lambda}$; $D_{min} = \frac{\beta}{2} = \frac{\lambda D}{2d}$]

6-15 In a YDSE, a parallel beam of light of wavelength 6000 Å is incident on slits at angle of incidence 30°. A & B are two thin transparent films, each of refractive index 1.5. Thickness of A is 20.4 μm. Light coming through A & B have intensities I & $4I$ respectively on the screen. Intensity at point O which is symmetric relative to the slits is $3I$. The central maxima is above O.

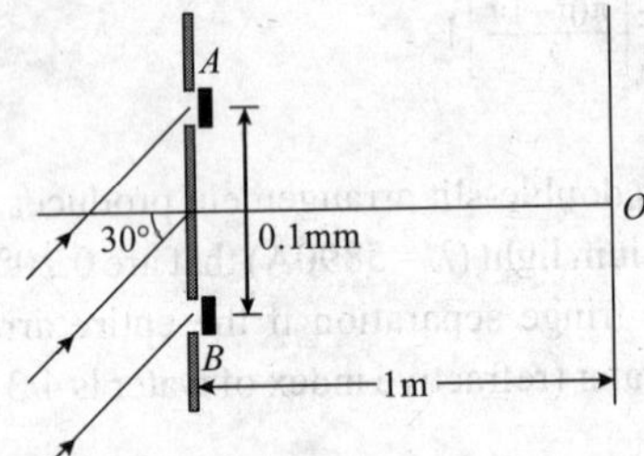

Figure 6.123

(a) What is the maximum thickness of B to do so ? Assuming thickness of B to be that found in part (a), answer the following parts :

(b) Find fringe width, maximum intensity & minimum intensity on screen.

(c) Distance of nearest minima from O.

(d) Intensity at 5 cm on either side of O.

Ans. [(a) t_B = 120 μm; (b) β = 6 mm; $I_{max} = 9I$, $I_{min} = I$; (c) β/6 = 1 mm (d) I (at 5 cm above 0) = $9I$]

6-16 A central portion with a width of $d = 0.5$ mm is cut out of a convergent lens having a focal length of 20 cm. Both halves are tightly fitted against each other and a point source of monochromatic light ($A = 2500$ Å) is placed in front of the lens at a distance of 10 cm. Find the maximum possible number of interference bands that can be observed on the screen.

Ans. [5]

6-17 A plastic film with index of refraction 1.80 is put on the surface of a car window to increase the reflectivity and thereby to keep the interior of the car cooler. The window glass has index of refraction 1.60.

(a) What minimum thickness is required, if light of wavelength 600 nm in air reflected from the two sides of the film is to interfere constructively?

(b) It is found to be difficult to manufacture and install coatings as thin as calculated in part (a). What is the next greatest thickness for which there will also be constructive interference?

Ans. [(a) 8.33×10^{-8} m; (b) 2.5×10^{-7}]

6-18 Two coherent monochromatic sources A and B emit light of wavelength λ. The distance between A and B is $d = 4\lambda$.

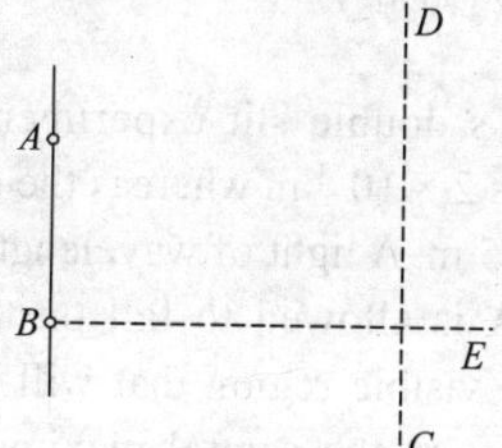

Figure 6.124

(a) If a light detector is moved along a line CD parallel to AB, what is the maximum number of minima observed ?

(b) If the detector is moved along a line BE perpendicular to AB and passing through B, what is the number of maxima observed ?

Ans. [(a) 8, (b) 4]

6-19 A beam of light consisting of two wavelengths, 6500 Å and 5200 Å is used to obtain interference fringes in a Young's double slit experiment. Find the distance of the third fringe on the screen from the central maximum for the wavelength 6500Å. What is the least distance from the central maximum at which the bright fringes due to both wavelengths coincide? The distance between the slits is 2 mm and the distance between the plane of the slits and the screen is 120 cm.

Ans. [1.17 mm, 1.56 mm]

6-20 In an experiment using Fresnel biprism, fringes of width 0.185×10^{-3} m are observed at a distance of 1 m from the slit. Images are of the coherent sources are then produced at the same distance from the slit by placing a convex lens at a distance of 0.3 m from the slit. The images are found to be separated by 0.7×10^{-2} m. Calculate the wavelength of the light used.

Ans. [5550 Å]

6-21 Two identical monochromatic light sources A and B of intensity 10^{-15} W/m^2 produce wavelength of light $4000\sqrt{3}$ Å. A glass of thickness 3 mm is placed in the path of the ray as shown in the figure-6.125. The glass has a variable refractive index $n = 1 + \sqrt{x}$ where x (in mm) is distance of plate from left to right. Calculate resultant intensity at focal point F of the lens.

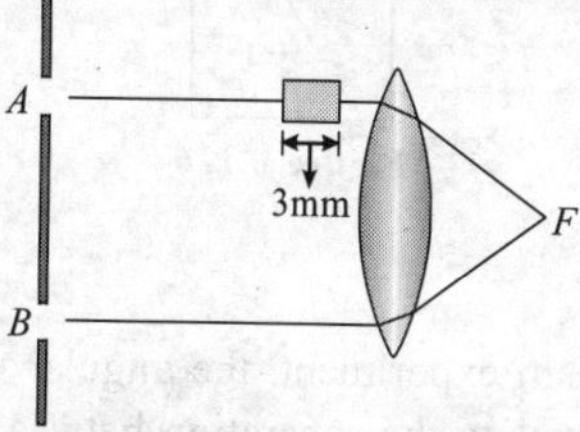

Figure 6.125

Ans. [4×10^{-15} W/m^2]

6-22 Two fine slits are placed very close to each other and they are illuminated by a strong beam of light of wavelength 5900 Å. Fringes are obtained at a distance of 0.3 m from the slits. The fringe width is found to be 5.9×10^{-5} m. Calculate the distance between the slits.

Ans. [3×10^{-3} m]

6-23 Biprism fringes are produced with the help of sodium light ($\lambda = 5893$ Å). The angle of the biprism is 179.5° and its refractive index 1.5. If the distance between the slit and the biprism is 0.4 m and the distance between the biprism and the screen is 0.6 m, find the distance between successive bright fringes. Also calculate the maximum width of the slit for which the fringes will still be sharp.

Ans. [3.376×10^{-4} m, 112 μm]

6-24 A glass plate 1.2×10^{-6} m thick is placed in the path of one of the interfering beams in a biprism arrangement using monochromatic light of wavelength 6000 Å. If the central band shifts by a distance equal to the width of the bands, find the refractive index of glass.

Ans. [1.5]

6-25 A monochromatic light of intensity I is incident on a glass plate. Another identical glass plate is kept close to it. Each glass plate reflects 25 per cent of the light incident on it and transmits the rest. Find the ratio of the maximum and minimum intensities in the interference pattern formed by the two beam obtained after reflection from each plate.

Ans. [49 : 1]

6-26 A plane light wave of wavelength $\lambda = 700$ nm falls normally on the base of a biprism made of glass (μ = 1.560) width refracting angle $\theta = 5°$. A plate is placed behind the biprism and the space between them is filled with a liquid of refractive index

($\mu' = 1.500$). Find the fringe width on a screen behind the biprism.

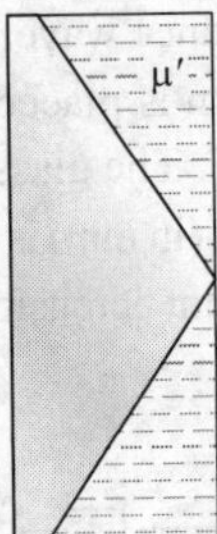

Figure 6.126

Ans. [66.8 μm]

6-27 In a biprism experiment, the angular width of fringes was $\theta = 2'$. Calculate the separation between the slits if the wavelength of the incident light was $\lambda = 700$ nm.

Ans. [1.2 mm]

6-28 In a biprism experiment, calculate the intensity of lights on the screen at a point $5\beta/6$ away from the central fringe in terms of the intensity of the central fringe, which is I_0. Here β is the fringe width.

Ans. [$3I_0/4$]

6-29 Two parallel beams of light P and Q (separation d and mutually coherent) are incident normally on a prism as shown. If the intensities of the upper and the lower beams, immediately after transmission from the face AC, are $4I$ and I respectively, find the resultant intensity at the focus of the lens which brings them into focus.

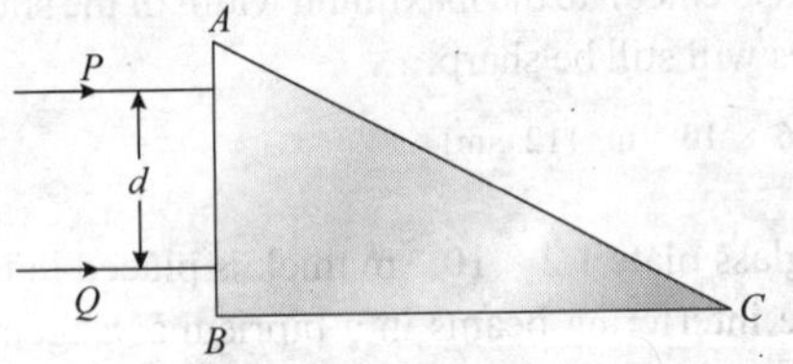

Figure 6.127

Ans. [$9I$]

6-30 Two point sources are $d = n\lambda$ apart. A screen is held at right angles to the line joining the two sources at a distance D from the nearer source. Calculate the distance of the point on the screen where the first bright fringe is observed. Assume $D >> d$.

Ans. [$\sqrt{\frac{2D(D+n\lambda)}{n}}$]

6-31 Two point coherent sources are $d = 4\lambda$ apart. Two light detectors are moved – one along the line parallel to the line joining the sources and the other along the line perpendicular to this line and passing through one of the sources. Find the maximum number of maxima registered by each detector.

Ans. [9, 9]

6-32 In a Young's arrangement, the distance between the slits is 1.5 mm and the distance of the screen from the slits is 2 m. At what minimum distance from the central fringe will red and violet bright fringes coincide if the slit is illuminated with white light? The wavelength range in white light is from 420 nm to 690 nm.

Ans. [12.88 mm]

6-33 A double-slit apparatus is immersed in a liquid of refractive index 1.33. It has slit separation of 1 mm, and distance between the plane of slits and screen is 1.33 m. The slits are illuminated by a parallel beam of light whose wavelength in air is 6300 Å.

(a) Calculate the fringe-width, (b) one of the slits of the apparatus is covered by thin glass sheet of refractive index 1.53. Find the smallest thickness of the sheet to bring adjacent minimum on the axis.

Ans. [0.633 mm, 1.58 mm]

6-34 In a Young's double slit experiment, the separation between the slits is 2×10^{-3} m whereas the distance of screen from the slits is 2.5 m. A light of wavelengths in the range of 2000 Å – 8000 Å is allowed to fall on the slits. Find the wavelength in the visible region that will be present on the screen at 10^{-3} m from the central maximum. Also find the wavelength that will be present at that point of the screen in the infrared as well as in the ultraviolet region.

Ans. [8000 Å, 4000 Å 2666.7 Å ... 8000 Å (infrared), 2666.7 Å (ultraviolet)]

6-35 A narrow slit of width 0.025 mm is illuminated by a parallel beam of light. The diffraction pattern is observed through a telescope. It is found that to reach the first minimum, the telescope has to be rotated through 1°24′ from the direction of the direct ray. Calculate the wavelength of light used.

Ans. [6100 Å]

6-36 Angular width of central maximum in the Fraunhofer diffraction pattern of a slit is measured. The slit is illuminated by another wavelength, the angular width decreases by 30%. Calculate the wavelength of this light. The same decrease in angular width of central maximum is obtained when the original apparatus is immersed in a liquid. Find the refractive index of the liquid.

Ans. [4200 Å, $\mu = 1.43$]

6-37 In a Young's double slit set up the wavelength of light used is 546 nm. The distance of screen from slits is 1 m. The slit separation is 0.3 mm.

(a) Compare the intensity at a point P distant 10 mm from the central fringe where the intensity is I_0.

(b) Find the number of bright fringes between P and the central fringe.

Ans. [(a) 3.0×10^{-6} m; (b) 3.0×10^{-4} I_0]

6-38 In a double slit pattern ($\lambda = 6000$ Å), the first order and tenth order maxima fall at 12.50 mm and 14.75 mm from a particular reference point. If λ is changed to 5500 Å, find the position of zero order and tenth order fringes, other arrangements remaining the same.

Ans. [12.25 mm, 14.55 mm]

6-39 An interference is observed due to two coherent sources S_1 placed at origin and S_2 placed at (0, 3λ, 0). Here λ is the wavelength of the sources. A detector D is moved along the positive x-axis. Find x-coordinates on the x-axis (excluding $x = 0$ and $x = \infty$) where maximum intensity is observed.

Ans. [1.25λ, 4λ]

6-40 A Young double slit apparatus is immersed in a liquid of refractive index μ_1. The slit plane touches the liquid surface. A parallel beam of monochromatic light of wavelength λ (in air) in incident normally on the slits.

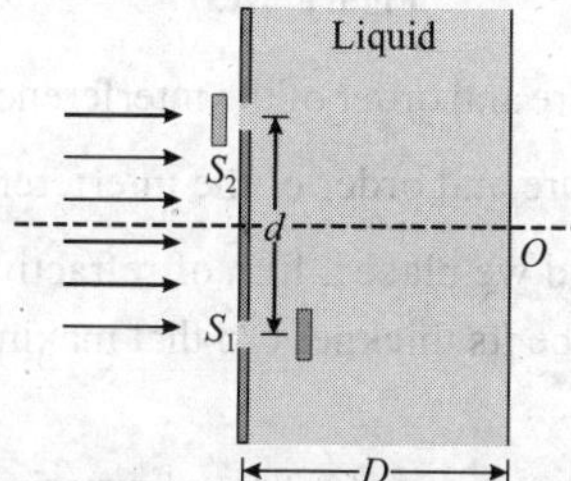

Figure 6.128

(a) Find the fringe width

(b) If one of the slits (say S_2) is covered by a transparent slab of refractive index μ_2 and thickness t as shown, find the new position of central maxima.

(c) Now the other slit S_1 is also covered by a slab of same thickness and refractive index μ_3 as shown in figure-6.128 due to which the central maxima recovers its position find the value of μ_3.

(d) Find the ratio of intensities at O in the three conditions (a), (b) and (c).

Ans.[(a) $\dfrac{\lambda D}{\mu_1 d}$; (b) $\dfrac{(\mu_2 - 1)tD}{d}$; (c) μ_1 μ_2; (d) $1{:}\cos^2\left\{\dfrac{\pi(\mu_2 - 1)t}{\lambda}\right\}{:}1$]

6-41 In a Young experiment the light source is at distance $l_1 = 20$ μm and $l_2 = 40$ μm from the slits. The light of wavelength $\lambda = 5000$Å is incident on slits separated at a distance 10 μm. A screen is placed at a distance $D = 2$ m away from the slits as shown in figure-6.129. Find

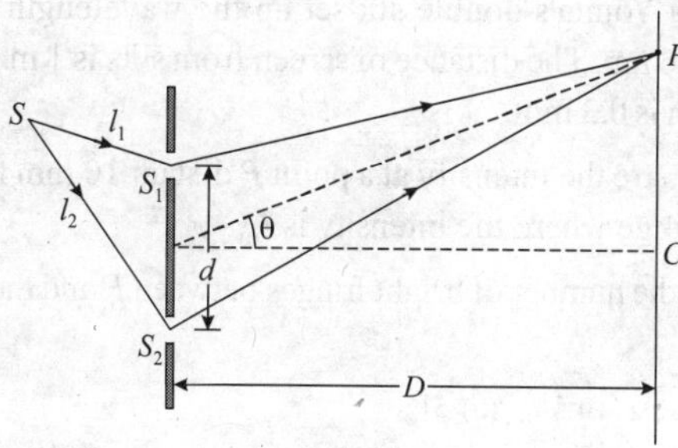

Figure 6.129

(a) The values of θ relative to the central line where maxima appear on the screen ?

(b) How many maxima will appear on the screen?

(c) What should be minimum thickness of a slab of refractive index 1.5 be placed on the path of one of the ray so that minima occurs at C?

Ans. [(a) $\sin^{-1}\left[2\left(\dfrac{n}{40} - 1\right)\right]$; (b) 40; (c) 5000Å]

6-42 A screen is placed 50 cm from a single slit, which is illuminated with 6000 Å light. If distance between the first and third minima in the diffraction pattern is 3.0 mm, what is the width of the slit ?

Ans. [0.2 mm]

6-43 In a double slit experiment the distance between the slits is 5.0 mm and the slits are 1.0 m from the screen. Two interference patterns can be seen on the screen one due to light with wavelength 480 nm, and the other due to light with wavelength 600 nm. What is the separation on the screen between the third order bright fringes of the two interference patterns?

Ans. [0.072 mm]

6-44 In a Young's double slit experiment using monochromatic light the fringe pattern shifts by a certain distance on the screen when a mica sheet of refractive index 1.6 and thickness 1.964 microns is introduced in the path of one of the interfering waves. The mica sheet is then removed and the distance between the slits and screen is doubled. It is found that the distance between successive maxima (or minima) now is the same as observed fringe shift upon the introduction of the mica sheet. Calculate the wavelength of the monochromatic light used in the experiment.

Ans. [589 nm]

6-45 Two very narrow slits are spaced 1.80 μm apart and are placed 35.0 cm from a screen. What is the distance between the first and second dark lines of the interference pattern when the slits are illuminated with coherent light of $\lambda = 550$ nm? (**Hint:** The angle θ is not small)

Ans. [12.6 cm]

6-46 In a Young's double slit set up the wavelength of light used is 546 nm. The distance of screen from slits is 1 m. The slit separation is 0.3 mm.

(a) Compare the intensity at a point P distant 10 mm from the central fringe where the intensity is I_0.

(b) Find the number of bright fringes between P and the central fringe.

Ans. [(a) $3.0 \times 10^{-4}\ I_0$; (b) 5]

6-47 Interference pattern with Young's double slits 1.5 mm apart are formed on a screen at a distance 1.5 m from the plane of slits. In the path of the beam of one of the slits, a transparent film of 10-micron thickness and of refractive index 1.6 is interposed while in the path of the beam from the other slit a transparent film of 15 micron thickness and the refractive index 1.2 is interposed. Find the displacement of the fringe pattern.

Ans. [3 mm]

6-48 A glass plate (n = 1.53) that is 0.485 μm thick and surrounded by air is illuminated by a beam of white light normal to the plate.

(a) What wavelengths (in air) within the limits of the visible spectrum (λ = 400 to 700 nm) are intensified in the reflected beam?

(b) What wavelengths within the visible spectrum are intensified in the transmitted light?

Ans. [(a) 424 nm, 594 nm; (b) 495 nm]

6-49 An oil film covers the surface of a small pond. The refractive index of the oil is greater than that of water. At one point on the film, the film has the smallest nonzero thickness for which there will be destructive interference in the reflected light when infrared radiation with wavelength 800 nm is incident normal to the film. When this film is viewed at normal incidence at this same point, for what visible wavelengths, if any, will there be constructive interference? (Visible light has wavelengths between 4000Å and 7000Å)

Ans. [5330Å]

6-50 A ray of light is incident on the left vertical face of the glass slab. If the incident light has an intensity I and on each reflection the intensity decreases by 90% and on each refraction the intensity decreases by 10%, find the ratio of the intensities of maximum to minimum in reflected pattern.

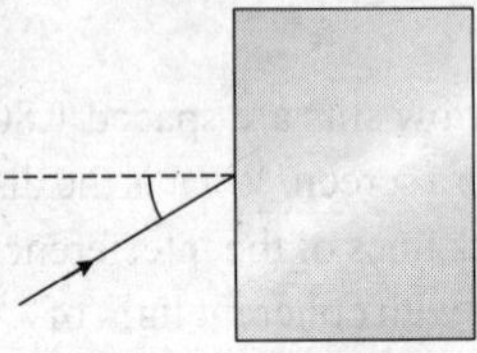

Figure 6.130

Ans. [361]

6-51 A convergent lens with a focal length of f = 10 cm is cut into two halves that are then moved apart to a distance of d = 0.5 mm (a double lens). Find the fringe width on screen at a distance of 60 cm behind the lens if a point source of monochromatic light (λ = 5000 Å) is placed in front of the lens at a distance of a = 15 cm from it.

Ans. [0.1 mm]

6-52 In the Young's double slit experiment a point source of λ = 5000 Å is placed slightly off the central axis as shown in the figure-6.131.

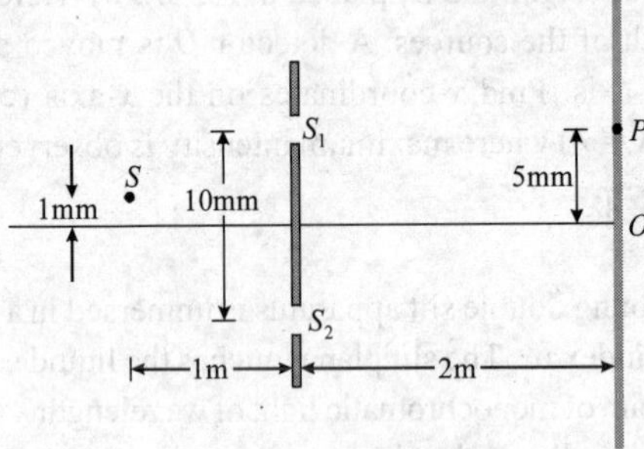

Figure 6.131

(a) Find the nature and order of the interference at the point P.

(b) Find the nature and order of the interference at O.

(c) Where should we place a film of refractive index μ = 1.5 and what should be its thickness so that maxima of zero order is obtained at O.

Ans. [(a) 70th order maxima; (b) 20th order maxima; (c) t = 20 μm, in front of S_1]

6-53 A convex lens of focal length f = 25 cm was cut along the diameter into two identical halves and was again set leaving a thin gap of width a = 0.10 cm. A narrow slit, emitting monochromatic light of wavelength λ = 0.60 μm was placed at the focus of the lens. A screen was placed behind the lens at a distance b = 50 cm. Find the width of the fringes on the screen and the possible number of fringes.

Ans. [1.5×10^{-4} m, 13]

6-54 A monochromatic beam of light of 6000Å is used in YDSE setup. The two slits are covered with two thin films of equal thickness t but of different refractive indices as shown in the figure-6.132. Considering the intensity of the incident beam on the slits to be I_0, find the distance of a point on the screen from O at which intensity is I_0 and is just above the central maxima. Assume that there is no change in intensity of the light after passing through the films.

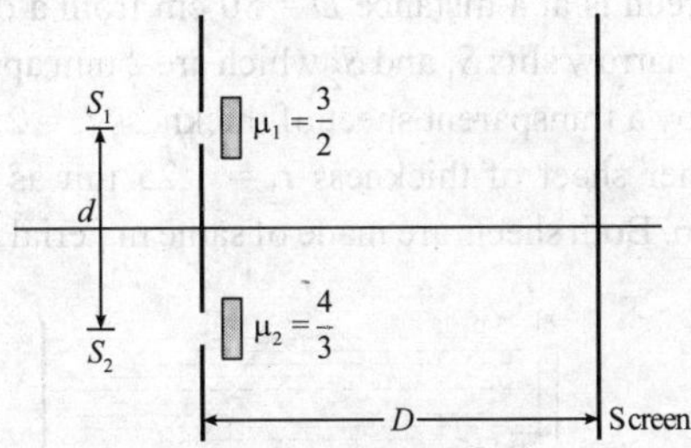

Figure 6.132

Consider $t = 6\ \mu m$, $d = 1$ mm, $D = 1$ m, where d and D have their usual meaning.

Ans. [3×10^{-4} m]

6-55 Light of wavelength $\lambda = 500$ nm falls on two narrow slits placed a distance $d = 50 \times 10^{-4}$ cm apart, at an angle $\phi = 30°$ relative to the slits as shown in figure-6.133. On the lower slit a transparent slab of thickness 0.1 mm and refractive index $\frac{3}{2}$ is placed. The interference pattern is observed on a distance $D = 2$ m from the slits. Then calculate :

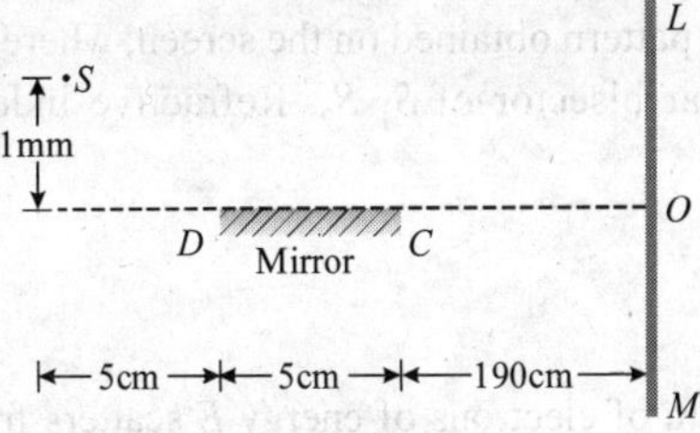

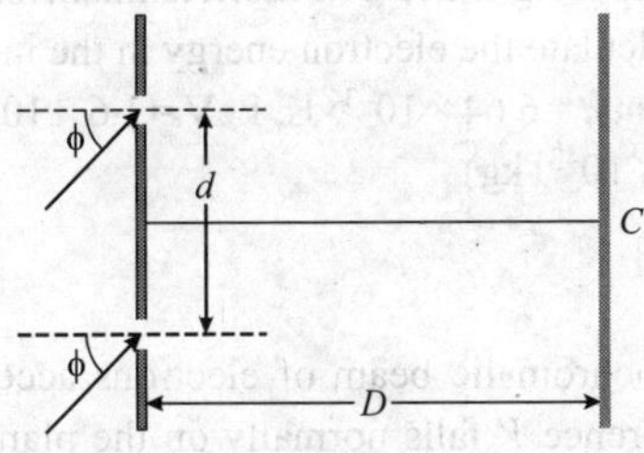

Figure 6.133

(a) Position of the central maxima?

(b) The order of maxima at point C of screen?

(c) How many fringes will pass C, if we remove the transparent slab from the lower slit?

Ans. [(a) At $\theta = 30°$ below C; (b) 50; (c) 100]

6-56 In a double-slit pattern ($\lambda = 6000$ Å), the zero-order and tenth-order maxima fall at 12.34 mm and 14.73 mm from a particular reference point. If λ is changed to 5000 Å, find the position of the zero order and tenth order fringes, other arrangements remaining the same.

Ans. [Zero-order at the same position but tenth-order maxima at 14.53 mm]

6-57 The distance between a slit and a biprism of acute angle 2° is 10 cm. Find the fringe width and the width of the entire band when observation is made on a screen at a distance of 90 cm from the biprism. The refractive index of the material of the biprism is 1.5 and $\lambda = 5890$ Å.

Ans. [0.168 mm, 31.5 mm]

6-58 In the *YDSE* the monochromatic source of wavelength λ is placed at a distance $\frac{d}{2}$ from the central axis (as shown in the figure-6.134), where d is the separation between the two slits S_1 and S_2.

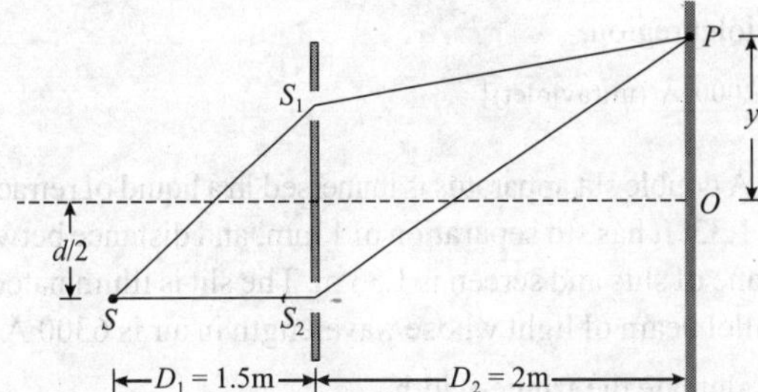

Figure 6.134

(a) Find the position of the central maxima

(b) Find the order of interference formed at O.

(c) Now S is placed on centre dotted line. Find the minimum thickness of the film of refractive index $\mu = 1.5$ to be placed infront of S_2 so that intensity at O becomes $\frac{3}{4}$th of the maximum intensity. Take $\lambda = 6000$ Å ; $d = 6$ mm

Ans. [(a) 4 mm above 0; (b) 20; (c) 2000 Å]

6-59 Fringes are produced by a Fresnel's biprism in focal plane of a reading microscope which is 100 cm from the slit. A lens inserted between the biprism and the eyepiece gives two images of the slit in two positions of the lens. In one case the two images of the slit are 0.45 mm apart in the other case 2.90 mm apart. If sodium light of wavelength 5893 Å used, find the width of the interference fringes. If the distance between the slit and biprism is 10 cm and refractive index of the material of the biprism is 1.5, calculate the angle in degrees which the inclined faces of the biprism makes with its base.

Ans. [2.91 or 1.73 mm]

6-60 In a biprism experiment with sodium light ($\lambda = 5893$Å), the micrometer reading is 2.32 mm when the eyepiece is placed at a distance of 100 cm from the source. If the distance between two virtual sources is 2 cm, find the new reading of micrometer when the eyepiece is moved such that 20 fringes cross the field of view.

Ans. [2°]

6-61 In two slit experiment with monochromatic light, fringes are obtained on screen placed at some distance from the slits. If the screen is moved by 5×10^{-2} m towards the slits, the change in fringe-width is 3×10^{-5} m. If the distance between the slits is 10^{-3} m, calculate the wavelength of the light used.

Ans. [6000 Å]

6-62 In a Young's double slit experiment, the separation between slits is 2×10^{-3} m whereas the distance of screen from the slits is 2.5 m. A light of wavelengths in the range of 2000 – 8000 Å is allowed to fall on the slits. Find the wavelength in the visible region that will be present on the screen at 10^{-3} m from the central maxima. Also find the wavelength that will be present at that point of screen in the infrared as well as in the ultraviolet region.

Ans. [2000 Å (ultraviolet)]

6-63 A double slit apparatus is immersed in a liquid of refractive index 1.33. It has slit separation of 1 mm, and distance between the plane of slits and screen is 1.33 m. The slit is illuminated by a parallel beam of light whose wavelength in air is 6300 Å.

(a) Calculate the fringe-width

(b) One of the slits of the apparatus is covered by a thin glass sheet of refractive index 1.53. Find the smallest thickness of the sheet to bring the adjacent minimum of the axis.

Ans. [(a) 0.63 mm; (b) 1.575 μm]

6-64 The Young's double slit experiment is done in a medium of refractive index 4/3. A light of 6000Å nm wavelength is falling on the slits having 0.45 mm separation. The lower slit S_2 is covered by a thin glass sheet of thickness 10.4 μm and refractive index 1.5. The interference pattern is observed on a screen placed 1.5 m from the slits as shown in figure-6.135.

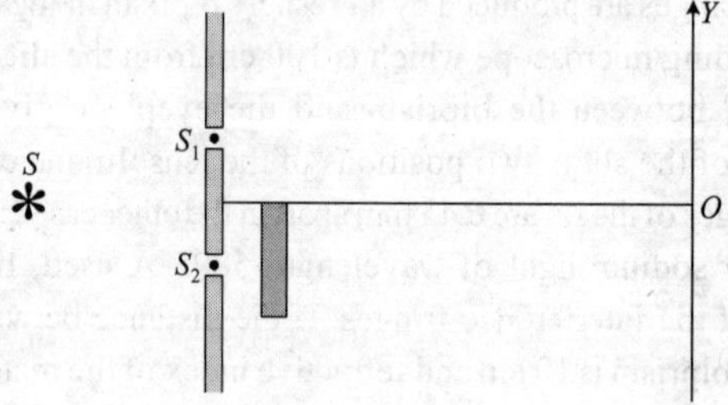

Figure 6.135

(a) Find the location of the central maximum (bright fringe with zero path difference) on the y-axis.

(b) Find the light intensity at point O relative to the maximum fringe intensity.

(c) Now, if 6000Å nm light is replaced by white light of range 4000 to 7000Å, find the wavelength of the light that form maxima exactly at point O. [All wavelengths in this problem are for the given medium of refractive index 4/3. Ignore dispersion]

Ans. [(a) 4.33 mm; (b) 0.75 I_{max}; (c) 1300Å, 650Å, 443.34Å, 260Å]

6-65 A screen is at a distance D = 80 cm from a diaphragm having two narrow slits S_1 and S_2 which are 2 mm apart. Slit S_1 is covered by a transparent sheet of thickness t_1 = 2.5 μm and S_2 by another sheet of thickness t_2 = 1.25 μm as shown in figure-6.136. Both sheets are made of same material

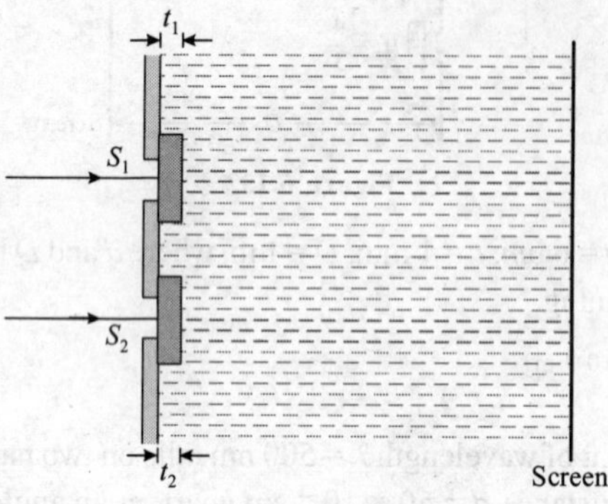

Figure 6.136

having refractive index μ = 1.40. Water in filled in space between diaphragm and screen. A monochromatic light beam of wavelength λ = 5000 Å is incident normally on the diaphragm. Assuming intensity of beam to be uniform and slits of equal width, calculate ratio of intensity at C to maximum intensity of interference pattern obtained on the screen, where C is foot of perpendicular bisector of $S_1 S_2$. Refractive index of water $\mu_w = 4/3$.

Ans. [$\frac{3}{4}$]

6-66 A beam of electrons of energy E scatters from a target having atomic spacing of 1 Å. The first maximum intensity occurs at θ = 60°. Calculate the electron energy in the incident beam. (Planck constant $h = 6.64 \times 10^{-34}$ Js, 1 eV = 1.6×10^{-19} J, electron mass $m = 9.1 \times 10^{-31}$ kg)

Ans. [50.47 eV]

6-67 A monochromatic beam of electrons accelerated by a potential difference V falls normally on the plane containing two narrow slits separated by a distance d. The interference pattern is observed on a screen parallel to the plane of the slits and at a distance of D from the slits. Fringe width is found to be β_1. When electron beam is accelerated by the potential difference $4V$ the fringe width becomes β_2. Find the ratio β_1/β_2. (Given $d << D$)

Ans. [2]

6-68 in a double-slit experiment, the separation between the slits is d = 0.25 cm and the distance of the screen D = 120 cm from the slits. If the wavelength of light used is λ = 6000 Å and I_0 is the intensity of the central bright fringe, what is the intensity at a distance $x = 4.8 \times 10^{-5}$ m from the central maximum ?

Ans. [$\frac{3I_0}{4}$]

* * * * *

ANSWERS & SOLUTIONS

CONCEPTUAL MCQS Single Option Correct

1	(D)	**2**	(D)	**3**	(C)
4	(B)	**5**	(A)	**6**	(B)
7	(A)	**8**	(D)	**9**	(A)
10	(A)	**11**	(B)	**12**	(C)
13	(A)	**14**	(D)	**15**	(D)
16	(B)	**17**	(D)	**18**	(A)
19	(A)	**20**	(C)	**21**	(B)
22	(C)	**23**	(A)	**24**	(A)
25	(C)	**26**	(B)	**27**	(B)
28	(C)	**29**	(B)	**30**	(B)
31	(A)				

NUMERICAL MCQS Single Option Correct

1	(C)	**2**	(A)	**3**	(D)
4	(B)	**5**	(D)	**6**	(C)
7	(A)	**8**	(B)	**9**	(D)
10	(B)	**11**	(B)	**12**	(C)
13	(B)	**14**	(C)	**15**	(B)
16	(D)	**17**	(B)	**18**	(B)
19	(D)	**20**	(D)	**21**	(B)
22	(A)	**23**	(C)	**24**	(D)
25	(B)	**26**	(C)	**27**	(C)
28	(A)	**29**	(C)	**30**	(B)
31	(C)	**32**	(D)	**33**	(C)
34	(B)	**35**	(D)	**36**	(B)
37	(D)	**38**	(B)	**39**	(D)
40	(D)	**41**	(B)	**42**	(A)
43	(D)	**44**	(A)	**45**	(C)
46	(A)	**47**	(D)	**48**	(C)
49	(A)				

ADVANCE MCQs One or More Options Correct

1	(D)	**2**	(D)	**3**	(B, C)
1	(All)	**2**	(B, C)	**3**	(A, D)
4	(A, C, D)	**5**	(All)	**6**	(A, D)
7	(A, D)	**8**	(A, C)	**9**	(B, C)
10	(A, C, D)	**11**	(B, C)	**12**	(A, C)
13	(A, B, D)	**14**	(A, B, C)	**15**	(A, B)
16	(B)	**17**	(B, C, D)	**18**	(B, D)
19	(A, B, C)	**20**	(C, D)	**21**	(A, B)
22	(A, B, C)	**23**	(A, C, D)	**24**	(A, C, D)
25	(B)	**26**	(A, C)	**27**	(A, C)
28	(A, B, D)	**29**	(A, D)	**30**	(B, D)

Solutions of PRACTICE EXERCISE 1.1

(i) As $r_n \propto n^2$

$$\Rightarrow \frac{r_1}{r_{10}} = \left(\frac{1}{10}\right)^2$$

$$\Rightarrow r_{10} = 100 \times 1.06 = 106\,\text{Å}$$

(ii) As $r_n \propto \dfrac{n^2}{Z}$ we use

$$\Rightarrow \frac{n_{Be}^2}{Z_{Be}} = \frac{n_H^2}{Z_{Be}}$$

$$\Rightarrow n_{Be}^2 = \frac{(1)^2}{1} \times 4 \Rightarrow n_{Be} = 2$$

(iii) As $E_n \propto \dfrac{Z^2}{n^2}$ we use

$$\Rightarrow \frac{E_{Be}}{E_H} = \frac{(4)^2/(2)^2}{(1)^2/(1)^2} = 4$$

(iv) $E = -3.4$ eV is for $n = 2$ state and we use

$$v_n \propto \frac{1}{n}$$

$$\Rightarrow \frac{v_1}{v_2} = \frac{1/1}{1/2} \Rightarrow v_2 = \frac{v}{2}$$

(v) As $E_n \propto \dfrac{Z^2}{n^2}$ we use

$$\left(\frac{Z_{Li}}{n_{Li}}\right)^2 = \left(\frac{Z_H}{n_H}\right)^2$$

$$\Rightarrow n_{Li}^2 = \left(\frac{1}{1}\right)^2 \times (3)^2$$

$$\Rightarrow n_{Li} = 3$$

(vi) As $KE_n = \dfrac{KZe^2}{2r_n}$ $TE_n = -\dfrac{KZe^2}{2r_n}$

$$\Rightarrow \frac{KE_n}{TE_n} = -1$$

(vii) As $KE_n = -TE_n$

$$\Rightarrow KE = +3.4\,\text{eV}$$

Solutions of PRACTICE EXERCISE 1.2

(i) Minimum wavelength is corresponding to transition from $\infty \to 1$ hence

$$\lambda_{min} = \frac{12431}{13.6}\,\text{Å}$$

and maximum wavelength is for transition $2 \to 1$

$$\Rightarrow \qquad \lambda_{max} = \frac{12431}{10.2} \text{ Å}$$

$$\Rightarrow \qquad \frac{\lambda_{min}}{\lambda_{max}} = \frac{3}{4}$$

(ii) We use $\lambda = \dfrac{12431}{13.6\left(\frac{1}{4}-\frac{1}{36}\right)} = 4113.2 \text{ Å}$

(iii) (a) We use

$$\lambda = \frac{12431}{13.6(3)^2\left(\frac{1}{1}-\frac{1}{9}\right)} = 114.26$$

(b) From $n = 3$ total spectral lines are ${}^3C_2 = 3$

(iv) We use $\Delta E = 13.6 Z^2\left(\frac{1}{4}-\frac{1}{9}\right)$

$$\Rightarrow \qquad Z^2 = \frac{68\times 36}{5\times 13.6} = 36$$

$$\Rightarrow \qquad Z = 6$$

KE in $h = 1$ is $KE_1 = +13.6 Z^2 = 489.6$ eV

and $\qquad \lambda = \dfrac{12431}{13.6\times 36} = 25.39 \text{ Å}$

(v) We use

$$\frac{12431}{10.2} = \frac{12431}{2.55Z_1^2}$$

$$\Rightarrow \qquad Z = 2$$

Energies of first four levels of X are

$$E_1 = -13.6\times 4 = -54.4 \text{ eV}$$
$$E_2 = -3.4\times 4 = -13.6 \text{ eV}$$
$$E_3 = -1.51\times 4 = -6.04 \text{ eV}$$
$$E_4 = -0.85\times 4 = -3.4 \text{ eV}$$

If for this atom is $+E_1 = 54.4$ eV

(vi) Given that

$$E_n - E_2 = 10.2 + 17.0 = 27.2 \text{ eV}$$

and $\qquad E_n - E_3 = 4.25 + 5.95 = 10.2$ eV

$$\Rightarrow \qquad E_3 - E_1 = 27.2 - 10.2 = 17 \text{ eV}$$

$$\Rightarrow \qquad 1.89 Z^2 = 17 \text{ eV}$$

$$\Rightarrow \qquad Z = 3$$

Now we use $27.2 = 13.6 Z^2\left(\frac{1}{4}-\frac{1}{n^2}\right)$

$$\Rightarrow \qquad n = 6$$

(vii) Incident photon energy $E = \dfrac{12431}{1218} = 10.2$ eV

When six wavelength are emitted that means electrons are excited to $n = 4$ and by absorption of 10.2 eV if electrons excite from n_1 to $n_2 = 4$ we use

$$10.2 = 13.6 Z^2\left(\frac{1}{n_1^2}-\frac{1}{16}\right)$$

for $Z = 1$ this is not possible

for $Z = 2$ we get $n_1 = 2$

for $Z = 3$ onward this is not possible

Thus $Z = 2$ and transition is from $n_1 = 2$ to $n_2 = 4$.

Minimum wavelength (maximum energy) emission is for transition $4 \to 1$

$$\Rightarrow \qquad \lambda_{min} = \frac{12431}{12.75\times 4} = 243.74 \text{ Å}$$

Maximum wavelength emission is for transition $4 \to 3$

$$\Rightarrow \qquad \lambda_{max} = \frac{12431}{0.66\times 4} = 4708.71 \text{ Å}.$$

Solutions of PRACTICE EXERCISE 1.3

(i) Frequency if e^- revolution in n^{th} orbit is

$$f_n = \frac{4\pi^2 K^2 Z^2 e^4 m}{n^3 h^3}$$

For transition from n to $n-1$ orbit radiation frequency is given by

$$\nu = \frac{\Delta E}{h} = \frac{2\pi^2 K^2 Z^2 e^4 m}{h^3}\left(\frac{1}{(n-1)^2}-\frac{1}{n^2}\right)$$

$$\Rightarrow \qquad \nu = \frac{2\pi^2 K^2 Z^2 e^4 m}{h^3}\left(\frac{Zn-1}{n^2(n-1)^2}\right)$$

For large n we can use $2n - 1 \simeq 2n$ and $n - 1 \simeq n$

$$\Rightarrow \qquad \nu = \frac{4\pi^2 K^2 Z^2 e^4 m}{n^3 h^3} \to f_n.$$

(ii) First line of Balmer series of H-atom is

$$\frac{1}{\lambda_H} = R\left(\frac{1}{4}-\frac{1}{9}\right)\times\frac{m_H}{m_e + m_H}$$

First line of Balmer series for T-atom is

$$\frac{1}{\lambda_T} = R\left(\frac{1}{4}-\frac{1}{9}\right)\times\frac{m_T}{m_e + m_T}$$

$$\Rightarrow \lambda_H - \lambda_T = \frac{36(m_e + m_H)}{5Rm_H} - \frac{36(m_e + m_T)}{5Rm_T}$$

$$\Rightarrow \lambda_H - \lambda_T = \frac{36}{5R}\left[\frac{(m_e + m_H)m_T - (m_e + m_T)m_H}{m_H m_T}\right]$$

$$\Rightarrow \lambda_H - \lambda_T = \frac{36}{5R}\left[\frac{m_e(m_T - m_H)}{m_H m_T}\right]$$

$$\Rightarrow \lambda_H - \lambda_T = \frac{36}{5 \times 10967800} \times \frac{9.109 \times 10^{-31} \times 2 \times 1.67 \times 10^{-27}}{3 \times (1.67 \times 10^{-27})}$$

$$\Rightarrow \lambda_H - \lambda_T = 2.387 \text{ Å}$$

(iii) 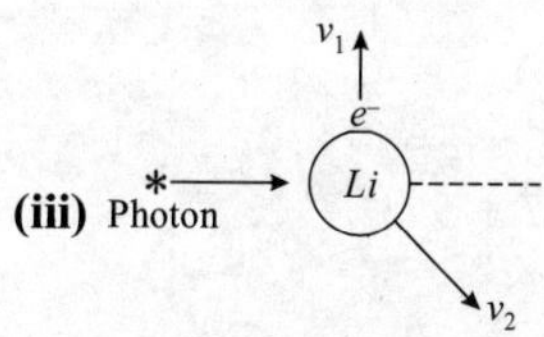

Wavelength of incident photon is

$$\lambda = \frac{12431}{5.4852} = 2266.28 \text{ Å}$$

Photon momentum is

$$P = \frac{h}{\lambda}$$

By conservation of energy we use

$$\Delta E = \frac{1}{2} m_e v_1^2 + \frac{1}{2} m_{Li} v_2^2 \quad \ldots(1)$$

By conservation of momentum we use

$$m_e v_1 = m_{Li} v_2 \sin\theta \quad \ldots(2)$$

and $$\frac{h}{\lambda} = m_{Li} v_2 \cos\theta \quad \ldots(3)$$

Squaring adding (2) and (3) we get

$$m_e^2 v_1^2 + \frac{h^2}{\lambda^2} = m_{Li}^2 v_2^2$$

$$\Rightarrow \frac{1}{2} m_e v_1^2 = \frac{1}{2m_e}\left(m_{Li}^2 v_2^2 - \frac{h^2}{\lambda^2}\right)$$

From equation-(1) we use

$$\Delta E = \frac{m_{Li}^2}{2m_e} v_2^2 - \frac{h^2}{2m_e\lambda^2} + \frac{1}{2} m_{Li} v_2^2$$

$$\Rightarrow v_2 = \sqrt{\frac{\Delta E + \frac{h^2}{2m_e\lambda^2}}{\frac{m_{Li}}{2}\left(\frac{m_{Li}}{me} + 1\right)}} = 14.2 \text{ m/s}$$

From equation-(3) we use

$$\cos\theta = \frac{h}{\lambda m_{Li} v_2} = 0.0178$$

$$\Rightarrow \theta = 88.9^\circ$$

(iv) For inelastic collision H-atom must at least excite from $n = 1$ to $n = 2$ by absorbing 10.2 eV energy. In given situation initial momentum is zero thus maximum possible energy loss can be $2 \times \frac{1}{2} mv^2$ so we use

$$mv^2 = 10.2 \text{ eV}$$

$$\Rightarrow v = \sqrt{\frac{10.2 \times 1.6 \times 10^{-19}}{1.67 \times 10^{-27}}} = 3.13 \times 10^4 \text{ m/s}$$

(v) (a) We use $mvr = \frac{h}{2\pi}$ for $n = 1$

$$\Rightarrow v = \frac{h}{2\pi mr}$$

and $$\frac{mv^2}{r} = evB$$

$$\Rightarrow \frac{m}{r}\left(\frac{h}{2\pi mr}\right) = eB$$

$$\Rightarrow r = \sqrt{\frac{h}{2\pi eB}}$$

(b) Using $mvr = \frac{nh}{2\pi}$ and $\frac{mv^2}{r} = evB$ we get

$$r = \sqrt{\frac{nh}{2\pi eB}}$$

(c) $$v = \frac{h}{2\pi m\sqrt{\frac{nh}{2\pi eB}}} = \sqrt{\frac{heB}{2\pi m^2 n}}$$

v is maximum when $n = 1$

$$\Rightarrow v_{max} = \sqrt{\frac{heB}{2\pi m^2}}$$

(vi) 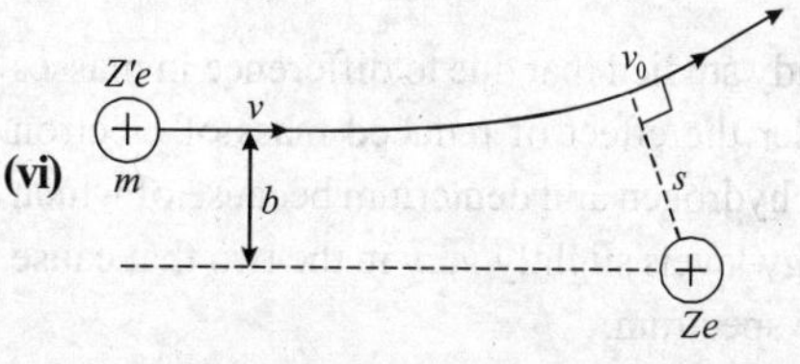

By angular momentum conservation we use

$$mvb = mv_0 s \quad \ldots(1)$$

by energy conservation we use

$$\frac{1}{2} mv^2 = \frac{1}{2} mv_0^2 + \frac{1}{4\pi\epsilon_0} \cdot \frac{ZZ'e^2}{s} \quad \ldots(2)$$

Substituting value of v_0 from (1) to (2) we get

$$\frac{1}{2}mv^2 = \frac{1}{2}m\left(\frac{vb}{s}\right)^2 + \frac{1}{4\pi\epsilon_0}\cdot\frac{ZZ'e^2}{s}$$

$$\Rightarrow \quad \frac{1}{2}mv^2\left(1-\frac{b^2}{s^2}\right) = \frac{1}{4\pi\epsilon_0}\cdot\frac{ZZ'e^2}{s}$$

For $b = 0$ we get

$$s = \frac{1}{4\pi\epsilon_0}\cdot\frac{2ZZ'e^2}{mv^2}$$

(vii) Using force on mass m is conservative field

$$F = -\frac{dU}{dr} = mb^2r$$

For circular orbit of particle

$$mb^2r = \frac{mv^2}{r} \quad \ldots(1)$$

and

$$mvr = \frac{nh}{2\pi} \quad \ldots(2)$$

$$\Rightarrow \quad m(br)r = \frac{nh}{2\pi}$$

$$\Rightarrow \quad r = \sqrt{\frac{nh}{2\pi mb}}$$

Solutions of CONCEPTUAL MCQS Single Option Correct

Sol. 1 (D) As energy in n^{th} Orbit of hydrogen atom is given as

$$E_n = -\frac{2\pi^2K^2Z^2e^4m}{h^2}\times\frac{Z^2}{n^2}$$

Hence option (D) is correct.

Sol. 2 (D) As radius of nth orbit of hydrogen atom is given as

$$r_n = \frac{h^2}{4\pi^2Ke^2m}\times\frac{n^2}{Z}$$

Hence option (D) is correct.

Sol. 3 (C) As already studied that due to difference in masses of nuclei we consider the effect of reduced mass of electron which is different in hydrogen and deuterium because of which energies of the energy levels slightly vary in the two that cause the difference in the spectrum.

Sol. 4 (B) The total energy of electron in hydrogen atom is given as

$$E_n = -\frac{1}{2}\frac{KZe^2}{r_n}$$

Hence option (B) is correct.

Sol. 5 (A) In Rydberg's formula the wave number is directly proportional to Z^2 and Balmer series of hydrogen atom is corresponding to the transition of electron from any level to $n = 2$. Shortest wave length for the spectrum of hydrogen like atom for transition to $n = 4$ level will be inversely proportional to n^2 and if it matches with that of the Balmer series of hydrogen atom then we use

$$\frac{Z^2}{n^2} = \frac{Z_H^2}{n_B^2}$$

$$\Rightarrow \quad Z^2 = \frac{1^2}{2^2}\times 4^2 = 4$$

$$\Rightarrow \quad Z = 2$$

Sol. 6 (B) Balmer series in the hydrogen atom has wavelength of most of its lines lying in the visible region of the electromagnetic spectrum and some are in infra red region.

Sol. 7 (A) It has already been discussed in theory that by the wave nature of electron and its De-Broglie wavelength we analyze for formation of stationary waves in an orbit the orbit circumference should be an integral multiple of the wavelength so for consistency of quantization postulate option (A) is correct.

Sol. 8 (D) Transition A is corresponding to infinity to $n = 1$ which is the last line (series limit) of Lyman series, transition B is from $n = 5$ to $n = 2$ which is third line of Balmer series and transition C is from $n = 5$ to $n = 3$ which is second line of Paschen series.

Sol. 9 (A) In lower energy levels kinetic energy is higher and potential energy and total energy is lesser hence option (A) is correct.

Sol. 10 (A) From conservation of momentum between the photon and the recoiling atom, we have

$$\vec{p}_H = |\vec{p}_{photon}|$$

$$\Rightarrow \quad \vec{p}_H = \frac{h}{\lambda} = hR\left(\frac{1}{1^2}-\frac{1}{2^2}\right) = \frac{3Rh}{4}$$

$$\Rightarrow \quad v_H = \frac{3Rh}{4M}$$

Sol. 11 (B) In Bohr's model the speed of the electron in n^{th} orbit is given as

$$v_n = \frac{2\pi Ke^2}{h}\times\frac{Z}{n}$$

Hence option (B) is correct.

Sol. 12 (C) We use

$$\frac{1}{4\pi \in_0} \frac{e^2}{a_0} = mv^2$$

$$\Rightarrow \qquad v = \frac{e}{\sqrt{4\pi \in_0 a_0 m}}$$

Sol. 13 (A) In n^{th} orbit maximum number of electrons can be $2n^2$ hence the possible electrons in energy levels 1, 2, 3 and 4 are 2, 8, 18 and 32 of which the sum is $2+8+18+32=60$. Hence option (A) is correct.

Sol. 14 (D) Because of the energy level differences in the hydrogen atom which explained that the energy level difference decreases as we go away from nucleus which explained the hydrogen spectrum which other models by that time couldn't explain hence option (D) is correct.

Sol. 15 (D) A quantum number gives the state of an electron in extranuclear part of an atom so according to Pauli's exclusion principle no two electrons can have same set of quantum numbers, hence option (D) is correct.

Sol. 16 (B) From the figure we can see that $\Delta E_3 = \Delta E_1 + \Delta E_2$ hence option (B) is correct as $\Delta E = hc/\lambda$.

Sol. 17 (D) At room temperature all atoms of hydrogen gas are in ground state in which only radiation of ultraviolet region can be absorbed to excite atoms from $n = 1$ to higher energy levels so visible light cannot excite any atom in ground state hence option (D) is correct.

Sol. 18 (A) The angular momentum of electron in hydrogen atom is quantized and according to Bohr's second postulate for n^{th} energy level it is given as $nh/2\pi$ so for two successive orbits option (A) is correct.

Sol. 19 (A) Hydrogen atoms at room temperature are in ground state and can only absorb radiation of ultraviolet region to excite from $n = 1$ to higher energy levels due to which in absorption spectrum of hydrogen gas only Lyman series is obtained hence option (A) is correct.

Sol. 20 (C) α-particle scattering occurs due to Coulomb repulsion of nucleus on incident α-particle hence option (C) is correct.

Sol. 21 (B) In any given orbit angular momentum of electrons are same as given by Bohr's second postulate and energies of electron in any hydrogen like ion is directly proportional to Z^2 hence option (B) is correct.

Sol. 22 (C) In case of electron we have studied that during collision it can transfer almost its complete energy to the particle it is colliding hence E_1 is the minimum required energy for ionization of hydrogen atom. In case of hydrogen and helium ion as helium is more massive than hydrogen it transfers less energy during inelastic collision compared to the case when hydrogen is colliding hence option (C) is correct.

Sol. 23 (A) The wavelength emitted is inversely proportional to the energy radiated hence option (A) is correct.

Sol. 24 (A) To excite the hydrogen atom the kinetic energy of neutron must be more than 20.4 eV so that in case of perfectly inelastic collision the energy loss which is half of the total kinetic energy (10.2 eV) may excite the hydrogen atom so in case if kinetic energy of neutron is less than 20.4 eV then collision must be perfectly elastic hence option (A) is correct.

Sol. 25 (C) As during de-excitation it is emitting six wavelengths that means the atom is excited to $n_2 = 4$ and the emitted energies have less, equal or more than the excitation energies then only option (C) can be correct.

Sol. 26 (B) Due to the effect of mass of nucleus we consider reduce mass of electron in analyzing the energies of energy levels of the atoms and due to this the binding energy of deuterium is more than that of hydrogen in ground state hence option (B) is correct. Bohr's model is valid for all one electron systems (hydrogen like) and some of the lines of Balmer series lie in infra red region thats why options (A) and (C) are not correct.

Sol. 27 (B) Balmer series is corresponding the de-excitation of electrons in hydrogen atom to $n = 2$ state hence option (B) is correct.

Sol. 28 (C) By using Rydberg's formula we can calculate the values of wavelengths emitted in above four cases and considering same value of Z for hydrogen and deuterium and will not consider the effect of nucleus as in given options we need to check for approximate relations, option (C) is correct.

Sol. 29 (B) As the total energy of electron in hydrogen atom is given as

$$E_n = -\frac{1}{2} \frac{KZe^2}{r_n}$$

hence option (B) is correct.

Sol. 30 (B) 12.1 eV is the difference in energies of $n = 1$ and $n = 3$ for hydrogen atom so the electron is excited to $n = 3$ state hence the angular momentum will become $3h/2\pi$ from $h/2\pi$ hence the increase in angular momentum is given in option (B).

Sol. 31 (A) In hydrogen atom the magnetic moment due to the motion of electron in n^{th} orbit is given as

$$M_n = \frac{enh}{4\pi m}$$

Hence option (A) is correct.

Solutions of NUMERICAL MCQS Single Option Correct

Sol. 1 (C) We use $\lambda = \dfrac{12431}{10.2} = 1218.72 \text{Å}$

Sol. 2 (A) We use

$$frL = \frac{v}{2\pi r} \times r \times \frac{nh}{2\pi} = \frac{nhv}{4\pi^2}$$

For Bohr's model we have

$$v = \frac{ke^2}{nh} \times 2\pi$$

$$\Rightarrow \quad frL = \frac{nh}{4\pi^2} \times \frac{ke^2}{nh} \times 2\pi = \frac{ke^2}{2\pi}$$

$$\Rightarrow \quad frL = \frac{ke^2}{2\pi} = \frac{ke^2 n^0}{2\pi} \Rightarrow x = 0$$

Sol. 3 (D) For first line of Balmer series

$$\frac{1}{\lambda} = R\left(\frac{1}{4} - \frac{1}{9}\right) = \frac{5R}{36} \quad \ldots(1)$$

For second line of Balmer series

$$\frac{1}{\lambda} = R\left(\frac{1}{4} - \frac{1}{16}\right) = \frac{3R}{16} \quad \ldots(2)$$

From equaion-(1) & (2)

$$\frac{\lambda'}{\lambda} = \frac{5/36}{3/16}$$

$$\Rightarrow \quad \lambda' = \frac{20}{27}\lambda$$

Sol. 4 (B) We know

$$[R] = L^{-1}$$

$$\Rightarrow \quad = \frac{1}{L} = \frac{1}{cT} = c^{-1} T^{-1}$$

Sol. 5 (D) All the transitions given in options (A), (B) and (C) give photons of energy more than by transition from $n = 4 \rightarrow 3$. Hence none of the transitions given in options (A), (B) and (C) give out infrared radiation.

Sol. 6 (C) First excitation energy of this atom is given as

$$\Rightarrow \quad eV = RhC\left(\frac{1}{1^2} - \frac{1}{2^2}\right) = \frac{3}{4} RhC$$

Thus ionization energy of this atom is

$$RhC = \frac{4V}{3}$$

Sol. 7 (A) As we have $E \propto \dfrac{Z^2}{n^2}$

$$\Rightarrow \quad \frac{E_{1H}}{E_{3Li}} = \frac{(1/1)^2}{(3/3)^2}$$

$$\Rightarrow \quad E_{3Li} = E_{1H} = E$$

Sol. 8 (B) First line of Lyman series

$$\lambda_1 = \frac{12431}{10.2} = 1218.7 \text{ Å}$$

Last time of Lyman series

$$\lambda_L = \frac{12431}{13.6} = 914 \text{ Å}$$

Hence option (B) is correct.

Sol. 9 (D) velocity of nth orbit is inversely proportional to n hence the excited state orbit is $n = 3$ and radius of nth orbit is directly proportional to square of n hence option (D) is correct.

Sol. 10 (B) We use $\lambda = \dfrac{h}{p} = \dfrac{h}{\sqrt{2mE}} \Rightarrow \dfrac{h}{\sqrt{2m(Vq)}}$

Thus for higher value of m and q; λ will be smaller and for an 'α' particle; both 'm' and 'q' are higher hence lesser is the wavelength.

As, we known (penetrating power) ∝ Energy ∝ $\dfrac{1}{\lambda}$

From above; penetrating power of an α-particle is more than that of a proton, hence option (B) is correct.

Sol. 11 (B) Time period of revolution is directly proportional to n^3 hence option (B) is correct.

Sol. 12 (C) Radius of nth orbit is proportional to n^2 hence the radius of first excited state ($n = 2$) will be four times that of the ground state hence its area will be 16 times that of ground state.

Sol. 13 (B) We use $\dfrac{1}{\lambda} = R\left(\dfrac{1}{16} - \dfrac{1}{n^2}\right) = \dfrac{9}{400}R$

Solving we get $n = 5$.

Sol. 14 (C) By the incident radiation electron will excite to $n = 3$ from which during de-excitation number of spectral lines will be ${}^3C_2 = 3$ lines.

Sol. 15 (B) Speed of electron is inversely proportional to n so for excitation from $n = 1$ to $n = 2$ the velocity will reduce to half.

Sol. 16 (D) After removal of one electron it becomes one electron system from which energy required to remove the second electron will be $13.6(2)^2 = 54.4$ eV so total energy required to remove both electrons will be $54.4 + 24.6 = 79.0$ eV.

Sol. 17 (B) The H like atom is in the third excited state i.e. $n = 4$.

$\Rightarrow$ Energy corresponding to this wave length

$$= \frac{12431 \times 51}{62000} = 10.2 \text{ eV}$$

This is the $E_2 - E_1$ for H and $E_4 - E_2$ for He^+

We get $Z = 2$ for $4 \rightarrow 2$ radiation

Hence the atom is Helium ion.

Sol. 18 (B) Let u be the speed of neutron before collision

m →u 4m

At end of the deformation phase (when the kinetic energy of (neutron + He^+) system is least)

m →u_{cm} 4m →u_{cm}

Where u_{cm} is velocity of centre of mass. From conservation of momentum

$$u_{cm} = \frac{mu}{m + 4m} = \frac{u}{5}$$

The loss of kinetic energy

$$\Delta K = \frac{1}{2}\text{mu}^2 - \frac{1}{2}\text{m}\left(\frac{u}{5}\right)^2 - \frac{1}{2}\,4\text{m}\left(\frac{u}{5}\right)^2$$

$$\Rightarrow \quad \Delta K = \frac{4}{5}\left(\frac{1}{2}mu^2\right)$$

It K is the kinetic energy of neutron then the maximum loss in K.E. of system is

$$\frac{4}{5}K = 12.75 \times 4 = 51 \text{ eV}$$

or $$K = \frac{51 \times 5}{4} = 63.75 \text{ eV}$$

Sol. 19 (D) For equilibrium of oil drop

$$3.2 \times 10^{-M} \times 10 = (\text{N} \times 1.6 \times 10^{-19}) \times \frac{1200}{6 \times 10^{-3}}$$

$$\Rightarrow \quad N = 10$$

Sol. 20 (D) We use

$$47.2 = 1.89\,Z^2$$

$$\Rightarrow \quad Z = 5$$

Sol. 21 (B)

H-atom ← ● E_1 (Case-I)

H-atom → ● E_2 (Case-II)

In the first case K.E. of H-atom increases due to recoil whereas in the second case K.E. decreases due to recoil

$$\Rightarrow \quad E_2 > E_1$$

Sol. 22 (A) Linear momentum $\Rightarrow mv \,\alpha\, \frac{1}{n}$

and angular momentum $\Rightarrow mvr \,\alpha\, n$

$\Rightarrow$ Product of linear momentum and angular momentum $\alpha\, n^0$.

Sol. 23 (C) For a Bohr atom velocity is proportional to Z/n hence option (C) is correct.

Sol. 24 (D) We use the concept of reduced mass so we have

$$\frac{Ke^2}{r^2} = \frac{m}{2}\omega^2 r \quad \ldots(1)$$

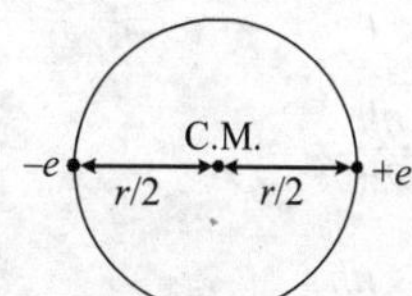

and $$\frac{m}{2}(\omega r) r = \frac{nh}{2\pi} \quad \ldots(2)$$

By (1) and (2) $$r = \frac{n^2h^2}{2\pi^2 mKe^2} = \left(\frac{n^2h^2}{4\pi^2 mKe^2}\right) \times 2$$

$$\Rightarrow \quad r = (0.529 \text{ Å}) \times 2n^2$$

For first excited state $n = 2$

$$\Rightarrow \quad r = 8 \times 0.529 \text{ Å}$$

$$\Rightarrow \quad r = 4.232 \text{ Å}$$

Sol. 25 (B) We use, kinetic energy $= \frac{1}{2}\text{m}\left(\omega\frac{r}{2}\right)^2$

$$\Rightarrow \quad K = \frac{1}{2} \cdot \frac{m \cdot \omega^2 r^2}{4} = \frac{Ke^2}{4r}$$

$$\Rightarrow \quad K = \frac{Ke^2}{4 \times (0.529 \text{Å} \times 2)} = \frac{13.6eV}{4} = 3.4 \text{ eV}$$

Sol. 26 (C) We use $\frac{1}{\lambda}=R\left(\frac{1}{1}-\frac{1}{n^2}\right)$

$$\Rightarrow \quad \frac{1}{\lambda R}=\frac{n^2-1}{n^2}$$

$$\Rightarrow \quad n^2=(n^2-1)\lambda R$$

$$\Rightarrow \quad n^2=\frac{\lambda R}{\lambda R-1}$$

$$\Rightarrow \quad n=\sqrt{\frac{\lambda R}{\lambda R-1}}$$

Sol. 27 (C) Energy of electron in hydrogen atom in n^{th} state is inversely proportional to n^2 hence option (C) is correct.

Sol. 28 (A) To get six spectral lines electron must be excited to $n = 4$ from $n = 1$ for which photon energy needed is 12.75 eV of which wavelength is given as

$$\lambda=\frac{12431}{12.75}=975\text{Å}$$

Sol. 29 (C) The maximum energy difference is for $n = 2$ to $n = 1$ hence option (C) is correct.

Sol. 30 (B) We use

$$\frac{GmM_P}{r^2}=\frac{mv^2}{r} \quad \ldots(1)$$

and
$$mvr=\frac{nh}{2\pi} \quad \ldots(2)$$

$$\Rightarrow \quad v=\frac{nh}{2\pi mr}$$

From (1) we have

$$\frac{GmM_P}{r}=m\left(\frac{nh}{2\pi mr}\right)^2$$

$$\Rightarrow \quad r=\frac{n^2h^2}{4\pi^2Gm^2M_P}$$

Sol. 31 (C) Radius of nth orbit is proportional to n^2 hence option (C) is correct.

Sol. 32 (D) Energy of nth sate in Hydrogen is same as energy of $3n^{th}$ state in Li^{++}

$\Rightarrow$ For $3 \rightarrow 1$ transition in H would it give same energy as the $3\times3 \rightarrow 1\times3$ transition in Li^{++}.

Sol. 33 (C) Total momentum of system is O hence maximum possible energy loss can be 10.5 eV out of which 10.2 eV can be absorbed hence option (C) is correct.

For completely inelastic collision both come to rest after collision and net energy of $4E + E = 10.5$ eV is lost. But electron in ground state of H-atom can accept only an energy of 10.2 eV. Hence the collision may be inelastic but it can never be perfectly inelastic.

Sol. 34 (B) Momentum of photon is given as

$$p=\frac{h}{\lambda}=\frac{h\nu}{c}=\frac{E}{c}$$

$$\Rightarrow \quad p=\frac{\left(13.6-\frac{13.6}{3^2}\right)\times1.6\times10^{-19}}{3\times10^8}$$

$$\Rightarrow \quad p=6.45\times10^{-27}\text{ kg m/s}$$

Sol. 35 (D) As the electron returns to ground state after emitting six different wavelengths in emission spectrum, there must be a difference of '2' between the ground and excited states. Also the ground state should be $n = 2$.

Hence $n_1 = 4$, $n_2 = 2$.

Sol. 36 (B) Longest wavelength corresponding to the transition from $n = 2$ to $n = 1$ for which we use

$$\frac{1}{\lambda}=4RZ^2\left(\frac{1}{1}-\frac{1}{4}\right)$$

$$\Rightarrow \quad \lambda=\frac{1}{3RZ^2}$$

Sol. 37 (D) For 2nd line of Balmer series in hydrogen spectrum

$$\frac{1}{\lambda}=R(1)\left(\frac{1}{2^2}-\frac{1}{4^2}\right)=\frac{3}{16}R$$

For Li^{2+}

Which is satisfied by only (D).

Sol. 38 (B) We use force on electron

$$F=\frac{dU}{dr}=Kr=\frac{mv^2}{r}$$

$$\Rightarrow \quad mv^2=Kr^2$$

and
$$mvr=\frac{rh}{2\pi}$$

$$mr\left(\sqrt{\frac{K}{m}}r\right)=\frac{nh}{2\pi}$$

$$\Rightarrow \quad r=\sqrt{\frac{nh}{2\pi\sqrt{Km}}}$$

Energy of nth orbit is

$$E_n=\frac{Kr^2}{2}+\frac{Kr^2}{2}=Kr^2$$

$$\Rightarrow \quad E_n=\frac{Knh}{2\pi\sqrt{Km}}=\frac{nh}{2\pi}\sqrt{\frac{K}{m}}$$

Sol. 39 (D) We use

$$\nu_1 = \frac{E_2 - E_1}{h} \quad \nu_2 = \frac{E_3 - E_1}{h};$$

$$\Rightarrow \quad \nu_2 - \nu_1 = \frac{E_3 - E_2}{h} = \nu_3$$

As $\nu_1 = k\nu_2$;

$$\Rightarrow \quad \nu_3 = \nu_2(1-k) = \left(\frac{1}{k} - 1\right)\nu_1$$

Hence the only incorrect option is $\nu = k^2\nu_2$.

Sol. 40 (D) The wavelength emitted in the first transition of electron from third excited state to the second excited state is calculated by Rydberg's formula, given as

$$\frac{1}{\lambda} = R\left(\frac{1}{n_f^2} - \frac{1}{n_i^2}\right)$$

Using $n_f = 4$ and $n_i = 3$, we have

$$\frac{1}{\lambda_1} = R\left(\frac{1}{3^2} - \frac{1}{4^2}\right)$$

$$\Rightarrow \quad \frac{1}{\lambda_1} = R\left(\frac{7}{9\times 16}\right) \quad \ldots(1)$$

For the second transition from second excited state to first excited state, we use $n_f = 3$ and $n_i = 2$, which gives

$$\frac{1}{\lambda_2} = R\left(\frac{1}{2^2} - \frac{1}{3^2}\right)$$

$$\Rightarrow \quad \frac{1}{\lambda_2} = R\left(\frac{5}{4\times 9}\right) \quad \ldots(2)$$

Dividing equation-(2) by (1) gives

$$\frac{\lambda_1}{\lambda_2} = \frac{\frac{5}{36}}{\frac{7}{9\times 16}} = \frac{20}{7}$$

Sol. 41 (B) Maximum energy of radiation incident on H-sample $= KE_{max}$ of electron + 13.6 eV = 51 eV this energy corresponds to the transition $n = 4 \rightarrow n = 1$ in Helium

For electrons of the He to get excited to $n = 4$

$$\lambda = \frac{12431}{51} = 243 \text{ Å}$$

Sol. 42 (A) For lower value of n the energy and hence the frequency is higher. Hence (A)

Sol. 43 (D) In the process of collision, the electron (because of very low mass in comparison to hydrogen atom) can loose upto 10 eV. 10 eV is sufficient to ionise the hydrogen atom or excite to higher excited state from first excited state.

Hence, the collision can be elastic, inelastic or perfectly inelastic.

Sol. 44 (A) Potential energy = 2 Total energy

$$\Rightarrow \quad = 2\times -21.76\times 10^{-19}$$

$$\Rightarrow \quad = -43.52\times 10^{-19}\text{ J}$$

Sol. 45 (C) The photon's with energies equal to that required for upward transition $A \rightarrow X$, $A \rightarrow B$ and $A \rightarrow C$ would be absorbed, hence only lines 1, 2 and 3 will be present in absorption spectrum.

Sol. 46 (A) Doubly ionised positively lithium ion is a hydrogen like atom so we use

$$L = mvr = \frac{nh}{2\pi}$$

Also for both $n = 1$ we have

$$L_1 = L_2 = \frac{h}{2\pi}$$

Hence option (A) is correct.

Sol. 47 (D) First line of Lyman series wavelength is

$$\lambda_1 = \frac{12431}{10.2} \text{ Å}$$

First time of Paschen series wavelength is

$$\lambda_2 = \frac{12431}{0.66} \text{ Å}$$

$$\Rightarrow \quad \frac{\lambda_1}{\lambda_2} = \frac{0.66}{10.2} = \frac{7}{108}$$

Sol. 48 (C) $\Delta E \propto Z^2$

Thus it is maximum for Li^{++} and minimum for H.

Sol. 49 (A) As radius of nth orbit is inversely proportional to the mass of electron for mesonic atom we use reduced mass of electron as

$$\mu = \frac{m_P(207m_e)}{m_p + 207m_e}$$

As $m_p = 1840\, m_e$

$$\Rightarrow \quad \mu = \frac{1840\times 207}{1840 + 207}\cdot m_e$$

$$\Rightarrow \quad \mu = 186\, m_e$$

Thus radius of first orbit of mesonic atom is

$$r = \frac{0.53\times 10^{-10}}{186} = 2.85\times 10^{-13}\text{ m}$$

ADVANCE MCQs One or More Options Correct

Sol. 1 (All) The potential energy in ground state is – 27.2 eV and that in first excited state is – 6.8 eV so the potential energy of first excited state is 20.4 eV higher than that of ground state so option (A) is correct. The kinetic energy of electron in first excited state is 3.4 eV so total energy becomes 23.8 eV hence options (B) and (C) are correct. In ground state total energy will be the kinetic energy which is 13.6 eV so option (D) is also correct.

Sol. 2 (B, C) In higher energy level Kinetic energy decreases hence speed or angular speed also decreases.

Sol. 3 (B, C) Energy required to excite the electron from second to third Bohr orbit is calculated as

$$\Delta E = 13.6Z^2\left(\frac{1}{n_1^2} - \frac{1}{n_2^2}\right)$$

$$\Rightarrow \quad 47.2 = 13.6Z^2\left(\frac{1}{2^2} - \frac{1}{3^2}\right)$$

$$\Rightarrow \quad Z = 5$$

Hence options (A) and (D) are NOT correct. The energy required to excite the electron from third to fourth Bohr orbit can be calculated as

$$\Delta E = 13.6 \times (5)^2\left(\frac{1}{3^2} - \frac{1}{4^2}\right) = 16{,}53 \text{ eV}$$

Hence option (B) is correct. Wavelength λ corresponding to first ionization energy of this element is for removing electron from first orbit to infinity, this is calculated as

$$\frac{hc}{\lambda} = 13.6Z^2$$

$$\Rightarrow \quad \lambda = \frac{hc}{13.6Z^2}$$

$$\Rightarrow \quad \lambda = \frac{6.626 \times 10^{-34} \times 3 \times 10^8}{13.6 \times 1.6 \times 10^{-19} \times (5)^2}$$

$$\Rightarrow \quad \lambda = 3.65 \text{ nm}$$

Hence option (C) is correct.

Sol. 4 (A, C, D) Wavelengths emitted in the two cases are

$$\lambda_{21} = \frac{\lambda_{32}}{\lambda_{21}} \text{ and } l_{32} = \frac{12431}{1.89eV}$$

$$\Rightarrow \quad a = \frac{\lambda_{32}}{\lambda_{21}} = \frac{10.2}{1.89} = \frac{27}{5}$$

Momentum ratio of photons is

$$b = \frac{\lambda/\lambda_{32}}{\lambda/\lambda_{21}} = \frac{5}{27}$$

Energy ratio of photons is

$$c = \frac{hc/\lambda_{32}}{hc/\lambda_{21}} = \frac{5}{27} = \frac{1}{a}$$

Hence options (A), (C) and (D) are correct.

Sol. 5 (All) Energy of electron in n^{th} orbit is

$$E = -\frac{2\pi^2 K^2 Z^2 e^4 m_e}{n^2 h^2}$$

Momentum of electron in n^{th} orbit is

$$P = mV_n = \frac{nh}{2\pi r}$$

where r is given as

$$r = \frac{n^2 h^2}{2\pi K Z e^2 m_e}$$

from above relations all options (A), (B), (C) and (D) are correct.

Sol. 6 (A, D) We use $\Delta E_3 = \Delta E_1 + \Delta E_2$

$$h\nu_3 = h\nu_1 + h\nu_2$$

$$\Rightarrow \quad \nu_3 = \nu_1 + \nu_2$$

$$\Rightarrow \quad \frac{c}{\lambda_3} = \frac{c}{\lambda_1} + \frac{c}{\lambda_2}$$

$$\Rightarrow \quad \lambda_3 = \frac{\lambda_1 \lambda_2}{\lambda_1 + \lambda_2}$$

Hence option (A) and (D) are correct.

Sol. 7 (A, D) Energy of He^+ ion is $Z^2 = 4$ times that of hydrogen atom for a given orbit so all transitions where square of n_2 and n_1 is a multiple of 4 for He^+ ion, it will match with some transition of hydrogen atom hence option (A) and (D) are correct.

Sol. 8 (A, C) From Bohr's Model we have

$$R = \frac{n^2 h^2}{2\pi^2 K Z e^2 m}$$

$$V = \frac{2\pi K Z e^2}{rh}$$

$$E = \frac{2\pi^2 K^2 Z^2 e^4 m}{n^2 h^2}$$

Hence option (A) and (C) are correct.

Sol. 9 (B, C) Any orbit the angular momentum of electron is an integral multiple of $h/2\pi$ so for any transition it can change by a factor integral multiple of $h/2\pi$ hence options (B) and (C) are correct.

Sol. 10 (A, C, D) In radiation *A* incident beam passes from which some of the wavelengths will be absorbed by the hydrogen gas hence option (A) is correct. Due to absorption of ultraviolet radiation electrons get excited and during reverse transition different spectral series of hydrogen atom are emitted in radiation *B* hence option (C) and (D) are correct.

Sol. 11 (B, C) Whenever a photon is emitted in Balmer series, it will be corresponding to the transition of electron to $n = 2$ state from where it will further transit to ground state and emit a line corresponding to the transition of $n = 2$ to $n = 1$ in Lyman series of which the wavelength can be given as $\lambda = 12431/10.2\text{ eV} \approx 122\text{ nm}$ hence options (B) and (C) are correct.

Sol. 12 (A, C) It is already been studied in spectral series of hydrogen atom that some of the lines of Balmer series are also lying outside the visible region hence options (A) and (C) are correct.

Sol. 13 (A, B, D) The ionization potential of this Hydrogen like atom is calculated as

$$IE = 13.6Z^2 = 54.4\text{ eV}$$

$$\Rightarrow \quad Z = 2$$

Hence option (B) is correct. The excitation energy of a Hydrogen like atom for first excitation is calculated as

$$\Delta E = 13.6Z^2\left[1 - \frac{1}{2^2}\right]\text{eV}$$

$$\Rightarrow \quad \Delta E = 13.6 \times 4 \times \frac{3}{4} = 40.8\text{ eV}$$

Hence option (A) is correct. An atom can only absorb a photon of energy more than or equal to that of its ionization energy or if the photon energy is equal to the difference between two energy levels of the atom in which in lower level there is an electron available for transition by absorption. In this case it is clear that by absorbing a photon of energy 56 eV, out of this 54.4 eV will be consumed as ionization energy and the electron will come out of atom with some kinetic energy equal to the remaining energy and 50 eV photon cannot be absorbed.

Sol. 14 (A, B, C) As we know

$$r_n \propto n^2$$

$$\Rightarrow \quad A_n \propto n^4$$

and $$f_n \propto \frac{1}{n^3}$$

$$\Rightarrow \quad T_b \propto n^3$$

$$\Rightarrow \quad \frac{r_n}{r_4} = n^2; \quad \frac{A_n}{A_1} = n^4; \quad \frac{f_n}{f_1} = \frac{1}{n^3}$$

Thus options (A), (B) and (C) are correct.

Sol. 15 (A, B) Energy, linear momentum and angular frequency of electron in Bohr's orbit are related to energy level *n* as

$E \propto \frac{1}{n^2}$, $P \propto \frac{1}{n}$ & $\omega \propto \frac{1}{n^3}$ so options (A) and (B) are correct.

Sol. 16 (B) Due to quantum nature, photon is absorbed only if its energy is equal to any of the transition energies other wise it will not be absorbed hence option (B) is correct.

Sol. 17 (B, C, D) With the standard data for kinetic energy, potential energy and angular momentum we can see that options (B), (C) and (D) are correct.

Sol. 18 (B, D) We use the given potential energy for calculation of force electron as

$$F = \frac{dU}{dr} = \frac{3}{2}\frac{Ke^2}{r^4}$$

$$\Rightarrow \quad KE\ \frac{1}{2}mv^2 = \frac{3}{4}\frac{Ke^2}{r^3}$$

Using Bohr's II Postulate $mvr = \frac{nh}{2\pi}$ we get

$$m\left(\frac{nh}{2\pi mr}\right)^2 = \frac{3}{2}\frac{Ke^2}{2\pi}$$

$$\Rightarrow \quad r \propto \frac{1}{n^2}$$

and $$r \propto m$$

Hence option (B) and (D) are correct as energy is inversely proportional to r^3.

Sol. 19 (A, B, C) For a hydrogen atom in second orbit the total energy of electron is – 3.4 eV hence options (A), (B) and (C) are correct.

Sol. 20 (C, D) As we know that radius of nth orbit $r_n \propto 1/Z$, velocity of electron in n^{th} orbit $v_n \propto Z$ and energy of electron in n^{th} orbit $E_n \propto Z^2$ so options (C) and (D) are correct.

Sol. 21 (A, B) Using the Rydberg's Formula for the given transition

$$\frac{1}{\lambda_0} = R\left[\frac{1}{1^2} - \frac{1}{n^2}\right]$$

Solving we get $n = 4$. Thus electron can come to ground state by emitting two or three photons such that the sum of energies of each transition remain same so we can use

$$\frac{hc}{\lambda_0} = \frac{hc}{\lambda_1} + \frac{hc}{\lambda_2}$$

$$\Rightarrow \quad \frac{1}{\lambda_0} = \frac{1}{\lambda_1} + \frac{1}{\lambda_2}$$

and
$$\frac{hc}{\lambda_0} = \frac{hc}{\lambda_1} + \frac{hc}{\lambda_2} + \frac{hc}{\lambda_3}$$

$$\Rightarrow \quad \frac{1}{\lambda_0} = \frac{1}{\lambda_1} + \frac{1}{\lambda_2} + \frac{1}{\lambda_3}$$

Hence options (A) and (B) are correct.

Sol. 22 (A, B, C) If the mass of striking particle is considered to be n times of mass of He^+ i.e. their masses are taken as m and nm. Before and after collision we consider p_1 and p_2 to be magnitude of momentum of particle P and p be the momentum of He^+ after collision. The collision is shown in figure below.

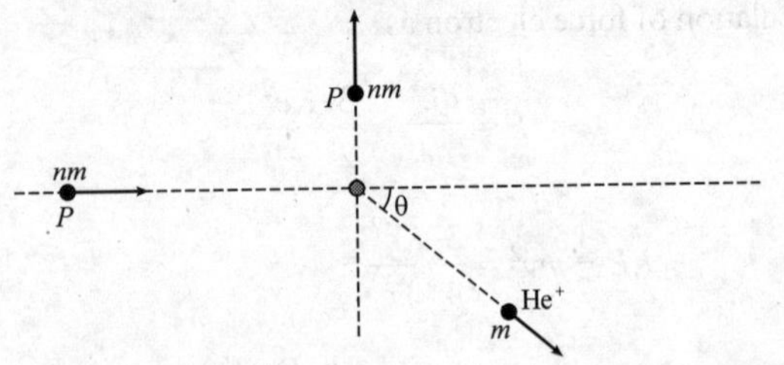

By conservation of momentum in above case, we have along x and y direction

$$p_1 = p\cos\theta$$

and
$$p_2 = p\sin\theta$$

It is specified in the question that kinetic energy of particle P and He^+ are equal after collision, so we can use

$$\frac{p_2^2}{2nm} = \frac{p^2}{2m}$$

$$\Rightarrow \quad p_2 = \sqrt{n}\,p$$

$$\Rightarrow \quad \sin\theta = \sqrt{n}$$

$$\Rightarrow \quad \cos\theta = \sqrt{1-n}$$

As some energy from the incident particle is being absorbed by the helium for excitation, the collision is inelastic so we use

$$\frac{p_1^2}{2nm} > 2\left(\frac{p^2}{2m}\right)$$

$$\Rightarrow \quad \frac{p^2\cos^2\theta}{2nm} > 2\left(\frac{p^2}{2m}\right)$$

$$\Rightarrow \quad \frac{p^2(1-n)}{2n} > p^2$$

$$\Rightarrow \quad 1-n > 2n$$

$$\Rightarrow \quad n < \frac{1}{3}$$

This means particle P is lighter than one third the weight of helium hence option (A) and (B) are correct.

As it is given that helium emits six radiations, means it gets excited to $n = 4$. Out of all the six radiations the transition corresponding to $n = 4$ to $n = 3$ will emit a photon of energy 2.64 eV which corresponds to wavelength 470.9 nm and it falls in visible region hence option (C) is correct.

Sol. 23 (A, C, D) Binding energy of hydrogen like atom is given as

$$E = -13.6\,\frac{Z^2}{n^2} = -122.4\text{ eV}$$

For $n = 1$ we get $Z = 3$ so option (A) is correct.

Excitation energy of this hydrogen like atom for excitation from $n = 1$ to $n = 2$ is given as

$$\Delta E_{12} = 10.2\,Z^2 = 10.2 \times 9 = 91.8\text{ eV}$$

Thus option (C) is correct.

When an electron of 125 eV collides with this atom, 122.4 eV energy is absorbed by the atom for ionization of electron and remaining energy 2.6 eV will get converged to kinetic energy of the ejected electron hence option (D) is correct.

Sol. 24 (A, C, D) For the given positronium atom Bohr model can be applied as explained in section-1.8. Here the reduced mass of revolving electron around positron in frame of positron is given as

$$\mu = \frac{m \times m}{m+m} = \frac{m}{2}$$

If Bohr model is applicable then the expressions of Rydberg's constant for positronium is written as

$$R_p = \frac{2\pi^2 K^2 e^4 \mu}{ch^3}$$

As $\mu = m/2$, we use

$$R_p = \frac{R_H}{2}$$

Hence option (A) is correct. The ionization energy of positronium is written as

$$IE_p = \frac{2\pi^2 K^2 e^4 \mu}{h^2}$$

As $\mu = m/2$, we use

$$IE_p = \frac{IE_H}{2}$$

Hence option (B) is NOT correct. The radius of orbit for positronium is written as

$$r_p = \frac{h^2}{4\pi^2 Ke^2\mu}$$

As $\mu = m/2$, we use

$$r_p = 2r_H$$

Hence option (C) is correct. The speed of revolving electron in the frame of positron will be same as that of H-atom because expression of speed doesn't depend on mass of revolving particle. But in the frame of centre of mass of positronium the radius of orbit of electron will be reduced to half so for same angular speed of motion, in this frame the speed of electron will be reduced to half due to which the kinetic energy of electron in this frame will become one fourth hence option (D) is correct.

Sol. 25 (B) On changing the reference potential energy in ground state to be zero, this will not affect the variation of energy with the energy levels as well as the difference in energies of any energy levels so total energy increases with higher energy levels hence statement given in option (B) is incorrect.

Sol. 26 (A, C) As discussed in the basic theory the affect of mass of nucleus is accounted by considering the reduced mass of electron in the orbital motion. So considering the effect of reduced mass in the expressions of radius and energy we can state that option (A) and (C) are correct.

Sol. 27 (A, C) For inelastic collisions the maximum possible energy loss in a collision should be more than the minimum energy required for excitation of any of the colliding atoms which in this case is 10.2 eV for hydrogen atom. As the hydrogen atom and neutron are of same mass, maximum kinetic energy loss can be the half of initial kinetic energy of the colliding particle hence in above case initial kinetic energy must be more than or equal to 20.4 eV for inelastic collision hence options (A) and (C) are correct.

Sol. 28 (A, B, D) For Balmer series,

$n_1 = 2, \quad n_2 = 3, 4, \ldots$

(lower) (higher)

In transition (VI), Photon of Balmer series is absorbed

In transition II

$$E_2 = -3.4\text{ eV}, E_4 = -0.85\text{ eV}$$

$$\Delta E = 2.55\text{ eV}$$

$$\Delta E = \frac{hc}{\lambda} \Rightarrow \lambda = \frac{hc}{\Delta E}$$

$$\Rightarrow \quad \lambda = 486\text{ nm}$$

Wavelength of radiation = 103 nm = 1030 Å

$$\Delta E = \frac{12400}{1030\text{Å}}$$

$$\Rightarrow \quad \Delta E \simeq 12.0\text{ eV}$$

So difference of energy should be 12.0 eV (approx)

Hence $n_1 = 1$ and $n_2 = 3$

(– 13.6) eV (– 1.51) eV

For longest wavelength, energy difference should be minimum. So in visible portion of hydrogen atom, minimum energy emitted is in transition IV.

Sol. 29 (A, D) The hydrogen atom is in $n = 5$ state

Thus maximum number of possible photons = $^5C_2 = 10$

To emit photon in ultra violet region, it must jump to $n = 1$, because only Lyman series lies in *UV* region. Once it jumps to $n = 1$ photon, it reaches to its ground state and no more photons can be emitted. So only one photon in u. v. range can be emitted. If H-atom emits a photon and then another photon of Balmer series, option *D* will be correct.

Sol. 30 (B, D) Any fraction of incident electron energy can be absorbed by the atom hence minimum energy required for excitation is 10.2 eV hence option (B) and (D) are correct.

* * * * *

ANSWERS & SOLUTIONS

CONCEPTUAL MCQS Single Option Correct

1	(D)	2	(A)	3	(D)
4	(D)	5	(B)	6	(A)
7	(D)	8	(A)	9	(B)
10	(A)	11	(D)	12	(A)
13	(B)	14	(A)	15	(C)
16	(C)	17	(D)	18	(A)
19	(A)	20	(C)	21	(D)
22	(D)	23	(C)	24	(C)
25	(C)	26	(A)	27	(C)
28	(B)	29	(C)	30	(B)
31	(C)	32	(D)	33	(C)
34	(A)	35	(D)	36	(D)
37	(B)	38	(D)	39	(B)
40	(B)	41	(A)	42	(D)
43	(D)				

NUMERICAL MCQS Single Option Correct

1	(B)	2	(A)	3	(B)
4	(B)	5	(B)	6	(B)
7	(D)	8	(B)	9	(D)
10	(C)	11	(C)	12	(C)
13	(D)	14	(B)	15	(C)
16	(A)	17	(D)	18	(A)
19	(C)	20	(A)	21	(D)
22	(B)	23	(A)	24	(B)
25	(B)	26	(C)	27	(B)
28	(B)	29	(A)	30	(A)
31	(C)	32	(A)	33	(D)
34	(A)	35	(C)	36	(A)
37	(B)	38	(A)	39	(C)
40	(B)	41	(B)	42	(A)
43	(D)	44	(A)	45	(B)
46	(B)	47	(D)	48	(A)
49	(C)	50	(A)	51	(B)
52	(D)	53	(B)	54	(A)
55	(B)	56	(A)	57	(C)
58	(B)	59	(C)	60	(A)

ADVANCE MCQs One or More Options Correct

1	(B, D)	2	(B)	3	(B)
4	(A, C)	5	(A, C)	6	(B, C)
7	(All)	8	(B)	9	(A, D)
10	(B, C)	11	(A, B, C)	12	(B, C)
13	(B, D)	14	(B)	15	(A, C)
16	(A, B, C)	17	(A, C)	18	(All)
19	(A)	20	(C)	21	(C)
22	(A, B, C)	23	(A, B)	24	(B, D)
25	(A, D)	26	(B, D)	27	(A, B, C)
28	(A, D)				

Solutions of PRACTICE EXERCISE 2.1

(i) Incident photon energy $E=\dfrac{12431}{4800}=2.59$ eV

$\Rightarrow\ KE_{max}=E-\phi=2.59-2.30=0.29$ eV

Threshold wavelength $\lambda=\dfrac{12431}{2.30}=5404.78$ Å

(ii) We use $\dfrac{hc}{\lambda}=\phi+KE_{max}$

$$\Rightarrow\quad \frac{h\times 3\times 10^8}{3310\times 10^{-10}}=\phi+3\times 10^{-19} \quad \ldots(1)$$

$$\text{and}\quad \frac{h\times 3\times 10^8}{5000\times 10^{-10}}=\phi+0.97\times 10^{-19} \quad \ldots(2)$$

Solving (1) and (2) we get

$$h\times 3\times 10^{18}\left[\frac{1}{3310}-\frac{1}{5000}\right]=2.03\times 10^{-19}$$

$$\Rightarrow\ h=\frac{2.03\times 10^{-19}}{3.06\times 10^{14}}=6.634\times 10^{-34}\text{ J-s}$$

and $\phi=3.01\times 10^{-19}$ J

$$=\frac{3.01\times 10^{-19}}{1.6\times 10^{-19}}\text{ eV}$$

$$=1.88\text{ eV}$$

(iii) $KE_{max}=10.4$ eV

$\Rightarrow$ Incident photon energy is $E=\phi+KE_{max}$

$$=1.7+10.4$$

$$=12.1\text{ eV}$$

Incident wavelength $\lambda=\dfrac{12431}{12.1}=1027.35$ Å

Energy gap 12.1 eV is corresponding to $n=3$ to $n=1$ energy level transition in hydrogen atom.

(iv)

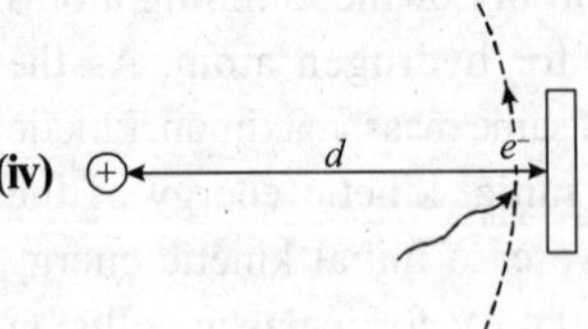

For circular motion of electrons around the ion we use

$$\frac{1}{4\pi\epsilon_0}\cdot\frac{e^2}{d^2}=\frac{mv^2}{d}$$

$$\Rightarrow\quad \frac{e^2}{8\pi\epsilon_0 d}=\frac{1}{2}mv^2=\frac{hc}{\lambda}-\phi$$

$$\Rightarrow\quad \lambda=\frac{8\pi\epsilon_0\, dhc}{e^2+8\pi\epsilon_0\,\phi d}$$

(v) (a) To ionize H-atom kinetic energy of photoelectrons must be atleast 13.6 eV

$$\Rightarrow \quad \frac{12431}{\lambda} = 1.7 + 13.6$$

$$\Rightarrow \quad \lambda = \frac{12431}{15.3} = 812.48\ \text{Å}$$

(b) To excite H-atom from $n = 1$ to $n = 2$ kinetic energy of photoelectrons must be atleast 10.2 eV

$$\Rightarrow \quad \frac{12431}{\lambda} = 1.7 + 10.2$$

$$\Rightarrow \quad \lambda = \frac{12431}{11.9} = 1044.62\ \text{Å}$$

(c) To emit visible light H-atom must be excited atleast from $n = 1$ to $n = 3$ so that in Balmer series it can emit visible light thus kinetic energy of photoelectrons must be atleast 12.09 eV

$$\Rightarrow \quad \frac{12431}{\lambda} = 1.7 + 12.09$$

$$\Rightarrow \quad \lambda = \frac{12431}{13.79} = 901.45\ \text{Å}$$

(iv) Initially we use

$$h\nu = \phi + 13.6\,\text{eV} \quad \ldots(1)$$

Later we use

$$h\left(\frac{5\nu}{6}\right) = \phi + \frac{12431}{1218}\,\text{eV} = \phi + 10.2\,\text{eV} \ldots (2)$$

Using (1) – (2), gives

$$\Rightarrow \quad \frac{h\nu}{6} = 3.4$$

$$\Rightarrow \quad \nu = \frac{3.4 \times 6 \times 1.6 \times 10^{-19}}{6.63 \times 10^{-34}}$$

$$= 4.923 \times 10^{15}\ \text{Hz}$$

From (1) we get

$$\phi = h\nu - 13.6\ \text{eV}$$

$$\Rightarrow \quad \phi = ((6.63 \times 10^{-34} \times 4.923 \times 10^{15})\, 1.6 \times 10^{-19}) - 13.6\ \text{eV}$$

$$\Rightarrow \quad \phi = 6.80\ \text{eV}$$

Solutions of PRACTICE EXERCISE 2.2

(i) Incident photon energy

$$E = \frac{12431}{5896} = 2.198\ \text{eV}$$

Maximum kinetic energy of photoelectrons

$$KE_{max} = 0.36\ \text{eV}$$

Work function $\quad \phi = E - KE_{max}$

$$\Rightarrow \quad \phi = 2.108 - 0.36 = 1.748\ \text{eV}$$

Threshold frequency $\quad \nu = \dfrac{\phi}{h} = \dfrac{1.748 \times 1.6 \times 10^{-19}}{6.63 \times 10^{-34}}$

$$\Rightarrow \quad \nu = 4.218 \times 10^{14}\ \text{Hz}$$

(ii) (a) Incident photon Energy

$$E = \frac{12431}{2300} = 5.4\ \text{eV}$$

Maximum kinetic energy of photoelectrons is

$$KE_{max} = 5.4 - 4.5 = 0.9\ \text{eV}$$

If V is the retarding potential we use

$$e(V - 0.6) = 0.9\ \text{eV}$$

$$\Rightarrow \quad V = 1.5\ V$$

(b) λ should be such that initial maximum kinetic energy of photoelectrons should be

$$KE_{max} = e(1 - 0.6) = 0.4\ \text{eV}$$

$$\Rightarrow \quad \lambda = \frac{12431}{4.5 + 0.4} = 2536.94\ \text{Å}$$

(iii) (a) Work function of metal is calculated as

$$\phi = \frac{hc}{621 nm}$$

When another wavelength incidents on the surface, we use

$$\frac{hc}{414 nm} = \frac{hc}{621 nm} + 1\ \text{eV}$$

$$\Rightarrow \quad h = \frac{1 \times 1.6 \times 10^{-19} \times 4140 \times 6210 \times 10^{-10}}{3 \times 10^{8} \times 2070}$$

$$\Rightarrow \quad h = 6.624 \times 10^{-34}\ \text{J-s}$$

(b) We use maximum kinetic energy of ejected electrons is given as

$$\frac{1}{2} m_e v^2 = 1\ \text{eV}$$

$$\Rightarrow \quad v = \sqrt{\frac{1 \times 1.6 \times 10^{-19} \times 2}{9.109 \times 10^{-31}}}$$

$$\Rightarrow \quad v = 5.927 \times 10^{5}\ \text{m/s}$$

(iv) We use $\quad KE_{max} = 2.5\ \text{eV}$

$$\Rightarrow \quad \frac{12431}{1980} = \phi + 2.5\ \text{eV}$$

$$\Rightarrow \quad \phi = 3.78\ \text{eV}$$

Threshold frequency $\nu = \dfrac{\phi}{h} = \dfrac{3.78 \times 1.6 \times 10^{-19}}{6.63 \times 10^{-34}}$

$$\Rightarrow \quad \nu = 9.122 \times 10^{14}\ \text{Hz}$$

(v) We use $\frac{12431}{6402} = \phi + 0.54\,\text{eV}$

$\Rightarrow \quad \phi = 1.402\,\text{eV}$

When λ changed to 4272 Å, we use

$$\frac{12431}{4272} = 1.402 + KE_{max}$$

$$\Rightarrow \quad KE_{max} = 1.508\,\text{eV}$$

$$\Rightarrow \quad V_0 = \frac{KE_{max}}{e} = 1.508\,\text{eV}$$

(vi) We use $\frac{hc}{\lambda_1} = \phi + 1.85\,\text{eV} \quad \ldots(1)$

and $\frac{hc}{\lambda_1} = \phi + 0.82\,\text{eV} \quad \ldots(2)$

Using, (1) – (2) gives

$$\Rightarrow \quad hc\left(\frac{1}{\lambda_1} - \frac{1}{\lambda_2}\right) = 1.03\,\text{eV}$$

$$h = \frac{1.03 \times 1.6 \times 10^{-19}}{3 \times 10^8} \times \frac{3000 \times 4300 \times 10^{-10}}{1300}$$

$$\Rightarrow \quad h = 5.451 \times 10^{-34}\,\text{J-s}$$

(vii) No of photons incident per second on plate are

$$N = \frac{P\lambda}{hc} = \frac{5 \times 4 \times 10^{-7}}{6.63 \times 10^{-34} \times 3 \times 10^8}$$

Photo current $I = \frac{Ne}{10^6}$

$$\Rightarrow \quad I = \frac{5 \times 4 \times 10^{-7} \times 1.6 \times 10^{-19}}{6.63 \times 10^{-34} \times 3 \times 10^8 \times 10^6}$$

$$\Rightarrow \quad I = 1.6 \times 10^{-6}\,\text{Å}$$

(viii) (a) Work function of metal is

$$\phi = \frac{hc}{6210\text{Å}}$$

We use $\frac{hc}{4140\text{Å}} = \frac{hc}{6210\text{Å}} + 1\,\text{eV}$

$$\Rightarrow \quad h = \frac{1 \times 1.6 \times 10^{-19} \times 4140 \times 6210 \times 10^{-10}}{3 \times 10^8 \times 2070}$$

$$\Rightarrow \quad h = 6.624 \times 10^{-34}\,\text{J-s}$$

(b) We use $\frac{1}{2} m_e v^2 = 1\,\text{eV}$

$$\Rightarrow \quad v = \sqrt{\frac{1 \times 1.6 \times 10^{-19} \times 2}{9.109 \times 10^{-31}}}$$

$$\Rightarrow \quad v = 5.927 \times 10^5\,\text{m/s}$$

Solutions of PRACTICE EXERCISE 2.3

(i) Number of photons emitted per second are given as

$$N = \frac{P\lambda}{hc} \times 0.6 = \frac{10 \times 5900 \times 10^{-10}}{6.63 \times 10^{-34} \times 3 \times 10^8} \times 0.6$$

$$= 1.78 \times 10^{-16}\,\text{photons/s}$$

(ii) Number of photons emitted per second are given as

$$N = \frac{P\lambda}{hc} \times 0.08 = \frac{150 \times 4500 \times 10^{-10}}{6.63 \times 10^{-34} \times 3 \times 10^8} \times 0.08$$

$$= 27.15 \times 10^{18}\,\text{photons/s}$$

(iii) Total heat required to convert ice into steam is

$$H = 0.05 \times 500 \times 20 + 0.05 \times 1000 \times 100 + 0.05 \times 8 \times 10^4 + 0.05 \times 5.42 \times 10^5$$

$$\Rightarrow \quad H = 500 + 5000 + 4000 + 27100 = 36600\,\text{cal}$$

$$= 36600 \times 4.2\,\text{J}$$

$$= 153720\,\text{J}$$

Heat supplied by heater is $H_1 = 420 \times 5 \times 60 = 126000\,\text{J}$

Heat supplied by infra red lamp is $H_2 = 153720 - 126000$

$$= 27720\,\text{J}$$

Total photons by infrared lamp are $N = \frac{H_2\lambda}{hc} \times \frac{1}{0.5}$

Photon striking rate is $r = \frac{N}{t} = \frac{2H_2\lambda}{hct}$

$$= \frac{2 \times 27720 \times 10000 \times 10^{-10}}{6.63 \times 10^{-34} \times 3 \times 10^8 \times 1400}$$

$$= 1.99 \times 10^{20}\,\text{s}^{-1}$$

(iv) Photon energies of incident wavelengths are

$$E_1 = \frac{12431}{5000} = 2.486\,\text{eV}$$

$$E_2 = \frac{12431}{6000} = 2.072\,\text{eV}$$

$$E_3 = \frac{12431}{7000} = 1.776\,\text{eV}$$

Thus only first and second radiation will cause photon emission. The incident light intensity of each wavelength is

$$I = \frac{P}{A} = \frac{\frac{1}{3} \times 10^{-3}}{3.14 \times (0.001)^2} = 106.16\,\text{W/m}^2$$

Electrons emitted per second per unit area are

$$N = \frac{I\lambda_1}{hc} + \frac{I\lambda_2}{hc}$$

$$N = \frac{106.16}{2.486 \times 1.6 \times 10^{-19}} + \frac{106.16}{2.072 \times 1.6 \times 10^{-19}}$$

Total charge emitted per second per unit area is

$$q = Ne = \frac{106.16}{2.486} + \frac{106.16}{2.072}$$

$$= 42.703 + 51.235$$

$$= 93.94 \text{ coul/m}^2\text{-s}$$

(v) Energy of each photon is

$$E = \frac{P}{N} = \frac{5\times10^{-3}}{8\times10^{15}} = 6.25\times10^{-19}\text{ J}$$

$$\Rightarrow \quad E = 3.9\text{ eV}$$

Given that maximum kinetic energy of ejected photoelectrons is 2 eV, we have

$$3.9 = \phi + 2.0$$

$$\Rightarrow \quad \phi = 1.9\text{ eV}$$

(vi) Energy absorbed by each potassium atom per second is given as

$$E = \frac{100\times0.05}{4\times3.14\times(0.75)^2}\times\frac{3.14\times(0.5\times10^{-10})^2}{1.6\times10^{-19}}\text{ eV/s}$$

$$E = 0.0347\text{ eV/s}$$

The time required to absorb 2.0 eV energy is

$$t = \frac{\phi}{E} = \frac{2.0}{0.0347} = 57.63\text{ s}$$

(vii) (a) Photon flux on earth surface is

$$\phi_\rho = \frac{I\lambda}{hc}$$

$$= \frac{1.4\times10^3\times5000\times10^{-10}}{6.63\times10^{-34}\times3\times10^8}$$

$$= 3.52\times10^{21}\text{ photon/s}$$

(b) Photon density on earth surface is

$$\rho_P = \frac{\phi_\rho}{c} = 1.17\times10^{13}\text{ photons/m}^3$$

(c) Total photons emitted by sun per second are

$$N = \phi_P\times4\pi r_{ES}^2$$

$$= 3.52\times10^{21}\times4\times3.14\times(1.5\times10^{11})^2$$

$$= 9.95\times10^{44}\text{ photons/s}$$

Solutions of PRACTICE EXERCISE 2.4

(i) In first Bohr orbit electron speed is

$$v = \frac{nh}{2\pi mr}$$

de Broglie wavelength is

$$\lambda = \frac{h}{mv}$$

$$\Rightarrow \quad \lambda = 2\pi r$$

(ii) At temperature T, de Broglie wavelength of any molecule is given as

$$\lambda = \frac{h}{\sqrt{3mkT}}$$

$$\Rightarrow \quad \frac{\lambda_H}{\lambda_{He}} = \sqrt{\frac{m_{H_e}T_{H_e}}{m_H T_H}} = \sqrt{\frac{4\times400}{2\times300}} = \sqrt{\frac{8}{3}}$$

(iii) Electron momentum initial

$$p_1 = \frac{h}{\lambda_1} = \frac{6.63\times10^{-34}}{10^{-10}}$$

$$\Rightarrow \quad p_1 = 6.63\times10^{-24}\text{ J-s}$$

Find $\quad p_2 = \frac{h}{\lambda_2} = \frac{6.63\times10^{-34}}{0.5\times10^{-10}}$

$$\Rightarrow \quad p_1 = 13.26\times10^{-24}\text{ J-s}$$

Kinetic energy of electron

$$E = \frac{P^2}{2m_e}$$

Energy added to electron is

$$\Delta E = \frac{P_2^2 - P_1^2}{2m_e}$$

$$\Rightarrow \quad \Delta E = \frac{[(13.26)^2-(6.63)^2]\times10^{-48}}{2\times9.109\times10^{-31}\times1.6\times10^{-19}}$$

$$\Rightarrow \quad \Delta E = 452.4\text{ eV}$$

(iv) Force on space vehicle is

$$F = \frac{P}{c} = \frac{100}{3\times10^8} = 3.33\times10^{-7}\text{ N}$$

Acceleration is

$$a = \frac{F}{m} = \frac{3.33\times10^{-7}}{50}$$

$$\Rightarrow \quad a = 6.66\times10^{-9}\text{ m/s}^2$$

(v) As 30% light is incident and reflected by mirror, force due to reflection of light on mirror is

$$F = 2\times\frac{0.3P}{c} = \frac{0.6P}{c}$$

To support the weight of mirror, we use

$$\frac{0.6P}{c} = mg$$

$$\Rightarrow \quad P = \frac{mgc}{0.6} = \frac{20\times10^{-3}\times10\times3\times10^8}{0.6}$$

$$\Rightarrow \quad P = 10^8\text{ watt}$$

(vi) By conservation of momentum

$$mv = mv' + \frac{hf}{c} \quad \ldots(1)$$

By conservation of energy

$$\frac{1}{2}mv^2 + \Delta E = \frac{1}{2}mv'^2 + hf \quad \ldots(2)$$

$$\Rightarrow \quad \Delta E = hf - \frac{1}{2}m(v^2 - v'^2)$$

$$\Rightarrow \quad \Delta E = hf - \frac{1}{2}m(v+v')\left(\frac{hf}{mc}\right)$$

$$\Rightarrow \quad \Delta E = hf - \frac{hf}{2}\frac{2v}{c} \quad (v \simeq v')$$

$$\Rightarrow \quad \Delta E = hf\left(1 - \frac{v}{c}\right)$$

When atom as at rest, we can use

$$\Delta E \cong hf_0$$

$$\Rightarrow \quad hf_0 = hf\left(1 - \frac{v}{c}\right)$$

$$\Rightarrow \quad f = f_0\left(1 + \frac{v}{c}\right)$$

(vii) Initial momentum of each particle is

$$\vec{P}_1 = \frac{h}{\lambda_1}\hat{i} \text{ and } \vec{P}_2 = \frac{h}{\lambda_2}\hat{j}$$

$$\Rightarrow \quad \vec{v}_1 = \frac{h}{m\lambda_1}\hat{i} \text{ and } \vec{v}_2 = \frac{h}{m\lambda_2}\hat{j}$$

Velocity of center of mass is gives as

$$\vec{v}_{cm} = \frac{m_1\vec{v}_1 + m_2\vec{v}_2}{m_1 + m_2} = \frac{h}{2m}\left(\frac{1}{\lambda_1}\hat{i} + \frac{1}{\lambda_2}\hat{j}\right)$$

Momentum of particles in frame of center of mass is

$$\vec{P}_{1c} = m(\vec{v}_1 - \vec{v}_{cm}) = \frac{h}{2}\left(\frac{1}{\lambda_1}\hat{i} - \frac{1}{\lambda_2}\hat{j}\right)$$

$$\text{and } \vec{P}_{2c} = m(\vec{v}_2 - \vec{v}_{cm}) = \frac{h}{2}\left(\frac{1}{\lambda_2}\hat{j} - \frac{1}{\lambda_1}\hat{i}\right)$$

$$|\vec{P}_{1c}| = |\vec{P}_{2c}| = \frac{h}{2}\frac{\sqrt{\lambda_1^2 + \lambda_2^2}}{\lambda_1\lambda_2}$$

de Broglie wavelength of particles in frame of their centre of mass is

$$\lambda_{1c} = \frac{h}{P_{1c}} = \frac{2\lambda_1\lambda_2}{\sqrt{\lambda_1^2 + \lambda_2^2}}$$

$$\text{and} \quad \lambda_{2c} = \frac{h}{P_{2c}} = \frac{2\lambda_1\lambda_2}{\sqrt{\lambda_1^2 + \lambda_2^2}}$$

Solutions of CONCEPTUAL MCQS Single Option Correct

Sol. 1 (D) As studied photoelectric current depends upon the intensity of incident light, work function of the emitter and the condition of its emission is that wavelength of incident light has to be less than the threshold wavelength of the metal hence option (D) is correct.

Sol. 2 (A) As work function of *B* is more than that of *A* the threshold frequency of *B* is more hence option (A) is correct.

Sol. 3 (D) Photoelectric effect starts when incident wavelength is less than that of the threshold wavelength of the metal. For the given threshold wavelength only ultraviolet wavelengths are less than this hence option (D) is correct.

Sol. 4 (D) Energy of a photon always remain same as in any optical phenomenon frequency of light does not change.

Sol. 5 (B) de-Broglie waves have wavelength inversely proportional to the momentum of the particle hence option (B) is NOT true for de-Broglie waves.

Sol. 6 (A) For same speed de-Broglie wavelength is inversely proportional to the mass of the particle hence option (A) is correct.

Sol. 7 (D) Photons having same momentum will have same de-Broglie wavelengths but photons having same wavelengths will have same magnitude of momentum but their directions may be different hence option (D) is correct.

Sol. 8 (A) For same speed de-Broglie wavelength is inversely proportional to the mass of the particle hence option (A) is correct.

Sol. 9 (B) As already discussed in theory that the electrons when ejected in photoelectric effect may loose their energy during emission process in collisions so the emitted electrons have their kinetic energy distributed from zero to $(h\nu - h\nu_0)$ hence option (B) is correct.

Sol. 10 (A) Photoelectric emission starts only when the frequency of incident light is more than the threshold frequency hence option (A) is correct.

Sol. 11 (D) Photoelectric effect explains the quantum nature of light particles called photons hence option (D) is correct.

Sol. 12 (A) Once photoelectric emission starts at frequency above threshold frequency the current is directly proportional to the photon flux in incident light which is proportional to the intensity of light hence option (A) is correct.

Sol. 13 (B) Due to collisions electrons may loose energy during the ejection process in photoelectric effect so the ejected electrons have their energy distributed between zero to the maximum possible kinetic energy of ejected electrons hence option (B) is correct.

Sol. 14 (A) Both momentum and energy of a photon are inversely proportional to the wavelength of radiation hence option (A) is correct.

Sol. 15 (C) From the relativistic relation $E^2 = p^2c^2 + m_0^2c^4$ only for a photon rest mass m_0 is zero thus the above relation is only valid for a photon hence option (C) is correct.

Sol. 16 (C) No. of photons emitted per second by a bulb of power P_{watt} *is*

$$N = \frac{P\lambda}{hc}$$

$$\Rightarrow \quad n_r = \frac{P\lambda_r}{hc} \text{ and } n_b = \frac{P\lambda_b}{hc}$$

As $\lambda_r > \lambda_b \Rightarrow n_r > n_b$

Sol. 17 (D) As already studied that in the process of ejection photoelectrons loose their kinetic energy in one or more collisions with other electrons hence option (D) is correct.

Sol. 18 (A) Among all the above options the photoelectric current is directly proportional to the incident light intensity hence option (A) is correct.

Sol. 19 (A) As X-rays have energy (and frequency) more than that of ultraviolet light option-(A) is correct.

Sol. 20 (C) As we have studied that the photoelectric effect equation obtained in experiment is

$$V_0 = \left(\frac{h}{e}\right)\nu - \frac{h\nu_{th}}{e}$$

Hence option (C) is correct.

Sol. 21 (D) As during ejection process an electron may loose energy in collision process the ejected electron can have kinetic energy less than the maximum possible energy ($h\nu - \phi$) hence option (D) is correct.

Sol. 22 (D) As maximum photocurrent in experiment depends upon light intensity hence option (D) is NOT true.

Sol. 23 (C) As energy of red light is less than that of blue and yellow light, no photoelectric emission will occur hence option (C) is correct.

Sol. 24 (C) At same potential difference, kinetic energy gained by both electron and proton will be same but momentum will be more that in photon hence its de-Broglie wavelength will be less hence option (C) is correct.

Sol. 25 (C) Kinetic energy of photoelectrons will increase if energy of incident light is increased hence option (C) is correct.

Sol. 26 (A) Based on experimental analysis studied in theory option (A) is correct.

Sol. 27 (C) As frequency of incident light is kept constant maximum kinetic energy of ejected photoelectrons will remain constant and intensity is increased which means photon flux is increased due to which more number of electrons are emitted hence option (C) is correct.

Sol. 28 (B) Due to increase in both frequency and photon flux by a factor of two, light intensity increases by four times. Due to doubling the frequency the maximum kinetic energy increases by a factor more than two and by doubling the photon flux the photo current increases by a factor of two hence option (B) is correct.

Sol. 29 (C) As kinetic energy of photoelectrons is related to wavelength of the incident light by a relation given as

$$K_{\text{max}} = hc/\lambda - \phi$$

hence in this case option (C) is correct.

Sol. 30 (B) At stopping potential the emitted photoelectrons are not able to reach the collected electrode and repelled back and absorbed by the emitter metal again hence option (B) is correct.

Sol. 31 (C) The relation of frequency of light and stopping potential is given as

$$eV_0 = h\nu - \phi$$

hence option (C) is correct.

Sol. 32 (D) As the distance of light source is doubled from the photo cell the light intensity which is inversely proportional to the distance will become one fourth hence option (D) is correct.

Sol. 33 (C) By changing the distance between source and emitter metal the photon flux changes and stopping potential depends upon frequency hence there will be no change in stopping potential in this case hence option (C) is correct.

Sol. 34 (A) As frequency of radiation is kept fixed there will be no change in maximum kinetic energy of the emitted photoelectrons hence option (A) is correct.

Sol. 35 (D) As photon flux and intensity of incident light is inversely proportional to the square of the distance from the light source from metal and saturation photocurrent is directly proportional to the photon flux, option (D) is correct.

Sol. 36 (D) The relation of frequency of light and stopping potential is given as

$$eV_0 = h\nu - \phi$$

hence option (D) is correct.

Sol. 37 (B) Due to downward direction of electric field the ejected electrons will experience upward acceleration due to this field and because of this the total kinetic energy of ejected electrons will increase.

Sol. 38 (D) In photoelectric effect the incident photon is absorbed by the free electrons of the metal in conduction band and these are emitted if incident light energy is more than the work function hence option (D) is correct.

Sol. 39 (B) The maximum kinetic energies of the ejected electrons from the two photons will be 1 – 0.5 = 0.5 eV and 2.5 – 0.5 = 2.0 eV hence option (B) is correct.

Sol. 40 (B) As the aperture of the lens is reduced to one fourth so photon flux coming out from lens will also become one fourth so current will also reduced to one fourth, hence option (B) is correct.

Sol. 41 (A) The relation in stopping potential and wavelength for a photoelectric effect experiment is given as

$$eV_0 = hc/\lambda - \phi$$

using above relation we can see that option (A) is correct.

Sol. 42 (D) In photoelectric effect electrons are ejected only when the photon energy is more than work function of metal and if photon energy is less than work function then electron will not be ejected no matter how much is the intensity. This fact supports the quantum nature of light hence option (A) is correct.

Sol. 43 (D) As studied in the theory of Einstein's photoelectric effect experiment, option (D) is correct.

Solutions of NUMERICAL MCQS Single Option Correct

Sol. 1 (B) We use

$$eV_S = \frac{hc}{\lambda} - \phi = \frac{1240(nm)eV}{400(nm)} - 1.9\text{ eV}$$

$$\Rightarrow \quad eV_S = 1.2\text{ eV}$$

$$\Rightarrow \quad V_S = 1.2\text{ V}$$

Thus the cesium ball can be charged to a maximum potential of 1.2 V.

Sol. 2 (A) We have

$$h\nu = eV$$

$$\Rightarrow \quad \nu = \frac{eV}{h}$$

$$\Rightarrow \quad \nu = \frac{1.6\times10^{-19}\times10\times10^3}{6.6\times10^{-34}}$$

$$\Rightarrow \quad \nu = 2.4\times10^{18}\text{ Hz}$$

Sol. 3 (B) No. of photoelectron emitted per second are

$$N = \frac{1.5\times10^{-3}W\times(10^{-3})}{\dfrac{1240(nm)(eV)}{400(nm)}\times e(V/5)} = \frac{0.48}{e}\times10^{-6}$$

$\Rightarrow$ Photo current $= ne = 0.48\ \mu\text{A}$

Sol. 4 (B) Change in momentum due to photon $= \dfrac{h}{\lambda}$

F = rate of change of momentum

$$\Rightarrow \quad F = n\frac{h}{\lambda} = ma$$

$$\Rightarrow \quad a = \frac{nh}{\lambda m}$$

Sol. 5 (B) We use $\phi = \dfrac{12431}{6000}\ eV$

$$\Rightarrow \quad \phi = 2.07\text{ eV}$$

$$\Rightarrow \quad \phi = 2.07\times1.6\times10^{-19}$$

$$\Rightarrow \quad \phi = 3.315\times10^{-19}\text{ J}$$

Sol. 6 (B) Number of photons per second are

$$N = \frac{P\lambda}{hc}$$

$$\Rightarrow \quad N = \frac{100\times0.05\times555\times10^{-9}}{6.63\times10^{-34}\times3\times10^8}$$

$$\Rightarrow \quad N = 1.39\times10^{-19}$$

Sol. 7 (D) The electron ejected with maximum speed v_{max} are stopped by electric field E = 4 N/C after travelling a distance d = 1 m. Thus we have

$$\frac{1}{2}mv_{max}^2 = eE\,d = 4\text{ eV}$$

The energy of incident photon $= \dfrac{12431}{2000} = 6.21$ eV

From equation of photo electric effect we use

$$\frac{1}{2}mv^2_{max} = h\upsilon - \phi_0$$

$\Rightarrow$ $$\phi_0 = 6.21 - 4 = 2.21 \text{ eV}$$

Sol. 8 (B) The radiation pressure depend on the intensity of light used and not on its wavelength and frequency.

Also, the radiation pressure depends on the nature of the surface on which light is falling. Hence (B).

Sol. 9 (D) The potential of anode with respect to the cathode must be – 5 V to repel fastest photoelectrons.

Sol. 10 (C) The maximum K.E. of ejected photoelectron is

$$(KE)_{max} = h\nu - \phi_0$$

If the frequency of photon is doubled, maximum kinetic energy of photon electron becomes

$$(KE)'_{max} = 2h\nu - \phi_0;$$

$\Rightarrow$ $$\frac{(KE)'_{max}}{(KE)_{max}} = \frac{2\left(h\nu - \frac{\phi_0}{2}\right)}{h\nu - \phi_0} > 2$$

$$\text{Photo current} \propto \frac{\text{intensity of beam}}{h\nu}$$

If intensity and frequency both are doubled, the photocurrent remains same.

Sol. 11 (C) Number of photons per second entering human eye are

$$N = \frac{P\lambda}{hc}$$

$\Rightarrow$ $$N = \frac{10^{-10} \times 660 \times 10^{-9}}{6.63 \times 10^{-34} \times 3 \times 10^8} \times 10^{-4}$$

$\Rightarrow$ $$N = 3.31 \times 10^4$$

Sol. 12 (C) At temperature T, average kinetic energy due to thermal motion is given as

$$\frac{1}{2}mv^2 = \frac{3}{2}kT$$

Momentum is given as

$$P = mv = \sqrt{3mkT}$$

de Broglie wavelength is given as

$$\lambda = \frac{h}{\sqrt{3mkT}}$$

Sol. 13 (D) Energy of a photon $= \frac{hC}{\lambda} = E; E' = 0.25\,E = \frac{hC}{4\lambda}$

So percentage change in wavelength $= \frac{4\lambda - \lambda}{\lambda} \times 100\% = 300\%$.

Sol. 14 (B) The net force on the plate is due to incidence of photons + due to emission of electrons

The number of photons incidents per second on the plate

$$= \text{number of electrons emitted per second}$$

$$= \frac{IS}{h\nu}$$

The momentum of each photon and electron respectively are $\frac{h}{\lambda}$ and $\sqrt{2m(h\nu - \phi)}$ where m is the mass of the electron. Hence the net force exerted on the metal plate is $\frac{IS}{h\nu}\left(\frac{h}{\lambda} + \sqrt{2m(h\nu - \phi)}\right)$.

Sol. 15 (C) Power percent area of wave is

$$P = \epsilon_0 E_0^2 C$$

Number of photons falling per unit area are

$$N = \frac{P\lambda}{hc} = \frac{\epsilon_0 E_0^2 C\lambda}{hc} = \frac{\epsilon_0 \lambda E_0^2}{h}$$

Sol. 16 (A) By conservation of momentum we use

$$\frac{h}{\lambda} = mV_R$$

$\Rightarrow$ $$V_R = \frac{h}{m\lambda}$$

Sol. 17 (D) Number of photons striking per second are

$$N = \frac{IA}{h\nu}$$

Area A here is the area perpendicular to the direction of intensity or direction of energy flow

Consider a ring of radius x and width dx on the disc. Intensity I on the ring due to source is $I = \frac{P}{4\pi r^2}$.

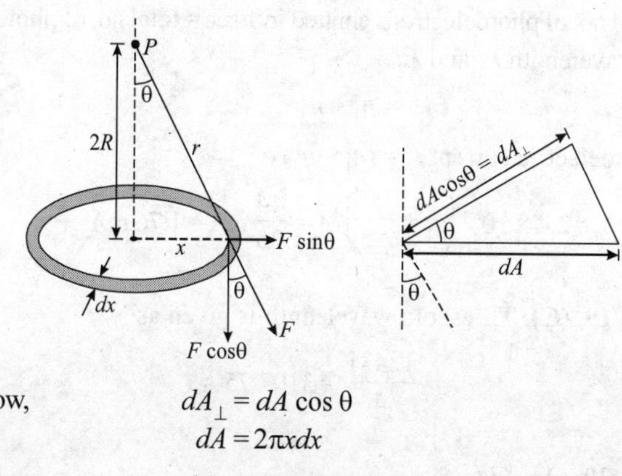

Now, $$dA_\perp = dA\cos\theta$$

$$dA = 2\pi x dx$$

Gives, $$dA_\perp = (2\pi x dx)\cos\theta$$

A photon will exert force F as shown, only the $F\cos\theta$ component will remain and $F\sin\theta$ will cancel out as we integrate on the ring

$$F = \frac{Nh}{\lambda}$$

[As N photons strike per second and this leads to less of $\frac{Nh}{\lambda}$ momentum per second]

As only $F\cos\theta$ component of force remains

$$dF = \left(\frac{IdA_{\perp}}{h\nu}\right) \times \frac{h}{\lambda} \cos\theta$$

$$\Rightarrow \int_0^F dF = \int_0^R \left[\frac{P}{4\pi(4R^2 + x^2)}\right] \times \frac{(2\pi dx \cos\theta)}{\left(\frac{hC}{\lambda}\right)} \times \frac{h}{\lambda} \cos\theta$$

[As $r = \sqrt{4R^2 + x^2}$]

Solving we get $F = \frac{P}{20c}$

Sol. 18 (A) We have

$$\lambda_1 = 4100\text{ Å}$$

$$\lambda_2 = 4960\text{ Å}$$

$$\lambda_3 = 6200\text{ Å}$$

$$\Rightarrow E_1 = \frac{12431}{410} = 3\text{ eV}$$

$$\Rightarrow E_2 = \frac{12431}{4960} = 2.5\text{ eV}$$

$$\Rightarrow E_3 = \frac{12431}{6200} = 2\text{ eV} < \phi$$

Hence only λ_1 and λ_2 can cause photoemission.

No. of photons of wavelength λ_1 incident on the sodium surface in 1 sec,

$$n_1 = \frac{P/3}{E_1} = \frac{IA\cos\theta/3}{E_1} = \frac{\frac{144}{3}\times 10^{-4}\times\frac{1}{2}}{E_1} = \frac{2.4\times 10^{-3}}{3e}$$

Similarly $n_2 = \frac{P/3}{E_2} = \frac{2.4\times 10^{-3}}{2.5e}$

Total no. of photoelectrons emitted in 1 sec = total no. of photons of wavelength λ_1 and λ_2

$$= n_1 + n_2$$

Photoelectric current $I_P = (n_1 + n_2)\, e$

$$\Rightarrow I_P = 2.4 \times 10^{-3}\left(\frac{1}{3} + \frac{1}{2.5}\right) A = \frac{44}{25}\text{ mA} = 1.76\text{ mA}$$

Sol. 19 (C) Threshold wavelength is given as

$$\lambda = \frac{12431}{4} = 3107.75\text{ Å}$$

Sol. 20 (A) We use

$$\frac{hc}{\lambda} = 5\,\text{eV}_0 + \phi$$

and $$\frac{hc}{3\lambda} = \text{eV}_0 + \phi$$

$$\Rightarrow \frac{2hc}{3\lambda} = 4\,\text{eV}_0$$

$$\Rightarrow \phi = \frac{hc}{6\lambda}$$

Sol. 21 (D) We use

$$\frac{1}{2}mv^2 = \frac{hc}{\lambda} - \phi$$

and $$\frac{1}{2}mv'^2 = \frac{hc}{(3\lambda/4)} - \phi = \frac{4hc}{3\lambda} - \phi$$

$$\Rightarrow v' > \sqrt{\frac{4}{3}}\, v$$

Sol. 22 (B) Potential of the sphere at any time

$$V(t) = \frac{Q_0 + Qt}{4\pi\varepsilon_0 R} = V + \frac{\eta\lambda Pet}{4\pi\varepsilon_0 Rhc}$$

Here we have $Qt = \frac{P\lambda}{hc}\eta e \times t$

Sol. 23 (A) Under the given condition energy of photon is made half the work function of the metal. Hence photoemission shall stop altogether.

Sol. 24 (B) Stopping potential $= \frac{KE_{\max}}{e} = 4\text{ V}$

Sol. 25 (B) We use $\frac{hc}{\lambda} = \phi + 3\,\text{eV}_0$ ...(1)

and $\frac{hc}{2\lambda} = \phi + \text{eV}_0$ ...(2)

Using 3 × (2)– (1) gives

$$\frac{hc}{2\lambda} = 2\phi \Rightarrow \phi = \frac{hc}{4\lambda}$$

Sol. 26 (C) The energy of incident photons is given by

$$h\nu = eV_s + \phi_0 = 2 + 5 = 7\text{ eV}$$

(V_s is stopping potential and ϕ_0 is work function)

$$\Rightarrow \text{Saturation current} = 10^{-5} A = \frac{\eta P}{h\nu} e = \frac{10^{-5} P}{7 \times e} e$$

Thus $P = 7\text{ W}$

Sol. 27 (B) Least detectable intensity for of eye is

$$I = 5 \times 10^4 \times \frac{hc}{\lambda}$$

$$\Rightarrow I = 5 \times 10 \times \frac{6.63\times 10^{-34} \times 3\times 10^8}{5\times 10^{-7}}$$

$\Rightarrow \quad I = 1.99 \times 10^{-19}\ \text{W/m}^2$

Thus eye is more sensitive power detector.

Sol. 28 (B) Threshold frequency

$$\nu = \frac{\phi}{h}$$

$$= \frac{3.3 \times 1.6 \times 10^{-19}}{6.63 \times 10^{-34}}$$

$$= 7.96 \times 10^{14}\ \text{Hz}$$

Hence (B) is most appropriate.

Sol. 29 (A) Incident photon energy

$$E = \frac{12431}{3000} = 4.14\ \text{eV}$$

$$KE_{max} = 4.14 - 3.3 = 0.84\ \text{eV}$$

Sol. 30 (A) Stopping potential $= \dfrac{KE_{max}}{e} = 0.84$ V.

Sol. 31 (C) Consider a ring of radius x and width dx. Power incident on the ring

$$dP = \frac{P}{4\pi[(nr)^2 + x^2]} \cdot 2\pi \times dx \cdot \cos\theta = \frac{Pxdx \cdot nr}{2[(nr)^2 + x^2]^{3/2}}$$

No. of photons falling (per unit time) on the area $= \dfrac{dP \cdot \lambda}{hC}$

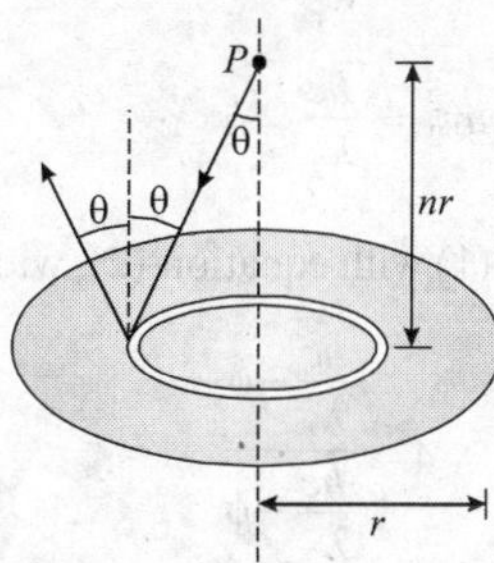

Momentum given by one photon $\Delta P = 2\,(h/\lambda)\cos\theta$

$\Rightarrow$ Force on the ring dF (in the downward direction)

$$= \frac{dP \cdot \lambda}{hC} \cdot \frac{2h}{\lambda}\cos\theta = \frac{2dP\cos\theta}{C}$$

$$\Rightarrow F = \int 2 \cdot \frac{Pxdxnr}{2[(nr)^2 + x^2]^{3/2}} \cdot \frac{\cos\theta}{C}\ \frac{Pn^2r^2}{C}\int_0^r \frac{xdx}{(n^2r^2 + x^2)^2};$$

$$\Rightarrow F = \frac{Pn^2r^2}{2C} \cdot \frac{1}{n^2r^2(n^2+1)} = \frac{P}{2C(n^2+1)}$$

Sol. 32 (A) Number of photons entering sensor are

$$N = \frac{P_i\lambda t}{hc} \qquad (P_i \rightarrow \text{incident power})$$

Where $\quad P_i = \dfrac{P}{4\pi l^2} \times \pi(2d)^2$

$$\Rightarrow \quad N = \frac{P\lambda d^2 t}{hcl^2}$$

Sol. 33 (D) We use

$$\frac{h}{mv} = \lambda$$

$$\Rightarrow \quad \frac{E_k}{E_{ph}} = \frac{\frac{1}{2}mv^2}{\frac{hc}{\lambda}} = \frac{m^2v^2\lambda}{2hcm} = \frac{v}{2c} = \frac{1}{4}$$

Sol. 34 (A) We use

$$h\nu_1 = \phi + eV_1 \qquad \dots(1)$$

and $\quad h\nu_2 = \phi + eV_2 \qquad \dots(2)$

Using (2) – (1) gives

$$V_2 = V_1 + \frac{h}{e}(\nu_2 - \nu_1)$$

Sol. 35 (C) Incident energy $E = h\nu$ and we use

$$KE_{max} = h\nu - \phi$$

$$\Rightarrow \quad \frac{1}{2}mv_{max}^2 = 6.63 \times 10^{-34} \times 3 \times 10^{15} - 4 \times 1.6 \times 10^{-19}$$

$$\Rightarrow \quad v_{max} = \sqrt{\frac{2 \times 13.49 \times 10^{-19}}{9.1 \times 10^{-31}}}$$

$$= 1.72 \times 10^6\ \text{m/s}$$

Sol. 36 (A) We use

$$hf_1 = \phi + \frac{1}{2}m\theta_1^2 \qquad \dots(1)$$

and $\quad hf_2 = \phi + \dfrac{1}{2}mv_2^2 \qquad \dots(2)$

Using (1) – (2) gives

$$v_1^2 - v_2^2 = \frac{2h}{m}(f_1 - f_2)$$

Sol. 37 (B) The maximum kinetic energy of the electrons immediately upon ejection is the difference between the energy of the incident photon and the threshold energy.

$$K = \frac{hc}{\lambda} - \frac{hc}{\lambda_0}$$

This kinetic energy of ejected electron is converted to

electrostatic potential energy, $\Delta U = eEd$, as electrons come to rest while moving in the direction of electric field. Therefore, $K = Eed$

and $$\lambda_0 = \left(\frac{1}{\lambda} - \frac{eEd}{hc}\right)^{-1}$$

Sol. 38 (A) Momentum of α particle is

$$p = \frac{h}{\lambda} = \frac{6.63\times10^{-34}}{0.004\times10^{-10}} = 1.66\times10^{-21}\text{ N-S}$$

Energy of α-particle is

$$E = \frac{P^2}{2m}$$

$$\Rightarrow \quad E = \frac{(1.66\times10^{-21})^2}{2\times4\times1.67\times10^{-27}\times1.6\times10^{-19}}\text{ eV}$$

$$= 1296.87\text{ eV}$$

Sol. 39 (C) If the source radiates uniformly in all directions, the intensity I of the light at a distance r is given by

$$I = \frac{P_0}{4\pi r^2} = \frac{1.0}{4\pi(0.5)^2} = 0.32\text{ W/m}^2$$

The target area A is $\pi(1.3\times10^{-10}\text{ m})^2$ or $5.3\times10^{-20}\text{ m}^2$, so that the rate at which energy falls on the target is given by

$$P = IA = (0.32)(5.3\times10^{-20})\text{ W}$$

$$\Rightarrow P = 1.7\times10^{-20}\text{ W}$$

If all this incoming energy is absorbed, the time required to accumulate energy for the electron to escape is

$$t = \left(\frac{1.8eV}{1.7\times10^{-20}\text{ J/s}}\right)\left(\frac{1.6\times10^{-19}\text{ J}}{1eV}\right) = 17\text{ s}$$

Sol. 40 (B) We use

$$E_e = \frac{P_e^2}{2m} = \frac{1}{2}mv^2$$

Given that $P_e = P_{Ph} = \frac{h}{\lambda}$ and $E_{Ph} = \frac{hc}{\lambda}$

$$\Rightarrow \quad E_{Ph} = P_{Ph}\cdot C = mvC$$

We use $\frac{E_e}{E_{Ph}} = \frac{v}{2C}$

Sol. 41 (B) Maximum kinetic energy of photoelectrons is

$$KE_{max} = \frac{1}{2}mv^2 = \frac{1}{2}\times\frac{9.1\times10^{-3}\times(1.8\times10^6)^2}{1.6\times10^{-19}}$$

$$\Rightarrow \quad KE_{max} = 9.21\text{ eV}$$

Stopping potential

$$V_0 = \frac{KE_{max}}{e} = 9.21\text{ V}$$

Sol. 42 (A) We use

$$\lambda_1 = \frac{h}{\sqrt{2mE_P}}$$

and $$\lambda_2 = \frac{hc}{E_P}$$

$$\Rightarrow \quad \frac{\lambda_1}{\lambda_2} \propto \sqrt{E_P}$$

Sol. 43 (D) For an accelerating voltage V de Broglie wavelength is

$$\lambda = \frac{h}{\sqrt{2meV}}$$

$$\Rightarrow \quad V = \frac{h^2}{2me\lambda^2}$$

$$\Rightarrow \quad V = \frac{(6.63\times10^{-34})^2}{2\times9.1\times10^{-31}\times1.6\times10^{-19}\times(0.4\times10^{-10})^2}$$

$$\Rightarrow \quad V = 943.4\text{ volt}$$

Sol. 44 (A) Using equation of photoelectric effect

$$K_{max} = E - W\,(K_{max} = eV_s)$$

$$\Rightarrow \quad 3\text{ eV} = \frac{12431}{\lambda} - \frac{12431}{5000} = \frac{12431}{\lambda} - 2.48\text{ eV}$$

$$\Rightarrow \quad \lambda = 2268\text{ Å}$$

Sol. 45 (B) Using equation for two wavelengths

$$\frac{1}{2}mv_1^2 = \frac{hc}{\lambda_1} - \phi \quad \ldots(1)$$

$$\Rightarrow \quad \frac{1}{2}mv_2^2 = \frac{hc}{\lambda_2} - \phi \quad \ldots(2)$$

Dividing equation-(1) with equation-(2), with $v_1 = 2v_2$, we have

$$4 = \frac{\frac{hc}{\lambda_1} - \phi}{\frac{hc}{\lambda_2} - \phi}$$

$$\Rightarrow \quad 3\phi = 4\left(\frac{hc}{\lambda_2}\right) - \left(\frac{hc}{\lambda_1}\right)$$

$$\Rightarrow \quad 3\phi = \frac{4\times12431}{5400} - \frac{12431}{3500} = 5.64\text{ eV}$$

$$\Rightarrow \quad \phi = 1.88\text{ eV}$$

Sol. 46 (B) For particle of mass m, charge q if accelerated at voltage V, its de-Broglei wavelength is given as

$$\lambda = \frac{h}{\sqrt{2mqV}}$$

$$\Rightarrow \quad \frac{\lambda_1}{\lambda_2} = \sqrt{\frac{V_2}{V_1}}$$

$$\Rightarrow \quad \lambda_2 = \sqrt{\frac{V_1}{V_2}} \times \alpha_1$$

$$\Rightarrow \quad \lambda_2 = \sqrt{\frac{150}{1350}} \times 1\,\text{Å}$$

$$\Rightarrow \quad \lambda_2 = \frac{1}{3}\,\text{Å}$$

Sol. 47 (D) For electron and proton we use

$$\lambda_e = \frac{h}{\sqrt{2meV}}$$

$$\lambda_P = \frac{h}{\sqrt{2MeV}}$$

$$\Rightarrow \quad \lambda_P = \lambda_e \sqrt{\frac{m}{M}}$$

Sol. 48 (A) As graphs '*a*' and '*b*' are starting at same point on potential axis, their stopping potential as well as frequency is same hence option (A) is correct.

Sol. 49 (C) Initial wavelength of electron is

$$\lambda = \frac{h}{P_i}$$

$$d\lambda = \frac{h}{P_i^2} dP_i$$

$$\Rightarrow \quad \frac{d\lambda}{h/P_i} = -\frac{dP_i}{P_i}$$

$$\Rightarrow \quad \frac{d\lambda}{\lambda} = -\frac{dP_i}{P_i}$$

$$\Rightarrow \quad \frac{0.5}{100} = \frac{P_m}{P_i}$$

$$\Rightarrow \quad P_i = 200\, P_m$$

Sol. 50 (A) The light contains two different frequencies. The one with larger frequency will cause photoelectrons with largest kinetic energy. This larger frequency is

$$\nu = \frac{\omega}{2\pi} = \frac{8\times10^{15}\,s^{-1}}{2\pi}$$

The maximum kinetic energy of the photoelectrons is

$$K_{max} = h\nu - W$$

$$= (4.14\times10^{-15}\,\text{eV-s}) \times \left(\frac{8\times10^{15}}{2\pi}\,s^{-1}\right) - 2.0\,\text{eV}$$

$$= 5.27\,\text{eV} - 2.0\,\text{eV} = 3.27\,\text{eV}$$

Sol. 51 (B) Since plate is in air, so gravitational force will act on this

$$F_{\text{gravitational}} = \text{mg} \quad \text{(downward)}$$

$$\Rightarrow \quad F_{\text{gravitational}} = 10\times10^{-3}\times10$$

$$\Rightarrow \quad F_{\text{gravitational}} = 10^{-1}\,\text{N}$$

For equilibrium force exerted by light beam should be equal to $F_{\text{gravitational}}$

$$F_{\text{photon}} = F_{\text{gravitational}}$$

If power of light beam be P, the photon force is

$$F_{\text{photon}} = \frac{P}{c}$$

$$\Rightarrow \quad \frac{P}{c} = 10^{-1}$$

$$\Rightarrow \quad P = 3.0\times10^8\times10^{-1}$$

$$\Rightarrow \quad P = 3\times10^7\,\text{W}$$

Sol. 52 (D) We use $\lambda = \frac{h}{p} = \frac{h}{\sqrt{2mE}}$

$$\Rightarrow \quad E = \frac{h^2}{2m\lambda^2}$$

Thus we have $\quad \Delta E = \frac{h^2}{2m}\left(\frac{1}{\lambda_1^2} - \frac{1}{\lambda_2^2}\right)$

Using $\quad \lambda_1 = 0.5\times10^{-9}\,\text{m}$

and $\quad \lambda_2 = 2\times10^{-9}\,\text{m}$

We get $\quad \Delta E = 5.67\,\text{eV}$

Sol. 53 (B) To produce the desired current in the cell, number of electrons needed per second are equal to 1.6% of the total electrons then we use

$$I = \left(\frac{P\lambda}{hc}\right) \times \frac{1.6}{100} \times 1.6\times10^{-19} = 3\,\text{mA}$$

$$\Rightarrow \quad P \approx 0.5\,\text{W}$$

Sol. 54 (A) From quantization condition we use

$$mvr = \frac{nh}{2\pi} \quad \text{for } n = 1$$

As we have $\quad mv = \frac{h}{\lambda} = \frac{h}{2\pi r}$

$$\Rightarrow \quad \lambda_{\text{de-Broglie}} = 2\pi r = 1.058\,\pi\,\text{Å}$$

Sol. 55 (B) We use $E = \frac{3}{2}kT$ & $P = \sqrt{2mE}$

$$\Rightarrow \quad \lambda_{\text{de-Broglie}} = \frac{h}{p} = \frac{h}{\sqrt{2m\left(\frac{3}{2}kT\right)}}$$

$$\Rightarrow \qquad \lambda_{\text{de-Broglie}} = \frac{h}{\sqrt{3mkT}}$$

Substituting values

$$\lambda_{\text{de-Broglie}} = 0.63\ \text{Å}$$

Sol. 56 (A) We use : K.E. $= \dfrac{P^2}{2m_e} = \dfrac{hc}{\lambda_{\min}}$

$$\Rightarrow \qquad P = \sqrt{\frac{2hcme}{\lambda_{\min}}}$$

We have $\quad \lambda_{\text{de-Broglie}} = \dfrac{h}{p} = \sqrt{\dfrac{h\lambda_{\min}}{2m_eC}}$

For $\lambda_{\min} = 10\text{Å}$ $\lambda_{\text{de-Broglie}} \cong 0.3\text{Å}$

Sol. 57 (C) Initial de Broglie wavelength $= \dfrac{h}{m_0 v_0}$

After any time t, $\quad \lambda = \dfrac{h}{m_0 v_0 + q_0 E_0 t}$

When λ becomes half of the initial value we use

$$\frac{h}{2m_0 v_0} = \frac{h}{m_0 v_0 + q_0 E_0 t}$$

$$\Rightarrow \qquad m_0 v_0 = q_0 E_0 t$$

$$\Rightarrow \qquad t = \sqrt{3}\,\frac{m_0 v_0}{q_0 E_0}$$

Sol. 58 (B) We use $h\nu = 13.6\,(3)^2 \left[\dfrac{1}{4^2} - \dfrac{1}{5^2}\right] = 2.75$ eV

and for $n = 4$ to $n = 3$

$$h\nu = (13.6) \times (3)^2 \left[\frac{1}{3^2} - \frac{1}{4^2}\right] = 5.95\ \text{eV}$$

$\Rightarrow$ for shorter wavelength we have

$$3.95 = 5.95 - \phi$$

$$\Rightarrow \qquad \phi = 2\ \text{eV}$$

For longer wavelength

$$eV_s = 2.75 - 2 = 0.75\ \text{eV}$$

Sol. 59 (C) We use

$$h\nu = h\nu_0 + \frac{1}{2} m v_{\max_1}^2$$

As $\nu = 2\nu_0$, we have

$$h\nu_0 = \frac{1}{2} m v_{\max_1}^2 \qquad \ldots(1)$$

$$5h\nu_0 = h\nu_0 + \frac{1}{2} m v_{\max_2}^2$$

$$\Rightarrow \qquad 4h\nu_0 = \frac{1}{2} m v_{\max_2}^2$$

Using (2) – (1) gives $4 = \dfrac{v_{\max_2}^2}{v_{\max 1}^2}$

$$\Rightarrow \qquad v_{\max_2} = 2 \times v_{\max_1}$$

$$\Rightarrow \qquad v_{\max_2} = 2 \times 4 \times 10^6$$

$$\Rightarrow \qquad v_{\max_2} = 8 \times 10^6\ \text{m/c}$$

Sol. 60 (A) For an electron with kinetic energy E we use

$$\lambda = \frac{h}{\sqrt{2mE}}$$

and for a photon we have

$$\lambda = \frac{hc}{E}$$

$$\Rightarrow \qquad \text{Ratio} = \frac{hc}{E} \cdot \frac{\sqrt{2mE}}{h} = \sqrt{\frac{2mc^2}{E}}$$

ADVANCE MCQs One or More Options Correct

Sol. 1 (B, D) Pressure on screen is given as

$$P = \frac{I}{c} = \frac{30 \times 10^3}{3 \times 10^8} = 10^{-4}\ \text{N/m}^2$$

Total momentum transferred in time t is given as

$$\Delta p = \frac{IAt}{c}$$

$$= \frac{30 \times 10^3 \times 100 \times 10^{-6} \times 1000}{3 \times 10^8}$$

$$= 10^{-5}\ \text{N-S}$$

Sol. 2 (B) Energy of photon $= \dfrac{12431}{2000}$ eV $= 6.21$ eV

Maximum KE of electron at emitter $= 6.2 - 4.5 = 1.7$ eV

Minimum KE of electron at emitter $= 0$

Maximum KE of electron at collector $= 1.7\ \text{eV} + 2\ \text{eV} = 3.7$ eV

Minimum KE of electron at collector $= 0 + 2\ \text{eV} = 2$ eV

If polarity is reversed, then Max KE of electron at emitter < 2 eV

So no electron will reach at the collector.

Sol. 3 (B) With the values of work functions of aluminium and sodium we can see that the threshold frequency of aluminimum is more than that of sodium.

Sol. 4 (A, C) In this case the maximum kinetic energy of ejected electrons is given as $K_{\max} = 10.4$ eV for the work function of the metal 1.7 eV. The incident energy of the radiation on the metal surface is

$$E = 10.4 + 1.7 = 12.1\ \text{eV}$$

Which is corresponding to the electron transition in hydrogen atom from $n = 3$ to $n = 1$

Thus wavelength of the incident ration is given as $\lambda = \frac{12423}{12.1}$ Å ≈ 1022 Å. Hence options (A) and (C) are correct.

Sol. 5 (A, C) In a given magnetic field the radius of the trajectory of a charge particle is given as $r = mv/qB$ hence option (A) and (C) are correct.

Sol. 6 (B, C) The energy of lower energy level is less than that of higher level but kinetic energy of electron is more at lower energy level hence option (B) and (C) are correct.

Sol. 7 (All) Due to momentum in the photons of incident light when these photons are absorbed by the opaque sheet so the energy and momentum are continuously transferred to the sheet hence all options are correct.

Sol. 8 (B) As it is evident that the orbiting electron does not radiate any energy while revolving around the nucleus in a specific orbit. We've studied that it happens because according to de Broglie the wave behaviour of electron is such that the wavelength of moving electron in an orbit is such that it forms stationary waves in the orbit and no energy is radiated. Thus the quantized angular momentum is obtained from the wave character of the electron in an orbit hence option (B) is correct.

Sol. 9 (A, D) If photon number is kept constant then intensity can be increased only by increasing the frequency of incident light due to which stopping potential increases. As saturation current in circuit depends only upon the total number of photons incident per unit time, it will remain same hence options (A) and (D) are correct.

Sol. 10 (B, C) From the given graphs in figure it is clear that photocathode 2 has higher work function and the ejected electrons from this photocathode have lesser energy so these are stopped by a lower stopping potential and as the area of photocathodes may be different so these can have different saturation currents.

Sol. 11 (A, B, C) Quantum nature of light states that the energy of light is quantized and the energy packets of light which are called photons cannot be combined with other packets or split in more packets which verifies that options (A), (B) and (C) are correct.

Sol. 12 (B, C) By using the relation of photon momentum as $p = h/\lambda$ we get options (B) and (C) are correct.

Sol. 13 (B, D) When the source is shifted a distance 3 times away then the intensity at the cell will drop by 9 times hence option (D) is correct. As stopping potential only depends upon the frequency of the incident light it does not change so option (B) is correct.

Sol. 14 (B) Work function is $\phi = 4.5$ eV

$$E = \frac{hc}{\lambda} = \frac{12423}{2000} \approx 6.2 \text{ eV}$$

Maximum kinetic energy of ejected electrons is

$$KE_{max} = 6.2 - 4.5 = 1.7 \text{ eV}$$

If collector is positive with respect to emitter then electron will reach the collector.

Accelerating potential is of collector is 2 V thus 2 eV work is done on electrons so maximum kinetic energy of electrons reaching the collector is $= 1.7 + 2 = 3.7$ eV

And if polarity is reversed then electron will not reaches to collector because 2 eV > 1.7 eV hence only option (B) is correct.

Sol. 15 (A, C) Radiation pressure $= \frac{Force}{Area}$

$$= \text{photon flux} \times \frac{2h}{\lambda}$$

$$= \frac{I\lambda}{h_c} \times \frac{2h}{\lambda} = \frac{2I}{c}$$

Hence option (A) is correct.

For equilibrium of mirror, we have

$$T \sin \theta = \frac{2IA}{c} \quad \ldots(1)$$

$$T \cos \theta = mg \quad \ldots(2)$$

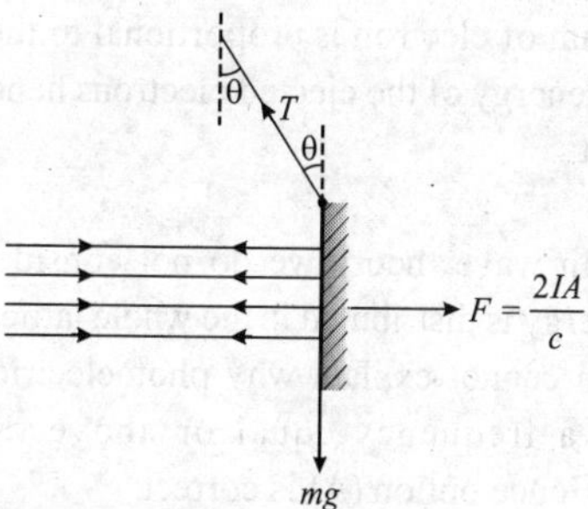

Dividing (2) by (1) we get

$$\tan \theta = \frac{2IA}{mgc}$$

Hence option (C) is correct.

Sol. 16 (A, B, C) By equation of photoelectric effect we have

$$4.25 = T_A + \phi_A \quad \ldots(1)$$

$$4.70 = T_B + \phi_B \quad \ldots(2)$$

de Broglie wavelength of the ejected electron in the two cases are given as

$$\lambda_A = \frac{12.27}{\sqrt{V_A}} \text{ and } \lambda_B = 2\lambda_A = \frac{12.27}{\sqrt{V_B}}$$

Dividing the above wavelength gives

$$\frac{1}{2}=\sqrt{\frac{V_B}{V_A}}$$

$$\Rightarrow \quad \frac{V_B}{V_A}=\frac{1}{4}$$

$$\Rightarrow \quad \frac{T_B}{T_A}=\frac{1}{4} \quad \ldots(3)$$

$$\Rightarrow \quad T_B=T_A-1.5\text{ eV} \quad \ldots(4)$$

By solving these equation gives we get

$$T_A=2\text{ eV};\ T_B=0.5\text{ eV}$$

and $\phi_A=2.25\text{ eV};\ \phi_B=4.20\text{ eV}$

Sol. 17 (A, C) Stopping potential of a metal surface in photoelectric effect experiment depends on frequency of incident light and work function of the metal surface which depends upon the characteristics of the emitter metal hence option (A) and (C) are correct.

Sol. 18 (All) From the graph it is clear that for the radiation B stopping potential is maximum which is corresponding to the maximum kinetic energy as well as maximum frequency of the radiation hence option (A) is correct. The stopping potential for the radiation C is minimum which is for the minimum frequency or longest wavelength of the radiation hence option (B) is also correct. Saturation current is maximum in case of radiation A which is corresponding to maximum rate of photons incident or maximum rate of electron emission from the surface. The momentum of electron is proportional to the square root of the kinetic energy of the ejected electrons hence option (D) is also correct.

Sol. 19 (A) In wave theory we do not consider the energy packets so energy is distributed in the whole lattice of the metal surface which cannot explain why photoelectric effect takes place on at a frequency equal or above the threshold frequencies. Hence option (A) is correct.

Sol. 20 (C) The stopping potential in the experiment of photoelectric effect is the reverse potential which stops the fastest emitted photoelectron to the collector plate. The fastest electron will be corresponding to the maximum energetic photon which is corresponding to the shortest wavelength in the radiation beam.

Sol. 21 (C) Photocurrent in an experiment of photoelectric effect is independent of the frequency of the incident light and depends only upon the rate at which photons incident on the metal surface.

Sol. 22 (A, B, C) If atom is moving initially then by conservation of momentum and energy we can find the frequency of emitted photon which will vary depending upon the direction of motion of atom and the direction in which the photon is ejected. A photon can be ejected in same, opposite or normal direction to the initial motion of the atom hence option (A), (B) and (C) can be correct.

Sol. 23 (A, B) Due to the pulse of light and its reflection it imparts some momentum to the mirror due to which it gains some momentum and starts to oscillate hence option (A) is correct. As some energy of the incident light is transferred to the mirror, the reflected light will have relatively lesser energy and slightly higher wavelength hence option (B) is correct.

Sol. 24 (B, D) For the metal plate A the stopping potential is calculated by the most energetic radiation in the incident beam by using the relation

$$eV_0=\frac{hc}{\lambda}-\phi$$

$$\Rightarrow \quad eV_0=\left(\frac{1240}{400}-1.5\right)\text{eV}$$

$$\Rightarrow \quad V_0=1.6\text{ V}$$

For metal plate B, it is calculated as

$$V_0=\frac{1240}{400}-2=1.1\text{ V}$$

Sol. 25 (A, D) Stopping potential is a reverse potential hence option (A) is correct. At stopping potential just before hitting the collector plate electrons are repelled away hence option (D) is also correct.

Sol. 26 (B, D) Due to increase in wavelength the incident energy decreases but if it is still higher than the work function of the metal photoelectric emission can take place hence option (B) is correct. Due to decrease in frequency of light the stopping potential will decrease hence option (D) is also correct.

Sol. 27 (A, B, C) Energy quanta or photo is considered a packet of energy which cannot be broken into parts as well as it cannot be combined with other quantas hence options A, B and C are correct.

Sol. 28 (A, D) $KE_{\max}=(5-\phi)\text{eV}$

When these electrons are accelerated through 5 V, they will reach the anode with maximum energy $=(5-\phi+5)$ eV

$$10-\phi=8$$

$$\Rightarrow \quad \phi=2\text{ eV}$$

Current is less than saturation current because if slowest electron also reached the plate it would have 5 eV energy at the anode, but there it is given that the minimum energy is 6 eV.

* * * * *

ANSWERS & SOLUTIONS

CONCEPTUAL MCQS Single Option Correct

1	(B)	**2**	(C)	**3**	(D)
4	(B)	**5**	(C)	**6**	(A)
7	(B)	**8**	(C)	**9**	(B)
10	(A)	**11**	(B)	**12**	(B)
13	(B)	**14**	(B)	**15**	(C)
16	(D)	**17**	(A)	**18**	(D)
19	(C)	**20**	(C)	**21**	(A)
22	(D)	**23**	(C)	**24**	(A)
25	(C)	**26**	(C)	**27**	(A)
28	(A)	**29**	(D)		

NUMERICAL MCQS Single Option Correct

1	(B)	**2**	(C)	**3**	(D)
4	(C)	**5**	(B)	**6**	(B)
7	(C)	**8**	(C)	**9**	(B)
10	(C)	**11**	(A)	**12**	(C)
13	(B)	**14**	(B)	**15**	(B)
16	(A)	**17**	(C)	**18**	(B)
19	(D)	**20**	(D)	**21**	(B)
22	(D)	**23**	(C)	**24**	(A)
25	(A)	**26**	(C)		

ADVANCE MCQs One or More Options Correct

1	(A, C)	**2**	(A, C)	**3**	(A, C, D)
4	(A, B, C)	**5**	(A)	**6**	(A, B, C)
7	(A, C, D)	**8**	(B)	**9**	(A, D)
10	(A)	**11**	(B, D)	**12**	(A, B, C)
13	(C, D)	**14**	(A, B)	**15**	(All)
16	(A, B)	**17**	(C)	**18**	(D)

Solutions of PRACTICE EXERCISE 3.1

(i) Given wavelength is $\lambda = 0.1 \times 10^{-9}\ \text{nm} = 1\text{Å}$

Photon energy $E = \dfrac{12431}{1} = 12.431\ \text{keV}$

Frequency $\nu = \dfrac{E}{h} = \dfrac{12.431\times10^3\times1.6\times10^{-19}}{6.63\times10^{-34}}$

$= 3\times10^{18}\ \text{Hz}$

Photon momentum $P = \dfrac{h}{\lambda} = \dfrac{6.63\times10^{-34}}{10^{-10}}$

$= 6.63\times10^{-24}\ \text{J-s}$

(ii) For $\lambda_c = 1\text{Å}$ we use

$$V = \frac{12431}{1} = 12.431\ \text{kV}$$

Photon energy $E = \dfrac{hc}{\lambda} = \dfrac{6.63\times10^{-34}\times3\times10^{8}}{10^{-10}}$

$= 1.99\times10^{-15}\ \text{J}$

(iii) Energy required to knockout L shell electron is 11.3 keV hence the potential difference across the tube must be less than 11.3 kV in case L shell electron is to be saved for no L series X-ray emission.

(iv) Wavelength of k_α photon is

$$\lambda = \frac{12431}{6400} = 1.942\ \text{Å}$$

Using momentum conservation we get

$$P = \frac{h}{\lambda} = mV_R$$

$\Rightarrow$ Recoil energy of atom is

$$E_R = \frac{P^2}{2m} = \frac{(h/\lambda)^2}{2m}$$

$$\Rightarrow E_R = \left(\frac{6.63\times10^{-34}}{1.942\times10^{-10}}\right)\times\frac{1}{2\times9.3\times10^{-20}\times1.6\times10^{-19}}$$

$\Rightarrow E_R = 3.91\times10^{-10}\ \text{eV}$

(v) Photons travel at speed of light so time taken by both photons is

$$t = \frac{d}{c} = \frac{3\times10^3}{3\times10^8} = 10^{-5}\ \text{s} = 10\ \mu\text{s}$$

(vi) Building energy of L-shell electron is 11.3 keV

Energy difference of $n = 2$ and $n = 1$ shell is

$$\Delta E = \frac{12431}{0.213} = 58.3615\ \text{keV}$$

$\Rightarrow$ Building energy of K-shell electron is

$$E_K = 58.3615 + 11.3$$
$$= 69.6615\ \text{keV}$$

Thus accelerating voltage required to knock out K-shell electron is 69.6615 V.

(vii) Energies required for below transition are

$n = 1$ to ∞ $\quad E_1 = 25.31$ KeV

$n = 2$ to ∞ $\quad E_2 = 3.56$ KeV

$n = 3$ to ∞ $\quad E_3 = 0.53$ KeV

$\Rightarrow$ Energy of K_α line is $\Delta E_{21} = 25.31 - 3.56 = 21.75$ KeV

$\Rightarrow$ Energy of K_β line is $\Delta E_{31} = 25.31 - 0.530 = 24.78$ KeV

$\Rightarrow$ Energy of L_α line is $\Delta E_{31} = 3.56 - 0.530 = 3.03$ KeV

Thus $\quad \nu_{K\alpha} = \dfrac{\Delta E_{21}}{h} = 5.249\times10^{18}\ \text{Hz}$

$$\nu_{K\beta} = \frac{\Delta E_{31}}{h} = 5.98 \times 10^{18}\text{ Hz}$$

$$\nu_{L\alpha} = \frac{\Delta E_{32}}{h} = 7.312 \times 10^{17}\text{ Hz}$$

Solutions of CONCEPTUAL MCQS Single Option Correct

Sol. 1 (B) In Coolidge tube high speed electrons are allowed to incident on the target anode metal for production of X-rays hence option (B) is correct.

Sol. 2 (C) In X-ray production the electric work done on electrons transformed to their kinetic energy and then this energy is radiated in form of X-rays during interaction of these high speed electrons with the field of nucleus of target anode atoms. Hence option (C) is most appropriate here.

Sol. 3 (D) If the incident energy allowed to emit K series of X-rays then K_α line frequency will remain same but the minimum wavelength of the continuous spectrum will get doubled hence option (D) is correct.

Sol. 4 (B) The minimum wavelength of X-rays emitted from an X-ray tube is given as

$$\lambda_c = \frac{hc}{eV} = \frac{12431}{V}\text{ Å}$$

Hence option (B) is correct.

Sol. 5 (C) Hard X-rays have higher energy and lower wavelength so the potential difference across the tube need to be increased hence option (C) is correct.

Sol. 6 (A) Molybdenum has high melting point due to higher value of its mass number so it can withstand against high energy electrons so this is preferred hence option (A) is correct.

Sol. 7 (B) As minimum wavelength of the continuous spectrum is inversely proportional to the applied voltage in the tube hence option (B) is correct.

Sol. 8 (C) Mosley's law is given as $\sqrt{\nu} = a\,(Z - \sigma)$ hence option (C) is correct.

Sol. 9 (B) From the spectrum of continuous X-rays the emitted radiation has wavelength above a minimum wavelength and extend upto infinite value hence option (B) is correct.

Sol. 10 (A) K_α line wavelength depends upon the atomic charge which is same in all isotopes hence option (A) is correct.

Sol. 11 (B) Sodium has less work function than copper so the kinetic energy of ejected electrons in case of sodium will be more hence the stopping potential will be more for sodium hence option (B) is correct.

Sol. 12 (B) The energy of X-ray photons is directly proportional to the radiation frequency with which the photons penetrate a physical substance hence option (B) is correct.

Sol. 13 (B) A good target for X-ray production must be able to withstand against high energy electron which looses energy to heat up the target so it should be a heavy element with high melting point hence option (B) is correct.

Sol. 14 (B) Continuous X-ray spectrum is produced due to loss of electron energies when these interact in the positive field of the target nuclei at different approach distances hence option (B) is correct.

Sol. 15 (C) X-rays are electrically neutral so these are not deflected by electric field hence option (C) is correct.

Sol. 16 (D) As the incident photon supplies some energy to the electron its energy decreases due to which its frequency decreases and wavelength increases, hence option (D) is correct.

Sol. 17 (A) X-rays are very high energy electromagnetic rays which can damage the target and receiver also over a period of time due to regular reflection and absorption thats why these are not used in RADAR hence option (A) is correct.

Sol. 18 (D) X-rays are electromagnetic radiation which travel at speed of light hence option (D) is correct.

Sol. 19 (C) X-ray photons have energy more than ultraviolet radiation but less than gamma radiation hence option (C) is correct.

Sol. 20 (C) X-rays are highly energetic electromagnetic radiation which will pass through the muscular organs and tissues of the body and no shadow is obtained hence option (C) is correct.

Sol. 21 (A) The energy differences in the shells of hydrogen are so less that the emitted photon energies do not fall in X-ray spectrum region hence option (A) is correct.

Sol. 22 (D) As X-rays are electrically neutral and does not produce any magnetic phenomenon, these are not deflected by magnetic field hence option (D) is correct.

Sol. 23 (C) White term is used to denote the mixture of several wavelengths in the continues spectrum of X-rays hence option (C) is most appropriate.

Sol. 24 (A) Wavelength of X-rays is inversely dependent upon the applied voltage in the tube hence among the options given (A) is correct.

Sol. 25 (C) K_α line has energy less than K_β line hence wavelength of K_α line is more than K_β hence option (C) is correct.

Sol. 26 (C) For higher energy levels in an atom screening constant cannot be precisely determined so the above relation mainly gives good approximated results for lower values of n_1 and n_2 hence option (C) is most appropriate here.

Sol. 27 (A) As X-rays wavelength is of the order of interatomic spacing, good level of diffraction pattern can be obtained by the lattice atoms for the study of structural analysis hence option (A) is correct.

Sol. 28 (A) As applied voltage across the tube increases, the cut off wavelength decreases thus the difference between λ_C and λ_K increases hence option (A) is correct.

Sol. 29 (D) From the figure it is clear the cut off wavelength of A is less than that of B so applied voltage for A is more than that of B and the characteristic K_α line wavelength of B is less than that of A that means the energy level difference of element B is more than that of A for $n = 1$ and $n = 2$ thus atomic charge of B is more than that of A hence option (D) is correct.

Solutions of NUMERICAL MCQS Single Option Correct

Sol. 1 (B) To knock out the innermost electron the voltage must be more than 40 kV then only a vacancy will be created in K shell and K series X-rays will be emitted.

Sol. 2 (C) The minimum wavelength is

$$\lambda_c = \frac{12431}{40000} = 031\text{Å}$$

Thus wavelengths lesser than 0.31 Å must not be present.

Sol. 3 (D) Minimum wavelength is

$$\lambda_c = \frac{12431}{80000} = 0.155\text{ Å}$$

As $\quad KE_{max} = 80\,keV > BE_K$

So characteristic X-rays will be there

Sol. 4 (C) We use

$$\frac{\lambda_1}{\lambda_2} = \left(\frac{Z_2 - 1}{Z_1 - 1}\right)^2$$

$$\Rightarrow \quad \lambda_2 = \lambda \times \left(\frac{56}{28}\right)^2 = 4$$

Sol. 5 (B) We use $\lambda_{min} = \dfrac{hc}{20000e}, \lambda'_{min} = \dfrac{hC}{10000e}$

Given that $4(\lambda_\alpha - \lambda_{min}) = (\lambda_\alpha - \lambda'_{min})$

$$\Rightarrow \quad 3\lambda\alpha = 4\lambda_{min} - \lambda'_{min}$$

$$\Rightarrow \quad \lambda_\alpha = \frac{hC}{30000e}$$

$$\Rightarrow \quad \frac{hC}{\lambda_\alpha} = 30000\,e$$

By using the formula of energy of electrons according to Bohr's model and considering shielding effect

$$30000 = (13.6)\left(\frac{1}{12} - \frac{1}{2^2}\right)(Z-1)^2$$

$$\Rightarrow \quad Z - 1 = 100\sqrt{\frac{5}{17}} = \frac{100}{\sqrt{3.4}} = 54$$

$$\Rightarrow \quad Z = 55$$

Sol. 6 (B) Initial kinetic energy of electron in X-ray tube is 50 keV. During first collision the energy of first photon released is 50% of initial kinetic energy of electron and 10% energy is dissipated as thermal energy which are given as

Energy of photon released in first collision = 25 keV

Energy dissipated in first collision = 5 keV

After first collision energy left in electron is

$$K_1 = (50 - 25 - 5)\text{ keV} = 20\text{ keV}$$

Now we can calculate the energy released as photon during second collision which is 50% of K_1 given as

Energy of the photon emitted during second collision is

$$E_{ph} = 10{,}000\text{ eV}$$

Wavelength of this emitted photon is given as

$$\lambda = \frac{hc}{E_{ph}} = \frac{1242}{10000} = 1.242\text{ Å}$$

Sol. 7 (C) We use

$$P = V_q$$

$$= 200\,(6.25 \times 10^{18} + 3.125 \times 10^{18}) \times 1.6 \times 10^{-19}$$

$$\Rightarrow \quad P = 300\text{ watt}$$

Sol. 8 (C) We use

$$E_{L_\alpha} = E_{K_\beta} - E_{K_\alpha}$$

$$\Rightarrow \quad E_{L_\alpha} = 12431\left(\frac{1}{1} - \frac{1}{2}\right)$$

$$\Rightarrow \quad E_{L_\alpha} = \frac{12420}{2} = 6215.5\text{ eV}$$

$$\Rightarrow \quad E_{L_\alpha} = 6.21\text{ KeV}$$

Sol. 9 (B) We use

$$\frac{\lambda_1}{\lambda_2} = \left(\frac{Z_2-1}{Z_1-1}\right)^2$$

$$\Rightarrow \quad Z_2 = (Z_1-1)\sqrt{\frac{\lambda_1}{\lambda_2}}+1$$

$$\Rightarrow \quad Z_2 = 50\times\sqrt{\frac{\lambda}{4\lambda}}+1$$

$$\Rightarrow \quad Z_2 = 26$$

Sol. 10 (C) We use

$$\lambda_c \propto \frac{1}{V}$$

$\Rightarrow$ as V charges to $V/2$ wavelength λ_c will get doubled.

Sol. 11 (A) For K_α line in X-ray spectrum, wavelength of line is related to the atomic number as

$$\frac{1}{\lambda} \propto (z-1)^2$$

$$\Rightarrow \quad \frac{1.5405}{0.7092} = \frac{(Z-1)^2}{(Z_{Cu}-1)^2}$$

$$\Rightarrow \quad Z = 42$$

Hence impurity is molybdenum.

Sol. 12 (C) Energy of photon is given by mc^2 now the maximum energy of photon is equal to the maximum energy of electron $= eV$

Hence, $mc^2 = eV$

$$\Rightarrow \quad m = \frac{eV}{c^2} = \frac{1.6\times10^{-19}\times18\times10^3}{(3\times10^8)^2} = 3.2\times10^{-32}\text{ kg}$$

Sol. 13 (B) We use

$$V = \frac{P}{i} = \frac{P}{ne}$$

$$\Rightarrow \quad V = \frac{1}{6.25\times10^{13}\times1.6\times10^{-19}}$$

$$\Rightarrow \quad V = 10^5\text{ volts}$$

$$\Rightarrow \quad \lambda_{min} = \frac{hc}{eV} = \frac{12431}{V}\text{ Å} \cong 0.12\text{ Å}$$

Sol. 14 (B) We use for K_α line

$$\frac{1}{\lambda_1} = R(Z-1)^2\left[1-\frac{1}{4}\right] \quad \ldots(1)$$

for K_β line we use

$$\frac{1}{\lambda_2} = R(Z-1)^2\left[1-\frac{1}{9}\right] \quad \ldots(2)$$

$$\frac{(1)}{(2)} \Rightarrow \frac{\lambda_2}{\lambda_1} = \frac{3}{4}\times\frac{9}{8}$$

$$\Rightarrow \quad \lambda_2 = \frac{27}{32}\lambda = \frac{27}{32}\times0.32\text{ Å} = 0.27\text{ Å}$$

Sol. 15 (B) Maximum photon energy is

$$E = \frac{12431}{0.33} = 37.67\text{ keV}$$

Sol. 16 (A) We use

$$\frac{1}{\lambda_\alpha} = \frac{3R}{4}(Z-1)^2$$

$$\Rightarrow \quad (Z-1) = \sqrt{\frac{4}{3R\lambda_\alpha}}$$

$$\Rightarrow \quad (Z-1) = \sqrt{\frac{4}{3\times1.1\times10^7\times1.8\times10^{-10}}}$$

$$\Rightarrow \quad (Z-1) = \frac{200}{3}\sqrt{\frac{5}{33}} = \frac{78}{3} = 26$$

$$\Rightarrow \quad Z = 27$$

Sol. 17 (C) Knock out an electron from K level, energy supplied must be enough to drive it to an unfilled higher level of negligible energy ($n \to \infty$)

$\Rightarrow$ Energy required = B.E. of K level = 69.5 keV

$\Rightarrow$ Acceleration potential = 69.5 kV

Sol. 18 (B) Power of electron beam is

$$P = V_i = 20\times10^3\times10\times10^{-3}$$

$$\Rightarrow \quad P = 200\text{ W}$$

$$\Rightarrow \quad P_{X\text{-ray}} = \frac{0.5}{100}\times200 = 1\text{ W}$$

Sol. 19 (D) On increasing the applied voltage across the tube the electrons which knock out the orbiting electrons will left over with extra energy and these may knock out more orbiting electrons in the target which leads to emission of more characteristic X-rays hence option (D) is correct.

Sol. 20 (D) Using $\frac{1}{\lambda} = R(z-1)^2\left[\frac{1}{n_2^2}-\frac{1}{n_1^2}\right]$

For α particle; $\quad n_1 = 2, n_2 = 1$

For metal A; $\quad \frac{1875R}{4} = R(Z_1-1)^2\left(\frac{3}{4}\right)$

$$\Rightarrow \quad z_1 = 26$$

For metal B; $675R = R(Z_2 - 1)^2 \left(\frac{3}{4}\right)$

$\Rightarrow$ $z_2 = 31$

Therefore, 4 elements lie between A and B.

Sol. 21 (B) Using Mosley's law for both cobalt and impurity

$$\sqrt{f} = K(Z-1)$$

$$\Rightarrow \sqrt{\frac{c}{\lambda}} = K(Z-1)$$

$$\Rightarrow \sqrt{\frac{c}{\lambda_{co}}} = K(Z_{co}-1) \text{ and } \sqrt{\frac{c}{\lambda_x}} = K(Z_x - 1)$$

$$\Rightarrow \sqrt{\frac{\lambda_{co}}{\lambda_x}} = \frac{Z_x - 1}{Z_{co} - 1} \Rightarrow Z_x = 40$$

Sol. 22 (D) Minimum wavelength emitted is

$$\lambda_c = \frac{12431}{66000} = 0.1883 \text{ Å}$$

Thus option (D) is correct.

Sol. 23 (C) Power dissipated in target anode is

$$P = V_i \times 0.01$$

$$\Rightarrow P = 150 N_0^3 \times 10 \times 10^{-3} \times 0.99$$

$$\Rightarrow P = 1485 \text{ watt}$$

$$\Rightarrow P = \frac{1485}{4.18} = 355.26 \text{ cal/sec}$$

Sol. 24 (A) No of electrons through the table per second are

$$N = \frac{3.2\times10^{-3}}{1.6\times10^{-19}} = 2\times10^{16}$$

Sol. 25 (A) Penetration power of X-rays depend upon the photon energies thus the photon energy is more for lesser wavelength radiation.

Sol. 26 (C) The energy of K_α X-ray photons is directly proportional to $(Z-1)^2$. The energy ratio of two K_α photons obtained in X-ray from two metal targets of atomic numbers Z_1 and Z_2 is $\left(\frac{Z_1 - 1}{Z_2 - 1}\right)^2$.

ADVANCE MCQs One or More Options Correct

Sol. 1 (A, C) With the frequency spectrum of electromagnetic waves, the rays in the short wavelength neighbourhood of X-rays are γ-rays and in the long wavelength neighbourhood of X-Rays are ultraviolet rays hence options (A) and (C) are correct.

Sol. 2 (A, C) K_α, K_β and L_α lines are corresponding to the electron transition from $n = 2$ to $n = 1$, $n = 3$ to $n = 1$ and $n = 3$ to $n = 2$ respectively. Thus we can use

$$\lambda_\alpha' > \lambda_\alpha > \lambda_\beta$$

By energy levels we can also use

$$\frac{hc}{\lambda_\alpha} = \frac{hc}{\lambda_\alpha} + \frac{hc}{\lambda_\beta}$$

Sol. 3 (A, C, D) If the potential difference is same, the electrons will gain same kinetic energy hence will have same speed (but may not be in same direction) so due to same magnitude of momentum they will have same de Broglie wavelengths. As these electrons have same energy they produce X-rays of same minimum wavelength as shortest wavelength of X-rays depends upon the accelerating voltage only.

Sol. 4 (A, B, C) When a high speed electron strikes a metal surface then, no amount of the energy dissipates initially. When electron passes in the field of nucleus, X-Rays are emitted and for any passing by electron its full energy can be converted into X-Ray photon or partially also partial energy can also be converted into the X-Ray photon energy hence options (A), (B) and (C) are correct.

Sol. 5 (A) As analyzed by de Broglie option (A) is the only correct option as given in question.

Sol. 6 (A, B, C) Shortest wavelength of X-rays emitted is given as

$$\lambda_C = \frac{12431}{20000} = 0.621 \text{ Å}$$

Hence option (A) is correct. As the incident energy 20 KeV is more then the energy of L shell L_α X-ray may be emitted which will have energy 19.9 KeV or less hence option (B) and (C) are correct.

Sol. 7 (A, C, D) The energy required to knock out K shell electron (from $n = 1$ to infinity) is more than that of L shell electron (from $n = 2$ to infinity) hence option (A) is correct. With the energy levels involved in transition of L_α, K_α and K_β X-rays it is clear that option (C) and (D) are correct.

Sol. 8 (B) The accelerating potential difference for the electrons to produce minimum wavelength 66.3 pm s given as

$$V = \frac{12431}{\lambda} \text{ volts} \approx 18.75 \text{ kV}$$

The de Broglie wavelength of the electrons reaching the anode is given as

$$\lambda = \frac{h}{\sqrt{2meV}} \approx 8.9 \text{ pm}$$

Hence only option (B) is correct.

Sol. 9 (A, D) As the potential difference applied to the tube increases, the energy of ejected X-ray photons increases due to which X-ray intensity increases and the minimum wavelength emitted which is inversely proportional to the applied voltage decreases. Hence options (A) and (D) are correct.

Sol. 10 (A) Cut off wavelength depends upon the accelerating potential difference so it will remain same and characteristic lines are dependent upon the energy gap between the energy levels of the element so these may change. Hence only option (A) is correct.

Sol. 11 (B, D) As we increase the applied potential difference, the electron energy increases which increases the frequency of the photons emitted hence option (B) is correct. With increase in filament current more electrons per second are incident on the target which increases the number of photons emitted per unit time hence intensity of X-rays increases but no effect will be there on the cut off wavelength due to this hence option (D) is correct.

Sol. 12 (A, B, C) As value of Z increases the difference of energies of energy levels also increase so wavelength corresponding to each characteristic line decreases hence option (A) is correct. As applied voltage across the tube increases, cut off wavelength decreases hence option (B) is correct. If power of cathode is increased which is done by increase in current or increase in number of electrons per unit time incident on the target, then due to this more X-ray photons are emitted per unit time from the target which increases the intensity of X-rays emitted hence option (C) is correct.

Sol. 13 (C, D) For the different characteristic X-rays given in options we know that the transitions for these X-rays are corresponding to the energy levels as given below

K_α $n=2$ to $n=1$
K_β $n=3$ to $n=1$
K_γ $n=4$ to $n=1$
L_α $n=3$ to $n=2$
M_α $n=4$ to $n=3$

For the above lines we know that correct energy and wavelength relations are

$$E(K_\alpha)<E(K_\beta)<E(K_\gamma) \text{ and } E(M_\alpha)<E(L_\alpha)<E(K_\alpha)$$

So we have $\lambda(K_\alpha)>\lambda(K_\beta)>\lambda(K_\gamma)$ and $\lambda(M_\alpha)>\lambda(L_\alpha)>\lambda(K_\alpha)$

Hence options (C) and (D) are correct.

Sol. 14 (A, B) The average rate of rise in temperature of target can be given by the power which is dissipated as heat. Here it is 99% of the incident power, which is given as

$$\frac{\Delta T}{\Delta t}=\frac{0.99P}{ms}=\frac{(0.99)(50\text{kV})(20\text{mA})}{(1kg)(495\text{ J kg}^{-1}{}^\circ C^{-1})}=2^\circ\text{C/s}$$

Hence option (A) is correct. The minimum wavelength of the X-rays emitted is given as

$$\lambda_{\min}=\frac{hc}{eV}=\frac{12400}{50\times10^3}=0.248\text{ Å}$$

Hence option (B) is correct. For fast conduction of heat and to protect the target from melting it should have high conductivity and high melting point hence options (C) and (D) are NOT correct.

Sol. 15 (All) X-ray is an electromagnetic radiation which carries energy and momentum, when it is incident on a substance and absorbed or reflected, it supplies energy and momentum to it hence all given options are correct.

Sol. 16 (A, B) As studied in basic theory of continuous X-rays are produced due to high kinetic energy of electrons because of applied potential difference across the tube is converted into radiation due to interaction with the nuclear charge and characteristic X-rays are produced due to excitation of lower shell electrons in the atom which creates a vacancy into which electrons of higher shell transits and emits characteristic lines hence options (A) and (B) are correct.

Sol. 17 (C) Characteristic X-rays have specific lines which are emitted corresponding to the transition of electron in the inner shells of the target atom in X-ray tube anode hence option (C) is false.

Sol. 18 (D) Characteristic X-rays wavelength are dependent upon the difference in energy levels of the target atoms hence among all the given options only option (D) is true.

* * * * *

ANSWERS & SOLUTIONS

CONCEPTUAL MCQS Single Option Correct

1	(D)	2	(A)	3	(A)
4	(B)	5	(D)	6	(D)
7	(D)	8	(B)	9	(A)
10	(D)	11	(D)	12	(A)
13	(D)	14	(B)	15	(C)
16	(A)	17	(C)	18	(B)
19	(B)	20	(C)	21	(A)
22	(C)	23	(D)	24	(A)
25	(D)	26	(C)	27	(B)
28	(B)	29	(A)	30	(C)
31	(D)	32	(D)	33	(B)
34	(A)	35	(D)	36	(A)
37	(B)	38	(A)	39	(C)
40	(D)	41	(B)	42	(B)
43	(A)	44	(B)	45	(B)
46	(D)	47	(C)	48	(C)

NUMERICAL MCQS Single Option Correct

1	(B)	2	(C)	3	(B)
4	(B)	5	(D)	6	(B)
7	(A)	8	(C)	9	(C)
10	(B)	11	(C)	12	(C)
13	(D)	14	(B)	15	(C)
16	(D)	17	(A)	18	(C)
19	(C)	20	(B)	21	(B)
22	(C)	23	(D)	24	(D)
25	(B)	26	(C)	27	(D)
28	(A)	29	(B)	30	(A)
31	(D)	32	(D)	33	(B)
34	(D)	35	(B)	36	(C)
37	(B)	38	(B)	39	(C)
40	(D)	41	(C)	42	(C)
43	(C)	44	(C)	45	(C)
46	(A)	47	(C)	48	(D)
49	(B)	50	(C)	51	(C)
52	(D)	53	(C)	54	(A)
55	(D)	56	(C)	57	(D)
58	(B)	59	(D)	60	(A)
61	(D)	62	(C)	63	(D)
64	(A)	65	(C)	66	(D)
67	(C)	68	(C)	69	(A)
70	(C)	71	(B)	72	(D)
73	(A)	74	(C)	75	(C)
76	(D)	77	(D)	78	(A)
79	(D)				

ADVANCE MCQs One or More Options Correct

1	(All)	2	(C, D)	3	(B, C)
4	(A, B)	5	(B, C)	6	(B, C)
7	(A)	8	(D)	9	(A, D)
10	(A, B, D)	11	(A, C)	12	(A, D)
13	(A, B, D)	14	(A, B)	15	(B, C, D)
16	(C, D)	17	(B, D)	18	(All)
19	(A, C, D)	20	(B, C, D)	21	(A, B, D)
22	(B, C)	23	(A, C)		

Solutions of PRACTICE EXERCISE 4.1

(i) **(a)** Mass defect is

$$\Delta m = 0.007 \times 10^{-3}\ \text{kg}$$

Energy released $\Delta E = \Delta mc^2 = 0.007 \times 10^{-3} \times (3 \times 10^8)^2$

$\Rightarrow$ $\Delta E = 63 \times 10^{10}\ \text{J}$

(b) Energy in *kwh* at 5% efficiency is

$$E = \frac{63\times10^{10}}{3600\times1000} \times 0.05 = 8.75\ \text{kwh}$$

(ii) Mass defect

$$\Delta m = 8(1.007825) + 8(1.008665)$$

$\Rightarrow$ -15.994915

$$\Delta m = 0.137005\ \text{amu}$$

Binding energy $\Delta E = 0.137005 \times 931.5\ \text{MeV}$

$\Rightarrow$ $\Delta E = 127.62\ \text{MeV}$

Binding energy per nucleon is

$$(\Delta E)_A = \frac{127.62}{16} = 7.976\ \text{MeV}$$

(iii) **(a)** Mass of nucleus $\simeq A$

(b) We use volume of nucleus

$$V = \frac{4}{3}\pi r^3$$

and $r = r_0 A^{1/3}$

$\Rightarrow$ $V = \frac{4}{3}\pi r_0^3 A$

(c) Density of nucleus

$\Rightarrow$ $\rho_n = \frac{M}{V} = \frac{Am}{\frac{4}{3}\pi r_0^3 A}$

$\Rightarrow$ $\rho_n = \frac{3m}{4\pi r_0^3}$

$\Rightarrow$ $\rho_n = \frac{3\times1.67\times10^{-27}}{4\times3.14\times(1.2\times10^{-15})^3}$

$\Rightarrow$ $\rho_n = 2.3 \times 10^{17}\ \text{kg/m}^3$

(iv) Mass defect $\Delta m = 1.007825 + 1.008665$

$$-2.014102$$

$\Rightarrow$ $\Delta m = 0.002388\ \text{amu}$

$\Rightarrow$ Binding energy $\Delta E = 0.002388 \times 931.5$

$\Rightarrow$ $\Delta E = 2.224\ \text{MeV}$

(v) Mass defect $\Delta m = 3(1.007825) + 4(1.008665) - 7.016005$

$\Rightarrow \Delta m = 0.04213$ amu

Binding energy $\Delta E = 0.04213 \times 931.5$ MeV

$\Rightarrow \Delta E = 39.231$ MeV

Binding energy per nucleus

$$(\Delta E)_A = \frac{39.231}{7} = 5.604 \text{ MeV}$$

(vi) Radius of C^{12} nuclei are

$$r = r_0(A)^{1/3}$$
$$= 1.2 \times 10^{-15} \times (12)^{1/3}$$
$$= 2.747 \times 10^{-15} \text{ m}$$

Electrical potential energy is

$$U = \frac{1}{4\pi \epsilon_0} \frac{(6e)^2}{(2r)}$$

$$\Rightarrow U = \frac{9\times10^9 \times 36 \times (1.6\times10^{-19})^2}{2\times 2.747\times10^{-15}}$$

$$\Rightarrow U = 9.435 \times 10^6 \text{ eV}$$

$$\Rightarrow U = 9.435 \text{ MeV}$$

(vii) Mass defect $\Delta m = 20(1.007825) + 36(1.008665) - 55.934939$

$= 0.533501$

$\Rightarrow$ Binding energy $= 0.533501 \times 931.5$ MeV

$= 496.95$ MeV

Solutions of PRACTICE EXERCISE 4.2

(i) (a) We use $m = m_0(2)^{-t/5}$

$$\Rightarrow 0.01 \times 10^{-3} = 10^{-3}(2)^{-t/1590}$$

$$\Rightarrow t = 1590 \times \frac{\log(10)}{\log(2)} = \frac{1590\times 2}{0.301}$$

$$\Rightarrow t = 10564.78 \text{ years}$$

(b) We use $0.99 \times 10^{-3} = 10^{-3}(2)^{-t/1590}$

$$\Rightarrow t = 1590 \times \frac{\log\left(\frac{100}{99}\right)}{\log(2)}$$

$$\Rightarrow t = \frac{1590 \times 0.004365}{0.301} = 23.05 \text{ years}$$

(ii) We use $A = A_0(2)^{-t/T}$

$$\Rightarrow 2700 = 4750\,(2)^{-5/T}$$

$$\Rightarrow T = \frac{5\times\log(2)}{\log\left(\frac{4700}{2700}\right)}$$

$$\Rightarrow T = \frac{5\times 0.301}{0.2453} = 6.135 \text{ min}$$

(iii) Activity of sample is

$$A = \lambda N$$

$$\Rightarrow A = \frac{0.693}{28\times86400\times365} \times \frac{6.023\times10^{23}}{90}$$

$$\Rightarrow A = 5.106 \times 10^{12} \text{ dps}$$

(iv) We use $A = A_0 2^{-t/T}$

$$A = (1 \text{ mCi})\, 2^{-1/5.3}$$

$$\Rightarrow A = 0.877 \text{ mCi}$$

(v) For substance A we use

$$m = m_0(2)^{-t/T}$$

$$\Rightarrow m_A = 10^{-2} \times (2)^{-16/4}$$

$$\Rightarrow m_A = \frac{6}{16}\times 10^{-2} = 6.25 \times 10^{-4} \text{ kg}$$

For substance B we use

$$m_B = 10^{-2} \times (2)^{-16/8}$$

$$\Rightarrow m_B = \frac{1}{4} \times 10^{-2} = 2.5 \times 10^{-3} \text{ kg}$$

(vi) **(a)** Half life = 10 s

$$\text{Mean life} = \frac{1}{\lambda} = \frac{T}{0.693} = 14.43 \text{ s}$$

(b) Further amount will reduce to half after next half life = 10 s

(vii) **(a)** Nuclear reaction for β decay is

$${}^{137}_{55}\text{Cs} \rightarrow {}^{137}_{56}\text{Cs} + {}^{0}_{-1}e$$

(b) We use $N = N_0(2)^{-t/T}$

$$\Rightarrow N = \frac{6.023\times10^{23}}{137} \times (2)^{-5/30}$$

$$\Rightarrow N = 3.913 \times 10^{21} \text{ atoms}$$

(c) We use $A = A_0(2)^{-t/T}$

$$\Rightarrow A = (1 \text{ mCi})\, 2^{-5/30} = 0.89 \text{ mCi}$$

(viii) Using $A = A_0(2)^{-t/T}$

$$\Rightarrow 6 = 15(2)^{-t/5730}$$

$$\Rightarrow t = \frac{5730\times\log\left(\frac{15}{6}\right)}{\log(2)}$$

$$\Rightarrow t = 7575.40 \text{ years}$$

(ix) **(a)** $\lambda = \dfrac{0.693}{3} = 0.231\ \text{sec}^{-1}$

(b) Using $N = N_0(2)^{-t/T}$

$\Rightarrow \quad 1000 = 8000(2)$

$\Rightarrow \quad t = 9\ \text{s}$

(c) $A = \lambda N = 0.231 \times 1000 = 231$ dps

Solutions of PRACTICE EXERCISE 4.3

(i) Explained in article 4.4.3

(ii) **(a)** Using charge and mass conservation equations are

$$^{213}_{83}Bi \rightarrow {}^{208}_{81}Tl + \alpha$$

and $$^{212}_{83}Bi \rightarrow {}^{212}_{84}P_0 + e^- + v$$

(b) Decay constant of α and β decay are

$$\lambda_\alpha = \frac{0.693}{1} \times \frac{7}{20}$$

and $$\lambda_\beta = \frac{0.693}{1} \times \frac{13}{20}$$

After 1 pm amount of Bi will reduce to half i.e. 0.5 gm and production rate of Tl and P_0 are in ratio of 7/13 hence the quantity after 1 pm are

$$m_{Tl} = 0.5 \times \frac{7}{20} = 0.175\ \text{gm}$$

$$mP_0 = 0.5 \times \frac{13}{20} = 0.325\ \text{gm}$$

(iii) Explained in article 4.4.3

(iv) If in time at total atoms inside the body are

$$N_{\text{body}} = N_0(2)^{-t/24}$$

If after time t $\quad N_A = \dfrac{N_0}{2}$

Total active atoms inside body at time t are

$$N_A = N_{\text{body}}\,(2)^{-t/6}$$

If after time t $\quad N_A = \dfrac{N_0}{2}$

we use $\quad \dfrac{N_0}{2} = N_0(2)^{-t/24}.(2)^{-t/6}$

$$\Rightarrow \quad t\left(\frac{1}{24} + \frac{1}{6}\right) = 1$$

$$\Rightarrow \quad t = \frac{24}{5} = 4.8\ \text{hrs}$$

(v) As half life of γ-decay is very small the amount of $^{57}C_0$ will only be governed by β-decay and γ-emission rate will be equal to β-emission rate only. Thus γ-emission rate will drop to half after half life of β-decay i.e. 270 days.

(iv) Explained in article 4.4.3

Solutions of PRACTICE EXERCISE 4.4

(i) 0.1% of mass of uranium is 0.001 gm

Thus energy released is

$$E = \frac{0.001 \times 10^{-3}}{1.66 \times 10^{-27}} \times 931.5 \times 10^6 \times 1.6 \times 10^{-19}$$

$$\Rightarrow \quad E = 8.978 \times 10^{10}\ \text{J}$$

(ii) Power output $= \dfrac{\text{Total released energy}}{\text{Time}}$

Total energy

$$= \frac{2 \times 10^3 \times 6.023 \times 10^{23}}{235} \times 185 \times 10^6 \times 1.6 \times 10^{-19}$$

$$= 1.517 \times 10^{14}\ \text{J}$$

$$\Rightarrow \quad \text{Power} = \frac{1.517 \times 10^{14}}{30 \times 86400} = 58.52\ \text{MW}$$

(iii) No of fissions required to produce 1000 J/3 energy are

$$N = \frac{1000}{200 \times 10^6 \times 1.6 \times 10^{-19}}$$

$$\Rightarrow \quad N = 3.125 \times 10^{13}\ \text{fissions/s}$$

(iv) Mass defect of reaction is

$$\Delta m = 2 \times 2.0141 - 4.0026$$

$$\Rightarrow \quad \Delta m = 0.0256\ \text{amu}$$

Energy released per fission is

$$\Delta E = 0.0256 \times 931.5\ \text{MeV}$$

$$\Rightarrow \quad \Delta E = 23.846\ \text{MeV}$$

Number of deuterium atoms needed per day are

$$N = \frac{200 \times 10^6 \times 86400}{23.846 \times 10^6 \times 1.6 \times 10^{-19}} \times 2$$

$$\Rightarrow \quad N = 9.058 \times 10^{24}\ \text{atoms}$$

Mass of deuterium needed per day is

$$m = \frac{9.058 \times 10^{24}}{6.023 \times 10^{23}} \times 2 \times \frac{100}{25}$$

$$\Rightarrow \quad m = 120.31\ \text{gm}$$

(v) Mass defect of reaction is

$$\Delta m = 2(2.014102) - 3.01605 - 1.007825$$

$$\Rightarrow \quad \Delta m = 0.004329\ \text{amu}$$

Energy released per reaction is

$$E_1 = 0.004329 \times 931.5$$

$\Rightarrow$ $$E_1 = 4.0324\,\text{MeV}$$

Number of D atoms required per day are

$$N = \frac{10^9 \times 86400}{4.0324 \times 10^6 \times 1.6 \times 10^{-19} \times 0.5} \times 2$$

$\Rightarrow$ $$N = 5.356 \times 10^{26}\,\text{atoms}$$

Mass of D atoms required per day is

$$m = \frac{5.356 \times 10^{26}}{6.023 \times 10^{23}} \times 2$$

$\Rightarrow$ $$m = 1778.5\,\text{gm}$$

(vi) Given reaction is

$${}^2_1\text{H} + {}^2_1\text{H} \rightarrow {}^4_2\text{He} + \Delta E$$

Released energy is

$$\Delta E = 4(7.0) - 4(1.1)$$

$\Rightarrow$ $$\Delta E = 23.6\,\text{MeV}$$

(vii) Fission reaction is

$${}^{235}_{92}U + {}^1_0n \rightarrow {}^{92}_{36}Kr + {}^{141}_{56}Ba + 3{}^1_0n + \text{energy}$$

mass defect of reaction is

$$\Delta m = 235.043925 - 91.8973 - 140.9139 - 2(1.008665)$$

$$\Delta m = 0.215395\,\text{amu}$$

Energy released $= 0.215395 \times 931.5\,\text{MeV}$

$\Rightarrow$ $$\Delta E = 200.64\,\text{MeV}$$

(viii) Reaction is

$${}^{41}_{20}Ca \rightarrow {}^{40}_{20}Ca + {}^1_0n$$

mass defect of reaction is

$$\Delta m = 40.962278 - 39.962591 - 1.008665$$

$\Rightarrow$ $$\Delta m = -0.008978\,\text{amu}$$

As mass defect is negative, this reaction requires energy for its completion and amount of energy required is

$$E = 0.008978 \times 931.5\,\text{MeV}$$

$\Rightarrow$ $$E = 8.363\,\text{MeV}$$

(ix) Mass defect of this reaction is

$$\Delta m = 1.007825 + 7.016004 - 2(4.002603)$$

$\Rightarrow$ $$\Delta m = 0.018623\,\text{amu}$$

As mass defect is positive, this reaction releases energy so it is exothermic reaction and its Q-value is

$$E = 0.018623 \times 931.5\,\text{MeV}$$

$\Rightarrow$ $$E = 17.347\,\text{MeV}$$

Solutions of PRACTICE EXERCISE 4.5

(i) Charge required for $2V$ potential can be given as

$$2 = \frac{1}{4\pi \epsilon_0} \cdot \frac{q}{R}$$

$\Rightarrow$ $$q = \frac{2 \times 0.01}{9 \times 10^9}C$$

time required to attain this charge is

$$t = \frac{q}{r_\beta \times 0.4 \times 1.6 \times 10^{-19}}$$

$\Rightarrow$ $$t = \frac{2 \times 0.01}{9 \times 10^9 \times 5 \times 10^{10} \times 0.4 \times 1.6 \times 10^{-19}}$$

$\Rightarrow$ $$t = 6.94 \times 10^{-4}\,\text{s}$$

(ii) Nuclear reaction is

$${}^{230}_{90}Th \rightarrow {}^{226}_{88}Ra + {}^4_2He + \text{energy}$$

Mass defect of reaction is

$$\Delta m = 230.033131 - 226.025406 - 4.002603$$

$\Rightarrow$ $$\Delta m = 0.005122\,\text{amu}$$

Energy released is $E = 0.005122 \times 931.5\,\text{MeV}$

$$E = 4.771\,\text{MeV}$$

Kinetic energy of α-particle is

$$E_\alpha = \left(\frac{A-4}{A}\right)E = \frac{226}{230} \times 4.771$$

$\Rightarrow$ $$E_\alpha = 3.267\,\text{MeV}$$

(iii) Energy γ-photon is

$$E_\gamma = \frac{12431}{0.125} = 0.09945\,\text{MeV}$$

Mass defect of reaction is

$$\Delta m = 239.052158 - 235.043925 - 4.002603$$

$\Rightarrow$ $$\Delta m = 0.00563\,\text{amu}$$

Energy released is

$$E = 0.00563 \times 931.5\,\text{MeV}$$

$\Rightarrow$ $$E = 5.24434\,\text{MeV}$$

Kinetic energy distributed in ${}^{235}_{92}U$ and ${}^4_2He$ is approximately

$$E_k = E - E_\gamma = 5.24434 - 0.09945$$

$$= 5.1449\,\text{MeV}$$

Thus kinetic energy of α-particle is

$$k_\alpha = \left(\frac{A-4}{A}\right)E_k = \frac{235}{239} \times 5.1449\,\text{MeV}$$

$$\Rightarrow \quad k_\alpha = 5.0588\text{ MeV}$$

Now we use

$$\frac{1}{2}m_\alpha v^2 = 5.0588\text{ MeV}$$

$$\Rightarrow \quad v = \sqrt{\frac{2\times 5.0588\times 10^6\times 1.6\times 10^{-19}}{4.002603\times 1.66\times 10^{-27}}}$$

$$\Rightarrow \quad v = 1.56\times 10^7\text{ m/s}$$

(iv) Mass defect of reaction is

$$\Delta m = 12.018613 - 12.0000 - 2(0.00055)$$

$$\Rightarrow \quad \Delta m = 0.017513\text{ amu}$$

Total energy released

$$E = 0.017513\times 931.5\text{ MeV}$$

$$\Rightarrow \quad E = 16.3133\text{ MeV}$$

Kinetic energy of ^{12}C and β-particle will be approximately

$$E_k = E - E_r$$

$$\Rightarrow \quad = 16.3133 - 4.43\text{ MeV}$$

$$\Rightarrow \quad = 11.88\text{ MeV}$$

As mass of e^+ is very small almost whole of this energy is carried by beta particle.

(v) Energy of decay for nuclei in two cases of α-emission are

$$E_{D_1} = \frac{4}{206}\times E_{\alpha 1} = \frac{4}{206}\times 5.3\text{ MeV}$$

$$\Rightarrow \quad E_{D_1} = 0.1029\text{ MeV}$$

$$E_{D_2} = \frac{4}{206}\times E_{\alpha 2} = \frac{4}{206}\times 4.5\text{ MeV}$$

$$\Rightarrow \quad E_{D_2} = 0.0873\text{ MeV}$$

Thus total energy released in first case reaction is

$$E_T = E_{D_1} + E_{\alpha_1} = 5.3 + 0.1029\text{ MeV}$$

$$= 5.4029\text{ MeV}$$

In second case when γ-photon is released, we use

$$E_T = E_{D_2} + E_{\alpha_2} + E_\gamma$$

$$\Rightarrow \quad E_\gamma = E_T - E_{D_2} - E_{\alpha_2} = 5.40 - 4.50 - 0.09$$

$$\Rightarrow \quad E_\gamma = 0.81\text{ MeV}$$

(vi) Mass defect of nuclear reaction is

$$\Delta m = M_P + M_{Li} - 2\,M_{He}$$

$$= 1.007825 + 7.016004 - 2\,(4.002603)$$

$$= 0.018623\text{ amu}$$

Total energy released is

$$\Delta E = 0.018623\times 931.5\text{ MeV}$$

$$= 17.347\text{ MeV}$$

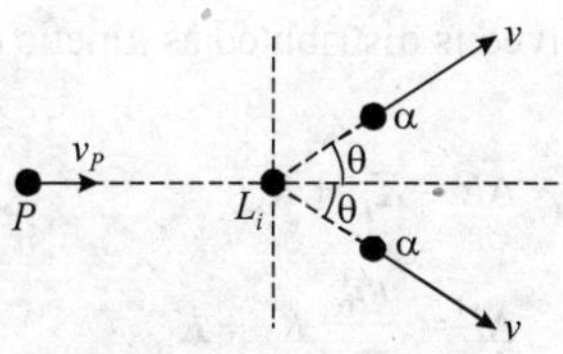

By conservation of momentum, we have

$$m_P\,v_P = 2m_\alpha v_\alpha \cos\theta \qquad \ldots(1)$$

By energy conservation, we have

$$T + \Delta E = 2\times \frac{1}{2}m_\alpha v_\alpha^2$$

$$\Rightarrow \quad k_\alpha = \frac{1}{2}(T+\Delta E) = \frac{1}{2}\,(1 + 17.347)\text{ MeV}$$

$$= 9.1735\text{ MeV}$$

From equation-(1) we have

$$\sqrt{2m_P T} = 2\sqrt{2m_\alpha k_\alpha}\,\cos\theta$$

$$\Rightarrow \quad \cos\theta = \frac{1}{2}\sqrt{\frac{m_P T}{m_\alpha k_\alpha}}$$

$$= \frac{1}{2}\sqrt{\frac{1.007825\times 1}{4.002603\times 9.1735}}$$

$$= \frac{0.1657}{2} = 0.08285$$

$$\Rightarrow \quad \theta = 85.25^\circ$$

⇒ Divergence angle $= 2\theta = 170.5^\circ$

(vii) Mass defect of reaction is

$$\Delta m = M_{Th} - M_{Ra} - M_\alpha$$

$$= 228.028726 - 224.020196 - 4.00260$$

$$= 0.00593\text{ amu}$$

Total energy released $\Delta E = 0.00593\times 931.5$ MeV

$$= 5.524\text{ MeV}$$

Energy distributed between ^{224}Ra* and α is given as

$$E_{Ra}^* + E_\alpha = \Delta E - E_r \qquad \ldots(1)$$

$$\Rightarrow \quad = 5.524\text{ MeV} - 0.217\text{ MeV}$$

$$= 5.307\text{ MeV}$$

From equation-(1) we have

$$\Rightarrow \quad \frac{m_\alpha}{m_{Ra}^*}\,E_\alpha + E_\alpha = 5.307\text{ MeV}$$

$$\Rightarrow \quad E_\alpha\left(\frac{4}{224}+1\right) = 5.307\text{ MeV}$$

$$\Rightarrow \quad E_\alpha = 5.305\times\frac{224}{228} = 5.214\text{ MeV}$$

(viii) Mass defect of the reaction is

$$\Delta m = M_B + M_n - M_{Li} - M_\alpha \qquad \ldots(1)$$

Total energy evolved is distributed as kinetic energy of Li and α so we have

$$\Delta E = K_{Li} + K_{\alpha}$$

$$\Rightarrow \quad \Delta E = \frac{m_{\alpha}}{m_{Li}} K_{\alpha} + K_{\alpha}$$

$$\Rightarrow \quad \Delta E = K_{\alpha}\left(\frac{m_{\alpha}}{m_{Li}} + 1\right)$$

$$\Rightarrow \quad \Delta m \times 931.5 = 1.83\left(\frac{4}{7} + 1\right) \text{MeV}$$

$$\Rightarrow \quad \Delta m = \frac{2.8757}{931.5} = 0.003087 \text{ amu}$$

From equation-(1) we have

$$0.003087 = 10.01167 + 1.00894 - M_{Li} - 4.00386$$

$$\Rightarrow \quad M_{Li} = 7.013663 \text{ amu}$$

Solutions of CONCEPTUAL MCQS Single Option Correct

Sol. 1 (D) If in above decay x alpha and y beta particles are emitted then we use

$$4x = 238 - 222 = 16$$

$$\Rightarrow \quad x = 4$$

and $\quad 2x - y = 7$

$$\Rightarrow \quad y = 1$$

Hence option (D) is correct.

Sol. 2 (A) Out of the above curie is the largest unit of activity hence option (A) is correct as 1 Ci = 3.7×10^{10} Bq and 1 Ru = 10^6 Bq.

Sol. 3 (A) Among the given radiations gamma rays are of highest energy hence option (A) is correct.

Sol. 4 (B) Due to each alpha emission Z reduces by 2 and for beta minus emission Z increases by 1 and for beta plus emission Z decreases by 1 hence for the given sequence option (B) is correct.

Sol. 5 (D) By conservation of charge and mass for the above reaction we have charge of x is 2 and mass is 4 hence option (D) is correct.

Sol. 6 (D) We have studied that for all stable nuclei average mean density of nuclear matter almost remain constant hence option (D) is correct.

Sol. 7 (D) By conservation of charge and mass for the above reaction we have charge of X is 0 and mass is 1 hence option (D) is correct.

Sol. 8 (B) As we have studied that in fusion binding energy per nucleon released is more than that compared to a fission reaction hence option (A) is correct.

Sol. 9 (A) Chemical properties of an element is dependent upon the valance electrons in an atom hence option (A) is correct.

Sol. 10 (D) Critical mass is the amount of fissionable material which can self sustain the chain reaction in it, this can be reduced by putting a surrounding shield from which the neutrons can get reflected and reused in the fission process hence option (D) is correct.

Sol. 11 (D) When in a nuclear reactor Cadmium rods are inserted, these absorb neutrons and slow down the rate of reaction and when pulled out, rate of reaction increases so by these rods the rate at which energy is being produced by the reactor can be controlled hence option (D) is correct.

Sol. 12 (A) A β^--particle carries -1 charge which is emitted when inside a nucleus a neutron transforms into a proton.

Sol. 13 (D) To start fusion nuclei must have very high kinetic energy to overcome the Coulomb repulsion between the nuclei and this high kinetic energy is obtained by thermal energy due to high temperature only hence option (D) is correct.

Sol. 14 (B) As studied in basic theory mass defect is referred to the difference in masses of the nucleons of a nucleus and the sum of masses of its independent nucleons which produces energy when the nucleus is produced by annihilation of nucleons hence option (B) is most appropriate here.

Sol. 15 (C) By basic definition of Packing fraction option (C) is correct.

Sol. 16 (A) Fusion of elements occur at very high temperature and pressure as at high temperature and pressure the closest distance of approach of nuclei during collision decreases to a level where fusion can start by appearance of nuclear attraction hence option (A) is correct.

Sol. 17 (C) As explained in article 4.6.1 of basic theory of fission of uranium nuclei option (C) is correct.

Sol. 18 (B) As already studied that majority of space in an atom is empty thats why in gold foil experiment most of incident alpha particles pass undeviated and very few gets deflected. Due to very small size of nucleus very few particles get reflected hence option (B) is correct.

Sol. 19 (B) C-13 and C-14 are not available in abundance so it is not possible to fuse these element nuclei with other whereas in option (D), the given reaction is a fission reaction hence option (B) is correct.

Sol. 20 (C) Carbon dating is a process in which age of a specimen is estimated by analyzing the amount of C-14 present in it as compared to C-12 hence option (C) is correct.

Sol. 21 (A) In radioactive elements from their nuclei protons are never emitted hence option (A) is correct. Protons can only transform into neutrons within the nuclei by emission of β^+ emission.

Sol. 22 (C) As studied in theory that beta minus decay occurs due to transformation of a neutron into a proton inside the nucleus hence option (C) is correct.

Sol. 23 (D) By conservation of charge and mass in the above reaction option (D) is the correct.

Sol. 24 (A) If in above decay x alpha and y beta particles are emitted then we use

$$4x = 200 - 168 = 32$$

$$\Rightarrow \quad x = 8$$

and $\quad 2x - y = 10$

$$\Rightarrow \quad y = 6$$

Hence option (A) is correct.

Sol. 25 (D) The activity of element X is the rate for formation of Y and the activity decreases exponentially according to radioactive decay law hence option (D) is correct.

Sol. 26 (C) By conservation of charge and mass we can see that charge of x is 2 and mass is 4 hence it is an alpha particle so option (C) is correct.

Sol. 27 (B) By conservation of charge and mass we can see that option (B) is correct.

Sol. 28 (B) According to Pauli's neutrino hypothesis an electron emission is accomplished by emission of an antineutrino and a positron emission is accomplished by emission of a neutrino hence option (B) is correct.

Sol. 29 (A) By conservation of charge and mass we can see that x is an electron hence option (A) is correct.

Sol. 30 (C) By conservation of charge and mass we can see that option (C) is correct.

Sol. 31 (D) Half life of a radioactive element is a nuclear property which does not depend upon external factors hence option (D) is most appropriate here.

Sol. 32 (D) From the given information we have

$$\ln(2)/\lambda_X = 1/\lambda_Y$$

$$\Rightarrow \quad \lambda_X > \lambda_Y$$

hence X is more active than Y hence option (D) is correct.

Sol. 33 (B) By conservation of charge and mass we can see that option (B) is correct.

Sol. 34 (A) In above reaction nuclear charge decreases by 1 hence it occurs due to an electron capture among the given options hence option (A) is correct.

Sol. 35 (D) After 200 minutes the number of X will reduce to 1/16 and that of Y will reduce to 1/4 hence option (D) is correct.

Sol. 36 (A) β^--particle is a fast moving electron emitted from the nucleus due to transformation of one neutron into a proton hence option (A) is correct.

Sol. 37 (B) By conservation of charge and mass we can see that option (B) is correct.

Sol. 38 (A) In a nuclear reactor moderator is used to slow down the neutrons to a level where fission can start hence option (A) is correct.

Sol. 39 (C) In path 3 it shows that the fired particle is attracted by the nucleus which is not possible as alpha particle is always repelled by the nucleus.

Sol. 40 (D) As studied in theory the radioactive property of an element is a nuclear process and not associated with any physical and chemical properties of the element hence option (D) is correct.

Sol. 41 (B) By conservation of charge and mass we can see that option (B) is correct.

Sol. 42 (B) By conservation of charge and mass we can see that option (B) is correct.

Sol. 43 (A) For the same energy alpha particles have largest in size due to which these cannot penetrate much in physical substances and have least penetration power and gamma radiation being electromagnetic radiation have maximum penetration depth hence option (A) is correct.

Sol. 44 (B) Due to emission of beta particle mass number does not change hence option (B) is correct.

Sol. 45 (B) Fast neutrons in a nuclear reactor are slowed down by use of moderator which are heavy water and lad shielding hence option (A) is most appropriate.

Sol. 46 (D) When a nucleus ruptures into two parts their velocities are in inverse ratio of their masses as linear momentum of the system remain conserved thus the mass ratio of the two parts will be 1 : 2 hence from the relation of fermi radius their size ratio will be $1 : 2^{1/3}$ hence option (D) is correct.

Sol. 47 (C) From the curve of variation of binding energy per nucleon with mass number it is clear that the two elements with mass number more than 100 when fuse the binding energy per nucleon of the resulting element is lower than the fusing elements hence energy must be supplied for this purpose hence option (C) is INCORRECT.

Sol. 48 (C) Energy is released in a process when the binding energy per nucleon of the product is less than that of initially reacting elements hence option (C) is correct.

Solutions of NUMERICAL MCQS Single Option Correct

Sol. 1 (B) We use $A_P = A_Q e^{-\lambda t} = A_Q e^{-\frac{1}{T}t}$

$$\Rightarrow \qquad t = T \ln \frac{A_Q}{A_P}$$

Sol. 2 (C) We use

$$N = N_0(2)^{-t/T}$$

$$\Rightarrow \qquad \frac{N_0}{8} = N_0(2)^{-t/5}$$

$$\Rightarrow \qquad t = 15 \text{ days}$$

Sol. 3 (B) No of atoms left after 10 years are

$$N = N_0(2)^{-10/5} = \frac{N_0}{4}$$

Thus $(3/4)^{\text{th}}$ of sample decay in 10 years thus probability of decay is 75%.

Sol. 4 (B) Rate of decay of A keeps on decreasing continuously because concentration of A decreases with time $\Rightarrow$ (A) is false.

Initial rate of production of B is $\lambda_1 N_0$ and rate of decay is zero. With time, as the number of B atom increase, the rate of its production decrease and its rate of decay increases. Thus the number of nuclei of B will first increase and then decrease. $\Rightarrow$ (B) is the correct choice

The initial activity of B is zero whereas initial activity of A is $\lambda_1 N_0 \Rightarrow$ (C) is false.

As time $t \to \infty : N_A = 0, N_B = 0$ and $N_C = N_0 \Rightarrow$ (D) is false

Sol. 5 (D) Using $N = N_0(2)^{-t/10}$ we have

at $t = 30$, $\qquad N = \dfrac{N_0}{8}$

and at $t = 40$, $\qquad N = \dfrac{N_0}{16}$

Hence option (D) is correct.

Sol. 6 (B) Using $N = N_0(2)^{-t/T}$

at $t = 1$ day

$$0.9N_0 = N_0(2)^{-1/T}$$

$$\Rightarrow \qquad \frac{1}{T} = \frac{\log\left(\frac{10}{9}\right)}{\log(2)}$$

at $t = 2$ days

$$N = N_0(2)^{-2/T}$$

$$\Rightarrow \qquad \frac{\log\left(\frac{N_0}{N}\right)}{\log(2)} = 2\frac{\log\left(\frac{10}{9}\right)}{\log(2)}$$

$$\Rightarrow \qquad \frac{N_0}{N} = \frac{100}{81}$$

$$\Rightarrow \qquad N = 0.81\,N_0$$

Sol. 7 (A) Using $10.81 = 10x + 11(1 - x)$

$$\Rightarrow \qquad 10.81 = 11 - x$$

$$\Rightarrow \qquad x = 0.19$$

$$\Rightarrow \qquad 1 - x = 0.81$$

Sol. 8 (C) We use

$$N = N_0(2)^{-t/T}$$

For A $\qquad N_A = N_0(2)^{-80/20}$

For B $\qquad N_B = N_0(2)^{-80/20}$

$$\Rightarrow \qquad \frac{N_A}{N_B} = \frac{1}{4}$$

Sol. 9 (C)

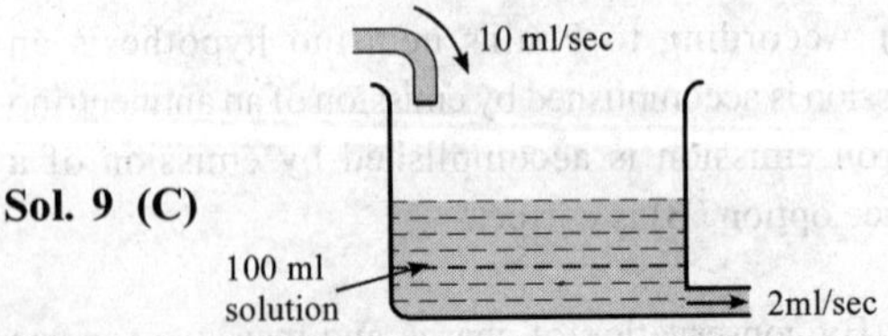

The volume of liquid in beaker at any instant of time t is

$$V = 100 + 8t$$

The volume of liquid ejected in t seconds is $2t$

Number of active atoms being taken out is

$$-dN = \frac{N}{V}\,2dt$$

$$\Rightarrow \quad -\frac{dN}{dt}=\frac{2N}{V}=\frac{2N}{100+8t}$$

Multiplying both sides with disintegration constant.

$$-\lambda\, dN=\lambda N\frac{2dt}{V} \quad \text{or} \quad -dA=A\cdot\frac{2dt}{V}$$

Where A is activity of the solution. The time taken for 10 ml solution to come out is 5 second.

$$\Rightarrow \quad \int_{A_0}^{A}\frac{dA}{A}=\int_{0}^{5}\frac{-2t}{100+8t}\,dt$$

$$\Rightarrow \quad A=A_0\left(\frac{5}{7}\right)^{1/4}$$

Thus required activity of the ejected solution is

$$A-A_0=A_0\left[1-\left(\frac{5}{7}\right)^{1/4}\right]$$

Sol. 10 (B) We use $A=A_0(2)^{-t/T}$

$$\Rightarrow \quad A_{safe}=16\,A_{safe}\,(2)^{-t/3}$$

$$\Rightarrow \quad t=12 \text{ hrs}$$

Sol. 11 (C) After four half lives $\frac{1}{16}$ of the sample will left undecayed.

Sol. 12 (C) At 300 K temperature most probable speed of thermal neutrons is

$$v=\sqrt{\frac{2kT}{m}}$$

Thus $$E_K=\frac{1}{2}mv^2\,kT$$

$$\Rightarrow \quad E_K=\frac{1.38\times10^{-23}\times300}{1.6\times10^{-19}}$$

$$\Rightarrow \quad E_K=0.026\,\text{eV}$$

Sol. 13 (D) After 4 hours the sample will contain 30 gm of isotope B and 12.5 gm of isotope A.

Mass of isotope A decayed to A' is 37.5 gm which will have a mass after four hours

$$m'=37.5\times\frac{146}{150}=36.5 \text{ gm}$$

Total mass $=30+12.5+36.5=79$ gm

Sol. 14 (B) No. of α-particles emitted $=\frac{37.5}{150}N_A$

$$\Rightarrow \quad N_\alpha=\frac{1}{4}N_A\approx1.5\times10^{23}$$

Sol. 15 (C) Energy released is

$$E=234(8.5)-236(7.6)$$

$$\Rightarrow \quad E=1989-1793.6$$

$$\Rightarrow \quad E=195.4\,\text{MeV}$$

Sol. 16 (D) If x amount is remaining then after three half tubes activity will be

$$\frac{1}{8}\times\frac{C}{100}\times(x)=\frac{C}{10}$$

$$\Rightarrow \quad x=10\,\text{cm}^3$$

Sol. 17 (A) After first half hrs $N=N_0\frac{1}{2}$

For $t=\frac{1}{2}$ to $t=1\frac{1}{2}$ $N=\left(N_0\frac{1}{2}\right)\left[\frac{1}{2}\right]^4=N_0\left(\frac{1}{2}\right)^5$

For $t=1\frac{1}{2}$ to $t=2$ hrs

[For both A and B $\frac{1}{t_{1/2}}=\frac{1}{1/2}+\frac{1}{1/4}=2+4=6\; t_{1/2}=1/6$ hrs]

$$N=\left[N_0\left(\frac{1}{2}\right)^5\right]\left(\frac{1}{2}\right)^3=N_0\left(\frac{1}{2}\right)^8$$

Sol. 18 (C) Energy released is

$$E=4(7.1)-2(1.15)$$

$$\Rightarrow \quad E=23.8\,\text{MeV}$$

Sol. 19 (C) We use $N=\frac{1}{\lambda}[\alpha-(a-\lambda N_0)\,e^{-\lambda t}]$ taken from example-4.24

$$\Rightarrow \quad 100=[200-(200)\,e^{-t}]$$

$$\Rightarrow \quad 100=200\,(1-e^{-t})$$

$$\Rightarrow \quad e^{-t}=\frac{1}{2}$$

$$\Rightarrow \quad t=\ln(2)$$

Sol. 20 (B) Rest mass energy of an electron is

$$E=0.00055\times931.5\,\text{MeV}$$

$$\Rightarrow \quad E=0.512\,\text{MeV}$$

Sol. 21 (B) $$\frac{dN_2}{dt}=\lambda N_1-2\lambda N_2$$

For N_2 to be maximum,

$$\frac{dN_2}{dt}=0$$

$$\Rightarrow \quad \lambda N_1=2\lambda N_2 \quad \text{or} \quad \frac{N_1}{N_2}=2$$

Sol. 22 (C) We use

$$N = N_0(2)^{-t/T}$$

$$\Rightarrow \quad \frac{N_0}{6} = N_0(2)^{-2/T}$$

$$\Rightarrow \quad T = 2\frac{\log 2}{\log 6}$$

$$\Rightarrow \quad T = 0.7736 \text{ hrs}$$

$$\Rightarrow \quad T = 46.41 \text{ min}$$

Sol. 23 (D) H after 5 half lives $\frac{1}{32}$ for the sample will remain hence it is

$$\frac{16}{32} = 0.5 \text{ gm}$$

Sol. 24 (D) $n = \lambda N$

$$\Rightarrow \quad \lambda = \frac{n}{N}$$

$$\Rightarrow \quad t_{1/2} = \frac{0.69}{\lambda} = \frac{0.69N}{n}$$

Sol. 25 (B) A ⟶ B ⟶ C

Let b be the number of nuclei of B $\frac{dB}{dt} = x - \lambda b$ or $y = x - \lambda b$

$$\Rightarrow \quad \lambda b = x - y$$

Activity of $B = -\lambda b = y - x$

Sol. 26 (C) After $t = 9$ yrs

$$\frac{A_0}{3} = A_0(2)^{-9/T}$$

$$\Rightarrow \quad T = 9\frac{\log(2)}{\log(3)}$$

at $t = 18$ yrs $A = A_0(2)^{-18/T}$

$$\Rightarrow \quad 18 \cdot \frac{\log(2)}{\log\left(\frac{A_0}{A}\right)} = 9 \cdot \frac{\log(2)}{\log(3)}$$

$$\Rightarrow \quad \left(\frac{A_0}{A}\right) = (9)$$

$$\Rightarrow \quad A = A_0/9$$

Sol. 27 (D) We use

$$A = A_0 e^{-t/\tau}$$

$$\Rightarrow \quad y = \times e^{-(t_2 - t_1)/\tau}$$

No of atoms disintegrated during $t_2 - t_1$ is

$$\Delta N = (x - y)\tau$$

Sol. 28 (A) $\frac{\lambda_1}{\lambda_2} = \frac{\lambda_1 N}{\lambda_2 N}$

$$\Rightarrow \quad \frac{\lambda_1}{\lambda_2} = \frac{\text{decay rate of } \alpha \text{ decay}}{\text{decay rate of } \beta \text{ decay}}$$

$$\Rightarrow \quad \frac{\lambda_1}{\lambda_2} = \frac{\text{probability of } \alpha \text{ decay}}{\text{probability of } \beta \text{ decay}}$$

$$\Rightarrow \quad \frac{\lambda_1}{\lambda_2} = \frac{\frac{75}{100}}{\frac{25}{100}} = 3$$

Sol. 29 (B) ${}_{92}U^{228}$ and ${}_{92}U^{234}$ are isotopes similarly ${}_{90}Th^{234}$ and ${}_{90}Th^{230}$ are isotopes.

Sol. 30 (A) Using $N = N_0(2)^{-t/T}$

$$\frac{N_0}{8} = N_0(2)^{-t/2}$$

$$\Rightarrow \quad t = 6 \text{ hrs}$$

Sol. 31 (D) No of fissions per second required are

$$N = \frac{3.2 \times 10^6}{200 \times 10^6 \times 1.6 \times 10^{-19}}$$

$$\Rightarrow \quad N = 10^{17}$$

Sol. 32 (D) Energy of γ photon

= Difference in energies of α particles = 0.4 MeV

Sol. 33 (B) ${}_{z}X^{A} \longrightarrow {}_{z-1}Y^{A} + e^{+} + \nu$

$$\downarrow$$

$$2\alpha + {}_{z-5}X'^{A-8}$$

Given $A - 8 = 224$

& $Z - 5 = 89$

$$\Rightarrow \quad A = 237, Z = 94$$

Sol. 34 (D) Using $N = N_0^{-\lambda t}$ we have

$$N = N_0 e^{-2}$$

$$\Rightarrow \quad N = \frac{N_0}{(2.71)^2} = 0.13\,N_0$$

Sol. 35 (B) $A = A_0 e^{-\lambda t}$

$$\Rightarrow \quad 100 = 800\, e^{-\lambda(6 \times 60)}$$

$$\Rightarrow \quad e^{-360\lambda} = 1/8$$

$$\Rightarrow \quad -360\lambda = \lambda n\frac{1}{8} = -\lambda n8$$

$$\Rightarrow \quad \lambda = \frac{ln2^3}{360} = \frac{ln2}{120}$$

$\Rightarrow \quad T_{1/2} = \frac{ln2}{\lambda} = \frac{ln2}{(ln2/120)} = 120 \text{ min}$

or $\quad T_{1/2} = 2 \text{ hrs}$

Sol. 36 (C) $\quad A = A_0 e^{-\lambda t}$

After one year : $\frac{A_0}{10} = A_0 e^{-\lambda}$

$\Rightarrow \quad e^{-\lambda} = \frac{1}{10}$

After further 9 years : (i.e. after 10 years)

$$A = A_0 e^{-10\lambda} = \frac{A_0}{10^{10}}$$

Sol. 37 (B) We use

$$m = m_0(2)^{-t/T}$$

$\Rightarrow \quad 1 = 256\,(2)^{-t/12.5}$

$\Rightarrow \quad t = 100 \text{ hrs}$

Sol. 38 (B) ${}_3Li^7 + {}_0n^1 \longrightarrow {}_{-1}e^0 + 2\,{}_2He^4$

Hence the unknown nuclide is ${}_3Li^7$.

Sol. 39 (C) After a very long time at equilibrium

$$\frac{dN}{dt} = 0$$

$\Rightarrow$ Rate of decay = rate of formation = 10^4 dps.

Sol. 40 (D) Using

$N = N_0(2)^{-t/T}$ we have

$$N = 10^8\,(2)^{-5/10} = \frac{10^8}{\sqrt{2}}$$

Sol. 41 (C) Nuclear Reaction are

$${}^{238}_{92}U \rightarrow {}^{234}_{90}Th + {}^{4}_{2}He$$

$${}^{234}_{90}Th \rightarrow {}^{234}_{91}Pa + {}^{0}_{-1}e$$

Sol. 42 (C) Explained in example 4.24

Sol. 43 (C) In above reaction four hydrogen nuclei are fusing to produce a helium nucleus so it is a fusion reaction.

Sol. 44 (C) In the mixture, initially $N = N_1 + N_2$

$\Rightarrow$ At any time (t) : $N(t) = N_1(t) + N_2(t)$

$N(t) = N_1 e^{-\lambda 1 t} + N_2 e^{-\lambda 2 t}$

$\Rightarrow$ Decay rate at time (t) (obtained by differentiating above) $= N_1\lambda_1 e^{-\lambda 1 t} + N_2\lambda_2 e^{-\lambda 2 t}$

Hence (C)

Sol. 45 (C) ${}^{226}_{88}Ra + n({}_2He^4) + m({}_{-1}\beta^0) \longrightarrow {}^{206}_{82}Pb$

Where n and m are respectively the required number of α and β particles. Clearly from the options given, only (C) satisfy the above reaction.

Sol. 46 (A) Since there is no change in atomic number and mass number due to the emission or absorption of a γ-ray photon $({}_0\gamma^0)$. Hence (A).

Sol. 47 (D) Energy released by 1 kg fuel is

$$E = \frac{1 \times 0.001 \times (3 \times 10)^2}{1000 \times 3600} = 2.5 \times 10^7 \text{ kwh}$$

Sol. 48 (D) Energy released is

$$E = 8(7.06) - 7(5.60) \text{ MeV}$$

$\Rightarrow \quad E = 56.48 - 39.20 \text{ MeV}$

$\Rightarrow \quad E = 17.28 \text{ MeV}$

Sol. 49 (B) For α-decay : ${}_xA^y \longrightarrow {}_{x-2}B^{y-4} + \alpha$

For β^- – decay : ${}_xA^y \longrightarrow {}_{x+1}B^y + {}_{-1}\beta^0$

For β^+ – decay : ${}_xA^y \longrightarrow {}_{x-1}B^y + {}_{+1}\beta^0$

For k - capture : there will be no change in the number of protons. Hence, only case in which no of protons increases is β^--decay Hence (B).

Sol. 50 (C) Rate of formation of Y is the decay rate of X which is given as

$$\frac{dN}{dt} = \lambda N_0 e^{-\lambda t}$$

If N_0 are no. of nuclei of X at $t = 0$.

Sol. 51 (C) Energy released in a nuclear reaction is proportional to C^2 so if C will reduce to half the energy released become one fourth and will reduced by $(3/4)^{th}$ of initial volume

Sol. 52 (D) From given graph we have

$$\ln(A) = -\left(\frac{2.5}{25}\right)t + 2.5$$

$\Rightarrow \quad A = e^{(-t/10 + 2.5)}$

$\Rightarrow \quad A = e^{2.5} \cdot e^{-0.1t}$

$\Rightarrow \quad A = 12\, e^{-0.1t}$

Sol. 53 (C) Activity of an element is

$$A = \lambda N$$

For same number of molecules

$$\frac{A_1}{A_2} = \frac{\lambda_1}{\lambda_2} = \frac{4}{3}$$

Sol. 54 (A) We use

$$A = A_0(2)^{-t/T}$$

$\Rightarrow$ $$5 = A_0(2)^{-4}$$

$\Rightarrow$ $$A_0 = 5 \times 16 = 80 \text{ dps}$$

Sol. 55 (D) Explained in article 4.4.2

Sol. 56 (C) We use

$$KE_\alpha = \frac{1}{4\pi \epsilon_0} = \frac{v_1 v_2}{r}$$

$$r = \frac{9\times10^9 \times 2\times92\times(1.6\times10^{-19})^2}{5\times10^6 \times1.6\times10^{-19}}$$

$\Rightarrow$ $$r = 5.29 \times 10^{-14} \text{ m}$$

$\Rightarrow$ $$r = 5.29 \times 10^{-12} \text{ cm}$$

Sol. 57 (D) We use

$$N_x = \frac{N_0}{2}\cdot e^{-\lambda_1 t} = 0.2\, N_0 \quad \ldots(1)$$

and $$N_y = \frac{N_0}{2}\cdot e^{-\lambda_2 t} = 0.8\, N_0 \quad \ldots(2)$$

Dividing equation-(2) by (1) we get

$$e^{(\lambda_1-\lambda_2)} = 4$$

$\Rightarrow$ $$t = 8 \times 10^9 \text{ years}$$

Sol. 58 (B) By conservation of momentum we use

$$A_1 : A_2 = 1 : 2$$

$\Rightarrow$ $$r_1 : r_2 = 1 : 2^{1/3}$$

Sol. 59 (D) Total no of decays,

$$\Delta N = N_0 - N(t)$$

$\Rightarrow$ $$= N_0(1 - e^{-\lambda t})$$

$\Rightarrow$ $$= N_0(1 - e^{-ln2.t/t_{1/2}})$$

$\Rightarrow$ $$= N_0(1 - 2^{-t/t_{1/2}})$$

This quantity is maximum for option (D)

Sol. 60 (A) Given that $\lambda_B = 2\lambda_A$. After n half lives of A their activities are

$$A_A = \lambda_A N_0(2)^{-n}$$

as $$T_B = \frac{T_A}{2}$$

and $$A_B = \lambda_B N_0(2) - 2n$$

As per given condition

$$A_A = A_B$$

$\Rightarrow$ $$\lambda_A N_0(2)^{-n} = 2\lambda_A N_0(2)^{-2n}$$

$\Rightarrow$ $$-n = 1 - 2n$$

$\Rightarrow$ $$n = 1$$

Sol. 61 (D) Reaction is ${}^{15}_{7}N + {}^{4}_{2}He \rightarrow {}^{18}_{8}O + {}^{1}_{1}P$

Sol. 62 (C) We use

$$N = N_0(2)^{-t/T}$$

So after time t we have

$$\frac{N_0}{5} = N_0(2)^{-t/2}$$

$\Rightarrow$ $$t = 2\frac{\log 5}{\log 2} = 4.64 \text{ hrs}$$

Sol. 63 (D) By radioactive decay law

$$N_1 = N_0\, e^{-10\lambda t}$$

and $$N_2 = N_0\, e^{-\lambda t}$$

$\Rightarrow$ $$\frac{N_1}{N_2} = \frac{1}{e} = e^{-9\lambda t}$$

$\Rightarrow$ $$t = \frac{1}{9\lambda}$$

Sol. 64 (A) $$\lambda_{eff} = \frac{\ln 2}{1620} + \frac{\ln 2}{810}$$

$\Rightarrow$ $$\frac{N_0}{4} = N_0\,(e)^{-\lambda_{eff}\, t}$$

$\Rightarrow$ $$t = \frac{2\ln(2)}{\frac{\ln 2}{1620} + \frac{\ln 2}{810}}$$

$\Rightarrow$ $$t = 1080 \text{ years}$$

Sol. 65 (C) Mass defect of reaction is

$$\Delta m = 3(2.014102) - 4.002603 - 1.008665 - 1.007825$$

$\Rightarrow$ $$\Delta m = 0.023213 \text{ amu}$$

Energy released

$$E = 0.23213 \times 931.5 \text{ MeV}$$

$\Rightarrow$ $$E = 21.623 \text{ MeV}$$

Total supply by 10^{40} deuterons will get exhausted in time

$$t = \frac{21.623\times10^6 \times1.6\times10^{-19} \times10^{40}}{3\times10^{16}}$$

$\Rightarrow$ $$t = 1.153 \times 10^{12} \text{ s}$$

Sol. 66 (D) Cu nucleus is heavier than Zn so it will decay through beta decay.

Sol. 67 (C) Number of nuclei of N_y will be maximum when its decay rate becomes equal to its production rate.

Sol. 68 (C) de-Broglie wavelengths ratio will be inversely proportional to the momentum of the two particles which will be same as parent particle was at rest so has initial zero momentum.

Sol. 69 (A) Number of nuclei will become maximum when the production rate of nuclei will be equal to their decay rate hence we use $\alpha = \lambda N$ thus option (A) is correct.

Sol. 70 (C) We use

$$N = N_0 (2)^{-t/T}$$

$$\Rightarrow \quad \frac{N_0}{8} = N_0 (2)^{-t/T}$$

$$\Rightarrow \quad t = 3 \times 1.37 \times 10^9$$

$$\Rightarrow \quad t = 4.11 \times 10^9 \text{ yrs}$$

Sol. 71 (B) For N_1 atoms of the radioactive element beta activity is N_2 dps hence we use $N_2 = \lambda N_1$.

Sol. 72 (D) Power of Sun is

$$P_S = 1.4 \times 10^3 \times 4\pi (1.5 \times 10^{11})^2$$

Energy released by Sun per day is

$$E_{\text{sun/day}} = P_S \times 86400$$

Mass lost by sun per day is

$$m = \frac{E_{\text{sun/day}}}{C^2}$$

$$\Rightarrow \quad m = \frac{1.4 \times 10^3 \times 4 \times 3.14 \times (1.5 \times 10^{11})^2 \times 86400}{(3 \times 10^8)^2}$$

$$\Rightarrow \quad m = 8.79 \times 10^{14} \text{ kg}$$

Sol. 73 (A) Energy released by 2 kg of uranium is

$$E = \frac{2000 \times 6.023 \times 10^{23}}{235} \times 185 \times 10^6 \times 1.6 \times 10^{-19} \text{ J}$$

Power output is

$$P = \frac{E}{t} = \frac{2000 \times 6.023 \times 10^{23} \times 185 \times 10^6 \times 1.6 \times 10^{-19}}{235 \times 30 \times 86400}$$

$$= 5.853 \times 10^6 \text{ W}$$

Sol. 74 (C) Given that present quantity are

$$\frac{A_1}{\lambda} \text{ and } \frac{A_2}{\lambda}$$

Quantity before time t_1 and t_2 are N_0 and $2N_0$

$$\Rightarrow \quad N_0 = \frac{A_1}{\lambda} e^{-\lambda t_1}$$

and

$$2N_0 = \frac{A_2}{\lambda} e^{-\lambda t_2}$$

$$\Rightarrow \quad 2A_1 e^{-\lambda t_1} = A_2 e^{-\lambda t_2}$$

$$\Rightarrow \quad e^{\lambda(t_2 - t_1)} = \frac{A_2}{ZA_1}$$

$$\Rightarrow \quad t_2 - t_1 = \frac{1}{\lambda} \ln\left(\frac{A_2}{ZA_1}\right)$$

$$\Rightarrow \quad t_2 - t_1 = \frac{T}{\ln 2} \ln\left(\frac{A_2}{ZA_1}\right)$$

Sol. 75 (C) We use

$$N = N_0 2^{-t/T}$$

$$\Rightarrow \quad N = N_0 2^{-\frac{63.5}{12.7}}$$

$$\Rightarrow \quad N = \frac{N_0}{32}$$

There total number of nuclei decayed will be $\frac{31}{32} N_0$.

Sol. 76 (D) To achieve kinetic energy of elements of the order of potential energy at fusion reparation we use

$$2kT = 7.7 \times 10^{-14}$$

$$\Rightarrow \quad T = \frac{7.7 \times 10^{-14}}{2 \times 1.38 \times 10^{-23}} = 2.78 \times 10^9 \text{ K}$$

Sol. 77 (D) Initial nuclei at time t_1 are

$$N_0 = A_1 \tau$$

at time $t_z = N = A_2 \tau$

Total nuclei decayed in time $t_2 - t_1$ are

$$N_0 - N = (A_1 - A_2)\tau$$

Sol. 78 (A) $\frac{dN}{dt} = t^2 - \lambda N$

For $\frac{dN}{dt}$ to be minimum; $\frac{d^2N}{dt^2} = 0$

$$\Rightarrow \quad \frac{d^2N}{dt^2} = 2t - \lambda \frac{dN}{dt} = 2t - \lambda(t^2 - \lambda N) = 0$$

$$\Rightarrow \quad N = \frac{2t_0 - \lambda t_0^2}{\lambda^2}$$

Sol. 79 (D) If day-1 N_D nuclei decay then are use

	Decayed	
Day-1	N_D	$= 2^0 N_D$
Day-2	$2N_D$	$= 2^1 N_D$
Day-3	$4N_D$	$= 2^2 N_D$
⋮		
Day-9	$256\, N_D$	$= 2^8 N_D$
Day-10	$512\, N_D$	$= 2^9 N_D$
Total Decayed	$1023\, N_D$	

Amount left after 9th day is

$$= \frac{512}{1023} \times 100$$

$$\cong 50\%$$

ADVANCE MCQs One or More Options Correct

Sol. 1 (All) In α-decay nuclear charge decreases by a factor of 2 and mass decreases by a factor of 4 and in β-decay no effect is there on the mass of nucleus but charge increases or decreases by a factor of 1 and in case of γ-decay no change will be there on charge or mass. Hence all the above given options are correct.

Sol. 2 (C, D) Only in γ-decay or *K*-capture process no charge is emitted from the atom hence options (C) and (D) are correct.

Sol. 3 (B, C) As we have studied in basic theory that a neutron decays radioactively to a proton but a proton can transform to a neutron only within the nucleus and cannot decay freely hence options (B) and (C) are correct.

Sol. 4 (A, B) From the basic definition of half life and mean life time options (A) and (B) are correct. If in decay equation we put t = mean life = $1/\lambda$ then we get $N = N_0/e = 0.37\, N_0$ hence option (C) is not correct similarly by substituting $t = 3T$ we can check that option (D) is also not correct.

Sol. 5 (B, C) Assuming β to be ${}_{+1}\beta^0$ the nuclear reaction with atomic numbers and mass numbers of the elements are written as

$${}_{69}E^{172} \xleftarrow{\gamma} {}_{69}D^{172} \xleftarrow{\alpha} {}_{71}C^{176} \xleftarrow{{}_{+1}\beta^0} {}_{72}B^{176} \xleftarrow{\alpha} {}_{74}A^{180}$$

Hence options (B) and (C) are correct.

Sol. 6 (B, C) Using radioactive decay equation $N = N_0 e^{-\lambda t}$ we have

At $t = 0$ number of nuclei are $N_1 = N_0$ and at time t number of nuclei left are $N_2 = N_0 e^{-\lambda t}$

Thus number of nuclei decayed in time t are $(N_1 - N_2) = N_0(1 - e^{-\lambda t})$

Probability that a radioactive nuclei does not decay in $t = 0$ to

$$t: \frac{N}{N_0} = \frac{N_0 e^{-\lambda t}}{N_0} = e^{-\lambda t}$$

Hence options (B) and (C) are correct.

Sol. 7 (A) In γ-decay no effect is there on atomic and mass numbers hence option (A) is correct.

Sol. 8 (D) As *A* and *B* are isotopes, these will have same atomic number and belong to same element. *B* and *C* are isobars so these will have same mass numbers but different atomic numbers so these will be different elements. By a radioactive process of alpha or beta decay atomic number always changes so *B* can change to *C* by any of these processes hence option (D) is correct.

Sol. 9 (A, D) As already discussed in basic theory that in α-emission the energy of all the emitted α-particles are same so these will have almost the same speeds but in case of β-emission due to emission of neutrino the energy is distributed among beta particle and neutrino so emitted β-particles have different speeds hence options (A) and (D) are correct.

Sol. 10 (A, B, D) In option (A) the reaction given is the fission reaction of U^{235} by a slow neutron hence option (A) is correct. Option (B) is correct as H atoms in ordinary water may capture neutrons, while Deuterium in heavy water does not capture neutrons. Option (C) is not correct as Cadmium rods decreases the reactor power by absorbing neutrons. Option (D) is correct as for U^{235} slow neutrons causes effective fission whereas in U^{238} fast neutrons causes effective fission.

Sol. 11 (A, C) We use decay equation $N = N_0 e^{-\lambda t}$

In a given time t the amount of radioactive substance decayed is given as

$$\Delta N = (N_0 - N_0 e^{-\lambda t})$$

In time $t = 1/\lambda$ we have

$$\Delta N = N_0\left(1 - \frac{1}{e}\right)$$

$$\Rightarrow \quad \Delta N = N_0(1 - 0.37) = N_0(0.63)$$

$$\Rightarrow \quad \frac{\Delta N}{N_0} = \left[\frac{N_0(0.63)}{N_0}\right] \times 100 = 63\%$$

Hence option (A) is correct

Half life time of the substance is given as $T_{1/2} = \dfrac{\log_e 2}{\lambda} = 4$ year

thus option (C) is correct.

Sol. 12 (A, D) We have studied that the stability of a nucleus is due to the mass defect in formation of a nucleus so the rest mass of a nucleus is less than the sum of rest masses of its nucleons considered independently hence option (A) is correct. In case of nuclear fission heavy elements disintegrate in smaller fragments by inducing the reaction through a neutron and due to the fragmentation of nucleus energy is released hence option (D) is correct.

Sol. 13 (A, B, D) According to the decay equation we have $N = N_0 e^{-\lambda t}$ hence option (A) and (D) are correct and according to radioactive decay law option (B) is correct.

Sol. 14 (A, B) The parameter represented by y-axis in the figure grows with time and becomes constant after a finite/long time interval. According to radioactive decay law the number of nuclei of a radioactive element left undecayed decreases exponentially with time so the total nuclei decayed can be represented like this curve hence option (B) is correct. If in a reactor a radionuclide is produced at a constant rate then these start decaying just after their production starts and after some time equilibrium comes when the decay rate becomes equal to the production rate then the number of such nuclei can also be represented by this curve, hence option (A) is correct.

Sol. 15 (B, C, D) By radioactive decay law we can find that options (B) and (C) are correct. The disintegration energy of the U^{235} nucleus is distributed among α-particle and the daughter nucleus hence option (D) is correct.

Sol. 16 (C, D) As Ca nucleus is more stable than Ne nucleus rest mass of former is less than twice the rest mass of the latter hence option (C) is correct. As Ne nucleus is a stable element its rest mass is less than the sum of rest masses of its nucleons hence option (D) is correct.

Sol. 17 (B, D) From the figure it can be seen clearly that energy is released in a nuclear reaction when the B/A of elements produced is more than that of the reactants or the nuclei present before the reaction. If two nuclei in the range $51 < A < 100$ will fuse then they will produce an element with mass number above 100 and less than 200 which has more B/A thus energy is released hence option (B) is correct. Similarly a nucleus in the range $200 < A < 260$ when broken into two equal fragments then the B/A of these fragments will be more than that of the nucleus hence option (D) is correct.

Sol. 18 (All) In a radioactive decay depending upon it is α, β or γ decay process all of the given options can be correct.

Sol. 19 (A, C, D) According to radioactive decay law $N = N_0 e^{-\lambda t}$ option (A) is correct. As we've studied in basic theory that the activity per nuclei remain constant and equal to the decay constant of the element, option (C) is correct. The rate at which daughter nuclei are produced is the activity of the element which decreases exponentially hence option (D) is also correct.

Sol. 20 (B, C, D) According to decay law for activity we use

$$A = A_0 (2)^{-200/T}$$

at $t = 200$ days $\quad 800 = A_0 (2)^{-200/T} \qquad \ldots(1)$

at $t = 300$ days $\quad \dfrac{8000}{\sqrt{2}} = A_0 2^{-300/T} \qquad \ldots(2)$

Dividing-(1) by (2) we get

$$\sqrt{2} = 2^{1/T(300-200)}$$

$$\Rightarrow \quad 2^{1/2} = 2^{100/T}$$

$$\Rightarrow \quad T = 200 \text{ days}$$

From equation-(1) we have

$$8000 = A_0 (2)^{-1}$$

$$\Rightarrow \quad A_0 = 16000 \text{ dps}$$

at $t = 400$ days we have

$$A = 16000 (2)^{-400/200}$$

$$\Rightarrow \quad A = \frac{16000}{4} = 4000 \text{ dps}$$

Hence options (B), (C) and (D) are correct.

Sol. 21 (A, B, D) As half life of the decay is 3.8 days so using radioactive decay equation we can calculate the amount left after 11.4 days, given as

$$m = m_0 (2)^{-t/T}$$

$$\Rightarrow \quad m = (1)(2)^{-3} = \frac{1}{8} = 0.125 \text{ mg}$$

Hence option (A) is correct. Activity of Rn after 7.6 days can also be calculated by radioactive decay equation for activity which is written as

$$A = A_0 (2)^{-t/T}$$

$$\Rightarrow \quad A = A_0 (2)^{-2} = \frac{A_0}{4}$$

Hence option (B) is correct. Radioactive laws can only be applied for very large number of particles in a group so option (C) is NOT correct. As Po is the daughter nucleus formed by alpha decay of Rn, it will be more stable hence option (D) is correct.

Sol. 22 (B, C) When α-decay occurs then by conservation of momentum both daughter nucleus and alpha particles have same magnitude of linear momenta but in opposite direction and for equal linear momentum the kinetic energy is inversely proportional to the mass of particle hence options (B) and (C) are correct.

Sol. 23 (A, C) As $\frac{1}{\lambda} = \frac{t_{1/2}}{ln2} \Rightarrow t_{(1/2)A} > t_{(1/2)B}$

at $t = 60\text{ min}$

$\Rightarrow \qquad \lambda_A N_A = \lambda_B N_B$

$\Rightarrow \qquad N_A > N_B$

Activity curves are $(T_{1/2\,(A)} > T_{1/2\,(B)})$

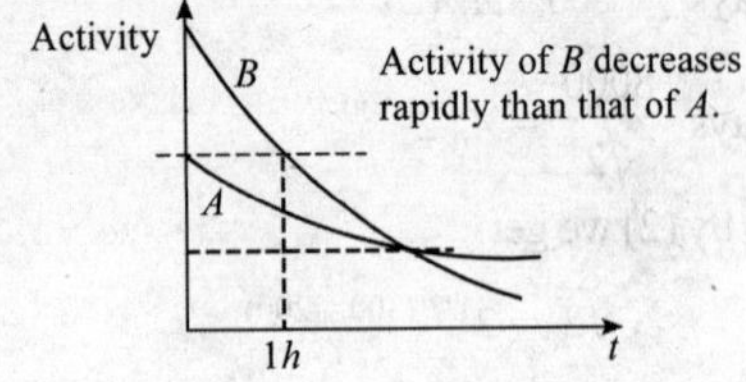

* * * * *

ANSWERS & SOLUTIONS

CONCEPTUAL MCQS Single Option Correct

1	(A)	2	(C)	3	(B)
4	(C)	5	(A)	6	(D)
7	(D)	8	(B)	9	(A)
10	(C)	11	(C)	12	(D)
13	(D)	14	(A)	15	(A)
16	(B)	17	(C)	18	(B)
19	(A)	20	(A)	21	(A)
22	(D)	23	(B)	24	(B)
25	(B)	26	(D)	27	(C)
28	(C)	29	(C)	30	(D)
31	(D)	32	(D)	33	(B)
34	(A)	35	(A)	36	(A)
37	(A)	38	(A)	39	(B)
40	(C)	41	(B)	42	(D)
43	(A)				

NUMERICAL MCQS Single Option Correct

1	(A)	2	(C)	3	(B)
4	(B)	5	(B)	6	(D)
7	(C)	8	(C)	9	(D)
10	(C)	11	(B)	12	(A)
13	(A)	14	(B)	15	(C)
16	(B)	17	(A)	18	(D)
19	(B)	20	(C)	21	(D)
22	(D)	23	(B)	24	(C)
25	(A)	26	(B)	27	(D)
28	(C)	29	(D)	30	(A)
31	(A)	32	(A)	33	(A)
34	(A)	35	(B)	36	(D)
37	(B)	38	(C)	39	(A)
40	(C)	41	(B)	42	(B)
43	(B)	44	(C)	45	(B)
46	(A)	47	(A)	48	(C)
49	(B)	50	(B)	51	(A)

ADVANCE MCQs One or More Options Correct

1	(B, C, D)	2	(A, D)	3	(A, B)
4	(A, D)	5	(A, C)	6	(A, C)
7	(All)	8	(A, C)	9	(A, C)
10	(A, D)	11	(B, C)	12	(B, C, D)
13	(A, B, D)	14	(A, C)	15	(A, D)
16	(C, D)	17	(A, D)	18	(A, B, D)
19	(B, C)	20	(B, C)	21	(A, B)
22	(B, C)	23	(B, C)	24	(All)
25	(A, C)	26	(B, C)	27	(B, C, D)
28	(B, C, D)	29	(B, C)	30	(A)
31	(B, C)				

Solutions of PRACTICE EXERCISE 1.1

(i) By Similarly in triangle ABC and DEC

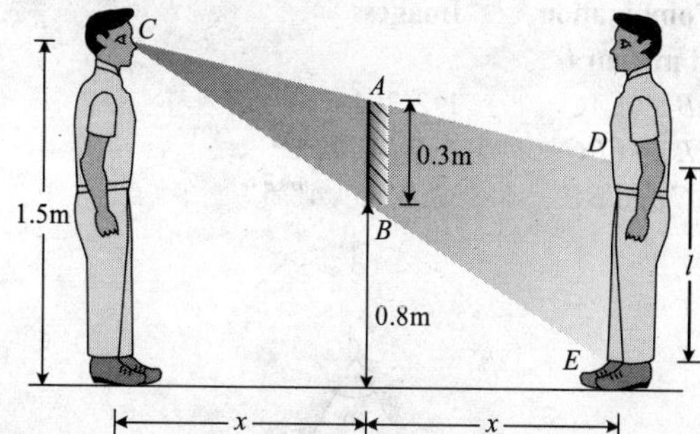

In the triangles ΔCDE and ΔCAB by similarity we have

$$\frac{l}{0.3} = \frac{2x}{x}$$

$$\Rightarrow \quad l = 0.6\,\text{m}$$

(ii) If the mirror center of curvature is considered on its left and object is placed on the right side of it, here for mirror formula we use

$$f = -20\text{ cm},\ u = ?$$

and $\quad m = (-v/u) = \dfrac{1}{4}$

or $\quad v = -(u/4)$

Using the mirror formula,

$$\frac{1}{f} = \frac{1}{u} + \frac{1}{v}, \text{ we have}$$

$$\Rightarrow \quad -\frac{1}{20} = \frac{1}{u} - \frac{4}{u}$$

Solving we get $u = 60$ cm

(iii) The figure below shows the incident angles on the mirrors M_1 and M_2 and in the triangle ABC, we have

In ΔABC we have

$$2i + 2(60 - i) + \theta = 180°$$

$$\Rightarrow \quad 120° + \theta = 180°$$

$$\Rightarrow \quad \theta = 60°$$

(iv) Figure below shows the multiple images formed by the combination of each pair of mirrors listed below. As studied earlier that two mirrors placed at an angle 60° produces 5 images, all of which lie on a circle, here we consider 5 images formed by each pair of images as shown.

Combination of mirrors	Images
AB and AC	$1, 2, 3, 4, 5$
AB and BC	$1', 2', 3', 4', 5'$
AC and BC	$1'', 2'', 3'', 4'', 5''$

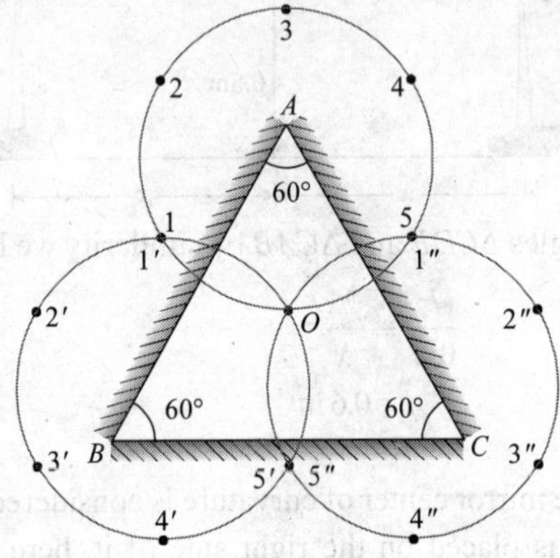

For the mirror AB and BC $\frac{360}{60} = 6$

Thus by three pair of mirrors total 15 images will be produced but three images out of these located at (1, 1′), (5, 1″) and (5′, 5″) are coinciding so total $15 - 3 = 12$ images are produced by the given configuration of mirrors.

(v) Figure shows the field of view IPQ of the image of light source B from the line along which the man is walking. In this figure from triangle IPQ and IMN we use

$$\frac{PQ}{MN} = \frac{3L}{L} \Rightarrow PQ = 3d$$

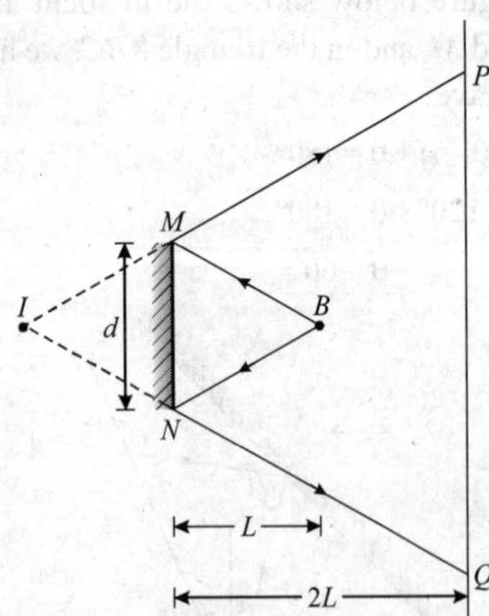

(vi) Due to object motion, image velocity components parallel to mirror remain same and the component normal to the mirror gets reversed hence we use along the surface of mirror image velocity components are

$$\vec{v}_{i_x} = 5\hat{i} \text{ m/s}$$

and $$\vec{v}_{i_y} = -3\hat{j} \text{ m/s}$$

Due to motion of mirror the image velocity in the direction normal to mirror the image velocity is increased by twice the velocity of mirror thus in direction normal to the mirror image velocity is given as

$$\vec{v}_{i_z} = 2\vec{v}_{m_z} - \vec{v}_{o_z}$$

$$\Rightarrow \quad \vec{v}_{i_z} = 2(-3\hat{k}) - (-11\hat{k}) = +5\hat{k}$$

Thus final velocity of image is given as

$$\vec{v}_i = 5\hat{i} - 3\hat{j} + 5\hat{k} \text{ m/s}$$

(vii) Different angles of incidence and reflection at mirrors M_1 and M_2 are as shown in Figure

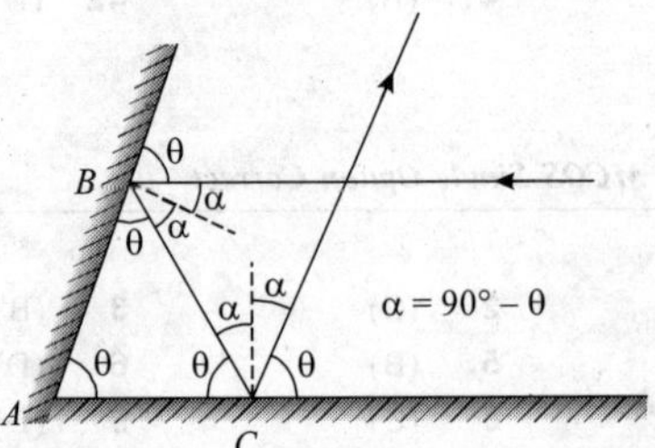

In triangle ΔABC we have

$$\theta + \theta + \theta = 180°$$

$$\Rightarrow \quad \theta = 60°$$

(viii) As we have studied that due to motion of object the image velocity component normal to mirror gets reversed and due to mirror motion the velocity of image in direction normal to mirror gets doubled in same direction so the final image velocity we will have here will be given as

$$v_i = 2v_m - v_0$$

$$\Rightarrow \quad v_i = -2 - 5 = -7 \text{ m/s}$$

Thus final speed of image is 7 m/s and direction is towards left.

(ix) We know that along the direction parallel to the mirror which is x and z directions in this case the velocity components of the image will remain same as that of object and along the normal to the mirror which is y direction here the image velocity is equal and opposite to the object velocity and added to twice the mirror velocity which becomes $-(-4) + 2(+5) = 14$ m/s thus the final velocity of image is given as

$$\vec{V_I} = -2\hat{i} + 14\hat{j} + 4\hat{k}$$

(x) The light ray retraces its path only when it falls on the mirror normally so the light ray in its third reflection falls on mirror M_1 normal to it as shown in the ray diagram shown in figure. Thus from triangle ΔOBC, we have

$$75° + \theta + 90° = 180°$$

$$\Rightarrow \quad \theta = 15°$$

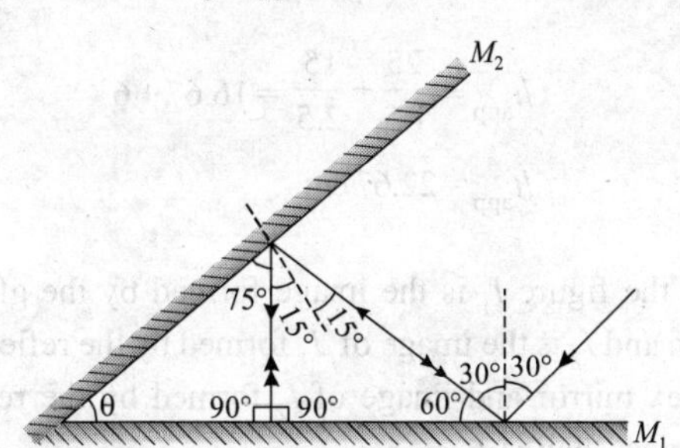

Solutions of PRACTICE EXERCISE 5.2

(i) Considering object placed to the left of mirror then by coordinate convention for mirror formula, we use

$$v = +35 \text{ cm and } f = +60 \text{ cm}$$

Using mirror formula, we have

$$u = \frac{vf}{v-f} = \frac{35 \times 60}{-25} = -84 \text{ cm}$$

Magnification $\quad m = -\frac{v}{u} = \frac{35}{84} = \frac{5}{12}$

Size of image = $m \times$ size of object

$$= \frac{5}{12} \times 12 = 5 \text{ cm}$$

Figure shows the position of object and image with respect to convex mirror.

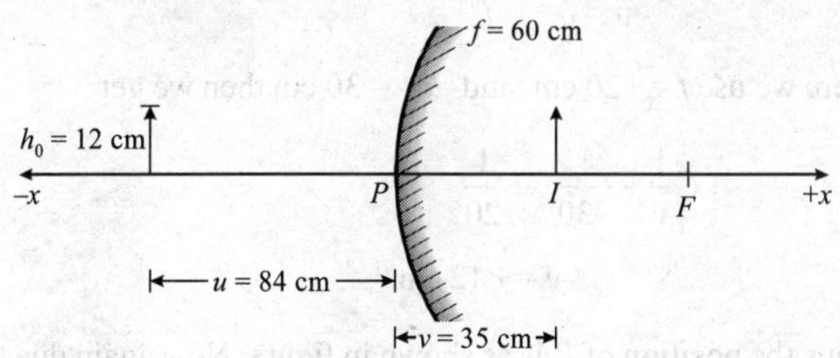

(ii) As object is real and image produced is inverted that means image is also real. In this case the magnification produced is given as

$$m = -\frac{v}{u} = -\frac{v}{-12} = -\frac{5}{2}$$

$\Rightarrow$ Image distance is $v = -12(2.5) = -30$ cm

Focal length of mirror is given by mirror formula as

$$f = \frac{uv}{u+v} = \frac{-12 \times -30}{-42} = -\frac{60}{7} = -8.6 \text{ cm}$$

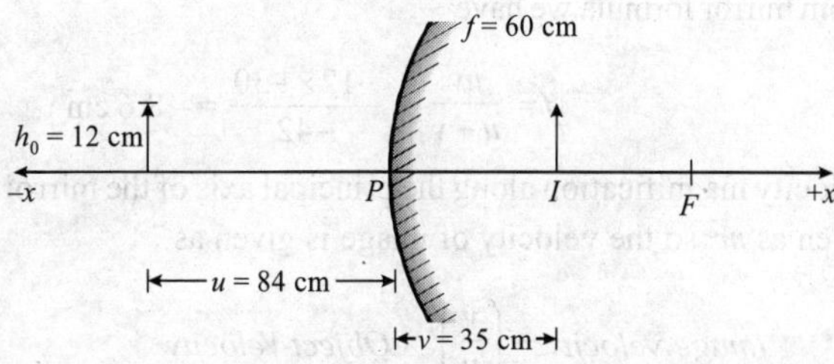

(iii) By coordinate convention for mirror formula we use

$$u = -25 \text{ cm}, f = -20 \text{ cm}$$

By mirror formula we have

$$v = \frac{uf}{u-f} = \frac{-25 \times -20}{-5} = -100 \text{ cm}$$

Thus magnification in this case is

$$m = -\frac{v}{u} = -\frac{-100}{-25} = -4$$

Image velocity along the principal axis is given as

$$v_{i(\text{along } PA)} = m^2 \times v_{o(\text{along } PA)}$$

$$\Rightarrow \quad v_{i(\text{along } PA)} = 16 \times \frac{5}{\sqrt{2}} = 40\sqrt{2} \text{ cm/s}$$

And image velocity normal to principal axis is given as

$$v_{i(\text{normal to } PA)} = m \times v_{o(\text{normal to } PA)}$$

$$\Rightarrow \quad v_{i(\text{normal to } PA)} = 4 \times \frac{5}{\sqrt{2}} = 10\sqrt{2} \text{ cm/s}$$

(iv) Here

$$u = -40 \text{ cm}$$
$$v = +80 \text{ cm}$$

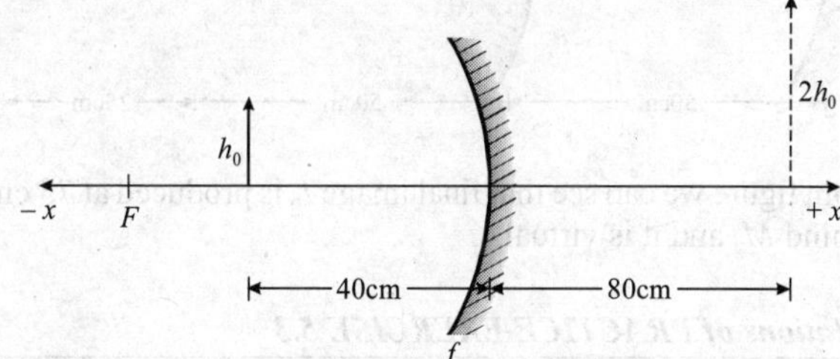

using mirror formula

$$f = \frac{uv}{u+v} = \frac{-40 \times 80}{-40+80} = \frac{-40 \times 80}{40}$$

$$f = -80 \text{ cm}$$

Thus focal length of mirror is 80 cm.

(v) Using magnification formula, if we consider both object and image are located on the left of the concave mirror, we use

$$-\frac{v}{u} = \frac{\text{size of image}}{\text{size of object}}$$

$$\Rightarrow \quad -\frac{v}{-12} = -\frac{5}{2}$$

$$\Rightarrow \quad v = -30 \text{ cm}$$

From mirror formula we have

$$f=\frac{uv}{u+v}=\frac{-12\times-30}{-42}=-8.6 \text{ cm}$$

Velocity magnification along the principal axis of the mirror is given as m^2 so the velocity of image is given as

$$\textit{Image velocity}=\left(\frac{v}{u}\right)^2\times \textit{Object Velocity}$$

$$\Rightarrow \quad \textit{Image velocity}=\left(\frac{30}{12}\right)^2\times 1.2=7.5 \text{ cm/s}$$

As object is moving toward the mirror, image must be moving in opposite direction as it is inverted so it must be moving away from center of curvature.

(vi) Considering first Reflection

$$u=+25 \text{ cm} \,\&\, f=+20 \text{ cm}$$

Using mirror formula

$$v\ I_1=\frac{uf}{u-f}=\frac{25\times 20}{5}=100 \text{ cm}$$

Considering second Reflection at convex mirror

$$u=+50 \,\&\, f=+30 \text{ cm}$$

$$v=\frac{uf}{u-f}=\frac{50\times 30}{20}=+75 \text{ cm}$$

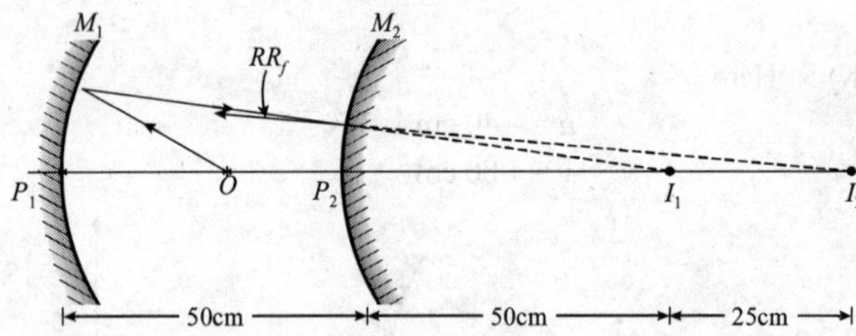

From figure we can see that final image I_2 is produced at 75 cm behind M_2 and it is virtual.

Solutions of PRACTICE EXERCISE 5.3

(i) The system now comprises of two slabs of different materials so the net shift of point of convergence is given as

$$\text{Shift}=t_1\left[1-\frac{1}{\mu_1}\right]+t_2\left[1-\frac{1}{\mu_2}\right]$$

$$=6\left[1-\frac{2}{3}\right]+4\left[1-\frac{1}{2}\right]=4 \text{ cm}$$

As the slabs are denser than surrounding the direction of the shift is in the direction of the incident rays which is to the right. Therefore, the rays will finally converge to a point at a distance equal to $(14-6-4)+4=8$ cm to the right of the second slab surface.

(ii) Apparent depth due to refraction by parallel sides glass slabs is given as

$$h_{\text{app}}=\frac{h_1}{\mu_1}+\frac{h_2}{\mu_2}$$

$$\Rightarrow \quad h_{\text{app}}=\frac{25}{1.5}+\frac{15}{2.5}=16.67+6$$

$$\Rightarrow \quad h_{\text{app}}=22.67 \text{ cm}$$

(iii) In the figure I_1 is the image formed by the glass slab refraction and I_2 is the image of I_1 formed by the reflection by the convex mirror and image of I_2 formed by the refraction through glass slab is I_3.

First we consider shift by glass slab in air which is given as

$$\text{Shift}=t\left(1-\frac{1}{\mu}\right)=6\left(1-\frac{1}{2}\right)=3 \text{ cm}$$

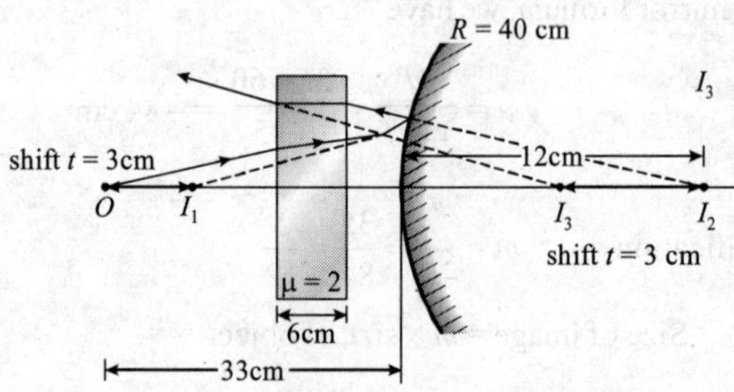

Now for reflection at convex mirror we use mirror formula

$$\frac{1}{v}+\frac{1}{u}=\frac{1}{f}$$

Here we use $f=+20$ cm and $u=-30$ cm then we get

$$\frac{1}{v}+\frac{1}{-30}=\frac{1}{20}$$

$$\Rightarrow \quad v=+12 \text{ cm}$$

Thus the position of I_2 is as shown in figure. Now again due to refraction through glass slab a shift of 3 cm is included so image I_3 is obtained at a distance of $12-3=9$ cm from the pole of mirror hence the distance between object and final image is $33+9=42$ cm.

(iv) Speed of light in glass is given as

$$v=\frac{C}{\mu}$$

The ray diagram in figure below shows the path of light ray in the glass slab

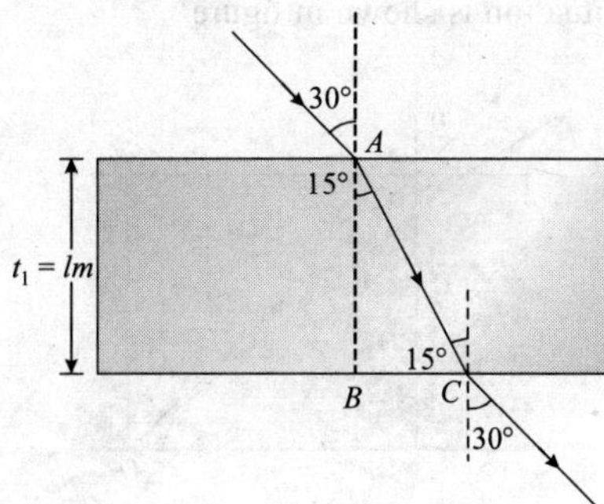

By Snell's law we use

$$1.\sin 30° = \mu \sin 15°$$

$$\Rightarrow \quad \mu = 2\cos 15°$$

Time taken by light to cross the slab

$$t = \frac{AC}{v} = \frac{t_1/\cos 15°}{C/\mu}$$

$$\Rightarrow \quad t = \frac{1}{\cos 15°} \times \frac{2\cos 15°}{3\times 10^8}$$

$$\Rightarrow \quad t = \frac{2}{3}\times 10^{-8}\ \text{s}$$

(v) Figure below shows the ray diagram of image produced at 5ft mark for both the marks - One at 4 inch by refraction and other at 17ft by reflection.

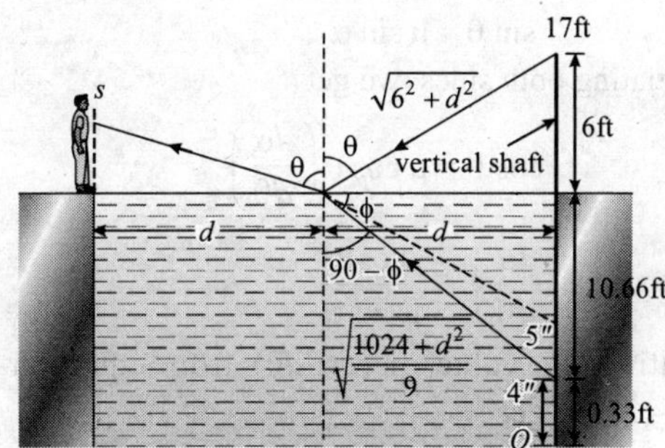

By using Snell's law we have

$$1 \times \sin\theta = \frac{4}{3}\sin(90-\varphi)$$

$$\Rightarrow \quad 1\times\frac{d}{\sqrt{36+d^2}} = \frac{4}{3}\times\frac{d}{\sqrt{\left(\frac{32}{3}\right)^2+d^2}}$$

$$\Rightarrow \quad \sqrt{1024+9d^2} = 4\sqrt{36+d^2}$$

On squaring both sides, we get

$$1024+9d^2 = 16(36+d^2)$$

$$\Rightarrow \quad 1024+9d^2 = 576+16d^2$$

$$\Rightarrow \quad 7d^2 = 448$$

$$\Rightarrow \quad d^2 = \frac{448}{7} = 64$$

$$\Rightarrow \quad d = 8\ \text{feet}$$

$\Rightarrow$ Width of canal is $2d = 16$ feet

(vi) Lateral displacement of height due to a glass slab is given as

$$\Delta = \frac{t\sin(i-r)}{\cos r}$$

$$\Rightarrow \quad \Delta = \frac{t[\sin i\cos r - \cos i \sin r]}{\cos r}$$

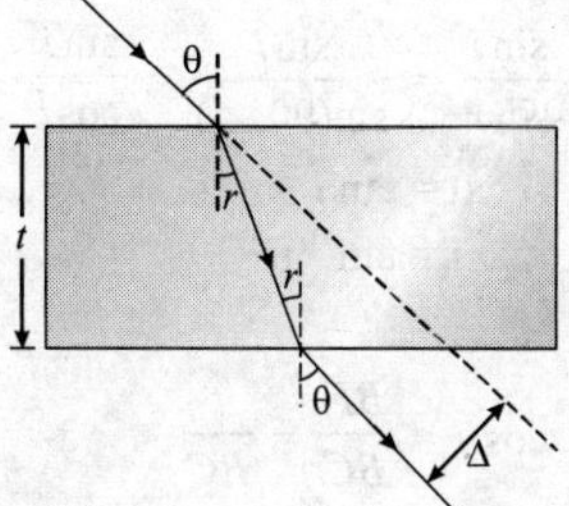

For small θ we use $\sin\theta = \theta$ and $\sin r = r$ and both cosine terms to be almost equal to unity so we have

$$\Delta = t(i-r) \qquad \ldots(1)$$

In the above figure shown, by Snell's law we have

$$\sin\theta = \mu\sin r$$

$$\Rightarrow \quad \theta = \mu r$$

$$\Rightarrow \quad r = \frac{\theta}{\mu}$$

Thus from equation-(1) we have

$$\Delta = t\left(\theta - \frac{\theta}{\mu}\right) = \frac{t\theta(\mu-1)}{\mu}$$

(vii) Figure shows the container filled with water upto a height x so that when observed from top, it appears to be half filled

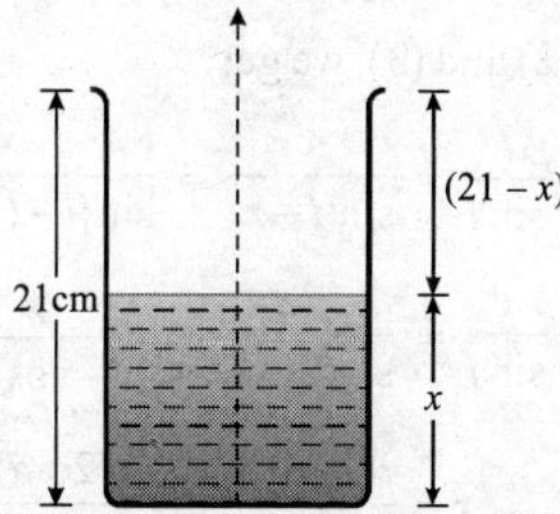

The apparent depth of container is such that it should be equal to the empty length of container for it to appear half filled, so we use

$$\frac{x}{\mu} = 21 - x$$

$$\frac{3x}{4}+x=21$$

$$\frac{7x}{4}=21$$

$$x=12\text{ cm}$$

(viii) The situation is shown in figure. As per given condition we use

$$i+r=90°$$

$$\Rightarrow \quad r=(90-i)$$

By Snell's law we have

$$\mu=\frac{\sin i}{\sin r}=\frac{\sin i}{\sin(90-i)}=\frac{\sin i}{\cos i}$$

$$\mu=\tan i$$

$$\Rightarrow \quad i=\tan^{-1}\mu \qquad \ldots(1)$$

From ΔBCF,

$$\cos r=\frac{BF}{BC}=\frac{t}{BC}$$

$$\Rightarrow \quad BC=\frac{t}{\cos r}=\frac{t}{\cos(90°-i)}$$

$$=\frac{t}{\sin i} \qquad \ldots(2)$$

From ΔBCE,

$$\sin(i-r)=\frac{x}{BC}$$

$$\Rightarrow \quad BC=\frac{x}{\sin(i-r)} \qquad \ldots(3)$$

From equations-(2) and (3), we get

$$\frac{t}{\sin i}=\frac{x}{\sin(i-r)}=\frac{x}{\sin\{i-(90-i)\}}$$

$$\Rightarrow \quad \frac{t}{\sin i}=\frac{x}{\sin(2i-90)}=\frac{x}{-\cos 2i}$$

$$\Rightarrow \quad x=\frac{t(-\cos 2i)}{\sin i}=\frac{t(2\sin^2 i-1)}{\sin i}$$

$$\Rightarrow \quad x=\frac{t\left[2\dfrac{\mu^2}{1+\mu^2}-1\right]}{\left[\dfrac{\mu}{\sqrt{(1+\mu^2)}}\right]}=\frac{t(\mu^2-1)}{\mu\sqrt{(1+\mu^2)}}$$

(ix) The situation is shown in figure

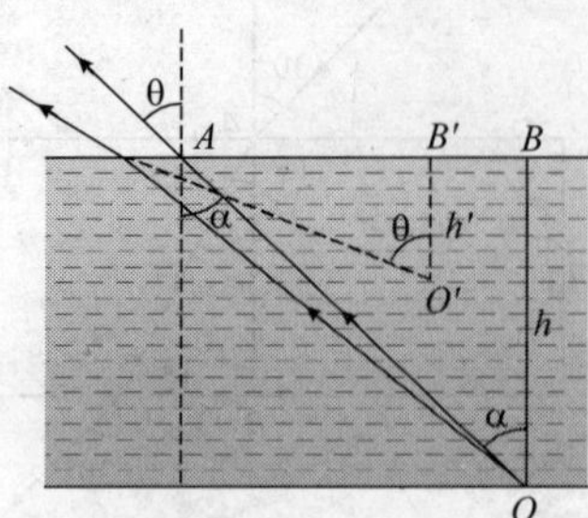

$$\text{From figure,} \quad AB=h\tan\alpha \qquad \ldots(1)$$

$$\text{Similarly,} \quad AB'=h'\tan\theta \qquad \ldots(2)$$

Now $h\tan\alpha-h'\tan\theta=$ constant

Differentiating both sides, we get

$$h\sec^2\alpha\frac{d\alpha}{d\theta}-h'\sec^2\theta=0$$

$$\Rightarrow \quad \frac{h}{\cos^2\alpha}\left(\frac{d\alpha}{d\theta}\right)=\frac{h'}{\cos^2\theta}$$

$$\Rightarrow \quad h'=\frac{h\cos^2\theta}{\cos^2\alpha}\left(\frac{d\alpha}{d\theta}\right) \qquad \ldots(3)$$

By Snell's law, we have

$$\mu=\frac{\sin\theta}{\sin\alpha}$$

$$\Rightarrow \quad \sin\theta=\mu\sin\alpha \qquad \ldots(4)$$

Differentiating both sides, we get

$$\cos\theta=\mu\cos\alpha\left(\frac{d\alpha}{d\theta}\right)$$

$$\Rightarrow \quad \left(\frac{d\alpha}{d\theta}\right)=\frac{\cos\theta}{\mu\cos\alpha} \qquad \ldots(5)$$

Substituting the value of $(d\alpha/d\theta)$ from equation-(5) in equation-(3), we get

$$h'=\frac{h\cos^2\theta}{\cos^2\alpha}\times\frac{\cos\theta}{\mu\cos\alpha}$$

$$\Rightarrow \quad =\frac{h\cos^3\theta}{\mu\cos^3\alpha} \qquad \ldots(6)$$

From equation-(4), $\sin\alpha=\dfrac{\sin\theta}{\mu}$

$$\Rightarrow \quad \cos\alpha=\sqrt{1-\left(\frac{\sin^2\theta}{\mu^2}\right)}$$

$$\Rightarrow \quad \cos^3\alpha=\left[1-\left(\frac{\sin^2\theta}{\mu^2}\right)\right]^{3/2}$$

$$\Rightarrow \quad \cos^3\alpha=\frac{(\mu^2-\sin^2\theta)^{3/2}}{\mu^3}$$

Substituting the value of $\cos^3 \alpha$ in equation-(6), we have

$$h' = \frac{\mu^2 h \cos^3 \theta}{(\mu^2 - \sin^2 \theta)^{3/2}}$$

(x) The situation is shown in figure. The length of shadow of pole AB at the bottom of river is given as

$$L = x_1 + x_2 \quad \ldots(1)$$

From ΔAPQ, we have

$$x_1 = AQ \tan 60° = \sqrt{3} \text{ m} \quad \ldots(2)$$

From ΔRPM, we have

$$x_2 = PM \tan r = 2 \tan r \quad \ldots(3)$$

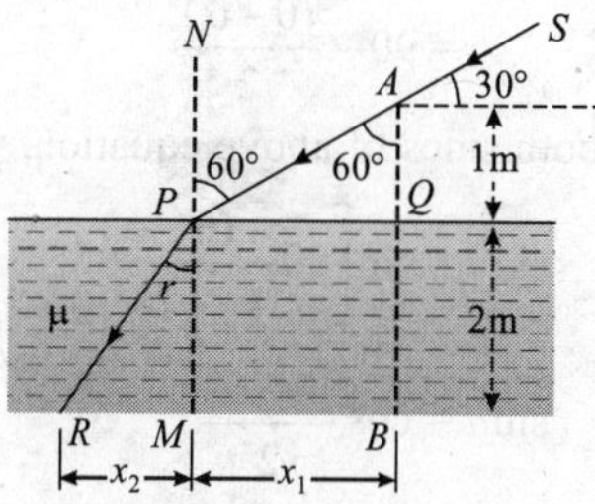

From Snell's law, at point P, we have

$$\frac{\sin 60}{\sin r} = \mu = \frac{4}{3}$$

$$\Rightarrow \quad \sin r = \frac{3}{4} \sin 60 = \frac{3\sqrt{(3)}}{8}$$

$$\Rightarrow \quad \cos r = \sqrt{(1 - \sin^2 r)} = \frac{\sqrt{(37)}}{8}$$

We substitute the value of r in equation-(3)

$$x_2 = 2 \tan r$$

$$\Rightarrow \quad x_2 = 2 \times \frac{(3\sqrt{3})/8}{\sqrt{(37)}/8} = \frac{6\sqrt{(3)}}{\sqrt{(37)}} = 1.708 \text{ m} \quad \ldots(4)$$

From equation-(1), (3) and (4)

$$L = \sqrt{3} + 1.708 = 3.44 \text{ m}$$

(xi) The focal length of the concave mirror is $100/2 = 50$ cm. In first case when the depth of water is 80 cm the situation is shown in figure. As the rays are incident normally on the mirror from infinity, the image I_1 is produced by mirror at its focal point i.e. at 50 cm from the pole of mirror.

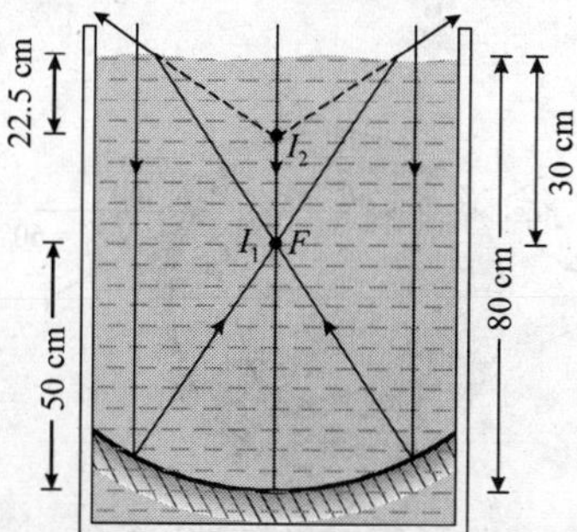

The light rays from this image I_1 will incident on the water surface at a height of 30 cm and gets refracted out in air. Due to refraction at water surface the final image is produced at an apparent depth $h/\mu = 30/(4/3) = 22.5$ cm below the water surface or at a height $80 - 22.5 = 47.5$ cm from the pole of mirror.

In second case when the depth of water is 40 cm after reflection from mirror, the reflected rays from will produce an image I_1 at its focal point at a distance 50 cm from the mirror pole as shown in figure. But before reaching the focus, light rays gets refracted from the water surface and produce image I_2 as shown in figure.

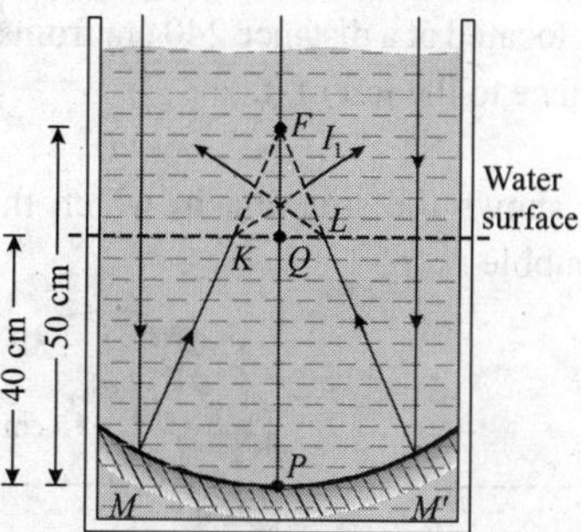

For refraction at water surface object will be taken as I_1 which is at a distance 10 cm from the surface and for this the image produced will be at a distance $h/\mu = 10/(4/3) = 7.5$ cm above the water surface or at a height $50 + 7.5 = 57.5$ cm from the pole of mirror.

(xii) Figure shows the ray diagram of the image formation as described in the given condition. By using Snell's law, we have

$$\mu_w \sin \theta = 1 \sin \phi$$

$$\Rightarrow \quad \frac{4}{3} \times \frac{3}{5} = \sin \phi \Rightarrow \phi = 53°$$

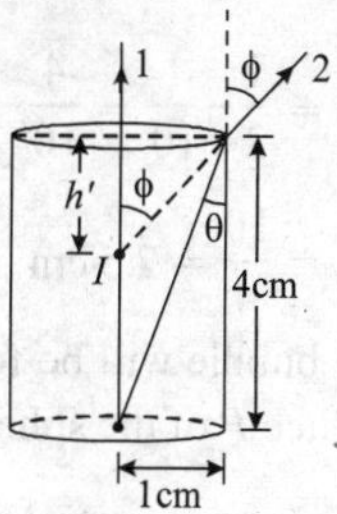

Here we have $\quad \tan \phi = \dfrac{3}{h'}$

$$\Rightarrow \quad h' = \frac{3}{4/3} = \frac{9}{4} = 2.25 \text{ cm}$$

Solutions of PRACTICE EXERCISE 5.4

(i) We use refraction formula for which we have

$$v = \infty; \ \mu_1 = \frac{4}{3}; \ \mu_2 = \frac{3}{2} \text{ and } R = +30 \text{ cm}$$

Using these values in refraction formula, we have

$$\frac{\mu_2}{v}-\frac{\mu_1}{u}=\frac{\mu_2-\mu_1}{R}$$

$$\Rightarrow \frac{3/2}{\infty}-\frac{4/3}{u}=\frac{3/2-4/3}{30}$$

$$\Rightarrow -\frac{4}{3u}=\frac{1}{180}$$

$$\Rightarrow u=-240 \text{ cm}$$

Thus object is located at a distance 240 cm from the pole of the refracting surface to the left of it.

(ii) Figure shows the situation in which the observer is viewing the bubble

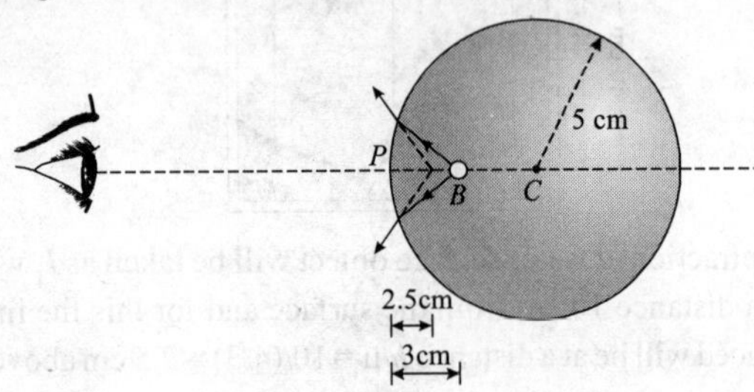

We use refraction formula

$$\frac{\mu_2}{v}-\frac{\mu_1}{u}=\frac{\mu_2-\mu_1}{R}$$

For refraction formula we use

$$R=+5 \text{ cm};\ u=+3 \text{ cm};\ \mu_1=1.5 \text{ and } \mu_2=1$$

Substituting the values in the formula, we get

$$\frac{1}{v}-\frac{1.5}{3}=\frac{1-1.5}{5}$$

$$\Rightarrow \frac{1}{v}=\frac{1}{2}-\frac{1}{10}=\frac{4}{10}$$

or $$v=\frac{10}{4}=2.5 \text{ cm}$$

Thus the image of the bubble will be formed at a distance of 2.5 cm behind the surface P of the sphere.

(iii) The ray diagram of the situation is shown in figure. Here we consider the total deviation of incident ray and emergent ray is α.

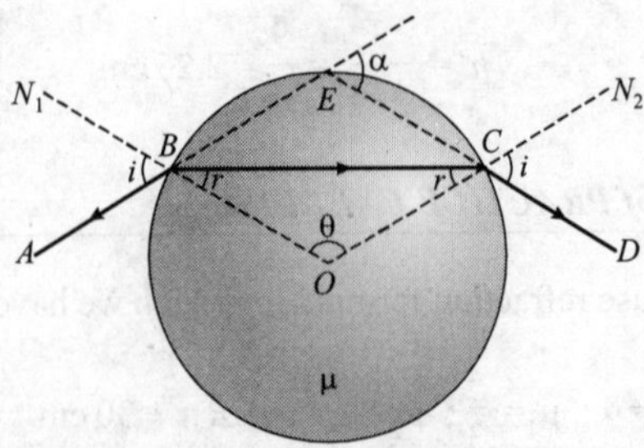

Here $BO=OC$ so from triangle OBC, we have

$$2r+\theta=180$$

$$\Rightarrow r=(180-\theta)/2$$

Taking sine on both sides of above equation, we get

$$\sin r=\sin\left(90-\frac{\theta}{2}\right)=\cos\frac{\theta}{2} \quad \ldots(1)$$

From figure, total deviation of light ray is given as

$$\alpha=\angle EBC+\angle EDB$$

$$\Rightarrow \alpha=(i-r)+(i-r)=2(i-r)$$

$$\Rightarrow i=\frac{\alpha}{2}+r=\frac{\alpha}{2}+90-\frac{\theta}{2}$$

$$\Rightarrow i=90-\frac{(\theta-\alpha)}{2}$$

Taking sine on both sides of above equation, we get.

$$\sin i=\sin\left[90-\frac{(\theta-\alpha)}{2}\right]$$

$$\Rightarrow \sin i=\cos\frac{(\theta-\alpha)}{2} \quad \ldots(2)$$

By Snell's law we have

$$\mu=\frac{\sin i}{\sin r}$$

Substituting the value of $\sin i$ and $\sin r$ from equations-(1) and (2), we get

$$\mu=\frac{\cos(\theta-\alpha)/2}{\cos\theta/2}$$

$$\Rightarrow \cos\frac{(\theta-\alpha)}{2}=\mu\cos\frac{\theta}{2}$$

(iv) Since, the distance of all the points lying on the sphere is constant from the centre, all the angles of refraction are same. Here we consider δ_1 is the deviation of the light ray at first refraction, δ_2 is the deviation of the transmitted ray through partially polished surface and δ_3 is the deviation of the light ray emerging out of the sphere at final refraction. Figure shows the ray diagram of the given situation then according to the given condition, we have from figure

$$(60-r)+(60-r)=\frac{1}{3}[(60-r)+(60-r)+(180-2r)]$$

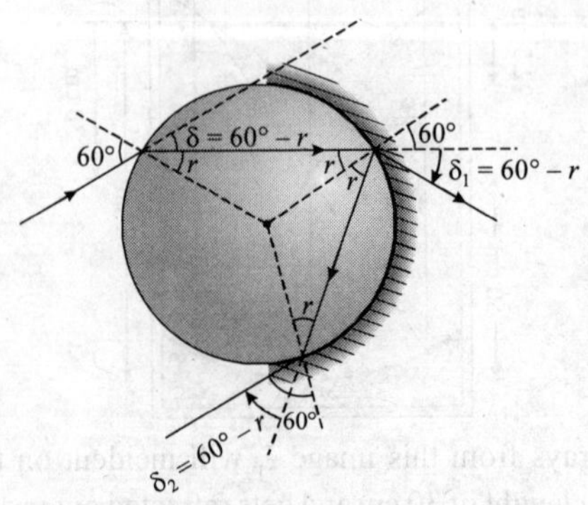

$$\Rightarrow \quad 120-2r=\frac{1}{3}[300-4r]$$

$$\Rightarrow \quad 360-6r=300-4r$$

$$\Rightarrow \quad 60=2r$$

$$\Rightarrow \quad r=30°$$

Now using Snell's law, we have

$$1.\sin 60° = \mu.\sin r$$

$$\Rightarrow \quad \frac{\sqrt{3}}{2}=\mu\times\frac{1}{2}$$

$$\Rightarrow \quad \mu=\sqrt{3}$$

(v) Figure shows the refraction of a parallel beam on a solid glass sphere at near normal incidence. At first refraction image I_1 is produced which acts as an object for second refraction at other surface of sphere at which after refraction final image I_2 is produced

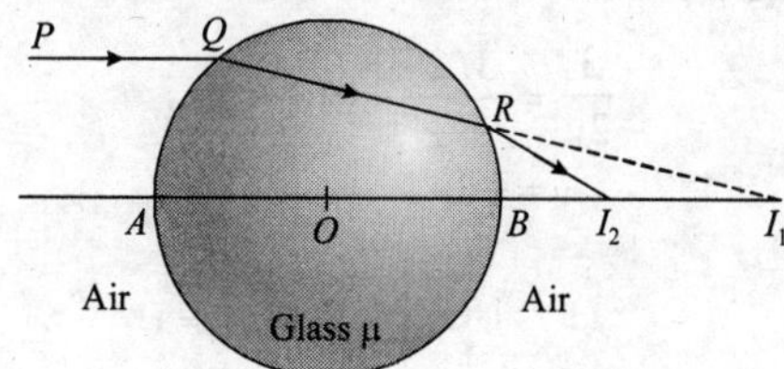

Using refraction formula at first surface we have

$$\frac{\mu_2}{v_1}-\frac{\mu_1}{u_1}=\frac{\mu_1-\mu_2}{R} \quad \ldots(1)$$

Here we use $\mu_1=1$; $\mu_2=\mu$; $u_1=\infty$ and $R=+R$

Substituting the values in refraction formula we get

$$v_1=\frac{\mu R}{(\mu-1)} \quad \ldots(2)$$

For the refraction at the second surface, we use

$$\mu_1=\mu;\ \mu_2=1;\ R=-R \text{ and}$$

$$u_2=+\frac{\mu R}{(\mu-1)}-2R=\frac{2R-\mu R}{(\mu-1)}=\frac{R(2-\mu)}{(\mu-1)}$$

For the second surface,

$$\frac{1}{v_2}-\frac{\mu}{u_2}=\frac{(1-\mu)}{-R}$$

$$\Rightarrow \quad \frac{1}{v_2}-\frac{\mu(\mu-1)}{R(2-\mu)}=\frac{(1-\mu)}{-R}$$

$$\frac{1}{v_2}=\frac{\mu(\mu-1)}{R(2-\mu)}-\frac{(1-\mu)}{R}$$

Simplifying, we get

$$v_2=\frac{R(2-\mu)}{2(\mu-1)}$$

(vi) The image formation is shown in figure. The mark considered as object is at point O. First refraction takes place from the inner surface and the image is produced at O_1. Now this image acts as the object for the second outer surface and second refraction takes place from this outer surface and final image is formed at O_2.

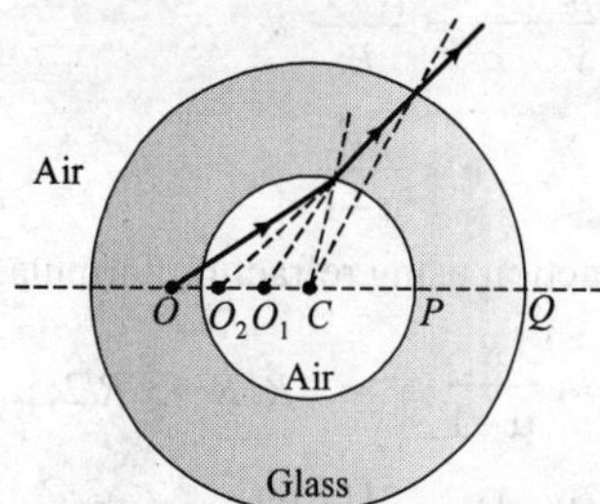

For the first refraction at inner surface for refraction formula we use,

$$u=-2R;\ R=-R;\ \mu_1=1 \text{ and } \mu_2=\mu$$

$$\frac{\mu_2}{v_1}-\frac{\mu_1}{u_1}=\frac{\mu_2-\mu_1}{R}$$

Substituting the values, we get

$$\frac{1}{2R}+\frac{\mu}{v_1}=\frac{\mu-1}{-R}$$

$$\Rightarrow \quad \frac{\mu}{v_1}=-\left[\frac{1}{2R}+\frac{(\mu-1)}{R}\right]=-\frac{(2\mu-1)}{2R}$$

$$\Rightarrow \quad v_1=-\frac{2\mu R}{(2R-1)}$$

For the refraction at second surface, we use,

$$\mu_1=\mu;\ \mu_2=1;\ R=-2R \text{ and}$$

$$u_2=-\left[R+\frac{2\mu R}{(2\mu-1)}\right]=-\frac{(4\mu-1)R}{(2\mu-1)}$$

Now using the refraction formula, we have

$$\frac{\mu_2}{v_2}-\frac{\mu_1}{u_2}=\frac{\mu_2-\mu_1}{R}$$

$$\Rightarrow \quad \frac{\mu(2\mu-1)}{(4\mu-1)R}+\frac{1}{v_2}=\frac{1-\mu}{-2R}$$

$$\Rightarrow \quad \frac{1}{v_2}=\left[-\frac{1-\mu}{2R}-\frac{\mu(2\mu-1)}{(4\mu-1)R}\right]$$

On solving we get $v_2=-\dfrac{2R(4\mu-1)}{(3\mu-1)}$ ...(1)

So the distance of the final image O_2 from O is given by equation-(1). The shift of object is given by

$$\text{Shift}=3R-\frac{2R(4\mu-1)}{(3\mu-1)}=R\left[3-\frac{2(4\mu-1)}{3\mu-1}\right]$$

$$\Rightarrow \quad \text{Shift}=R\left[\frac{9\mu-3-8\mu+2)}{(3\mu-1)}\right]=\frac{(\mu-1)R}{(3\mu-1)}$$

(vii) We consider refractive index of glass to be μ and after first refraction, image is produced at v then by refraction formula, we use

$$\frac{\mu_2}{v_1}-\frac{\mu_1}{u_1}=\frac{\mu_2-\mu_1}{R}$$

$$\Rightarrow \quad \frac{\mu}{v}-\frac{1}{\infty}=\frac{\mu-1}{R}$$

$$\Rightarrow \quad v=\frac{\mu R}{\mu-1}$$

For second refraction using refraction formula, we have

$$u_1=\frac{\mu R}{\mu-1}-R=+\frac{R}{\mu-1};\ v_1=+R;\ R=+R/2;\ \mu_1=\mu \text{ and } \mu_2=1$$

$$\Rightarrow \quad \frac{1}{R}-\frac{\mu(\mu-1)}{R}=\frac{2(1-\mu)}{R}$$

$$\Rightarrow \quad \mu^2-3\mu+1=0$$

Solving we get $\quad \mu=\dfrac{3+\sqrt{5}}{2}$

(viii) Figure shows the ray diagram of the given situation. By Snell's law, we have

$$\sin 60^\circ=\mu \sin\theta$$

$$\Rightarrow \quad \sin\theta=\frac{\sin 60^\circ}{\sqrt{3}}$$

$$\Rightarrow \quad \sin\theta=\frac{\sqrt{3}/2}{\sqrt{3}}=\frac{1}{2}$$

$$\Rightarrow \quad \theta=30^\circ$$

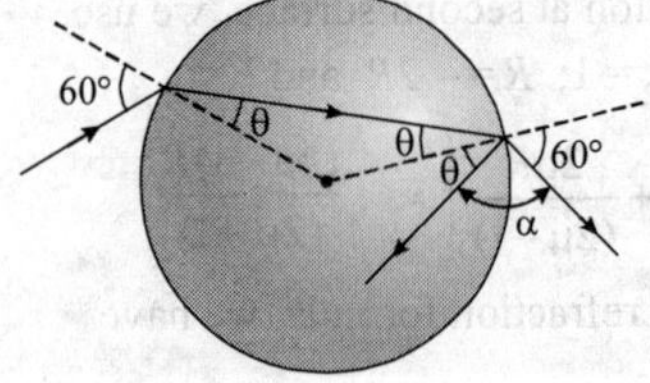

The angle between reflected and refracted ray at the second surface can be calculated from figure which is given as

$$\alpha=180-60-\theta$$

$$\Rightarrow \quad \alpha=120^\circ-30^\circ$$

$$\Rightarrow \quad \alpha=90^\circ$$

(ix) Figure below shows the situation described in the question

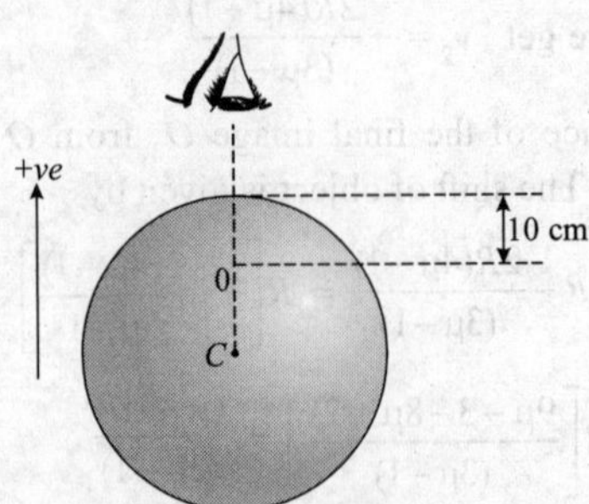

We apply refraction formula

$$\frac{\mu_2}{v}-\frac{\mu_1}{u}=\frac{\mu_2-\mu_1}{R}$$

Here we use $u=-10$ cm; $R=-15$ cm; $\mu_1=1.5$ and $\mu_2=1$

Substituting the values, we have

$$\frac{1}{v}-\frac{1.5}{-10}=\frac{1-1.5}{-15}$$

Solving we get $\quad v=-8.57$ cm

Thus the apparent depth of bubble will be 8.57 cm from the top of the sphere.

(x) For refraction formula we use

$$u=\infty;\ \mu_1=1;\ \mu_2=\frac{3}{2} \text{ and } R=+r$$

$$\frac{\mu_2}{v}-\frac{\mu_1}{u}=\frac{\mu_2-\mu_1}{R}$$

Substituting the values we have

$$\frac{3}{2v}=\frac{3/2-1}{r}=\frac{1}{2r}$$

$$\Rightarrow \quad v=+3r$$

By similarity, we can write

$$\frac{d}{d'}=\frac{3r}{2r}$$

$$\Rightarrow \quad d'=\frac{2d}{3}$$

(xi) For refraction formula, we use

$$u=+15\text{ cm};\ \mu_1=\frac{4}{3};\ \mu_2=1 \text{ and } R=+10\text{ cm}$$

$$\frac{\mu_2}{v}-\frac{\mu_1}{u}=\frac{\mu_2-\mu_1}{R}$$

Substituting the values, we get

$$\frac{1}{v}-\frac{4}{3\times 15}=\frac{1-\frac{4}{3}}{10}=-\frac{1}{30}$$

$$\Rightarrow \quad \frac{1}{v}=\frac{4}{45}-\frac{1}{30}=\frac{1}{18}$$

$$\Rightarrow \quad v=+18\text{ cm}$$

Velocity magnification along optic axis is given as

$$m=\frac{\mu_1 v^2}{\mu_2 u^2}=\frac{\frac{4}{3}\times(18)^2}{1\times(15)^2}=1.92$$

Velocity of image of fish

$$=1.92\times 2=3.84 \text{ mm/s}$$

(xii) By Snell's law at surface AB we have

$$\frac{\mu_2}{\mu_1}=\frac{\sin i}{\sin r}$$

$$\Rightarrow \quad \frac{\sqrt{2}}{1}=\frac{\sin 45°}{\sin r}$$

$$\Rightarrow \quad \sin r=\frac{1}{\sqrt{2}\sqrt{2}}=\frac{1}{2}$$

$$\Rightarrow \quad r=30°$$

It shows that the refractive ray thus becomes parallel to AD inside the block. So parallel ray is incident on spherical surface CD. Now for refraction formula we have

$$u=\infty;\ R=0.4 \text{ m};\ \mu_1=\sqrt{2} \text{ and } \mu_2=1.514$$

$$\frac{\mu_2}{v}-\frac{\mu_1}{u}=\frac{\mu_2-\mu_1}{R},$$

Substituting values we get

$$\Rightarrow \quad \frac{1.514}{v}-\frac{\sqrt{2}}{\infty}=\frac{1.514-\sqrt{2}}{0.4}$$

Solving, we get $v=6.06$ m

$$\Rightarrow \quad OE=6.06 \text{ m}$$

Solutions of PRACTICE EXERCISE 5.5

(i) Here ${}_a\mu_g=1.66$ and ${}_a\mu_w=1.33$

$$\Rightarrow \quad {}_w\mu_g=\frac{{}_a\mu_g}{{}_a\mu_w}=\frac{1.66}{1.33}$$

We know that $\mu=\dfrac{\sin(A+\delta_m)/2}{\sin A/2}=\dfrac{1.66}{1.33}$

$$\Rightarrow \quad \frac{\sin\left(\frac{72+\delta_m}{2}\right)}{\sin 36°}=\frac{1.66}{1.33}$$

$$\Rightarrow \quad \sin\left(\frac{72+\delta_m}{2}\right)=\frac{1.66\sin 36°}{1.33}$$

$$\Rightarrow \quad =1.248\times 0.5878=0.7336$$

$$\Rightarrow \quad \frac{72+\delta_m}{2}=47°\,11'$$

$$\Rightarrow \quad \delta_m=22°\,22'$$

(ii) Using Snell's law, we have

$$\sin i=\mu \sin r_1$$

$$r_1+r_2=A$$

$$\Rightarrow \quad \sin i=2\times\sin 30°=2\times\frac{1}{2}=1$$

$$\Rightarrow \quad i=90°$$

Thus, it will happen at grazing incidence.

(iii) We draw a tangent at any point (x, y) on the trajectory which makes an angle θ with optical normal parallel to y-axis as shown in figure.

By using Snell's law at the initial point and at the general point of the trajectory of light, we have

$$\sin 90°=\mu \sin\theta$$

$$\Rightarrow \quad \sin\theta=\frac{1}{\mu}=\frac{1}{\sqrt{1+y}} \quad \ldots(1)$$

Slope of tangent is

$$\frac{dy}{dx}=\tan(90-\theta)$$

$$\Rightarrow \quad \frac{dy}{dx}=\cot\theta \quad \ldots(2)$$

From equation-(1) and (2) we get,

$$\frac{dy}{dx}=y^{1/2}$$

$$\Rightarrow \quad \int_0^y \frac{dy}{y^{1/2}}=\int_0^x dx$$

$$\Rightarrow \quad 2\sqrt{y}=x \ \Rightarrow y=\frac{x^2}{4}$$

(iv) Figure shows the situation in which from the top circular area light will come out in air. The light rays falling on the circumference of the circle make an angle equal to critical angle so all the light rays falling on the water surface out of this circular area will internally reflected into water

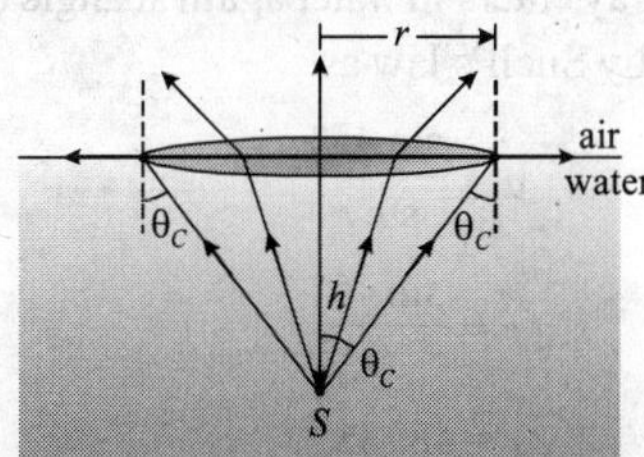

From the figure we have

$$\tan\theta_C=\frac{r}{h}$$

$$\Rightarrow \quad r=h\tan\theta_C$$

Area of circle through which light comes out from water is

$$A = \pi r^2 = \times \pi h^2 \tan^2 \theta_C$$

Where critical angle θ_C is given as

$$\theta_C = \sin^{-1}\left(\frac{1}{\mu}\right) = \tan^{-1}\left(\frac{1}{\sqrt{\mu^2-1}}\right)$$

(v) Figure shows the ray diagram of the light ray incident on the given prism. Here from the given conditions, we have

$$\angle E = \angle F = 45°$$

As at point B the light ray AB is reflected we have

$$\angle i = \angle r = 45°$$

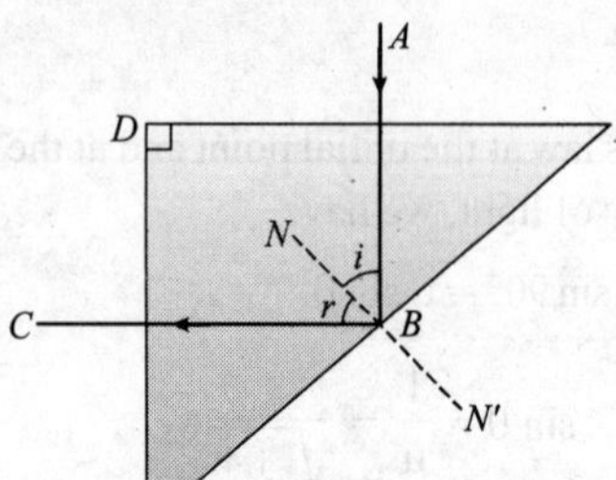

For internal reflection of the light ray at face EF, we use

$$\sin i \geq \sin \theta_C \geq \frac{1}{\mu} \geq \frac{1}{\sin 45°}$$

$$\Rightarrow \qquad \mu_{min} = 1.414$$

When the prism immersed in water, then path of the light ray is shown in figure

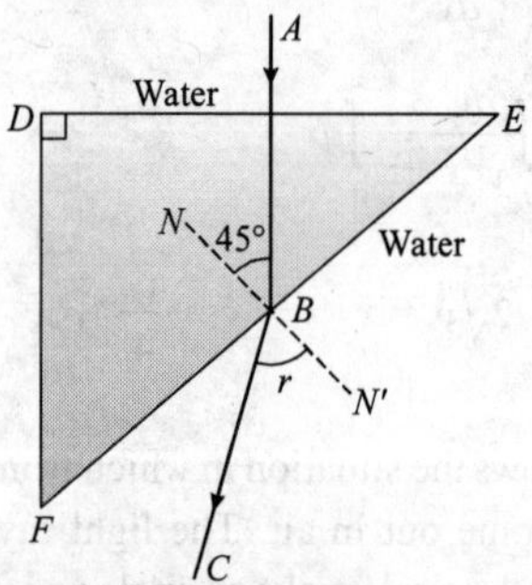

As the incident ray is normal to the prism, it passes undeviated through water and glass at first refraction but at point B after refraction light ray enters in water again at angle of refraction r which is given by Snell's law as

$$\mu = \frac{\sin 45°}{\sin r}$$

$$\Rightarrow \qquad \sin r = \frac{\sin 45°}{{}_g\mu_w}$$

$$\Rightarrow \qquad \angle r = 48° \, 35'$$

(vi) **(a)** Using Snell's law, we have

$$\sin \theta = \mu \sin \theta_2 \qquad \ldots(1)$$

$$\mu \sin \theta_3 = \sin 90°$$

$$\Rightarrow \qquad \mu \cos \theta_2 = 1 \qquad \ldots(2)$$

Squaring and adding equation-(1) and (2), we get

$$\mu^2 = 1 + \sin^2 \theta$$

$$\Rightarrow \qquad \mu = \sqrt{1+\sin^2\theta}$$

(b) Maximum value of θ can be 90° for which $\theta_2 = \theta_3 = 45°$

Thus $\qquad \mu_{max} = \sqrt{1+1} = \sqrt{2}$

(c) If angle θ is slightly increased, θ_2 will increase and θ_3 will decrease so light ray emerges out in air and it will no longer be grazing emergence.

(d) If angle θ is slightly decreased, θ_2 will decrease and θ_3 will increase beyond critical angle and it point Q total internal reflection of light will take place.

(vii) For glass critical angle is given as

$$\theta_c = \sin^{-1}\left(\frac{1}{\mu}\right)$$

$$\Rightarrow \qquad \theta_c = \sin^{-1}\left(\frac{2}{3}\right) \simeq 42°$$

As incident light is normal to the face, this light incident on other face of prism at 60° which is more than critical angle so light will be internally reflected as shown in figure

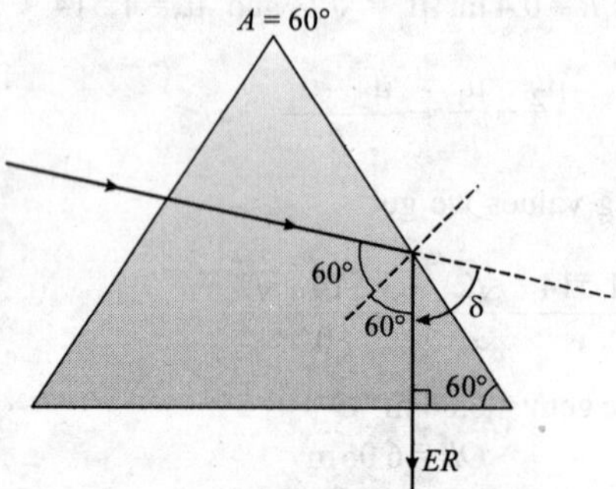

Thus angle between incident emergent ray is

$$\delta = 60°$$

(viii) $\mu \sin \theta = 1 \times \sin 90°$

$$\Rightarrow \qquad \sin \theta = \frac{1}{\mu}$$

$$\Rightarrow \qquad \tan \theta = \frac{1}{\sqrt{\mu^2-1}} = \frac{1}{\sqrt{1+e^{x/d}-1}} = e^{-x/2d}$$

$$\Rightarrow \qquad \frac{dy}{dx} = e^{-x/2d}$$

$$\Rightarrow \qquad y = 2d(1 - e^{-x/2d})$$

When $y = d$, then $\qquad \frac{1}{2} = 1 - e^{\frac{x}{2d}}$

$$\Rightarrow \qquad e^{\frac{x}{2d}} = 2$$

$$\Rightarrow \qquad x = 2d \ln 2$$

$$\Rightarrow \qquad \mu = \sqrt{1+e^{\frac{2d\ln 2}{d}}} = \sqrt{1+4} = \sqrt{5}$$

(ix) For minimum deviation of a light ray through a trihedral prism we use

$$\mu = \frac{\sin\left(\frac{A+\delta}{2}\right)}{\sin A/2}$$

The refractive index μ is a function of λ. Thus a change in wavelength λ corresponds to a change in refractive index of the material and it also causes change in δ. Therefore, δ is a function of μ. A differential change in refractive index Δμ causes a differential change Δδ in δ. If the rate of change of μ with respect to δ be ($d\mu/d\delta$), then we use

$$\Delta\mu = \frac{d\mu}{d\delta}\Delta\delta$$

$$\Rightarrow \quad \Delta\mu = \frac{d}{d\delta}\left[\frac{\sin\left(\frac{A+\delta}{2}\right)}{\sin A/2}\right]\Delta\delta$$

$$\Rightarrow \quad \Delta\mu = \frac{1}{2}\left[\frac{\cos\left(\frac{A+\delta}{2}\right)}{\sin A/2}\right]\Delta\delta$$

$$\Rightarrow \quad \Delta\delta = \left[\frac{2\sin A/2}{\left\{1-\sin^2\left(\frac{A+\delta}{2}\right)\right\}^{1/2}}\right]\Delta\mu$$

$$\Rightarrow \quad \Delta\delta = \left[\frac{2\sin A/2}{\sqrt{(1-\mu^2\sin^2 A/2)}}\right]\Delta\mu$$

$$\Rightarrow \quad \Delta\delta = \frac{2\sin 60/2[1.520-1.515]}{\sqrt{\{1-1.555\sin^2(60/2)\}}}$$

$$\Rightarrow \quad \Delta\delta = \frac{2\sin 30\times(0.005)}{\sqrt{\{1-1.555\sin^2 30\}}}$$

$$\Rightarrow \quad \Delta\delta = 0.5° \text{ approx}$$

(x) Using the given conditions the deviation angle of light after passing through the prism is

$$\delta = A(\mu-1) = \frac{5}{4} \qquad \ldots(1)$$

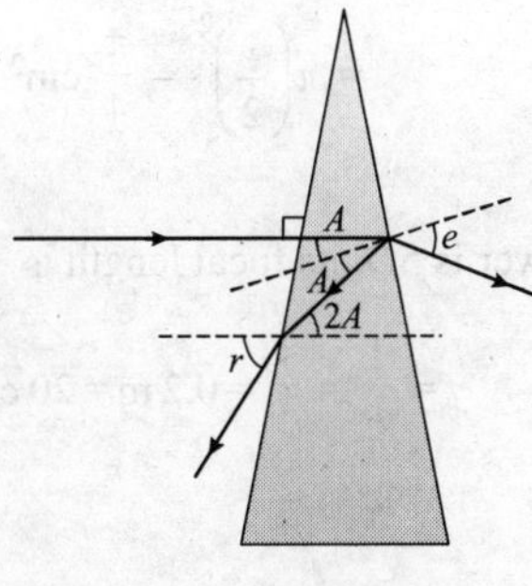

By Snell's law

$$\mu \sin A = \sin e$$

and $$\mu \sin 2A = \sin r$$

For small angles, we use

$$e = \mu A$$

and $$r = 2\mu A = 6.5$$

Now we have

$$A(\mu-1) = \frac{5}{4}$$

$$\Rightarrow \quad 3.25 - A = 1.25$$

$$\Rightarrow \quad A = 2°$$

$$\Rightarrow \quad \mu = \frac{13}{8}$$

(xi) From the given condition we use the deviation angle of light ray which passes through the prism is given as

$$\delta = i_1 + i_2 - A$$

$$30° = 60° + i_1 - 30°$$

$$\Rightarrow \quad i_2 = 0 \text{ or } r_2 = 0$$

$$\Rightarrow \quad r_1 = A = 30°$$

Now by using Snell's law we have

$$\mu = \frac{\sin i_1}{\sin r_1} = \frac{\sin 60°}{\sin 30°} = \sqrt{3}$$

(xii) In the given situation as incidence angle is 0° for the prism if light ray incident on the other inside face of prism at an angle r then we use

$$r = A = 30°$$

Now by using Snell's law we have

$$\mu = \frac{\sin i_2}{\sin r_2}$$

$$\Rightarrow \quad 1.5 = \frac{\sin i_2}{\sin 30°}$$

$$\Rightarrow \quad \sin i_2 = 1.5 \sin 30°$$

$$\Rightarrow \quad \sin i_2 = 1.5 \times \frac{1}{2} = 0.75$$

$$\Rightarrow \quad i_2 = \sin^{-1}(0.75) = 48.6°$$

The deviation angle of light passing through the prism is given as

$$\delta = (i_1 + i_2) - A$$

$$\Rightarrow \quad \delta = (0 + 48.6) - 30$$

$$\Rightarrow \quad \delta = 18.6°$$

(xiii) Suppose θ is the angle of incident ray at any point (x, y) on trajectory of light in the medium as shown in the figure. The slope of the trajectory at this point is given as

$$\frac{dy}{dx} = \tan(90° - \theta)$$

$$\Rightarrow \quad \frac{dy}{dx} = \cot\theta$$

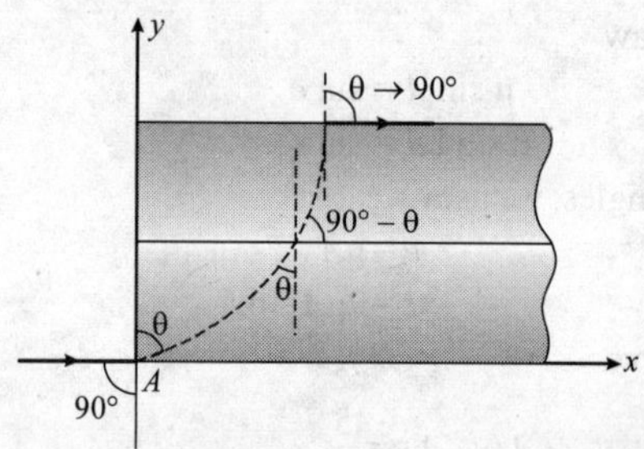

(a) By Snell's law at initial point and the general point we have

$$\mu \sin\theta = 1 \sin 90° \quad \ldots(1)$$

$$\Rightarrow \quad \sin\theta = \frac{1}{\mu}$$

$$\Rightarrow \quad \cos\theta = \sqrt{1-\sin^2\theta}$$

$$\Rightarrow \quad \cos\theta = \sqrt{1-\frac{1}{\mu^2}} = \frac{\sqrt{\mu^2-1}}{\mu}$$

Slope of tangent is given as

$$\cot\theta = \frac{\cos\theta}{\sin\theta}$$

$$\Rightarrow \quad \cot\theta = \frac{\frac{\sqrt{\mu^2-1}}{\mu}}{\frac{1}{\mu}}$$

$$\Rightarrow \quad \cot\theta = \sqrt{\mu^2-1}$$

(b) From equation-(1) we have

$$\mu \sin\theta = 1$$

$$\Rightarrow \quad \mu^2 \sin^2\theta = 1$$

$$\Rightarrow \quad \mu^2 = \frac{1}{\sin^2\theta} = \operatorname{cosec}^2\theta$$

$$= 1 + \cot^2\theta$$

$$\Rightarrow \quad (ky^{3/2}+1) = 1+\left(\frac{dy}{dx}\right)^2$$

$$\Rightarrow \quad ky^{3/2} = \left(\frac{dy}{dx}\right)^2$$

$$\Rightarrow \quad \frac{dy}{dx} = k^{1/2}\, y^{3/4}$$

$$\Rightarrow \quad \frac{dy}{y^{3/4}} = k^{1/2}\, dx$$

On integrating the above relation, we get

$$4y^{1/4} = k^{1/2}\, x + c$$

At $x = 0$, $y = 0$ and so $c = 0$,

$$\Rightarrow \quad k^{1/2}x = 4y^{1/4}$$

(c) At $y = 1$, from equation of trajectory we have

$$x = \frac{4(1)^{1/4}}{1^{1/2}} = 4$$

Thus coordinates of the upper surface, where ray intersect are (4, 1)

(d) At upper interface, we have

$$\mu \sin e = 1$$

$$\Rightarrow \quad \sin e = \frac{1}{\mu} = \frac{1}{1} = 1$$

$$\Rightarrow \quad e = 90°$$

Thus the emergent ray will be grazing out from the upper surface of the medium.

Solutions of PRACTICE EXERCISE 5.6

(i) Applying lens formula for the given case with

$$u = -15 \text{ cm and } f = +10 \text{ cm}$$

$$\Rightarrow \quad \frac{1}{v} - \frac{1}{-15} = \frac{1}{10}$$

$$\frac{1}{v} = \frac{1}{10} - \frac{1}{15} = \frac{3-2}{30}$$

$$\Rightarrow \quad v = +30 \text{ cm}$$

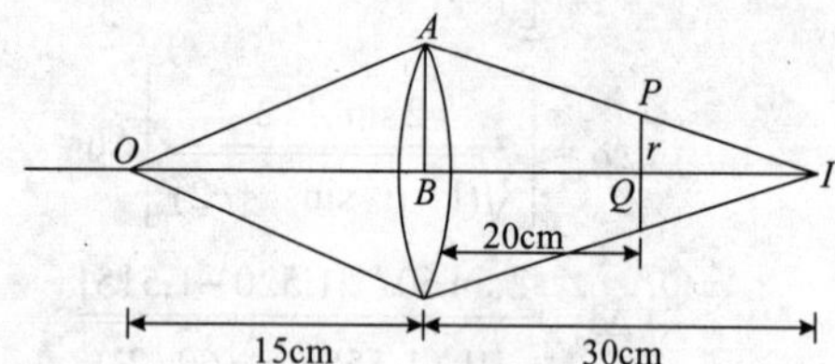

$$AB = \frac{\text{diameter}}{2} = 1.5 \text{ cm}$$

r = radius of the illuminated part

Using similar triangle $\Delta PQI \sim \Delta ABI$, we have

$$\frac{1.5}{r} = \frac{30}{10} \Rightarrow r = \frac{1}{2} \text{ cm},$$

So, Area of illuminated part $= \pi r^2$

$$= \pi\left(\frac{1}{2}\right)^2 = \frac{\pi}{4} \text{ cm}^2$$

(ii) As lens power is $5D$, its focal length is

$$f = \frac{1}{P} = \frac{1}{5} = 0.2 \text{ m} = 20 \text{ cm}$$

Given condition is $\quad v = 4u$

As image is virtual, we use

$$|u| < |f|$$

Here we consider $u = x$

$\Rightarrow$ $v = -4x$

By using lens formula, we have

$$\frac{1}{v} - \frac{1}{u} = \frac{1}{f}$$

$$\Rightarrow -\frac{1}{4x} + \frac{1}{x} = \frac{1}{20}$$

$$\Rightarrow \frac{3}{4x} = \frac{1}{20}$$

$$\Rightarrow x = 15 \text{ cm}$$

(iii) For final image at infinity object must at focal point of lens i.e., 20 cm

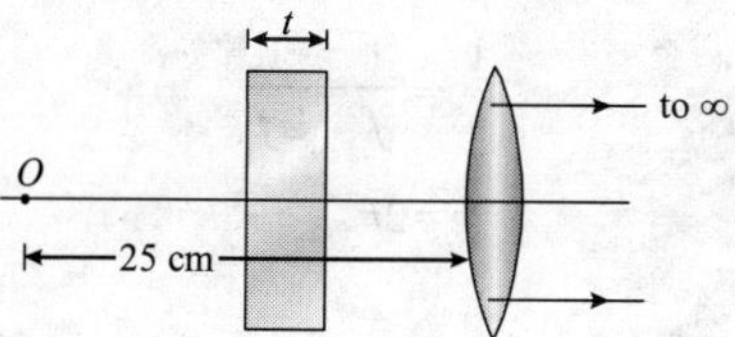

As actual object is kept at 25 cm so 5 cm is the shift due to glass slab, given as

$$\text{Shift} = t\left(1 - \frac{1}{\mu}\right)$$

$$\Rightarrow 5 = t\left(1 - \frac{1}{1.5}\right)$$

$$\Rightarrow t = 15 \text{ cm}$$

(iv)

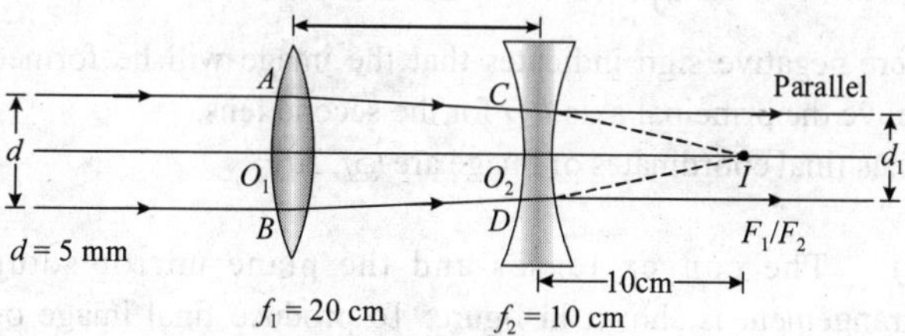

By similarity of ΔABI and CDI, we have

$$\frac{AB}{O_1F_1} = \frac{CD}{O_2F_1}$$

$$\Rightarrow \frac{d}{20} = \frac{d_1}{10}$$

$$\Rightarrow d_1 = \frac{d}{2} = 2.5 \text{ mm}$$

(v) The convex lens and the convex mirror are shown in the figure. As we know to produce image on object reflected light rays retrace the path of incident rays so here for the ray to retrace its path it should be incident normally on the convex mirror, or the rays should pass through the center of curvature of the mirror.

From the diagram we see that for the lens

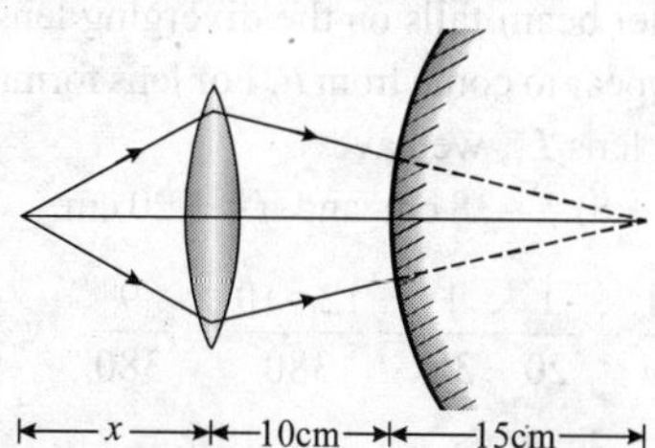

If object is considered to be placed at a distance x from lens then for lens formula we use

$$u = -x;\ f = +20 \text{ cm and } v = +10 + 15 = +20 \text{ cm}$$

From the lens formula, we get

$$\frac{1}{v} - \frac{1}{u} = \frac{1}{f}$$

$$\Rightarrow \frac{1}{25} - \frac{1}{-x} = \frac{1}{20}$$

$$\Rightarrow x = 100 \text{ cm}$$

(vi) Figure show the image formation when light beam falls first on the converging lens. In the absence of lens L_2, the rays will be focussed at F at a distance 20 cm from lens L_1. This point F acts as virtual source for lens L_2. Its image is formed at P.

Thus for lens formula at lens L_2, we use

$$u = +12 \text{ cm and } f = -30 \text{ cm}$$

Substituting in $\frac{1}{v} - \frac{1}{u} = \frac{1}{f}$

We have $\frac{1}{v} - \frac{1}{12} = -\frac{1}{30}$

$$\Rightarrow v = 20 \text{ cm}$$

Thus the rays converge to a point P, 20 cm from L_2.

Second case when parallel beam falls first on diverging lens is shown in figure.

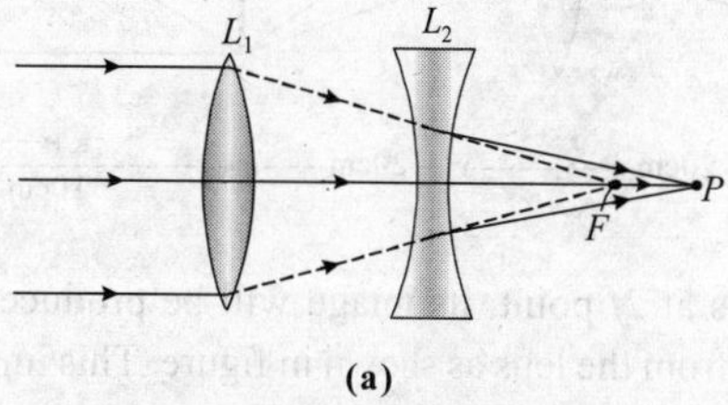

(a)

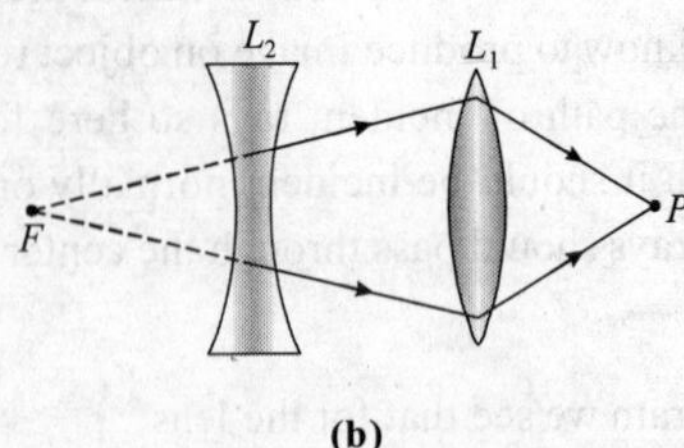

(b)

When a parallel beam falls on the diverging lens L_2, the rays diverge and appear to come from F. For lens formula to be used at converging lens L_1, we have

$$u = -(30+8) = -38 \text{ cm} \text{ and } f = +20 \text{ cm}$$

$$\Rightarrow \quad \frac{1}{v} = \frac{1}{20} - \frac{1}{38} = \frac{12-10}{380} = \frac{9}{380}$$

$$\Rightarrow \quad v = \frac{380}{9} = 42.2 \text{ cm}$$

Thus the point P in this case is located at a distance 42.2 cm from Lens L_1.

(vii) Focal length of an equiconvex lens is given as

$$f = \frac{R}{2(\mu - 1)}$$

For lenses A & B, we use

$$\frac{R_A}{2(\mu_A - 1)} = \frac{R_B}{2(\mu_B - 1)}$$

$$\Rightarrow \quad \frac{\mu_A - 1}{0.9} = \mu_B - 1$$

$$\Rightarrow \quad \frac{0.63}{0.9} = \mu_B - 1$$

$$\Rightarrow \quad \mu_B = 1 + 0.7 = 1.7$$

(viii) If AB is the object placed at a distance of 20 cm from the convex lens L as shown in figure then we can calculate the position of the final image after first refraction through the lens and then reflection from the concave mirror then again refraction from the lens.

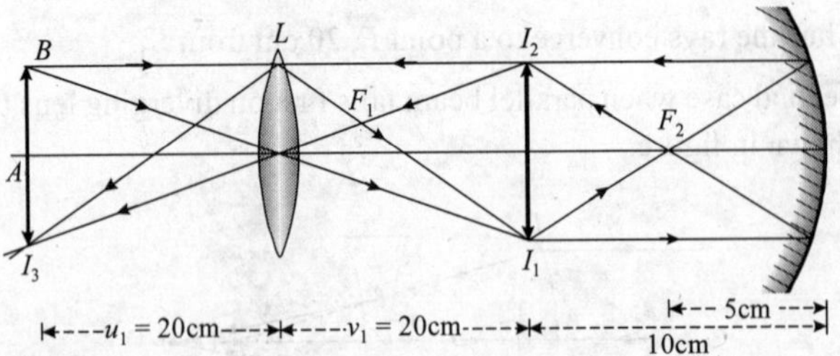

As object is at $2f$ point, its image will be produced at same $2f = 20$ cm from the lens as shown in figure. This image I_1 acts as object for the concave mirror and it is located at a distance 10 cm from the mirror which is the center of curvature of the mirror so again image I_2 is produced at this point only after refraction as shown in ray diagram.

Further refraction takes place through the lens and we can see that image I_2 is at $2f$ point of the lens and its final image is produced at the original object which is of same size but inverted as shown.

(ix) The x-axis is the principal axis for first lens & PQ is the principal axis for second lens. First lens produces image at its focal point at a distance f on x-axis.

Now for second lens, we use lens formula as

$$\frac{1}{v} - \frac{1}{-2f} = \frac{1}{f}$$

$$\Rightarrow \quad \frac{1}{v} = \frac{1}{f} - \frac{1}{2f}$$

$$\Rightarrow \quad v = 2f$$

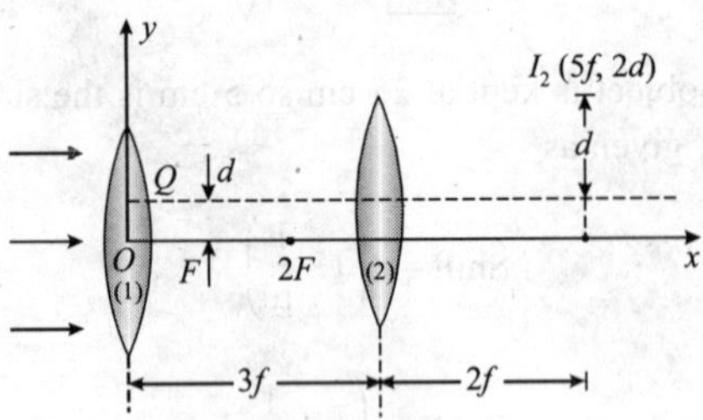

Magnification for the second lens is given as

$$m = \frac{h_i}{h_0} = +\frac{v}{u} = \frac{+2f}{-2f} = -1$$

Here negative sign indicates that the image will be formed above the principal axis PQ for the second lens.
Thus final coordinates of image are $(5f, 2d)$

(x) The convex lenses and the plane mirror setup arrangement is shown in figure. To produce final image on object itself, all the reflected rays are to retrace their path or the rays should be incident normally on the plane mirror.

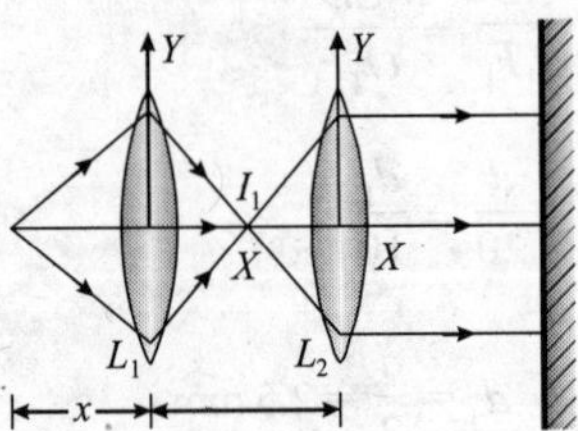

For light rays to fall normally on mirror the image I_1 produced by first lens must be located at the focal point of the second lens which is at a distance 10 cm from it. From the diagram if we use lens formula for lens L_1, we have

$$v = 30 - 10 = +20 \text{ cm},$$
$$f = +10 \text{ cm}, u = -x$$

From the lens equation we get

$$\frac{1}{v} - \frac{1}{u} = \frac{1}{f}$$

$$\Rightarrow \quad \frac{1}{20} - \frac{1}{-x} = \frac{1}{10}$$

$$\Rightarrow \quad x = 20 \text{ cm}$$

(xi) For lens formula, we have

$$u = -11 \text{ cm}$$
$$f = +6 \text{ cm}$$

$$\Rightarrow \quad \frac{1}{v} - \frac{1}{u} = \frac{1}{f}$$

$$\Rightarrow \quad \frac{1}{v} + \frac{1}{11} = \frac{1}{6}$$

$$\Rightarrow \quad \frac{1}{v} = \frac{1}{6} - \frac{1}{11} = \frac{5}{66}$$

$$\Rightarrow \quad v = \frac{66}{5} \text{ cm}$$

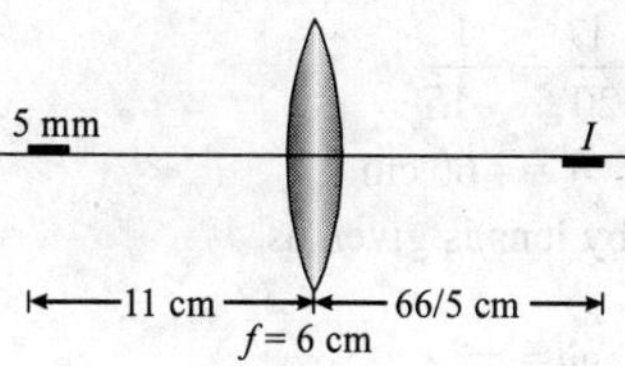

Magnification by lens is given as

$$m = \frac{v}{u} = \frac{66}{5 \times 11} = \frac{6}{5}$$

Longitudinal magnification is

$$m_L = m^2 = \frac{36}{25}$$

$$\text{Image size} = \frac{36}{25} \times 5 \text{ mm}$$

$$\Rightarrow \quad \text{Image size} = \frac{36}{5} \text{ mm} = 7.2 \text{ mm}$$

(xii) As per the condition given in the question, magnifications for the two are same in magnitude. If first case when image is real its distance is taken positive and in second case when image is virtual its distance is taken negative so the two magnifications are taken as

$$m_1 = \frac{h_i}{h_0} = \left|\frac{+v_1}{-u_1}\right| = \frac{v_1}{16}$$

$$m_2 = \frac{h_i}{h_0} = \left|\frac{-v_2}{-u_2}\right| = \frac{v_2}{6}$$

As magnifications are same, we use

$$\frac{v_1}{16} = \frac{v_2}{6}$$

$$\Rightarrow \quad 6v_1 = 16v_2 \quad \ldots(1)$$

by lens formula we have in the two cases

$$\frac{1}{v_1} - \frac{1}{-16} = \frac{1}{f} \quad \ldots(2)$$

$$\frac{1}{-v_2} - \frac{1}{-6} = \frac{1}{f} \quad \ldots(3)$$

By solving above equations we get,

$$f = 11 \text{ cm}$$

Here positive sign indicates that the lens is a convex (or converging) lens.

(xiii) We first find the image produced by mirror using mirror formula as

$$\frac{1}{v} + \frac{1}{u} = \frac{1}{f}$$

We use u = – 12.5 cm and f = – 10 cm, we get

$$\frac{1}{v_1} + \frac{1}{-12.5} = \frac{1}{-10}$$

$$v_1 = -50 \text{ cm}$$

$$m_1 = -\frac{v}{u} = -\frac{(-50)}{(-12.5)} = -4$$

Hereimage formed by the mirror is at a distance of 50 cm from the mirror to the left of it. It is inverted and four times enlarged. Image formed by mirror acts as an object for lens. It is located at a distance of 25.0 cm to the left of lens for the light rays incident on it from right so using the lens formula with $u = -25$ cm and $f = +16.7$ cm, we have

$$\frac{1}{v} - \frac{1}{u} = \frac{1}{f}$$

$$\Rightarrow \quad \frac{1}{v_2} - \frac{1}{-25} = \frac{1}{+16.7}$$

$$\Rightarrow \quad v_2 = +50.3 \text{ cm}$$

Magnification by lens is given as

$$m_2 = \frac{v}{u} = \frac{50.3}{-25} = -2.012$$

overall magnification by the system is

$$m = m_1 \times m_2 = 8.048$$

Thus, the final image is produced at a distance 25.3 cm to the right of the mirror, virtual, upright enlarged 8.048 times. Positions of the intermediate and final images are shown in figure.

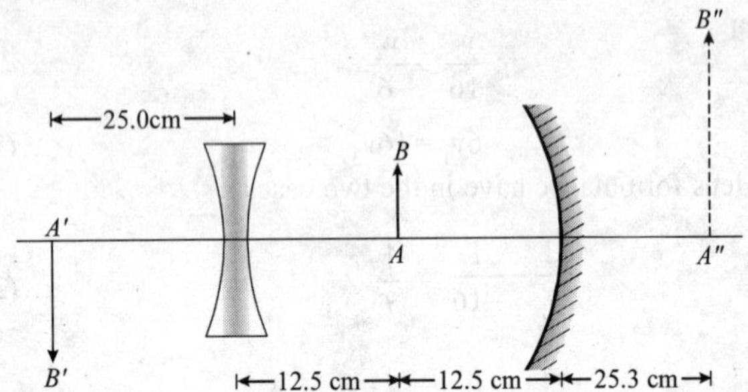

(xiv) If the second lens is not present, the parallel incident rays will focus at F_1, at a distance f_1 from the first lens on its principal axis. These rays now intercepted by second lens, and finally focus at some point P which is obtained by lens formula for second lens. Thus for second lens, we use

$$u_2 = +(f_1 - d) \text{ and } f = +f_2$$

By lens formula,

By lens formula we have

$$\frac{1}{v} - \frac{1}{u} = \frac{1}{f}$$

$$\Rightarrow \quad \frac{1}{v} - \frac{1}{(f_1 - d)} = \frac{1}{f_2}$$

Solving, we get

$$v = \frac{f_2(f_1 - d)}{(f_1 + f_2 - d)}$$

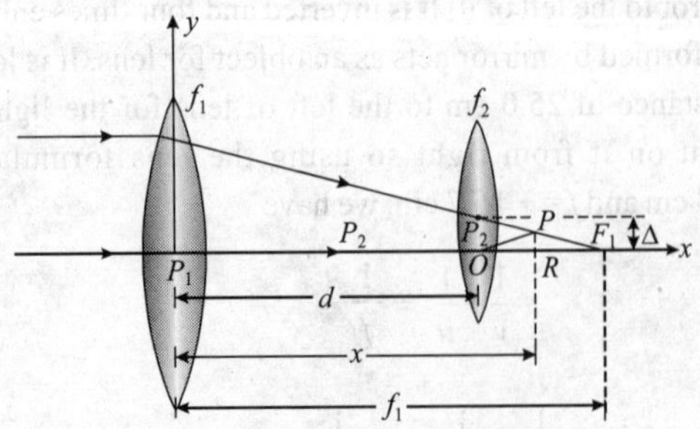

The x coordinate of the final image at point P is

$$x = d + v$$

$$\Rightarrow \quad x = d + \frac{f_2(f_1 - d)}{(f_1 + f_2 - d)}$$

$$\Rightarrow \quad d = \frac{f_1 f_2 + d(f_1 - d)}{(f_1 + f_2 - d)}$$

The y-coordinate of the focus F can be obtained by using magnification by second lens as

$$m = \frac{v}{u} = \frac{f_2}{(f_1 + f_2 - d)}$$

For second lens the image produced at F_1 by first lens acts as an object which is located at a distance Δ in y direction from the principal axis of the second lens. So the distance of final image at point P from principal axis of second lens can be given as

$$\Delta_1 = m.\Delta = \frac{f_2 \Delta}{(f_1 + f_2 - d)}$$

The y-coordinate of point P thus can be written as $\Delta - \Delta_1$

$$y_P = \Delta - \Delta_1 = \frac{\Delta(f_1 - d)}{(f_1 + f_2 - d)}$$

(xv) For refraction through lens, we use

$$u = +20 \text{ cm}, f = -15 \text{ cm}$$

From lens formula, we have

$$\frac{1}{v} - \frac{1}{u} = \frac{1}{f}$$

$$\Rightarrow \quad \frac{1}{v} - \frac{1}{20} = \frac{1}{-15}$$

$$\Rightarrow \quad v = -60 \text{ cm}$$

Magnification by lens is given as

$$m = \frac{v}{u}$$

$$\Rightarrow \quad \textit{Image size} = \frac{v}{u}\ \textit{Object size} = \frac{-60}{20} \times 1.2$$

$$= -3.6 \text{ cm}$$

The image formed by lens acts as an object for mirror. It is located $(3.6 - 0.6)$ cm below the principal axis of the mirror and 0.6 cm lies above principal axis. Let image of C_1B_1 is $C'B'$, and that of C_1A_1 is $C'A'$.

Now we use mirror formula for reflection at concave mirror as

$$\frac{1}{v} + \frac{1}{u} = \frac{1}{f}$$

$$\Rightarrow \quad \frac{1}{v} + \frac{1}{-30} = \frac{1}{+30}$$

$$\Rightarrow \quad v = -15 \text{ cm}$$

Magnification by mirror is given as

$$\frac{C'B'}{3.0} = \frac{v}{u}$$

$$\Rightarrow \quad \frac{C'B'}{3.0} = -\frac{15}{30} = -\frac{1}{2}$$

$$\Rightarrow \quad C'B' = -1.5 \text{ cm}$$

Also we have for same magnification

$$\frac{C'A'}{0.6} = \frac{v}{u}$$

$$\Rightarrow \quad \frac{C'A'}{0.6} = \frac{15}{30}$$

$$\Rightarrow \quad C'A' = -0.3 \text{ cm}$$

We use $\quad A'B' = C'B' + C'A'$

$$\Rightarrow \quad A'B' = 1.5 + 0.3 = 1.8 \text{ cm}$$

Then 1.5 cm of image lies above principal axis and 0.3 cm lies below principal axis

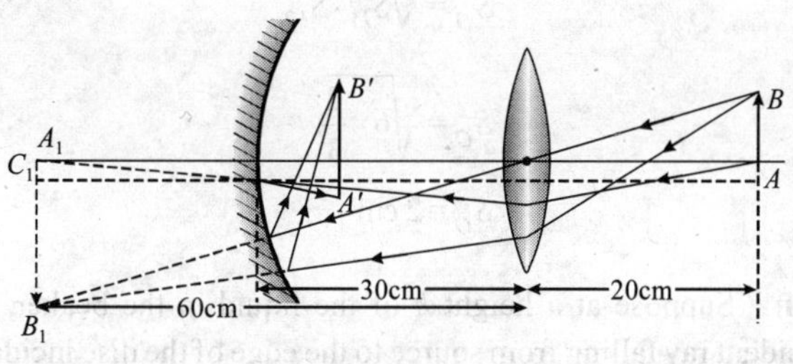

(xvi) Figure shows optical setup as described in the question.

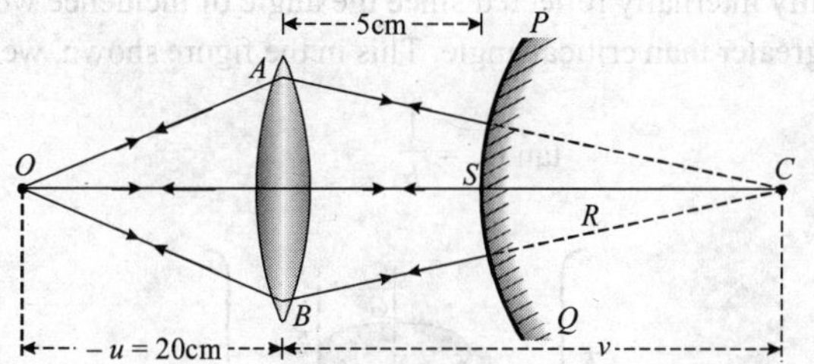

Here convex mirror PQ is separated at a distance of 5 cm from the lens. An object O is placed at a distance 20 cm from the lens. The rays after refraction through lens form an image at C so that the light rays fall normally on the mirror and reflected rays will retrace the path of incident rays to produce image on the object position.

For refraction at lens we use

$$u = -20 \text{ cm} \text{ and } f = +15 \text{ cm}$$

By lens formula, we have

$$\frac{1}{v} - \frac{1}{u} = \frac{1}{f}$$

$$\Rightarrow \quad \frac{1}{v} = \frac{1}{15} - \frac{1}{20} = \frac{4-3}{60} = \frac{1}{60}$$

$$\Rightarrow \quad v = +60 \text{ cm}$$

Thus radius of curvature of the mirror is given as

$$R = v - 5 = 60 - 5 = 55 \text{ cm}$$

Solutions of PRACTICE EXERCISE 5.7

(i) If object is placed at focus of lens, light rays become parallel and fall normal on plane mirror. So, rays retrace their path.

(ii) Focal length of thin concavo convex lens is given as

$$f_L = \frac{R_1 R_2}{(\mu-1)(R_1 - R_2)} = \frac{30 \times 60}{1/2 \times 30}$$

$$\Rightarrow \quad f_L = 120 \text{ cm}$$

Focal length of mirror is given as

$$f_M = \frac{30}{2} = 15 \text{ cm}$$

Equivalent focal length of lens mirror combination is given as

$$\frac{1}{f_{eq}} = \frac{2}{f_L} + \frac{1}{f_M} = \frac{2}{120} + \frac{1}{15} = \frac{1}{12}$$

$$\Rightarrow \quad f_{eq} = 12 \text{ cm}$$

Thus for image to be produced on object, it should be kept at a distance $2f_{eq} = 24$ cm.

(iii) (a) For the combination of two lenses and a plane mirror, the equivalent focal length is given as

$$\frac{1}{f_{eq}} = \frac{2}{f_{L1}} + \frac{2}{f_{L2}} + \frac{1}{f_M}$$

Focal length of the plano concave lens is

$$f_{L1} = \frac{R}{\mu_1 - 1} = \frac{30}{1.5-1} = 60 \text{ cm}$$

Focal length of the plano convex lens is

$$f_{L2} = \frac{R}{\mu_1 - 1} = \frac{30}{1.25-1} = 120 \text{ cm}$$

Focal length of plane mirror is $f_M = \infty$

Equivalent focal length of the combination is given as

$$\frac{1}{f_{eq}} = 2\left(\frac{-1}{60} + \frac{1}{120}\right) + 0 = -\frac{1}{60}$$

$$\Rightarrow \quad f_{eq} = -60 \text{ cm}$$

As equivalent focal length is negative, thus nature of equivalent mirror diverging or convex.

(b) For the equivalent mirror, we can apply the mirror formula to find the final position of the image. Thus we use

$$\frac{1}{v}+\frac{1}{u}=\frac{1}{f_{eq}}$$

$$\Rightarrow \quad \frac{1}{v}+\frac{1}{-15}=\frac{1}{60}$$

$$v=+12 \text{ cm}$$

Thus magnification by the combination is

$$m=-\frac{v}{u}=\frac{+12}{-15}=\frac{4}{5}$$

(iv) If f_{eq} is the focal length of combination, we use

$$u=-12.5 \text{ cm}$$

For real image $\quad v=mu=+50 \text{ cm}$

$$\frac{1}{v}-\frac{1}{u}=\frac{1}{f_{eq}}$$

$$\Rightarrow \quad \frac{1}{50}+\frac{1}{12.5}=\frac{1}{f_{eq}}$$

$$\Rightarrow \quad \frac{1}{f_{eq}}=\frac{1}{10}$$

$$\Rightarrow \quad f_{eq}=10 \text{ cm}$$

Equivalent power of the lens system is

$$P_{eq}=\frac{1}{0.1}=10\,D=2P_{\text{eqch}}$$

Optical power of each lens is

$$P_{\text{eqch}}=5D$$

(v) Figure shows the ray diagram for image formation

For lens L_1 we use $u_1=-20$ cm and $f_1=+25$ cm

$$\Rightarrow \quad \frac{1}{v_1}=\frac{1}{25}-\frac{1}{20}=\frac{4-5}{100}=-\frac{1}{100}$$

$$v_1=-100 \text{ cm}$$

So the lens L_1 forms a virtual image A_1B_1 at 100 cm behind the lens. For lens L_2, this image A_1B_1 acts as a real object for which we use

$$u_2=-(100+10)=-110 \text{ cm, and } f_2=+20 \text{ cm}$$

$$\Rightarrow \quad \frac{1}{v_2}=\frac{1}{20}-\frac{1}{110}=\frac{11-2}{220}=\frac{9}{220}$$

$$\text{or} \quad v_2=+\frac{220}{9}=+24.4 \text{ cm}$$

Thus final image A_2B_2 is real and is formed at a distance 24.4 cm from lens L_2

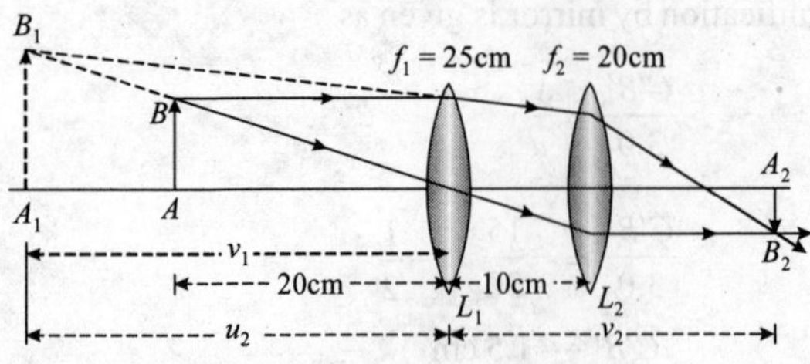

$$\text{Magnification of lens } L_1=\frac{v_1}{u_1}=\frac{100}{20}=5$$

$$\text{Magnification of lens } L_2=\frac{v_2}{u_2}=\frac{220/9}{110}=\frac{2}{9}$$

$$\text{Total magnification}=5\times\frac{2}{9}=\frac{10}{9}$$

(vi) In displacement method experiment, as explained in article 5.18.2, the size of object is given as

$$S_O=\sqrt{S_{I1}\cdot S_{I2}}$$

$$\Rightarrow \quad S_O=\sqrt{6\times\frac{2}{3}}$$

$$\Rightarrow \quad S_O=2 \text{ cm}$$

(vii) Suppose at a height h of the liquid in the beaker, an incident ray falling from source to the edge of the disc incident at critical angle so it gets refracted at grazing manner as shown in figure. Any other light ray falling on water surface will be totally internally reflected since the angle of incidence would be greater than critical angle. This in the figure shown, we use

$$\tan\theta_C=\frac{1}{h} \quad \ldots(1)$$

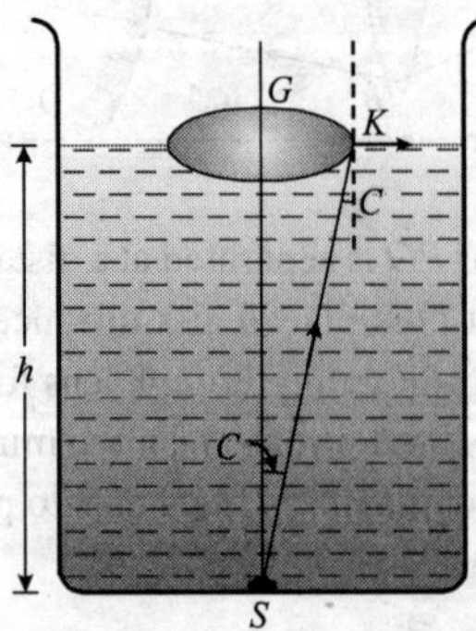

By Snell's law we have

$$\sin\theta_C=\frac{1}{\mu}=\frac{3}{5} \quad \ldots(2)$$

$$\Rightarrow \quad \cos\theta_C=\sqrt{\left(1-\frac{9}{25}\right)}=\frac{4}{5} \quad \ldots(3)$$

$$\Rightarrow \qquad \tan\theta_C = \frac{3/5}{4/5} = \frac{3}{4}$$

$$\Rightarrow \qquad \frac{1}{h} = \frac{3}{4}$$

$$\Rightarrow \qquad h = 1.33 \text{ cm}$$

(viii) Figure below shows the given situation and for solving the above problem.

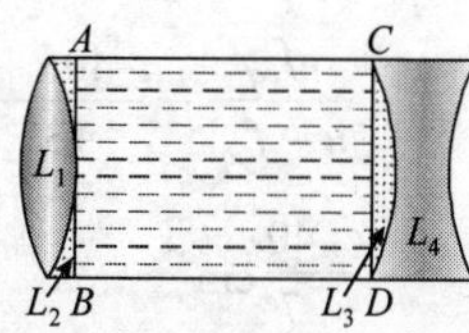

In figure we consider whole system may be considered to consist of two equivalent lens combinations separated by a fix distance in air.

First combination is on the left end of the optical setup

(i) double convex lens (glass) L_1

(ii) plano-concave lens (water) L_2

The above two lenses form one group of lens, say of focal length f_{eq1}.

Second combination is on the right end of the optical setup

(iii) plano convex lens (water) L_3

(iv) double concave lens (glass) L_4

The above two lenses form one group of lens, say of focal length f_{eq2}.

The above two groups are separated by parallel plane water slab of thickness 4 cm. The apparent thickness of water slab will be $4/\mu = 4/(4/3) = 3$ cm. Thus the above two groups can be considered to be separated by air of thickness 3 cm.

By lens makers formula, the focal-length of lens L_1 with respect to air is given as

$$f_1 = \frac{R}{2(\mu-1)} = \frac{4}{2(1.5-1)}$$

$$\Rightarrow \qquad f_1 = 4 \text{ cm} \qquad \ldots \text{(i)}$$

Now with respect to air, focal length of lens L_2 is given as

$$f_2 = \frac{R}{\mu-1} = \frac{4}{4/3-1}$$

$$\Rightarrow \qquad f_2 = -12 \text{ cm} \qquad \ldots \text{(ii)}$$

Equivalent focal length of this combination is given as

$$\frac{1}{f_{eq1}} = \frac{1}{f_1} + \frac{1}{f_2} = \frac{1}{4} - \frac{1}{12}$$

$$= \frac{1}{6}$$

$$\Rightarrow \qquad f_{eq} = 6 \text{ cm} \qquad \ldots \text{(a)}$$

With respect to air, focal length of lens L_3 is given as

$$f_3 = \frac{R}{\mu-1} = \frac{8}{4/3-1}$$

$$\Rightarrow \qquad f_3 = 24 \text{ cm}$$

With respect to air, focal length of lens L_4 is given as

$$f_4 = \frac{R}{2(\mu-1)} = \frac{8}{2(1.5-1)}$$

$$= -\frac{1.2}{8}$$

$$\Rightarrow \qquad f_4 = -6.67 \text{ cm}$$

Equivalent focal length of lenses L_3 and L_4 is given as

$$\frac{1}{f_{eq2}} = \frac{1}{24} - \frac{1.2}{8}$$

$$\Rightarrow \qquad f_{eq} = -\frac{120}{13} \text{ cm} \qquad \ldots \text{(b)}$$

Lens combinations of which focal lengths are given by equations-(a) and (b) are separated by air distance 3 cm so combined focal length F of the system is given by

$$\frac{1}{F} = \frac{1}{f_{eq1}} + \frac{1}{f_{eq2}} - \frac{d}{f_{eq1} f_{eq2}}$$

$$\Rightarrow \qquad \frac{1}{F} = \frac{1}{6} - \frac{13}{120} + \frac{3}{6 \times (120/13)}$$

$$\Rightarrow \qquad \frac{1}{F} = \frac{120 - 78 + 39}{6 \times 120}$$

$$\Rightarrow \qquad F = 8.9 \text{ cm}$$

(ix) The plane mirror forms a virtual image at a distance $(a + b)$ behind it. Given that there is no parallax between the images formed by mirror and lens and so both the images are formed at a distance $(a + b)$ behind mirror.

The distance of the image from lens

$$v = (a + b) + b = (a + 2b)$$

Here the lateral magnification produced by the lens is 2 because it is given that the transverse length of final image formed by lens is twice that of image formed by mirror and the mirror forms an image of same length of the object.

As the distance of the object from lens is a, hence distance of image from lens should be equal to $2a$.

$$\Rightarrow \quad (a+2b)=2a$$

$$\Rightarrow \quad b=a/2 \qquad \ldots(1)$$

The silvered lens may be regarded as a combination of equiconvex lens and a concave mirror in contact. Thus for an equiconvex lens, focal length is given as

$$f_1=\frac{R}{2(\mu-1)}$$

$$\Rightarrow \quad f_1=40\text{ cm}$$

For concave mirror, focal length is given as

$$f_m=\frac{R}{2}=-20\text{ cm}$$

The combined focal length of the lens mirror system is given as

$$\frac{1}{F}=\frac{2}{f_1}+\frac{1}{f_m}=\frac{1}{20}+\frac{1}{20}$$

$$\Rightarrow \quad F=-10\text{ cm}$$

For the combination for mirror formula, we have

$$u=-a,\ v=+2a$$

and $$F=-10\text{ cm}$$

Using the mirror formula in this case,

$$\frac{1}{v}+\frac{1}{u}=\frac{1}{F}$$

$$\Rightarrow \quad \frac{1}{2a}+\frac{1}{(-a)}=\frac{1}{-10}$$

$$\Rightarrow \quad a=5\text{ cm}$$

and $$b=a/2=5/2=2.5\text{ cm}$$

(x) The optical setup is shown in figure. For a plano convex lens the focal length of the lens is given as

$$f=\frac{R}{\mu-1}$$

$$\Rightarrow \quad R=f(\mu-1)$$

$$\Rightarrow \quad R=30\left(\frac{3}{2}-1\right)=15\text{ cm}$$

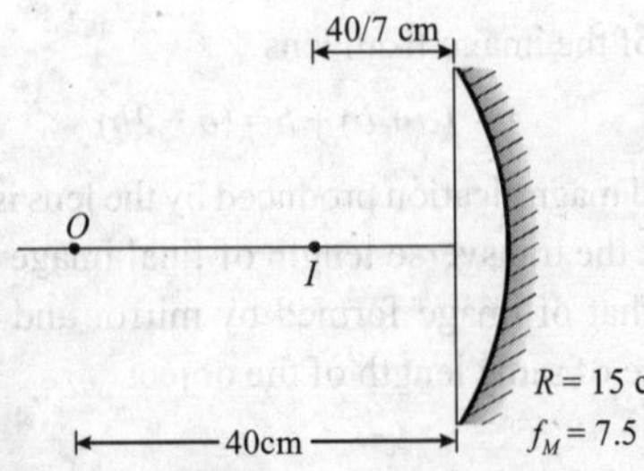

If f_{eq} is equivalent focal length of lens-mirror combination then we use

$$\frac{1}{f_{eq}}=\frac{2}{f_L}+\frac{1}{f_M}=\frac{2}{30}+\frac{1}{7.5}$$

$$\Rightarrow \quad \frac{1}{f_{eq}}=\frac{6}{30}=\frac{1}{5}$$

$$\Rightarrow \quad f_{eq}=5\text{ cm}$$

Using mirror formula, we have

$$u=-40\text{ cm}$$

$$f_{eq}=-5\text{ cm}$$

$$v=\frac{uf_{eq}}{u-f_{eq}}=\frac{-40\times+5}{+35}$$

$$\Rightarrow \quad v=-\frac{40}{7}\text{ cm}$$

(xi) For two thin lenses kept in contact the equivalent focal length of the combination is given as

$$\frac{1}{F}=\frac{1}{f_1}+\frac{1}{f_2} \qquad \ldots(1)$$

When lenses are immerged in water, their individual focal lengths are given as

$$f_1=\frac{R}{2\left(\frac{\mu_1}{\mu_w}-1\right)}$$

and $$f_2=\frac{R}{2\left(\frac{\mu_2}{\mu_w}-1\right)}$$

$$\Rightarrow \quad \frac{1}{F}=\frac{1}{f_1}+\frac{1}{f_2}=\frac{2}{R}\left[\frac{\mu_1-\mu_2}{\mu_w}\right]$$

$$\Rightarrow \quad F=\frac{\mu_w R}{2(\mu_1-\mu_2)}$$

$$\Rightarrow \quad F=\frac{4}{3}\times\frac{10}{2(1.7-1.5)}=33.3\text{ cm}$$

(xii) If the distance of the lens from the object be L when a real image is formed on the screen. Then by lens formula we have

$$\frac{1}{100-L}-\frac{1}{-L}=\frac{1}{23}$$

On solving, we get

$$L=(50\pm 10\sqrt{2})\text{ cm}$$

Now, as lens is executing SHM and a real image is formed after a fixed time gap then this time gap must be such that real image is obtained when the lens passes through two positions at same distance from the mean position and having separated by a time gap of on fourth of the period of SHM.

Thus phase difference between the two positions of real image formation must be $\frac{\pi}{2}$. As the two position are symmetrically located about the mean position, phase difference of any of these positions from origin must be $\frac{\pi}{4}$. If A is the amplitude of SHM then we have

$$\Rightarrow \quad 10\sqrt{2}\text{ cm} = A\sin\frac{\pi}{4}$$

$$\Rightarrow \quad A = 20\text{ cm}$$

Velocity of lens at mean position in this case is

$$v_0 = A\omega = A\sqrt{\frac{K}{m}}$$

Required impulse to attain this speed is

$$J = mv_0 = A\sqrt{Km} = 8\text{ kgm/s}$$

NOTE : Students can also think that real images are obtained on screen at two extreme positions of lens in SHM when time gap becomes half of the time period !!!

Solutions of PRACTICE EXERCISE 5.8

(i) As we know that for achromatic combination we use

$$D = D'$$

$$\Rightarrow \quad (\mu_V - \mu_R)A = (\mu_V' - \mu_R')A'$$

$$\Rightarrow \quad A' = \frac{(1.42-1.35)4°}{1.9-1.7} = 1.4°,$$

Net deviation of light for achromatic combination of prism is given as

$$\delta_{Net} = \delta \sim \delta' = (\mu_Y - 1)A \sim (\mu_Y' - 1)A'$$

$$\Rightarrow \quad \delta_{Net} = (1.40-1)4° \sim (1.8-1)1.4°$$

$$\Rightarrow \quad \delta_{Net} = 0.48°$$

(ii) For blue light, by Snell's law, we have

$$\mu = \frac{\sin i_1}{\sin r_1}$$

$$\Rightarrow \quad 1.68 = \frac{\sin 65°}{\sin r_1}$$

$$\Rightarrow \quad r_1 = 32.6°$$

Other refraction angle of light ray at second surface of prism is given as

$$r_2 = A - r_1 = 27.4°$$

If e_B is the emerging angle for blue light, we use Snell's law at other surface of prism, we get

$$\mu = \frac{\sin e}{\sin r_2}$$

$$\Rightarrow \quad 1.68 = \frac{\sin i_2}{\sin 27.4°}$$

$$\Rightarrow \quad e = 50.6°$$

Deviation angle for red light when it passes through prism is

$$\delta_B = i_1 + e_B - A$$

$$\Rightarrow \quad \delta_B = 65° + 50.6° - 60° = 55.6° \quad \ldots(i)$$

For red light, by Snell's law we have

$$1.65 = \frac{\sin 65°}{\sin r_1}$$

$$\Rightarrow \quad r_1 = 33.3°$$

$$\Rightarrow \quad r_2 = A - r_1 = 26.7°$$

If e_R is the emerging angle for red light, we use Snell's law at other surface of prism, we get

$$1.65 = \frac{\sin e}{\sin 26.7°}$$

$$\Rightarrow \quad e_R = 47.8°$$

Deviation angle for red light when it passes through prism is

$$\delta_R = i_1 + e_R - A$$

$$\Rightarrow \quad \delta_R = 65° + 47.8° - 60° = 52.8° \quad \ldots(ii)$$

From equations-(i) and (ii) we get angular dispersion as

$$\delta_B - \delta_R = 2.8°$$

(iii) If the angles of crown and flint prisms be taken as A and A' then the dispersive power of prism materials is given by

$$\omega = \frac{\mu_v - \mu_r}{\mu - 1}$$

$$\Rightarrow \quad \mu_v - \mu_r = (\mu - 1)\omega$$

Angular dispersion produced by the prism is given by

$$(\mu_v - \mu_r)A = (\mu - 1)\omega A$$

So the angular dispersions produced by crown and flint prisms respectively will be $(\mu - 1)\omega A$ and $(\mu' - 1)\omega' A'$ for achromatic combination

$$(\mu - 1)\omega A = (\mu' - 1)\omega' A'$$

$$\Rightarrow \quad \frac{A'}{A} = \frac{(\mu-1)\omega}{(\mu'-1)\omega'} = \frac{0.517 \times 0.03}{0.621 \times 0.05}$$

$$= 0.50 \quad \ldots(1)$$

Total deviation produced is $(\delta - \delta')$, given as

$$\Rightarrow \quad \delta - \delta' = (\mu - 1)A - (\mu' - 1)A'$$

$$1° = 0.517A - 0.621A' \quad \ldots(2)$$

Solving equations-(1) and (2), we get

$$A = 4.8° \text{ and } A' = 2.4°$$

(iv) The deviation produced by the crown prism is

$$\delta = (\mu - 1)A$$

and that produced by the flint glass prism is

$$\delta' = (\mu' - 1)A'$$

The prisms are placed with their angles inverted with respect to each other. The deviations are also in the opposite directions. Thus, the total deviation of light ray is

$$\delta_T = \delta - \delta' = (\mu - 1)A - (\mu' - 1)A' \quad \ldots(1)$$

(a) If the net deviation for the mean ray is zero,

$$\Rightarrow \quad (\mu - 1)A = (\mu' - 1)A'$$

$$\Rightarrow \quad A' = \frac{(\mu - 1)}{(\mu' - 1)}A = \frac{1.517 - 1}{1.620 - 1} \times 5° = 4.169°$$

(b) The angular dispersion produced by the crown prism is :

$$\delta_v - \delta_r = (\mu_v - \mu_r)A$$

and that by the flint prism is,

$$\delta'_v - \delta'_r = (\mu'_v - \mu'_r)A$$

The net angular dispersion is, $(\mu_v - \mu_r)A - (\mu'_v - \mu'_r)A$

$$= (1.523 - 1.514) \times 5° - (1.632 - 1.613) \times 4.2° = -0.0348°$$

The angular dispersion is 0.0348°.

(v) The condition for the combination to be achromatic is given as

$$(\mu_F - \mu_C)A = (m'_F - \mu'_C)A'$$

$$(1.523 - 1.515) \times 20° = (1.664 - 1.644)\alpha'$$

$$\Rightarrow \quad \alpha' = \frac{0.008}{0.02} \times 20° = 8°$$

(vi) (a) As it is given that instrument is set to give minimum deviation for red light, the refractive index of the material for red light is given as

$$\mu = \frac{\sin\left(\dfrac{A + \delta_m}{2}\right)}{\sin A/2} = \frac{\sin\left(\dfrac{60 + \delta_m}{2}\right)}{\sin 30°}$$

$$\Rightarrow \quad \sin\left(\frac{60 + \delta_m}{2}\right) = 1.514 \times \frac{1}{2} = 0.7570$$

$$\Rightarrow \quad \left(\frac{60 + \delta_m}{2}\right) = \sin^{-1}(0.7570) = 49°12'$$

$$\Rightarrow \quad \delta_m = 2(49°12') - 60 = 38°24'$$

and $\quad i = 49°12'$

(b) While considering the refraction for violet colour through the prism, we use at first surface of prism

$$\frac{\sin i_1}{\sin r_1} = \frac{\sin 49°12'}{\sin r_1} = 1.53$$

$$\Rightarrow \quad \sin r_1 = \frac{\sin 49°12'}{1.53} = \frac{0.7570}{1.53} = 0.4948$$

$$\Rightarrow \quad r_1 = 29°39'$$

and other refraction angle is given as

$$r_2 = 60° - 29°39'$$

$$\Rightarrow \quad r_2 = 30°21'$$

By Snell's law at other surface of prism, we have

$$\frac{\sin e}{\sin r_2} = 1.53$$

$$\Rightarrow \quad \frac{\sin e}{\sin 30°21'} = 1.53$$

$$\Rightarrow \quad \sin e = \sin 30°21' \times 1.53 = 0.7732$$

$$\Rightarrow \quad e = \sin^{-1}(0.7732) = 50°38'$$

(c) Angular width = angle of emergence for red – angle of emergence for violet

$$= 50°38' - 49°12'$$

$$= 1°26'$$

(vii) For achromatism of two lenses in contact, the condition is

$$\frac{\omega_1}{f_1} + \frac{\omega_2}{f_2} = 0$$

$$\Rightarrow \quad \frac{\omega_2}{\omega_1} = -\frac{f_2}{f_1} \quad \ldots(1)$$

The dispersive power of crown glass is given by

$$\omega_1 = \frac{\mu_V - \mu_R}{\dfrac{\mu_V + \mu_R}{2} - 1}$$

$$\Rightarrow \quad \omega_1 = \frac{1.55 - 1.53}{1.54 - 1} = 0.037$$

For the equiconvex lens, its focal length is given as

$$f_1 = \frac{R}{2(\mu_Y - 1)}$$

$$\Rightarrow \quad f_1 = \frac{0.54}{2(1.54 - 1)} = \frac{0.54}{2 \times 0.54} = 0.5\text{ m}$$

If the combination has a focal length F, then we use

$$\frac{1}{F} = \frac{1}{f_1} + \frac{1}{f_2}$$

$$\Rightarrow \quad \frac{1}{f_2} = \frac{1}{F} - \frac{1}{f_1}$$

$$\Rightarrow \quad \frac{1}{f_2}=\frac{1}{1.5}-\frac{1}{0.5}=-\frac{2}{1.5}$$

From equation-(1), we use

$$\frac{\omega_2}{0.037}=-\frac{0.5}{0.75}$$

$$\Rightarrow \quad \omega_2=-\frac{0.5}{0.75}\times 0.037$$

$$\Rightarrow \quad \omega_2=0.055$$

(viii) Condition for minimum chromatic aberration is that the distance between lenses = mean of the focal lengths of the component lenses

$$=\frac{0.06+0.04}{2}=0.05\text{ m}$$

So for the desired eyepiece the lenses must be placed coaxially 0.05 m apart. The first lens (0.06 m focal length) will be the field lens and the other the eye-lens.

$$\Delta=f_1+f_2-x=0.06+0.04-0.05=0.05\text{ m}$$

$$F=\frac{f_1f_2}{\Delta}=\frac{0.06\times 0.04}{0.05}=0.048\text{ m}$$

Magnifying power for normal vision

$$=\frac{D}{F}=\frac{0.25}{0.048}=5.2$$

The distance of the first principal plane from the field lens towards the eye-lens is

$$\alpha=\frac{x}{\Delta}f_1=\frac{0.05}{0.05}\times 0.06=0.06\text{ m}$$

The first principal focus is at a distance of 0.048 m from the first principal plane towards the object. With reference to the field lens, it is at a distance of (0.06 – 0.048) = 0.012 m on the other side. Hence it is a negative eyepiece.

$$\Delta=f_1+f_2-x=0.06+0.04-0.05=0.05\text{ m}$$

$$F=\frac{f_1f_2}{\Delta}=\frac{0.06\times 0.04}{0.05}=0.048\text{ m}$$

Magnifying power for normal vision

$$\frac{D}{F}=\frac{0.28}{0.048}=5.2$$

The distance of the first principal plane from the first lens (field lens) towards the eye-lens is given by

$$\alpha=\frac{x}{\Delta}f_1=\frac{0.05}{0.05}\times 0.06=0.06\text{ m}$$

The first principal focus is at a distance 0.048 m from the first principal plane towards the object. With reference to the field lens it is at a distance of (0.06 – 0.048) = 0.012 m on the other side. Hence it is a negative eyepiece.

(ix) (a) Condition for achromatic combination is given as

$$\frac{\omega_1}{f_1}+\frac{\omega_2}{f_2}=0$$

$$\Rightarrow \quad \omega_2=\left(-\frac{f_2}{f_1}\right)\omega_1$$

$$\Rightarrow \quad \omega_2=-\frac{(-30)}{(+20)}(0.18)=0.27$$

(b) Equivalent focal length of lens doublet can be given as

$$\frac{1}{F}=\frac{1}{f_1}+\frac{1}{f_2}=\frac{1}{20}-\frac{1}{30}$$

$$\Rightarrow \quad F=+60\text{ cm}$$

Solutions of PRACTICE EXERCISE 5.9

(i) We are given that the focal length of the lens is $f=10$ cm and distance between the screen and lens is $v=500$ cm. Using the lens formula, we have

$$\frac{1}{v}-\frac{1}{u}=\frac{1}{f}$$

$$\Rightarrow \quad \frac{1}{u}=\frac{1}{v}-\frac{1}{f}$$

$$\Rightarrow \quad \frac{1}{u}=\frac{1}{500}-\frac{1}{10}=-\frac{49}{500}$$

$$\Rightarrow \quad u=-\frac{500}{49}\text{ cm}$$

Now the linear magnification is given by

$$\frac{\text{Size of Image}}{\text{Size of Object}}=\frac{v}{u}$$

$$\Rightarrow \quad \textit{Image size}=\frac{v}{u}\times \textit{Object size}=\frac{500\times 49}{500}\times 2=98\text{ cm}$$

$$\Rightarrow \quad \text{Size of the image}=98\text{ cm}\times 98\text{ cm}$$

Suppose the illuminating power of the source be P, then

$$\text{Illumination of slide}=\frac{P}{2\times 2}$$

$$\text{Illumination of picture}=\frac{P}{98\times 98}$$

$$\frac{\text{Illumination of slide}}{\text{Illumination of picture}}=\frac{P}{2\times 2}\times\frac{98\times 98}{P}=2401$$

(ii) For the objective, we use

$$u_o=-0.31\text{ cm and } f_o=0.3\text{ cm}$$

Using lens formula, we have

$$\frac{1}{v_o}-\frac{1}{u_o}=\frac{1}{f_o}$$

$$\Rightarrow \quad \frac{1}{v_o}-\frac{1}{-0.31}=\frac{1}{0.3}$$

$$\Rightarrow \quad v_o=+9.3\text{ cm}$$

For the eyepiece, we use

$$v_e=-25\text{ cm and } f_e=+5\text{ cm}$$

Using lens formula, we have

$$\frac{1}{v_e}-\frac{1}{u_e}=\frac{1}{f_e}$$

$$\Rightarrow \quad \frac{1}{-25}-\frac{1}{u_e}=\frac{1}{5}$$

$$\Rightarrow \quad u_o=-25/6\text{ cm}=-4.166\text{ cm}$$

Magnifying power of telescope is given as

$$M=\frac{v_0}{u_0}\left(1+\frac{D}{f_e}\right)=\frac{9.3}{0.31}\left(1+\frac{25}{5}\right)=180$$

Separation between lenses $= v_0+u_e=9.3+4.166=13.466$ cm

(iii) For the eyepiece, we use

$$v_e=-25\text{ cm and } f_e=5\text{ cm}$$

Using lens formula for eyepiece, we have

$$\frac{1}{v_e}-\frac{1}{u_e}=\frac{1}{f_e}$$

$$\Rightarrow \quad \frac{1}{u_e}=\frac{1}{-25}-\frac{1}{5}=-\frac{6}{25}\text{ cm}$$

$$\Rightarrow \quad u_e=-\frac{25}{6}\text{ cm}$$

Magnification of eyepiece is

$$M_e=\frac{v_e}{u_e}=\frac{25}{(25/6)}=6$$

The magnification of microscope is given as

$$50=M_e\times M_0$$

$$\Rightarrow \quad 50=6\times M_0$$

$$\Rightarrow \quad M_0=\frac{50}{6}=\text{Magnification of objective}$$

The magnifying power of objective is given by

$$M_0=\frac{v_o}{u_o}=\frac{v_o-f_o}{f_o}$$

$$\Rightarrow \quad M_0f_0=v_0-f_0$$

$$\Rightarrow \quad v_0=M_0f_0+f_0=f_0(M_0+1)$$

$$\Rightarrow \quad v_0=f_0\left(\frac{50}{6}+1\right)=\frac{56}{6}f_0=\frac{56}{6}$$

When the distance is increased by 2 cm, then new value of v_0 will become

$$v_0'=\frac{56}{6}+2=\frac{68}{6}$$

Now magnification by objective will be

$$M_0'=\frac{(68/6)}{1}-1=\frac{62}{6}$$

As magnification by eyepiece will remain same, total magnification will now be

$$M_T=M_0'\times M_e=\frac{62}{6}\times 6=62$$

(iv) Using lens formula for objective, we have

$$\frac{1}{v_0}-\frac{1}{-5}=\frac{1}{+0.25}$$

$$\Rightarrow \quad v_0=-0.2632\text{ m}$$

Now using lens formula for eyepiece, we have

$$\frac{1}{-0.25}-\frac{1}{-u_e}=\frac{1}{+0.025}$$

$$\Rightarrow \quad \frac{1}{u_e}=4+40=44$$

$$\Rightarrow \quad u_e=0.0227\text{ m}$$

Tube length of the telescope is $=0.2632+0.0227=0.2859$ m

$$\text{magnifying power}=\frac{v_0}{u_e}=\frac{0.2632}{0.0227}=11.6$$

(v) When the telescope is focussed on a distant object and the final image is also at infinity, the distance between lenses

$$L=f_0+f_e$$

$$=50+5=55\text{ cm}$$

When it is turned on a nearer object, the image formed by the objective will not be at its focus, but a little away from it. The eyepiece has to be shifted exactly by the same distance through which the image is shifted from focus of objective because the final image is at the same distance without change in accommodation of eye. Figure below shows the ray diagram of this situation.

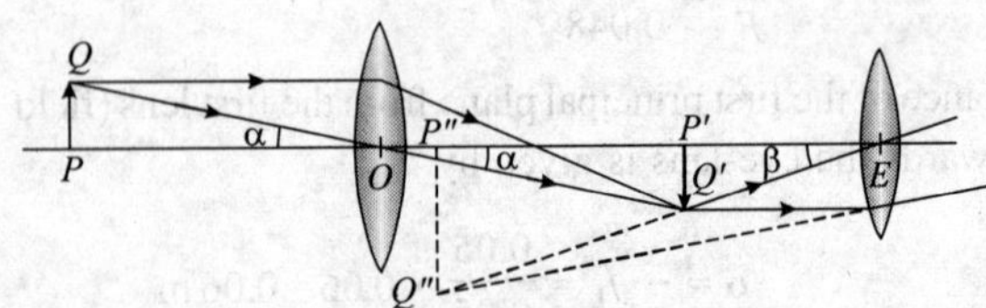

Using lens formula for the objective, we have

$$\frac{1}{v_0}-\frac{1}{-10}=\frac{1}{+0.5}$$

$$\Rightarrow \quad v_0 = +\frac{50}{95}\,\text{m} = +52.63\text{ cm}$$

The distance by which the eyepiece is to be shifted is

$$s = 52.63 - 50$$

$$\Rightarrow \quad s = 2.63\text{ cm}$$

When the object is at a finite but large distance then the Magnifying power of telescope is given as

$$M = \frac{\beta}{\alpha} = \frac{v_0}{u_e}$$

For the case of focussing the telescope in both cases, using lens formula for eyepiece, we have

$$\frac{1}{\infty} - \frac{1}{-u_e} = \frac{1}{+5}$$

$$\Rightarrow \quad u_e = 5\text{ cm}$$

Thus Magnification of telescope for the case of focussing on object located at a distance of 10 m is

$$M = \frac{52.63}{5} = 10.52$$

Previous magnification when telescope is focussed on Moon, we know magnification is given as

$$M' = \frac{f_0}{f_e} = \frac{50}{5} = 10$$

(vi) We know that the magnification M is given by the formula

$$M = \frac{v_0}{u_0}\left(1 + \frac{D}{f_e}\right)$$

In first case, $$M_1 = \frac{(v_0)_1}{u_0}\left(1 + \frac{D}{f_e}\right)$$

Where $f_e = 0.03$ m $= 3$ cm and $D = 25$ cm

$$\Rightarrow \quad M_1 = \frac{(v_0)_1}{u_0}\left(1 + \frac{25}{3}\right)$$

$$\Rightarrow \quad = \frac{(v_0)_1}{u_0} \times \frac{28}{3} \quad \ldots(1)$$

Similarly in second case

$$M_2 = \frac{(v_0)_2}{u_0}\left(1 + \frac{25}{4}\right)$$

$$\Rightarrow \quad M_2 = \frac{(v_0)_2}{u_0} \times \frac{29}{4} \quad \ldots(2)$$

Given that $\quad M_1 = M_2$

$$\Rightarrow \quad \frac{(v_0)_1}{u_0} \times \frac{28}{3} = \frac{(v_0)_2}{u_0} \times \frac{29}{4}$$

$$\Rightarrow \quad (v_0)_2 = \frac{112}{87}(v_0)_1 \quad \ldots(3)$$

If in the first arrangement, the distance of the object from eyepiece be x. Then by lens formula for eyepiece, we have

$$\Rightarrow \quad -\frac{1}{25} + \frac{1}{x} = \frac{1}{3} \text{ or } x = \frac{75}{28}\text{ cm}$$

$$\Rightarrow \quad (v_0)_1 = 20 - \frac{75}{28} = \frac{485}{28}\text{ cm} \quad \ldots(4)$$

and $$(v_0)_2 = \frac{112}{87} \times \frac{485}{28} = \frac{1940}{87}\text{ cm} \quad \ldots(5)$$

Let, in the second arrangement, the distance of the object from eyepiece be y. Then

$$-\frac{1}{25} + \frac{1}{y} = \frac{1}{4}$$

$$\Rightarrow \quad y = \frac{100}{29} \quad \ldots(6)$$

Now, distance between lenses in the second case must be

$$\frac{1940}{87} + \frac{100}{29} = \frac{2240}{87} = 25.75\text{ cm}$$

$$= 0.2575\text{ m}$$

(vii) In the normal adjustment, magnification (angular) produced by telescope is

$$M = \frac{f_0}{f_e} = 30$$

$$\Rightarrow \quad f_0 = 30 f_e$$

and tube length $= f_0 + f_e = 93$

$$\Rightarrow \quad f_e = \frac{93}{31} = 31\text{ cm}$$

and $$f_0 = 90\text{ cm}$$

$$\Rightarrow \quad \frac{1}{\infty} - \frac{1}{-u_e} = \frac{1}{+3} \text{ and } u_e = 3\text{ cm}$$

Then $$v_0 = 90 + 3 = 93\text{ cm}$$

$$\Rightarrow \quad \frac{1}{+93} - \frac{1}{-u_0} = \frac{1}{+90}$$

$$\Rightarrow \quad \frac{1}{u_0} = \frac{1}{90} - \frac{1}{93} = \frac{3}{90 \times 93}$$

$$\Rightarrow \quad u_e = 30 \times 93 = 2790\text{ cm} = 27.9\text{ m}$$

$$\text{Magnification} = \frac{v_0}{u_e} = \frac{93}{3} = 31$$

Solutions of CONCEPTUAL MCQS Single Option Correct

Sol. 1 (A) In first case, the apparent depth of the liquid

$$= (b - a)$$

$$\Rightarrow \quad \text{Real depth} = \mu(b - a)$$

In second case, apparent depth = $(d - c)$

$$\Rightarrow \quad \text{Real depth} = \mu(d - c)$$

The difference in depth of liquid

$$= \mu(d - c) - \mu(b - a)$$

Here we use $\mu(d - c) > \mu(b - a)$

from experimental data, the difference is equal to $(d - b)$

Hence

$$\mu(d - c) - \mu(b - a) = d - b$$

$$\Rightarrow \quad \mu = \frac{d - b}{(a + d - c - b)}$$

Sol. 2 (C)

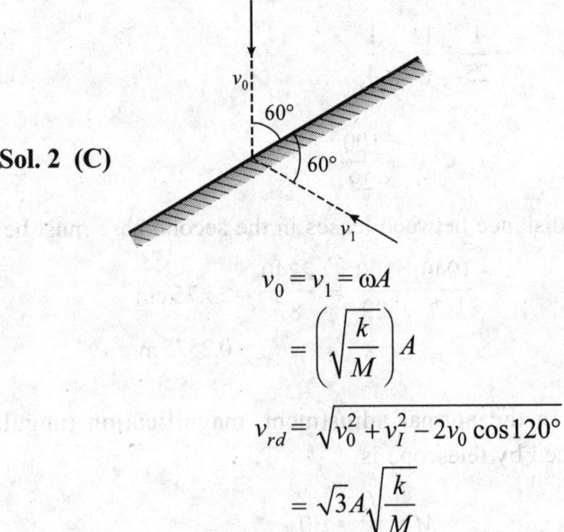

$$v_0 = v_1 = \omega A$$

$$= \left(\sqrt{\frac{k}{M}}\right) A$$

$$v_{rd} = \sqrt{v_0^2 + v_I^2 - 2v_0 \cos 120°}$$

$$= \sqrt{3}A\sqrt{\frac{k}{M}}$$

Sol. 3 (B) If O is the centre and A is the point source for the light ray incident at any point P on surface of sphere to angle have maximum angle of incidence i, then situation of maximum i is shown in figure. It happens when OA and AP are perpendicular, for which we have

$$i = \sin^{-1}\frac{OA}{OP} = \sin^{-1}\frac{x}{R}$$

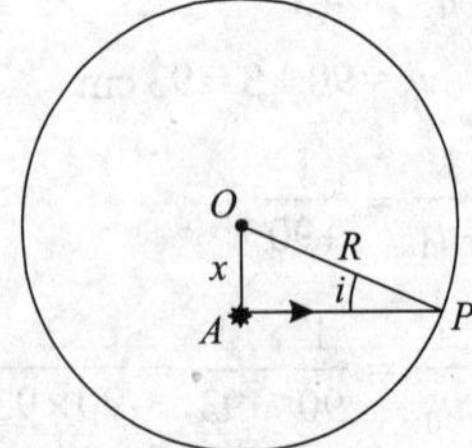

Sol. 4 (C) When the man M_1 is in the region RP and SQ, then man M_1 sees the image of M_2.

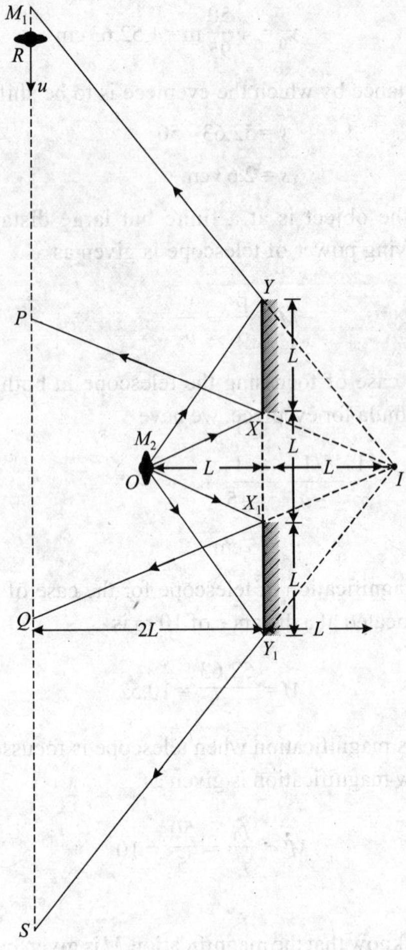

From the similar triangle PIQ and XIX_1

$$\Rightarrow \quad \frac{PQ}{XX_1} = \frac{3L}{L} \Rightarrow PQ = 3L$$

From the similar triangle, RIS and PIQ

$$\Rightarrow \quad \frac{RS}{YY_1} = \frac{3L}{L} \Rightarrow RS = 9L$$

Then $\quad RP + QS = RS - PQ = 9L - 3L = 6L$

$$\Rightarrow \quad \text{Time} = \frac{6L}{u}$$

Sol. 5 (A) Here, PQ is the length of reflected light from the mirror. From the similar triangles, PMA and MXS'

$$\Rightarrow \quad \frac{PA}{XS'} = \frac{3H}{H}$$

Then, $\quad PA = 3\,(XS') = 3H$

From the similar triangles QNA and XNS'

$$\frac{QA}{XS'} = \frac{2H}{2H}$$

$\Rightarrow \qquad QA = H$

$\Rightarrow \qquad PQ = PA - QA = 3H - H = 2H$

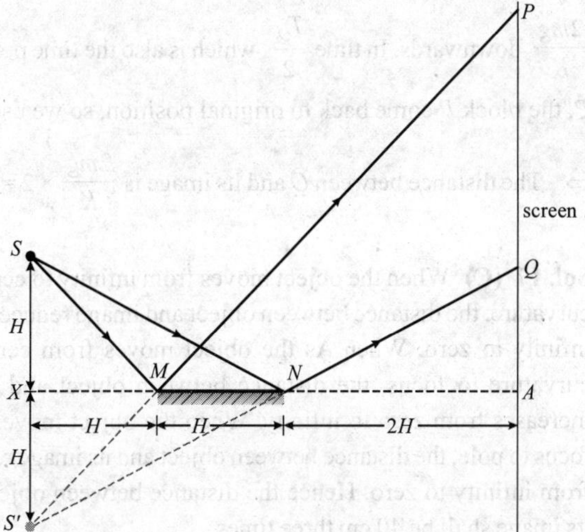

Sol. 6 (D) Focal length of lens does not depend on the aperture of lens. It depends on the refractive index of lens and that of surrounding and the radius of curvature of its surfaces.

For intensity of image, we have

$I \propto (\text{aperture diameter})^2$

$\Rightarrow \quad I_{\text{blocked}} \propto \left(\frac{d}{2}\right)^2$ and $I_0 \propto d^2$

Hence, $\quad I_{\text{blocked}} = \frac{I_0}{4}$

Final image intensity

$$I_f = I_{\text{original}} - I_{\text{blocked}}$$

$$\Rightarrow \quad I_f = I_0 - \frac{I_0}{4} = \frac{3I_0}{4}$$

Sol. 7 (D) If mirror is turned, about an axis perpendicular to plane of mirror, then there will be no change in incident angle and reflected angle so angle between incident & reflected rays after rotation will be same as before.

Sol. 8 (B) Let the critical angle of interface between media 1 and 2 is c_1 and between 1 and 3 is c_2

Then $\sin c_1 = \frac{\mu_2}{\mu_1}$ and $\sin c_2 = \frac{\mu_3}{\mu_1}$

From *TIR* at second interface $90 - c_1 > c_2$. Taking sine of both sides, we get

$$\cos c_1 > \sin c_2$$

or $\quad \sqrt{1-\left(\frac{\mu_2}{\mu_1}\right)^2} > \frac{\mu_3}{\mu_1}$

$$\mu_1^2 - \mu_3^2 > \mu_2^2$$

Sol. 9 (A) Using refraction formula for spherical surface taking '*B*' as object, if its image to be at ∞, we have

$$\frac{\mu_2}{\infty} - \frac{\mu_1}{(-2R)} = \frac{\mu_2 - \mu_1}{-R}$$

$$\Rightarrow \quad \frac{\mu_1}{\mu_2} = 2$$

Sol. 10 (C) If we draw an incident ray along the top side of rectangular strip, which happens to be parallel to the principal axis. After reflection this ray passes through focus. Thus image of all points on the top surface of the strip $O_1, O_2, O_3, \ldots$ etc. lie on this reflected ray at locations $I_1, I_2, I_3, \ldots$etc. in between focus and centre of curvature. Thus the image of this strip is a triangle as shown in figure :

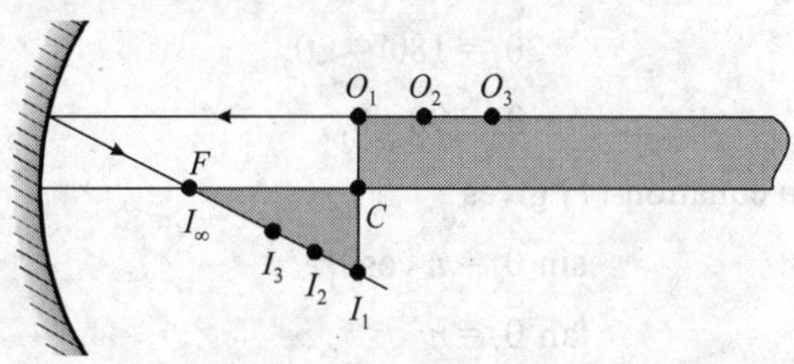

Sol. 11 (C) If we consider two point objects O_1 and O_2, as shown in figure on the two sides of the center of curvature C of the surface. Figure also shows the incident rays from O_1 and O_2 at point P and as the other medium is denser both incident rays bend towards normal and thus the corresponding refracted rays will be diverging hence in both cases the image produced due to refraction will always be virtual.

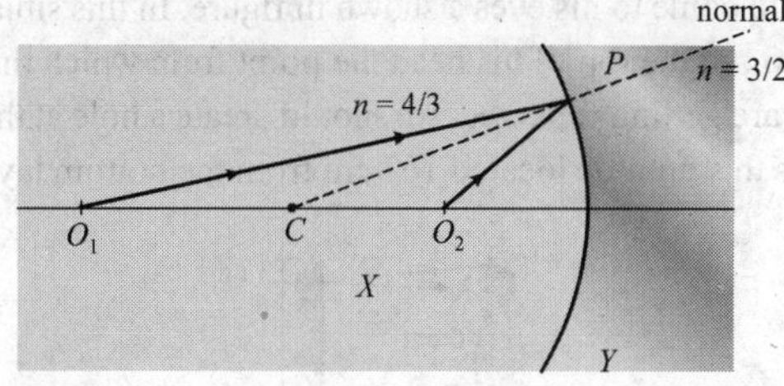

Sol. 12 (D) Slab only shifts the image of point *P* by some distance which will remain constant and does not depend upon the location of slab so the final image formed by slab has a fixed separation from '*O*' and will not move.

Sol. 13 (D) We use $v = c/n$. For air, we consider the index of refraction $n_{\text{air}} = 1$. The Snell's law is given by the equation :

$$\sin\theta_1 = n \sin\theta_2 \qquad \ldots(1)$$

We see that for the normal component of velocity to be constant,

$$v_1 \cos\theta_1 = v_2 \cos\theta_2$$

$$\Rightarrow \quad c \cos\theta_1 = \frac{c}{n} \cos\theta_2 \qquad \ldots(2)$$

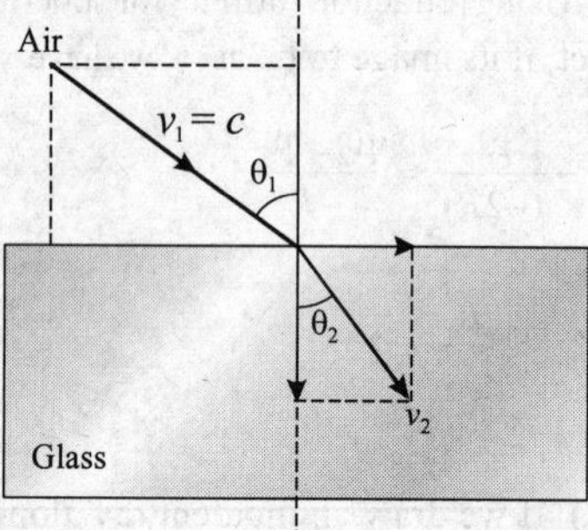

We multiply equations-(1) and (2), obtaining

$$\sin\theta_1 \cos\theta_1 = \sin\theta_2 \cos\theta_2$$

$$\Rightarrow \quad \sin 2\theta_1 = \sin 2\theta_2$$

The solution $\theta_1 = \theta_2$ does not satisfy equation-(1) and must be rejected. The other solution is

$$2\theta_1 = 180° - 2\theta_2$$

$$\Rightarrow \quad \theta_2 = 90 - \theta_1$$

Then equation-(1) gives

$$\sin\theta_1 = n \cos\theta_1,$$

$$\Rightarrow \quad \tan\theta_1 = n$$

$$\Rightarrow \quad \theta_1 = \tan^{-1} n$$

Sol. 14 (A) The image 'I_1' of object 'O' formed by plane mirror moves towards left. Here I_1 acts a real object for concave mirror. As I moves towards left, its image formed by concave mirror whether real or virtual will always move towards right.

Sol. 15 (A) To see head, the light ray from head after reflection should come to his eyes a shown in figure. In this situation for not to see the top of his head the point from which these light rays are getting reflected, we should create a hole at this point. Thus this point is located 167 cm from the bottom layer.

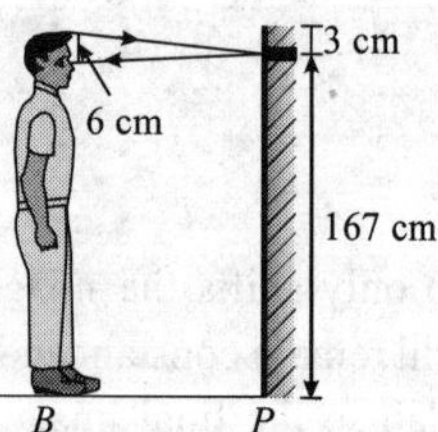

Sol. 16 (B) Both blocks loose contact immediately after the release as the springs are different and net forces on the two blocks are also not equal. The time period of oscillations of the two blocks is given as

$$T_P = 2\pi\sqrt{\frac{m}{4K}}, \quad T_Q = 2\pi\sqrt{\frac{m}{K}}$$

$$\Rightarrow \quad T_Q = 2T_P$$

Q comes at lowest position at time $\frac{T_Q}{2}$ travelling a distance $\frac{2mg}{K}$ downwards. In time $\frac{T_Q}{2}$, which is also the time period of P, the block P come back to original position, so we use

$\Rightarrow$ The distance between Q and its image is $\frac{2mg}{K} \times 2 = \frac{4mg}{K}$

Sol. 17 (C) When the object moves from infinity to centre of curvature, the distance between object and image reduces from infinity to zero. When As the object moves from centre of curvature to focus, the distance between object and image increases from zero to infinity. When the object moves from focus to pole, the distance between object and its image reduces from infinity to zero. Hence the distance between object and its image shall be 40 cm three times.

Sol. 18 (B) In the situation given in question, we can see that after third reflection the reflected ray becomes parallel to mirror M_2 after which no more reflections will take place. Thus light ray can reflect maximum three times in this case.

Sol. 19 (A) Focal length is minimum in case I, therefore power is maximum. In cases given in options (C) and (D) the focal length and power remain same.

Sol. 20 (A) If distance of image is v from lens, we use

$$\frac{1}{v} = \frac{1}{f} + \frac{1}{f} + \frac{1}{f} + \left(\frac{2}{R_1} + \frac{2}{R_2}\right)$$

Here we used that ray of light passes through lens thrice and reflected twice from the two spherical surfaces of lens

$$\Rightarrow \quad \frac{1}{v} = \frac{3}{f} + 2\left(\frac{1}{R_1} + \frac{1}{R_2}\right)$$

By lens maker's formula, we have

$$\frac{1}{f} = (\mu - 1)\left(\frac{1}{R_1} + \frac{1}{R_2}\right)$$

$$\Rightarrow \quad \frac{1}{v} = \left(\frac{1}{R_1} + \frac{1}{R_2}\right)(3\mu - 3 + 2)$$

$$\Rightarrow \quad v = \frac{f(\mu - 1)}{3\mu - 1} = \frac{f}{7}$$

Sol. 21 (A) As we know in direction normal to mirror we use

$$\vec{V}_{Image} = \vec{V}_{Object}$$

No effect of $V\cos\theta$ as its in the plane of mirror

$\Rightarrow$ $V_I = 2V\sin\theta$

Sol. 22 (D) For no ray to emerge out of side PR, we use

$$A > 2\theta_C$$

$$\Rightarrow \quad \sin\frac{A}{2} > \sin\theta_C$$

$$\Rightarrow \quad \sin\frac{A}{2} > \frac{\sqrt{3}}{2}$$

$$\Rightarrow \quad A > 120°$$

Sol. 23 (B) As AB is common and $O_1B = BI$ and triangles ΔO_1BA and ΔBAI are congruent so

By symmetry AI is normal to O_1 to O_2 and $\angle O_1AB = \angle BAI$

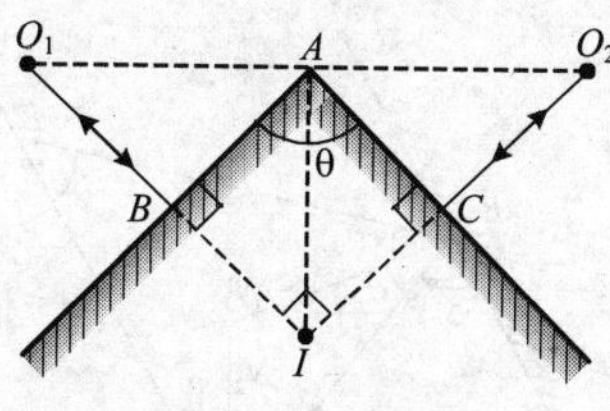

$$\Rightarrow \quad \angle BAI = 45°$$

and $\quad \angle BAC = 90°$

Sol. 24 (B) The line joining O and I crosses principal axis of the mirror at centre of curvature. In a convex mirror, for a real object image is always virtual.

Hence the given situation can be achieved only by using a concave mirror with object placed a distance 'a' above centre of curvature C on principal axis as shown.

Sol. 25 (B) Figure shows the image formation in focal plane. In ΔOAB, we use

$$\tan\theta = \frac{AB}{OB} = \frac{r}{f}$$

$$\Rightarrow \quad r^2 \propto f^2$$

$$\Rightarrow \quad \text{Area} \propto f^2$$

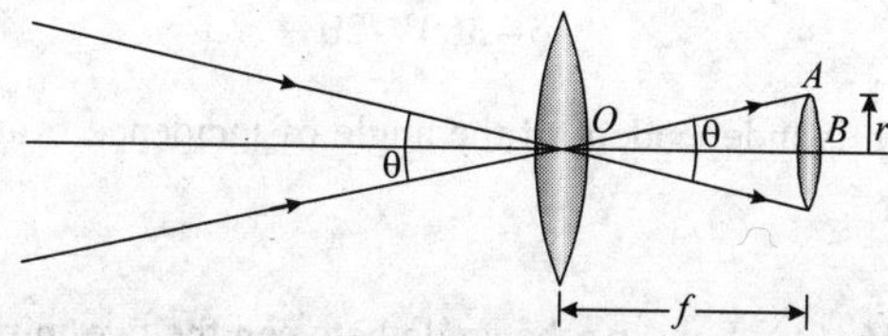

Sol. 26 (D) The optic axis of a lens does not change even on cutting it so in this case as magnification is 2, image of P will be produced 1 cm below optic axis of lens which is 1.5 cm below line XY.

Sol. 27 (C) The acceleration of the elevator does not affect the apparent depth.

Sol. 28 (C) For first case, we use

$$\frac{1}{v_1} + \frac{1}{u_1} = \frac{1}{f} \qquad \ldots(1)$$

and for second case, we use

$$-\frac{1}{v_2} + \frac{1}{u_2} = \frac{1}{f} \qquad \ldots(2)$$

$$\Rightarrow \quad \frac{v_2}{u_2} = \frac{f}{f - u_2}$$

But $\frac{v_1}{u_1} = \frac{v_2}{u_2}$, thus we use

$$\frac{f}{u_1 - f} = \frac{f}{f - u_2}$$

$$\Rightarrow \quad f = \frac{u_1 + u_2}{2}$$

Sol. 29 (C) In P a biconcave lens of $\mu = 1.33$ is formed. In Q, we have a combination of two convex and one plano-concave lenses but overall the converging power is more so both cases are convergent.

Sol. 30 (D) For image of center of mass of A and B, we have

$$\vec{v}_{\text{cm}\,x} = \frac{m_1 v_1}{m_1 + m_2}(-\hat{i})$$

$$\vec{v}_{\text{cm}\,y} = \frac{m_2 v_2}{m_1 + m_2}(+\hat{i})$$

$$\Rightarrow \quad |\vec{v}_{\text{cm}}| = \sqrt{\frac{m_1^2 v_1^2}{(m_1 + m_2)^2} + \frac{m_2^2 v_2^2}{(m_1 + m_2)^2}}$$

$$\Rightarrow \quad |\vec{v}_{\text{cm}}| = \frac{1}{m_1 + m_2}\sqrt{m_1^2 v_1^2 + m_2^2 v_2^2}$$

Sol. 31 (D) For the image of mango when it is located at a distance x from the water surface, apparent distance of mango appear to tortoise is,

$$x_{app} = \mu x$$

$$\Rightarrow \quad \frac{d^2 x_{app}}{dt^2} = \mu\frac{d^2 x}{dt^2}$$

$$\Rightarrow \quad a_{app} = \mu g$$

Thus the acceleration of falling mango with respect to tortoise is given as

$$a_{\text{relative}} = a + a_{\text{app}} = g + \mu g = g(1 + \mu)$$

Sol. 32 (D) Maximum separation will be $4A$ when A is the amplitude which is given as

$$A\omega = v$$

$$\Rightarrow \quad A\sqrt{\frac{k}{m}} = v$$

$$\Rightarrow \quad A = v\sqrt{\frac{m}{k}}$$

Therefore the maximum separation is $4v\sqrt{\frac{m}{k}}$.

Sol. 33 (B) By Snell's law, we have

$$\frac{\sin i}{\sin r} = \frac{1}{\mu}$$

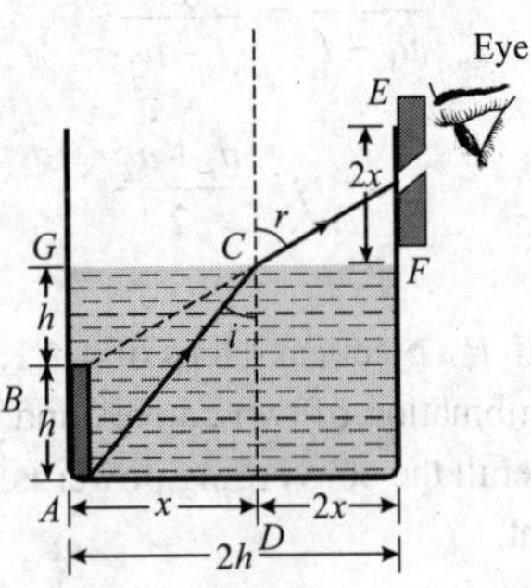

In triangles ΔACD and ΔCEF

$$\frac{\dfrac{x}{\sqrt{x^2+4h^2}}}{\dfrac{2h-x}{\sqrt{(2h-x)^2+h^2}}} = \frac{1}{\mu} \quad \ldots \text{(i)}$$

In ΔBCG, we have

$$\sin r = \frac{2h-x}{\sqrt{(2h-x)^2+h^2}} = \frac{x}{\sqrt{h^2+x^2}} \quad \ldots \text{(ii)}$$

We also have by similarity of triangles

$$\frac{h}{x} = \frac{2h-x}{h} \quad \ldots \text{(iii)}$$

Solving equation-(i), (ii) and (iii), we get

$$\mu = \sqrt{\frac{5}{2}}$$

Sol. 34 (A) Consider Point A on which by Snell's law, we have

$$\mu_1 \sin\theta_1 = \mu_2 \sin\theta_2 \quad \ldots (1)$$

and angle of incidence on top face is

$$\theta_2 = 90° - \theta_c$$

For total internal reflection at top face we use

$$\theta_2 > \theta_c$$

$$\Rightarrow \quad \cos\theta_2 = \sin\theta_c = \frac{\mu_1}{\mu_2} \quad \ldots (2)$$

Elimination of θ_2 between (1) and (2), we get

$$\sin\theta_1 = \sqrt{\left(\frac{\mu_2}{\mu_1}\right)^2 - 1}$$

Sol. 35 (A) A ray AB is incident on mirror OM_1 at angle α and is reflected along BC suffering a deviation $\delta_1 = \angle FBC$

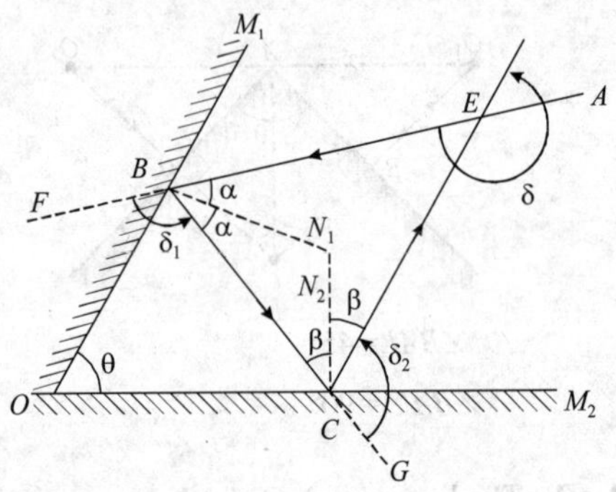

The ray BC falls on mirror OM_2 at an angle of incidence β and is reflected along CD suffering another deviation

$$\delta_2 = \angle GCD$$

The total deviation is $\delta = \delta_1 + \delta_2$

It is clear from the diagram that

$$\delta_1 = 180° - 2\alpha \text{ and } \delta_2 = 180° - 2\beta$$

$$\Rightarrow \quad \delta = \delta_1 + \delta_2 = 360° - 2(\alpha + \beta)$$

Now, in triangle OBC, we can use

$$\alpha + \beta = \theta$$

$$\Rightarrow \quad \delta = 360° - 2\theta$$

Which is independent of the angle of incidence α at the first mirror.

Sol. 36 (A) Let θ be the angle between the two mirrors OM_1 and OM_2. The incident ray AB is parallel to mirror OM_2 and strikes the mirror OM_1 at an angle of incidence equal to α. From figure we have

$$\angle M_1BA = \angle OBC = M_1OM_2 = \theta$$

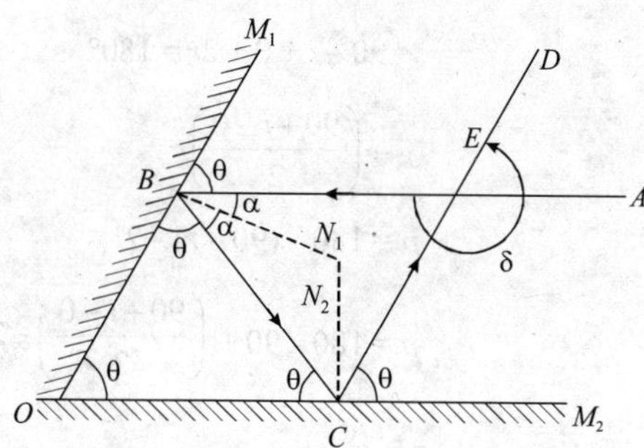

Similarly for reflection at mirror OM_2, we have

$\angle M_2CD = \angle BCO = \angle M_2OM_1 = \theta$

Now in triangle OBC, $3\theta = 180°$, therefore $\theta = 60°$.

Sol. 37 (A) There is no effect on the spot. Rotating the glass slab will shift a ray parallel to axis. The direction of a ray before and after the glass slide is unaffected. All parallel rays are focussed at the focal point of the lens according to ray optics, and there is no effect on the focussed spot.

Sol. 38 (A) The slab does not object for minimum deviation by prism, thus for minimum deviation, we use

$$r_1 = r_2 = 30° \text{ as shown in figure}$$

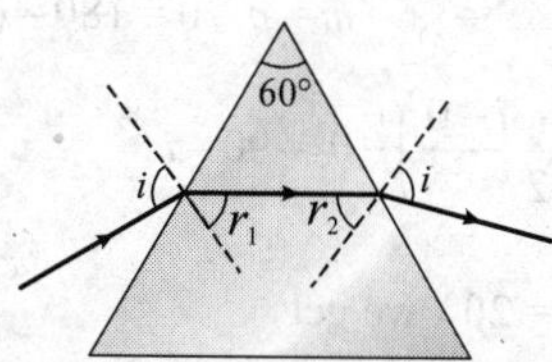

$\Rightarrow \sin i = \sqrt{2}\sin 30°$ or $i = 45°$

Thus minimum deviation $= 2i - A = 90° - 60° = 30°$

$\Rightarrow \sin i = \sqrt{2}\sin 30°$ or $i = 45°$

Sol. 39 (B) As mirror is moving parallel to itself, it does not affect the position of image so length of spot on ground will remain same. This can also be seen by similar triangles in figure.

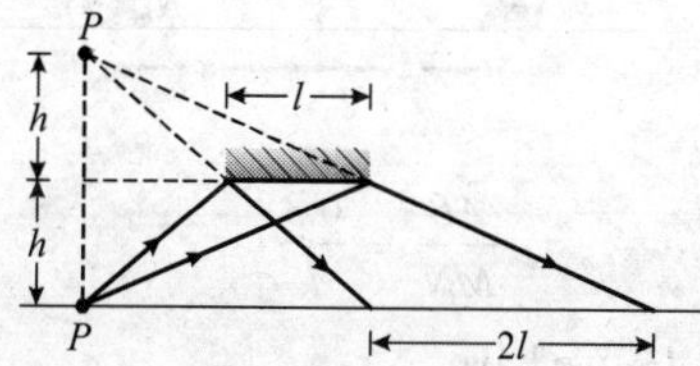

Sol. 40 (C) When the lens is tilted by θ, the image is formed at the intersection point P of focal plane of lens in tilted position and x-axis.

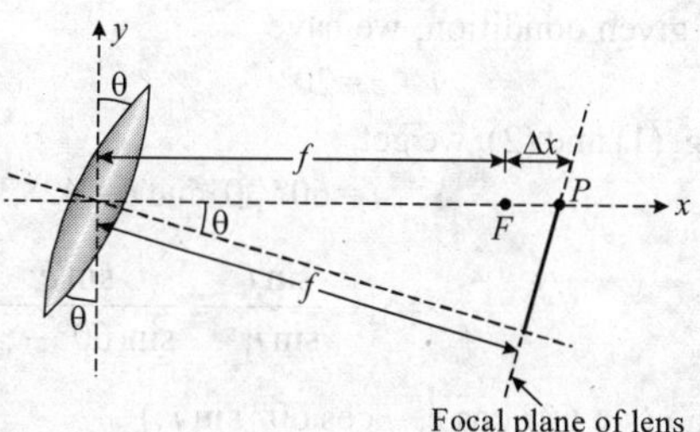

As the lens oscillates. The image shifts on x-axis in between F and P.

Thus distance between two extreme position of the oscillating image is

$$\Delta x = PF = \frac{f}{\cos\theta} - f = f(\sec\theta - 1)$$

Sol. 41 (B) We use magnification

$$\frac{v}{u} = \frac{f}{u-f} = \frac{f}{\text{distance of object from focus}} = \frac{f}{x}.$$

Sol. 42 (D) As we know that a light ray after successive reflections from two mutually perpendicular mirrors reverses its direction. Thus as the finally reflected ray is having same slope as that of the given incident light ray so only option (D) can be the correct answer for a given set of mirrors.

Sol. 43 (A) If the angle of emergence from the first prism is 'e' calculating step by step by Snell's law, we get

$$e = \sin^{-1}\frac{2}{3}$$

Then for net deviation to be double, the incident ray on side $A'B'$ of second prism should make angles i or e with normal.

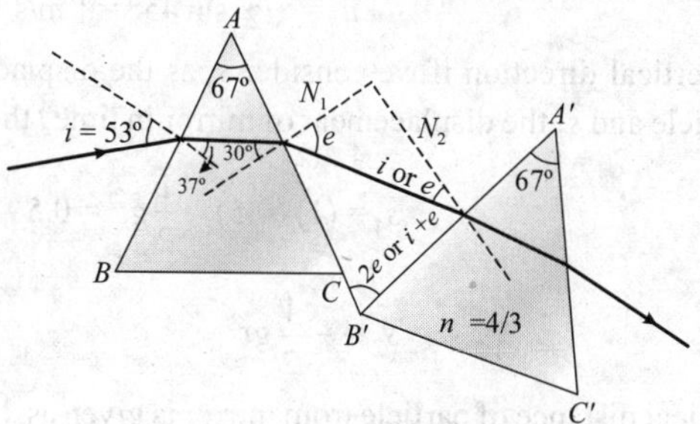

Thus the angle between the given situation be $2e$ or $i + e$.

Solutions of NUMERICAL MCQS Single Option Correct

Sol. 1 (A) We know that for a prism deviation angle is given as

$$\delta = i + e - A$$

$$\Rightarrow \quad 45° = i + e - 60°$$

$$\Rightarrow \quad i + e = 105° \quad \dots(1)$$

As per given condition, we have

$$i - e = 20° \quad ...(2)$$

Solving. (1) and (2), we get

$$i = 60° 30' \text{ and } e = 42° 30'$$

Now $$\mu = \frac{\sin i}{\sin r_1} = \frac{\sin e}{\sin(60° - r_1)}$$

$$\Rightarrow \sin i (\sin 60° \cos r_1 - \cos 60° \sin r_1) = \sin e \sin r_2$$

$$\Rightarrow 0.8870 (0.866 \cos r_1 - 0.5 \sin r_1) = 0.6756 \sin r_1$$

Solving we get

$$\Rightarrow \tan r_1 = \frac{0.8870 \times 0.866}{1.1191}$$

$$r_1 = 34° 28'$$

$$\Rightarrow \mu = \frac{\sin i_1}{\sin r_1} = \frac{0.8870}{0.5659} = 1.567$$

Sol. 2 (C)

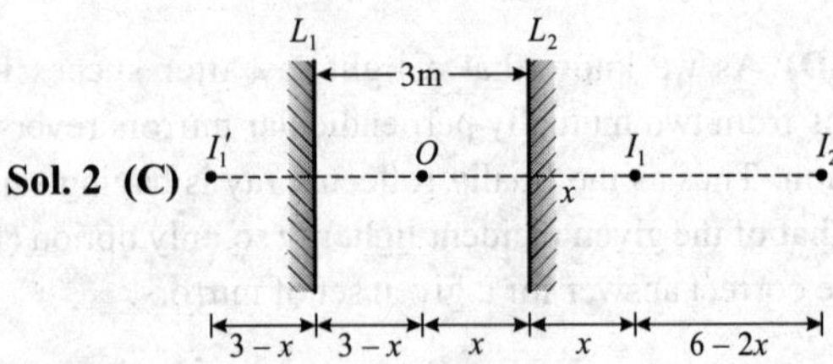

Distance between images I_1 and I_2 is given as

$$I_1 I_2 = 6 - 2x = 4 \text{ m}$$

$$\Rightarrow x = 1 \text{ m}$$

Sol. 3 (B) After projection of the particle its velocity component in vertical direction is given as

$$u_y = \sqrt{2} \sin 45° = 1 \text{ m/s}$$

In vertical direction if we consider s_1 as the displacement of particle and s_2 the displacement of mirror in time t then we use

$$s_1 = (1)(0.5) - \frac{1}{2}gt^2 = 0.5 - \frac{1}{2}gt^2$$

and $$s_2 = -\frac{1}{2}gt^2$$

Vertical distance of particle from mirror is given as

$$s = s_1 - s_2 = 0.5 \text{ m}$$

Thus, distance between particle and its image is

$$\Delta s = 2s = 1 \text{ m}$$

Sol. 4 (B) As we know that along the normal the velocity of image is double the velocity of mirror and opposite to the velocity of image and along the surface of mirror image velocity components are same as that of object, so velocity of image is given as $(3\hat{i} + 4\hat{j} + 11\hat{k})$.

Sol. 5 (B) From the figure in triangle QRS, we have

$$90 - i + \theta + 2r = 180°$$

$$\Rightarrow r = \left(\frac{90 + i - \theta}{2}\right)$$

$$\Rightarrow p = 180 - (90 - r) - 2i$$

$$\Rightarrow p = 180 - 90 + \left(\frac{90 + i - \theta}{2}\right) - 2i$$

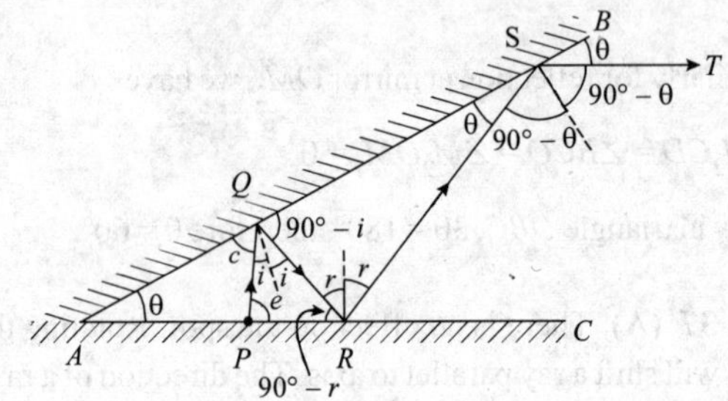

$$\Rightarrow p = \frac{180 - 4i + 90 + i - \theta}{2}$$

$$\Rightarrow p = \left(\frac{270 - 3i - \theta}{2}\right)$$

$$\Rightarrow m = p - \theta = 180 - (90 - i) - 2i$$

$$\Rightarrow \left(\frac{270 - 3i - \theta}{2}\right) - \theta = 90 - i$$

Substituting $\theta = 20°$, we get

$$i = 30°$$

Sol. 6 (D) In the figure MN is the length of image he sees in the mirror. From the similar triangles EAB and EMN, we have

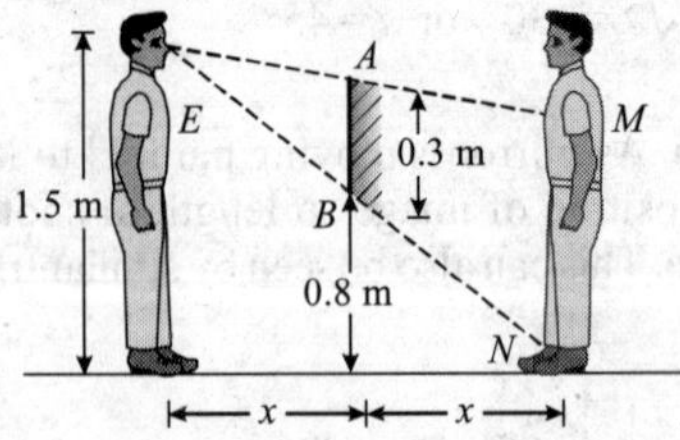

$$\frac{AB}{MN} = \frac{0.3}{l}$$

As $MN = 2AB$, we have

$$l = 0.6 \text{ m}$$

Sol. 7 (C) Here, PQ is the size of spot formed on the wall. From the similar triangles $\Delta PS'Q$ and $\Delta MS'N$, we have

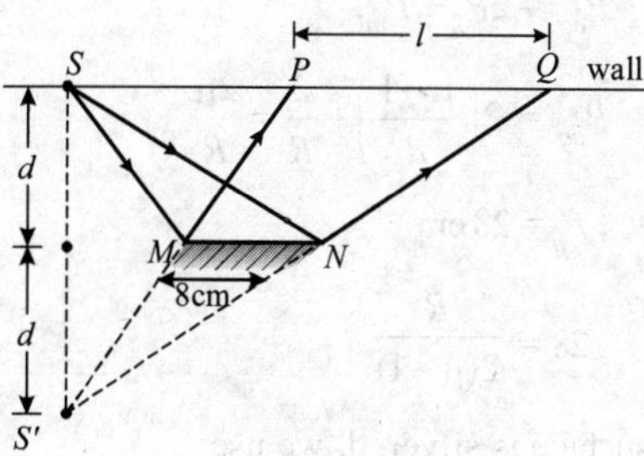

$$\frac{PQ}{MN} = \frac{2d}{d}$$

$\Rightarrow \quad PQ = 2 \times 8 = 16 \text{ cm}$

Sol. 8 (C) Using refraction formula for air-glass interface, we use

$$u = -x; \; R = +10 \text{ cm}; \; \mu_1 = 1 \text{ and } \mu_2 = 3/2$$

By refraction formula, we use

$$\frac{\mu_2}{v} - \frac{\mu_1}{u} = \frac{\mu_2 - \mu_1}{R_1}$$

$$\Rightarrow \quad \frac{\mu_2}{\infty} - \frac{1}{-x} = \frac{1.5 - 1}{10}$$

$$\Rightarrow \quad x = -20 \text{ cm}$$

As the second surface is flat, rays must become parallel after first refraction only as from flat surface rays will not suffer any deviation when falls normally.

Sol. 9 (D) Using lens formula we can see that first image after refraction through lens is obtained 10 cm behind the lens from which when light rays are reflected from plane mirror next image will be obtained at a distance 20 cm behind the plane mirror which will act as an object for the next refraction at lens so we use

$$u = +30 \text{ cm and } f = +10 \text{ cm}$$

Using lens formula, we have

$$\frac{1}{v} - \frac{1}{u} = \frac{1}{f}$$

$$\Rightarrow \quad \frac{1}{v} - \frac{1}{30} = \frac{1}{10}$$

$$\Rightarrow \quad \frac{1}{v} = \frac{1}{10} + \frac{1}{30} = \frac{4}{30}$$

$$\Rightarrow \quad v = +7.5 \text{ cm}$$

Thus final image is obtained 7.5 cm to the right of lens.

Sol. 10 (C) Here nose of the boy is the object & fish is observer. So for refraction formula, we use

$$u = +R; \; \mu_2 = 4/3; \; \mu_1 = 1 \text{ and } R = -R$$

Using refraction formula, we have

$$\frac{\mu_2}{v} - \frac{\mu_1}{u} = \frac{\mu_2 - \mu_1}{R}$$

$$\Rightarrow \quad \frac{4}{3v} - \frac{1}{R} = \frac{\frac{4}{3} - 1}{-R}$$

$$\Rightarrow \quad v = +2R$$

Thus the image of child's nose will appear at a distance $3R$ from the center of the bowl. The ray diagram is shown in below figure.

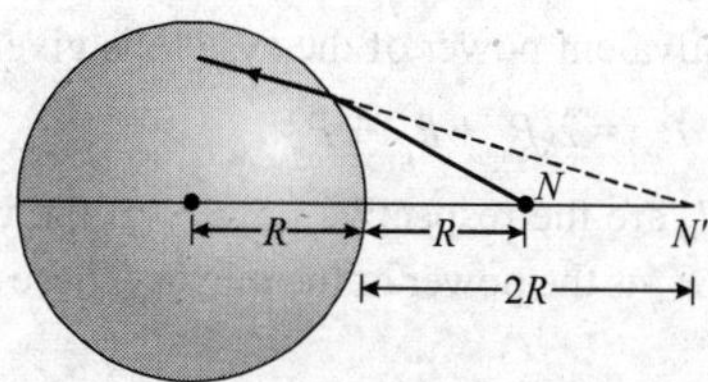

Sol. 11 (B) Final image coincides with the object when the image produced by lens is formed at centre of curvature of mirror or itself on the pole of mirror. So there are two possible conditions here.

For the lens, we use $u = -15$ cm and $f = +10$ cm so in lens formula, we use

$$\frac{1}{v_1} - \frac{1}{u} = \frac{1}{f}$$

$$\Rightarrow \quad \frac{1}{v_1} - \frac{1}{-15} = \frac{1}{10}$$

$$\Rightarrow \quad v_1 = +30 \text{ cm}$$

Thus image produced must be at the centre of curvature of the mirror as it is not possible at the pole because the distance of pole to lens is only 10 cm

$$\Rightarrow \quad R = 20 \text{ cm}$$

$$\Rightarrow \quad f = 10 \text{ cm}$$

Sol. 12 (A) Equivalent focal length of the system of three lenses in contact is given as

$$\frac{1}{f_{eq}} = \frac{1}{f_G} + \frac{1}{f_W} + \frac{1}{f_G} \quad \ldots(1)$$

Where focal length of glass lenses is given as

$$f_G = \frac{R}{\mu - 1} = 2R$$

$$\Rightarrow \quad R = 5 \text{ cm}$$

Focal Length of water lens is given as

$$f_W = \frac{R}{2(\mu-1)} = \frac{3R}{2} = 7.5 \text{ cm}$$

Now from equation-(1), we have

$$\Rightarrow \quad \frac{1}{f_{eq}} = 2\left(\frac{1}{10}\right) + \left(-\frac{2}{15}\right) = \frac{1}{15}$$

Equivalent optical power of the given system is given as

$$P_e = \frac{1}{15} \times 100 = 6.67 \text{ D}$$

Sol. 13 (A) Equivalent power of the system is given as

$$P_{eq} = 2(P_w + P_g) + P_m$$

Where P_w and P_g are the respective powers of the water and glass lenses and P_m is the power of the mirror. These are given as

$$\frac{1}{f_w} = (\mu_w - 1)\left(\frac{1}{\infty} - \frac{1}{-60}\right)$$

$$\Rightarrow \quad P_w = \frac{1}{180} \text{ cm}^{-1}$$

and $P_g = \frac{1}{f_g}$, where we use

$$\frac{1}{f_g} = (\mu_g - 1)\left(\frac{1}{-60} - \frac{1}{-20}\right)$$

$$\Rightarrow \quad P_g = \frac{1}{60} \text{ cm}^{-1}$$

and $$P_m = \frac{1}{f_m} = \frac{2}{20} \text{ cm}^{-1}$$

Equivalent power of the system is now given as

$$P_{eq} = 2(P_w + P_g) + P_m,$$

$$\Rightarrow \quad P_{eq} = 2\left(\frac{1}{180} + \frac{1}{60}\right) + \frac{2}{20}$$

$$\Rightarrow \quad P_{eq} = \frac{13}{90}$$

$$\Rightarrow \quad f_e = \frac{90}{13} \text{ cm}$$

Sol. 14 (B) When plane surface is silvered, we use

$$P_{eq} = 2P_L = 2\left(\frac{\mu-1}{R}\right)$$

Then in case when curved surface is silvered, we use

$$P_{eq}' = 2P_L + P_m,$$

$$\Rightarrow \quad P_{eq}' = 2\left(\frac{\mu-1}{R}\right) + \frac{2}{R} = \frac{2\mu}{R}$$

Given that, $f_{eq} = 28$ cm

So we use $$28 = \frac{R}{2(\mu-1)} \quad \ldots(1)$$

When curved surface is silvered, we use

$$f_{eq}' = \frac{R}{2\mu} = 10 \quad \ldots(2)$$

From equation-(1) and (2) we get,

$$\mu = \frac{14}{9}$$

Sol. 15 (C) For the minimum angle of deviation produced by the prism, $i = e$ and $r_1 = r_2$,

$$\Rightarrow \quad r_1 + r_2 = A \text{ then, } r = 45° \text{ (since } A = 90°),$$

Using Snell's law for the 1st interface, we have

$$1. \sin i = \mu \cdot \sin r$$

$$\Rightarrow \quad \sin i = \sqrt{\frac{3}{2}} \times \frac{1}{\sqrt{2}}$$

$$\Rightarrow \quad i = 60°,$$

Then $$\delta_{min} = (i - r) + (e - r) = (60 - 45) + (60 - 45),$$

$$\Rightarrow \quad \delta_{min} = 30°$$

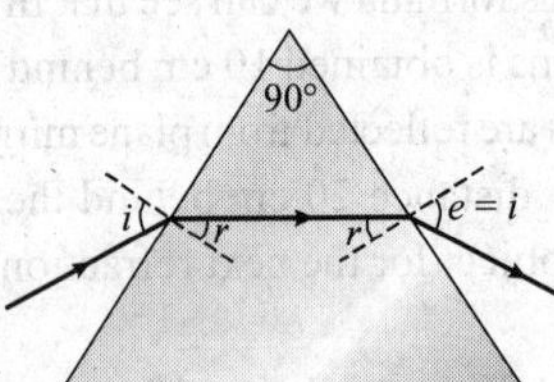

Sol. 16 (B) Graph between $(\delta - i)$ for the prism is shown in figure. Here i = Angle of incidence when it is undergoes minimum deviation, we have deviation angle

$$\delta = i + e - A$$

$$\Rightarrow \quad 44° = 42° + 62° - A$$

$$\Rightarrow \quad A = 60°$$

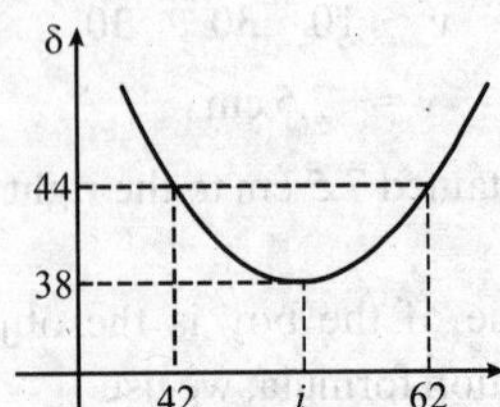

For the condition of minimum deviation

$$r_1 + r_2 = A$$

$\Rightarrow$ $r = 30°$ (As $r_1 = r_2 = r$)

$$\delta_{min} = 2(i - r)$$

$\Rightarrow$ $38 = 2(i - 30°)$

$\Rightarrow$ $i = 49°$

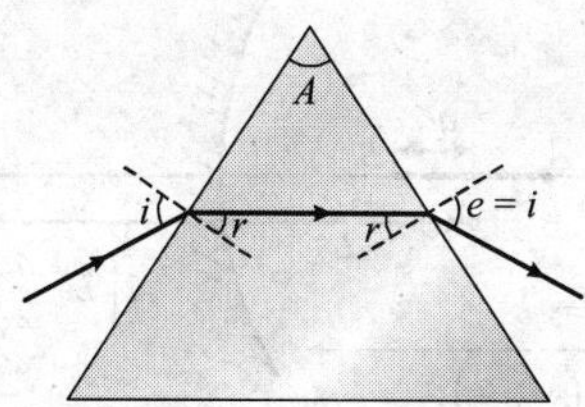

Sol. 17 (A) Ray diagram of the grazing emergence is shown in figure

Here we have $r + \theta_c = A$

$\Rightarrow$ $r + \theta_c = 60$

Using Snell's law at the second surface, we have

$$\sqrt{2}\sin\theta_c = 1 \sin 90$$

$\Rightarrow$ $\sin\theta_c = \dfrac{1}{\sqrt{2}}$; $\theta_c = 45°$

Then, we have $r = A - \theta_c = 15°$

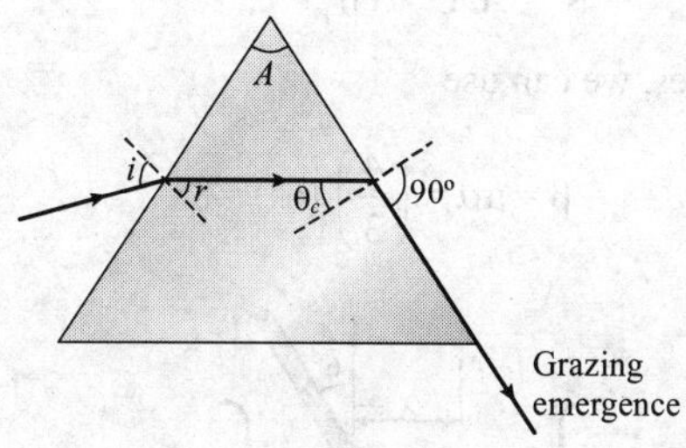

Using Snell's law at the 1st surface, we have

$$1 \sin i = \sqrt{2}\sin r$$

and $\sin i = \sqrt{2}\sin 15$

$\Rightarrow$ $i = \sin^{-1}\left(\dfrac{\sqrt{3}-1}{2}\right)$

(As $\sin 15° = \dfrac{\sqrt{3}-1}{2\sqrt{2}}$)

Sol. 18 (D) For refraction formula at spherical surface, we use

$$v = 2R;\ u = \infty;\ \mu_1 = 1 \text{ and } \mu_2 = \mu$$

Using refraction formula, we have

$$\frac{\mu_2}{v} - \frac{\mu_1}{u} = \frac{\mu_2 - \mu_1}{R}$$

$\Rightarrow$ $\dfrac{\mu}{2R} - \dfrac{1}{\infty} = \dfrac{\mu - 1}{R}$

$\Rightarrow$ $\mu = 2\mu - 2$

$\Rightarrow$ $\mu = 2$

Sol. 19 (B) Apparent shift in the object O due to three slabs S_1, S_2 and S_3 with respect to the medium of $\mu = \dfrac{4}{3}$ is given as

$$\Rightarrow \text{Shift} = 45\left(1 - \frac{1}{\frac{3/2}{4/3}}\right) + 24\left(1 - \frac{1}{\frac{1}{4/3}}\right) + 54\left(1 - \frac{1}{\frac{3/2}{4/3}}\right)$$

$$\Rightarrow \text{Shift} = 45\left(1 - \frac{8}{9}\right) + 24\left(1 - \frac{4}{3}\right) + 54\left(1 - \frac{8}{9}\right)$$

$$\text{Shift} = 5 + (-8) + 6 = 3 \text{ cm}$$

$\Rightarrow$ Object distance $u = 150$ cm

Thus image will be formed on the object itself as light rays fall on mirror normally as the object appears to be located at its center of curvature.

Sol. 20 (C) As, we know

$$\frac{dv}{dt} = -\frac{v^2}{u^2}\frac{du}{dt}$$

We use $\dfrac{1}{f} = \dfrac{1}{u} + \dfrac{1}{v}$

$\Rightarrow$ $\dfrac{1}{-12} = \dfrac{-1}{20} + \dfrac{1}{v}$

$\Rightarrow$ $v = -30$ cm/s

$\Rightarrow$ $\dfrac{dv}{dt} = -\left(\dfrac{30}{20}\right)^2 \times 4 = -9$ cm/s

i.e., 9 cm/s away from the mirror.

Sol. 21 (D) Acceleration of block $AB = \dfrac{3mg}{3m + m} = \dfrac{3}{4}g$;

acceleration of block $CD = \dfrac{2mg}{2m + m} = \dfrac{2g}{3}$

Acceleration of image in mirror AB

= 2 acceleration of mirror

$$= 2\cdot\left(\frac{-3g}{4}\right) = \frac{-3}{2}g$$

Acceleration of image in mirror $CD = 2\cdot\left(\dfrac{2g}{3}\right) = \dfrac{4g}{3}$

$\Rightarrow$ Acceleration of the two image w.r.t. each other is given as

$$a_{rd} = \frac{4g}{3} - \left(\frac{-3g}{2}\right) = \frac{17g}{6}$$

Sol. 22 (D) The situation described in the question is shown in the ray diagram below

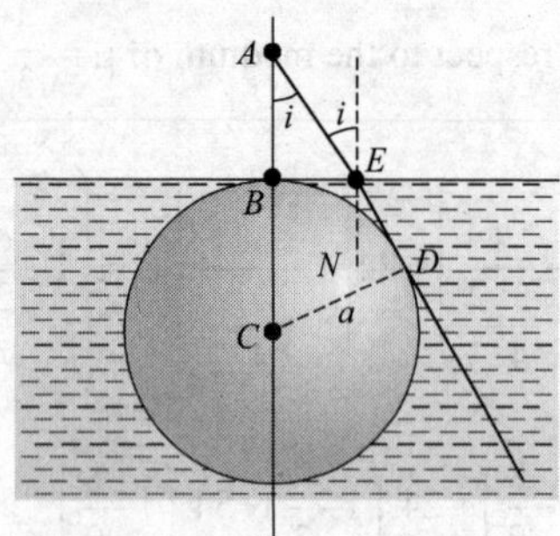

We are given that

$$\angle NED = 30^\circ$$

$\Rightarrow$ $\angle BED = 120^\circ$

As $BCDE$ is a cyclic quadrilateral, we have

$$\angle BCD = 60^\circ$$

The line CE will be angle bisector of $\angle BCD$

$\Rightarrow$ $BE = a \tan 30^\circ = \frac{a}{\sqrt{3}}$

We use $\tan i = \frac{BE}{AB} = \frac{a\sqrt{3}}{a/2} = \frac{2}{\sqrt{3}}$

$\Rightarrow$ $\sin i = \frac{2}{\sqrt{7}}$

Using Snell's law, we have

$$1. \sin i = n \sin r$$

$\Rightarrow$ $\frac{2}{\sqrt{7}} = n \times \frac{1}{2}$

$\Rightarrow$ $n = \frac{4}{\sqrt{7}}$

Sol. 23 (B) Incidence angle on face BC is

$$i = 90 - \theta$$

$$i = A = 90 - \theta > \theta_C \text{ (for light not to cross } BC)$$

$$\cos\theta > \sin\theta_C = \frac{6/5}{3/2} = \frac{4}{5}$$

$\Rightarrow$ $\theta < \cos^{-1}\frac{4}{5} = 37^\circ$

Sol. 24 (C) If the length of rod be 'a'. The magnitude of transverse magnification of ends A and B is 2 each. The image of B is virtual and that of A is real.

Applying mirror formula to B and A, we have

$$\frac{1}{2\left(L-\frac{a}{2}\right)} - \frac{1}{\left(L-\frac{a}{2}\right)} = -\frac{1}{f} \quad \ldots(1)$$

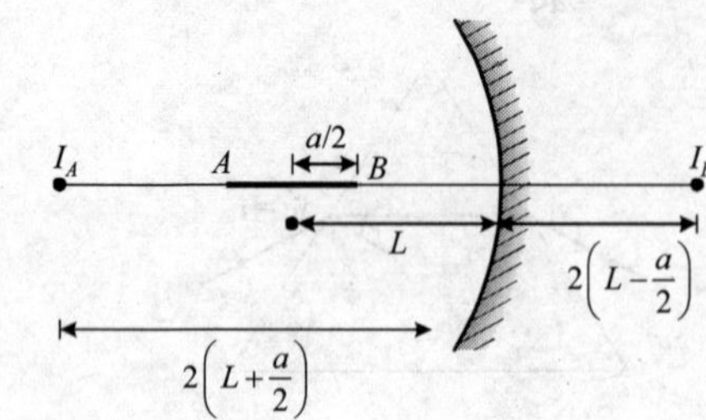

$$-\frac{1}{2\left(L+\frac{a}{2}\right)} - \frac{1}{\left(L+\frac{a}{2}\right)} = -\frac{1}{f} \quad \ldots(2)$$

Solving equation-(1) and (2) we get $a = L$.

Sol. 25 (A) As shown in figure, we use

$$\alpha = \frac{x}{OC} \text{ and } \beta = \frac{x}{OC'}$$

$\Rightarrow$ $\frac{\alpha}{\beta} = \frac{OC'}{OC} = \frac{1}{\mu}$

For small angles, we can use

$$\beta = \mu\alpha = \left(\frac{4}{3}\right)(6^\circ) = 8^\circ$$

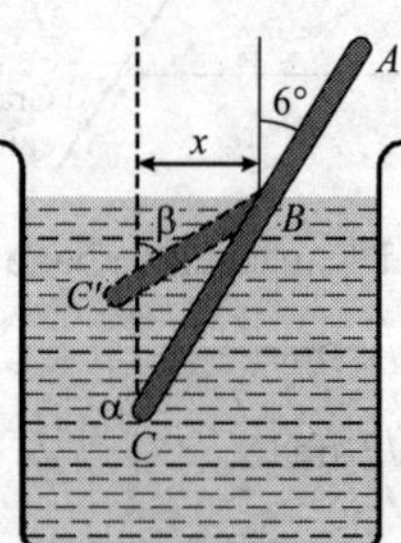

$\Rightarrow$ Bending angle $= \beta - \alpha = 2^\circ$

Sol. 26 (B) This is a case of total internal reflection, we use

$\Rightarrow$ $\theta > \theta_C \left(= \sin^{-1}\frac{1}{\mu}\right)$

$$\frac{1}{\mu} < \sin\theta$$

As at point B angle of incidence of light ray is maximum, we use

$$\frac{1}{\mu} < \sin 45^\circ$$

$\Rightarrow \quad \mu > 1/\sin 45°$

$\Rightarrow \quad \mu > \sqrt{2}$

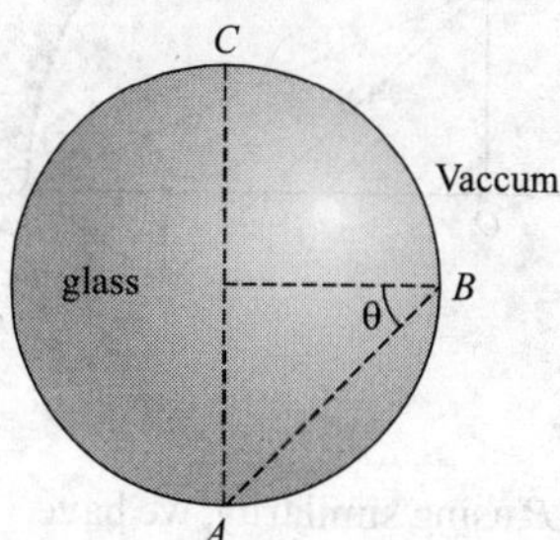

As $\quad v = \dfrac{c}{\mu}$

$\Rightarrow \quad v < \dfrac{c}{\sqrt{2}} = \dfrac{3\times10^8}{\sqrt{2}}$

$\Rightarrow \quad v < 2.1 \times 10^8$

$\Rightarrow$ only (B) is not possible.

Sol. 27 (D) For the reflection from mirror, we use

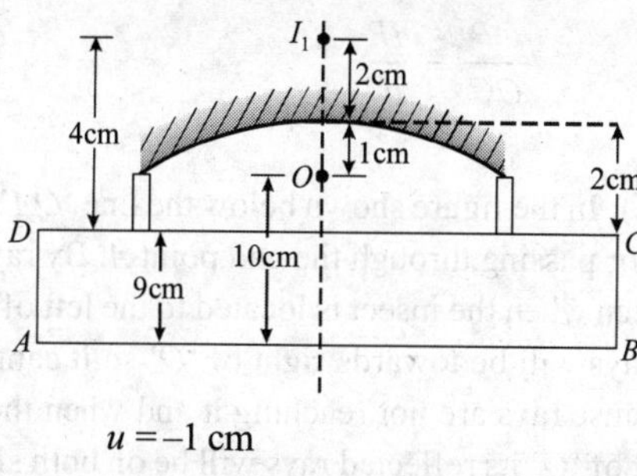

$u = -1$ cm

$f = -2$ cm

using $\quad \dfrac{1}{v} + \dfrac{1}{u} = \dfrac{1}{f}$

$$\frac{1}{v} = \frac{1}{f} - \frac{1}{u} = \left(\frac{1}{-2}\right) - \left(\frac{1}{-1}\right) = 1 - \frac{1}{2}$$

$\Rightarrow \quad v = 2$ cm

Now for the slab image I_1 can be taken as the object. Here we use

$$h_{app} = \left(\frac{d_1}{\mu_1} + \frac{d_2}{\mu_2}\right)\mu_3$$

Where $\quad d_1 = 9$ cm, $d_2 = 4$ cm, $\mu_1 = 3/2$, $\mu_2 = 1$, $\mu_3 = 1$

$$\Rightarrow \quad h_{app} = \left(\frac{9}{3/2} + \frac{4}{1}\right).1 = 10 \text{ cm}$$

i.e. the final image formed at 10 cm from side AB of the slab. Thus at the object itself as shown in figure. Here the image is virtual.

Sol. 28 (C) Image due to plane mirror will be produced at a distance of 20 cm left of the mirror. As image formed by two mirrors lie adjacent to each other, of convex mirror, image position has to be at a distance 15 cm towards left. So for mirror formula, we use

$$u = +25 \text{ cm and } v = -15 \text{ cm}$$

By mirror formula, we have

$$\frac{1}{v} + \frac{1}{u} = \frac{1}{f}$$

$$\Rightarrow \quad \frac{1}{-15} + \frac{1}{25} = \frac{2}{R}$$

$$\Rightarrow \quad R = -75 \text{ cm}$$

Sol. 29 (D) The rays just above x-axis which are considered paraxial to the given axis after refraction at curved surface intersect x axis at point A which is at a distance x_1 from O. By refraction formula, we have

$$\frac{1}{x_1} = \frac{\mu - 1}{R}$$

or $\quad x_1 = \dfrac{R}{\mu - 1} = \dfrac{15}{2}$ cm

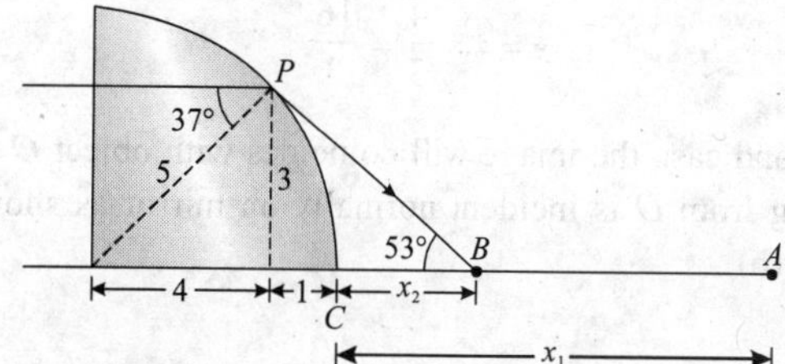

The critical angle for air-glass interface is $\theta = \sin^{-1}\dfrac{3}{5} = 37°$. The rays above the ray incident on curved surface at $i = 37°$ will suffer total internal reflection and will not be considered. The light ray which incident on curved surface at $\theta = 37°$ after refraction intersect curved surface at point B a distance x_2 from O location of which can be obtained from ΔPCB, as

$$\frac{3}{1 + x_2} = \tan 53° = \frac{4}{3} \text{ or } x_2 = \frac{5}{4}$$

$\Rightarrow$ Required width of region AB is

$$\Delta x = x_1 - x_2 = \frac{15}{2} - \frac{5}{4} = \frac{25}{4} \text{ cm}$$

Sol. 30 (A) This case is the referring to the setup of displacement method experiment as product of the two magnifications is unity. This is shown in figure below.

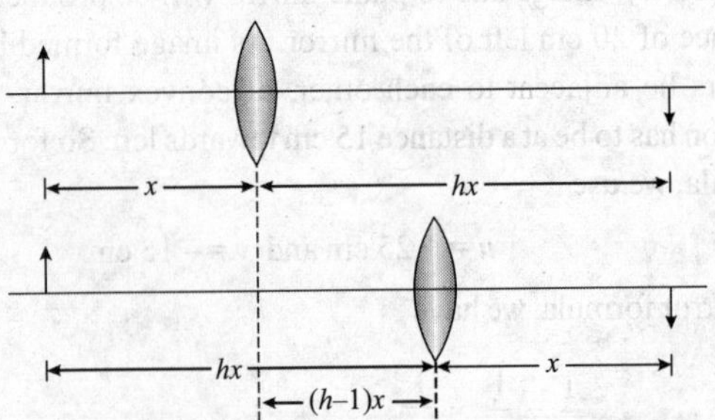

Using lens formula, we have

$$\frac{1}{\eta x}+\frac{1}{x}=\frac{1}{f}$$

$$\Rightarrow \qquad f=\frac{\eta x}{\eta+1}$$

So we get the given ratio is $\frac{(\eta^2-1)}{\eta}$.

Sol. 31 (A) The image coincides with object O if the ray starting from O is incident normally on mirror as shown in figure-(a)

Here the image is located at

$$x=4\times\frac{4}{3}=\frac{16}{3}$$

In second case the image will coincides with object O if ray starting from O is incident normally on mirror as shown in figure-(b)

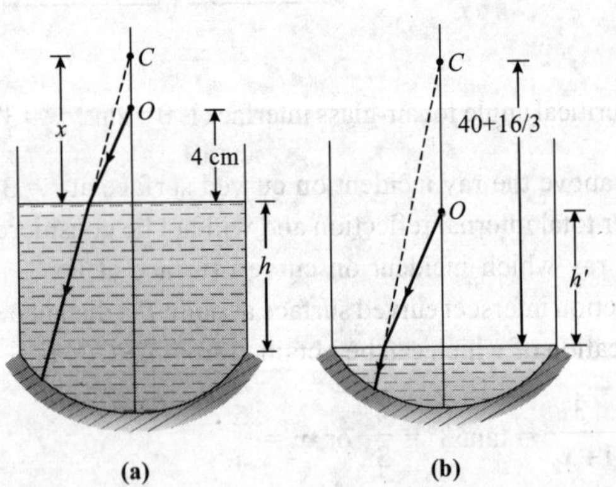

Thus here we use

$$\frac{136}{3}=h'\times\frac{4}{3}$$

$$\Rightarrow \qquad h'=\frac{136}{3}\times\frac{3}{4}=34\text{ cm}$$

Sol. 32 (A) In the figure shown

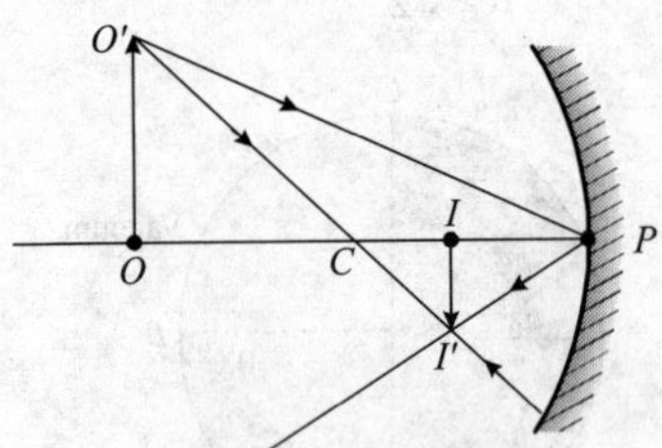

In $\Delta OO'P$ & $\Delta II'P$ using similarity, we have

$$\frac{OO'}{II'}=\frac{OP}{IP} \qquad \ldots(1)$$

also in $\Delta OO'C$ & $\Delta II'C$ using similarity, we have

$$\frac{OO'}{II'}=\frac{OC}{IC} \qquad \ldots(2)$$

By equation-(1) and (2)

$$\frac{OP}{IP}=\frac{OC}{IC}$$

$$\Rightarrow \qquad \frac{OP}{OC}=\frac{IP}{IC}$$

Sol. 33 (A) In the figure shown below the line 'OA' is normal to the mirror passing through the end point A. By ray diagram it can be seen when the insect is located to the left of 'O' all its reflected rays will be towards right of 'O' so it cannot see its image because rays are not reaching it and when the insect is to the right of 'O' its reflected rays will be on both sides of the insect that means the insect will be in the field of view of its own image so it can see its image.

So it will be able to see its image till it reaches the point 'B' of the mirror from point 'O', if t is the time for which it will be in field of view of its own image, we use

$$2\times t=\left(\frac{3}{\cos 60°}\right)\times 100$$

$$\Rightarrow \qquad t=300\,r$$

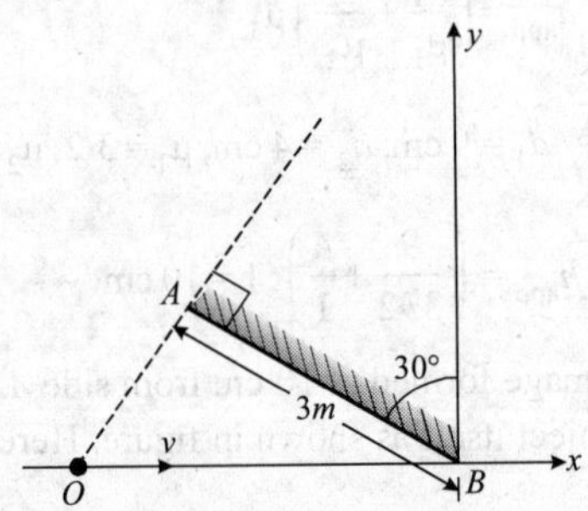

Sol. 34 (A) By using mirror formula, we have

$$\frac{1}{v}+\frac{1}{-10}=\frac{1}{10}$$

$$\Rightarrow \quad v=+5\text{ cm}$$

Thus magnification by mirror is

$$\Rightarrow \quad m=+\frac{1}{2}$$

So the image revolves in circle of radius $\frac{1}{2}$ cm. Image of a radius is erect so particle will revolve in the same direction as the particle. The image will complete one revolution in the same time 2s so velocity of image will be given as

$$v=\omega r=\frac{2\pi}{2}\times\frac{1}{2}=\frac{\pi}{2}\text{ cm/s}=1.57\text{ cm/s}$$

Sol. 35 (B) If cable of an elevator breaks then elevator will be in free fall at acceleration g

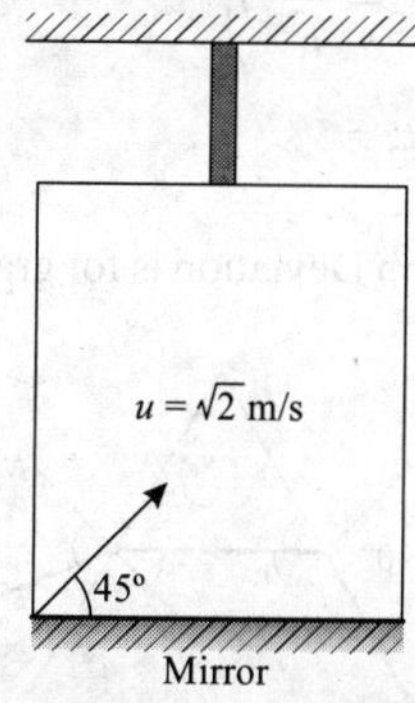

And particle starts moving vertically up at speed $u \sin\theta$ which will be constant with respect to elevator as both elevator and particle both are in free fall. Thus separation between particle and floor after time t is

$$s=u\sin\theta.t=\sqrt{2}.\sin 45^\circ\frac{1}{2}=\frac{1}{2}\text{ m}$$

Thus separation between the particle and it's image is given as

$$s'=2s=\frac{1}{2}+\frac{1}{2}=1\text{ m}$$

Sol. 36 (D) Using mirror formula, we have

$$\frac{1}{v}+\frac{1}{10}=\frac{1}{-20}$$

$$\Rightarrow |v|=\frac{20}{3}\text{ cm in front of mirror.}$$

Sol. 37 (B) From the given vectors for the direction of light rays we can use

For the first medium $\sin\theta_1=\frac{a}{\sqrt{a^2+b^2}}$

and for the second medium $\sin\theta_2=\frac{c}{\sqrt{c^2+d^2}}$

By Snell's law, we have $\mu_1\sin\theta_1=\mu_2\sin\theta_2$

$$\Rightarrow \quad \frac{\mu_1 a}{\sqrt{a^2+b^2}}=\frac{\mu_2 a}{\sqrt{c^2+d^2}}$$

Sol. 38 (C) Using mirror formula, we have

$$\frac{1}{v}+\frac{1}{u}=\frac{1}{f}$$

$$\Rightarrow \quad \frac{1}{v}+\frac{1}{-90}=\frac{1}{-30}$$

$$\Rightarrow \quad v=-45\text{ cm}$$

For velocity of image we use velocity magnification along the principal axis as

$$\left|\frac{dv}{dt}\right|=\left|\frac{v^2}{u^2}\right|\left|\frac{du}{dt}\right|=\left(\frac{45}{90}\right)^2 4=1\text{ cm/sec}$$

Sol. 39 (A) In first case, we use

$$\frac{1}{p}+\frac{1}{q}=\frac{1}{f}$$

and $$\frac{q}{p}=m_1$$

$$\Rightarrow \quad 1+m_1=\frac{q}{f} \quad \ldots(1)$$

In the second case, we use

$$\frac{1}{q+x}+\frac{1}{p'}=\frac{1}{f}$$

and $$\frac{q+x}{p'}=m_2$$

$$\Rightarrow \quad m_2=\frac{q+x}{f} \quad \ldots(2)$$

From equations-(1) and (2), we have

$$\Rightarrow \quad m_2-m_1=x/f$$

$$\Rightarrow \quad f=\frac{x}{m_2-m_1}$$

Sol. 40 (C) In the ray diagram shown in figure, we can see that at refraction at point P, by Snell's law, we have

$$\frac{\sin 60^\circ}{\sin r_1}=\sqrt{3}$$

$$\Rightarrow \quad \sin r_1 = \frac{1}{2}$$

$$\Rightarrow \quad r_1 = 30°$$

Since $r_2 = r_1$

$$\Rightarrow \quad r_2 = 30°$$

Now considering refraction at point Q, by Snell's law, we have

$$\frac{\sin r_2}{\sin i_2} = \frac{1}{\sqrt{3}}$$

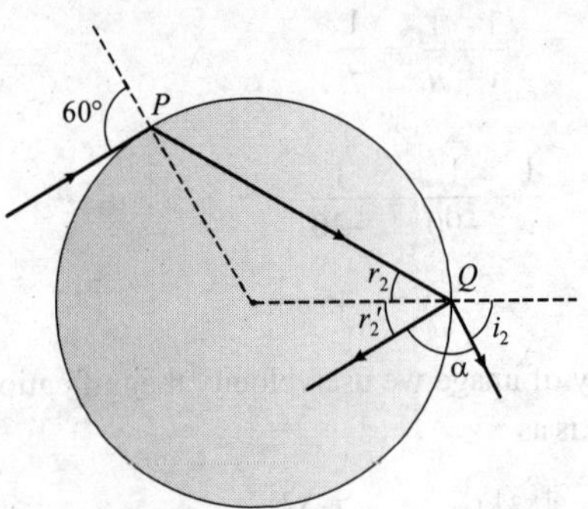

Putting $r_2 = 30°$ we get $i_2 = 60°$

The angle between reflected and refracted ray at point Q is given as

$$\alpha = 180° - (r_2' + i_2)$$

$$\Rightarrow \quad \alpha = 180° - (30° + 60°) = 90°$$

Sol. 41 (B) For multiple layers of parallel sided media, apparent depth is given as

$$h_{app} = \frac{t_1}{\mu_1} + \frac{t_2}{\mu_2}$$

$$\Rightarrow \quad \frac{36}{7} = \frac{5}{5/3} + \frac{3}{\mu_2}$$

$$\Rightarrow \quad \frac{3}{\mu_2} = \frac{36}{7} - 3 = \frac{15}{7}$$

$$\Rightarrow \quad \mu_2 = \frac{7}{5} = 1.4$$

Sol. 42 (B) As object is located at center, all the incident rays will be normal to both the inner and outer glass surfaces of the spherical shell and will not suffer any deviation, so final image as seen from outside will be produced at the center only.

Sol. 43 (B) By lens makers formula, the focal length of the lens is given as

$$\frac{1}{f} = (\mu - 1)\left(\frac{1}{R_1} - \frac{1}{R_2}\right)$$

$$\Rightarrow \quad \frac{1}{f}\ (1.5-1)\left(\frac{1}{20} - \frac{1}{20}\right) = \frac{0.5 \times 2}{20} = \frac{1}{20}$$

$$\Rightarrow \quad f = 20\text{ cm}$$

Thus the light rays will converge at 20 cm from the optical centre of the lens.

Sol. 44 (C) If prints are similar, total light energy required for the exposure will be same, so we use

$$I_1 t_1 = I_2 t_2$$

Where I_1 & I_2 are the intensities reception on print area. If P_1 and P_2 are the light intensities when the source is at a distance r_1 and r_2, we have

$$\Rightarrow \quad \frac{P_1}{r_1^2} t_1 = \frac{P_2}{r_2^2} t_2$$

As we have $\quad P_1 = P_2$

$$\Rightarrow \quad t_2 = \frac{r_2^2}{r_1^2} t_1$$

$$\Rightarrow \quad t_2 = 5\text{ s}$$

Sol. 45 (B) Maximum Deviation is for grazing incidence

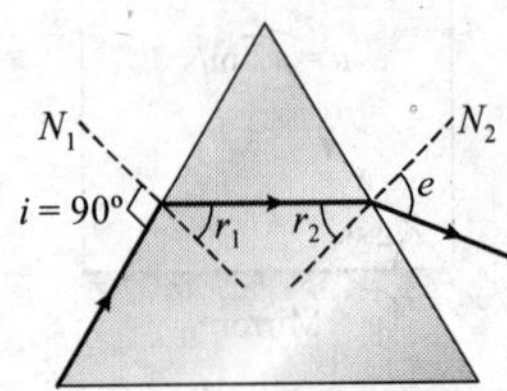

The deviation is maximum when $i = 90°$ or $e = 90°$ that is at grazing incidence or grazing emergence.

Let $\quad i = 90°$

$$\Rightarrow \quad r_1 = C \sin^{-1}(1/\mu)$$

$$\Rightarrow \quad r_1 = \sin^{-1}(2/3) = 42°$$

$$\Rightarrow \quad r_2 = A - r_1 = 60° - 42° = 18°$$

By Snell's law

$$\frac{\sin r_2}{\sin e} = \frac{1}{\mu}$$

$$\sin e = u \sin r_2 = 1.5 \sin 18°$$

$$\Rightarrow \quad \sin e = 0.463$$

$$\Rightarrow \quad e = 28°$$

$$\text{Deviation} = \delta_{max}$$

$$= i + e - A$$

$$= 90° + 28° - 60°$$

$$= 58°$$

Sol. 46 (A) As the sun is very far away, the incident rays are considered parallel.

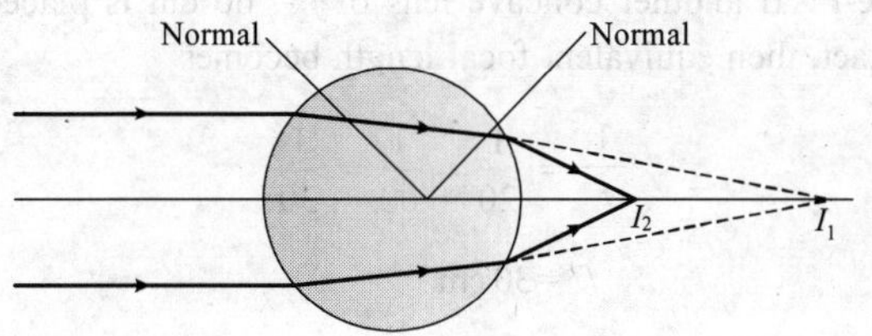

For refraction at first surface of sphere we use refraction formula as

$$\frac{\mu_1}{u}+\frac{\mu_2}{v}=\frac{\mu_2-\mu_1}{R}$$

$$\Rightarrow \quad \frac{1}{\infty}+\frac{1.5}{v_1}=\frac{1.5-1}{+8}$$

$$\Rightarrow \quad v_1=24\text{ cm} \qquad \text{... [18 (A)]}$$

The rays will converge at I_1 which will act as an object for the second surface, so using refraction formula for the second surface, we have

$$\frac{\mu_1}{u}+\frac{\mu_2}{v}=\frac{\mu_2-\mu_1}{R}$$

$$\Rightarrow \quad \frac{1.5}{-8}+\frac{1}{v_2}=\frac{1-1.5}{-8}$$

$$\Rightarrow \quad v_2=4\text{ cm}$$

Sol. 47 (A) By lens makers formula power of a lens is given as

$$P=(\mu-1)\left[\frac{1}{R_1}-\frac{1}{R_2}\right]$$

If P_a is the lens power in air and P_L is the lens power when submerged in the liquid we can use

$$\frac{P_a}{P_L}=\frac{\left(\frac{\mu_g}{\mu_a}-1\right)}{\left(\frac{\mu_g}{\mu_L}-1\right)}=\frac{5}{-100/100}=-5$$

$$\Rightarrow \quad \mu_L=\frac{5}{3}$$

Sol. 48 (C) By lens makers formula, we can find the radius of curvature of the lens surface as

$$\frac{1}{10}=\left(\frac{3}{2}-1\right)\left(\frac{1}{R}-\frac{1}{\infty}\right)$$

$$\Rightarrow \quad \frac{1}{2R}=\frac{1}{10}$$

$$\Rightarrow \quad R=5\text{ cm}$$

For image to be obtained on object, light rays on mirror must fall normally to retrace the path of incident rays after reflection. So by refraction formula, we have

$$\Rightarrow \quad \frac{3/2}{\infty}-\frac{1}{-d}=\left(\frac{1}{-d}-\frac{1/2}{5}\right)$$

$$\Rightarrow \quad \frac{1}{d}=\frac{1}{10}$$

$$\Rightarrow \quad d=10\text{ cm}$$

Sol. 49 (B) By lens formula, we have

$$\frac{1}{v}-\frac{1}{u}=\frac{1}{f}$$

$$\Rightarrow \quad \frac{1}{20}=\frac{+1}{+30}+\frac{1}{v}$$

$$\Rightarrow \quad \frac{1}{v}=\frac{1}{20}-\frac{1}{30}=\frac{1}{60}$$

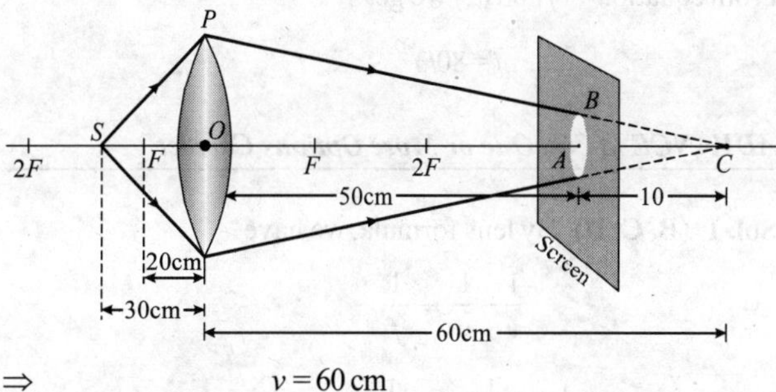

$$\Rightarrow \quad v=60\text{ cm}$$

As triangles OPC & ABC are similar

$$\Rightarrow \quad \frac{2}{60}=\frac{x}{10}$$

$$\Rightarrow \quad x=\frac{1}{3}=0.3\text{ cm}$$

Sol. 50 (B) By lens makers formula, we have

$$\frac{1}{f}=(\mu-1)\left(\frac{1}{R_1}-\frac{1}{R_2}\right)$$

Differentiating both sides, we get

$$\Rightarrow \quad -\frac{df}{f^2}=\left(\frac{1}{R_1}-\frac{1}{R_2}\right)d\mu$$

$$\Rightarrow \quad -\frac{df}{f^2}(\mu-1)\left(\frac{1}{R_1}-\frac{1}{R_2}\right)=\left(\frac{1}{R_1}-\frac{1}{R_2}\right)dn$$

$$\Rightarrow \quad -df=f\frac{d\mu}{\mu-1}$$

But $\qquad d\mu=\mu_v-\mu_R$

$$\Rightarrow \quad -df=\frac{\mu_V-\mu_R}{\mu-1}f$$

$\Rightarrow \quad df = -\omega f$

$\Rightarrow \quad f_v - f_R = -\omega f$

$= -0.4 \times 10 = 4$ mm

Sol. 51 (A) For object O_1, by lens formula, we have

$$\frac{1}{v} + \frac{1}{20} = \frac{1}{f} \quad \ldots(1)$$

For object O_2, we have

$$\frac{1}{v} - \frac{1}{40} = -\frac{1}{f} \quad \ldots(2)$$

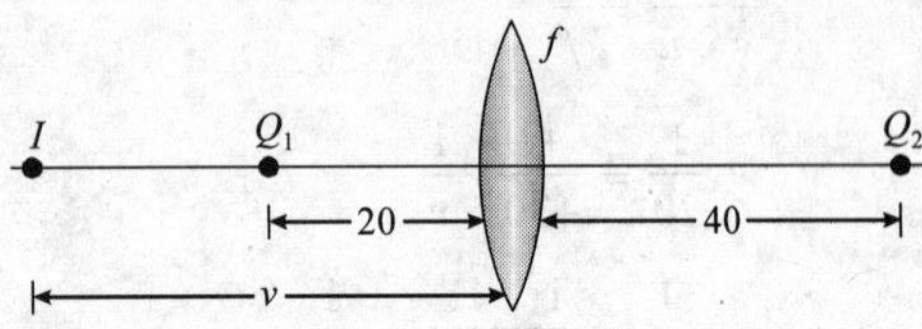

From equation-(1) and (2) we get

$$f = 80/3$$

ADVANCE MCQs One or More Options Correct

Sol. 1 (B, C, D) By lens formula, we have

$$\frac{1}{v} - \frac{1}{u} = \frac{1}{f}$$

$$\Rightarrow \quad \frac{1}{v} - \frac{1}{(-25)} = \frac{1}{20}$$

$$\Rightarrow \quad \frac{1}{v} = \frac{1}{20} - \frac{1}{25} = \frac{1}{100}$$

$$\Rightarrow \quad v = 100 \text{ cm}$$

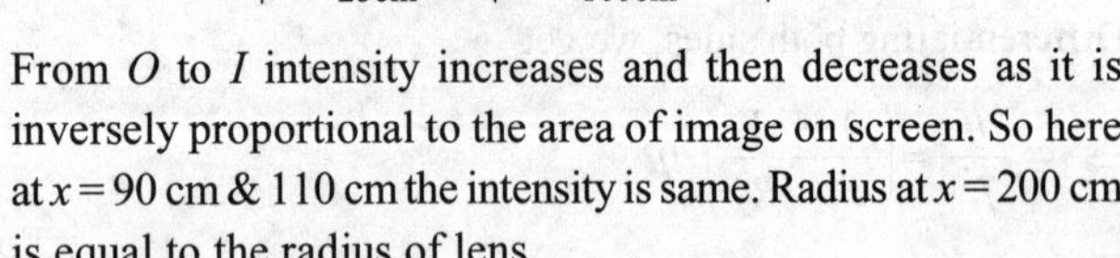

From O to I intensity increases and then decreases as it is inversely proportional to the area of image on screen. So here at $x = 90$ cm & 110 cm the intensity is same. Radius at $x = 200$ cm is equal to the radius of lens.

Sol. 2 (A, D) For the given lens $f = 20$ cm and $\mu_g = \frac{3}{2}$, we use

$$\Rightarrow \quad \left(\frac{3}{2} - 1\right)\frac{2}{R} = \frac{1}{20}$$

$$\Rightarrow \quad R = 20 \text{ cm}$$

Now $u = 30$ cm. If f will change to 30 cm, image will be at infinity that is possible in two ways.

Case-I: If another concave lens of $f = 60$ cm is placed in contact, then equivalent focal length becomes

$$\frac{1}{f'} = \frac{1}{20} - \frac{1}{60} = \frac{1}{30}$$

$$\Rightarrow \quad f' = 30 \text{ cm}$$

(ii) If this lens is immersed in a liquid of refractive index $\frac{9}{8}$, then its focal length becomes

$$\frac{1}{f'} = \left(\frac{\frac{3}{2} - \frac{9}{8}}{\frac{9}{8}}\right)\frac{2}{20} = \frac{1}{30}$$

$$\Rightarrow \quad f' = 30 \text{ cm}$$

Hence options (A) and (D) are correct.

Sol. 3 (A, B) For given condition the incident light rays after refraction from lens should fall at mirror normally.

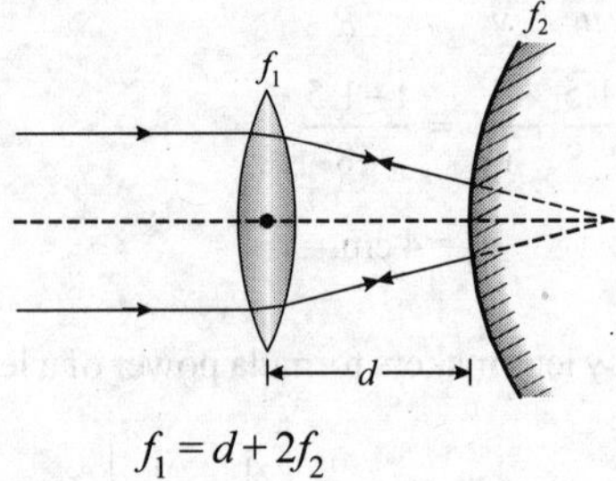

So $\quad f_1 = d + 2f_2$

$\Rightarrow \quad d = |f_1| - 2|f_2|$

As the light beam is reflected as it is, the beam diameter will be same as it is retracing it's original path.

If whole arrangement is submerged in water then focal length of lens would change as it depends upon surrounding medium also but that of mirror, f_2 will remain same.

Sol. 4 (A, D) First three images on M_1 are formed at distances 5 cm, 35 cm and 45 cm. First three images on M_2 are formed at distances 15 cm, 25 cm and 55 cm.

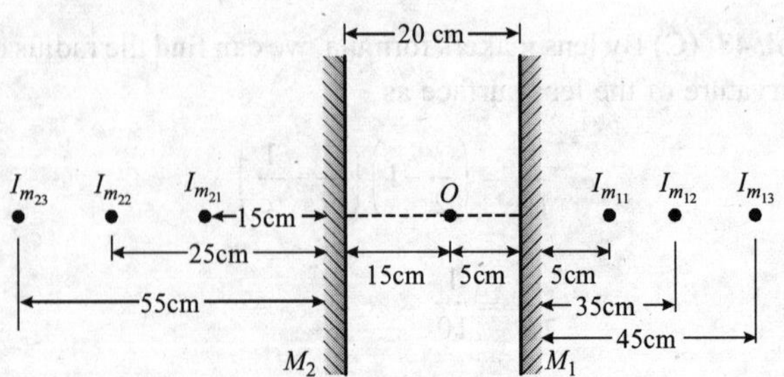

Sol. 5 (A, C) Using Snell's law at point Q, we have

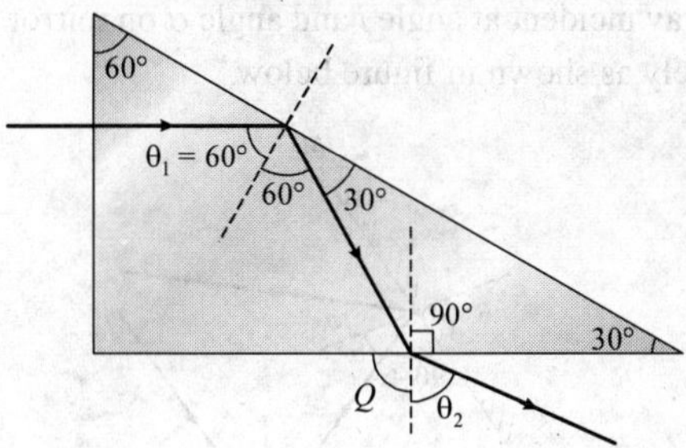

$$\mu_1 \sin\theta_1 = \mu_2 \sin\theta_2$$

$$\Rightarrow \quad \frac{5}{3}\cdot\sin 30^\circ = \frac{4}{3}\cdot\sin\theta_2$$

$$\Rightarrow \quad \theta_2 = \sin^{-1}\left(\frac{5}{8}\right)$$

For total internal reflection at P, we use

$$\frac{5}{3}\sin 60^\circ = \mu_2 \cdot 1$$

$$\Rightarrow \quad \mu_2 = \frac{5}{2\sqrt{3}}$$

Sol. 6 (A, C) The image of a point closer to the focus will be farther. As the transverse magnification of B will be more than A, the image of AB will be inclined to the optical axis.

Sol. 7 (All) Figure explains how deviation angle varies with the incidence angle. With this figure we can analyze that all given options are correct.

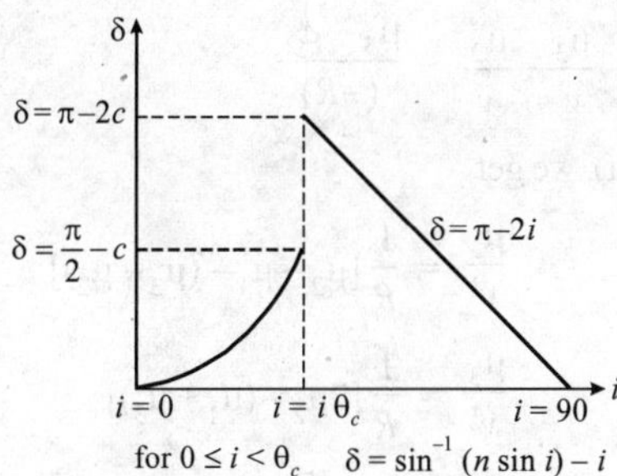

Sol. 8 (A, C) For convex mirror always $|m| < 1$ for any real object

As we know that $V_{image} = -m^2 V_{object}$

$\Rightarrow \quad |V_{image}| < |V_{object}|$

Sol. 9 (A, C) A concave or convex mirror is to be placed left of the object. The object and the image both will be real for concave mirror and virtual for convex mirror.

Sol. 10 (A, D) Let the bubble B is at distance h from the face A of the cube which appears to be at 5 cm so we use

$$h_1 = \frac{h}{\mu} = 5 \text{ cm} \qquad \ldots(1)$$

Similarly when looking from opposite face B, we have

$$h_2 = \frac{12-h}{\mu} = 3 \text{ cm} \qquad \ldots(2)$$

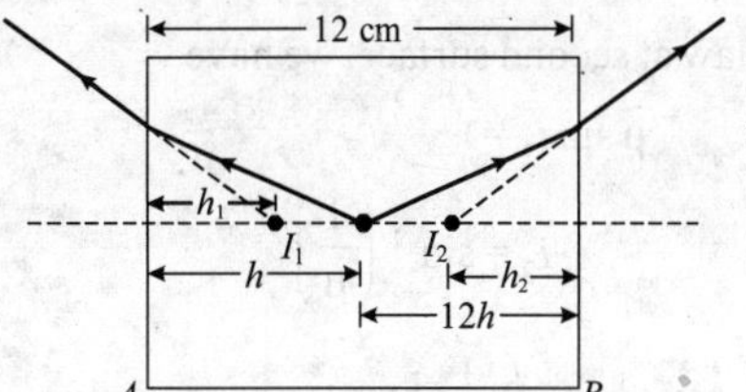

Solving equations-(1) and (2), we get $h = 7.5$ cm and $\mu = 1.5$.

Sol. 11 (B, C) A plane mirror always produces an image of nature opposite to that of object and the nature of rays after reflection on a plane mirror remain same as that of before incidence hence options (B) and (C) are correct.

Sol. 12 (B, C, D) This is a case of displacement method experiment in which we have studied that the object height is given as

$$S_o = \sqrt{I_1 I_2} = \sqrt{9\times 4} = 6 \text{ cm}$$

Magnification in first situation of lens is

$$m = \frac{3}{2}$$

$$\Rightarrow \quad \frac{v}{u} = \frac{3}{2} \Rightarrow v = \frac{3}{2}u$$

and $\quad v + u = 90$

$$\Rightarrow \quad \frac{5}{2}u = 90 \Rightarrow u = 36 \text{ cm}$$

By lens formula, we have

$$\frac{1}{v} - \frac{1}{u} = \frac{1}{f}$$

$$\Rightarrow \quad \frac{1}{54} - \frac{1}{(-36)} = \frac{1}{f} \Rightarrow f = 21.6 \text{ cm}$$

Sol. 13 (A, B, D) Figure below shows the ray diagram and path of light ray after refraction through the prism

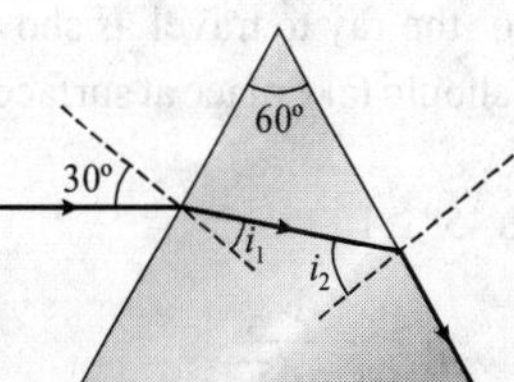

In above figure, we have

$$i_1 + i_2 = \frac{\pi}{3} \qquad \ldots(1)$$

By Snell's law at first surface, we have

$$1 \cdot \sin 30° = \mu \sin i_1$$

$$\Rightarrow \quad i_1 = \sin^{-1}\left(\frac{1}{2\mu}\right) \quad \ldots(2)$$

By Snell's law at second surface, we have

$$\mu \sin i_2 = 1$$

$$\Rightarrow \quad i_2 = \sin^{-1}\left(\frac{1}{\mu}\right) \quad \ldots(3)$$

$$\Rightarrow \quad \sin^{-1}\left(\frac{1}{\mu}\right) + \sin^{-1}\left(\frac{1}{2\mu}\right) = \frac{\pi}{3}$$

Sol. 14 (A, C) By lens formula, we have

$$\frac{1}{v} - \frac{1}{u} = \frac{1}{f}$$

Initially as magnification is 0.5, we have

$$\Rightarrow \quad v = \frac{u}{2}$$

$$\Rightarrow \quad \frac{1}{u/2} - \frac{1}{-u} = \frac{1}{f}$$

$$\Rightarrow \quad u = 3f$$

When displaced by 20 cm, real image of equal size is formed. Therefore object must have been moved from $3f$ to $2f$ so the focal length of lens must be 20 cm

$$\Rightarrow \quad f = 20\,\text{cm}$$

and $\quad u = 3f = 60\,\text{cm}$

Sol. 15 (A, D) As shown in diagram the plane mirror should be placed at 12° with horizontal

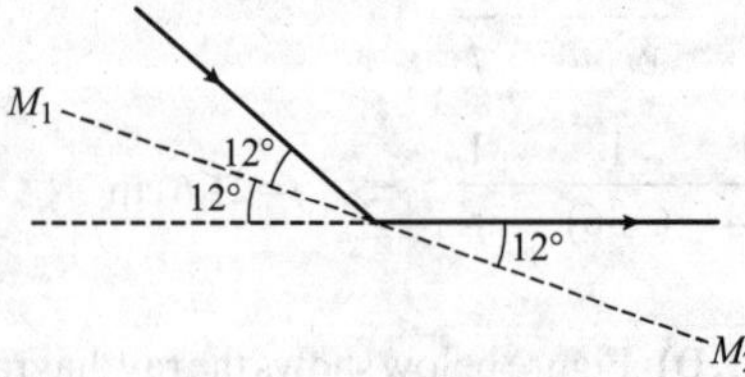

Sol. 16 (C, D) For the ray to travel as shown in figure, total internal reflection should take place at surface AB, for which we use

$$\mu \sin 45° \geq 1$$

$$\Rightarrow \quad \mu \geq \frac{1}{\sin 45°}$$

$$\Rightarrow \quad \mu > 1.414$$

Therefore for refractive index greater than 1.414 (which is the case for C and D) total internal reflection takes place.

Sol. 17 (A, D) If the angle between the two plane mirror be θ, the light ray incident at angle i and angle α on mirror M_1 & M_2 respectively as shown in figure below.

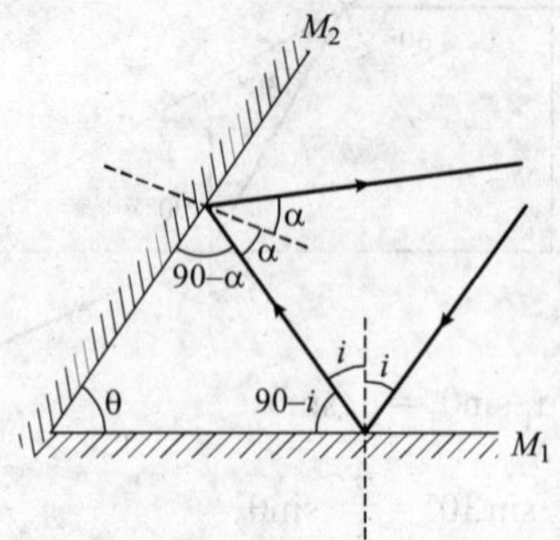

The deviation of light ray due to M_1 is $\delta_1 = 180° - 2i$

and the deviation of light ray due to M_2 is 'δ_2' $= 180° - 2\alpha$

Total deviation $\delta = \delta_1 + \delta_2 = 360° - 2(i + \alpha)$

But $\theta + (90 - i) + (90 - \alpha) = 180°$

As we use from figure

$$i + \alpha = \theta$$

$$\Rightarrow \quad \delta = 360° - 2\theta$$

Sol. 18 (A, B, D) If a parallel beam of light incident on lens then for refraction at first surface of lens, we have

$$\frac{\mu_2}{v} - \frac{\mu_1}{\infty} = \frac{\mu_2 - \mu_1}{R} \quad \ldots(i)$$

Then for refraction at second surface of lens, we have

$$\frac{\mu_3}{v'} - \frac{\mu_2}{v} = \frac{\mu_3 - \mu_2}{(-R)} \quad \ldots(ii)$$

From (i) & (ii), we get

$$\frac{\mu_3}{v'} = \frac{1}{R}[\mu_2 - \mu_1 - (\mu_3 - \mu_2)]$$

$$\Rightarrow \quad \frac{\mu_3}{v'} = \frac{1}{R}[2\mu_2 - (\mu_1 + \mu_3)]$$

$$\Rightarrow \quad \frac{1}{v'} = \frac{2}{\mu_3 R}\left[\mu_2 - \frac{(\mu_1 + \mu_3)}{2}\right]$$

If $\mu_2 > \left(\frac{\mu_1 + \mu_3}{2}\right) \Rightarrow v' = +\text{ve}$ (converging lens)

$\mu_2 < \left(\frac{\mu_1 + \mu_3}{2}\right) \Rightarrow v' = -\text{ve}$ (diverging lens)

$\mu_2 = \left(\frac{\mu_1 + \mu_3}{2}\right) \Rightarrow v' = \infty$ (neither diverging nor converging)

Sol. 19 (B, C) As already studied for emergent ray to exist, refracting angle at surface AC in side the prism must be less than critical angle and maximum value of angle r in figure can also be critical angle so for this to happen $A < 2\theta_C$

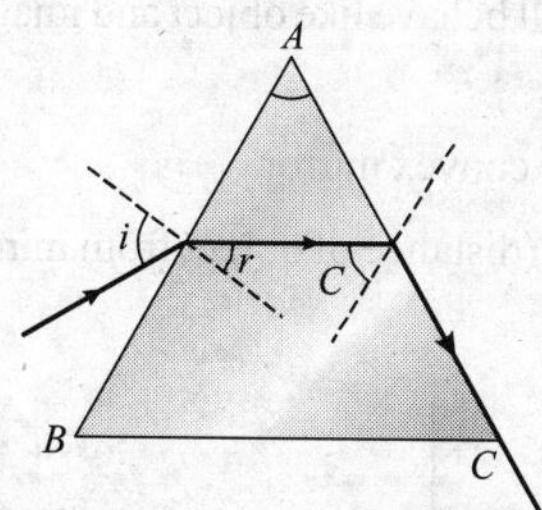

If light incident at angle i. For emergent ray to exist, we must have

$$r > (A - \theta_C)$$

$$\Rightarrow \quad \sin i > \mu \sin (A - \theta_C)$$

$$\Rightarrow \quad \sin i > \frac{\sin(A - \theta_C)}{\sin \theta_C}$$

Sol. 20 (B, C) If P is the power of the source. Then energy emitted from water surface

$$= \frac{P}{4\pi} 2P(1 - \cos\theta_c)$$

Fraction of light $\quad f = \frac{1}{2}(1 - \cos\theta_c)$

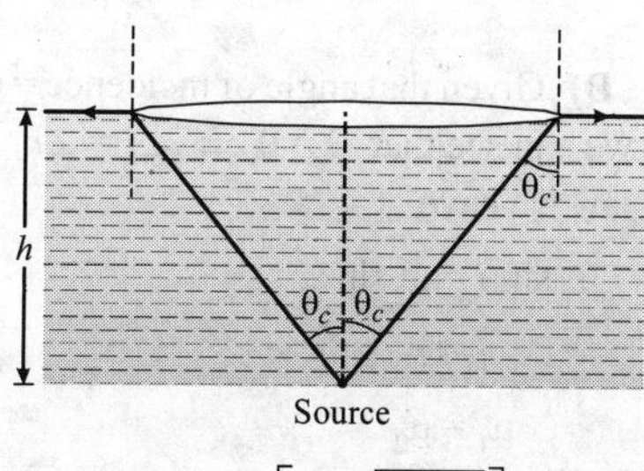

$$f = \frac{1}{2}\left[1 - \sqrt{1 - \frac{1}{\mu^2}}\right]$$

Sol. 21 (A, B) If $d_1 = 120$ cm then by refraction at curved surface, by refraction formula, we have

$$\frac{3}{2v} - \frac{1}{-120} = \frac{\left(\frac{3}{2} - 1\right)}{60}$$

$$\Rightarrow \quad v = \infty$$

Thus parallel light incident normally on mirror and hence image will form on object itself, hence option (A) is correct.

If $d_1 = 240$ cm then using refraction formula we get $v = 360$ cm so if $d_2 = 360$ cm, then plane mirror form image at same place and again final image form on object itself hence option (B) is also correct.

Sol. 22 (B, C) Distance of fish as observed by bird is given as

$$= \frac{0.8}{\left(\frac{4}{3}\right)} + 6 = 6.6 \text{ m}$$

And distance of bird as observed by fish is given as

$$\left(\frac{6}{1} + 0.8\right)\frac{4}{3} = 6.8 \times \frac{4}{3} = 8.8 \text{ m}$$

Sol. 23 (B, C) From figure we can see that

$$AB = \frac{HT}{2} = \frac{170}{2} = 85 \text{ cm}$$

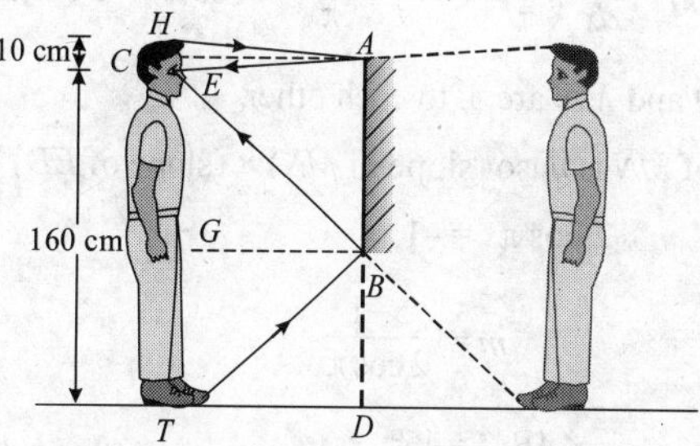

and ΔEBT we have $EG = GT = BD = \frac{160}{2} = 80$ cm

Sol. 24 (All) If the mirrors OM and ON make an angle θ with each other as shown in figure, then we have

$$\angle BLC = 240 - 180 = 60°$$

In ΔABC, we have

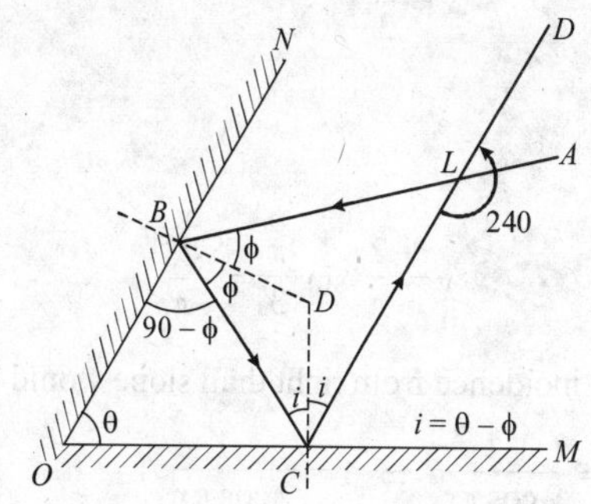

$$2\phi + 2(\theta - \phi) + 60° = 180°$$

$$\Rightarrow \quad 2\phi + 2\theta - 2\phi + 60° = 180°$$

$$\Rightarrow \quad \theta = 60°$$

$$\text{Number of images} = \left(\frac{360°}{60°} - 1\right) = 5$$

Hence all option are correct.

Sol. 25 (A, C) Let us assume that incident ray is AB and Reflected ray is BC

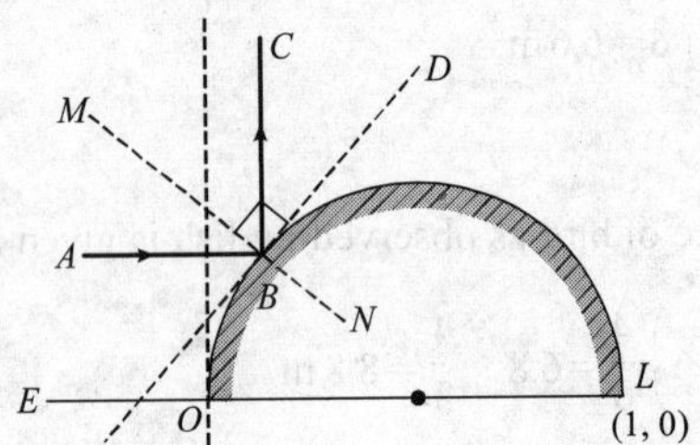

Point of incidence is B

Let as calculate the slope of tangent at point B

$$\frac{d}{dx}(y) = \frac{d}{dx}\left(\frac{2}{\pi}\sin \pi x\right) = \frac{2}{\pi} \times \pi \cos \pi x = 2\cos \pi x$$

Since ED and MN are $\perp$ to each other

If slope of MN is m so (slope of MN) × (slope of ED) = –1

If $\quad m \times 2\cos \pi x = -1$

$$m = \frac{-1}{2\cos \pi x}$$

$$\angle ABM = 45°$$

and $\quad \angle MBC = 45°$

$$\Rightarrow \quad m = \tan 135°$$

$$\tan 135° = \frac{-1}{2\cos \pi x} \quad \Rightarrow \quad \cos \pi x = \frac{1}{2}$$

$$\pi x = \frac{\pi}{3}$$

$$\Rightarrow \quad x = \frac{1}{3}$$

At $x = \frac{1}{3}$

$$\Rightarrow \quad y = \frac{2}{\pi}\sin\frac{\pi}{3} = \frac{\sqrt{3}}{\pi}$$

If light ray is incidence from right than slope would be 45°

$$\Rightarrow \tan 45° = \frac{-1}{2\cos \pi x} \Rightarrow 1 = \frac{-1}{2\cos \pi x}$$

$$\Rightarrow \quad x = \frac{2}{3}$$

$$\Rightarrow \quad y = \frac{2}{\pi}\sin\frac{\pi \times 2}{3} = \frac{\sqrt{3}}{\pi}$$

So points are $\left(\frac{1}{3}, \frac{\sqrt{3}}{\pi}\right)$ and $\left(\frac{2}{3}, \frac{\sqrt{3}}{\pi}\right)$

Sol. 26 (B, C) Since first reflection should be at plane mirror then image of AB would be $A'B'$ which will be equal distance from mirror.

Now image $A'B'$ will behave like object and image will be formed by convex mirror

$f = +60$ cm for convex mirror

$u'_A = -60$ cm (distance of object from mirror)

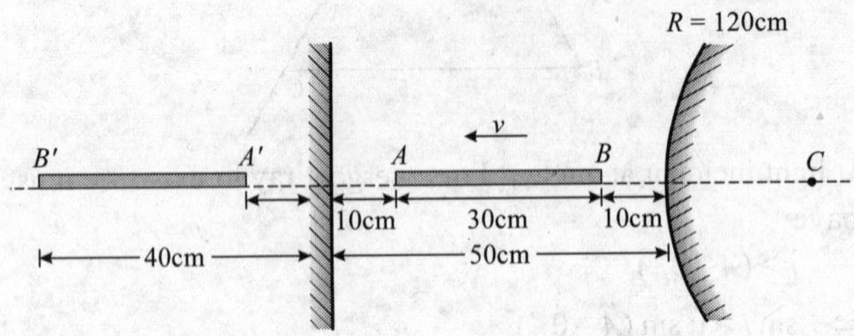

$u'_B = -90$ cm (distance of object from mirror)

$$\Rightarrow \quad v'_A = \frac{uf}{u-f} = \frac{-60 \times 60}{-60-60} = \frac{-60 \times 60}{-120} = 30 \text{ cm}$$

$$\Rightarrow \quad v'_B = \frac{uf}{u-f} = \frac{-90 \times 60}{-90-60} = \frac{-90 \times 60}{-150} = 36 \text{ cm}$$

size of image = 36 – 30 = 6 cm

size of object = 30 cm

overall magnification $= \frac{6}{30} = \frac{1}{5}$.

Sol. 27 (B, C, D) Given that angle of incidence = 60°

When $k = k_0$, we can see that $\theta = 0 \Rightarrow \angle i = \angle r$

Using Snell's law we have

$$\mu_1 \sin i = \mu_2 \sin r$$

If $\quad i = r$

$$\Rightarrow \quad \mu_1 = \mu_2$$

$$\Rightarrow \quad \frac{\mu_1}{\mu_2} = 1$$

$$\Rightarrow \quad k_0 = 1$$

Before k_1 i.e. $k < k_1$ value of $\theta = 0$

So this is the condition of total internal reflection

So $\quad \sin\theta_C = \frac{\mu_1}{\mu_2} = \sin\frac{\pi}{3}$

$$\Rightarrow \quad k_1 = \frac{\mu_1}{\mu_2} = \frac{\sqrt{3}}{2}$$

Value of $\theta_1 = |r - i| = |90° - 60°| = \frac{\pi}{6}$

When $k = \infty$ then $\theta = \theta_2$ In this situation after refraction ray will travel along the normal

So, we have $\quad i = \frac{\pi}{3};\ r = 0$

$$\Rightarrow \quad \theta_2 = |r - i| = \left|0 - \frac{\pi}{3}\right| = \frac{\pi}{3}$$

Sol. 28 (B, C, D) For deviation angle δ to be minimum, we need

$$i = e$$

$$\Rightarrow \quad r_1 = r_2$$

$$\Rightarrow \quad r_1 + r_2 = A$$

$$\Rightarrow \quad r_1 = 30°$$

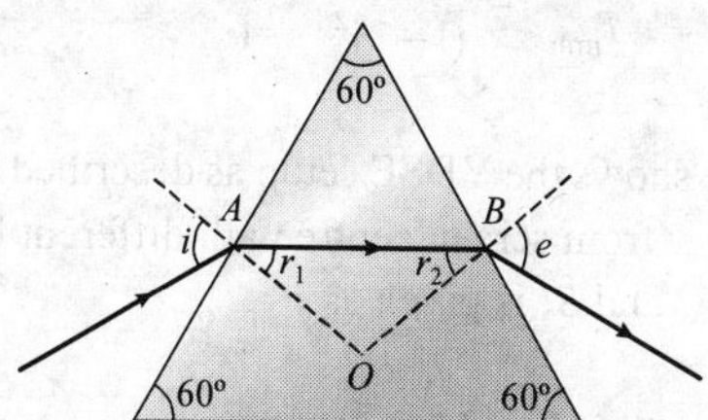

If r_1 = 30° then ray AB must be parallel to base of prism for minimum deviation so there can be only single angle of deviation but for other deviation angles there can be two angle of incidence (θ_1, θ_3). Figure below shows the variation of deviation angle with angle of incidence.

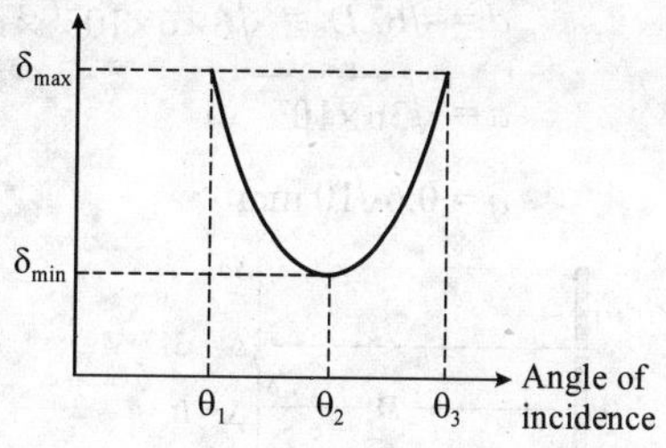

In general for small angled prism, we have

$$\delta = (\mu - 1)A$$

Where we can see that as μ increases, δ also increases.

Sol. 29 (B, C) Using lens formula for refraction through the lens, we have

$$\frac{1}{v} - \frac{1}{u} = \frac{1}{f}$$

$$\Rightarrow \quad v = \frac{uf}{u+f} = \frac{-15\times 30}{-15+30} = \frac{-15\times 30}{15} = -30 \text{ cm}$$

By reflection at plane mirror image would be produced at a distance 45 cm behind the mirror which is 60 cm from lens and it will again act as an object for refraction through the lens, so again by lens formula we use

$$v = \frac{uf}{u+f} = \frac{60\times -30}{60-30} = -60 \text{ cm}$$

Thus final image will be real and located 60 cm to the left of lens.

Sol. 30 (A) For $u = \frac{-3F}{4}$ image position can be obtained by lens formula as

$$\frac{1}{v} - \frac{1}{u} = \frac{1}{f}$$

$$\Rightarrow \quad v = \frac{uf}{u+f} = \frac{-(3F/4)\times(F)}{-3F/4+F} = \frac{-3F/4\times F}{F/4} = -3F$$

Now for $u = -\frac{F}{2}$, image position will be given as

$$v = \frac{uf}{u+f} = \frac{-f/2\times F}{-f/2+F} = \frac{-F^2/2}{+F/2} = -F$$

$$\text{Speed of image} = \left(\frac{-3F+F}{t}\right) = -\frac{2F}{t}$$

We can find the image coordinate for $\frac{F}{2}$ and $\frac{F}{4}$ and we can find that image speed will be more in previous case.

Statement-(ii) we have already studied in displacement method experiment and is correct.

Sol. 31 (B, C) The given case is that of displacement method experiment in which we have studied that minimum distance between a real object and its real image produced by a convex lens is $4f$ so we have $d > 4f$.

In experiment there are two positions of the lens for which sharp images are obtained on the screen for which the product of magnification is unity, thus we have

$$M_1 M_2 = 1$$

* * * * *

ANSWERS & SOLUTIONS

CONCEPTUAL MCQS Single Option Correct

1	(D)	2	(C)	3	(B)
4	(A)	5	(C)	6	(C)
7	(B)	8	(A)	9	(B)
10	(C)	11	(A)	12	(A)
13	(D)	14	(C)	15	(A)
16	(D)	17	(B)	18	(C)
19	(A)	20	(C)	21	(A)
22	(C)	23	(C)	24	(A)
25	(B)	26	(B)	27	(B)
28	(C)	29	(B)	30	(B)
31	(C)	32	(B)	33	(C)
34	(D)	35	(A)		

NUMERICAL MCQS Single Option Correct

1	(B)	2	(A)	3	(C)
4	(D)	5	(C)	6	(C)
7	(C)	8	(B)	9	(B)
10	(D)	11	(B)	12	(A)
13	(B)	14	(A)	15	(B)
16	(C)	17	(B)	18	(C)
19	(D)	20	(D)	21	(B)
22	(D)	23	(C)	24	(A)
25	(B)	26	(C)	27	(C)
28	(D)	29	(C)	30	(B)
31	(A)	32	(A)	33	(C)
34	(D)	35	(B)	36	(A)
37	(B)	38	(D)	39	(B)
40	(D)	41	(B)	42	(D)
43	(D)	44	(C)	45	(A)
46	(C)	47	(C)	48	(D)
49	(B)				

ADVANCE MCQs One or More Options Correct

1	(A, C, D)	2	(B, D)	3	(B, C, D)
4	(A, C)	5	(B, C)	6	(C)
7	(A, D)	8	(C)	9	(A, C)
10	(B, C)	11	(All)	12	(A, C, D)
13	(A, C, D)	14	(B, C)	15	(A, C)

Solutions of PRACTICE EXERCISE 6.1

(i) The intensity of the wave is proportional to the area of the slit. Thus we can use the intensities I_1 and I_2 from the slits on screen are in ratio

$$\frac{I_1}{I_2} = \frac{b_1 l}{b_2 l} = \frac{b_1}{b_2} = \frac{1}{4}$$

If a_1 and a_2 are the amplitudes of the waves, then we have

$$\frac{I_1}{I_2} = \frac{a_1^2}{a_2^2} = \frac{1}{4}$$

$$\Rightarrow \quad \frac{a_1}{a_2} = \frac{1}{2}$$

The ratio of maximum to minimum intensity is given as

$$\frac{I_{max}}{I_{min}} = \frac{(a_1+a_2)^2}{(a_1-a_2)^2}$$

$$\Rightarrow \quad \frac{I_{max}}{I_{min}} = \frac{(1+2)^2}{(1-2)^2} = \frac{9}{1}$$

(ii) Figure shows the YDSE setup as described in question. At a distance x from screen centre path different between the waves from S_1 and S_2 is given as

$$\Delta = \frac{dx}{D}$$

As it is given that at $x = d/2$, path difference is given as 3λ because third bright fringe is located in front of one slit on screen. Thus we use

$$\frac{d^2}{2D} = 3\lambda$$

$$\Rightarrow \quad d = \sqrt{6\lambda D} = \sqrt{6\times 6\times 10^{-7}\times 1}$$

$$\Rightarrow \quad d = \sqrt{36\times 10^{-7}} \text{ m}$$

$$\Rightarrow \quad d = 0.6\sqrt{10} \text{ mm}$$

(iii) **(a)** Just above point O the direct waves from source and reflected waves have a phase difference π due to reflection from mirror so these wave interfere destructively so there will be dark fringe at O, therefore intensity of light at O will be zero.

(b) From the figure, we can see that the distance of first maximum (first bright fringe) from O will be located at half fringe width above, so we have

$$y = \frac{\beta}{2} = \left(\frac{D\lambda/2d}{2}\right)$$

$$\Rightarrow \quad y = \frac{D\lambda}{4d}$$

(iv) We know that intensities due to slits is directly proportional to the area of slits or proportional to the width of slits as these are of equal lengths hence we use

$$\frac{I_1}{I_2} = \frac{9}{4}$$

Ratios of maximum to minimum intensity on screen is given as

$$\frac{I_{max}}{I_{min}} = \left(\frac{\sqrt{I_1}+\sqrt{I_2}}{\sqrt{I_1}-\sqrt{I_2}}\right)^2 = \left(\frac{3+2}{3-2}\right)^2$$

$$\Rightarrow \quad \frac{I_{max}}{I_{min}} = 25$$

(v) (a) Figure shows the calculation of path difference on screen at a general point R which is located at a distance y_2 from the center Q

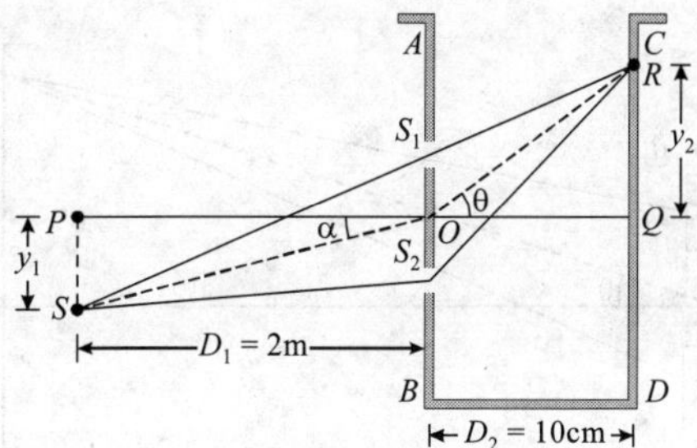

In above figure angles α and θ are given as

$$\tan\alpha = \frac{1}{5} \text{ and } \tan\theta = \frac{y_2}{10}$$

As slit separation is small compared to D_1 and D_2 in figure, we can use that difference between SS_1 and SS_2 is

$$\Delta_1 = SS_1 - SS_2$$

$$\Rightarrow \quad \Delta_1 = d\sin\alpha = (0.8\text{ mm})\left(\frac{1}{5}\right)$$

$$\Rightarrow \quad \Delta_1 = 0.16\text{ mm} \qquad \ldots(1)$$

If at point R on the screen, central bright fringe is observed then at this point the path different in waves before slit plane and after slit plane must cancel each other.

Path difference between S_2R and S_1R would be

$$\Delta_2 = S_2R - S_1R$$

$$\Rightarrow \quad \Delta_2 = d\sin\alpha \qquad \ldots(2)$$

Central bright fringe will be observed when net path difference is zero, thus we use

$$\Rightarrow \quad \Delta_2 - \Delta_1 = 0$$

$$\Rightarrow \quad d\sin\theta = 0.16$$

$$\Rightarrow \quad \sin\theta = \frac{0.16}{0.8} = \frac{1}{5}$$

$$\Rightarrow \quad \tan\theta = \frac{1}{\sqrt{24}}$$

Thus we use

$$\tan\theta = \frac{y_2}{D_2} = \frac{1}{\sqrt{24}}$$

$$\Rightarrow \quad y_2 = \frac{D_2}{5} = \frac{10}{\sqrt{24}} = 2.04\text{ cm}$$

Thus, central bright fringe is observed at 2.04 cm above point Q on side CD of the vessel.

(b) The central bright fringe will be observed at point Q if the path difference created by the liquid of thickness $t = 10$ cm is equal to Δ_1, so that the net path difference at Q becomes zero. Figure shows the situation after vessel is filled with the liquid.

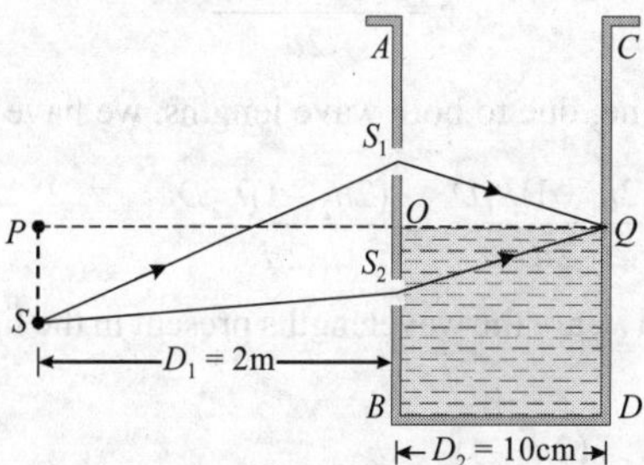

The path difference in waves reaching at Q after the slit plane is given as $(\mu - 1)t$, thus to obtain central bright fringe at Q, we have

$$(\mu - 1)t = \Delta_1$$

$$\Rightarrow \quad (\mu - 1)(100) = 0.16$$

$$\Rightarrow \quad \mu - 1 = 0.0016$$

$$\Rightarrow \quad \mu = 1.0016$$

(vi) (a) Phase difference in the two waves reaching at C from the two slits must be zero for central bright fringe to be obtained at C. Here the phase difference is given as

$$\Delta\phi = \frac{2\pi}{\lambda} d\sin\phi - \frac{2\pi}{\lambda} t\,({}_{w}\mu_m - 1)$$

Where first term in above expression is the phase difference due to the path difference d sin f which is there before the slit plane due to inclined incidence of the light beam as shown in figure. The second term here is the phase difference due to the path difference introduced by the thin mica film. Thus for central maxima at C, we use

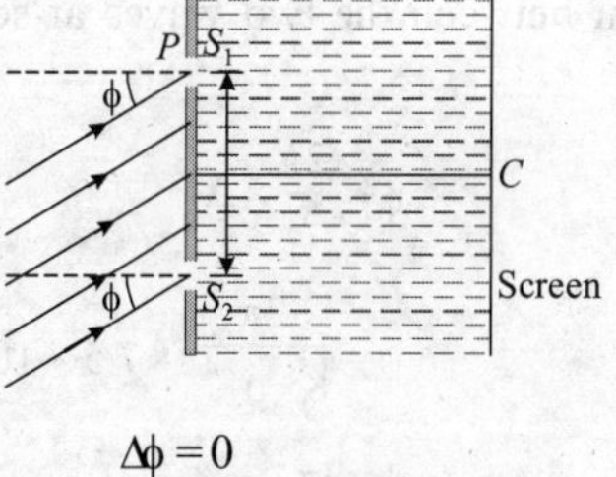

$$\Delta\phi = 0$$

$\Rightarrow \quad t = \dfrac{d\sin\varphi}{({}_w\mu_m - 1)}$

$\Rightarrow \quad \dfrac{2\times10^{-3}\times\sin 30°}{({}_w\mu_m - 1)} = 5\times10^{-3}$

$\Rightarrow \quad {}_w\mu_m = 1.2$

$\Rightarrow \quad \mu_m = 1.2\times\mu_w = 1.2\times(4/3) = 1.6$

Hence refractive index of mica slab = 1.6

(b) A black line is formed at the position where dark fringe is formed for both the wavelength. Thus distance of the first dark fringe from center bright fringe is

$$y = \frac{(2n-1)\lambda D}{2d} \quad \ldots(i)$$

For black line, due to both wave lengths, we have

$$\frac{(2n_1-1)\lambda_1 D}{2d} = \frac{(2n_2-1)\lambda_2 D}{2d}$$

Here λ_1 and λ_2 are the wavelengths present in the light beam in the water

$\Rightarrow \quad \dfrac{(2n_1-1)}{(2n_2-1)} = \dfrac{\lambda_2}{\lambda_1};$

Where $\quad \lambda_1 = \dfrac{\lambda_{10}}{\mu_\omega}$ and $\lambda_2 = \dfrac{\lambda_{20}}{\mu_\omega}$

$\Rightarrow \quad \dfrac{(2n_1-1)}{(3n_2-1)} = \dfrac{7}{5}$

For first line we choose minimum values of n_1 and n_2, taken as

$$n_1 = 4 \text{ and } n_2 = 3$$

Hence distance of the first black line from center is

$$y = \frac{(2\times4-1)4000\times10^{-10}\times40\times10^{-2}\times3}{2\times2\times10^{-3}\times4}$$

$\Rightarrow \quad y = 2.1\times10^{-4}\,\text{m} = 210\,\mu\text{m}$

(vii) Path difference due to insertion of a thin film at screen centre is given as

$$\Delta = t(\mu-1)$$

$\Rightarrow \quad \Delta = 1.5\times10^{-6}\times0.5$

$\Rightarrow \quad \Delta = 7.5\times10^{-7}\,\text{m}$

Phase different between the two waves at screen centre is given as

$$\phi = \frac{2\pi}{\lambda}\times\Delta$$

$\Rightarrow \quad \phi = \dfrac{2\pi}{8\times\mu^{-4}}\times7.5\times10^{-7}$

$\Rightarrow \quad \phi = 3\pi$

Thus resulting intensity at C is given as

$$I_R = 4I_0\cos^2(\phi/2) = 0$$

(viii) Figure shows the two waves from the two slits reaching point P on screen. If this point is the position of zero order maxima and the distance of P from the centre O of the screen is y_0, so the optical path of light waves from source S_1 is given as

$$x_1 = S_1P + (\mu_1 - 1)t_1$$

The optical path of light waves from source S_2

$$x_2 = S_2P + (\mu_2 - 1)t_2$$

The path difference between the two waves reaching at P is

$$\Delta x = x_2 - x_1$$

$$= (S_2P - S_1P) + (\mu_2 - 1)t_2 - (\mu_1 - 1)t_1$$

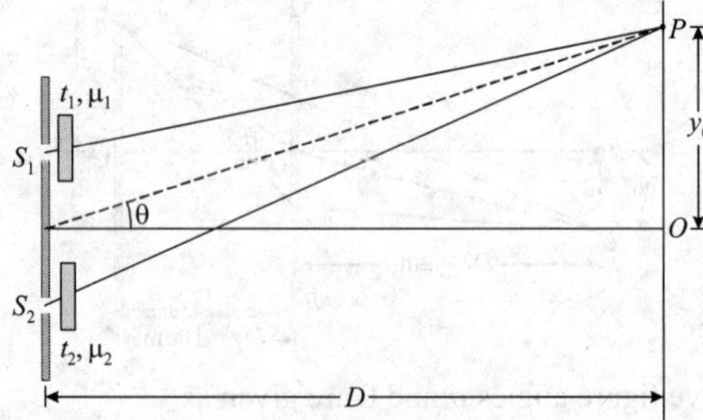

As we know the physical path difference from slits to a point on screen is given as

$$S_2P - S_1P = d\sin\theta \simeq \frac{dy_0}{D}$$

$\Rightarrow \quad \Delta x = \dfrac{dy_0}{D} + (\mu_2 - 1)t_2 - (\mu_1 - 1)t_1$

For zero order maxima, $\Delta x = 0$

$\Rightarrow \quad 0 = \dfrac{dy_0}{D} + (\mu_2 - 1)t_2 - (\mu_1 - 1)t_1$

$\Rightarrow \quad y_0 = \dfrac{D[(\mu_1-1)t_1 - (\mu_2-1)t_2]}{d}$

For find the condition for zero order maxima at the centre O, we use

$$y_0 = 0$$

$\Rightarrow \quad 0 = \dfrac{D[(\mu_1-1)t_1 - (\mu_2-1)t_2]}{d}$

$\Rightarrow \quad (\mu_1 - 1)t_1 = (\mu_2 - 1)t_2$

(ix) In this setup of *YDSE*, we can use

$$d = 2\,\text{mm} = 2\times10^{-3}\,\text{m}$$

$$D = 1.2\,\text{m}$$

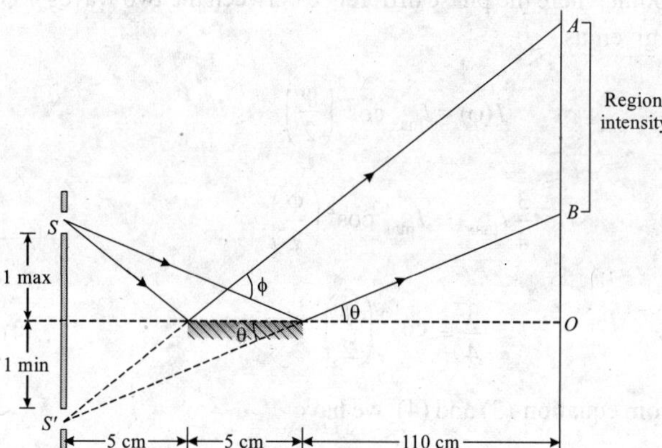

Fringe width in *YDSE* or similar setup is given as

$$\beta = \frac{\lambda D}{d} = \frac{6\times10^{-7}\times1.2}{2\times10^{-3}m}$$

$$\Rightarrow \qquad \beta = 3.6\times10^{-4}\,\text{m}$$

$$\Rightarrow \qquad \beta = 0.36\,\text{mm}$$

Width of interference pattern on screen is given as

$$AB = OA - OB \qquad \ldots(1)$$

Here by similar triangles, we use

$$\frac{OB}{110} = \frac{0.1}{10}$$

$$\Rightarrow \qquad OB = 1.10\,\text{cm}$$

And we also have

$$\frac{OA}{115} = \frac{0.1}{5}$$

$$\Rightarrow \qquad OA = 2.3\,\text{cm}$$

Now from equation-(1), we have

$$AB = 2.3 - 1.1$$

$$= 1.2\,\text{cm}$$

(x) (a) For the lens formula, we use

$u = -0.15$ m and $f = +0.10$ m

By using lens formula, we have

$$\frac{1}{v} - \frac{1}{u} = \frac{1}{f}$$

$$\Rightarrow \qquad \frac{1}{v} = \frac{1}{u} + \frac{1}{f} = \frac{1}{(-0.15)} + \frac{1}{(0.10)}$$

$$\Rightarrow \qquad v = +0.3\,\text{m}$$

In this case lateral magnification by the lens is

$$m = \frac{v}{u} = \frac{0.3}{-0.15} = -2$$

Thus by the two lenses, two images S_1 and S_2 of S will be formed at 0.3 m from the lens as shown in the figure. Image S_1 is due to part 1 which will be formed at 0.5 mm above its optical axis ($m = -2$). Similarly the image S_2 which is due to part 2 is formed 0.5 mm below the optical axis of this part as shown.

Now the light waves from S_1 and S_2 will interfere on screen like a *YDSE* or an equivalent setup for which the separation between S_1 and S_2 is 1.5 mm and separation between the sources and screen is given as

$$D = 1.30 - 0.30 = 1.0\,\text{m} = 10^3\,\text{mm};$$

Light wavelength is

$$\lambda = 500\,\text{nm} = 5\times10^{-4}\,\text{mm}$$

Thus fringe width is given as

$$\beta = \frac{\lambda D}{d} = \frac{(5\times10^{-4})(10^3)}{(1.5)}\,\text{mm} = \frac{1}{3}\,\text{mm}$$

As it is given that the point A is at the third maxima, we use

$$OA = 3\beta = 3\,(1/3)\,\text{mm}$$

$$\Rightarrow \qquad OA = 1\,\text{mm}$$

(b) If the gap between L_1 and L_2 is reduced, d will decrease. Hence, the fringe width will increase so the distance OA will increase.

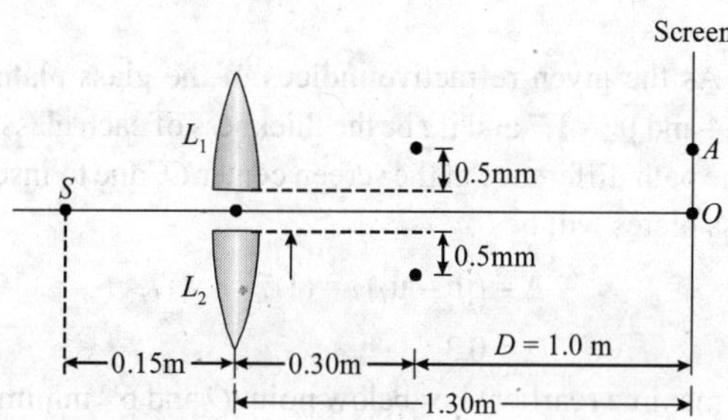

(xi) (a) Path difference due to insertion of the glass slab is given as

$$\Rightarrow \qquad \Delta = (\mu - 1)t = (1.5 - 1)t = 0.5t$$

Due to this slab, 5 red fringes have been shifted upwards so we use

$$\Delta = 5\lambda_{red}$$

$$\Rightarrow \qquad 0.5t = (5)(7\times10^{7}\,\text{m})$$

$$\Rightarrow \qquad t = 7\times10^{-6}\,\text{m}$$

(b) Let μ' be the refractive index of glass for green light then we have

$$\Delta' = (\mu' - 1)t$$

Now shift is equal to that of 6 fringes of red light so we use

$$\Delta' = 6\lambda_{red}$$

$$\Rightarrow \qquad t(\mu - 1) = 6\lambda_{red}$$

$$\Rightarrow \quad (\mu'-1)=\frac{(6)\times(7\times10^{-7})}{7\times10^{-6}}=0.6$$

$$\Rightarrow \quad \mu'=1.6$$

(c) In part (a), shifting of 5 bright fringes was equal to 10^{-3} m, which implies that

$$5\beta_{red}=10^{-3}\text{ m}$$

$$\Rightarrow \quad \beta_{red}=\frac{10^{-3}}{5}\text{ m}=0.2\times10^{-3}\text{ m}$$

As fringe width is given as

$$\beta=\frac{\lambda D}{d}$$

We can use

$$\frac{\beta_{green}}{\beta_{red}}=\frac{\lambda_{green}}{\lambda_{red}}$$

$$\Rightarrow \quad \beta_{green}=\beta_{red}\frac{\lambda_{green}}{\lambda_{red}}=(0.2\times10^{-3})\left(\frac{5\times10^{-7}}{7\times10^{-7}}\right)$$

$$\Rightarrow \quad \beta_{green}=0.143\times10^{-3}\text{ m}$$

$$\Rightarrow \quad \Delta\beta=\beta_{green}-\beta_{red}=(0.143-0.2)\times10^{-3}\text{ m}$$

$$\Rightarrow \quad \Delta\beta=-5.71\times10^{-5}\text{ m}$$

(xii) As the given refractive indices of the glass plates are $\mu_1=1.4$ and $\mu_2=1.7$ and if t be the thickness of each glass plate then the path difference at the screen center O, due to insertion of glass plates will be

$$\Delta=(\mu_2-\mu_1)t=(1.7-1.4)t$$

$$\Rightarrow \quad \Delta=0.3t \quad \ldots(1)$$

As 5th maxima (earlier) lies below point O and 6th minima lies above point O, this path difference must lie between 5λ and 5.5λ. This situation is shown in figure.

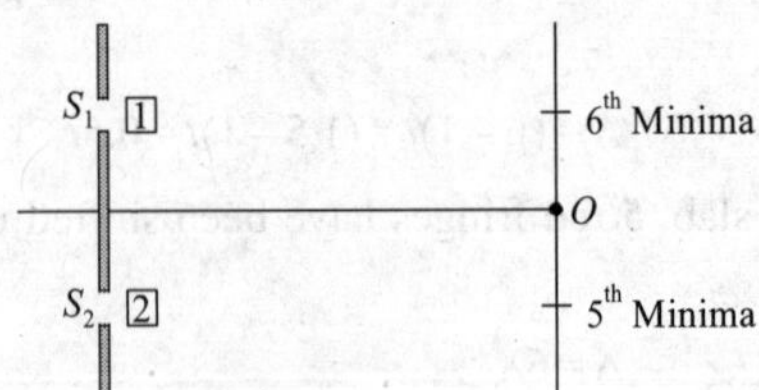

Due to the path difference Δ, the phase difference at O will be

$$\phi=\frac{2\pi}{\lambda}\Delta=\frac{2\pi}{\lambda}(5\lambda+\Delta_1)$$

$$\Rightarrow \quad \phi=\left(10\pi+\frac{2\pi}{\lambda}\Delta_1\right) \quad \ldots(3)$$

In above equation Δ_1 is considered less than $\lambda/2$.

Intensity at point O is given $\frac{3}{4}I_{max}$ so we use the intensity at a point where the phase difference between the two waves is φ is given as

$$I(\varphi)=I_{max}\cos^2\left(\frac{\varphi}{2}\right)$$

$$\Rightarrow \quad \frac{3}{4}I_{max}=I_{max}\cos^2\left(\frac{\varphi}{2}\right),$$

$$\Rightarrow \quad \frac{3}{4}=\cos^2\left(\frac{\varphi}{2}\right) \quad \ldots(4)$$

From equation-(3) and (4), we have

$$\Delta_1=\frac{\lambda}{6}$$

$$\Rightarrow \quad \Delta=5\lambda+\frac{\lambda}{6}=\frac{31}{6}\lambda=0.3t$$

Solving, we get

$$t=\frac{31\lambda}{6(0.3)}=\frac{(31)(5400\times10^{-10})}{1.8}\text{ m},$$

$$\Rightarrow \quad t=9.3\times10^{-6}\text{ m}=9.3\ \mu\text{m}$$

(xiii) For the setup given values are – $\lambda=0.5$ mm, $d=1.0$ mm and $D=1$ m

(a) When the incident beam falls normally the path difference between the two waves S_2P and S_1P is,

$$\Delta=S_2P-S_1P\approx d\sin\theta$$

For minimum intensity, we use

$$d\sin\theta=(2n-1)\frac{\lambda}{2},\ n=1,2,3,\ldots$$

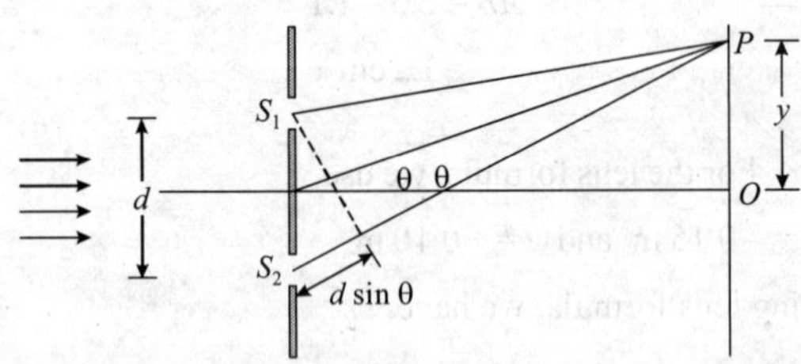

$$\Rightarrow \quad \sin\theta=\frac{(2n-1)\lambda}{2d}=\frac{(2n-1)0.5}{2\times1.0}=\frac{2n-1}{4}$$

As $\sin\theta\le1$ therefore $\frac{(2n-1)}{4}\le1$ or $n\le2.5$,

$\Rightarrow$ So, n can be either 1 or 2

For $n=1$, we have

$$\sin\theta_1=\frac{1}{4}$$

$$\Rightarrow \quad \tan\theta_1 = \frac{1}{\sqrt{15}}$$

When $n = 2$, we have

$$\sin\theta_2 = \frac{3}{4}$$

$$\Rightarrow \quad \tan\theta_2 = \frac{3}{\sqrt{7}}$$

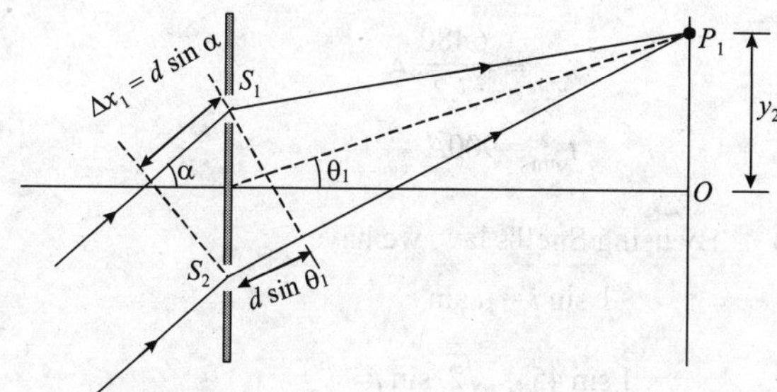

[In this case, net path difference $\Delta x = \Delta x_1 - \Delta x_2$]

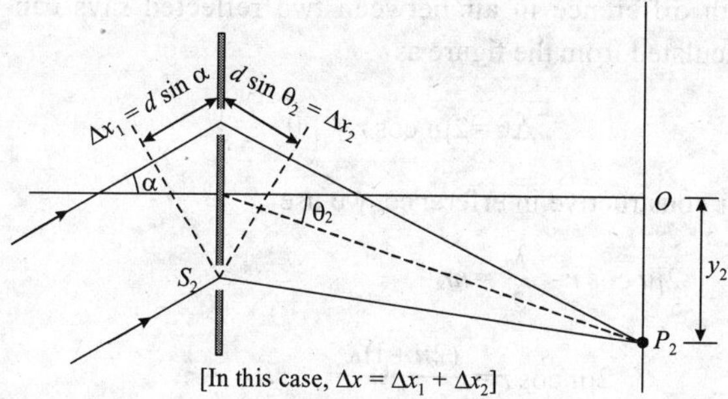

[In this case, $\Delta x = \Delta x_1 + \Delta x_2$]

$$\Rightarrow \quad y = D\tan\theta = \tan\theta \; (D = 1\text{ m})$$

So, the position of minima will be :

$$y_1 = \tan\theta_1 = \frac{1}{\sqrt{15}}\text{ m} = 0.26\text{ m}$$

and
$$y_2 = \tan\theta_2 = \frac{3}{\sqrt{7}}\text{ m} = 1.13\text{ m}$$

And as minima can be on either side of centre O. Therefore there will be four minimas at position ± 0.26 m and ± 1.13 m on the screen.

(b) When $\alpha = 30°$, path difference between the rays before reaching S_1 and S_2 is

$$\Delta_1 = d\sin\alpha = (1.0)\sin 30° = 0.5\text{ mm} = \lambda$$

So, there is already a path difference of λ between the rays. Central maximum is defined as a point where net path difference is zero. So we use

$$\Delta_1 = \Delta_2$$

$$\Rightarrow \quad d\sin\alpha = d\sin\theta$$

$$\Rightarrow \quad \theta = \alpha = 30°$$

$$\Rightarrow \quad \tan\theta = \frac{1}{\sqrt{3}} = \frac{y_0}{D}$$

$$\Rightarrow \quad y_0 = \frac{1}{\sqrt{3}}\text{ m} \; [D = 1\text{ m}]$$

$$y_0 = 0.58\text{ m}$$

At point P, $\quad \Delta x_1 = \Delta x_2$

Above P $\quad \Delta x_2 > \Delta x_1$ and

Below point P $\quad \Delta x_1 > \Delta x_2$

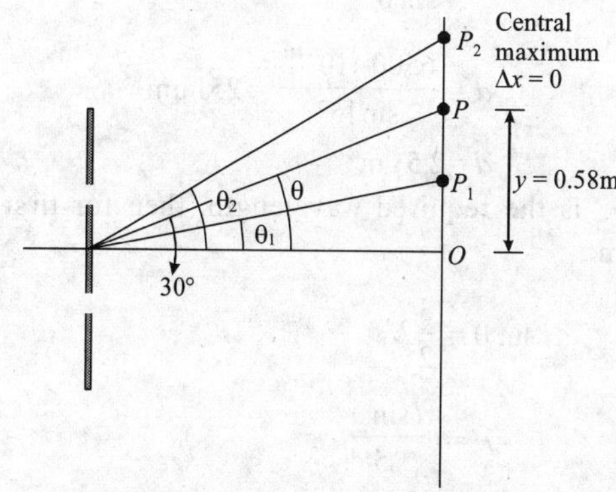

Now, let P_1 and P_2 be the minimas on either side of central maxima. Then, for P_2

$$\Delta_2 = \Delta_1 + \frac{\lambda}{2}$$

$$\Rightarrow \quad \Delta_2 = \Delta_1 + \frac{\lambda}{2} = \lambda + \frac{\lambda}{2} = \frac{3\lambda}{2}$$

$$\Rightarrow \quad d\sin\theta_2 = \frac{3\lambda}{2}$$

$$\Rightarrow \quad \sin\theta_2 = \frac{3\lambda}{2d} = \frac{(3)(0.5)}{(2)(1.0)} = \frac{3}{4}$$

$$\Rightarrow \quad \tan\theta_2 = \frac{3}{\sqrt{7}} = \frac{y_2}{D}$$

$$\Rightarrow \quad y_2 = \frac{3}{\sqrt{7}}\text{ m} = 1.13\text{ m}$$

Similarly for point P_1, we use

$$\Delta_1 - \Delta_2 = \frac{\lambda}{2}$$

$$\Rightarrow \quad \Delta_2 = \Delta_1 - \frac{\lambda}{2} = \lambda - \frac{\lambda}{2} = \frac{\lambda}{2}$$

$$\Rightarrow \quad d\sin\theta_1 = \frac{\lambda}{2}$$

$$\Rightarrow \quad \sin\theta_1 = \frac{\lambda}{2d} = \frac{(0.5)}{(2)(1.0)} = \frac{1}{4}$$

$$\Rightarrow \quad \tan\theta_1 = \frac{1}{\sqrt{15}} = \frac{y_1}{D}$$

$$\Rightarrow \quad y_1 = \frac{1}{\sqrt{15}}\text{ m} = 0.26\text{ m}$$

Therefore, y-coordinates of the first minima on either side of the central maximum are

$$y_1 = 0.26\text{ m} \text{ and } y_2 = 1.13\text{ m}$$

Note : In this problem the relation

$$\sin\theta \approx \tan\theta \approx \theta \text{ is not valid as } \theta \text{ is large}$$

(xiv) (a) For first minima, we have

$$d\sin\theta = \lambda$$

$$d = \frac{\lambda}{\sin\theta}$$

$$\Rightarrow \quad d = \frac{6500\times10^{-10}}{\sin 15^\circ} = 251\ \mu\text{m}$$

$$\Rightarrow \quad d = 2.5\ \mu\text{m}$$

(b) If λ' is the required wavelength, then for first order maximum

$$d\sin\theta = \frac{3}{2}\lambda'$$

$$\lambda' = \frac{d\sin\theta}{1.5}$$

$$\Rightarrow \quad \lambda' = \frac{2511\times\sin 15^\circ}{1.5}$$

$$\Rightarrow \quad \lambda' = 4300\text{Å}$$

Solutions of PRACTICE EXERCISE 6.2

(i) Incident ray AB is partly reflected as ray 1 from the upper surface and partly reflected as ray 2 from the lower surface of the layer of thickness t and refractive index μ_1 = 1.8 as shown in the figure. Path difference between the two rays would be given as

$$\Delta = 2\mu_1 t$$

$$\Rightarrow \quad \Delta = 2(1.8)t = 3.6\,t$$

Ray 1 is reflected from a denser medium, therefore, it undergoes a phase change of π, whereas the ray 2 gets reflected from a rarer medium, therefore, there is no change in phase of ray 2. Hence, phase difference between rays 1 and 2 would be $\phi = \pi$. Therefore, condition of constructive interference would be

$$\Delta = \left(n - \frac{1}{2}\right)\lambda$$

Where $\quad n = 1, 2, 3 \ldots$

$$\Rightarrow \quad 3.6t = \left(n - \frac{1}{2}\right)\lambda$$

Least values of t is corresponding to $n = 1$ so we get

$$t_{\min} = \frac{\lambda}{2\times3.6}$$

$$\Rightarrow \quad t_{\min} = \frac{6480}{7.2}\text{Å}$$

$$\Rightarrow \quad t_{\min} = 900\text{Å}$$

(ii) By using Snell's law, we have

$$1\sin i = \mu\sin r$$

$$\Rightarrow \quad 1\sin 45 = \sqrt{2}\,\sin r$$

$$\Rightarrow \quad r = 30^\circ$$

Path difference in air between two reflected rays can be calculated from the figure as

$$\Delta x = 2\mu t\cos r + \left(0 - \frac{\lambda}{2}\right)$$

For constructive interference, we use

$$2\mu t\cos r - \frac{\lambda}{2} = n\lambda$$

$$\Rightarrow \quad 2\mu t\cos r = \frac{(2n+1)\lambda}{2}$$

$$\Rightarrow \quad t = \frac{(2n+1)\lambda}{4\mu\cos r}$$

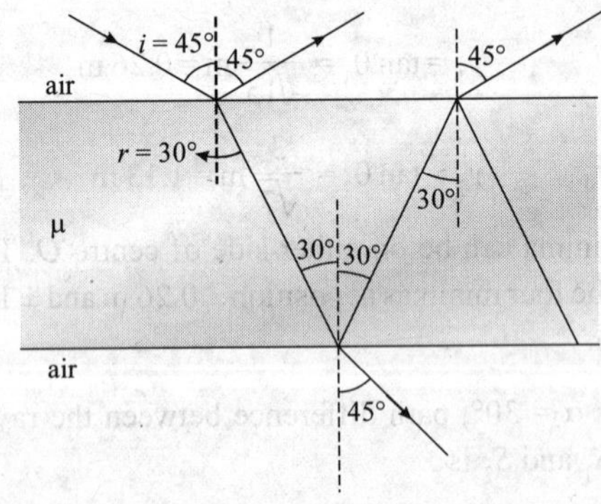

For minimum thickness we use $n = 0$, so we get

$$\Rightarrow \quad t_{\min} = \frac{\lambda}{4\mu\cos r} \quad \text{for minimum thickness}$$

$$\Rightarrow \quad t_{\min} = \frac{\lambda}{4\sqrt{2}\times\frac{\sqrt{3}}{2}} = \frac{\lambda}{2\sqrt{6}} = 1224\text{Å}$$

(iii) Path difference in the two waves constituting the reflected light at normal incidence is given as

$$\Delta = 2\mu t - \frac{\lambda}{2}$$

For destructive interference when the film appears dark we use

$$\Delta = 2\mu t - \frac{\lambda}{2} = (2N-1)\frac{\lambda}{2}$$

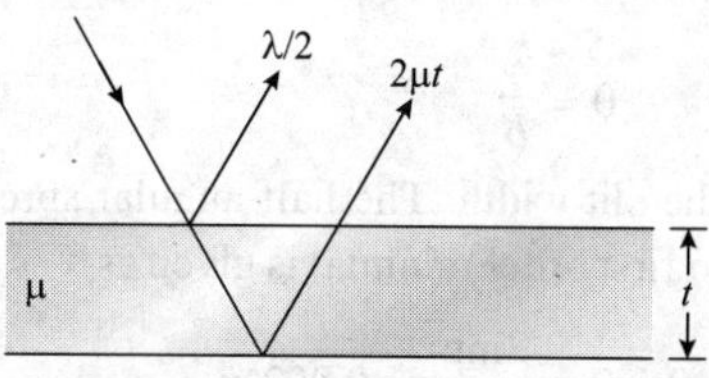

$\Rightarrow \quad 2\mu t = N\lambda$

$\Rightarrow \quad \mu = \frac{N\lambda}{2t} = \frac{N \times 5800 \times 10^{-7}}{2 \times 1.1 \times 10^{-6}}$

$\Rightarrow \quad \mu = 0.263\, N$

Where we use $\quad N = 1, 2, 3,$

As per the given condition on refractive index $1.2 < \mu < 1.5$

We get refractive index in the given range at $N = 5$

$$\mu = 1.318$$

(iv) As indicated in the figure only one of the reflected ray suffers a phase inversion. As already discussed we ignore the reflections from top surface of top plate and bottom surface of bottom plate due to plate thickness. At the thin end of the wedge, where the thickness is negligible, the two rays interfere destructively. This region is dark in the reflected light. The condition for destructive interference in the reflected light is

$$2t = N\lambda$$

Where $\quad N = 0, 1, 2, \ldots$

The change in thickness between adjacent dark fringes is $\Delta t = \lambda/2$. The horizontal spacing between fringes is given as $d = 1/12$ cm $= 8.3 \times 10^{-4}$ m. From figure we can see by similarity in triangles that $D/L = \Delta t/d$, thus we have

$$\Delta = \frac{\lambda L}{2d} = \frac{(5.5 \times 10^{-7} m)(0.2m)}{16.6 \times 10^{-4} m}$$

$\Rightarrow \quad D = 6.6 \times 10^{-5}$ m

(v) For strong reflection of a colour, its wavelength reflected from top and bottom surface of film must interfere constructively fo which the path difference in the two waves must be an integral multiple of the wavelength

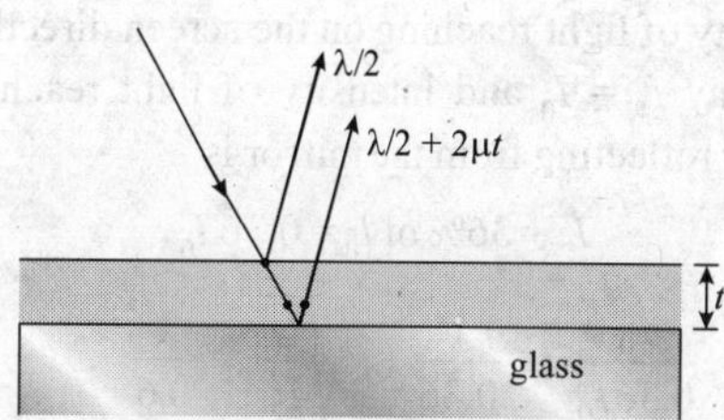

As shown in figure, the path difference in the two waves reflected from the film is given as

$$\Delta = 2\mu t = N\lambda$$

$\Rightarrow \quad \lambda = \frac{2\mu t}{N} = \frac{2 \times 1.5 \times 3 \times 10^{-7}}{N}$

$\Rightarrow \quad \lambda = \frac{9000 \text{Å}}{N}$ for $N = 1, 2, 3\ldots$

$\Rightarrow \quad \lambda = 9000$Å, 4500Å, 3000Å …

White light approximately ranges from 4000Å to 8000Å so here light of wavelength 4500Å will be strongly reflected by this film.

(vi) According to the given condition in question, Intensity of ray AB, $I_1 = \frac{I_0}{5}$, and Intensity of ray $A'B'$ is given corresponding to 20% reflection at each surface as

$$I_2 = \frac{16 I_0}{125}$$

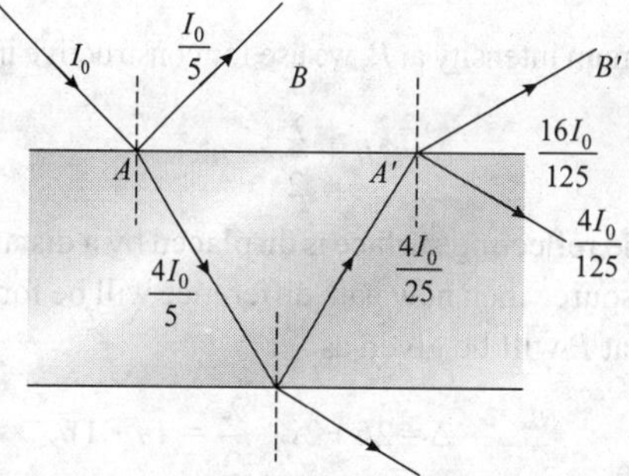

For light rays AB and $A'B'$, after interference maximum and minimum intensities are given as

$$I_{max} = (\sqrt{I_1} + \sqrt{I_2})^2 = \frac{81}{125} I_0,$$

and $\quad I_{min} = (\sqrt{I_1} - \sqrt{I_2})^2 = \frac{I_0}{125}, \quad \frac{I_{max}}{I_{min}} = 81$

(vii) (a) Shape of the interference fringes will be concentric circles with center at point P. This is because at a point on a circle with center at P on the screen, the path difference in the light waves coming from source and from its image remain constant.

(b) Intensity of light reaching on the screen directly from the source is say $I_1 = I_0$ and intensity of light reaching on the screen after reflecting from the mirror is

$$I_2 = 36\% \text{ of } I_0 = 0.36\, I_0$$

$$\Rightarrow \quad \frac{I_0}{0.36 I_0} = \frac{1}{0.36} \text{ or } \sqrt{\frac{I_1}{I_2}} = \frac{1}{0.6}$$

$$\Rightarrow \quad \frac{I_{min}}{I_{max}} = \frac{\left(\sqrt{\frac{I_1}{I_2}}-1\right)^2}{\left(\sqrt{\frac{I_1}{I_2}}+1\right)^2} = \frac{\left(\frac{1}{0.6}-1\right)^2}{\left(\frac{1}{0.6}+1\right)^2} = \frac{1}{16}$$

(c) Initially path difference P between two waves reaching from S and S' is

$$\Delta = 2h + \frac{\lambda}{2}$$

Here $\lambda/2$ is the path difference added in reflected light due to reflection from the mirror which is a denser medium.

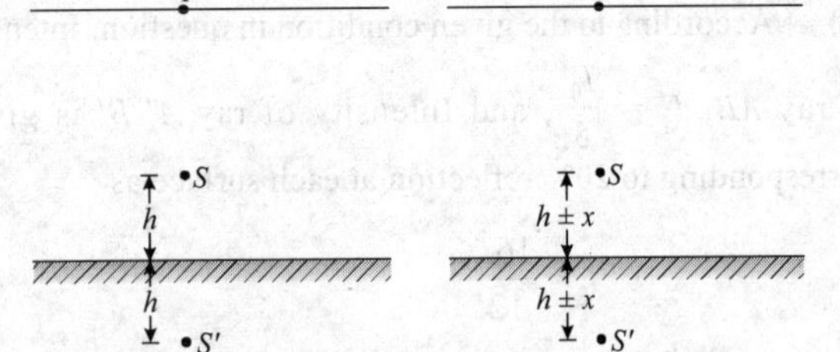

For maximum intensity at P, we use for constructive interference

$$\Delta = 2h + \frac{\lambda}{2} = n\lambda \quad \ldots(1)$$

Now, if the reflecting surface is displaced by a distance x away from the source then new path difference will be for maximum intensity at P will be given as

$$\Delta = 2h + 2x + \frac{\lambda}{2} = (n+1)\lambda \quad \ldots(2)$$

$$\Rightarrow \quad 2h + 2x = \left[n + 1 - \frac{1}{2}\right]\lambda \quad \ldots(3)$$

Solving equation-(1) and (3), we get

$$x = \frac{\lambda}{2} = \frac{6000}{2}\text{Å} = 3000\text{Å}$$

Solutions of PRACTICE EXERCISE 6.3

(i) This is a case of Fraunhofer diffraction by a narrow rectangular slit in which condition for minima, we use,

$$b \sin\theta = n\lambda$$

Where $n = 1, 2, 3, \ldots$

$$\Rightarrow \quad 0.025 \times 10^{-3} \sin 1°24' = 1 \times \lambda$$

$$\Rightarrow \quad \lambda = 0.025 \times 10^{-3} \times 0.0244$$

$$\Rightarrow \quad \lambda = 6100 \times 10^{-10}\,\text{m} = 6100\,\text{Å}$$

(ii) First order minima on either side of the central maxima are at an angular separation θ from the screen center, which is given as

$$b \sin\theta = \lambda$$

For small θ, we use $\sin\theta = \theta$, so we have

$$\theta = \frac{\lambda}{b}$$

Where b is the slit width. The half angular spread of central maxima (upto first order minima) is given as

$$\tan\theta \approx \theta = \frac{2\text{mm}}{1\text{m}} = 0.002\,\text{m}$$

Thus we have

$$b = \frac{\lambda}{0.002} = \frac{600 \times 10^{-9}}{0.002} = 0.3\,\text{mm}$$

(iii) The condition of minima due to single slit diffraction is

$$b \sin\theta = \lambda$$

$$\Rightarrow \quad \lambda = 0.05 \times \sin 30°$$

$$\Rightarrow \quad \lambda = 0.05 \times 0.5 = 0.025\,\text{m} = 2.5\,\text{cm}$$

(iv) The angular spread of central bright spot on the screen is given as

$$\sin\theta = \frac{1.22\lambda}{b}$$

For small θ, we use $\sin\theta = \theta$, so we have

$$\theta = \frac{1.22\lambda}{b}$$

The radius of the central bright spot on screen can be given as

$$r = d\theta = d \times \frac{1.22\lambda}{b}$$

$$\Rightarrow \quad r = 20 \times 10^{-2} \times \frac{1.22 \times 5900 \times 10^{-10}}{10 \times 10^{-2}}\,\text{m}$$

$$\Rightarrow \quad r = 1.4396 \times 10^{-6}\,\text{m}$$

Solutions of PRACTICE EXERCISE 6.4

(i) (a) Using Malus' law for the second Polaroid, we have

$$I_1/I_2 = \cos^2\phi = \cos^2 30° = (0.866)^2 = 0.75$$

Thus three-fourth of the light striking the second Polaroid is transmitted. As we know that the first Polaroid allows only half the intensity of unpolarized light through it, thus we have total intensity which passes through the second polaroid is

$$\frac{1}{2} \times \frac{3}{4} = \frac{3}{8}$$

thus $(3/8)^{th}$ of the original light is transmitted out from the second polaroid.

(b) Now the final intensity is 10 percent of the intensity of the light entering the first polaroid thus the light coming out from the second Polaroid is having 20% intensity of the light entering this second polaroid, so we use

$$I_2/I_1 = 0.2 = \cos^2 \phi,$$

$$\Rightarrow \quad \phi = 63.4°$$

(ii) Suppose angle between first and second nicol's prisms is θ. Then the angle between second and third nicol's prisms becomes 90° – θ. If I_0 is the intensity of the incident light on the first prism, then intensity of emerging light from this will be $I = \frac{I_0}{2}$. The intensity of light emerging from second and third nicol's prisms be $\left(\frac{I_0}{2}\right)\cos^2\theta$ and $\left[\left(\frac{I_0}{2}\right)\cos^2\theta\right]\sin^2\theta$ respectively.

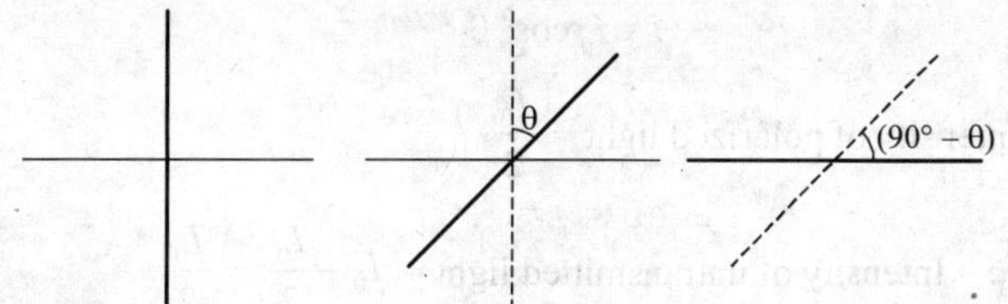

Thus according to the given condition

$$\frac{I_0}{2}\cos^2\theta\sin^2\theta = \frac{I_0}{16}$$

$$\Rightarrow \quad (\sin\theta\cos\theta)^2 = \frac{1}{8}$$

$$\Rightarrow \quad (2\sin\theta\cos\theta)^2 = \frac{1}{2}$$

$$\Rightarrow \quad \sin^2(2\theta) = \frac{1}{2}$$

$$\Rightarrow \quad \sin 2\theta = \frac{1}{\sqrt{2}}$$

$$\Rightarrow \quad 2\theta = 45°$$

$$\Rightarrow \quad \theta = 22.5°$$

(iii) The intensity of the light after passing through the first polarizer is $I = I_0\cos^2\theta_1$. This light is polarized in the direction of the axis of the first sheet, and so its axis makes the angle $\theta_2 - \theta_1$ with the axis of the second sheet. Consequently, the intensity of the light after passing through the second polarizer is

$$I' = I\cos^2(\theta_2 - \theta_1) = I_0\cos^2\theta_1\cos^2(\theta_2 - \theta_1)$$

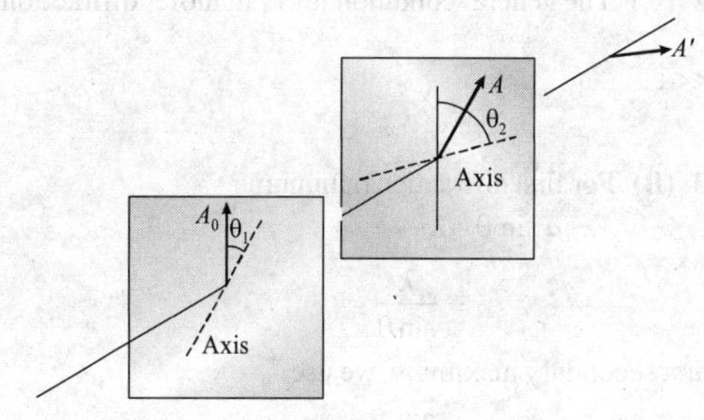

(iv) Is should be remembered that the transmitted intensity of unpolarised light will be $I_0/2$ for all orientation of polariser sheet whereas the intensity of polarised light varies from zero to I_p. Thus intensity of emerging light from polarising sheet will be

$$I_{min} = I_0/2,$$

and $$I_{max} = \frac{I_0}{2} + I_p$$

According to given condition;

$$I_{max} = 4I_{min}$$

$$\Rightarrow \quad \frac{I_0}{2} + I_p = 4\frac{I_0}{2}$$

$$I_p = \frac{3I_0}{2}$$

$$\Rightarrow \quad \frac{I_p}{I_0} = \frac{3}{2}$$

For θ = 45°, $$I = \frac{I_0}{2} + I_p\cos^2 45°$$

$$\Rightarrow \quad I = \frac{I_0}{2} + \frac{I_p}{2}$$

$$\Rightarrow \quad I = \frac{I_0}{2} + \frac{3I_0/2}{2} = \frac{5I_0}{4}$$

Solutions of CONCEPTUAL MCQS Single Option Correct

Sol. 1 (D) The phase difference (ϕ) between the wavelets from the top edge and the bottom edge of the slit is $\phi = \frac{2\pi}{\lambda}(d\sin\theta)$ where d is the slit width. The first minima of the diffraction pattern occurs at

$$\sin\theta = \frac{\lambda}{d},$$

So $$\phi = \frac{2\pi}{\lambda}\left(d \times \frac{\lambda}{d}\right) = 2\pi$$

Sol. 2 (C) The general condition for Fraunhofer diffraction is $\frac{b^2}{L\lambda} << 1$.

Sol. 3 (B) For first diffraction minimum

$$a \sin\theta = \lambda$$

$$\Rightarrow \quad a = \frac{\lambda}{\sin\theta}$$

For first secondary maximum, we use

$$a \sin\theta' = \frac{3\lambda}{2}$$

$$\Rightarrow \quad \sin\theta' = \frac{3\lambda}{2} \times \frac{1}{a} = \frac{3\lambda}{2} \times \frac{\sin\theta}{\lambda}$$

$$= \frac{3}{2} \times \sin 30° = \frac{3}{4}$$

$$\Rightarrow \quad \theta' = \sin^{-1}\left(\frac{3}{4}\right)$$

Sol. 4 (A) The first diffraction minima of light waves of wavelength λ diffracted by a single, long narrow slit of width b is given by

$$b \sin\theta = \lambda$$

$$\sin\theta = \frac{\lambda}{b}$$

When b is decreased for same wavelength, sin θ increases, hence θ increases. Thus, width of central maxima will increase.

Sol. 5 (C) For a slit of width b, light of wavelength λ, when light falls on the slit, the diffraction patterns is obtained. The first diffraction minimum occurs at the angles given by

$$\sin\theta = \frac{\lambda}{b}$$

From the equation, it is clear that width of the central diffraction maximum is inversely proportional to the width of the slit. One increasing the width size b, the angle θ at which the intensity first becomes zero decreases, resulting in a narrower central band and if the slit width is made smaller, the angle θ increases, giving a wider central band.

Sol. 6 (C) Brewster's angle is given as

$$\tan i = \frac{1}{\sin\theta_C}$$

$$\Rightarrow \quad \cot i = \sin\left[\sin^{-1}\left(\frac{3}{5}\right)\right]$$

$$\Rightarrow \quad \tan i = \frac{5}{3}$$

$$\Rightarrow \quad i = \tan^{-1}\left(\frac{5}{3}\right)$$

Sol. 7 (B) Ultrasonic waves cannot be polarized as these are longitudinal waves.

Sol. 8 (A) As explained in article 6.8.8, if an unpolarised light is converted into plane polarised light by passing through a polaroid its intensity becomes half.

Sol. 9 (B) Some crystals such as tourmaline and sheets of iodosulphate of quinine have the property of strongly absorbing the light with vibrations perpendicular to a specific direction (called transmission axis) transmitting the light with vibrations parallel to it. This selective absorption of light is called dichroism.

Sol. 10 (C) According to Malus' law, we use

$$I = I_0 \cos^2\theta = I_0(\cos^2 60°)$$

$$\Rightarrow \quad = I_0 \times \left(\frac{1}{2}\right)^2 = \frac{I_0}{4}$$

Sol. 11 (A) According to Malus' law, we use

$$I = I_0 \cos^2\theta$$

Intensity of polarized light $= \frac{I_0}{2}$

$\Rightarrow$ Intensity of untransmitted light $= I_0 - \frac{I_0}{2} = \frac{I_0}{2}$

Sol. 12 (A) Optical rotation or optical activity is the rotation of linearly polarized light as it travels through certain materials. It occurs in solutions of chiral molecules, solids with rotated crystal planes and spin polarized gases of atoms or molecules.

Sol. 13 (D) For liquid A, we have

$$L_1 = 20 \text{ cm}, \theta_1 = 38; \text{concentration} = C_1$$

Specific rotation is given as

$$\alpha_1 = \frac{\theta_1}{L_1 C_1} = \frac{38°}{20 \times C_1}$$

Similarly, for liquid B, we have

$$L_2 = 30 \text{ cm}, \theta_2 = -24°, \text{concentration} = C_2$$

Specific rotation is given as

$$\alpha_2 = \frac{\theta_2}{L_2 C_2} = \frac{(-24°)}{30 \times C_2}$$

The mixture has 1 part of liquid A and 2 parts of liquid B,

$$\Rightarrow \quad C_1' : C_2' = 1 : 2$$

$$\Rightarrow \quad \theta = \{\alpha_1 C_1' + \alpha_2 C_2'\} l$$

$$\Rightarrow \quad \theta = \left\{\frac{38°}{20 \times C_1} \times \frac{C_1}{3} + \frac{(-24°)}{30 \times C_2} \times \frac{2C_2}{3}\right\} \times 30$$

$\Rightarrow$ $\theta = 19^3 - 16° = 3°$

Thus, the optical rotation of mixture is + 3° in right hand direction.

Sol. 14 (C) The strength of solution is given by

$$C = \frac{\theta}{l \times s}$$

Where the symbols have their usual meanings.

Here, $\theta = 19°, l = 20\text{ cm} = 0.20\text{ m}$

$S = 0.5\text{ deg m}^2\text{ kg}^{-1}$

$$\Rightarrow C = \frac{19}{0.20 \times 0.5} = 190\text{ kg-m}^{-3}$$

The sugar sample dissolved in a m^3 of water is 200 kg in which 190 kg is pure sugar. Therefore, purity is given as

$$\frac{190}{200} \times 100 = 95\%$$

Sol. 15 (A) If initial intensity of incident light is $I_0$the intensity of light after transmission from first polaroid will be $\frac{I_0}{2}$ and intensity of light emitted from P_3 is given by Malus' law as

$$I_1 = \frac{I_0}{2}\cos^2\theta$$

Intensity of light transmitted from last polaroid will be given by Malus' law as

$$P_2 = I_1\cos^2(90° - \theta)$$

$$\Rightarrow P_2 = \frac{I_0}{2}\cos^2\theta\sin^2\theta$$

$$\Rightarrow P_2 = \frac{I_0}{8}(2\sin\theta\cos\theta)^2$$

$$\Rightarrow P_2 = \frac{I_0}{8}\sin^2 2\theta$$

Sol. 16 (D) The resulting amplitude in the given four cases are $4a_0$, $2a_0$, $2a_0$ and $4a_0$. Thus in case I and IV intensity will be maximum and equal.

Sol. 17 (B) Resulting intensity at points A is given as

$$\Rightarrow I_A = I_1 + I_2 + 2\sqrt{I_1 I_2}\cos\theta_1$$

$$\Rightarrow I_A = I_1 + I_2 + 2\sqrt{I_1 I_2}\cos\frac{\pi}{2}$$

$$\Rightarrow I_A = I_1 + I_2$$

$$\Rightarrow I_A = 5I$$

Similarly resulting intensity at point B is given as

$$I_B = I_1 + I_2 + 2\sqrt{I_1 I_2}\cos\theta_2$$

$$\Rightarrow I_B = I_1 + I_2 + 2\sqrt{I_1 I_2}\cos\pi$$

$$\Rightarrow I_B = I$$

Difference in light intensities at points A and B is given as

$$I_A - I_B = 5I - I = 4I$$

Sol. 18 (C) Frequency of electromagnetic waves going towards the approaching mirror is given by Doppler's effect as

$$w' = \frac{c + v}{c} \cdot w_0$$

Frequency of waves reflected from mirror and moving towards source is also given by Doppler's effect as

$$w'' = \frac{c}{c - v} \cdot w'$$

$$\Rightarrow w'' = \frac{c}{c - v} \times \frac{c + v}{c} \cdot w_0 = \left(\frac{c + \upsilon}{c - \upsilon}\right) w_0$$

$$\Rightarrow w'' = \frac{c\left(1 + \frac{v}{c}\right)}{c\left(1 - \frac{v}{c}\right)} w_0$$

$$\Rightarrow \frac{\left(1 + \frac{v}{c}\right)}{\left(1 - \frac{v}{c}\right)} w_0 = \left(\frac{1 + \beta}{1 - \beta}\right) w_0 \text{ where } \beta = \frac{v}{c}$$

Sol. 19 (A) Path difference in the two lights from the slits at a point in front of one of the slits is given as

$$\Delta = \frac{\left(\frac{b}{2}\right) \cdot b}{d} = \frac{b^2}{2d}$$

For missing wavelength, light waves should destructively interfere at this point so we should have path difference between waves to be

$$\Delta = \frac{\lambda_1}{2}, \frac{3\lambda_2}{2}, \frac{5\lambda_3}{2}, \frac{7\lambda_4}{2}, \ldots\ldots$$

$$\Rightarrow \frac{\lambda_1}{2} = \frac{b^2}{2d} \quad \text{or} \quad \lambda_1 = \frac{b^2}{2d}$$

$$\text{and} \quad \frac{3\lambda_2}{2} = \frac{b^2}{2d} \quad \text{or} \quad \lambda_2 = \frac{b^2}{3d}$$

$$\text{and} \quad \frac{5\lambda_3}{2} = \frac{b^2}{2d} \quad \text{or} \quad \lambda_3 = \frac{b^2}{5d}$$

Sol. 20 (C) Central fringe will have maximum intensity which is four times the intensity due to each of individual slits, and if intensity at point A is considered as I_R then we have

$$\frac{I_R}{I_{max}}=0.853$$

$$\Rightarrow \quad I_R=0.853\,I_{max}=0.853\times 4I$$

The intensity at point A is given as

$$I_R=I+I_0+2I\cos\phi=2I(1+\cos\phi)=0.853\times 4I$$

$$\Rightarrow \quad \phi=\frac{\pi}{4}$$

Thus corresponding to the above phase difference the path difference is $\frac{\lambda}{8}$.

Sol. 21 (A) It is already discussed that intensity at maxima is four times the individual intensity if both waves are of equal intensities. In this situation the intensity at minima is zero.

Sol. 22 (C) If each of the sources is producing an intensity I' at the point of interference then at the central maximum, intensity will be due to constructive interference of the light due to these two sources which will be $4I'$ and this is given as I, thus we have

$$I'=\frac{I}{4}$$

Sol. 23 (C) In *YDSE*, we know fringe width is given as

$$\beta=\frac{\lambda D}{d}=\frac{\lambda(2D)}{2d}=\beta$$

$$\Rightarrow \quad D'=2D$$

Sol. 24 (A) Here we use

$$n_1\lambda_1=n_2\lambda_2$$

$$\Rightarrow \quad n_2=\frac{n_1\lambda_1}{\lambda_2}=\frac{12\times 600}{400}=18$$

Sol. 25 (B) As we know maximum and minimum amplitudes at locations of bright and dark fringes are given as

$$a_{max}=a_1+a_2 \text{ and } a_{min}=a_1-a_2$$

$$\Rightarrow \quad \frac{I_{max}}{I_{min}}=\frac{(a_1+a_2)^2}{(a_1-a_2)^2}=\frac{9}{1} \Rightarrow a_1=2 \text{ and } a_2=1$$

$$\Rightarrow \quad \frac{a_1}{a_2}=\frac{2}{1}=2$$

Sol. 26 (B) For a point source of light we use

$$I\propto\frac{1}{r^2}$$

and as we use $A\propto\sqrt{I}$

$$\Rightarrow \quad A\propto\sqrt{\frac{1}{r^2}}$$

$$\Rightarrow \quad A\propto\frac{1}{r}$$

Sol. 27 (B) For a line source of light, we use

$$I\propto\frac{1}{r^2}$$

$$\Rightarrow \quad A\propto\sqrt{I}$$

$$\Rightarrow \quad A\propto r^{-1/2}$$

Sol. 28 (C) As we know at the point of superposition, resulting amplitude is given as

$$A_R=\sqrt{A^2+A^2+2A\cdot A\cos\theta}$$

$$\Rightarrow \quad A_R=\sqrt{A^2+A^2+2A^2\cos\left(\frac{2\pi}{3}\right)}$$

$$\Rightarrow \quad A_R=\sqrt{A^2+A^2+2A^2\left(-\frac{1}{2}\right)}$$

$$\Rightarrow \quad A_R=\sqrt{A^2+A^2-A^2}=\sqrt{A^2}=A$$

Sol. 29 (B) In a *YDSE* setup the light intensity on screen due to any slit is directly proportional to its slit width, so we use

As Intensity $\propto$ slit width

$$\frac{I_1}{I_2}=\frac{4}{1}$$

$$\Rightarrow \quad \frac{a_1}{a_2}=\sqrt{\frac{I_1}{I_2}}=2$$

Sol. 30 (B) Since there is no shift in central maxima the path difference introduced by the two sheets should be equal and nullify each other, so we have

$$(\mu_1-1)\,t_1=(\mu_2-1)\,t_2$$

Where μ_1 and μ_2 are refraction indices of the two sheets

$$\Rightarrow \quad \frac{t_1}{t_2}=\frac{(\mu_2-1)}{(\mu_1-1)}=\frac{(1.5-1)}{(1.25-1)}=\frac{0.5}{0.25}=2$$

Sol. 31 (C) Increase in optical path is given as

$$\Delta=\mu t-t=(\mu-1)t$$

Sol. 32 (B) $PR=d$

and $\quad PO=d\sec\theta$

and $\quad CO=PO\cot 2\theta=d\sec\theta\cos 2\theta$

Path difference between the two rays is,

$$\Delta x=CO+PO=(d\sec\theta+d\sec\theta\cos 2\theta)$$

Path difference between the two rays is,

$\Delta\phi = \pi$(one is reflected, while another is direct)

Therefore, condition for constructive interference should be

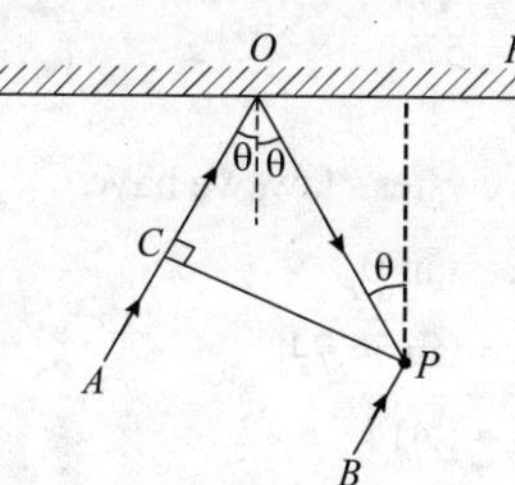

$$\Delta x = \frac{\lambda}{2}, \frac{3\lambda}{2} \ldots$$

$$\Rightarrow \quad d \sec\theta\,(1 + \cos 2\theta) = \frac{\lambda}{2}$$

$$\Rightarrow \quad \left(\frac{d}{\cos\theta}\right)(2\cos^2\theta) = \frac{\lambda}{2}$$

$$\Rightarrow \quad \cos\theta \frac{\lambda}{4d}$$

Sol. 33 (C) In such type of question, we should obtain phase difference ($\Delta\phi$) at the given point

$$I = 4I_0 \cos^2\frac{\Delta\varphi}{2}$$

$$\Rightarrow \quad I_0 = 4I_0 \cos^2\frac{\Delta\varphi}{2}$$

($\because$ $I = I_0$ Given in the question)

$$\Rightarrow \quad \Delta\phi = \frac{2\pi}{3}$$

We know that, $\Delta\phi = \frac{2\pi}{\lambda}\Delta x$

In the YDSE setup, we have

$$\Delta x = \frac{yd}{D}$$

$$\Rightarrow \quad \frac{yd}{D} = \frac{\lambda}{3} \quad \text{[From the above relation]}$$

$$\Rightarrow \quad y = \frac{\lambda D}{3d}$$

Sol. 34 (D) If a parallel beam of white light is incident on the plane, then there is only one point where all light falls on the screen, which in the central maxima. Hence, position of the central maxima is at bisector of the two slits, which is at $\frac{d}{6}$ distance above the point 'O'.

Sol. 35 (A) Path difference in air at point O, is given as

$$\Delta x = [(S_1 - O - t)\,n_2 + tn_3 - (S_2\,O)]t$$

$$\Rightarrow \quad \Delta x = [S_1O - S_2O)\,n_2 + (n_3 - n_2)t],$$

$$\Rightarrow \quad \Delta x = (n_3 - n_2)\,t$$

Phase difference, $\Delta\phi = \frac{2\pi}{\lambda_a} \times$ Path difference in air,

$$\Delta\phi = \frac{2\pi}{n_1\lambda}(n_3 - n_2)t \qquad \left(\because\ n_1 = \frac{\lambda_a}{\lambda}\right)$$

Solutions of NUMERICAL MCQS Single Option Correct

Sol. 1 (B) In *YDSE* setup angular width of fringes on screen is given as

$$\theta = \frac{\lambda}{d}$$

$$\Rightarrow \quad d = \frac{6\times10^{-7}\times180\times7}{0.1\times22} = 0.344\text{ mm}$$

Sol. 2 (A) In *YDSE* setup fringe width is given as

$$\beta = \frac{\lambda D}{d} = \frac{5893\times10^{-8}\times200}{0.08} = 0.1473\text{ cm}$$

Sol. 3 (C) Diffraction Limit of resolution of the telescope is given as

$$\alpha = \frac{1.22\lambda}{a} = \frac{d}{x}$$

$$\Rightarrow \quad d = \frac{1.22\lambda x}{a}$$

$$\Rightarrow \quad d = \frac{1.22\times5\times10^{-7}\times8\times10^{16}}{0.25}$$

$$\Rightarrow \quad d = 1.95\times10^{11}\text{ m}$$

Sol. 4 (D) In single slit diffraction pattern, angular separation of first dark fringe from central bright fringe is given as

$$b\sin\theta = \lambda$$

For small angle we can use

$$\sin\theta = \theta$$

Separation distance of first dark fringe from central maxima is given as

$$x = D\theta$$

$$\Rightarrow \quad x = \frac{D\lambda}{b} = \frac{600\times10^{-9}\times2}{1\times10^{-3}} = 12\times10^{-4}\text{ m}$$

So, distance between the first dark fringes on either side of the central bright fringe

$$s = 2x$$

$$\Rightarrow \quad s = 2\times12\times10^{-4}\text{ m}$$

$$\Rightarrow \quad s = 24\times10^{-4}\text{ m} = 2.4\text{ mm}$$

Sol. 5 (C) Width of central maxima is given as

$$y = \frac{2D\lambda}{b}$$

If slit width is reduced to half and wavelength is changed to 6000Å, new width of central maxima is given as

$$y' = \frac{2D}{(b/2)} \times \frac{6000}{4000} = 3y$$

Sol. 6 (C) After first polaroid the intensity reduces to half. If I_0 is the initial incident intensity then after next four polaroids, intensity will become

$$I = \frac{I_0}{2} \cdot \cos^4(60°)$$

$$\Rightarrow \quad I = \frac{I_0}{2} \cdot \frac{1}{(4)^4}$$

$$\Rightarrow \quad I = \frac{I_0}{512}$$

Sol. 7 (C) From Brewster's law, we have

$$\mu = \tan i_b$$

$$\Rightarrow \quad \frac{c}{v} = \tan 60° = \sqrt{3}$$

$$\Rightarrow \quad v = \frac{c}{\sqrt{3}} = \frac{3 \times 10^8}{\sqrt{3}}$$

$$\Rightarrow \quad v = \sqrt{3} \times 10^8 \text{ m/s}$$

Sol. 8 (B) For the path difference due to plate is compensated by the physical path difference, we use

$$(\mu - 1)t = \frac{xd}{D}$$

$$\Rightarrow \quad \mu = 1 + \frac{xd}{Dt}$$

$$\Rightarrow \quad \mu = 1 + \frac{0.5 \times 0.2}{10 \times 0.05} = 1 + 0.2 = 1.2$$

Sol. 9 (B) We use, from the figure

$$i_b = r + \delta$$

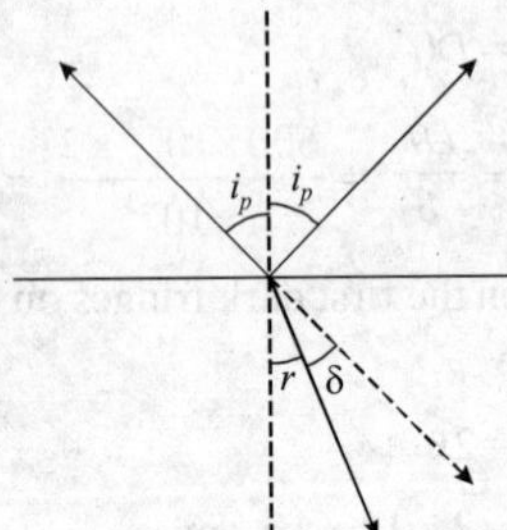

$$i_b = r + 24 \quad \ldots(1)$$

Moreover, $\quad i_b + r = 90° \quad \ldots(2)$

From equations (1) and (2), we get

$$i_b + (i_b - 24) = 90°$$

$$\Rightarrow \quad i_b = 57°$$

Sol. 10 (D) By Brewster's law, we have

$$\mu = \tan \theta_P$$

$$\Rightarrow \quad \mu = \tan 54.74°$$

$$\Rightarrow \quad \mu = 1.414$$

For an equilateral prism, we use prism angle 60° and the angle of minimum deviation is given by the relation

$$\mu = \frac{\sin\left(\frac{A + \delta_m}{2}\right)}{\sin\left(\frac{A}{2}\right)}$$

$$\Rightarrow \quad 1.414 = \frac{\sin\left(\frac{60° + \delta_m}{2}\right)}{\sin\left(\frac{60°}{2}\right)}$$

$$\Rightarrow \quad \frac{1.414 \times 1}{2} = \sin\left(\frac{60° + \delta_m}{2}\right)$$

$$\Rightarrow \quad \frac{\sqrt{2}}{2} = \sin\left(\frac{60° + \delta_m}{2}\right)$$

$$\Rightarrow \quad \frac{1}{\sqrt{2}} = \sin\left(\frac{60° + \delta_m}{2}\right)$$

$$\Rightarrow \quad 45° = \left(\frac{60° + \delta_m}{2}\right)$$

$$\Rightarrow \quad \delta_m = 30°$$

Sol. 11 (B) Distance of fifth bright fringe is given as

$$x_{5B} = n\frac{\lambda D}{d} = \frac{5 \times 6.5 \times 10^{-7} \times 1}{10^{-3}} = 32.5 \times 10^{-4} \text{ m}$$

Distance of third dark fringe is given as

$$x_{3D} = (2n - 1)\frac{\lambda}{2}\frac{D}{d} = \frac{5 \times 6.3 \times 10^{-7} \times 1}{2 \times 10^{-3}} = 16.25 \times 10^{-4} \text{ m}$$

$$\Rightarrow \quad x_{5B} - x_{3D} \approx 1.63 \text{ mm}$$

Sol. 12 (A) As ratio of slit widths = Ratio of intensities

$$\Rightarrow \quad \frac{I_1}{I_2} = \frac{9}{4}$$

$$\Rightarrow \quad \frac{a_1^2}{a_2^2} = \frac{9}{4}$$

$$\Rightarrow \quad \frac{a1}{a2} = \frac{3}{2}$$

Maximum and Minimum amplitude are given as

$$a_{max} = a_1 + a_2 = 3 + 2 = 5$$

and $$a_{min} = 3 - 2 = 1$$

$$\Rightarrow \quad \frac{I_{max}}{I_{min}} = \frac{(a1+a2)^2}{(a1-a2)^2} = \frac{(3+2)^2}{(3-2)^2} = \frac{25}{1}$$

Sol. 13 (B) In case of moving light source, apparent frequency will be

$$v' = \frac{c+v}{c} \cdot v$$

and $$\frac{v'}{v} = \frac{c+v}{c} = \frac{\lambda}{\lambda'}$$

$$\Rightarrow \quad \lambda' = \frac{\lambda c}{c+v} = \frac{5500 \times c}{c+0.5c} = \frac{5500 \times 2}{3} = 3667 \text{Å}$$

$$\Rightarrow \quad \Delta\lambda = (5500 - 3667) \text{ Å} = 1833 \text{ Å}$$

Sol. 14 (A) If shift of fringes is x then we use

$$\frac{xd}{D} = (\mu - 1)t$$

$$\Rightarrow \quad x = \frac{(\mu-1)tD}{d}$$

$$\Rightarrow \quad x = \frac{(1.5-1) \times 10^{-3} \times 100}{0.25} = 0.2 \text{ cm}$$

Sol. 15 (B) Angular width of central maxima in diffraction pattern is given as

$$2\theta = 30^\circ$$

Where we have

$$\sin 30^\circ = \frac{\lambda}{b}$$

$$\Rightarrow \quad b = \frac{\lambda}{\sin 30^\circ} = \frac{6000 \times 10^{-10}}{1/2} = 12000 \times 10^{-10} \text{ m}$$

$$\Rightarrow \quad b = 12 \times 10^{-7} \text{ m}$$

Sol. 16 (C) For angular positions of central minima, we use

$$b \sin \theta = n\lambda$$

$$\Rightarrow \quad b \cdot \frac{x}{D} = n\lambda$$

$$\Rightarrow \quad b = n\lambda \frac{D}{x}$$

$$\Rightarrow \quad D = \frac{a \cdot x}{n\lambda}$$

$$\Rightarrow \quad D = \frac{3 \times 10^{-4} \times 4 \times 10^{-3}}{1 \times 6000 \times 10^{-10}} = 2.0 \text{ m}$$

Sol. 17 (B) By Doppler's effect in light we use

$$\frac{v}{c} = \frac{\Delta\lambda}{\lambda}$$

$$\Rightarrow \quad \Delta\lambda = \frac{v}{c} x\lambda$$

$$\Rightarrow \quad \frac{\Delta\lambda}{\lambda} = \frac{1.2 \times 10^6}{3 \times 10^8} = \frac{12}{3} \times \frac{10^5}{10^8} = 4 \times 10^{-3}$$

$$\Rightarrow \quad \frac{\Delta\lambda}{\lambda} \times 100 = 0.4 \text{ i.e., } 0.4\%$$

Sol. 18 (C) Diffraction minima on either side of central maxima is given as

$$b \sin \theta = n\lambda$$

$$\Rightarrow \quad b \cdot \frac{x}{D} = n\lambda$$

$$D = \frac{bx}{n\lambda} = \frac{2 \times 10^{-4} \times 5 \times 10^{-3}}{1 \times 5000 \times 10^{-10}} = 2.0 \text{ m}$$

Sol. 19 (D) Doppler shift is given as

$$d\lambda = \frac{v}{c} \times \lambda = R\omega\left(\frac{\lambda}{c}\right)$$

$$\Rightarrow \quad R\left(\frac{2\pi}{T}\right)\frac{\lambda}{c} = d\lambda$$

Substituting values, we get

$$T = \frac{R \times 2\pi}{d\lambda} \times \frac{\lambda}{c}$$

$$\Rightarrow \quad T = 25 \text{ days}$$

Sol. 20 (D) Shift in no. of fringes is given by

$$n\lambda = (\mu - 1)\,t$$

$$\Rightarrow \quad n = \frac{(\mu-1)t}{\lambda} = \frac{(1.5-1) \times 2 \times 10^{-6}}{5000 \times 10^{-10}} \text{ fringes} = 2$$

Sol. 21 (B) When source is fixed and observer is moving towards it, by Doppler's effect the apparent frequency is given as

$$\nu' = \frac{c+a}{c} \cdot \nu$$

When source is moving towards observer at rest, we use

$$\nu'' = \frac{c}{c-a}\nu' = \frac{c+a}{c-a} \cdot \nu = c\left[\frac{1+\frac{a}{c}}{1-\frac{a}{c}}\right]\nu$$

$$\Rightarrow \quad \nu'' = c\left[1+\frac{a}{c}\right]\left[1-\frac{a}{c}\right]^{-1}\nu \approx \left[1+\frac{2a}{c}\right]\nu$$

$$\Rightarrow \quad \Delta\nu = \nu' - \nu = \frac{2a\nu}{c} = \frac{2a}{\lambda}$$

$$\Rightarrow \quad a = \lambda\frac{\Delta\nu}{2} = \frac{0.5\times1000}{2} = 250\ \text{ms}^{-1}$$

$$\Rightarrow \quad a = 900\ \text{km/hr}$$

Sol. 22 (D) In single slit diffraction pattern, n^{th} order minima is given as

$$b\sin\theta = n\lambda$$

$$\Rightarrow \quad 0.3\times10^{-3}\times\theta = 6000\times10^{-10}$$

$$\Rightarrow \quad \theta = 2\times10^{-3}\ \text{rad}$$

Sol. 23 (C) By Doppler's effect, we have

$$\frac{\Delta\lambda}{\lambda} = \frac{\nu}{c}$$

$$\Rightarrow \quad \Delta\lambda = \frac{\lambda\Delta}{c}$$

Change in wavelength for two edges = ± Δλ

⇒ Total change is

$$\delta\lambda = 2\Delta\lambda = 2\frac{\lambda\nu}{c}$$

$$\Rightarrow \quad \nu = \frac{c\delta\lambda}{2\lambda}$$

Time period of revolution is given as

$$T = \frac{2\pi R}{\nu} = 2\pi Rx\frac{2\lambda}{c\delta\lambda} = \frac{4\pi R\lambda}{c\delta\lambda}$$

$$\Rightarrow \quad T = \frac{4\times3.14\times6.95\times10^{8}\times0.59\times10^{-6}}{3\times10^{8}\times8\times10^{-12}\times86400}\ \text{days}$$

$$\Rightarrow \quad T = 24.8\ \text{days} \approx 25\ \text{days}$$

Sol. 24 (A) For first diffraction minima at angle θ, we can use

$$d(\sin\theta - \sin\theta_0) = \pm\lambda$$

Here θ_0 is the angle at which central maxima is obtained

For one side of central maxima, we use

$$\sin\theta_1 = \sin\theta_0 + \frac{\lambda}{d}$$

$$\Rightarrow \quad \sin\theta_1 = 0.5 + \frac{0.5}{10} = 0.55$$

$$\Rightarrow \quad \theta_1 = 33.37^\circ$$

Sol. 25 (B) For first diffraction min. $d\sin\theta = \lambda$

and if angle is small, $\sin\theta = \theta$

$$\Rightarrow \quad d\theta = \lambda$$

Angular width of first dark fringe from central maxima is

$$\theta = \frac{\lambda}{d}$$

Full angular width of central maxima is

$$w = 2\theta = \frac{2\lambda}{d}$$

Also we can use

$$w' = \frac{2\lambda'}{d}$$

$$\Rightarrow \quad \frac{\lambda'}{\lambda} = \frac{w'}{w}$$

$$\Rightarrow \quad \lambda' = \lambda\frac{w'}{w}$$

$$\Rightarrow \quad \lambda' = 6000\times0.7 = 4200\text{Å}$$

Sol. 26 (C) By Snell's law we have

$$\mu = \frac{\sin i}{\sin r}$$

$$\Rightarrow \quad \sin r = \frac{\sin i}{\mu} = \frac{0.788}{1.33} = 0.6$$

$$\Rightarrow \quad \cos r = \sqrt{1-\sin^2 r} = \sqrt{1-(0.6)^2} = 0.8$$

For constructive interference on reflection

$$2\mu t\cos r = (2n+1)\frac{\lambda}{2}$$

$$\Rightarrow \quad t = \frac{(2n+1)\lambda}{4\mu\cos r} = \frac{(2n+1)\times0.6}{4\times1.33\times0.8}$$

$$\Rightarrow \quad t = 0.14(22+1)\ \mu\text{m}$$

Sol. 27 (C) For diffraction minima due to a single slit of width b, we use

$$b\sin\theta = n\lambda$$

$$\Rightarrow \quad b = \frac{n\lambda}{\sin\theta} = \frac{2\times6000\times10^{-10}}{\sin 30^\circ}$$

$$\Rightarrow \quad b = \frac{2\times6000\times10^{-10}}{1/2} = 4\times6000\times10^{-10}$$

$$\Rightarrow \quad b = 24\times10^{-7}\ \text{m} = 24\times10^{-5}\ \text{cm}$$

Sol. 28 (D) Fringe width in *YDSE* setup is given as

$$\beta = \frac{\lambda D}{d}$$

Angular fringe width is given as

$$\theta = \frac{\beta}{D} = \frac{\lambda}{d}$$

Angular widths of two wavelengths are given as

$$\theta_1 = \frac{\lambda_1}{d},\ \theta_2 = \frac{\lambda_2}{d}$$

$$\Rightarrow \quad \frac{\theta_1}{\theta_2} = \frac{\lambda_1}{\lambda_2}$$

$$\Rightarrow \quad \lambda_2 = \lambda_1 \cdot \frac{\theta_2}{\theta_1}$$

$$\Rightarrow \quad 5890 \times \frac{0.22}{0.20} = 6479 Å$$

Sol. 29 (C) Shift in fringe pattern due to insertion of a sheet in front of slits is given as

$$\frac{xd}{D} = (\mu - 1)t$$

$$\Rightarrow \quad x = \frac{(\mu - 1)tD}{d}$$

When distance between screen and slit is doubled, them fringe width becomes

$$\beta = \frac{2\lambda D}{d}$$

As per the given condition, we have

$$\beta = x$$

$$\Rightarrow \quad \frac{2\lambda D}{d} = \frac{(\mu - 1)tD}{d}$$

$$\Rightarrow \quad \lambda = \frac{(\mu - 1)t}{2} = \frac{(1.6 - 1) \times 1.964 \times 10^{-6}}{2}$$

$$\Rightarrow \quad \lambda = 0.5892 \times 10^{-6} \text{ m} = 5892 Å$$

Sol. 30 (B) Fringe width in *YDSE* setup is given as $\beta = \frac{\lambda d}{d}$

Difference in fringe widths is given as

$$\beta_1 - \beta_2 = \frac{\lambda(D_1 - D_2)}{d} \text{ or } \lambda = \frac{d(\beta_1 - \beta_2)}{D_1 - D_2}$$

$$\Rightarrow \quad \lambda = \frac{3 \times 10^{-5} \times 10^{-3}}{5 \times 10^{2}} = 6000 Å$$

Sol. 31 (A) Fringe width on screen is given as

$$\beta = \frac{\lambda D}{d} = \frac{5000 \times 10^{-10} \times 1}{5 \times 10^{-4}} = 0.001 \text{ m} = 1 \text{ mm}$$

Shift in fringe pattern x due to insertion of glass plate is given as

$$\frac{xd}{D} = (\mu - 1)t$$

$$\Rightarrow \quad x = \frac{(\mu - 1)Dt}{d} = \frac{(1.5 - 1) \times 1.5 \times 10^{-6} \times 1}{5 \times 10^{-4}}$$

$$= 1.5 \times 10^{-3} \text{ m} = 1.5 \text{ mm} = 1.5\,\beta$$

Thus after insertion, at screen center there will be a dark fringe so intensity will be zero.

Sol. 32 (A) Path difference at a distance x from the central maxima on screen is given as

$$\Delta = \frac{xd}{D} = \frac{10^{-3} \times 2 \times 10^{-3}}{2.5} = 8000 Å$$

For bright line at this position, we use

$$8000 = n_1 \lambda_1$$

If $\quad n_1 = 2,$

We get $\quad \lambda_1 = 4000 Å$

Thus second bright line for visible region is present.

Sol. 33 (C) In a liquid the wavelength of light changes to

$$\lambda_L = \frac{\lambda_{air}}{\mu_L}$$

In *YDSE* setup the fringe width is given as

$$\beta = \frac{\lambda D}{d}$$

When the setup is submerged in a liquid fringe width changes to

$$\beta = \frac{\lambda_L D}{d} = \frac{\lambda_{air} D}{\mu_L d}$$

$$\Rightarrow \quad \beta = \frac{6300 \times 10^{-10} \times 1.33}{1.33 \times 10^{-3}} = 0.63 \text{ mm}$$

Sol. 34 (D) On screen distinguished fringes are seen until the bright fringe of one wavelength overlaps with the dark fringe of other so we use

$$n\lambda_2 = \left(n + \frac{1}{2}\right)\lambda_1$$

$$\Rightarrow \quad \frac{\left(n + \frac{1}{2}\right)}{n} = \frac{\lambda_2}{\lambda_1}$$

$$\Rightarrow \quad \frac{1}{2n} = \frac{\lambda_2 - \lambda_1}{\lambda_1} = \frac{5895 - 5890}{5890} = \frac{5}{5890}$$

$$\Rightarrow \quad n = \frac{5890}{10} = 589$$

Sol. 35 (B) For maximum reflection of a specific wavelength, we use

$$2\mu t = (2n + 1)\frac{\lambda}{2}$$

$$\Rightarrow \quad \mu = \frac{\lambda}{2}\frac{(2n+1)}{2t} = \frac{(2n+1) \times 5320 \times 10^{-10}}{2 \times 5 \times 10^{-5} \times 10^{-2}}$$

$$\Rightarrow \quad \mu = 1.33$$

Sol. 36 (A) By Brewster's law, we use

$$\mu = \tan i_p$$

$\Rightarrow \quad \tan i_p = 1.54$

$\Rightarrow \quad i_p = \tan^{-1} 1.54 = 57^\circ$

At polarizing angle we use

$$r + i_p = 90^\circ$$

$\Rightarrow \quad r = 90^\circ - i_p$

$\Rightarrow \quad = 90^\circ - 57 = 33^\circ$

Sol. 37 (B) For diffraction minima by a single slit of width b, we use

$$b \sin\theta = n\lambda$$

$\Rightarrow \quad \lambda = \dfrac{a \sin\theta}{n}$

$\Rightarrow \quad \lambda = 1.0 \times 10^{-5} \times \sin 30^\circ$

$\Rightarrow \quad \lambda = 1.0 \times 10^{-5} \times \dfrac{1}{2}$

$\Rightarrow \quad \lambda = 0.5 \times 10^{-5} = 5 \times 10^{-6}$ cm

$\Rightarrow \quad \lambda = 500$ Å

Sol. 38 (D) Diffraction minima on either side of central maxima is given as

$$b \sin\theta = n\lambda$$

$\Rightarrow \quad \sin\theta = \dfrac{n\lambda}{a} = \dfrac{6328 \times 10^{-10} \times 1}{0.2 \times 10^{-3}}$

$\Rightarrow \quad \sin\theta = 3164 \times 10^{-6}$ rad $= 0.003164$ radian

Angular width of central maxima is given as

$$2\theta = 2 \times 0.003164 \times \frac{180^\circ}{\pi} = 0.36^\circ$$

Sol. 39 (B) Location of diffraction minima in single slit diffraction pattern is given as

$$b \sin\theta = n\lambda$$

$\Rightarrow \quad b \cdot \dfrac{x}{D} = n\lambda$

$\Rightarrow \quad \lambda = \dfrac{bx}{nD}$

$\Rightarrow \quad \lambda = \dfrac{2 \times 10^{-4} \times 6 \times 10^{-3}}{1 \times 2} = 6000$ Å

Sol. 40 (D) Angular spread of central maxima in a single slit diffraction pattern with slit width b and for light of wavelength λ on either side is given by

$$\theta = \frac{\lambda}{b} = \frac{1}{5} \text{ rad}$$

Sol. 41 (B) Fringe width in *YDSE* setup is given as

$$\beta = \frac{\lambda D}{d} = \frac{5 \times 10^{-7} \times 2}{10^{-3}} = 10^{-3} \text{ m} = 1 \text{ mm}$$

Sol. 42 (D) By Doppler's effect in light shift in wavelength is given as

$$\Delta\lambda = \frac{v}{c}\lambda$$

$\Rightarrow \quad v = \dfrac{c\Delta\lambda}{\lambda}$

$\Rightarrow \quad v = \dfrac{3 \times 10^{8} \times 1.9 \times 10^{-10}}{5700 \times 10^{-10}} = 100 \text{ km s}^{-1}$

Sol. 43 (D) Fringe width in *YDSE* setup is given as

$$\beta = \frac{\lambda D}{d}$$

As in both setups fringe widths are equal, we use

$$\beta = \frac{\lambda_1 D_1}{d_1} = \frac{\lambda_2 D_2}{d_2}$$

$\Rightarrow \quad \dfrac{D_1}{D_2} = \dfrac{d_1}{d_2} \times \dfrac{\lambda_2}{\lambda_1} = \dfrac{2}{1} \times \dfrac{2}{1} = 4 : 1$

Sol. 44 (C) Distance of nth bright fringe in a *YDSE* pattern from central maxima is given as

$$x = n\lambda\frac{D}{d} = (n+1)\lambda'\frac{D}{d}$$

$\Rightarrow \quad n \times 12000 = (n+1) \times 10000$

$\Rightarrow \quad n = 5$ and $x = n\lambda\dfrac{D}{d}$

$\Rightarrow \quad d = \dfrac{n\lambda D}{x} = \dfrac{5 \times 12000 \times 10^{-10} \times 2}{6 \times 10^{-3}}$ m

$\Rightarrow \quad d = 2 \times 10^{-3}$ m $= 2$ mm

Sol. 45 (A) Fringe widths β and β' in a *YDSE* setup is given as

$$\beta = \frac{\lambda D}{d} \text{ and } \beta' = \frac{\lambda D'}{d}$$

$\Rightarrow \quad \beta - \beta' = \dfrac{\lambda(D - D')}{d}$

$\Rightarrow \quad d = \dfrac{\lambda(D - D')}{(\beta - \beta')}$

$\Rightarrow \quad d = \dfrac{6000 \times 10^{-10} \times 5 \times 10^{-2}}{3 \times 10^{-5}} = 10^{-3} \text{ m} = 1 \text{ mm}$

Sol. 46 (C) First polariser, polarises the light and hence intensity of light reduces by 50%.

Sol. 47 (C) The concentration of solution is given as

$$C = \frac{\theta}{lS}$$

$\Rightarrow \quad S = \dfrac{\theta}{iC} = \dfrac{9.9}{2 \times 0.075}$

$\Rightarrow \quad S = 66^\circ$

Sol. 48 (D) The angular width of interference fringes in *YDSE* setup for the two wavelengths are given as

$$\theta_1 = \frac{\lambda_1}{d} \text{ and } \theta_2 = \frac{\lambda_2}{d}$$

$$\Rightarrow \frac{\theta_1}{\theta_2} = \frac{\lambda_1}{\lambda_2}$$

$$\Rightarrow \lambda_2 = \lambda_1 \times \frac{\theta_2}{\theta_1}$$

$$\Rightarrow \lambda_2 = 5890 \times \frac{0.22}{0.20} = 6479 \text{ Å}$$

Sol. 49 (B) Fringe width,

$$\omega = \frac{\lambda D}{d} \propto \lambda$$

When the wavelength is decreased from 600 nm to 400 nm, fringe width will also decrease by a factor of $\frac{4}{6}$ or $\frac{2}{3}$ or the number of fringes in the same segment will increase by a factor of 3/2. Therefore, number of fringes observed in the same segment $= 12 \times \frac{3}{2} = 18$

Concept :
Since $\omega \propto \lambda$, and if *YDSE* apparatus is immersed in a liquid of refractive index μ, the wavelength λ and thus the fringe width will decrease μ times.

ADVANCE MCQs One or More Options Correct

Sol. 1 (A, C, D) Glass slab introduces extra path difference o fringe pattern will get shifted towards covered slit. Due to reduced intensity of one of the slits, intensity of bright fringe decreases and that of dark fringe increases. Fringe width is given as

$$\beta = \frac{\lambda D}{d}$$

Hence fringe width will remain constant.

Sol. 2 (B, D) For sustained interference the phase difference must remain constant between the interfering waves, if it varies with time then the resulting intensity at the point of interference will change with time so the interfering waves must be coherent. With change in amplitude and intensity of the two waves, only the resulting intensity will be affected but it does not change, hence option (B) and (D) are not necessary for sustained interference.

Sol. 3 (B, C, D) As analyzed in article 6.4.5 options (B), (C) and (D) are correct.

Sol. 4 (A, C) The path difference in the two waves from S_1 and S_2 is given as

$$\Delta = d \sin\theta$$

and frequency of the waves is $f = 10^6$ Hz and wavelength is given as

$$\lambda = \frac{3\times10^8}{10^6} = 300 \text{ m}$$

Case-1 : If $\theta = 90°$, we have

$$\Delta = d$$

Thus phase difference between waves is

$$\Delta\phi = \frac{2\pi}{\lambda}\Delta x$$

$$\Rightarrow \Delta\phi = \frac{2\pi}{300} \times 150 = \pi$$

Thus resulting intensity is given as

$$I = I_0 \cos^2\frac{\theta}{2}$$

$$\Rightarrow I = 0$$

Case-2 : If $\theta = 30°$, we have

$$\Delta = d\sin 30° = \frac{d}{2}$$

Thus phase difference between waves is

$$\Delta\phi = \frac{2\pi}{\lambda} \times \Delta x = \frac{\pi}{2}$$

Thus resulting intensity is given as

$$I(\theta) = I_0 \cos^2\frac{\pi}{4} = \frac{I_0}{2}$$

Case-3 : If $\theta = 0°$, we have

$$\Delta = 0$$

$$\Rightarrow \Delta\phi = 0$$

$$\Rightarrow I = I_0$$

Sol. 5 (B, C) As fringe width in *YDSE* is directly proportional to the wavelength of light used, fringe width will decrease due to which overall fringe pattern will shrink. As the fringe pattern is obtained only within the central diffraction maxima of each slit on screen, due to reduced fringe width, total number of bright fringes will increase.

Sol. 6 (C) For a wavefront, we know that time taken by all points on it from one position to another of same wavefront are equal. If t is the time taken by the wavefront in travelling from position *AB* to position *MN* as shown in figure, then we use

$$tv_m = d$$

$$tv_{\text{air}} = b$$

Where v_m is the speed of light in water and v_{air} is the speed of light in air. Dividing the above two equations, we get

$$\frac{V_m}{V_{air}} = \frac{d}{b}$$

$$\frac{\mu_m}{\mu_{air}} = \frac{b}{d}$$

Sol. 7 (A, D) When light is reflected from the boundary of a denser medium, it suffers an addition of extra path $\lambda/2$ or an additional phase π. Reflected light from top surface of film will have constructive interference with the reflected light from its bottom surface when at any reflection it will not suffer an extra path of half wavelength to interfere constructively hence option (A) is correct. Similarly in transmitted beams, one is directly transmitting and other is reflecting from bottom surface of film then its top surface, again it will constructively interfere with the directly transmitted light when its reflection is from the boundary of rarer media hence option (D) is also correct.

Sol. 8 (C) As light is travelling along Y direction (+ or −), its wavefront must be parallel to XZ plane as wavefront is always normal to the direction of propagation of light, hence only option (C) can be correct.

Sol. 9 (A, C) The angular positions of diffraction minima in single slit diffraction pattern is given by the relation

$$b \sin\theta = n\lambda$$

In above relation as b decreases $\sin\theta$ increases so width of central maxima will increase hence option (B) is correct. As slit width becomes equal to the light wavelength then fringe pattern will disappear and central maxima will spread upto infinity hence option (C) is correct.

Sol. 10 (B, C) For equal intensity waves, after interference, resulting intensity is given as

$$I = I_0 \cos^2 \frac{\theta}{2}$$

If resulting intensity is $I_0/2$ then solving we get options (B) and (C) are correct.

Sol. 11 (All) When each polaroid is placed with its optic axis at 90° with the previous and next polaroid then no light will come out.

Sol. 12 (A, C, D) The path difference between the two slits S_1 and S_2 is half of wavelength so the waves from the slits will emit in opposite phase. The physical path difference between waves emitting from slits and reaching the screen centre O is zero so at point O the waves will interfere in opposite phase hence at O destructive interference will take place and a minima will be obtained at O hence option (B) is INCORRECT and it will be chosen as one correct option. At point P the physical path difference from the slits is equal to the path difference between waves from the slits so it will nullify the total path difference and waves will meet at point P in same phase hence at point P a maxima (central maxima as path difference is zero) will be formed and resulting intensity at P will be $4I_0$ hence options (A) and (D) are correct and will not be chosen as correct options. Here option (C) is INCORRECT so it will be chosen as a correct option.

Sol. 13 (A, C, D) As the sources are point monochromatic sources, the fringes obtained on the screen will be alternate bright and dark circular rings corresponding to maxima and minima.

The path difference between the waves arriving from the two sources at O is d. If d is a multiple of λ then there will be a constructive interference between waves at O and there will be a maxima obtained. Hence option (C) is correct. If $d = N\lambda$ then between O and infinite distance on screen there will be $N-1$ maxima (bright circular fringes) hence option (D) is correct. When the path difference at O is 4.3λ there will be four maxima on screen corresponding to path differences λ, 2λ, 3λ, 4λ and four minima corresponding to path differences 0.5λ, 1.5λ, 2.5λ, 3.5λ hence option (B) is NOT correct. For $d = 7\lambda/2$, waves will produce destructive interference at point O hence option (A) is correct.

Sol. 14 (B, C) The interference setup shown in figure is similar to the Lloyd's mirror as explained in section 6.4.9. Fringe width obtained on screen is given as

$$\beta = \frac{\lambda D}{2h}$$

$$\Rightarrow \quad \frac{1}{4} = \frac{\lambda(1)}{2h} \quad \ldots(1)$$

$$\text{and} \quad \frac{1}{6} = \frac{\lambda(1)}{2(h+0.6)} \quad \ldots(2)$$

$$\Rightarrow \quad \frac{\frac{1}{4}}{\frac{1}{6}} = \frac{h+0.6}{h}$$

$$\Rightarrow \quad \frac{3}{2} = \frac{h+0.6}{h}$$

$$\Rightarrow \quad h = 1.2 \text{ mm}$$

From equation-(1), we have

$$\frac{1}{4} mm = \frac{\lambda(1m)}{2\times(1.2)mm}$$

$$\Rightarrow \quad \lambda = 6000 \text{Å}$$

Sol. 15 (A, C) For a point P on screen at a distance y from screen centre, the physical path difference in light waves from slits after slit plane is calculated as

$$S_1P - S_2P = \frac{dy}{D}$$

Due to medium between slit plane and screen and due to inclined incidence of incident beam, the optical path difference between waves at point P is given as

$$\Delta x = (\mu_0 + kt)\frac{dy}{D} - d\sin\phi$$

For central maxima to be obtained at P,

$$\Delta x = 0$$

$$\Rightarrow \qquad \Delta x = (\mu_0 + kt)\frac{dy}{D} - d\sin\phi = 0$$

$$\Rightarrow \qquad y = \frac{D\sin\phi}{\mu_0 + kt}$$

Hence option (A) is correct. The velocity of fringe pattern is given as

$$\frac{dy}{dt} = -\frac{kD\sin\phi}{(\mu_0 + kt)^2}$$

Hence option (C) is correct.

* * * * *